Teaching Individuals with Physical or Multiple Disabilities

Teaching Individuals with Physical or Multiple Disabilities

Fifth Edition

Sherwood J. Best
California State University, Los Angeles

Kathryn Wolff Heller
Georgia State University

June L. Bigge
San Francisco State University

Upper Saddle River, New Jersey
Columbus, Ohio

Library of Congress Cataloging in Publication Data
Best, Sherwood J.
Teaching individuals with physical or multiple disabilities / Sherwood J. Best, Kathryn Wolff Heller, June L. Bigge.—5th ed.
p. cm.
Rev. ed. of: Teaching individuals with physical, health, or multiple disabilities / June L. Bigge. 4th ed. c2001.
Includes bibliographical references and index.
ISBN 0-13-112122-7
1. Children with disabilities—Education—United States. I. Heller, Kathryn Wolff. II. Bigge, June L. III. Bigge, June L. Teaching individuals with physical, health, or multiple disabilities. IV. Title.
LC4231.B53 2005
371.91—dc22

2003068861

Vice President and Executive Publisher: Jeffery W. Johnston
Acquisitions Editor: Allyson P. Sharp
Editorial Assistant: Kathleen S. Burk
Production Editor: Linda Hillis Bayma
Production Coordination: Ann Mohan, WordCrafters Editorial Services
Design Coordinator: Diane C. Lorenzo
Cover Designer: Jeff Vanik
Cover image: John Best
Production Manager: Laura Messerly
Director of Marketing: Ann Castel Davis
Marketing Manager: Autumn Purdy
Marketing Coordinator: Tyra Poole

This book was set in Garamond by Carlisle Communications, Ltd. It was printed and bound by Courier Kendallville, Inc. The cover was printed by Coral Graphic Services, Inc.

Photo Credits: pp. 15, 16, 17, 23 by John Best; pp. 19, 329 (left), 330, 357 by Penny Silva Musante; p. 97 by John Hinderer; pp. 99, 101 by Beverly Cusik; pp. 77, 102, 260, 322, 324, 375 (left), 395, 447 (left) by Marvin L. Silverman; pp. 103, 327 (right), 329 (right), 332 by Addie Adom; p. 105 by Carol Fusco; pp. 175, 326, 375 (right) by John Stripeika; pp. 201, 207, 209, 210, 212, 213, 214, 216, 217 courtesy of Sammons Preston; pp. 205, 361, 362 courtesy of Sports 'n Spokes/Paralyzed Veterans of America; p. 235 by Manni Mason's Pictures; p. 251 by Jane Kelly; pp. 288, 289, 296, 297, 300, 301, 302, 304, 305 by Kate Bobrowicz; pp. 314, 315, 316, 321, 325, 448, 455 by Kathryn Wolff Heller; p. 327 (left) by Terry Caldwell; p. 331 by J. Mark Rainz; p. 447 (right) courtesy of American Printing House for the Blind, Louisville, Kentucky; p. 454 by Keytime, Inc.

Pearson Education Ltd.
Pearson Education Singapore Pte. Ltd.
Pearson Education Canada, Ltd.
Pearson Education—Japan
Pearson Education Australia Pty. Limited
Pearson Education North Asia Ltd.
Pearson Educación de Mexico, S.A. de C.V.
Pearson Education Malaysia Pte. Ltd.

10 9 8 7 6 5 4 3 2
ISBN: 0-13-112122-7

The fifth edition of *Teaching Individuals with Physical or Multiple Disabilities* is dedicated to Mr. Matthew Rudes and Ms. Natalie Tumlin, two young adults who possess great courage, inner strength, and the will to succeed. You are the inspiration for our work.

Contributors

Rona Alexander, Ph.D., CCC-SP
Rona Alexander Ltd.
Wauwatosa, Wisconsin

Peggy Allgood
Teacher
Atlanta Area School for the Deaf
Atlanta, Georgia

Sherwood J. Best, Ph.D.
Professor
Division of Special Education
Charter College of Education
California State University, Los Angeles
Los Angeles, California

June L. Bigge, Ph.D.
Professor Emerita
Department of Special Education
San Francisco State University
San Francisco, California

Gary M. Clark, Ph.D.
Professor
Department of Special Education
University of Kansas
Lawrence, Kansas

Kathryn Wolff Heller, Ph.D.
Professor
Department of Educational Psychology and Special Education
Georgia State University
Atlanta, Georgia

Catherine Mary Macias
Teacher
Pasadena, California

Penny Musante
Program Director
ALIVE
Antioch, California

Penny Reed
Assistive Technology Consultant
Juneau, Wisconsin

Colleen Shea Stump, Ph.D.
Program Specialist
Seattle Public Schools
Seattle, Washington

Preface

This text was originally authored by June L. Bigge with invited contributors; Sherwood J. Best and Kathryn Wolff Heller joined her in the fourth edition. It has become the preeminent text for teachers of students who have physical, health, or multiple disabilities. This edition builds on the foundation of the previous editions, and June Bigge continues to guide and inspire our efforts. The book is designed for use by family members, educators, related-service providers, administrators, paraprofessionals, and others who provide services to individuals with physical, health, or multiple disabilities. It meets the needs of service providers in three ways. First, it describes specific physical and health impairments with attention to their educational and psychosocial implications. Second, it illustrates accommodations and modifications that promote access to the curriculum and participation in home and community environments. Third, it addresses curricular issues in a comprehensive manner, thereby serving as a resource for family members and service providers.

This edition contains both similarities to and differences from the fourth edition. The focus on assistive technology has been retained, as have most chapters from the previous edition. Knowledge and skill statements, questions for discussion, and "Focus on the Net" remain to extend the reader's interaction with the subject matter. The differences are in the conceptual and structural improvements to this edition.

ORGANIZATION OF THE BOOK

This fifth edition contains 16 chapters organized within four major parts. Part I, "Impact and Implications of Physical, Health, and Multiple Disabilities," provides foundational knowledge and describes a variety of specific physical and health impairments and their implications. Chapter 1 provides definitions, explains current laws, and explores issues in the lives of individuals with physical, health, or multiple disabilities. This chapter orients educators and others to historical and current perspectives on disability that shape policy and practice in education. Chapters 2, 3, and 4 introduce specific physical and health disabilities, with definitions; descriptions of associated medical conditions; and discussions of the impact of disability on physical, cognitive, and psychosocial development. Readers are urged to explore these and other disabilities further through Internet resources.

Part II, "Accommodations for Curricular Access," contains information that assists educators in individualizing curricula for individuals with physical or multiple disabilities, with an emphasis on improved academic access and quality of life. Chapter 5 introduces the theme of accommodation by providing a model for planning and designing courses of study for students with disabilities. It includes accommodations and modifications of the general education curriculum and curricula in modified means of communication and task performance. Chapter 6 adds explanatory power to the model presented in the previous chapter by providing strategies for developing task and situation analyses to individualize curricula. An important aspect of this chapter is differentiating task difficulties that arise from either motor or cognitive challenges. Chapter 7 incorporates materials from two chapters in the previous edition. The first half of the chapter is focused on assistive technology (AT) assessment, and the second half provides practical AT solutions. This chapter also addresses the critical need for appropriate positioning, seating, and mobility. Chapter 8 concludes this part of the book with a focused discussion of augmentative and alternative communication (AAC), one of the fastest-growing knowledge areas in special education and related services.

Part III, "Specialized Curricula," focuses on unique needs of individuals with physical, health, or multiple disabilities. Feeding and swallowing issues are addressed in Chapter 9. A discussion of the connection between feeding/swallowing and speech development provides valuable information to educators and others. This knowledge is paired with strategies assessment and appropriate feeding interventions. Chapter 10 describes techniques that enable individuals with disabilities to function with maximum independence. A unique perspective in this chapter is attention to strategies for teaching students to manage their own care, which reinforces autonomy and self-determination. Chapter 11 describes adapted physical education, recreation, and leisure options for individuals with physical, health, or multiple disabilities. Chapter 12 focuses on the topic of transition, with an overview of career education, development and implementation of the individual transition plan, and description of activities to support effective transition from school to work and community.

Finally, Part IV, "Core Curriculum Adaptations and Instructional Strategies," helps educators align student learning needs with curricula in general education. Chapter 13 begins the discussion on core curriculum adaptations with a focus on literacy. A critical aspect of this chapter is assisting educators to provide meaningful literacy experiences for students with motor and speech disabilities. Chapter 14 extends this discussion to the topic of writing, with emphasis on practical, low-tech adaptations in addition to computer-based options. Chapter 15 offers suggestions for modifying social studies and science curricula. Chapter 16 addresses mathematics. Every chapter in Part IV includes information on appropriate software to ensure accessibility and add meaning to content areas. Functional academic skills are also incorporated into all chapters in this part of the book.

The organization and content of this text provide educators and others with general information, specialized knowledge, and specific strategies that result in meaningful, high-quality educational experiences for students with physical, health, or multiple disabilities. The text prepares readers for providing direct or consultative services in a variety of educational arenas, including general education classes, special education classes, and hospital settings.

ACKNOWLEDGMENTS

As principal authors of this edition, we retained, edited, and supplemented considerable amounts of June Bigge's original work. In addition, we guided the work of invited contributors, who collaborated on chapters with the principal authors or updated entire chapters they had written for the previous edition. The following authors made major contributions to the book: Rona Alexander, Gary Clark, Penny Reed, and Colleen Shea Stump. In addition, we thank Peggy Allgood, Catherine Mary Macias, and Penny Musante for their foundational work in the fourth edition that was retained in this edition.

Input from reviewers was greatly appreciated. Many thanks to the following for their instructive suggestions: Lisa Battaglino, Bridgewater State College; Lawrence A. Beard, Jacksonville State University; Joseph Domaracki, Indiana University of Pennsylvania; and Patrick McCaffrey, California State University, Chico.

Educators and other service providers made critical contributions to this book. Students enrolled in special education credential programs where we teach or have taught and teachers who have worked in the field of physical and health impairments for many years provided personal anecdotes and teaching strategies that enliven and enrich the book. Publishers, product vendors, and others provided materials that make the book especially useful. Finally, we sincerely thank John Best and the late Marvin Silverman for their sensitive and instructive photography.

No book can be completed without a great deal of technical support. We thank Allyson Sharp, Kathy Burk, and Linda Bayma at Merrill/Prentice Hall for the three "Ps": patience, perfectionism, and persistence. Ann Mohan at WordCrafters Editorial Services is to be commended for transforming the original manuscript into a book that is inviting to the senses and the mind. Friends provided assistance with library research and proofreading. Special thanks to Cheryl Wilkinson for her contributions to Chapters 2 and 3.

Finally, our thanks go to special individuals and family members for their support throughout the completion of this edition. June Bigge is appreciative and relieved because she both enjoys her retirement years and knows that her efforts will be continued and updated through the expertise of the two colleagues she chose to undertake the revisions: Sherwood Best and Kathryn Wolff Heller. Sherwood Best thanks two members of her family who always support her work: her daughter Sarah and her husband John. Kathryn Wolff Heller thanks her husband Ed and her son Daniel. To our families and friends, who provided the time to listen, the space to let us work, and the dedication to teaching individuals with physical or multiple disabilities, we are forever grateful.

Sherwood J. Best
Kathryn Wolff Heller
June L. Bigge

Discover the Companion Website Accompanying This Book

THE PRENTICE HALL COMPANION WEBSITE: A VIRTUAL LEARNING ENVIRONMENT

Technology is a constantly growing and changing aspect of our field that is creating a need for content and resources. To address this emerging need, Prentice Hall has developed an online learning environment for students and professors alike—Companion Websites—to support our textbooks.

In creating a Companion Website, our goal is to build on and enhance what the textbook already offers. For this reason, the content for each user-friendly website is organized by topic and provides the professor and student with a variety of meaningful resources. Common features of a Companion Website include:

FOR THE PROFESSOR—

Every Companion Website integrates **Syllabus Manager**™, an online syllabus creation and management utility.

- **Syllabus Manager**™ provides you, the instructor, with an easy, step-by-step process to create and revise syllabi, with direct links into Companion Website and other online content without having to learn HTML.
- Students may logon to your syllabus during any study session. All they need to know is the web address for the Companion Website and the password you've assigned to your syllabus.
- After you have created a syllabus using **Syllabus Manager**™, students may enter the syllabus for their course section from any point in the Companion Website.
- Clicking on a date, the student is shown the list of activities for the assignment. The activities for each assignment are linked directly to actual content, saving time for students.
- Adding assignments consists of clicking on the desired due date, then filling in the details of the assignment—name of the assignment, instructions, and whether it is a one-time or repeating assignment.
- In addition, links to other activities can be created easily. If the activity is online, a URL can be entered in the space provided, and it will be linked automatically in the final syllabus.
- Your completed syllabus is hosted on our servers, allowing convenient updates from any computer on the Internet. Changes you make to your syllabus are immediately available to your students at their next logon.

FOR THE STUDENT—

- **Overview and General Information**—General information about the topic and how it will be covered in the website.
- **Web Links**—A variety of websites related to topic areas.
- **Content Methods and Strategies**—Resources that help to put theories into practice in the special education classroom.
- **Reflective Questions and Case-Based Activities**—Put concepts into action, participate in activities, examine strategies, and more.
- **National and State Laws**—An online guide to how federal and state laws affect your special education classroom.
- **Behavior Management**—An online guide to help you manage behaviors in the special education classroom.
- **Message Board**—Virtual bulletin board to post and respond to questions and comments from a national audience.

To take advantage of these and other resources, please visit the *Teaching Individuals with Physical or Multiple Disabilities* Companion Website at

www.prenhall.com/best

EDUCATOR LEARNING CENTER: AN INVALUABLE ONLINE RESOURCE

Merrill Education and the Association for Supervision and Curriculum Development (ASCD) invite you to take advantage of a new online resource, one that provides access to the top research and proven strategies associated with ASCD and Merrill—the Educator Learning Center. At **www.EducatorLearningCenter.com** you will find resources that will enhance your students' understanding of course topics and of current educational issues, in addition to being invaluable for further research.

How the Educator Learning Center will Help Your Students Become Better Teachers

With the combined resources of Merrill Education and ASCD, you and your students will find a wealth of tools and materials to better prepare them for the classroom.

Research

- More than 600 articles from the ASCD journal *Educational Leadership* discuss everyday issues faced by practicing teachers.
- A direct link on the site to Research Navigator™ gives students access to many of the leading education journals, as well as extensive content detailing the research process.
- Excerpts from Merrill Education texts give your students insights on important topics of instructional methods, diverse populations, assessment, classroom management, technology, and refining classroom practice.

Classroom Practice

- Hundreds of lesson plans and teaching strategies are categorized by content area and age range.
- Case studies and classroom video footage provide virtual field experience for student reflection.
- Computer simulations and other electronic tools keep your students abreast of today's classrooms and current technologies.

Look into the Value of Educator Learning Center Yourself

A four-month subscription to Educator Learning Center is $25 but is **FREE** when used in conjunction with this text. To obtain free passcodes for your students, simply contact your local Merrill/Prentice Hall sales representative, and your representative will give you a special ISBN to give your bookstore when ordering your textbooks. To preview the value of this website to you and your students, please go to **www.EducatorLearningCenter.com** and click on "Demo."

Brief Contents

PART I
Impact and Implications of Physical, Health, and Multiple Disabilities 1

1 Definitions, Supports, Issues, and Services in Schools and Communities 3

2 Physical Disabilities 31

3 Health Impairments and Infectious Diseases 59

4 Cerebral Palsy 87

PART II
Accommodations for Curricular Access 111

5 Curricular Options for Individuals with Physical or Multiple Disabilities 113

6 Task and Situation Analysis 151

7 Assistive Technology 179

8 Augmentative and Alternative Communication 227

PART III
Specialized Curricula 275

9 Feeding and Swallowing 277

10 Adaptations for Personal Independence 309

11 Adaptations in Physical Education, Leisure Education, and Recreation 337

12 Transition and Self-Determination 367

PART IV
Core Curriculum Adaptations and Instructional Strategies 399

13 Adaptations and Instruction in Literacy and Language Arts 401

14 Adaptations and Instruction in Writing 441

15 Adaptations and Instruction in Science and Social Studies 471

16 Adaptations and Instruction in Mathematics 501

Contents

PART I
Impact and Implications of Physical, Health, and Multiple Disabilities 1

1 Definitions, Supports, Issues, and Services in Schools and Communities 3

Historical Perspectives 4
Past and Present Perspectives 4
The Disability Rights Movement 5
Coming to Terms with Terminology 6
Impairment, Disability, Handicap 6
DisABILITY 7
Federal Categories and Definitions 8
Legal Supports and Mandates 9
PL 93-112: The Rehabilitation Act of 1973 10
PL 94-142: The Education for All Handicapped Children Act of 1975 10
PL 100-407: Technology-Related Assistance for Individuals with Disabilities Act of 1988 10
PL 101-336: Americans with Disabilities Act of 1990 10
PL 101-392: Carl D. Perkins Vocational and Applied Technology Education Act of 1990 11
PL 101-476: The Individuals with Disabilities Education Act (IDEA) of 1990 11
PL 105-17: The IDEA Amendments of 1997 11
Critical Issues for Individuals with Physical, Health, or Multiple Disabilities 12
Alike and Different 12
Visible and Invisible 12
Acute and Chronic 13
Appropriate Accommodation 13
Service Intensity and Personal Independence Issues 15
Educational Goals and Expected Outcomes 16
Teaching and Learning Environments 16
Education Service Delivery Systems 16
Challenges to Effective Service Delivery 18
Teacher Competencies and Evolving Roles 20
Knowledge and Skills 20
Professional Roles 21
Summary and Conclusion 26
Questions for Discussion 26
Focus on the Net 27
References 28

2 Physical Disabilities 31

Neuromotor Impairments 32
Neural Tube Defects 32
Descriptions and Characteristics 32
Associated Medical Conditions 33
Medical and Therapeutic Treatments 34
Impact on Physical, Cognitive, and Psychosocial Development 34
Implications for Education and Personal Autonomy 35
Implications for Career and Adult Outcomes 37
Traumatic Brain Injury 38
Descriptions and Characteristics 38
Associated Medical Conditions 39
Medical and Therapeutic Treatments 39
Impact on Physical, Cognitive, and Psychosocial Development 40
Implications for Education and Personal Autonomy 45
Implications for Career and Adult Outcomes 46
Degenerative Diseases 46
Muscular Dystrophy 46
Definitions and Descriptions 46
Associated Medical Conditions 48
Medical and Therapeutic Treatments 48
Impact on Physical, Cognitive, and Psychosocial Development 49
Implications for Education and Personal Autonomy 50
Implications for Career and Adult Outcomes 51
Orthopedic and Musculoskeletal Conditions 51
Limb Deficiencies 51
Definitions and Descriptions 51
Associated Medical Conditions 52
Medical and Therapeutic Treatments 52

Impact on Physical, Cognitive, and Psychosocial Development 53
Implications for Education and Personal Autonomy 53
Implications for Career and Adult Outcomes 54
Summary and Conclusion 54
Questions for Discussion 55
Focus on the Net 55
References 56

3 Health Impairments and Infectious Diseases 59

Health Impairments 60
Asthma 61
Definitions and Descriptions 61
Associated Medical Conditions 62
Medical and Therapeutic Treatments 62
Impact on Physical, Cognitive, and Psychosocial Development 63
Implications for Education and Personal Autonomy 63
Implications for Career and Adult Outcomes 64
Cystic Fibrosis 65
Definitions and Descriptions 65
Associated Medical Conditions 66
Medical and Therapeutic Treatments 66
Impact on Physical, Cognitive, and Psychosocial Development 66
Implications for Education and Personal Autonomy 67
Implications for Career and Adult Outcomes 67
Cancer 68
Definitions and Descriptions 68
Associated Medical Conditions 68
Medical and Therapeutic Treatments 68
Impact on Physical, Cognitive, and Psychosocial Development 69
Implications for Education and Personal Autonomy 70
Implications for Career and Adult Outcomes 70
Infectious Diseases 70
Cytomegalovirus 71
Definitions and Descriptions 71
Associated Medical Conditions 71
Medical and Therapeutic Treatments 71
Impact on Physical, Cognitive, and Psychosocial Development 71
Implications for Education and Personal Autonomy 72
Implications for Career and Adult Outcomes 72
HIV/AIDS 72
Definitions and Descriptions 72
Associated Medical Conditions 73
Medical and Therapeutic Treatments 73
Impact on Physical, Cognitive, and Psychosocial Development 74
Implications for Education and Personal Autonomy 74
Implications for Career and Adult Outcomes 75
Special Topics in Health Care 76
Meeting Specialized Health Care Needs 76
Preventing Infectious Disease Transmission and Implementing Universal Precautions 79
Summary and Conclusion 81
Questions for Discussion 81
Focus on the Net 82
References 82

4 Cerebral Palsy 87

Cerebral Palsy 88
Definitions and Descriptions 88
Classification of Cerebral Palsy 89
Location—Topography 89
Movement—Motor Pattern 89
Function—Level of Severity 90
Conditions Associated with Cerebral Palsy 90
Sensory Impairments 91
Communication Impairments 91
Orthopedic Deformities 92
Nutrition and Feeding Needs 92
Cognitive Deficits 92
Learning Disabilities 92
Seizures 93
Therapeutic Management of Cerebral Palsy 93
Physical Therapy 93
Occupational Therapy 93
Medical Treatment of Cerebral Palsy 97
Orthotics 97
Medication and Injections 97
Surgery 98
Developmental Issues in Cerebral Palsy 98
Physical Development 98
Physical Management Strategies 98
Communication Development 102
Social/Emotional Development 103
Implications for Education 104
Educational Segregation 104
Learning Disabilities 104
Personal Autonomy 105
Career and Adult Function 106

Summary and Conclusion 106
Questions for Discussion 106
Focus on the Net 107
References 107

PART II Accommodations for Curricular Access 111

5 Curricular Options for Individuals with Physical or Multiple Disabilities 113

Curricular Options and Fundamental Curricular Domains 115
Option 1: General Education Curriculum with Accommodations 115
Option 2: General Education Curriculum with Accommodations and Modifications 120
Option 3: Life Skills Curriculum 126
Option 4: Curriculum with Modified Means of Communication and Task Performance 129
Fundamental Curricular Domain 1: Self-Determination 136
Fundamental Curricular Domain 2: Transition Education 137
Working Collaboratively to Determine Curriculum Needs for Individuals 143
Developing Courses of Study and Crafting a Curricula Map 145
Summary and Conclusion 147
Questions for Discussion 148
Focus on the Net 148
References 149

6 Task and Situation Analysis 151

Purposes of Task and Situation Analysis 152
Process and Product 152
Task Analysis as an Assessment Tool 152
Order of Tasks 153
Task Analysis Process 153
Using Typical Sequences as Guides 155
Defining Results of Unsuccessful Trials 157
Differentiating Motor from Cognitive Difficulties 158
Identifying Student Response Difficulties and Needs in Lessons 160
Determining Kinds and Amounts of Assistance Needed 161
Task Analysis as a Product 167
Screening Performances 167
Comparing Skills of Different Students 167
Developing Specialized Curricula 167
Situation Analysis 169
Teacher Recollections 171
Questionnaire for Similar-Age Peers 172
Student Strategies 173
Learning and Practicing Self-Care Routines 173
Analyzing Bodies of Information 174
Solving Personal Access Problems 174
Summary and Conclusion 176
Questions for Discussion 176
Focus on the Net 177
References 177

7 Assistive Technology 179

Definitions and Legal Basis for Assistive Technology 180
Assistive Technology Devices and Services 181
Determining the Need for Assistive Technology 184
Considering the Need for Assistive Technology 184
Assistive Technology and Assessment 186
Assessing an Individual's Need for Assistive Technology 186
Team Assessment Principles and Practices 186
Extended Assessment or Trial Use 190
Selecting and Acquiring Assistive Technology 192
Determination of Desired Product Features 193
Product Specifications and Demonstrations 193
Product Searches and Ordering 193
Writing Assistive Technology into the IEP 194
Positioning and Seating 196
Positioning 196
Seating 198
Assistive Devices for Positioning and Seating 201
Safe Transfers 203
Location 203
Mobility 204
Manual Wheelchairs 204
Power Wheelchairs 205
Travel Stroller Chairs 207
Mobility Variations 207
Architectural Access Modifications 211
Environmental and Object Modification 211
Location of Materials and Equipment 211
Work Surface Modifications 213
Object Modifications 214

Environmental Control 217
Assistive Technology for Sensory Impairments 220
Assistive Technology and Hearing Loss 220
Assistive Technology and Visual Impairments 221
Summary and Conclusion 221
Questions for Discussion 222
Focus on the Net 223
References 224

8 Augmentative and Alternative Communication 227

Nonsymbolic Communication 228
Form, Function, and Content of Nonsymbolic Communication 228
Recognizing Nonsymbolic Communication 229
Moving from Noncommunicative Behaviors to Nonsymbolic Communication 231
Utilizing Nonsymbolic Expressive Communication 232
Utilizing Nonsymbolic Receptive Communication 232
Moving to Symbolic Communication 234
Symbolic Communication 234
Unaided Symbolic Communication 234
Aided Symbolic Communication 235
Selecting the Communication System 236
Aided Considerations: Symbol Type 238
Aided Considerations: Means of Access 240
Direct Selection 240
Scanning 242
Encoding 243
Aided Considerations: Vocabulary and Retrieval 245
Levels 245
Picture-Based Acceleration Techniques 245
Abbreviation Expansion 246
Predictive Techniques 246
Output Methods 247
Voice Outputs 247
Visual Outputs 247
Hard Copy 248
Content of Augmentative and Alternative Communication 248
Ecological Inventory for Task-Specific Content 248
School Topic Content 250
Non-Task-Related (or Social) Communication 250
Verifying Content 251
Board Arrangement 253
Symbol Placement 253
Vocabulary Organization 253
Vocabulary Arrangement for Receptive Communication 258
Types of Displays 259
Displays for Nonelectronic Communication Devices 259
Displays on Dedicated Devices and Computers 262
Instructional Strategies 262
Establishing Want/No 263
Response Prompt Strategies 264
Milieu Teaching Procedures 265
Environmental Arrangement Strategy 266
Interrupted-Chain Strategy 267
Conversational Skill Training 267
Breakdown Strategies 267
Summary and Conclusion 270
Questions for Discussion 271
Focus on the Net 271
References 272

PART III
Specialized Curricula 275

9 Feeding and Swallowing 277

Why Are We Concerned with Feeding and Swallowing? 279
Typical Feeding and Swallowing Development 281
Characteristics of Typical Oral-Motor Development 281
Characteristics of Typical Respiratory Development 284
Typical Respiratory Coordination with Oral and Pharyngeal Activities 285
Feeding and Swallowing in Children with Neuromotor Involvement 287
Atypical Oral-Motor Activity 287
Atypical Respiratory Function 290
The Comprehensive Evaluation Process 290
Feeding and Swallowing Intervention 293
Carryover Activities 293
Positioning for Mealtime Feeding 293
Selection of Feeding Utensils 298
Choosing Appropriate Foods and Liquids 298
Preparation of the Oral Mechanism 299
Direct Help for the Jaw, Lips, and Tongue 300
Cup Drinking 302
Spoon-Feeding 303
Solid Food 303

Stimulating Respiratory Coordination with Oral and Pharyngeal Activities 305
Summary and Conclusion 306
Questions for Discussion 306
Focus on the Net 306
References 307

10 Adaptations for Personal Independence 309
Assessment and Instruction of Personal Management Skills 310
Hygiene Skills 312
Hand Washing 313
Face and Body Washing 313
Hair Brushing 314
Oral Hygiene 314
Tissue Use 316
Feminine Hygiene 316
Basic Self-Help Skills: Eating and Toileting 317
Tube Feeding, Catheterization, and Colostomy Care 319
Tube Feeding 320
Catheterization 320
Colostomy Care 321
Students Performing Their Own Health Care Procedures 321
Dressing 322
Helping Individuals Learn Dressing Skills 322
Adapted Clothing and Adapted Dressing Devices 323
Home Care and Management 326
Kitchen Tasks 327
Housecleaning 329
Technology and Environmental Control 330
Community-Based Instruction 330
Anticipating Architectural Barriers 330
Shopping 332
Summary and Conclusion 333
Questions for Discussion 333
Focus on the Net 334
References 334

11 Adaptations in Physical Education, Leisure Education, and Recreation 337
Adapted Physical Education 338
Collaboration with Adapted Physical Education Specialists 339
Assessment 340
Individualized Education Program Planning 342
Adapting Physical Education Activities 343
Planning for Adaptations 344
Instructional Program 346
Instructional Strategies 346
Safety Issues 348
From the Classroom to the Community 348
Leisure Education and Recreation 348
Leisure Education Program Development 349
Leisure Education Program Areas 350
Creative Domains 350
Special Interests 351
Science and Technology Domains 353
Recreation Domains 356
Travel 359
Sports 360
Wheelchair Racing 360
Racquet and Arm Sports 361
Winter or Summer 361
Summary and Conclusion 362
Questions for Discussion 362
Focus on the Net 363
References 365

12 Transition and Self-Determination 367
Surmounting Barriers to Employment 369
Physical Self-Reliance 369
Valid Self-Evaluation 370
Enhanced Self-Adaptability and Self-Determination 370
Teaching Career and Transition Education from Early Childhood 372
Career Awareness 373
Career Exploration 373
Career Preparation 378
Career Placement/Follow-up and Continuing Education 383
Making the Transition from School to Employment 384
Students with High Abilities 384
Students with Severe Physical and/or Multiple Disabilities 386
Assessment for Transition Planning 386
Summary and Conclusion 394
Questions for Discussion 395
Focus on the Net 396
References 397

PART IV
Core Curriculum Adaptations and Instructional Strategies 399

13 Adaptations and Instruction in Literacy and Language Arts 401

Literacy Barriers 401
Restricted Language and Participation 401
Lack of Motor Ability 402
Individual Factors 402
Lack of Experiences 402
Learning Environment and Instruction 402

Addressing Literacy Barriers 403
Addressing Communication Barriers 403
Addressing Physical Efficiency Areas 405
Addressing Individual Considerations 408
Addressing Experiential Deficits 409
Addressing the Learning Environment and Instructional Barriers 409

Emergent and Beginning Literacy 410
Book and Print Awareness 410
Storybook Reading with Adaptations 412
Repeated Reading and Promoting Choice 413
Phonemic Awareness 414
Letter–Sound Correspondence 415
Software Programs Addressing Beginning Literacy Skills 416

Conventional Literacy: Approaches and Assessment 416
Assessment of Conventional Reading Skills 417

Conventional Literacy: Phonics 418
Adapting Phonic Instruction: The Nonverbal Reading Approach 419
Teaching Multiple-Syllable Words 424

Conventional Literacy: Vocabulary Instruction 424
Promoting Vocabulary Development with Symbols 424

Conventional Literacy: Fluency 426

Conventional Literacy: Text Comprehension 426
Teaching Comprehension 427
Basic Comprehension Strategy 428

Software and Specialized Curricula for Reading 430

Functional Literacy: Reading 431
Vocabulary Selection: Ecological Assessment 431
Instructional Strategies 432

Summary and Conclusion 435

Questions for Discussion 435

Focus on the Net 435

References 436

14 Adaptations and Instruction in Writing 441

Identifying and Addressing Writing Barriers 441

Literacy Skills: Accessing Writing Tools 443
Handheld Writing Tools and Paper Adaptations 444
Handwriting Skills 446
Electronic Writing Tools: Computers 449
Keyboarding Skills and Computer Tools 456

Literacy Skills: Spelling 457
Assessing Spelling 457
Spelling Instruction 458
Spelling Tools 459
Computer Programs for Spelling 459

Literacy Skills: Written Expression 459
Assessing Written Expression 459
Early Written Expression 461
Written Expression Instruction 462
Software Support for Written Expression 464

Literacy Skills: Functional Writing 464
Assessment of Functional Writing 464
Functional Writing Strategies 465

Summary and Conclusion 465

Questions for Discussion 466

Focus on the Net 466

References 467

15 Adaptations and Instruction in Science and Social Studies 471

Lesson Preparation 471
Determining Content 472
Evaluating and Adapting Instructional Material 472
Assessing Students' Background Knowledge 475
Determining Modifications for Students with Physical or Multiple Disabilities 476

Lesson Presentation 479
Prelesson Activities 479
Presenting New Materials and Guided Practice 481
Independent Practice of Material 486

Evaluating Content Knowledge 486

Social Studies Curriculum Considerations 487
Social Studies Defined 487
Process Skills for Social Studies 487
Social Studies Curriculum Design and Adaptations 488
Social Studies Software 489

Science Curriculum Considerations 489
Science Defined 489
Process Skills for Science 490
Science Curriculum Design and Adaptations 490
Science Software 496

Summary and Conclusion 496
Questions for Discussion 497
Focus on the Net 497
References 497

16 **Adaptations and Instruction in Mathematics 501**

Barriers in Mathematics 501
Assessing Math Skills 502
Standardized Achievement Tests for Mathematics 504
Diagnostic Tests of Math Performance 504
Curriculum-Based Measurement 505
Informal Teacher-Constructed Tests 505
Portfolio Assessment 505
Error Analysis 505
General Approaches and Principles of Math Instruction 507
Building on Previous Learning 507
Systematic and Explicit Instruction 507
Active Involvement of Students 508
Learning Strategies 508
Computer-Assisted Instruction 509
Adaptations and Attitudes 509
Beginning Math Skills 510
Prenumber Skills 510
Counting 511
Numerals and Place Values 514
Software for Early Math Skills 518
Computational Skills: Addition and Subtraction 518
Math Rules for Addition and Subtraction 521
Addition and Subtraction Algorithms 521
Addition and Subtraction Sequences 524
Computational Skills for Multiplication and Division 525
Multiplication and Division Rules 525
Heuristic Strategies 526
Multiplication and Division Algorithms 526
Multiplication and Division Sequences 529
Software for Computational Skills 529
Calculator Use 530
Word Problems 530
General and Advanced Math Skills 531
Functional Math Skills 531
Money 534
Time 536
Calendar Use 538
Summary and Conclusion 539
Questions for Discussion 539
Focus on the Net 540
References 541

Author Index 545

Subject Index 553

Note: Every effort has been made to provide accurate and current Internet information in this book. However, the Internet and information posted on it are constantly changing, and it is inevitable that some of the Internet addresses listed in this textbook will change.

PART I

IMPACT AND IMPLICATIONS OF PHYSICAL, HEALTH, AND MULTIPLE DISABILITIES

CHAPTER 1 Definitions, Supports, Issues, and Services in Schools and Communities

CHAPTER 2 Physical Disabilities

CHAPTER 3 Health Impairments and Infectious Diseases

CHAPTER 4 Cerebral Palsy

Definitions, Supports, Issues, and Services in Schools and Communities

SHERWOOD J. BEST

CHAPTER 1

KNOWLEDGE AND SKILLS

After you have read this chapter, you will be able to:

1. **Understand past and present perspectives on individuals with physical, health, or multiple disabilities;**
2. **Differentiate among the terms *impairment, disability,* and *handicap;***
3. **Identify federal disability categories for special education and related services;**
4. **Use disability classifications that are objective, appropriate, and dignified;**
5. **Appreciate the utility *and* the limits of disability classifications;**
6. **Appreciate the implications of legislation for supporting educational, social, and vocational inclusion of individuals with physical or multiple disabilities;**
7. **Explore critical issues in the lives of individuals with physical or multiple disabilities;**
8. **Evaluate educational service delivery systems and the challenges of effective educational inclusion for students with physical or multiple disabilities;**
9. **Identify teacher competencies specific to serving students with physical, health, or multiple disabilities and apply them to the evolving roles of special education teachers.**

Individuals with physical, health, or multiple disabilities live on your block or in your community, go to school with you or your children, worship in your churches, synagogues, or mosques, volunteer in your community organizations and activities, pay taxes, shop in supermarkets, enjoy public and private recreational facilities, and partake of society in every way imaginable. They are your lawyers, gardeners, homemakers, students, accountants, grocery store stockers and baggers, doctors, salespersons, and teachers. Sometimes their disabilities are visible and identifiable, and sometimes you are unaware that they have a disability. At certain times the impact of disability makes more difference in a person's life than at other times. Individuals with physical, health, or multiple disabilities are people in your neighborhood who come from all walks of life, who serve society in many ways, and whose roles and opportunities continue to expand.

Disability may occur from injury or illness or may result from the aging process. The normal process of aging results in degrees of loss of physical agility and mobility, visual acuity, hearing, and cognitive abilities such as memory. As Covey (1997) stated, "We all become physically disabled to a degree as we age" (p. 45). The recognition that people with physical or multiple disabilities live, work, and play in all communities, that anyone could become disabled through accident or disease, and that disability is a natural part of the human condition leads to the logical conclusion that disability should not be perceived as "them" versus "us" or as a dehumanizing condition. However, readers should not assume that disability has little functional impact on education, activities, and life outcomes.

Teachers and others who work with individuals with physical, health, or multiple disabilities must develop knowledge and skills that extend beyond standard pedagogy. Their knowledge and skills should include the ability to modify the general education curriculum and to incorporate a specialized life skills curriculum. They should also be able to modify the means of communication and performance through (a) modified physical task performance, (b) intensive speech and language development, (c) operation and use of assistive technology, (d) augmentative and alternative communication, and (e) modified means of information acquisition and management (see chapter 5, p. 115).

Teachers of students with physical, health, or multiple disabilities must have more than curricular knowledge and strategies for effective instruction. They must have knowledge about a variety of disabling conditions and their implications for function. They must understand the legal mandates for providing education, supplementary supports, and services. They must interact successfully with personnel from many disciplines, including therapists, doctors, nurses, speech/language specialists, and others. They must have the empathy and knowledge required for working with families who may be coping with issues including chronic illness, frequent hospitalizations, and perhaps terminal outcomes. They must function as a resource for teachers in general education. Teachers must also be advocates for their students, and they must always envision the goal of self-advocacy for students and their families.

The purpose of this chapter is to provide a clear and comprehensive overview of the uniqueness and commonalities of individuals with physical, health, or multiple disabilities. First, readers will become acquainted with historic and contemporary perspectives on disability and the disability rights movement. These perspectives provide the backdrop for a discussion of terminology and of the legal mandates in education and broader civil rights. Major issues and challenges in the lives of these individuals will be addressed. Readers will become aware of a variety of educational service delivery systems and teacher competencies specific to working with people with disabilities. Finally, the evolving roles of teachers in direct service provision and consultation will be explored, as well as the vital contributions of support personnel who help to create a comprehensive educational team.

This chapter provides a foundation and background information about individuals with physical, health, or multiple disabilities. Teachers will gain from it a deeper appreciation of disability through the lenses of philosophy, history, psychology, and sociology.

HISTORICAL PERSPECTIVES

Individuals with disabilities have made numerous contributions to science, the arts, literature, sports, and all other areas of endeavor. However, opportunities and supports for people with disabilities have not always been readily available, as the following overview of perspectives suggests.

Past and Present Perspectives

Individuals with disabilities have evoked recognition and reaction throughout time and across cultures (Covey, 1997; Scheer & Groce, 1988). Social reactions to physically disabling conditions and health impairments have ranged from extermination and abandonment to education and care (Nikiforuk, 1993; Park, 1991). These reactions varied with environmental circumstances, individual and group beliefs, social and economic conditions, religious influences, legal attention, and medical knowledge (Covey, 1997; Shapiro, 1994; Treanor, 1993). A brief review of historical responses to and interactions with individuals with physical, health, or multiple disabilities supports the understanding of current perspectives and issues.

In ancient civilizations, the harshness of the physical environment shaped public and private reaction to individuals with disabilities. Individuals who could not contribute to group survival through their physical strength or ability to bear children would not be viewed as an asset. Appropriate medical care of people with severe disabilities would not have been possible in the absence of life-saving technology. Under such basic and harsh conditions, many individuals died in infancy or early childhood. Those who suffered illness or injury later in life fared little better. However, written artifacts revealed that attempts were made in ancient times to heal or ease the effects of illness (Lubkin, 1995).

During the Middle Ages, the evolving authority of religion in Western Europe gave rise to the concept of humanitarian care, a form of spiritual "treatment."

People with developmental disabilities might be perceived as "children of God" and afforded Church protection. Conversely, they were sometimes perceived as possessed by evil spirits (Scheerenberger, 1982) or as being the offspring of fairies, elves, or demons (Covey, 1997). While the developmentally disabled "child of God" was venerated (or at least tolerated) as a blessing, the individual whose behaviors were influenced by evil spirits was believed to have willfully chosen this path. The concept of internal ("God given," medically determined, etc.) versus external (environmental, social, etc.) factors as causative has a modern corollary in viewpoints of medical versus sociocultural bases for defining disability.

From the late 1600s to the present, developing medical inquiry and discovery in Western Europe supported treatment of physical, health, and multiple disabilities from a scientific perspective. Understanding of linkages between contagion and some diseases contributed to reforms in hospital care, although the notion persisted that some disabilities (e.g., epilepsy) were also contagious (Covey, 1997). Social reform resulting from political events also influenced community reactions toward disability. For example, the French Revolution instilled a sense of community responsibility that resulted in social reform and education. The efforts of such pioneers in special education as Louis Braille, Thomas Hopkins Gallaudet, Jean Marc Gaspard Itard, and Edouard Seguin resulted in specialized instructional and behavioral adaptations for people with disabilities (MacMillan & Hendrick, 1993). Along with the efforts of these individuals came the establishment of large residential institutions to provide training and protection. However, the original vision that residential institutions for specialized training would cure people of their disabilities was not fulfilled, and they degenerated into places of custodial care and little habilitation. Eventually, residential institutions became places to "protect" society from so-called "undesirables" (MacMillan & Hendrick, 1993).

Individuals with disabilities did not necessarily enjoy the benefits of industrialized commerce, the rise of large cities, and improved medical care. More rural, less industrial communities may have provided opportunities or niches for social participation and acceptance that were not available in organized residential institutions or highly technological societies.

Living situations for individuals with disabilities have moved away from segregated institutions toward independent living, pair living, and supported living in small, community-based residential facilities. The inclusion of students with disabilities in general education parallels this shift and reflects the acknowledgment that individuals with physical, health, or multiple disabilities contribute positively to their families and society. The perception that a disability represents a deficit that must be treated is being replaced with the notion that a disability is but one aspect of an individual. Self-determination is also gaining prominence in the lives of individuals with disabilities, largely due to the influence of the disability rights movement.

The Disability Rights Movement

In 1917, Congress passed legislation designed to address the vocational needs of disabled World War I veterans (Cimera, 2003). However, President Franklin Delano Roosevelt is credited with bringing disability issues into federal politics through promotion of his "New Deal." The 1935 Social Security Act provided funds for vocational rehabilitation for people with disabilities as well as retirement and insurance benefits (Treanor, 1993). However, Roosevelt was reluctant to incorporate his own disability (polio) into his public image. His behavior has been criticized by current scholars as an effort to promote the concept of "overcoming" disability rather than confronting its impact through political and social means (Treanor, 1993).

After World War II, disabled veterans added a powerful voice to demands for civil rights in vocational rehabilitation and physical access to jobs, services, and other life activities. Individuals with disabilities also gained from the *Brown v. Board of Education* decision in 1954. This decision, which prohibited racial segregation in education, provided the foundation for inclusion of students with disabilities in schools with peers without disabilities. A notable event in the 1960s was the passage of the Civil Rights Act of 1964, which provided the model for the Americans with Disabilities Act of 1990. Another important piece of legislation was the Architectural Barriers Act of 1968. This law was followed by the creation of the Architectural and Transportation Barriers Compliance Board, which established minimal guidelines for physical accessibility. Independent Living Centers were established during this time. Their services include advocacy programs, job training, and attendant care registries.

Treanor (1993) proposed an explanation for why the civil rights protest movements so prevalent during the 1960s did not involve people with disabilities. He suggested that the interests and energies of individuals with disabilities were most closely connected to specific groups such as the March of Dimes and United Cerebral Palsy. These groups, while providing a much-needed focus on specific disability areas, also had the effect of fragmenting the voice and political power of people with disabilities. The passage of the Rehabilitation Act of 1973, followed by many other disability-focused laws, unified issues of educational and civil rights of individuals with disabilities. Several of these laws will be discussed later in this chapter. The interested reader is referred to legal references at the end of this chapter and to Treanor (1993) and Shapiro (1994) for detailed accounts of the disability rights movement in the United States.

COMING TO TERMS WITH TERMINOLOGY

The definition of *disability* is not as simple as it initially appears (Smith, 2001). The very notion of what constitutes a disability shifts with differences in attitudes, beliefs, orientations, and culture (Smith, p. 7). As a result, many labels are used to describe individuals with physical, health, or multiple disabilities (e.g., "orthopedic impairment," "physical disability," "other health impairment"). The World Health Organization (WHO) has set forth international definitions of *impairment, disability,* and *handicap* that are useful benchmarks and that facilitate professional communication (1993). Federal definitions used to categorize individuals with physical, health, or multiple disabilities provide a framework for understanding nationally mandated educational service delivery and will be described later in this chapter.

Using labels to describe people may lead to stereotyping, false assumptions about capability, and promotion of negative images. Elimination of formal labeling, however, can also lead to miscommunication and support the development of informal (and even more negative) labels (e.g., "dummy," "spaz," "cripple"). The use of labels or categories to broadly describe persons with disabilities should be approached with great sensitivity; they should never be used in a manner that does not recognize the individual as a person first.

Impairment, Disability, Handicap

In 1980 WHO published an innovative classification scheme that remains a benchmark system for assessing and describing the consequences of disease in cause–effect relationships. WHO differentiated among the terms *impairment, disability,* and *handicap* in ways that distinguished them as organic, functional, and personal/social consequences of disease or injury (Fougeyrollas & Gray, 1998). Table 1–1 presents the WHO definitions.

Impairment indicates the presence of a specific condition that affects the individual at the organ or system level. For example, spina bifida is a birth defect that affects the musculoskeletal and central nervous systems, and cystic fibrosis is a disease of the exocrine glands. Impairment does not necessarily mean that the individual is sick or has a disease. For example, a person born without an arm (congenital limb deficiency) has an impairment of the musculoskeletal system but is not sick. In their relationship to each other, impairment and disability are hierarchical in nature. This means that *disability is related to levels of performance based on functional limitation* and occurs as a direct consequence of impairment. Using the previous example of the spina bifida, a disability related to this impairment would be loss of mobility and/or control of the bladder and bowels.

Disability may be temporary or permanent, static or progressive, reversible or irreversible (WHO, 1993, p. 28). Both impairment and disability are objective and observable terms (Badley, 1993; WHO, 1993). This means that they describe actual conditions and resulting loss of function that, by themselves, are not stigmatizing. However, *handicap represents the value attached to a condition that departs from the norm* (Badley, 1993). It presupposes impairment, but is less focused on attributes of individuals and more focused on circumstances that may create barriers to function. The label *handicap* can be applied by others to

TABLE 1–1
World Health Organization Classification for Impairment, Disability, and Handicap

Term	Definition
Impairment	Any loss or abnormality of psychological, physiological, or anatomical structure or function (p. 27)
Disability	Any restriction or lack (resulting from an impairment) of ability to perform an activity in the manner or within the range considered normal for a human being (p. 28)
Handicap	A disadvantage for a given individual, resulting from an impairment or a disability, that limits or prevents the fulfillment of a role that is normal (depending on age, sex, and social or cultural factors) for that individual (p. 29)

Note. From "Definitions of Impairment, Disability, and Handicap." *International Classification of Impairments, Disabilities, and Handicaps* (pp. 22–27). Geneva, Switzerland: World Health Organization. Copyright 1993 by the World Health Organization. Reprinted with permission.

a person with an impairment, or it can be self-imposed. When we think about impairments and disabilities, we think about *conditions*. When we think about handicaps, we think about *perceptions*. Impairments, disabilities, and handicaps may all result in barriers, but they must be approached in different ways.

In examining these terms, it is apparent that an individual can have an impairment without a disability or have a disability without a handicap. However, the individual cannot have a disability without an impairment. In addition, a person can be handicapped without having either an impairment or a disability. Some examples will provide clarification of these seemingly confusing statements. For example, a person with asthma has an impairment due to the physiological response of the lungs to a stimulus, causing them to constrict and the person to wheeze. If the asthma is well controlled and function is normal, there is no disability. There is a disability if the asthma is uncontrolled and occurs for days at a time, resulting in frequent absenteeism from school and poor grades. Asthma becomes a handicap if others view the person as unable to fully participate on sports teams due to the possibility of an asthma attack (whether justified or not), resulting in reduced opportunities for participation.

Handicaps may also be situational. For example, if the lights went out in a windowless room, a person who is blind could maneuver far better than any sighted person. The stigma of "handicap" would be eliminated for the individual with the impairment.

Debating the finer points among labels such as *impairment, disability,* and *handicap* may initially appear to be an intellectual exercise with little application in reality. However, these subtle differences among terms are magnified in practice. For example, *impairment* is a clinical term that suggests a medical approach, while *disability* suggests remediation and rehabilitation. *Handicap,* however, may be relative to the perceptions of others and can be modified as circumstances and environments change (remember the person who is blind in the dark room). Since the concept of "handicap" frequently arises from social values attached to a norm embraced by the individual or society, it is possible to change either the norm or the perception of what is "normal."

DisABILITY

Throughout the text, the term *disability* is used, suggesting that functional performance differences brought about by impairment have educational, social/emotional, and vocational impacts. The difficulty with any label is that it acquires meaning apart from its descriptive intent. Treanor (1993) noted that the prefix *dis* (as in *dis*ability), is from the Latin, meaning "not" or "unable" (pp. 190–191). The term *handicap* is thought to have originated in a wagering game involving the "cap-in-the-hand" and has a more contemporary meaning of assigning extra weight (a handicap) to better performers to "level the field" and enhance wagering. Treanor (1993) further speculated that the term *impairment* may derive from the Latin for "unequal" and refer specifically to a system of the body. While these labels have been used to varying extents, the term *disability* is used in this text because it is consistent with contemporary legal usage and refers to the functional effects of impairment. Throughout this text, the phrase "individuals with physical or multiple disabilities" is used to reflect person-first language, and to reinforce the belief that disability is but one aspect of individuality. As early as 1976, Bigge used person-first language for the first edition of this text in recognition of the importance of this concept.

Despite their usefulness for communication, public recognition, funding, and service delivery categorization, labels frequently become established as stereotyped images. Group stereotyping, which occurs when a phrase such as "the disabled" is used, should be avoided. Phrases such as "confined to a wheelchair," "cerebral palsy sufferer," and so forth are unacceptable because they portray persons as helpless victims. Acceptable substitute phrases would be "wheelchair user" and "a person with cerebral palsy." Terms such as *cripple* and *spastic,* which were once considered neutral descriptors, are stigmatizing and unacceptable for general usage. Teachers and other professionals must always practice appropriate etiquette in the areas of language, behavior, and attitudes.

While it may be necessary for service providers to use labels for communication, they must also look past labels to avoid underestimating the capabilities and potentials of individuals with physical, health, or multiple disabilities. The teacher should never describe individuals in a classroom by saying "I have two wheelchairs and one nonspeaker" or "There is a CP in my class." People are *never* equipment; neither are they the result of their disability.

Federal Categories and Definitions

In 1975, the enactment of Public Law (PL) 94–142 established 11 categories of exceptionality for the purpose of providing educational and related services. In 1990, passage of PL 101–476 added the categories of traumatic brain injury and autism. Prior to the enactment of PL 101–476, children with autism were often categorized as health impaired, based on the belief that their condition had a biochemical basis. Increasing survival of individuals with traumatic brain injury promoted creation of a separate category for this group. Orthopedic impairments, other health impairments, multiple disabilities, and traumatic brain injury are four federal categories whose members have needs addressed in this text. Although these categories have specific definitions, and a variety of conditions within the categories of orthopedic and health impairments will be described in Chapters 2, 3, and 4, readers need to remember that an individual may have a disability that crosses categories.

Orthopedic Impairments. The term *orthopedic impairments* is used to refer to "impairments caused by congenital anomaly (e.g., club foot, absence of some member, etc.), impairments caused by disease (e.g., poliomyelitis, bone tuberculosis, etc.), and impairments from other causes (e.g., cerebral palsy, amputations, and fractures or burns that cause contractures" (34 C.F.R. § 300.7[c][8], 1999). This definition hints at the variety of impairments that are classified as orthopedic. Individuals who have orthopedic impairments may have functional limitations of movement and/or sensation and may also have health impairments. Most orthopedic impairments are stable, some are progressive, and a few are terminal.

In this text, the authors use the term *physical* instead of *orthopedic* for several reasons. First, the term *physical* is more inclusive of a broader number of categories, including neuromotor impairments, degenerative diseases, and orthopedic and musculoskeletal disorders (Heller, Alberto, Forney, & Schwartzman, 1996). These categories are either specific to a system of the body (e.g., central nervous system/neuromotor) or process (e.g., disease). Second, the federal definition of "orthopedic impairments" contains a subcategory labeled "other," which includes examples as divergent and unrelated as cerebral palsy, burns, and amputation. Further examination of the federal definition reveals that "absence of some body part" (i.e., limb loss) is listed as a disability of congenital origin, while "amputation" is specifically identified in the "other" category. This overlap has resulted from using noncomparable categories that are based on time of disablement (congenital) versus miscellaneous categories (other).

Other Health Impairments. *Other health impairment* means

> having limited strength, vitality, or alertness, including a heightened alertness to environmental stimuli, that results in limited alertness with respect to the educational environment, that (i) Is due to chronic or acute

> health problems such as asthma, attention deficit or attention deficit hyperactivity disorder, diabetes, epilepsy, a heart condition, hemophilia, lead poisoning, leukemia, nephritis, rheumatic fever, and sickle cell anemia: and (ii) Adversely affects a child's educational performance. (34 C. F. R. § 300.7[c][9][i][ii], 1999)

As with orthopedic impairments, there are a variety of health impairments, which can be stable, progressive, or terminal in nature. This category was recently amended to include attention deficit disorder and attention deficit hyperactivity disorder.

Multiple Disabilities. Persons with multiple disabilities have more than one impairment "the combination of which causes such severe educational needs that they cannot be accommodated in special education programs solely for one of the impairments. The term does not include deaf-blindness" (34 C.F.R. § 300.7[c][7], 1999). The effects of multiple disabilities are not the result of adding one impairment to another; they interact with each other.

The interaction effects of multiple disabilities can be illustrated through examples. Individuals who have cerebral palsy and mental retardation have motor disabilities associated with their orthopedic impairment, which can compromise their ability to physically perform activities of daily living such as meal preparation. Adaptations to accommodate the physical disability might include using a computer to develop a grocery list and providing directions for others to prepare the meal. However, deficits in memory and sequencing that may accompany mental retardation could hinder the ability to conceptualize the steps in preparing a meal. In this situation, individuals may need training to select from a prepared list of food items and be able to partially participate in meal preparation. Understanding the difference between motor (physical) and discrimination (cognitive) difficulties is critical to planning an appropriate educational response for individuals with multiple disabilities. Chapter 4 is devoted to the topic of cerebral palsy as a forum for describing the impact of multiple disabilities.

Traumatic Brain Injury. A *traumatic brain injury* (TBI) is defined as

> an acquired injury to the brain caused by an external physical force, resulting in total or partial functional disability or psychosocial impairment, or both, that adversely affects a child's educational performance. The term applies to open or closed head injuries resulting in impairments in one or more areas, such as cognition; language; memory; attention; reasoning; abstract thinking; judgment; problem-solving; sensory, perceptual, and motor abilities; psychosocial behavior; physical functions; information processing; and speech. The term does not apply to brain injuries that are congenital or degenerative, or to brain injuries induced by birth trauma. (34 C.F.R. § 300.7[c][12], 1999)

This definition clearly reflects variability in the nature and degree of impairment in persons who have sustained a TBI. In 1990, TBI was recognized as a separate disability category in PL 101-476, highlighting the requirement to provide appropriate services for this population of individuals.

LEGAL SUPPORTS AND MANDATES

Since the early 1970s, numerous laws have been passed by the United States Congress to protect the civil and educational rights of individuals with disabilities. These federal laws are referred to as *Public Laws,* since they apply to the "public," or population of the United States. Any reference to a public law begins with the letters *PL,* followed by the session of Congress in which the law was passed, followed by a number that indicates the chronological order in which the law was passed. For example, PL 94-142 was the 142nd piece of legislation passed by the 94th Congress. Public laws are placed into codes and regulations that assist in their interpretation. State laws are then enacted to comply with federal legislation, and local education agencies use both federal and state laws to develop educational policy.

The major aspects of several federal laws will be presented in chronological order from the time of their passage. Lengthy discussion of legislation is beyond the scope of this chapter, but readers may want to gain a deeper understanding of federal legislation from the text and Web-based references at the end of this chapter or by consulting the governmental documents sections of their public or university libraries. Terminology within legal documents has changed over time, reflecting greater sensitivity to issues of language and labeling. Therefore, earlier legislation used terms such as "handicapped individuals," while more recent legislation uses phrases such as "individuals with disabilities."

PL 93–112: The Rehabilitation Act of 1973

In 1973, Congress passed PL 93–112, also known as the Rehabilitation Act of 1973. Notable in this legislation was Section 504, which stated that

> no otherwise qualified handicapped individual in the United States . . . shall, solely by reasons of . . . handicap, be excluded from the participation in, be denied the benefits of, or be subjected to discrimination under any program or activity receiving Federal financial assistance. (1, United States Code Congressional and Administrative News, Sec. 504, p. 454)

This statement means that all recipients of financial assistance from the federal government (such as state education agencies, schools, colleges and universities, libraries, vocational schools, and state rehabilitation agencies) are subject to Section 504 provisions. In practice, passage of PL 93–112 means that programs must provide opportunities to achieve equal results through accommodation and accessibility. For individuals with physical, health, or multiple disabilities, this might mean removal of architectural barriers, provision of information in accessible formats (such as computer-based math problems, use of augmentative communication, or low-tech academic materials adaptations), provision of accessible test and other evaluation materials, a shortened day to accommodate fatigue, and many other possibilities.

In 1986 and 1992, PL 93–112 was amended to include assistive technology as part of vocational rehabilitation plans. PL 93–112 and its amendments represent important civil rights legislation for people with disabilities in schools, because it reinforces nondiscrimination and supports equal access through adaptation of curriculum and assessment and through appropriate accommodation.

PL 94–142: The Education for All Handicapped Children Act of 1975

Readers may be acquainted with PL 94–142, the Education for All Handicapped Children Act of 1975. This landmark piece of educational legislation was enacted to ensure free, appropriate, public education for individuals with disabilities (then called "handicapped individuals"). PL 94–142 mandated the individualized education program (IEP) for every student who was found to be eligible for special education. The IEP identified educational services for eligible children and young adults (ages 3–21) and provided a system for procedural safeguards for children and their parents in identification, assessment, and educational placement. This law also mandated the provision of "related services," which included physical and occupational therapy, adaptive physical education, and speech/language therapy. Related services were critical to achieving maximum benefit from educational experiences.

PL 100–407: Technology-Related Assistance for Individuals with Disabilities Act of 1988

As Radabaugh (1988) noted, "For Americans without disabilities, technology makes things easier. For Americans with disabilities, technology makes things possible" (p. a.1). Individuals with disabilities received significant support through passage of PL 100–407, the Technology-Related Assistance for Individuals with Disabilities Act (Tech Act) of 1988, and its amendments in 1994 (PL 103–218). These laws have their roots in the concept of reasonable accommodation embodied by Section 504 of PL 93–112, the Americans with Disabilities Act (ADA; PL 101–336), and in those aspects of the Individuals with Disabilities Education Act (IDEA; PL 101–476) and its amendments of 1997 (PL 105–17) that mandate special education, related services, and placements in least restrictive environments.

While the Tech Act does not provide funds for direct purchase of assistive technology equipment for persons with disabilities, it requires states to work toward laws, regulations, policies, practices, or organizational structures that promote consumer-responsive programs, increase access to assistive technology devices, and empower individuals with disabilities to achieve greater independence and integration into the community workforce. Passage of the Tech Act acknowledged the powerful role that assistive technology can play in maximizing independence of persons with disabilities. Attention will be paid to the role of assistive technology in discussions of adaptations of teaching materials throughout this text. Assistive technology is pivotal for enhancing the lives of individuals with physical or multiple disabilities.

PL 101–336: Americans with Disabilities Act of 1990

Congress enacted PL 101–336 in 1990. This piece of civil rights legislation carried the mandates of PL 93–112 further by addressing discrimination in private sector employment, housing, public accommodations, education, transportation, communication, recreation, institutionalization, health services, voting, and access to public services. People protected by the ADA were those with impairments that substantially limited them in one or more major life activities. All provisions of the ADA were implemented by 1996.

As an antidiscrimination and equal opportunity law, the ADA has far-reaching implications. Among these are the mandate for reasonable accommodation and provision of public/private sector services. For school-age individuals, reasonable accommodation must be provided for students to benefit from education. This may mean modification of equipment or school buildings so that students can physically go where other students go and engage in the same (or similar) activities. For example, installing a ramp to an auditorium stage means that a student in a wheelchair can sit with peers during graduation exercises rather than being placed in front of the stage on the auditorium floor. In the workplace, employers must provide "reasonable accommodation" for disabilities of their employees, unless such accommodation results in undue hardship. Employers cannot inquire whether someone has a disability or use job selection criteria to screen out a person with a disability unless the criteria are job related and necessary. For students with disabilities, this law makes jobs more attainable.

While terms such as *reasonable accommodation* sound unnecessarily vague, they provide wide latitude for interpretation in different situations, which is a positive and flexible aspect of the law. Requiring that services be provided in both public and private sectors moved the ADA beyond PL 93–112 and means that even private businesses (such as restaurants, hotels, etc.) must be accessible. Transportation accommodation, another aspect of the ADA, enhances the ability of persons with disabilities to enjoy all aspects of community participation. For persons with disabilities, the ADA means they can benefit from all aspects of community life that are enjoyed by anyone else.

PL 101–392: Carl D. Perkins Vocational and Applied Technology Education Act of 1990

The Carl D. Perkins Vocational and Applied Technology Education Act of 1990 (PL 101–392) provides secondary schools and community colleges with funds to strengthen vocational/technical education. It applies to individuals with disabilities and those who are educationally or economically disadvantaged, those who have limited English proficiency, those who participate in programs designed to eliminate sex bias, and/or those who are in correctional institutions. Through funding provided by this act, school districts can:

- Purchase occupationally relevant equipment and vocational curricula;
- Purchase materials for learning labs;
- Support curriculum development and modification;
- Provide career counseling and guidance and supplemental services for special populations;
- Support academic-vocational integration;
- Hire vocational staff;
- Provide remedial classes; and
- Expand their technical preparation programs.

Students with physical or multiple disabilities who are involved in programs funded under this act receive training that assists them to compete in a society that is becoming more technologically advanced.

PL 101–476: Individuals with Disabilities Education Act (IDEA) of 1990

In 1990, an amendment to PL 94–142 changed its title to the Individuals with Disabilities Education Act, or IDEA. IDEA was amended to include traumatic brain injury and autism as separate federal disability categories. Rehabilitation counseling and social work services were added as "related services." The label *handicapped* was replaced with the term *disability*. Moreover, the authors of IDEA recognized the importance of person-first language by using the phrase "individuals with disabilities" instead of "disabled individuals."

PL 105–17: The IDEA Amendments of 1997

In 1997, IDEA was amended by PL 105–17 (sometimes called the IDEA Amendments of 1997). While some of its amendments resulted in significant policy changes, others represented subtle shifts to fine-tune law that has been in place since PL 94–142 was passed in 1975. Under the IDEA Amendments of 1997, children with disabilities must now be included in district-wide assessments (with accommodations as necessary), and alternative forms of assessment are to be developed for children who cannot participate in standardized assessment. States and local education agencies have the responsibility to develop alternative assessments.

One significant change brought about by PL 105–17 is its interpretation of the least restrictive environment (LRE). The IDEA Amendments of 1997 require a statement of how the disability impedes performance in general education and an explanation of the extent to which the child will *not* be participating in general education. This change in focus strongly supports education in general education unless an appropriate alternative educational placement is justified. In addition, general education teachers are to be included on the IEP team.

The implications of the IDEA Amendments of 1997 are too numerous to discuss in detail. The role of special education teachers in supporting the education of students with special needs in the least restrictive environment will continue to expand into areas of consultation and collaboration with general education teachers. In addition, special education teachers must provide direct instruction based on individual need, regardless of the educational setting. The impact of learning, behavior, language and communication, and equipment/technology needs of students with disabilities in all school programs heightens the need for professionals with specific expertise.

Many laws have been enacted by Congress to protect the civil rights and enhance the educational experiences of individuals with disabilities. Legislation can be conceptualized as a framework that provides support and direction for specific outcomes. However, a framework does not always address all concerns of individuals with specific disabilities. The following section identifies representative issues that are especially important for individuals with physical, health, or multiple disabilities.

CRITICAL ISSUES FOR INDIVIDUALS WITH PHYSICAL, HEALTH, OR MULTIPLE DISABILITIES

The issues of alike/different, visible/invisible, acute/chronic, service intensity, and educational goals and expected outcomes are especially important for individuals with physical, health, or multiple disabilities. Each of these issues will be explored briefly, followed by its implications for teachers. It is important to remember that not all aspects of each issue will apply to every individual, nor can all important issues be addressed in this chapter.

Alike and Different

In most respects, people with disabilities have many of the same interests and life goals as people who do not have disabilities. These goals include education, personal relationships, satisfying careers, and community contributions. However, the presence of disability may have an impact on these goals, necessitating adjustment and adaptation for their successful attainment. Smith (2001) noted that the overemphasis on "sameness" when applied to educational and social needs of persons with disabilities may obscure the supports that are necessary for them to achieve best outcomes (p. 7). Teachers who work with individuals with physical or multiple disabilities need to recognize and appreciate similarities and differences, which will allow them to experience the *person* without either applying stereotypes or ignoring vital individual needs.

Visible and Invisible

Disability may be obvious or invisible to the observer. When disability is apparent to others, either through some aspect of the body or through use of equipment, the individual with a disability is confronted with the meaning others attach to the disability. The visibility of physical disability necessitates acknowledgment, as well as adjustment to changes in social interaction patterns related to acknowledgment of difference. In his classic work on disability and social identity, Goffman (1963) noted that disability visibility had a profound impact on social encounters. Individuals with visible disabilities have no choice regarding concealment and must make immediate decisions about responding to reactions of others.

Visible disability may generate inappropriate perceptions and reactions by others. For example, individuals with cerebral palsy who may not be able to walk or to use speech for communication may be treated as chronologically younger or intellectually less able by persons who do not know them well. Another factor to consider is disability relevance. While the disability itself may have no relevance to a particular social encounter, it may become the focus of perception simply because it is *there.* The individual with a visible disability is therefore frequently confronted with managing the reactions of others in social situations.

Goffman (1963) noted that a different series of personal decisions and social encounters occur when a disability is invisible. For example, a person who has epilepsy may choose not to reveal this condition in a casual conversation, either because this disclosure is irrelevant to the interaction or because the individual does not wish to be exposed to potential explanations and possible rejection by acquaintances. In the event of a seizure, however, every participant will be confronted with the condition in an immediate fashion and with no preparation. It is true that knowledge of a disability condition may result in appropriate easing of expectations (restricted physical activity for a person with asthma, for example). However, if the condition remains invisible (e.g., an individual with a cardiac condition does not wish to disclose this condition), the individual may be subjected to unhealthful expectations ("You will run a lap around the track or receive a demerit") or risk rejection by peers ("You are a slacker"). The individual with an invisible disability is challenged by decisions about whether to reveal information that may be held against him or her or not disclose and be subjected to inappropriate expectations.

Teachers who work with individuals with physical or multiple disabilities must not only be sensitive to the dynamics of visibility/invisibility, they must also actively assist students to develop effective social interaction strategies. Effective strategies for managing stress and coping with potentially negative social interactions should be part of a specialized curriculum plan for individuals with physical or multiple disabilities.

Acute and Chronic

When most people think of illness, they conceptualize a period of discomfort and certain symptoms, such as nausea, loss of appetite, gastrointestinal upset, rash, and fever. These conditions are acute. After a period of time (and sometimes with medication or hospitalization), the illness dissipates and the person recovers. Although some acute illnesses can be very serious, they are characterized by resolution in some form. Some conditions do not resolve. These conditions are referred to as *chronic.*

By its definition, chronic illness is not curable. Toombs, Barnard, and Carson (1995) stated that chronic illness is "not simply a discrete episode in the course of a life narrative but rather a permanent feature of that narrative. To live with chronic illness and disability is to live a certain kind of life" (p. xi). The impact of chronic illness extends to family, educational experiences, social adjustment, career functioning, and overall quality of life in ways that are profound and lasting. Persons with chronic illness must cope with issues related to the impact of the illness, which may include altered growth and development, managing the trajectory of the illness, illness roles, stigma, altered mobility, pain, social isolation, body image, compliance with medical regimens, coping with fear and grief, receiving care, and sexuality (Lubkin, 1995).

Chronic illness includes conditions such as asthma, diabetes, congenital heart disease, epilepsy, cystic fibrosis, sickle cell anemia, cancer, HIV infection, rheumatoid arthritis, and kidney disease (Edwards & Davis, 1997). It is estimated that 10% to 15% of children under the age of 16 have chronic conditions (Weiland, Pless, & Roghmann, 1992). In 1991, the World Health Organization estimated that 8 to 10 million persons have been infected with HIV (WHO, 1992). Clearly, chronic illness poses major concerns at individual, community, and national levels.

Teachers will encounter the challenges of chronic illness experienced by individuals with physical, health, or multiple disabilities. They must be alert to changes in physical condition that may signal the need for medical treatment. They may need to alter the intensity or amount of coursework to match the fatigue caused by a chronic condition, medication, or medical regimen. Close communication with parents is a necessity. Students may become so ill that they die, at home or even at school. Teachers must be able to support other students, school personnel, and themselves in the grief and coping that follow death. Parallel to all the physical, psychological, and social alterations created by chronic illness, the teacher must strive to provide a learning environment that is as typical and predictable as possible.

Appropriate Accommodation

Federal law mandates that reasonable accommodation be provided for individuals with physical, health, or multiple disabilities in order for them to gain access to those aspects of their lives that may be altered by disability. Accommodations may need to be provided on a long-term or permanent basis.

Assistive Technology. Assistive technology is a critical form of accommodation. The definition of *assistive technology* from the Tech Acts of 1988 and 1994 was incorporated into IDEA as "any item, piece of equipment, or product system, whether acquired commercially off the shelf, modified, or customized, that is used to increase, maintain, or improve functional capabilities of a child with a disability" (20 U.S.C., 1401 § 602 [1]). Assistive technology encompasses many areas, including positioning and mobility, augmentative communication, visual aids, computer access, physical education, leisure, play, self-care, and environmental control.

Male (2003) proposed a shift from accommodation for individuals to applying principles of universal design that apply to all individuals. Originally a concept from the field of architecture, universal design, when applied to teaching, is based on four differences in thinking:

1. Students with disabilities fall along a continuum of learner differences, like other students do.
2. Teachers can and do make adjustments for all students, not just those with disabilities.
3. Curricular materials should be as varied and diverse as the needs in the classroom.
4. Rather than adjust students to learn a specific curriculum, the curriculum should be flexible to accommodate a range of student differences (Male, 2003, p. 21).

While accommodation in the form of assistive technology makes significant improvements for individuals with physical or multiple disabilities, Malouf (2001) warned that "introducing technology into education gives the impression of innovation and effectiveness for no other reason than technology is involved" (p. 1). This means that technology used to enhance the lives of individuals with disabilities must be carefully tailored to meet individual needs and not applied in a "one size fits all" manner. Teachers who provide services to students with physical or multiple disabilities must therefore develop expertise in assistive technology that extends beyond more traditional pedagogy.

When teachers examine all the areas addressed by assistive technology, they will be tempted to wonder whether assistive technology isn't really the specialty of a related-service provider such as a physical or occupational therapist, rehabilitation engineer, adaptive physical education specialist, or speech/language specialist. While the contributions of these professionals are crucial to successful outcomes for individuals with disabilities, it is the teacher with specialized expertise who provides the instructional link that focuses assistive technology on classroom applications. Because of its importance to meeting the needs of individuals with physical or multiple disabilities, assistive technology will be addressed in a separate chapter in this text, and examples of assistive technology will be infused throughout all text chapters.

Illness Accommodation. One area that requires programmatic sensitivity is illness accommodation. Many situations contribute to decreased school participation, including student absenteeism, pain management, fatigue, and the necessity of following medical regimens during school hours. Although virtually all students occasionally miss school due to illness or doctor appointments, students with physical, health, or multiple disabilities may have multiple and/or prolonged absences that result in the need for special accommodation to maintain school performance. Some conditions are associated with increased pain and/or fatigue. If their disability is invisible, students may be perceived as healthy even when they feel bad or experience fatigue. For example, a student with a severe cardiac condition may appear healthy but experience chest pain and exhaustion after even mild exercise. Reduced performance related to illness, pain, and/or fatigue may result in teacher perception that students are inattentive to activities at school. Finally, some students must follow very strict medical treatments that require absence from class. An example would be the student with diabetes who must test for blood glucose levels and then administer insulin. Another example would be the student with paralysis who must be excused from class to receive bladder catheterization.

Accommodations for absenteeism, pain, fatigue, and other situations that result in reduced performance include modifying homework assignments, reformulating school absence and grading policies, scheduling rest periods, rescheduling academic instruction or allowing a peer to take notes while a student is out of class, and providing home/hospital instruction.

Service Intensity and Personal Independence Issues

Individuals with physical or multiple disabilities receive education and related services from many persons. While the roles of educators, therapists, nurses, and others frequently overlap, services should be provided or supervised by specifically assigned and trained professionals. Consistency of assistance provides important reassurance to students that the persons who assist them are familiar with physical routines and will not harm them. Any reader who has experienced prolonged hospitalization will appreciate the efficiency and security afforded by consistent assistance from a trusted individual.

Peer Assistance. Occasionally a recommendation is made that a classroom peer provide assistance to a student with a disability. While peers can be very helpful in areas such as notetaking, obtaining materials, and other classroom activities, using peers to feed a friend, push a wheelchair, or provide instruction should be undertaken only after specific training and under adult guidance and for a specified, limited time period. Accidents can happen quickly and leave persistant feelings of guilt and blame. Even under carefully controlled circumstances, peer assistance is not always advisable. When peers are used in the role of assistants, their social interaction changes and may limit friendships available to the student with a disability. In Figure 1–1, a student receives assistance from a peer during an art project. Although she cannot squeeze the glue bottle independently, she can give directions. Taking charge of learning situations is an important self-advocacy tool.

FIGURE 1–1
Self-advocacy is supported when students take charge of learning situations

In the area of self-care, individuals with physical or multiple disabilities may require services beyond developmental and social expectations. For example, assistance may be required in the bathroom or for dressing. The need for intensive and personal assistance means that the person who is disabled must take intellectual and emotional control of situations in which physical control is lacking. This dynamic extends into areas of life management, including experiences such as managing personal assistants, negotiating medical treatment, and so on (Heller, Forney, Alberto, & Schwartzman, 2000). For example, a child may be unable to pull up his or her pants but can tell an assistant when and how this task should be accomplished. If it is not necessary for the assistant to take control (as would be the case with very young children), allowing the child to make decisions supports positive emotional growth.

The issues of service intensity and personal independence have important implications for teachers. First, teachers must acquire collaboration skills with personnel representing many disciplines. They must frequently coordinate their educational schedules with others who provide service and assistance. Scheduling must be accomplished with minimal disruption for students and their families and without compromising classroom learning experiences. Second, whoever is assigned to assist students with self-care must do so with the greatest respect for personal dignity and privacy. When physical care must be provided on a level that is more typical for very young children (e.g., wiping the nose, assisting with toilet paper, feeding) it is important not to respond to the recipient as immature.

As stated earlier, individuals who require personal assistance should receive it from adults specifically assigned and trained for that purpose and upon the request of the individual needing assistance. Besides the need for continuity of assistance and maintenance of dignity, receiving physical assistance and being handled by many different adults can break down boundaries of appropriate and inappropriate handling and place the student at risk for physical injury or sexual exploitation.

Educational Goals and Expected Outcomes

Individuals with physical or multiple disabilities may be intellectually gifted or academically typical. They may have intellectual or learning disabilities. They may have a combination of disabilities (and also, perhaps, be gifted). They may demonstrate average physical stamina or varying degrees of fatigue. They may be totally independent in gross and fine motor function while performing tasks, require some physical assistance, or have such severe motor and communication problems that they require support to achieve academic outcomes and the most basic self-care skills. Educational goals for students with physical, health, or multiple disabilities should correspond to their potential and not any preconceptions based on appearance. Teaching and learning environments that are responsive to the range of needs of these students afford them the greatest potential for intellectual and social growth.

TEACHING AND LEARNING ENVIRONMENTS

Teachers who serve individuals with physical or multiple disabilities provide support in a variety of educational systems and must possess specific knowledge and skills. In addition, their roles continue to evolve to include increased collaboration and consultation within education and related disciplines. Finally, they must function as a resource beyond the field of teaching for families and professionals. Contemporary teachers do more than instruct; they are learners, leaders, and advocates.

Educational services for students with physical or multiple disabilities traditionally were aligned with a medical and deficit model, which emphasized physical care and attention to specialized health needs. This position was reflected in the locations for their educational service delivery, including hospitals, convalescent homes, and residential facilities for "delicate" children with conditions such as diabetes, poliomyelitis, or pre-tuberculosis (Best, Bigge, & Sirvis, 1990). Segregation of students in separate classes and schools was justified on the basis of centralized therapy and related services, architectural accessibility, and social acceptance by a peer group with disabilities.

Current educational service delivery trends for students with physical or multiple disabilities have broadened to include an array of placement options. Educational service delivery decisions should be made after consideration of the unique needs of students and may involve more than one placement at a time (e.g., general education classes plus specific support in special class or with an assistant). Special education is *what* and *how* teaching occurs, not *where* teaching occurs. Sometimes the impact of a disability dictates educational placement, as happens in hospitalization or home instruction. Systems for instruction must represent the least restrictive and best educational environment for the specific student in relation to his or her unique needs, abilities, and goals.

Education Service Delivery Systems

Most students with physical or health disabilities are educated in **general education class** (inclusive) settings with supplementary aids and services as appropriate. (Best, Hemsley, & Best, 1986) (see Figure 1–2). General education teachers may be supported through

FIGURE 1–2
Three friends enjoy a computer activity in their general education class

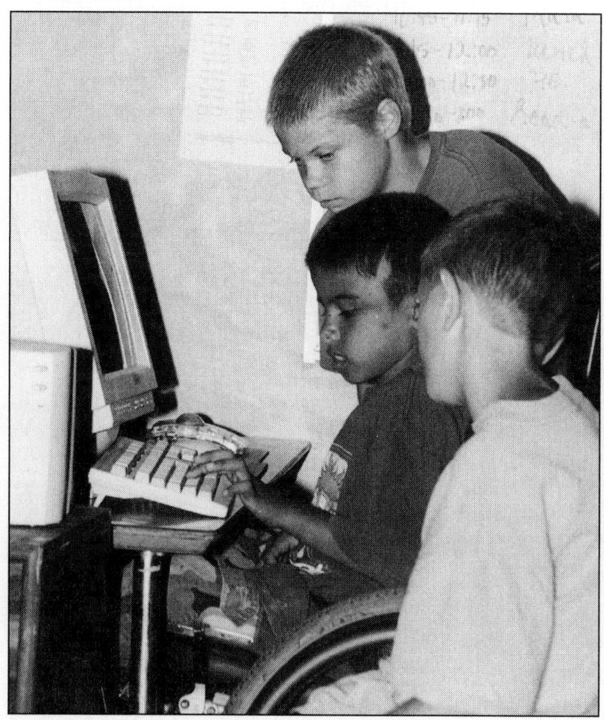

collaborative and consultive services from a special education teacher in order to implement a variety of specific instructional strategies. Students may receive direct services from an **itinerant special education instructor,** who goes to different schools and who provides direct instruction to students in the general education classroom. In a third model, the special education teacher may provide **resource services** to students with physical, health, or multiple disabilities, either in the general education classroom ("clustering"), or by providing intensive educational support in a separate area ("pull-out") (see Figure 1–3).

Some students require an educational environment outside of general education classes. They may be taught in **special day classes**, which are usually located on general education campuses with provisions for inclusion with same-age peers. In some cases, students are educated on **special sites** that are separate from general education campuses. Even if these options are selected, every effort should be made to ensure interaction with nondisabled peers.

With the exception of special sites, the models just described are part of the general education service system. One unique aspect of educating students with physical, health, or multiple disabilities is the existence of options for instruction that are not typical in general education. Students with acute or chronic illnesses may receive instruction in **hospital-based programs**. Hospital-based educators provide direct services in classrooms located in the hospital. For students whose physical conditions makes classroom attendance impossible, teachers work with students at their bedsides. Hospital instruction may require that universal precautions be used, including the use of physical barriers such as surgical gowns, gloves, and masks. If children are in the process of bone marrow transplantation or other procedures that suppress their immune systems, the teacher must "scrub" before providing services, and educational materials must be sterilized before use. Figure 1–4 describes the experiences of a teacher in a large metropolitan hospital.

Students who are recuperating from recent surgery, or whose condition prohibits school attendance, may be educated through special **itinerancy services at home**. Home teachers are itinerants with a student caseload who maintain contact with students and their assigned classroom teachers to foster successful educational progress and reintegration into the general education program after their health stabilizes.

Instructional systems for students unable to attend a classroom-based program have been changed by the rapid advances in technology and the availability of alternative learning environments. One alternative to home instruction is **distance education**. The teacher makes contact with several students through a school site-based telephone system, e-mail, or the Internet. This model eliminates the travel time and one-to-one requirements of home teaching while retaining the advantage of multi-student service and direct, immediate contact. The use of e-mail and the Internet (including school Web postings) adds print output to visual interaction. Students must have corresponding systems to send and receive e-mail, receive and download Internet information, and be down-linked for distance education services. Systems for individual students may be provided by the family, school district, communication company, community agency, or a combination of resources.

Finally, some models of educational service include a primary emphasis on the **community as an**

FIGURE 1–3
This teacher tries a variety of strategies to stabilize materials so her student can be more independent

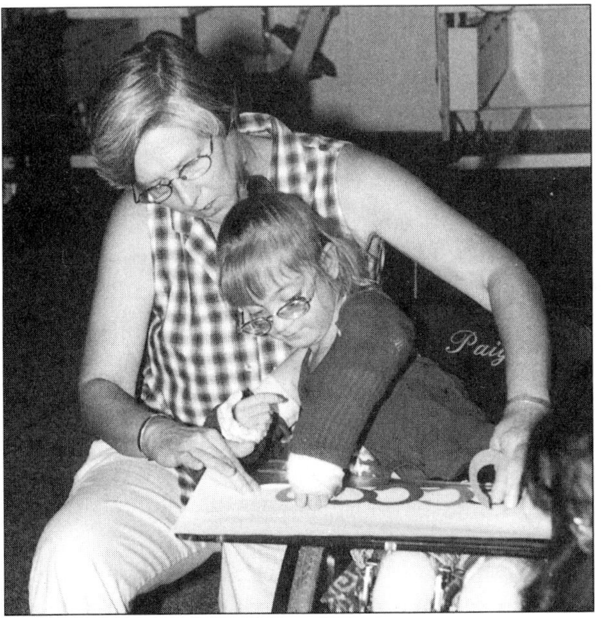

FIGURE 1–4
Thoughts on hospital teaching: Where everything else seems more important than learning

Hospital teaching fascinates many observers. I can work on a one-to-one basis with my kids, choose my own books and often the classes I teach, develop a close relationship with every student, and fulfill many of their individual needs. I have time to build rapport with families and have access to full medical records. This all leads to quality teaching where individualization, task analysis, and a humanistic approach can flourish.

And then there's the flip side to all this merriment. These kids are sick. That's why they are hospitalized. They often don't feel good and cannot work during the allotted time set aside for them. They may be on strong medication and feel drowsy. Often they are not in the room when you arrive—books, puzzles, laptop in hand. Where are they? They're having a bone scan or an X-ray, perhaps they're getting a new cast, or an MRI, or an EEG. A common phrase I hear is "Come back in a few hours."

Flexibility, empathy, and sensitivity to individual needs are the hallmarks of hospital teaching. If a teacher has an issue with "being in control," hospital teaching is not the place to be. When working in a hospital, the teacher is always in the way. In I walk, materials in hand. I may have to go hunting for something to sit on, seat myself on the side opposite the blood pressure cuff, and watch out for the IV tubing. If the child is in isolation, a mask, gloves, and gown may be in order. Finally, I'm nestled next to the bed with all my equipment and we begin the lesson. All of a sudden a telephone rings, the nurse comes in, the social worker arrives, and the child is transported to whirlpool. "Come back later, Teacher."

The essentials for the traveling classroom vary with the students. If the child is able to write, pens, pencils, markers, paper, and a clipboard are necessities. I cannot leave textbooks with students in case they are discharged and take them home, never to be recovered. Younger and more developmentally delayed children benefit from manipulatives. This can present a transportation problem, and disinfectant spray must be used on toys and books to make this system safe. I try to plan all lessons in conjunction with the child's general education teacher.

In the sad event of a child's passing away, we call the student's home school and communicate with staff personally. I have stopped asking "Why?" and take the attitude that if I can bring a little relief and sunshine to these kids while helping them learn, my role is complete.

As you can see, my milieu is vastly different from the typical classroom setting. Bulletin boards, yard duty, parent conferences, and group lessons do not exist for the bedside hospital teacher. The core knowledge and values for the teaching profession remain the same. Commitment to educational excellence, sensitivity to the needs of individual students, and interpersonal skills assist me to be the best teacher to the children I serve.

Note. Adapted from "Thoughts on Hospital Teaching: Where Everything Else Seems More Important Than Learning," by E. Raikhy, 1998, *DPHD Newsletter*, pp. 2, 7. Reprinted with permission.

educational setting. For many students with physical or multiple disabilities, the career and vocational aspects of curricula, daily living skills, and leisure pursuits would most appropriately occur in the community. In Figure 1–5, a young man practices mobility skills in a community environment that is close to his home.

Educational placement decisions should *always* be based on the unique needs of individual students. It is inappropriate to presuppose that specific service delivery options are linked to disability severity. For instance, one cannot assume that a student with multiple disabilities must be educated in a special day class or separate site. Neither is it appropriate to assume that all students with health impairments are best served in general education settings. Some students are educated in more than one service placement at a time, and placement should change as student need changes. Family members play an integral part in making education placement decisions.

Challenges to Effective Service Delivery

Even after issues of educational service delivery are successfully addressed, many challenges exist for providing effective education. These may be broadly conceptualized as architectural, tangible, philosophical, and training-based. These barriers are not mutually exclusive, and they can be interactive. For example, renovating bathroom facilities to meet architectural accommodation requirements is a positive step toward physical integration, but it does not address the need for appropriately trained personnel who provide physical assistance to use adapted facilities. Furthermore, if such adaptations are perceived as an encroachment on

FIGURE 1–5
Many important skills can be acquired in community environments

available bathroom space (as happens when two toilet stalls are combined to provide one wider space or the faculty restroom is used for particular students because it is more accessible), fully adapted bathroom facilities and trained personnel still do not address resentment and possible backlash against integration attempts.

1. *Architectural barriers.* Architectural and other tangible barriers may be easy to remove if they are obvious and correctable. Installing a ramp, lowering a drinking fountain, and widening a doorway are simple examples. While federal and state regulatory codes and uniform accessibility requirements provide guidance, and legislation such as the Americans with Disabilities Act adds legal reinforcement, identifying an architectural accommodation is only an initial step.

2. *Tangible barriers. Lack of adequate equipment and lack of service provision* are examples of tangible barriers that are logistical. Even when all parties have agreed on materials and services, significant time may elapse before materials arrive or repairs occur. Stories abound in which a wheelchair or other equipment had been ordered but was finally delivered after it was outgrown or a wheelchair had been broken for a year before agency funds were made available for its repair.

Failure to schedule and deliver services when and where they are most needed results in ineffective education. Consider the following situations:

- A general education teacher takes students for an out-of-classroom excursion and fails to leave a message for related-services or special education personnel who were scheduled to work with a student during that time.
- A special education teacher has pulled out students from general education classrooms at the teacher's convenience and ignored the goals of the general education program.
- A student who is fully included and uses a wheelchair for mobility misses an educational excursion because no one remembers to schedule a bus with a lift.
- A teacher has scheduled appointments with parents and others who then failed to honor those appointments.

The consequences of these experiences are wasted time and effort, abandonment of a collaborative education effort, and reduced learning time for students.

Material portability is another tangible barrier to successful school experiences. Augmentative communication devices, mobility devices, therapy equipment, adapted classroom furniture, and other equipment may consume considerable classroom space. In addition, if the student moves between classrooms, such equipment must be moved or duplicated. Some equipment is transported from home to school and back again on a daily basis. Equipment must be maintained in proper working order, be moved carefully, and be available where and when it is needed. Preplanning and ongoing communication are key elements in successful use of adapted materials.

Finally, individuals themselves must move through their environments. Students who use wheelchairs may be seated closest to the exit door to decrease class disruption if they must exit the class frequently for health procedures. However, placement at the back of the class should not be a default situation because it is easier for the teacher and does not interfere with furniture arrangement.

Accessibility must be provided to all areas of the classroom and the larger school environment. Materials must be placed at a height to facilitate independent access and manipulation. Extra space may be necessary for specialized equipment. If the student moves among classrooms, sufficient passing time must be allowed to avoid tardiness. Failure to provide opportunities for independent movement fosters a sense of failure and helplessness.

3. *Competing philosophies.* Competing philosophies regarding effective educational service delivery can present another barrier. If strong opinions exist about issues such as appropriate educational placement, curricula, discipline, and so on, the immediate educational, social, and vocational needs of the student may be sacrificed to ideology. Development and maintenance of open communication, willingness to come together to listen and compromise, and mutual appreciation of differences form the basis for making effective changes.

Individuals with disabilities require support and services from families and personnel whose tasks and job requirements overlap, but whose goals for the individual may be in conflict. For example, a child may be receiving feeding instruction from an occupational therapist who has established a goal of transition to varied textures and finger feeding. The parent may wish for the child to remain on pureed foods to ensure adequate nutritional intake and ease of feeding. At school, the child is primarily fed by an instructional assistant, who receives conflicting input from both sources. Inevitably, issues of "turf" arise in multi-person systems and must be resolved through respectful communication and the ability of those involved to look beyond their particular professional roles and activities. Often the teacher must act as a case manager in bringing together all parties for mutual problem solving.

4. *Appropriate training.* After architectural and philosophical barriers are addressed, there remains the critical need for well-trained instructional personnel. While it is impossible in this text to fully describe the training requirements of all personnel who provide services to individuals with physical, health, or multiple disabilities, teacher competencies merit detailed attention.

TEACHER COMPETENCIES AND EVOLVING ROLES

Teachers who instruct individuals with physical, health, or multiple disabilities must possess specific competencies that encompass instruction, physical management of students and the educational environment, health maintenance, use of assistive technology and augmentative communication, and curricular adaptation (Council for Exceptional Children, 1998; Heller, Fredrick, Dykes, Best, & Cohen, 1999; Heller & Swinehart-Jones, 2003). In a recent national competency survey, special education teachers who lacked concentrations or disability-specific credentials to teach in the physical/health disabilities area reported that they did not feel well trained or comfortable in providing direct services (Heller et al., 1999). This uncertainty regarding training was shared by special education directors and university personnel. The fact that students with orthopedic disabilities, health impairments, and multiple disabilities are increasingly served in general education programs places greater pressure on teachers who do not have specialized certification to meet the unique educational needs of this population (U.S. Department of Education, 2000).

The authors contend that evolution toward more inclusive educational environments, school attendance of children with severe and complex health needs, and the rising prevalence of students with physical disabilities support the importance of teachers' having specific competencies for meeting the needs of students with physical, health, or multiple disabilities (Heller et al., 1998; Heller & Swinehart-Jones, 2003). These knowledge and skill areas are related to direct instruction and competencies that allow teachers to fulfill many roles in the field of special education.

Knowledge and Skills

With a growing trend toward less disability-specific teacher certification in special education and increasing placement of individuals with physical, health, or multiple disabilities into general education classrooms, specialist teachers report pressure from their colleagues to respond to questions about curriculum adaptation, assistive technology, postsecondary supports and services, and development of skills for self-determination. In 1995, the Council for Exceptional Children (CEC) published *What Every Special Educator Must Know: The International Standards for the Preparation and Certification of Special Education Teachers.* This document included a common core of essential knowledge and skills for special education teachers, plus specialized knowledge and skills related to disability categories. CEC identifies three broad categories within which the Standards are distributed: Field Experiences/Clinical Practice, Assessment System, and Special Education Content.

In 2003, Heller and Swinehart-Jones grouped the specialized knowledge and skills in the area of physical and health disabilities from the CEC Special Education Content Standards into the following categories:

- Physical and health monitoring and maintaining a safe, healthy environment;
- Adapted and specialized assessment and evaluation;
- Modifications and assistive technology;
- Specialized instructional strategies;
- Disability-specific core curricula;
- Setting the affective and learning environment.

Many accommodations require the use of *assistive technology,* a broad term that encompasses both devices and specialized services (Osborne & Russo, 2003). Readers are referred to Heller and Swinehart-Jones (2003) for numerous examples within each of these knowledge and skill categories.

Professional Roles

Teachers of individuals with physical or multiple disabilities must be prepared to fulfill several educational and service roles. Not only do they provide direct instruction, they frequently collaborate with related-services personnel in the implementation of goals and objectives that are derived from their assessment. An increasingly important role is consultation to teachers in general education, where specialist teachers are perceived as the necessary link for specialized instruction, resources, and information.

Direct Instruction and Collaborative/Consultant Roles. This text devotes several chapters to adaptations and instructional strategies for teaching academic subject matter and specialized curricula to students with physical or multiple disabilities. In addition to providing direct instruction to students, teachers must be prepared to provide other direct and indirect services. For example, the specialist teacher might be asked to adapt assessments and provide information about making accommodations and/or modifications regarding the student's learning environment. Figure 1–6 highlights questions that teachers with specialized training in physical or multiple disabilities might be asked by other personnel.

Collaboration and transdisciplinary service provision are necessary for teachers who serve individuals

FIGURE 1–6
Questions to ask the consultant/teacher specializing in physical, health, or multiple disabilities

Consultant/Teacher in Physical/Health Disabilities: This consultant/teacher has specialized knowledge in meeting the educational needs of students with physical and health disabilities. Some areas of expertise include: curriculum modification and design; assessment and evaluation adaptations; instructional techniques and modifications; arranging and adapting the learning environment; use of assistive technology and augmentative communication systems; instructing students in physical health care procedures; implications and implementation of the student's individual health plan; and interpreting, relaying, and implementing information from medical and related service reports.

GENERAL QUESTIONS REGARDING THE AREA OF PHYSICAL/HEALTH DISABILITIES

What is the current educational definition of students with physical or health disabilities?

What are the criteria for a student to be considered to have a physical or health disability?

What are the service delivery options for students with physical or health disabilities?

What are the laws and policies related to providing specialized health care in educational settings?

What are the roles and responsibilities of all the team members?

What additional resources and information are available to address the needs of students with physical/health disabilities?

(Continued)

FIGURE 1–6
(Continued)

QUESTIONS REGARDING THE CHARACTERISTICS OF THE PHYSICAL/HEALTH DISABILITY

What do I need to know about the student's physical/health condition?
Is the physical/health condition progressive or terminal?
Are there possible emergency situations that can occur? What do I need to watch for and do?
Are there any activity or diet restrictions?
Are there any medication side effects or treatment effects that will affect the student's learning?
Will the student fatigue easily and need rest breaks?
Will the student's condition predispose him or her to frequent absences?
Will the student need assistance to do certain activities or require assistive devices?
Does the student have any additional disabilities (e.g., cognitive, sensory)?

QUESTIONS REGARDING THE IMPACT OF THE PHYSICAL/HEALTH DISABILITY ON LEARNING

Has the physical/health condition impacted the student's quantity and quality of life experiences?
Has the physical/health disability affected concept development?
How does the physical/health condition impact the student's learning?
How can I enhance the student's learning?
What types of technology and assistive devices does the student require to enhance learning?

QUESTIONS REGARDING STUDENT EVALUATIONS

What pertinent information do I need to know from the medical evaluation(s) and related service evaluation(s)?
Could the student's physical/health disability interfere with the accuracy of certain educational and psychological evaluations?
Does the student require an alternate form of response (e.g., AAC device, pointing, eye gaze)?
What are the following specialized assessments and their implications for instruction:
  adaptive technology assessment?
  augmentative/alternative communication assessment?
  movement and mobility assessment?

QUESTIONS REGARDING THE LEARNING ENVIRONMENT

How does the learning environment need to be adapted to accommodate the needs and abilities of students with physical or health disabilities?
How do I promote a positive environment for the student with a physical/health disability?
What are the implications of the individual health care plan and how is it integrated into daily programming?
How are the activities of the related service personnel coordinated to maximize direct instruction time?
What are the optimal positioning options for the student and the material?
How is the adaptive equipment used to facilitate positioning, mobility, communication, and learning?
How do I maintain universal precautions in the classroom?
How do I address the needs of a student with a chronic illness or terminal illness?

QUESTIONS REGARDING CURRICULUM CONTENT AND INSTRUCTIONAL STRATEGIES

What type of curriculum is being provided for the student (e.g., identical, parallel, lower grade level, functional)?
Will the student's curriculum include expanded content areas in addition to the regular curriculum?
Does the student require modifications to instruction, material, or curriculum?
What instructional techniques will be most helpful to this student?
What adaptations and assistive devices are needed for the student to benefit from the lesson?
How can the instructional lesson be adapted to minimize physical exertion?
How can the instructional lesson be adapted to allow the student to actively participate?
How will the student ask questions?

QUESTIONS REGARDING ASSIGNMENTS AND TESTS

How do I modify tests for the student?
How do I modify assignments for the student?
How do I grade the student's work?

Note. From "Questions to Ask the Consultant/Teacher Specializing in Physical and Health Disabilities," by K. W. Heller, in *Including Learners with Special Needs Related to Hearing, Physical/Health, or Vision in All Classrooms,* by M. R. Byrne, S. R. Easterbrooks, A. R. Powers, M. K. Dykes, K. W. Heller, S. J. Best, C. Holbrook, R. C. Davidson, and A. L. Com. Presentation at the conference of the Council for Exceptional Children, Salt Lake City, Utah, April 1997. Reprinted with permission.

with physical or multiple disabilities. Figure 1–7 shows students receiving services from a therapist, a school nurse, and an adapted physical education specialist. These services may be provided by professionals who work at the school site where students receive their services or who travel to several different school sites. In some cases, the students may travel to another school site to receive therapy on an "outpatient" basis.

FIGURE 1–7
Children receive related services from (a) a therapist, (b) a school nurse, and (c) an adapted physical education specialist

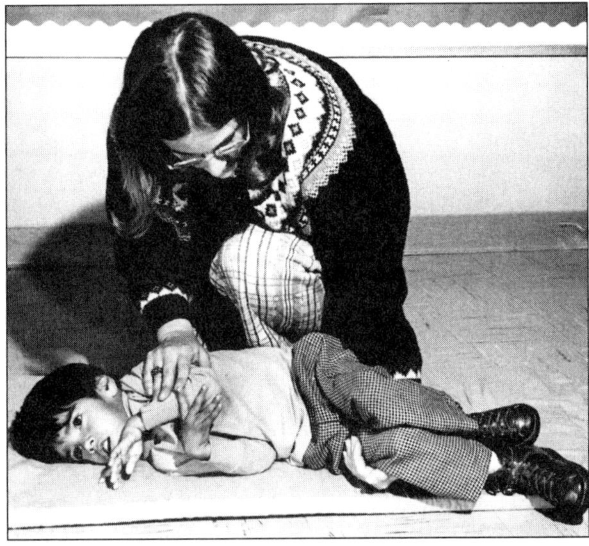
(a)

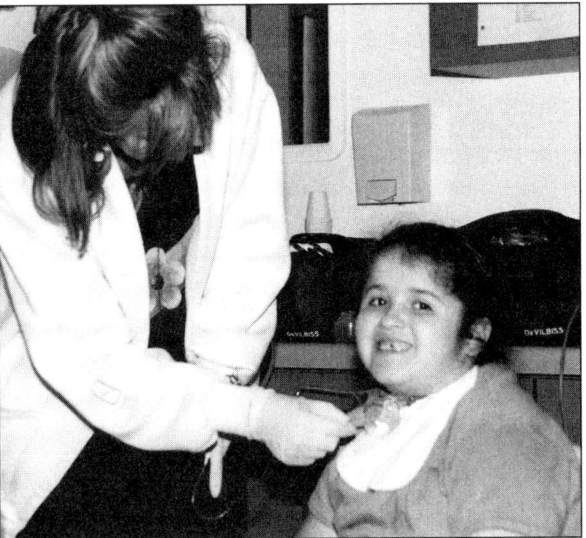
(b)

(c)

Bigge and Stump (1999) have provided an extensive description of personnel who typically provide services for students with disabilities in educational and community settings (see Figure 1–8). Descriptions of several of these professionals (e.g., occupational therapist, physical therapist, augmentative and alternative communication specialist, inclusion specialist) reveal the complementary nature of their roles. Therefore, it is important to compare the roles of related-services personnel with that of educators who serve individuals with physical or multiple disabilities.

Therapists cannot take the place of professional educators, even though they assist in equipment modification and training that increases functional skills in educational settings. Conversely, educators cannot provide direct therapy services, although they frequently follow through on therapeutic management regimens established by occupational therapists and physical therapists. The emphasis on collaboration is particularly critical for meeting support in all areas of functioning for individuals with physical, health, or multiple disabilities.

The personnel descriptions listed in Figure 1–8 are not presented in order of their importance, but to illustrate the intensity of service needs. Certain service providers may at some times play a greater role than others, depending on student needs. Figure 1–9 identifies key questions specific to the needs of individuals

FIGURE 1–8
Related services personnel in education systems

- **Special Education Teacher.** An educator who is qualified to design and provide instruction to students with disabilities and "has met . . . approved or recognized certification—that applies to the area in which he or she is providing special education" (34 C.F.R. §300.15).
- **Resource Room Teacher.** An educator who provides resource room instruction for individuals with disabilities by either pulling students out of a general education class for one or more hours/periods a day to receive this support in a special education resource classroom, or by working in general education classrooms; may also serve as collaborator with general education teachers for arranging modifications in general education classrooms.
- **Itinerant Teacher.** "A teacher or resource consultant who travels between schools or homes to teach or [to] provide instructional materials" (Esterson & Bluth, 1987, p. 148) to students with disabilities.
- **Speech-Language Pathologist.** "A professional who evaluates and develops programs for individuals with speech or language problems" (Anderson, Chitwood, & Hayden, 1990, p. 220).
- **Occupational Therapist.** A professional who delivers "activities focusing on fine motor skills and perceptual abilities that assist in improving physical, social, psychological, and/or other intellectual development; e.g., rolling a ball, finger painting" (Anderson, Chitwood, & Hayden, 1990, p. 218).
- **Augmentative and Alternative Communication Specialist.** A specialist who is qualified to meet the needs of individuals who have communication difficulties and who will benefit from special educators and speech-language pathologists providing services that prepare them to use augmentations and alternatives to speaking and writing.
- **Physical Therapist.** A professional "primarily concerned with preventing or minimizing [motor] disability, relieving pain, improving sensorimotor function, and assisting an individual to his or her greatest physical potential following injury, disease, loss of body part, or congenital disability" (Esterson & Bluth, 1987, p. 79).
- **Audiologist.** "A nonmedical specialist who measures hearing levels and evaluates hearing defects" (Esterson & Bluth, 1987, p. 147).
- **Educational Psychologist.** A professional with expertise in test administration and interpretation; may also have expertise in counseling and working with students in crisis situations.
- **District Special Education Administrator or Coordinator.** A professional who oversees special education programs in a school district; may assist with assessment, attend IEP/ITP meetings, and provide teacher support.
- **Diagnostician.** A professional with expertise in test administration and interpretation; the term may be used interchangeably with *educational psychologist,* although an educational psychologist's role generally requires skills beyond assessment and its interpretation.
- **Inclusion Specialist/Inclusion Facilitator.** A professional prepared in a special education field (e.g., learning disabilities) who manages programs of students participating in inclusion programs; responsibilities range from consulting with general education teachers to team planning and co-teaching with general education teachers in inclusion settings.
- **Educational Therapist.** A professional who works with individuals who exhibit learning problems and is also skilled in formal and informal assessment procedures, synthesizing assessment findings, developing and implementing remedial programs and strategies for addressing social and emotional aspects of learning problems. The educational therapist also serves as a case manager, and builds and supports communication links among the individual, family, school, and other professionals (Association of Educational Therapists, 1982).
- **Orientation and Mobility Specialist.** A specialist who prepares individuals who are visually impaired or blind to "orient themselves to their environments and move about independently" (Hazekamp & Huebner, 1989, p. 113).
- **Adaptive Physical Educator.** A person who designs and carries out "a physical education program that has been modified to meet the specific needs" of students with disabilities (Anderson, Chitwood, & Hayden, 1990, p. 211).
- **Social Worker.** "In an educational context, a school social worker provides a link between school personnel and the families of . . . children [with disabilities] through activities such as individual pupil evaluation, parent interviews, and contact with community support services" (Anderson, Chitwood, & Hayden, 1990, p. 220).
- **Counselor[s].** "Qualified social workers, psychologists, guidance counselors, or other qualified personnel [who work to] . . . generally . . . improve a child's behavioral adjustment and control skills in order to make the child more available for participation in the educational program" (Esterson & Bluth, 1987, p. 27).
- **Rehabilitation Counselor.** An accredited counselor who assists individuals with disabilities in making transitions from school to work.

Note. From *Curriculum, Assessment, and Instruction for Students with Disabilities,* 1st edition, by J. L. Bigge and C. S. Stump. © 1999. Reprinted with permission of Wadsworth Publishing, a division of Thomson Learning. Fax 800 730–2215.

FIGURE 1–9
Questions to ask select members of the educational team for students with physical, health, or multiple disabilities

CONSULTANT/TEACHER IN PHYSICAL AND HEALTH DISABILITIES

This consultant/teacher has specialized knowledge in meeting the educational needs of students with physical and health disabilities. (See earlier description).

PHYSICAL THERAPIST (PT)

The physical therapists provides essential information regarding the optimal physical functioning in instructional activities, especially as they relate to gross motor skills and mobility.

Types of questions to ask the physical therapist:

Is the student properly positioned for this activity?
Is the adaptive positioning equipment being used correctly?
How do we safely help the student to move from area to area?
Are we using correct lifting and transferring techniques?
Are the splints/orthosis being properly applied?

OCCUPATIONAL THERAPIST (OT)

The occupational therapist provides essential information regarding physical functioning in instructional activities, particularly as they relate to fine motor skills, visual-motor skills, and self-care activities.

Types of questions to ask the occupational therapist:

How can we improve the student's handwriting?
What is the best placement of this material?
How can we best promote dressing skills?
What feeding techniques are most appropriate to encourage eating and feeding?
Are the hand splints being properly applied?
What is the most appropriate adaptive equipment for this activity?

SPEECH AND LANGUAGE PATHOLOGIST (SLP)

The SLP provides essential information in speech and language. Depending upon the SLP's background, the SLP may also have expertise in augmentative communication and feeding skills.

Types of questions to ask the speech and language pathologist:

What forms of communication does the student have?
Will the student's speech improve?
What do I do if I cannot understand what the student is saying?
Are alternative forms of communication being used?
How do you program the augmentative communication device for instruction?

NURSE

The nurse provides vital information for the educational team concerning students' physical and medical conditions and their effects on the students' educational programs. The nurse can also provide information on specialized health procedures.

Types of questions to ask the nurse:

What type of physical/health condition does the student have?
What do I need to know about the student's physical/health condition?
What are the side effects of the medications the student is taking?
What is the individualized health plan for the student?
What health care procedures are being done at school?

PARENT AND CHILD

The parent(s) and child are critical members of the educational team who provide important information regarding history, goals, and objectives.

Types of questions to ask the parent and/or child:

What do we need to know about your child's (or your) condition?
How has your child (or how have you) liked school so far?
What has worked well for your child (or you) in school?
What are some of the problems found by your child (or you) at school?
How do you think these problems could be eliminated?
What goals are most important for your child (or you) to learn?
Does the physical or health disability interfere with doing homework?
Are there typically a lot of absences due to the physical/health disability?

Note. From "Questions to Ask the Consultant/Teacher Specializing in Physical and Health Disabilities," by K. W. Heller, in *Including Learners with Special Needs Related to Hearing, Physical/Health, or Vision in All Classrooms,* by M. R. Byrne, S. R. Easterbrooks, A. R. Powers, M. K. Dykes, K. W. Heller, S. J. Best, C. Holbrook, R. C. Davidson, and A. L. Com. Presentation at the conference of the Council for Exceptional Children, Salt Lake City, Utah, April 1997. Reprinted with permission.

with physical or multiple disabilities that general and specialist teachers could ask select members of the educational team.

Resources. Teachers who serve individuals with physical, health, or multiple disabilities must possess critical skills in direct service and interaction with other personnel. However, they must recognize that they cannot reasonably expect to master all aspects of education and support. The gap between one's current knowledge base and needed information can be met through resourceful exploration and lifelong learning. Being resourceful means that teachers need to think beyond the classroom, and educate themselves and others through information related to disability, parent resources, education, community agencies, and other services. Teachers have many opportunities to gain additional expertise through resources provided by expanding technology. One of the most useful resources available to educators is the Internet. At the conclusion of every chapter, several specific organizations will be profiled in the section titled "Focus on the Net." However, teachers and others should use caution when gathering information from Web sites, because not all Web-based material is accurate. It is best to consult sites that are current, valid, and professionally supervised, such as those from recognized health agencies or government-sponsored institutions.

SUMMARY AND CONCLUSION

In this chapter, readers were acquainted with perceptions of individuals with physical, health, or multiple disabilities and gained knowledge related to important terminology, legal mandates, and major issues. Readers were provided with an overview of educational service delivery systems and teacher competencies and roles specific to working with individuals with physical, health, or multiple disabilities. An important goal of this chapter was to show how disability may have an impact on function and on the accomplishment of individual activities but is not the defining characteristic of any individual.

The current emphasis on inclusive education, the expanding knowledge base in assistive technology (including augmentative and alternative communication), the importance of specific teacher competence and disability-specific certification at the national, state, and local levels, and the range and complexity of instructional strategies and related services provision for this population have changed how teachers serve individuals with physical, health, or multiple disabilities. Teachers who work with these students must be able to modify curricula and use specialized strategies, apply knowledge of disability conditions to educational outcomes, work collaboratively with a range of personnel, and provide resources for family and service providers.

QUESTIONS FOR DISCUSSION

1. What are some examples that illustrate the difference between an impairment, a disability, and a handicap?
2. How do you feel that the image of individuals with physical, health, or multiple disabilities is changing? Do you feel that discrimination still exists? Discuss your position in terms of issues of "alike and different," "visible and invisible," and "acute and chronic."
3. Design a public service commercial for television that would clarify the following labels: *impairment, disability,* and *handicap.* Explain why it is important for members of the general public to understand the subtle effects of labels.
4. Some individuals are served under the Individuals with Disabilities Education Act, while others are served under Section 504 of the Rehabilitation Act of 1973. Discuss the difference between these two laws, providing examples of when one person may be served under one versus the other. Incorporate into your response the meaning of *reasonable accommodation.*
5. Discuss the various educational delivery systems available to students with physical, health, or multiple disabilities. Include in your discussion the advantages and disadvantages of each system and the need to select the least restrictive environment.

6. Provide examples of competing philosophies that affect special education services and how they might be resolved.
7. Discuss the key competencies and skills that a teacher qualified to teach students with physical/health disabilities should have and how these skills differentiate this teacher from other teachers and therapists.

FOCUS ON THE NET

The National Information Center for Children and Youth with Disabilities (NICHCY)
http://www.nichcy.org/index.html

NICHCY is the national information and referral center for families, educators, and other professionals interested in the needs of children (birth to age 22) with disabilities and special health care needs. A variety of services and information is available online, including information related to specific disabilities, early intervention, special education and related services, IEPs, and family issues. In addition, NICHCY publishes a variety of disability-related materials. Many resources are now available in Spanish, and all are also available online. Perhaps one of NICHCY's most important services is their availability to personally answer questions regarding children with disabilities, either online or through e-mail.

The Council for Exceptional Children (CEC)
http://www.cec.sped.org

CEC was established in 1922 and remains the largest international professional organization for individuals with exceptional needs. CEC contains divisions that address special interest categories, including the Division for Physical and Health Disabilities (DPHD). CEC sponsors national and regional conferences and workshops for parents, teachers, and related-service providers that highlight the latest in instruction, technology, policy, and other services for individuals with exceptional needs. CEC members receive three different publications several times a year: a monthly newsletter entitled *CEC Today,* a practice-based publication entitled *Teaching Exceptional Children,* and *Exceptional Children,* a research-based publication.

Educational Resources Information Center (ERIC)
http://www.aspensys.com/eric/

ERIC is a national information system designed to provide users with ready access to an extensive body of education-related literature. Established in 1966, ERIC is supported by the U.S. Department of Education, Office of Educational Research and Improvement, and the National Library of Education.

National Clearinghouse for Professions in Special Education (NCPSE)
http://www.specialedcareers.org

NCPSE, affiliated with the Council for Exceptional Children, provides materials regarding career information, supply-and-demand data, university program listings, financial aid resources, licensure/certification standards, job search, and other information for individuals who are interested in a career in special education and related services. Teachers and administrators will appreciate NCPSE's materials related to teacher recruitment and retention. A special feature of this organization is that it provides resources for educators with disabilities.

Office of Special Education Programs (OSEP)
http://www.ed.gov/offices/OSERS/OSEP/osep.html

OSEP currently funds over 1,200 projects in 18 programs authorized by federal legislation, including "formula grant" programs that provide funding to states on the basis of child count or census data and "discretionary" programs that award funds on a competitive basis to state and local agencies, universities, and other appropriate organizations and entities.

Office of Special Education and Rehabilitative Services (OSERS)
http://www.ed.gov/offices/OSERS/

OSERS supports programs that assist in educating children with special needs, provides for the rehabilitation of youth and adults with disabilities, and supports research to improve their lives.

United States Department of Education
http://www.ed.gov/

Become familiar with your state department of education and its involvement in special education issues.

REFERENCES

Americans with Disabilities Act of 1990, PL 101-336, 42 U.S.C.A. § 12101 *et seq.* (West 1993).

Badley, E. M. (1993). An introduction to the concepts and classifications of the international classification of impairments, disabilities, and handicaps. *Disability and Rehabilitation, 15*(4), 161–178.

Best, S. J., Bigge, J. L., & Sirvis, B. (1990). Physical and health impairments. In N. G. Haring & L. McCormick (Eds.), *Exceptional children and youth: An introduction to special education* (pp. 284–324). Upper Saddle River, NJ: Merrill/Prentice Hall.

Best, S. J., Hemsley, R. E., & Best, G. A. (1986). *P.L. 94-142: Characteristics of children with physical disabilities and implications for service delivery.* Unpublished manuscript.

Bigge, J. L. (1976). *Teaching individuals with physical and multiple disabilities.* Upper Saddle River, NJ: Merrill/Prentice Hall.

Bigge, J. L., Stump, C. S., with Spagna, M. E., & Silberman, R. K. (1999). *Curriculum, assessment, and instruction for students with disabilities.* Belmont, CA: Wadsworth.

Carl D. Perkins Vocational and Applied Technology Education Act of 1990, PL 101–392, U.S.C.A.

Cimera, R. E. (2003). *Preparing children with disabilities for life.* Lanham, MD: Scarecrow Press.

Council for Exceptional Children. (1995). *What every special educator should know: The international standards for the preparation and certification of special education teachers.* Reston, VA: Author.

Council for Exceptional Children. (1998). *What every special educator should know: The international standards for the preparation and licensure of special educators* (3rd ed.). Reston, VA: Author.

Covey, H. C. (1997). *Social perception of people with disabilities in history.* Springfield, IL: Charles C. Thomas.

Education for All Handicapped Children Act of 1975, PL 94-142, 20 U.S.C.A. 1401 *et seq.* (West 1990).

Edwards, M., & Davis, H. (Eds.). (1997). *Counselling children with chronic medical conditions.* Baltimore: Brookes.

Fougeyrollas, P., & Gray, D. B. (1998). Classification systems, environmental factors, and social change. In D. B. Gray, L. A. Quatrano, & M. L. Lieberman (Eds.), *Designing and using assistive technology: The human perspective* (pp. 13–29). Baltimore: Brookes.

Goffman, E. (1963). *Stigma: Notes on the management of spoiled identity.* New York: Simon & Schuster.

Heller, K. W., Alberto, P. A., Forney, P. E., & Schwartzman, M. N. (1996). *Understanding physical, sensory, and health impairments.* Pacific Grove, CA: Brooks/Cole.

Heller, K. W., Forney, P. E., Alberto, P. A., & Schwartzman, M. N. (2000). *Meeting physical and health needs of children with disabilities: Teaching student participation and management.* Belmont, CA: Wadsworth.

Heller, K. W., Fredrick, L. D., Dykes, M. K., Best, S. J., & Cohen, E. L. (1999). Competencies in physical/health disabilities: A national perspective. *Exceptional Children, 65,* 219–234.

Heller, K. W., & Swinehart-Jones, D. (2003). Supporting the educational needs of students with orthopedic impairments. *Physical Disabilities: Education and Related Services, 22*(1), 3–25.

Individuals with Disabilities Education Act (IDEA) of 1990, PL 101–476, 20 U.S.C.A. § 1400 *et seq.* (West 1998).

Individuals with Disabilities Education Act (IDEA) of 1997, PL 105–17, 20 U.S.C.A. § 1400 *et seq.* (West 1998).

Lubkin, I. M. (1995). *Chronic illness: Impact and interventions* (3rd ed.). Boston: Jones and Bartlett.

MacMillan, D. L., & Hendrick, I. (1993). Evolution and legacy. In J. I. Goodlad & T. C. Lovitt (Eds.), *Integrating general and special education* (pp. 23–48). New York: Merrill.

Male, M. (2003). *Technology for inclusion: Meeting the special needs of all students.* Boston: Allyn & Bacon.

Malouf, D. B. (2001). Special education technology and the field of dreams. In J. Woodward and L. Cuban (Eds.), *Technology, curriculum, and program development: Adapting schools to meet the needs of students with disabilities* (pp. 1–2). Thousand Oaks, CA: Corwin Press.

Nikiforuk, A. (1993). *The fourth horseman: A short history of epidemics, plagues, famine and other scourges.* New York: M. Evans.

Osborne, A. G. & Russo, C. J. (2003). *Special education and the law: A guide for practitioners.* Thousand Oaks, CA: Corwin Press.

Park, K. (1991). Healing the poor: Hospitals and medical assistance in Renaissance Florence. In J. Barry & C. Jones (Eds.), *Medicine and charity before the welfare state* (pp. 26–45). London: Routledge.

Radabaugh. (1988). *Controls and choices for students with multiple disabilities: Assistive technology series.* San Diego City Schools Integrated Life Skills Program (p. a.1). San Diego, CA: Author.

Rehabilitation Act of 1973, PL 93–112, 29 U.S.C.A. § 701 *et seq.* (West 1999).

Scheer, J., & Groce, N. (1988). Impairment as a human constant: Cross-cultural and historical perspectives on variation. *Journal of Social Issues, 44*(1), 23–37.

Scheerenberger, R. C. (1982). Treatment from ancient times to the present. In P. T. Cegelka & H. J. Prehm (Eds.), *Mental retardation: From categories to people* (pp. 44–75). Upper Saddle River, NJ: Merrill/Prentice Hall.

Shapiro, J. P. (1994). *No pity: People with disabilities forging a new civil rights movement.* Chicago: Times Books.

Smith, D. D. (2001). *Introduction to special education: Teaching in an age of opportunity* (5th ed.). Boston: Allyn & Bacon.

Technology-Related Assistance for Individuals with Disabilities Act Amendments of 1994, PL 103–218, 29 U.S.C.A. § 2201 *et seq.* (West, 1999).

Technology-Related Assistance for Individuals with Disabilities Act of 1988, PL 100–407, 29 U.S.C.A. § 2201 *et seq.* (West, 1999).

Toombs, S. K., Barnard, D., & Carson, R. A. (Eds.). (1995). *Chronic illness: From experience to policy.* Bloomington: Indiana University Press.

Treanor, R. B. (1993). *We overcame: The story of civil rights for disabled people.* Falls Church, VA: Regal Direct.

U.S. Department of Education (2000). To assure the free appropriate public education of all children with disabilities. *21st annual report to Congress on the implementation of the Individuals with Disabilities Education Act.* Washington, DC: U.S. Government Printing Office.

Weiland, S., Pless, I., & Roghmann, K. (1992). Chronic illness and mental health problems in pediatric practice. Results of a survey of primary care providers. *Pediatrics, 89,* 445–449.

World Health Organization (WHO). (1992). *World health statistics annual 1991.* Geneva, Switzerland: Author.

World Health Organization (WHO). (1993). *International classification of impairments, disabilities, and handicaps.* (ICIDH). Geneva, Switzerland: Author.

Physical Disabilities

SHERWOOD J. BEST

CHAPTER 2

This chapter briefly describes several frequently encountered physical disabilities, any of which can affect the educational performance of students. Readers learned in Chapter 1 that physical disabilities may include neuromotor impairments, degenerative diseases, and orthopedic and musculoskeletal disorders (Heller, Alberto, Forney, & Schwartzman, 1996). Physical disabilities can be either congenital or acquired, and may be accompanied by other conditions. **Congenital disabilities** refer to those conditions that are present at birth, regardless of their cause. **Acquired disabilities** are not genetic or due to a birth defect, but are caused by illness or accident. Readers also learned that physical disabilities may be either **acute** or **chronic.**

Several specific physical disabilities are profiled in this chapter to provide basic information for educators and others about the nature of the disability and its impact. First, the physical disability itself will be defined and described. Second, medical conditions associated with the primary disability will be discussed. Third, readers will be provided with information regarding current medical and therapeutic treatments related to each physical disability. Readers will learn about the impact of each disability for physical, cognitive, and psychosocial development, accompanied by strategies for enhancing developmental outcomes. Finally, implications of each disability will be discussed for education, personal autonomy, and career/adult function.

The information in this chapter was especially chosen to introduce the most basic elements considered to be crucial to readers' understanding of certain physical disabilities, but more importantly to assist readers to understand the ways in which disability may have an impact on development, education, and pursuit of life goals. It is not the intent of the author to provide

KNOWLEDGE AND SKILLS

After you have read this chapter, you will be able to:

1. **Describe several physical disabilities that are caused by neuromotor impairments, degenerative diseases, and/or orthopedic and musculoskeletal disorders.**
2. **Describe secondary or associated conditions that frequently accompany some physical disabilities.**
3. **Appreciate the impact of different physical disabilities on physical and psychosocial development.**
4. **Understand the implications of different physical disabilities for education, personal autonomy, and adult/career outcomes.**
5. **Incorporate strategies for moderating the effects of physical disabilities into teaching activities and social interactions.**

either exhaustive descriptions or short but inadequate overviews of many physical disabilities. Further in-depth study about these and other conditions resulting in physical disability is critical for teachers and other service providers. Readers are referred to references at the conclusion of this chapter for more detailed information about specific conditions. Readers can also benefit by contacting disability-specific agencies, foundations, and information resources. Finally, the proliferation of information available on the Internet enables the exploration of current disability-specific resources. Readers are encouraged to explore a variety of resources to become informed in greater depth regarding specific physical disabilities.

*

NEUROMOTOR IMPAIRMENTS

Neuromotor impairments include conditions that originate in the central nervous system (i.e., the brain and spinal cord) and that affect the nerves and muscles (Heller et al., 1996). Neuromotor impairments include cerebral palsy, seizure disorders, neural tube defects, and traumatic brain injury. This chapter addresses neural tube defects and traumatic brain injury in depth. Chapter 4 provides an in-depth discussion of cerebral palsy and seizure disorders. Since cerebral palsy is usually accompanied by other impairments (including seizure disorders), it best illustrates the impact of multiple disabilities.

NEURAL TUBE DEFECTS

Descriptions and Characteristics

Sometimes babies are born with malformations of the brain, spinal cord, and/or vertebrae. These defects are collectively called **neural tube defects (NTDs),** although many people commonly refer to them as **spina bifida** (*bifid* means "divided in two"). Neural tube defects occur when the bones of the spinal column (vertebrae) fail to close properly (Liptak, 1997). A variety of environmental factors may contribute to neural tube defects, including nutrition, medication, and temperature. Many physicians now recommend folic acid supplements during pregnancy to reduce the possibility of neural tube defects (Liptak, 1997). Evidence of genetic links to neural tube defects must also be considered, since the condition is significantly higher in some ethnic groups than others (Disabato & Wulf, 1994; Shurtleff & Lemire, 1995). Neural tube defects also occur more frequently in females than males (Liptak, 1997).

The major types of neural tube defects are **encephalocele** (en-sef′-ah-low-seal), **anencephaly** (an-en-sef′-ally), and **spina bifida** (spy′-na bif′-ah-da). An encephalocele occurs when the skull is malformed and a portion of brain material **herniates** (pushes out) through the malformation. Children with encephalocele have multiple disabilities. In anencephaly, there is an absence of brain development beyond the brainstem. If an infant with anencephaly survives to be born, it rarely lives beyond infancy (Liptak, 1997).

The most common of the three types of neural tube defects is spina bifida, which is further classified into the categories of **spina bifida occulta** (o-cul′-ta), **meningocele** (mah-nin′-joe-seal), and **myelomeningocele** (my′-low-mah-nin′-joe-seal) (Heller et al., 1996). Figure 2–1 illustrates lateral and cross-section views of the normal spine and variations of spina bifida (Mitchell, Fiewell, & Davy, 1983, p. 118).

Spina bifida occulta is the mildest form of neural tube defect. In this condition, only a few vertebrae are bifid (not closed) and there is no protrusion of the spinal cord or its covering (Figure 2–1[b]). The defect is not externally visible, although the individual may have a patch of hair or dimple in the skin over the bifid vertebrae. Another type of spina bifida is called **meningocele** (*meninges* are the membranes that envelop the brain and spinal cord, and *cele* means the protruding sac or hernia). The meninges protrude through the open defect in the spine (Figure 2–1[c]). There is no resulting paralysis in either spina bifida occulta or meningocele. **Myelomeningocele** (sometimes called meningomyelocele) is the most common and severe form of spina bifida. It is characterized by the protrusion of the spinal cord and its coverings (meninges) through the defective vertebral opening (Figure 2–1[d]). Presence of a myelomeningocele results in varying degrees of paralysis and loss of sensation in the lower trunk and lower limbs. Since

FIGURE 2–1
Views of the normal spine and variations of neural tube defects

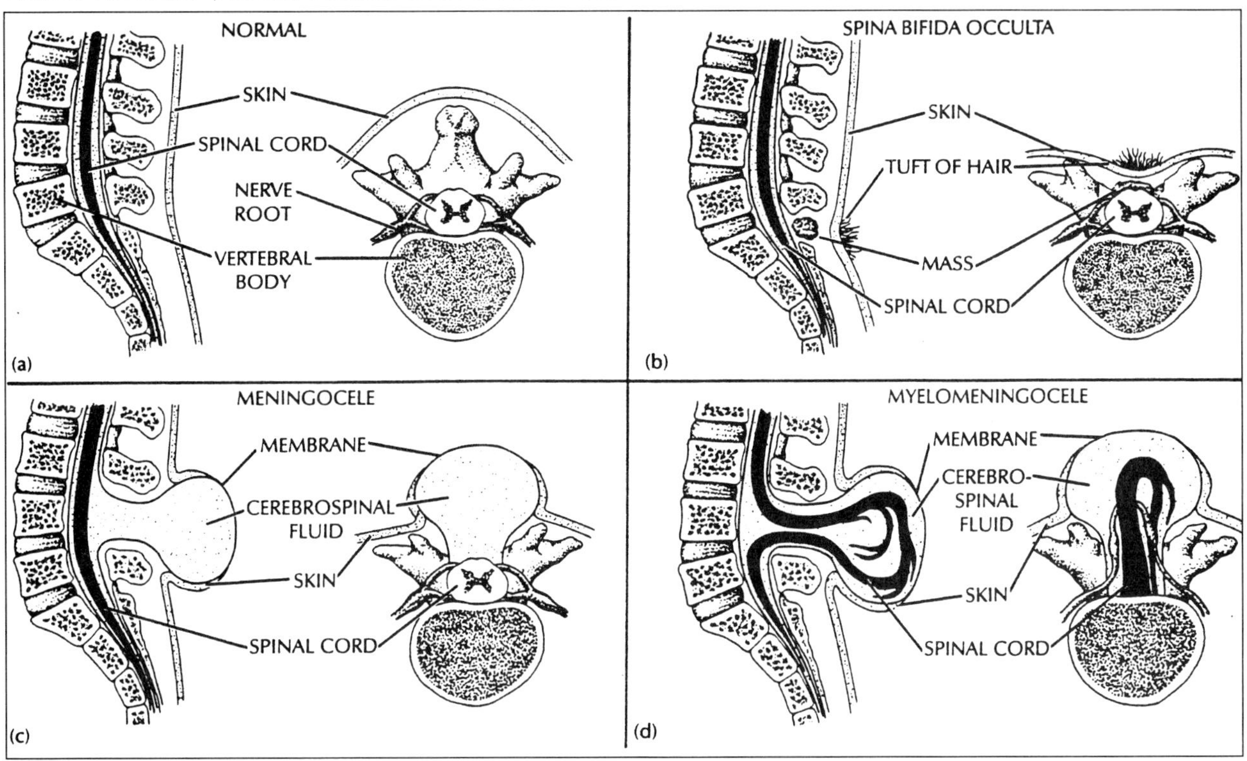

A. *Normal spine*—lateral and cross-section views.
B. *Spina bifida occulta*—fatty mass and hair may or may not be present.
C. *Meningocele*—no nerves from the spinal cord are displaced.
D. *Myelomeningocele*—note disrupted, abnormal spinal cord and nerves.
Note. From "Spina Bifida" by D. C. Mitchell, E. Fiewell, and P. Davy, in *Physical Disabilities and Health Impairments: An Introduction,* ed. J. Umbreit, © 1983 by Prentice-Hall, Inc., Upper Saddle River, NJ. Reprinted by permission of the author.

myelomeningocele is both the most common form of spina bifida and has the greatest negative impact on function, it will be the focus of the remainder of the discussion of neural tube defects.

Associated Medical Conditions

The extent of functional disability in spina bifida is associated with the type of defect (spina bifida occulta, meningocele, or myelomeningocele) and its location. The location of the defect on the spinal column has a direct impact on muscle paralysis and loss of sensation. If the protrusion occurs in the lower back (lumbar and sacral areas), only the spinal nerves may be affected. However, if the defect occurs higher up the spinal column in the thoracic area, the spinal cord itself may be involved.

Individuals with myelomeningocele experience **decreased or absent sensation** to touch, temperature, pressure, or pain, and partial or complete weakness may occur in the lower extremities. There is an accompanying **loss of bladder or bowel control.** Because the urge to void the bladder or bowel is frequently absent, individuals with myelomeningocele may neglect proper techniques for elimination. Frequently the bladder becomes overfull and urine backs up (refluxes) into the kidneys. Failure to properly empty the bladder causes infections and an overstretched bladder. Infections may not be noticed because the pain that accompanies them is absent due to paralysis. Kidney damage may result from repeated infections, and the individual may have urinary incontinence (dribbling) because the bladder is no longer able to properly contain urine. Bowel incontinence may also occur.

Many individuals with myelomeningocele have associated **hydrocephalus** characterized by head enlargement, brain abnormalities, and seizures (Liptak, 1997). Hydrocephalus (hy-dro-sef'-ah-lus) is caused by blocked cerebrospinal fluid (CSF) drainage. Fluid accumulates within the cavities or ventricles inside the brain rather than flowing to the meninges and into the bloodstream where the kidneys filter it out of the body. Hydrocephalus occurs in approximately 60–95% of individuals with myelomeningocele and may be congenital or develop later (Griebel, Oakes, & Worley, 1991). Surgical intervention is necessary to achieve proper elimination of cerebral spinal fluid, and may be repeated during the individual's life.

Joint deformities and spinal curvature such as **scoliosis** and **kyphosis** are commonly noted in individuals with spina bifida (Banit, Iwinski, Talwalkar, & Johnson, 2001; Eule, Erikson, O'Brien, & Handler, 2002; Rowley-Kelly & Reigel, 1993; Westcott, Dynes, Remer, Donaldson, & Dias, 1992). Some individuals with myelomeningocele have a condition known as **tethered cord,** in which the cord is "caught" on the vertebrae or restricted by scar tissue from earlier surgery. The cord is abnormally stretched, causing spinal curvature and nerve damage (Accardo & Whitman, 1996; Pierz, Banta, Thompson, Gahm, & Hartford, 2000). Finally, the individual with myelomeningocele may experience cognitive impairments and/or learning disabilities (Friedrich, Lovejoy, Shaffer, Shurtleff, & Beilke, 1991).

Medical and Therapeutic Treatments

Surgery. Surgical treatment of myelomeningocele is initiated shortly after birth. The protruding sac is removed so that the open area along the spinal column can be closed. The purpose of this surgery is to prevent infection and protect exposed nerves from injury (Charney, Weller, Sutton, Bruce, & Schut, 1985). Within days, this surgery is frequently followed by another to place a **shunt** into the brain (McLone, 1992). The shunt is a plastic tube that is inserted into the ventricles to drain CSF from the ventricles of the brain to the abdominal cavity (Charney, 1992; Liptak, 1997). Without surgery to correct hydrocephalus, infants with myelomeningocele may suffer brain damage as the CSF pushes brain matter against the inside of the skull. Other surgeries may involve release of tethered cord (Pierz et al., 2000) and spinal fusion (Eule et al., 2002).

Orthopedic Treatment. Orthopedic care is essential to prevent deformities of the spine, hips, and legs that interfere in achieving independent mobility. Frequent standing sessions and/or time spent in the prone (on-the-stomach) position are helpful in preventing contractures (muscle tightness) in the hips. Surgery, braces, and splints can also help correct or reduce deformities. Surgery may also be indicated if the child develops a severe spinal curvature, which may interfere with sitting and walking (Banit et al., 2001; Liptak, 1997). Braces are usually required to support the lower extremities and trunk, and to assist in ambulation (walking). Whether the child with myelomeningocele becomes ambulatory will depend on the location and extent of paralysis, cognitive function, and diligence in following the therapy program (Liptak, 1997). Individuals may be fully functional **community ambulators, household ambulators,** who are limited to essential movement at home, **nonfunctional ambulators,** who walk only for weight-bearing maintenance of hip joints, or **nonambulators,** who require wheelchairs at all times.

Therapeutic Contributions. Physical therapists are important members of the multidisciplinary team who assist children with gait training, use of mobility aids, and other aspects of independent function. Occupational therapists are instrumental in the area of self-care. They may work with educators to teach self-care skills such as independent dressing and provide suggestions to enhance fine-motor eye-hand skills. They may work with families and school personnel to assist with **clean intermittent catheterization (CIC)** of the bladder and special programs to achieve regular bowel movements. Establishing a manageable personal hygiene program for students with myelomeningocele is extremely important for fostering independence and avoiding feelings of embarrassment that would occur with a toilet accident.

Impact on Physical, Cognitive, and Psychosocial Development

There is great developmental variation in infants and children with myelomeningocele. Early intervention must be individualized and focus on sensorimotor and social development (Williamson, 1987). When children begin to attend school programs, motor development will be focused on functional skills such as self-care and mobility.

Physical and Cognitive Development. Infants and children with myelomeningocele may be delayed in rolling, sitting, and crawling. Depending on the extent of their impairment, they may only stand and walk with extensive bracing or mobility equipment (Liptak, 1997). Loss of movement means that children with myelomeningocele are more dependent on others for physical care and mobility than more typically developing children. Restricted mobility may impair interaction with play materials or engagement in games and other physical activities with peers. Physical activities (such as diving, contact sports, etc.) that might result in shunt blockage are contraindicated (not advisable). As adults, persons with myelomeningocele will probably require adapted equipment for activities such as driving.

Myelomeningocele may also affect cognitive development. Although individuals with myelomeningocele score below norms on tests of intelligence (Friedrich et al., 1991), this outcome may be due to many factors. Impairment in physical ability will restrict opportunities for interactions with the environment and individuals/objects in the environment, which delays cognitive growth. Damage to brain tissue that may occur as a result of malformation and/or surgical procedures may further inhibit cognitive function.

Whenever possible, educators and others should modify activities in ways that support achievement in cognitive and motor areas. Infants and children should be encouraged to be as active as possible; this can be fostered by placing enticing play materials just out of reach or modifying them for easier grasp and manipulation. Seating devices can be placed on the floor to allow children to sit beside their peers during group activities. Game rules can be adapted to allow greater participation, including an emphasis on games that involve the upper body. Therapists and physical disability specialists provide excellent guidance on equipment and materials adaptations.

Psychosocial Development. Positive psychosocial development depends on an environment that is supportive and predictable and that provides a variety of experiences. During the years when they develop the motivation to independently perform skills such as toileting, walking, and dressing, children with myelomeningocele may experience frustration if they cannot achieve mastery. Lack of mastery may extend to adolescence, particularly if individuals remain dependent upon their parents for personal care (Blum, Resnick, Nelson, & St. Germaine, 1991). Odor associated with bladder and bowel incontinence has a stigmatizing effect on peer relationships. For adolescents and adults, sexual dysfunction related to paralysis and loss of sensation may contribute to poor self-esteem and body image (Blum et al., 1991).

Task mastery is important to good psychosocial adjustment. Children with myelomeningocele must be encouraged to appropriately participate in all school activities. Mastery in self-care is also important, even though it means a commitment of time and extra effort by family members and service providers. In addition to providing a sense of achievement, opportunities to care for oneself provide the opportunity to discuss bodily differences and coping/compensatory strategies.

Implications for Education and Personal Autonomy

Students with myelomeningocele encounter academic challenges in addition to their physical needs. They may experience frequent absences from school due to hospitalization for orthopedic surgeries, shunt revisions, bladder/kidney infections, bone fracture treatment, or pressure-sore treatment. Teachers and other service providers need to balance the time spent in school among competing goals of academic achievement, self-care training, and therapy activities. In addition, psychosocial development must not be neglected.

Academic Impact of Myelomeningocele. Perceptual and other learning disabilities are frequently observed in students with myelomeningocele. According to Mitchell et al. (1983), "Specific learning disabilities are common and include problems in visual-motor perception, motor planning, and visual and auditory discrimination. Some youngsters have attention deficits and others have emotional disorders that complicate their education" (p. 122). Deficiencies in sensation result in disruption of information from touch, movement, position in space, and monitoring one's motor experience (motor planning). The results are problems in "spatial judgment, concepts of direction, distance, and motor organizational skill" (Mitchell et al., 1983, p. 120) that affect writing, reading, and mathematical skills.

Language Issues of Children with Myelomeningocele. The language pattern of some individuals with hydrocephalus in addition to myelomeningocele is characterized by a behavior called "cocktail party language." Students are social and chatty, but their conversation is often superficial and cliché-ridden (Hurley, Dorman, Laatsch, Bell, & D'Avignon, 1990). This chatter may create a false impression of academic or cognitive ability, leading to unreasonable expectations of intellectual performance (Bleck, 1982). Strategies that help educators and others respond to cocktail party chatter include maintaining an academic focus and organized classroom routines, resisting the impulse to respond in ways that reinforce this conversation, and pairing the student with a peer who is task oriented.

Strategies to Enhance Personal Autonomy. Service providers must be alert to the possibility of malfunction of the shunt. Physical symptoms such as headache, lethargy, nausea, or vomiting could indicate shunt malfunction, and require immediate medical investigation. Other signs are more subtle. When teachers detect changes in school performance, difficulty with handwriting, or social withdrawal in students with myelomeningocele, they need to explore the possibility of shunt malfunction or other physical problems. Figure 2–2 provides a list of indicators of possible shunt malfunction.

The teacher and classroom aides are important facilitators in the daily care of children with myelomeningocele for whom paralysis and loss of sensation are major problems. Personal autonomy is supported through consistent management and strategies for the following needs.

Skin care. Cusick (1991)[1] emphasizes the importance of maintaining good skin care. A lack of sensation to touch, pressure, pain, and temperature can result in catastrophic episodes of skin breakdown on the buttocks (because of pressure while sitting) and under ill-fitting braces. Even small children who drag themselves on the floor can unwittingly suffer rug burns and lacerations. Ripped or rough wheelchair upholstery can injure the skin. It is important to remove braces and check skin at regular intervals and to remind the child to do push-ups at regular intervals to relieve pressure in sitting. Positioning alternatives, such as standing frames, also relieve pressure on the buttocks but must be used with close and frequent skin inspections. The child needs to participate in and

FIGURE 2–2
Indicators of possible shunt malfunction

- Lethargy or generalized weakness or tiredness
- Difficult in waking or staying awake
- Dizziness or confusion
- Personality disturbances
- Increasing restlessness or irritability
- Lack of motivation or loss of interest in personal care
- Loss of appetite
- Vomiting (sometimes projectile)
- Fever
- Swelling or redness around the shunt path (side of neck or in abdomen)
- Recurrent headaches and back or neck pain or stiffness, particularly in the morning, that results from increased CSF pressure that occurs when the person is lying down asleep
- Enlargement of the head (in infants and toddlers)
- Visual disturbances (e.g., loss of vision; strabismus; blurred or double vision; pupil changes)
- A downward deviation of the eyes (in young infants)
- Increased sensitivity to noise
- Deteriorating school performance
- Development of spasticity in muscles that previously were normal
- Periods of total body rigidity
- Difficulties in maintaining balance
- Unsteady gait
- Ascending motor loss in lower extremities
- Tremors of the hands or eyelids
- Loss of upper extremity strength
- Deteriorating fine motor skills
- Increasing spinal curvature above the spinal defect
- Seizures
- Alterations in consciousness

Note. From *Meeting the Needs of Students with Special Physical and Health Care Needs* by Hill, © 1999. Reprinted by permission of Prentice-Hall, Inc., Upper Saddle River, NJ.

[1]Some of the material on skin care, fractures, bladder and bowel management, fostering of independence, orthopedic treatment, and therapeutic contributions are from Cusick (1991).

eventually assume primary responsibility for skin care, management, and inspection, including brace removal and attachment.

One important aspect of skin care is awareness of latex allergy. Many individuals with myelomeningocele are allergic to latex (Meeropol, 1997; Pearson, Cole, & Jarvis, 1994), possibly because of continued exposure. Care should be taken to avoid skin contact with products that contain latex, including balloons, rubber toys, art supplies, clothing with elastic rubber bands around the waist and legs, wheelchair tires or cushions, and bandages (Liptak, 1997; Meeropol, 1997). Service providers must wear nonlatex gloves during diapering and cleaning (Gleeson, 1995). Balloons and latex gloves have been identified as causing the majority of allergic reactions, possibly because they are powdered (which releases the proteins in latex), they come in contact with mucous membranes, and they are commonly used (Pearson et al., 1994).

Students should also learn to recognize latex products and what action to take in the event of an allergic reaction. If there is any suspicion that latex is present in a product, consult with your school nurse.

Fractures. The bones of the legs are often somewhat fragile from the lack of appropriate stresses of muscle pull and weight bearing. Fractures and bone cracks can occur, and these require prompt orthopedic attention. Students and their care providers need to rely on fracture indicators such as swelling and inflammation, since the paralysis associated with myelomeningocele means that the students may not experience the pain associated with fractures. Transfers and lifting should be undertaken with care to protect against fractures.

Bladder and bowel management. Clean intermittent catheterization (CIC) is a preferred method of emptying the bladder for students with myelomeningocele. Students using CIC will use a specific schedule (often every 3 to 4 hours) of when they need to be catheterized. Age, ability to sequence steps in the process, and fine motor skills are important considerations for determining the best time to teach CIC skills to students. The health care team will determine the best time to formally teach the student to perform the CIC procedure. Privacy is critical, and teachers and other care providers need to provide sufficient time for the student to practice CIC. For students who are not good candidates for CIC, alternatives include use of diapers or use of external urinary catheters and surgical options (Heller et al., 1996).

Bowel management programs are frequently initiated at home. It is important for school personnel and families to work together to establish a regular schedule for bowel management. Bowel management alternatives include use of diapers, scheduled toilet time, straining to increase intra-abdominal pressure (grunting), use of suppository and stool softener, and the colostomy option.

Fostering independence. Independence in locomotion, transfers from chair to other support systems, toileting, dressing, and equipment management (including braces) are important features of self-care. Time should be provided for students to use these skills while in school. There are several ways to facilitate and reinforce initiative and independent function. First, students should be taught to master tasks through consistent practice and positive response. Mastery motivation is a normal aspect of development, but students who depend on others for self-care skills may have lost initiative. Teachers and others may need to provide praise and encouragement for attempts and slowly require more-refined skill levels. Task efficiency should be stressed once a skill is established. Efficiency must never be sacrificed for safety, however. Developing and maintaining independence in personal care must occur with cooperation from family members.

Implications for Career and Adult Outcomes

Spina bifida is a chronic condition, which means that individuals with this physical disability will encounter challenges throughout their lives. Adolescents with myelomeningocele must maintain hygiene regimens to avoid body odor and skin breakdown. Physical exercise is essential to develop upper body fitness and avoid excessive weight gain. Adaptations will be necessary for individuals who wish to drive a car but cannot use their legs. Further adjustments are required for other aspects of independent physical function. Individuals with spina bifida are assisted by the Americans with Disabilities Act in dealing with issues such as transportation and access.

Adaptations and adjustments are not confined to overcoming physical limitations and architectural barriers. In a study that examined psychosocial aspects of classroom placement, it was reported that adolescents with spina bifida described themselves as significantly more lonely than their peers who were nondisabled (Lord, Varzos, Behrman, Wicks, & Wicks, 1990). It is critical that the issues of social isolation, realization of the permanence of this disability, and sexual dysfunction associated with spina bifida are addressed in ways that promote positive psychosocial functioning (Friedrich et al., 1991; Liptak, 1997).

In order to meet life goals, careful planning must begin during the school years. Academic education, job exploration, and vocational training provide the initial links for adult independence. Career development is only one aspect of adulthood, however. Life management skills (i.e., acquiring independence in personal care skills, independent travel, consumer awareness and practice, selecting personal care attendants, etc.) are more specific to disability and are a vital aspect of preparation for adult life. Separate chapters have been devoted to personal management and career/transition issues for individuals with physical or multiple disabilities.

TRAUMATIC BRAIN INJURY

Descriptions and Characteristics

There are several ways to describe an injury to the brain. The term **head injury** is used to describe either closed or open injuries/traumas. When there is no fracture to the skull, the injury is classified as a closed injury. If the skull is penetrated, the injury is classified as open (Heller et al., 1996). The term **brain injury** includes traumas (closed and open) that are acquired by an external physical force or nontraumatic events such as strokes, vascular accidents, infectious diseases, injuries such as near drowning and suffocation, and metabolic disorders such as insulin shock (Savage & Wolcott, 1994). In this chapter, **traumatic brain injury (TBI)** will be the focus of discussion.

By federal definition, "traumatic brain injury means an acquired injury to the brain caused by external physical force, resulting in total or partial functional disability or psychosocial impairment, or both, that may adversely affect a child's educational performance. The term applies to open or closed head injuries resulting in impairments in one or more areas, such as cognition; speech and language; memory; attention; reasoning; abstract thinking; judgment; problem solving; sensory, perceptual, and motor abilities; psychosocial behavior; physical functions; and information processing. The term does not apply to brain injuries that are congenital or degenerative, or brain injuries caused by birth trauma" (34 C.F.R. § 300.7 [c][12]).

Unlike neural tube defects, TBI is an acquired condition. TBI occurs most frequently as the result of a car accident, bicycle/motorcycle accident, sports injury, or fall (DiScala, Osberg, & Savage, 1997). Child abuse and gunshot wounds may also result in TBI. Enforcement of motor vehicle seat belt and motorcycle helmet use, restricted adolescent vehicle licensure, and advancements in emergency care have reduced death and serious injury from severe brain injury (Davis, 2000; Marshall, 2000). However, enough children continue to suffer severe TBI that it has become the most common acquired disability in childhood (Kraus, Rock, & Hemyari, 1990).

Mild TBIs (which may include **concussion**) are frequently the result of a fall or sports injury (Barth & Macciocchi, 1983; Koch, Merz, & Lynch, 1995; Kushner, 2001; Michaud, Duhaime, & Lazar, 1997). Some individuals who sustain mild TBIs appear to suffer no immediate damage, and their injuries therefore may go unreported. However, damage is still a possibility. For example, athletes are at risk for **second impact syndrome** (increased brain swelling and bleeding) if they return to sports activities before an earlier concussion is completely healed (Kushner, 2001).

Injuries may occur even when the head does not strike an object. For example, when an individual slams forward in the seat during an automobile accident, the brain travels forward in the skull even while the body is being held stationary. The brain then connects with the rough surface of the inside of the skull, causing a **contusion** (bruise). Then the head snaps back again as the body stabilizes, sending the brain back against the skull on the opposite side. This front-and-back impact pattern is referred to as **coup and contracoup.** At the same time, the brain may twist on the brain stem (Folzer, 2001).

Injuries may also be unreported if they are caused by physical abuse. If an individual suffers a severe TBI in conjunction with other bodily injuries (such as organ injury, lacerations, or fractures), the TBI may not be reported as the dominant injury. However, it is estimated that head trauma occurs in the general population at the rate of 1.5 to 2 million injuries per year (Davis, 2000) and in pediatric population group (1 month to 15 years) at the rate of approximately 1 million per year (Heller et al., 1996). Approximately 5% of individuals who experience a TBI sustain long-term physical, emotional, behavioral, and cognitive damage (Davis, 2000; National Institutes of Health, 1999). Even individuals with mild TBI may experience these problems (Folzer, 2001).

Coma, which is a loss of consciousness triggered by brain injury, is one criteria used as an indication of severe trauma. Brain injuries associated with coma have a mortality rate 10 times higher in children than in adults. Under 2 years of age, the mortality rate associated with severe TBI is extremely high.

Associated Medical Conditions

Traumatic brain injury can cause impairments in cognition, sensation, motor ability, and other functions. Intellectual and academic deficits are associated with the severity of the TBI (Jaffe et al., 1992; Jaffe, Polissar, Fay, & Liao, 1995). These include deficits in long- and short-term memory; deficits in organization, perception, and attention; poor judgment, problem solving, and reasoning; and decreased ability to learn (Davis, 2000; Hanson & Clippard, 1992). Seizures may result from TBI, and these can have a negative impact on cognitive function (Chadwick, 2000).

Depending on the type and degree of trauma, the individual may experience damage to vision and/or hearing. Direct damage to the eye or inner ear can result in visual or hearing impairment. Indirect damage from brain swelling or stroke can lead to **cortical visual impairment (CVI).** While the eye itself is intact, the brain can no longer interpret visual messages due to damage of the visual cortex. Brain damage may also lead to **nystagmus** (involuntary lateral eye movement) or **diplopia** (double vision) (Michaud et al., 1997).

Motor impairments related to TBI will depend on the location and severity of the injury. The individual may experience spasticity, ataxia, or tremors. Readers are referred to Chapter 4 for a more complete description of these motor deficits.

In addition to impairments in cognition, sensation, and motor function, individuals who experience a TBI may develop feeding and communication impairments. TBI can also disrupt behavioral or emotional functioning. The individual may be aggressive or apathetic or behave in a socially uninhibited manner. Impairments may be temporary or permanent and cause partial or total functional disability or psychosocial maladjustment.

Medical and Therapeutic Treatments

Surgery and Medical Care. The immediate result of brain injury includes lacerations and contusions (bruises) of the brain, shearing of axons in the brain, and bleeding. Secondary damage occurs when the brain receives inadequate oxygen (Wong, 2000). Initial medical treatments for injuries are designed to support vital functions, and must be prompt and comprehensive. Michaud et al. (1997) describe the first step in medical response as the "ABCs" of pediatric advanced life support: airway, breathing, and circulation (p. 602). Wong (2000) recommends a specific protocol that includes appropriate head and neck positioning, medication management, and reduction of stimulation in the environment to address secondary injury (p. 26). After immediate attention, a thorough neurological assessment is conducted. Neurosurgery may be required to reduce intracranial pressure and/or remove foreign objects. Associated injuries such as internal organ damage and fractures must also be treated (Michaud et al., 1997).

Once new patients have passed initial medical crises, they must continue to be examined and monitored for respiratory and neurological status. Medication may be given to control fluid buildup and prevent further damage to the brain. Testing such as a **computerized tomography scan (CT scan)** or **magnetic resonance imagery (MRI)** is conducted to determine the extent of brain tissue damage. Individuals who have experienced a TBI must also be monitored for seizures.

Therapeutic Contributions. Even while the individual remains in a coma, supportive, multidisciplinary therapy should begin. Medical treatment will continue to be directed at prevention and/or treatment of complications and seizures. Pressure sores should be prevented by providing passive range-of-motion exercises.

Rehabilitation after coma helps to establish compensatory abilities, prevent complications from the injury, and promote residual abilities. Early and vigorous rehabilitation has been shown to improve long-term functional outcome (Beaulieu, 2002). Physical, occupational, speech, and behavior therapy may all be required if the individual recovers from the coma (Hall, Johnson, & Middleton, 1990). Physical therapy, including the use of casts or splints (orthotics), may be necessary to prevent joint contractures. A sensory stimulation program may be beneficial. Occupational therapy will assist the individual to recover self-care and fine motor skills and learn compensatory skills. Communication needs will require speech/language therapy. Individuals must also learn to cope with the differences between their functional ability and possibly unrealistic expectations, as well as adjust to their "new self" (Folzer, 2001, p. 248). Psychotherapy is an important aspect of positive adjustment and recovery.

Some individuals who experience TBI will remain dependent and require a lifelong plan for structure and support to function in the community. When long-term care is provided, the individual may need to be followed indefinitely by the treatment team. Some may also require specialized health procedures (Heller, Forney, Alberto, Schwartzman, & Goeckel, 1999), and therapy may be continued after the patient returns to school.

Coma Recovery. Throughout the discussion related to treatment, the term **coma** has been mentioned. A coma is a loss of consciousness that can last for hours, days, or months. Individuals in a coma are unresponsive to attempts to awaken them (Heller et al., 1996). A scale (assessment) can be helpful to determine the depth of the coma and therefore the seriousness of the brain injury. Scales also provide a baseline of responses for future comparison and assist professionals to match current functioning with therapy and rehabilitative techniques. The **Glascow Coma Scale (GCS)** is a widely used scale in which points are assigned for specific responses (Jennett et al., 1977). A score of 13–15 indicates mild TBI, a score of 9–12 indicates moderate TBI, and a score below 8 indicates severe TBI (Jaffe et al., 1992). A rating below 7 indicates coma. Table 2–1 indicates the responses and point assignment on the Glascow Coma Scale.

TABLE 2–1
Glascow Coma Scale

Response	Score
Eye opening	
Spontaneous	4
To speech	3
To pain	2
Nil	1
Best motor response	
Obeys	6
Localizes	5
Withdraws	4
Abnormal flexion	3
Extensor response	2
Nil	1
Verbal response	
Oriented	5
Confused conversation	4
Inappropriate words	3
Incomprehensible sounds	2
Nil	1

Note. From "Severe Head Injuries in Three Countries," by B. Jennett, G. Teasdale, S. Galbraith, J. Pickard, H. Grant, R. Braakman, C. Avezaat, A. Maas, J. Minderhoud, C. J. Vecht, J. Heiden, R. Small, W. Caton, and T. Kurze, 1977, *Journal of Neurology, Neurosurgery, and Psychiatry, 40,* p. 293. Reprinted with permission.

Emerging from a coma (also called **lightening**) does not follow a smooth progression. Individuals do not awaken as if from sleep and find themselves possessed of all the abilities they had before their injury. Instead, they move in and out of consciousness. Levels of consciousness may be accompanied by changes in behavior. Initial behavior is not purposeful and may be marked by confusion, distraction, and/or agitation. The **Rancho Los Amigos Cognitive Scales** (Savage & Wolcott, 1995) is a useful tool for recognizing and responding to individuals in the initial stages of recovery from TBI (see Table 2–2). Teachers can use this scale to adjust curricular content and instructional approach to the individual's ability to respond. For example, a hospital teacher who is providing educational services to a school-age student (5 years and older) whose behavior is consistent with Level III on the Rancho Los Amigos Cognitive Scales would not attempt to introduce complex subject matter or expect the student to attend to more than the briefest of stimuli. It is very important that professional personnel reassure families that many of the behaviors associated with coma recovery will evolve with time and a consistent, predictable approach. However, it is impossible to predict the absolute extent of recovery, and individuals may have residual effects of brain injury throughout life.

Impact on Physical, Cognitive, and Psychosocial Development

Physical and Cognitive Development. Many factors influence long-term outcomes for individuals who experience a TBI. **Injury-related factors** include the severity, location, and extent of the injury, as well as depth and length of time spent in coma. - **Treatment-related factors** include immediacy of rescue and trauma care, complications, and rehabilitation. **Patient-related factors** include chronological

TABLE 2–2
Rancho Los Amigos Cognitive Scales: Level of Consciousness Records—Head Trauma Patients

Infants—6 Months to 2 Years

Level I: Interacts with Environment
a) Shows active interest in toys; manipulates or examines before mouthing or discarding.
b) Watches other children at play; may move toward them purposefully.
c) Initiates social contact with adults; enjoys socializing.
d) Shows active interest in bottle.
e) Reaches or moves toward person or object.

Level II: Demonstrates Awareness of Environment
a) Responds to name.
b) Recognizes mother or other family members.
c) Enjoys imitative vocal play.
d) Giggles or smiles when talked to or played with.
e) Fussing is quieted by soft voice or touch.

Level III: Gives Localized Response to Sensory Stimuli
a) Blinks when strong light crosses field of vision.
b) Follows moving object passed within visual field.
c) Turns toward or away from loud sound.
d) Gives localized response to painful stimuli.

Level IV: Gives Generalized Response to Sensory Stimuli
a) Gives generalized startle to loud sound.
b) Responds to repeated auditory stimulation with increased or decreased activity.
c) Gives generalized reflex response to painful stimuli.

Level V: No Response to Stimuli
a) Complete absence of observable change in behavior to visual, auditory, or painful stimuli.

Preschool—2 to 5 Years

Level I: Oriented to Self and Surroundings
a) Provides accurate information about self.
b) Knows he or she is away from home.
c) Knows where toys, clothes, etc., are kept.
d) Actively participates in treatment program.
e) Recognizes own room, knows way to bathroom, nursing station, etc.
f) Is potty trained.
g) Initiates social contact with adult. Enjoys socializing.

Level II: Is Responsive to Environment
a) Follows simple commands.
b) Refuses to follow commands by shaking head or saying "no."
c) Imitates examiner's gestures or facial expressions.
d) Responds to name.
e) Recognizes mother or other family members.
f) Enjoys imitative vocal play.

Level III: Gives Localized Response to Sensory Stimuli
a) Blinks when strong light crosses field of vision.
b) Follows moving object passed within visual field.
c) Turns toward or away from loud sound.
d) Gives localized response to painful stimuli.

Level IV: Gives Generalized Response to Sensory Stimuli
a) Gives generalized startle to loud sound.
b) Responds to repeated auditory stimulation with increased or decreased activity.
c) Gives generalized reflex response to painful stimuli.

Level V: No Response to Stimuli
a) Complete absence of observable change in behavior to visual, auditory, or painful stimuli.

School Age—5 Years & Older

Level I: Oriented to Time & Place: Is Recording Ongoing Events
a) Can provide accurate, detailed information about self and present situation.
b) Knows way to and from daily activities.
c) Knows sequence of daily routine.
d) Knows way around unit; recognizes own room.
e) Can find own bed; knows where personal belongings are kept.
f) Is bowel and bladder trained.

Level II: Is Responsive to Environment
a) Follows simple verbal or gestured requests.
b) Initiates purposeful activity.
c) Actively participates in therapy program.
d) Refuses to follow request by shaking head or saying "no."
e) Imitates examiner's gestures or facial expressions.

Level III: Gives Localized Response to Sensory Stimuli
a) Blinks when strong light crosses field of vision.
b) Follows moving object passed within visual field.
c) Turns toward or away from loud sound.
d) Gives localized response to painful stimuli.

Level IV: Gives Generalized Response to Sensory Stimuli
a) Gives generalized startle to loud sound.
b) Responds to repeated auditory stimulation with increased or decreased activity.
c) Gives generalized reflex response to painful stimuli.

Level V: No Response to Stimuli
a) Complete absence of observable change in behavior to visual, auditory, or painful stimuli.

Note. "Rancho Los Amigos Cognitive Scales." Reprinted from *An Educator's Manual: What Educators Need to Know About Students with Brain Injury,* edited by Ronald C. Savage, Ed.D., and Gary F. Wolcott, M.Ed., for the Brain Injury Association. Reprinted by permission of the Brain Injury Association. Copyright © 1995.

age, educational history prior to injury, and family issues (Beaulieu, 2002). Physically, students with TBI may experience sensory problems such as loss of taste or smell. Damage may affect vision or hearing. Because of brain tissue damage, the student with TBI may move slowly or clumsily. Balance may also be compromised. The student may experience seizures which add to cognitive confusion (Chadwick, 2000; Hill, 1999).

Cognitive changes in students with TBI are often subtle and occur in combination. Table 2–3 enumerates possible cognitive problems following brain injury and how these problems may affect functioning in school.

Teachers can employ numerous strategies to aid students whose cognition is compromised by TBI. First, it is important to remember that inability to attend or respond to instruction is not deliberate. Teachers need to modify the classroom environment to control stimuli. This may mean placing the student away from doors and windows to reduce visual and auditory distractions. Creating worksheets with fewer problems also reduces visual distraction. Allowing students to place a marker under a line of text may assist them to track more efficiently. Teachers must also modify instruction. Breaking lessons into small, component parts (see Chapter 6 on task and situation analysis) allows students to understand each aspect of the lesson before the next is presented. Teachers need to be prepared to repeat or rephrase to assist students with memory deficits. Cues in the form of written task sheets and key points or phrases help students stay organized and follow the steps in a sequence. Localized brain damage often impairs the ability to learn specific skills, while widespread **(diffuse)** damage may impair the ability to acquire new skills (Beaulieu, 2002). Therefore, the teacher must be prepared to teach compensatory skills and/or use familiar knowledge to assist the student to acquire new skills. Tyler and Grandinette (2003) provide a series of additional instructional strategies for assisting students with cognitive impairments.

Psychosocial Development. One of the greatest challenges faced by individuals who have experienced a TBI is adjusting psychologically to the changes resulting from their impairments. Students who have a good recollection of their lives before injury may be especially vulnerable to negative psychosocial outcomes. A mild injury may result in poor adjustment because the effects of the injury are felt even when they are not obvious to others (Folzer, 2001). Readers will remember that TBI has a direct effect on behavioral function. Teachers and others who provide services to students with TBI need specific strategies to facilitate appropriate behaviors.

Students with TBI may be agitated or aggressive. They may experience **emotional lability** (emotional "ups" and "downs"). If a student becomes agitated, teachers can help by physically redirecting him or her away from the source of irritation or gently changing the subject. With experience, teachers will learn to recognize factors that contribute to agitation (such as fatigue or frustration), and change **antecedents** (prior experiences, activities, etc.) so behaviors do not escalate. Another strategy is to establish a phrase or tactile cue to alert the student that control needs to be regained. For example, the teacher could say, "Eyes on me, breathe deep." An example of a tactile or touch cue would be to place a hand on the student's shoulder. These cues can be used without directly confronting the student about a specific behavior. Finally, teachers need to monitor their own behavior. Modeling is a powerful tool for managing behavior. The teacher can model frustration reactions by acting calmly, or by deliberately making an error and responding with a problem-solving approach. Students can be reinforced for "assisting" the teacher to correct an error. It is important to avoid sarcasm or ridicule. Sarcasm is often confusing to students who may have trouble separating actual words from their intent, and ridicule erodes trust and sensitizes students to their errors. Neither is an appropriate behavior management strategy.

Not all students with TBI are aggressive. The student may lose confidence and become overly depressed or self-critical. Classroom activities may be met with apathy or denial of the limitations imposed by disability. In these situations, teachers need to stress student strengths, emphasize activities that capitalize on the student's strongest learning modality, and provide goals that are attainable. Students who are apathetic and lack initiation need to be provided with choices (providing two choices that both attract the student is a good initial strategy). Using a rewarding experience or activity to reinforce a less preferred activity can be helpful. For example, a student had trouble maintaining interest in a group social studies project. The teacher responded by breaking the project into segments and allowing the

TABLE 2–3
Possible Cognitive Problems Following Head Injury

Aspect of Cognition	Possible Problems Following Brain Injury	Illustration of Problems in a School Setting
Component Cognitive Processes		
Attentional processes	• reduced arousal; sleepiness; fatigue; • difficulty focusing attention and filtering out distractions; • difficulty maintaining attention; • difficulty shifting easily from topic to topic or class to class; • difficulty dividing attention between two or more topics or activities.	1. A student may fail to follow the teacher's instruction or comprehend a lesson, not because of a willful failure to attend or an inability to understand, but rather because of an inability to filter out environmental distractions or internal feelings or thoughts. 2. Attentional problems may result in the student talking out of turn, introducing irrelevant topics, or responding inappropriately.
Perceptual processes	• difficulty seeing objects in part of the visual field; • difficulty perceiving the spatial orientation of objects; • difficulty separating the object of perception from background stimuli; • difficulty recognizing objects if too much is presented at once or too rapidly; • difficulty scanning and visually searching in an organized manner.	1. A student may be unable to do otherwise easy math problems if they are presented on a worksheet page filled with other math problems. 2. A student may be overwhelmed by classrooms that are overly stimulating visually or auditorily. 3. Without a line marker of enlarged print, reading comprehension may appear to be weak.
Memory/learning processes	• difficulty recalling events from earlier in the day or previous days; • difficulty staying oriented to a schedule or to activities; • difficulty registering new information or words that have been learned, particularly when under stress; • difficulty searching memory in an organized way and retrieving stored information and words.	1. A student may fail to complete assignments, not because of negligence or lack of desire to comply, but rather because the assignment, if not written or repeated several times, is not remembered. 2. A student may miss classes or do assignments incorrectly because of difficulty remaining oriented. 3. A student may require an unexpectedly large number of repetitions to learn simple motor sequences (e.g., tying shoes), classroom routines and rules, and textbook information. 4. A student may need to be reminded to repeat information over and over in order to place it in memory, and to "search memory" in order to find information that has been previously learned, or a student may need compensatory strategies to enhance memory.

(Continued)

student to choose a preferred activity (listening to music) after each segment was completed. The student drew a mural as his contribution to the group. Organizing the project for group activities also allowed the student to interact with peers through a structured activity, and allowed the teacher to comment on positive contributions and discuss different perspectives that arose during group interactions. Even when teachers carefully structure activities and maintain an emphasis on strengths, there may be times when student depression or withdrawal requires intervention by a school psychologist or other specially trained professional.

TABLE 2–3
Continued

Aspect of Cognition	Possible Problems Following Brain Injury	Illustration of Problems in a School Setting
Organizing processes	• difficulty analyzing a task into component parts; • difficulty seeing relationships (e.g., similarities/differences) among things; • difficulty organizing objects into appropriate groups or events into appropriate sequences; • difficulty organizing information into larger units (e.g., main ideas or themes); • difficulty grasping the major concept from detailed information.	1. A young student, faced with the task of getting ready for gym class, may be unable to break the task into parts and decide what to do first. 2. A high school student may understand each part of a text, but be unable to integrate the information to determine the main ideas and write a short summary. 3. A student may move unexpectedly from topic to topic in conversation because of an unusual set of associations; this may be interpreted as social strangeness or as resulting from a lack of knowledge about the subject.
Reasoning/abstract thinking processes	• difficulty understanding abstract levels of meaning (e.g., figures of speech, metaphors); • difficulty drawing conclusions from facts presented; • difficulty considering hypothetical explanations for events.	1. A student who does well with basic mathematical operations may have great difficulty with his/her application in solving word problems or with the more abstract relationships involved in algebra. 2. A student may lose the train of conversation when a figure of speech is used (e.g., "She was climbing the walls").
Problem-solving processes	• difficulty perceiving the exact nature of the problem; • difficulty considering information relevant to solving the problems; • difficulty considering a variety of possible solutions; • difficulty weighing the relative merits of alternative solutions.	1. Having forgotten his/her locker combination and not having ready access to his/her homeroom teacher, a student may simply become upset rather than considering carefully who else may be able to help. 2. Students who fail to comprehend a text with one or two readings may not use strategies to enhance comprehension (e.g., outlining the text, underlining key points, asking themselves questions as they read, discussing the text).
Component Cognitive Systems		
Working memory	• difficulty holding several words or thoughts or intentions in mind at one time.	1. A student may not be able to follow a two- or three-step command, even though comprehension of language is adequate. 2. A student may not be able to think about a compensatory strategy (e.g., "I must repeat this information in order to remember it"), and listen to the presented information at the same time.

Students with TBI may lack impulse control or age-appropriate social skills. Maintaining a consistent focus through structured daily plans and lessons, keeping materials organized and storing extraneous materials out of sight, and providing a quiet learning environment assist impulsive students to gain and maintain control. Students can facilitate self-control through developing a to-do list or schedule of activities to assist with cognitive

TABLE 2–3
Continued

Aspect of Cognition	Possible Problems Following Brain Injury	Illustration of Problems in a School Setting
Knowledge base	• recall of pre-traumatically acquired information, academic skill, social rules, etc., may have major gaps; islands of preserved high-level knowledge may convey an overly optimistic picture of the student's level; conversely, knowledge gaps at a low level may suggest an overly pessimistic picture of the student's level.	1. Occasionally, a student gains access to pre-traumatically acquired knowledge long after the injury. This may lead the teacher to infer that new learning is occurring at a more rapid rate than is actually the case. Alternatively, the inconsistency in learning rates may lead the teacher to infer that the student is often not trying.
Executive system	• difficulty setting goals; • difficulty perceiving strengths and needs in an objective manner; • difficulty planning activities; • difficulty initiating and/or inhibiting behavior; • difficulty monitoring one's own behavior; • difficulty evaluating one's own behavior.	1. Students who lack even a rudimentary awareness of current cognitive limitations commonly complain about tasks that are at too low a level and about restrictions on their activity that they perceive as unnecessary. 2. Organized studying (knowing how to divide the task, how to check one's understanding, how to organize the information for easy learning) relies on intact executive functioning, rarely found following severe head injury. 3. Students with initiation problems appear unmotivated and are easily categorized by teachers as resistive, "behavior problems," or as simply lazy. 4. Students who have difficulty monitoring their own behavior and who do not profit from the feedback of others behave in a socially awkward way.

Note. Reprinted from *An Educator's Manual: What Educators Need to Know About Students with Brain Injury*, edited by Ronald C. Savage, Ed.D., and Gary F. Wolcott, M.Ed., for the Brain Injury Association. Reprinted by permission of the Brain Injury Association. Copyright © 1995.

organization. Assigning an emotionally mature classroom work partner can facilitate social behavior. Teachers can help students who become disoriented in the busy school environment by encouraging the student to use verbal rehearsal before commencing an activity or traveling on school grounds, employing a buddy system, and helping the student recognize landmarks (Blosser & DePompei, 1994; Mira, Tucker, & Tyler, 1992; Ylvisaker, Szekeres, Hartwick, & Tworek 1994).

Implications for Education and Personal Autonomy

In 1997, the Individuals with Disabilities Education Act (IDEA) identified TBI as a separate federal disability category. Students with TBI may be identified as a distinct group for special education services, but their needs are individualized.

School Reentry. Besides modifying the classroom environment and employing specific instructional strategies, teachers and others must remember that students with TBI will face considerable challenges in addition to mastering academic content. Prior to school reentry, the student may have spent months in a hospital and/or rehabilitation center. Priorities of rehabilitation may have focused on motor function, speech/language, and other basic goals. Consequently, reentry to school is characterized by a lag in academic skills. Home instruction is one option for transition from hospital to school that provides academic support while allowing maximum opportunities for continued rehabilitation and rest. Upon return to school, students often realize that their educational goals have changed considerably. Altered behaviors and social skill deficits can interfere with peer relationships, creating more difficulties. Flexible and realistic short-term educational goals and objective must be established. Steensma (1991) recommends attendance in **transition or reentry classes** as a solution to the academic and social adjustment needs of students with TBI. Low teacher-student ratios, distraction control, behavior support strategies, and carefully structured instruction in transition classes will assist the students toward an ultimately successful school adjustment. Careful preparation of students for school reentry includes appropriate preparation of school personnel. Figure 2–3 provides a sample checklist for assisting students with TBI to make successful transitions into school.

Implications for Career and Adult Outcomes

Many of the challenges that face younger students with TBI must also be addressed by adolescents and adults. Deficits in problem solving, attention, and concentration may seriously interfere with employment potential. Wulz (1993) notes that the physical, cognitive, and social components of a job must be considered in job analysis and training. Job requirements may include data analysis and interpretation, decision making, planning and implementing projects, responding and adapting, and performing these requirements under stressful conditions (Wulz, 1993, p. 485). Social aspects of a job include coworker interactions and the complexity, number, and speed of those interactions. It is important that employees avoid work situations that cause excessive fatigue, which lowers performance. Employers should be guided by the Americans with Disabilities Act in providing "reasonable accommodations" to adults with TBI. One of the greatest tasks for adolescents and adults with TBI is to learn to "be" the person they have "become."

DEGENERATIVE DISEASES

Degenerative diseases result in progressive loss of motor movement (Heller et al., 1996). The progressive nature of these conditions distinguishes them from the other conditions discussed in this chapter. Deterioration of physical function will be accompanied by increasingly restricted ability to perform physical activities. Individuals with degenerative diseases are at risk for psychosocial crises as they confront issues of loss of bodily control, increasing fatigue and discomfort, and their mortality. Although there are many other degenerative diseases (e.g., spinal muscular atrophy, multiple sclerosis, Parkinson's disease, etc.), muscular dystrophy is better known to most people. It is a disease of muscle tissue and not the neurological system, affects school-age children, and is generally progressive.

MUSCULAR DYSTROPHY

Definitions and Descriptions

Muscular dystrophy is a group of primary muscle diseases characterized by progressive (increasing) weakness and death of muscle fibers. There is no associated change in the central nervous system in the muscular dystrophies. The most common form of muscular dystrophy is **Duchenne muscular dystrophy (DMD),** which was named after the neurologist Guillaume Benjamin Amand Duchenne. DMD occurs as a result of the absence or alteration of a protein called **dystrophin;** the gene for dystrophin production is located on one of the female's X chromosomes. As a result of its location, DMD is a "sex-linked" disease, and it affects approximately one in every 3,500 live male births (Do, 2002; Emery, 2002). Females transmit ("carry") the condition to 50% of their male offspring but are not affected themselves. It is possible to detect "carrier status" in women with a family history of DMD and to screen for DMD in children through blood sample analysis for elevation of the enzyme creatine kinase (CK) (Emery, 2002; Heller et al., 1996; Iannaccone, 1992). About one third of DMD cases occur by mutation with no family history of the disease.

Symptoms of Duchenne muscular dystrophy are observable between the ages of 2 and 6 years, although symptoms progress at varying rates. Initially, the child will have difficulty climbing stairs and running. Weakness generally begins in the lower legs and pelvic girdle muscles. The lower legs appear muscular and large when, in fact, muscle tissue is being replaced with fat and fibrous tissue (called **pseudohypertrophy**). When the pelvic girdle muscles become significantly weak, the child will need to push against his thighs with his hands to gain an upright

FIGURE 2–3
Entry/reentry checklist for students with TBI

Student's Name ____________________

Student's Teacher ____________________ School ____________________

Grade ____________________ School Year ____________________

Please ✔ box when completed. If not applicable, mark with an X.

	DATE	PERSON RESPONSIBLE	✔ OR X
REFERRAL RECEIVED			
Hospital Health Care Coordinator assigned	______	______	❑
School Coordinator assigned	______	______	❑
Education Coordinator assigned	______	______	❑
HEALTH TEAM ESTABLISHED			
Initial meeting held	______	______	❑
Additional meetings scheduled	______	______	❑
ASSESSMENT AND PLANNING			
Medical and educational information obtained	______	______	❑
Assessment data reviewed	______	______	❑
HEALTH CARE PLAN (HCP) DEVELOPED			
Orders (medication and procedures) obtained from physician	______	______	❑
HCP integrated into child's IEP	______	______	❑
Placement options reviewed	______	______	❑
Placement determined	______	______	❑
Personnel training plans developed	______	______	❑
Emergency care plans (plus backup) developed	______	______	❑
Transportation plan developed	______	______	❑
Equipment ordered and obtained	______	______	❑
Supplies ordered and obtained	______	______	❑
TRAINING OF STAFF AND STUDENTS			
Training schedule determined	______	______	❑
General training (staff and students)	______	______	❑
Child-specific training	______	______	❑
Training of child	______	______	❑
Follow-up in-service schedule determined	______	______	❑
Training of backup personnel arranged	______	______	❑
ENTRY/REENTRY			
Ongoing communication process developed	______	______	❑
Final authorization obtained (HCP signed)	______	______	❑
Final review of preceding steps	______	______	❑
FOLLOW-UP AND EVALUATION			
Periodic reevaluation meetings scheduled	______	______	❑
Follow-up inservice conducted (as needed)	______	______	❑

Case Manager ____________________ Date ____________________

Note. From *Meeting the Needs of Students with Special Physical and Health Care Needs* by Hill, © 1999, Reprinted with permission of Prentice-Hall, Inc.: Upper Saddle River, NJ.

FIGURE 2–4
Gower sign in boys with Duchenne muscular dystrophy

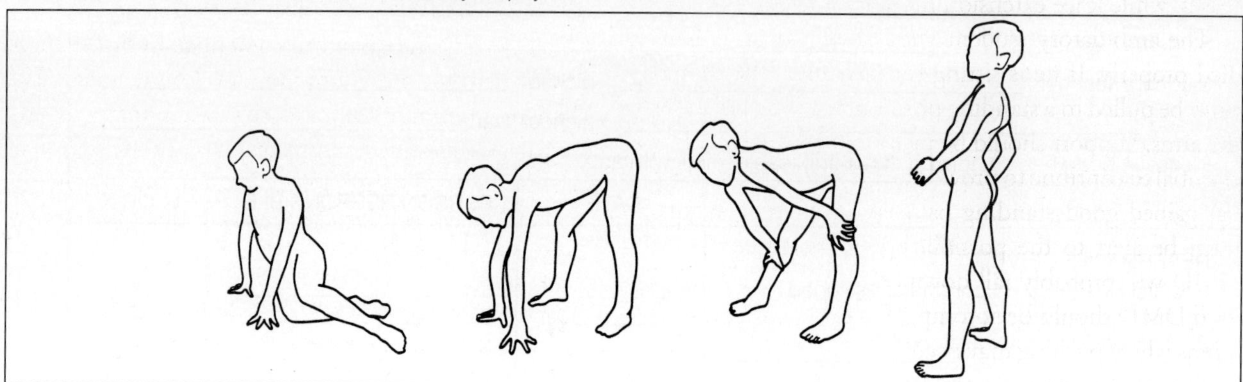

Note. From *Meeting the Needs of Students with Special Physical and Health Care Needs* by Hill, © 1999, Reprinted with permission of Prentice-Hall, Inc.: Upper Saddle River, NJ.

position (Figure 2–4). The child will walk with a sway back to compensate for weak leg muscles, and often develops **scoliosis** (spinal curvature) resulting from weak back muscles. Eventually ambulation will no longer be possible, and the child will need a manual wheelchair. Continuing muscle weakness will necessitate the use of an electric wheelchair. Muscle control will become limited to use of the fingers; even the ability to hold up the head will be lost.

In the final stages of muscular dystrophy, there is an increased incidence of respiratory infections. Individuals with Duchenne muscular dystrophy often live until adolescence or young adulthood. Death is usually caused by respiratory failure due to weakness of the chest muscles or heart failure due to weakened heart muscles. Life expectancy is constantly revised upward with advances in scoliosis treatment and pulmonary care.

Associated Medical Conditions

Gradual loss of respiratory function is secondary to weakness of the abdominal and thoracic muscles. Muscle weakness prevents the individual from coughing up secretions and may result in pneumonia. Teachers and others must remain alert to signs of respiratory failure and safeguard against transmission of infections.

Although it is not as common as respiratory involvement, a second consequence of muscle weakness is involvement of cardiac muscle in adolescents with DMD (Iannaccone, 1992). Finally, muscle weakness and atrophy leads to increasing difficulties in walking. Prolonged sitting and the inequality of strength of muscles lead to development of contractures in the hips, knees, ankles, and feet. Individuals require orthotics (braces), crutches, and supports to facilitate standing and to prevent lower limb deformities. Eventually, surgery may be required to prevent the progression of spinal curvatures (Miller, Moseley, & Koreska, 1992).

Medical and Therapeutic Treatments

Surgery. Since there is presently no cure for DMD, treatment is aimed at maintaining function and slowing the progression of symptoms. Surgery is indicated in order to prolong ambulation by release of contractures. After students with Duchenne muscular dystrophy begin to use wheelchairs, they may develop severe spinal curvatures that require **fusion** (surgically stabilizing vertebrae by attaching them to metal rods or wiring them together). While fusing the spine improves respiratory function and makes sitting easier, it also decreases independent mobility. Making the decision as to whether to lessen mobility in order to achieve improved function in other vital areas is only one challenge faced by families of individuals with muscular dystrophy.

Orthopedic Treatment. Because physical inactivity can speed the progression of symptoms, it is desirable for students with DMD to remain ambulatory as long as possible (Heller et al., 1996). A walker can be useful in prolonging walking with leg braces on tiled floors and thin carpeting and in maintaining strength in unaffected muscles in the arms and hands. Students with muscular dystrophy should begin to use standing equipment after leg braces are introduced and before walking ceases, while knee extension mobility is available.

The ambulatory student with DMD must be handled properly. If he is sitting (or has fallen), he should *never* be pulled to a standing position by lifting up under the arms. Support should be provided to the trunk. It is essential to continue to provide support until the student has gained good standing balance. In addition, adults must be alert to the possibility that the student with DMD will probably fall down if pushed. The student with DMD should be accompanied by an adult in situations where pushing may occur (such as cafeteria lines).

Eventually, a power-operated wheelchair will replace ambulation as the means of mobility. Wheelchairs should be comfortable to sit in, sturdy, and designed with thick, inflatable tires for use on outdoor terrain. However, a power chair generally requires the added purchase of a van (with a lift) for transport. The feasibility of using such a system at home should be examined. If the family cannot maintain the wheelchair at home, it may need to be stored and its battery charged at school. Students with DMD generally respond to a power wheelchair with pleasure at its speed and maneuverability. However, educational and therapeutic personnel must realize that wheelchair use also signals loss of function, and be sensitive to the conflicting feelings expressed by other family members for whom the wheelchair signals the progression of this disease.

Therapeutic Contributions. The management team struggles against the rapid progression of DMD by attempting to maintain active, upright mobility and positioning. Braces will be used to provide stability for walking and to prevent contractures (Do, 2002). Standing equipment is used to avoid knee or ankle contractures and to delay the onset of scoliosis. Swimming and other forms of water exercise may be recommended since the individual's increasing fat-to-muscle ratio make him more buoyant in water.

Students with Duchenne muscular dystrophy will need increased amounts of physical assistance with some school activities and with most, if not all, activities of daily living as their disease progresses. Therapists may recommend adaptive equipment to enhance hand function, including special eating utensils with grips or mobile arm supports. These are ball-bearing devices that support the arm in space so that the child may properly place the hand for activities such as feeding and writing.

Impact on Physical, Cognitive, and Psychosocial Development

Of all the physical disabilities described in this chapter, DMD is the most unique developmentally. The changes in motor function that accompany DMD have important implications that require adaptation of the environment. As important as environmental adaptations is acknowledgment of the psychosocial impact of this progressive disease.

Physical Development. The child with DMD has a different physical development experience than typically developing children. Physical development is initially normal; some children are not diagnosed until they begin to attend school. Initial physical mastery is followed by slow, progressive loss of function. Unlike the child with a congenital but stable disability (like myelomeningocele or cerebral palsy), students with DMD can remember when they were able to walk, run, and jump. To facilitate their physical and psychosocial adjustment, students with DMD should be encouraged to remain as active and autonomous as possible within the boundaries of their condition.

Three important ways to meet the physical needs of students with DMD are to (a) understand the condition and its typical progression, (b) periodically monitor student status, and (c) match student status with an appropriate level of assistance. It is very important to include input from family members, therapists, and school nurses in determining the best practices for physical support. One key to supporting physical capabilities in the student with DMD is to provide assistance that allows for maximum independence while conserving endurance. Therapists and dietitians will need to work with the student and his family to avoid obesity, which will make ambulation more difficult. Students should be encouraged to walk, but this goal must be balanced against fatigue. For example, a student who is too tired to participate with peers in a board game after walking out to the playground has lost the social benefit of recess. Instead, he might walk only part of the way and be pushed the remainder of the distance in his wheelchair.

Cognitive Development. Research indicates that cognition is impaired in some males with DMD, especially in verbal performance (Emery, 2002; Polakoff, Morton, Koch, & Rios, 1998). However, poor school performance may also be the result of low performance expectations, absence due to illness, or psychological stress. It is important for teachers to remain focused on academic proficiency while maintaining realistic expectations as the disease progresses.

Psychosocial Development. Individuals with Duchenne muscular dystrophy experience the psychosocial implications of terminal illness. In addition to their weakening physical condition, they eventually come to realize that their prognosis for a long life is not good. Increasing dependence for care, social isolation, and changes in body image might lead to depression (Polakoff et al., 1998).

Working and living with a child who has a terminal illness presents difficult situations leading to discomfort and withdrawal by service providers and even family members. The situation can be especially difficult if the family wishes to "spare" the older child or adolescent from the reality of his condition. One outcome of this situation is to isolate the student from open communication with his family, which may lead to significant emotional trauma. Teachers need to seek assistance from professionals such as school social workers or psychologists to negotiate this difficult situation. Teachers must also be careful about providing information if they are not familiar with the extent of what the student already knows. In the event that a student asks a teacher, "What is wrong with me?" the teacher should suggest a conversation with the parents or doctor instead of offering an explanation for which the student is unprepared.

For students with progressive conditions, "the psychological problems . . . manifested in youngsters with terminal illnesses are more difficult to cope with. The affected students, their peers, families, and teachers all need the perspectives that can be gained from death education programs" (Best, Bigge, & Sirvis, 1994, p. 327). Families, teachers, and others need to understand that age is an important variable in how children conceptualize death, and that children react to their mortality in different ways (Corr, Nabe, & Corr, 1994). It is most important for teachers and others to maintain an attitude that the student is a valued, useful, and vital person. Demonstrating separate expectations for the student with DMD (e.g., altering classroom discipline or ignoring inappropriate behavior) heightens the risk of estranging the student from his peers and sends the undesirable message that he is not as important as others. Providing structure with the expectation of achievement to the best of one's ability supports good mental health.

Implications for Education and Personal Autonomy

It is of paramount importance that students with DMD remain active and engaged in the educational process. School is the place where they meet their friends and stay connected to typical aspects of their lives. Teachers and others must strive to maintain academic rigor while anticipating the course of the disease.

Adaptation Strategies. There are numerous simple and effective ways to adapt educational materials for students with DMD. Low-technology adaptations include elevating work papers by using a desk podium, and providing a pencil with a soft lead or a marker for ease of use. Other simple adaptations include assigning homework that can be audiotaped instead of written, allowing use of the calculator (once the concept of a particular calculation is mastered), and distributing homework assignments across several days. Teachers can modify or eliminate time qualifiers on tests, classroom assignments, and games.

Computers can be very important for students with DMD. Individuals who have lost head and body control can have full access to computers and complete their schoolwork with switches that require very light movement or are even respiration-controlled. Computers can be used also for art projects, leisure activities, jobs, and environmental control. Software that eliminates keystrokes and otherwise reduces muscle use helps to reduce fatigue while boosting efficiency.

Strategies to Enhance Personal Autonomy. Teachers must be creative to reduce fatigue and enhance personal autonomy. The authors know one teacher who made a personalized signature stamp for a student to eliminate his need to sign his name to each of his papers. Some students benefit by placing the forearms on a shallow elevation of the table and lowering the keyboard under the wrists, so they can rest their arms and continue to use their hands to hit the keys. Miniature keyboards are perfect for the student with DMD. Teachers and other students can agree on a method for acknowledgment that does not involve raising the hand. Scheduling more rigorous academic activities for morning and allowing rest periods capitalizes on student performance capabilities. The student's desk can be positioned in the classroom to reduce the amount of effort needed to negotiate the distance.

Whatever the adaptation, it is important to maintain academic rigor. When teachers and others lower their expectations as the medical condition progresses, they are sending a message that the student is fundamentally different. School experiences may represent the most typical activity in the life of an adolescent whose physical condition is changing.

Implications for Career and Adult Outcomes

For all the reasons previously noted, adolescents with DMD may not have high expectations for themselves as functional adults. However, life expectancy in DMD is constantly being revised upward, and emphasis should be placed on career and vocational interests and skills. Since there is little evidence to indicate a negative association between DMD and academic ability (Heller et al., 1996), adolescents with DMD should consider postsecondary education.

ORTHOPEDIC AND MUSCULOSKELETAL CONDITIONS

Curvature of the spine, congenital hip dislocations and deformities, limb deficiencies, juvenile arthritis, osteogenesis imperfecta, and arthrogryposis all are categorized as orthopedic and musculoskeletal conditions. In this chapter, the authors have chosen to discuss limb deficiencies to represent this diverse category of physical disabilities.

LIMB DEFICIENCIES

Definitions and Descriptions

Limb deficiency is defined as an absence or partial loss of a limb. This can be **congenital** or **acquired.** Congenital deficiencies occur in about 1 in every 2,000 births, and acquired amputations occur less frequently (Scott, 1989). Congenital limb deficiencies may be due to chromosome defects or constriction within the uterus during pregnancy. Many times the cause is not known. **Thalidomide,** an antiemetic (antinausea) drug widely popular in Europe during the late 1950s to early 1960s and currently becoming available in the United States, is linked to limb deficiency. Other drugs may also be associated with congenital limb deficiency (Goldberg, 1981). Acquired limb deficiencies may be the result of accidents in which the limb was crushed, torn, or burned. Explosions also account for acquired limb deficiencies. Limbs may be lost due to bone tumors or cysts (Boos, Janvier, McIlvain-Simpson, Sanford, & Wade, 1993). Finally, acquired limb deficiencies (or amputations) may be surgically planned to prepare a partial limb for a **prosthesis** (artificial limb).

Limb deficiencies may further be classified as **terminal** or **intercalary.** Terminal deficiencies occur when the limb is correctly developed at its origin but is incomplete further down the limb. Intercalary deficiencies mean that all or part of the mid-portion of the limb is missing. Other terms include **amelia** (missing limb) and **phocomelia** (partial or complete limb attached to a shortened limb) (Williams, Heller, Alberto, Forney, & Schwartzman, 1996). Figure 2–5 illustrates one type of limb deficiency.

FIGURE 2–5
This girl has a condition called *phocomelia,* in which most of the arm and forearm bones are missing.

Note. From E. E. Bleck & D. A. Nagels (Eds.), *Physically Handicapped Children: A Medical Atlas for Teachers* © 1982. Published by Allyn and Bacon, Boston, MA. Copyright © 1982 by Pearson Education. Reprinted by permission of the publisher.

Associated Medical Conditions

There are no specific conditions associated with limb deficiencies, unless the condition that gives rise to the limb deficiency is part of a condition characterized by multiple anomalies. Readers are probably familiar with the effects of the drug thalidomide. Thalidomide was popular in Western Europe and Canada in the late 1950s to early 1960s for treatment of morning sickness, although it was not available in the United States for that purpose. Many of the pregnant women who took thalidomide gave birth to children with a range of congenital limb deficiencies. Thalidomide apparently interfered with formation of the bones of the arms and legs. Presently, thalidomide has reentered the medical market for treatment of nausea in persons with cancer and AIDS.

Medical and Therapeutic Treatments

Surgery. Medical treatment of limb deficiencies usually involves a surgical amputation procedure (when necessary), corrective procedures to improve the function of the existing partial limb, skin grafts, and preparing a limb for a prosthetic device. It is generally recommended that prosthetic fitting be carried out as soon as possible after the surgery.

Orthopedic Treatments. The field of prosthetics has developed rapidly in the areas of appearance and function (see Figure 2–6). Prostheses range from glovelike cosmetic hands to myoelectric devices that open and close by muscle activation in the stump via electrodes placed on the skin (Challenor, 1992). They extend the length, reach, and motion of the limb. However, because they block incoming sensation, some individuals prefer to use the stump (remainder of the limb). The apparatus that is used to secure the prosthesis can be awkward and heavy. Finally, some individuals will prefer to use their feet and mouth to perform specific activities.

Therapeutic Contributions. Children with congenital limb deficiencies will receive training to use the prosthesis at a very young age. Students who have a lower-limb deficiency may have difficulties with balance and footing and may experience fatigue from the weight of the prosthesis. Individuals with complete bilateral leg amputation (no legs at all) can wear a pelvic bucket with two full leg prostheses attached (Challenor, 1992).

FIGURE 2–6
Types of prosthetic devices

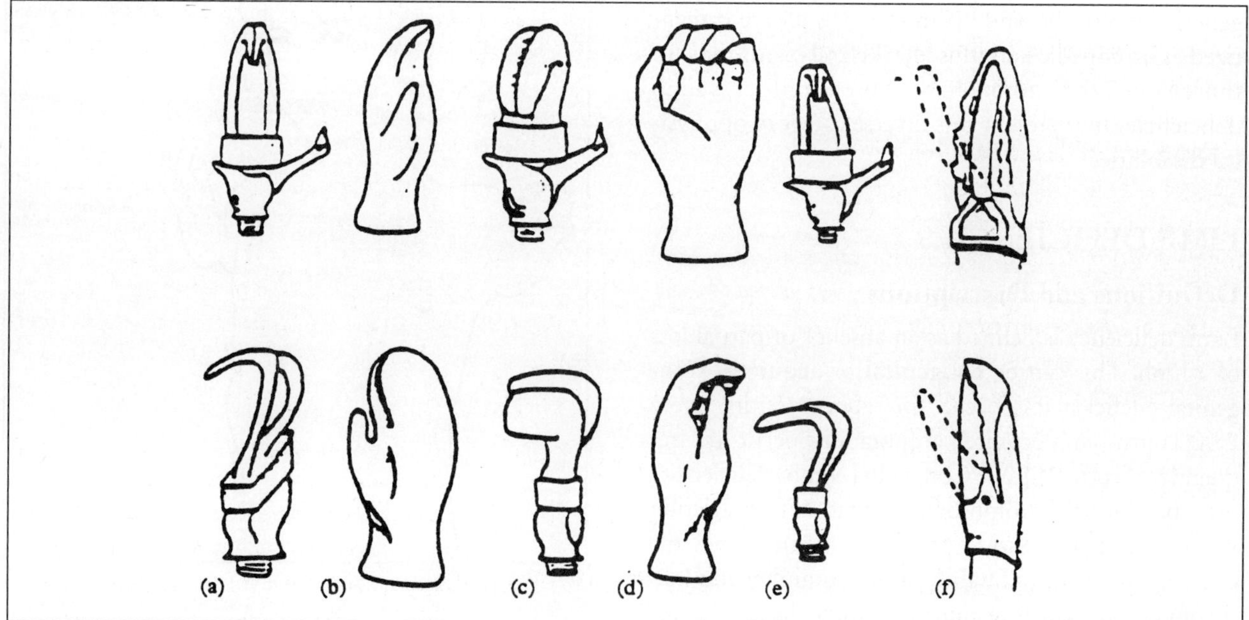

Note. From Y. B. Challenor (1992). "Limb Deficiencies in Children." In G. E. Molnar (Ed.), *Pediatric Rehabilitation* (2nd ed., pp. 400–424). Copyright © 1992 Lippencott Williams & Wilkins. Reprinted by permission.

Crutches will be needed to provide balance (Cusick, 1991). Children with complete bilateral arm amputation (no arms at all) can use their feet to perform many tasks.

Most children with one arm or one leg adapt by using the intact arm for hand-use activities in school. Classroom accommodations will be determined by the student's acceptance of the prosthesis and willingness to learn to operate it. Limitations on physical activities are caused only by the general state of health (as in cancer recovery) or the development of skin sores under the socket (where the prosthetic limb attaches). Any problems of fit or tolerance should be reported for prosthetic adjustment or replacement (Cusick, 1991).

Impact on Physical, Cognitive, and Psychosocial Development

Physical and Cognitive Development. Unless the limb deficiency is related to a specific syndrome or occurred secondary to a head injury, there is no correlation between limb deficiency and cognitive development. However, infants explore their environments through movement, and mobility must be encouraged even in the absence of limbs. Infants missing a hand or arm can be positioned in a car seat or seating device with a tray so that the remaining limb can be used to bring objects closer for exploration. Play materials can be stabilized by clamping them onto surfaces or made easier to grasp with loops. Older children must be encouraged to use their prostheses to stabilize materials. Teachers must challenge themselves to find creative ways for children with limb deficiencies to engage in the same activities as other children.

Temperature is an important health consideration for individuals with limb deficiencies. The mechanism for regulating body temperature is perspiration. If much skin surface area is lost (for example, if a leg is missing), the individual may have trouble regulating body temperature and become dehydrated. Skin under the prosthesis may also perspire and become irritated. Teachers can keep extra clothing at school and encourage the child to add or remove clothes as necessary (Mason & Wright, 1994). They should also be alert for any signs that the stump has become sore or that the skin on the stump is irritated or infected.

Psychosocial Development. Age is an important variable in psychosocial adjustment to limb deficiency. Children who are born with limb deficiencies face the need to make compensatory physical adaptations immediately. Attitudes within the family are very important. Parents may experience a sense of loss. In addition, they will be faced with the efforts involved in multidisciplinary team management. They will need to work with medical and therapeutic personnel, including doctors, prosthetists, physical and occupational therapists, and others in optimizing their child's functional abilities. They may respond with overprotection.

Children with acquired limb deficiencies face a slightly different situation. They may have attained motor milestones (walking, grasping, finger manipulation, etc.), only to lose that ability with the loss of a limb. If their limb was lost as a result of an accident, there may be feelings of guilt and anger. Family members may also experience these emotions.

Children with limb deficiencies must learn to negotiate questions by peers. It is important for teachers and others to understand that curiosity is a normal response, and the student with a limb deficiency can be helped to respond by having an opportunity to show other students how the prosthesis operates. For children who are shy, a good strategy is to practice skills. For example, the therapist can take a child to the school playground (when other children are not present) to practice getting onto a swing, gripping the chains, moving the swing back and forth, and getting off again. Once these skills are mastered, the child may feel more confident about playing in public. Similar strategies can be employed in classroom activities and even driver training.

Implications for Education and Personal Autonomy

Students with limb deficiencies should progress through academic grades with their nondisabled peers. If the limb deficiency occurred as a result of trauma, time may be lost from school while the student recovers from trauma, is fitted with a prosthesis, and receives rehabilitative therapy. Most educational concerns are related to adaptations of materials and psychosocial considerations.

Adaptations for Education. Therapists provide vital assistance to teachers and others who provide services to students with limb deficiencies in school. They can demonstrate the use and maintenance of the prosthesis. In addition, therapists can teach the child foot and mouth skills that have application for classroom activities.

There are many strategies for facilitating the use of prostheses. A student might be encouraged to use a prosthetic arm to stabilize a piece of paper for cutting or writing. If their stumps are long enough and/or if there are digits on the stump, some children choose to hold a pencil with the stumps or digits. Alternatives include mouth writing and foot writing. Using a computer is an alternative to written materials, and the same mechanisms apply—mouth, foot, stump, or prosthesis, depending upon the feasibility of each.

For the student who is missing a limb above the elbow, be sure that the height of the desk does not interfere with the function of the prosthesis. Because it is tiring to operate the device with the back muscles, lowering the desk will help to avoid fatigue.

Students should be encouraged to engage in any playground or sports activities unless prohibited by doctor's orders. For example, a student with weak leg bones following a cancer surgery or a student whose prosthesis is new needs gradually increased wear time to allow the skin to toughen. Skin damage can lead to infection, and teachers need to check where the prosthesis fits onto the limb for problems (skin that is irritated, broken, or bleeding, etc.). Keep crutches available for those occasions when the lower-extremity prosthesis breaks or when wearing it causes too much pain to withstand long-distance walking outside the classroom (Cusick, 1991).

Supporting Personal Autonomy. The child with a congenital limb deficiency will begin adjusting and adapting immediately. Care must be taken to encourage personal autonomy, even when the resulting behaviors look awkward or "less than normal." For example, the child may be able to feed himself or brush his teeth very efficiently with his feet. Not only does this behavior look different, it may remind observers that feet should not go near someone's mouth. However, using foot skills to perform functional activities is a better option than relying on others to perform the same task.

An important key to promoting personal autonomy and good psychosocial health is to encourage the student to assume care of the prosthesis as he or she would any other part of the body. The author remembers an instance in which a student was preparing for a swim class. Just like his peers, he prepared to go into the swimming pool by first removing his shoes and socks and placing the socks inside the shoes—although he wore prostheses on both legs! This behavior reflected how well the child had integrated his artificial limbs into his body awareness, and how naturally he responded to the situation.

Teachers can assist students to gain personal autonomy by allowing them to try physical activities (and even struggle a little). It is also important for teachers and others to approach the prosthesis as a part of that student. Reacting with disgust, dismay, or hesitation conveys a very negative message and undermines positive body image. A parent, therapist, and even the student can be instrumental in showing the teacher (and other students) how a prosthesis is operated and maintained.

Implications for Career and Adult Outcomes

Career possibilities improve with functional limb use, whether function is attained through use of the prosthesis or the partial/residual limb. Individuals with lower-limb deficiencies may be more comfortable if they are not required to stand or move frequently. Individuals with arm or hand loss may have some problems with fine motor dexterity and speed (Clark, 1993). However, these possibilities are very individual, and assumptions should not be made automatically about career options.

SUMMARY AND CONCLUSION

Students whose physical disabilities are the result of neuromotor impairments, degenerative diseases, and orthopedic and musculoskeletal disorders experience many challenges to development and functional skill acquisition. They may not receive the motor and sensory feedback that comes with moving their bodies through space. They may have acquired many skills, only to lose them as a result of an accident that injured their brain or resulted in removal of a limb. They may remember when they could do things (such as walk, ride a bicycle, or visit the bathroom independently) that are now impossible as a degenerative disease slowly encroaches on their abilities. Teachers who work with individuals with physical disabilities need to remember these issues as they strive to make the school experience exciting, challenging, and stimulating. Their job will be to understand the nature of the disability and its effect on function, but not allow this knowledge to become a disincentive or an excuse. Much creativity and energy will be required to adapt materials, adjust lesson length and intensity, work with other professionals, and communicate with families. Putting the child first also means supporting the outcome of independent function, whether it is in equipment maintenance, homework follow-through, or maintaining balance while sitting at a desk. Above all, children need to incorporate their impairments into daily function to ensure maximum autonomy.

QUESTIONS FOR DISCUSSION

1. A student with myelomeningocele has recently joined your elementary class. What adaptations might that student need to become independent in self-care in the bathroom? How can the student be accommodated at school?
2. Describe three ways that you could assist a child who displays "cocktail party syndrome" to remain focused on academic classroom assignments.
3. In your high school there is a boy with myelomeningocele who uses a wheelchair. In the teacher's lounge you overhear one of his teachers talking about this student's interest in learning to drive a car. Where could you direct this teacher for more information?
4. Students who have experienced a TBI react in different ways as their consciousness becomes less impaired. Using the Rancho Los Amigos Cognitive Scales, describe how you might alter a lesson in math for a student who is functional at Level II (responsive to environment).
5. Duchenne muscular dystrophy is a progressive disease. How would you prepare *yourself* to welcome an adolescent with DMD into your classroom?
6. A little girl has just moved into your kindergarten class. She is missing her right arm entirely and has only two fingers on the end of the other arm. She wears a prosthesis but can also use her fingers. What questions will you ask her parents, her physical and occupational therapists, and her to help her make a good transition into class?

FOCUS ON THE NET

National Organization of Rare Disorders
http://www.rarediseases.org

Begun in 1983, the National Organization of Rare Disorders (NORD) is considered to be the primary nongovernmental, nonprofit clearinghouse for information regarding rare disorders, related organizations, and orphan drug information. Internet users will find a variety of exceptionally useful types of information located on the NORD Web site. The general public, patients, family members, and medical personnel all profit from NORD's information.

1. "Rare Disorders Database" (RDB), the "heart" of NORD's program, is a delivery system providing understandable information specifically related to a variety of conditions. Currently, over 1,000 rare disorders are catalogued in this database. A "rare" disorder is defined as a condition that affects fewer than 2,000 people in the United States. With more than 5,000 rare disorders identified, approximately 28 million Americans (1 in 12) are affected by some kind of rare disorder. Topics covered include symptoms, causes, affected population(s), related disorders, standard therapies, and resources. The complete database is available by subscription only. Individuals or organizations interested in accessing the full text of the database must pay a fee. Abstracts for each of the rare disorders are available online, however.
2. "Resources database" is available free online and is an exhaustive listing of resources that correspond to the rare disorders catalogued in RDB.
3. "Orphan Drug Database" provides drug-related information according to specific diseases and conditions, generic and trade names of drugs, and disease sponsors.

Each of the databases is keyword searchable.

The American Academy of Neurology
http://www.aan.com/

The American Academy of Neurology (AAN) is a worldwide professional organization that provides information on neurology to both medical professionals and the public. Knowing more about neurology can not only be empowering for families and education professionals, but can make all the difference in the treatment and improvement of people's health.

Children with Spina Bifida: A Resource Page for Parents
http://www.waisman.wisc.edu/~rowley/sb-kids/index.htmlx

Developed by the mother of a child with spina bifida, this Web site shows how to connect with other parents, provides stories and pictures from other families, and lists current research articles and links to other spina bifida Web sites.

Karolinska Institute Library/Musculoskeletal Diseases
http://www.mic.ki.se/Diseases/c05.html

Karolinska Institute Library/Nervous System Diseases
http://www.mic.ki.se/Diseases/c05.html

An exhaustive, exceptionally well organized Web site that is organized according to musculoskeletal diseases and disorders of the nervous system. This is an excellent place to search for disability-specific information.

REFERENCES

Accardo, P. J., & Whitman, B. Y. (1996). *Dictionary of developmental disabilities terminology.* Baltimore: Paul Brookes.

Banit, D. M., Iwinski, H. J., Talwalkar, V., & Johnson, M. (2001). Posterior spinal fusion in paralytic scoliosis and myelomeningocele. *Journal of Pediatric Orthopaedics, 21,* 117–125.

Barth, J., & Macciocchi, S. (Eds.). (1983). Mild traumatic brain injury. *Journal of Head Trauma Rehabilitation, 8*(3), 1–12.

Beaulieu, C. L. (2002). Rehabilitation and outcome following pediatric traumatic brain injury. *Surgical Clinics of North America, 82,* 393–408.

Best, S., Bigge, J., & Sirvis, B. (1994). Physical and health impairments. In N. Haring & L. McCormick, *Exceptional children and youth* (6th ed., pp. 300–341). New York: Macmillan.

Bleck, E. E. (1982). Myelomeningocele, meningocele and spina bifida. In E. E. Bleck & D. A. Nagel (Eds.), *Physically handicapped children: A medical atlas for teachers* (pp. 345–362). New York: Grune & Stratton.

Blosser, J. L., & DePompei, R. (1994). Creating an effective classroom environment. In R. Savage & G. Wolcott (Eds.), *Educational dimensions of acquired brain injury* (pp. 413–454). Austin, TX: Pro-Ed.

Blum, R. W., Resnick, M. D., Nelson, R., & St. Germaine, A. (1991). Family and peer issues among adolescents with spina bifida and cerebral palsy. *Pediatrics, 88,* 280–285.

Boos, M. L., Janvier, K. W., McIlvain-Simpson, G. R., Sanford, C. C., & Wade, G. (1993). Nursing planning, intervention, and evaluation for altered musculoskeletal function. In D. B. Jackson and R. B. Saunders (Eds.), *Child health nursing: A comprehensive approach to the care of children and their families* (pp. 1679–1745). Philadelphia: Lippincott.

Chadwick, D. (2000). Seizures and epilepsy after traumatic brain injury. *The Lancet, 355,* 334–335.

Challenor, Y. B. (1992). Limb deficiencies in children. In G. E. Molnar (Ed.), *Pediatric rehabilitation* (2nd ed., pp. 400–424). Baltimore: Williams and Wilkins.

Charney, E. B. (1992). Neural tube defects: Spina bifida and myelomeningocele. In M. Batshaw & Y. M. Perret (Eds.), *Children with disabilities: A medical primer* (3rd ed., pp. 471–488). Baltimore: Brookes.

Charney, E. B., Weller, S. C., Sutton, L. N., Bruce, D. A., & Schut, L. B. (1985). Management of the newborn with myelomeningocele: Time for a decision making process. *Pediatrics, 75,* 58–64.

Clark, D. R. (1993). Orthotics and prosthetics. In M. G. Brodwin, F. Tellez, & S. K. Brodwin (Eds.), *Medical, psychosocial, and vocational aspects of disability* (pp. 407–420). Athens, GA: Elliott & Fitzpatrick.

Corr, C., Nabe, C., & Corr, D. (1994). *Death and dying: Life and living.* Pacific Grove, CA: Brooks/Cole.

Cusick, B. (1991). Therapeutic management of sensorimotor and physical disabilities. In J. L. Bigge, *Teaching individuals with physical and multiple disabilities* (3rd ed., pp. 16–50). New York: Macmillan.

Davis, A. (2000). Cognitive impairments following traumatic brain injury. *Critical Care Nursing Clinics of North America, 12*(4), 447–455.

Disabato, J., & Wulf, J. (1994). Altered neurologic function. In C. L. Betz, M. M. Hunsberger, & S. Wright (Eds.), *Family-centered nursing care of children* (2nd ed., pp. 1717–1814). Philadelphia: Saunders.

DiScala, C., Osberg, J., & Savage, R. (1997). Children hospitalized for traumatic brain injury: Transition to postacute care. *Journal of Head Trauma Rehabilitation, 12*(3), 1–10.

Do, T. (2002). Orthopedic management of the muscular dystrophies. *Current Opinions in Pediatrics, 14,* 50–53.

Emery, A. E. H. (2002). The muscular dystrophies. *The Lancet, 359,* 687–695.

Eule, J. M., Erikson, M. A., O'Brien, M. F., & Handler, M.(2002). Chiari I malformation associated with syringomyelia and scoliosis. *SPINE, 27*(13), 1431–1455.

Folzer, S. M. (2001). Psychotherapy with "mild" brain-injured patients. *American Journal of Orthopsychiatry, 71*(2), 245–251.

Friedrich, W. N., Lovejoy, M. C., Shaffer, J., Shurtleff, D. B., & Beilke, R. L. (1991). Cognitive abilities and achievement status of children with myelomeningocele: A contemporary sample. *Journal of Pediatric Psychology, 16,* 423–428.

Gleeson, R. M. (1995). Use of non-latex gloves for children with latex problems. *Journal of Pediatric Nursing, 10*(1), 64–65.

Goldberg, M. J. (1981). The pediatric amputee: An epidemiologic survey. *Orthopedic Review, 10*(10), 49–54.

Griebel, M. L., Oakes, W. J., & Worley, G. (1991). The Chiari malformation associated with myelomeningocele. In H. L. Rekate (Ed.), *Comprehensive management of spina bifida* (pp. 67–92). Boca Raton, FL: CRC Press.

Hall, D. M., Johnson, S. L., & Middleton, J. (1990). Rehabilitation of head injured children. *Archives of Disease in Childhood, 65,* 553–556.

Hanson, S. L., & Clippard, D. (1992). Assessment of children with traumatic brain injury: Planning for school reentry. *Physical Medicine and Rehabilitation: State of the Art Reviews, 6,* 483–494.

Heller, K. W., Alberto, P. A., Forney, P. E., & Schwartzman, M. N. (1996). *Understanding physical, sensory, and health impairments: Characteristics and educational implications.* Pacific Grove, CA: Brooks/Cole.

Heller, K. W., Forney, P. E., Alberto, P. A., Schwartzman, M. N., & Goeckel, T. M. (1999). *Meeting physical and health needs of children with disabilities.* Belmont, CA: Wadsworth.

Hill, J. L. (1999). *Meeting the needs of students with special physical and health care needs.* Upper Saddle River, NJ: Prentice Hall.

Hurley, A. D., Dorman, C., Laatsch, L. K., Bell, S., & D'Avignon, J. (1990). Cognitive functioning in patients with spina bifida, hydrocephalus, and the cocktail party syndrome. *Developmental Neuropsychology, 6,* 151–172.

Iannaccone, S. T. (1992). Current status of Duchenne muscular dystrophy. *Pediatric Clinics of North America, 39,* 879–894.

Jaffe, K. M., Fay, G. C., Polissar, N. L., Martin, K. M., Shurtleff, H., Rivara, J. M., & Winn, H. R. (1992). Severity of pediatric brain injury and early neurobehavioral outcome: A cohort study. *Archives of Physical Medicine and Rehabilitation, 73,* 540–547.

Jaffe, K. M., Polissar, N. L., Fay, G. C., & Liao, S. (1995). Recovery trends over three years following pediatric traumatic brain injury. *Archives of Physical Medicine and Rehabilitation, 76,* 17–26.

Jennett, B., Teasdale, G., Galbraith, S., Pickard, J., Grant, H., Braakman, R., Avezaat, C., Maas, A., Minderhoud, J., Vecht, C. J., Heiden, J., Small, R., Caton, W., & Kurze, T. (1977). Severe head injuries in three countries. *Journal of Neurology, Neurosurgery, and Psychiatry, 40,* 291–298.

Koch, L., Merz, M., & Lynch, R. (1995). Screening for mild traumatic brain injury: A guide for rehabilitation counselors. *Journal of Rehabilitation, 61*(4), 50–56.

Kraus, J. F., Rock, A., & Hemyari, P. (1990). Brain injuries among infants, children, adolescents, and young adults. *American Journal of Diseases of Children, 144,* 684–691.

Kushner, D. S. (2001). Concussion in sports: Minimizing the risk for complication. *American Family Physician, 64,* 1007–1015.

Liptak, G. S. (1997). Neural tube defects. In M. L. Batshaw (Ed.), *Children with disabilities* (4th ed., pp. 529–552). Baltimore: Brookes.

Lord, J., Varzos, N., Behrman, B., Wicks, J., & Wicks, D. (1990). Implications of mainstream classrooms for adolescents with spina bifida. *Developmental Medicine and Child Neurology, 32,* 20–29.

Marshall, L. F. (2000). Head injury: Recent past, present, and future. *Neurosurgery, 47*(3), 546–561.

Mason, K. J., & Wright, S. (1994). Altered musculoskeletal function. In C. L. Betz, M. M. Hinsberger, & S. Wright (Eds.), *Family centered nursing care for children* (2nd ed., pp. 1825–1873). Philadelphia: Saunders.

McLone, D. G. (1992). Continuing concepts in the management of spina bifida. *Pediatric Neurosurgery, 18,* 254–256.

Meeropol, E. (1997). Alert: Latex allergy. In S. Porter, M. Haynie, T. Bierle, T. H. Caldwell, & J. Palfrey (Eds.), *Children and youth assisted by medical technology in educational settings* (2nd ed., pp. 79–82). Baltimore: Brookes.

Michaud, L., Duhaime, A., & Lazar, M. F. (1997). Traumatic brain injury. In M. Batshaw (Ed.), *Children with disabilities: A medical primer* (4th ed., pp. 595–617). Baltimore: Brookes.

Miller, F., Moseley, C. F., & Koreska, J. (1992). Spinal fusion in Duchenne muscular dystrophy. *Developmental Medicine and Child Neurology, 34,* 775–786.

Mira, M., Tucker, B., & Tyler, J. (1992). *Traumatic brain injury in children and adolescents: A sourcebook for teachers and other school personnel.* Austin, TX: Pro-Ed.

Mitchell, C. C., Fiewell, E., & Davy, P. (1983). Spina bifida. In J. Umbreit (Ed.), *Physical disabilities and health impairments: An introduction* (pp. 117–131). Upper Saddle River, NJ: Merrill/Prentice Hall.

National Institutes of Health. (1999). *Report of the NIH consensus development conference on the rehabilitation of persons with traumatic brain injury.* Bethesda, MD: U.S. Department of Health and Human Services.

Pearson, M. L., Cole, J. S., & Jarvis, W. R. (1994). How common is latex allergy? A survey of children with myelodysplasia. *Developmental Medicine and Child Neurology, 36,* 64–69.

Pierz, K., Banta, J., Thompson, J., Gahm, N., & Hartford, J. (2000). The effect of tethered cord release on scoliosis in myelomeningocele. *Journal of Pediatric Orthopaedics, 20,* 362–365.

Polakoff, R. J., Worton, A. A., Koch, K. D., & Rios, C. M. (1998). The psychological and cognitive impact of Duchenne's muscular dystrophy. *Seminars in Pediatric Neurology, 5*(2), 116–123.

Rowley-Kelly, F. C., & Reigel, D. (1993). *Teaching the student with spina bifida.* Baltimore: Brookes.

Savage, R. C., & Wolcott, G. (Eds.). (1994). *Educational dimensions of acquired brain injury.* Austin, TX: Pro-Ed.

Savage, R. C., & Wolcott, G. (Eds.). (1995). *An educator's manual: What educators need to know about students with traumatic brain injury.* Washington, DC: Brain Injury Association.

Scott, C. I. (1989). Genetic and familial aspects of limb defects with emphasis on the lower extremity. In A. Kalamachi (Ed.), *Congenital lower limb deficiencies* (pp. 46–57). New York: Springer-Verlag.

Setoguchi, Y. (1982). Amputations in children. In E. Bleck & D. Nagel (Eds.), *Physically handicapped children: A medical atlas for teachers* (pp. 17–26). New York: Grune & Stratton.

Shurtleff, D. B., & Lemire, R. J. (1995). Epidemiology, etiologic factors, and prenatal diagnosis of open spinal dysraphism. *Neurosurgery Clinics of North America, 6,* 183–193.

Steensma, M. (1991). Getting the student with head injuries back to school: Strategies for the classroom. *Intervention in School and Clinic, 27,* 207–210.

Tyler, J., & Grandinette, S. (2003). Effective teaching strategies. *Brain Injury Source,* 38–41.

Westcott, M. A., Dynes, M. C., Remer, E. M., Donaldson, J. S., & Dias, L. S. (1992). Congenital and acquired orthopedic abnormalities in patients with myelomeningocele. *Radiographics, 12,* 1155–1173.

Williams, S. M., Heller, K. W., Alberto, P. A., Forney, P. E., & Schwartzman, M. N. (1996). Limb deficiency. In K. W. Heller, P. A. Alberto, P. E. Forney, & M. N. Schwartzman (Eds.), *Understanding physical, sensory, and health impairments: Characteristics and educational implications* (pp. 179–193). Pacific Grove, CA: Brooks/Cole.

Williamson, G. G. (Ed.). (1987). *Children with spina bifida: Early intervention and preschool programming.* Baltimore: Brookes.

Wong, F. W. H. (2000). Prevention of secondary brain injury. *Critical Care Nurse, 20*(5), 18–27.

Wulz, S. V. (1993). Acquired traumatic brain injury. In M. G. Brodwin, F. Tellez, & S. K. Brodwin (Eds.), *Medical, psychosocial, and vocational aspects of disability* (pp. 473–489). Athens, GA: Elliott & Fitzpatrick.

Ylvisaker, M., Szekeres, S. F., Hartwick, P., & Tworek, P. (1994). Cognitive intervention. In R. C. Savage & G. Wolcott (Eds.), *Educational dimensions of acquired brain injury* (pp. 121–184). Austin, TX: Pro-Ed.

Health Impairments and Infectious Diseases

SHERWOOD J. BEST

CHAPTER 3

KNOWLEDGE AND SKILLS

After you have read this chapter, you will be able to:

1. **Define and describe the following health impairments: asthma, cystic fibrosis, and cancer.**
2. **Define and describe the following infectious diseases: cytomegalovirus and HIV/AIDS.**
3. **Describe secondary or associated conditions that frequently accompany specific health impairments and infectious diseases.**
4. **Appreciate the impact of different health impairments and infectious diseases on physical, cognitive, and psychosocial development.**
5. **Understand the implications of different health impairments and infectious diseases for education, personal autonomy, and career/adult outcomes.**
6. **Incorporate strategies for moderating the effects of health impairments and infectious diseases into teaching activities and social interactions.**
7. **Implement universal precautions and infectious disease transmission prevention in educational environments.**

This chapter briefly describes several health impairments and infectious diseases (see Figure 3–1). Using the same organizational structure as in Chapter 2, information related to the nature and evolution of each disability is presented through discussion of (a) definitions and descriptions, (b) associated medical conditions, and (c) medical and therapeutic treatments. Readers will learn about the impact of specific health impairments and infectious diseases on physical, cognitive, and psychosocial development, including strategies for enhancing developmental outcomes. Implications of each disability will be discussed for education, personal autonomy, and career/adult function. The chapter concludes with a discussion of infectious disease transmission prevention, universal precautions, and development of health care plans.

Health impairments can occur in conjunction with physical or multiple disabilities. The co-occurrence of disabilities may be coincidental, as would be the case for an individual with cerebral palsy who also has asthma. Sometimes a physical disability is linked to health impairment, which would be the case for an individual who must have a leg amputated as a consequence of diabetes. Infectious disease may also occur together with physical and health disabilities, or occur in individuals with no other disabilities. For this reason, it is important for readers to acquire a firm understanding of the dynamics of a variety of disabilities and how they interact to influence development and other outcomes.

In parallel fashion to Chapter 2, the information in this chapter should be viewed as introductory in content. Further study about these and other conditions resulting in physical, health, or multiple disabilities is encouraged. Readers can contact specific agencies, foundations, and information resources that are disability-specific, or explore resources via the Internet. To begin

FIGURE 3–1
Categories of health impairments

Major Health Impairments
Heart disorders
Blood disorders
Asthma
Cystic fibrosis
Juvenile diabetes
Chronic renal failure
Childhood cancer

Infectious Diseases
Hepatitis B
Human immunodeficiency virus and AIDS
Other infectious diseases

Note. Adapted from *Understanding Physical, Sensory, and Health Impairments: Characteristics and Educational Implications,* 1st edition, by Heller/Alberto/Schwartzman/Forney. © 1996. Reprinted with permission of Wadsworth, a division of Thomson Learning: *www.thomsonrights.com.* Fax 800–730–2215.

this exploration, several organizations are profiled in "Focus on the Net" at the end of this chapter.

HEALTH IMPAIRMENTS

Health impairments represent a major category of diverse conditions that can result in disability. As defined in Chapter 1, health impairments are conditions that limit strength, vitality, and alertness (including heightened alertness). Health impairments may be chronic or acute and may have an adverse effect. The number of individuals with health impairments in schools is increasing (DePaepe, Garrison-Kane, & Doelling, 2002).

Increasingly, students with health impairments are educated in their neighborhood schools. To help meet the educational needs of this population, the Council for Exceptional Children (2000) has identified specific knowledge and skills required of educators who work with students with health impairments. These include knowledge of the condition and its effects on development, psychological and emotional characteristics that accompany the condition, and lesson adaptation to accommodate effects of the condition. In addition, educators needs to understand roles and responsibilities of medical providers, appreciate and practice universal precautions and confidentiality policies, and be aware of professional organizations that support individuals with health impairments (Council for Exceptional Children, 2000). These requirements are addressed throughout this chapter.

A major difference between health impairments and physical disabilities is visibility. Many health impairments are not apparent from simple observation, but their developmental effects can be devastating. Since the impairment does not usually provide a visible reminder, adaptations that would facilitate development, academic learning, and social skills may not be readily provided. In addition, some individuals with health impairments may not be perceived as really ill. This perception is nurtured by the reality that the individual functions normally much of the time. As a result, the individual with a health impairment might be challenged to engage in activities that are harmful (e.g., participation in very active physical education activities by students with asthma or cardiac conditions).

Another consequence of invisible disability is the option to conceal it. If the individual chooses not to disclose a health impairment, there is always a possibility that others will become aware under circumstances that are not optimal. For example, observers who are acquainted with a friend with a limb deficiency would know immediately if that individual failed to wear a prescribed prosthesis. However, there would be no immediate outward manifestation of failure to take the proper amount of insulin for a person with diabetes until there was a medical crisis.

Third, many health impairments are chronic in nature. Although they may have acute phases or periods of exacerbation, most chronic conditions must be managed throughout the life span. For example, individuals with diabetes manage their disease through appropriate diet, exercise, and use of insulin. Management must be consistent, or the individual may experience the consequences of excessive or inadequate amounts of insulin. Crises may occur within minutes and be fatal without appropriate and swift action. Individuals with asthma must be ready to respond to changes in the environment that could trigger an acute episode. Individuals with cystic fibrosis and cancer must sometimes undergo aggressive antibiotic treatment to prevent or inhibit infections. Even when management is excellent, outcomes are not assured. Treatments may be painful and physically exhausting or lead to symptoms that may feel more uncomfortable than the disease itself. Under these circumstances it is sometimes difficult to motivate individuals to follow through with medical regimens (Brown, Lourie, & Pao, 2000).

The health impairments described in this chapter include asthma, cystic fibrosis, and cancer. These health impairments were chosen for discussion for several reasons. First, each illustrates how a disability can alter the function of different systems of the body. Asthma affects the respiratory system, while cystic fibrosis is an impairment of the exocrine system. Cancer can occur in several body systems, including the musculoskeletal system (bone cancer), the central nervous system (brain cancer), or the lymphatic system (leukemia). Second, these health impairments were chosen for discussion because they may be familiar to teachers and others who do not necessarily provide services in the field of special education, but who may have had personal experience with the impairment. Finally, these health impairments are interesting to compare because they have different **trajectories** (clinical outcomes). For example, asthma is a chronic condition that is potentially lethal, but can frequently be managed with an excellent functional outcome. Cancer is a disease whose treatment can lead to remission or a less favorable outcome in which life is prolonged, but not saved. Cystic fibrosis is also treatable, but remains a progressive and terminal disease. Finally, each of these health impairments will have a greater impact on development and function at some times than at others. A balanced perspective for teachers and others who provide educational and therapeutic support is that a health impairment is only one aspect of an individual.

ASTHMA

Definitions and Descriptions

Asthma is the most common pulmonary disease of childhood, although estimates of its incidence and prevalence vary widely (Bloomberg & Strunk, 1992; Kraemer & Bierman, 1983). As many as 4.3% of school-age children are affected by asthma (Weitzman, Gortmaker, Sobol, & Perrin, 1992), and this number may be an underestimate (Raj, Mishra, Feinsilver, & Fein, 2000). Asthma can begin in infancy or develop later in life, and its symptoms range from mild to life threatening (Heller, Alberto, Forney, & Schwartzman, 1996). It can occur as a result of extreme sensitivity to tiny particles of dust and other debris (such as cigarette smoke or cat fur) that enters the lungs, causing a respiratory reaction (asthma attack). Other contributing causes include respiratory infections, sensitivity to allergens, a reactive airway, a family history of asthma, and gender (Heller et al., 1996; Morgan & Martinez, 1992). Asthma is classified by causes of lung irritation, including extrinsic, intrinsic, mixed, aspirin-induced, exercise-induced, and occupation-induced causes (Heller et al., 1996).

Asthma occurs as a result of the body's immune response. **Antigens** are the foreign substances that enter the lungs. The body responds by producing **antibodies,** which act to suppress the antigen (Heller et al., 1996). In asthma, the individual has a large number of IgE antibodies that react to antigens through the release of chemicals that cause swelling, mucus secretion, and muscle tightening in the lungs. The result is an obstructed airway and difficulty breathing. Symptoms include wheezing, coughing, sweating, and chest constriction. Repeated exposure to the offending substance can heighten sensitivity. An individual having an asthma attack may appear unimpaired or may show signs of extreme distress (as in Figure 3–2).

FIGURE 3–2
Extreme distress during an asthma attack

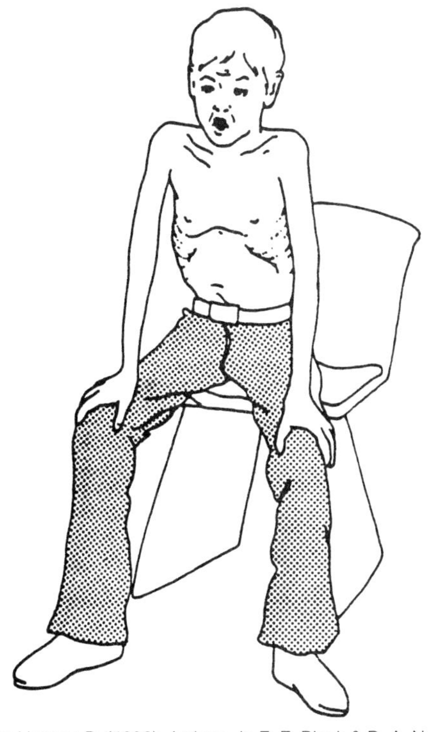

Note. From Harvey, B. (1982). Asthma. In E. E. Bleck & D. A. Nagels (Eds.), *Physically handicapped children: A medical atlas for teachers* (p. 36). Copyright © 1982 by Allyn & Bacon. Reprinted by permission.

Diagnosis is reached through chest X-rays, lung-function tests, blood and sweat tests, and skin-based allergy tests (Avery & First, 1994; Haggerty, 1990; Mueller & Eigen, 1992). Some of these tests are administered to identify the presence of asthma, while others are used to rule out other conditions (such as cystic fibrosis).

Associated Medical Conditions

For individuals with repeated asthma episodes, air may become trapped in the **alveoli** (tiny air sacs in the lungs). Trapped air results in overinflated lungs and difficulty exhaling. Over time, the chest may become barrel shaped (Heller et al., 1996). In some cases, asthma may delay the onset of puberty, which has contributed to the myth that asthma retards physical growth. When puberty is reached, however, growth resumes (Reid, 1992).

Medical and Therapeutic Treatments

Treatment of asthma involves prevention of attacks or moderating the strength of an attack. Drugs such as Singulair and Accolade prevent asthma from occurring, while others are used for acute situations. Substituting a long-term medication during an acute attack will not reduce symptoms. Teachers and others need to know the type of medication, its immediate purpose, and side effects.

Prevention. The first step in preventing asthma attacks is detecting its cause. Once the substance or situation that triggers the attack is isolated, one of the best preventative measures is avoidance. Removing pets from the house, rigorous housecleaning, and substituting area rugs and blinds for carpeting and drapes can control substances such as pet dander and dust. Household air-cleaning systems can be installed to reduce the amount of ambient (surrounding) allergens. However, it is clearly not possible to control the environment to such an extent that all asthma-inducing triggers are eliminated. For example, the author's daughter experienced mild asthma attacks in response to cat hair. Her pediatrician suggested that the family cat be given away. However, it was felt that the emotional turmoil generated by losing her pet would outweigh the benefits of reducing cat hair in the house. The solution was to reduce the amount of ambient cat dander through frequent carpet cleaning, removing the cat from furniture, training it to sleep on the porch, and reminding the daughter not to kiss her pet.

Preventative treatment may also involve exposing the individual to low doses of the allergen (**immunotherapy,** or allergy shots), in an effort to produce tolerance (O'Connell & Heilman, 1996). In addition to environmental control measures and immunotherapy, individuals may take medications to reduce inflammation and phlegm (mucus) in the lungs (Hill, 1999). Long-term inhaled medications that target the underlying process of inflammation appear to be the best approach, particularly for individuals who experience symptoms more than twice a week (Hogan & Wilson, 2003).

Intervention. In the event of an attack, medications to open the airways (**bronchodilators**) can be very effective. Medication can be taken via inhaler, or through a breathing machine (**nebulizer**) that delivers medication-laden mist straight to the lungs. Inhalers are useful because they are administered in small doses and directly to the source of the problem (the lungs). Using a nebulizer may be a better option for individuals who cannot coordinate breathing with delivering the dose from the inhaler. Sometimes these measures are inadequate to counteract the attack. Teachers and others who work with children with asthma must be alert to signs of a serious asthma episode. If the child fails to respond to medication, experiences excessive shortness of breath, is unresponsive, or has cyanosis (blue or blue-gray coloration of the lips and nail beds), emergency medical treatment is indicated.

Because asthma is a common condition and its symptoms are often reversible, it may be perceived as nonthreatening or even trivial. Recent accounts of self-treatment with over-the-counter bronchodilators by individuals who subsequently suffered fatal asthma attacks attest to the public perception that asthma is no cause for concern—until it is too late.

Other Treatments. In addition to prevention and medication-based intervention, other treatments may reduce the effects of asthma. The individual can breathe moist air to reduce congestion caused by mucus in the lungs. Another technique is **pulmonary percussion** paired with **postural drainage.** The back and chest areas are "clapped" by another person, using cupped hands and striking firmly and rhythmically. The effect is to loosen mucus so that it can be coughed up. During percussion, the person being treated may be positioned to facilitate gravity flow of mucus from the lungs. The individual may be taught coughing techniques to clear the lungs. Finally, breathing exercises can be used to facilitate good breathing patterns and reduce anxiety.

Impact on Physical, Cognitive, and Psychosocial Development

Asthma is a chronic condition whose symptoms are reversible. However, prolonged asthma attacks can lead to changes in the lungs (Heller et al., 1996). While the physical effects of asthma are minimal, psychosocial function may be greatly affected.

Physical and Cognitive Development. There is no specific connection between asthma and physical development. Children whose asthma is exercise-induced must be careful about engaging in activities that overexert them. If their stamina is affected, they would benefit from modified physical education. However, exercise is important in maintaining physical fitness and preventing obesity. There is no connection between asthma and level of cognitive function.

Psychosocial Implications. Asthma was once believed to be behavioral/emotional in origin. Parents were blamed for precipitating asthma attacks in their children through overprotective behaviors. Asthma episodes were perceived as resulting from emotional disturbance, and children were blamed for "causing" their attacks. It is now known that asthma is biochemical and metabolic in origin. However, heightened emotional reactions such as excessive laughing or crying can alter respiration sufficiently that an attack is triggered (Hill, 1999). Emotional reactions during an episode can also interfere with return of normal respiration. Repeated asthma attacks can produce negative emotional and social reactions from others. Frightening episodes may lead to parental and teacher overprotection. Frequent absences from school can also lead to lower academic achievement.

Becoming knowledgeable about the dynamics of asthma is the first step in its physical and psychosocial management. Students benefit from learning about the nature of asthma, medication administration, and trigger avoidance (Lehrer, Feldman, Giardino, Song, & Schmaling, 2002). Teachers who are confident about assisting with medication administration and who remain calm during an acute episode inspire confidence in their students. Full participation in school and community activities is a desirable outcome for individuals with asthma and is achievable when its dynamics and treatment are kept in mind.

Implications for Education and Personal Autonomy

It is estimated that children lose between 10 million and 130 million school days every year to asthma (Majer & Joy, 1993; McLoughlin & Nall, 1994). Absences may increase if the student is uncomfortable about asthma management in the school environment or uses the condition as an excuse to avoid school. Teachers and others should be proactive about addressing these issues and should strive to make the educational experience as typical as possible for the student with asthma.

Education. Students with asthma can achieve at levels that are academically commensurate with their peers (Lindgren et al., 1992). However, asthma can interfere with school performance. For example, students whose asthma keeps them awake at night are especially at academic risk due to fatigue and poor attendance (Diette, Markson, Skinner, Nguyen, Algatt-Bergstrom, & Wu, 2000). The following discussion addresses how teachers and others can assist in asthma prevention and intervention to facilitate physical health, academic achievement, and psychosocial adjustment.

Irritant reduction can be achieved by carefully evaluating the classroom environment. Area rugs (low pile) should be vacuumed regularly, and other floor areas kept clean of dust by damp mopping. Room cleaning should occur when students are not present to breathe in dust or the fumes of cleaning products. Adequate ventilation should be provided if students are sensitive to materials such as solvents, paints, or glues. Students may need to sit away from boards to avoid chalk dust or felt-tip pen fumes. Fur-bearing classroom pets (such as rabbits or guinea pigs) and even stuffed animals may need to be avoided. Students can be seated away from open windows to avoid cold air and/or during seasons when pollen is prevalent. Some students benefit from using their inhalers before participating in physical activities. Teachers should consult with parents and their school nurses about which foods might need to be avoided.

If environmental control is insufficient to prevent an asthma attack, it is important to practice good intervention techniques. First, the student's breathing should be observed. The irritant should be removed from the vicinity. The student should be seated and assisted to take medication. Clear fluids can be given to thin mucus. Appropriate school personnel (the school nurse) should be contacted and summoned if necessary. A record should be kept regarding the episode and the parents informed in a manner that is mutually acceptable (National Institutes of Health, 1994; Silkworth & Jones, 1986). By responding in an organized manner during an acute asthma attack, teachers and other service providers can reduce anxiety and achieve an efficient response.

Sometimes students may experience severe asthma episodes that become life threatening or do not respond to treatment. To meet the challenge of medical emergencies, school personnel should develop plans for responding to acute medical situations. Plans should always be developed in conjunction with parents and medical personnel, be student-specific, and include components such as (a) who remains with the student; (b) how assistance (on and off the campus) is summoned; (c) who administers medication and performs other medical responses; (d) specific medical intervention techniques; and (e) how parents or guardians are informed. Steps in the plan should be clear and readily accessible. Guidelines for creating an emergency-care plan and responding to urgent-care situations are provided later in this chapter.

The teacher is instrumental in maintaining a supportive emotional climate during a medical emergency. Using a calm and controlled voice is reassuring to all students in the classroom. Students who witness an acute medical emergency need to move away from the immediate vicinity, either by going to their desks or to another predetermined location. If medical personnel are summoned to the classroom, they will need to have a clear space for assisting the student. Handling student reactions after a medical emergency is also critical. Students must have an opportunity to discuss their feelings and be provided with age-appropriate explanations about what they witnessed. Exploring their emotions will reduce fear and help them to respond positively when their classmate returns to school.

Personal Autonomy. As with all chronic illnesses, it is important for the student with asthma to understand the dynamics of medication and take control of medical self-management as soon as appropriate. Young students should be assisted to take their medication, since nebulizers require measuring and inhalers must be used correctly to deliver adequate amounts of medication. Older students can be taught to self-medicate. Medication should be kept at school and be easily available for quick administration. Some schools have established policies that medication must be kept in a central location, usually the school administrative office or nurse's office. This creates a conflict between the need of the student to self-medicate in a timely manner and the need of school personnel to keep medications secure. Whenever a student leaves the school area (on a field trip, for example), the medication should be taken (Heller et al., 1996).

A compromise may be necessary between the student's need for privacy and the adult's need to provide supervision. Some students may want to be excused to leave the room to take their medication, while others will be embarrassed by this "publicity." Finally, there is the problem with students who either over- or undermedicate. Signs of overmedication include drowsiness, fine-motor tremors, irritability, heightened motor behavior, and loss of attentiveness (Klein & Timmerman, 1994). These effects may also occur when children are correctly medicated, so teachers must know which are common side effects for each individual and which indicate overmedication. Incorrect use of inhalers may result in inadequate amounts and delivery of asthma medication. This is a serious situation, since medication taken to stop an acute attack will be ineffective. If medication is taken as a preventative measure, undermedication will result in increased asthma episodes. Teachers and others can assist by making sure children are correctly using their inhalers. It is important to gain knowledge about *why* an adolescent is undermedicating. The solution may be as simple as allowing the adolescent to choose where to take medication, or may require a more complex approach, such as counseling by a professional who can assist the adolescent with the unique issues related to chronic illness.

Implications for Career and Adult Outcomes

Individuals with asthma need to carefully consider employment options that compromise their respiration. This may include working away from environments that contain asthma triggers. Some individuals may need to avoid outdoor work that would expose the individual to pollen, molds, or other allergens. For individuals who work inside, use of humidifiers (where air is too dry) or dehumidifiers (where air is too moist) may be needed to help maintain correct air moisture. However, molds and fungus grow in more humid conditions. When these are triggers, humidifiers and vaporizers must be cleaned periodically. For individuals whose asthma is exercise-induced, strenuous work may be inappropriate. Even when these factors are considered, there are almost limitless career choices and life activities available for individuals with asthma. Having asthma does not need to present a barrier to any aspects of adult life.

CYSTIC FIBROSIS

Definitions and Descriptions

Cystic fibrosis (CF) is a hereditary and progressive disease that affects the lungs and other major body organs. It is the most common hereditary terminal disease among Caucasians, although it occurs in lower numbers in other ethnic groups. Cystic fibrosis occurs in 1 in every 2,000 live births (Thompson, Gustafson, Hamlett, & Spock, 1992). It is estimated that approximately 30,000 persons in the United States have CF, while approximately 1 in 31 are "carriers" (Cystic Fibrosis Foundation, 2001a; Hill, 1999). Cystic fibrosis occurs equally in males and females.

The gene for CF is located on chromosome 7 (Weinberger, 1993). Transmission can occur only if each parent is a "carrier" of the gene for cystic fibrosis. In this type of inheritance, there is a one-in-four chance that a child of parents with the CF gene will have the disease (inherit the gene from both parents), a one-in-four chance that a child of parents with the CF gene will not inherit the gene from either parent, and a two-in-four chance that a child of parents with the CF gene will be a carrier (inherit the gene from only one parent).

Cystic fibrosis is a disease of the exocrine system. This system consists of those glands that secrete fluid through ducts (or openings) to the surface of the body (such as sweat glands) or to organs that empty into a body cavity that secretes outside the body (such as respiratory mucus or pancreatic juice). Exocrine glands throughout the body are affected by CF (Heller et al., 1996; Hill, 1999). One effect of CF is excessive secretion of sticky mucus in the respiratory system. The result is blockage of tiny airways in the lungs, causing them to become less efficient. Oxygen can become trapped in the lungs by mucous plugs, which will cause parts of the lungs to overinflate. Without proper treatment, trapped mucus will also cause parts of the lungs to collapse. Cystic fibrosis also affects the digestive system. Mucus in the pancreas prevents efficient release of pancreatic juice for food digestion. Without digestive enzymes, food is poorly digested, and the individual suffers from chronic malnourishment. The combination of overinflated lungs and distended abdomen can result in an appearance that includes abdominal distension and lack of subcutaneous fat on limbs (see Figure 3–3). Mucus also

FIGURE 3–3
Appearance of a child with cystic fibrosis

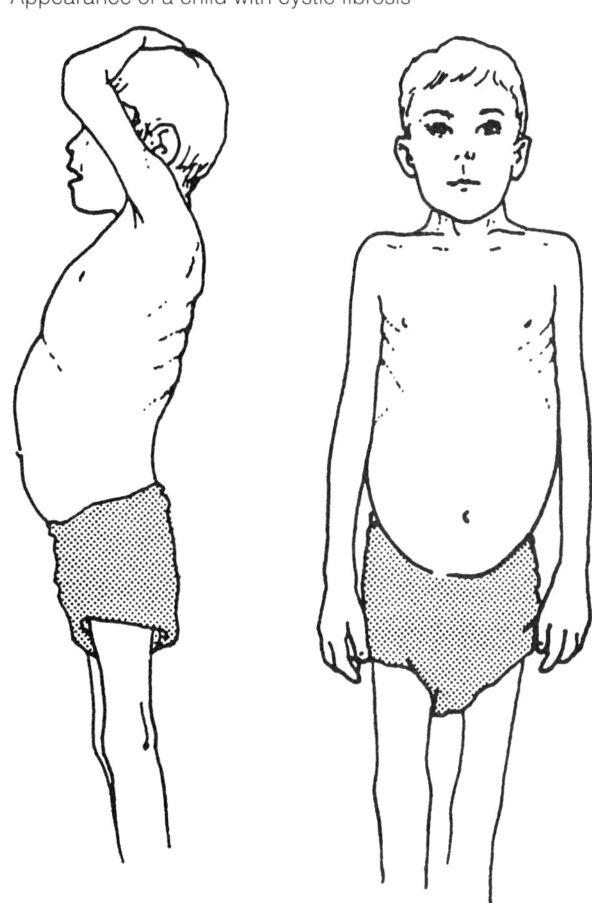

Note. From Harvey, B. (1982). Cystic fibrosis. In E. E. Bleck & D. A. Nagels (Eds.), *Physically handicapped children: A medical atlas for teachers* (p. 261). Copyright © 1982 by Allyn & Bacon. Reprinted by permission.

interferes with the function of other bodily organs, including the liver, intestines, and testicles. Even when they are blocked by mucus, the organs continue to produce secretions. The secretions get trapped inside the organs and develop into cysts surrounded with scarred tissue (hence "cystic fibrosis").

Cystic fibrosis is a progressive and terminal condition. Ultimately the individual will die from pneumonia or other respiratory complication. Life-span prognosis ranges from the teens until the thirties (with some ranging into the fifties). With aggressive antibiotic therapy, medication, and even lung transplants, individuals with cystic fibrosis are living longer than ever before.

Cystic fibrosis may be detected at birth, or later in childhood when the child fails to gain sufficient weight for age. Diagnosis in childhood is confirmed through a "sweat test," in which sweat is collected and analyzed for salt content. Other diagnostic means include lung X-rays and enzyme evaluations.

Associated Medical Conditions

It is clear from the preceding description that cystic fibrosis is a **systemic** condition; that is, it affects the body generally and has an impact on many organs. People with cystic fibrosis do not digest food properly. Fats are especially difficult to digest for people with cystic fibrosis, and their stools may be bulky, greasy, and foul smelling. Some infants with cystic fibrosis are born with bowel obstruction related to digestive deficiencies. Ingesting adequate amounts of calories, and the appropriate proportions of nutrients, becomes a lifelong struggle. Infants and young children with cystic fibrosis are at increased risk for malnutrition and reduced pulmonary function. Calories need to be increased by between 22 and 32% to maintain normal nutritional needs (Powers et al., 2002). In addition, because people with cystic fibrosis produce an abundance of excessively salty sweat, they must be careful to replace salt and fluids lost through sweating. If damage occurs to those areas of the pancreas that produce insulin, individuals with cystic fibrosis may also develop diabetes. Males with cystic fibrosis are usually sterile, since the vas deferens (the duct that transports semen) becomes blocked. Females with cystic fibrosis may experience thickened vaginal secretions. Both males and females may have late onset of puberty, which can create psychosocial problems.

Medical and Therapeutic Treatments

Treatments for cystic fibrosis have progressed tremendously, including the exciting possibility of gene therapy (Cystic Fibrosis Foundation, 2001b). However, medical treatments are primarily aimed at addressing symptoms of the disease. The most important medical treatment outcomes are maintaining lung and digestive functions.

Medical. Respiratory infections are treated with antibiotics, which may be taken orally, in aerosol form, or intravenously. The individual will also take expectorants to rid the lungs of mucus. Chest physiotherapy is a routine aspect of pulmonary maintenance. It consists of percussion or vibration techniques to loosen mucus, followed by positioning the body to drain secretions. Recently, heart-lung transplants are available to prolong the lives of people with cystic fibrosis (Cropp & Shames, 1994).

Due to their digestive dysfunctions, individuals with cystic fibrosis require vitamin and mineral supplements to maintain adequate nutrition. To aid in food absorption, they must also take digestive enzymes. The individual must be encouraged to eat often and well of a healthful, low-fat diet.

Impact on Physical, Cognitive, and Psychosocial Development

Physical and Cognitive Development. Many infants with cystic fibrosis are not diagnosed until a series of respiratory infections and failure to gain weight alert their parents and pediatrician that something is wrong. Other infants are born with a bowel obstruction that requires surgical intervention. Because digestion is compromised, children with cystic fibrosis may be malnourished and not grow as rapidly as their peers. Frequent respiratory infections will further retard physical development. Short stature, slow sexual development, and physical abnormalities (such as barrel chest and distended abdomen) all contribute to altered physical appearance (Hill, 1999). Children with cystic fibrosis do not have cognitive delays, but may miss many school days and experience gaps in their academic experience. Attendance problems will become worse as the student grows older and the disease progresses.

Psychosocial Implications. The treatment regimens of daily chest physiotherapy, eating certain foods (and avoiding others), and taking a variety of medications becomes a part of life for families of children with cystic fibrosis. Despite all these medical precautions, individuals with cystic fibrosis will continue to experience respiratory difficulties. As a result, children and their families can become discouraged and even exhausted by the treatment demands of this chronic illness. The routines required to meet medical needs may consume family time and energy and leave little space for other activities. Conversely, routines may be ignored because they impose excessive demands.

Meeting the medical needs of cystic fibrosis at school can impose psychosocial hardship. It is very important that students with cystic fibrosis cough frequently to rid their lungs of mucus. In addition, they may need to visit the restroom frequently. At school, students may suppress their coughing rather than face the embarrassment of disrupting others or asking permission to leave the classroom. Teachers need to create the dynamic that coughing is permissible in public places. Some teachers help students to manage their need to cough by developing a signal system for being excused to a more private area. In addition, frequent hospitalizations can disrupt friendships and school social activities. The student with cystic fibrosis is at risk for feeling disassociated from important aspects of school life. Altered physical appearance, including slow physical and sexual maturation, presents a particular challenge for adolescents.

Implications for Education and Personal Autonomy

Teachers and other service providers must work closely with family members to provide whatever medical treatments are necessary during school hours. Chest physiotherapy may be performed before and after school, but an immediate response is necessary if the child develops a mucous plug. A good strategy is to keep digestive enzymes, other medications, and oral supplements (such as salt tablets and vitamins) where the student can take them in privacy but under supervision. Quietly excusing the student to the nurse's office a few minutes before lunch and snack times will meet medication and privacy needs.

Privacy is also necessary when considering restroom needs. Undigested fat contributes to frequent, bulky, and foul-smelling stools in individuals with cystic fibrosis. Teachers and others must allow the student to visit the restroom whenever necessary. If embarrassment is an issue, the student should be allowed to use a restroom when other students are not present, or a restroom in another location (such as the nurse's or principal's office). Special deodorizers should be made available.

When in school, the child should be encouraged to cough. Teachers may need to explain to other students and adults that coughing does not necessarily indicate an infectious condition. Rigorous physical exercise assists in loosening mucus, but should be undertaken cautiously. Students may need to take salt tablets after exercise to replace salt lost through perspiration. Increased salt intake will also increase the need for fluids.

It is important to provide academic support if the student requires hospitalization or home instruction for antibiotic therapy. Many hospitals provide educational services for students who require sustained hospital care, and teachers must maintain close contact with hospital teachers (see Chapter 1 for a vignette on hospital teaching). Arranging a telephone call between peers and their hospitalized friend can be immensely supportive. Peers can also maintain friendships through e-mail and other forms of technology-based contact. Making an effort to provide similar academic assignments supports feelings of normality. The key to successful school/hospital/home instruction is continuity and flexibility.

Personal Autonomy. It is not unusual for individuals who require intensive medical attention to develop feelings of separation from the normal patterns of life. This may be reflected in "patterns of learned helplessness" (Heller et al., 1996, p. 295). Individuals with cystic fibrosis must be encouraged to participate in their medical treatments, exercise with their peers, and follow the same rules as others. The pertinent guideline is "appropriateness." For example, it is appropriate to provide a student extra time to complete a homework assignment in class if that student becomes fatigued later in the day. It is not appropriate to excuse that student from homework entirely.

Implications for Career and Adult Outcomes

Individuals with cystic fibrosis have all the typical interests of people their age. Conservation of energy, in the face of normal adolescent desire to maintain an active academic and social life, may present challenges for the student, family, and service providers. Although there are no cognitive barriers to career possibilities for individuals with cystic fibrosis, fatigue and increasing respiratory involvement limits options to less-physical arenas. Adults with cystic fibrosis marry, although males are usually not able to father children.

Cystic fibrosis is a progressive and terminal condition. However, this does not mean that individuals should not be encouraged to strive for a full and abundant life, nor explore the pleasures and responsibilities of adulthood. New treatments have dramatically increased life expectancy. The key to facing the challenges of cystic fibrosis lies in managing the pulmonary and digestive complications of this disease, while not allowing it to dominate all aspects of life.

CANCER

Definitions and Descriptions

Cancer is a term used for a variety of diseases characterized by the growth and spread of abnormal cells (Elmayan, 1993). Masses of these abnormal cells are called **tumors** or **neoplasms.** If their growth is localized and more controlled, tumors are referred to as **benign.** If growth is rampant, invades surrounding tissues, and reoccurs, the tumor is referred to as **malignant** or **cancerous** (Heller et al., 1996). When cancer cells travel to other regions of the body in blood and lymph, cancer is said to **metastasize.** Cancer is a dynamic disease; without treatment, the individual will eventually die. However, it should not be perceived as inevitably fatal either. The goals of treatment are tumor elimination, disease remission, and even cure.

Cancer occurs in approximately 14 in every 100,000 children; in the United States, about 25,000 per year die of this disease (Behrman, 1992). It is the second most common cause of death in children between the ages of 1 and 14 (Parker, Tong, Bolden, & Wingo, 1997). Cancers that occur in adults are more likely to involve organ tissue (breast, lung, colon, etc.), while cancers in children usually involve connective or supporting tissue (bone, muscle, lymphatic tissues, etc.). Some children's cancers are more common than others.

There are several ways to detect cancer. Blood tests allow doctors to assess whether numbers of red cells, white cells, and platelets in the blood are normal; abnormal numbers may indicate cancer such as leukemia. Spinal fluid may also be removed for analysis. X-rays and scanning techniques can be used to detect tumors (Behrman, 1992). Detection of a tumor is normally followed by biopsy (removal of some or all of the tumor) for analysis of malignancy (Heller et al., 1996). These tests are usually performed after the individual experiences certain symptoms, such as persistent fever, localized pain, changes in appearance of the eye or skin, or a mass.

Associated Medical Conditions

Medical problems that accompany cancer are dependent on the type of malignancy. In cancers where the spinal cord is involved, loss of sensation, gait changes, impaired bladder function, and even paralysis can occur. Brain tumors have the effect of causing pressure within the skull. This can cause nausea, dizziness, lack of balance and coordination, headache, visual problems, and even behavior changes (Heller et al., 1996). Individuals with leukemia are often anemic due to a decrease in red blood cells. They will feel tired, bruise easily, and may experience bone and joint pain.

If cancer cells metastasize to other areas of the body, tissues and organs in those places will also be affected. Some forms of cancer metastasize to certain areas. Bone cancer, for example, spreads to the lungs and central nervous system (Heller et al., 1996).

Medical and Therapeutic Treatments

Medical Treatment. The prognosis for cancer survival has improved tremendously through early detection and a variety of medical treatments. Following biopsy, malignant tumors may be treated with a combination of treatment approaches. Surgery may involve removal of the tumor only or may be more radical in nature. For example, in retinoblastoma (cancer of the eye), treatment may involve removal of the eyeball. Bone cancers are also often treated with amputation. Surgery is generally followed by chemotherapy (medication therapy) for malignant tumors. **Chemotherapy** consists of the administration of powerful drugs whose effect is to prevent cancer cells from dividing. The side effects of chemotherapy can be very unpleasant. These include nausea, weight gain or loss, growth retardation, hair loss, mouth sores, delayed onset of puberty, and learning disabilities (Crooks et al.,

1991). Additional drugs are used to counteract some of the effects of chemotherapy. Chemotherapy leaves the individual in a depressed immune state, which results in vulnerability to opportunistic infections. **Radiation** (designed to attack the atomic structure of cancer cells) is often used with chemotherapy. It can be administered externally or via implants. Finally, individuals with leukemia (cancer of the blood-producing structures) can receive **bone marrow transplants.** Response to any of these treatments depends on the type of cancer, how early it was detected, and the general health of the individual.

Therapeutic Treatment. Following acute (immediate) treatment for the malignancy, the individual may receive therapy. For example, osteosarcoma (bone cancer) most frequently occurs in the long bones of the leg. Surgical removal would be followed by prescription for a prosthesis (artificial limb) and physical therapy to teach ambulation.

Impact on Physical, Cognitive, and Psychosocial Development

Physical and Cognitive Development. Cancer and its treatments can alter physical development. Central nervous system tumors can alter gross and fine motor ability. Children with leukemia may develop leukemic meningitis, which leaves bones thin and weak and prone to fracture (Hill, 1999). Medication can damage dental enamel, resulting in discoloration. Some types of childhood cancer are associated with additional physical abnormalities and cognitive delay.

If the cancer progresses, physical deterioration will occur. The presence of pain interferes with concentration and heightens fatigue. If medication has suppressed the immune system, the student will be vulnerable to infection. Teachers must be alert for signs of communicable diseases in peers who might pass their infections to the student with cancer.

It is important for educators and others to know the specific type of cancer, its current treatment, and physical limitations imposed by the disease and its treatment. The student will benefit from reduced physical exercise and even a shortened school day if there is considerable physical discomfort. Teachers also must be aware that "some days are better than other days," and that students should be encouraged to participate to the extent possible at that time. Since radiation treatment has been associated with learning disabilities (Brown & Madan-Swain, 1993; Williams, Berry, Caldwell, Zolten, & Spence, 1992), academic accommodations may be required to meet learning needs.

Psychosocial Implications. Cancer causes a great deal of irrational fear in others, including the mistaken belief that it is contagious. Psychosocial difficulties arise when fear, avoidance, and rejection are communicated to the individual with cancer. Therefore, psychosocial support for the student with cancer must include peer education. Families of students with cancer should be consulted about what (and how much) will be communicated to peers. One successful method of peer education is implementing a "(dis)Ability awareness program." Such programs provide an excellent avenue for promoting empathy, understanding, and increased contact between students with and without disabilities. They have the added benefit of reducing teasing or avoidance behavior (Denti & Meyers, 1997).

Any effects of the disease or its treatment that alter physical appearance (skin problems, mouth sores, hair loss, amputation, etc.) have implications for psychosocial adjustment. The individual may wish to wear a wig or hat to conceal hair loss, although situations have occurred where classmates have shaved their heads in solidarity with their peer. Contact with a social worker, child life specialist, and/or psychologist at the hospital where the student receives treatment will provide teachers with strategies for successful school reentry. It is important to remember that students who experience cancer treatment at a critical developmental age may experience depression and related symptoms such as fatigue (Visser & Smets, 1998).

Although cancer is more treatable than ever before, the outcome is not positive in all cases. In the event that the student dies, teachers will need to convey this information to classmates and others at the school. Some families are comforted when students and school personnel attend the funeral. Other activities of remembrance include assembling a photo book with written anecdotes by peers or sending a card or letter on the anniversary of the student's death. Sometimes families appreciate a telephone call, letter, or visit several weeks after the death. The author remembers being asked to assist one family to clean their son's bedroom and sort his clothing for donation because, as his mother said, "You knew and loved S__________ as well as we did."

Implications for Education and Personal Autonomy

Education. As they do for all students with chronic conditions, teachers and others must maintain consistency in educational programming, while assisting the student to cope with missed school time, social and academic reintegration after hospitalization, or altered appearance as a result of treatment and/or disease progression. The key educational response to cancer and its treatment is *flexibility.* Knowledge of the student's treatment schedule is helpful for planning academic activities and anticipating absences. Returning to school after hospitalization gives students a sense of control and return to normality. Therefore, academic expectations should also parallel achievement before hospitalization, with flexibility for the possibility that function may be altered.

Personal Autonomy. Flexibility extends to issues of autonomy. Students must be encouraged to be independent and to participate in school-based activities, but not feel that they failed to meet expectations if they lack physical or psychological energy.

Students with cancer may require specialized health care services at school. Service providers must establish appropriate schedules for services that will interfere as little as possible with school routines. Research has long shown that children cope more positively with physical discomfort and unfamiliar situations such as hospitalization when they are prepared and feel in control (Melamed & Siegel, 1975). One strategy is to allow young children to perform "procedures" on dolls in preparation for their own hospital experiences. Older children benefit from explanations of their disease and its treatment. Optimal coping occurs when the child develops a good relationship with the individual who performs procedures. In school settings, this means that students should be able to count on a certain person (whom they trust) to provide specialized health care procedures. To develop mastery, the student should be allowed to assist with procedures whenever possible and appropriate.

If the cancer leads to physical deterioration, students may require care in meeting their daily living needs as well as specific cancer treatments. At all times, their dignity must be preserved.

Implications for Career and Adult Outcomes

This chapter has focused on cancers that are more likely to occur in childhood. Advances in cancer treatment have resulted in increasing survival rates (Parker et al., 1997; Schwenn, 1996), so teachers and others should anticipate that children with cancer will grow up, enter the workforce, and assume adult roles and responsibilities. A rehabilitation counselor can help the adolescent to explore career options and develop a realistic plan for attaining life goals.

INFECTIOUS DISEASES

Infectious diseases can be transmitted directly or indirectly from one person to another. Infectious disease transmission can occur through four modes. The first is through **airborne** water or dust particles (such as in the case of viral or bacterial infections). The second transmission mode is **contact** (such as in the case of chicken pox or sexually transmitted diseases). The third mode of contact is the **vehicle route** (such as through contaminated water or food). **Vectorborne** contamination, which occurs via an organism that carries the disease-causing microorganism from one host to another (such as the tick whose bite causes Lyme disease), is the final contamination route. Common childhood diseases (such as chicken pox, measles, and mumps) are considered infectious, but are acute in nature and usually have no lasting effect if the course of the infection is normal and the individual is otherwise healthy at the time of the infection. Chronic infectious diseases often have residual (lasting) effects.

Two chronic infectious diseases are described in this chapter: cytomegalovirus infection (CMV) and human immunodeficiency virus and acquired immune deficiency syndrome (HIV/AIDS). These infectious diseases were chosen for discussion for several reasons. First, they are infections that can be transmitted congenitally (in utero or during birth) or be acquired after birth. Second, these infectious diseases have associated medical, developmental, and educational implications that require careful attention. A section of this chapter has been devoted to discussion of infection transmission prevention and universal precautions, which can significantly decrease infectious disease in educational settings. Third, these two diseases reflect opposite levels of knowledge in the general population. Although HIV/AIDS receives more public attention, CMV has the potential for greater health risk in educational settings. In all cases, the intensive needs of individuals with CMV and HIV/AIDS necessitate a team management response to meet medical, developmental, and educational needs.

CYTOMEGALOVIRUS

Definitions and Descriptions

Cytomegalovirus (sy-toe-meg′-ah-lo-virus), or CMV, is one of a group of infections that can result in serious malformations if the disease is contracted in the uterus. The other infections in this group are syphilis, toxoplasmosis, rubella, and herpesvirus (Batshaw & Perret, 1992; Heller et al., 1996). When grouped with other infections such as varicella zoster (chicken pox) and polio, these are called the **STORCH**—S (syphilis), T (toxoplasmosis), O (other), R (rubella), C (CMV), and H (herpes)—infections.

CMV is believed to be one of the primary causes of congenital mental retardation and microcephaly (a condition characterized by an abnormally small head) (Hanshaw, 1981). It can be transmitted through direct contact with CMV-contaminated individuals or objects. An acute episode of CMV lasts about two weeks, with flu-like symptoms. Sometimes the individual is asymptomatic (has no symptoms). However, the danger of CMV lies in exposure to this virus during pregnancy. CMV may cross the placenta at any time during pregnancy, although the result to the infant will depend on whether the infection enters the central nervous system and on the time of infection (Heller et al., 1996). Infants who were prenatally exposed to CMV and show evidence of damage are described as having cytomegalic inclusion disease (CID). The number of infants born with CMV is higher than the combined totals of prenatal infection from herpes, toxoplasmosis, and rubella (Sever, Larsen, & Grossman, 1988).

Associated Medical Conditions

There are many associated medical complications of CID, including organ damage, skin rash, microcephaly, sensorineural (inner ear) hearing loss, visual impairments, seizures, and cerebral palsy (Andersen, Bale, Blackman, & Murph, 1986; Hanshaw, 1981; Heller et al., 1996). Infants exposed prenatally to CMV but born without symptoms may develop conditions later in life such as progressive sensorineural hearing loss (Williamson, Demmler, Percy, & Catlin, 1992).

Medical and Therapeutic Treatments

Treatment for CMV is geared toward correcting existing damage to organs, but the effects of CMV are irreversible. One important aspect of CMV is that this virus can be periodically "shed" (secreted) for up to eight years after the primary infection (Heller et al., 1996). All liquid secretions (blood, vomitus, tears, saliva, sweat, semen, bronchial secretions, urine, feces, etc.) may contain CMV. There is no indication from observation whether a student is shedding the virus. In addition, CMV remains active on environmental surfaces for several hours. Therefore, the greatest preventative measure that can be taken against CMV infection is proper infection control measures.

Impact on Physical, Cognitive, and Psychosocial Development

Physical and Cognitive Development. As stated earlier, CMV is one of the STORCH infections, all of which are associated with birth defects. CMV is characterized by organ and tissue damage; children with CMV are very often multiply disabled. The occurrence of cerebral palsy indicates damage to the central nervous system (see Chapter 4), with resulting delays in gross and fine motor development. Seizures and microcephaly can affect cognition. Sensorineural hearing loss and visual impairments reduce the individual's ability to gather and respond to information from the environment. If sensory impairments are paired with low cognition, functioning is severely impaired.

Psychosocial Development. In addition to any implications for psychosocial development that are associated with their physical and cognitive disabilities, children with CMV may evoke fear and rejection in educators and others who provide services to them in educational settings. Although most individuals will have CMV during their lifetime, service providers who are pregnant must be especially careful in handling children with CMV, because of the risk of acquiring CMV and transmitting it to the fetus (Giardina & Psota, 1997).

Implications for Education and Personal Autonomy

Transdisciplinary service delivery is critical for meeting the needs of students with CMV. If they have cognitive delays and learning disabilities, provision of special education services will be necessary. They may receive related services from occupational, physical, and speech therapists, and adapted physical educators. They may also receive specialized health care services from a nurse or health care aide. When a student has such an array of needs (and therefore services), regular and coordinated communication provides the avenue for appropriate service delivery.

Educators and others must be especially alert to avoid transmission of CMV to other individuals. For example, a young child who picks up and mouths a toy before moving to another play area has transmitted the CMV to that object. The virus can live for several hours on environmental surfaces and is undetectable, so the next child who plays with the same toy may spread the virus to the hands and then possibly the mouth. Another example would be CMV transmission from one child to another if they are both in diapers and are changed on a surface that is not properly cleaned after each diaper change. Although a child infected with CMV may become mildly ill, the real danger is the possibility of CMV exposure of pregnant women or individuals with depressed immune systems.

Care must be taken not to exclude children with CMV from educational settings for fear that others will contract the virus. They do not shed the virus constantly, the virus itself is not considered to be highly contagious, and CMV symptoms are mild (Cordell, Solomon, & Hale, 1996). Appropriate staff in-service training is essential for educating service providers about avoiding CMV transmission and universal precautions.

Implications for Career and Adult Outcomes

Career and adult outcomes for individuals with congenital CMV will depend on the extent of associated disabilities. Since individuals with CMV may have normal intelligence, learning disabilities, or severe/profound cognitive involvement, planning for adulthood will necessarily be individualized.

HIV/AIDS

Definitions and Descriptions

Acquired Immunodeficiency Syndrome (AIDS) "is the final stage of immune system breakdown in a person infected with the human immunodeficiency virus (HIV)" (Hale, 1997, p. 83). These words clearly describe the relationship between an infection that can exist for many years in the body, slowly evolving with increasing amounts of virus and concurrent bodily symptoms, and its final diagnosis, heralded by the appearance of opportunistic infections and ending in death. AIDS is considered a new chronic childhood illness that is more frequently occurring than several of the disabilities previously discussed, including cystic fibrosis, leukemia, and muscular dystrophy (Meyers & Weitzman, 1991). It is estimated that every year in the United States, 7,000 infants are born at risk for developing HIV infection (Rutstein, Conlon, & Batshaw, 1997, p. 66). In some states, HIV/AIDS is surpassed only by injury as a leading cause of death in children (Simonds & Rogers, 1992).

Transmission of HIV can occur through several avenues, which are broadly categorized as perinatal, sexual, or parenteral. **Perinatal transmission** occurs from an HIV-infected mother to her fetus or infant, through the uterus, at delivery via contact with infected blood or vaginal secretions, or through breastfeeding. **Sexual transmission** occurs as a result of contact with infected blood, semen, or vaginal secretions during sexual activity. Finally, **parenteral transmission** refers to infection acquired through exposure to infected blood, blood products, or tissue. Examples include transfusion, organ transplantation, needle sharing during intravenous drug use, and accidental needle "sticks" (Simonds & Rogers, 1992). It is important to note that blood-screening techniques for transfusion and organ transplantation are sufficiently sophisticated that HIV transmission from transfusion or organ transplantation is now extremely unlikely.

Most young children who contract HIV infection do so prenatally or through the process of birth (perinatally). However, not all children born to HIV-positive mothers will themselves contract HIV (Rutstein et al., 1997, p. 66). The risk of transmission during birth is significantly decreased if AZT (zidovudine) is administered to the mother and the baby is delivered via cesarean section (National Institute of Allergy and Infectious Diseases [NIAID], 2003). Another option is providing the mother with an oral dose of NVP (nevirapine) during labor and another to the baby within three days of birth (National Institute of Allergy and Infectious Diseases [NIAID], 2003).

The HIV passes through several stages before a diagnosis of AIDS is appropriate. After initial infection, 6 to 12 weeks may pass before blood tests "positive" for the HIV antibody. For infants less than 15 months, there is the possibility of testing HIV positive while actually not being infected, due to the mother's antibody status. In the next stage, the HIV is multiplying, but there are no manifestations. This stage may last up to several years, but appears to be shorter in children (Hale, 1997). In the third stage, symptoms appear with the continued proliferation of HIV in the body. The lymph nodes, liver, and spleen may be swollen. The individual may experience fever, nausea, vomiting, and weight loss. The final stage is characterized by the appearance of opportunistic infections such as CMV, oral thrush, certain cancers, and pneumonia (Heller et al., 1996). These symptoms constitute "AIDS-defining illnesses," resulting in the label of AIDS (Hale, 1997; NIAID, 2001). Children at this stage may experience **failure to thrive** and **encephalopathy** (disorders in cognition). In children who acquire HIV perinatally, those who were infected in utero usually have symptoms before they are one year old, while children who were infected during the birth process do not have symptoms for several years (Barnhart et al., 1996).

Associated Medical Conditions

Associated conditions that are most likely to occur in children with a diagnosis of AIDS include involvement of the central nervous system, opportunistic infections, and nonspecific symptoms. Central nervous system disorders may include motor problems such as ataxia and spasticity, microcephaly, and dementia. Opportunistic infections include pneumocystis carinii pneumonia. Karposi's sarcoma (a rare form of cancer) also occurs in individuals with AIDS. Individuals may also easily contract strep or flu. CMV may reappear with severe symptoms due to the impaired immune system of individuals with AIDS. Other symptoms include chronic diarrhea, thrush, failure to thrive, and upper respiratory infections (Heller et al., 1996).

Medical and Therapeutic Treatments

Medical Responses. HIV/AIDS is treated with a variety of medications that slow replication of the virus (antiretroviral drugs), counteract bacterial infections (prophylactic antibiotics), and support the immune system (intravenous immunoglobulin). A "cocktail" consisting of numerous drugs is effective in reducing the level of detectable HIV, although effective dosage levels for children are still being explored. New antiretroviral drugs are being developed in response to drug resistance. The use of AZT in HIV-positive pregnant women reduces transmission of HIV to their infants (Rutstein et al., 1997). One medical goal for addressing HIV/AIDS is to produce a vaccine that would prevent infection. Another possibility is a vaccine that reduces the effects of HIV in infected individuals. HIV should be managed as a chronic illness and not a terminal disease (Rutstein et al., 1997). It is important for educators to appreciate the dangers of poor medication compliance. When the medical regimen is complex (involving taking various medications in certain dosages at certain times), doses may be missed. As a result, the medication is less effective and the individual may even develop dosage resistance (Brown, Lourie, & Pao, 2000).

One complication of medical treatment is the issue of vaccination of children who are immunosupressed. Although children with HIV should be vaccinated against common childhood diseases, using a live virus vaccine may actually induce the illness against which the child is being vaccinated. For example, the child should receive the injectable polio vaccine (IPV) instead of oral polio vaccine (OPV), because the IPV is a killed virus. Unfortunately, the vaccine against measles, mumps, and rubella (MMR) is a live vaccine. Many families choose vaccination, because the alternative is risk of infection with a childhood illness that can be fatal to the child with HIV. The new varicella (chicken pox) vaccination is currently not being recommended for children with HIV infection (Rutstein et al., 1997).

Perhaps one day a vaccine will be developed for HIV/AIDS. Presently, advances in medical treatment have added years of life to infected individuals. However, prevention remains the most effective approach to HIV/AIDS. Teachers and others need to join in coordinated efforts to reduce (and eventually prevent) HIV/AIDS.

Therapeutic Treatment. Individuals with HIV/AIDS may benefit from therapeutic interventions such as exercise programs to build and maintain physical endurance. As the effects of the virus progress, self-care activities such as eating, personal hygiene, and dressing may be negatively affected. Occupational and physical therapists can assist teachers and others with strategies for maintaining independent self-care, which has a positive effect on the individual's psychological health.

Impact on Physical, Cognitive, and Psychosocial Development

Physical and Cognitive Development. Many children with HIV/AIDS experience a slight lag in physical and cognitive development early in the disease process (Rutstein et al., 1997). For some individuals, physical and cognitive effects of HIV infection are subtle and include a higher-than-typical incidence of poor expressive language skills (Brouwers, Belman, & Epstein, 1994), learning disabilities, and attention-deficit/hyperactivity disorders (Grubman et al., 1995). As they enter school, these children may require special education services when a learning disability is present. Development is less positive for other infants, who display a pattern of deterioration and then plateau (level off) in physical and cognitive development. In 10–20% of cases, deterioration is rapid. The head fails to grow, and the brain begins to deteriorate. Physically, the infant exhibits muscle weakness, abnormal muscle tone, tremors, and eventual quadriplegia (decreased use in all four limbs). Death usually occurs before 4 years of age (Brouwers et al., 1994).

Psychosocial Implications. If the child contracted HIV through prenatal transmission, then other family members are also likely to be infected. A great deal of social stigma continues to cling to a diagnosis of HIV infection. As a result, families may not disclose its presence in their children to school personnel or to their own children. Guilt may also play a part in nondisclosure. When parents are involved with managing their own illness, it will be difficult to attend adequately to their children's physical and psychosocial well-being. Changes in physical function and appearance as a result of opportunistic infections can also have a negative impact on psychosocial adjustment. Finally, neurological deterioration may also affect behavior in children and adolescents with HIV/AIDS.

Implications for Education and Personal Autonomy

Education. The educational implications of HIV/AIDS parallel the progression of the disease. When children are asymptomatic, they feel good and are able to attend school and fully participate in educational activities. Modifications are necessary if the virus asserts itself and other symptoms appear. Physical symptoms such as fever, nausea, vomiting, and physical discomfort can be managed with medication, but can result in considerable fatigue. Fatigue can be managed through strategies such as shifting academic emphasis to times of greatest endurance, providing in-school areas in which to rest, and/or implementing a decreased attendance schedule.

The neurological effects of HIV/AIDS have significant educational and behavioral consequences. Cognitive impairments may include deficits in organization, attention, and expressive language. Reducing visual and auditory distractions and providing outlines and other visual cues assists students to organize school materials and attend to relevant aspects of tasks. Teachers can employ task analysis to break new material into manageable steps. Advance organizers (indicating upcoming subject matter) can be provided through outlines, key words or phrases, or other formats. Use of choral reading or recitation supports expressive language attempts. A consistent response is critical to curbing impulsive behaviors.

HIV/AIDS is not transmitted through casual contact, although sharing any equipment that may allow blood-to-blood exchange (including a toothbrush or a safety razor) is a dangerous practice. There is no medical, public health, or social justification for excluding a child with HIV infection from school. In fact, the educational environment may pose a substantial health threat for the individual with HIV/AIDS whose immune system is compromised. Educators and others must be alert to signs of illness in other individuals in order to protect the student with HIV.

HIV/AIDS demands a response that is compassionate, sensitive, and supportive of the evolving needs of the student and family. LeRoy, Powell, and Kelker (1994, pp. 40–44) suggest 12 components for providing an optimal educational environment for students with HIV/AIDS:

- Inclusion in schools;
- Interdisciplinary team management;
- Early/frequent assessment;
- Family focus;
- Sensitive and nonjudgmental services;
- Responsibility and confidentiality;
- Safety;
- Keeping current;
- Prevention programs;
- Preparing the educational team;
- Quality of life;
- Advocacy.

It is particularly important that teachers honor confidentiality and behave responsibly regarding HIV status in students. Teachers must establish a climate of mutual respect and compassion. The absence of respect results in the abandonment of trust. Respect is modeled when teachers include students with HIV/AIDS in all aspects of the curriculum, refuse to accept any level of teasing or ridicule, and keep physical assistance subtle. They must also refrain from any information disclosure. How teachers respond provides the foundation for appropriate behavioral interactions.

HIV/AIDS education, coupled with clear and consistent infection-control policies and practices, is the most effective weapon against HIV/AIDS. Many states have included HIV/AIDS education in their health curricula for students in high school. Heightened awareness through education is effective in prevention and has the added benefit of reducing misconceptions and stigma.

Personal Autonomy. As HIV/AIDS advances, independent performance of self-care and other personal management activities may be affected due to extreme fatigue or illness. Physical autonomy exists along a continuum; it is not necessary for a student to independently complete all aspects of self-care. For example, a student who is no longer able to perform independent dressing can direct the service provider by choosing certain clothing items and ask that they be put on the body in certain ways and in a particular order. Another strategy is assisting in care. In the dressing example, the student can give clothing items to the service provider as they are needed. Even pointing to items involves active participation. Finally, cooperating in routines by moving the body preserves a measure of physical autonomy.

Progression of HIV/AIDS has psychological consequences of loss of autonomy, feelings of "being different" from others, and fear of the future. The combination of physical deterioration and social isolation places the individual at risk for reduced psychological well-being. Three strategies for confronting loss of autonomy and reduced social contact for students with HIV/AIDS are providing choices, implementing respite care, and maintaining peer linkages. As students with HIV/AIDS become physically weaker and more susceptible to opportunistic infections, they may choose to receive educational services at home. Later, if they feel better, they may choose to return to school. The educational system must remain flexible in regard to where services are received. Even when they are very ill, students with AIDS may wish to remain at home surrounded by familiar objects, people, and routines. Respite care provides relief for families who may become exhausted and who would otherwise be unable to keep the individual at home. Teachers can facilitate autonomy by providing updated packets of schoolwork to complete at home and encouraging peer contact. The availability of computers in classrooms makes transmission of e-mail a feasible option for contact. Electronic mail is simple to send and receive, and has the added advantage of immediacy. Another strategy is videotaping. Making tapes of class and school activities and viewing them in the home of the student with HIV/AIDS provides a link with events, is focused in the present, and provides further material for conversation and social interaction.

Implications for Career and Adult Outcomes

Since individuals with HIV/AIDS are living longer and healthier lives, there is no reason why adolescents should not plan for postsecondary education and careers. As is the case with other disabilities, federal law protects individuals with HIV/AIDS against discrimination in employment and other aspects of adult life (such as housing). Any career restrictions should be related to physical aspects of HIV/AIDS and not the perceptions of what an individual "can" or "should" accomplish.

SPECIAL TOPICS IN HEALTH CARE

Chapters 2, 3, and 4 provide information on a variety of physical, health, and multiple disabilities. Within these broad groups are individuals with special health care needs. Although not all individuals with special health care needs require medical technology and treatments, they need particular considerations for optimal outcomes in school (Porter, Haynie, Bierle, Caldwell, & Palfrey, 1997). In a comprehensive national study by Heller, Fredrick, Best, Dykes, and Cohen (2000), teachers and paraprofessionals reported that they regularly performed specialized health care procedures (e.g., suctioning mucus, performing clean intermittent catheterization), but only half that number felt very knowledgeable about these procedures. Most respondents also indicated interest in receiving more training, assistance in policy development, and technical assistance. Based on these data, it is clear that support provision for individuals with special health care needs is an important topic for teachers and others who provide services to individuals with physical, health, or multiple disabilities. Developing an individualized health care plan (IHCP) will be discussed as a critical aspect of support for individuals with specialized health care needs in educational environments.

While medical research and technology continue to be directed toward primary disease prevention, much can be done by educators and other service providers to maintain a clean environment and prevent the spread of infectious disease. Practice of infectious disease transmission prevention and implementation of universal precautions is an important special topic for educators and others who provide services for students with health impairments and infectious diseases.

Meeting Specialized Health Care Needs

Caldwell, Todaro, and Gates (1991, p. 51) note that students with special health care needs can be categorized within these five groups:

- Students who have special health conditions;
- Students whose conditions are infectious;
- Students whose conditions require technology;
- Students whose conditions cause changes in neurological functioning;
- Students who are medically fragile.

Of course, it is possible for a specific student to have needs across several categories. For example, students who are medically fragile are a subset of students with specialized health care needs. They may experience a temporary medical crisis, be consistently fragile, or have a condition that is progressive and will lead to a fragile state (Caldwell et al., 1991, p. 71). An example in which a student has specialized health care needs across categories is when a student has HIV/AIDS. This individual has an infectious disease which may eventually cause changes in neurological functioning.

Children with special health care needs may be intimidating to teachers and other service providers. Their equipment may be bulky and may necessitate physical accommodation in classrooms. Even if teachers are not responsible for equipment maintenance, they should learn how it operates and pay attention to signs of malfunction. Frequently, trained providers are available to meet special health care needs at school. However, the teacher must also become aware of health care procedures and remain alert for signs that the student is in distress or needs immediate attention. Most important, teachers and others must remind themselves that equipment and procedures enhance function, but that the student has the same academic and psychosocial needs as anyone else. Many students with special health care needs perform well in general education classes with adequate support (Figure 3–4).

It is impossible in this chapter to provide detailed information related to specific medical technologies such as tube feeding, dialysis, or clean intermittent catheterization. Readers are referred to sources such as *Meeting Physical and Health Needs of Children with Disabilities: Teaching Student Participation and Management* (Heller, Forney, Alberto, Schwartzman, & Goeckel, 2000) and *Children and Youth Assisted by Medical Technology in the Classroom: Guidelines for Care* (Porter et al., 1997) for complete descriptions of a variety of specialized health care procedures. Even if teachers are not directly responsible for performing

FIGURE 3–4
(a) Portable ventilator and suctioning equipment allow this sixth grader to attend regular class. (b) It is easy to be overwhelmed by the equipment and not see the child

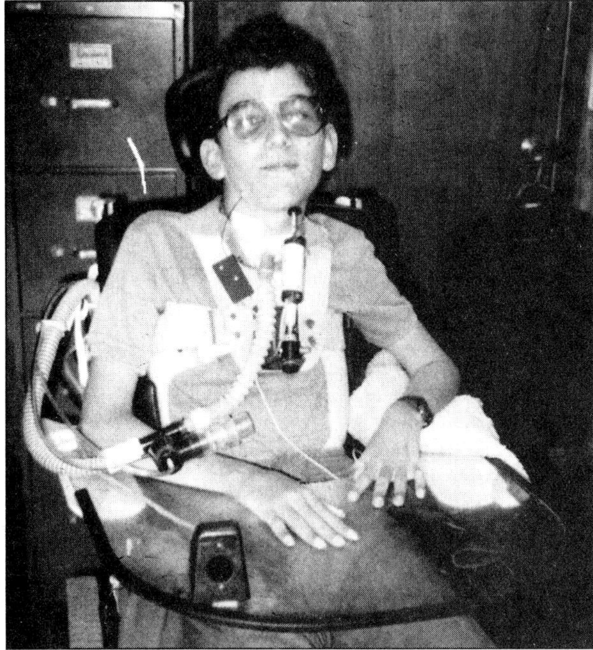

(a)

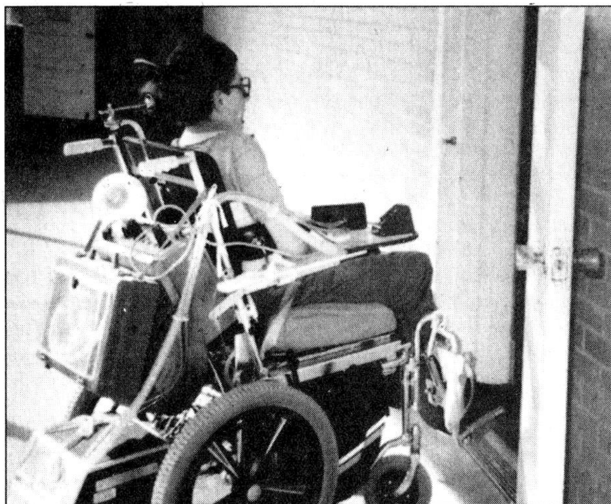

(b)

these procedures, it is important for them to have current knowledge of best practices for meeting specialized health care needs. Pertinent information can be transmitted through development of an individualized health care plan (IHCP).

Developing Individualized Health Care Plans. There are several reasons to develop an IHCP for any individual with special health care needs (Porter et al., 1997). First, having an IHCP provides continuity of care within educational environments and ensures the quality of services (Haas, 1993). Second, the IHCP provides documentation that could be used to request further assistance and to assess the success of current practices. Third, the IHCP can be used to defend existing policy in the event of a legal dispute. Finally, if an IHCP is included as part of the IEP, teachers and others will be exposed to the child's heath care needs in a direct, understandable, and accessible manner.

The IHCP should be developed under the leadership of health professionals and include a description of the condition, a brief health history, basic health status and health care needs, treatments or medications and their side effects, transportation concerns, equipment needs, emergency plans, and specific precautions and/or activity restrictions (Caldwell et al., 1991; Porter et al., 1997). It is also important to indicate the extent of independent health care, including whether the individual can self-medicate or recognize the signs and symptoms of potential health crises (Caldwell et al., 1991). Involving individuals in their own health care fosters personal and psychological autonomy, as does the promotion of any other self-care skill. The level of independence should be guided by the student's developmental ability (Heller et al., 2000). Figure 3–5 provides a sample IHCP.

Planning and implementing an IHCP is only one aspect of support for students with specialized health care needs. Heller et al. (2000) state that infection control, cardiopulmonary resuscitation (CPR), first aid, appropriate documentation strategies, and equipment responsibility are important components of a safe environment for students with specialized health care needs. Other areas include understanding legal rules and constraints, developing emergency plans, establishing/maintaining communication among family, school personnel, and medical providers, meeting special transportation needs, and accommodating educational needs of students who miss a substantial amount of school because of absences (Caldwell et al., 1991, pp. 52–53; Porter et al., 1997). Teachers will be involved in many aspects of the IHCP and in promoting safe environments for students with specialized health care needs.

FIGURE 3–5
Sample individualized health care plan (IHCP)

Student Individualized Health Care Plan

❑ 504
❑ Special Education

Student's Name ____________ Birth Date ____________
Student's Teacher ____________ School ____________
Grade ____________ School Year ____________

Physician's Name ____________
Address ____________ Telephone Number ____________
Parents/Guardians ____________ Home Phone ____________
Work Phone (Mother) ____________ Emergency Phone ____________
Work Phone (Father) ____________ Emergency Phone ____________
Work Phone (Guardian) ____________ Emergency Phone ____________
Hospital Health Care Coordinator ____________ Phone ____________
School Health Care Coordinator ____________ Phone ____________
Education Coordinator ____________ Phone ____________

MEDICAL OVERVIEW

Brief Medical History ____________

Known Allergies ____________

Medications ____________

Medication Authorization Form Attached for Each Medication ❑ Yes ❑ No

Specific Health Care Needs ____________

Procedure Authorization Form Attached for Each Procedure ❑ Yes ❑ No

ADDITIONAL NEEDS/PLANS

Emergency Plan Attached ❑ Yes ❑ No
Recreational Activity Permission Form Attached ❑ Yes ❑ No

Transportation Plan Attached ❑ Yes ❑ No
Personnel Training Plan Attached ❑ Yes ❑ No
Entry/Reentry Checklist Completed ❑ Yes ❑ No
Other: ____________

ADDITIONAL INFORMATION

Special Diet ____________

Additional Information Attached ❑ Yes ❑ No

Special Safety Measures ____________

FIGURE 3–5
(Continued)

Additional Information Attached ❑ Yes ❑ No
Special Equipment ______________________________

____

Additional Information Attached ❑ Yes ❑ No
Other: ______________________________

____

Additional Information Attached ❑ Yes ❑ No

PARENT/GUARDIAN AUTHORIZATION

We (I) ____________ hereby request and approve this Individualized Health Care Plan for our (my) child
(name)

____________ as prescribed by our (my) child's physician ____________ .
(name) *(name)*

We (I) will notify the school immediately if there is any change to or cancellation of these orders. We (I) release school personnel from liability should reactions result from any treatments given.

Signature ____________ Date ____________

Signature ____________ Date ____________

Next IHCP Review Date ______________________________

Note. From *Meeting the Needs of Students with Special Physical and Health Care Needs* by Hill, © 1999. Reprinted by permission of Prentice-Hall, Inc., Upper Saddle River, NJ.

Students with special health care needs include those with infectious diseases. Within their own classrooms, teachers can do much to prevent the spread of infectious disease through the implementation of universal precautions and infection control techniques. Adoption of universal precautions represents current best practices for *all* teachers and others who work in health care settings.

Preventing Infectious Disease Transmission and Implementing Universal Precautions

Growing concern with transmission of bloodborne diseases such as HIV and hepatitis B resulted in the 1987 recommendations by the Centers for Disease Control (CDC) for contact with blood and body fluids. Since teachers and others may not be aware that a particular student has a bloodborne disease, the CDC adopted the term *universal precautions* to reinforce their recommendation that certain precautions be adopted with all individuals. The use of universal precautions provides the following benefits: (a) protecting infected individuals from further infection; (b) protecting the privacy of infected individuals; (c) protecting the health of service providers; and (d) protecting the health of other students. Universal precautions include handwashing; use of personal protective equipment (barrier protection); safe methods of disposing of waste, cleaning up spills, and handling laundry; and procedures for dealing with accidental exposure to potentially infectious materials.

In 1991, the Occupational Safety and Health Administration (OSHA) created a standard for prevention of infection by bloodborne diseases. This standard requires employers to provide a written exposure control plan, training about exposure prevention, procedures for evaluating incidents of exposure, and a schedule for implementation (Bradley, 1994; Occupational Exposure to Blood-Borne Pathogens, 1991). Some states have adopted this standard for implementing universal precautions in educational environments (Porter et al., 1997).

Universal precautions should be followed if there is contact with blood or serum, semen, vaginal secretions, or other fluids found within the body (such as cerebral spinal fluid). Universal precautions also apply to the following body fluids if they contain visible blood: feces, nasal secretions, sputum, saliva, sweat, tears, urine, vomitus, and breast milk (Centers for Disease Control and Prevention, 1987). Not all diseases are transmitted by blood and blood products, however. Conditions such as hepatitis A, pinworms, and common diarrhea can be transmitted through contact with contaminated feces. The best defense against contamination with potentially infectious materials is proper handwashing.

Handwashing. Handwashing is an ordinary procedure that people follow daily, often without thinking about the steps in this process. However, proper handwashing is the key to prevention of infection transmission. Hands should be washed before and after contact with students, after touching or cleaning objects that have been contaminated with bodily secretions *even if gloves are worn,* after cleaning up blood spills or other potentially infectious materials *even if gloves are worn,* after contamination of hands by bodily secretions, blood, or other potentially infectious materials *even if gloves are worn,* after removal of gloves or other personal protective equipment, before taking breaks, and before leaving the workplace (Giardina & Psota, 1997, p. 75). Figure 3–6 provides specific handwashing techniques.

What can service providers do when standard equipment for handwashing is not immediately available? One strategy is to equip a waist or fanny pack with supplies that can be taken out of the classroom.

FIGURE 3–6
Handwashing techniques

1. Inspect your hands for any visible soiling, breaks, or cuts in the skin or cuticles.
2. Remove any jewelry.* If you have a watch on, push it up your arm as high as possible. Also push up the sleeves of your blouse or jacket so that they are well above the wrist.
3. Turn on the water and adjust water flow and temperature to ensure that it is not too hot or has too much flow. Warm water is needed to ensure proper action of the soap. Use cold water only if warm water is not available. Water that is too hot will remove the protective oils of the skin and will dry the skin, making it vulnerable to damage. Water that comes out of the tap with too much force is more likely to splash onto the floors and walls, possibly spreading the microorganisms.
4. With the water running, wet your hands and wrists. Ensure that your hands are lower than your elbows so that the water flows from the least contaminated areas (i.e., the wrists) to the most contaminated areas (i.e., the hands). Lather hands with soap. Liquid soap is preferable to bar soap, which can be a reservoir for bacteria. Use bar soap only when dispensed soap is not available.
5. Wash thoroughly for at least 30 seconds. If you have just handled a contaminated object (e.g., a dirty glass), wash for 1 minute. If you have been in direct contact with any type of bodily fluid (e.g., you have just changed a diaper), you should wash for up to 2 minutes. Use a firm, circular motion and friction and ensure that you wash the back of hands, palms, and wrists. Wash each finger individually, making sure that you wash between fingers and knuckles (i.e., interlace fingers and thumbs and move hands back and forth) as well as around the cuticles. Do not use too much pressure, as this may result in the skin being damaged.
6. Rinse thoroughly with warm water. Use a fingernail file or orange stick and clean under each fingernail while the water is still running. If a file or stick is not available, use the fingernails of the opposite hand.
7. Shake hands to remove excess water. Dry your hands thoroughly using a paper towel, working upward from fingertips, to hands, to wrists, and finally to forearms. When drying, rather than rub vigorously, it is best to pat the skin. It is important that the hands be dried well to prevent chapping.
8. Turn off the taps using the paper towel you used to dry your hands. Use the paper towel to wipe the surfaces surrounding the sink. Dispose of the paper towel in a covered, child-proof receptacle with a disposable plastic liner.
9. Apply lotion, if desired, to keep skin soft, to reduce the risk of chapping, and to act as a barrier for invasion of microorganisms.

*Since microorganisms can lodge in the settings or stones of rings, it is recommended by some that staff working with students who need physical care do not wear *any* jewelry (Silkworth, 1986); others have suggested that it is permissible to leave on a plain wedding band (Sitler, 1991).

Note. Adapted from Silkworth, (1998b); Sitler, (1991); and Utah State Office of Education, (1995).

The pack can be filled with disposable gloves, Band-Aids, gauze, elastic wrap, tweezers, and disposable wipes. Taking a waist pack on field trips, to the playground, and other outings is convenient and accessible. Follow-up would consist of thorough handwashing and other appropriate cleanup procedures as soon as facilities are available (Making It Work: Always Be Prepared, 1995).

Waterless skin antiseptics have become popular to use when traditional handwashing means are not available. They are portable and scented and are advertised as antibacterial. The danger with antibacterial skin preparations lies in *substituting* them for standard handwashing. Since they frequently contain alcohol, continued use can irritate skin. Use of a waterless skin antiseptic should be followed up with standard handwashing.

Waste Disposal. Disposing of soiled materials is a critical step in preventing infection transmission. Liquid secretions should be wiped up with disposable towels, and all disposable soiled materials placed into a plastic bag whose top is then tied shut. Nondisposable items (e.g., clothing) should also be bagged until it can be properly cleaned. After secretions are removed, the areas should be cleaned with a solution of nine parts water to one part of household bleach. The water/bleach solution can be mixed in a spray bottle for easy dispensing. A fresh solution should be made every day. During every aspect of cleanup, disposable gloves must be worn. If everyone who performs these procedures uses the same techniques, no overt attention is paid to particular children who are infected. Universal precautions have the additional benefit of reducing infection transmission for everyone by ensuring a cleaner environment.

SUMMARY AND CONCLUSION

The health impairments and infectious diseases described in this chapter represent a sampling of these clinically diverse categories. Although health impairments involve different systems of the body, have different outcomes, and require different treatments, all have the potential to disrupt physical, cognitive, psychosocial, and educational functioning. Understanding the dynamics of health impairments allows service providers to better understand their impact and make appropriate accommodations.

Implementing universal precautions and infection control in school settings is critical to preventing disease transmission. Readers were provided with standards and techniques for appropriate universal precautions and infection control.

A key concept for teachers and others who provide services for students with health impairments and infectious diseases is to *strive for a typical instructional atmosphere.* Chronic conditions invade many aspects of life and can be emotionally as well as physically exhausting. When educational services are provided in an atmosphere of acceptance and appropriate accommodation, students with health impairments and infectious diseases are physically safe and more emotionally able to confront their realities. When they are overprotected, when their medically related needs are ignored, or when service providers are unaware of the implications of their disabilities for development, the outcomes are decreased psychosocial and physical well-being.

QUESTIONS FOR DISCUSSION

1. Why do "invisible disabilities" such as asthma place individuals at risk for psychosocial problems?
2. What steps can teachers take to reduce possible asthma triggers in their classrooms?
3. A 15-year-old adolescent with cystic fibrosis has moved into the school district where you provide consultant services. In conjunction with the school nurse, what would you tell this adolescent's general education teacher about accommodating her medical needs using strategies that are effective but unobtrusive?
4. How can teachers and others facilitate personal autonomy in children and adolescents with cancer?
5. A child in your special day class recently died of cancer. How can you continue to provide support for the child's family, for the other children in your class, and for yourself?
6. You have been asked to provide an in-service training program entitled "Practical Strategies for Universal Precautions and Infection Prevention in Educational Settings." Please prepare an outline of this presentation.

FOCUS ON THE NET

Asthma Information Center

http://www.ama-assn.org/special/asthma

Sponsored by the American Medical Association, the Asthma Information Center is intended for health care professionals, journalists, researchers, patients, and parents of children with asthma. It is intended to facilitate communication among researchers and provide information to consumers about the latest developments in asthma care and treatment.

Centers for Disease Control and Prevention

http://www.cdc.gov

Federally funded and operated, the Centers for Disease Control and Prevention (CDC) has many "departments" within its main system. For example, the CDC National Center for Infectious Diseases can be accessed via the CDC main site. This highly specialized site can provide answers to numerous health-related questions. Examples of links to the National Center for Infectious Diseases include:

- Health Topics A–Z
- Data and Statistics
- Traveler's Health

The CDC is perhaps the most extensive organization for disease research and information.

Cystic Fibrosis Foundation

http://www.cff.org

"65 Roses: Why Do Children Give Such a Beautiful Name to Such a Terrible Disease?" Readers may be aware of the story of the child who mistook the name "cystic fibrosis" for "65 roses." The Cystic Fibrosis Foundation is dedicated to a cure for cystic fibrosis and improvement of the quality of life for persons who have this disease.

Medhelp International

http://www.medhelp.org

Medhelp International is a nonprofit organization dedicated to helping people to find qualified medical information and support for their medical conditions and questions. With information from Medhelp International, people are empowered to make healthier lifestyle choices through high-quality medical information and support. This site helps patients make informed treatment decisions within the short timelines dictated by their illness or disease.

National Pediatric AIDS Network

http://www.npan.org

The National Pediatric AIDS Network offers a resource site for children and adolescents with HIV/AIDS. It is a nonprofit group that provides information for families, and its site includes an excellent listing of further sites for children, teens, and caregivers, plus links to related health organizations and Web sites.

REFERENCES

Andersen, R. D., Bale, J. F., Blackman, M. D., & Murph, J. R. (1986). *Infections in children: A sourcebook for educators and care providers.* Rockville, MD: Aspen.

Avery, M. E., & First, L. R. (1994). *Pediatric care.* Baltimore: Williams & Wilkins.

Barnhart, H. X., Caldwell, M. B., Thomas, P., Mascola, L., Ortiz, I., Hsu, H., et al. (1996). Natural history of human immunodeficiency virus disease in perinatally infected children: An analysis from the pediatric spectrum of disease project. *Pediatrics, 97,* 710–716.

Batshaw, M. L., & Perret, Y. M. (1992). *Children with disabilities: A medical primer* (3rd ed.). Baltimore: Brookes.

Behrman, R. E. (1992). *Nelson handbook of pediatrics.* Philadelphia: Saunders.

Bloomberg, G. R., & Strunk, R. C. (1992). Crisis in asthma care. *Pediatric Clinics of North America, 39,* 1225–1241.

Bradley, B. (1994). *Occupational exposure to bloodborne pathogens: Implementing OSHA standards in school settings.* Scarborough, ME: National Association of School Nurses.

Brouwers, P., Belman, A. L., & Epstein, L. (1994). Central nervous system involvement: Manifestation, evaluation, and pathogenesis. In P. A. Pizzo & C. M. Wilfert (Eds.), *Pediatric AIDS: The challenge of HIV infection in infants, children, and adolescents* (2nd ed., pp. 433–455). Baltimore: Williams & Wilkins.

Brown, L. K., Lourie, K. J., & Pao, M. (2000). Children and adolescents living with HIV and AIDS: A review. *Journal of Child Psychiatry and Allied Disciplines, 41*(1), 81–96.

Brown, R. T., & Madan-Swain, A. (1993). Cognitive, neuropsychological and academic sequelae in children with leukemia. *Journal of Learning Disabilities, 26,* 74–90.

Caldwell, T. H., Todaro, A. W., & Gates, A. J. (1991). Special health care needs. In J. L. Bigge, *Teaching individuals with physical and multiple disabilities* (pp. 50–74). Upper Saddle River, NJ: Merrill/ Prentice Hall.

Centers for Disease Control and Prevention. (1987). Recommendations for prevention of HIV transmission in health care settings. *Morbidity and Mortality Weekly Report, 36*(Suppl.), 3S–18S.

Cordell, R. L., Solomon, S. L., & Hale, C. M. (1996). Exclusion of mildly ill children from out-of-home child care facilities. *Journal of Infectious Medicine, 13*(1), 41, 45–48.

Council for Exceptional Children (2000). *The standards for the preparation and licensure of special educators* (4th edition). Reston, VA: Author.

Crooks, G. M., Baron-Hay, G. S., Byrne, G. C., Cameron, F. G., Hookings, P., Keogh, E. J., et al. (1991). Late effects of childhood malignancies seen in Western Australia. *American Journal of Pediatric Hematology/Oncology, 13*(4), 442–449.

Cropp, G. J., & Shames, R. S. (1994). Respiratory and allergic diseases. In A. M. Rudolph & R. K. Kamei (Eds.), *Rudolph's fundamentals of pediatrics* (pp. 537–582). Norwalk, CT: Appleton & Lange.

Cystic Fibrosis Foundation (2001a, December). *Facts about cystic fibrosis.* Bethesda, MD: Cystic Fibrosis Foundation.

Cystic Fibrosis Foundation (2001b, December). *Gene therapy and cystic fibrosis.* Bethesda, MD: Cystic Fibrosis Foundation.

Denti, L. G., & Meyers, B. S. (1997). Successful ability awareness programs: The key is in the planning. *Teaching Exceptional Children, 29*(4), 52–54.

DePaepe, P., Garrison-Kane, L., & Doelling, J. (2002). Supporting students with health needs in schools: An overview of selected conditions. *Focus on Exceptional Children, 35*(1), 1–24.

Diette, G. B., Markson, L., Skinner, E. A., Nguyen, T. T. H., Algatt-Bergstrom, P., & Wu, A. W. (2000). Nocturnal asthma in children affects school attendance, school performance, and parents' work attendance. *Archives of Pediatric and Adolescent Medicine, 134,* 923–928.

Elmayan, M. M. (1993). Cancer. In M. G. Brodwin, F. A. Tellez, & S. K. Brodwin (Eds.), *Medical, psychosocial, and vocational aspects of disability* (pp. 233–249). Athens, GA: Elliot & Fitzpatrick.

Giardina, R. G., & Psota, C. E. (1997). Universal precautions and infection control in a school setting. In S. Porter, M. Haynie, T. Bierle, T. H. Caldwell, & J. S. Palfrey (Eds.), *Children and youth assisted by medical technology in the classroom: Guidelines for care* (2nd ed., pp. 74–78). Baltimore: Brookes.

Grubman, S., Gross, E., Lerner-Weiss, N., Hernandez, M., McSherry, G. D., Hoyt, L. G., et al. (1995). Older children and adolescents living with perinatally acquired human immunodeficiency virus infection. *Pediatrics, 95,* 657–663.

Haas, M. B. (1993). Individualized healthcare plans. In M. B. Haas (Ed.), *The school nurse's sourcebook of individualized healthcare plans* (pp. 41–45). North Branch, MN: Sunrise River Press.

Haggerty, M. C. (1990). Asthma. In D. L. Sexton (Ed.), *Nursing care of the respiratory patient* (pp. 137–168). Norwalk, CT: Appleton & Lange.

Hale, A. R. (1997). Human immunodeficiency virus and acquired immunodeficiency syndrome. In S. Porter, M. Haynie, T. Bierle, T. H. Caldwell, & J. S. Palfrey (Eds.), *Children and youth assisted by medical technology in the classroom: Guidelines for care* (2nd ed., pp. 83–93). Baltimore: Brookes.

Hanshaw, J. B. (1981). CNS infections. *Pediatrics in Review, 2*(8), 245–251.

Heller, K. W., Alberto, P. A., Forney, P. E., & Schwartzman, M. N. (1996). Asthma. In K. W. Heller, P. A. Alberto, P. E. Forney, & M. N. Schwartzman (Eds.), *Understanding physical, sensory, and health impairments: Characteristics and educational implications* (pp. 277–295). Pacific Grove, CA: Brooks/Cole.

Heller, K. W., Forney, P. E., Alberto, P. A., Schwartzman, M. N., & Goeckel, T. M. (2000). *Meeting physical and health needs of children with disabilities: Teaching student participation and management.* Belmont, CA: Wadsworth.

Heller, K. W., Fredrick, L. D., Best, S. J., Dykes, M. K., & Cohen, E. T. (2000). Providing specialized health procedures in the schools: Training and service delivery. *Exceptional Children, 66,* 173–186.

Hill, J. L. (1999). *Meeting the needs of students with special physical and health care needs.* Upper Saddle River, NJ: Prentice Hall.

Hogan, M. B., & Wilson, N. W. (2003). Asthma in the school-aged child. *Pediatric Annals, 32*(1), 20–25.

Klein, G. L., & Timmerman, V. (1994). *Keys to parenting the asthmatic child.* Hauppauge, NY: Barron's.

Kraemer, M. J., & Bierman, C. W. (1983). Asthma. In J. Umbreit (Ed.), *Physical disabilities and health impairments: An introduction* (pp. 159–166). Upper Saddle River, NJ: Merrill/Prentice Hall.

Lehrer, P., Feldman, J., Giardino, N., Song, H. S., & Schmaling, K. (2002). Psychological effects of asthma. *Journal of Consulting and Clinical Psychology, 70*(3), 691–711.

LeRoy, C. H., Powell, T. H., & Kelker, P. H. (1994). Meeting our responsibilities in special education. *Teaching Exceptional Children, 26*(4), 37–44.

Lindgren, S., Lokshin, B., Stromquist, A., Weinberger, M., Nassif, E., McCubbin, M., et al. (1992). Does asthma or treatment with theophylline limit children's academic performance? *New England Journal of Medicine, 32,* 926–930.

Majer, L. S., & Joy, J. H. (1993). A principal's guide to asthma. *Principal, 73*(2), 42–44.

Making it work: Always be prepared. (1995). *Child Care Plus, 5*(3), 2.

McLoughlin, J. A., & Nall, M. (1994). Allergies and learning/behavior disorders. *Intervention in School and Clinic, 29,* 198–207.

Melamed, B. G., & Siegel, L. G. (1975). Reduction of anxiety in children facing hospitalization and surgery by use of filmed modelling. *Journal of Consulting and Clinical Psychology, 43,* 511–521.

Meyers, A., & Weitzman, M. (1991). Pediatric HIV disease: The newest chronic illness of childhood. *Pediatric Clinics of North America, 38,* 169–194.

Morgan, W. J., & Martinez, F. D. (1992). Risk factors for developing wheezing and asthma in childhood. *Pediatric Clinics of North America, 39,* 1185–1203.

Mueller, G. A., & Eigen, H. (1992). Pediatric pulmonary function testing in asthma. *Pediatric Clinics of North America, 39,* 1243–1259.

National Institute of Allergy and Infectious Diseases (NIAID), National Institute of Health (2003, June). *HIV infection and AIDS: An overview.* Retrieved on October 12, 2003, from http://www.niaid.nih.gov/factsheets/hivinf.htm

National Institutes of Health; National Asthma Education Program. (1994). *Executive summary: Guidelines for the diagnosis and management of asthma.* (Publication No. 94–3042A). Bethesda, MD: U.S. Department of Health and Human Services, National Heart, Lung, and Blood Institute.

Occupational Exposure to Blood-Borne Pathogens: Final Rule. 56 Fed. Reg. 64004–64182 (1991) (to be codified at 29 C.F.R. § 1910.1030).

O'Connell, E. J. & Heilman, D. K. (1996). Asthma. In F. D. Burg, W. R. Wald, J. R. Inglefinger, & R. A. Polin (Eds.), *Gellis & Kagan's current pediatric therapy* (15th ed., pp. 708–713). Philadelphia: Saunders.

Parker, S. L., Tong, T., Bolden, S., & Wingo, P. A. (1997). Cancer statistics, 1997. *Cancer Journal for Clinicians, 47,* 5–27.

Porter, S., Haynie, M., Bierle, T., Caldwell, T. H., & Palfrey, J. S. (Eds.), (1997). *Children and youth assisted by medical technology in the classroom: Guidelines for care* (2nd ed.). Baltimore: Brookes.

Powers, S. W., Patton, S. R., Byars, K. C., Mitchell, M. J., Jelalian, E., Mulvihill, M. H., et al. (2002). Caloric intake and eating behavior of infants and toddlers with cystic fibrosis. *Pediatrics, 109*(5), E75.

Raj, A., Mishra, A., Feinsilver, S. H., & Fein, A. M. (2000). An estimate of the prevalence and impact of asthma and related symptoms in a New York City middle school. *Chest, 118*(4), 84S.

Reid, M. J. (1992). Complicating features of asthma. *Pediatric Clinics of North America, 39,* 1327–1341.

Rutstein, R. M., Conlon, C. J., & Batshaw, M. L. (1997). HIV and AIDS. In M. L. Batshaw (Ed.), *Children with disabilities* (4th ed., pp. 163–181). Baltimore: Brookes.

Schwenn, M. R. (1996). The child cured of cancer. In F. D. Burg, J. R. Ingelfinger, E. R. Wald, & R. A. Polin (Eds.), *Gellis & Kagan's current pediatric therapy* (15th ed., pp. 306–307). Philadelphia: Saunders.

Sever, J. L., Larsen, J. W. Jr., & Grossman, J. H., III, (1988). *Handbook of perinatal infections* (2nd ed.). Boston: Little, Brown.

Silkworth, C. S., & Jones, D. (1986). Helping the student with asthma. In G. Larson (Ed.), *Managing the school-age child with a chronic health condition: A practical guide for schools, families, and organizations* (pp. 75–93). Wayzata, MN: DCI.

Simonds, R. J., & Rogers, M. F. (1992). Epidemiology of HIV in children and other populations. In A. C. Crocker, H. J. Cohen, & T. A. Kastner (Eds.), *HIV infection and developmental disabilities: A resource for service providers* (pp. 3–13). Baltimore: Brookes.

Sitler, A. (1991). Medical asepsis. In B. L. Christensen & E. O. Kockrow (Eds.), *Foundations of nursing* (pp. 212–239). St. Louis: Mosby.

Thompson, R. L., Gustafson, K. E., Hamlett, K. W., & Spock, A. (1992). Psychological adjustment of children with cystic fibrosis: The role of child cognitive processes and maternal adjustment. *Journal of Pediatric Psychology, 17,* 741–755.

Utah State Office of Education. (1995). *Utah guidelines and procedures for serving students with special health care needs.* Salt Lake City: Author.

Visser, M. R., & Smets, E. M. (1998). Fatigue, depression, and quality of life in cancer patients: How are they related? *Supportive Care in Cancer, 6,* 101–105.

Weinberger, S. E. (1993). Recent advances in pulmonary medicine. *New England Journal of Medicine, 328,* 1389–1397.

Weitzman, M., Gortmaker, S. L., Sobol, A. M., & Perrin, J. M. (1992). Recent trends in the prevalence and severity of childhood asthma. *Journal of the American Medical Association, 268,* 2673–2677.

Williams, J., Berry, D. H., Caldwell, D., Zolten, A. J., & Spence, G. T. (1992). A comparison of neuropsychological and psychosocial functioning after prophylactic treatment for childhood leukemia in monozygotic twins. *American Journal of Pediatric Hematology/Oncology, 14*(4), 289–296.

Williamson, W. D., Demmler, G. J., Percy, A. K., & Catlin, F. I. (1992). Progressive hearing loss in infants with asymptomatic congenital cytomegalovirus infection. *Pediatrics, 90,* 862–866.

Cerebral Palsy

SHERWOOD J. BEST
JUNE L. BIGGE

CHAPTER 4

KNOWLEDGE AND SKILLS

After you have read this chapter, you will be able to:

1. **Define and describe cerebral palsy.**
2. **Understand that cerebral palsy is frequently accompanied by other disabilities, and that multiple disabilities have effects on development that are greater than the sum of their individual parts.**
3. **Identify risk factors associated with occurrence of cerebral palsy.**
4. **Classify types of cerebral palsy by location, movement patterns, and function.**
5. **Identify a variety of conditions commonly associated with cerebral palsy.**
6. **Describe the roles of physical and occupational therapists in assisting with physical management for individuals with cerebral palsy.**
7. **Describe current medical and therapeutic treatments for individuals with cerebral palsy.**
8. **Develop strategies to support individuals with cerebral palsy for optimal physical, social/emotional, and communication development.**
9. **Understand the implications of cerebral palsy for education, personal autonomy, and career and adult function.**

In Chapters 2 and 3, readers become acquainted with several physical disabilities, health impairments, and infectious diseases. However, it is important to understand that separating conditions into categories such as physical or health disabilities is somewhat arbitrary. It is logical to assume that individuals with physical disabilities may also have health or other impairments. Thus, many individuals are considered to have multiple disabilities.

Readers will remember from Chapter 1 that individuals may have two or more disabilities whose combination results in severe educational problems due to the interaction effects of the disabilities. For example, individuals who have severe cerebral palsy have motor disabilities that can compromise their physical ability to perform activities of daily living such as meal preparation or driving a car. To compensate, they could use a computer to develop a grocery list and provide directions for others to prepare the meal. With the assistance of adaptive technology, they could possibly drive a car using hand controls. While dependent for some aspects of daily living, they retain considerable independence and control of outcomes. However, the impact of the disability becomes more complex when sensory, cognitive, or health disabilities are also present. For example, the effect of cognitive disabilities on memory and reasoning might prevent the individual from even conceptualizing the steps in preparing a meal, operating a computer, or driving a car. If cognition and motor function are both impaired, individuals may need training to select from a prepared list of food items, partially participate in meal preparation, and substitute public transportation for independent driving. The connections among physical, health, and multiple disabilities highlight the importance of acquiring a firm understanding of the dynamics of a variety of conditions, and their interaction effects.

The condition of cerebral palsy was chosen to illustrate the complexities of multiple disabilities. Although it is primarily a "disorder of movement and posture" (Pellegrino, 1997, p. 499), cerebral palsy is frequently accompanied by visual impairments (Schenk-Rootlieb, van Nieuwenhuizen, van der Graff, Wittebol-Post, & Willemse, 1992), hearing impairments (Nehring & Steele, 1996), communication impairments (Alexander & Bauer, 1988), and orthopedic deformities (Jones, 1983). Many individuals with cerebral palsy have feeding problems, including weak sucking ability, abnormal tongue movement, gagging, choking, and spitting up (Azcue, Zello, Levy, & Pencharz, 1996; Murphy & Caretto, 1999). Feeding problems may contribute to nutritional problems (Koontz-Lowman & Murphy, 1999). Other impairments include learning disabilities (Hill, 1999), cognitive disabilities (Pellegrino, 1997), and seizures (Aksu, 1990). Although individuals with cerebral palsy may have any or all of these associated conditions, readers should *never make assumptions about cognition, potential, or outcomes for individuals with cerebral palsy or any multiply disabling condition.*

In this chapter, cerebral palsy will be defined and described, followed by discussion of conditions that frequently occur with this disability. The reader will become acquainted with how physical and occupational therapists support the management of individuals with cerebral palsy. Medical treatments designed to maintain and improve physical and health function will be reviewed. The authors will describe the impact of cerebral palsy on physical, social/emotional, and communication development. Implications of cerebral palsy for education, personal autonomy, and career and adult function will be discussed.

CEREBRAL PALSY

Many people have heard the term *cerebral palsy* and developed a personal perception about the appearance and effects of this impairment. As we shall see from its definition, *cerebral palsy* is a descriptive category, which means that this condition may be mild for some individuals and severe for others. There is no "typical" individual with cerebral palsy or typical constellation of impairments that accompany cerebral palsy.

Definitions and Descriptions

Cerebral palsy is "a disorder of movement and posture that is due to non-progressive abnormality of the immature brain" (Kurtz, 1992, p. 441). This description means that cerebral palsy affects the way people move, the tension or "tone" of their muscles, and the control they exert over their bodies' position in space. Second, cerebral palsy is considered to be nonprogressive; the brain does not deteriorate with a resulting change in function. Third, cerebral palsy is a "developmental disability" because the term applies to damage that occurs while the brain is still immature—either before birth or during early childhood (Pellegrino, 1997).

Approximately 5,000 babies are born annually with cerebral palsy. Each year, another 1,200 to 1,500 infants or young children acquire cerebral palsy through accidents, injury, or other postbirth traumas (Heller, Alberto, Forney, & Schwartzman, 1996). These numbers support the belief that most causes of cerebral palsy are due to problems in intrauterine (within the uterus) development (Scher, Balfar, & Martin, 1991). These intrauterine, or **prenatal**, situations include infection, brain malformation, genetic syndromes associated with brain damage, and lack of oxygen (anoxia). Infants who are premature or who have low birth weight are also at risk for cerebral palsy (O'Shea & Dammann, 2000). Another significant risk factor is the situation of multiple births (Blickstein, 2002; Pharoah & Cooke, 1996; Williams, Hennessy, & Alberman, 1996). Blickstein (2002) reported that risk for cerebral palsy is three to six times greater in multiple births, which are increasing due to the influence of assisted reproductive technologies. Cerebral palsy can also occur in the **perinatal** period (during birth) due to abnormal birth presentation, maternal infection, abnormalities of the placenta, and other situations that reduce or prevent oxygenation of the infant's brain (Heller et al., 1996; Krebs, Topp, & Langhoff-Roos, 1999; Nelson & Grether, 1998; O'Shea & Dammann, 2000). Finally, cerebral palsy can occur during the **postnatal** period (after birth) as a result of traumatic brain injury, poison, infection of the central nervous system (such as en-

TABLE 4–1
Causes and Risk Factors Associated with Cerebral Palsy

Causes	Risk Factors
Prenatal	Toxemia
Brain malformation	Maternal bleeding
Genetic syndrome	Placental insufficiency
Prenatal infection	Maternal infection
Severe anoxia	Multiple births
	Maternal bleeding
Perinatal	Maternal mental retardation
Asphyxia	
CNS infection	
Postnatal	
CNS infection	
Traumatic brain injury	
Poison	
Anoxia	

Note: Adapted from *Understanding Physical, Sensory and Health Impairments: Characteristics and Educational Implications,* 1st edition, by Heller/Alberto/Schwartzman/Forney. © 1996. Reprinted with permission of Wadsworth, a division of Thomson Learning: www.thomsonrights.com. Fax 800-730-2215.

cephalitis), or any situation in which there is a lack of oxygen to the brain (near drowning, suffocation, or electrocution). In postnatal cases, the brain was damaged because it was directly injured and became less functional due to lack of oxygen. Table 4–1 indicates common conditions that may contribute to cerebral palsy.

Cerebral palsy clearly does not occur from a single situation or risk factor. Because there are many possible circumstances that result in cerebral palsy, the amount of damage to the brain varies. The location of the damage in the brain varies among individuals, which means that different brain functions may be affected. For these reasons, a diagnosis of cerebral palsy is not descriptive of how any particular individual is affected. A more precise classification scheme must be used.

CLASSIFICATION OF CEREBRAL PALSY

There are several ways to classify cerebral palsy: by which limb is affected (**location** or **topography**), by which area of the brain is involved (**neuroanatomy**), by motor patterns (**movement**), and by levels of severity (**function**). Classification of cerebral palsy by location, movement, and function are most useful, since these schemes allow teachers to plan for specific adaptations.

Location—Topography

Classifying cerebral palsy by location (topography) involves description of which limbs are affected. The major categories of classification by location are as follows:

- **Diplegia**: involving all four limbs, but the legs more than the arms;
- **Hemiplegia**: involving one side of the body;
- **Quadriplegia**: involving all four limbs (Howle, 2002).

In addition, the term **double hemiplegia** is sometimes used to describe persons with quadriplegia with greater impairment on one side of the body (Scherzer, 2001). From this description, the reader can visualize the possible adaptations that may be needed to support function. For example, the individual with hemiplegia will rely on one half of the body for postural support and movement more than the other in gross-motor activities. To assist the individual in fine-motor activities (such as handwriting), papers may need to be secured to the desktop. If the computer is used, a one-handed access system may be needed. Other adaptations might be necessary for the individual with quadriplegia, including powered mobility (a wheelchair, scooter, or other device), computer access involving a switch instead of a keyboard, peer notetaking, and other supports.

Movement—Motor Pattern

Another way to classify cerebral palsy is by specific motor patterns. The most common motor classification categories are **spastic, dyskinesia, ataxia,** and **mixed** (McMurray, Jones, & Khan, 2002). Readers are referred to Howle (2002), Pellegrino (1997), and Heller et al. (1996), for more detailed descriptions of categories of cerebral palsy by motor pattern.

Spastic Cerebral Palsy. Spastic cerebral palsy is the most common form of cerebral palsy, and is characterized by increased muscle tone (hypertonia) and exaggerated reflexes. Spasticity results in tight, "contracted" muscles and shortened ligaments. The contracted muscles may pull the legs together and across each other in a "scissors" position. Muscle contractions also result in gradual limitations of joint mobility and restricted range of motion. Contractures can contribute to deformities of the spine and hip dislocation, which will interfere with the ability to walk. Individuals with spastic cerebral palsy have difficulty with voluntary and coordinated movements and have abnormal movement and posture. Approximately 75% of children with cerebral palsy have the spastic classification (Howle, 2002).

Dyskinetic Cerebral Palsy. Dyskinetic cerebral palsy consists of a group of disorders that includes athetosis, rigidity, and tremor. Athetosis is associated with damage in the deep structures of the brain and occurs in 15–20% of all cases (McMurray et al., 2002). It is characterized by involuntary nonpurposeful movements, particularly in the arms, hands, and facial muscles. When movement is attempted, it "overflows" to other muscle groups, resulting in movements that range from writhing to jerking, tremors, and shaking (Russman, 1992). Tone (muscle tension) may shift so that the individual experiences more rigid tone when awake and more relaxed tone when asleep (Pellegrino, 1997). In addition, the individual can become "stuck" in abnormal positions or postures and require specific positioning to maintain more normal tone and movement. Rigidity is less common than athetosis, and is characterized by stiffness throughout the range of movement. Tremor typically occurs along with athetosis or ataxia (Howle, 2002).

Ataxic Cerebral Palsy. Ataxic cerebral palsy occurs when there is damage to the cerebellum, an organ at the base of the brain (Jones, 1983). It is found in only 10% of children with cerebral palsy, but can occur in conjunction with spasticity and athetosis (Esscher, Flodmark, Hagberg, & Hagberg, 1996). The main feature of ataxia is lack of coordination in balance and equilibrium. The individual with ataxia may walk with a wide-based gait, holding the arms out for balance. The constant effort to stabilize can eventually result in more rigid quality of movement, as the person consistently exerts effort to compensate for lack of stability (Bly, 1999; Bly & Sterne, 1981).

Mixed Cerebral Palsy. Brain damage is often **diffuse** (occurring throughout the brain) in situations where individuals experience postnatal trauma or an extended period of anoxia (Hill, 1999). The result is mixed cerebral palsy. The individual may experience spasticity in the legs and athetosis in the arms (Hill, 1999) or spasticity in all four limbs with low tone in the trunk and neck.

Many infants born with cerebral palsy have initial **hypotonia** (low tone) and muscle weakness, particularly in the neck and trunk. Hypotonia is frequently the first motor symptom in children who are later diagnosed with spastic, athetoid, or ataxic cerebral palsy. In all types of cerebral palsy, tone can fluctuate, further complicating the situation.

Function—Level of Severity

A third method of classification can be used to indicate severity of motor involvement and level of function. For teachers who are unfamiliar with more medically oriented terms related to location and motor patterns in cerebral palsy, functional criteria are useful for making direct comparisons with typical behaviors and activities. Functional descriptions also provide guidelines which foster consistency in communication among professionals. Criteria for mild, moderate, and severe levels of functional limitation are listed in Figure 4–1.

Level of function, type of motor pattern, and location are frequently used together to communicate what level of physical support will be needed. For example, a diagnosis of "moderate spastic diplegia" allows the reader to visualize an individual with tight or contracted leg muscles who may require braces to walk, but who probably has adequate arm and hand use. A description of "severe mixed spastic/athetoid quadriplegia" suggests an individual with motor involvement in all four limbs, who may use a wheelchair and require significant support to perform most functions independently. Appearances are deceiving, however. Readers should *never assume that degree of physical impairment is directly related to level of cognition or learning potential.* Care must be taken to refrain from developing preconceived notions about an individual's academic or cognitive potential, based on outward appearance.

CONDITIONS ASSOCIATED WITH CEREBRAL PALSY

Cerebral palsy is caused by damage to the central nervous system (CNS), which consists of the brain and the spinal cord. One can imagine the brain as the lo-

FIGURE 4–1
Classification of cerebral palsy by levels of severity

MILD FUNCTIONAL IMPAIRMENT
1. Ambulation and speech are present.
2. Head and neck control are present.
3. Limitation of activity is slight to unimpaired.
4. Activities of daily living or other useful physical activity are achieved independently.

MODERATE FUNCTIONAL IMPAIRMENT
1. Impairments affect ambulation and speech.
2. Head and neck control are affected.
3. Limitation of activity is moderate to severe.
4. Activities of daily living or other useful physical activity are limited without assistive technology.

SEVERE FUNCTIONAL IMPAIRMENT
1. Impairments are incapacitating.
2. Head and neck control are absent or severely limited.
3. Physical deformities and contractures are present.
4. Individuals are unable to complete activities of daily living or other useful physical activity without assistive technology.

Note. Adapted from "Cerebral Palsy" in *Understanding Physical, Sensory and Health Impairments: Characteristics and Educational Implications* 1st edition by Heller/Alberto/Schwartzman/Forney. © 1996. Reprinted with permission of Wadsworth, a division of Thomson Learning: *www.thomsonrights.com. Fax 800-730-2215.*

cation where messages are generated and sent out through the spinal cord and nerves to all systems of the body. Sensation returns to the brain for interpretation and reaction. When the brain is damaged, these messages may be incomplete, distorted, or absent. As a result, functions related to movement, sensation, and cognition can be affected.

What are the conditions commonly associated with cerebral palsy? Cerebral palsy may have a direct effect on vision, hearing, and speech. Individuals with cerebral palsy may have difficulties with nutrition and eating. Musculoskeletal impairments occur when contractures and muscle tightness around joints cause deformities in the spine and extremities. Cognitive deficits, learning disabilities, or seizures may also be present.

Sensory Impairments

Individuals with cerebral palsy frequently experience impairments in vision and/or hearing. For example, the eyes are able to track smoothly back and forth and converge (focus) on objects through the coordinated movement of the oculomotor muscles. If these muscles receive distorted messages due to brain damage, eye movement may be abnormal and result in a visual impairment such as **strabismus** (eyes crossed in or turned out) and/or **nystagmus** (eyes flickering back and forth). **Retinopathy of prematurity (ROP)** (vision loss related to premature birth) can occur in individuals with cerebral palsy. Hearing loss can occur in children with cerebral palsy, especially when it was related to intrauterine infection (such as congenital rubella, i.e., German measles).

As a first step in meeting sensory needs, teachers must work with the school nurse to be sure that students have adequate vision and hearing assessments. If a sensory impairment is present, services from a specialist in visual and/or hearing impairments will provide many strategies for enhancing educational achievement. Assistive technology devices and services are available to enhance function when a visual impairment is present.

Communication Impairments

Speech is a motor act that occurs through the coordinated efforts of breathing and movement of the muscles that control the mouth, tongue, and lips. When muscles are affected by CNS damage, speech may be slurred, distorted, or absent. Language, which requires receiving and expressing information, may be affected if the individual with cerebral palsy has cognitive deficits. If speech and language are involved, the individual may have trouble understanding what is said, formulating a response, and using speech to communicate the response. If the individual is unable to communicate through speech, **augmentative or alternative communication (AAC)** may be required.

Orthopedic Deformities

Cerebral palsy is different from conditions that are progressive and/or unstable. The brain damage that causes cerebral palsy does not heal, but neither does it worsen. However, changes that occur through normal maturation can have an effect on physical function. Continuing muscle tightness can cause skeletal deformities in the spine and extremities (hips, legs, feet, arms, hands, fingers, etc.). Orthopedic deformities may require corrective surgeries and therapeutic rehabilitation. However, muscles can also be negatively affected if braces are overused, leading to atrophy (Howle, 2002). Ongoing collaborative effort among therapists, teachers, and family members is necessary to achieve optimal therapeutic outcomes.

Nutrition and Feeding Needs

Individuals with cerebral palsy place high energy demands on their bodies to maintain balance and to ambulate. Consequently they may have trouble gaining weight. Nutritional supplements may be used to augment a regular diet. When eating capability is limited due to motor impairment in the oral (mouth) area or in swallowing, the individual may need to receive nutritional supplements via a device known as a **G-tube,** which is placed directly into the stomach. Care must be taken to keep the tube placed and to follow correct protocols for tube feeding. The reader is urged to consult references in this chapter and in Chapter 3 for additional information related to tube feeding and other specialized health care procedures (Heller et al., 2000; Koontz-Lowman & Murphy, 1999; Porter, Haynie, Bierle, Caldwell, & Palfrey, 1997).

Many individuals with cerebral palsy may not require tube feeding, but still have significant oral-motor feeding problems (Reilly, Skuse, & Poblete, 1994). Teachers and others who provide educational services will need to follow appropriate feeding programs (Koontz-Lowman & Murphy, 1999). Consultation with the occupational therapist and speech/language specialist will assist the teacher to use feeding techniques that are appropriate and safe. Readers can refer to Chapter 9 for in-depth coverage of the important topic of swallowing and feeding.

Cognitive Deficits

Individuals with cerebral palsy may be gifted, have normal intelligence, or experience significant cognitive deficits (Heller et al., 1996). Although the degree of intellectual impairment may vary according to the type of cerebral palsy, there is no exact relationship. Individuals with spastic hemiplegia are more likely to have typical intelligence than individuals with spastic quadriplegia (Pellegrino, 1997). Individuals with athetoid or ataxic cerebral palsy are less likely to have cognitive deficits than those with spastic cerebral palsy (Hill, 1999). The relationship between expected cognitive ability and type of cerebral palsy is further complicated by the fact that many individuals have more than one type of cerebral palsy. If epilepsy is present, cognition may be further compromised (Wallace, 2001).

It is often difficult to assess intelligence in individuals with cerebral palsy using standardized measures. Many of the tasks in these assessments are based on experiences or motor and verbal responses that are impossible for the individual with cerebral palsy to reproduce. Care should be taken *never to infer intellectual deficits solely on the basis of motor and/or speech disabilities.*

Learning Disabilities

Students with cerebral palsy may have learning disabilities, which include visual processing, auditory processing, and proprioception difficulties. **Visual processing** disabilities mean that students will have difficulty finding words on a page, creating and maintaining a visual memory of what specific words "look like," keeping their place while reading, copying material from the board to a piece of paper, aligning columns for math computation, and other visual skills. If there are **auditory processing** disabilities, students have difficulty following oral directions, retelling a story, and answering comprehension questions. Students with problems of **proprioception** have difficulty with the position of their bodies in space. This results in difficulties distinguishing left/right and other directional concepts, finding their place in line or on a page, and even knowing when to stop moving when they encounter a solid surface (such as a wall). Students whose cerebral palsy includes learning disabilities require specific compensatory strategies for coping with processing and proprioception deficits.

Seizures

Central nervous system damage may trigger abnormal excessive electrical impulses, resulting in a seizure. A **seizure** is a sudden occurrence of altered consciousness, behavior, sensation, and/or movement due to disruption of normal electrochemical activity in the brain (Clancy, 1990). It is estimated that between 25% and 50% of children with cerebral palsy have seizure disorders (Aksu, 1990; Brown, 1997). Epilepsy is more common in individuals with spastic cerebral palsy than in individuals with athetosis or ataxia (Wallace, 2001). Seizures may last for a few seconds or many minutes and are classified according to whether they involve the entire brain or are confined to certain areas (Behrman, 1992).

Teachers must be ready to follow the appropriate steps in caring for a student when a seizure occurs. The Epilepsy Foundation of America (1994), with additions by Heller et al. (1996), provides a series of guidelines for responding to seizures in the classroom (see Table 4–2). The teacher who understands and has skills in seizure management and can calmly and appropriately respond to a seizure conveys confidence and a positive attitude to students.

Seizure medication can have an impact on function. Teachers must be knowledgeable about medication dosage and effects. They must also watch for medication effects such as drowsiness and clumsiness. Communication with the school nurse or other health care provider and parents is critical for correct medication administration and monitoring.

THERAPEUTIC MANAGEMENT OF CEREBRAL PALSY

Because of its complex nature, a diagnosis of cerebral palsy indicates the need for a transdisciplinary approach to education, medical treatment, and physical management. Although many professionals contribute to successful service delivery for individuals with cerebral palsy, the activities of physical and occupational therapists will be emphasized in this chapter. Readers may refer to the "Focus on the Net" section at the end of this chapter for more information related to these professions.

Physical Therapy[1]

The **physical therapist (PT)** is a licensed health professional whose primary attention is focused on evaluation and program planning for posture and balance, deformity prevention, and gross-motor function, including walking. The pediatric PT usually attends to the trunk and lower extremities in the following areas:

- Alignment of the spine, legs, and feet;
- Fitting and monitoring positioning equipment, braces, prostheses, or casts;
- Postoperative rehabilitation;
- Physical management at home.

The PT in the school uses these skills to maximize the student's independent function in the classroom, on the school grounds, and with transport vehicles.

Occupational Therapy

The **occupational therapist (OT)** is a licensed health professional who attends to the following areas:

- Coordination of eye-hand skills;
- Facilitation of use of the arms and hands for self-feeding, writing or typing, and self-care;
- Prevention of deformity in the arms and hands;
- Assessment and remediation of perceptual skills such as figure-ground discrimination;
- Evaluation of sensory integration (the capacity to organize and respond appropriately to incoming sensory information from all channels);
- Promotion of independence in activities of daily living (ADL) such as toileting, dressing, and food preparation;
- Prevocational assessment.

Although they embrace different therapeutic goals, occupational and physical therapists regard many issues with equal concern. For example, the OT would evaluate poor sitting balance as it interferes with achieving precision in handwriting, while the PT would be more concerned with the relationship between poor

---

[1]The material on physical therapy and occupational therapy is from Cusick (1991).

TABLE 4–2
Seizure Recognition and First Aid

Seizure Type	What It Looks Like	What It Is Not	What to Do	What Not to Do
Generalized tonic-clonic (also called Grand mal)	Sudden cry, fall, rigidity, followed by muscle jerks, shallow breathing or temporarily suspended breathing, bluish skin, possible loss of bladder or bowel control. The seizure usually lasts a couple of minutes. Normal breathing then starts again. There may be some confusion and/or fatigue, followed by return to full consciousness.	Heart attack; stroke.	Look for medical identification. Protect from nearby hazards. Loosen ties or shirt collars. Protect head from injury. Turn on side to keep airway clear. Reassure when consciousness returns. If single seizure lasted less than 5 minutes, ask if hospital evaluation wanted. If multiple seizures or if one seizure lasts longer than 5 minutes, call an ambulance. If person is pregnant, injured, or diabetic, call for aid at once.	Don't put any hard implement in the mouth. Don't try to hold tongue. It can't be swallowed. Don't try to give liquids during or just after seizure. Don't use artificial respiration unless breathing is absent after muscle jerks subside or unless water has been inhaled. Don't restrain.
Absence (also called Petit mal)	A blank stare, beginning and ending abruptly, lasting only a few seconds, most common in children. May be accompanied by rapid blinking, some chewing movements of the mouth. Child or adult is unaware of what's going on during the seizure but quickly returns to full awareness once it has stopped. May result in learning difficulties if not recognized and treated.	Daydreaming; lack of attention; deliberate ignoring of adult instructions.	No first aid necessary, but if this is the first observation of the seizure(s), medical evaluation should be recommended.	

TABLE 4–2
Continued

Seizure Type	What It Looks Like	What It Is Not	What to Do	What Not to Do
Simple partial	Jerking may begin in one area of body, arm, leg, or face. Can't be stopped, but patient stays awake and aware. Jerking may proceed from one area of the body to another and sometimes spreads to become a convulsive seizure.	Acting out; bizarre behavior.	No first aid necessary unless seizure becomes convulsive, then follow *Generalized Tonic-Clonic Seizures* first aid (described above).	
	Partial sensory seizures may not be obvious to an onlooker. Person experiences a distorted environment. May see or hear things that aren't there, may feel unexplained fear, sadness, anger, or joy. May have nausea, experience odd smells, and have a generally "funny" feeling in the stomach.	Hysteria. Mental illness. Psychosomatic illness. Parapsychological or mystical experience.	No immediate action needed other than reassurance and emotional support. Medical evaluation should be recommended.	
Complex partial (also called Psychomotor or Temporal lobe)	Usually starts with blank stare, followed by chewing, followed by random activity. Person appears unaware of surroundings, may seem dazed and mumble. Unresponsive. Actions clumsy, not directed. May pick at clothing, pick up objects, try to take clothes off. May run, appear afraid. May struggle or flail at restraint. Once pattern established, same set of actions usually occurs with each seizure. Lasts a few minutes, but postseizure confusion can last substantially longer. No memory of what happened during seizure period.	Drunkenness. Intoxication on drugs. Mental illness. Disorderly conduct.	Speak calmly and reassuringly to patient and others. Guide person gently away from obvious hazards. Stay with person until he or she is completely aware of environment. Offer to help person get home.	Don't grab hold unless sudden danger (such as a cliff edge or an approaching car) threatens. Don't try to restrain. Don't shout. Don't expect verbal instructions to be obeyed.

(Continued)

TABLE 4–2
Continued

Seizure Type	What It Looks Like	What It Is Not	What to Do	What Not to Do
Atonic (also called Drop attacks)	A child or adult suddenly collapses and falls. After 10 seconds to a minute he or she recovers, regains consciousness, and can stand and walk again.	Clumsiness. Normal childhood "stage." In a child, lack of good walking skills. In an adult, drunkenness, acute illness.	No first aid needed unless child is hurt in a fall, but the child should be given a thorough medical evaluation.	
Myoclonic	Sudden brief, massive muscle jerks that may involve the whole body or parts of the body. May cause person to spill what they were holding or fall off a chair.	Clumsiness. Poor coordination.	No first aid needed but a thorough medical evaluation is needed.	
Infantile spasms	These are clusters of quick, sudden movements that start between 3 months and 2 years of age. If a child is sitting up, the head will fall forward, and the arms will flex forward. If lying down, the knees will be drawn up, with arms and head flexed forward as if the baby is reaching for support.	Normal movements of the baby. Colic.	No first aid but doctor should be consulted.	

Note. Columns 1, 2, 4, and 5 adapted in format from *Information and Education Sheets—Seizure Recognition and First Aid.* Copyright © Epilepsy Foundation of America, 1994. Format from Heller et al. (1996).

sitting balance and potential for deformity. This example illustrates the complementary nature of their skills. Because both PTs and OTs are concerned with postural alignment and stability, some people assume that their functions are interchangeable. PTs and OTs, however, have very different perspectives and educational backgrounds. They represent a valuable resource to the teacher, who frequently implements therapeutic procedures in the classroom. As stated in Chapter 1, however, therapists cannot take the place of teachers, and teachers are not therapists. Members of every professional discipline must appreciate their unique contribution to a successful educational outcome for students with cerebral palsy.

FIGURE 4–2
Orthotic devices

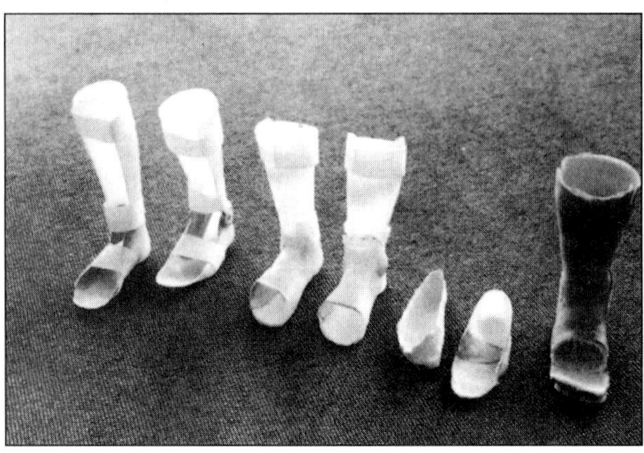

MEDICAL TREATMENT OF CEREBRAL PALSY

Therapists work closely with physicians to manage the orthopedic complications that frequently accompany cerebral palsy. Medical treatment of cerebral palsy may involve the use of orthotics, medications, and surgeries (Heller et al. 1996; Pellegrino, 1997; Morris, 2002).

Orthotics

Orthotic devices include braces, splints, and other appliances that are used to support weak or inefficient muscles. Braces not only support muscles but also hold them in correct positions to prevent contractures and the need for future surgery. In contrast to previous braces constructed of metal with leather cuffs and straps, modern braces are lightweight and unobtrusive (see Figure 4–2). Readers are encouraged to review Morris (2002) for a thorough review of the effectiveness of different orthotic devices, including dynamic and hinged varieties. It is important for children with cerebral palsy to wear their braces as prescribed by a therapist. Service providers should learn from therapists how to correctly position limbs in braces.

Individuals with cerebral palsy may wear splints on their hands to reduce tone (hold the fingers in a more open and relaxed position) and improve grip. They may wear a body jacket if their trunk muscles are weak (Pellegrino, 1997). Braces, splints, and body jackets are always custom-made and must be replaced when outgrown. Because they are made from plastic and are worn close to the body, these appliances can irritate the skin and cause the wearer to feel uncomfortably warm. A cotton shirt worn under a body jacket will help to absorb perspiration. Socks should always be worn with braces and should be wrinkle-free, dry, and clean. Any redness, soreness, or other indication of poor fit or skin breakdown should be reported to the therapist and nurse immediately.

Medication and Injections

Medications may be used to relax muscles. One commonly prescribed medication is **diazepam (Valium),** which affects how the brain controls muscle tone. Another medication is **baclofen (Lioresal),** which inhibits the central nervous system. A third is **dantrolene (Dantrium),** which inhibits contractions of muscle cells (Pellegrino, 1997). These medications may cause drowsiness, increased drooling, muscle weakness, and upset stomach.

A recent innovation that reduces medication side effects involves delivering baclofen through a tube into the cerebral spinal fluid in the lower back (**intrathecal baclofen therapy**). The amount of baclofen is regulated by a pump that is worn externally or placed below the skin in the abdomen. The baclofen pump bypasses the need for repeated injections and ensures correct dosage (Albright, 1996). Use of baclofen appears to reduce spastic tone in the lower limbs, but is less conclusive for reducing spastic tone in the upper limbs, enhancing functional activity, and improving range of motion (Butler & Campbell, 2000). In addition, mechanical complications of the pump and catheter (tube) leading to the spine, as well as concern of school staff related to pump management, require heightened awareness toward individuals who have had this procedure (Butler & Campbell, 2000).

Another medication innovation is the use of **botulinum toxin (Botox),** which is injected into spastic muscles to reduce their tension (Pellegrino, 1997). A review of several medical studies about the usefulness of Botox injections in children with cerebral palsy indicated that this medication reduces spasticity and decreases pain associated with spasticity. However, pain at the injection site and the cost of injections are negative issues in the use of Botox (Roscigno, 2002).

Surgery

Orthopedic surgery may be indicated for individuals with cerebral palsy to prevent or release contractures, correct muscle imbalance, and improve function (Sprague, 1992). Surgery is usually used in conjunction with other techniques, such as positioning and bracing. A recent neurosurgical technique is **selective dorsal (posterior) rhizotomy,** which involves severing certain sensory nerve fibers to relieve spasticity (Berman, Vaughan, & Peacock, 1990; Park & Owen, 1992; Roscigno, 2002). This surgery is used for individuals with spastic diplegia. Reported side effects include back pain and spinal deformity (Steinbok, 2001, Steinbok & Schrag, 1998), so this surgery is not without risk. Teachers must provide appropriate, physician-directed care for all children who return to their classrooms following surgery.

DEVELOPMENTAL ISSUES IN CEREBRAL PALSY

It is clear from the previous descriptions that individuals with cerebral palsy require collaborative treatment from professionals in many disciplines, often over extended time periods. Understanding the impact of cerebral palsy on physical, communication, and social/emotional development allows teachers and others to provide services that maximize individual potential.

Physical Development

Readers were acquainted with the concept of developmental maturation in Chapter 2. Because individuals with cerebral palsy have experienced damage to the CNS, they will also experience alterations in motor development and function.

Movement dysfunction has great significance for development and learning. Researchers in human cognitive development commonly acknowledge the significance of sensorimotor (sensation and movement) activity in the early years of life. Through movement, it is presumed that babies learn about spatial relations, the limits and proportions of their own bodies, and balance. They also learn the properties of objects and mass by moving about in space, exploring, experimenting, and remembering consequences. It is important for teachers and others to provide opportunities for sensorimotor experiences.

Sensorimotor dysfunction affects learning and classroom performance in many ways. The struggle for balance and movement control may deplete the energy supply needed for attending to learning tasks, studying, and homework. Poor postural control also interferes with breathing and alertness, which has a negative impact on proficiency in handwriting, drawing, the capacity to hold books and utensils, listening, and responding. Although it is important for teachers to understand the role of movement patterns in individuals with cerebral palsy, they should not be expected to fill the role of diagnostician or therapist in developing therapeutic interventions in the classroom. Nevertheless, teachers spend much time in close proximity to each student during the school day and often follow through on therapy programs. The following information provides strategies for physical management of cerebral palsy.

Physical Management Strategies[2]

As noted earlier in this chapter, cerebral palsy is characterized by disorders of movement that include spasticity, athetosis, and ataxia. Children with spasticity generally have high muscle tone and limited range of motion, while children with athetosis have involuntary and disorganized movement. Children with ataxia have disorders of balance and equilibrium. In some cases, children with cerebral palsy may also exhibit hypotonia, or low tone. Often infants with hypotonia develop subsequent spasticity or athetosis. The following strategies will assist teachers to manage individuals with spasticity, athetosis, ataxia, and mixed cerebral palsy.

---

[2]Most of the material on physical management strategies is from Cusick (1991).

Managing Spastic Cerebral Palsy. Teachers need to adjust sensory input as appropriate for each student with spastic cerebral palsy in order to calm their overexcitable nervous systems, reduce their fear of falling, and help them attend to motor tasks. Activities that modify sensory input include mobilizing and weight-bearing activities, slow, rotary movements of the trunk and shoulders, deep pressure and massage, and stroking techniques to specific areas of the hand and fingers (Perin, 1989). In addition, the appropriate use of massage can reduce muscle tension, promote circulation, and increase flexibility (Stewart, 2000). These techniques are readily incorporated into classroom activities (see Figures 4–3 and 4–4). Teachers should seek the assistance of occupational and physical therapists for appropriate training.

Students with spastic hemiplegia present a special challenge, since they are less likely to move or use their involved side. They need to be encouraged to bring both hands together in front of them (the midline position). This brings both hands into the visual field and encourages use of the involved hand as a "helper" to assist in picking up and manipulating objects. Older children can use the involved arm and hand to stabilize a piece of paper on their desks for drawing or handwriting. They also must practice actively moving their bodies through increasing **range of motion (ROM)** without losing their balance.

FIGURE 4–3
Preparation for hand use: Loosening the elbow and wrist

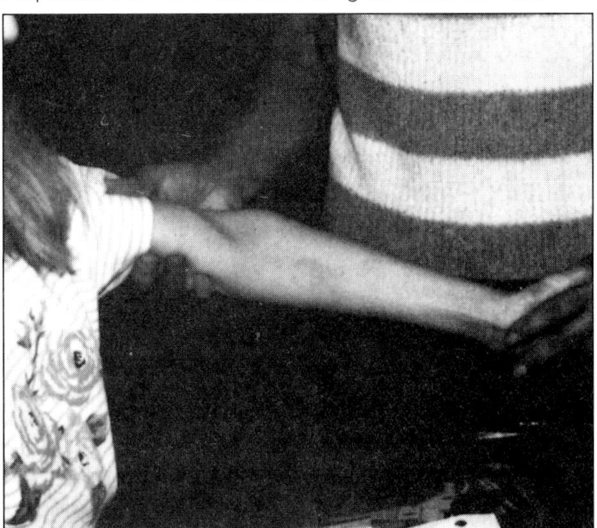

If the more involved limbs are completely insensitive to touch, pressure, pain, and temperature, functional gain cannot be expected. Intervention then focuses on prevention of deformity. Teachers can help by consulting the OT about proper techniques and schedules for moving limbs, by seeing that arm and hand splints are worn appropriately, and by checking the skin daily for injuries (swelling, bruises, redness, and blisters). Teachers can also consistently draw attention to the affected arm in games and classroom activities by applying stickers, selecting activities that require an appropriate level of bilateral skill, and incorporating play activities that raise sensory awareness. Such activities might include having the child smear the affected arm with hand cream, mineral oil, or finger paints. Students with spastic quadriplegia are affected in all four limbs. Spasticity may interfere with independent ambulation (walking). Teachers need to work closely with occupational and physical therapists,

FIGURE 4–4
Preparation for hand use: Loosening the elbows and shoulders

who will help them recognize appropriate movements and provide strategies for positioning and ambulation.

Many students with spasticity have low tone (hypotonia) when they are young. Hypotonia may persist in the trunk after the limbs have become tight (hypertonic). The primary goals with hypotonia are to excite and activate the sluggish nervous system, reduce response-time lags, and facilitate the use of trunk and pelvic muscles needed to enhance balance and hand-use skills. The teacher might be instructed to use preparation techniques, such as tapping certain areas of the trunk and shoulders and compressing the joints of the neck, trunk, or shoulder, to increase and sustain the activation of supporting muscles.

Students with hypotonia have problems with joint alignment in the trunk and legs. For example, the feet should be adequately supported against internal collapse with custom-molded shoe inserts to prevent unnecessary fatigue from walking and to prevent long-term deformity of the feet and legs. Teachers participate by observing ankle and foot alignment when the child is seated or standing, and by ensuring that proper foot support is available.

The hypotonic student must be challenged regularly (within reasonable limits) to maintain an upright position and make quick and appropriate motor responses. Unnecessary external supports, such as head rests, trunk straps, and carrying in a fully reclined position, are not appropriate. The following suggestions might be useful in the classroom:

- Students who are unable to sit independently on a classroom chair might need seating modifications to assure a sense of security and appropriate sensory input. These modifications can range from technologically sophisticated seating systems to the simple addition of rolled towels to keep the shoulders rotated slightly inward and a security strap across the pelvis.
- Weak trunk muscles can be strengthened by sitting the student periodically on a wedged seat, padded to increase friction, which gently inclines up toward the back of the chair. This system tips the student slightly forward and activates the lower trunk extensor muscles to push back against gravity.
- Children who rely too much on positional stability sit and stand with their legs spread apart. The consulting therapist might apply a soft thigh-connector splint to reduce the child's base of support and encourage development of internal stability skills. This splint should be worn consistently, with the supervision of the therapist, for most routine activities, including floor play, walking, and sitting.
- Teachers can provide weighted toys, such as bean bags or balls partially filled with sand. These offer resistance to movement and can improve hand strength, body sense, and grasping patterns.
- Hand and wrist strength and sensory awareness can be enhanced by having the student wring wet towels or grip a substance such as clay or dough before proceeding to finer hand skills, such as writing.

Managing Athetoid Cerebral Palsy. Athetosis is primarily characterized by involuntary, somewhat explosive, disorganized movements. Young children with athetosis need to learn to organize movement in the **midrange** (between extremes) through the repetition of actively elicited, effective midrange movements. Clear and precise feedback about the correctness or accuracy of their motions is necessary for them to be able to self-regulate their own sensorimotor circuitry. For example, the verbally spoken "Good!" is not adequate feedback if a motion is better than the preceding one, but still grossly inadequate for function. Precise verbal feedback details the components of an activity that are both correct and incorrect and compares performances, specifying features of improvement. In addition to repetition, placing a weight around the wrist of the child with athetosis provides extra proprioceptive feedback and assists the student to achieve smoother movements.

The main physical management goal for older students with athetosis is optimum independent function, sometimes using switch adaptations to operate power wheelchairs, computers, and other environmental controls. Most children with severe athetosis will not become functional walkers. The alternative of a power-driven wheelchair should be explored, and a system of mobility provided as early as possible, such as in preschool, so that the child can achieve a needed measure of independence and control. Sitting for long periods of time in a power wheelchair each day will result in too much leg **flexion** (bending) and result in deformities. Standing equipment is an alternative positioning method that improves bone health and prevents flexion contractures in the legs. Therapists will assist teachers by selecting appropriate standing equipment.

Managing Ataxic Cerebral Palsy. The student with ataxia needs enhanced sensory input about body and joint position in order to respond with more-accurate movements. Weighted vests sometimes help to achieve this increased proprioceptive input through the trunk and hips. Weighted shoes, however, should not be used; they are tiring to the student, and when they are removed, the unloaded limb might be even more difficult to place on the ground precisely. Students with ataxic cerebral palsy have difficulty moving through space, or **motor planning.** Teachers can help facilitate more-precise motor planning by arranging the classroom environment. Desks can be moved to create wider aisles, and the student's seat can be positioned so that it is accessible.

Managing Mixed Cerebral Palsy. Students with mixed involvement require unique and variable applications of the principles of altering sensory input to improve motor output. For example, movement and positioning interventions to reduce the effects of spasticity may trigger athetoid movements. Common denominators in the management of each type must be identified, such as seating adaptations, frequent standing sessions, symmetry (mirror image positioning on both sides of the body), deep pressure to enhance postural sensory input, eye contact with people and the task at hand, and close monitoring of postural adjustment and movement. Therapists are critical participants in selecting and modifying the most effective individual interventions.

In all cases where mobility is affected, the individual with cerebral palsy is at increased risk for respiratory infections. Teachers need to monitor students with cerebral palsy for signs of upper respiratory conditions. In addition, they should frequently reposition individuals with cerebral palsy to reduce muscle fatigue and counteract inappropriate muscle tone. Upright positioning also enhances respiration and weight bearing. Specialized equipment allows for appropriate sitting, standing, and prone (on-the-stomach) positioning. Readers are encouraged to consult resources that provide a broad range of strategies for physical management in classroom and home environments (Finnie, 1997).

Body Mechanics. Teachers who assist in physical management of students with cerebral palsy are at risk for injuring themselves or their students. To provide protection from muscle strain and back injury, therapists must instruct all appropriate staff in the use of proper body mechanics for transferring or lifting and carrying children. The therapist can assist educational personnel to resolve specific problems such as transfers from the chair to the floor, the toilet, or onto positioning equipment. If the student is wearing casts, special handling techniques are likely to be needed.

Following the primary rules of body mechanics ensures safe and effective lifting and transfers. Steps include the following:

- Directly approach the individual or item to be lifted (i.e., "square up").
- Keep your trunk erect and bend with your legs rather than your back (Figure 4–5).

FIGURE 4–5
Body mechanics

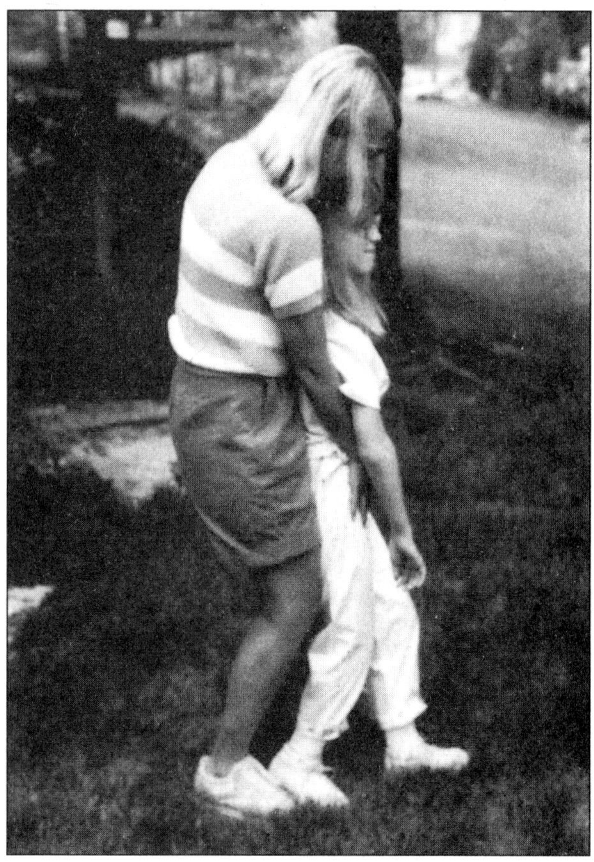

FIGURE 4–6
Transferring and positioning

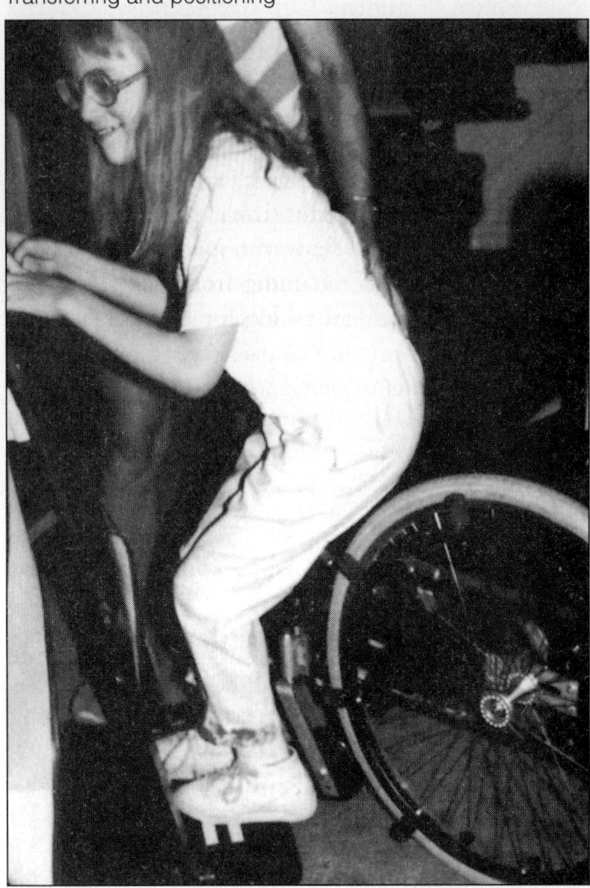

- Keep the child close to your body (Figure 4–5).
- Approach the child without rotating your own trunk.
- Keep your feet flat on the floor and comfortably separated with one foot slightly in front of the other for stability.
- Let the child bear as much weight as is possible (or appropriate) when transferring (Figure 4–6).
- Get help if you need it. A two-person lift should be used for children who are difficult to lift or who weigh over 35 pounds.

Communication Development

Earlier in this chapter the authors noted that the mechanical aspects of speech may be negatively affected by cerebral palsy. If receptive language is affected by cognitive or learning disabilities, individuals with cerebral palsy may be unable to formulate what they want to say or how they want to say it. Imagine the frustrations that result from an inability to understand and apply the concept of choice making (cognitive deficit), retrieve the appropriate vocabulary (language deficit), or formulate a verbal response (speech deficit).

Communication is not entirely speech based. Gestural communication develops much earlier, as readers will agree when they remember seeing a baby wave "bye-bye." Even before an infant learns to pair a certain hand movement with the word "bye-bye," facial expressions are used to communicate a variety of emotions and needs. Crying and basic physiological responses such as respiration and skin color changes signal caregivers to respond with a variety of strategies (offer the bottle or breast, check the diaper, rock or pat the infant, make soothing sounds, etc.). Very quickly these behaviors become transactional in nature, with the infant and caregiver attending to each other's signals and modifying their own responses.

Typical avenues of communication may be distorted or absent for individuals with cerebral palsy. Facial grimacing (instead of smiling) may be interpreted as rejection by caregivers. Infants who are hypotonic (floppy) or hypertonic (stiff) may not be able to "cuddle" in the caregiver's arms. Feeding problems that result in spitting up, gagging, and tongue thrust may convince caregivers that the infant does not like being fed. As a result of these and other behaviors exhibited by infants with cerebral palsy, important communication cues are misinterpreted. Caregivers may respond inappropriately ("The baby doesn't like me") or withdraw ("I am a poor parent"). The important early communication link is disrupted (Light, 1989).

Later in development, individuals who cannot communicate effectively through speech may be perceived as less intellectually capable. Many formal cognitive assessments rely on language and motor skills. The child with cerebral palsy who makes movements that lack purpose and sounds that are uninterpretable may be perceived as uninterested, disruptive, or unintelligent. Their conversation may be shortened to yes/no responses, which further limits vocabulary acquisition and complex language use.

Fortunately, the development of assistive technology has created new opportunities for individuals with cerebral palsy. Augmentative and alternative communication strategies have made complex communication possible for individuals whose speech is not

FIGURE 4–7
Eye gaze, effective listening, and specialized interaction strategies enhance communication.

effective for them (Beukelman & Mirenda, 1992; Glennen & DeCoste, 1997). For assistive technology to be effective, teachers and other communication partners must use effective listening and specialized interaction strategies to facilitate comprehension (Figure 4–7). Chapter 8 is devoted entirely to the topic of augmentative and alternative communication for individuals with physical or multiple disabilities.

Social/Emotional Development

Although the physical impact of cerebral palsy can be moderated with specialized therapeutic and/or medical interventions, assistive technology, and other management techniques, differences are inevitable. Most children do not wish to be perceived as "different" in ways that cause peers to avoid them. This need is especially important in the adolescent years.

Fostering Social Communication. Teachers and others can reduce the emotional/social impact of cerebral palsy in many ways. First, *it is important for teachers to understand the link between communication and social/emotional development.* Communicating with others allows for exchange of ideas, feelings, and opinions. It is an important link through which we convey that which is unique about ourselves.

Many individuals with cerebral palsy have speech that is difficult to understand or even unintelligible. They may require augmentative communication technology to meet their communication needs. If communication devices are used, they should not be reserved for conversations between the student and the speech/language specialist. Teachers must become proficient in operating AAC devices, and can model social conversation by incorporating their use into classroom routines and encouraging conversational initiation from students who use AAC. Teachers must also appreciate that students with speech difficulties have important things to say. Appropriate interaction behavior includes waiting for students with speech difficulties to complete statements, refraining from finishing their words or sentences, and asking for rephrasing when they are difficult to comprehend. Peers should also be encouraged to imitate good listening behaviors. These strategies encourage active participation from students with speech difficulties and provide them and their peers with ways to maintain important social/communication links.

Assistance with Dignity. Individuals with cerebral palsy may need considerable physical assistance with activities of daily living. If students need medication, it can be administered discreetly in the nurse's office or other private area prior to recess or other normal breaks in class routines. Physical care routines (particularly those related to the bathroom and other intimate functions) should never be publically discussed or initiated.

Assistance in classroom activities is frequently needed by individuals with cerebral palsy. It is not unnatural for teachers and others to "overassist" students because it is easier and faster to provide help rather than watch students struggle. However, the time and energy expended to complete tasks fosters feelings of maturity, self-control, and mastery. Chapters 7 and 10 address many issues and strategies related to functional participation and adaptations for independence.

Social and Physical Encounters. To reach maturity, people must learn to interact with their peers and others in many social situations. Too often children with cerebral palsy are "protected" from social encounters that may hurt their feelings, such as teasing or staring. While the authors do not advocate that teasing is desirable for anyone, it is important for *all* children to learn social mediation strategies. In addition, age-inappropriate social behaviors should not be tolerated in individuals with cerebral palsy, since they create a barrier to social interactions.

Social mediation extends into arenas such as dating, sexual behavior, marriage (or partnering), and child rearing. Adolescents with cerebral palsy may not feel as attractive or appealing as their peers. These feelings may be especially acute if they have difficulty walking or speaking, if they drool, or if they experience significant movement in the facial areas. However, it should never be assumed that the presence of cerebral palsy indicates poor self-concept or emotional maladjustment. Just as readers have learned that there is no absolute connection between severity of disability and learning potential, it is also true that there is no absolute connection between severity of disability and social/emotional adjustment.

IMPLICATIONS FOR EDUCATION

The authors wish to express again that judgments about intellectual function or learning potential should never be based on the presence of a physically disabling condition. It is clear that individuals with cerebral palsy are at risk for being identified as intellectually disabled due to poor outcomes on tests that are motor and/or speech based. In addition, it is important for educators to resist the impulse to exclude students with cerebral palsy from important educational experiences on the basis of their motor challenges.

Educational Segregation

True educational integration is a matter of providing support that matches the level of need as well as adapting curricula for access and function. How many students with cerebral palsy have been positioned at an activity table (or at the back of the room) and watched their peers complete a science lab or assemble the ingredients for a cooking project? How many have been scorekeepers during game time rather than players? How many have been told they are participating in art when the instructional assistant completes a painting for which the student has selected the colors but never handled the brush? The motor deficits of cerebral palsy must not be allowed to interfere with meaningful participation in educational experiences. Throughout this text readers are presented with strategies for adapting assessment, curricula, and activities for students with motor impairments, including cerebral palsy.

Learning Disabilities

As noted earlier, students with cerebral palsy may have sensory impairments that inhibit learning. They may also experience processing deficits that contribute to learning disabilities. If visual processing disabilities are present, teachers can assist students to locate specific words on a page of writing by numbering each line. A reminder to "look on line 25" will alert the student to scan down the page to the number, then across to the appropriate word. Sometimes it helps to cover some lines of text in order to reduce visual complexity. For students who lose their place on a page of written material, a slot the width of the line of print can be cut in a file folder. The paper is then slipped into the folder and positioned so that only the written material being studied is visible. Gradually the slot in the folder can be widened and more material exposed. Sometimes folding a paper in half reduces visual complexity and aids in visual discrimination. Other strategies include using graph paper to align columns of numerals in mathematics problems and posting sequences of steps in tasks if visual memory is impeded.

Students with auditory processing disabilities need practice in skills such as following directions and telling a story. Providing visual prompts to aid auditory memory is a common strategy. Examples include allowing the student to sequence pictures that accompany a story and then use the pictures to assist in recall, accompanying a written recipe with pictures that depict each step, and providing a skeleton outline for notetaking.

Some learning disabilities involve proprioception difficulties, which is the feedback we feel relative to our position in space. For example, when individuals walk down a crowded corridor, they automatically adjust their bodies to cause the least friction and bumping against others. Of course the issue of "personal space" is influenced by individual and cultural differences. However, most people would not care to crash into others. Individuals with cerebral palsy do not move their muscles in a smooth or coordinated fashion. Consequently, they receive distorted physical perceptions of what it feels like to move. If they use wheelchairs, this equipment presents a further barrier between themselves and the tactile world. In classroom situations, proprioception difficulties may mean the individual has difficulty maneuvering around the room without bumping into peers, desks, or the teacher. It may be difficult to negotiate the straightest distance from one's desk to the door. In fine-motor activities, there may be confusion with direction and position in space. Teachers can help by arranging the classroom environment so the student can get to parts of the room without complex maneuvering. For example, a line of tape may be placed on the floor or carpeting to facilitate decisions about maneuvering the wheelchair. Time spent out of the wheelchair assists the students to really "feel" his or her body in relation to regular chairs, the carpet, and so on.

Personal Autonomy

Independence is a critical goal for everyone. For individuals with cerebral palsy, autonomy is often a matter of gaining as much physical control as possible rather than absolute physical independence. Two areas that foster autonomy are training in equipment use and training in the activities of daily living.

Equipment Use. Individuals with cerebral palsy use a variety of assistive equipment to maximize function. Early instruction and use of this equipment aids in mobility and communication and boosts autonomy. Teachers need to become familiar with the function of orthotic devices, wheelchairs, and augmentative/alternative communication equipment. They need to assist the individual to incorporate equipment care into classroom routines and develop a matter-of-fact attitude about equipment use. Equipment should be perceived as necessary and useful to the individual, and not as a bulky nuisance that clutters classroom space.

Activities of Daily Living. Bigge, Stump, Spagna, and Silberman (1999, p. 88) use the term *life skills curriculum* to refer to areas of functional academics, daily and community living skills, and transition education that are practiced across domestic, community, leisure, and vocational domains. Intensive fundamental life skills curricula are not typical aspects of the school experience for most students, but contribute to independent outcomes for many students with disabilities. Chapters 10 and 12 in this text are devoted to discussion of adaptations for independence and career/transition for individuals with physical or multiple disabilities. Chapters 13–16 address general education curricula and functional academics in the content areas of literacy and language arts, writing, social studies and science, and mathematics.

Learning personal-care and daily-living skills is an important developmental goal for everyone. For individuals with cerebral palsy, personal-care activities such as eating, dressing, and bathing take considerable practice and frequently require the use of assistive technology in the form of adapted equipment (see Figure 4–8). Even with practice, self-care skills may not be achieved at the chronological age they are usually acquired or at a level sufficient for independence. Teachers must provide time in their daily schedules for appropriate self-care practice and work closely with occupational therapists, physical therapists, nurses, and others to establish self-care routines and promote function. It is never appropriate to react with disgust or avoidance when children are attempting to master a skill such as independent feeding, even when they are messy or slow.

In addition to providing practice time, teachers must be aware of the time and effort involved in acquiring basic self-care skills for individuals with significant motor disabilities. Teachers are often faced with the competing demands of the many goals that must be addressed during valuable class time. For example, a teacher may be aware that a student needs to practice independent mobility using a walker. Should the teacher insist that the student practice this skill during transitions to the playground for recess, even if it means that recess is over by the time the student

FIGURE 4–8
Practice promotes independence, even when the process is time-consuming or messy

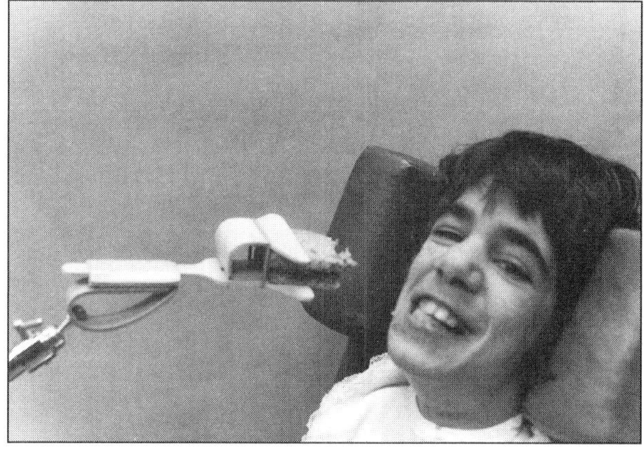

arrives? This decision sacrifices valuable recreational and social experiences. Better strategies might be to excuse the student a few minutes early to begin the walk to the playground, push the student in a wheelchair to the playground and have him or her use the walker to return, or practice mobility skills in the classroom where distances aren't as great.

Career and Adult Function

Children with cerebral palsy grow up to be adults with cerebral palsy, so lifelong needs and challenges become critical issues. Since cerebral palsy is an ongoing condition, planning for the future is an important goal. Students with cerebral palsy must be encouraged to achieve to their highest potential academically and to gain mastery in life skills. They must be able to appraise their abilities, which involves acknowledging their strengths and limitations and making a commitment to work toward what can be achieved. Teachers can assist students by providing experiences in the student's area(s) of strength, by providing realistic feedback regarding needs, and by helping the student to develop alternatives or modified strategies for successful outcomes.

Cerebral palsy has different implications for different stages in life (McCuaig & Frank, 1992). Families of young children with cerebral palsy may be focused on self-care, therapy, and medical issues. Later, adaptations for educational participation become paramount. Adolescents with cerebral palsy are interested in their peers, social interactions, and evolving independence. Transition into adulthood means that careers, living accommodations, community participation, and starting a family become central concerns. Although these outcomes are generalizations, they reflect the "typical" interests of all individuals. Chapter 12 is devoted to the topic of career and transitions for individuals with physical or multiple disabilities, including individuals with cerebral palsy.

SUMMARY AND CONCLUSION

The effects of multiple disabilities are often both multiplicative and interactive. Cerebral palsy is a disability that originates from damage to the central nervous system, but which is often accompanied by sensory, communication, orthopedic, learning, and cognitive disabilities. In addition to the presence of accompanying disabilities, the complex nature of cerebral palsy is related to differences in causation and the nature and degree of motor involvement.

Individuals with cerebral palsy receive a variety of educational and related services. Teachers and related service providers must work together to provide appropriate educational and therapeutic programming. Care must be taken to avoid educational segregation, in which the individual is physically present, but not actually involved in curricular or social activities. Teachers must be creative in adapting activities to facilitate meaningful participation of individuals with cerebral palsy.

QUESTIONS FOR DISCUSSION

1. Define cerebral palsy, and discuss why it is important for teachers to understand that cerebral palsy is a "developmental disability."
2. Cerebral palsy is seldom a "single-syndrome" condition. Describe at least three disabilities that may accompany cerebral palsy, and explain why the presence of multiple disabilities has interactive effects on academic and communication functions.
3. Cerebral palsy can occur during the prenatal, perinatal, or postnatal periods. Discuss how postnatally caused cases of cerebral palsy could be reduced.
4. Cerebral palsy is classified by location, movement patterns, and function. What information is conveyed to a teacher who is told that a student has "severe quadriplegic spastic cerebral palsy"? What positioning strategies might a teacher employ to support more functional movement for a student who is described this way?
5. Describe the roles of physical and occupational therapists in assisting with physical management for individuals with cerebral palsy. Why is it important for therapists and teachers to work collaboratively in areas that are therapeutic and/or educational in nature?

6. If you had a student with spastic hemiplegia and an auditory processing deficit, how might you assist this student to complete a book report?
7. Why is the acquisition of life skills particularly important for individuals with cerebral palsy? If independent function is not a possible outcome, should life skills curricula still be taught? Why or why not?
8. Respond to this statement: Low-tech solutions frequently work as well as high-tech solutions for individuals with cerebral palsy.

FOCUS ON THE NET

American Occupational Therapy Association
http://www.aota.org

The American Occupational Therapy Association (AOTA) promotes quality occupational therapy (OT) services by providing accreditation of educational programs, professional development, public education, and advocacy on programs related to national health care issues. Information is available to the general public about OT as a career and schools that offer professional programs in OT. A variety of print and audiovisual materials for the OT practitioner are published and sold by the organization.

AOTA has professional information packets on numerous subject areas, sponsors regional workshops, and publishes a professional journal entitled *The American Journal of Occupational Therapy,* in addition to other publications.

American Physical Therapy Association
http://www.apta.org

The American Physical Therapy Association (APTA) is a national professional organization representing more than 75,000 members, whose goal is to foster advancement in physical therapy practice, education, and research.

Epilepsy Foundation of America
http://www.efa.org

The Epilepsy Foundation of America is the largest organization that provides support, research, and advocacy services to individuals with epilepsy. Founded in 1968, the EFA has more than 60 affiliated foundations nationwide. A member of the National Health Council as well as the International Bureau for Epilepsy, the EFA has an extensive Web site that serves children and adult needs. Topics include:

- Advocacy;
- Kid's Club;
- Local services.

National Easter Seals Society
http://www.seals.com

Founded in 1919, Easter Seals is a nationwide network of 109 affiliate societies serving 50 states, the District of Columbia, and Puerto Rico. The societies operate nearly 500 program service sites to meet the needs of more than 1 million people annually.

United Cerebral Palsy
http://www.ucpa.org/html/index.html

For more than 45 years, United Cerebral Palsy (UCP) has been committed to change and progress for people with disabilities. The national organization and its nationwide network of 153 affiliates strive to ensure the inclusion of people with disabilities in every facet of society—from the Web to the workplace, from the classroom to the community. As the second largest health charity in America, United Cerebral Palsy's mission is to advance the independence, productivity, and full citizenship of people with cerebral palsy and other disabilities, through their commitment to the principles of independence, inclusion, and self-determination.

REFERENCES

Aksu, F. (1990). Nature and prognosis of seizures in patients with cerebral palsy. *Developmental Medicine and Child Neurology, 32,* 661–668.

Albright, A. L. (1996). Intrathecal baclofen in cerebral palsy movement disorders. *Journal of Child Neurology, 11*(1), S29–S35.

Alexander, M. A., & Bauer, R. E. (1988). Cerebral palsy. In V. B. Van Hasselt, P. Strain, & M. Hersen (Eds.), *Handbook of developmental and physical disabilities* (pp. 215–226). New York: Pergamon.

Azcue, M. P., Zello, G. A., Levy, L. D., & Pencharz, P. B. (1996). Energy expenditure and body composition in children with spastic quadriplegic cerebral palsy. *Journal of Pediatrics, 129,* 870–876.

Behrman, R. E. (1992). *Nelson handbook of pediatrics.* Philadelphia: Saunders.

Berman, B., Vaughan, C. L., & Peacock, W. J. (1990). The effect of rhizotomy on movements in patients with cerebral palsy. *American Journal of Occupational Therapy, 44,* 511–516.

Beukelman, D. R., & Mirenda, P. (1992). *Augmentative and alternative communication: Management of severe communication disorders in children and adults.* Baltimore: Brookes.

Bigge, J. L. (1991). Accompanying disabilities. In J. L. Bigge, *Teaching individuals with physical, and multiple disabilities* (3rd ed, pp. 75–101). Upper Saddle River, NJ: Merrill/Prentice Hall.

Bigge, J. L., Stump, C. S., Spagna, M. E., & Silberman, R. K. (1999). *Curriculum, assessment, and instruction for students with disabilities.* Belmont, CA: Wadsworth.

Blickstein, I. (2002). Cerebral palsy in multifoetal pregnancies. *Developmental Medicine and Child Neurology, 44,* 352–255.

Bly, L., (1999). *Baby treatment based on NDT principles.* San Antonio, TX: Therapy Skill Builders.

Bly, L., & Sterne, F. (1981). *Baby treatment: Advanced training in neurodevelopmental treatment* (lecture and instructional materials). New York: Neurodevelopmental Treatment Association, New York Hospital.

Brown, L. W. (1997). Seizure disorders. In M. L. Batshaw (Ed.), *Children with disabilities* (4th ed., pp. 553–593). Baltimore: Brookes.

Butler, C., & Campbell, S. (2000). Evidence of the effects of intrathecal baclofen for spastic and dystonic cerebral palsy. *Developmental Medicine and Child Neurology, 42,* 634–645.

Clancy, R. R. (1990). Valproate: An update: The challenge of modern pediatric seizure management. *Current Problems in Pediatrics, 20*(4), 161–233.

Cusick, B. (1991). Therapeutic management of sensorimotor and physical disabilities. In J. L. Bigge, *Teaching individuals with physical and multiple disabilities* (3rd ed., pp. 16–49). Upper Saddle River, NJ: Merrill/Prentice Hall.

Epilepsy Foundation of America. (1994). *Information and education sheets: Seizure recognition and first aid.* Landover, MD: Author.

Esscher, E., Flodmark, O., Hagberg, G., & Hagberg, B. (1996). Non-progressive ataxia: Origins, brain pathology and impairments in 78 Swedish children. *Developmental Medicine and Child Neurology, 38,* 285–296.

Finnie, N. R. (1997). *Handling the young child with cerebral palsy at home* (3rd ed.). Oxford, England: Butterworth-Heinemann.

Glennen, S. L., & DeCoste, D. C. (1997). *Handbook of augmentative and alternative communication.* San Diego, CA: Singular.

Heller, K. W., Alberto, P. A., Forney, P. E., & Schwartzman, M. N. (Eds.). (1996). *Understanding physical, sensory, and health impairments: Characteristics and educational implications.* Pacific Grove, CA: Brooks/Cole.

Hill, J. L. (1999). *Meeting the needs of students with special physical and health care needs.* Upper Saddle River, NJ: Prentice Hall.

Howle, J. (2002). *Neuro-developmental treatment approach: Theoretical foundations and principles of clinical practice.* Laguna Beach, CA: Neuro-Developmental Treatment Association.

Jones, M. H. (1983). Cerebral palsy. In J. Umbreit (Ed.), *Physical disabilities and health impairments: An introduction* (pp. 41–58). Upper Saddle River, NJ: Merrill/Prentice Hall.

Koontz-Lowman, D. K., & Murphy, S. M. (1999). *The educator's guide to feeding children with disabilities.* Baltimore: Brookes.

Krebs, L., Topp, M., & Langhoff-Roos, J. (1999). The relation of breech presentation at term to cerebral palsy. *British Journal of Obstetrics and Gynecology, 106,* 943–947.

Kurtz, L. A. (1992). Cerebral palsy. In M. L. Batshaw & Y. M. Perret (Eds.), *Children with disabilities: A medical primer* (3rd ed., pp. 441–469). Baltimore: Brookes.

Light, J. (1989). Toward a definition of communicative competence for individuals using augmentative and alternative communication systems. *Augmentative and Alternative Communication, 5*(2), 137–144.

McCuaig, M., & Frank, G. (1992). The able self: Adaptive patterns and choices in independent living for a person with cerebral palsy. *American Journal of Occupational Therapy, 45,* 224–234.

McMurray, J. L., Jones, M. W., & Khan, J. H. (2002). Cerebral palsy and the NICU graduate. *Neonatal Network, 21*(1), 53–57.

Morris, C. (2002). A review of the efficacy of lower-limb orthoses used for cerebral palsy. *Developmental Medicine and Child Neurology, 44,* 205–211.

Murphy, S. M., & Caretto, V. (1999). Anatomy of the oral and respiratory structures made easy. In D. Koontz-Lowman & S. M. Murphy (Eds.), *The educator's guide to feeding children with disabilities* (pp. 35–48). Baltimore: Brookes.

Nehring, W. M., & Steele, S. (1996). Cerebral palsy. In P. L. Jackson & J. A. Vessey (Eds.), *Primary care of the child with a chronic condition* (2nd ed., pp. 232–254). St. Louis, MO: Mosby.

Nelson, K. B., & Grether, J. K. (1998). Potentially asphyxiating conditions and spastic cerebral palsy in infants of normal weight. *American Journal of Obstetrics and Gynecology, 179,* 505–513.

O'Shea, T. M., & Dammann, O. (2000). Antecedents of cerebral palsy in very low-weight infants. *Clinics in Perinatology, 27*(2), 285–299.

Park, T. S., & Owen, J. H. (1992). Surgical management of spastic diplegia in cerebral palsy. *New England Journal of Medicine, 326,* 745–749.

Pellegrino, L. (1997). Cerebral palsy. In M. L. Batshaw (Ed.), *Children with disabilities* (4th ed., pp. 499–528). Baltimore: Brookes.

Perin, B. (1989). Physical therapy for the child with cerebral palsy. In J. S. Tecklin (Ed.), *Pediatric physical therapy* (pp. 68–105). Philadelphia: Lippincott.

Pharoah, P. O., & Cooke, T. (1996). Cerebral palsy and multiple births. *Archives of Disability in Childhood and Fetal Neonatal Education, 75,* 174–177.

Porter, S., Haynie, M., Bierle, T., Caldwell, T. H., & Palfrey, J. S. (Eds.). (1997). *Children and youth assisted by medical technology in the classroom: Guidelines for care* (2nd ed.). Baltimore: Brookes.

Reilly, S., Skuse, D., & Poblete, X. (1994). Prevalence of feeding problems and oral motor dysfunction in children with cerebral palsy: A community survey. *Journal of Pediatrics, 129,* 877–882.

Roscigno, C. I. (2002). Addressing spasticity-related pain in children with spastic cerebral palsy. *Journal of Neuroscience Nursing, 34*(3), 123–132.

Russman, B. S. (1992). Disorders of motor execution. I: Cerebral palsy. In *Pediatric neurology for the clinician* (pp. 469–480). Norwalk, CT: Appleton & Lange.

Schenk-Rootlieb, A. J. F., van Nieuwenhuizen, O., van der Graaf, Y., Wittebol-Post, D., & Willemse, J. (1992). The presence of cerebral visual disturbance in children with cerebral palsy. *Developmental Medicine and Child Neurology, 34,* 473–480.

Scher, M. S., Balfar, H., & Martin, J. (1991). Destructive brain lesions of presumed fetal onset: Antepartum causes of cerebral palsy. *Pediatrics, 88,* 898–906.

Scherzer, A. L. (2001). *Early diagnosis and intervention therapy in CP* (3rd ed.). New York: Marcel Dekker.

Sprague, J. B. (1992). Surgical management of cerebral palsy. *Orthopaedic Nursing, 11*(4), 11–18.

Steinbok, P. (2001). Outcomes of selective dorsal rhizotomy for spastic cerebral palsy. *Child's Nervous System, 17*(1–2), 1–18.

Steinbok, P., & Schrag, C. (1998). Complications after selective posterior dorsal rhizotomy for spasticity in children with cerebral palsy. *Pediatric Neurosurgery, 28,* 300–313.

Stewart, K. (2000). Massage for children with cerebral palsy. *Nursing Times, 96*(1), 50–51.

Wallace, S. J. (2001). Epilepsy in cerebral palsy. *Developmental Medicine and Child Neurology, 43,* 713–717.

Williams, K., Hennessy, E., & Alberman, E. (1996). Cerebral palsy: Effects of twinning, birthweight, and gestational age. *Archives of Disability in Childhood and Fetal Neonatal Education, 75,* 178–182.

PART II

ACCOMMODATIONS FOR CURRICULAR ACCESS

CHAPTER 5 Curricular Options for Individuals with Physical or Multiple Disabilities

CHAPTER 6 Task and Situation Analysis

CHAPTER 7 Assistive Technology

CHAPTER 8 Augmentative and Alternative Communication

Curricular Options for Individuals with Physical or Multiple Disabilities

COLLEEN SHEA STUMP
JUNE L. BIGGE

CHAPTER 5

KNOWLEDGE AND SKILLS

After you have read this chapter, you will be able to:

1. **Identify four primary curricular options and two fundamental curricular domains available for individuals with physical or multiple disabilities.**
2. **Describe kinds of content and outcomes that can be taught in each of the options and in the fundamental curricular domains.**
3. **Describe modifications and accommodations within and across these curricular options and domains to meet the needs of individuals with physical or multiple disabilities.**
4. **Discuss the advantages of each of the options and domains when designing a course of study or curriculum map for individuals with physical or multiple disabilities.**
5. **Identify steps for determining for individuals the appropriateness of the general education curriculum with accommodations and/or modifications, and for aligning IEP goals with general education standards.**
6. **Explore strategies for working collaboratively with IEP team members, including parents, in the selection and design of these curricular options and domains for students with physical or multiple disabilities.**

Curriculum embraces the broader meanings and purposes of education and represents the knowledge and skills identified as significant for students' success and participation in their daily lives. In this text we have focused on the intended curriculum (Nolet & McLaughlin, 2000) and define it as the "what" students are to know and be able to do as a result of their education. The "what" can be expressed through knowledge and skill domains and includes skills and performance areas that are important for meeting school and other major life demands and challenges. The intended curriculum does not include instructional methods or strategies; the intended curriculum is the "what" that is targeted as essential for teachers to teach and students to learn.

For students with disabilities, the intended curriculum includes both the general education curriculum, as set forth by the state and/or the district, as well as additional curricular options (e.g., life skills) and fundamental curricular domains (e.g., self-determination). Goals, standards, and student learning outcomes or benchmarks serve as the frame for the intended general education curriculum and guide educators in selecting learning targets for students. **Goals** are broad statements of a philosophy or mission of schooling (e.g., "All students will be readers and writers"). **Standards** specify what students are to learn and be able to do as a result of their schooling (e.g., "All students will be critical readers"). **Student learning outcomes or benchmarks** specify the level and types of performance expected of students and many times are presented as grade-level performance indicators designed to assist teachers in determining what students at the various grade levels are to know and be able to do (e.g., "All students will read and critique editorials in a variety of media and identify the author's position, support for the position, and possible outcomes associated with the position").

In addition to the intended general education curriculum represented through goals, standards, and student learning outcomes or benchmarks, many students with disabilities will need a much more deliberately planned and implemented curriculum in the very basic functional "life skills," including community-based experiences in collaboration with their families and teachers (Sitlington, Clark, & Kolstoe, 2000). In addition, those students with physical or multiple disabilities who cannot use spoken or written words as their primary mode of communication would not have a chance to succeed in school without specialized and intensive curriculum in modified means of communication and task performance (e.g., skills for using communication boards and systems). These students often require an intensive and specialized curriculum to learn alternatives to the usual approaches (e.g., curriculum, including goals, in the use of an alternative, augmentative communication device). Student curricular experiences in these areas should be as planned and as deliberate as any other curriculum. Additionally, curricula in self-determination (e.g., self-advocacy and goals setting) and transition (e.g., movement from elementary to middle school, from service provider to service provider) are essential components of a comprehensive curriculum plan for students with disabilities.

Therefore, there are at least four curricular options and two fundamental curricular domains that should be made available to students with physical or multiple disabilities. The four options are (1) general education curriculum with accommodations, (2) general education curriculum with accommodations and modifications, (3) life skills curriculum, and (4) curriculum in modified means of communication and task performance (adapted from Bigge, Stump, Spagna, & Silberman, 1999). The two fundamental curricular domains are self-determination and transition.

The intended curriculum for most students with disabilities encompasses these entities, but all options and fundamental curricular domains may not be identified as separate options. The amount and kind of curriculum needed for some students with disabilities, however, may vary significantly from those of other students and merit recognition. Consideration of all four options plus the fundamental curricular domains results in the development of an intended curriculum that is comprehensive and takes into consideration not only students' needs today, but also future needs as well (Polloway, Patton, & Serna, 2001).

Figure 5–1 displays the four curricular options and the two fundamental curricular domains that should be considered for the intended curriculum for students with physical or multiple disabilities, as well as for all students with disabilities.

This chapter describes each option and domain. **Option 1: General education curriculum with accommodations** is the primary curriculum offered in schools. It includes core classes, electives, and basic skills, as well as accommodations needed to access this curriculum. **Option 2: General education curriculum with accommodations** and modifications is the general education curriculum that includes accommodations and has been adapted to meet the needs of students with disabilities. **Option 3: Life skills curriculum** consists of knowledge and skills that typically developing peers develop through observation and participation in everyday activities, but in which students with disabilities may require specialized instruction (e.g., daily-living skills and career and vocational education). **Option 4: Curriculum in modified means of communication and task performance** represents intensive and/or specialized skills and knowledge students with disabilities require in order to participate in and benefit from instruction and other major life experiences. **Fundamental Curricular Domain 1: Self-determination** includes knowledge and skills in self-advocacy and goal setting. **Fundamental Curricular Domain 2: Transition** includes curricula embedded in all forms of transition, including movement from setting to setting, from service provider to service provider, and from one school level (e.g., elementary school) to another. All components are to be considered when developing a course of study or curricular map for students with physical or multiple disabilities.

*

FIGURE 5–1
Curricular options

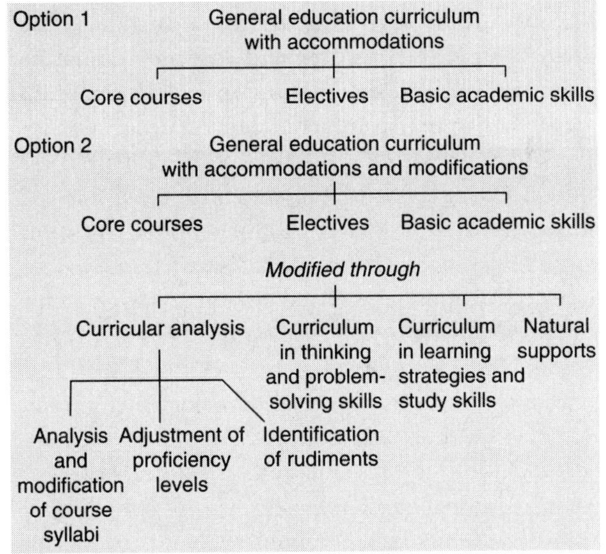

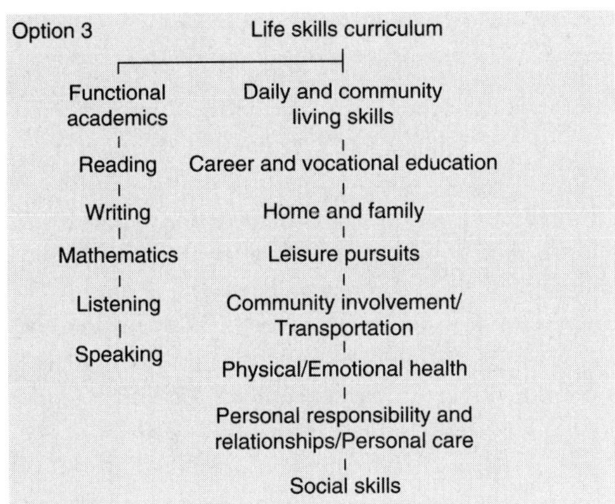

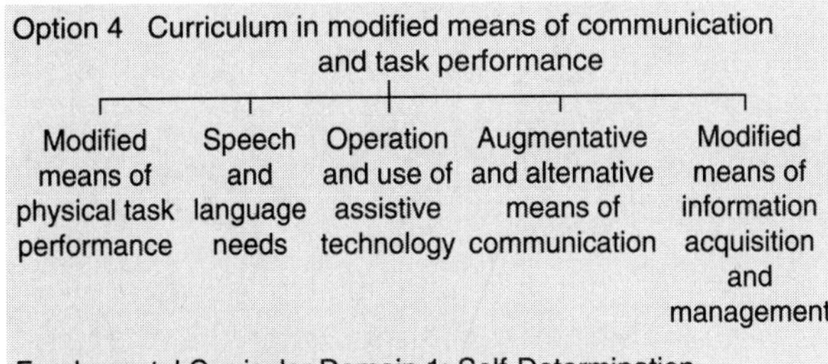

Note. Adapted from *Assessment, Curriculum, and Instruction for Students with Disabilities*, 1st edition, by J. L. Bigge and C. S. Stump. © 1999. Reprinted with permission of Wadsworth, a division of Thomson Learning: *www.thomsonrights.com*. Fax 800–730–2215.

CURRICULAR OPTIONS AND FUNDAMENTAL CURRICULAR DOMAINS

Option 1: General Education Curriculum with Accommodations

General education curriculum with accommodations, in this chapter, refers to curriculum that is organized and delivered with the needs of typical learners in mind and is adjusted, through accomodations, to meet the individual needs of students. This curriculum is specified in state, district, and national standards and is generally provided to students in general education learning environments. Individually based accommodations are provided to assist students in accessing the curriculum (e.g., providing more time to complete assignments, having fewer spelling words on the weekly test, having preferential seating, providing sign-language interpreters), but the curriculum itself (the "what") is not changed in content, outcomes, or levels of complexity to meet the unique learning challenges of students with disabilities—the students are expected to achieve the same outcomes and meet the same standards as their nondisabled peers, with the addition of accommodations as appropriate.

The reauthorization of IDEA '97 continues to place the general education curriculum at the center of curricular planning for all students, including students with disabilities. The intended general education curriculum is typically presented through goals, standards, and student learning outcomes or benchmarks. Using the intended general education curriculum as a starting point ensures that students with disabilities are provided opportunities to progress in the general education curriculum. Focus on the general education curriculum also ensures that curricular goals for students with disabilities will be consistent, to the maximum extent appropriate, with what is expected of typical students (Polloway, Patton, & Serna, 2001).

Using the general education curriculum as a starting point is essential because it is important to expose individuals with significant disabilities to a "range of general education curricular activities" (Giangreco,

1997, p. 54), rather than to automatically restrict their curricular options to life skills and work-related content. This broadening of curricular considerations may be most critical for students with physical or multiple disabilities because many of these students are capable of achieving general education standards when provided appropriate accommodations and modifications over time.

As a result, it is essential for IEP teams to begin with the general education curriculum and to align IEP goals with general education student learning outcomes/benchmarks. Although states and districts may have their own way of specifying standards and desired learning outcomes, the majority do have written documents from which teachers can draw when determining curricula for students and when setting IEP goals. Alignment is significant because if IEP goals are aligned with the general education curriculum, there is greater assurance that the IEP (a) will reflect long-term planning, (b) will support student access to the general education curriculum and learning environment, (c) will ease communication and collaboration with general education staff because teachers are using the same language when discussing learning outcomes, and (d) will provide a more consistent curricular map for students with IEPs. Walsh (2001) and Matlock, Fielder, and Walsh (2001) provide some beginning guidelines for aligning IEP goals with general education standards.

Curriculum Elements. The general education curriculum includes three key elements. These three elements are (a) core courses, (b) electives, and (c) basic skills.

Core courses. Core courses are those specified in the course of study for all students. Generally, core courses consist of a specified number of units or hours in key curricular areas, including the following:

- Language Arts (Reading and Written Expression);
- Mathematics;
- Physical and Health Education;
- Fine Arts;
- Science;
- History/Social Science;
- Technology.

At the elementary level, the core courses are offered across the school day, with all students, as a unit, moving through the curriculum together. The day may begin with reading and writing/spelling instruction, followed by instruction in mathematics. The afternoon may consist of science and social studies instruction, with the addition of fine arts or physical education. At this level, the curriculum may be the same for all students. At the middle and high school levels, an array of courses may be offered to meet core course requirements (e.g., biology, earth science, chemistry).

Core course requirements are prescribed at all levels, with a specified number of hours or units in each area established for all students. At the high school level, these core courses and requirements reflect graduation requirements. Generally, schools specify how many hours/units in, or outcomes from, core courses are requisite to graduation.

Electives. Electives are courses and experiences in which students choose to participate. Electives vary greatly across schools and can include experiences in the fine arts (e.g., drawing, pottery, drama, photography, orchestra), in vocationally related activities (e.g., welding, woodworking, accounting, auto shop), and other areas (e.g., foreign language, computers, computer-aided design, business). The purpose of electives is to broaden the curricular base of students by offering opportunities for exploration in areas of interest and possible future careers.

For students with physical or multiple disabilities, participation in electives with general education peers may provide significant avenues for self-exploration and expression and be an arena in which students excel. They may provide opportunities for development of friendships and community-based skills as well.

Basic skills. What is identified as a basic skill is generally locally determined and reflected in the standards adopted by a given school, district, or state. Basic skills may include skills in reading, writing, speaking, and listening; computer skills; interpersonal skills; and thinking/problem-solving skills. These skills cross all disciplines, as well as core and elective courses, and are designated as essential outcomes for all graduates. For students with physical or multiple disabilities, participation in activities that target basic skills may ensure the skills necessary for participation in college, technical training, or employment opportunities following graduation.

Accommodations. Students with physical or multiple disabilities can participate in an array of these general education curriculum elements when provided appropriate accommodations. **Accommodations** are supports provided to students to aid their access to the curriculum. Accommodations do not modify what the child is to know or do (i.e., do not change the "what" students are to learn), but rather, support access to the curriculum. For example, Manuel, a student with mild cerebral palsy, achieves success in a general education mathematics class with accommodations that include having someone read the problems to him and extending the time allowed for completing tests. Another student, Alicia, who has a spinal cord injury that involves all four limbs to some degree, requires mobility assistance but makes great gains in the general education curriculum. Alicia's mobility accommodations include leaving the class early in order to be on time to the next class, and riding the school elevator. Jeff, a boy in middle school who works at near-grade level, uses two assistive technology devices as accommodations. He uses a small device that allows him or his teacher to scan tests or lesson documents into a word-processing application. Jeff then types his responses into the spaces where his peers write theirs. The document, with his additions, can then be printed like any word-processed document and handed in to the teacher. Again, the curriculum has not been modified or changed, but rather, the student has been provided accommodations for accessing and participating in that curriculum.

Accommodations can include preferential seating (e.g., a student with a hearing loss sits in the middle and to the side of the classroom to maintain better eye contact with the teacher), use of assistive devices (e.g., word-processing software, communication systems, spell-checkers, books on tape), and reduction in workload (e.g., the student writes two paragraphs instead of three). Table 5–1 presents a representative list of accommodations.

One powerful way to accommodate students with disabilities in the general education curriculum is to provide natural supports. Natural supports are supports and assistance provided by individuals and technologies found in the learning environment that lead to the achievement of goals (Butterworth, Hagner, Kiernan, & Schalock, 1996). According to Butterworth et al. (1996), natural supports consist of "assistance provided by people, procedures, or equipment in a given workplace or group that: (a) lead to desired personal and work outcomes, (b) are typically available or culturally appropriate in the workplace, and (c) are supported by resources from within the workplace, facilitated to the degree necessary by human service consultation" (p. 106). Examples of natural support involving peers include when a typical peer assists a student in turning pages when engaged in a paired reading activity, and when a peer delivers classroom supplies to the student. It is through the provision of these supports that students with physical, health, or multiple disabilities gain access to and participate in the general education curriculum and in their workplaces. According to Sitlington et al. (2000), "(1) the major purpose of engaging natural networks and resources is to enhance the community inclusion and quality of life of the individual; (2) the need for support may be of lifelong duration and may fluctuate during different stages of the individual's life; and (3) the goal is to maximize natural supports without any assumption or requirement that they will be fully adequate" (p. 164). Students may also need external support services.

Figure 5–2 describes how natural supports were introduced to enhance Yen's inclusion with peers and his quality of life in learning and participation at school. Yen, a student with spastic cerebral palsy, benefits from these natural supports when in a sixth-grade science classroom. Of course, natural supports can also be provided across all settings, including the workplace.

All or parts of the general education curriculum with accommodations may be viable for some students with physical or multiple disabilities when appropriate accommodations are provided.

TABLE 5–1
Representative List of Accommodations

Environmental Considerations • Ramps provide accessibility throughout the school site. • Classrooms are in accessible locations. • Classroom furniture is provided to meet unique positioning/seating needs. • Classroom furniture is arranged to promote positive behavior and limit distractions (e.g., study carrels, quiet corners, etc.). • Group and individual learning needs are arranged in the classroom (e.g., places for group work and quiet places for individual work and activities). • There is a "safe place" where a child can go as necessary. • Modified locations for storage and retrieval of personal learning and study materials and for assistive devices are provided. • Accessible surfaces are available for writing and other communications. • Plans are available for evacuation of wheelchair users. • Classroom furniture is placed to promote access to adaptive technologies where needed in lessons.
Physical/Sensory-Related Accommodations • Special transportation is provided. • Mobility aids are available for individual students. • Optical aids are available for individual students. • Adaptive equipment is available to enhance learning (e.g., pencil grips, book holders, raised line paper, page turners, computer with alternative input method, etc.). • Physical assistance for motor tasks is available (e.g., student peers are allowed to manipulate materials for the target student, scribes/notetakers, etc.). • Materials are provided in large print or other altered format (e.g., color contrast, spacing, etc.). • Preferential seating to aid seeing/hearing of information is provided. • Assistive technology is available that allows for participation in different curricular options (including augmentative and alternative communication). • Adapted feeding and eating equipment is available.
Health-Related Accommodations • Individualized Health Plan is in place (including appropriately posted medication/procedure regimens). • Qualified personnel are available to provide specialized health care routines. • Universal precautions are followed. • Increases in the number of excused absences is allowed. • Early release or later arrival times are established. • Modified daily schedules are established to include therapies, adapted physical education, etc. • Break time/resting times are allowed during the day. • Specific allergic reactions are monitored for and precautions taken (e.g., allow student to have own snacks). • Snacks are available in the classroom for students who are hungry. • Students are allowed to rest if fatigued. • An air purifier is used in the classroom. • Temperature is controlled. • Special diets are accommodated.
Curricular and Instructional Accommodations • Assignments are adjusted for optimal success (e.g., more time, fewer items, reduced complexity of curricular content, etc.). • Information is presented in multiple formats (e.g., visual, auditory, tactile, kinesthetic). • Instruction is clustered into short learning segments with breaks. • Instruction is broken down into steps (task analysis of instruction). • Instruction is presented in writing or with the use of icons. • Instructions are presented orally and in writing, with check-ins for student understanding. • Instructional approaches are varied to reflect multiple intelligences and learning styles/needs. • Students are offered choices. • Important information is highlighted through a variety of strategies (e.g., advanced organizers, repetition, key words, etc.). • Hands-on learning or concrete learning experiences are provided. • Alternative methods for providing information are used (e.g., line drawings, clip art, or graphics in place of writing or speech in text). • Alternative access materials are available (e.g., screen-reading software, playback machines, "talking books," etc.). • Alternative forms and response modes are used. • Assignment length is reduced; students are to strive for quality rather than quantity. • Directions are given one at a time and are quietly repeated to target students after they have been given to the rest of the class.

TABLE 5–1
(Continued)

Curricular and Instructional Accommodations (*Continued*)
- A student is told in advance the question he/she will be asked so that he/she has time to prepare a response.
- Student is allowed to begin an assignment and then go to the teacher after a few problems for confirmation the work is being done correctly.
- Assignments are folded to reveal small segments at a time or cut into strips.
- Students are provided with a card to pull down as they move through the work.

Rules and Consequences
- Schoolwide and classwide rules are posted and frequently reviewed.
- The number of rules are reduced to only essential items.
- Rules are written at student's comprehension level and modified as appropriate (e.g., pictures or other graphics are used to represent rules).
- Extra time is allowed to travel between classes.
- Schedules and rules for medication regimens are available and followed.
- Rules during physical education and recess are modified as appropriate.

Behavioral Accommodations
- A consistent, predictable schedule is provided; the schedule is posted in the classroom.
- Behavior management system are in place that promote, reinforce, and reward positive behaviors.
- Students are prepared for transitions.
- Students have permission to leave the group when anxious, frustrated, angry, etc.
- Students are allowed to move about the room or stand when completing work.
- Students are positively reinforced for initiating communications.
- Self-management techniques are implemented.
- Daily/weekly charting of behaviors is paired with reinforcement.
- Praise and reinforcement is consistent and common.
- Tasks are paired with positive consequences.
- Students are given frequent feedback about their behavior.
- Behavioral contracts are implemented between home and school.
- Attention is rewarded.
- Students are rewarded for timely accomplishments.
- Materials are housed in specific locations.
- Teachers inform students of behavioral expectations.
- Students are given responsibilities or leadership roles.

FIGURE 5–2
Natural supports (with Yen)

Yen is a bright and inquisitive boy with spastic cerebral palsy. He uses a wheelchair for mobility, an AAC device and eye-gaze for communicating, and an adapted computer for generation of school papers and projects. He is performing at grade level and greatly enjoys school.

The sixth-grade science curriculum is inquiry based and involves extensive cooperative learning work and the conducting of experiments. Yen's general and special education teachers have been working collaboratively to identify and incorporate natural supports that support Yen's active participation in the science curriculum.

Today the class is working with simple machines. They are to develop a pulley system for moving certain objects. Yen is sitting with his cooperative group at a specially adapted table that allows Yen to pull up close to it and to easily view all objects and equipment.

The students in his group serve as natural supports for his participation. His peers have been provided strategies for how to include Yen in the manipulation of the science equipment. They ask him for suggestions and follow his eye-gaze when selecting and positioning pieces. They ask him questions and wait for his input through the AAC device and, several times, follow his suggestions for building the pulley system. The students manipulate the materials for him, based on his input.

Option 2: General Education Curriculum with Accommodations and Modifications

The term "general education curriculum with accommodations and modifications" refers to a general education curriculum in which the student receives both accommodations (i.e., adjustments) and curricular modifications (i.e., significant changes in content, outcomes, and levels of complexity). The primary difference between this option and "general education with accommodations" is that in this option, in addition to accommodations, modifications are made in content, outcomes, or levels of complexity.

Curricular Modifications. Curricular modifications change or adapt the "what" being taught. One way to deliver curricular modifications is to employ a multilevel curriculum approach (Giangreco & Putnam, 1991) in which students work in the same curricular area, but the curricular outcomes are modified for students with disabilities. For example, all students are working on money skills, with general education students working on determining discounts while students with IEPs learn the names and values of coins and bills. Another curricular delivery approach, curriculum overlapping (Giangreco & Putnam, 1991), also modifies the curriculum for students with disabilities by having students learn side by side, working toward different learning outcomes (e.g., general education peers may be learning about photosynthesis while a student with an IEP is working on eye contact and fine-motor skills). In these scenarios, the curriculum has been changed, or modified, with students with IEPs focusing on different knowledge and skills and working toward different outcomes. Modifications change the "what" students are learning and represent specially designed instruction captured through IEP goals.

There are at least two considerations when selecting general education curriculum with modifications: (a) determining whether the general education curriculum needs to be modified for particular learners and, when appropriate, (b) selecting and applying an approach for modifying the curriculum.

Determining a Need for Modifications. Determining if the general education curriculum should be or needs to be modified for a particular learner can be done in a multitude of ways. We present three options.

Question and analysis approach. This approach is presented by Westling and Fox (1995), drawing from the work of Snell (1993). The approach involves the asking of five questions. Responses to these questions assist teams in determining whether the general education curriculum should be modified for a particular student.

Figure 5–3 presents the five questions (Westling & Fox, 1995, pp. 134–135) and discusses how the team, working with Namita (a student with mild cerebral palsy and mild cognitive impairment), determines whether to modify the general education English curriculum to best serve her needs.

Question and choice approach. This three-question approach is presented by Falvey and Grenot-Scheyer (1995) and is similar to the first approach in that it is structured by questions. However, the approaches differ because in the question and choice approach, the response to the final question leads to the determination of whether the general education curriculum will be modified, and if so, how it will be modified.

Figure 5–4 presents three questions and choices (from Falvey and Grenot-Scheyer, 1995, p. 153), and discusses how a team working with Amanda (a student with upper limb deficiencies) determines whether to modify the general education mathematics curriculum to serve her needs. Note that in this example, the application of the questioning approach led the team to determine that Amanda requires only accommodations to be successful in the general education curriculum; thus, she will be participating in Curricular Option 1: General Education Curriculum with Accommodations.

Objective evaluation approach. This approach is more prescriptive and involved than the previous two and outlines specific steps a team may move through to determine whether particular general education standards, student learning outcomes, or benchmarks should be modified to meet the needs of an individual learner. Figure 5–5 outlines the seven primary steps of

FIGURE 5–3
Question and analysis approach (with Namita)

Namita is a junior in high school who has mild cerebral palsy and a mild cognitive impairment. She wears leg braces to assist her in walking. Her cerebral palsy makes it difficult for her to express herself using verbal communication. She relies on gestures and her communication device to communicate with others. Her mild cognitive impairment presents challenges in her ability to organize information and to remember information from day to day.

1. **What is the age of the student and how much time does he or she have remaining in school?** Namita is a high school junior. She intends to remain in high school through the age of 21 and at that point transfer to a community college to gain skills for working in a retail office, doing basic filing and copying tasks.
2. **What amount of success has the student had thus far in learning academic skills?** Namita reads at the fourth-grade level. She enjoys listening to novels and is able to identify the main characters, story events, and story outcomes. She has done well in her previous general education literature classes with accommodation and modifications. Primary accommodations have been books on tape, outlines of chapters, having a classroom partner with whom to complete assignments, and using her assistive technology devices. Modifications have included working on vocabulary at the fourth-grade level, working in basic paragraph writing, and identifying major story elements of setting, character, and problem.
3. **What type of academic skills are needed for functioning in relevant environments and also for leisure and recreational activities?** Namita's goal of working in a retail office requires basic reading and writing skills, and interpersonal skills for working with coworkers.
4. **What is the relative value or significance of academic skills when compared to other skills? Are there other skills that will reduce dependence or increase independence?** Namita participates in a specialized reading and writing class in addition to participation in the general education English class. As a result, she participates in two periods of instruction focused on the development of reading and writing skills: one with a focus on the general education curriculum, and one with a focus on functional reading skills at her current reading level. The combination appears most appropriate for her at this time with skills learned in both environments leading to skill enhancement and greater independence.

   Namita's interpersonal and communication skills have significantly improved with her participation in general education curriculum/classes. She socializes with peers and has established a peer friendship outside of school. The skills she is learning from participation in the general education curriculum and classes are increasing her independence.
5. **What are the wishes of the student and the student's parents regarding instruction in academic skills?** Namita would like to remain in the general education class because she enjoys working with peers. She also wishes to continue in the functional reading class, expressing that it is providing her skills needed for admission to the community college. Her parents support her continued participation in the general education curriculum/class, with accommodations, but want to closely monitor her reading and writing skills to ensure she has the skills necessary for the community college program.

The team determined Namita would participate in the general education curriculum, with modifications that include peer supports, book outlines, and books on tape. Modifications include continuing to work in vocabulary and story elements at her current reading level and working on basic paragraph writing. She will also continue to participate in the functional reading curriculum course.

the process. Figure 5–6 follows one example through each step. For more information and examples of this approach in practice, refer to pages 70 through 77 in the Bigge, Stump, Spagna, and Silberman (1999) text.

Selecting and Applying an Approach for Modifying the Curriculum. Once it is determined that the general education curriculum should be modified, the team has a multitude of options available for how to make those curricular modifications. Three curricular modification approaches may be most relevant for students with health, physical, or multiple disabilities: (1) curricular analysis, (2) addition of curriculum in thinking and problem-solving skills, and (3) addition of curriculum in learning strategies and study skills. Teachers can use a combination of these curricular modification approaches to meet individual student needs.

Curricular analysis. When conducting a curricular analysis, teachers, support providers, and parents work together to identify essential skills and understandings

FIGURE 5–4
Question and choice (with Amanda)

Amanda is a second-grade student with limb deficiencies that leave her with one short right arm and no right hand and one left arm of normal length and a left hand with only two fingers and no thumb. Her limb deficiencies makes it difficult for her to manipulate objects and to write. To date, she has done well in the general education curriculum.

1. **What do students need to learn?** Students are to develop skills in problem solving.
2. **How do students need to learn?** Students work in cooperative learning groups. They are expected to use manipulatives to solve the problem. Each student is to use paper and pencil to sketch the group solution and to draft a group description of their problem-solving procedures.
3. **What modifications or adaptations are necessary for student learning?**
   a. leave curriculum as is
   b. provide physical assistance
   c. provide adapted materials
   d. provide a multilevel curriculum (Giangreco & Putnam, 1991)
   e. provide for curriculum overlap (Giangreco & Putnam, 1991)
   f. provide a substitute curriculum

The team compares the ways in which students are expected to learn and demonstrate understanding with Amanda's learning profile. Although the team agrees that Amanda has the ability to participate and gain from the general education curriculum and does well in cooperative learning groups, they reject choice *a* because it fails to address her difficulties with manipulatives, handwriting and entry of information on the computer. They also reject choices *d, e,* and *f* because they believe Amanda can achieve the core understandings of the general education curriculum. The team identifies choice *b* (provide physical assistance) and *c* (provide adapted materials) as most relevant for meeting Amanda's needs. They decide to provide the following accommodations to support Amanda's participation in the general education curriculum:

1. Provide Amanda and the group with adapted manipulatives. They will be provided larger versions of cubes and counters when possible, and be provided a sheet of nonslip material to prevent the manipulatives from moving or sliding on their own.
2. Provide Amanda with software selected because of its ease of use in making line drawings.
3. Allow Amanda to make verbal presentations of the problem-solving process from her point of view after listing key words on the computer as reminders. This would decrease the writing load and, because she is extremely slow in word processing, would allow her to contribute about the problem-solving process when the others contribute their ideas. Frequently, Amanda will be participating in the general education curriculum with accommodations—option1.

represented by the curriculum—what is most important for teachers to teach and for students to learn. The purpose of curricular analysis is, first, to take apart the curriculum as it is proposed; next, to identify the key understandings represented; and last, to determine if these key understandings need to be modified to reflect the learning needs and goals of a student with a disability.

This analysis can occur in many ways, including (1) analyzing and modifying course syllabi or course outlines, (2) adjusting proficiency levels students are expected to achieve to demonstrate competence and achievement, and (3) identifying rudiments and teaching to the mastery of these rudiments. For example, a student outcome or benchmark for reading may be to identify the primary story elements of setting, characters, problem, resolution, and conclusion. Through a curricular analysis of rudiments, the team may determine that for a general education student, the curriculum requires (a) the identification and description of all primary characters, (b) the description of all settings of the story, (c) a detailed analysis of the problem faced by the characters, (d) an analysis of the resolution in terms of the actions the characters took toward that resolution and why, and (e) how all of these elements were tied together at the conclusion of the story. For a student with a disability, the curriculum may be modified to emphasize the following rudiments: (a) identification of the main character and the primary setting in which the story takes place, and (b) the sequencing of primary story events. The curriculum is modified because the learning outcomes have been changed for the student with the IEP.

FIGURE 5–5
Objective evaluation approach

Procedure A: Identify important target objective(s) stated for peers in the general education curriculum for which individual students with disabilities may need modifications in complexity.

Procedure B: Create a checklist of knowledge and skill competencies that lead to the accomplishment of each target objective.

Procedure C: Use the knowledge and skill checklists to determine those competencies a student does and does not possess.

Procedure D: Identify the one or more competencies on the knowledge and skills list that are critical (C) to accomplishment of the target objective at even the most elemental level of complexity.

Procedure E: Use information about student possession of those competencies considered critical to determine whether to keep, modify, or change the objective and related content.

- **Option E1:** *If* a student possesses the critical competencies . . . *then* follow general education curriculum by keeping the original objective(s) and content and maintain or increase their level complexity.
- **Option E2:** *If* a student possesses some critical competencies but still has difficulty meeting the objective, or *if* a student possesses some but not all of the en route competencies with the probability that the student can learn the rest of the critical and other en route competencies in a reasonable amount of time . . . *then* consider keeping the original objective(s) and content and reducing their level of complexity.
- **Option E3:** *If* a student does *not* possess the critical competencies, and *if* there is some probability that the student can learn one or more en route competencies on the checklist in a reasonable amount of time and those competencies would be useful to the student . . . *then* substitute different but related objectives and content (e.g., one or more of the competencies on the checklist).
- **Option E4:** *If* a student does not possess the critical competencies, and *if* totally different objectives would be more useful to the student . . . *then* substitute an alternative objective (e.g., objectives for life skills outcomes; objectives for modified means of communication and performance).

Procedure F: Develop appropriate objectives tailored to the needs of specific students, keeping the general education curriculum in mind as a point of reference.

Procedure G: Plan curriculum to help students attain or advance toward meeting the stated objectives.

Note. Adapted from *Curriculum, Assessment and Instruction for Students with Disabilities, 1st edition* by J. L. Bigge and C. S. Stump, © 1999. Reprinted with permission of Wadsworth, a division of Thomson Learning: *www.thomsonrights.com*. Fax 800–730–2215. Also adapted from California Department of Education (1978) "Steps in Devising Differential Standards," in *Developing Proficiency Standards for Pupils in Special Education Programs: Workshop Outline and Agenda*. Sacramento, CA: Author.

These three approaches of curricular analysis are explained in Table 5–2. Each offers unique advantages, depending on the learning profiles of individual students.

Addition of curriculum in thinking and problem-solving skills. For many students with physical or multiple disabilities, the inclusion of thinking and problem-solving skills into the curriculum can significantly increase the likelihood of their accessing the general education curriculum and gaining skills and understandings. Identifying curriculum in strategies for how to think about content and approach problems may provide the scaffolding students need to achieve success in the general education curriculum, including that at a modified level of complexity. The explicit targeting of thinking and problem-solving skills modifies the curriculum provided to typical peers because this curricular content is in addition to what typical students are taught. It may be that typical students gain these skills through day-to-day experiences or teacher modeling, but for students with disabilities, explicit and systematic curricula are needed in order for them to gain and apply these skills in meaningful ways.

For example, students may greatly benefit from developing decision-making skills and strategies for engaging in inquiry and for approaching multistep problems. Figure 5–7 describes how this approach to curricular analysis was applied to the needs of Emanuel, a student with cystic fibrosis enrolled in a general education art class. The explicit teaching of problem-solving strategies represents curriculum specially developed to address Emanuel's learning needs.

FIGURE 5–6
Example steps of the objective evaluation approach in relation to one general education objective approach

Procedure A: (target GE objective)
Application Given a topic sentence and series of up to four related sentences containing time-order words, students will first locate the topic sentence, write it down, then continue to write the detail sentences in logical order in paragraph form. Students meet the criteria when they correctly sequence 10 sets of sentences correctly into written paragraphs.

Procedure B: (checklist of student knowledge and skill competencies leading to accomplishment of target objective)
Application
- Knows that a paragraph is a group of related sentences, all dealing with a particular idea.
- Summarizes the main idea of a group of related sentences.
- Knows that a topic sentence expresses the main idea of a paragraph.
- Identifies the topic sentence in a group of related sentences.
- Knows that detail, or supporting, sentences tell about the main idea.
- Identifies supporting sentences in a group of sentences.
- Knows the meaning of time-ordered words (e.g., first, next, last, etc.).

Procedure C: (competencies a student does and does not possess)
Application
\+ Knows that a paragraph is a group of related sentences, all dealing with a particular idea.
− Summarizes the main idea of a group of related sentences.
\+ Knows that a topic sentence expresses the main idea of a paragraph.
− Identifies the topic sentence in a group of related sentences.
− Knows that detail, or supporting, sentences tell about the main idea.
− Identifies supporting sentences in a group of sentences.
\+ Knows the meaning of time-ordered words (e.g., first, next, last, etc.).

Procedure D: (critical competencies: **C**)
Application
\+ Knows that a paragraph is a group of related sentences, all dealing with a particular idea.
− Summarizes the main idea of a group of related sentences.
\+ Knows that a topic sentence expresses the main idea of a paragraph.
C− Identifies the topic sentence in a group of related sentences.
− Knows that detail, or supporting, sentences tell about the main idea.
− Identifies supporting sentences in a group of sentences.
\+ Knows the meaning of time ordered words (e.g., first, next, last, etc).

Procedure E: (decision to keep, modify, or change the objective and related content)
Application

Option E 1: Keep the original objective(s) and content and maintain or increase their level of complexity. *Given a topic sentence and series of up to four related sentences containing time-order words, students will first locate the topic sentence, write it down, then continue to write the detail sentences in logical order in paragraph form. Students meet criteria when they correctly sequence 10 sets of sentences correctly into written paragraphs.*

Option E 2: Keep the original objective(s) and content and reduce their level of complexity: *Given a topic sentence and two related sentences containing time-order words, students will first locate the topic sentence, write it down, then continue to write the detail sentences in logical order in paragraph form. Students meet the criteria when they sequence 10 sets of the sentences correctly in paragraph order.*

(Sample exercise):
First, she looked in her yard.
Then she found the dog under her bed.
Sarah lost her dog, Mr. Buster.

Option E 3: Substitute different but related objective(s) and content (e.g., one or more of the competencies on the checklist):
\+ Knows that a paragraph is a group of related sentences, all dealing with a particular idea.
− Summarizes the main idea of a group of related sentences.
\+ Knows that a topic sentence expresses the main idea of a paragraph.
− **Identifies the topic sentence in a group of related sentences:**
Given a mixed order of a topic sentence and up to three related sentences containing time-order words, students will identify the topic sentence. Students meet criteria when they correctly locate the topic sentence and write it down.

Option E 4: Substitute an alternative objective (e.g., objectives for life skills outcomes; objectives for modified means of communication and task performance): *Given verbal instruction, written information to copy, and lined envelopes to accommodate the information, students will address envelopes to the addressee and write their names and addresses as senders. Students meet the criteria when they correctly complete a stack of 20 envelopes.*

Procedure F: Application Select the most appropriate options from Option E. Develop appropriate objectives tailored to the needs of specific students, keeping the general education curriculum in mind as a point of reference.

Procedure G: Application Plan curriculum to help students attain or advance toward meeting the stated objectives. Use this text as a resource for planning the curriculum.

Note. Adapted from *Curriculum, Assessment and Instruction for Students with Disabilities, 1st edition* by J. L. Bigge and C. S. Stump, © 1999. Reprinted with permission of Wadsworth, a division of Thomson Learning: www.thomsonrights.com. Fax 800–730–2215. Also adapted from, California Department of Education (1978). "Steps in Devising Differential Standards," in *Developing Proficiency Standards for Pupils Special Education Programs: Workshop Outline and Agenda*. Sacramento: CA: Author.

TABLE 5–2
Approaches to Curricular Analysis

Approach	Description
Analyze and modify course syllabi or course outlines	Review a syllabus or course outline and adjust what is taught, how it is taught, and how students demonstrate understanding
Adjust proficiency levels students are expected to achieve to demonstrate competence and achievement	Develop rubrics that indicate different levels of performance: • Basic (uses complete simple sentences, makes few spelling and mechanical errors, stays on topic) • Proficient (uses blend of simple and more complex sentences, makes few spelling or mechanical errors, develops topic sentence and support sentences that explore a single topic) • Advanced (uses varied sentence structure, makes few spelling and mechanical errors, thoroughly develops topic sentences, support sentences, and concluding sentences that include descriptive words and phrase)
Identify rudiments and teaching to the mastery of these rudiments	Review the curriculum to identify key concepts and skills to be developed. Select the rudiments that are most important for the individual's development. This can be accomplished by • looking through different resources to identify what is taught in a particular area • looking for the sequence in which concepts and skills are taught • identifying key vocabulary • identifying key concepts to be learned • completing a task analysis

FIGURE 5–7
Teaching thinking and problem-solving skills (with Emanuel)

Emanuel is a high school junior with cystic fibrosis. Because of this health impairment, he has missed a great deal of school. Teachers have made accommodations in the number of assignments he must submit to earn a passing grade and have allowed extended time for project completion. Emanuel's IEP goals focus on developing problem-solving skills, especially in the areas of long- and short-term planning. Emanuel has received specially designed curriculum in 5-step problem-solving procedures.

In art, Emanuel is required to participate in a show at the end of the term. He is to contribute a minimum of three pieces for the show (general education peers are required to submit a minimum of five pieces). He has two of the pieces started and has not yet decided on the third. All projects are to be submitted in three weeks.

Emanuel with the assistance of his teachers, decides to apply this problem-solving approach to help him complete his art assignment. He outlines how he will apply the 5-step approach to his art class situation.

1. **Identify the problem.**
   Need to complete three art projects in three weeks.
2. **Brainstorm possible solutions.**
   Solution A: Complete one project per week.
   Solution B: Work a little on each project each day.
   Solution C: Decide what needs to be done with each project, sequence the tasks, and put them into a timeline.
3. **Analyze each solution and select the best one.**
   Solution A: Two of the projects are already started and could possibly be finished in a week, but the third project may take longer than a week because it has not been started yet.
   Solution B: Sometimes it takes a whole period to get something done on a project, so he may never get to all three in a period, or over the course of a week.
   Solution C: May be best because it will specify what needs to be done and Emanuel can set a timeline for getting tasks completed.
4. **Implement the selected solution.**
   Emanuel selects Solution C and outlines what needs to be done to complete each of the projects. He writes the components on a grid and adds dates for each to be completed. He makes a contingency plan in case he misses some school days.
5. **Evaluate how things are going and make needed adjustments.**
   The teacher and Emanuel decide they will meet in three more days to evaluate how the plan is working.

FIGURE 5–8
Study strategies (with Melanie)

Melanie is a fourth-grade student with spina bifida. She uses crutches to get around in the classrooms and a wheelchair for mobility on the school campus. She also has learning disabilities and experiences difficulties in reading and with organization and attention.

Melanie has been having difficulties in her social studies class. She is having a hard time reading and comprehending the text and staying on task during independent work time. Many times she fails to turn in completed assignments.

As part of the social studies curriculum, the general and special education teachers have been team-teaching a study skills curriculum to aid all students in comprehension. As part of this curriculum, they have introduced the RCRC (Archer & Gleason, 1994) method for reading text. The study skill is as follows:

R: Read (Read a paragraph or section and identify important information.)
C: Cover (Cover the paragraph or section with your hand or a piece of paper.)
R: Recite (Restate the information in your own words.)
C: Check (Uncover the section and check your ideas against what is written.)

Melanie has been using the study strategy when reading her assignments. The physical movement of covering and uncovering the text and displaying a limited amount of text at a time has greatly aided her in comprehending the text. Having a structured and strategic approach to reading has also aided her in maintaining her attention when reading.

Addition of curriculum in learning strategies and study skills. As with thinking and problem-solving skills, some students can make great gains in the general education curriculum if provided specially designed curricula in learning strategies and study skills. The addition of learning strategies and study skills to the general education curriculum serves to modify the curriculum that is provided to typical students and can enhance students' ability to access the general education curriculum.

One example of a learning strategy is instruction in how to approach a writing task. The curriculum may include skills in (a) identifying a topic, (b) brainstorming ideas to write about, (c) organizing these ideas into an outline or web, (d) generating topic sentences for each main idea, (e) generating details and examples for each topic, and (f) writing the information in paragraph form.

Study skills are sometimes identified as a separate curriculum designed to support success in the general education classroom. The study skills curriculum may include organizational skills, notetaking skills, test-taking skills, and use of resources. Figure 5–8 shows how study strategies were included in the curriculum plan for Melanie, a student with spina bifida.

Option 3: Life Skills Curriculum

Life skills curriculum includes the knowledge and skills individuals need for successful and meaningful participation in community and life experiences. These skills complement those developed in the general education curriculum and expand the curricular options available for students with disabilities. Life skills may be identified in domestic, community, leisure, and vocational domains (Wehman, 1996) and should be included in as an option in curriculum planning across the age span. Table 5–3 presents some examples of life skills that can be introduced at different grade levels.

Curricula in this area do not need to supplant student participation in general education, nor become the sole curriculum of students with physical or multiple disabilities. The life skills curricula can be considered an addition to the other three curricular options and serve to address the individual and unique learning needs of students.

Functional Academics. Functional academics are fundamental academic skills directly related to daily life activities. Examples include purchasing items, balancing a checkbook, reading cooking instructions, reading labels on medicine labels, writing shopping lists, producing a signature, and using a computer. The purpose of a functional academics curriculum is to address skills students will need to live as independently as possible as adults.

Cronin and Patton (1993) identify specific, embedded functional academic skills of reading, writing, listening, speaking, and math applications. Examples of these functional academic skills are presented in

TABLE 5–3
Life Skills Across the Grades

Student	Domestic	Community	Leisure	Vocational
Tim (elementary age)	—Picking up toys —Washing dishes —Making bed —Dressing —Grooming —Practicing eating skills —Practicing toileting skills —Sorting clothes —Vacuuming	—Eating meals in a restaurant —Using restroom in a local restaurant —Putting trash into container —Choosing correct change to ride city bus —Giving the clerk money for an item he wants to purchase —Recognizing and reading pedestrian safety signs —Participating in local scout troop —Going to a neighbor's house for lunch	—Climbing on swing set —Playing board games —Playing tag with neighbors —Tumbling activities —Running —Playing kickball —Playing croquet —Riding bicycles —Playing with age-appropriate toys	—Picking up plate, silverware, and glass after a meal —Returning toys to appropriate storage spaces —Cleaning the room at the end of the day —Working on a task for a designated period (15–30 minutes) —Wiping tables after meals —Following two- to four-step instructions —Answering the telephone —Emptying trash —Taking messages to people
Mary (junior high age)	—Washing clothes —Preparing simple meals (e.g., soup, salad, sandwich) —Keeping bedroom clean —Making snacks —Mowing lawn —Raking leaves —Making grocery lists —Purchasing items from a list —Vacuuming and dusting living room	—Crossing streets safely —Purchasing an item from a department store —Purchasing a meal at a restaurant —Using local transportation system to get to and from recreational facilities —Participating in local scout troop —Going to a neighbor's house for lunch on Saturday	—Playing volleyball —Taking aerobics classes —Playing checkers with a friend —Playing miniature golf —Cycling —Attending high school or local basketball games —Playing softball —Swimming —Attending craft class at city recreation center	—Waxing floors —Cleaning windows —Filling lawn mower with gas —Hanging and bagging clothes —Busing tables —Working for 1–2 hours —Operating machinery (e.g., dishwasher, buffer) —Cleaning sinks, bathtubs, and fixtures —Following a job sequence
Sandy (high school age)	—Cleaning all rooms in place of residence —Developing a weekly budget —Cooking meals —Operating thermostat to regulate heat and air conditioning —Doing yard maintenance —Maintaining personal needs —Caring for and maintaining clothing	—Utilizing bus system to move about the community —Depositing checks into bank account —Using community department stores —Using community restaurants —Using community grocery stores —Using community health facilities (e.g., physician, pharmacist)	—Jogging —Archery —Boating —Watching college basketball games —Playing video games —Playing card games (e.g., Uno) —Attending athletic club swimming class —Gardening —Going on a vacation trip	—Performing required janitorial duties at J.C. Penney —Performing housekeeping duties at Days Inn —Performing groundskeeping duties at college campus —Performing food service at K Street cafeteria —Performing laundry duties at Moon's Laundromat —Performing photocopying at Virginia National Bank headquarters —Performing food-stocking duties at Farm Fresh —Performing clerical duties at electrical company —Performing job duties at company standards

Note. Adapted from *Life Beyond the Classroom: Transition Strategies for Young People with Disabilities,* (3rd ed.), by P. Wehman. Copyright 2001 by Paul H. Brookes Publishing Company, Inc. Adapted with permission of the publisher and the author.

TABLE 5–4
Specific, Embedded Functional Academic Skills

	Employment/ Education	Home and Family	Leisure Pursuits	Community Involvement	Emotional/ Physical Health	Personal Responsibility/ Relationships
Reading	Read library books on various occupations	Read directions to prepare brownies from a mix	Look for ads in the newspaper for toys	Read road signs and understand what they mean	Locate poison control numbers in the phone book	Read a story to a younger child
Writing	Write to the school board about a pot-hole in the school driveway	Make a list of items needed from the grocery store	Fill out a magazine order form completely	Complete an application to play little league [ball]	Keep a daily diary of food you eat in each food group	Write a thank-you note to a relative for a gift
Listening	Listen to a lecture by a bank official on savings accounts	Listen to a lecture on babysitting tips	Listen to radio/TV to see if a ball game is rained out	Listen to a lecture on how children can recycle	Listen to the school nurse explain the annual eye exam for your class	Listen to a friend describe their family vacation
Speaking	Discuss reasons we work	Ask parents for permission to stay at a friend's house	Invite friends over to play Monopoly	Discuss park and playground improvements with the mayor	Ask the school nurse how to care for mosquito bites	Discuss honesty, trust, and promise. Define them.
Math Applications	Calculate how much you would make babysitting at $1.25 an hour for 3 hours	Compute the cost of a box of cereal using a coupon	Compute the cost of going to the movies	Compute tax on a video game	Calculate and compare the cost of different types of Band-Aids. Include tax.	Ask a friend to share a candy bar. Calculate your part of the cost.

Note. Adapted from *Life Skills Instruction for All Students with Special Needs: A Practical Guide for Integrating Real-Life Content into the Curriculum* (p. 32), by M. E. Cronin and J. R. Patton, 1993.. Austin, TX: PRO-ED. Copyright 1993 by PRO-ED.Adapted with permission.

Table 5–4 (which is only a portion of the table in the Cronin and Patton book). Notice the need for functional academics throughout these domains.

Students with physical or multiple disabilities can greatly benefit from participation in a functional academic curriculum. The curriculum can provide the avenue for the development of skills and understandings that will result in greater independence upon school exit. The only caution in adopting a functional academics curriculum is that it not become the entire curriculum for students and thus limit their exposure to other understandings and experiences represented in the general education curriculum. Functional academics may become more relevant and significant as a student progresses in school, but creating a holistic, comprehensive curriculum may be ultimately most beneficial for the student. Figure 5–9 presents an example of how this curricular suboption assisted Brenda, a student with multiple disabilities, in achieving academic goals and greater independence.

Daily and Community Living Skills. Students with physical or multiple disabilities can greatly benefit from inclusion of curriculum that assists them in learning what other students learn easily. Planning and preparing snacks may be a major undertaking for some students with disabilities, but is something that children without disabilities can typically learn without a great deal of special instruction and effort. What are simple tasks for some students may not be learned by other students without spe-

FIGURE 5–9
Functional academics (with Brenda)

Brenda is a high school senior with multiple disabilities. In addition to the athetoid form of cerebral palsy Brenda has a moderate cognitive impairment and is deaf. Brenda communicates through hand gestures, sign, and the use of her adaptive communication device.

Brenda spends part of her instructional day developing functional academic skills in mathematics, reading, and writing. In mathematics, the curriculum is focused on the understanding of money (e.g., paying for public transportation, purchasing items at a local store). Reading curriculum has focused on the reading of labels in the community and emergency vocabulary (e.g., Women; poison). Writing has focused on Brenda's ability to supply needed information for job applications using a job reference cue card. Participation in this functional academics curriculum forms the base of Brenda's course of study, which is augmented through participation in employment and life skills, communication and task performance skills, and general education curriculum with modifications in the areas of art and career education.

Brenda continues to participate in sign language instruction to increase her fluency in American Sign Language.

cialized curricular programming in cooperation with families of students.

Cronin and Patton (1993) and others (Loyd & Brolin, 1997) identify areas of living skills curricula that are similar to the suboptions of the Life Skills Curriculum Option in the Bigge-Stump model introduced earlier in this chapter, in Figure 5–1. Cronin and Pattons's (1993) Domains of Adulthood Model identifies six domains of adulthood, each with subdomains and accompanying lists of real-life demands. These suggest desired outcomes for a daily and community living skills curriculum that would prepare students not only for adulthood but also for their current lives. These daily and community living skills fall into domains of (a) employment/education (b) home and family, (c) leisure pursuits, (d) community involvement, (e) physical/emotional health, and (f) personal responsibility and relationships (including social skills and self-determination). Table 5–5 lists specific life demands for each of these domains.

Formalized inclusion of life skills curriculum in a student's course of study may lead to greater independence and overall satisfaction with life. Figure 5–10 presents an example of how this Domains of Adulthood Model by Cronin and Patton (1993) assisted teachers with helping Danielle, a student with multiple disabilities, in achieving life goals and greater independence.

It is advisable to include some life skills curriculum throughout a student's course of study, or curricula map. Creating a course of study that includes some degree of formalized life skills curriculum from early childhood may be ultimately beneficial for many students with physical, health, or multiple disabilities. This curricular option may become more relevant and significant for some students as they progress up the grades in school and approach adulthood. As highlighted by Myles and Simpson (2001), the explicit inclusion of social skills into a child's curriculum may be the child's key to a successful school experience, and should not be relegated to a position of the "hidden curriculum" that is expected but not systematically or explicitly planned for.

Option 4: Curriculum with Modified Means of Communication and Task Performance

The fourth curricular option, modified means of communication and task performance, represents knowledge and skills some students with disabilities require in order to be communicators and participants in family, school, and community experiences. Some students with disabilities require unique and different means for communication and participation, and teachers must be specifically trained to provide curriculum in these key areas. Communication skills include expressive skills (e.g., speaking, augmentative and alternative communication, gesturing, signing) and receptive skills (e.g., comprehension of the spoken word, sign reading, and speech reading when hard-of-hearing). The term "task performance" refers to how students complete tasks (e.g., through gesturing, drawing, mobilizing, etc.).

We have identified five skill areas of modified means of communication and task performance for students with disabilities, with a focus on students with physical or multiple disabilities (see Figure 5–1).

TABLE 5–5
Domains of Adulthood

Domain	Subdomain	Life Demands
EMPLOYMENT/ EDUCATION	*General Job Skills*	Seeking and securing a job Learning job skills Maintaining one's job Understanding fundamental and legal issues
	General Education/Training Considerations	Knowing about education/training options Gaining entry to postsecondary education/training settings (higher education, adult education, community education, trade/technical schools, military service) Finding financial support Utilizing academic and system survival skills (e.g., study skills, organizational skills, and time management) Requesting employment services when needed (e.g., Department of Vocational Rehabilitation, unemployment) Accessing support services of training setting
	Employment Setting	Recognizing job duties and responsibilities Exhibiting appropriate work habits/behavior Getting along with employer and coworkers Understanding company policies (e.g., fringe benefits, wages, sick/personal leave, advancement procedures) Understanding take-home pay/deductions Managing employment-related expenses (travel, clothes, dues) Understanding OSHA regulations
	Career Refinement and Reevaluation	Revitalizing career choice Exploring alternative career options Pursuing career change
HOME AND FAMILY	*Home Management*	Setting up household operations (e.g., initiating utilities, rerouting mail delivery) Arranging furniture and equipment Identifying and implementing security provisions and safety procedures Cleaning dwelling Maintaining and landscaping a yard Laundering and maintaining clothes and household items Performing/contracting for home repairs/improvements and regular maintenance Storing household items Maintaining automobile(s) and equipment, appliances, etc. Reacting to environmental dangers (e.g., pollution, extreme weather conditions)
	Financial Management	Creating a general financial plan (e.g., savings investments, retirement) Maintaining a budget Using banking services Paying bills Establishing a good credit rating Purchasing day-to-day items (clothes, food, etc.) Renting an apartment Selecting and buying a house (building new/purchasing existing) Making major purchases (e.g., auto, computer) Determining payment options for major purchases (cash, credit, layaway, debit card, finance plan, etc.) Preparing and paying taxes Buying insurance Purchasing specialty items throughout the year (e.g., birthday gifts, Christmas gifts, etc.) Planning for long-term financial needs (e.g., major purchases, children's education) Obtaining government assistance when needed (e.g., Medicare, food stamps, student loans)

TABLE 5–5
(Continued)

Domain	Subdomain	Life Demands
HOME AND FAMILY	*Family Life*	Preparing for marriage, family Maintaining physical/emotional health of family members Maintaining family harmony Scheduling and managing daily, weekly, monthly, yearly family events (e.g., appointments, social events, leisure/recreational pursuits) Planning and preparing meals (menu, buying food, ordering take-out food, dining out) Arranging for/providing day care (children or older relatives) Managing incoming/outgoing mail
	Child Rearing	Acquiring realistic information about raising children Preparing for pregnancy and childbirth Understanding childhood development (physical, emotional, cognitive, language) Managing children's behavior Preparing for out-of-home experiences (e.g., day care, school, camp) Helping children with school-related needs Hiring and training in-home babysitter
LEISURE PURSUITS	*Indoor Activities*	Playing table/electronic games (e.g., cards, board games, puzzles, Nintendo, arcades, etc.) Performing individual physical activities (e.g., weight training, aerobics, dance, swimming, martial arts) Participating in group physical activities (e.g., racquetball, basketball) Engaging in individual hobbies and crafts (e.g., reading, handicrafts, sewing, collecting)
	Outdoor Activities	Performing individual physical activities (e.g., jogging, golf, bicycling, swimming, hiking, backpacking, fishing) Participating in group physical activities (e.g., softball, football, basketball, tennis) Engaging in general recreational activities (e.g., camping, sightseeing, picnicking)
	Community/ Neighborhood Activities	Going to various ongoing neighborhood events (e.g., garage sales, block parties, BBQs) Attending special events (e.g., fairs, trade shows, carnivals, parades, festivals)
	Travel	Preparing to go on a trip (e.g., destination, transportation arrangements, hotel/motel arrangements, packing, preparations for leaving home) Dealing with the realities of travel via air, ground, or water
	Entertainment	Engaging in in-home activities (e.g., TV, videos, music) Attending out-of-home events (e.g., theaters, spectator sports, concerts, performances, art shows) Going to socially oriented events (e.g., restaurants, parties, nightclubs)
COMMUNITY INVOLVEMENT	*Citizenship*	Understanding legal rights Exhibiting civic responsibility Voting in elections Understanding tax obligations Obeying laws and ordinances Serving on a jury Understanding judicial procedures (e.g., due process, criminal/civil courts, legal documents) Attending public hearings Creating change in the community (e.g., petition drives)
	Community Awareness	Being aware of social issues affecting community Knowing major events at the local, regional, national, world levels Using mass media (TV, radio, newspaper)

(Continued)

TABLE 5–5
(Continued)

Domain	Subdomain	Life Demands
COMMUNITY INVOLVEMENT	*Community Awareness*	Understanding all sides of public opinion on community issues Recognizing and acting on fraudulent practices
	Services/ Resources	Knowing about the wide range of services available in a specific community Using all levels of government agencies (tax office, driver's license [DMV], permits, consumer agencies [BBB]) Accessing pubic transportation (trains, buses, subways, ferries, etc.) Accessing private services (humane society, cable services, utilities [phone, water, electric, sewage, garbage]) Accessing emergency services/resources (police, EMS, hospital, fire, civil defense, [911]) Accessing agencies that provide special services (advocacy centers, child protective services) Securing legal representation (e.g., lawyer reference service)
PHYSICAL/ EMOTIONAL HEALTH	*Physical*	Living a healthy lifestyle Planning a nutritional diet Exercising regularly as part of lifestyle Having regular physical/dental checkups Understanding illnesses and medical/dental needs across age levels Using proper dental hygiene/dental care Preventing illness and accidents Recognizing health risks Recognizing signs of medical/dental problems Reacting to medical emergencies Administering simple first aid Using medications Providing treatment for chronic health problems Recognizing and accommodating physical changes associated with aging Recognizing and dealing with substance use/abuse
	Emotional	Understanding emotional needs across age levels Recognizing signs of emotional needs Managing life changes Managing stress Dealing with adversity and depression Dealing with anxiety Coping with separation/death of family members and friends Understanding emotional dimensions of sexuality Seeking personal counseling
PERSONAL RESPONSIBILITY AND RELATIONSHIPS	*Personal Confidence/ Understanding*	Recognizing one's strengths and weaknesses Appreciating one's accomplishments Identifying ways to maintain or achieve a positive self-concept Reacting appropriately to the positive or negative feedback of others Using appropriate communication skills Following one's religious beliefs
	Goal Setting	Evaluating one's values Identifying and achieving personal goals and aspirations Exercising problem-solving/decision-making skills Becoming independent and self-directed
	Self-Improvement	Pursuing personal interests Conducting self-evaluation Seeking continuing education Improving scholastic abilities Displaying appropriate personal interaction skills Maintaining personal appearance

TABLE 5–5
(Continued)

Domain	Subdomain	Life Demands
PERSONAL RESPONSIBILITY AND RELATIONSHIPS	*Relationships*	Getting along with others Establishing and maintaining friendships Developing intimate relations Deciding upon potential spouse or partner Being sensitive to the needs of others Communicating praise or criticism to others Being socially perceptive (e.g., recognizing contextual clues) Dealing with conflict Nurturing healthy child/parent interactions Solving marital problems
	Personal Expression	Sharing personal feelings, experiences, concerns, desires with other people Writing personal correspondence (e.g., letters, notes, greeting cards)

Note. From *Life Skills Instruction for All Students with Special Needs: A Practical Guide for Integrating Real-Life Content into the Curriculum* (pp. 16–19), by M. E. Cronin and J. R. Patton, 1993, Austin, TX: PRO-ED. Copyright 1993 by PRO-ED. Reprinted with permission.

FIGURE 5–10
Life skills and independence (with Danielle)

Danielle is a high school freshman with multiple disabilities. She is visually impaired and has cerebral palsy. Her current course of study includes (1) general education curriculum with modifications, (2) life skills curriculum, and (3) curriculum in modified means of communication and task performance.

Danielle's life skills curriculum content is focused on two key elements from the Domains of Adulthood Model: Employment/Education, and Personal Responsibility and Relationships with emphasis on self-determination and social skills. Danielle has experienced difficulties in advocating for herself and communicating her needs at school, in the home, and in the community. She also has difficulty forming relationships with others and tends to withdraw in social situations.

Goals and outcomes for each of these curricular subareas are listed below.

Employment/Education

- job awareness (e.g., visiting job sites, interviewing employers and workers)
- self-evaluation of interests to determine possible careers and jobs
- working at a community work site one day a week for a minimum of two hours to gain job experience

Personal Responsibility and Relationships

Self-determination

- self-advocacy (e.g., learning how to ask for assistance when appropriate, learning to ask questions when on the job)
- decision making (e.g., learning to apply a decision-making strategy when confronted with a conflict situation on the job)

Social Skills

- interacting with coworkers on the job (e.g., strategies for greeting coworkers, strategies for entering a conversation)
- socializing with coworkers during breaks and lunch

They include (1) modified means of physical task performance, (2) speech and language needs, (3) operation and use of assistive technology, (4) augmentative and alternative means of communication, and (5) modified means of information acquisition and management. Each of these areas represents opportunities for specialized curriculum for students with disabilities, which should be reflected in IEP objectives.

Modified Means of Physical Task Performance. Bigge (1988) identifies six means of physical task performance students are commonly required to use in school subjects. The six include (1) gesturing, (2) speaking, (3) drawing, (4) handwriting, (5) showing dexterity, and (6) mobilizing. Curriculum that provides an adaptive approach to a specific type of physical task performance, or an alternative means for completing the task, is developed to address a student's specific need.

This topic is covered directly and indirectly throughout this text, since it is a major need for intervention with the population of students of concern here. In particular, Chapters 6, 7, 8, and 10 describe modified means of physical task performance through specific topics: task analysis, assistive technology, augmentative and alternative communication, and adaptations for personal independence. Readers are also challenged to consider modified means of task performance in all chapters that address different school subjects (e.g., literacy, mathematics, etc.).

Speech and Language Needs. Traditional curriculum in speech and language focuses on development and use of speech (e.g., articulation, voice, and fluency) and language (e.g., phonology, morphology, syntax, semantics, pragmatics). Many students with disabilities experience difficulties in one or more of these areas and may benefit from curriculum delivered by a speech/language pathologist as well as from teachers.

Speech and language curriculum may be broadened further and be described as curriculum needed by English-language learners. Gersten and Baker (2000) use the term "English-language learners" identified by Rivera (1994) to replace terms such as "limited-English proficient" and "language minority" and to include those learners whose conversational English is or may be adequate, but who struggle with the abstract language of academic disciplines.

The term "English-language development" (ELD) refers to "all types of instruction that promote the development of either oral or written English-language skills and abilities.... It is intentionally broad ... encompassing not only traditional instruction which often focused heavily on grammar, syntax, and proper usage, but also attempts to merge ELD with academic content instruction" (Gersten & Baker, 2000, p. 455). By its definition, we assume ELD covers the teaching of competence in a range of expressive and receptive skills, many of which students need to meet various life demands.

The term "English-language learners" can be applied to students with disabilities and language development difficulties. Those with physical disabilities may not only have speech impairments, but may have language difficulties due to any number of reasons. Some may be limited in speech and language development because of their difficulties in making others understand them and the consequent limitation of idea and information exchange; others may not have the practical experiences upon which to build language; still others may have cognitive difficulties that influence speech and language learning; and others may have English as their second language. Special education, general education, and career education teachers, as well as parents and speech/language pathologists, can work collaboratively to support a student's English-language development through articulation of a curriculum focused on language developed and expressed through the student's primary mode(s) of communication.

Operation and Use of Assistive Technology. As stated in IDEA '97, an assistive technology device is any item, piece of equipment, or product system, whether produced commercially and bought off the shelf, modified, or custom-made, that is used to increase, maintain, or improve functional capabilities of a child with a disability (PL 105-17, 20 U.S.C. 1401 § 602[1]). Chapters 1 and 7 provide additional information related to the law and provision of assistive technology.

Assistive technologies, again, are used to (a) augment a sense of movement, (b) circumvent a sense of movement, (c) provide alternatives or adaptation for means of communication and information expressed and received, and (d) provide means of performance in learning demonstrations and in a variety of educational life activities (34 C.F.R. § 300.5 2000). Chapter 7 covers assessment for assistive technology needs and facilitation of participation with a variety of assistive technologies.

Bigge, Stump, et al. (1999) identify three areas of assistive technology curriculum. Students using devices will most likely need curriculum and instruction in each of these areas. They include:

1. Access: starting up using direct selection (e.g., using hands, fingers, head-wand to activate on/off buttons) and voice recognition systems (e.g., use of voiced commands take the place of direct selection as input);
2. Operation: understanding how to operate the device;
3. Functional use: developing competence in using the device to accomplish functional life tasks such as using voice recognition to produce a paper.

Students, family members, teachers, and peers should also become familiar with the access, operation, and functional use of these technologies so that they may assist. For peers, familiarity helps them to develop a better understanding of how and why students need to use the devices. As with the introduction of any device, teachers and service providers must be sensitive to the feelings, attitudes, and beliefs of the student and his/her family about how and when to use the device.

Curriculum in the access, operation, and use of assistive technology can facilitate the participation of students with physical or multiple disabilities across school, family, and community environments. The degree of students' proficiency as users may depend on the amount and quality of the curriculum that they receive to learn and perfect their knowledge and skills in access, operation, and functional use.

Augmentative and Alternative Means of Communication. Curriculum in augmentative and alternative means of communication offers students with disabilities viable avenues and alternatives. "*Augmentative* communication refers to ways to augment or supplement partially intelligible speech. *Alternative* communication refers to means of communication other than by speech and writing" (Bigge, Stump, et al., 1999, p. 130). Examples of augmentative and alternative communication include aid and symbol use for communication (e.g., communication boards or books with picture symbols that represent vocabularies students need to express themselves, specially designed microprocessor-based communication devices, braille, signs, and finger spelling). New technologies and devices are being created almost daily, and with the creativity of teachers, support providers, parents, and students, these tools can be adapted and used to support student access and participation in school curriculum, and greater independence in all life activities. Students require specialized curriculum that specifies the knowledge and skills students need to access, operate, and functionally use these tools.

Modified Means of Information Acquisition and Management. As defined by Bigge, Stump, Spagna, and Silberman (1999), "methods for acquiring and managing information include reading, speaking, listening, touching, moving the body, and observing" (p. 142). For some students, these channels for gaining and working with information are unavailable, or are inefficient, and they require different and adapted means for achieving the goal of acquiring and managing information. Modified means of information acquisition and management, a component of the fourth curricular option, Modified Means of Communication and Task Performance, can be subdivided into three subcategories: (1) information acquisition, (2) information storage and retrieval, and (3) communication of printed information to others.

Information acquisition. Students with movement impairments benefit from specialized procedures, materials, and assistive technologies to acquire information in school (Bigge, Stump, Spagna, & Silverman, 1999). Some may need physical guidance as they attempt to gain information through touch and movement in first-hand experiences such as feeling the scales of a fish for a science experiment or describing some object. Some may need learning materials strategically placed for easy access. Book holders, lessons presented in enlarged print, outlines of chapters, and other specialized materials may be helpful. Computers with usual or modified means of physical operation provide sources of information when independence in handling reference books is not possible. Computer and other assistive technologies transcribe print into spoken words so students can hear the information when they have difficulty acquiring information from print.

Students who also have visual or hearing impairments may require further adaptation in means for acquiring information. Use of amplification devices, speech reading, interpreters, and forms of manual communication are examples for students who are deaf or hard of hearing. Use of residual vision, enlarged text, braille, cassette tapes, optical devices, and conversions from text to speech on computer disks are examples for students with visual impairment.

Information storage and retrieval. In school, students and teachers use writing and keyboarding as means for managing information—students take notes during lectures, students write papers and answer questions to demonstrate understanding, and students use computers to produce hard-copy documents. In family and community settings, individuals use written communication to manage grocery lists, to communicate messages to others, to organize their time through development of calendars and activity lists, and do tasks at work.

For some students with physical or multiple disabilities, the act of using paper and pencil for storing and managing information may not be viable. They may not have the strength or dexterity required, or they may have a sensory impairment that prevents them from seeing and using text. Therefore, they need modified means for storing and retrieving information.

Assistive technologies and augmentative and alternative communication devices can play a critical role in assisting students in storing and retrieving information. The use of portable word processors, modified computers (e.g., voice-recorded input and output on computer; synthesized speech; voice activation), alternative keyboards, and tape recorders are some basic considerations. A student may also elicit the aid of a peer for notetaking and related activities. The use of these technologies and devices allows students means for organizing and storing this information in ways that ease their ability to retrieve it when desired. Students will require specialized curriculum in order to develop necessary knowledge and skills.

Communication of printed information to others. The most common means for communicating information to others in schools is through handwritten assignments, essays, or reports. As previously mentioned, many students with disabilities experience significant difficulties in communicating via writing, and curriculum that represents alternative knowledge and skills needs to be developed and implemented. Again, assistive technologies and augmentative and alternative communication devices can play a major role in overcoming the barriers to learning and achievement in school, family, and community activities. The use of computers and printers comes to mind first, if students can keyboard at a speed and with accuracy that is functional. Accommodations may be as basic as allowing students to tape-record their assignments, allowing them to give oral rather than written presentations, or allowing students to act something out rather than having to write it on paper. These accommodations not only serve to address the communication needs of the students, but also are responsive to the multiple intelligences (Gardner, 1983) present in the classroom. Students may require specialized curriculum in the access, operation, and functional use of these tools. Again, this specialized curriculum is represented in students' course of study or curricula map, and through IEP goals.

Students with physical or multiple disabilities may participate in curriculum in modified means of communication and task performance, the fourth option, on a daily basis. The curriculum may include all five areas outlined here under Option 4, or a selected few. Teachers', service providers', and parents' willingness to work collaboratively to support students' access to and participation in this highly specialized curriculum, and their openness to trying new technologies and devices, are key ingredients to students' success in this curriculum. Their willingness also greatly increases the likelihood of the skills and understandings developed in this curricular area being generalized to support students' active participation and learning in the general education curriculum, in the life skills curriculum, and in different life roles.

Fundamental Curricular Domain 1: Self-Determination

Field and Hoffman (1994) define self-determination as "one's ability to define and achieve goals based on a foundation of knowing and valuing oneself" (p. 164). They present a model of the kinds of affective, cognitive, and behavioral activity that affect the extent of self-determination that a person will achieve (Figure 5–11). It serves as a guide for curriculum development and implementation in self-determination. The model includes five major components: (1) know yourself, (2) value yourself, (3) plan, (4) act, and (5) experience outcomes and learn. Through consideration of each, the IEP team can work with students to develop affective, cognitive, and behavioral knowledge and skills to strengthen the extent of self-determination.

One instructional way to support student development of self-determination is student use of a Self-Advocacy Notebook. The notebook can be based on the questions presented in Figure 5–12 with the student responding to the items as appropriate. The notebook can be used as a means of introduction to the new case manager and special education support team when a student moves to a new program or school, or is working with a new service provider. The student can use it as a basis for making presentations to peers and teachers in which the student explains his/her disability and how it has affected his/her life. The items

FIGURE 5–11
Self-determination

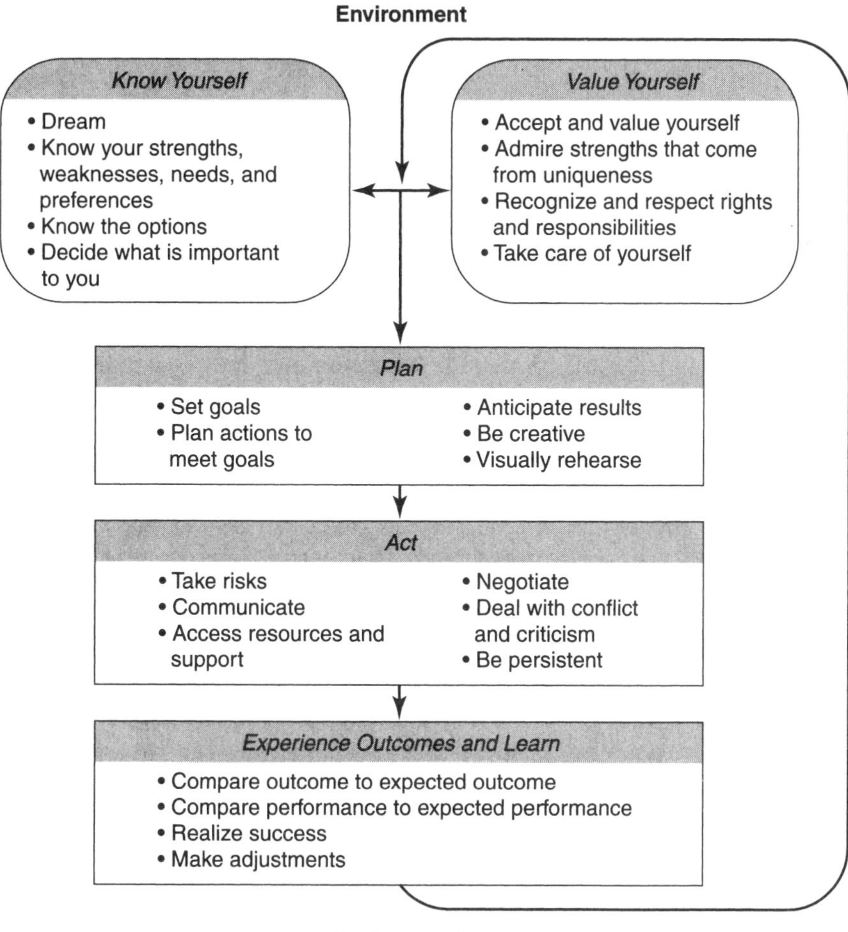

Note. From "Development of a Model of Self-Determination," by S. Field and A. Hoffman, 1994, *Career Development for Exceptional Individuals, 17*(2), p. 16. Copyright 1994 by CDEI. Reprinted with permission.

included in Figure 5–12 can be used as a basis for developing a self-determination curriculum for students and for determining IEP goals.

Fundamental Curricular Domain 2: Transition Education

Many students with physical or multiple disabilities experience significant difficulties generalizing and transferring what they have learned to new environments. For example, students may learn to demonstrate specific knowledge and skills when working with a special education support provider in a protective environment but may have extreme difficulty transferring or generalizing that skill in community-based work environments or some other transition point (e.g., can make change when purchasing items in a classroom store, but have difficulty making change when purchasing items in a community store). Because of the difficulties with transfer and generalization, formal transition curriculum becomes of extreme importance to these students.

Transition as a component of the life skills curriculum represents all forms of transition, not just transition from school to work. Views of transition in the schools are now widening to encompass the view that there is not just one transition in life that deserves attention, but many transitions. Emerging models (Bigge, Stump, et. al., 1999; Sitlington, Clark, & Kolstoe, 2000; and others) contend that transition from the K–12 school program to adult living in the community is but one of these many transitions.

Sitlington, Clark, and Kolstoe (2000) present a "Comprehensive Transition Education Model" to

FIGURE 5–12
Framework for a personal self-advocacy book

SECTION I
All About Me

_______________ full name
_______________ age
_______________ persons I live with
_______________ city of residence
_______________ school attending (year of attendance)
_______________ favorite color
_______________ favorite food
_______________ favorite school subject
_______________ name of homeroom teacher
_______________ classes I am taking
_______________ best person to call in an emergency
_______________ phone number where I can reach this contact
_______________ hobbies and things I collect
_______________ special interests I enjoy
_______________ favorite television program
_______________ types of music I enjoy
_______________ what kind of pets I have, if any
_______________ household responsibilities

_____ I do/don't know my complete address and telephone number from memory
_____ It is safe/not safe for me to be left alone in a room unattended for brief periods of time
_____ I need to wear/don't need to wear eyeglasses to improve my vision
_____ My hearing is normal/has problems
_____ My balance is adequate/good/of concern
_____ I am able/not able to manage stairs
_____ I need/do not need assistance for walking
_____ I need/do not need assistance for bathrooming
_____ I need/do not need assistance with eating
_____ I am allergic to _______________ / no known allergies
_____ I have a fear of _______________
_____ One thing about me you should know in order to work with me better is _______________

SECTION II
Helpful Information at School

_____ I am able/not able to write independently
_____ I am able/not able to copy off the board
_____ I am able to take notes in class/need a note-taker or copy of peer notes
_____ I rely on a computer for completing written assignments
_____ I rely on dictating my answers to an adult or another student
_____ I need/do not need my assignments modified in length
_____ I often/seldom need extra time allowed for me to complete and turn in assignments
_____ I am better at giving verbal/written answers
_____ I am able to use a computer independently/with a little assistance/with a great deal of assistance
_____ I am able to use a computer after it is loaded and booted up
_____ I am able to use a standard keyboard/modified keyboard
_____ I am able/not able to use a mouse
_____ I am able to read along in classes with the existing materials/need to be read to by an adult or peer
_____ It is easier/not easier for me to see enlarged print
_____ I am able to find my way to classes on my own/need assistance getting to my classes
_____ I learn best in small groups/one-to-one
_____ I am able/not able to concentrate in large groups
_____ I learn best by doing/seeing/listening
_____ I remember best by saying it aloud to myself/having it repeated to me aloud/having it demonstrated to me over and over
_____ I am able/not able to keep track of my belongings at school

Note. Courtesy of Cheryl Katz, Plymouth, Minnesota.

FIGURE 5–12
(Continued)

_____ I am able/not able to keep track of my assignments
_____ I feel responsible for getting my assignments to and from school each day/need help getting assignments back and forth
_____ I am able/not able to get things out of my backpack without assistance
_____ I feel I am able/not able to ask questions when I am not clear on what I am supposed to do

SECTION III
Personal Care Management
_____ I would like a man/woman/either to help me with managing my personal needs
_____ I am able/not able to get myself out of bed in the morning
_____ I am able to wake to an alarm clock/I need another person to wake me up in the morning
_____ I am/am not at my best in the morning (I am quick or slow to wake up completely)
_____ I am able/not able to wash my face and brush my teeth (need minimal or a great deal of assistance)
_____ I know/don't know how to use mouthwash
_____ I am able/not able to schedule my own dental appointments
_____ I am able/not able to wash and dry my own hands (need minimal or a great deal of assistance)
_____ I am able/not able to use the toilet on my own (I need help with managing clothing, getting on or off toilet, wiping, flushing)
_____ I can/can't use a urinal
_____ I need/don't need a urinal bottle
_____ I feel/do not feel secure being left alone on the toilet (I need someone or a bar to hold on to for stability)
_____ I do/don't need assistance with bathing/showering (need equipment such as a shower chair, backbrush)
_____ I do/don't need assistance with washing my hair
_____ I do/don't need assistance with combing, brushing, and styling my hair
_____ I am able/not able to make good independent choices about what clothes to wear for school and play
_____ I am/am not fully aware of special clothing to wear during the winter months
_____ I am/am not aware of color choices in clothes that go well together without being told by others
_____ I can/cannot choose my own clothing
_____ I need/do not need help getting dressed and/or undressed
_____ I need/do not need help with outer garments (boots, hat, gloves, coat)
_____ I am/am not able to access the school lunch line
_____ I am able/not able to feed myself (special needs: food must be cut up, milk/juice containers need to be opened, need specific utensil and or cup/straw, must avoid certain foods, food allergies, history of choking, more time allotted for eating)
_____ I manage to keep food off my face, using my napkin, with or without being reminded or encouragment from others around me
_____ I am able/not able to manage caring for my nose when it is running
_____ I recognize/do not recognize when my face and/or hands are dirty and need washing without being told by an adult
_____ I am able/not able to manage shaving
_____ I can/cannot take medications independently
_____ I am able/not able to manage feminine hygiene needs
_____ I am capable/not capable of using deodorant
_____ I can/cannot clean my eyeglasses
_____ I can/cannot manage caring for my hearing aids
_____ I feel/do not feel capable of purchasing my own health and beauty products without assistance
_____ I am able/not able to apply makeup
_____ I recognize/do not recognize when my clothing needs washing or repair

SECTION IV
Responsibilities and Community Access
_____ I am able/not able to work on homework assignments without assistance
_____ I am able/not able to recall what subjects I have homework in without relying on other adults
_____ I attempt/do not attempt to get my homework completed daily and returned the next day
_____ I remember/do not remember to study for tests without reminding
_____ I currently have/do not have a part-time job
_____ I am interested/not interested in working at this time

(Continued)

FIGURE 5–12
(*Continued*)

_____ I have/do not have specific career interests
_____ I have/have not used public transportation independently
_____ I plan/do not plan to learn to drive
_____ I am able/not able to call Metro Mobility for a ride
_____ I currently do/do not stay home alone without the presence of a caretaker
_____ I do/do not access my local neighborhood alone
_____ I do/do not access a local shopping mall independently
_____ I feel/do not feel comfortable being out in the local community with a friend
_____ I would/would not like the opportunity to access the neighborhood or local community on my own
_____ I am aware/not aware of where to go in the community to purchase various goods and services (post office, grocery store, hardware store, department store, etc.)
_____ I attend/do not attend school functions and events
_____ I go/do not go to movies
_____ I have/do not have a library card
_____ I know/do not know how to access a public library
_____ I am able/not able to use an elevator independently (need help pushing the button to my floor)
_____ I can/cannot find my way around in a grocery store and make simple purchases
_____ I have/do not have experience cooking simple foods (e.g., hard-boiled egg, spaghetti)
_____ I can/cannot read a simple recipe and fix a simple meal
_____ I know/do not know how to use a measuring cup and measuring spoons
_____ I know/do not know how to operate the stove, oven, microwave
_____ I am able/not able to fix a frozen dinner independently
_____ I can/cannot fix a sandwich
_____ I can/cannot pour liquids from bottles and containers
_____ I can/cannot locate expiration dates on foods and/or medications
_____ I am able/not able to clean up spills
_____ I have/have not been able to wash the floor
_____ I have/have not been able to vacuum
_____ I can/cannot select an item to eat at a restaurant from the menu independently
_____ I recognize/do not recognize the need to get exercise regularly
_____ I am/am not aware of the types of foods that are good and not good for me nutritionally
_____ I am aware/not aware of my weight gains and losses
_____ I am responsible/not responsible for helping to care for a pet or younger sibling
_____ I know/do not know how to do laundry (separate dark- and light-colored clothing, load a washing machine, add soap, and turn on)
_____ I know/do not know how to determine which clothes are machine washable and which ones need dry cleaning
_____ I know/do not know how to operate a clothes dryer
_____ I am able/not able to fold clothes coming out of the dryer
_____ I am able/not able to put away my own clothes
_____ I have/have not been to a laundromat
_____ I have/have not used vending machines for soda, candy, to make change
_____ I am able/not able to identify the values of coins and dollar bills
_____ I am able/not able to add up combinations of money
_____ I am able/not able to make change (use next-dollar-up strategy)
_____ I am able/not able to tell time as it relates to my day
_____ I am able/not able to read a schedule to locate specific information (*TV Guide,* bus, train, and plane schedules)
_____ I am able/not able to use a newspaper to find out information about movies and events (locations and scheduling)
_____ I am able/not able to locate dates on a calendar (special occasions, appointments)
_____ I am able/not able to use a telephone independently to make local calls
_____ I am able/not able to use a telephone independently to make long-distance calls
_____ I know/don't know how to locate information in a telephone book
_____ I know/don't know how to dial operator, information (411) and/or emergency assistance (911)
_____ I am able/not able to speak clearly enough to be understood over the phone
_____ I am capable/not capable of selecting appropriate clothes to purchase at the store (size, fit, machine washable vs. dry clean only)
_____ I am aware/not aware of services available to the disabled (e.g., books on tape, Department of Rehabilitation Services, SSI)

guide families, teachers, and transition teams when they are contemplating and implementing a transition curriculum for their students. It prepares teachers and others for "determining what a student needs to meet his or her transition services needs in the areas of instruction, community experiences, employment, and other postschool adult living activities" (p. 26). These transition education specialists direct family and teacher attention to multiple "exit points and outcomes." Focus on life transitions needs to begin as early as possible (Clark, Carlson, Fisher, Cook, & D'Alonzo, 1991; Clark, Field, Patton, Brolin, & Sitlington, 1994; Halpern, 1994). Rather than focusing only on transitions from high school, or exit outcomes for high school, the Comprehensive Transition Education Model (Sitlington, Clark, & Kolstoe, 2000) identifies exit outcomes to target along the way to high school and even after high school. It defines "exit points" (e.g., exit to preschool programs; exit to middle/junior high school) and to these expected exit points adds outcomes such as community participation and age-appropriate self-determination that correspond to certain developmental/life phases of the individual as shown in Table 5–6.

This model directs teacher and family attention to an organization and implementation of curriculum and services that focus on "knowledge and skills domains." The knowledge and skills domains specified are almost identical to the areas identified in Figure 5–1, the model of curricular options. There is a high degree of agreement in the field as to the categories of knowledge and skills content and outcomes that should be the focus of transitional school curriculum for students with disabilities. Here the focus is on:

> knowledge and skill *outcomes* rather than knowledge and skill curriculum *content*. . . . Nine domains are proposed as the framework for responding to the Individualized Education Program (IEP) requirement under the IDEA for determining what a student needs to meet his or her transition services needs in the areas of instruction, community experiences, employment, and other postschool adult living activities . . . :
>
> **Knowledge and skills domains**
>
> Communication and Academic Performance
> Self-Determination
> Interpersonal Relationships
> Integrated Community Participation
> Health and Fitness
> Independent/Interdependent Daily Living
> Leisure and Recreation
> Employment
> Further Education and Training (Sitlington, Clark, & Kolstoe, 2000, pp. 26–27, emphasis added)

To accompany the Comprehensive Transition Education Model, Sitlington, Clark, and Kolstoe (2000) identify education and service delivery systems that might be appropriate, as the situation determines. The model also "reflects the connection between knowledge and skill domains and the multiple service delivery alternatives that can be considered in any individual's transition planning" (p. 29). The model identifies representational education and service delivery systems that might be involved in collaborative responsibilities

TABLE 5–6
Developmental/Life Phases and Corresponding Exit Points

Developmental/Life Phases	Exit Points
Infant/toddler/and home training	Exit to preschool programs and integrated community participation
Elementary school	Exit to middle school/junior high school programs and integrated community participation
Middle school/junior high school	Exit to high school programs, entry-level employment, age-appropriate self-determination, and integrated community participation
High school	Exit to postsecondary education or entry-level employment, adult and continuing education, full-time homemaker, self-determined quality of life, and integrated community participation
Postsecondary education	Exit to specialized, technical, professional, or managerial employment, graduate or professional school programs, adult and continuing education, full-time homemaker, self-determined quality of life, and integrated community participation

Note. From *Transition Education and Services for Adolescents with Disabilities*, (p. 28) by P. L. Sitlington, G. M. Clark, and O. P. Kolstoe, 2000. Boston: Allya & Bocon.

and efforts to plan and support the transition processes, as needed, for the various phases:

Education and service delivery systems
Home and neighborhood
Family and friends
Public and private infant/toddler programs
General education with related and support services
Special education with related and support services
Generic community organization and agencies (employment, health, legal, housing, financial)
Specific community organizations and agencies (crisis services, time-limited services, ongoing services)
Apprenticeship programs
School and community work-based learning programs
Postsecondary vocational or applied technology programs
Community colleges
Four-year colleges and universities
Graduate or professional schools
Adult and continuing education/transition (p. 28)

This model is appropriate for students with physical or multiple disabilities with some additions for consideration. We find that students who have mobility, dexterity, communication, health, learning, and other accommodation needs benefit from transition education and services at other times as well (Bigge, Stump, et al., 1999). Some special circumstance transitions include:

- Moving between hospital teaching, home teaching, and school classroom teaching;
- Moving between learning face-to-face with teachers to learning online from teachers and through the Internet;
- Moving between special education and general education learning environments;
- Moving between school-based and community-based learning experiences;
- Moving between related service providers (e.g., physical therapists, occupational therapists, speech therapists) and their schooling.

Figure 5–13 illustrates the first kind of transition for Nicholas, a student moving between hospital teaching, home teaching, and school classroom teaching. It illus-

FIGURE 5–13
Transition from hospital and home teaching (with Nicholas)

Nicholas is an eighth grader who has suffered a traumatic brain injury. Prior to his accident, Nicholas was the photographer for the school yearbook, vice president of the computer club, and a member of the wrestling squad. Last year he fell off his skateboard while riding at a high speed on an obstacle course. The accident resulted in his need to use a wheelchair for mobility. He communicates verbally, but speaks with great effort and in more basic language. He becomes extremely agitated because he has forgotten how to do schoolwork and computer tasks he used to do easily. He also tires easily.

Nicholas has received hospital and then home teaching for the past eight months. He is now making the transition back to school, and classes. The IEP team has met and determined that he will be able to participate in his traditional program, with modifications, if a transition plan is in place to ensure gradual reintegration into the school program.

Nicholas is extremely worried about returning to the school campus. He has met with the special education teacher and his homeroom, general education teacher to plan his transition back to the school campus. Together, with Nicholas's parents, they have developed a transition plan:

(a) The eighth-grade team, in collaboration with the special education teacher, Nicholas, and his parents, will prepare an informational assembly (delivered to individual classes) for Nicholas's peers on what it means to have a brain injury. Nicholas will play as major a role as possible in explaining his situation to his peers.
(b) Nicholas will begin by attending morning classes, periods 1 through 4.
(c) Classroom accommodations will be provided (e.g., time-and-a-half for in-class assignments and tests, extended time lines for long-term assignments, in-class note-taker, use of a portable word processor for writing assignments across his curriculum).
(d) Nicholas will receive specially designed curriculum in communication, mobility, use of assistive devices, and in all core curricular areas from the special education staff, in collaboration with the general education staff.
(e) Nicholas will be allowed to leave classes 5 minutes prior to dismissal to ensure on-time arrival at the next class.
(f) Nicholas will be provided transportation to participate in after-school activities of his choice (e.g., yearbook, computer club)
(g) Nicolas will develop strategies for asking for different kinds of assistance from teachers, peers, bus drivers, and others.
(h) The team will meet in three weeks to discuss progress.

trates how transition efforts on the part of the teacher and team as well as transition education delivered to the student assisted that student in reintegrating into his school and classes and reestablishing friendship with peers.

Chapter 12 in this text emphasizes one of the kinds of transitions undertaken by students with and without disabilities: exiting from high school and exiting to community-based entry-level employment. Because of the magnitude of the transition from school to postschool employment, we devote a chapter to career and transition education. This chapter gives teachers some important pointers about teaching career and transition education. It ends with the recognition and appreciation of the wide range of knowledge and skills gained from all other curricular options that assist with career and transition education.

WORKING COLLABORATIVELY TO DETERMINE CURRICULUM NEEDS FOR INDIVIDUALS

Probably the most important considerations in designing curriculum for students are a child's current strengths, needs, and wishes, his/her parent's dreams for the child now and in the future, and state/local goals and standards set for all students. Working collaboratively with teachers, support providers, and community members is one way to ensure that curriculum is inclusive and relevant for the student. Priority performance goals for students that relate to both present performances and future goals should be identified at the outset. A multiyear matrix worksheet (Bigge, Stump, et al., 1999; Bigge, 1988 and 1991) combines these elements for curricular planning.

The multiyear matrix worksheet (Figure 5–14) guides teams into a collaboration process to provide information about an individual student for three time frames of the student's life: (a) current activities, (b) activities one year from present, and (c) projected activities three years from present or at some other point in the future. A matrix format guides thinking for each of these stages. These time frames are identified along the top of the Figure 5–14 matrix. In addition, this matrix guides teams into a systematic exploration of a student's performances and needs in various areas of curriculum. Therefore, the major curriculum options and

FIGURE 5–14
Multiyear matrix worksheet

CURRICULUM OPTIONS:	A. Present Level(s) of Performance	B. Performance Goals for One Year in the Future (IEP Goals)	C. Performance Goals for Three Years in the Future
General Education *with* Accommodations			
General Education *with* Accommodations and Modifications			
Life Skills Curriculum			
Curriculum in Modified Means of Communication and Task Performance			
Self-Determination			
Transition			

Note. Adapted from *Curriculum Based Instruction for Special Education Students* (p. 318), by J. L. Bigge, 1988, Mountain View, CA: Mayfield. Copyright 1988 by June L. Bigge. Adapted with permission.

fundamental curricular domains introduced in this text are identified along the left margin to remind readers to address them.

The use of the multiyear matrix worksheet with the team begins with describing a student's *Present Levels of Performance* (Column A). The team considers student performances, activities, or outcomes in each of the options and domains. Those items related to unique needs stemming from a student's disability are considered priority, along with related strengths of the student. By collaboratively generating this information, a holistic profile of the student is created that reflects a child's performance across home, school, and community. For example, teachers and the student may provide information concerning school performance; the parents and family members may provide information concerning community leisure activities and the student's role in family life; and the speech pathologist, teachers, parents, the student, and community members provide information concerning communication skills at home, in school, and in the community.

Next, the team skips over to Column C and identifies *Performance Goals for Three Years in the Future.* Here the procedure guides a team's attention to several years in the future in order to determine what is important for a student to be accomplishing at that time. The team uses this "futures" information (Column C) when appropriate and helpful along with information about the student's present level of performance (Column A) to determine goals for the upcoming year (Column B). This sequence resembles the concept of outcome-based education and curricular mapping in which what you teach each year builds toward designated future outcomes. In more traditional approaches, teams move directly from present levels of performance (represented by Column A) to goals for the upcoming year (represented by Column B). This more traditional approach may result in more goals set for splinter, or isolated, skills, without attention given to long-range goals and plans.

The purpose of Column C is to determine what the child should be able to do at a certain point in the future. The team collaborates to identify desired performances, activities, or outcomes for the child to accomplish by "three years into the future" or at some identified exit point. Exit points may include "upon exit from elementary school to middle school," "upon exit from high school," "in adulthood," or some other designated point in time. By looking to the future, the team's planning becomes more relevant and meaningful. Completion of these cells in the matrix may be triggered by questions such as "What kinds of performances will same-age peers display three years from the present?" "Which of these performances will present the greatest challenge to this child because of his or her disability?" "What life demands (living a healthy lifestyle, understanding legal rights, learning job skills) will this child want to be able to meet?" "What recommendations do we have for this particular student three years from the present or at some other point in the future?"

Shared information, comments, and suggestions help the student, family members, teachers, and other team members to make links between current performance and projected performance a few years in the future. These links assist the team in the immediate task of setting realistic and achievable goals for one year from the present, which, in turn, assists with attainment of goals for several years in the future.

Finally, the team works back from the information presented in this "futures" time frame in the matrix to determine *Performance Goals for One Year in the Future* (Column B). The primary questions here become "Knowing what the child does at the present time, what do we want the child to accomplish a year from now?" and "What does this student need to learn this next year that would contribute to accomplishing the projected three-year activities?" (Bigge, Stump, et al., 1999, p. 244).

Figure 5–15 presents a portion of the three-year matrix for Angie, age 10, a beginning fourth-grade student. Angie has moderate cerebral palsy of the athetoid type that causes some dexterity difficulty and requires her to use an electric wheelchair for mobility. She uses an assistive device for communication because few beyond her family, school personnel, and peers understand her speech. She experiences learning disabilities in reading and spelling. So far the team has collaborated and derived information on two of the three columns—Columns A and C, or the "current" and "three years in the future" time frames in the multiyear matrix worksheet process.

The immediate task of this team was to determine priority goals, objectives, and benchmarks for this child for the upcoming year. Because this was an effort on be-

FIGURE 5–15
Multiyear matrix worksheet for Angie

	A. Present Level(s) of Performance	B. Goals for One Year in the Future (IEP Goals)	C. Performance Goals for Three Years in the Future
1. General Education *with* Accommodations	• Achieves success in GE grade level (beginning fourth grade) curriculum in math when word problems are read to her • Incorporates art into varieties of assignments or projects once materials are specially set up • Loves to draw and paint with feet at home; will not use feet in school		• Meet grade level standards in math and read own short word problems • Draw, paint, and do other art work with feet at school, if better skilled with feet • Use computer for a variety of projects in art
2. Life Skills Curriculum	• Rarely attempts to use academics in the community, except for math • Has no consistent responsibilities for chores in the home • Loves to draw and to study about fish. Has fish tank. • Enjoys outings with family and depends on them for pushing the wheelchair, making financial transactions, and making decisions • Enjoys friends of the family; has few friends of her own away from school		• Find sales and use own money for special purchases • Select, order, and buy own food at fast food restaurants when out with family and friends • Work twice a week in the cafeteria or elsewhere in school; evaluate herself • Participate in special-interest activities in the community without the presence of family • Use public transportation • Initiate and plan activities with family and friends • Visit worksites of parents and family • Describe her own strengths and need for doing well in high school

Note. From *Curriculum Based Instruction for Special Education Students* (p. 318), by J. L. Bigge, 1988, Mountain View, CA: Mayfield. Copyright 1988 by J. L. Bigge. Adapted with permission.

half of a student with possible special education needs, the team concentrated on curriculum options and domains where it was suspected that Angie would experience difficulties. The team also noted information about some of Angie's strengths that might be useful in their deliberations. They found themselves identifying pieces of relevant information about Angie's current level of performance in Column A and then jumping to Column C to identify where they hoped Angie would be three years from then in regard to that piece of information. Next was the challenge of studying information in Columns A and C to determine which performance goals would be among the priorities to meet the child's unique needs through curriculum for the upcoming year. Some of these goals for the upcoming year would be translated into IEP goals.

DEVELOPING COURSES OF STUDY AND CRAFTING A CURRICULA MAP

Awareness of the curricular components available to students creates a knowledge base from which courses

TABLE 5–7
Course of Study (with GW)

	Curricular Areas	Sources of Curriculum	Service Delivery
General Education *with* Accommodations	Mathematics with assistance in reading the material. Art with physical assistance as student requests.	General education curriculum and local standards	General education classroom
General Education *with* Accommodations and Modifications	General education objectives at reduced levels of complexity in: English, Language Arts, History, Social Science, Science; Junior Band/Drum	General education curriculum with standards for a lower grade level Supplemental district syllabi Special remedial programs	General education classroom with collaboration of general education and special education teachers
Life Skills Curriculum	Functional academics in reading, writing, listening, speaking, and math applications Daily and community living skills Transition education	Embedded functional academic skills outcomes from Cronin & Patton (1993) IEP goal/objectives for daily and community living skills Career education	Integrated real-life content into general education Special education community-based learning expeditions Special education career/vocational education program and parents
Curriculum in Modified Means of Communication and Performance	Operation /use of variety of assistive technologies to "proof" typed work; Augmentative and alternative communication strategies in work settings	Simplified *WYNN Handbook* written by special education teacher Benchmarks designed by AAC specialists for community participation	Special education resource program; physical therapy evaluation for positioning & seating Collaboration of special education teacher and speech-language specialist
Self-Determination	Goal setting	Goal setting curriculum	Special education resource program
Transition	Communication skills with 10 workers	Transition curiculum/ communication	Community work setting

Note. Adapted from *Assessment, Curriculum, and Instruction for Students with Disabilities, 1st edition,* by J. L. Bigge and C. S. Stump © 1999. Reprinted with permission of Wadsworth, a division of Thomson Learning: www.Thompsonrights.com. Fax 800-730-2215.

of study for students are created, or for which curricula maps can be developed. For students with disabilities, documentation of their courses of study might include summaries of (a) curricular areas (e.g., the four options and two domains), (b) sources of the curriculum, (c) service delivery system(s) for relevant components of curriculum, and (d) extracurricular activities of the student (Bigge, Stump, et al., 1999). A curricula map can assist IEP teams in connecting current goals with long-term goals in ways that will lead to desired student outcomes in the near as well as distant future (Nolet & McLaughlin, 2000). Application of one or both of these approaches can prevent teams from only planning curriculum on a year-to-year basis and from creating an inconsistent plan that fails to embrace long-term needs and aspirations. A course of study or curricula map can guide the team as the child moves through his or her school career, and can ensure that teaching and learning is strategic and in alignment with overall desired outcomes of schooling for the individual student.

Table 5–7 is an example of a course of study for GW, a student who has a severe coordination problem that affects his right arm, shoulder, and leg, as well as having moderate cognitive impairment and partially

TABLE 5–8
Curricula Map for Selected Area

OPTION 3: LIFE SKILLS CURRICULUM			
	Beginning Skills	Intermediate Skills	Advanced Skills
Area: Financial Management	• Create a simple budget • Use bank services • Purchase items and maintain a checkbook	• Create a more sophisticated budget that includes rent, day-to-day purchases and loans • Use a credit card and establish a good credit rating • Plan for and make major purchases involving layaway and loans	• Manage a sophisticated budget • Plan for long-term financial needs • Maintain credit and good standing with bank and loaning institutions

intelligible speech. GW is a high school sophomore. Notice that his life skills curriculum to meet his unique needs is infused into the general education curriculum as well as being taught in a special education resource room. This is made possible through collaborations between general and special education teachers, student, and parents.

Table 5–8 presents a curricula map in the area of financial management for a student with multiple disabilities.

The establishment of courses of study or curricula maps will guide IEP and Individualized Transition Program (ITP) teams in setting goals and objectives that are inclusive and reflect a systematic curriculum. Without a course of study or curricula map, the curriculum for students with disabilities may lack a goal-centered approach and be strongly influenced by teachers or programs. Proceeding without a cohesive curriculum that builds skills and understandings from year to year and that is based on long-term goals for a student will most likely result in a failure to achieve desired outcomes.

SUMMARY AND CONCLUSION

This chapter addressed four curricular options and two fundamental curricular domains available to students with physical, health, or multiple disabilities. The four options are (1) general education curriculum with accommodations, (2) general education curriculum with accommodations and modifications, (3) life skills curriculum, and (4) curriculum in modified means of communication and performance, and the two fundamental curricular domains are (1) self-determination and (2) transition. All components represent viable curricular considerations for students with disabilities.

At the base of all curricular decision-making is the general education curriculum. Putting the general education intended curriculum at the base of curricular planning allows students with disabilities to meet, to the degree possible, the standards expected of other students who participate in the general education curriculum. For students with physical or multiple disabilities, it may mean doing this with appropriate accommodations. If and when appropriate, the complexity of the general education curriculum can be modified to meet the learning needs of students with disabilities. In addition to participating with nondisabled peers and other peers with disabilities in the general education curriculum to different degrees, students with disabilities may benefit from participation in other curricula that address their unique needs or that are taught more directly and intensely. Therefore, life skills curriculum, with subcomponents of functional academics and daily and community living skills, becomes an option to consider. Additionally, a curriculum in modified means of communication and performance enhances students' abilities to effectively use their supplementary aids and other technologies to participate in, and gain from, the other curricular options—and the range of major life experiences. Finally, the inclusion of curriculum in self-determination and transition for all students with disabilities is essential.

Special educators are encouraged to take leadership in guiding consideration of all curricular components when designing a course of study or curricula map for a student with disabilities. In combination, the curricular components create curricula reflective of life demands, commonly accepted goals and outcomes for schooling, and the unique learning profiles of students with disabilities.

QUESTIONS FOR DISCUSSION

1. How will you ensure that a student's IEP and course of study or curricula map will be the result of consideration of curriculum from the four curricular options and two curricular domains, as appropriate?
2. How will you work with general educators to ensure the inclusion of accommodations and, as appropriate, modifications, in the general education curriculum?
3. Beginning with a general education standard or an associated student learning outcome or benchmark in a curricular domain of your choice, identify possible difficulties a student with a physical or multiple disabilities may experience in meeting the outcome stated. Next, identify the types of accommodations a student may need to access the standard. Now, identify how you would modify that standard to reflect the student's learning needs and the elements of the other curricular components that could be considered to support student achievement of the modified standard.
4. What steps would you take to ensure that a student has curricula that allow him or her to gain expertise in the use of assistive or adapted devices for activities at school, in the home, and in the community?
5. How would you ensure that curricular plans for all students with disabilities include outcomes in self-determination and transition?

FOCUS ON THE NET

Association for Supervision and Curriculum Development
http://www.ascd.org/

This site includes the ASCD Education Bulletin, press releases, hot topics, and tutorials on curriculum integration, performance assessment, and inclusion.

CEC: ERIC Clearinghouse on Disabilities and Gifted Education
http://ericec.org/abouterc.htm

ERIC CEC gathers and disseminates the professional literature, information, and resources on the education and development of individuals of all ages who have disabilities and/or who are gifted. ERIC stands for Educational Resources Information Center.

Center for Change in Transition Services
http://www.depts.washington.edu/transctr/trs_links.htm

This site focuses on changing practices in the transition from school to adult roles for students with disabilities. Includes student stories of transition from school to work, and descriptions of exemplary programs.

Education World
http://www.education – world.com/

This site provides extensive information concerning lesson planning, curriculum, teacher lessons, sites, cutting-edge schools and their programs, technology, school issues, administrators, site review, books in education, and financial planning.

ERIC/CASS
http://www.uncg.edu/edu/ericcass/libhome.htm

This site leads to ERIC (Educational Resource Information Center) and Internet access to the ERIC database. The ERIC/CASS Virtual Library is an online collection of full-text materials developed in order to provide relevant research and materials on current topics of interest. It is intended as a resource for anyone concerned about education issues: educators, administrators, parents, students, and community members.

Guide for Educators
http://school.discovery.com/schrockguide/

This is one of the most extensive sites providing resources for teachers. Resources, curricula suggestions, lesson plans, and other activities are provided across grade levels and disciplines.

National Center for Educational Outcomes
http://www.coled.umn.edu/NCEO

The National Center of Educational Outcomes site at the University of Minnesota offers extensive information on how the performance of students with disabilities is being assessed as related to established general education curricular standards and what can be done to accommodate students with disabilities in the curriculum and in testing situations.

National Institute for Urban School Improvement
http://www.educ.org/urban/publicat.html

This site is sponsored by the National Institute for Urban School Improvement and offers a library, e-news, and listing of activities specifically addressing educational practice in urban settings. A special section is provided on working with students with disabilities, and the adoption of inclusive practices.

REFERENCES

Archer, A., & Gleason, M. (1994). *Skills for school success: Teacher guide.* North Billerica, MA: Curriculum Associates.

Bigge, J. L. (1988). *Curriculum based instruction for special education students.* Mountain View, CA: Mayfield.

Bigge, J. L. (1991). *Teaching individuals with physical and multiple disabilities* (3rd ed.). Upper Saddle River, NJ: Merrill/Prentice Hall.

Bigge, J. L., Stump, C. S., Spagna, M. E., & Silberman, R. K. (1999). *Curriculum, assessment, and instruction for students with disabilities.* Belmont, CA: Wadsworth.

Butterworth, J., Hagner, D., Kiernan, W. E., & Schalock, R. L. (1996). Natural supports in the work-place: Defining an agenda for research and practice. *JASH, 21*(3), 103–113.

Clark, G. M., Carlson, B. C., Fisher, S., Cook, I. D., & D'Alonzo, B. J. (1991). Career development for students with disabilities in elementary schools. A positions statement of the Division on Career Development and Transition. *Career Development for Exceptional Individuals, 14,* 109–120.

Clark, G. M., Field, S., Patton, J. R., Brolin, D. E., & Sitlington, P. L. (1994). Life skills instruction: A necessary component for all students with disabilities. A position statement of the Division on Career Develoment and Transition. *Career Development for Exceptional Individuals, 17,* 125–134.

Cronin, M. E., & Patton, J. R. (1993). *Life skills instruction for all students with special needs: A practical guide for integrating real-life content into the curriculum.* Austin, TX: PRO-ED.

Falvey , M. A., & Grenot-Scheyer, M. (1995). Instructional strategies. In M.A. Falvey (Ed.), *Inclusive and heterogeneous schooling: Assessment, curriculum, and instruction* (pp. 131–158). Baltimore: Brookes.

Field, S., & Hoffman, A. (1994), Development of a model for self-determination. *Caveer Development for Exceptional Individuals, 17*(2), 8–21.

Gardner, H. (1983). *Frames of mind: The theory of multiple intelligences.* New York: Basic Books.

Gersten, R., & Baker, S. (2000) What we know about effective instructional practices for English-language learners. *Exceptional Children, 66*(4), 454–470.

Giangreco, M. E. (1997). Persistent questions about curriculum for students with severe disabilities. *Physical Disabilities: Education and Related Services, 15*(2), 53–56.

Giangreco, M. E., & Putnam, J. (1991). Supporting the education of students with severe disabilities in regular education environments. In L. H., Meyer, C. A. Peck, & L. Brown (Eds.), *Critical issues in the lives of people with severe disabilities* (pp. 245–270). Baltimore: Brookes.

Halpern, A. S. (1994). The transition of youth with disabilities to adult life. A position statement of the Division on Career Development and Transition. *Career Development for Exceptional Individuals, 17,* 115–124.

Hitchcock, C. G. (2001). Balanced instructional support and challenge in university-designed learning environments. *Journal of Special Education Technology, 16*(4), 23–30.

Individuals with Disabilities Education Act (IDEA) of 1997, PL 105-17, 20 U.S.C.A. § 1400 *et seq.* (West 1998).

Loyd, R. J., & Brolin, D. E. (1997). *Life centered career education: Modified curriculum for individuals with moderate disabilities.* Reston, VA: Council for Exceptional Children.

Matlock, L., Fielder, K., & Walsh, D. (2001). Building the foundation for standards-based instruction for all students. *Teaching Exceptional Children, 33*(5), 68–73.

Myles, B. S., & Simpson, R. L. (2001). Understanding the hidden curriculum: An essential social skills curriculum for children and youth with Asperger syndrome. *Intervention in School and Clinic, 36*(5), 279–286.

Nolet, V., & McLaughlin, M. J. (2000). *Accessing the general curriculum: Including students with disabilities in standards-based reform.* Thousand Oaks, CA: Corwin Press.

Polloway, E. A., Patton, J. R., & Serna, L. (2001). *Strategies for teaching learners with special needs.* Upper Saddle River, NJ: Prentice Hall.

Rivera, C. (1994). Is it real for all kids? *Harvard Educational Review, 64,* 55–75.

Sitlington, P. L., Clark, G. M., & Kolstoe, O. P. (2000). *Transition education and services for adolescents with disabilities.* Boston: Allyn and Bacon.

Snell, M. (Ed.) (1993). *Instruction of students with severe disabilities.* New York: Merrill.

Walsh, J. M. (2001). Betting the "big picture" of IEP goals and state standards. *Teaching Exceptional Children, 33*(5), 18–26.

Wehman, P. (1996). *Life beyond the classroom: Transition strategies for young people with disabilities* (2nd ed.). Baltimore: Brookes.

Westling, D. L., & Fox, L. (1995). *Teaching students with severe disabilities.* Upper Saddle River, NJ: Prentice Hall.

Task and Situation Analysis

SHERWOOD J. BEST
JUNE L. BIGGE

CHAPTER 6

KNOWLEDGE AND SKILLS

After you have read this chapter, you will be able to:

1. **Understand the relationship of curricular scope and sequence to task and situation analysis.**
2. **Use task analysis as a process and a product.**
3. **Use task analysis for formative and summative assessment purposes.**
4. **Determine the kinds and amounts of assistance needed for promoting independent function.**
5. **Use shaping as a technique to promote independent function.**
6. **Create task and situation analyses for a variety of curricular areas.**
7. **Assist students with physical or multiple disabilities in using task analyses to learn self-care routines, analyze bodies of information, and solve personal access challenges.**

Teachers and others who provide services to students with physical, health, or multiple disabilities may be familiar with specific curricula in content areas such as language arts, mathematics, social studies, and/or science. Different content areas present specific concepts at certain grade levels, which is called the **scope** of the curriculum. For example, students in fourth grade are frequently introduced to the concept and computation of fractions, which would be part of the scope of mathematics curriculum in that grade. However, *fractions* is a global term that includes a number of skills. The hierarchy of skills that are needed to master a specific concept is called the **sequence**. Mastering computation of fractions would follow this sequence:

- Addition and subtraction of simple fractions with common denominators;
- Addition and subtraction of simple fractions with mixed denominators;
- Addition and subtraction of mixed fractions with common denominators;
- Addition and subtraction of mixed fractions with mixed denominators;
- Multiplication and division of fractions;
- Decimal fractions. (Bartel, 1990, pp. 305–306)

However, teachers know that students who enter fourth grade may have already acquired some of the skills necessary to master fraction computation. Other students may lack prerequisite skills, including defining fractions and using a number line, an array, or a geometric figure as ways to conceptualize fractions (Bartel, 1990, p. 305). Teachers need to determine which students possess a knowledge base in a particular content area and which students would benefit from additional instruction. To assist in this determination and provide instruction that most closely matches the needs of the learner, **task analysis** is an important technique.

*

PURPOSES OF TASK AND SITUATION ANALYSIS

Process and Product

Task analysis is among the most valuable tools available to teachers of individuals with physical, health, or multiple disabilities—and to the students themselves. It is defined as "*the content and sequence of skills, behaviors, and activities to be taught through instruction*" (Bigge & Best, 2001, p. 122) and involves breaking skills, behaviors, or activities into teachable units. Examination of this definition reveals that task analysis is both a process and a product. As a process, task analysis is a way to break complex skills or activities into smaller steps. The process of task analysis may result in something that is organized as a product. As a product, task analysis is a written series of steps which reflect the content and order of instruction of a complex skill or activity.

Because task analysis is based on the notion that learning is cumulative (skills are built upon one another), it is compatible with curricular sequences frequently found in grade-level textbooks (Mercer & Mercer, 2001). It performs the additional function of providing a means whereby teachers can examine a skill area within a sequence-based text and break that skill into subskills (a sequence within a sequence). Therefore, performing task analyses assists teachers and others to identify student strengths and needs, observe and record the learning process, prioritize instructional goals and objectives, and plan for the sequence of instruction (Downing, & Demchak, 2002; Rivera & Smith, 1997).

Most people use task analysis processes and products in their everyday lives but do not necessarily label them as such. For example, one of the authors recently taught her daughter to drive a car. Although the outcome was for the daughter to drive a car successfully, safely, and independently, many steps had to be mastered before this complex goal was reached. Initial tasks included learning the sequence of steps involved in handling the clutch, accelerator, and brake on a car with a standard shift mechanism. This skill had been practiced until it had become automatic to the author, but it was an unfamiliar and unnatural experience for the daughter. To assist in the teaching/learning process, the steps in using the brake, clutch, and accelerator were taught in sequence and then practiced. This sequence of skills was first mastered in a large empty parking lot where little attention had to be directed toward other vehicles. Later, shifting gears, steering, and maneuvering the car through traffic were added to the larger goal of driving. In this example, leaving out necessary steps in the task analysis could have had serious consequences!

If the goal of driving a car was applied to an adolescent with a physical disability, the sequence of using the clutch, accelerator, and brake would need to be modified if the student was unable to use the lower body. Hand controls would be substituted for foot pedals, and the sequence of skills would be adjusted to fit this adapted technology. However, the outcome would remain the ability to drive a car successfully, safely, and independently.

Task Analysis as an Assessment Tool

Task analysis can be considered an extension of assessment. It is used when we assume that the reason someone is not accomplishing or may not be able to accomplish a particular task or activity is because of the inability to accomplish one or more of its parts. Sometimes it is not always obvious which part is problematic. By breaking down a task into its component parts, teachers can determine the problem more precisely. It is important to remember that task analysis also provides a profile of student strengths by revealing what a student *can* do. Task analysis, therefore, is not always about uncovering deficits.

Every task, simple or complex, can be broken down into as many components and subcomponents as is necessary. The key to the number of components and subcomponents corresponds to the **size of steps (response units)** that are teachable to certain individuals. When a student has a physical disability, for instance, the steps of a motor task may be broken into smaller steps than the same task might be for someone who does not have as much trouble with motor tasks. However, task parts need not always be written as a product; they may be present only in the mind.

Task analysis has value as a **formative assessment**. Formative assessments "are used to inform instructional practice [and] provide information about how a student is doing as instruction is delivered and [they inform teachers] about needed instructional modifications" (Bigge, Stump, Spagna, & Silberman, 1999, p. 182). Task analysis also functions as **summative assessment,** which tells "what a student has learned as a result of instruction" (Bigge, Stump, et al., 1999, p. 182). Many standardized achievement tests, published diagnostic tests, criterion-referenced instruments, and developmental scales are themselves the result of task analysis. Administration of such instruments may yield records about what tasks or kinds of tasks students performed and did not perform. Results of unsuccessful trials are pinpointed as areas needing some other intervention.

Order of Tasks

Generally, task analyses are developed so that the order of instruction is in logical order, from top to bottom or from first to last (**forward chaining**). For example, a teacher might establish the goal of teaching students how to perform subtraction problems involving three-digit minuends (the numeral from which a numeral is subtracted) and two-digit subtrahends (the numeral being subtracted). Instruction would begin with basic single-digit subtraction facts and proceed in first-to-last order until the goal was reached. Table 6–1 provides an inventory of subtraction problems that could be used as a task analysis whose steps would be taught in first-to-last order.

At times, depending on the individual situation of the student, instruction may be given in a different order (Meier, 1992). Instruction may begin at the bottom of the series of steps and proceed, in order, to the top (**backward chaining**). For example, a teacher might want to instruct a student to perform the self-care skill of pulling up a pair of elastic-waist pants. First, the steps in the sequence leading to the goal of having the pants pulled up would be developed. Upon examining the task analysis, the instructor would notice that adjusting the pants around the waist is the last step in the process. Instruction would begin with the teacher performing all steps but adjusting the pants, which would be completed by the student. After this step was mastered, the student would be required to perform the next-to-last step, followed by the last step. Instruction would proceed in this "backwards" manner. Backwards chaining is particularly useful for students who require more immediate gratification of task mastery. Figure 6–1 provides a task analysis whose steps would be taught in last-to-first order.

Task analysis is a tool that can be used with different theoretical approaches. It is a basic strategy that teachers use regardless of their theoretical positions about assessment, curriculum, and instruction for children and adults with physical or multiple disabilities.

Task analysis examples in this chapter are grouped by some broad similarities. The first group of five examples illustrates how the task analysis process can be helpful to teachers of students with physical or multiple disabilities. The second group of three examples illustrates task analysis as a product. The third group introduces the concept of situation analysis and introduces two variations of the ecological inventory strategy. Finally, the last four examples illustrate task analysis uses to be taught to the students themselves as tools for their life management.

TASK ANALYSIS PROCESS

Task analysis, in the first group of examples, facilitates the identification of (a) the performance of children with disabilities in relation to typical milestones and intermediary steps; (b) which aspects of a task pose difficulty for the student; (c) difficulties that are motor versus difficulties that are cognitive in nature; (d) which student response requirements cause difficulties or require modifications; and (e) what kind and amount of assistance a student needs and could benefit from in different task attempts. Specifically, topics are:

- Using typical sequences as guides;
- Defining results of unsuccessful trials;
- Differentiating motor from cognitive difficulties;
- Identifying student response difficulties and needs in lessons;
- Determining kinds and amounts of assistance needed.

To conduct the process of task analysis (as illustrated in the first group of examples), users learn to isolate and identify the components of tasks and organize them into

TABLE 6–1
Task Analysis of Subtraction Problems

Problem Type	Exercises for Child to Complete			
Basic subtraction facts without zero	1. 4 −2	2. 8 −1	3. 17 −3	4. 15 −6
Basic subtraction facts involving zero		5. 7 −7	6. 9 −0	
Higher-decade subtraction fact requiring no regrouping		7. 79 −6		
Higher-decade subtraction fact requiring regrouping		8. 75 −9		
Higher-decade subtraction fact, with difference in ones' place		9. 25 −23		
Higher-decade subtraction fact; zero in ones' place in minuend		10. 20 −3		
Subtraction of ones and tens with no regrouping required		11. 47 −24		
Three-digit minuend minus two-digit subtrahend; no regrouping		12. 169 −45		
Subtraction of ones, tens, hundreds; no regrouping		13. 436 −215		
Two-digit minuend minus two-digit subtrahend; regrouping tens and ones in minuend required		14. 46 −38	15. 72 −34	
Three-digit minuend minus two-digit subtrahend; regrouping tens and ones in minuend required (zero in difference)		16. 272 −64		
Three-digit minuend minus two-digit subtrahend; regrouping hundreds and tens of minuend required		17. 528 −54		
Subtraction of ones, tens, hundreds; regrouping tens and ones in minuend required		18. 742 −208	19. 750 −374	
Subtraction of ones, tens, hundreds; regrouping hundreds and tens in minuend required		20. 724 −183	21. 307 −121	
Subtraction of ones, tens, hundreds; regrouping entire minuend required		22. 531 −173		
Four-digit minuend minus three-digit subtrahend; regrouping entire minuend required		23. 1076 −247	24. 5254 −968	25. 5805 −978
Subtraction of ones, tens, hundreds, thousands; regrouping hundreds, tens, and ones of minuend required		26. 4553 −1258		
Subtraction of ones, tens, hundreds, thousands; regrouping entire minuend required		27. 9563 −2687		
Five-digit minuend minus four-digit subtrahend; regrouping entire minuend required		28. 23238 −3879		
Five-digit minuend minus four-digit subtrahend; regrouping entire minuend (involving zeros) required		29. 10000 −7192		
Five-digit minuend minus five-digit subtrahend; regrouping entire minuend required		30. 30503 −19765		

Note. From "Problems in Mathematics Achievement," by N. R. Bartel, in *Teaching Students with Learning and Behavior Problems* (pp. 308–309), by D. D. Hammill and N. R. Bartel (Eds.), 1990, Boston: Allyn & Bacon. Copyright 1990 by Allyn & Bacon. Reprinted with permission.

teachable steps in a logical order. What some people call major or target tasks, others might identify as subtasks of a larger task or activity. Task descriptions and parts are made relative to each other by the person constructing the task analysis. There is no single way to divide tasks and to establish size of steps other than what is helpful to a particular group or individual. Identifying teachable components, or steps, is generally the goal.

Some individuals prefer to construct task analysis around generalized situations or activities, such as

FIGURE 6–1
Task analysis of self-care skills: Pulling up pants

SETTING
Student is seated on the edge of a chair with pants turned right-side out and within reach.

PREREQUISITE PHYSICAL SKILLS
- Maintenance of upright sitting posture
- Grasp with both hands
- Ability to stand and maintain upright standing position
- Range of motion to pull pants upwards

PREREQUISITE COGNITIVE SKILLS
- Concept of "up"
- Concept of "left/right"
- Concept of "back/front"

1. Pulls pants up and adjusts pants around waist
2. Stands while grasping waistband of pants
3. Grasps waistband of pants and pulls pants upwards toward hips
4. Pulls left pant leg over left foot
5. Pushes left leg down the length of left pant leg
6. Bends left knee and inserts left leg into left pant leg
7. Pulls right pant leg over right foot
8. Pushes right leg down the length of right pant leg
9. Bends right knee and inserts right leg into right pant leg
10. Positions pants against legs with label in the back*

*More steps may be added to the task analysis.

"shopping for food at any of three local groceries." These are analyzed for accomplishment in different situations and with different people. These task analyses are in contrast to more traditional tasks that consist of functional skills such as "putting on one's own coat" or "opening a can using only one hand."

Using Typical Sequences as Guides

To develop appropriate instruction and goals for students with physical, health, or multiple disabilities, teachers can compare performance and programming for young children in relationship to some systematic sequence. Using available information about the sequences through which most children progress helps teachers to understand how complex skills or activities associated with outcomes of typical growth and development are made up of a series of simpler skills.

When appropriate, descriptions of typical developmental sequences and timelines can guide analysis of student performance and progress. Descriptions of these developmental milestones typically cover several areas of human development, including fine motor, gross motor, speech and language, cognitive, social, and self-care.

Teachers and other professionals can use descriptions of developmental milestones or sequences derived from the study of typically developing children to gain understanding of the relative status and progress of a child with physical or multiple disabilities. For those children not progressing in relatively typical sequences and at usual rates, observers may realize that all developmental information will not be appropriate to guide task analysis. In this situation, three different strategies may be employed for using developmental milestones. First, milestones may be used with *modified expectations*. These milestones may be reached behind the usual schedule, but still guide instruction. Second, *certain typical milestones may be inappropriate* for certain individuals. The gross-motor skills of crawling and walking, for instance, may be impractical for a child with a severe physical impairment. Third, in conducting task analysis, observers learn that some students with disabilities employ *different methods of accomplishment* for certain milestones. Language milestones, for example, may be accomplished with augmentative communication systems rather than primarily by speech.

Developing Intermediary Steps. Sequences of typical development and standardized instruments do not always identify some of the small intermediary steps between milestones. From the information given, teachers and others may find need to define intermediate steps. A visual schema, such as a representation of a series of steps to the top of a ladder, assists with task identification and analyzing. The "task ladder" (see Figure 6–2), for instance, gives a visual representation for organizing the task-analysis information-gathering process.

Many teachers rely on developmental information for the identity of some "target tasks" and intermediary subtasks on a task ladder. Once a student has accomplished a target task by completing all the subtasks, teachers can choose the next target task and list its subtasks based upon data about what generally comes next (see Figure 6–2). The result highlights and clarifies usual sequences.

FIGURE 6–2
Target tasks and subtasks

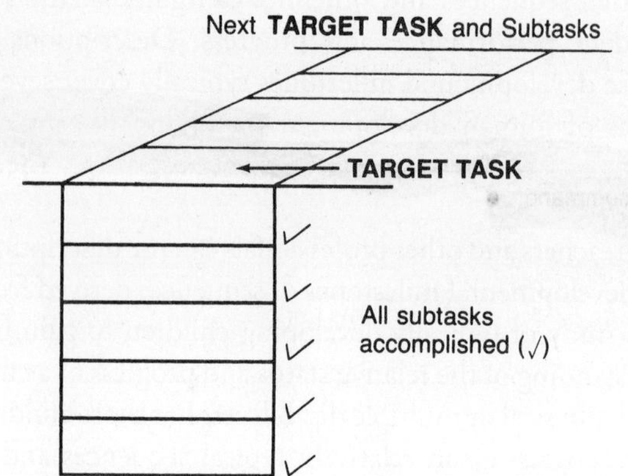

Note. From *Teaching individuals with Physical and Multiple Disabilities* (3rd ed., p. 249), by J.L. Bigge, 1991, Upper Saddle River, NJ: Merrill/Prentice Hall.

Cautions about Using Developmental Sequences. Students with severe physical or multiple disabilities often score poorly on developmental scales that are normed on a typically developing sample (Brown & Snell, 2000; Downing & Demchak, 2002). These scales usually contain subscales that address areas such as fine- and gross-motor development, self-care (dressing, eating, self-toileting, etc.), speech, and social/emotional skills. Frequently these assessments rely on motor performance. For example, one might wish to assess performance of specific self-care skills, such as dressing and undressing. However, children with severe cerebral palsy may be unable to coordinate movements of their arms and hands to perform tasks such as buttoning, lacing, or pulling up pants.

Students with severe physical disabilities are also at a significant disadvantage on many tests of intellectual potential, even when they are aware of the appropriate response. For example, a student who is asked to assemble a series of blocks to make a pattern may understand the task and be able to visualize the correct pattern, but remain unable to push the blocks into position. Frequently, motor-based tests also contain a time element, resulting in a higher score for students who can complete the pattern more rapidly. A student who can complete a block assembly task independently but slowly (because of motor disabilities) would be at a disadvantage. If speech is also impaired, the student would be unable to describe how the blocks should be assembled.

Requiring students to demonstrate a skill that is removed from the normal context in which it would typically be performed does not account for individual motivation or interest (Downing & Demchak, 2002). For example, the child might be asked to complete a lacing-board activity. A lacing board is constructed of two flaps of stiff fabric attached to a surface (such as cardboard). Each flap has a series of grommet holes along its length. The object of the activity is to push a large shoelace through the holes in the fabric and "lace" the flaps together. This activity appears to have utility—teaching a child to lace with the eventual outcome of lacing shoes. However, completing a lacing board has no functional outcome, as lacing a real shoe would. It is also possible that children with cognitive disabilities would be unable to "generalize" the skills involved in completing a lacing board to lacing real shoes. Finally, lacing may be an inappropriate task for some students with motor disabilities. Shoe lacing could be circumvented by using Velcro® shoe closures or "curly laces" that twine around each other and never need tying. When evaluating developmental tasks, teachers and others must always ask themselves if there is an appropriate alternative that supports mastery and independence.

Task analysis can be used successfully with developmental sequences. Figure 6–3 illustrates a developmental sequence superimposed upon a task ladder. This method directs attention to many of the steps (subtasks) between more commonly recognized milestones. In this example, subtasks have been identified that lead to the target task "respond to requests of one-step direction." Analysis of these subtasks indicates that the individual can make directional body movements in response to requests (typically performed at 9–28 months), but does not yet point to objects, body parts, and pictures upon request (15–60 months) nor place objects in response to requests of one-step directions (17.8–24 months). The subtask of pointing to objects, body parts, and pictures upon request would be an appropriate skill to master. This skill could be taught in the context of interesting and motivating activities, such as pointing to familiar objects in the environment, playing imitation games that include body part identification, and looking at picture books with peers. Teachers must employ modified expectations and different methods of accomplishment when ap-

FIGURE 6–3
Sequence of developmental subtasks superimposed on a task ladder

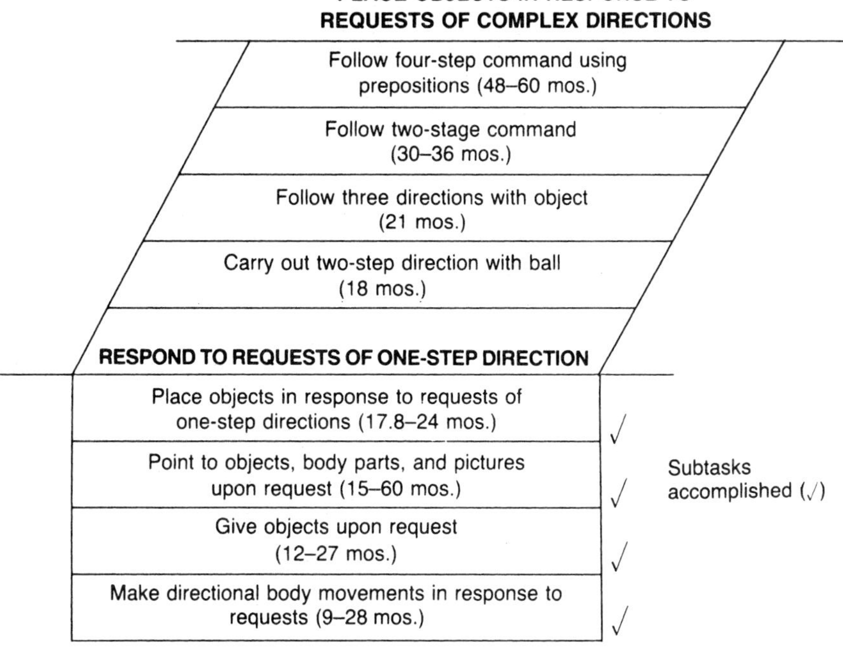

Note. From "Developmental pinpoints," by M. Cohen, P. Gross, and N. Haring, in *Teaching the Severely Handicapped* (pp. 63–64), N. Harring and L. Brown (Eds.), 1976, Boston: Allyn & Bacon. Copyright © 1976 by Allyn & Bacon. Reprinted by permission.

plying task analysis to developmental sequences. Finally, remember that typical milestones may be inappropriate for some individuals with physical or multiple disabilities.

Defining Results of Unsuccessful Trials

Task analysis is a helpful strategy when observing an individual attempting a functional task in a natural situation but experiencing difficulty. Observers are able to analyze what parts, or steps, pose the difficulties through noting which subtasks were performed successfully and which were not. Once observers isolate subtasks and designate those "performed" and those "not performed," unaccomplished subtasks can be targeted for future learning as temporary target tasks (see Figure 6–4).

FIGURE 6–4
Sample task and temporary target task

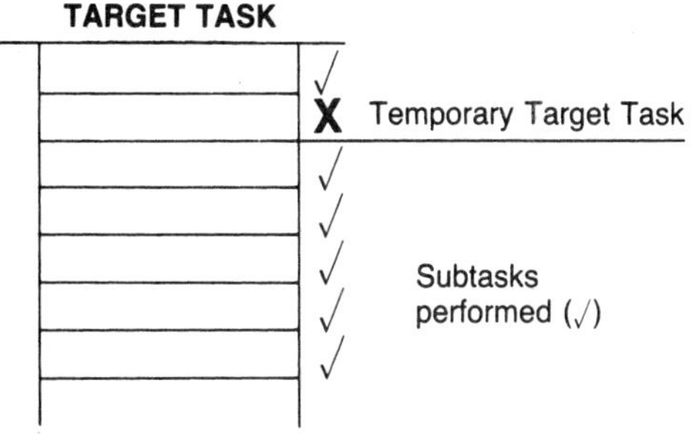

Note. From *Teaching Individuals with Physical and Multiple Disabilities* (3rd ed., p. 250), by J. L. Bigge, 1991, Upper Saddle River, NJ: Merrill/Prentice Hall.

Figure 6–5 shows a task analysis that employs the strategy of identifying unaccomplished subtasks and using them as the basis for temporary tasks. Lisa, a first grader with cerebral palsy, was able to participate in the regular first grade. However, she was unable to move independently into class through the classroom door. The teacher watched her as she tried to accomplish the task and then completed a task analysis based on the observation. Note in Figure 6–5 the definition of the actual target task in bold at the top of the ladder. Notice also that possible reasons for Lisa's repeated failures to get through the door are eliminated by checking off what she did perform. What she needs to be taught is clearly indicated by the subtasks she did not perform, and then is projected as temporary objectives for instruction, or temporary target tasks.

FIGURE 6–5
Using subtasks as temporary target tasks

OPENING THE CLASSROOM DOOR AND WALKING THROUGH IT WHILE USING CRUTCHES

Subtask		
11. Keep door open while walking through doorway	X	
10. Grasp released crutch and hold door open	X	Temporary Target Task
9. Released doorknob	√	
8. Pulled door open	√	
7. Turned knob	√	
6. Grasped knob	√	
5. Reached doorknob	√	
4. Maintained left crutch under left armpit	√	
3. Released hand from crutch to reach for knob	√	
2. Stood in position to open the door	√	
1. Walked to the door	√	

Note. From *Teaching Individuals with Physical and Multiple Disabilities* (3rd ed., p. 251) by J. L. Bigge, 1991, Upper Saddle River, NJ: Merrill/Prentice Hall.

FIGURE 6–6
Relationship between unaccomplished subtasks and temporary target tasks

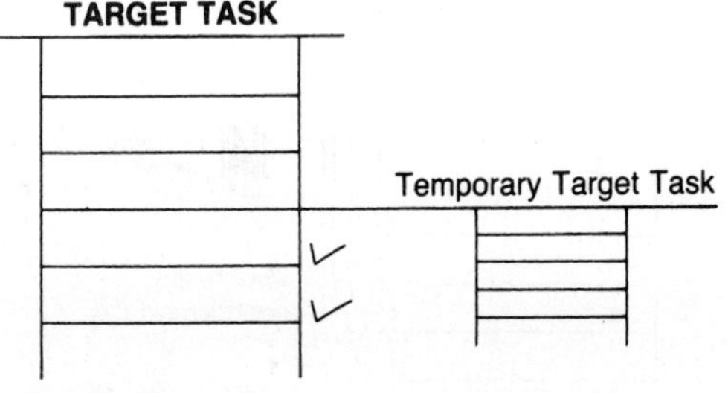

Note. From *Teaching Individuals with Physical and Multiple Disabilities* (3rd ed., p. 251) by J. L. Bigge, 1991, Upper Saddle River, NJ: Merrill/Prentice Hall.

Sometimes, when a difficulty is isolated as a temporary target task, a solution becomes obvious and perhaps even immediate. Sometimes more deliberation is necessary. The temporary target task can be broken into its own subtasks (see Figure 6–6). With this structure of analysis, teachers can decide whether to teach the subtasks or to consider major or minor adaptations.

Each temporary target task was broken into its subtasks after Lisa's teacher tried to duplicate Lisa's attempts as closely as possible. Using Lisa's crutches and walking on her knees, the teacher worked out a series of steps that would enable her to get through the door. This series of steps, or subtasks of the temporary target task, were taught to Lisa. Eventually, she was able to complete the target task (Figure 6–7) of opening the classroom door and walking through.

Differentiating Motor from Cognitive Difficulties

Teachers and others who educate individuals with physical or multiple disabilities face challenges with students whose greatest training needs are created by **motor impairment**. The training needs of individuals with cognitive disabilities are often more focused on **discrimination skills**. Where should teachers proceed with students whose abilities to interact with or operate on the environment motorically is impaired? How can teachers differentiate motor from cognitive impairments? Task analysis can provide a useful strategy.

Using the usual procedures of task analysis, teachers and others can complete a data collection process that identifies whether persons are having motor difficul-

FIGURE 6–7
Developing subtasks of a temporary target task

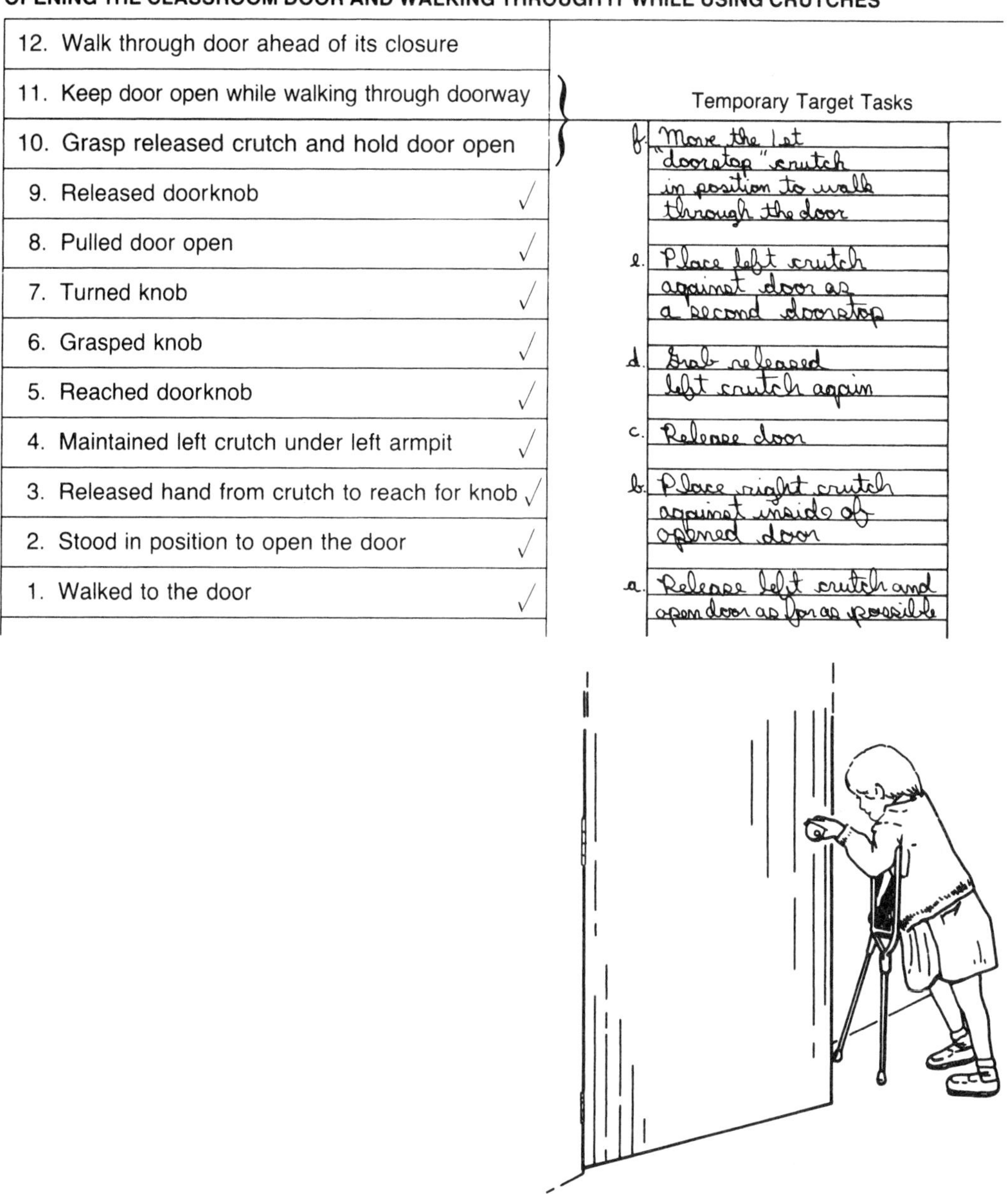
OPENING THE CLASSROOM DOOR AND WALKING THROUGH IT WHILE USING CRUTCHES
12. Walk through door ahead of its closure
11. Keep door open while walking through doorway
10. Grasp released crutch and hold door open
9. Released doorknob √
8. Pulled door open √
7. Turned knob √
6. Grasped knob √
5. Reached doorknob √
4. Maintained left crutch under left armpit √
3. Released hand from crutch to reach for knob √
2. Stood in position to open the door √
1. Walked to the door √
Temporary Target Tasks
f. Move the 1st "doorstop" crutch in position to walk through the door
e. Place left crutch against door as a second doorstop
d. Grab released left crutch again
c. Release door
b. Place right crutch against inside of opened door
a. Release left crutch and open door as far as possible

Note. From *Teaching Individuals with Physical and Multiple Disabilities* (3rd ed., p. 252) by J. L. Bigge, 1991, Upper Saddle River, NJ: Merrill/Prentice Hall.

ties (M), discrimination difficulties (D), or both (see Figure 6–8). The data in Figure 6–8 show that Sara

always attempted to initiate the correct step. However, she had difficulty completing several steps correctly because of motor problems. In step 2, she had difficulty removing paper clips because of the necessity to grasp, pull, and hold the paper in place, all simultaneously. In steps 3 and 14—when she carried papers from the table to the machine and back—she would crumple the paper. Sara was only able to grasp the papers with one hand while walking, and this hand had a fairly high degree of tension spasticity in it. In step 7, she couldn't

FIGURE 6–8
Differentiating motor from discrimination difficulties

Student: Sara Trainer: Rich
Date: 9/10/04 Task: Photocopying

STEP	D	M	D	M
1. Obtain original from request basket on worktable	+	+	+	+
2. Remove paper clip	+	−	+	−
3. Carry original to machine	+	−	+	−
4. Turn quantity knob to number of copies requested	+	+	+	+
5. Open copier door	+	+	+	+
6. Place original on window	+	+	+	+
7. Align paper	+	−	+	−
8. Close door	+	+	+	+
9. Push start button	+	+	+	+
10. Open copier door	+	+	+	+
11. Remove original	+	+	+	+
12. Repeat steps 5–11 until all pages are copied				
13. Remove copies	+	+	+	+
14. Take copies back to worktable	+	−	+	−
15. Even copy/original stacks	+	−	+	−
16. Place clip on each copy/original	+	−	+	−

get the paper aligned and then remove her hand without pushing or knocking it out of alignment. In step 15, she would drop papers when she tried to even the papers in a copy or original group. In step 16, she could not get the clip around the pages. Thus, the trainer recorded a (1) under the D and a (2) under the M for each of these steps. (Sowers, Jenkins, & Powers, 1988, p. 403)

To see the importance of the process, check the information in the data and find the patterns. What do these data indicate for intervention? This is a situation when the data indicate that training procedures should be employed to reduce or eradicate difficulties caused by motor disability. It is an example of how important it is to use the task analysis strategy to identify the need for training on specific steps of tasks and to differentiate whether teaching should address motor impairments, discrimination deficits, or both. The form also guides the task analysis process when planning for teaching new skills, including modified student response methods, self-care skills, and other life management skills.

Identifying Student Response Difficulties and Needs in Lessons

Different school assignments and other tasks have different motor-based response requirements for students. Students with motor impairments frequently experience difficulty in participating in curricular and extracurricular activities because their motor impairments prevent them from exhibiting the necessary control and speed for performing activities in usual ways. When these difficulties are not identified and modifications are not made, students are unable to demonstrate what they know and can do.

There is a further risk that assumptions will be made about students' potential to comprehend and complete tasks based on what they can perform without modification. Students with motor impairments may not be assigned more-complex tasks, on the assumption that what they cannot perform they cannot comprehend. Loss of opportunity will eventually result in loss of academic knowledge and skills. Another danger arises when teachers "solve" this situation by relegating the student with motor impairments to the role of observer. *Students with physical, health, or multiple disabilities must be actively engaged in activities.*

Teachers responsible for helping these students to benefit from educational experiences must analyze the educational environment in which students are participating. Conducting task analyses within or across situations can be used to identify which motor tasks or activities within assignments present difficulties.

Analysis can take place relative to a classroom in which the student currently participates, or be applied to future educational settings. Analysis can reflect immediate response needs in one or more of the student's classes or deal with more generalized needs. Whichever the case, teachers need to identify the method of participation required (e.g., handwriting) and the specific qualities of participation (e.g., amount and speed desired). Particular attention is given to **lesson response requirements** (e.g., handwriting and speaking) and **performance requirements** (e.g., making something with clay, making a model, conducting a science experiment) that may pose problems for students with motor impairments.

Teachers can conduct their own student response needs analysis or use an existing inventory as a guide. Bigge (1988, 1991) developed an Inventory of Task Performance that rates student performance "in relation to physical performance demands of the curriculum" (Bigge, Stump, et al., 1999, p. 209). The inventory is arranged in four columns. Column 1 lists typical task requirements in school and life activities and the means by which they are usually performed (i.e., the typical task requirement of drawing includes the task performance requirements of drawing lines, marking choices, drawing shapes, creating artistic works, and coloring/painting). Column 2 is a numerical rating scale to analyze performance. Column 3 provides space for observational notes about physical performance and targets for intervention. This provides information about student performance that requires immediate intervention. The last column is an action plan for recommendations for additional instruction or assessment. Teachers and others can use this information to establish goals, benchmarks, and objectives for instruction (Bigge, Stump, et al., 1999, p. 212). Figure 6–9 provides the complete Inventory of Task Performance and rating scale.

With this kind of task analysis, teachers can identify activities in which students can participate fully and activities in which students are having difficulty with participation. Interventions may include any one of several modifications of student response and performance method, such as:

- Instructing students in *more effective uses* of the usual response and performance methods;
- Using the *usual response and performance method with adaptations* (pencil with pencil grip);
- Providing *augmentations or supplements* to usual response and performance methods (picture communication board to augment unintelligible speech);
- Providing *different or alternative response and performance methods* (keyboarding instead of handwriting).

Determining Kinds and Amounts of Assistance Needed

It is always important to promote independence in students with physical or multiple disabilities. Maximum independence is supported when teachers know how much and what kind of assistance is needed by students in order to partially or fully accomplish tasks. In some instances, the kinds and amounts of assistance are described for a target task or activity. Mostly, assistance needs are identified in relation to subtasks. Assistance, if well chosen, can contribute information helpful to task learning and accomplishment. If overused, assistance can be detrimental and contribute to learned helplessness. Task analysis of natural activities provides the framework for rating the kinds and amounts of assistance given to each subtask. The goal is to use assistance when it is needed and then to fade the assistance and eventually eliminate it whenever possible (Downing & Demchak, 2002). Two kinds of assistance are prompting and shaping.

FIGURE 6–9
Inventory of means of task performance

Name: ______________________ Age/Grade ________ Date ________

Typical Task Requirements by Typical Means of Task Performance	Numerical Descriptions of Present Means of Performance	Observations and Explanations (e.g., can speak but chooses not to)	Action Plan Ideas (e.g., individualized or additional instruction; further assessment to identify needs)
GESTURING			
1. Points to indicate, looks to indicate: people, places, and things 2. Gives a sign to direct attention to something: boys in a fight; an example of the concept "hard" 3. Makes movements of body to express or emphasize ideas, emotions: dramatizes			
SPEAKING			
4. Replies *yes, no, I don't know,* etc. 5. Names personal needs and wants, peoples, places, and things 6. Reads aloud 7. Initiates and replies using short phrases 8. Engages in basic conversational dialogues 9. Expresses thoughts, questions, feelings, etc. 10. Makes oral presentations, reports, debates, etc.			
DRAWING AND RELATED MEANS			
11. Draws lines to connect, to underline, etc. 12. Marks choices, marks to eliminate items, etc. 13. Draws shapes 14. Creates artistic works 15. Colors or paints			
HANDWRITING			
16. Writes letters of the alphabet 17. Writes own signature 18. Writes short exercises: answers, lists, note taking, stories, etc. 19. Writes long exercises: formal reports, compositions, letters, etc. 20. Writes numerals, math problems, calculations, and answers			
HOLDING, MANIPULATING, AND MANEUVERING			
21. Holds and steadies objects 22. Manipulates common school and work tools: scissors, measuring devices, staplers, papers 23. Handles equipment in sports and recreation activities: game pieces, balls, ropes			

FIGURE 6–9
(Continued)

Typical Task Requirements by Typical Means of Task Performance	Numerical Descriptions of Present Means of Performance	Observations and Explanations (e.g., can speak but chooses not to)	Action Plan Ideas (e.g., individualized or additional instruction; further assessment to identify needs)
HOLDING, MANIPULATING, AND MANEUVERING (*Continued*)			
24. Manages common household items: brooms, silverware, trash cans 25. Manages common educational, vocational, domestic tasks: clearing desktop, using the phone, washing dishes, etc. 26. Runs common electrical appliances: household, vocational, personal care, etc. 27. Sets up and operates aids and devices: communication aids, TTY telephone units for deaf 28. Operates machines: car, washing machine, vending machines 29. Makes things: exhibits, displays, crafts 30. Maneuvers things: carries, pushes, pulls, lifts			
MOBILIZING SELF			
31. Maneuvers self: from one position or posture to another, etc. 32. Moves about safely in a variety of environments: school, home, workplace, shopping center, etc. 33. Uses transportation system: car, bus, train, plane 34. Completes physical routines: washing dishes 35. Uses steps, elevators and escalators			
OTHER			
36. Other:			

5 = Satisfactorily uses means typically used by peers
4 = Needs individualized/additional instruction in use of typical means
3 = Satisfactorily uses modified means for performance (e.g., adaptations, alternatives, or augmentations to the typical means)
2 = Needs individualized/additional instruction in uses of modified means of performance
1 = Needs assessment to determine best means of performance in different school and life activities
0 = Not applicable

Note. From *Assessment, Curriculum, and Instruction for Students with Disabilities*, 1st edition, by J. L. Bigge and C. S. Stump. © 1999. Reprinted with permission of Wadsworth, a division of Thomson Learning: *www.thomsonrights.com* Fax 800-730-2215.

Prompting. Teachers and others who provide services to individuals with physical or multiple disabilities use a variety of prompting techniques. These include:

- Verbal instructions (telling what should be done);
- Modeling/demonstration (showing what should be done);
- Gestures (pointing to what should be done);
- Visual cues (showing pictures of what should be done);
- Physical assistance (moving the body of the student through the movements required by a response). (Downing & Demchak, 2002, p. 50)

In addition to these prompting techniques, Downing and Demchak (2002) recommend several prompting procedures that are particularly useful for students with severe disabilities (including multiple disabilities). These procedures include increasing assistance, decreasing assistance, graduated guidance, constant time delay, and progressive time delay. Table 6–2 describes different procedures for prompting.

Prompting can be applied to different learning situations and levels of student need. For example, using the decreasing assistance strategy is most helpful for students who are unfamiliar with or lack skills to perform behaviors in a particular task analysis. The initial level of teacher assistance is high to support an accurate response. However, if students already have some of the skills to perform behaviors in a particular task analysis, the increasing-assistance strategy is more appropriate. Only the least amount of teacher prompting is used to ensure an accurate response (Westling & Fox, 2000). Whenever prompting is used, it should be unobtrusive and faded as soon as possible.

Students must always be allowed a sufficient time to respond after any prompt (Bigge & Best, 2001; Downing & Demchak, 2002). Using "**wait time**" allows students to think about the task (cognition), formulate a response (cognition), and execute the response (motor or motor/speech). For students with motor impairments, wait time is critical. Teachers must resist the impulse to immediately provide additional prompts or physical assistance, which may confuse the student or lead to the expectation that they will be "rescued" if they remain passive. Teachers must also assist other students to refrain from providing unneeded assistance in the form of verbal cues (answers). To test your wait time, position yourself near a clock with a second hand and ask a friend to keep time. At a predetermined signal, close your eyes and imagine that you are working with a group of students, one of whom was just asked a question. The student you asked is looking at you but has not responded. Raise your hand at the moment when you think you would need to provide another prompt to assist the student's response. Your friend can then tell you how long you were able to employ "wait time." Most teachers are surprised to learn that they cannot wait more than a few seconds before providing assistance. However, some students with motor and cognitive disabilities may need several minutes to respond!

Shaping. Different kinds of assistance can be augmented with the strategy of **shaping**. Shaping is the technique of accepting behaviors that are only **approximations** to the desired behavior, then gradually requiring behaviors that are closer to a desired outcome. The following example uses a variety of types of prompts with shaping to achieve a desired skill. A stu-

TABLE 6–2
Procedures for Prompting Students with Severe Disabilities

Increasing assistance	Consists of a hierarchy of prompts arranged in order from presumed least informative to most informative assistance for a given activity; also known as system of least prompts or least-to-most prompts
Decreasing assistance	Begins with the most informative prompt needed for the individual to respond in a given activity and moves through a specified hierarchy to less-informative levels of assistance; also known as most-to-least prompts
Graduated guidance	Degrees of physical assistance provided from most intrusive to least intrusive, with amount of assistance varying within a teaching instance as the student responds (i.e., teacher makes moment-to-moment decisions regarding amount of assistance) and if appropriate
Constant time delay	Initial tracing opportunities provided at a 0-second delay, with all subsequent teaching trials provided at a predetermined delay interval (e.g., 5 seconds)
Progressive time delay	Initial teaching opportunities provided at a 0-second delay, with the amount of time between the natural cue and the prompt gradually increased (e.g., increments of 2 seconds) to allow the student to respond

Note. From *Including Students with Severe and Multiple Disabilities in Typical Classrooms: Practical Strategies for Teachers* (p. 47) by J. E. Downing, Baltimore: Brookes. Copyright 1996 by Paul H. Brookes Publishing Company, Inc. Reprinted with permission.

dent with mild fine-motor impairments is learning to make letters. The teacher may begin by telling the student how the letter "l" is formed (verbal instructions) and writing the formation of the letter on the chalkboard or whiteboard (**demonstration**). The student may then be encouraged to come to the board and practice making the letter. Occasionally the teacher may reposition the student's hand to facilitate writing (physical assistance). The student may then begin to **practice** the letter "l" on a piece of paper that has several sample letters with arrows indicating the direction for starting and finishing the letter (**visual cues**). The paper may contain samples of the letter for tracing, followed by samples in which the letter is formed from dotted lines, and finally blank lines for independent letter formation (**cue fading**). Initially the teacher will accept attempts to form the letter (an approximation), even if the result is imperfect. After sufficient practice and corrective feedback, the teacher will only accept perfectly formed letter "l's" that do not loop below or above the line on the paper.

Determining Amounts of Assistance. Prompting and shaping are powerful strategies for building and refining student responses. How do teachers determine how much assistance to provide to students? Falvey (1989) provides a formula for determining percentages for the levels of assistance provided when individuals engage in different activities. Falvey presents a scale in which the heaviest weighting (6) is given to those skills or subtasks of activities which are accomplished in response to natural cues in the environment, without any physical assistance or verbal and gestural cues. The more assistance needed, the less the weighting. Therefore, a low rating is given if full physical assistance is needed. It is assumed that increases in a percentage of independence in skills within an activity reflect an overall increase in independence in the activity. Readers may recognize that this weighting scale is itself a task analysis of amount of assistance.

The weighting-scale items chosen by Falvey (1989) for the methods of assistance are as follows:

1 = Physical guidance (hand-guided manipulation).
2 = Modeling (demonstration followed by imitation from the learner; always face the task from same direction as the learner would).
3 = Direct verbal ("Flip it over"; "Other hand").
4 = Indirect verbal ("Where does it go?").
5 = Gestural (Pointing; making a straight line motion; tapping near where it goes).
6 = Natural cue. (p. 55)

Two kinds of information are needed to calculate percentage of independence: level of student performance and independence level (Falvey, 1989). Level of student performance is the total rating of each skill at any one attempt at a particular activity. A student rating of 30 would have been attained by a person who completed five skills with ratings of 6 on each response to natural cues. For a student who performed five skills with ratings of 3, 2, 3, 4, and 6, the student level would be 18. Independence level is the total representing the performance of all skills in response to natural cues (all 6's). If there are five skills, the independence level is 30 (5 × 6); if nine skills, the independence level is 54 (9 × 6). Percentage of independence is determined by the student level divided by the independence level, multiplied by 100.

Figure 6–10 illustrates this use of task analysis. A high school student with significant impairment in hand use and in cognition is learning to wash clothes at a laundromat. The highest possible independence level score for doing this task based on the 10 steps is 60. This student's initial score on using a washing machine in a laundromat was 43, thus giving her a 72% level of independence. The goal then set for her was a score of 60, or a 100% level of independence on this activity.

Such a system provides a teacher with a tool for recording amounts and kinds of assistance used in more-objective terms. It "tightens the data" by providing more-specific information than do statements such as "Joey has increased his independence in ___________." It allows comparison of present function with the overall level of independence level in carrying out the entire activity (present levels of functioning). It also allows comparisons of changes in performance over time (which reflects the effectiveness of teaching). Using task analysis, this system pinpoints which skills within an activity needed or received which method of assistance. Kinds and amounts of assistance needed and their continuance depend upon the improving performance of the student.

FIGURE 6–10
Scoring-by-levels data sheet

Location: Hogan High School

SCORING-BY-LEVELS DATA SHEET

Student: Mary Ann

Skills	Dates: 10/14										
1. Open machine	6										
2. Load clothes, distributing weight	6										
3. Measure detergent	6										
4. Pour detergent	6										
5. Select water temperature	3										
6. Select water level/load size	3										
7. Select speed	3										
8. Select cycle	0										
9. Close lid	6										
10. Start machine	4										
Student's Total	43										
Independence level = # of skills performed in response to natural cues × 6 (i.e.,10 skills: 10 × 6)	60										
Percentage of independence (Student's level ÷ independence level × 100)	72										
Code: physical guidance = 1; model = 2; direct verbal = 3; indirect verbal = 4; gesture= 5; natural cue = 6.											

Note. Adapted from *Community-Based Curriculum: Instructional Strategies for Students with Severe Handicaps* (p. 29), by M. Falvey, 1989, Baltimore: Brookes. Copyright 1989 by Mary Falvey. Reprinted with permission.

TASK ANALYSIS AS A PRODUCT

Results of the process of task analysis such as those illustrated in this section become products that can be used as a sequence for students to learn. If applied during the instructional process, these products can function as **formative assessments** of specific skills. If applied after instruction, they can also function as **summative assessments**. As mentioned earlier in the chapter, components of standardized achievement tests, published diagnostic tests, criterion-referenced instruments, and developmental scales are themselves the result of task analysis. Products of task analysis are used for screening, describing, evaluating, clarifying student performances, comparing skills of different students, and developing specialized curricula. Three of these products will be discussed.

Screening Performances

To determine where to begin instruction, it is helpful to find out what a person already knows. Teachers can do this quickly by giving a child a chance to try at least one subskill that represents a group of subskills. Teacher-made inventories and criterion-referenced curriculum guides provide quick screening of learning needs.

Each arithmetic computation or operation (addition, multiplication, subtraction, and division), for instance, has several different subskills. Looking at arithmetic computation from a task analysis viewpoint, one teacher used the process to select representative problems and make an informal inventory (see Figure 6–11). Computations are divided into components or subskills based on the four major operations. Within each operation are smaller components or subskills. The same process can be done for different school subjects.

Comparing Skills of Different Students

To find patterns in students' skills and to discover students' strengths and weaknesses for purposes of grouping them for instruction, teachers can tally student errors or problem areas (see Figure 6–12). Those students with similar instructional needs can be grouped. Rolo, Linda, and Rich might be grouped because of similar needs to learn certain practical academic skills for use in community-based exercises. Bette, Jo, and George have a different need than the other three students. When the profile was shared with other teachers, it was revealed that these students have needs for instruction in common with two similar-age students having difficulty in a regular class. Perhaps some collaborative instruction could be arranged to benefit the students and teachers. Ruth Mary's skills do not fit the patterns of either group of students. Perhaps she will be taught individually in this particular curricular component and work with others in cooperative learning situations so she can learn from others and share strengths in other areas with them.

Developing Specialized Curricula

Task analyses can be used to assist teachers to instruct students in academic content areas. However, students with physical or multiple disabilities require additional, specialized curricula. One of the most critical products that result from the task analysis strategy is the set of skills that students with disabilities need to learn in order to manage their lives. It is possible to expedite the education of students by determining if they possess the vital competencies that may be viewed as foundational tools for life management. Task analysis for developing specialized curricula in life management concentrates on *fundamental skills and adaptive behaviors* that simultaneously build foundations for effective functioning in almost any current and subsequent environment. For students with physical or multiple disabilities to achieve independence and quality in their lives, and find satisfaction and happiness, it is important for them to learn to use life management tools such as:

- Tools for interpersonal effectiveness;
- Tools for self-care and personal needs;
- Tools for practical academic knowledge;
- Tools for good work habits;
- Tools for self-reliance in transportation and mobility;
- Tools for selection of either paid or voluntary work;
- Tools for adaptation to working environments.

It is helpful for teachers to employ a screening process to identify foundational life management tools that are considered important for use by individuals with physical or multiple disabilities.

Task analysis has many advantages. First, its emphasis on sequential skill development reinforces task and instructional organization. This organization is useful for students, whose learning is facilitated as they

FIGURE 6–11
Using task analysis to screen for operational difficulties with whole numbers

Addition

Simple facts

5	6	4	2	8	5	6+2=	3+4=	5+3=
+2	+3	+5	+9	+4	+8			

Column addition

4	3	7
2	5	7
+3	8	9
	+2	+7

No carrying

24	50	47
+43	+2	+300

Carry from ones' place

27	16	58
+35	+4	+139

Carrying from tens' place

142	57	490
+293	+352	+90

Carrying from consecutive places

273	316	4806
+258	+89	+2998

Carrying in alternate places

2582	87060
+3908	+38479

Subtraction

Simple facts

5	8	7	7−1=
−3	−8	−2	9−0=
			8−3=

No regrouping necessary

47	89	302
−26	−40	−102

Regrouping in tens' and ones' places

42	48	72
−36	−19	−6

Regrouping in hundreds' and tens' places

470	473	500	7863
−129	−183	−70	−7793

Regrouping in consecutive places

526	800	9012
−378	−73	−8236

Regrouping in alternate places

4238	60402
−3919	−15192

Multiplication

Simple facts

4	3	6	9×9=
×2	×3	×9	4×3=
			5×6=
			7×8=

No carrying

42	21	30
×2	×6	×3

Carrying from ones' to ten's place

46	58	209
×2	×3	×4

Carrying from tens' to hundreds' place

705	150	371	3051
×7	×5	×7	×9

Carrying in consecutive places

195	286	4857
×7	×9	×8

Carrying in alternate places

2519	6807
×3	×3

Multiplying by numbers ending in zero

43	267	487
×10	×50	×600

Multiplying by two- and three-place numbers

25	358	469
×12	×347	×408

move from familiar skills to more challenging tasks. It is also useful for teachers, who can use task analysis to ensure that curricular scope and sequence is followed. Second, task analysis provides a vehicle for individualizing instruction. Teachers can identify specific student strengths and needs within a particular skill or content area. Third, task analysis partitions outcomes into smaller segments that are less complicated and therefore easier to learn. Successful accomplishment of a series of tasks reinforces positive self-esteem and

FIGURE 6–11
(Continued)

Division—One-place Divisors

One-place divisors

$2\overline{)8}$ $6\overline{)54}$ $4\overline{)24}$

$8 \div 1 =$
$16 \div 8 =$
$9 \div 3 =$
$6 \div 2 =$

Even division

$3\overline{)96}$ $2\overline{)180}$ $4\overline{)2408}$

Uneven division—no remainders

$4\overline{)72}$ $3\overline{)174}$ $5\overline{)3925}$

Uneven division—remainders

$5\overline{)57}$ $4\overline{)163}$ $7\overline{)6934}$

Division—Two-place Divisors

Easy types

$25\overline{)575}$ $43\overline{)519}$ $34\overline{)714}$

Complex types

$92\overline{)3423}$ $45\overline{)2393}$ $56\overline{)8456}$

Estimation difficulties

$37\overline{)15928}$ $26\overline{)2376}$ $18\overline{)13410}$

Zeroes in quotients

$43\overline{)1720}$ $97\overline{)4859}$ $85\overline{)680439}$

Note. Adapted from *Teaching Individuals with Physical and Multiple Disabilities* (3rd ed., pp. 261–262), by J. L. Bigge, 1991, Upper Saddle River, NJ: Merrill/Prentice Hall.

FIGURE 6–12
Error analysis of a group of students

Skills	Betty	Rolo	Jo	Linda	Rich	Ruth Mary	George	Class Totals
Skill 1	X	X	X	X	X	X	X	
Skill 2	X	X	X	X	X	X	X	
Skill 3		X	X		X	X		
Skill 4	X			X		X		
Skill 5	X	X	X		ab	X	X	
Skill 6			X		ab	X		
Skill 7	X		X		X	X		
Skill 8	X		X			X		
Skill 9	X					X	X	
Skill 10						X		
Skill 11						X		
Skill 12								

Note. Adapted from *Teaching Individuals with Physical and Multiple Disabilities* (3rd ed., p. 262), by J. L. Bigge, 1991, Upper Saddle River, NJ: Merrill/Prentice Hall.

boosts motivation. In addition, implementing task analysis provides the student with many opportunities to practice and learn skills. Finally, task analysis has value as an assessment tool that reflects outcomes of instruction (summative) and provides data regarding ongoing progress (formative).

SITUATION ANALYSIS

Educational assessment and curriculum development for students with physical or multiple disabilities generally depend, at least in part, upon examining situations in the home, school, and community in which students participate. Careful analysis of these situations results in identification of skills that can be further task-analyzed for direct instruction. The assessments that are used to examine situations are called **ecological inventories**. Ecological assessment "allows an examiner to evaluate a student's status in the various **ecologies** or **environments** in which the student functions" (Brown, 1990, p. 347). Sequences of behaviors in various environments (ecologies) are clustered to form ecological inventories. Ecological inventories allow a broader and more natural picture of student function than formal, norm-referenced assessments. Using ecological inventories allows teachers to individualize program content, using established content or curriculum as a base. Because they are conducted in the student's environment, ecological inventories may also provide direction for altering environments to improve student function.

Alper (1996) and Ryndak and Alper (2003) list steps for identifying curricular content using the ecological inventory approach. These are:

1. Select a domain or skill category (domestic, leisure, school, community, or vocational).
2. Identify all the environments in that domain.
3. Delineate the subenvironments within each environment.

4. Identify the activities that are performed within each subenvironment.
5. Use task analysis to determine what skills are needed to perform the activities. (Ryndak & Alper, p.26)

Family members, coworkers, and peers can all provide information to develop an ecological inventory. In addition, a variety of ecological inventories can be used to develop curriculum content. Figure 6–13 demonstrates how a variety of inventories was used to create a leisure education program.

Two other examples of using ecological inventories will be presented next to illustrate its importance. These are ecological inventories of formalizing teacher recollections and questionnaires with peer groups,

FIGURE 6–13
Using inventories to identify content for a leisure education program

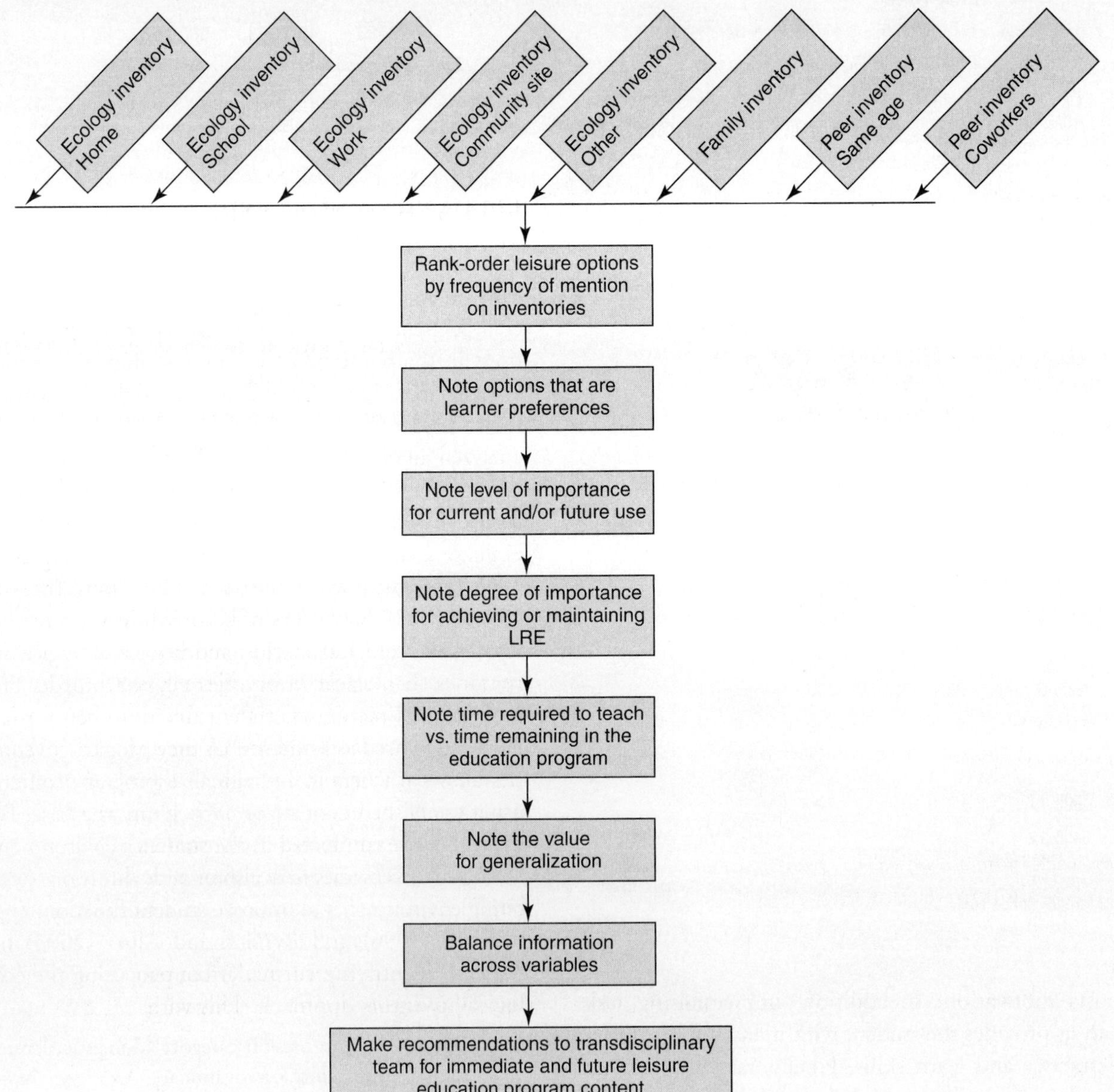

Note. From "Leisure Education for Positive Life Styles," by D.L. Ryndak, B.P. Sirvis, and D.S. Alcoulo loumre, in *Instructional Methods for Adolescents with Learning and Behavior Problems* (p. 317), P.J. Schloss, M.A. Smith, and C.N. Schloss (Eds.), 1997, Boston: Allyn & Bacon. Copyright © 1997 by Allyn & Bacon. Reprinted with permission.

which will be applied to the situation of participating in music-related activities. Different versions of the ecological inventory strategy will be used depending upon the situation and the teacher's style. Some inventories are conducted on-site in natural situations, some are conducted through teacher recollections from a lifetime of experience, and some use information from student peers.

Information and examples here are designed to help teachers conduct ecological inventories to determine what their students know and need to know in order to pursue and participate in activities in the community. In this case the specific environment such as a local concert hall and subenvironment such as the concert for a particular kind of music are yet to be determined. This is because the teacher is not yet aware of how similar-age peers in the community are participating in music-related activities.

Teacher Recollections

Recollections, or personal knowledge, of teachers can become a time-saving strategy. Teachers and others conducting ecological inventories need not always be on-site. Personal knowledge of audience etiquette, for instance, is one place to start for teacher analysis. This is indeed one of the rudiments, because if students do not know how to act in concerts or other performances, they are not appreciated by others and will not be happy with themselves. For some students, the following might be a short-term objective; for others it might be a multiple-year skills objective.

Objective: Demonstrate appropriate audience behavior at musical performances given in different situations.

- Find seat.
- Clap at proper places.
- Refrain from making unnecessary odd noises.

Another part of attending music events is finding the place in the program or advertisements that tells about the musical instrumentation used and the people playing the instruments. Skills might be stated in this way:

- Locate and read printed matter in newspapers and other advertisements which identifies instruments and players.
- Identify parts of printed programs which tell about instruments and performers in the events attended.
- Read programs for information or ask someone to tell about the content of the printed program if unable to physically hold it or if unable to read it for some reason.

In addition to enjoying the music at different levels of sophistication, many people enjoy making observations at the concert. Many seem to enjoy identifying by name some of the different instruments they see or finding instruments that all belong to the same family. Many enjoy finding the different instruments and where their players are seated in different kinds of ensembles and music groups. Sometimes it is hard to discriminate and identify sounds of individual instruments; however, many people learn to discriminate the sounds of families of instruments. Some skills to learn in this area might be:

- Identify some of the different instruments seen in a variety of musical events.
- Identify large groups, smaller ensembles, duets, and solo presentations.
- Identify those instruments seen in musical ensembles which belong to the same family.
- Identify the sounds of instruments heard in live and recorded performances.

People generally choose to go to concerts or other kinds of performances because they like particular kinds of music. Children learn early how to discriminate one kind of music from another. In determining the interests of students of different ages, notice that the students usually know the place on the radio (or television) to find the music that they prefer. Many respond to music in some way with their bodies. They, of course, must know how much bodily response, if any, is appropriate at live performances.

Much conversation in hallways and at lunch centers around the music interests and experiences of students. They enjoy sharing the enjoyment of listening to the same thing at the same time. Often people enjoy sharing knowledge and musical skills with others who are interested. This is important because too often children with physical or multiple disabilities do not have opportunities for these kinds of experiences in natural situations. Consequently, they have limited opportunities to become what others perceive as interesting persons.

Questionnaire for Similar-Age Peers

Development of a questionnaire to give peers is one of the best strategies for determining content for different components of curricular domains designed to teach life skills. Life management curriculum can be based partially on feedback from peers who are in general education classes and who represent what the majority of students with and without disabilities like in various aspects of community life. Figure 6–14 provides a sample music questionnaire about music activities of peers.

FIGURE 6–14
Sample questionnaire to inventory student interests and experiences

MUSIC QUESTIONNAIRE

YOUR AGE? _____

1. What is your favorite kind of music (techno, classical, rap, rock, etc.)? ______
2. How do you hear this music (radio, TV, live concerts, videos, etc.)? ______
3. Who are your favorite performers of your favorite type of music? ______
4. What instruments are used mostly with this kind of music (electric guitar, orchestra, etc.)? ______
5. What is it about the music that makes you like it best (the tune, lyrics, friends like it, etc.)? ______
6. How would you describe this music to someone who doesn't know what it is? ______
7. What are some of your favorite tunes? ______
8. Who are some of your favorite singers (in addition to any listed above)? ______
9. What kinds of lyrics do you like best? ______
10. When do you usually listen to music? ______
11. What makes music special to you and your friends? ______
12. Where, when, and how have you learned new things about music? ______
13. How have you participated in music (read and write music, piano lessons for 3 years, music appreciation class at school, etc.)? ______
14. Do you have access to recording equipment? If so, what kind? ______
15. If you answered Yes on #14, would you be willing to volunteer to make a short cassette tape for us if we supply the tape and describe which samples of music we want in order to teach music to student with disabilities? ______
16. If you answered Yes on #15, please give us your name, address, and telephone number or e-mail address so we can get in touch with you. Thank you, ______
(name of teacher)

Note. Adapted from *Teaching Individuals with Physical and Multiple Disabilities* (3rd ed., pp. 271–272), by J.L. Bigge, 1991, Upper Saddle River, NJ: Merrill/Prentice Hall.

Duplicate such a questionnaire, field-test it on a few students, duplicate with revision, present it to a teacher or present it directly to a general education class, and make sure a deadline is designated for its return. Try to use the opportunity to elicit assistance after the questionnaire. Students who participated now have a direct interest and are perfect resources. They often have tape-recording equipment and can make demonstration tapes of certain kinds of music to help uninformed students learn about that music.

When analyzing questionnaire results, notice patterns in responses for each question. Also consider the cultural and linguistic influence on students. What are the sources of musical interests and experiences? Do students in this community listen to a limited number of local radio stations? A wide variety? What is available in terms of selection? Do these students watch nationwide television shows on popular music such as MTV? Do the students attend concerts that are advertised on TV and radio? Do touring musical groups regularly appear in the community? If so, what kinds of music do they offer? What do local music sources provide?

By reading the answers and analyzing patterns of responses, teachers should be able to gain a strong idea of the musical preferences of similar-age students. Gathering the same information from students receiving special education provides information that allows teachers to identify noticeable discrepancies. Once the discrepancies are identified, the teacher can provide the content and objectives of some components of a life management curriculum. Pay special attention to how the music is accessible to the students. A resulting challenge may arise in making adaptations to equipment such as radios, tape recorders, and CD players so students with poor upper extremity control can use them independently. Transportation and architectural accessibility issues involved in attending concerts become reasons for additional ecological inventories.

STUDENT STRATEGIES

Finally, the following set of task analysis strategies meets special needs of both the educators and the students they teach. Too often textbooks underemphasize the importance of task analysis. While authors acknowledge its worth as a valuable tool for professionals who work with students with disabilities, they often do not recognize that task analysis is perhaps one of the most valuable tools that instructors can teach their students. Therefore, the fourth and final group of examples of task analyses in this chapter are techniques recommended for professionals and also for the strategy repertoire of individuals with physical or multiple disabilities. These topics are:

1. Learning and practicing self-care routines.
2. Organizing bodies of information.
3. Solving personal access problems.

Learning and Practicing Self-Care Routines

Students with physical or multiple disabilities frequently must depend upon others for care of their personal needs. Before they realize it, students have slipped into a state of learned helplessness or learned dependence.

One way to avoid this and to help students with disabilities to prepare themselves for self-sufficiency in life is to teach students self-care, learning, and problem-solving strategies. Students should be taught to generate their own written or mental task analyses to determine everything they would have to be able to do to complete a particular task. For tasks not yet attempted or ones without any established subtasks, students need to learn how to specify what they will need to do to complete the entire task, noting each necessary step.

One teacher helped a 7-year-old girl prepare to transition from a special program to a regular class in her neighborhood school. The girl was incontinent (had no bladder control) because of spina bifida. The teacher and the girl knew the transition might be possible if the pupil could change her own diaper. The girl was already able to close the door behind her, lower herself to the floor, and propel herself to the cot carrying a diaper bag over one shoulder. A classroom health-care assistant or parent had always completed the entire diaper-changing procedure. Now the student needed to learn to complete the task herself. The teacher first watched the classroom health-care assistant complete the procedure. Next she and the student identified each step the student would need to learn to take complete care of herself. Figure 6–15 is a portion of the routine in the task ladder format.

FIGURE 6–15
Task analysis for self-care routine

TARGET TASK: PUT ON DIAPER WITH NO ASSISTANCE
ETC.
ETC.
Roll to left and straighten diaper.
Pull fresh diaper and cover under buttocks with left hand.
Roll to right.
Lie on back.
Place on floor.
Pull diaper and plastic cover away with right hand.
Roll body to the left.
Place tissue between legs on soiled diaper.
Wipe self.
Reach into bag for tissue.
Unsnap used diaper.
Pull pants down farther.
Lie on back.
Pull other side down.
Roll to right.
Pull pants with elasticized waistband down.
Roll to left.
Place diaper to left at level of buttocks.
Turn and lie down with legs extended.
Raise legs to cot with hands.
Place bag near cot on floor.
Take fresh diaper out of bag and place it on cot.
Put crutches on floor.
Sit on a cot.

Note. From *Teaching Individuals with Physical and Multiple Disabilities* (3rd ed., p. 274), by J.L. Bigge, 1991, Upper Saddle River, NJ: Merrill/Prentice Hall.

Because of physical impairment, some students cannot make the movements to actually accomplish tasks for themselves. In these situations, the strategy of **partial participation** helps to promote independence and reduces unnecessary dependence. Students should be allowed to complete as much of a task as they can independently achieve, with assistance to complete the rest of the task. When they cannot complete a step in a task, they can provide step-by-step instruction to others who are trying to help them. Heller, Forney, Alberto, and Schwartzman (2000) have described how students can assist in their own physical care needs or direct others to assist them. "Taking charge" in this manner supports physical and emotional independence.

Analyzing Bodies of Information

To develop proficiency with unfamiliar subjects, any student needs to use strategies that will help him or her find the most salient characteristics of new material. For students with physical or multiple disabilities, this becomes even more important.

Laborious, weak, and uncoordinated body movements or physical fatigue interferes with student attempts to take copious notes in their classes. Even if they can write or type, students may have to concentrate so much on the act of writing that they cannot concentrate on the material to be remembered. They may write too slowly to be functional. Depending on notes taken by peers is efficient, but students must remain engaged with the content that is presented.

For those students who need an efficient method of extracting the most salient ideas, concepts, and facts from unfamiliar material, a strategy for taking notes can be learned. A classic approach is using a **pattern method** or **graphic organizer** that combines pictures and words (Buzan, 1976). This strategy works well for students who can write and draw a little but cannot write quickly enough to take sufficient notes in class, at lectures, and in personal study.

On one sheet of paper students make a configuration of key words representing groups of key ideas extracted from source materials. Main ideas, concepts, and facts are graphically recorded with the key words to provide emphasis, information, and relationships (see Figure 6–16). This method has some advantages over traditional outlining. In one glance students can see important ideas and their relationships. This graphic approach adds interest and provides easy-to-remember cues. The result allows students a quick review of the salient points studied and provides a basis for lesson learning.

Solving Personal Access Problems

If individuals with physical, health, or multiple disabilities wait for others to develop ways they can do things independently, they may be losing precious time. Some solutions are so personal that even well-intentioned helpers do not have the appropriate perspective to propose satisfactory solutions. Hence, it is

FIGURE 6–16
Task analysis for analyzing information

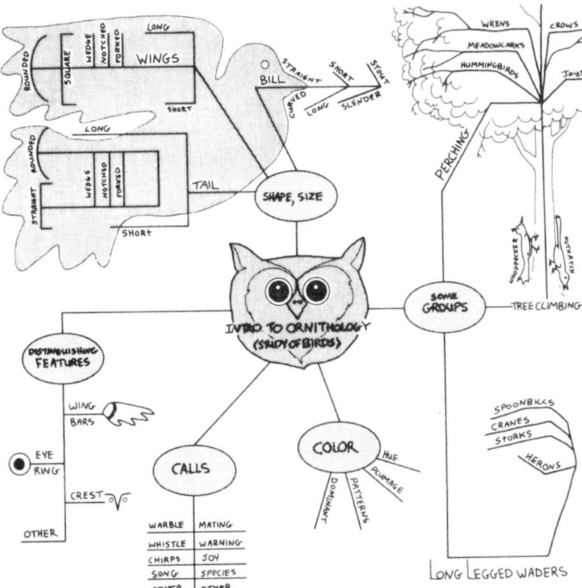

Note. From *Teaching Individuals with Physical and Multiple Disabilities* (3rd ed., p. 274), by J. L. Bigge, 1991, Upper Saddle River, NJ: Merrill/Prentice Hall.

FIGURE 6–17
Task analysis can be used to solve personal access problems.

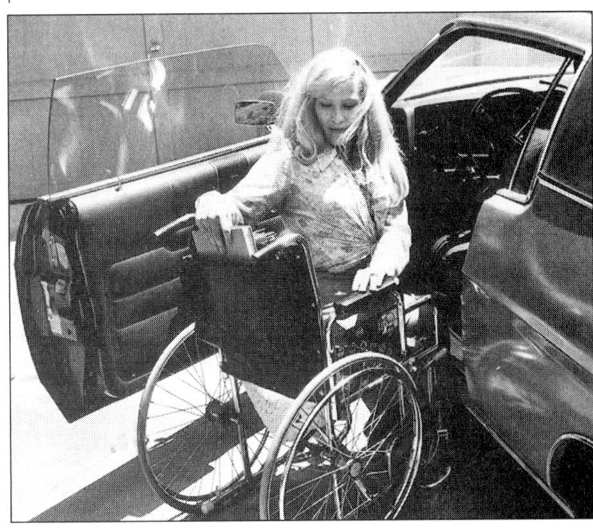

desirable to make every effort to encourage students to develop their own strategies for solving their own problems.

Take the example of a secondary student who was preparing for transition to the world of work. This youth, with paralysis of the legs (paraplegia), had a job offer. Since she had to provide her own transportation, her immediate goal was to find a way to get herself and her wheelchair into and out of a car (Figure 6–17). After considering the specifications of various cars, she chose one with adequate clearance between the rear door and the front seat. She made sure the front door opened to at least a 60-degree angle and that there was enough floor space behind the driver's seat for a wheelchair. She then had hand controls installed for the car. Next, she had to devise a way to get herself and her wheelchair in and out without help from others. She analyzed the necessary tasks and how they could be negotiated. Then the contemplated subtasks were tried out. With some minor changes in her original plan, she found she could accomplish her goal with the following sequence of steps:

1. Take books out of the book bag on the chair.
2. Lock the wheelchair brakes.
3. Place left arm on the car seat and right arm on the right wheelchair arm.
4. Push with arms to lift trunk and swing from the wheelchair onto the bottom door frame.

But each time she collapsed the chair and tried to pull it into the car, the chair opened up again. After much experimentation and with the help of friends, she worked out a plan. They designed a clamp for the chair handles to prevent its reopening. Now she completed the task this way:

5. Collapse the chair.
6. Push the clamp down over the second handle grip to keep the chair closed.
7. Turn the chair so the front wheels will go in first.
8. Pull the front wheels over the bottom door frame and rest it there.
9. Use arms to lift body from the door frame onto the car seat.
10. Use arms to lift legs inside the car.
11. Slide to the passenger side of the car.
12. Push the driver's seat back forward; reach over the back of the driver's seat and pull the chair into the car behind the driver's seat.
13. Slide back to the driver's seat.
14. Fasten the seat belt.
15. Drive using hand controls.

The outcome of this task analysis was a solution to a problem of personal access, resulting in greater autonomy and independent achievement of an age-appropriate skill (accessing the automobile for employment).

SUMMARY AND CONCLUSION

This chapter illustrates the many ways that task analysis strategies are central to the education of students with physical or multiple disabilities. It recounts that goals and objectives are generally based upon knowledge of a student's present performance, which task analysis, among other procedures, can help to assess. Task analysis can define the intermediary steps between present performance and full accomplishment of goals. Selected intermediary steps, in turn, often become the focus of instructional objectives. Task analysis also can help define as criteria the degree of independence and conditions under which the steps will be trained and performed. The written product of the task analysis may well provide lists of skills and activities in such a format that allows data to be easily collected during instruction and training. The written product may also become the description of specialized curricula. It can reflect the results of ecological inventories of natural situations in which students might find themselves. Finally, as the chapter concludes, task analysis is a valuable strategy to be learned and used by individuals with physical or multiple disabilities.

Remember that task analysis does not take place in a vacuum but is one of many strategies teachers use to reach desired goals and objectives. Once teachers have analyzed tasks, they will have new information to apply in the instructional program. Teachers, however, need not feel responsible for knowing everything (the entire scope of the problem, its future ramifications, specialized knowledge) that will affect the analysis and performance of a task. Working with expert professionals and with parents or guardians who are themselves experts with a particular student is important for a teacher who uses task analysis as a framework for examining, evaluating, and programming student performance.

QUESTIONS FOR DISCUSSION

1. Describe two examples in which task analysis can be used as a process. Describe two examples in which task analysis can be used as a product.
2. Discuss the advantages and disadvantages of developmental sequences for developing task analyses.
3. Describe a teaching/learning situation in which a teacher could employ the assistance strategies of verbal instructions, modeling/demonstration, and visual cues.
4. Why should teachers employ "wait time" with students with physical or multiple disabilities? Give an example in which a teacher can effectively use "wait time."
5. How do task analyses differ from situation analyses? If you were going to evaluate student skills for successfully ordering a meal in a restaurant, would you use task or situation analysis? Why? If you were going to analyze student skills for appropriate behavior in group social activities, would you use task or situation analysis? Why?

FOCUS ON THE NET

Low Incidence Unit

http://www.ged.gld.gov.au/tal/liu

The Low Incidence Unit (LIU) is a comprehensive source of instruction, ideas, and specific disability-related teaching systems for educators of students with specific low-incidence disabilities. One important feature of this site is its explanations for adapting instruction for students with physical disabilities. The LIU site has been produced through the government of Australia, but provides ideas that have universal application. The following areas can be located on the home page of LIU and lead the reader to useful information:

- Disabilities
- Therapy in Education
- Adaptive Technology

Disability Information for Students and Professionals

http://www.abilityinfo.com

This excellent site offers discussion forums, over 200 web links, and newswire information to continue to support development and knowledge in instruction of students with disabilities.

Maddux Special Education Homepage

http://www.unr.edu/homepage/maddux

The University of Reno produces the Maddux Special Education Homepage, which offers a variety of assessment and analysis ideas for educators and parents.

REFERENCES

Alper, S. (1996). An ecological approach to identifying curricular content for inclusive settings. In D. L. Ryndak & S. Alper (Eds.), *Curricular content for students with moderate to severe disabilities in inclusive settings* (pp. 19–31). Boston: Allyn & Bacon.

Bartel, N. R. (1990). Problems in mathematics achievement. In D. D. Hammill & N. R. Bartel (Eds.), *Teaching students with learning and behavior problems* (pp. 289–343). Boston: Allyn & Bacon.

Bigge, J. L. (1988). *Curriculum based instruction for special education students.* Mountain View, CA: Mayfield.

Bigge, J. L. (1991). *Teaching individuals with physical and multiple disabilities* (3rd ed.). Upper Saddle River, NJ: Merrill/Prentice Hall.

Bigge, J. L., & Best, S. J. (2001). Test and situation analysis. In J. L. Biggs, S. J. Best, & K. W. Heller, *Teaching individuals with physical, health, or multiple disabilities* (4th ed., pp. 121–148). Upper Saddle River, NJ: Merrill/Prentice Hall.

Bigge, J. L., Stump, C. S., Spagna, M. E., & Silberman, R. K. (1999). *Curriculum, assessment, and instruction for students with disabilities.* Belmont, CA: Wadsworth.

Brown, F., & Snell, M. E. (2000). Meaningful assessment. In M. E. Snell & F. Brown, *Instruction of students with severe disabilities* (pp. 67–114). Upper Saddle River, NJ: Merrill/Prentice Hall.

Brown, L. (1990). Evaluating and managing classroom behavior. In D. D. Hammill, & N. R. Bartel (Eds.), *Teaching students with learning and behavior problems* (pp. 345–415). Boston: Allyn & Bacon.

Buzan, T. (1976). *Use both sides of your brain.* New York: Dutton.

Cohen, M., Gross, P., & Haring, N. (1976). Developmental pinpoints. In N. Haring & L. Brown (Eds.), *Teaching the severely handicapped* (pp. 35–110). New York: Grune & Stratton.

Downing, J. E., & Demchak, M. A. (2002). Determining individuals' abilities and how to support students. In J. E. Downing, *Including students with severe and multiple disabilities in typical classrooms: Practical strategies for teachers* (pp. 15–61) (2nd ed.). Baltimore: MD Brookes.

Falvey, M. (1989). *Community-based curriculum: Instructional strategies for students with severe handicaps.* Baltimore: Brookes.

Hammill, D. D., & Bartel, N. R. (1990). *Teaching students with learning and behavior problems.* Boston: Allyn & Bacon.

Heller, K. W., Forney, P. E., Alberto, P. A., & Schwartzman, M. N. (2000). *Meeting physical and health needs of children with disabilities: Teaching student participation and management.* Belmont, CA: Wadsworth.

Meier, F. E. (1992). *Competency-based instruction for teachers of students with special learning needs.* Boston: Allyn & Bacon.

Mercer, C. D., & Mercer, A. R. (2001). *Teaching students with learning problems.* Upper Saddle River, NJ: Prentice Hall.

Rivera, D. P., & Smith, D. D. (1997). *Teaching students with learning and behavior problems* (3rd ed.). Boston: Allyn & Bacon.

Ryndak, D. A., & Alper, S. (2003). *Curriculum and instruction for students with significant disabilities in inclusive settings* (2nd ed.). Boston: Allyn & Bacon.

Ryndak, D. L., Sirvis, B. P., & Alcouloumre, D. S. (1997). Leisure education for positive life styles. In P. J. Schloss, M. A. Smith, & C. N. Schloss (Eds.), *Instructional methods for adolescents with learning and behavior problems* (pp. 305–329). Boston: Allyn & Bacon.

Sowers, J., Jenkins, C., & Powers, L. (1988). Vocational education of persons with physical handicaps. In R. Gaylord-Ross (Ed.), *Vocational education for persons with handicaps* (pp. 387–414). Mountain View, CA: Mayfield.

Westling, D. L., & Fox, L. (2000). *Teaching students with severe disabilities* (2nd ed.). Upper Saddle River, NJ: Merrill/Prentice Hall.

Assistive Technology

SHERWOOD J. BEST
PENNY REED
JUNE L. BIGGE

CHAPTER 7

KNOWLEDGE AND SKILLS

After you have read this chapter, you will be able to:

1. **Define assistive technology (AT) devices and services.**
2. **Describe the legal mandates for AT devices and services.**
3. **Discuss appropriate positioning, seating, and mobility for facilitating physical function and AT use for individuals with physical or multiple disabilities.**
4. **Evaluate AT product features for specific individuals across several areas of function.**
5. **Work as a member of a collaborative team to assess students' needs for AT.**
6. **Make informed choices about purchasing commercial AT devices.**
7. **Incorporate AT into IEP documents.**
8. **Incorporate a variety of modifications into classroom and community learning environments.**

Impairments become disabilities when they have a negative impact on the individual's participation in curricular, extracurricular, and other major life activities. One of the greatest challenges faced by teachers and others who work with individuals with physical or multiple disabilities is to assist with adaptations that reduce this negative impact. If these adaptations consist of specific items, pieces of equipment, or product systems, they are called **assistive technology devices.** If an individual with a disability requires assistance with assistive technology devices, they are eligible for **assistive technology services.**

Providing assistive technology (AT) so that students with physical or multiple disabilities can demonstrate what they think, know, and do comprises a large part of special education for this population. Teachers are integrally involved in identifying barriers to participation and solutions that will increase the amount and quality of participation. They must constantly identify ways in which students can participate in a variety of academic and functional activities. Two kinds of information are important to optimize participation: (1) the circumstances that give students difficulty when they try to participate and (2) the adaptations that might present helpful solutions. Assistive technology provides many answers to how student participation can be enhanced.

Sometimes identification of the problem and the nature of the needed assistive technology is obvious. In many cases, however, information is needed to develop and support avenues to participation for individuals with physical or multiple disabilities. Identification of the salient problems and generation of useful solutions stem from understanding the individual nature of each student, as well as knowledge related to specific physical conditions, therapeutic management of the conditions, and implications for management by teachers and others. Chapters 2 through 4 provided readers with this knowledge base. The next step is the addition of a broad background of information about types of adaptations and/or assistance. This chapter provides readers with a broad scope of information about various AT devices, services, and applications. First, legal definitions are presented and general areas of AT are explored. Assessing individuals for AT devices and services, using a multidisciplinary team approach, is addressed next. The second half of this chapter is devoted to application of AT. Proper positioning and seating introduce the discussion of AT, since they provide the foundation for participation in school and life activities. The topics of mobility, architectural access, environmental and object modification, and environmental control include a variety of strategies for supporting physical and sensory capabilities through AT.

Confining discussion of AT to a single chapter would not provide the emphasis that this topic deserves. Therefore, separate chapters devoted to the topics of writing, augmentative/alternative communication, literacy, mathematics, recreation/leisure, and personal independence are infused with discussions of assistive technology.

*

DEFINITIONS AND LEGAL BASIS FOR ASSISTIVE TECHNOLOGY

In 1988, Congress passed the Technology-Related Assistance for Individuals with Disabilities Act (commonly called the Tech Act). The Tech Act provided grants to states to "facilitate access to, provision of, and funding for assistive technology devices and services for individuals with disabilities" (Protection and Advocacy, Inc., 1995, p. 1). These grants were extended through reauthorization of the Tech Act in 1994.

Although the Tech Act did not provide direct funding to specific individuals with disabilities, it was designed to create a climate in which states would make changes in their structures, policies, and laws to provide access to AT devices and services. In 1990 the legal definitions of assistive technology devices and services developed under the Tech Act were incorporated into the Individuals with Disabilities Education Act (IDEA) and applied to infants, toddlers, children, and youth with disabilities. Both assistive technology devices and services are defined in IDEA.

> The term **assistive technology devices** means any item, piece of equipment or product system, whether acquired commercially off the shelf, modified, or customized, that is used to increase, maintain, or improve the functional capabilities of a child with a disability. (20 U.S.C. 1401 § 602 [1])

This broad definition indicates that assistive technology devices can range from very simple to very complex, depending on individual needs and circumstances.

Providing AT devices alone does not address the entire issue. AT services must also be guaranteed to support their use. These services are defined in the IDEA as follows:

> The term **assistive technology services** means any service that directly assists a child with a disability in the selection, acquisition, or use of an assistive technology device. These services include:
>
> - *evaluation* of the needs of such child including a functional evaluation of the child in the child's customary environment;
> - *purchasing, leasing, or otherwise providing for the acquisition* of assistive technology devices by such child;
> - *selecting, designing, fitting, customizing, adapting, applying, maintaining, repairing, or replacing* of assistive technology devices;
> - *coordinating and using other therapies, interventions, or services* with assistive technology devices, such as those associated with existing education and rehabilitation plans and programs;
> - *training and technical assistance for such child,* or, where appropriate, the family of such child; and
> - *training or technical assistance for professionals* (including individuals providing education and rehabilitation services), employers, or other individuals who provide services to, employ, or otherwise are substantially involved in the major life functions of such child. (20 U.S.C. 1401§ 602 [2]) (emphasis added)

The specific requirements for school districts to provide assistive technology are found in the IDEA regulations, as follows:

> § 300.308 Assistive technology.
>
> (a) Each public agency shall ensure that assistive technology devices or assistive technology services, or both, as those terms are defined in §§300.5–300.6,

are made available to a child with a disability if required as a part of the child's

(1) Special education under §300.26;

(2) Related services under §300.24; or

(3) Supplementary aids and services under §§300.28 and 300.550(b)(2).

(b) On a case-by-case basis, the use of school-purchased assistive technology devices in a child's home or in other settings is required if the child's IEP team determines that the child needs access to those devices in order to receive FAPE [free appropriate public education]. (20 U.S.C. 1412[a][12][B][i]).

In addition to the assistive technology services defined in IDEA in 1990, the reauthorization of IDEA in 1997 added the requirement that members of the IEP team consider the child's need for assistive technology when developing the IEP. This requirement is part of a set of "Special Factors" which must be considered.

Section 614 (d)(3)(B) Consideration of Special Factors. The IEP team also shall . . . . (v) Consider whether the child requires assistive technology devices and services.

Consideration was a new term in IDEA '97 and caused many school districts to search for ways to facilitate and document AT use. Close examination of IDEA reveals that AT is defined separately from the definitions of "special education" and "related services." However, it can be considered within the definition of special education as "specially designed instruction" and within the definition of related services as "a developmental, corrective, or supportive service." Therefore, AT can be considered as a special education service, a related service, or a supplementary aid or service that must be provided to assist students to be educated in the least restrictive environment (Osborne & Russo, 2003, p. 48).

While IDEA is the primary law affecting the provision of assistive technology services in schools, Golden (1998) notes that both the Americans with Disabilities Act (ADA) and Section 504 of the Rehabilitation Act of 1973 must not be overlooked. Under IDEA, schools are required to provide a free appropriate public education (FAPE). The focus in deciding if assistive technology is needed is to determine whether the use of the device is within the basic requirement of "appropriate." This is often challenging enough, but Golden (1998) reminds us that Section 504 has a different standard. This law requires schools to provide "equal access" to an education as well as FAPE. The ADA has a third standard. It also requires equal access, but it goes beyond Section 504 and requires "effective communication" and "consideration of consumer preference." Assuring FAPE under IDEA or FAPE and equal access under Section 504 may not satisfy the effective communication requirement of the ADA, especially when examining the need for AT. Case law will continue to determine and define these and other fine points of the requirements for provision of AT devices and services by school districts, as hearing officers and judges hear cases.

ASSISTIVE TECHNOLOGY DEVICES AND SERVICES

Assistive technology devices can be very simple or very complex. One way to approach this very diverse group of items is to think about the functional capabilities that are addressed. In the **Wisconsin Assistive Technology Checklist** (Wisconsin Assistive Technology Initiative, 2004), assistive technology is divided into a number of categories and subcategories (see Figure 7–1). Within each of these categories, suggested AT devices and strategies are arranged in a hierarchy from simple, low-tech alternatives to more complex or high-tech items. This is because the developers shared a belief that it is important to select the simplest alternative that successfully assists the student. It is not unusual for teachers, therapists, or parents to immediately select the most complex solution or the one they just heard about on television, without first trying other alternatives. The hierarchical arrangement of the items in the Assistive Technology Initiative Checklist is designed to promote thinking from the simplest to the most complex. For example, voice recognition might not be the first AT option to try with a student who has difficulty with writing. While it is an exciting and very appealing technology, there are simpler tools that might be tried first.

Each section in the Assistive Technology Checklist also includes a space for new AT options, since many new products are introduced each year. The final section of the Assistive Technology Checklist provides a place for comments by team members. In this way, the checklist is flexible and capable of expansion. It is also important to remember that students with physical or

FIGURE 7–1
Wisconsin Assistive Technology Checklist

Writing

Mechanics of Writing

Assessment form: Mechanics of writing
- ❑ Pencil/pen with adaptive grip
- ❑ Adapted paper (e.g., raised line, highlighted lines)
- ❑ Slantboard
- ❑ Typewriter
- ❑ Portable word processor
- ❑ Computer
- ❑ Other:

Alternate Computer Access

Assessment form: Fine motor related to computer access
- ❑ Keyboard w/ Easy Access or Access DOS
- ❑ Word Prediction, abbreviation/expansion to reduce keystrokes
- ❑ Keyguard
- ❑ Arm support (e.g., Ergo Rest)
- ❑ Track ball/track pad/joystick w/ on-screen keyboard
- ❑ Alternate keyboard (e.g., IntelliKeys, Disc. Board, TASH)
- ❑ Mouth stick/head pointer w/ standard/alternate keyboard
- ❑ Head Mouse/Head Master/Tracker w/ onscreen keyboard
- ❑ Switch with Morse Code
- ❑ Switch with scanning
- ❑ Voice recognition software
- ❑ Other:

Composing Written Material

Assessment form: Composing written material
- ❑ Word cards/word book/word wall
- ❑ Pocket dictionary/thesaurus
- ❑ Electronic/talking electronic dictionary/thesaurus/spell checker (e.g., Franklin Bookman)
- ❑ Word processing w/ spell checker/grammar checker
- ❑ Word processing w/ word prediction (e.g., Co:Writer) to facilitate spelling and sentence construction
- ❑ Talking word processor for multisensory typing
- ❑ Multimedia software for expression of ideas (assignments)
- ❑ Voice recognition software
- ❑ Other:

Communication

Assessment form: Communication
- ❑ Communication board/book with pictures/objects/ letters/words
- ❑ Eye gaze board/frame
- ❑ Simple voice output device (e.g., BIGmack, Cheap Talk, Voice in a Box, MicroVoice, talking picture frame, Hawk)
- ❑ Voice output device w/ levels (e.g., 6 Level Voice in a Box, Macaw, Digivox)
- ❑ Voice output device w/ icon sequencing (e.g., AlphaTalker Liberator, Chatbox)
- ❑ Voice output device w/ dynamic display (e.g., Dynavox, Speaking Dynamically w/ laptop computer/Freestyle)
- ❑ Device w/ speech synthesis for typing (e.g., Cannon Communicator, Link, Write:Out Loud w/ laptop)
- ❑ Other:

Reading, Studying, and Math

Reading

Assessment form: Reading
- ❑ Changes in text size, spacing, color, background color
- ❑ Book adapted for page turning (e.g., page fluffers, 3-ring binder)
- ❑ Use of pictures with text (e.g., Picture It, Writing with Symbols)
- ❑ Talking electronic device to pronounce challenging words (e.g., Franklin Bookman, American Heritage Dictionary)
- ❑ Scanner w/ OCR and talking word processor
- ❑ Electronic books
- ❑ Other:

Detailed assessment form:

Learning/Studying

Assessment form: Learning and studying
- ❑ Print or picture schedule
- ❑ Low tech aids to find materials (e.g., index tabs, color coded folders)
- ❑ Highlight text (e.g., markers, highlight tape, ruler, etc.)
- ❑ Voice output reminders for assignments, steps of task, etc.
- ❑ Software for manipulation of objects/concept development (e.g., Blocks in Motion, Toy Store)
- ❑ May use alternate input device, e.g., switch, touch window
- ❑ Software for organization of ideas and studying (e.g., Inspiration, Claris Works Outline, PowerPoint, etc.)
- ❑ Recorded material (books on tape, taped lectures with numbered coded index, etc.)
- ❑ Other:

Math

Assessment form: Math
- ❑ Abacus/ Math Line
- ❑ Calculator/calculator with print out
- ❑ Talking calculator
- ❑ Calculator w/ large keys and/or large LCD print out
- ❑ On-screen calculator
- ❑ Software with cueing for math computation (may use adapted input methods)
- ❑ Tactile/voice output measuring devices (e.g., clock, ruler)
- ❑ Other:

FIGURE 7–1
(Continued)

Recreation & Leisure

Assessment form: Recreation and leisure

- ❑ Adapted toys and games (e.g., toy with adaptive handle)
- ❑ Use of battery interrupter and switch to operate a toy
- ❑ Adaptive sporting equipment (e.g., lighted/bell ball, velcro mitt)
- ❑ Universal cuff to hold crayons, markers, paint brush
- ❑ Modified utensils (e.g., rubbers, stampers, scissors.)
- ❑ Ergo Rest to support arm for drawing/painting
- ❑ Drawing/graphic program on computer (e.g., Kid Pix, Blocks in Motion)
- ❑ Playing games on the computer
- ❑ Music software on the computer
- ❑ Other:

Activities of Daily Living (ADLs)

- ❑ Nonslip materials to hold things in place
- ❑ Universal cuff/strap to hold items in hand
- ❑ Color coded items for easier locating and identifying
- ❑ Adaptive eating utensils (e.g., foam handles, deep sides)
- ❑ Adaptive drinking devices (e.g., cup with cut out rim)
- ❑ Adaptive dressing equipment (e.g., button hook, elastic shoe laces, Velcro® instead of buttons, etc.)
- ❑ Adaptive devices for hygiene (e.g., adapted toothbrushes, raised toilet seat, etc.)
- ❑ Adaptive bathing devices
- ❑ Adaptive equipment for cooking
- ❑ Other:

Mobility

Assessment form: Mobility

- ❑ Walker
- ❑ Grab bars and rails
- ❑ Manual wheelchair including sports chair
- ❑ Powered mobility toy (e.g., Cooper Car, GoBot)
- ❑ Powered scooter or cart
- ❑ Powered wheelchair joystick, head switch, sip/puff or other control
- ❑ Adapted vehicle for driving
- ❑ Other:

Environment Control

- ❑ Light switch extension
- ❑ Use of Powerlink and switch to turn on electrical appliances (e.g., radio, fan, blender, etc.)
- ❑ Radio/ Ultrasound/ remote controlled appliances
- ❑ Other:

Positioning & Seating

Assessment form: Seating and positioning

- ❑ Non-slip surface on chair to prevent slipping (e.g. Dycem)
- ❑ Bolster, rolled towel, blocks for feet
- ❑ Adapted/alternate chair, side lyer, stander
- ❑ Custom fitted wheelchair or insert
- ❑ Other:

Vision

Assessment form: Vision

- ❑ Eye glasses
- ❑ Magnifier
- ❑ Large print books
- ❑ CCTV (closed circuit television)
- ❑ Screen magnifier (mounted over screen)
- ❑ Screen magnification Sftwr. (e.g., CloseView, Zoom Text)
- ❑ Screen color contrast (e.g., CloseView)
- ❑ Screen reader (e.g., OutSpoken), text reader
- ❑ Braille translation software
- ❑ Braille printer
- ❑ Enlarged or Braille/tactile labels for keyboard
- ❑ Alternate keyboard with enlarged keys
- ❑ Braille keyboard and note taker (e.g., Braille N Speak)
- ❑ Other:

Hearing

Assessment form: Hearing

- ❑ Pen and paper
- ❑ Computer/portable word processor
- ❑ TTY for phone access w/ or w/o relay
- ❑ Signaling device (e.g., vibrating pager)
- ❑ Closed captioning
- ❑ Real time captioning
- ❑ Computer aided notetaking
- ❑ Screen flash for alert signals on computer
- ❑ Personal amplification system
- ❑ Hearing aid
- ❑ FM system
- ❑ Loop system
- ❑ Infrared system
- ❑ Phone amplifier
- ❑ Other:

Comments:

Note: Wisconsin Assistive Technology Checklist by Wisconsin Assistive Technology Initiative, 2004, Oshkosh, WI. Copyright 2000–2001 by WATI. Reprinted with permission.

multiple disabilities may need AT from more than one of these categories and that their needs may change over the years. The contents of the checklist are also available in a "user friendly" format from the Council for Exceptional Children (CEC). The AT "Quick Wheel" contains the list of tools in Figure 7–1 as well as a brief summary of the law related to AT and numerous resources for quick reference. The AT Quick Wheel is particularly useful to practitioners at IEP meetings. Readers can view the AT Quick Wheel on the Internet at *www.ideapractices.org/resources/tam* and order it online from the Technology and Media Division of CEC at *www.tamcec.org*.

DETERMINING THE NEED FOR ASSISTIVE TECHNOLOGY

Based on IDEA, it is clear that the school district (which is a public agency) must ensure that AT devices or services or both are provided if "required." It is the determination of whether or not the AT is required that is often challenging for school personnel. Under IDEA the standard used to determine whether something is "required" is whether it is needed for a student to receive a free appropriate public education (FAPE). Free appropriate public education includes a variety of components such as special education services, related services, supplementary aids and services, and modifications to the program. The IEP team must consider FAPE when they are trying to determine whether a particular AT device or service would just be a "nice" thing to have or whether it is really necessary—that is, without it, the child would not be receiving FAPE. Frequently IEP teams will find it necessary to implement AT use on a trial basis to determine its impact on the child's performance and progress in the curriculum. Like all other aspects of FAPE, AT must be provided at no cost to parents.

Considering the Need for Assistive Technology

In order for an IEP team to appropriately and effectively consider the student's need for AT, they must collectively have enough knowledge to make a good determination. This includes some knowledge about AT devices and services that might be appropriate and applicable for the student they are discussing. In addition, they will need a process or procedure to efficiently make a good decision. How should team members "consider" the need for AT?

- Consideration is a brief process that can take place within every IEP meeting.
- Consideration is more than someone saying, "Oh, that doesn't apply to my students."
- At least one person on the IEP team must have some knowledge about AT, because you cannot "consider" something about which you know nothing.
- In order to think about whether AT would be helpful, the bulk of the IEP must be developed in order for team members to evaluate the student's goals.
- The annual goals which the child is expected to accomplish will be the focus of the discussion about what AT might assist or allow the child to accomplish them.

The following situations might lead team members to consider AT as a solution:

- Standard print size is too small to read;
- A student is unable to hear all that is being said;
- Manipulative materials are too difficult to utilize;
- The student often needs text read to him or her in order to complete an assignment;
- The child's handwriting is so illegible that the meaning is impossible to decipher;
- The effort of writing is so slow or so exhausting that assignments do not get completed;
- The student is not able to communicate effectively or efficiently;
- Current modifications are not working;
- The student is "stuck," making little progress; or
- Decoding reading assignments is so difficult that the student loses track of the meaning.

Figure 7–2 illustrates the four general types of outcomes that may be reached after AT consideration (Reed, 1998).

Most state education agencies have developed a set of questions in their IEP forms to ensure that IEP teams respond to the question "Does the student need AT devices or services?" If the answer is yes, the IEP team members must specify the particular device(s) that are needed. Because some IEP teams need more guidance than that single question provides, the Wisconsin Assistive Technology Initiative has developed

FIGURE 7–2
Wisconsin Assistive Technology Initiative AT Consideration Outcomes

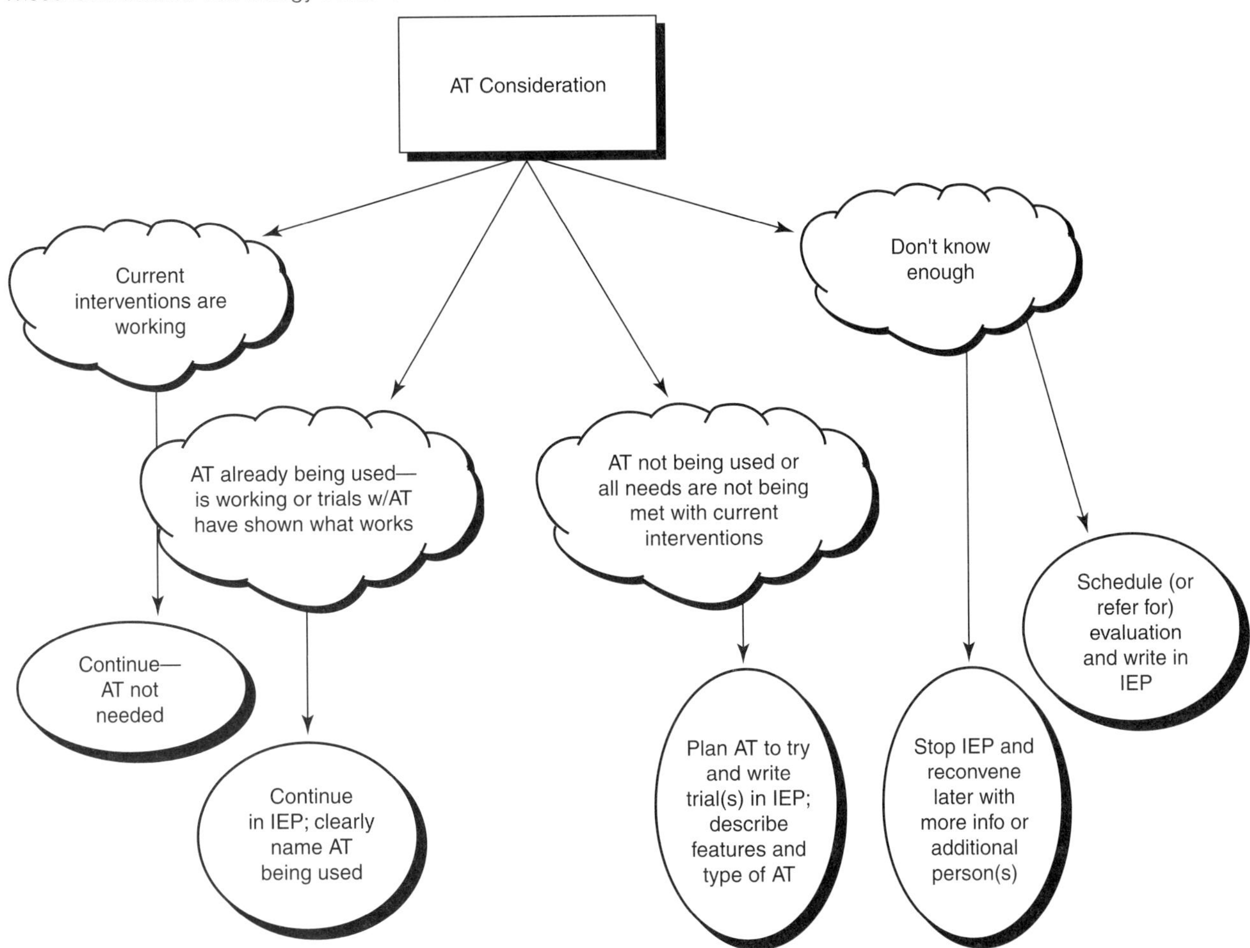

Note. From *AT Consideration Outcomes* by P. Reed, 1998, Oshkosh Wisconsin Assistive Technology Initiative. Copyright 1998 by WATI. Reprinted with permission.

the AT Consideration Guide (Wisconsin Assistive Technology Initiative, 2002a). The AT Consideration Guide leads the IEP team through the following questions to help them determine whether the student does or does not "need" AT devices or services:

1. What task is it that we want this student to do, that s/he is unable to do at a level that reflects his/her skills/abilities (writing, communicating, reading, seeing, hearing, etc.)?
2. Is the student currently able to complete tasks with special strategies or accommodations?
3. Is AT (devices, tools, hardware, or software) currently used to address this task?
4. Would the use of AT help the student perform this skill more easily or efficiently, in the least restrictive environment, or perform successfully with less personal assistance?

The AT Consideration Guide also provides the place to describe results when a new AT device or service is tried. It is important to plan one or more formal trials to actually determine what AT will work for a specific student. *Only after successful trial use should the permanent use of AT be written into the IEP.* Readers are encouraged to download the AT Consideration Guide and the Trial Use Forms at *www.wati.org/assessmentforms.htm.*

Assistive Technology and Assessment

As noted earlier, one of the outcomes of "consideration" may be the determination that some kind of assessment or evaluation of the child's need for AT is needed. The need for an AT assessment may occur at any time during the provision of services to children with disabilities. It may come up during the official "consideration" during the IEP meeting, during referral, or at any time while a student is receiving special education and related services (Bowser & Reed, 1995, 1998). Generally the need for an AT assessment is brought up either by the parents or the therapists, teachers, paraeducators, or other individuals who provide services to the student in the school. It may be a formal request for an "Assistive Technology Evaluation" or more of a realization that the routine problem-solving that is a normal part of service delivery is not sufficient to answer this question and something more is needed.

The question may be broad: "Jennifer struggles with trying to do all of the required reading and writing in sixth grade. She understands the concepts, but decoding the printed word and trying to spell what she wants to write are so difficult that she is feeling overwhelmed and frustrated. She is falling further behind. Is there any assistive technology that could help with this?" Or it can be very specific: "Matt is not able to understand the graphics in the social studies book due to limited vision." In Jennifer's case there may be a whole range of hardware (from low-tech to computer based) and software that will need to be tried for specific reading and writing tasks in her various classes. In Matt's case only one or two things may need to be tried before a workable solution will be found. In either situation, the team of service providers who work with that child needs to have a systematic approach to begin to answer the question.

Bowser and Reed (1995, 1998) recommend that school districts make AT services, including assessment of the need for AT, an integral part of their system of referral, evaluation, plan development, and implementation of special education and related services at designated points in the delivery of special education services. Of course, teachers and therapists who are new to AT or teams new to the role of "assessing" a student's need for AT may struggle at first. They struggle to figure out where to start, what questions to ask, what commercial tests, if any, they might need to use, and what AT might be helpful. They require specific training and a systematic approach to this task. The Wisconsin Assistive Technology Initiative has developed a set of forms to help the team and its individual members through these difficulties and to help them focus on the specific issues that must be addressed (Wisconsin Assistive Technology Initiative, 2002b). Each form can be used to guide the team through specific steps of the assessment process. The forms include:

- The **WATI Student Information Guide,** which provides the questions necessary for the team to describe the student's abilities and needs;
- The **WATI Environmental Observation Guide,** a form used during classroom observations;
- The **WATI Assistive Technology Decision-Making Guide,** which leads the team through a decision-making process;
- The **WATI Trial Use Guide,** which organizes periods of trial use of assistive technology; and
- The **Assistive Technology Trial Use Summary,** which provides a concise summary of the outcomes of the AT trials. (Wisconsin Assistive Technology Initiative, 2002b).

It is recommended that readers download these forms from the Wisconsin Assistive Technology Initiative Web site and refer to them throughout the remainder of this chapter discussion on AT assessment. A manual is also available for assessing students' need for AT (Reed & Lahm, 2004).

ASSESSING AN INDIVIDUAL'S NEED FOR ASSISTIVE TECHNOLOGY

Team Assessment Principles and Practices

The IEP team or an identified AT team may decide to complete the assessment. In some cases there is no AT team or only one person has been designated as a "specialist" or "consultant" in AT for the district. In this case a team of people with sufficient knowledge to make an appropriate and useful decision must be assembled. The process used to complete the assessment can be divided into two main components—*gathering information* and *decision making.* Each component has several subcomponents. The final component is *trial implementation.*

Step 1.0: Gathering Information.

Step 1.1: Assemble team. A brief meeting may be held to identify and assign specific tasks, or a team leader may assign tasks without a meeting if team members can function effectively without this "organizational" meeting.

While the number of team members and their specific expertise will vary with the magnitude and complexity of the questions to be answered, there are some specific considerations in selecting the members of the team. It is important that someone on the team understand curriculum. This expertise is provided by a special or general education teacher. If the questions related to AT involve speech or language, then someone with expertise in language development is needed. This is most typically a speech/language pathologist, but might also be a teacher of the hearing impaired, if appropriate. Often there are questions about positioning or motor ability. In this case a physical and/or occupational therapist is needed. And, of course, one or more of these individuals must have knowledge about specific assistive technologies that might be appropriate to address the child's needs. There may be any number of other individuals in the AT assessment team. For example, if the child has a visual impairment, there would need to be a vision specialist involved. Even when a core group of people in a school district routinely addresses questions about AT, the specific team working together to determine an AT solution should include individuals who collectively can address all of the student's unique needs. Finally, one or both of the parents should be active participants in the information gathering and decision making. Students who can contribute and understand information should participate in meetings with family members. Typically a group of three to seven individuals will meet to begin the information-gathering and decision-making stages of the AT assessment process.

Step 1.2: Team members gather information. Team members review existing information regarding the student's abilities, difficulties, environment, and tasks. This includes a thorough file review, sharing information with each other, and one or more observations in relevant environments. If questions remain unanswered, team members will need to complete formal or informal tests that yield the information needed (e.g., receptive language ability).

The **WATI Student Information Guide** is an excellent tool for gathering information from many possible sources. This guide is a collection of questions that the team will need to be able to answer in order to match the student's needs with appropriate AT devices and services. The first section of the WATI Student Information Guide contains questions about what AT is currently being used and what has been used in the past. This is important information because one service provider may be using AT without others being aware of it. For example, the Language Arts teacher may have discovered that the quality of Samantha's writing is much better with voice output on the computer. This may occur because all of the computers in her classroom are equipped with speech cards and talking word processing. She observes over the course of several months that Samantha regularly chooses to work with talking word processing and that it has improved both the spelling and grammar in her written assignments. Documenting and sharing that kind of information is essential.

The next section requires a file review to determine what AT has been tried in the past and the outcome of that use. Changes in staff can cause them to lose track of valuable information. Perhaps the most extreme example of this is the case of a team who spent several weeks trying to determine what augmentative communication device might work for a nonspeaking student. They were all new and neglected to thoroughly review the file until late October, when they were startled to learn that a $6,000 dynamic-display, voice-output communication aid had been purchased for the student two years earlier. It was in a box, at the back of the classroom closet, safely stored away. Had someone not reviewed the file, they would have spent money on another device, when they already had a very powerful one available. The parent had told them on several occasions that there "used to be something that talked for him," but they had not tracked down the critical information.

The team then consults the WATI Student Information Guide and selects the other sections that they feel they will need to complete. It is recommended that a team new to AT assessment concentrate on only one area of concern at a time. For example, perhaps the child has a learning disability and team members are most concerned about writing. They would proceed to the Writing section and answer the questions in that section. If they are concerned about more than one task, they may decide to complete more than one section of the WATI Student Information Guide. The team must determine how many and which sections of the Guide will be helpful. The following sections are included in the WATI Student Information Guide:

- Motor Aspects of Writing;
- Fine Motor Related to Computer Access;
- Composing Written Material;
- Communication;
- Reading;
- Learning and Studying;
- Math;
- Recreation and Leisure;
- Activities of Daily Living;
- Mobility;
- Positioning and Seating;
- Control of the Environment;
- Vision;
- Hearing.

Once the desired sections of the WATI Student Information Guide are completed, the team moves to the section on general information. The questions on this page apply to every child. They include questions about behaviors that might impact the child's use of AT and other significant factors that should be noted, such as learning style, coping strategies, or interests that the team should remember and consider as they move on with the assessment process.

The next step in the process is to observe the student in the settings where he or she is experiencing difficulties. The **WATI Environmental Observation Guide** is a simple form that draws the observer's attention to what is going on in the activity and setting. First the activity or task being observed is noted. Then the observer is asked to describe the way that typical students participate in that activity. The observer is asked to note how the target student participates and record any apparent barriers to the target student's participation. This might include the position or location of the student, the position or location of instructional materials, lighting, noise level, or any other factor. Finally the observer is asked to note any potential accommodations or AT that comes to mind right then as a potential solution.

Figure 7–3 is an example of a completed Environmental Observation Guide. Although some of the observations are common sense, others require a minimal knowledge of AT. For example, in order to suggest a "prerecorded message," one would need to know that having some device with a prerecorded message is possible, but would not necessarily need to know any certain type or brand. If they did know types and brands, they could also note that. If they knew where one was available in the school, they could include that information. Decisions or even formal recommendations come later in the assessment process.

In this example, Jeff is a 5-year-old child with moderate cerebral palsy. He utilizes a wheelchair for mobility and positioning and is minimally speaking. His utterances are understood better by his family than by his peers and service providers at school. The observer noted that Jeff was looking away from the teacher to avoid the bright light in his eyes. He was not being inattentive. The other children were seated at a lower level and were not bothered by the sunlight. The teacher changed her position the next day so that her back was not to a window.

Step 1.3: Schedule meeting. Schedule the meeting with the full team, including the parents (and students if appropriate).

Step 2.0: Decision Making. Using an effective decision-making process requires team members to acquire and use a variety of skills that are separate from the technical skills of data gathering. These include communication skills and group process skills. Communication skills include, but are not limited to, active listening, negotiation, providing nonthreatening feedback, and accepting criticism without becoming defensive. Group process includes following a schedule, reaching consensus, and effectively making formal group decisions.

The value of using a clearly defined decision-making process in team decision making has been identified within the field of education (Dettmer, Thurston, & Dyck, 1993; Gordon, 1977; Schmuck & Runkel, 1994), and early intervention (Prentice & Spencer, 1985). Although awareness of the importance of this training has been evident in the literature for more than two decades, most teachers and therapists are still not receiving training in this

FIGURE 7–3
Completed Wisconsin Assistive Technology Initiative Environmental Observation Form

Student/Child: Jeff **Date:**

Location: Kindergarten classroom **Observer(s):**

Activity: Opening circle time

Activity/task(s) being observed	Ways that typical students participate	Ways the target student participates	Barriers to target student's participation	Potential accommodation(s) and/or AT
Teacher sits on chair with back to low bookcase with materials. Talks about day of week, month, weather; uses props; talks about how they are dressed for the weather; reads story about rain.	Students sit on floor in semicircle. They point at items on magnet board, answer questions, choose day of week, month, etc. During story, they attend, answer questions, point to things in book, chant words in repeated lines.	Wheeled over in wheelchair, placed directly in front of teacher. Sometimes looks at items, other times looks away. Attempts to point when magnet board is held close enough. During story time turns head away.	At different height from other children, no voice output device, sun shining in eyes during story.	Positioning device for floor, sitting, prerecorded message about weather or day, move teacher to other wall to solve sun/bright light in eyes, prerecorded repeated lines from book being read that day.

Note. From Wisconsin Assistive Technology Initiative, 9/97, Oshkosh, WI. Reprinted with permission.

area before they are employed (Reed, 1997c). As a result, most teams do not use a clearly defined process and may not even be aware of the need for formalizing or organizing their decision making. The meetings where important decisions are made may be very free flowing and disorganized, with no agenda, no process for assuring everyone has input, and no formal determination of agreement or disagreement among members.

The key elements or steps of an effective decision-making process include:

1. **Problem Identification:** The identification and definition of a specific problem;
2. **Solution Generation:** The suggestion of possible solutions;
3. **Solution Selection:** The evaluation of suggestions and choosing of a solution, to create an action plan;
4. **Implementation:** The carrying out of the plan; and
5. **Follow-up:** Meeting again to evaluate the solution.

The challenge comes in having all members of the team recognize the steps and follow the sequence together. Because it is not unusual for team meetings to be conducted in an informal manner with information presented verbally and with little attention to specific steps of the decision-making process, individual styles of thinking and communicating can lead to problems. One team member may be seeking very specific and minute details of the problem, while another team member is thinking of great solutions, and still another is wondering how soon the meeting will be over or what assignment to use in class tomorrow.

The **WATI Assistive Technology Decision-Making Guide** provides a simple but effective structure for making AT decisions.

Step 2.1: Identify problems using the WATI assistive technology decision-making guide. The emphasis in Problem Identification is to identify tasks the child needs to be able to do and the relationship of the child's abilities/difficulties and environment to the child's performance of the tasks.

The team should move quickly through the first two areas of Problem Identification: "Student's Abilities/Difficulties Related to Tasks" and "Environmental Considerations." The third area of Problem Identification is to identify the tasks the child needs to be able to do, which will help to generate AT solutions.

Step 2.2: Choose tasks for solution generation. The team must select one critical task for which they will generate solutions. If there are multiple needs, they will work on them one at a time.

Step 2.3: Solution generation. This portion of the problem-solving process is brainstorming. All possible solutions are written so all can see them. There is no discussion. The specificity of the solutions will vary depending on the knowledge and experience of the team members. Some teams may generate names of specific devices with features that will meet the child's needs; other teams may simply talk about features that are important, e.g., "needs voice output," "needs to be portable," "needs few [or many] messages," "needs input method other than hands," etc. If needed, the team can use specific resources (such as the WATI checklist) to assist with Solution Generation.

If the solutions generated by the team are primarily teaching strategies and include little or no AT, then the team may need to utilize additional resources. These resources can provide an overview of the types of AT solutions that would be appropriate for the child and task of concern.

Step 2.4: Solution selection. At this step, the team discusses the solutions listed during Solution Generation, thinking about which have the most potential to be effective for the student. Team members should combine, sequence, and prioritize solutions, then obtain consensus.

Step 2.5: Develop implementation plan. Utilizing the items selected in Solution Selection, the team will develop an "Implementation" or Action Plan (including any needed trials with specific hardware or software). At this step the team must assign specific names of individuals who are responsible to complete tasks and the dates by which they need to be completed.

Step 2.6: Plan for follow-up. The team will arrange to meet again to review progress. Follow-up should reflect the number of steps to be completed in the Implementation Plan.

Step 3.0: Implementation

Step 3.1: Implement the Plan. If part of the plan is a series of trials with a variety of hardware or software, they will need to be scheduled as the AT is purchased, borrowed, or rented for trial use. Any training needed by the staff implementing the plan will need to be provided immediately to prevent delays. The plan should be followed completely to assess whether the solutions that were selected are good ones.

Step 3.2: Follow Up on Planned Date. The follow-up meeting will involve a review of all actions to date, including specific data collected, and a discussion of whether the AT is working. Recycling to Step 2 of the decision-making process may be necessary if changes are needed. At a set interval after implementation, follow-up or monitoring must take place. This is a critical area that cannot be bypassed.

Figure 7–4 shows a completed Wisconsin Assistive Technology Decision-Making Guide. Following these simple but effective steps can be extremely useful to teams as they strive to make appropriate and effective AT decisions for the students with physical or multiple disabilities.

Extended Assessment or Trial Use

It may be necessary to have one or more extended trials with various assistive technologies in order to gather data about their effectiveness for a particular student. If several questions remain unanswered, a longer time period may be needed. For example, if team members are not sure whether the student is intentionally activating a device, specific data on preferred reinforcers, type of switch, location of switch, and many other questions may need to be collected. The process of organized trials with AT is called **extended assessment.**

The **Assistive Technology Trial Use Guide** (Wisconsin Assistive Technology Initiative, 2002b) is a tool for planning an effective extended assessment. It leads the team through a discussion of the overall goal for the assessment period, the environments where AT will be used, and plans for obtaining specific devices.

FIGURE 7–4
Completed Wisconsin Assistive Technology Initiative Decision-Making Guide

Date of Meeting: September 24
Team Members Present:

Mr. & Mrs. Smith—Parents
Mrs. Jones—Special Education Support Teacher
Mrs. Frost—Fifth-Grade Teacher
Mrs. Kelly—Paraprofessional
Ms. Trent—Occupational Therapist
Ms. Williams—Assistive Technology Consultant

PROBLEM IDENTIFICATION		
Student's Abilities/Difficulties	**Environmental Considerations**	**Tasks**
Writing—Legible, but not at level of peers Takes extra time Laborious Tried adaptive grip Able to isolate fingers for typing Can use mouse Composing—Difficulty w/spelling Frustrating Difficulty staying on task Communication—Very verbal Reading—A strength in some ways At or below grade level Sometimes frustrating Math—Has difficulty Mobility—Independent in manual wheelchair Vision—20/30 with glasses Functional at school Hearing—Not a concern Behavior—Attention deficit, No concerns about throwing or abusing equipment	PC in 5th gr. classroom available at all times Has word processor; not sure if it has sound card No educational software Mac computer in Resource Rm	Produce legible written material Reading Studying Math Rec/leisure at school **Task selected:** Producing legible written material

Solution Generation	Solution Selection	Implementation Plan
Adaptive pencil grips Laptop computer Keyboarding instruction Use computer in classroom Alpha Smart 3000 More writing practice Software that reduces keystrokes and helps with spelling Spell checking Abbreviation/expansion Computer speak text	Start with low expectations w/keyboarding, index fingers Teach traditional keyboarding Teach use of word prediction More cursive writing practice; try adaptive pencil grips again Start with computer in Resource Rm. Do journal and assignments Work on keyboarding in OT time Check on sound card Try talking word processing	Start using keyboard—index fingers only Familiarization—Trent, start 10/1 Journaling—Jones, start 10/15. Word prediction & talking word processing—Jones 11/15 after training and loan from Williams Check on sound card—Frost 11/1; req. from Tech Comm if needed Cursive writing: During creative writing—Frost 10/1 During OT—Trent, start 10/5 Try adaptive pencil grips—Trent-10/5 Teach traditional keyboarding: Start this year—Trent-10/19 6th grade keyboarding class next year **Follow Up Meeting:** 11/22

Note. Wisconsin Assistive Technology Initiative, 9/97, Oshkosh, WI. Reprinted with permission.

It ends with a summary of the results of the trial period. The data generated by the Assistive Technology Trial Use Guide can then be utilized by the team members if they need to seek a funding source for the device, because it provides the answers to questions that third-party payers ask when considering funding AT.

During an extended assessment, the team is usually implementing a series of trials with several different devices to see if any one of them provides a better solution. Extended assessment is often needed when the child has more complex or severe disabilities where extensive training and experience are required to gather the data needed to make a decision (Reed, Bowser, & Korsten, 2002).

There are several steps necessary to conduct an extended assessment. First, specific devices that will be used during the trial period must be identified. The next step is to identify specific goals and timelines for the trials. Team members need to clarify expectations for the student and define what they consider to be a successful trial. For example, a team that was problem-solving for Keith, a fifth-grade student with mild cerebral palsy and a learning disability, decided that they needed a trial with talking word processing to see if it would make a difference in his written work. They did not discuss goals or expectations. They borrowed talking word processing software and used it for one month. At the end of that month, the teachers and therapists thought it was a failure and the parents thought it was a success. How could that happen? Easily! At first the software really slowed him down because he stopped and thought about what he heard and what he actually wanted to write. It fascinated him. It also allowed him to become aware of mistakes as he wrote them. For instance, he typically typed *saw* when he meant *was.* It astounded him when the computer said "saw." He often had it repeat it several times and then struggled to change the letters around. Although he was starting to work faster, at the end of the month, he had still not reached the same length of written assignments that he had produced prior to using the talking word processing software. Therefore the staff felt that it was not a useful tool. At the same time, his family saw a big change in Keith. For the first time ever, he brought home one of his written assignments and put it on the refrigerator door himself. He was more pleasant on the mornings that he knew were going to include a long writing assignment at school. His demeanor was noticeably different when talking about written work. They felt the talking word processing was a fabulous success. Who was right? They both were, of course, but the decreased length of assignments would correct itself when given more practice, so the parents were actually looking at the more significant data. However, the full team took many weeks of arguing to arrive at that conclusion. This could have been avoided if they had discussed goals and criteria for success before beginning the trial.

The third step is to acquire the AT for the extended assessment. Although borrowing equipment from vendors, lending libraries, or disability organizations is optimal to determine if particular AT hardware or software will meet student needs (National School Boards Association and U.S. Department of Education, 1997), this process may take several weeks to arrange and depend upon product availability. It may require the reorganization of the trials to reflect the dates the specific AT hardware or software can be obtained. The fourth step is to implement the trial period. Each piece of hardware or software must be systematically tried to determine what works.

Once trials have been implemented, the final step is decision making based upon the trial data. Some data can be difficult to interpret and require much discussion. When a student has a clear preference for one of the alternatives, that preference must be an important part of decision making. Long-term research on abandonment of AT supports the importance of preference, ease of use, ease of training, versatility, durability, and portability in continued use (Scherer, 1993).

SELECTING AND ACQUIRING ASSISTIVE TECHNOLOGY

Numerous commercial products that can be used as assistive devices are sold to the general public (referred to as generic or standard products). These products range from low-tech items, such as the wide range of pens with special soft grips, to high-tech, expensive items such as computers with voice recognition and speech output. Commercial products that are mass-produced for the general public are the least expensive. Other products are specially designed for individuals with particular disabilities (customized or dedicated specialized products). The information in this section will expedite searches for both the generic and the specialized commercial products that can help meet the identified needs of students with physical or multiple disabilities.

Determination of Desired Product Features

Selecting the best features of an AT product is illustrated through the following example. Assume that a team has completed the assessment process and determined that communicating wants and needs and answering questions in class are the main concern for Mary. After brainstorming, it was agreed that she needs a voice output device with at least 15 messages. Unless someone on the team is knowledgeable about AT products, how does the team decide what devices are available and which ones might work for Mary? The process used to determine which product or products might work for an individual student is called **feature match.** Feature match involves identifying the unique needs of the student and identifying a device or devices that have features "matching" those needs. The student's unique abilities have been identified using the information-gathering process previously discussed, including the WATI Student Information Guide. Now the task is to utilize that knowledge to find devices with the physical features that match the student's unique abilities and needs. Some of the main components of features of products include **element placement** (e.g., location of on/off switch, spacing between keys) and **element dimensions** (e.g., size of unit, size of switch, size of keys, width). Another important component is **input method,** which is the method by which users may be capable of accessing or operating a device (e.g., directly touching or activating it versus needing to use scanning with a specially placed switch and adapter to activate it). Another component is **processing,** which involves a user's ability to perceive a stimulus and make an appropriate response. The last major component is **output.** Outputs are described in terms of modalities (e.g., speech, visual display, printer, Braille, etc.). Other features that may be considered include portability, weight, color, versatility, and battery life. Software tools are available to assist with feature match.

Product Specifications and Demonstrations

The specifications of a product are detailed, precise, written descriptions of commercially available equipment. Specifications of commercial products are printed for public review. The ABLEDATA database is a good source of this type of information and can be accessed from the Web site listed at the end of this chapter. Selecting the best options is based upon comparing strengths and weaknesses of the features in relation to the identified student needs. Product demonstration followed by hands-on experience and training on product functions is important. Training may be provided from the product vendor, but it also may be available from a variety of consumer groups or consultants within a school district, region, or state.

Product Searches and Ordering

Products are identified by different kinds of information (e.g., size, features, brand, etc.). In finding products, people may have some but not all the information they need. They may have only some specifications. Whatever the case, they can search for products on the Internet, in catalogs, and at AT conferences using what information they have. To actually order products, very specific information is needed. When searching for AT products, the following factors are important:

- Generic name (common names of product);
- Brand name (trade name of product);
- Manufacturer (manufacturing source);
- Distributor (distribution source);
- Address (address of manufacturer or distributor);
- Cost per year (list price with date);
- Description (physical description of the product with specific features needed, e.g., 8 message versus 32 message, two level versus four level, etc.);
- Identifiers (descriptive terms used to classify product, e.g., augmentative communication devices, word prediction software, assistive listening devices, etc.).

Commercially available products do not always meet the unique needs of students with physical or multiple disabilities. Products with the needed specifications are not always available and can be expensive. In some cases, changes in the specifications are needed so frequently that commercial products are not feasible. Sometimes hand-constructed equipment and devices using locally available and low-cost materials are a viable option. The valuable resources of time and imagination can sometimes produce AT that compares with the most useful commercial products. Unfortunately, the cost in staff time and effort may make it as expensive as the commercial product. In addition, homemade items are typically not as sturdy as commercially available ones. All of these factors must be considered when deciding whether to make or purchase an item.

Writing Assistive Technology into the IEP

Following either consideration, assessment, or extended assessment, the IEP team frequently decides that some type of AT will need to be written into the IEP. Although AT devices or services may be a related service, a supplementary aid or service, or a part of a child's special education program, writing it in the IEP continues to be a challenge for many. The following vignettes provide examples of AT that has been included in the IEP document in each of these three ways.

Assistive Technology as Part of Special Education. When AT is provided as part of specially designed instruction (special education), it will be described in the goals and objectives. In some cases the child will need training and instruction on the use of the AT and in others it will be a material that the child is using to achieve a specific goal or objective. In writing annual goals using AT, it is important to include three components: the area of need, the direction of change, and the level of attainment. In addition, it is critical to relate it to the functional task that the child needs to complete. For instance, a technically correct annual goal might be, "Bobby will activate a single switch 75% of the time." However, it fails the "So what?" test. Why is it that you want Bobby to activate a switch in the first place? What will he accomplish? To operate a toy? To operate a computer? To call for help? To indicate he is ready to be moved to a new position? To greet a friend? If we always relate the use of the technology to a functional outcome, we will avoid the mistake of focusing on the equipment as an end in itself rather than a means to an end.

EXAMPLE:

Present Level of Educational Performance: Sarah can use eye gaze successfully to indicate her wants and needs when items are displayed so that her communication partner can tell where she is gazing. She currently makes a grunting sound to greet others, to get attention, and to represent both yes and no. She has recently tried using a four-message output device and is having some success at making choices. Sarah travels independently about the school in a power chair.

Annual Goal: Sarah will interact with others in the school environment in four out of five opportunities to indicate her preferences and needs using a voice output device and eye-gaze strategies.

Short-Term Objective 1: When provided with a preprogrammed single message voice output device on her wheelchair with a message and corresponding symbol, Sarah will use it to greet peers in the hallways, lunchroom, and classroom 100% of the time.

Short-Term Objective 2: Using an eye-gaze frame mounted on her wheelchair with appropriate symbols or pictures, Sarah will indicate her preference between four choices 80% of the time on three random trials.

Short-Term Objective 3: When asked "yes/no" questions, Sarah will indicate "yes" with a smile and eye contact with communication partner, and "no" by looking down at her wheelchair tray for at least three seconds 90% of the time on three random trials.

Short-Term Objective 4: When provided with a preprogrammed four-message voice output device with symbols/pictures, Sarah will participate in story time by using repetitive phrases, requests to "hear more," "turn the pages," etc., appropriately at least 80% of the time during three random trials.

EXAMPLE:

Present Level of Educational Performance: Eric participates in regular education programs for all academic subjects. His hand strength is limited and he fatigues quickly when doing any handwriting task. Social Studies and English homework are a particular problem because of lengthy assignments and reports that need to be completed.

Annual Goal: Eric will use a computer or portable word processor to complete assignments in 10th-grade English and Social Studies classes.

Short-Term Objective 1: Eric will review and practice keyboarding skills to input information into a computer or portable word processor at a functional rate of at least 15 words per minute when tested on a standard keyboarding assignment.

Short-Term Objective 2: Eric will use a portable word processor at home or school to complete 100% of English and Social Studies homework assignments each day as reported by respective teachers.

Short-Term Objective 3: Eric will learn to transfer documents from portable word processor to computer, use spell-checker, use other computer features to reformat appropriately (e.g., cut, paste, bold, tab, etc.), and operate printer 100% of time as reported by respective teachers.

AT as a Related Service. A related service is a service that a child needs in order to benefit from his or her specially designed instruction. Assistive technology most typically appears as a related service when it is not an integral part of a student's educational program, but is needed in order to benefit from that educational program. Examples of AT as a related service include walkers, wheelchairs, and various positioning devices. Augmentative communication devices and computers are also sometimes listed there. The amount/frequency, duration, and location of the AT must be specified.

EXAMPLE:

Stephanie is in the third grade. She has cerebral palsy and is ambulatory, but her motor impairments make it difficult for her to walk long distances. It is so fatiguing that she does not recover from the exertion for 30 to 45 minutes and is not able to concentrate on school activities if long walks are required. She is able to walk short distances with no ill effects if enough time is provided.

Related Services	*Frequency*	*Duration*	*Location*
Other (specify): Walker	Daily during lunch	Entire school year	Classroom/ lunchroom

Because of the specificity of frequency, duration, and location required for a related service, many people prefer to use the Related Services section of the IEP to document AT. However, the provision of AT is equally binding when it is described under Supplementary Aids and Services or in goals and objectives of the specially designed instruction. It is important to note here that IDEA does not automatically *require* that an IEP include separate annual goals and short-term objectives/benchmarks for related services. For example, typically goals are not written for services like transportation. However, a goal could be written if the student was learning to access public transportation to get to a work site during transition. The determination of whether annual goals and short-term objectives/benchmarks are needed is contingent upon the related service itself. If the related services include the learning of new skills that are not already part of an existing annual goal or short-term objective, then there would need to be goals and/or objectives in addition to the details of frequency, duration, and location listed under Related Services.

AT as Supplementary Aids and Services. Supplementary aids and services are those aids, services, and other supports that are provided to enhance or allow the student's placement in the least restrictive environment (LRE), especially when the LRE is the general education classroom. Assistive technology is most logically included in the IEP as a supplementary aid when it provides more independence and requires little instruction in order to be used effectively. Items such as portable word processors, talking spellcheckers, and other small, portable devices are often included under Supplementary Aids and Services.

EXAMPLE:

Jacob is in kindergarten. He likes to do the coloring and writing activities with the other children. He has difficulty with these activities because he is subject to an STNR (symmetric tonic neck reflex), which causes him to round his shoulders and flex his arms whenever he bends his head down to look at the paper. It is very fatiguing for him to look down and back up at the teacher. It is important to Jacob to participate in the same way as the other students.

Supplementary Aids & Services	*Frequency*	*Duration*	*Location*
Slant-top table for all writing, coloring, drawing, and painting activities	Daily	Entire school year	Kindergarten

EXAMPLE:

Carl uses his personal hearing aid to good advantage in quiet environments. However, he is confused when the background noise is elevated, as often occurs in active classroom situations and large-group activities. He has therefore not been able to effectively participate in many important school activities.

Supplementary Aids & Services	*Frequency*	*Duration*	*Location*
FM classroom amplification system to assist with auditory discrimination	Daily	Entire school year	5th grade class

Support for School Personnel. IDEA '97 requires that each IEP include a statement of the "supports for school personnel that will be provided for the child." Needed supports may include training, technical assistance, access to materials, or anything else that the service providers who work with the student may need in order to provide necessary services. This applies to AT as much as to any other intervention or strategy. For example, if a student using a voice output communication aid moved to a school where the classroom teacher, speech/language pathologist, and paraeducator did not know how to operate, program, and troubleshoot that device, they must receive appropriate training.

As AT solutions are implemented in the various environments, new decisions will need to be made. As the student acquires new skills, as the tasks and environments change, as new technology becomes available, the AT for the student will also need to be changed. Each time new decisions are required, the team members can utilize the WATI Student Information Guide and WATI Environmental Observation Guide, plus any formal or informal tests that are necessary to gather information. Then they can meet together and follow the WATI Assistive Technology Decision-Making Guide once again to direct them through the making of a new decision and the WATI Assistive Technology Checklist to remind them of available AT options. As team members become more sophisticated, they may find that they may wish to adapt these tools to meet their unique needs. Assistive technology consideration, assessment, extended assessment or trials, and implementation can be performed successfully by school district teams.

POSITIONING AND SEATING

The first part of this chapter demonstrated the critical nature of AT for individuals with physical or multiple disabilities. However, without proper positioning, AT cannot be used to its best advantage. Teachers need to understand the principles of positioning and seating in order to provide appropriate access to the curriculum for students with physical or multiple disabilities. The need for positioning equipment will vary according to age, disability, and intended use, but the principles remain the same.

Physical and occupational therapists, in collaboration with seating specialists and rehabilitation engineers, have the major responsibility for evaluating, selecting, and adapting positioning equipment. However, teachers should be included in the evaluation process to provide information regarding the student's activities, schedule, needed positions to facilitate attending to instruction, room arrangements, and furniture shape and height in the classroom, computer lab, and other environments. Teachers have the advantage of observing a student's position throughout the day, every day. For example, a student may consistently tire near the end of the day and lean over the side of his wheelchair. This problem needs to be identified during the seating evaluation to determine what components must be included in the seat to provide a more upright posture. Information will be needed not only about a student's position but also about the equipment itself. An example is Melissa, who needs a new positioning insert and a new wheelchair. The teacher realizes that Melissa will be moving from class to class next year and needs a seat height that will allow her to access the desks, computer work stations, and library tables. A lower seat height will allow her to fit at all of these desks and tables and to be more independent. It is also important that she maintains her independence in transfers in and out of the wheelchair. If she needs positioning straps at her chest, pelvis, or ankles, they must be designed in such a way that she can manage the straps independently. The teacher is often in a position to provide the type of information that will assist in the selection of the most appropriate seating and mobility equipment for the student.

Positioning

The importance of positioning cannot be understated. The individual's position will always affect the quality and precision of movement and ability to accomplish tasks. That effect is either positive or negative, depending on its appropriateness.

Positioning Affects Muscle Tone and Posture. Individuals with physical disabilities are often affected by problematic muscle tone, especially if their disability includes neurological components. When there is too much tone, voluntary movements become difficult, particularly in the extremities such as the hands (Radell, 1997). For example, a student with spastic cerebral palsy who is improperly positioned will experience increased muscle tone and may not be able to separate his fingers in order to strike the keys on a keyboard.

Good Positioning Results in Alignment and Proximal Support of the Body. A positioning device usually provides alignment with support near the body's center of gravity unless the child already has a fixed deformity that must be accommodated. This support, if fit properly, provides trunk stability, which is the key to good positioning.

Many individuals with motor impairment lack the inward stability to maintain an upright position against gravity because balance/equilibrium responses and muscle tone do not function optimally. Therefore, they may require the use of positioning components such as outside supports or pads at the trunk, head, hips, and feet to provide them with stability. (See Figure 7–5 for a sample of improper positioning and proper positioning in seating with the aid of positioning components). As a teacher, your role is to monitor the child's position throughout the activities of the day and alert the occupational or physical therapist if further adjustments are necessary.

Stability Positively Affects Uses of the Upper Body. Positioning will directly affect the ability of individuals to use their head, arms, and hands in a functional way. **Proximal stability** (close to the body's center of gravity) is necessary before **distal stability** (far from the body's center of gravity) can occur. To demonstrate, try this experiment using a pen and a piece of paper. Try to write your name while holding the pen at its top end with your arm extended away from your body and suspended above the writing surface. Notice that accurate distal finger movements are difficult because you have eliminated the proximal stability of your arm against your body and against the tabletop. Now imagine trying to write in this

FIGURE 7–5
Improper and proper positioning: (a) bad posture, (b) posture improved by appropriate pads and cushions

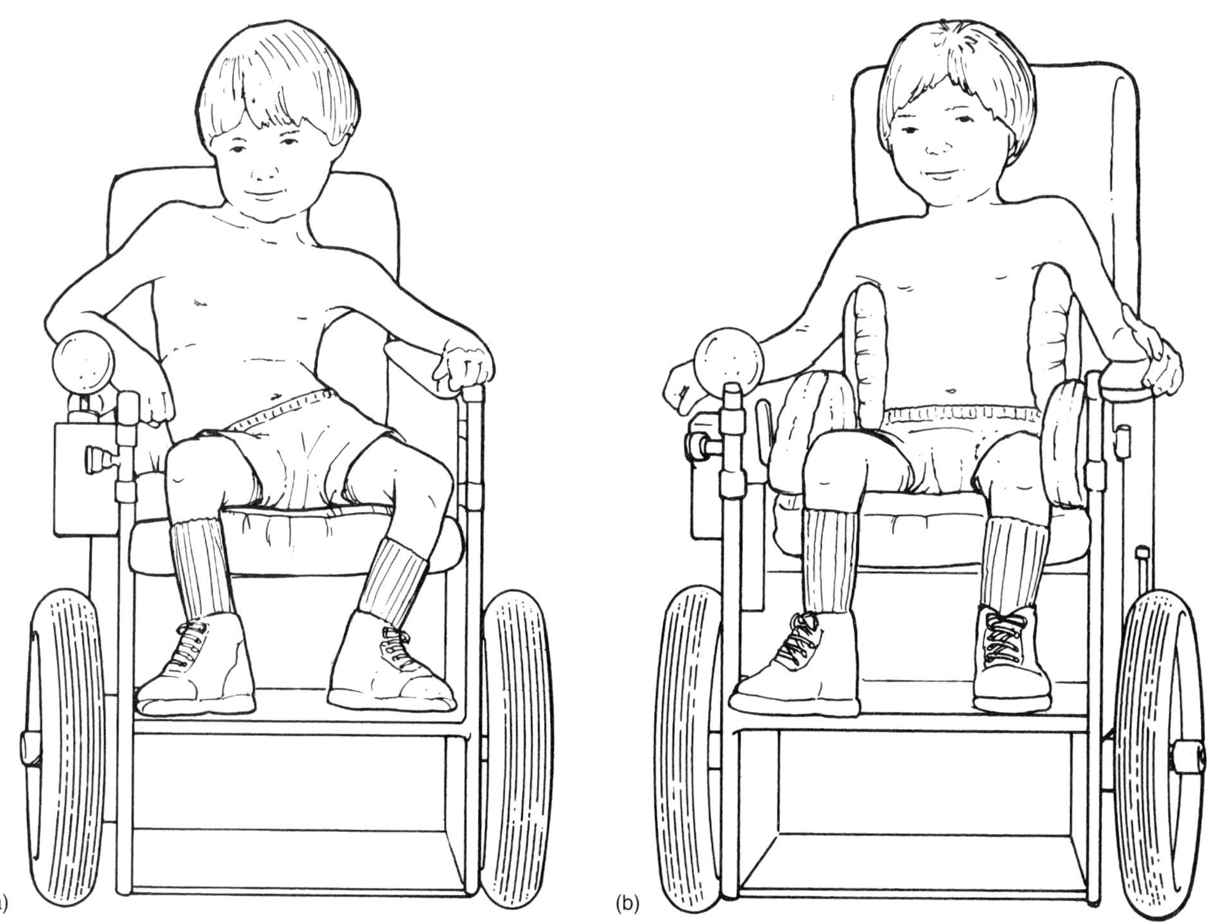

Note. From *The Child with a Handicap* (p. 350), by D. M. B. Hall, 1984, Oxford: Blackwell Scientific Publications Limited. Used with permission.

manner while you are sitting on a narrow edge of a high wall without foot support (lack of sitting stability). The task would be nearly impossible. Proximal stability can affect distal motor control, whether the child is writing with a pen or adapted pencil, or using a joystick to move a motorized wheelchair. Accuracy of the arm and other body movements will be influenced by the body's position and consequent stability.

Stability Promotes Feelings of Physical Security and Safety. Because stability provides a person with a greater sense of physical security while using positioning equipment, the fear of using this equipment is decreased. Fear can increase muscle tone, which further impairs motor control and range of movement. Muscle tone can also increase if the child is not adequately supported, because he or she learns to hold himself or herself artificially, or "fixes" against gravity. This fixing can interfere with motor development and lead to later contractures or deformities. Caution must be taken, however, to provide adequate stability without too much restriction. Excessive restriction can occur when unnecessary supports are used or when straps are too tight.

Good Positioning Can Reduce Deformity. Individuals with neurologically based motor disabilities have a tendency to adopt postures that become fixed (habitual) on one part or side of the body (Radell, 1997). The result is loss of movement and eventual deformity. Deformity occurs because of asymmetry (unequal distribution) of muscle tone. Positioning is used to help maintain symmetry and range of motion and to allow movement, which assists with prevention of deformity.

Positions Must be Changed Frequently. With prolonged periods in any one position, students may acquire such bodily problems as red marks, pressure sores, and stiffness. Changing positions is especially important to students with severe physical disabilities, particularly those who cannot express their discomfort or change their own position at will. The sitting position is the position most frequently used, but there are alternatives for students who cannot sit and for students who need position changes. The same positioning principles apply. Stability is necessary in any position and is provided through good support of the trunk and pelvis. Position alternatives include supported standing, side lying, lying prone (on the stomach) on a wedge, and lying supine (on the back). In addition, the proper position should also be maintained on wheel toys (e.g., tricycles, riding cars) and other pieces of gross-motor equipment (see Figure 7–6). Teachers should consult with physical and occupational therapists for the most appropriate positions for each student. In addition, positions should be changed often to avoid boredom, promote health, and ensure comfort.

Seating

Seating directly influences posture, muscle tone, and coordination. Desired sitting positions have specific features. Radell (1997) and others (Harryman & Warren, 1992; Levin & Scherfenberg, 1987; Myhr, von Wendt, Norrlin, & Radell, 1995) identify key points

FIGURE 7–6
Alternatives to allow change of position throughout the day: (a) sidelyer, (b) wedge, (c) tricycle with built-up back and pedals. Adult three-wheeled bikes are available for larger children and adolescents.

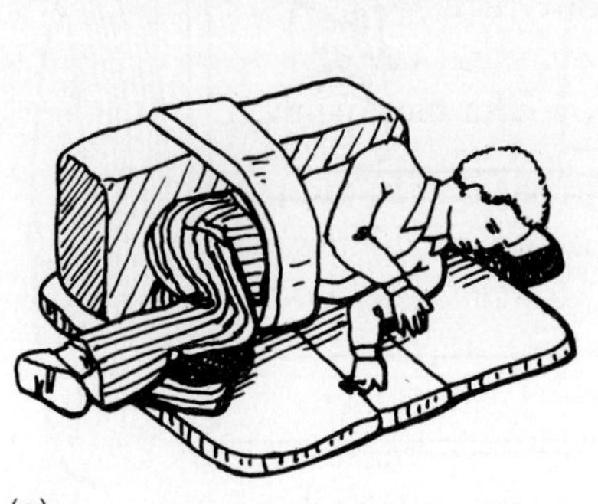
(a)

(b)

(c)

for achieving an appropriate sitting position, including the pelvis, feet, and shoulders/upper trunk.

Pelvic Position. The pelvis serves as the base for head and trunk control. The pelvis must be in neutral position, and not tilted forward, rotated, or tipped. The position is optimal when the pelvis is parallel to the back of the back surface and perpendicular to the seat surface (see Figure 7–7). When the pelvis is appropriately positioned, the student is able to keep the trunk and head erect with less effort. The pelvis can be stabilized with a seat belt, which must be placed at a 45-degree angle and below the front of the iliac spine to prevent further deformity (Harryman & Warren, 1992). The student's hips should be shifted as far back in the chair as possible and weight should be distributed evenly on both sides of the buttocks. In this position, the individual will not be sitting on the sacrum (backbone). If the pelvis shifts to the side or moves forward, additional adaptations may be required. Some seating devices are better than others in maintaining this position, but most individuals in wheelchairs will need seating adjustments throughout the day.

FIGURE 7–7
Components of normal seating

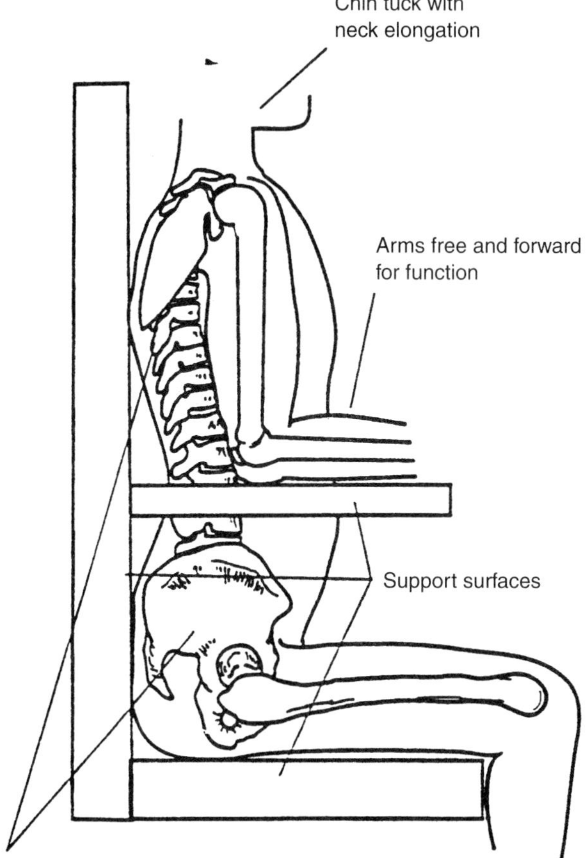

Note. From *The Handbook of Assistive Technology, 1st edition,* by Church © 1992. Reprinted with permission of Delmar, a division of Thomson Learning. Fax 800-730-2215.

Conventional wisdom might dictate that the chair seat be tilted up slightly in front to keep the hips back in the seat and the head from slumping forward. In this position, the child is reclined slightly backward. However, this position actually encourages spasticity and decreases postural control (Myhr et al., 1995; Radell, 1997). Myhr et al. (1995) suggest that, once the pelvis and hips are appropriately positioned, the individual must be encouraged to lean forward slightly. This is important because it positions the center of gravity in front of the hip joint. Children who need additional support when leaning forward can be seated in front of a table and use its surface to rest their arms. The height of the table should be high enough to accommodate a wheelchair. Sometimes a small "book podium" or slant board can be placed on the table to raise and position materials to prevent the individual from sitting with a rounded back or dropping the head too far down on the chest. Examples of book podium and other slant-top surfaces are provided later in this chapter in Figure 7–20.

Foot Support. The student's feet should be level and supported on the floor or wheelchair foot pedals. The feet provide stability through the thighs and keep the pelvis in the correct position. Heel loops, ankle straps, and toe straps may also be used to help keep the feet in place. It is very important to avoid "dangling" feet when a student is seated in a chair. Something as simple as a telephone book wrapped with duct tape can be placed in front of the chair to act as a foot support. Wooden or cardboard boxes can also be used to provide an elevated surface for foot stability.

Shoulder and Upper Trunk Support. Students with more severe physical disabilities may need upper trunk support to maintain an upright position. Also, support at the shoulders provides a base for head control. Supports for the upper trunk include "H straps," vest-type supports, and straps that start under the chair trunk supports and go over the shoulder in a backpack fashion. The straps are designed to bring the shoulders back, keeping the trunk up and against the back of the chair. Shoulder pommels usually provide slight pressure in the pectoral (chest) region to bring the upper trunk back. Some H straps have extra padding in the pectoral area to provide similar pressure. All supports should allow for freedom of arm movement. When the pelvis, hips, and shoulders/upper trunk are correctly positioned, the arms can come forward and together. If the body is tilted backward, the arms flex at the elbow and the hands come up and close into fists, thus preventing useful motion. Figure 7–8 provides samples of shoulder and upper trunk support.

One type of support may be preferable over another for a given child. For example, some children lean into shoulder straps, causing the shoulders to come forward and the head to drop. Shoulder pommels may provide a better base of support for both head and arm movement. While the occupational and physical therapists will take the lead in determining appropriate supports, it is up to the teacher, who is there throughout the day, to monitor their effectiveness and efficiency.

Inadequate Seating Has Negative Consequences. Whenever teachers suspect inadequate seating positions, they should describe these observations to therapists and obtain instruction about what to do. When prolonged, inadequate seating can result in negative consequences. The following positions contribute to spinal deformity and interfere with respiration, phonation, eating, digestion, visual field, and motor control of upper body and head:

- Rounded back;
- Sliding out of seat;
- Leaning of the body to either side or forward; and
- Head leaning to the side, tilted forward, or thrown far back.

Other inadequate positions and their negative consequence include:

- Too much total body movement. Lack of stability contributes to greater difficulty isolating controlled movements.
- Legs maintain a "windswept" position. The hips and knees are not aligned and the knees lean to the opposite side of the hips (contributes to hip dislocation and spinal deformity).
- Backs of knees are more than one inch from the edge of the seat. Wheelchair size may be inappropriate and contributing to poor positioning elsewhere in the body.

FIGURE 7–8
Samples of shoulder and upper trunk support

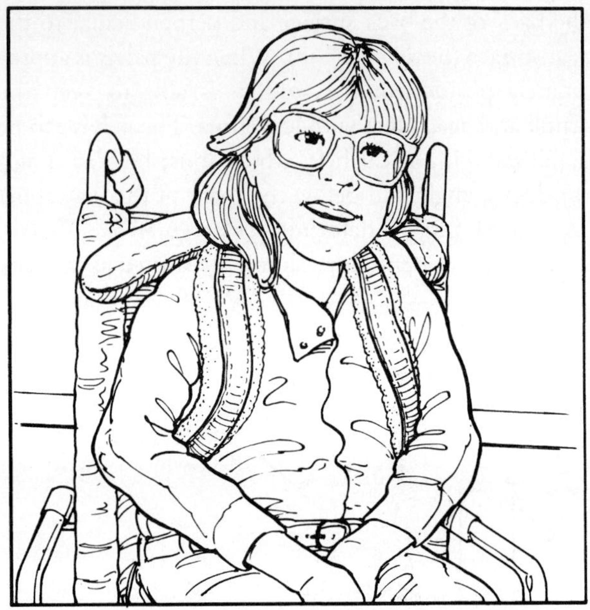

Using shoulder straps

Using shoulder pommels

Note. From *Selection and Use of Simple Technology in Home, School, Work and Community Settings* (p. 22) by J. Levin and L. Scherfenberg, 1987, Minneapolis, MN: ABLENET. Used with permission.

- Plantar flexed feet that maintain pointed-toes position. Possible deformity of foot may prevent bearing weight during standing transfers or ambulation.
- Legs are flexed or bent under the seat and off the footrests. Tight hamstring muscles may contribute to pelvic and spinal deformity and prevent an adequate weight-bearing position due to flexion contractures. Lack of foot support also contributes to lack of stability elsewhere in the body.

Assistive Devices for Positioning and Seating

The seat belt is usually the key to good positioning because it holds the pelvis, which is an anchor point for the rest of the body. Pads at the sides of the hips may also provide stability to the pelvis. The pelvis should be positioned correctly by sliding the buttocks back into the seat until they touch the back cushion. The seat belt should be located either at a 45-degree angle across the pelvis or across the thighs close to the body. The belt should then be comfortably tightened, and the buckle should not press against the pelvis unless it is padded.

An **abductor** or leg separator can provide stability to the pelvis and trunk by maintaining alignment in the legs. The abductor may be a separate piece of equipment or be an integral part of the seat. It should never be positioned too close to the crotch in order to hold the child in the chair; rather, it should be placed between the knees to prevent crossing of the legs and to maintain symmetry. If the individual has low muscle tone and the legs open too wide, rolled towels or soft padding can be placed between the wheelchair sides and the legs to keep them aligned. Figure 7–9 shows three types of abductors.

Shoulder and chest straps should not be too close to the sides or front of the neck. They also should not be

FIGURE 7–9
Three types of abductors: (a) feeder seat with floor sitter wedge; (b) foam-padded plastic knee separator; (c) foam knee separator with strap

(a)

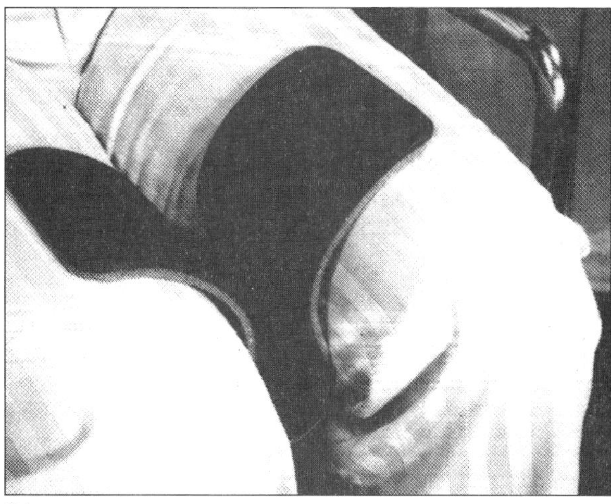

(b)

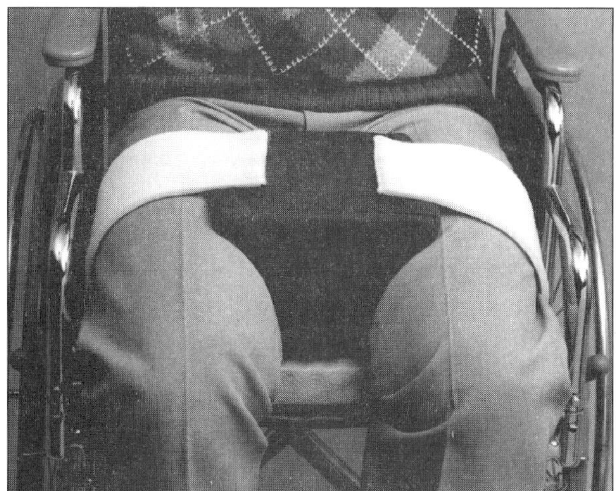

(c)

FIGURE 7–10
Alternative seating: (a) chair without legs and with added post in front of chair to promote abduction of hips; (b) chair with arms and footrests—runners or skis can be added to keep chair from tipping; (c) sandbags as supports; (d) and (e) corner seats (with lap straps, leg positioners and perhaps a tray)

(a)

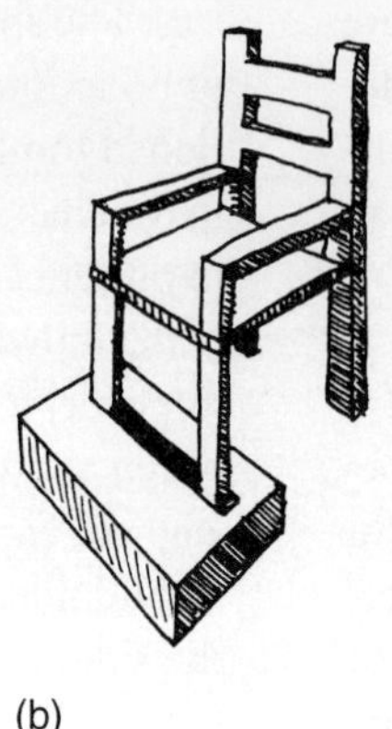
(b)

(c)

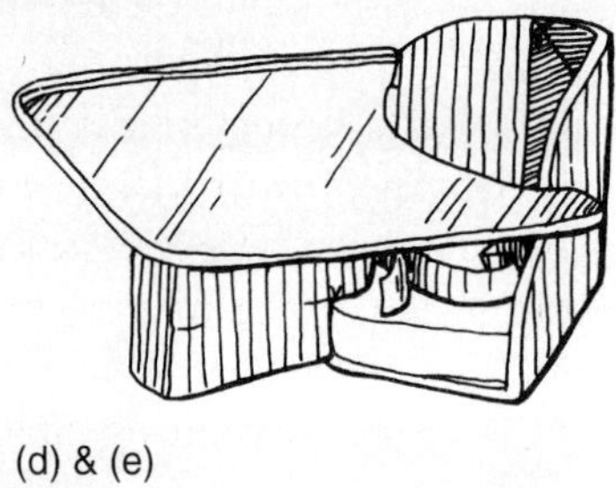
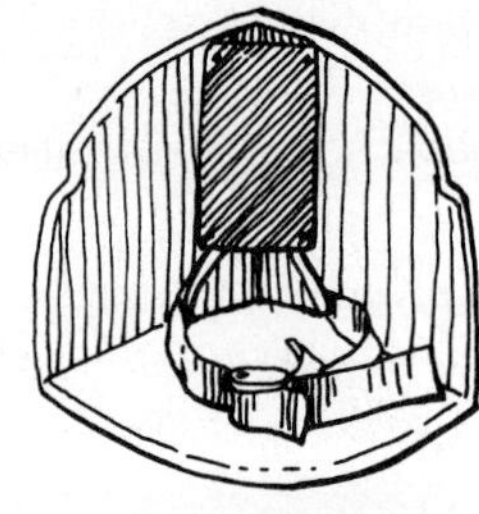
(d) & (e)

attached to the seat belt as an anchor point. However, students who require the use of straps to minimize extraneous movements should be less restricted when motor control is not as important, such as during recess time.

Seating equipment often requires the fabrication of custom adaptations to provide adequate support. Therapists can use temporary inserts made of wood, foam, cushions, toweling, or triwall (a three-layer dense cardboard). This provides an inexpensive means to fabricate an insert and evaluate its effectiveness over a period of time until a permanent seat can be selected and provided. Inserts should always be checked to make sure they are not rubbing against skin, pinching, or causing other tissue damage.

Various types of adapted chairs can be employed to support the trunk and to bring the arms forward and for functional activities. Corner chairs and floor sitters (chairs without legs) allow children to sit on the floor with their legs extended forward. These help develop trunk posture and reduce hamstring contractures. Platforms can be added to the bottom of chairs to provide a footrest and prevent tipping. Many types of commercial chairs and other seating systems are available, but inexpensive alternatives can also be devised (see Figure 7–10). The reader is encouraged to review the texts by Campbell and Truesdell (2000), Packer (1995), and Stoller (1998) for low-tech seating solutions, including adaptive equipment made from paper.

Teachers who serve individuals with physical or multiple disabilities must work collaboratively with parents and therapists to set goals to gradually modify and eventually eliminate some of the positioning and seating components so that the student has an opportunity to improve motor development whenever possible. However, for individuals with severe impairment, this is not always possible. The goal then becomes one of maintaining motor function and reducing deformities during the child's growth and development. If positioning and seating equipment is used throughout the individual's life, it should be as functional, typical-appearing, and unobtrusive as possible.

Once a piece of equipment is selected, it must be monitored for correct fit and safety. Positioning equipment should be comfortable, provide stability for the body, and maintain alignment. This is more difficult to achieve when several students share the same equipment and adjustments must be made to accommodate each student. Equipment that can be easily adjusted (e.g., side-lyer, prone stander) can become easily unadjusted. An improper fit may be subtle at first, but can lead to pain and discomfort, decreased motor abilities, pressure sores, and future deformities.

Since teachers and paraprofessionals are often responsible for placing students in equipment, they must know why the equipment is being used, how to properly place the students in it, and how to observe for signs of improper fit and discomfort. Students who cannot easily communicate, and those with paralysis who cannot feel pain, are especially dependent upon others for help in determining if a positioning device is fitting properly. Therapists should demonstrate how to properly place a student into the equipment, establish a frequency-of-use schedule, and determine the time limit for use of the equipment. In most circumstances a static position should not be maintained for longer than 30-minute intervals. Students may also benefit from being taken out of positioning equipment periodically. Removing students from equipment has the benefit of allowing them to practice maintaining appropriate positions and appreciate how their bodies feel without constraint of equipment. It also allows air to circulate around the body and perspiration to evaporate, which helps to maintain proper hygiene and dissipate body odor. Teachers and others should always be guided by therapists' instructions before they remove students from positioning devices.

Safe Transfers

It is imperative for staff to be aware of the proper way to transfer a student into and out of a wheelchair and other positioning devices. This will assist in preventing injuries and also assure that the student is sitting in the optimum position. Before transferring a heavy or awkward student, always ask for assistance from another adult and from the student. Many students can learn to control extraneous body movements if they know when and how you plan to move them. Always prepare students by telling them when and why you are going to move them. During transfers, be certain to maintain your own good body posture and mechanics by bending at the knees and hips while keeping the back straight and the stomach and hip muscles tight. Move slowly and do not twist your back. Rather, pivot with your feet to turn.

Location

Discussion of the individual's position is not complete without addressing the location of the individual in the classroom and the location of the items he or she needs to utilize. It is important that the student be placed where he can see and hear what he needs to see and hear and reach the items that are needed throughout the day. This sounds simplistic and obvious, yet students with a physical or multiple disability are often placed at the back of a classroom because there is more space for the wheelchair or other equipment. Another perception is that the student will be less disruptive to others when a paraprofessional or therapist works with him "out of sight." Due to the high incidence of vision and hearing problems that accompany many physical and multiple disabilities, it is imperative that vision and hearing needs are considered in determining the student's location within the classroom.

Other things to consider are the source of light and sound that may interfere with the ability to see or hear. As much as possible, the student should be positioned with his back to the window so that the light source comes from behind. At the same time, if the student is working on a computer, it is important to check to see that there is no glare or reflection on the screen. Glare can come from both windows and overhead lights. Light source is an important consideration in planning location. Also, the height of the computer monitor needs to be at an appropriate level for the student's eyes, so that he or she is not required to scrunch down or throw his or her head back in order to see the screen.

If the room includes an activity area where talking or playing will occur, consideration should be given to the potential for that sound to distract or interfere with the student's ability to pay attention or complete work independently. If the student needs to work independently, then locate the student away from those distractions as much as possible during independent work time. However, when the student needs to participate in an activity, ensure that he or she is positioned to be able to participate. Nothing is more segregating than to walk into a classroom and find all of the students seated in a circle on the floor engaged in an activity while one student in a wheelchair sits alone above others.

Mobility

Mobility, or the ability to move from place to place when unable to walk independently, is another area in which modifications may be necessary in order for individuals to participate as fully as possible in their education and other major life activities. Movement enhances development in cognition, perception, communication, and socialization. Exciting technological advances in mobility equipment have made independent mobility an outcome for many individuals with physical and multiple disabilities.

As stated by Kermoian (1998), "Self-directed mobility, by expanding children's opportunities to interact with their social and physical world, promotes integration into society at an earlier age" (p. 251). When infants or young children are able to move independently, they gain experiences about which aspects of their environments are stable and which are novel. With practice, they can focus their attention on new and interesting aspects of their environments. For example, the infant or young child who is ambulatory may ignore aspects of a room that are unchanging (walls, floor, etc.) and concentrate instead on what is novel and interesting, such as toys in the room (Kermoian, 1998).

As infants and children gain mobility, they encounter the world in new and different ways. If their mobility is impaired, experiences and opportunities for interaction are reduced. If their mobility is enhanced, positive outcomes include greater independence, self-confidence (Thiers, 1994), and self-initiation (Butler, 1986). Therefore, mobility should be augmented through AT devices at the earliest possible opportunity (Deitz, 1998).

The selection of devices to assist individuals with mobility needs must take into account many factors. These include age, motor abilities, physical endurance, environmental situation at home and in the community, funding of the equipment, school placement needs (e.g., a student is fully included in general education and has a need for quick mobility), therapy, and educational goals. Selection of the most appropriate primary mobility aid is the responsibility of the therapists, physician, and parent or guardian. Young students typically use a variety of methods to achieve mobility: creeping, rolling, and crawling, plus the use of scooter boards, tricycles, walkers, strollers, and wheelchairs. Older students may use one form of mobility for rapid movement (a wheelchair), but may choose to use another (walk with crutches) when they are in familiar surroundings that don't require rapid mobility (at home). However, one form of mobility generally will be selected as the primary one.

The goal of any primary mobility aid is to provide a means of movement with the greatest amount of independence, using the best quality of movement patterns in the most efficient manner. For example, a student might be able to push herself in a manual wheelchair. However, upon doing this, she leans to one side and bends forward, rounding her back, and expending a lot of energy to turn the wheels. This movement pattern promotes poor posture that could lead to a future deformity of her spine and hips. An alternative and more efficient means of mobility should be considered, unless a better position can be attained while she actively pushes the wheelchair. She might sit up straighter and use less energy if she utilized an electric wheelchair. Selection of the appropriate mobility aid and optimum position requires a thorough evaluation and much consideration.

The exertion of propelling a manual wheelchair or walking with crutches or a walker should also be considered. Franks, Palisano, and Darbee (1991) demonstrated that students with a physical disability who struggle to ambulate with a walker or crutches are exerting energy equivalent to strenuous exercise. This may also be true of wheelchair propulsion for some individuals. Exertion may require an extended period of recovery and interfere with the student's ability to attend to and benefit from instruction immediately following exertion. Teachers are the professionals who are best able to monitor the student's ability to participate in instruction, recess, or sports during the time period following therapy or physical education sessions.

Manual Wheelchairs

Manual wheelchairs have improved over the past few years due to the introduction of durable but lightweight models. These chairs are easy to maneuver and handle

FIGURE 7–11
Manual wheelchairs have improved and are light but durable

FIGURE 7–12
Parts of the motorized wheelchair that are generally covered

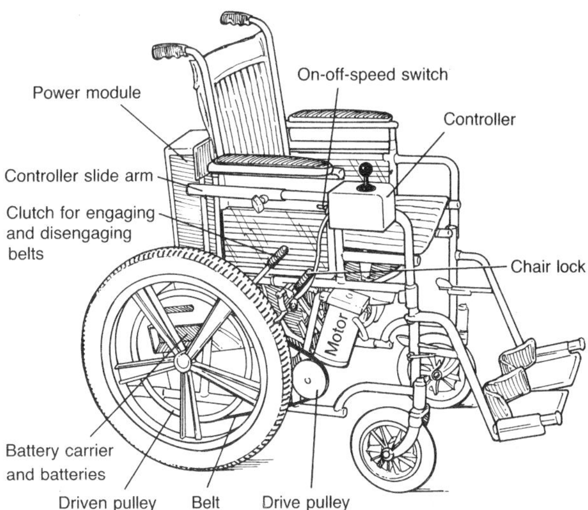

Note. Courtesy of Medical Equipment Distributors, Lubbock, Texas.

(see Figure 7–11). Users may require seating/positioning supports or inserts in the wheelchairs. Most manual wheelchairs require the user to push using both hands. Hemi-drive wheelchairs allow the user to manipulate the chair using only one hand. Safety considerations include making certain the student's hands are not near the spokes when another person pushes, making certain the safety belt is latched securely, and locking the brakes before transferring a student. Students who operate their own wheelchairs might want to use special gloves that protect their hands and keep them clean.

Students may have a manual wheelchair as a backup to their power wheelchair. This is necessary because the power wheelchair will at times be out for repairs and cannot be used at all in some environments. In addition to the chair, students can benefit from different kinds of wheelchair accessories such as wheelchair trays, crutch and cane holders, communication-aid mounting systems, backpacks, and transfer boards.

Power Wheelchairs

Power (electric, motorized) wheelchairs make it possible for people with severe movement impairment to gain independence in mobility. Microchips in the electronics of the control system have added to the sophistication of power wheelchairs. These advancements make the electronic operation of the chair more efficient and provide more options for the user, such as controlling speed, joystick sensitivity, and access to environmental controls. Unfortunately, this also makes it more difficult for nontechnicians to repair problems in the wheelchair's operation. Power wheelchairs are also big, heavy, hard to operate for some children, and must be charged to deliver optimal performance (Todis, 2001). Teachers and others must familiarize themselves with parts of power chairs and with battery care so that they can assist in locating problems and making minor adjustments. Knowing the name, location, and function of wheelchair parts is helpful for communicating about repair and maintenance (see Figure 7–12).

To operate the chair, all plugs must be tightly connected, the brakes off, the clutch engaged, and the control box power switch turned on. The battery supplies the power that makes the motors operate. The motors drive the chair when they are engaged to the wheels. A clutch mechanism tightens and loosens a drive belt around a drive pulley. The user engages the wheels by moving a knob or lever to activate the clutch

FIGURE 7–13
(a) Conventional power wheelchair, (b) typical power-base unit, (c) typical three-wheel scooter

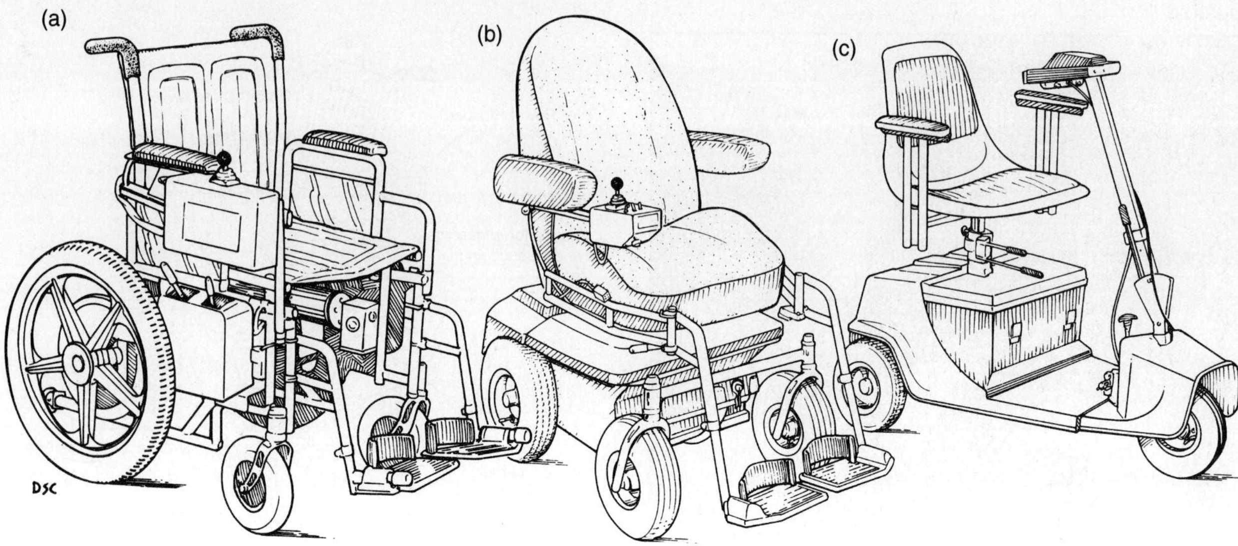

Note. Courtesy of Medical Equipment Distributors, Lubbock, Texas.

and to tighten the belt around the drive pulley. Friction makes the wheels move when the control box switch is turned on and the motors activated. If a wheelchair is not working and the power switch light is blinking, the battery most likely needs recharging (most problems with power chairs are battery related). In the meantime, the wheelchair will need to be pushed by another person. Most electric wheelchairs can be pushed manually by disengaging the wheels. The user or an assistant disengages the motors from the wheels by using the knobs or levers that loosen the belt, so that the unit can freewheel. When the motors are disengaged, an assistant can push the chair as they would a manual chair.

It is better to turn off the wheelchair, disengage the wheels, and push it manually than to let the battery become completely dead. Proper care of the battery includes consistently charging it (according to the manufacturer's specifications) and maintaining the water level.

The three basic types of power chairs include (1) conventional, (2) power base, and (3) three-wheel, or scooter. Each is illustrated in Figure 7–13. The conventional power chair looks like a regular wheelchair but has a motor. A power-base wheelchair has a power base onto which any one of several special seating systems can be mounted. These chairs have heavier, smaller, and wider wheels. They provide mobility outdoors over relatively rough surfaces. Three-wheel power scooters have handlebars and a swivel seat. They look like miniature golf carts. Some can be quickly disassembled and transported in a car.

Power wheelchairs are driven by a variety of joysticks and alternatives to joysticks. Even students who have the most severe motor impairments can learn to operate a power chair using alternative methods of driving it. Options include a joystick operated by the chin, mouth, or foot; a switch operated by a sip and puff of the breath stream; an array of push switches; a single switch to control an automatic scanning display of lights that indicate direction; and even a voice-operated controller. Safety precautions for power wheelchairs include making certain that:

- Seat belts are used;
- The power switch is off and cannot be easily turned on during transfers;
- The speed of the chair is appropriately set for the student; and
- The student receives training in driving skills prior to trying to maneuver the chair in small, crowded, and dangerous places.

Certain prerequisites for driving a power wheelchair are assumed, such as adequate vision, the ability to under-

FIGURE 7–14
Travel stroller chairs

(a)

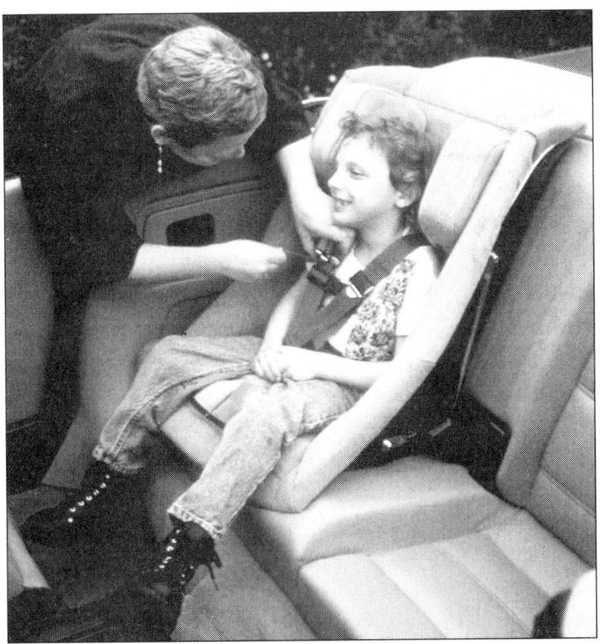
(b)

stand and follow directions, and an awareness of environmental factors. However, it is a mistake to withhold opportunities for individuals to experience powered mobility, since physical manipulation of their environment (including being mobile) contributes to visual-perceptual skills, socialization, self-esteem, communication, and motor function (Wright-Ott, 1998). Children as young as 14 months have learned to drive electric mobility devices (Wright-Ott, 1998). Because of their small size and weight, it is often possible to adapt toy cars with a joystick to test the potential for powered mobility. However, children with severe motor disabilities commonly require considerable trial-and-error practice and training in controlling an electronic mobility device. Teachers and paraprofessionals are often involved in implementing some of this training on a daily basis in conjunction with the physical therapist. Part of that training may include utilizing software that provides virtual training in addition to actual training.

Travel Stroller Chairs

These are often the first wheelchairs children receive. They are intended to make life more convenient for caregivers when transporting a young child. The chairs fit into the seat of a car and can be used as a car seat. The child can sit in the chair while the chair is being put in the car (see Figure 7–14). This has the advantage of reducing the amount of equipment needed and may provide an incentive for including children in more activities. However, travel stroller chairs can be heavy and are often difficult to maneuver. Another disadvantage with these chairs is that the child must depend upon others for mobility. The chair also looks like a stroller, which may not be socially appropriate for older children. It is important that children who use travel stroller chairs are not overlooked as possible candidates for some form of independent mobility.

Mobility Variations

The importance of evaluating the potential of a child to achieve independent mobility, by any means, should not be overlooked. Since mobility affects development in perception, cognition, communication, and interactive skills, children learn by exploring their

FIGURE 7–15
Planned mobilization for children with physical handicaps

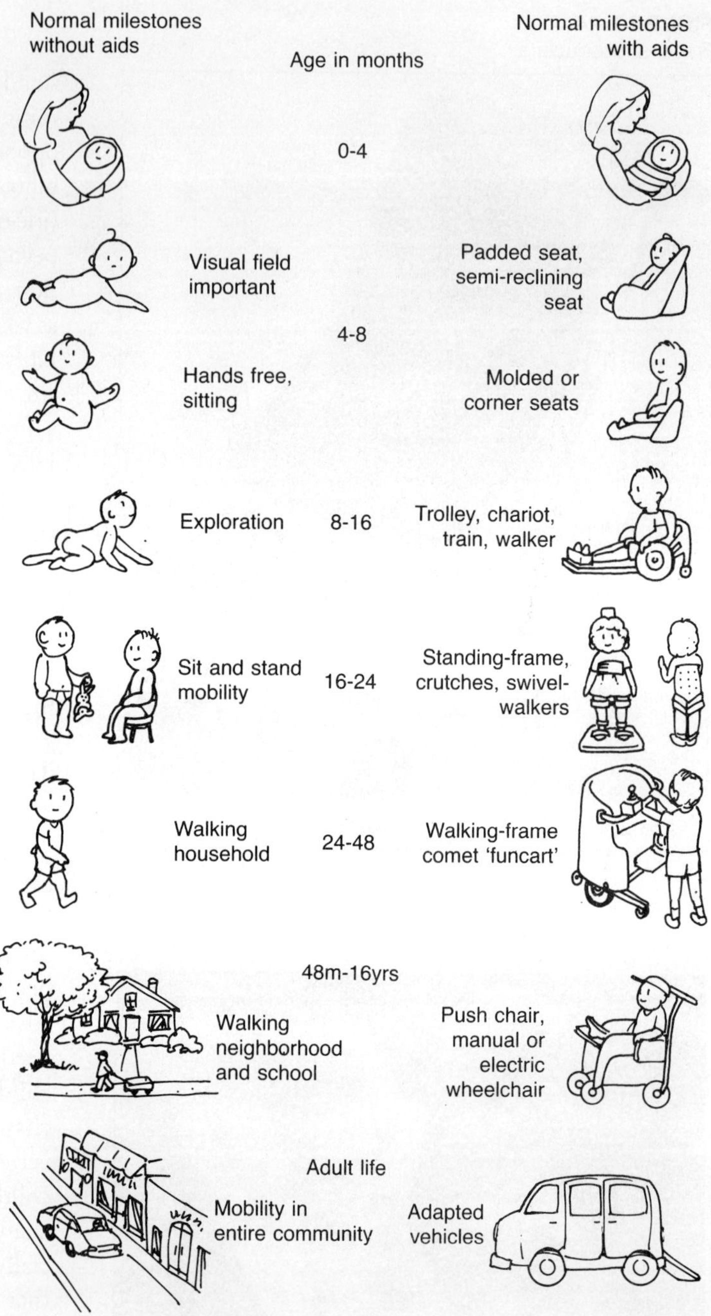

Note. From *The Child with a Handicap* (p. 337) by D. M. B. Hall, 1984, Oxford: Blackwell Scientific Publications Limited. Used with permission.

environment. At 5 months of age an infant begins to roll, and typically by 12 months the child has achieved independent mobility. Because it supports development and independence, determining how a child with a disability can best achieve mobility is worth the time and effort spent. The importance of positioning and mobility is summarized in Figure 7–15. In this figure, assistive technology is used to support approximations of developmental milestones at each age.

Wheelchairs and strollers are not the only AT devices that support mobility. Tricycles and various styles of "go-carts" are exciting means of mobility that al-

FIGURE 7–16
Toys as mobility aids: (a) prone scooter board; (b) hand-propelled wheeler

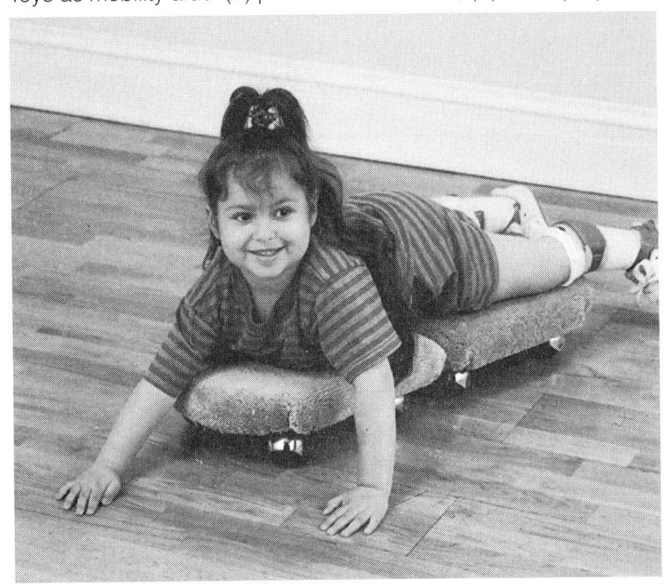

(a)

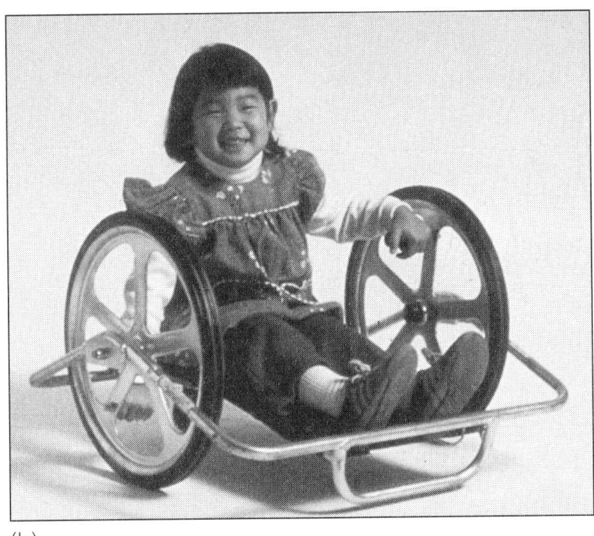

(b)

low children with physical and multiple disabilities to engage in age-appropriate play activities (see Figure 7–16). In these examples, mobility is achieved for children in sitting and prone (on-the-stomach) positions. The two mobility aids in Figure 7–16 (a and b) are designed for children who may need to use their arms to propel themselves. Other mobility aids provide enough stability to allow upright seating or walking, and are propelled by the legs.

Walkers also assist with mobility (see Figure 7–17). Some require weight bearing, while others are designed for movement from a seated position. Some walkers are designed to be in front of the user, and others are designed to fit behind for a more upright

FIGURE 7–17
Different assistive walking devices: (a) reverse walker; (b) nonfolding walker; (c) forearm crutches; (d) aluminum crutches

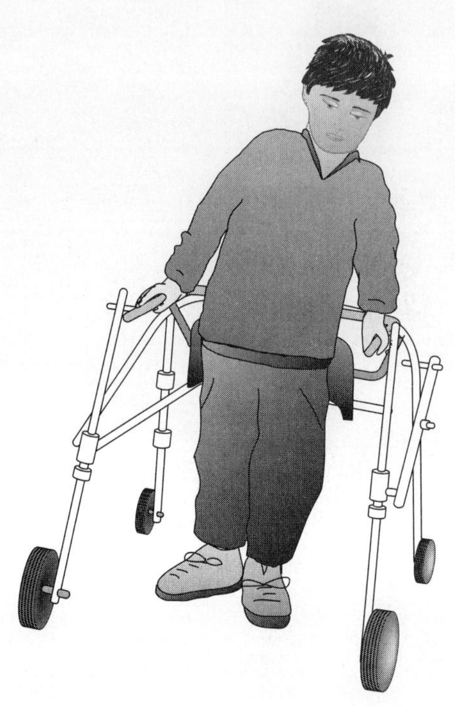

(a)

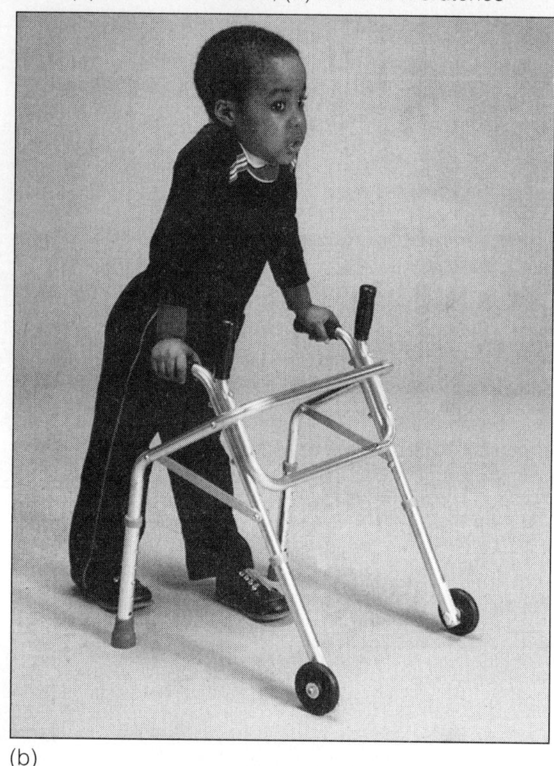

(b)

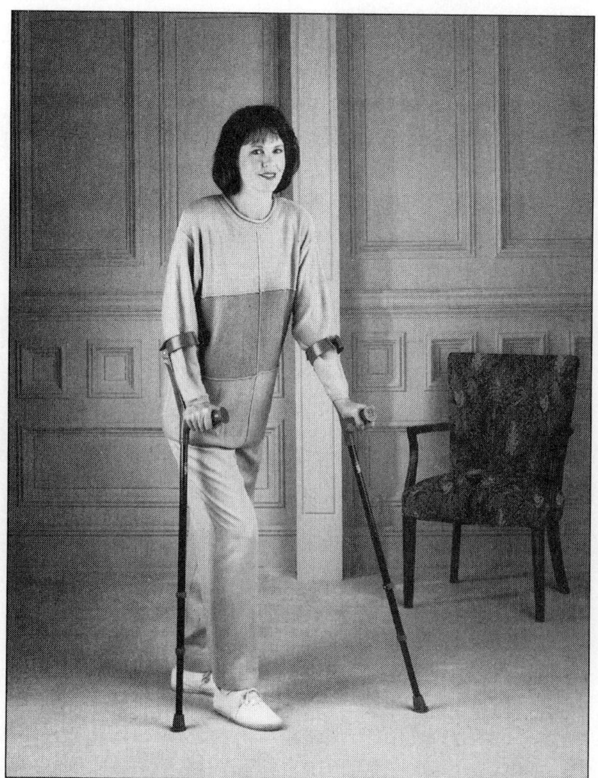

(c)

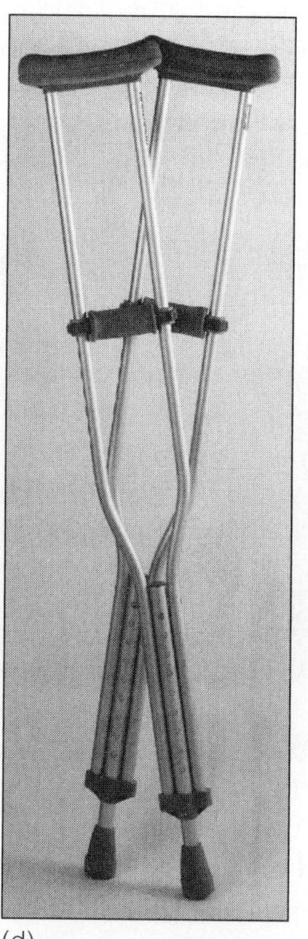

(d)

posture. Walkers may have rigid frames for stability or be folded for portability.

Individuals with greater stability may use crutches. There are several types of crutches (see Figure 7–17). Walkers and crutches are customized for individual students depending on their mobility needs.

ARCHITECTURAL ACCESS MODIFICATIONS

Students who use various means of conveyances or mobility devices must be able to move in and out of buildings safely and independently. They must be provided access to bathrooms, lunchrooms, classrooms, and other areas of the school and community. The Americans with Disabilities Act (ADA) has provided standards for uniform accessibility of public and private accommodations. What is meant by "uniform accessibility"? The *Accessibility Guidelines for Buildings and Facilities* specified by the U.S. Architectural and Transportation Barriers Compliance Board (ATBCB) (1998) provides regulations for design and placement of many items. Examples include drinking-fountain height, slope of ramps, handrail heights, door and walkway width, door lever installation, and restroom facility modifications such as sink heights (see Figure 7–18). These specifications include an addendum that provides accessibility rules for children ages 2–12. Another useful guideline is the *Recommendations for Accessibility Standards for Children's Environments* (U.S. Architectural and Transportation Barriers Compliance Board, 1992). Teachers and others who serve individuals with physical and multiple disabilities are advised to obtain copies of such uniform accessibility documents from the ATBCB.

Contingency plans must be arranged in advance for problems with architectural accessibility, including emergencies and building evacuation. For example, elevator failure might mean students on crutches and even a few who generally use wheelchairs would need to safely maneuver themselves by sitting down and scooting on the stairs. Procedures during various types of emergencies should be specifically defined for individuals with mobility impairment. Care should be taken to ensure that everyone is informed of the procedures, including all teachers and paraprofessionals, rescue companies, students, and substitute teachers.

FIGURE 7–18
Designing for accessibility

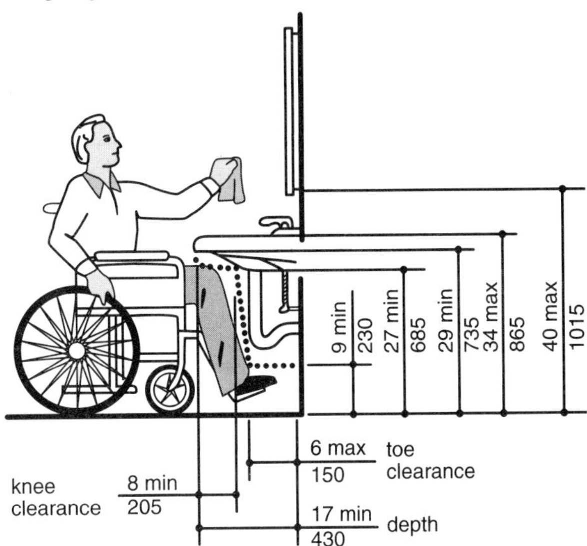

Note. U.S. Architectural and Transportation Barriers Compliance Board (1998). Americans with Disabilities Act accessibility guidelines. *Federal Register,* January 13, p. 2080.

Cots and blankets should be kept on the upper floors so that they can be used in case of emergency to transport students to safety.

ENVIRONMENTAL AND OBJECT MODIFICATION

As defined by Sowers, Jenkins, and Powers (1988), environmental modifications can be used to "change the work environment by modifying equipment used as part of the task, or by actually modifying the manner in which the task is done" (p. 408). Environmental modifications, as described in this chapter, include (a) changes in location of material and equipment, (b) work surface modifications, (c) object modifications, and (d) manipulation aids.

Location of Materials and Equipment

Whether students use a tray as a tabletop or some other table arrangement, it is important for them to be able to obtain and put away their own materials whenever possible. If students do not have desks for storage, boxes can be attached to the side of a table so that the opening is at the table height and materials are dropped into the box from the top. Another option is to use plastic modular office stacking trays and

FIGURE 7–19
Three ways to store materials on a wheelchair: (a) side pocket; (b) back pack; (c) beverage caddy

(a)

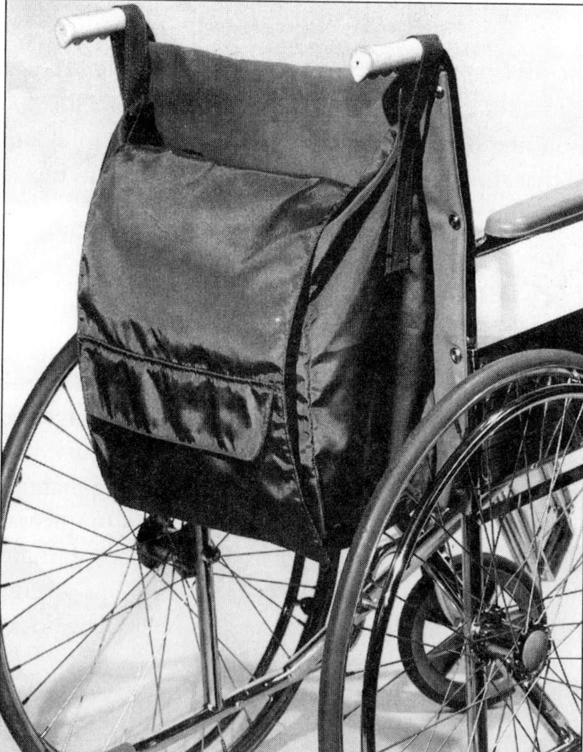
(b)

(c)

crates that can be attached to the side of a desk or rest on the desk surface. In addition to providing an accessible place for materials, plastic crate, box, or tray storage provides a useful organization tool. Some containers for student materials can be attached to the front, side, or back of the wheelchair or attached to a swivel arm so that they can ride behind the wheelchair when not in use (see Figure 7–19). If, for physical reasons, students cannot obtain and put away their own materials, they should learn to ask others for help. By pausing to wait for the student's request, teachers and classmates encourage the student to take responsibility in this area, and help enhance the student's self-esteem.

It is important that students learn to put away their mobility equipment. Crutches that are carelessly left on classroom floors and in aisles are a liability for everyone. An example is Lee, a student who let his crutches fall onto the classroom floor after he seated himself at his desk. In this class, desks accommodated two people and were arranged in long rows facing the front of the classroom. Lee was placed near the front of the room and in an aisle seat. He was taught to lay his crutches to the side of his desk and parallel to the aisle after he was seated. The teacher made the aisle sufficiently wide so that other students did not need to step over his crutches. Another strategy would be to secure a Velcro® strap to the edge of the desk and use it to secure the crutches. This leaves the crutches upright and within easy access.

Students who use mobility equipment must be responsible for keeping it safely stored, but others must also help. Sufficient storage space must be provided for large equipment such as wheelchairs and walkers. In classrooms, furniture placement should allow access to all areas of the room. Slippery papers must never be left on the floor. Courtesy and common sense should be practiced by everyone.

Work Surface Modifications

Features of tabletops, including wheelchair lap trays, can influence how a child uses arm and head movements. The size, position, slant, and height are characteristics that may be adjusted to the needs of the student. To counteract a slumping (or flexion) pattern, a higher table height is desirable, since it requires the student to sit taller. Children with low muscle tone and athetoid cerebral palsy typically benefit from a high working surface that provides elbow support. However, for those with a limited range of movement, such as children with spastic cerebral palsy or those who hyperextend the body, a lower tabletop is better, since the lower working surface area does not interfere with their limited movements. Many children with physical disabilities also benefit from using a tabletop that extends behind their elbows, such as a table with a U-shaped cutout area for the chest, because it provides additional arm support (see Figure 7–20).

Wheelchair arms present problems when choosing table height. Sometimes if a table is high enough for the wheelchair arms to fit underneath, it is too high for adequate use by the student. There are different ways to counteract this problem. First, a student might utilize a wheelchair with arms that are removable, or "desk arms." Another possibility is to cut away the desk compartment under the table and then lower the whole table as far as it will go before it interferes with the wheelchair arms.

Arranging the height of the work surface often is not enough. The slant or angle of surface areas may need to be adapted. This can be accomplished with a slant board or book easel that comes in a variety of angles. Another way to create a slanted work surface is to use a

FIGURE 7–20
Work surface modifications using (a) stander with cut-out tray and (b) raised table surface

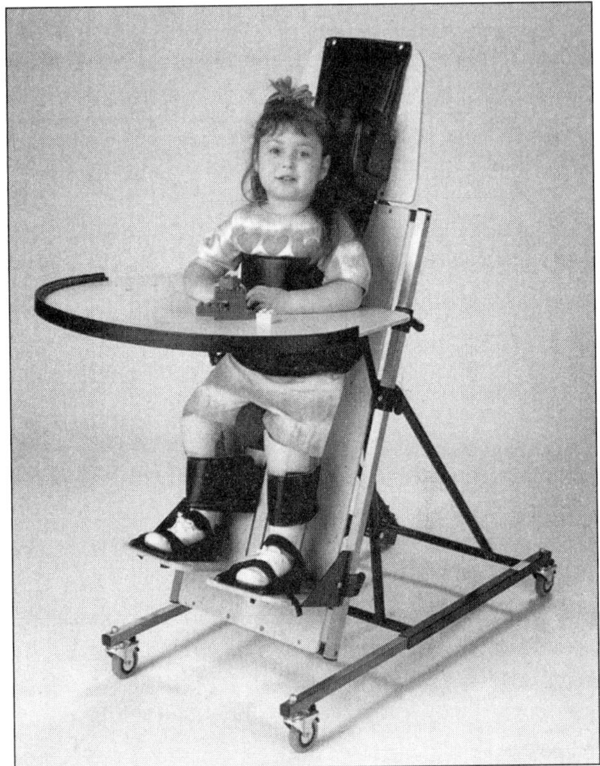

(a)

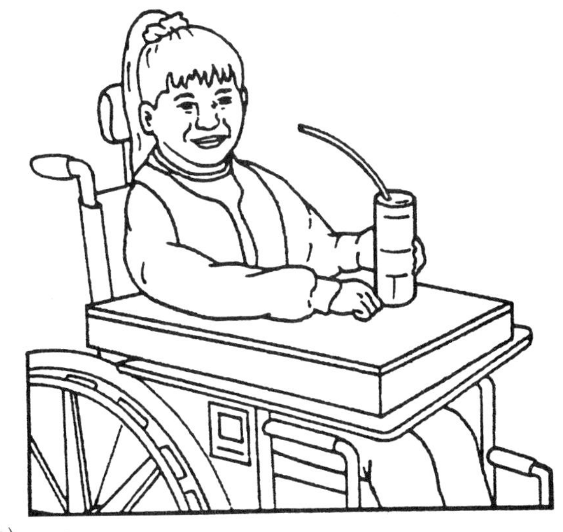

(b)

FIGURE 7–21
Slant devices: (a) desktop storage box with slant top; (b) high-tech convertible slant table; (c) notebook and ruler; (d) low-tech wooden back podium

(a)

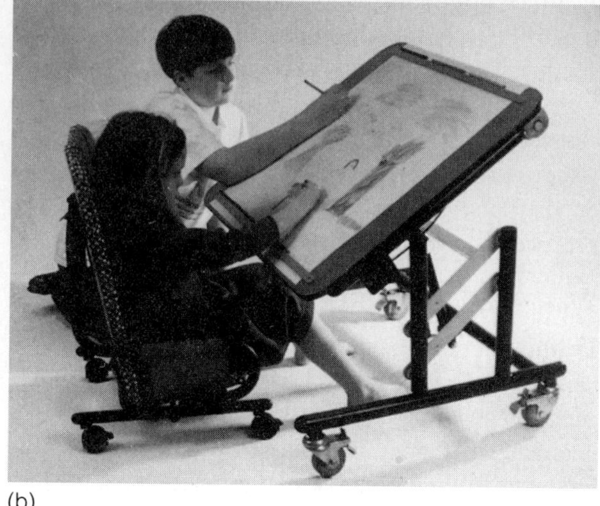
(b)

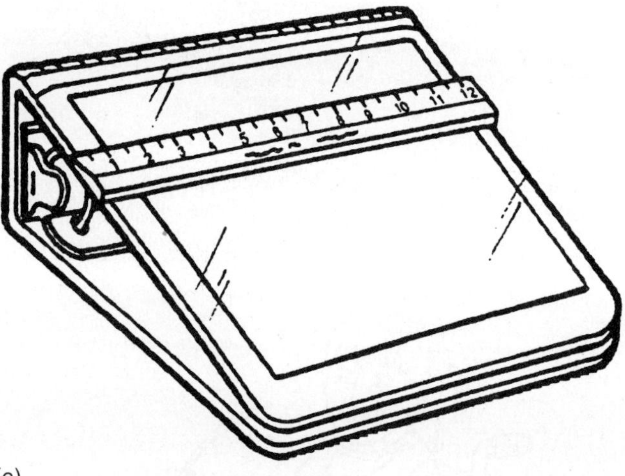

(c)

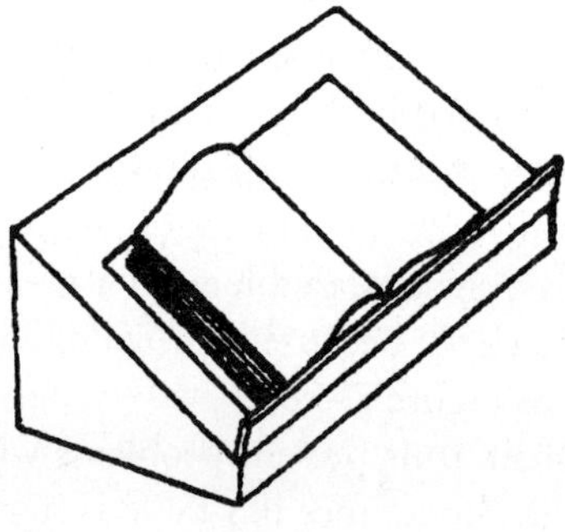
(d)

Note. (c) Reprinted with permission of Therapro, Inc., Framingham, MA, from *Low-Tech Assistive Devices: A Handbook for the School Setting* © 1998. (d) from *Creative Constructions: Technologies That Make Adaptive Design Accessible, Affordable, Inclusive, and Fun* (p. 88) by M. Campbell and A. Truesdell, 2000, Cambridge, MA: Creative Constructions. Reprinted with permission.

notebook binder placed on its side and secured to the work surface. Materials can be secured to the surface of the binder with a plastic "chip clip" commonly found in retail stores that has been glued to the side of the binder. Slanted work surfaces should be evaluated for individual students. An angle that works for one student might not be the proper angle for another. Figure 7–21 displays several angled work surfaces of varying complexity.

Object Modifications

In their discussions of making toys and other play materials accessible for children with cerebral palsy, Finnie (1997, pp. 127–160) and Schaeffler (1988, pp. 26–28) categorize specialized modification techniques that include (1) object stabilization, (2) boundary creation, (3) grasping aids, (4) manipulation aids, and (5) switches. Because of their relevance to modification strategies and student performance, the first four techniques are summarized here. The fifth specialized technique for object modification, using switches, is covered in the environmental control section of this chapter.

Object Stabilization. The hand functions commonly affected by physical control and coordination difficulties are grasp and manipulation (Church & Glennen, 1992; Finnie, 1997; Heller & Swinehart-Jones, 2003; Schaeffler, 1988). Stabilization keeps items in position so that individuals with problems directing their hands will not knock them off or away and therefore do not have to redirect their reach toward displaced items. Stabilization of items assists bimanual tasks, or those in which a person needs one hand to hold an object and the other to manipulate it. Stabilization strategies include:

- Clamping the bases of items to tables;
- Using masking tape to secure items to surfaces (2-inch width provides the strongest bond);
- Placing hook-type Velcro® on the item and loop-type Velcro® on the clean surface;
- Using textured paper or other materials with adhesive properties underneath the item to be secured;
- Using adhesive-backed Velcro® or foam tape to adhere directly to a table or on a board that is clamped to a table;
- Attaching a wood or plastic pipe frame to a wheelchair surface and attaching objects to the frame; and
- Using suction cups to stabilize objects for short periods of time (use on clean nonwood surface and moisten the edges of the cup for best results).

Boundaries. Many students with physical or multiple disabilities accidentally push items out of reach and cannot retrieve them. Physical boundaries can be created to keep items in a limited area but within reach. Boundaries are also useful for students with visual impairments because they can be used to secure materials within visual range. Boundary strategies include:

- Creating tracks to confine items when appropriate (make tracks for pull toys);
- Placing items inside boxes, trays, or other compartments;
- Placing an edge on a wheelchair tray;
- Placing cooking or art materials inside a sturdy plastic zip-lock bag and mix by shaking the bag; and
- Placing the child within an enclosed play area (such as a ball pit) to keep materials within physical reach and visual field.

Figure 7–22 shows a variety of object stabilization and boundary devices.

Grasping Aids. Grasping aids are useful for those who are unable to grasp, hold, and feel objects. Grasping can be facilitated by:

- Using a cuff designed for holding crayons and other stick-shaped items;
- Placing Velcro® on the palm of a glove and on a toy that can then be picked up;
- Attaching small magnets on the palm or finger of a glove for picking up metal objects such as toy cars, blocks, etc; and
- Enlarging items to make them easier to hold by wrapping foam and/or tape around the item.

Manipulation Aids. Manipulation aids help students who find it difficult to move the parts on objects such as toys because they lack the "required isolated finger movements, use of a pincers grasp, and controlled movement of the wrist for [the toys'] operation" (Schaeffler, 1988, p. 27). Manipulation aids can also extend the reach of students whose range of motion is restricted. Techniques include:

- Enlarging the pieces to be held to make the grasp easier;
- Extending and widening pieces of objects to make pushing easier;
- Attaching flat extensions, knobs, or dowels to increase surface areas (prosthetic pieces);
- Attaching a crossbar or dowel to an object to compensate for the inability to rotate the wrist;
- Placing a longer handle on objects to extend range of motion;
- Placing a tongue depressor between book pages to function as "handles" for page turning; and
- Widening the space between book pages with double-sided foam tape or cardboard.

Figure 7–23 shows a variety of devices that facilitate grasp and manipulation.

FIGURE 7–22
Object stabilization and boundary devices: (a–c) keeping small objects confined; (d) paintbrush holder; (e) lotion or soap stabilizer; (f) bowl holder

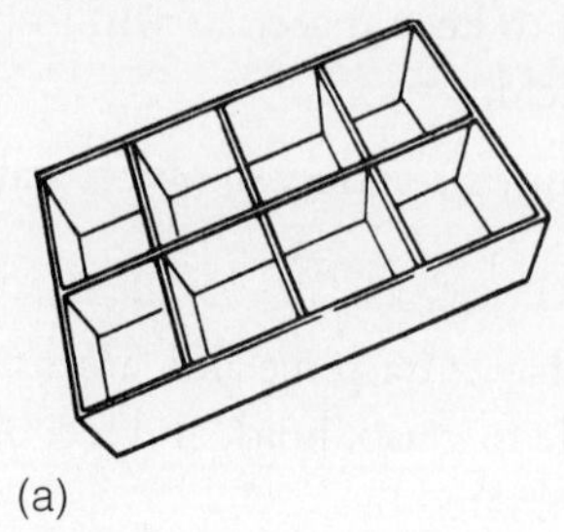

(a)

(b)

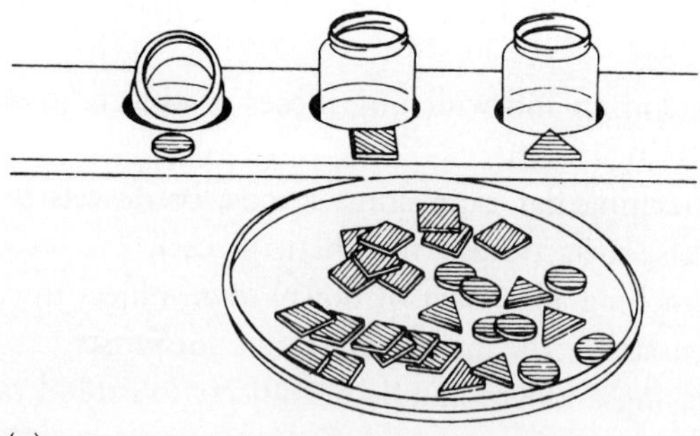

(c)

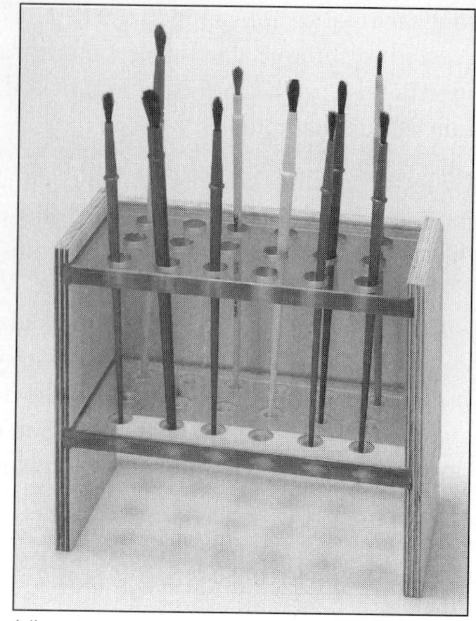

(d)

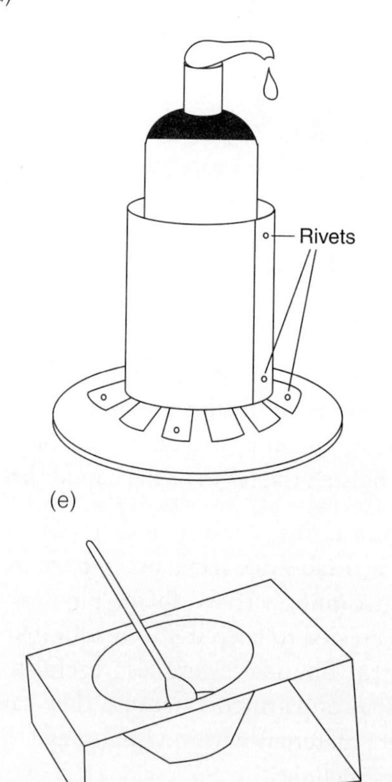

(e)

(f)

Note. (e) and (f) from *Creative Constructions: Technologies That Make Adaptive Design Accessible, Affordable, Inclusive, and Fun* (p. 113) by M. Campbell and A. Truesdell, 2000, Cambridge, MA: Creative Constructions. Reprinted with permission.

FIGURE 7–23
Grasp and manipulation aids: (a) tabbed communication notebook; (b) no-slip scissors; (c) long-handle brushes and combs; (d) large-handle eating utensils

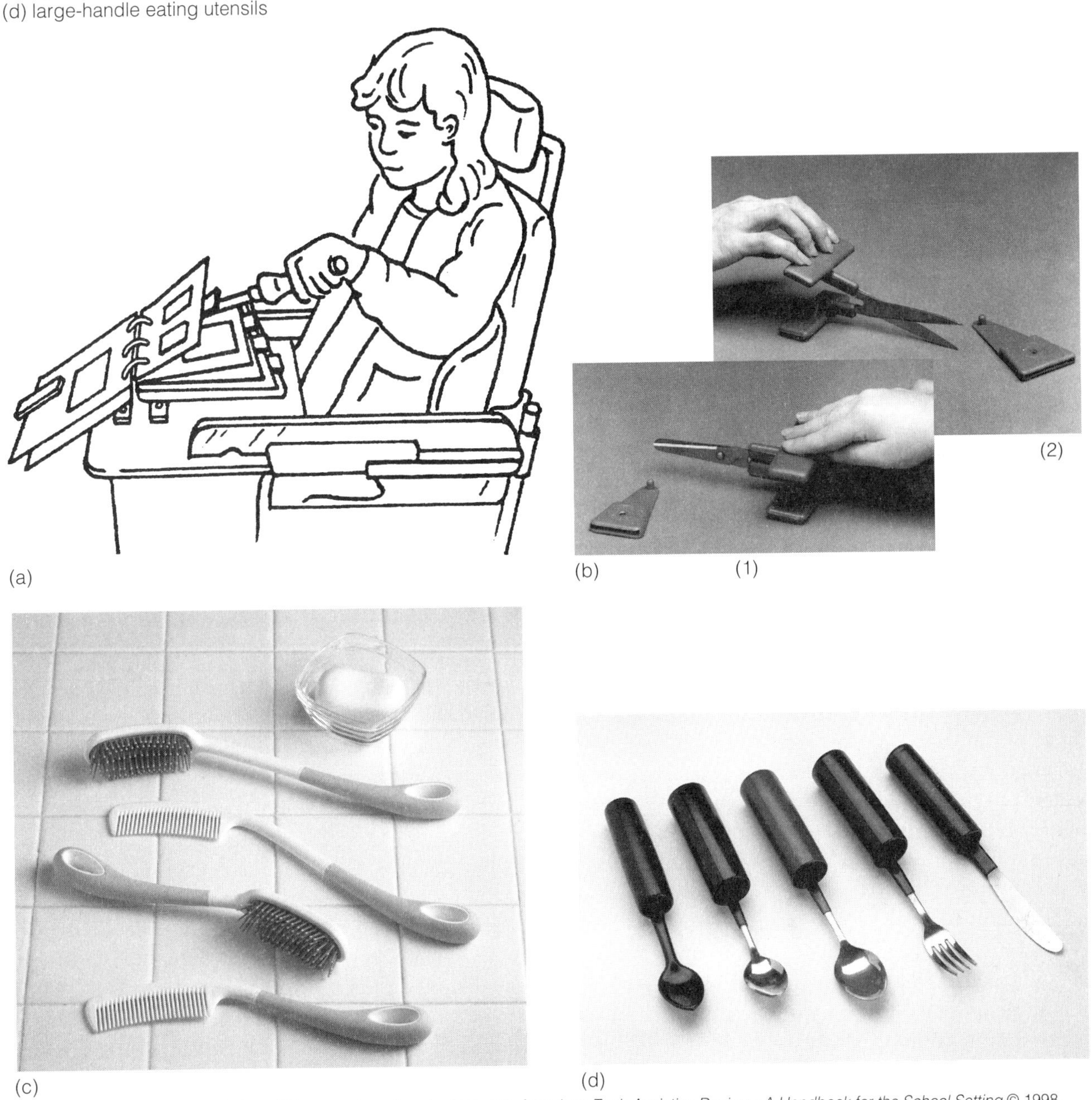

Note. (a) Reprinted with permission of Therapro, Inc., Framingham, MA, from *Low-Tech Assistive Devices: A Handbook for the School Setting* © 1998.

ENVIRONMENTAL CONTROL

Individuals with physical or multiple disabilities often lack the physical ability to operate appliances in their environments. Appliances they may need to control include communication devices, computers, home security systems, home lighting devices such as lamps and overhead lighting, electric wheelchairs, AC (alternating current) appliances (e.g., TV, stereo, blender), and various DC (direct current) appliances (e.g., tape recorders, battery-operated toys, battery-powered radios). AT devices that allow individuals to control their environments are referred to as electronic aids to daily living (EADLs). Discussion will focus on simple technology whose purpose is to allow people to operate appliances and battery-operated devices using EADLs. When using an EADL, the full electrical system includes (a) an electrical appliance (used for housekeeping, personal care, leisure, or work), (b) a switch, and (c) the EADL. An EADL is a device that provides the user with programmed or spontaneous control over one or more electrically operated appliance. More-sophisticated EADL systems include infrared, radio control, ultrasound control, and AC power line control systems. These systems can be used to operate home electronic units such as televisions, stereos, automatic door openers, VCRs, burglar alarms, and other appliances. Older texts referred to these devices as environmental control units (ECUs). Readers are referred to Church and Glennen (1992) for a detailed description of additional ECU/EADLs.

For classroom use, an EADL is a unit that reduces the voltage from the appliance at the electrical outlet to a lower voltage at the switch, where the person accesses the appliance (Levin & Scherfenberg, 1987). Figure 7–24 shows a variety of appliances and an ECU/EADL.

FIGURE 7–24
Components of a system to allow persons to use a switch to operate electrical appliances

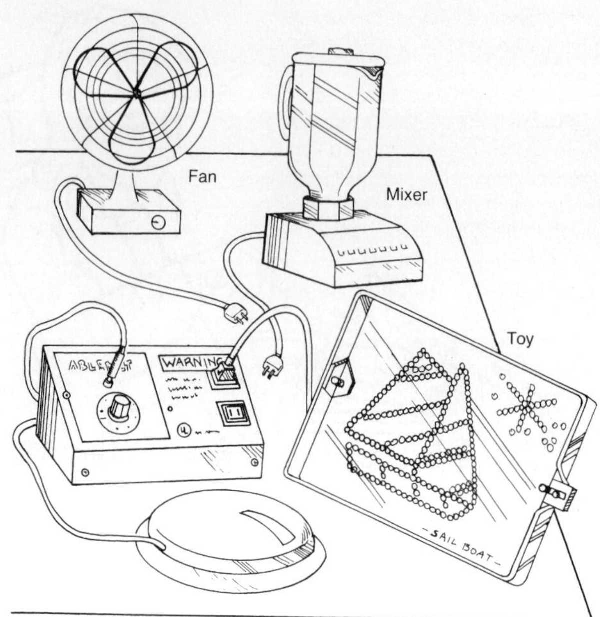

Note. Adapted from *Selection and Use of Simple Technology in Home, Schoolwork, and Community Settings* (p. 7) by J. Levin and L. Scherfenberg, 1987, Minneapolis, MN: ABLENET. Used with permission.

EADLs may also be used to control battery-operated systems. A battery-operated system includes (a) a battery-operated toy or device (radio, tape recorder, etc.), (b) a switch, and (c) a battery device adapter. A battery interrupter is used to operate a battery-powered device with an external switch rather than the built-in on-off switch. It consists of a metal wafer on one end of an electric cord and a switch on the other end of the cord. The wafer is inserted between the batteries and their metal contacts to interrupt the circuit and allow the circuit to be completed by someone pressing the switch. Battery interrupters must be selected or made to fit the size of the batteries (D, C, AA, etc.). They are easy to make if readers choose to do so (Burkhart, 1980, 1982), but are also commercially available.

Switches. Individuals who can make at least one voluntary motion with their bodies can activate a switch to gain some control over their environment. A switch is a "hardware device that either opens or closes an electronic circuit, controlling the flow of electricity to an electronic device much like a light switch in the home turns on (open circuit) or off (closed circuit)" (Glennen & DeCoste, 1997, p. 778). To use a switch effectively, individuals should (a) be properly positioned if nonambulatory, (b) demonstrate nonreflexive response stimulation, and (c) exhibit voluntary movement on cue.

Switch Selection. Any switch prescribed must be safe, accommodate a workable activation point and/or movement, mount successfully, be durable and consistent, and be easily replaced or duplicated. Switches vary by the type of movement and pressure needed to activate them. Switches also differ by the feedback they provide to the user. Some provide tactile feedback, while others produce a sound. Visual feedback (such as light activation) can also be produced with switches (Glennen & DeCoste, 1997).

Switch activation is an important consideration. Switch types include push action, pull action, tilt action, sip/puff action, brow-wrinkle/eye-blink action, flex/constrictive action, and squeeze action. Switches can be positioned in dozens of locations to be activated by use of the hands, feet, elbows, knees, head, eyebrow, etc. Experimentation is required to determine which

FIGURE 7–25
Adaptive switches. (a) Zygo Tread Switch: requires downward pressure on the plate surface and gives audible feedback. (b) Zygo Leaf Switch: bending the wire in the plastic casing to the right or left activates the switch. (c) Prentke Romich Wobble Switch: moving the ball minimally in any direction activates the switch, which gives audible click feedback. (d) Zygo Lever Switch: requires minimal downward pressure on the padded foam surface. (e) Toys for Special Children 5 × 8 Plate Switch: minimally pressing on the surface activates the switch. (f) Prentke Romich Rocking Lever Switch: pressing downward on the right or left side activates selections on the device. (g) TASH Plate Membrane Switch: minimal pressure in the circled area activates the switch. (h) Able Net Big Red Switch: downward pressure on the large circular surface activates the switch

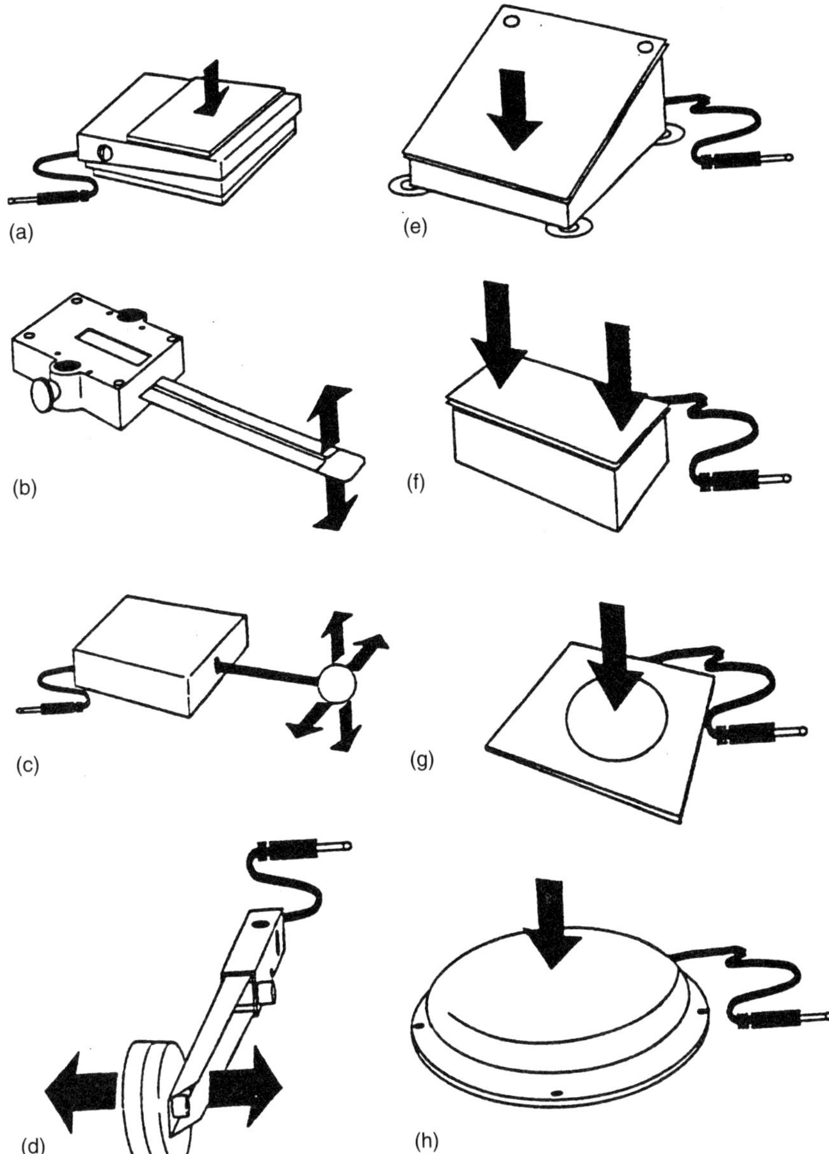

Note. From The Handbook of Assistive Technology, 1st edition, by Church © 1992. Reprinted with permission of Delmar, a division of Thomson Learning. Fax 800-730-2215.

site provides the most reliable movement with the least fatigue and the least likelihood of causing future contractures or pain from repetitive movement. The occupational therapist is the team member with the most knowledge in this area and will most likely take the lead in helping to determine switch placement and activation site. Before a switch is purchased for long-term use, it should be tried with the student in the environments in which it will be used to ensure that it works as intended. As a teacher, you will be involved in helping identify environments and tasks in which switches are needed and in monitoring use to help determine functionality. Although there are now dozens of commercially available switches, they can also be constructed. For those interested in building switches, Burkhart (1980, 1982) discusses the design and construction of simple switches. There are also directions for building switches and other items on her Web site, listed in "Focus on the Net" at the end of this chapter. Several switches are displayed in Figure 7–25.

Switch Mounting. Mounting a switch for use by a student can be a simple or frustrating task. There are several potential reasons for different switch mounts. The switch may need to be mounted in order to properly position it at the activation point, secure it to the desired position, or protect it and others when used by a student who accidentally dislodges or intentionally throws objects. An example is Lourdes, a student with mixed spastic and athetoid cerebral palsy. Attempts to activate a switch for scanning on her computer using her hands met with frustration, since she knocked her hands and arms against the switch and frequently sent it flying off her wheelchair tray. In addition, she lacked sufficient motor control to activate the switch reliably with her hands or arm. The switch was then mounted under her wheelchair tray. The clear plastic tray allowed her visual access to the switch, and her more reliable leg control allowed her to activate the switch by pushing her knee against it. The switch stayed in place and became a useful way to activate AT devices.

Never overlook the impact of making the transition from a relatively passive role to one of being able to control the physical environment. Selection of tasks, appliances, and EADLs is only part of the process of controlling the environment. Training in all aspects of the system will still be required.

ASSISTIVE TECHNOLOGY FOR SENSORY IMPAIRMENTS

Individuals with physical disabilities and sensory impairment (visual, hearing, or both) may also require AT devices. For a student with a mild to moderate impairment in either vision or hearing, that source of sensory input is still usable, but is limited in some way. The most frequent type of limitation is one of intensity (Cook & Hussey, 1995). For visual input, this means that the size of object is too small to be seen by the student and must be magnified in some way. This may be with glasses, a magnifying glass, or enlarged print. For auditory input, this means that the volume of the sound is too weak to be heard by the student and must be intensified in some way. This may be with hearing aids, FM system, or some other means of amplification. The second type of limitation is one of frequency or wavelength limitation (Cook & Hussey, 1995). In visual input this may mean a lack of contrast between figure and background or a problem discriminating color. It may require filters or overlays to vary the colors to produce greater contrast. In hearing, this may mean a specific frequency loss that will require hearing aids designed to compensate for that specific loss. The third type of loss is a field limitation (Cook & Hussey, 1995). In hearing, this usually means unequal hearing in the two ears, and binaural hearing aids are used. In vision, a field loss may be partially accommodated for with special lenses.

When the sensory loss is so significant there is no useful input of information via that channel, then we must provide input via a different channel. For example, sign language can be used for children who are deaf, or Braille for students who are blind. Leadership in the provision and management of AT services for these technologies will be provided by specialists trained in the respective areas of visual impairment/blindness, hearing impairment, or dual sensory impairment as needed. The responsibility of the teacher is to become familiar with the AT, know when and how it is to be used, how to recognize that it is malfunctioning, and whom to contact.

Assistive Technology and Hearing Loss

Assistive technology for students with hearing loss falls into three categories: (1) assistive listening devices, (2) telecommunication equipment and peripherals, and (3) alerting devices.

Assistive Listening Devices. Assistive listening devices (ALDs) are special amplifying devices and systems that can be utilized with or without hearing aids. In difficult listening situations, particularly noisy environments, or environments where the student is at a distance from the source of the sound, hearing aids do not always provide enough help to make speech recognizable. ALDs are designed to help the student hear better in a variety of difficult listening situations by "bridging" the distance between the sound source and the student with the hearing loss and by improving the student's ability to hear when there is background noise. There are two major categories of ALDs. The first are personal infrared or FM (frequency modulated) systems that are worn by the student and receive speech input from a teacher-worn microphone connected to a receiver worn by the child or a group of children. The second are sound field FM systems that provide amplified speech from a teacher-worn microphone to a speaker directed into an entire room or parts of a room. Both types of ALDs may be used alone or in conjunction with a student's hearing aid.

Telecommunication Equipment. This form of AT encompasses portable amplifiers that can be plugged into standard phones, amplified handsets, amplified headsets, extra-loud ringers, cell phones that vibrate when they ring, and, of course, adapted telephones that allow the user to type in words (TDDs or TTYs). *TTY* ("teletypewriter") is the older terminology, but is still commonly used in the deaf community. *TDD* (which stands for "telecommunication devices for the deaf") will be used here. TDDs allow the deaf or severely hard-of-hearing individual to type in a message and receive a response that is printed out on a liquid crystal display (LCD) or printer. The TDD may be used to communicate with another TDD user or with a relay operator who speaks the message to a hearing communication partner. Of course, a TDD can be used by students with physical or multiple disabilities only if they are able to activate the keyboard either directly or with additional assistive technology. Another type of telecommunication equipment is the closed-caption television, which provides a print conversion of the words being spoken on screen. It is called "closed" captioning because the words are not visible unless the viewer has a closed-caption decoder. All televisions currently being produced have a built-in decoder.

Alerting or Warning Devices. These devices may utilize a visual or tactile signal or an amplified auditory signal to notify the deaf or hard-of-hearing student that something has happened or needs their attention. A student who is deaf or has a severe hearing loss will require the visual or tactile signals to get their attention. Alerting devices are available for a variety of items, including alarm clocks, doorbells, telephones, fire alarms, and smoke or carbon monoxide detectors. There are also units that alert a person to someone knocking on the door, a baby's cry, or any other sounds in the environment.

Assistive Technology and Visual Impairments

Two of the major problems for students with vision impairments are accessing print materials and moving about safely in their environments (orientation and mobility). For students with low vision who require AT to access print, devices include optical or electronic magnifiers, handheld or spectacle-mounted magnifiers or telescopes, large-print books, and closed-circuit television (CCTV). The CCTV is a device that is used to enlarge the print on existing books and papers. The print material is placed under the camera eye that magnifies the print and displays it on a screen or monitor. There are small handheld sizes with displays that are approximately 3 inches by 7 inches and larger ones that can display the text on full-size monitors up to 25 inches. Low-tech, handheld magnifiers tend to magnify something up to 4 or 5 times its actual size. The smaller CCTVs typically magnify print up to 12 or 13 times. However, the large-screen monitors can magnify print up to 65 times its actual size. In addition to size, the quality of the magnification varies with different products, and usually a variety will be tried in order to determine which works best for the individual. (See Figure 14–6, Chapter 14.)

Computer-based tools include screen enlargers, software that changes the color of text and the color of the background to enhance the contrast, and screen-reading software that reads the text aloud using synthesized voice. Assistive technology for persons who cannot read print at all due to their vision includes Braille materials, screen-reading software, optical-character-reading software, reading machines, Braille writers, and electronic notetaking devices.

There are many other types of AT for individuals who are blind or have limited vision. Examples include beeping balls, talking watches and clocks, talking and large-display calculators (including scientific calculators), talking thermometers and thermostats, talking money identifiers, talking rulers and dice, large-print or Braille key caps for keyboards, and large-key illuminated remote controls for operating televisions and VCRs. Even talking microwave ovens are available. The best way to find out about these items is to request a catalog from specific product vendors or to attend a product show designed to promote a variety of commercial AT devices.

SUMMARY AND CONCLUSION

Individuals with physical or multiple disabilities face ongoing challenges to improve their participation in all facets of daily life. That challenge can often be met through appropriate use of assistive technology devices and services. There is now an AT solution for virtually every possible disability and every possible task. A range of AT options exists for all types of tasks. It is the job of the IEP team and others who serve the student to determine what, if any, AT might help a particular student. If AT will make a significant difference, then it is necessary in order for the student to receive a free, appropriate public education.

The first step in appropriate intervention through AT is to identify the problems encountered during activities; the second step is to look for adaptations. If an educator is familiar with available AT and adaptation possibilities, it is a much easier task to intervene or to contribute ideas to interdisciplinary deliberations when a problem occurs. To understand AT, to collaborate with others in appropriate AT assessment, and to guide or initiate decisions about intervention options are common goals of educators who work with students with physical or multiple disabilities. Information about the application of AT is provided throughout the remainder of this text.

Before leaving the discussion of AT, it is important to mention the practice of anticipating student needs whenever possible. Rather than waiting to see how a student gets along in a particular situation and then developing solutions for future times, it is more prudent to anticipate and be prepared with potential adaptations. The same basic process for identification of student difficulties described early in this chapter should be used proactively so that students do not unnecessarily miss any opportunities for participation. The successful analysis of a student's need, coupled with application of knowledge about appropriate AT and the timing of its provision, can give the student with a physical or multiple disability access to the total educational experience.

QUESTIONS FOR DISCUSSION

1. What is assistive technology? What is the difference between AT devices and AT services, according to federal law?
2. Why should AT assessment have a multidisciplinary focus? Describe how the following contribute to AT assessment: speech/language therapist, occupational therapist, physical therapist, special or general education teacher.
3. Describe the basic considerations for appropriately positioning and seating an individual for AT access.
4. Describe three "low-tech" devices that could be built to facilitate sitting.
5. Under what circumstances would an individual want to use a power wheelchair instead of a manual wheelchair? When is a manual wheelchair a better option than a power wheelchair?
6. Take an "accessibility walk" around your classroom, school, or neighborhood. List six modifications that could be made to make these environments more accessible for an individual who uses a wheelchair for mobility.
7. Describe how you would use AT to make the following activities more accessible for students with motor and sensory impairments: a classroom reading activity, a board game, doll play, math homework (algebra or geometry).
8. An 11-year-old girl is beginning sixth grade in your classroom. She has athetoid cerebral palsy and limited use of her limbs. She uses a power wheelchair. Her speech is intelligible only to people who know her well. She is eager to make friends. How would you adapt your classroom to provide her with access to materials and activities?
9. A 15-year-old boy has just enrolled in your class. He has multiple disabilities that include visual and hearing impairments. He is ambulatory but only uses his right hand. He uses gestures and sounds to communicate. You have noticed that he follows two-step directions. He occasionally resorts to physical self-aggression when he is unable to convey his needs and wants to others. He lacks many activities of daily living skills, including the ability to independently feed and dress himself. How would you adapt your classroom to provide him with access to materials and activities?

FOCUS ON THE NET

AbleData

http://www.abledata.com

This site provides a searchable database of AT that contains over 25,000 products. In addition to descriptions, it also contains information on cost of items, capabilities, and ordering information. It covers everything from wheelchairs to reachers to computer keyboards. In some cases there are pictures. It is updated regularly and also contains a variety of other resource information.

Adaptive Design Association, Inc.

http:www.adaptivedesign.org

"The mission of Adaptive Design Association, Inc., is to ensure that children with disabilities get the customized equipment they need to fully participate in home, school, and community life." The creators of this organization recognize that children with disabilities need adaptive equipment to interact, and that they should never go without such equipment. To this end, they train a variety of professionals and community volunteers to design and build adaptive equipment. Their focus is on "appropriate technology," the reliance on basic tools, simple techniques, and low-cost materials.

Alliance for Technology Access

http://www.ataccess.org

The Alliance for Technology Access (ATA) is a network of not-for-profit centers throughout the United States that provides assistive technology training. Readers are urged to visit their Web site to learn the location of assistive technology centers in their states. This site also provides a wealth of information for families, including links to other Web sites.

Linda Burkhart's Web Site

http://www.lburkhart.com

This Web site has a variety of excellent resources about using the Internet as an instructional tool for students with disabilities in school. It includes tips for the "one-computer classroom" as well as advanced information on student search tools, student start pages, and teacher resources. It also contains her directions for making your own switches and your own adapted mouse. Her list of Web links is extremely large and well organized. It contains several links to sites with activities and setups to download. This is a good place to start if you are new to AT or instructional technology uses for students with physical, health, or multiple disabilities.

Closing the Gap

http://www.closingthegap.com

One extremely useful tool is the *Closing the Gap* Resource Directory, which is published each spring as the February/March issue of the *Closing the Gap* newsletter. It is also available as a searchable database on their Web site. It is an excellent tool for school teams. The directory is divided into five sections: Hardware, Software, Producers, Organizations, and Glossary. The Producers section lists over 250 vendors. This can be used in a variety of ways. Suppose, for example, that a teacher hears that Don Johnston is one of the commonly used vendors for talking word-processing software. Looking up Don Johnston, Inc., in the Producers, she finds a long list of products. Scanning that list, she sees Write: OutLoud, which sounds like it might be talking word processing. Turning to the Software section of the Resource Directory, she finds a description of this talking word-processing software, including price, type of computer it runs on, system requirements, and other valuable information.

DisAbility Information and Resources

http://www.makoa.org

DisAbility Information and Resources (DIR) is run by Jim Lubin, P.O. Box 82433, Kenmore, WA 98028-0433, and is organized alphabetically by categories. It focuses on physical disabilities and addresses every access need to achieve independence, including AT. Consumers can find an athletic guide, education and job training resources, information on service animals, mailing lists, and resources for caregivers. The following is a sample of resources available through DIR:

- Travel and Recreation Resources
- Accessibility Design Resources
- Legal and Advocacy Resources

IntelliTools
http://www.IntelliTools.com

The IntelliTools Web site contains over 100 overlays and activities that can be downloaded to use with children. While these overlays are designed to be used with the IntelliKeys and other IntelliTools products, many of these can be used without those products. They also provide a downloadable IntelliPics player that allows the individual to use the software created with IntelliPics even though they don't have that software.

National Rehabilitation Information Center
http://www.naric.com/nairc

This site provides information on many low- and high-technology products and services for individuals with disabilities.

Switch In Time
http://www.switchintime.com

This Web site offers several freeware programs that are very useful and easy to use. These include CD Juke Box, Single Switch Bingo, Switch Hitter, Word Search, and Scan 'n Read. All are for the Macintosh, except Scan 'n Read, which is available in both platforms. Scan 'n Read is a wonderful productivity tool for teachers that allows you to make electronic storybooks that can be operated with a single switch.

Wisconsin Assistive Technology Initiative
http://www.wati.org

The Wisconsin Assistive Technology Initiative (WATI) offers a variety of online resources. The Web site has eight sections, including Best Practices in AT Service Delivery, WATI assessment forms (which can be downloaded as pdf files), Assistive Technology and Adapted Art, special buys on various assistive technology, and information on AT training.

The Hattie B. Monroe Barkley Memorial Augmentative and Alternative Communication Centers
http://www.aac.unl.edu

This Web site has a rich variety of resources in AAC, including YAACK: Augmentative and Alternative Communication Connecting Young Kids. YAACK was created by Ruth Ballinger as a master's degree project at the University of Hawaii and is a very useful beginner's tool. Other information on this Web site includes virtual resources and PowerPoint presentations about research projects in AAC.

REFERENCES

Bowser, G., & Reed, P. (1995). Education tech points for assistive technology planning. *Journal of Special Education Technology, 7,* 325–338.

Bowser, G., & Reed, P. (1998). *Education tech points: A framework for assistive technology planning.* Winchester: Coalition for Technology in Oregon.

Burkhart, L. J. (1980). *Homemade battery-powered toys and educational devices for severely handicapped children.* College Park, MD: Author.

Burkhart, L. J. (1982). *More homemade battery-powered toys and educational devices for severely handicapped children.* College Park, MD: Author.

Butler, C. (1986). Effects of powered mobility on self-initiated behaviors of very young children with locomotor disability. *Developmental Medicine and Child Neurology, 28,* 472–474.

Campbell, M., & Truesdell, A. (2000). *Creative constructions: Technologies that make adaptive design accessible, affordable, inclusive, and fun.* Cambridge, MA: Author.

Church, G., & Glennen, S. R. (1992). *The handbook of assistive technology.* San Diego, CA: Singular.

Cook, A., & Hussey, S. (1995). *Assistive technologies: Principles and practice.* St. Louis, MO: Mosby—Year Book.

Deitz, J. C. (1998). Pediatric augmented mobility. In D. B. Gray, L. A. Quantrano, & M. L. Leiberman (Eds.), *Designing and using assistive technology: The human perspective* (pp. 269–283). Baltimore: Brookes.

Dettmer, P., Thurston, L., & Dyck, N. (1993). *Consultation, collaboration, and teamwork for students with special needs.* Boston: Allyn & Bacon.

Finnie, N. (1997). *Handling the young child with cerebral palsy at home.* Oxford, England: Butterworth-Heinemann.

Franks, C., Palisano, R., & Darbee, J. (1991). The effects of walking with an assistive device and using a wheelchair on school performance in students with myelomeningocele. *Physical Therapy, 71,* 570–577.

Glennen, S. L., & DeCoste, D. C. (1997). *Handbook of augmentative and alternative communication.* San Diego, CA: Singular.

Golden, D. (1998). *Assistive technology in special education: Policy and practice.* Albuquerque, NM: Council of Administrators of Special Education.

Gordon, T. (1977). *Leader effectiveness training. LET: The no-lose way to release the production potential in people.* Toronto: Bantam.

Harryman, S., & Warren, L. (1992). Positioning and power mobility. In G. Church & S. Glennen (Eds.), *The handbook of assistive technology* (pp. 55–92). San Diego, CA: Singular.

Heller, K. W., & Swinehart-Jones, D. (2003). *Promoting literacy in students with physical disabilities.* Atlanta: Bureau for Students with Physical and Health Impairments, Georgia State University.

Individuals with Disabilities Education Act, PL 101–476, 20 U.S.C. 33, § 1401 *et seq.*

Kermoian, R. (1998). Locomoter experience facilitates psychological functioning. In D. B. Gray, L. A. Quantrano, & M. L. Leiberman (Eds.), *Designing and using assistive technology: The human perspective* (pp. 251–268). Baltimore: Brookes.

Levin, J., & Scherfenberg, L. (1987). *Selection and use of simple technology in home, school, work, and community settings.* Minneapolis, MN: ABLENET.

Lynch, K., & Reed, P. (1997). *Assistive technology checklist.* Oshkosh: Wisconsin Assistive Technology Initiative.

Myhr, U., von Wendt, L., Norrlin, S., & Radell, U. (1995). A 5-year follow-up on the functional sitting position in children with cerebral palsy. *Developmental Medicine and Child Neurology, 37,* 587–596.

National School Boards Association and U.S. Department of Education, Office of Special Education Programs. (1997). *Technology for students with disabilities: A decision maker's resource guide.* Alexandria, VA: Author.

Osborne, A. G., & Russo, C. J. (2003). *Special education and the law: A guide for practitioners.* Thousand Oaks, CA: Corwin Press.

Packer, B. (1995). *Appropriate paper-based technology (APT): A manual.* London: Intermediate Technology Publications.

Prentice, R., & Spencer, P. (1985). *Project BRIDGE: Decision-making for early services: A team approach.* Elk Grove Village, IL: American Academy of Pediatrics.

Protection and Advocacy, Inc. (1995). *Accessing assistive technology: The rights of persons with disabilities.* Sacramento, CA: Author.

Radell, U. (1997). Augmentative and alternative communication assessment strategies: Seating and positioning. In S. L. Glennen & D. C. DeCoste (Eds.), *Handbook of augmentative and alternative communication* (pp. 193–241). San Diego, CA: Singular.

Reed, P. (1997a). *Environmental observation guide.* Oshkosh: Wisconsin Assistive Technology Initiative.

Reed, P. (1997b). Unpublished survey. Oshkosh: Wisconsin Assistive Technology Initiative.

Reed, P. (1998). *AT Consideration Outcomes.* Oshkosh: Wisconsin Assistive Technology Initiative.

Reed, P., Bowser, G., & Korsten, J. (2002). *How do you know it? How do you show it? Making assistive technology decisions.* Oshkosh: Wisconsin Assistive Technology Initiative.

Reed, P., & Lahm, E. (Ed.). (2004). *Assessing students' need for assistive technology: A resource manual for school district teams.* Oshkosh: Wisconsin Assistive Technology Initiative.

Schaeffler, C. (1988). Making toys accessible for children with cerebral palsy. *Teaching Exceptional Children, 20*(3), 26–28.

Scherer, M. (1993). *Living in the state of stuck.* Cambridge, MA: Brookline.

Schmuck, R., & Runkel, P. (1994). *The handbook of organization development in schools.* Palo Alto, CA: Mayfield.

Sowers, J., Jenkins, C., & Powers, L. (1988). Vocational education of persons with physical handicaps. In R. Gaylord-Ross (Ed.), *Vocational education for persons with handicaps* (pp. 387–416). Mountain View, CA: Mayfield.

Stoller, L. C. (1998). *Low tech assistive devices: A handbook for the school setting.* Framingham, MA: Therapro.

Technology-Related Assistance for Individuals with Disabilities Act of 1988, PL 100–407, 29 U.S.C. § 2201 *et seq.*

Thiers, N. (1994). Hope for rehab's forgotten child. *OT Week,* May, pp. 16–18.

Todis, B. (2001). It can't hurt: Implementing AAC technology in the classroom for students with severe and multiple disabilities. In J. Woodward & L. Cuban (Eds.), *Technology, curriculum, and professional development: Adapting schools to meet the needs of students with disabilities* (pp. 27–46). Thousand Oaks, CA: Corwin Press.

U.S. Architectural and Transportation Barriers Compliance Board. (1992). *Recommendations for accessibility standards for children's environments.* Washington, DC: Author.

U.S. Architectural and Transportation Barriers Compliance Board. (1998). *Accessibility guidelines for buildings and facilities.* Washington, DC: Author.

Wisconsin Assistive Technology Initiative. (2002a). *Assistive Technology Consideration Guide.* Oshkosh: Author.

Wisconsin Assistive Technology Initiative. (2002b). *WATI Assistive Technology Assessment Forms.* Oshkosh: Author.

Wisconsin Assistive Technology Initiative. (2004). Assistive Technology Checklist. Oshkosh: Author.

Wright-Ott, C. (1998). Designing a transitional powered mobility aid for young children with physical disabilities. In D. B. Gray, L. A. Quantrano, & M. L. Leiberman (Eds.), *Designing and using assistive technology: The human perspective* (pp. 285–295). Baltimore: Brookes.

Augmentative and Alternative Communication

KATHRYN WOLFF HELLER
JUNE L. BIGGE

CHAPTER 8

KNOWLEDGE AND SKILLS

After you have read this chapter, you will be able to:

1. **Understand early communication development and its importance to augmentative communication instruction and selection of the form(s) of communication.**
2. **Define augmentative and alternative communication (AAC).**
3. **Differentiate between form, function, and content of communication and give examples of each.**
4. **Promote nonsymbolic communication, both expressively and receptively.**
5. **Describe different aided and unaided forms of symbolic communication.**
6. **Describe types of symbol systems, different storage and retrieval systems, and three main ways to access symbols.**
7. **Determine the appropriate content of a communication system.**
8. **Discuss board arrangement and types of displays that may be used.**
9. **Implement several instructional strategies for promoting AAC use.**

Perhaps one of the greatest teaching challenges is instructing students who have severe speech and physical impairments. The impact of having both physical and speech impairments can affect a student's ability to learn, participate, and interact with others. Basic wants and needs can go unmet, and isolation and frustration can occur. With an estimated 4% to 6% of the special education population having severe speech impairments that are often accompanied with a physical or multiple disability (DeCoste, 1997; Lafontaine & DeRuyter, 1987; Matas, Mathy-Laikko, Beukelman, & Legresley, 1985), it is imperative that these students be taught effective means of communication. This involves enhancing students' current forms of communication and systematically teaching them to effectively use augmentative and alternative communication.

Augmentative communication is needed when listeners unfamiliar with the student are unable to understand a student's verbalization. Sometimes it is difficult to determine whether others can understand the student, due to the teacher's or parent's own high familiarity with the student. School personnel will often select three persons unknown to the student (such as another student, a secretary, and a teacher who does not instruct the student) and determine whether they are able to understand what the student is saying. If they are unable to understand the student, an augmentative communication system needs to be taught. Students then have a means to communicate to individuals who are unfamiliar with their speech. There is also no need to be concerned over the use of augmentative communication, since it has been found that augmentative communication does not in any way inhibit speech production (Romski & Sevcik, 1993).

Augmentative and alternative communication (AAC) is defined as the combination of all methods of communication available to an individual, including any speech, vocalization, gestures, and communication behaviors as well as specific communication methods and devices (Doster & Politano, 1996). Students will typically use several different forms (or types) of AAC. For example, it is not unusual for a student to use facial expression, pointing, vocalization, and a communication device all within one communication interaction with another person. This is similar to a student without disabilities talking, gesturing, and using facial and body expressions while communicating. Having a variety of means to communicate across different people and environments will make the student a more effective communicator. The types of communication that a student uses will depend upon the student's physical, sensory, and cognitive abilities as well as the ability to understand the student's communication partners and the environment in which communication is occurring.

When developing a student's communication options, a team of individuals is needed. Collaboration of general and special educators, parents, the student, speech/language pathologists, physical and occupational therapists, and other school personnel and communication partners will help assure that the student learns to effectively communicate with others across a range of environments. Collaborating teams, with the active involvement of students with severe speech impairments and their families, are necessary to prepare users of AAC to participate as fully as possible in education and other major life activities. Often individuals with severe speech impairments have something to say, but need a more effective way of communicating it. Teaching students to effectively communicate should be an educational priority.

When planning for instruction in AAC, there are several factors that must be carefully considered. The first is the *form* (i.e., type) of communication to teach. Forms of communication range from those that are nonsymbolic (e.g., gestures, body positions) to those that are symbolic (e.g., sign language, electronic communication system). Careful selection of the appropriate forms will depend upon a thorough evaluation of the student. The second factor to consider is the *function* (i.e., intent or reason) of the communication. Students should be provided with communication that allows several communicative functions, such as commenting, requesting, questioning, and refusing. The third factor to consider is the selection of the communicative *content.* Content refers to what the communication is about (i.e., the vocabulary being used). Each of these three factors will be discussed in this chapter, as well as several additional considerations, such as symbol types, means of access, vocabulary storage and retrieval, and symbol display arrangement. The final section of the chapter will present several major instructional strategies to effectively teach whatever augmentative communication the student is learning.

NONSYMBOLIC COMMUNICATION

To understand the different forms of communication, it is important to have a basic understanding of early communication development. Communication can be seen as developing across three stages. In the first stage (**perlocutionary** stage), the child engages in behaviors that have an effect on the listener without intending to do so. For example, an adult may interpret an infant's crying as meaning that the infant wants to be carried. In this stage, the infant is displaying behaviors without intentionally communicating with another person. After several months, the second stage of communication begins (**illocutionary** stage). In this stage, the child does intentionally communicate to a person using presymbolic or nonsymbolic communication. For example, the child may point to a desired toy. In the last stage (**locutionary** stage), the child begins to use words to communicate, which is a symbolic form of communication (Austin, 1962; Bates, 1979). This model has been adapted and used to explain communication in students with severe disabilities who are unable to communicate in the last stage of communication, but who can communicate using nonsymbolic forms of communication.

Form, Function, and Content of Nonsymbolic Communication

Nonsymbolic communication consists of the behaviors, basic gestures, expressions, and/or object manipulations used to intentionally communicate with another person. This type of communication is not symbolic, because symbols (i.e., words or pictures) are not being used. These behaviors are considered communicative, and not a display of behavior as in the perlocutionay stage, because the person is intentionally transmitting information to another person.

There are several different nonsymbolic forms of communication. These include pointing, holding up an empty glass, frowning, leaning away, groaning, screaming, and pulling someone over to something. In each case, the child intentionally communicates to another person about something. Nonsymbolic forms may be used in combination with symbolic forms of communication or used alone. For example, nonsymbolic communication is used with symbolic communication when a child points to a toy (nonsymbolic communication) and says "want" (symbolic communication). An adult smiling and saying "I agree" is also using a combination of nonsymbolic and symbolic forms of communication. However, nonsymbolic communication may be used as the primary or only means of communication for some students with multiple disabilities who do not understand symbolic forms of communication.

Nonsymbolic communication may occur across several different functions of communication. One type of communication function is requesting an item or action. For example, a student may look at a glass of juice and the teacher, indicating he wants the teacher to give him the juice. In this example, the form of communication is eye gaze and the function of the communication is request. Another function is rejecting or protesting, such as turning away from an unpleasant spoonful of vegetables. Other types of functions include greeting, commenting, questioning, and acknowledging an action or replying.

Communicative functions have been divided into the three categories of behavior regulation, social interaction, and joint attention. In **behavior regulation,** the purpose of the communication is to get another person to do something or to stop doing something. This is done through the child's requesting or protesting an item or action. In **social interaction,** the purpose of the communication is to get others to notice or interact with oneself. This is accomplished through such functions as requesting a routine, greeting another person, acknowledging another person's action, or showing off. In **joint attention,** the purpose of the communication is to get others to look at an item or action. This is accomplished through such functions as commenting on an item or action, requesting information about an event, or clarifying a previous communication (Westling & Fox, 2004; Wetherby, Yonclass, & Bryan, 1989).

The content of the communication refers to what the communication is about. Did the communication have to do with a favorite toy or a cookie at snack time? The content of the communication is very critical, since a child will communicate only about things he or she is interested in communicating. For example, if a child was presented with some milk and she didn't care about having it, she may not be interested in communicating anything about it. However, if the child's favorite toy is across the room, she may be motivated to communicate by pointing and vocalizing (using nonsymbolic forms of communication) that she wants (request function) the toy (content of the communication). With this kind of information, teachers can create many communication opportunities in classroom and community environments.

Recognizing Nonsymbolic Communication

When nonsymbolic communication is the only form of communication used by students with physical or multiple disabilities, communication can easily be overlooked or misinterpreted. This is especially the case when the student has limited or abnormal movements. In these instances, nonsymbolic communication such as leaning toward another, slight hand movement that is not necessarily toward the desired item, or distorted facial expressions may be overlooked as forms of communication. Nonsymbolic communication may also be misinterpreted as behavior problems. For example, students may moan to indicate they are thirsty or hit themselves to gain attention. It is therefore important to carefully observe the student's behavior for communicative intent. This is done by observing the student's form, function, and content of communication.

The student should be observed in naturally occurring situations as well as arranged situations to determine the different nonsymbolic forms and communicative functions the student has in his or her repertoire. The student should be observed across a variety of environments and activities with a communication partner (e.g., peer, teacher) present. Some situations may be arranged, such as showing the child his or her favorite toy and placing it out of reach and noting how the student indicates he or she wants it. One possible form that may be used to record the student's use of nonsymbolic

FIGURE 8–1
Checklist of communicative functions and nonsymbolic forms

Student: ________

Date: ________ Setting: ________

Context: ________

____

Observer: ________

Nonsymbolic Forms

Communicative Functions	Generalized Movements or Tone Changes	Vocalizations	Facial Expressions	Orientation	Touching or Manipulating Objects	Acting on Objects or Using Objects	Pause	Assuming Positions or Mobility	Conventional Gestures	Depictive Actions	Aggressive or Self-Injurious Behavior	Withdrawal	Other: ____	Other: ____	Other: ____	Other: ____
Behavioral Regulation																
Request Object/Action																
Protest Object/Action																
Social Interaction																
Request Social Routine																
Request Comfort																
Greet																
Call																
Showing Off																
Request Permission																
Joint Attention																
Comment on Object/Action																
Request Information																
Other Functions																

Note. From "Nonsymbolic Communication" by E. Siegel/A. Wetherby in *Instruction of Students with Severe Disabilities* 5/e edited by Snell/Brown, © 2000. Reprinted by permission of Pearson Education, Inc., Upper Saddle River, NJ.

communication is the Checklist of Functions and Nonsymbolic Forms (see Figure 8–1). As the student is observed, it is noted what forms and functions the child uses. Sometimes it is difficult to determine whether the student is communicating or what function is being used. In these instances the communication partner will need to try a variety of actions to see how the student responds. For example, a teacher may ask the student, "Do you want this?" and guide the student's hand to feel the slimy snail toy. In response, the child's arm jerks back, hitting the toy as her arm passes by. It may be difficult to determine whether this was a startle reaction due to the cerebral palsy and not communicative at all; whether the student was trying to request the item by moving her hand farther toward it to get a good grasp, but was unable to do so due to the cerebral palsy; or whether the child was protesting and rejecting the item. The teacher needs to systematically reintroduce the item and closely observe the student response. What happens if the item is shown and then taken away? How does the student react? What happens if the item is given back to the child? Knowing that the student uses the nonsymbolic behavior of trying to touch an object to request it, but that her physical disability may make it appear that she is rejecting it, is important information for communication partners to have in order to avoid misinterpreting the student's intent.

An inverse relationship between communication ability and severity of aberrant behavior has been found in which lower levels of communication are associated with higher levels of aberrant behavior (and vice versa) (Sigafoos, 2000). Not only does this indicate a need to teach communication, but some problem behaviors may have communicative intent. When the student lacks formal, symbolic behavior, it is important to determine whether the behavior is a means of nonsymbolic communication. For example, Mary, a student with severe speech and physical impairments, periodically moaned throughout the day. Her previous teacher had assumed that Mary was displaying inappropriate behavior and would put her in time-out when this occurred. Her new teacher, however, thought it could be communicative. She would carefully take data on what would occur before and after the moaning occurred. She would also try a variety of things when the moaning occurred to see what the student would do. After a few days the teacher noted a pattern that the student moaned any time she was near water. After giving her water, the moaning stopped. It was determined that her moaning was serving as a request for something to drink. Over time, Mary was taught a different form of communication that was more acceptable and easier for others to understand. This aligns with Hetzroni and Roth's study (2003) in which challenging behavior decreased with the implementation of positive behavior support plans that were accompanied with augmentative and alternative communication intervention.

After careful observation and interviewing others, it may appear that the student does not have any nonsymbolic communication. In these instances, it is important to implement strategies to assist the student to move from behaviors (as in the perlocutionary stage) to nonsymbolic communication (as in the illocutionary stage) to facilitate learning how to communicate.

Moving from Noncommunicative Behaviors to Nonsymbolic Communication

In some instances, students with very severe disabilities may be operating in the beginning stage of communication development, in which the student does not interact with another communicatively. Instead, the student displays certain behaviors without communicative intent. To help develop nonsymbolic communication, the teacher assigns meaning to a student's behavior and consistently responds to the behavior as if it were communicative. Through the teacher's repeated efforts, the student will learn to react communicatively. Development of communication is based on the communication partner's actions and is a transactional process between two individuals.

Goossens and Crain (1986) outlined a series of steps to assist students to move from perlocutionary to nonsymbolic communication. This is as follows:

Step 1. Select several activities that the student appears to like and that are associated with increased vocalizations, smiling, or motor activity. These can include activities that are proprioceptive (e.g., rocking, bouncing), tactile (e.g., feeling a vibrating toy or interesting texture), visual (e.g., interesting toy), auditory (e.g., music), gustatory (e.g., favorite food), or olfactory (e.g., pleasant-smelling item).

Step 2. Engage the student in one of the pleasurable activities and pause intermittently. Observe the student's behavior during the pauses to determine if the student engages in some behavior (motor movement, vocalization) to anticipate the possible continuation of the activity. If the student does not do so, instruction should be aimed at engaging the student in a variety of activities, with pauses, and encouraging the student to make a movement (e.g., move his or her hand) when the activity stops.

Step 3. Once the student can anticipate the reinstatement of an activity, emphasis shifts to teaching the student that the behavior he or she was using in Step 2 can serve as a nonsymbolic communication signal for "more." After briefly engaging the student in the pleasurable activity and then pausing the activity, the teacher will say "more" (or, for example, "more music") upon the student's making his vocalization, motor movement, or eye contact, and the teacher will immediately resume the activity. If the student does not produce a movement after waiting a sufficient amount of time and it appears that the student would like the activity continued, the student may be guided to make the targeted movement. In this example, music is only provided when the targeted communicative movement is made (independently or with prompting).

Step 4. The teacher will continue to pause throughout the activity, pairing the verbal word "more" with the targeted communicative behavior. Over time, the student will learn that upon performing the targeted nonsymbolic communicative behavior, he or she receives more of the activity. Although the student may not understand the spoken word, the word will acquire meaning with the consistent pairing.

Utilizing Nonsymbolic Expressive Communication

How the student communicates to another individual is the student's expressive communication. After observing what forms of nonsymbolic expressive communication are currently used by the student, the teacher may teach additional forms of nonsymbolic communication. Instruction may target several different forms of communication, such as objects or gestures. When objects are used for communication at the nonsymbolic stage, the actual object is used in the desired activity. Students are taught to look at, touch, or hand the object to a person to express their wants and needs. For example, a student may be taught to hand another person a juice glass to indicate she wants a drink. The teacher would then fill that same glass and give it back. Students often have a difficult time generalizing at this stage. If a different glass is used to represent the student's own glass, the student may view the glasses as two distinct objects and have difficulty understanding that one glass represents a different glass (Daehler, Perlmutter, & Myers, 1976). Because of this, initial communication systems using objects usually start with using the actual object involved in the activity. In this example the student would indicate she wants to drink by touching her own glass and then would receive a drink with this same glass. (At a more advanced symbolic level, the student may touch a glass and then receive a different glass [her own] with something in it. In this instance the glass used for communication was a symbolic representation of her own glass with the drink in it.)

Gestures may also be taught as a form of nonsymbolic communication. Students may be taught to communicate using such gestures as pointing, opening and closing the hand to indicate "want," or waving in the form of a greeting. Some of the gestures may be very idiosyncratic due to a physical impairment. Since gestures may be created, or difficult to interpret, it is important that a "dictionary" be made explaining what the gesture looks like and means, so that everyone will understand the student's gestures. More-formalized gestures may also be taught. One example of a formal gestural system is Amer-Ind, which is adapted from American Indian Hand Talk (Skelly & Schinsky, 1979). This system has been found to be 80% intelligible to people who have not been trained in this system (Duncan & Silverman, 1977).

Utilizing Nonsymbolic Receptive Communication

Consideration must also be given to how others are communicating to the student, also referred to as receptive communication. Students who are functioning on a nonsymbolic level of communication may not necessarily understand the teacher's (or other communication partner's) speech. Although the student may learn to understand some words over time, the student may have difficulty understanding what the teacher is referring to when only speech is used. It has been shown that students with mental retardation could more readily understand what the teacher was referring to when the teacher used nonsymbolic communication in addition to speech, rather than speech alone (Heller, Alberto, & Romski, 1995). Pairing a nonsymbolic form of communication with speech can help the student understand what is being said to him or her.

There are several forms of nonsymbolic communication that may be paired with speech to promote receptive communication for the student with disabilities. Some of these include gestures, movement cues, touch cues, and object cues. A **gesture** is a concrete, natural, nonsymbolic motion to give receptive information to the student. For example, the teacher may do a scooping motion when she says to the student, "It is time to eat," or gesture putting on headphones to indicate it's time to listen to music. In some instances, teachers may use **movement cues,** which are guided movements representing some movement used in the activity. For example, a teacher may guide a student's arm through the scooping motion used in eating to indicate they are going to eat, or guide a student through the motion of putting on headphones to indicate it's time to listen to music. Some teachers may use **touch cues,** which are minimal physical-contact cues on certain parts of the student's body to provide specific information. For example, the teacher may touch the student's mouth to mean "eat" or touch the student's ear to mean "music." An **object cue** is an object that is placed into the student's hand to provide receptive communication. For example, the teacher may hand the student a spoon as they leave to go to the lunchroom as she says, "It's time to go eat," or hand the student headphones for music (Heller, Alberto, & Bowdin, 1995).

Objects may also be arranged in the form of an **object calendar** (also known as anticipation shelves)

FIGURE 8–2
Creating/Using a calendar/schedule system

Organizing the Calendar/Schedule System

The *first* step in putting together a schedule system is to identify the individual's daily schedule across relevant home, school and community environments. This schedule should include all of the activities he or she does every day or during a relevant portion of the day. Make a list of the activities in order as they occur.

Second, symbols that can be used to represent each of these activities should be identified. For most beginning communications, these symbols will probably be real object or partial object symbols although they may be photographs, line drawings, or any other type of symbols the individual can recognize. Once you have identified the appropriate types of symbols, you should gather symbols representing each of the activities in the schedule. For example, if you use real objects, a brush might represent morning grooming activities, a milk container might represent eating breakfast, and socks might represent getting dressed. Collect the symbols in one place (such as a cardboard box) so that they are readily available. The same objects should represent the activities every time.

Third, a container for the schedule system should be constructed. You can place real objects in a series of shallow containers arranged in a left-to-right order. These can be a series of empty shoe boxes or cardboard magazine holders taped together, a series of transparent plastic bags hung on cup hooks, or maybe just a long cardboard box with cardboard dividers taped into it at intervals. If you chose photographs or other graphic symbols, you can place them in the slots of a slide projector page, on the pages of a photo album, or in some other portable carrier.

Fourth, you should devise a system for identifying finished activities. If you use real objects, this system can be a "discard box" into which the individual can deposit each object after finishing the activity. If you selected photographs or other graphic symbols the individual can simply turn them over at the end of each activity.

Using the Calendar/Schedule System

Before each activity, you should prompt the individual to go to the schedule box or to open the schedule book. The symbol for the first activity should be selected or identified. If real objects are used, the object should be taken to the related activity and used during the activity. For example, the symbol for breakfast (a milk container) might have been selected because the first thing that happens at breakfast is that someone pours the milk. Perhaps the individual could be assigned this task as his or her way of participating in breakfast preparation. This will help him or her make the connection between the symbol and the activity.

When the activity is completed, the person should discard the symbol in the manner determined. The discarded symbols should be readily accessible to the individual at all times. He or she thus has the option of going to the box and taking out a symbol of an activity that has been completed if he or she wants to ask to do that activity again. If this ever happens, facilitators should make every attempt to respond to the request—let the individual do the activity the symbol represents, if at all possible!

Positive signs that might indicate that the person is making the connection between a symbol and the activity it represents include 1) taking a symbol and then wheeling or walking to the room or area where the activity typically occurs (e.g., to the bathroom for grooming, to the table for eating) and 2) smiling or laughing when the individual picks up a symbol for something he or she likes to do.

Note. From *Augmentative and Alternative Communication: Management of Severe Communication Disorders in Children and Adults* (2nd ed., p. 296) by D. R. Beukelman and P. Mirenda, 1998, Baltimore: Brookes. Copyright 1998 by Paul H. Brookes Publishing Co. Used with permission.

(Sternberg & McNerney, 1988; Stillman & Battle, 1984). Object calendars provide information to the student about the sequence of the day. The teacher selects objects to represent the major activities of the day. The objects are attached to the table or wall with Velcro® or placed in a series of shoeboxes or containers. The student learns to go to the first box (or item) and remove the item. The student then proceeds to go to where the object is indicating the next activity is occurring. (For example, if the first object was something used in the activity related to calendar time, the student would pick up the object and take it to where calendar time occurs.) After the activity is over, the student would put the object in a "finished" box and select the next item. Object calendars help students know what activity is occurring next and help students transition from one activity to the next. See Figure 8–2 for a description of how to organize an object calendar/schedule box.

Regardless of the form of nonsymbolic communication being used, there is no standardized set of these nonsymbolic forms. School personnel and family members need to determine what receptive forms of communication to use and use them consistently. Over time, students may also use these forms of communication to communicate expressively. For example, the teacher may have been using a movement cue for "eat" by guiding the student's hand in a scooping motion to tell the student it is time to eat. Over time, the student may learn to perform this movement to tell others he or she wants to eat.

Moving to Symbolic Communication

Students who are functioning on a nonsymbolic level of communication can often move to a more symbolic form of communication, such as pictures, symbols, or signs. When moving from nonsymbolic to symbolic forms of communication, the teacher will want to pair the nonsymbolic form of communication with the symbolic form of communication and, over time, gradually fade the nonsymbolic form. For example, if the student knows that a spoon represents "eat," the spoon may be presented along with a picture of a spoon. Over time, the teacher would fade the actual spoon by gradually moving it behind the communication picture or moving it farther away and having the picture up close. Eventually, just the picture would be presented.

SYMBOLIC COMMUNICATION

Symbolic communication refers to using forms of communication that represent something else. Saying the word "ball," for example, stands for an actual ball. As with nonsymbolic communication, communication may occur through a movement or through the use of an object or item. The different forms of symbolic communication can be classified as either **unaided** (which is more movement based) or **aided** (which uses some sort of aid, such as a picture or print). Both aided and unaided forms of augmentative communication can be expressed using the same functions (i.e., the intent of communication). Functions include initiating an interaction (e.g., "What are you up to?"), greeting (e.g., "Hi"), responses (e.g., "I'm fine), requests (e.g., "May I have some?), information exchange (e.g., "I'm going to a movie this weekend"), commenting (e.g., "That's gross"), wrap-up farewell (e.g., "See ya later"), and conversation repair (e.g., No, that's not what I mean) (Cook & Hussey, 2002).

Unaided Symbolic Communication

When communication occurs through some type of movement or vocalization that the person makes, and does not require a physical aid or device, it is referred to as an unaided form of augmentative communication (Vanderheiden & Lloyd, 1986). There are many different symbolic forms of communication that are unaided. Some of these include oral language, manual sign languages, and/or individualized communicative behavior. These forms of communication may range from simple movements such as one blink for "yes" and two blinks for "no" to using specific hand positions with arm movements to indicate such things as colors, actions, names, objects, or needs. Children who have the ability to individualize finger movements and to perform a sequence of meaningful movements may use sign language to express their needs.

Sign languages are formalized gestural symbols with relatively abstract meanings and specific rules for production (Lloyd & Karlan, 1984). There are several different sign languages. American Sign Language (ASL) is used extensively in the deaf community. It is a language distinctly different from English, with its own syntax and signs. Often whole concepts are conveyed using certain signs, instead of multiple words as used in English. Other sign languages, such as Signing Exact English (SEE), parallel English in their structure and format. SEE is often taught in the schools to promote reading and writing English.

When unaided forms of communication are being considered for instruction, it is important that the child has the ability to display different types of movements and display them consistently, in order to establish readable messages. For unaided communication to be effective, the user will need to combine cognitive and motor skills by being able to (a) remember the meaning and the sequence of the movements, (b) execute the movement motorically, and (c) perform the movement at the appropriate time (Doster & Politano, 1996). Children with motoric problems affecting their arms and fingers may have difficulty executing movements that are found in traditional sign language, but may be able to make sign approximations. However, these may be highly idiosyncratic and unrecognizable to personnel familiar with sign language. When this occurs, the IEP team decides whether signing is appropriate.

Aided Symbolic Communication

Aided forms of augmentative communication refer to the use of any device or item that children may use beyond their bodies to communicate to other persons. Examples include pencil and paper, communication boards, eye-gaze boards, and electronic communication devices. The device or item may contain any number of symbols, such as printed words, objects, pictures, and/or symbols.

Aided forms of communication are typically divided into three categories: nonelectronic devices, dedicated communication devices, and computer-based communication systems. Nonelectronic communication devices are also referred to as "low or light technology." They can be as simple as having pictures, symbols, or words placed on a single sheet of paper or inserted into a notebook or wallet. Depending on what is holding the pictures, nonelectronic communication devices may be referred to as communication boards, communication notebooks, or wallet inserts.

Dedicated augmentative communication devices are electronic devices that are usually portable units designed specifically for communication (Struck, 1996). All of the components are contained on one unit. Dedicated devices can range from those designed to provide a few messages (e.g., BIGmack Communication Aid, manufactured by AbleNet, Inc.; and Cheap Talk 4-Direct, manufactured by Enabling Devices) to advanced programmable devices with hundreds of stored words, phrases, and sentences (e.g., DynaMyte 3100, manufactured by DynaVox Systems; and Pathfinder, manufactured by Prentke Romich Company). Other devices may be more in between, such as the Macaw (manufactured by Zygo) and AlphaTalker III (manufactured by Prentke Romich Company.) Dedicated devices usually have voice output and are custom-designed to meet the student's vocabulary needs. More-advanced systems contain the alphabet to allow the student to spell words not on the device. Devices vary in shape and design and many can be carried or mounted on a wheelchair.

Computer-based communication systems typically consist of a computer with standard or alternative input options, communication software, and a speech synthesizer. One example of this is Speaking Dynamically Pro (manufactured by Mayer-Johnson, Inc.), which is a software program designed for making color, customized, multilevel picture or word communication displays on the computer with speech output. The advantage of a computer-based system is that it provides easy accessibility to other computer programs as well as the communication program itself. These computer-based communication systems are usually placed on a laptop computer that can be mounted to wheelchair or carried.

The effectiveness of providing augmentative communication through computer-based speaking and writing systems is demonstrated by Stephen Hawking. Dr. Hawking is an internationally known physicist who has lost speech ability and control of most of his body because of ALS (amyotrophic lateral sclerosis). He has a single-switch scanning program and laptop computer with special software to allow it to function as a speech output aid. With this, he is able to conduct formal presentations and lectures at scientific conferences and to participate in impromptu televised interviews (see Figure 8–3).

FIGURE 8–3
Stephen Hawking with his AAC device

FIGURE 8–4
Requirements of an overall multicomponent communication system: A checklist

A multi-component system is a system of different symbols, techniques (with aids as required) and strategies that are used together to meet an individual's overall needs and constraints. The following checklist is useful in evaluating the systems of individual clients. Remember that the questions apply to the overall system of symbols, techniques and strategies, not just to a single symbol/technique.

Checklist for client's system

MULTI-COMPONENT COMMUNICATION SYSTEM REQUIREMENTS

Yes	No	
		A. Provides full range of communicative functions
		■ Communication of basic needs
		■ Conversation
		■ Writing and messaging
		■ Drawing
		■ Computer access (electronic communication, learning, & information systems)
		B. Compatible with other aspects of individual's life
		■ Seating system & *all* other positions
		■ Mobility
		■ Environmental controls
		■ Other devices, teaching approaches, etc., in the environment
		C. Does not restrict communication partners
		■ Totally obvious yes/no for strangers (from 3–5 feet away)
		■ Useable/understandable with strangers and those not familiar with special techniques
		■ Promotes face-to-face communication
		■ Useable with peers/community
		■ Useable with groups
		D. Useable in all environments and physical positions
		■ Always with the person (always working)
		■ Functions in noisy environments
		■ Withstands physically hostile environments (sandbox, beach, travel, classroom)

Individuals often use both low-tech and high-tech communication devices in order to effectively communicate across different settings, activities, and communication partners. When individuals are proficient in both, they have a more comprehensive and serviceable multicomponent communication system. Students need to be taught the skills necessary to use a variety of augmentative communication devices—from the simplistic attention-getting buzzer activated by a switch to a more elaborate system such as a dedicated communication aid or computer.

Selecting the Communication System

When selecting the student's forms of communication, the idea of a communication system should be targeted. The concept "communication system" refers to a collection of techniques, aids, symbols, and strategies that the individual can use interchangeably (Vanderheiden & Lloyd, 1986). It is also important to remember that AAC devices must be individually selected based on the student's needs. Students will vary in their ability to use certain devices due to physical or cognitive demands. Not all devices are suitable for all students. Communication devices should be selected that are usable for the student in current environments with consideration as to their feasibility in future environments.

When an electronic communication device is selected, a nonelectronic system should be devised to serve as a backup system when the electronic device is low on energy, is not available due to repair, or is not available for quick access due to a change in the child's position or activity. Consideration should also be given

FIGURE 8–4
(Continued)

Yes	No	
		E. Does not restrict topic or scope of communication ■ Any topic, word, idea can be expressed ■ Open vocabulary ■ User definable vocabulary
		F. Effective ■ Maximum possible rate (for both Quicktalk & Exacttalk) ■ Very quick method for key messages (phatic, emergency, control) ■ Yes/no communicable from a distance ■ Basic needs communicable from a distance ■ Ability to interrupt ■ Ability to secure and maintain speaking turn (e.g., override interruptions) ■ Ability to control message content (e.g., not be interpreted) ■ Ability to overlay emphasis or emotion on top of message ■ Low fatigue ■ Special superefficient techniques for those close to individual
		G. Allows and fosters growth ■ Appropriate to individual's current skills ■ Allows growth in vocabulary, topic, grammar, uses ■ New vocabulary, aspects easily learned
		H. Acceptable and motivating to user and others ■ Individual ■ Family ■ Peers/friends ■ Education or employment environment
		I. Affordable ■ Purchase ■ Maintenance

Note. From "Communication Systems and Their Components," by G. C. Vanderheiden and L. L. Lloyd, in *Augmentative Communication: An Introduction* (p. 54), editors S. W. Blackstone and D. M. Bruskin, Rockville, MD: American Speech-Language-Hearing Association. Used with permission.

to the effect of the communication system on communicative interactions. Some students will be able to use their communication systems well, but at a very slow rate of speed. Additional training will be required to encourage the communication partner to wait and for the student to understand why someone might walk away in the middle of message construction.

An individual using an electronic communication aid may also have a manual communication board to use in hostile environments (rain, beach); may use signing or limited vocal communication for expressing basic needs to familiar individuals; may use signals (for bathroom and other important needs) that can be quickly and easily performed; and may employ a battery of skills and strategies for gaining and maintaining listener attention, communicating with total strangers, talking about topics not represented on the communication board or device, and so forth.

Vanderheiden and Lloyd (1986) identify and describe requirements of an overall multicomponent communication system. The checklist in Figure 8–4 provides a profile of the requirements against which to evaluate an individual's communication system. This comprehensive checklist serves as a reminder of the necessity for multidisciplinary collaborations on behalf of students with severe speech impairment.

When selecting the communication system, it is also important to consider the types of communication partners the student will be encountering. Communication partners may be divided into four categories, based upon the amount of contact the partner has with the student: (1) primary communication partners (e.g., teacher, classmates, family members), (2) regular communication partners (e.g., student in class one period a day, cafeteria worker), (3) irregular communication partners (e.g., classmates passed in hall, out-of-town relative), and (4) stranger (e.g., observer from another school, repair person) (Heller, Alberto, & Bowdin, 1995). This is similar to Blackstone and Hunt-Berg's (2003) circles-of-communication-partners paradigm in which various types of partners (i.e., lifelong communication partners, close friends/relatives, acquaintances, paid workers, and unfamiliar partners) and the student's communicative needs related to these partners change over time.

The ability to provide training to communication partners varies depending upon the type of communication partner. Communication partners who typically have high contact with the student (e.g., primary communication partners and some regular communication partners) will have greater opportunity for training than those with little or minimum contact, such as the irregular and stranger communication partners. Because of this, primary and some regular communication partners will typically have high familiarity with the student's communication system and have ample opportunity to learn it. Since this is not the case with irregular communication partners or strangers, the student may need to also learn "partner-friendly" forms of communication to be able to effectively communicate with a full range of communication partners. For example, the customer at the grocery store (a stranger) may have no idea what the sign language or gestures mean when communicating with a student with a disability, and there is limited to no time for instruction of this communication partner. To effectively communicate with the customer, the student will need to learn to expand his or her current communication system to include some type of communication system with symbols and printed words that would be easier for the customer to understand (e.g., alphabet board).

AIDED CONSIDERATIONS: SYMBOL TYPE

There are a wide variety of symbols that may be used in aided-communication systems. Symbols can include objects, parts of the objects, miniatures, photographs, line drawings, letters, words, or other symbols (Doster & Politano, 1996). The type of symbol selected will depend upon the student's sensory, motor, and cognitive skills. For example, a young child may use a spoon to indicate hunger, while an older, more advanced child may use a line drawing of a sandwich to indicate what he or she would prefer for lunch.

When objects or three-dimensional items are used for communication, they are often referred to as **tangible symbols.** Tangible symbols may be composed of identical entire objects, parts of objects, associated objects, objects with one or two shared features of the targeted item, or created associations (Rowland & Schweigert, 2000). For example, to indicate it is time for P.E., the student may be given a tennis shoe to represent P.E. (since he has to change into tennis shoes for P.E.). This would be an example of an **entire object cue.** Sometimes using an entire object cue is too cumbersome and a **partial object cue** may be used. For example, instead of being given a shoe, he may be given part of the shoe, such as the shoelaces, or some Velcro that is used on the shoes. In some instances, an **associated-object cue** may be used, such as handing the student a coat hook to indicate "coat." A **shared-feature cue** of a basketball could be a ping-pong ball that has the shared feature of shape. **Created-associations cues** may have some feature associated with the target or be abstract, but in either case, an association is created between the tangible symbol and what it represents. For example, a placemat may be placed on a table where the student sits and part of the mat serves as the symbol of the table, or a wooden cat shape may be attached to the door to the classroom and the student uses a similar wooden cat shape to represent this classroom. Regardless of which type of tangible symbol is used, the object is often mounted onto cardboard, with its meaning written on the cardboard. Mounting the item helps the student distinguish that it is a communication symbol representing an actual object, rather than the object itself.

Sometimes photographs are used for communication. Care must be taken that the photographs are clear and without a distracting background. Some students learn better with photographs of only the object they represent (such as a cup representing "drink"), while others do better with a picture that include themselves drinking with the cup. Teachers will need to determine which is most understandable for their students.

FIGURE 8–5
An example of how different symbol systems represent select words

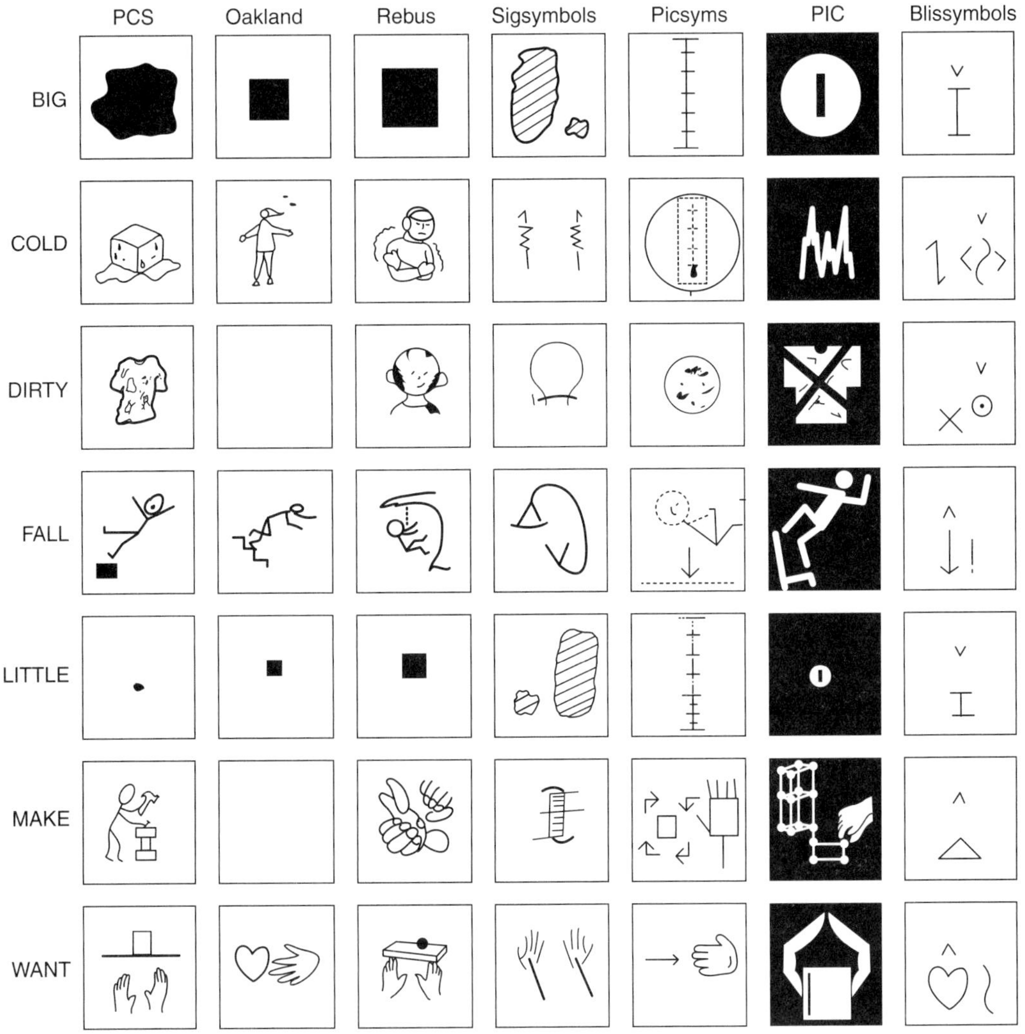

Note. From *Augmentative Communication: An Introduction* (Figure 3–5, p. 74), editor S. Blackstone, Rockville, MD: American Speech-Language-Hearing Association. Reprinted by permission.

Line drawings are another type of symbol used for communication. These can vary from black-and-white handmade drawings to drawings that are commercially made. One popular product is Boardmaker (Mayer-Johnson Company), which uses Picture Communication Symbols (PCS). This software program allows teachers to quickly construct communication boards and overlays for communication devices. It consists of a library of symbols (clip art) that can be selected and arranged to meet the student's own communication needs. The symbols can also be modified or redrawn for individualization.

Other symbol systems may be selected, such as Rebus, Picsyms, Blissymbols, Lexigrams, or traditional orthography. As seen in Figure 8–5, these vary as to their **transparency** (how easily the untrained observer can guess the symbols' meaning) or their **translucency** (how readily guessable the symbols are once the relationship between the symbol and its referent are explained) (Millikin, 1997). For example, in Figure 8–5, the PCS symbol for "fall" has high transparency (it's easy to guess its meaning), while the Rebus symbol for "cold" is highly translucent (becomes obvious) once the untrained observer realizes the person is shivering. The ability of the communication partner to understand the symbol becomes as important as the ability of the student to learn the symbol. Most symbol sets show the written word above the symbol, for clarity. If an electronic AAC device is used and the voice output malfunctions, low-transparency symbols can be difficult to interpret.

When determining which symbols to select for a student, it is important to remember that the more iconic the symbol, the easier it is to learn (Clark, 1981; Yovetich & Young, 1988). **Iconicity** refers to the degree a symbol (or sign) resembles what it represents. For example, using a cup to represent the student's own cup is more iconic than using a line drawing of a cup or using the written word *cup*. Mirenda and Schuler (1988) summarize results of several studies (Hurlbut, Iwata, & Green, 1982; Mirenda & Locke, 1987; Sevcik & Romski, 1986) that indicate "persons with limited language abilities . . . follow a rather predictable sequence in their ability to recognize various types of symbols as representations of particular objects" (p. 38). Mirenda and Schuler (1988) summarize the predicted sequence from easiest to most difficult:

1. Identical objects.
2. Nonidentical objects.
3. Colored photographs.
4. Black and white photographs.
5. Miniature objects.
6. Black and white line drawing symbols (Rebus, picture communication symbols).
7. Blissymbols.
8. Written words. (p. 38)

Symbol sets are chosen for their appropriateness in relation to each student's current cognitive and conceptual abilities. Mirenda and Schuler (1988) clarify that the level of symbol selected for use as a result of assessment is usually the "highest level . . . that the child is able to readily recognize as representative of the vocabulary items necessary for functional communication. This may mean that, for some individuals, several different symbol sets are used on the initial communication device" (p. 38).

If there is a problem with the match between symbol and user, Verberg (1987) suggests the weakness may be in one or more of three areas: (1) the symbol itself (or in the choice of symbol), in which case the symbol and its features need to be made more meaningful to the individual through the graphic information provided; (2) the student's opportunity to acquire knowledge of the external world, which could be eliminated by providing opportunities for a student to explore, experiment with, and construct what is in his or her external world; or (3) the student's internal representations, or memories, of things that parallel the external world. The more a student knows about how things sound, smell, look, feel, and what they can do and be used for, the more a student can build a network of internal representations, thereby adding names and symbols for them. Verberg concludes, "Symbols that are not tied to a child's world or to his/her internal representation are meaningless and unusable" (p. 18).

AIDED CONSIDERATIONS: MEANS OF ACCESS

When using an aided system, students must be provided with some mechanism for selecting the symbols. Some students will be able to point at the symbol they want with their finger, while others will not have the physical capability to do so. Different ways of accessing a communication system can be divided into three main categories: direct selection, scanning, and encoding.

Direct Selection

Using direct selection means directly indicating, by pointing or some other mechanism, the desired symbol or item. "Direct selection techniques are the most straightforward and cognitively simple techniques. They are, therefore, more obvious both to users and message receivers" (Vanderheiden & Lloyd, 1986, p. 120). They also tend to be one of the fastest ways to communicate. This tends to make them the top choice, when physically possible. The most common direct selection technique is pointing with the finger, but this may not be feasible for some students due to the extent of their physical impairment. In these cases, students using direct selection may use a different body part (e.g., toe), splint, head/mouth stick, eye pointing, or optical pointer or sensor, among others. Speech recognition software can also fall into this category as well.

Splints and **head or mouth sticks** are a way of providing direct selection access. A plastic splint with an extension to serve as the pointer can be attached to the hand. Head sticks or chin sticks (also known as wands) can be used to point to an aided-communication system. A head or chin stick is a wooden or metal dowel approximately 5 to 8 inches long that is attached to a helmet and is angled to extend from the user's forehead or chin. Similarly there are mouth sticks that may be embedded in a plastic mouthpiece and held in the teeth. Some attachments are permanent; only one dowel at one angle may be used. Other attachments allow insertion of dowels of different lengths and angles for different purposes. A dowel for easel painting may be straight, whereas a dowel for indicating choices on a communication board may be curved.

Eye pointing is frequently used to make direct selections. Eye movements are not as useful as other methods when several items are closely spaced. They are generally used with a limited number of selections that are widely spaced. In this way confusion is eliminated over what is being indicated. Students are taught to look at the item or symbol and then look back at the communication partner to indicate that the last thing looked at is the selection. This avoids confusion when a student is looking at a variety of symbols to find the one he or she wants. By looking back at the communication partner after looking at the desired symbol, the student lets the partner know he or she has made a selection.

Optical pointers or sensors are another form of direct select. Some optical pointers use a laser light pointer that shines a small focused beam of light on the device to make a selection. For example, when the Optical Headpointer is directed at the array of miniature lights (light-emitting diodes, or LEDs) on a device, the device highlights that location to tell the user what location he or she is currently pointing to. After a user pauses on a target for 1/2 to 1 second, or is pointing to a particular target the most (for those who cannot hold it steady), the device presumes that this location is being chosen. It then registers that selection as a "keystroke." When one or more "keystrokes" have been registered (or accepted) by the device, the device retrieves, displays, and speaks the message that had been stored there. (See Figure 8–6.) However, newer technologies often use

FIGURE 8–6
Student using an Optical Headpointer to access her AAC device

wireless optical sensors that track a small dot (or a different item depending on the manufacturer) placed on the forehead or glasses. An example of this is the Headmouse (manufactured by Origin Instruments) that is designed to replace the standard mouse.

Speech recognition is the final selection technique described in this chapter. Using speech recognition, individuals can "train" a computer program to accept different user vocalizations to mean different inputs to the keyboard. Vocalizations to indicate a specific input to the keyboard need only be consistent; they need not resemble the actual spoken keyboard letter name or other piece of information to be typed. Therefore, the technique is quite suitable for individuals who do not speak in a way that others can understand but who can make a different vocalization for each desired input.

Scanning

Scanning techniques involve presenting choices to the student one at a time or in a sequential pattern and having the student indicate the choice by activating a switch or making a body movement. Scanning may be presented as visual or auditory scanning. In visual scanning, the choices are presented visually, such as a series of pictures, objects, or symbols. In auditory scanning, the student listens to the choices and makes the selection. Auditory scanning is often used with individuals who have a visual and physical impairment. Scanning considerations include determining the type of switch and number of switches, the switch activation method, and the scanning pattern.

Type of Switch. The student will need to be carefully evaluated to determine which type of switch the student can best control. Switches may be activated by pressing on them with any part of the body, such as the hand, cheek, knee, or any other usable body part (Levin & Scherfenberg, 1987). A switch may also be designed to be activated in other ways besides pressing on it, such as through a pull action, sip/puff action, tilt action, squeeze action, or contraction of a muscle. The scanning system may utilize one or more switches.

Switch Activation Methods. Switches may be activated in many different ways. **Automatic scanning** refers to the presentation of the symbol or word choice (by highlighting each choice with a light or sound) in a sequential pattern. Upon having the desired symbol or word highlighted, the student activates the switch (e.g., by pushing on it) to make a choice. **Directed or reverse scanning** refers to continuous switch activation (pressing) by the student until the desired symbol or word is highlighted. The switch is then released (i.e., deactivated). **Step scanning** refers to pressing the switch each time to move the device forward to highlight each selection in a sequential pattern (e.g., press the switch once and the first item is highlighted, then press the switch again and the second item is highlighted). Upon reaching the desired symbol, the user stops pressing the switch. In two-step scanning, the user moves the scanning process forward by repeatedly activating the switch, and, upon reaching the desired symbol, activates a second switch to make a selection.

Scanning Patterns. There are three main scanning techniques: (1) linear or circular scanning, (2) row–column or group-item scanning, and (3) directed scanning (see Figure 8–7).

Linear or circular scanning highlights each of the choices in a sequential order by light, speech output, or someone pointing. When the desired symbol is highlighted, the student indicates that that is his or her choice. Pointing to each item on a communication display until the student indicates the desired symbol is a type of linear scanning.

Group-item scanning addresses more than one dimension in the scanning process. Row-column scanning is the most commonly used group-item scanning technique. First, each row of symbols is scanned as a group. When the light or assistant reaches the row in which the choice is located, the student indicates with a switch or a sign to the assistant to stop on that row. Then the scanning proceeds across the columns, targeting one item at a time on that row, until a choice is made. Other types of group scanning may allow the user to select which section of the display to begin scanning first.

For directed scanning, both the type or direction of movement and the timing of the movement influence item selection. For example, a joystick might be used to move the indicator up, down, left, right, or diagonally, with the user activating a switch to make the selection when the indicator is over the target item.

FIGURE 8–7
AAC scanning patterns

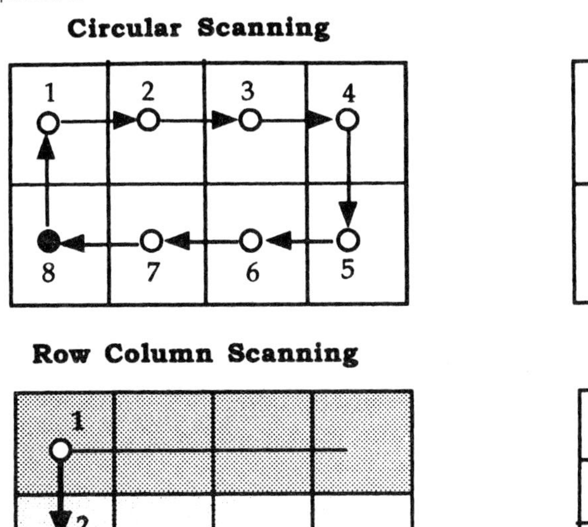

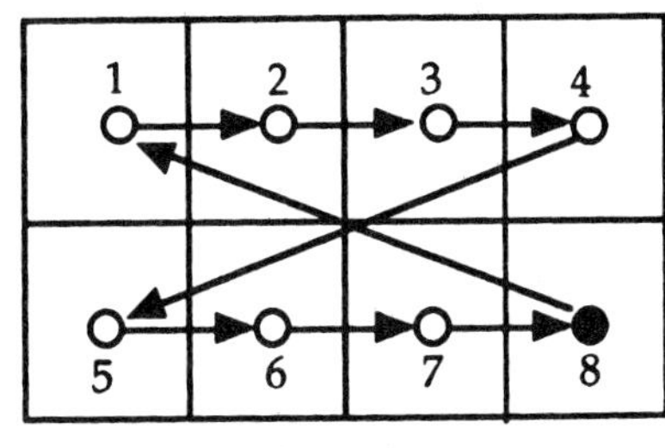

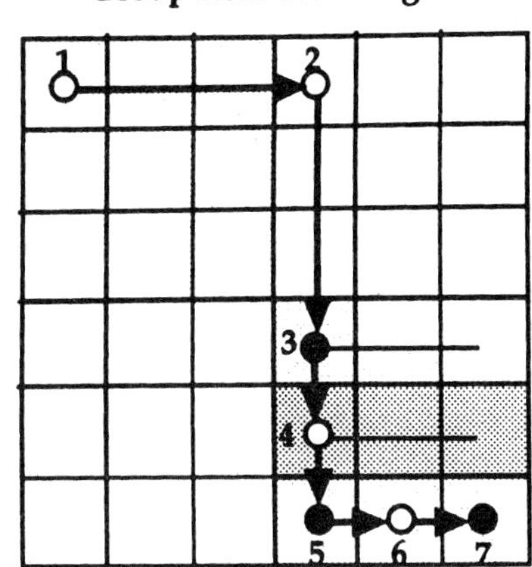

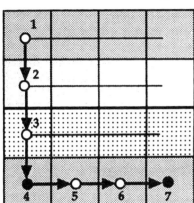

○ White dots indicate "wait" scanning locations to reach the last display symbol during automatic scanning.

● Black dots indicate switch activation locations to reach the last display symbol during automatic scanning.

Note. From *Handbook of Augmentative and Alternative Communication* 1st edition, by GLENNEN. © 1997. Reprinted with permission of Delmar Learning, a division of Thomson Learning: *www.thomsonrights.com*. Fax 800 730–2215.

Encoding

The encoding technique is particularly useful for students who have severe motor impairments. When students are only able to point to a few widely spaced choices or slowly scan through choices, encoding may be a viable alternative to increase the size of the vocabulary a person can access. "The term *encoding* is used with any technique where the individual gives multiple signals which, taken together, specify the desired item from the individual's selection vocabulary" (Vanderheiden & Lloyd, 1986, p. 124). Encoding is a technique of using codes to direct partners to messages. Originally developed for students using eye-gaze boards, it can be used in combination with direct selection or scanning techniques.

Encoding can use very simple combinations or more complex ones, such as Morse code. Actually, any series of codes can be used, from numerals to colors to symbols. An example of encoding using direct selection and numerals is a student eye-gazing a number 1 and a number 3 on an eye-gaze board to indicate that she wants to communicate the 13th phrase on her list of 30 communication phrases, which are displayed on a sheet of paper for reference.

Another common encoding technique is based upon a simple pairing of items (two numbers, two letters, a letter and a number, a number and a color, etc.) with the various vocabulary listings on a reference card. The pairs of items are codes for printed messages on a reference, or master, list (see Figure 8–8). A stu-

FIGURE 8–8
(a) Student indicates the color and then, on the same display, indicates a number to cue the communication partner to a location on a list of coded messages (b)

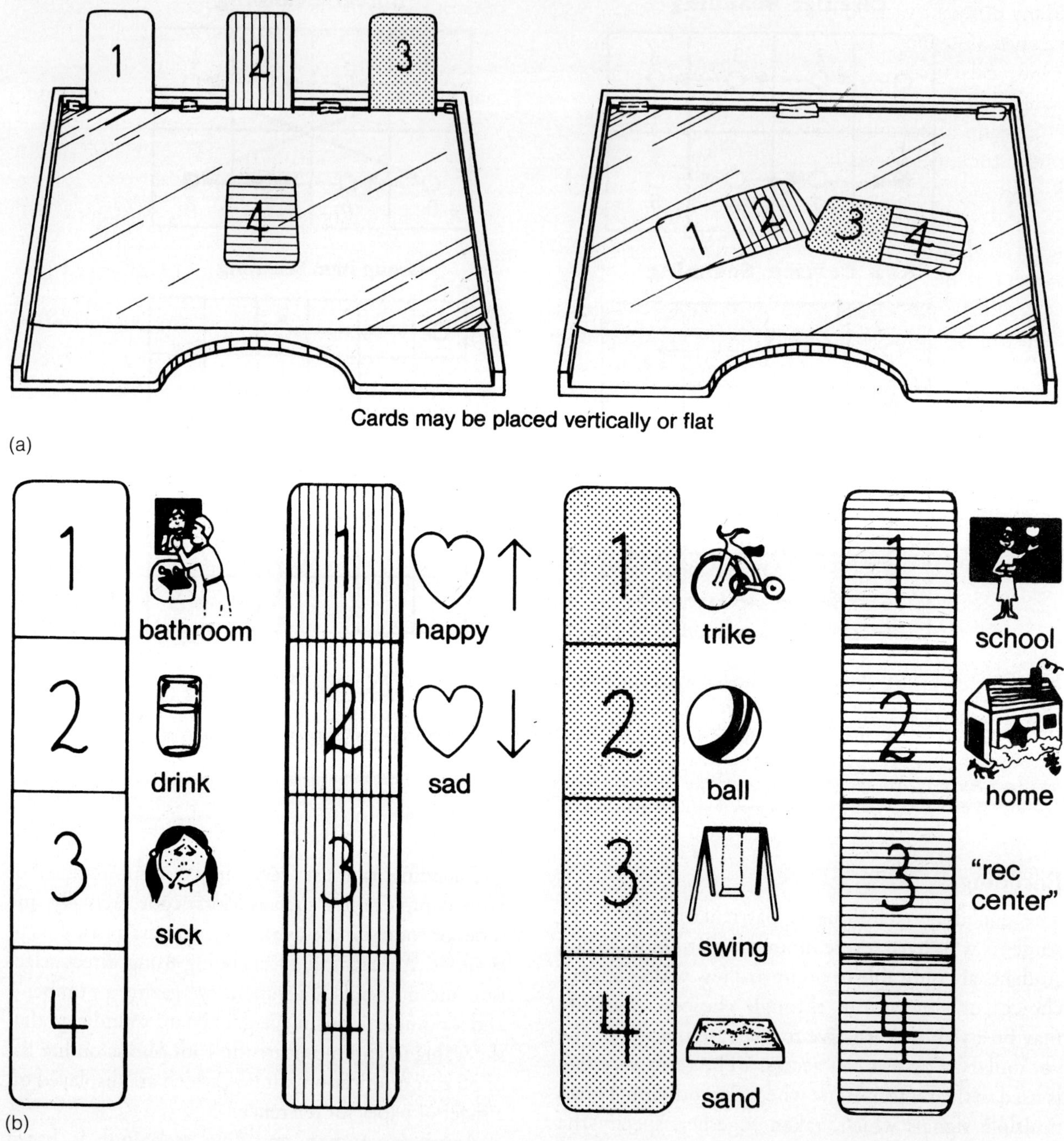

dent may be able to touch only four targets because of physical difficulties. Yet, by using this encoding technique of pairing a color and a number, the student can choose from more than four messages. A communication partner need only ask, "What color?" and the child chooses one of four colors. The communication partner knows the child is sending the message from a group coded by that color. Next the communication partner asks, "What number?" and the child indicates a number (e.g., one to four). It now becomes obvious which number on that color houses the message the child is sending. This is a very simple use of encoding. Many different variations of encoding have been developed (Glennen, 1997; Musselwhite & St. Louis, 1988; Silverman, 1980; Vanderheiden & Lloyd, 1986).

Selection techniques may not come easily for some students, especially encoding techniques. Motor, sensory, and cognitive factors influence student methods and efficiency of indicating messages in a functional manner. A constant goal of the professional is to help each individual user of augmentative communication to learn selection techniques that are highly reliable and accurate and as easy to use as possible. Practice is one of the best ways to improve in using selection techniques for communication in life activities.

AIDED CONSIDERATIONS: VOCABULARY AND RETRIEVAL

Aided communication rates are typically between 2 and 26 words per minute, with most below 12 words per minute (Kraat, 1985), as compared to the average spoken communication rate of 126 to 172 words per minute (Foulds, 1980). Because of this, communication breakdowns, frustration, and limited communication options are bound to ensue. This is further compounded by the amount of vocabulary a system can display. By the time children are 2 years of age, they often know 150 to 300 words (Owens, 1988). A child using a basic AAC system is unable to have 200 choices displayed at one time, nor could the young child access a system complex enough to hold that many choices. In order to address problems of speed, fatigue, and number of choices, various vocabulary storage and retrieval techniques have been developed.

Storage and retrieval techniques are designed to deliver maximum communication while decreasing the number of symbols that a student needs to access to deliver a message. One way to address this is to have a symbol mean an entire message. For example, pointing to the symbol of the hamburger could result in the message "I want a hamburger." This does decrease the amount of time and effort by having an entire message in one symbol rather than having the student select three symbols: "I," "want," "hamburger." However, the student can lose the ability to express other functions and really say what he means. For example, the student loses the ability to say "I like the hamburger," "I had a hamburger yesterday," "Do you want a hamburger?" and "I want mustard on my hamburger" if by pushing the hamburger symbol, the one message indicating request of a hamburger occurs. Using one symbol to equal one message limits the individual to a small number of messages. Although this system may be used with some very young students or some students with severe intellectual disabilities, it will not be appropriate for many students with physical and multiple disabilities. Storage and retrieval systems that may be more appropriate include (a) levels, (b) picture-based acceleration techniques, (c) abbreviation expansion (alphanumeric acceleration), and (d) predictive techniques.

Levels

In order to have more symbols available, additional levels or pages of symbols may be used. These levels consist of additional symbols, which may be accessed by the student by touching or accessing a specific area on the communication device or display. For example, one student's communication device may allow him to display 36 symbols at one time and have 10 levels (or pages) of 36 symbols each that he can access.

For beginning students, the levels approach means the use of a different overlay for each of the different levels. In this way the symbol on the overlay relates directly to the message retrieved when a certain level has been activated. Advanced students are able to use a single overlay with content of different levels coded on it. They also have access to the keys that change levels, so that they can change levels whenever they need. There are many AAC devices that offer levels. Some of these include the Macaw3 (Zygo), 7 Level Communication Builder (Enabling Devices), and MessageMate (Words^{+}). Devices using picture-based acceleration techniques (see the next section), such as the Spring Board (Prentke Romich), Vanguard (Prentke Romich), and DynaVox (DynaVox Systems), can also use several levels.

Picture-Based Acceleration Techniques

Picture-based acceleration techniques refer to the technique of storing messages under combinations of two or three symbols (Glennen, 1997). Combinations can be very concrete, such as the symbols "I" and "drink" are combined to produce the message "I'm thirsty." Messages can also be very abstract, such as when the symbols "kitchen," "mountain," and "adjective" are combined to produce the word "cold."

One of the most common picture acceleration techniques is known as Minspeak, which stands for minimum effort speech (Baker, 1982). In this system, a symbol does not have a one-to-one correspondence to its meaning, but can have multiple meanings, depending upon the combination used. For example the symbol "apple" can mean "red," or "fruit," or even "ball." When a student accesses the symbol for "apple," followed by the symbol for "morning sunrise," the combination can mean "breakfast." This is because "apple" can represent food and a sunrise indicates morning. Minspeak is used by the Prentke Romich Company in a variety of communication devices, such as the Vanguard. A newer language based on Minspeak, known as Unity, has been recently developed and is used in many of their AAC devices, such as the Pathfinder.

Another picture acceleration technique is referred to as a dynamic display method of symbol sequencing. In this method, the display of picture symbols constantly changes based upon what the student touches. For example, if a student pushed the food symbol, the entire display would change to show a variety of foods. The DynaVox communication device uses this form of dynamic display. This type of system may be easier for students who have difficulty making abstract associations on a static display, such as those using Minspeak (Glennen, 1997). However, some students may find this difficult if they are unable to categorize.

Abbreviation Expansion

The abbreviation expansion approach allows students to use abbreviations and short codes to recall longer words, phrases, and sentences. Abbreviations are automatically expanded by the microcomputer-based communication device into words, phrases, or sentences. This encoding technique has the advantage of reducing the number of keystrokes needed or characters selected.

Abbreviation expansion is most commonly done using letter-coding techniques. Word abbreviation expansion techniques allow users to provide shorter letter-coded spellings for words, since the device automatically "looks up" the shorter spellings and then replaces the abbreviation with the fully spelled word (e.g., "bcs" for the word "because") (Vanderheiden & Kelso, 1987). Letter-encoding techniques can be divided into two principal varieties, **salient letter encoding** and **semantic letter encoding.** Salient letter coding derives its codes from initial or visually significant letters in the target language unit. For instance, "TRO" could be used to encode the sentence "Turn the radio on." "TRF" could be used to encode the sentence "Turn the radio off." Semantic letter encoding might take the letter "H" to refer to "homework." If the prestored message to be retrieved is about books, then a "B" could be added to the "H" to encode the sentence "I need help with my books, please." The user enters the abbreviation "HB" and the device outputs the desired sentence. Another example would have "F" represent items dealing with food. All sentences on the food topic would begin with "F". Thus "FH" could mean "I would like a hamburger, please."

Letter coding is used with a variety of devices. The RealVoice, for example, is an AAC device that uses letter-based abbreviation. Several computer programs also use this technique, including EZ Keys (Words$^+$), Abbreviate! (Words$^+$), and Co-Writer (Don Johnston).

Predictive Techniques

Prediction strategies are another form of storage and retrieval that is aimed at increasing the speed of communication. Predictive strategies guess the student's message by displaying a variety of choices that change as the student enters more letters. When the correct choice is displayed, the student can select it instead of continuing to type the remainder of the letters in the word. This saves time and energy.

Letter prediction and word prediction are two variations of predictive techniques (see Figure 8–9). In letter prediction, the letters most likely to complete the sequence of letters are displayed on a scanning panel for selection. Students using this strategy can accept the predicted letter sequence because it was what they had intended, or they can type more until the correct letter appears, or until they are finished. A more common prediction strategy is word prediction. As a student types a word, various word choices are displayed based upon what is already typed. The display continues to change based upon the next letter that the student types. When the correct word is displayed, the student can select it by typing in the number to which

FIGURE 8–9
Letter and word prediction strategies

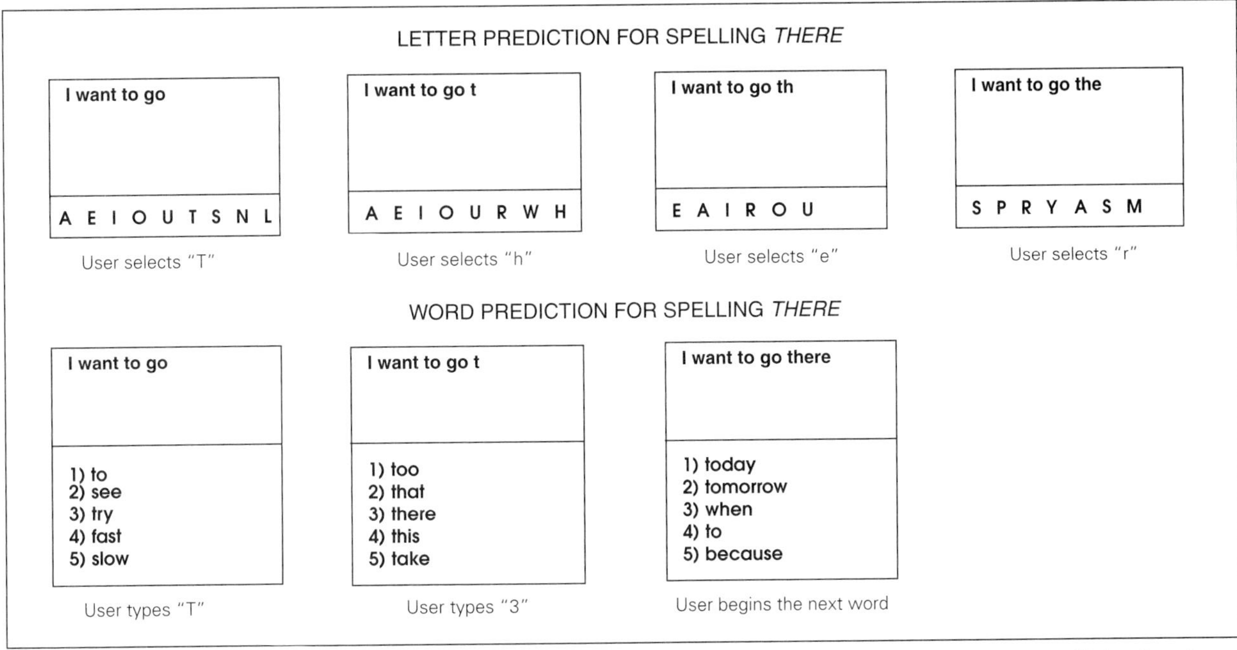

Note. From *Handbook of Augmentative and Alternative Communication* 1st edition by GLENNEN. © 1997. Reprinted with permission of Delmar Learning, a division of Thomson Learning: *www.thomsonrights.com*. Fax 800 730–2215.

it corresponds rather than typing the entire word. Word prediction is useful for students who have slow input rates, but is not useful for students who input very quickly, because the visual scanning required to look at the choices can slow them down (Glennen, 1997; Vanderheiden & Lloyd, 1986). Word prediction may also be used as a technique for poor spellers.

OUTPUT METHODS

Output capabilities of communication systems include voice output, visual output, hard copy, and a combination of these. It is important to decide which type or types of output are needed for each individual student. Equally important is to determine what type of output is needed for the communication partner across a variety of environments.

Voice Outputs

Most electronic systems have voice output. However, they vary as to the type of voice output they provide. Typically they fall into two categories. The first is **digitized speech.** This works similar to a tape recording in that the voice output is a prerecorded human voice. This allows the selection of a child of the same age and gender to program the device using his or her voice. Devices using this form of output may have 30 or more minutes of recording time. The other type of voice output is **synthesized speech.** This type of voice output is programmed into the device already and is usually phonetically based, so that new words can be constructed. Most devices using synthesized speech offer a wide variety of voices to choose from (e.g., gender choices, age choices, various voice characteristics).

Visual Outputs

Most AAC devices have some type of visual output. This may vary from a light indicating the choice on a device, to visual displays that show all or parts of generated words, phrases, or sentence messages. Communication partners therefore do not have to be present as each letter is indicated. Some computerized aids have memory options so that displayed messages can be saved, retrieved, shown on the display, spoken, and perhaps printed when needed at a later time.

Hard Copy

Some AAC devices come with printers or can be connected to printers to provide hard-copy printouts of what is being communicated. The value of hard-copy outputs lies in the user's ability to prepare lengthy messages in advance of conversations and to maintain some amount of confidentiality to messages because they can be transmitted in print and not be "overheard."

CONTENT OF AUGMENTATIVE AND ALTERNATIVE COMMUNICATION

In order for a communication system to be effective, the actual content, or vocabulary, must match the student's individual needs. The content of a communication system is dynamic, changing and expanding to meet the student's individual needs across various activities, interests, and individuals. The educational team needs to continually determine the need for new symbols and to delete symbols that are not used in order for the system to remain current. Whenever possible, the student should participate in this process by helping determine new vocabulary, as should various communication partner(s).

There are three primary approaches for determining vocabulary: developmental, functional, and environmental (Banajee, Dicarlo, & Stricklin, 2003). In a developmental approach, vocabulary words are often chosen from developmental language inventories. Drawing from the different word forms and number of words typically used at different ages helps in determining vocabulary for the communication system. A functional approach is based on utilizing the various types of communication functions (e.g., requesting, protesting, commenting, and greeting). In an environmental approach, an ecological inventory process is used to select vocabulary needed in various settings. All three approaches are often used in combination when selecting vocabulary.

When developing a beginning communication system, the content must be something about which the student wishes to communicate, otherwise the student has no reason to use the communication system. Often, beginning systems will target developmentally appropriate vocabulary consisting of items that the student really likes and that are reinforcing to the student. For example, if Sally really likes music, then an initial communication system will include an object, gesture, or symbol for "music." If Joe really likes chocolate pudding, then the communication system includes that in the content. These reinforcing items are usually taught as part of a requesting routine in which the student is presented with the item and taught to request it. By including these highly reinforcing items as part of the content of the AAC system, the student will be motivated to learn how to communicate using AAC to obtain the desired item or action.

After targeting highly reinforcing items, the communication system needs to be expanded to include a greater variety of content. There are several techniques to help determine vocabulary. Some of these, reported by Blackstone (1988), are as follows:

1. Conduct structured, face-to-face interviews with caregivers (family, speech-language pathologists, and teachers). For example, caregivers are asked "If __________ could talk, what would __________ say?" Questions are structured by context/environment, communicative function ("How does __________ get information?"), semantic category (places, people, foods), etc.
2. Conduct a structured interview with the individual. Note: responses are dependent on client's age and abilities.
3. Directly observe the individual in a natural-context/role-playing activity.
4. Review vocabulary from an available source list or lists.
5. Ask caregivers to complete a questionnaire.
6. Observe the speech of individuals without disabilities while they are conducting the same activity.
7. Ask the caregiver to maintain a communication diary. (p. 3)

After using these techniques, the team needs to base decisions about the student's vocabulary on (a) what others in similar situations use, (b) what communication partners think needs to be used, (c) what is already being used, and (d) what the contextual demands are (Blackstone, 1998). The team should also consider an ecological inventory to assist in determining vocabulary that is needed in specific settings.

Ecological Inventory for Task-Specific Content

To help identify the communicative content needed for specific activities, an ecological inventory (or ecological assessment) is often performed (Brown,

FIGURE 8–10
Communication Ecological Inventory Worksheet

1. Where does the student spend time?
   Environment: Community: McDonald's
   Subenvironment: McDonald's counter area
   Activities: Ordering food, waiting in line, socializing in line

2. Select activities: Ordering Food

3. List expressive vocabulary used in the activity:

   <u>I want</u>
   <u>hamburger</u>
   fish sandwich
   <u>small,</u> medium, large
   <u>Coke</u>
   chocolate
   milkshake
   Yes, No
   <u>That's all</u>
   <u>Thank you</u>
   My order is wrong
   I need
   extra ketchup
   For here
   Please repeat that
   How much?

4. List receptive vocabulary used in the activity:

   May I help you?
   Is that all?
   Here or to go?
   Your order will be ready soon
   I don't understand
   Your total is ________

5. Review listed words and determine which words are above, which are below, and which are at the student's level; which are within and which are outside of the student's experience; and which are necessary for the task. Circle/underline content to target.

Branston-McLean, Baumgart, Vincent, Falvey, & Schroeder, 1979; Westling & Fox, 2004). In an ecological inventory, the environment, subenvironment, and activities in which the student participates are identified. Activities are selected and the expressive vocabulary identified that is typically used in that activity. (If the student requires receptive vocabulary other than speech, the receptive vocabulary needed in that environment is also identified.) The listed messages/words are then reviewed, and the words/messages that are determined to be important for the task and are within the student's ability are targeted. Readers are encouraged to review Chapter 6 for more information on ecological inventories.

One way to help derive the vocabulary is to use a communication ecological inventory worksheet (Figure 8–10). To demonstrate using an ecological inventory following the outline of the sheet, we'll use Mary, who participates in community-based instruction and often goes to eat at McDonald's. The environment is the community; the subenvironment is McDonald's. In McDonald's there are several activities, such as ordering food, finding a place to sit, and socializing with friends over lunch. The activity targeted for communication in this example is ordering food. The teacher (with the student) lists all of the expressive vocabulary that is typically needed when ordering. If they are unsure, they can go to McDonald's and work out what the student would likely choose as well as listen to customers ordering. Some of the items that they might list are "I want," "hamburger," "small," "medium," "large," "Coke," "fish sandwich," "chocolate," "milk shake," "Yes," "No," "That's all," "Thank you," "My order is wrong," "I need," and "extra ketchup." If Mary required the McDonald's employee to point to symbols because Mary did not understand spoken words readily, the receptive vocabulary might be "May I help you?" "Is that all?" "Here or to go?" "Wait a minute," "I don't understand," and "Your total is ___________ " (with a place to write in the amount). Short and simple directions would need to be written out for the employee to understand how to use the communication system. After writing down all of the vocabulary, the words are reviewed and marked as to which are above the student's level, within the student's experience, and necessary for the task. In Mary's case the expressive words that were targeted (underlined in Figure 8–10) may have included "I want," "small Coke," "hamburger," "That's all," and "Thank you." She does not require receptive vocabulary. Another student who is just beginning communication may target only the symbols that indicate "hamburger" and "Coke" and a symbol for the employee to point to that indicates "What do you want?" The vocabulary selected will depend upon what the appropriate content, communicative functions, and number of new symbols are at that time for the specific student. Future vocabulary on the list may be targeted for subsequent instruction.

Consideration of the form of communication being used in this particular environment must also occur. If the student uses objects, each must be labeled so that the employee clearly understands their meaning. If the student signs, the student may need to learn an additional form of communication that is more readily understandable to the McDonald's employee (e.g., pictures, letters, words).

School Topic Content

Content may also be derived for specific lessons in a classroom. The process is similar to an ecological inventory, but in this instance the teacher is targeting what the student needs to be able to communicate to participate in the class discussion on the specific lesson being taught that day or week. An example of a social studies symbol set can be seen in Figure 8–11. It is a teacher-selected set of symbols that are lesson-specific. Often added to lesson-specific content are symbols needed to function across classrooms, such as "I don't understand," "Please repeat that," and "I know the answer." If the child has the ability to spell, the alphabet should always be available to allow the student to spell out novel messages not contained in the communication system.

Non-Task-Related (or Social) Communication

Equally important to task-specific communication (that occurs during specific activities and school classes) is non-task-related communication. Non-task-related communication refers to the communication that occurs between individuals that is not related to the activity, such as greetings, conversations, and social interactions. When determining content for non-task-related communication, vocabulary selection should take into account typical conversations that occur in that environment between students, family members, coworkers, or whoever else is in that environment; students' interests; communication partner interests; opening and closing phrases; and symbols that allow a variety of functions (such as commenting, questioning, requesting, or negation). Obtaining the communication partner's input, student's input, and the educational team's input will help ensure success. As with any communication system, the content will need to be changed over time to keep the communication current.

One example of a non-task-related communication board is shown in Figure 8–12. This was used by a student with moderate intellectual disabilities, sensory impairments, and mild cerebral palsy during community-based vocational training. It was noted that the students were communicating well during their job, but during break times and other non-working times, there was minimal to no communication occurring with coworkers. After interviewing the coworkers and each student, and taking data regarding the types of topics usually discussed between

FIGURE 8–11
Lesson-specific vocabulary was prepared in advance

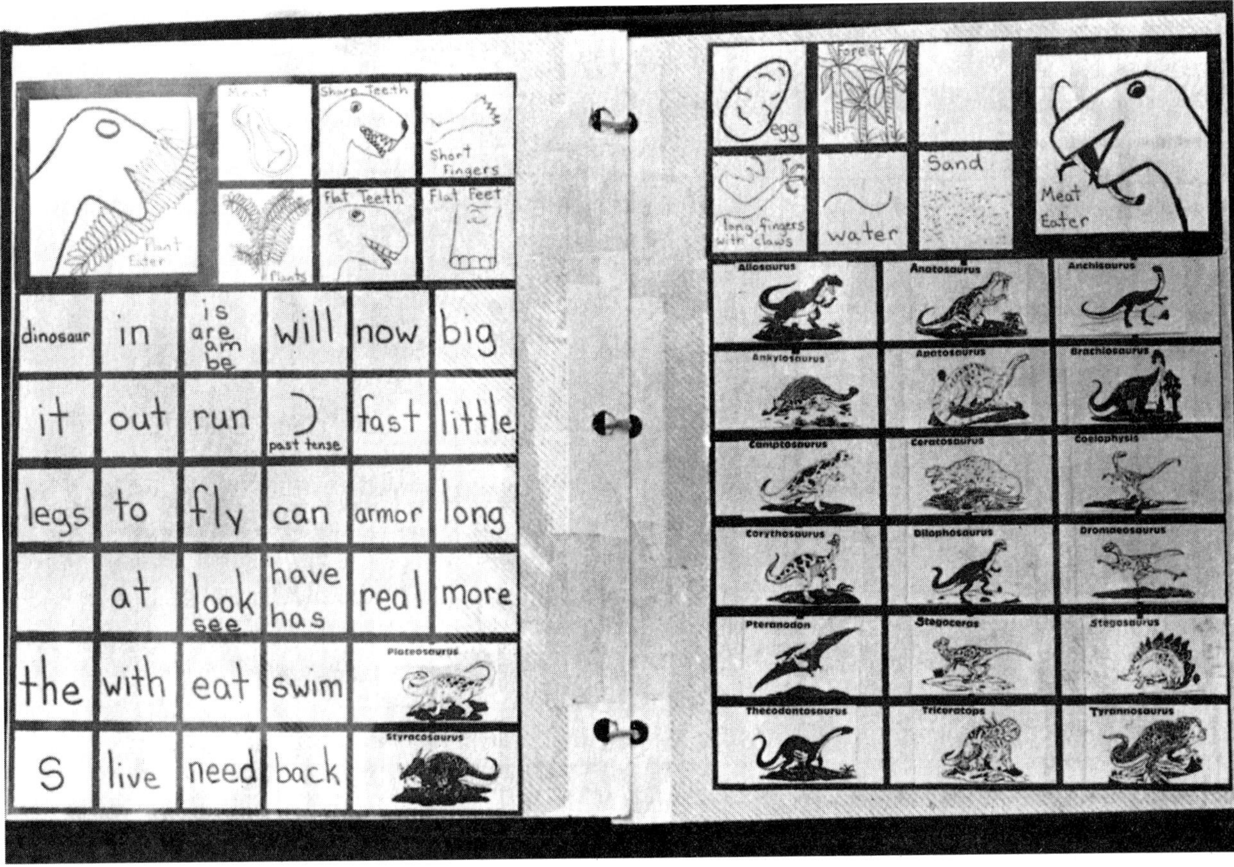

coworkers during lunch, non-task-related communication boards were developed. In this communication page, the student is able to wave and ask "How are you?" as well as close a conversation with "Have a nice day." In between, the student has many options. He can ask "How is work going?" and answer that question if the communication partner asks in return. He can ask, "What" "did you do last night?" He can ask the communication partner if he "watched" "football," if he "likes" "football," if he "wants" to "play" "football," and if "football" is "fun." This board allows flexibility across functions (requests, comments, questions) and several key content areas. Use of this non-task-related communication board increased communication between targeted students and coworkers, and high satisfaction was reported. (Heller, Allgood, Davis, Arnold, Castelle, & Taber, 1996).

Verifying Content

Once the content is determined, it is important that the teachers try communicating with each other using the selected content before presenting it to the student. Questions teachers should ask themselves are "How effective is the content in telling others what I want to say?" and "How long can someone maintain a conversation with the selected content?" Often key words or phrases may have been overlooked. A final test is to invite peers without speech involvement to role-play communicating with another using the selected content. Trying out the content will help teachers find what additional content may need to be added.

FIGURE 8–12
Example of a non-task communication overlay

Note. Made with Boardmaker and the Picture Communication Symbols: Mayer-Johnson Co., P.O. Box 1579, Solana Beach, CA 92075–1579.

BOARD ARRANGEMENT

Once symbols and vocabulary have been determined, decisions must be made about the way to display them so that users have easy access. Two major considerations are symbol placement and vocabulary organization.

Symbol Placement

Placement of symbols on a display or in the natural environment (e.g., affixed onto a wall, TV, car seat) depends upon such factors as physical capabilities, visual impairment, and need for the symbols to be key locations in the environment. In regard to physical capabilities, symbols need to be placed where they can be easily accessed physically. This includes carefully determining the student's positioning, range of motion, and fine-motor control (if that is the means of access) in regard to accessing the communication system.

Chapter 7 highlighted the importance of positioning to maximize function. It is important that the student have good positioning to effectively access the communication system. This includes determining how the communication system needs to be placed when the student is in optimal positions, as well as in various positions the student is in during the day (e.g., in wheelchair, prone over wedge, supported sitting in the sandbox). Considerations regarding the slant, height, and location of the system become important. Sometimes different heights and placements are necessary depending upon the position. In some cases different communication systems and access modes may also be needed. Systematically providing the communication system in various locations, heights, and slants while the student is in different positions and observing where to best place the system in regard to these different positions will help determine optimal placement.

In regard to the student's range of motion, the placement of the device and the symbols of the device need to be examined. The student should be able to easily access all symbols on the device. Sometimes this requires moving the device to a particular position (e.g., left of midline of the student and slanted 30 degrees). In some situations the student may be able to access only certain locations on the device. The areas that are easy to access will have symbols, while those that they cannot reach will need to remain blank.

For students who are accessing the communication system by pointing, poor fine-motor control will affect symbol placement. Selections should have enough space between them to reduce the likelihood that a user will select the wrong one because of a lack of refined motor control (head, arm-and-hand, or eye movement control). To help prevent errors due to motor limitations, the teacher should increase the spacing between the symbols. Another strategy is to separate possible choices on the display by noncompeting selections, so that if the student accidentally indicates a choice near the desired one, context clues can guide communication partners to realize it is a wrong choice. It should also be noted that if a student has good motor control, but an extremely limited range of motion and limited strength, it is best not to spread selections apart but to put all the selections within a small area.

Another consideration to symbol placement is the student's visual abilities. A student's visual acuity and visual field dictate the size, angle, color, and number of symbols that can be used in close proximity and still be visually discriminated. Systematically trying different variables and critically observing how well a student does is the best approach to use. One way to help determine symbol size is through a matching process. Figure 8–13 explains an easy way to determine print size that can also be used to determine symbol size.

Whether to place symbols in one central location or throughout the student's environment is another area to consider. The team must carefully consider what would be most appropriate for the student. If symbols are placed throughout the student's environment, it is important that on the student's main communication system that stays with him or her, there are symbols indicating the activity/location of the other needed symbols so that he or she can communicate about needing to go to these areas to construct a message. Since it is important that the student has a means to communicate with him or her at all times, it is important not to unintentionally restrict communication by not having needed symbols with the student.

Vocabulary Organization

For many users and communication partners, the conceptual organization of the symbols on a communication display becomes a source of cues to guide them.

FIGURE 8–13
Teacher tips: How do I know what size font to use?

Teachers often must determine what size print (or symbol) is appropriate to use for their students with orthopedic impairments. Font size is determined based on visual acuity and ability to point to words in a line of print. When the print is too small, many students have difficulty seeing it and are unable to point to each word due to their physical disability.

When considering the appropriate size to use to accommodate a visual impairment, the teacher will need to first print out various sized letters. The idea is to have the student match a letter to decreasingly smaller letters. The student does not need to know the name of the letters, only be able to match. For example, first show the student a large letter "c" and give three choices of letters that are the same size. Ask the student to find the same letter as the top one. If the student is successful, decrease the size of the choices as shown below. When the student can no longer correctly match the letters, the font size is too small and you need to use the next larger size that the student could successfully match. This should be repeated with other letters and then full words. It is important to check full words, since some students have difficulty seeing letters next to each other and will benefit from having the spacing between the letters adjusted. You might want to try bolding the letters and words, since many students can see smaller sizes when they are bolded. This assessment can also be used with symbols for communication systems.

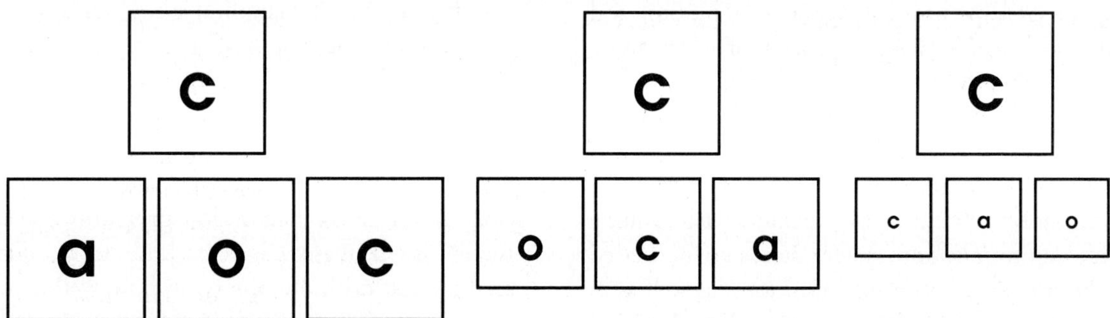

For students who need to point to each word as they read, the words may need to be further enlarged to accommodate the student's motoric ability. Print out increasingly larger font sizes of words in a sentence for the student to point to as he or she reads. Also experiment with having increased spacing between the lines. The easiest size to which the student can accurately point as he or she reads should be selected.

Note. From "How Do I Know What Size Font to Use?" by K. W. Heller, *Bureau for Students with Physical and Health Impairments, 1*(1), 3. Reprinted with permission.

Organization of the vocabulary needs to make sense to the student, so their participation in the arrangement of the vocabulary should be encouraged. An adult-generated vocabulary arrangement may not reflect the cognitive organization of young children who use augmentative communication systems. For example, in a study by Fallon, Light, and Achenbach (2003), young children were found to arrange vocabulary according to activity or event schema.

Vocabulary organization, or layout, can be organized in several conceptual formats. When electronic devices are used, some of the organization will depend upon the particular storage and retrieval method used. Some major categories of formats include (a) category-based formats, (b) activity-based formats, (c) theme-related formats, and (d) language-development-based formats.

Category-Based Format. In a category-based format, symbols are placed together within categories. This format is illustrated by communication displays that are "designed individually for foods, toys, people, places/positioning, body parts, and clothing . . . to provide . . . opportunities for requesting and thereby controlling the direction of interactions within routine home activities" (Goossens, 1989, p. 17). For example, a student could have a communication system that contains the symbols for her leisure activities of "music," "computer," and "book."

Some symbols will be arranged so that the first page indicates the categories, and the following pages show several symbols in each category. Indexes to additional vocabularies, such as in Figure 8–14, are helpful for individuals who can physically indicate a few locations but have more to say. A user maintains control of the conversation by indicating a category, which directs the conversation to a category-specific board, overlay, or display with symbols appropriate to the current situation.

Although a category-based format is appropriate for students with limited communicative ability, it can restrict an individual's ability to choose different functions besides requesting. Unless there are symbols indicating other functions, the student will be limited. Another approach is using an activity-based format.

Activity-Based Format. An activity-based format is an arrangement that places together a range of concepts, such as descriptors and function words, that can be used within the targeted activity. An example of this format is to supplement words denoting clothing items with symbols such as "dirty," "more," "all gone," "take off," and "put on" (Goossens, 1989, p. 18). This format provides more functional options for participating in activities. An added benefit is that communication partners can use the student's display to model new combinations of vocabulary. By actually making selections on the student's display, communication partners model interactive uses of single symbols as well as model two- and three-symbol combinations.

In order to efficiently arrange an activity-based format, it is important to determine the **core vocabulary.** A core vocabulary consists of those words or phrases that are commonly used across activities, while the specific content vocabulary is dependent upon that specific task. Common words, such as "want," "more," "no," "help," and "you," often comprise core vocabulary and are often composed of verbs, pronouns, prepositions, and demonstratives (Banajee, Dicarlo, & Stricklin, 2003). Core vocabulary may also consist of short phrases. For example, a communication system used across classes would probably have a core vocabulary consisting of such messages as "I know the answer," "I don't understand," "Could you please repeat that," and so forth. However, the specific content vocabulary used in an English class would be different from that used in a math class. The student would then have the core vocabulary displayed so that it was always present, easy to access, and ready to use in combination with the content-specific vocabulary.

An example of using a core vocabulary and a content-specific vocabulary is found in a study by Heller, Ware, Allgood, and Castelle (1996). Core vocabulary was identified across community-based vocational sites and incorporated both expressive and receptive vocabulary. This vocabulary was always visible on the top of the communication board; on the bottom of the board was the vocabulary needed for that workplace (e.g., a drugstore) (see Figure 8–15). Upon going later in the week to a different job site, the students would have the same core vocabulary on top, but would have a different job-specific vocabulary on the bottom for the second workplace (e.g., a nursery). This system had multiple pages with the same core vocabulary on top of each page and all of the specific content vocabulary for the same site across multiple pages at the bottom. In the figure, for example, the student would communicate such phrases as "What do I do with . . . security stickers," or "Finished . . . unload truck," or "I need . . . price gun." The supervisor at the job site could communicate, "Good job . . . dust" or "Get . . . cart."

Theme-Related Format. A theme-related format can be considered a subset of an activity-based format. In this case, the selected communication symbols involve a specific theme. Theme-specific boards can be used for such events as holidays, field trips, vacations, birthday parties, medical visits, and shopping. For example, a student may have a communication overlay or board that only has symbols depicting different activities and items associated with Christmas, Hanukkah, or Kwanza.

Language-Development-Based Format. People sometimes decide to organize vocabulary according to syntactic strategies. This organization encourages acquisition and use of syntactic patterns. Symbols are grouped from left to right by categories of people (including pronouns), actions, descriptive words, objects, times, and places. When constructing messages,

FIGURE 8–14
Index of vocabulary boards available for different situations

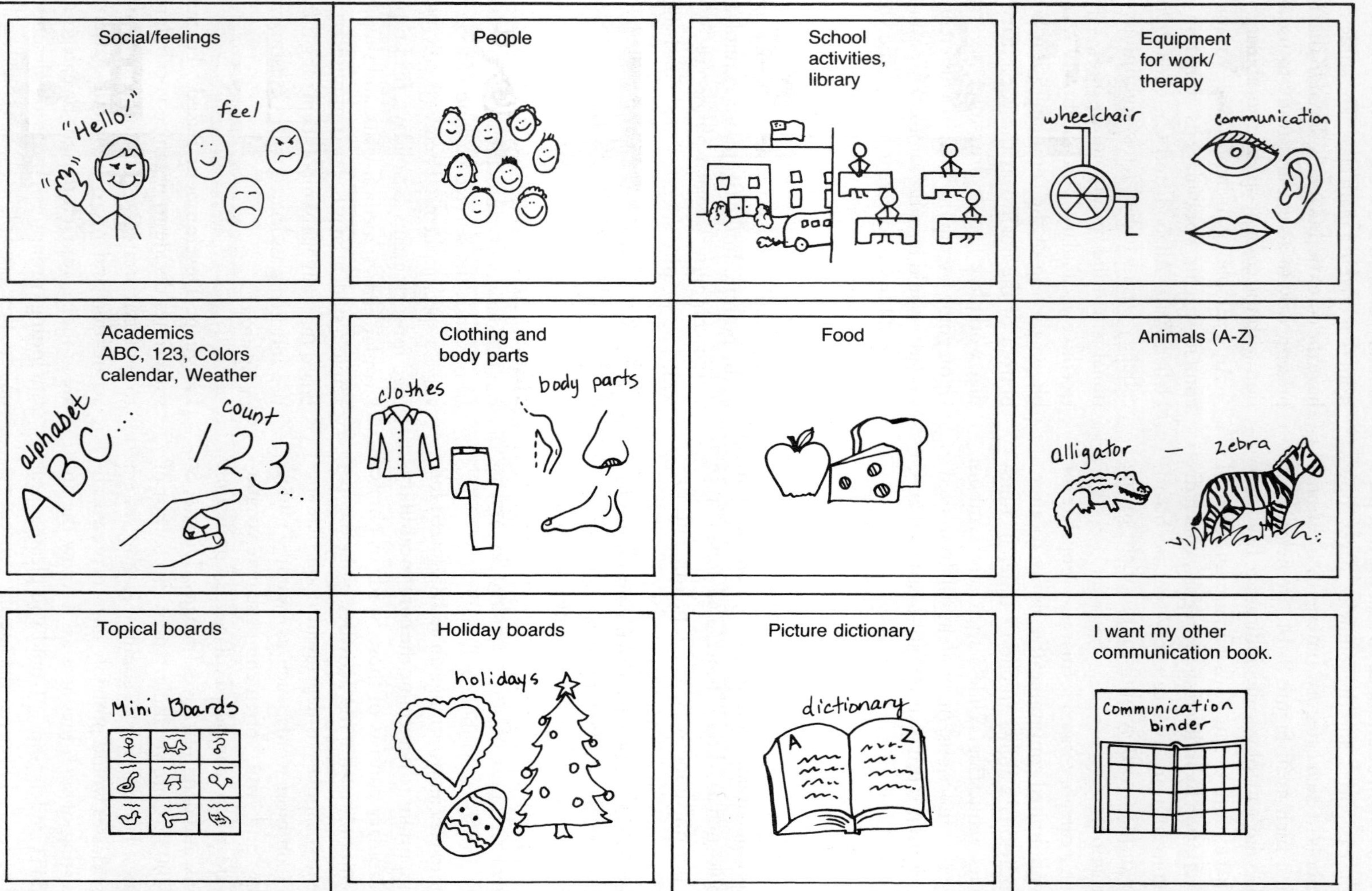

Note. Communication board configuration courtesy of Meg Mowry-Evans; communication symbols adapted with permission from the Picture Communication Symbols (PCS), Mayer-Johnson Co., P.O. Box 1579, Solana Beach, CA, 92075–1579.

FIGURE 8–15
Example of (a) core vocabulary and (b) specific content vocabulary at a job site

(a)

(b)

Note. Made with Boardmaker and the Picture Communication Symbols: Mayer-Johnson Co., P.O. Box 1579, Solana Beach, CA 92075–1579.

FIGURE 8–16
This language-development-based format allows the student to construct messages from left to right in a sentence format

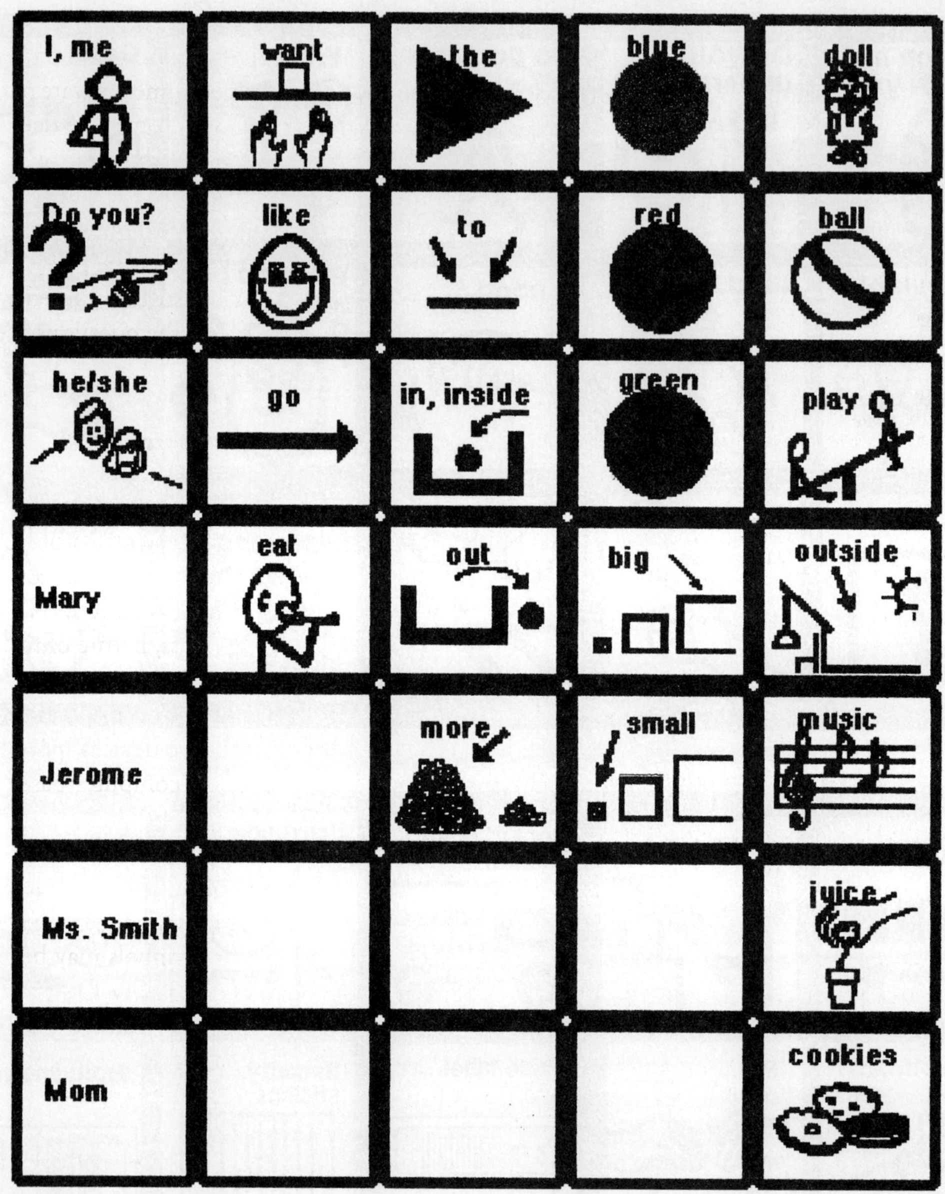

students select a subject, verb, adjectives, and nouns as they would when writing out a sentence. Figure 8–16 is an example of vocabulary arranged syntactically, with words grouped from left to right: nouns, pronouns, verbs, and descriptors. Phrases needed most often are written beside the communication system. Alphabet letters are provided to allow the student to say anything he or she wishes to say by spelling it out. As with all types of communication systems, content on this type of display is unique to each individual.

Vocabulary Arrangement for Receptive Communication

Some students will require receptive communication (what the communication partner is saying to them) in addition to the expressive communication on their aided system. This requires consideration as to the arrangement of the receptive communication symbols. There are several ways receptive communication symbols may be arranged. Some of the main ones are: (a) intermixed with the expressive communication symbols, (b) dual communication boards (systems), and (c) segregated to some part of the communication display.

In the first arrangement, receptive communication symbols are placed along with the expressive symbols, with no division between them. For example, in an activity-based arrangement, receptive communication is placed with the expressive communication, and in a language-development-based format, subjects, verbs, and nouns intended for the communication partner to use for receptive communication would be added. This has the advantage of using the same arrangement system that the student is accustomed to, which can assist the student in learning the receptive symbols as well as encourage the student to use them at a later time. However, this arrangement has the drawback of requiring the communication partner to scan for what he or she wants to say.

The second arrangement, dual communication boards, is similar to the first arrangement in that the communication symbols for receptive communication are placed along those symbols used for expressive communication. The difference is that two communication systems (e.g., boards, notebooks, overlays) are used. The student gives the communication partner a communication board (or notebook, overlay, etc.) that is identical to her own upon being approached to communicate. In this arrangement, the communication partner points to what he wants to say on his own board, and the student answers on the student board. This has been found to be preferred by communication partners because it gives them a chance to easily find their questions and responses, and it provides the option of allowing communication partners to take the board with them to examine the content and arrangement of the board at their leisure to become more familiar with them. Dual communication boards have also been found to make the flow of conversation smoother. Students also found this system less confusing, since it is clear that when a communication partner points to the partner board, he is addressing a question or response to the student. If the communication partner points to the student board, the partner is providing instruction by modeling a correct response (Heller, Ware, Allgood, & Castelle, 1994, 1996).

The third arrangement is having the receptive communication symbols on some separate part of the communication system (which may be detachable or just placed in a separate area). This strategy is often used in environments such as where a student is interacting with an employee at a store. For example, the receptive communication symbols may be placed at the top of a communication system so that the employee at McDonald's can easily find the questions he needs to ask (e.g., "Here or to go?").

TYPES OF DISPLAYS

Symbols used to relay information to others are displayed in many different forms. Display form is determined by such factors as the placement requirements of selections, organizational patterns of vocabulary, selection techniques of users, nature of the communication devices chosen, and situations in which displays are needed. Communication displays may be housed on nonelectronic assistive devices, portable dedicated communication aids, or computer-based systems.

Displays for Nonelectronic Communication Devices

There are numerous ways to display the vocabulary selected for the student. Symbols may be placed in wallet inserts for ease of portability. Other formats used to display symbols include binders, folders, flaps of purses, and sheets of paper. Communication boards may be placed on something portable for use on a lap, table, or wheelchair tray. They may be placed or designed so that they can be tilted at various angles. The selections may be placed, or attached to, several items, such as the top of the wheelchair tray, the top of a stand-up table, or the top of a worktable.

Portable communication boards can be designed with symbol sets on sheets inserted between a transparent plastic sheet and a stiff backing. Symbol sets vary depending on the information to be conveyed during a pending situation. A sheet may have only one symbol for a young child or a student who is just learning to use communication boards. That one choice may be something such as the picture side of an actual cereal box of

FIGURE 8–17
Given choices of block play, painting, and "something else," the student chooses painting

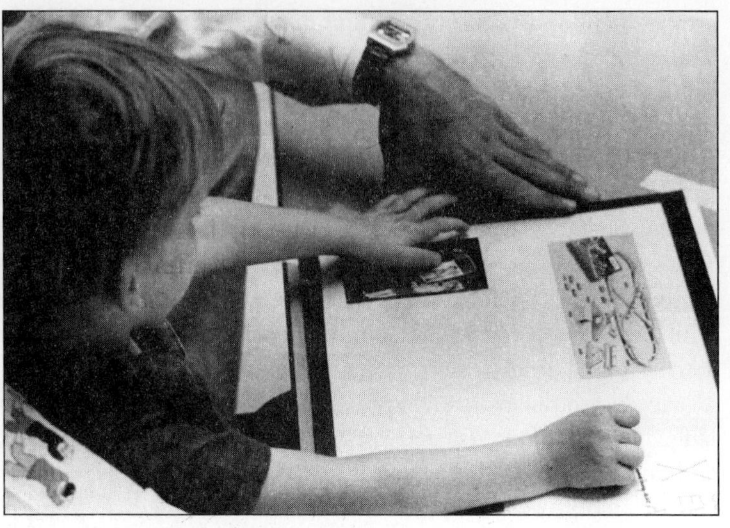

FIGURE 8–18
Examples of communication books with areas for continuous display of specific symbols

a. "Always" section on sides.

b. "Always" section on top.

c. "Always" section on top and sides.

d. "Always" section surrounds pages.

Note. From *Handbook of Augmentative and Alternative Communication* 1st edition by GLENNEN. © 1997. Reprinted with permission of Delmar Learning, a division of Thomson Learning: *www.thomsonrights.com.* Fax 800 730–2215.

her favorite kind of cereal. Touching the symbol results in a bite of cereal. Sheets may have several choices for one situation. A sheet depicting pictures of choices of play activities, for instance, could be inserted just before a young student goes out to the playground. He can place his fist on a picture or in some other manner indicate his choice (see Figure 8–17). The sheet can then be changed before lunch and a new one inserted so that he can communicate whether he wants milk or juice.

For students using a core vocabulary, the vocabulary must be present at all times. This can be done by having a foldout section that can always be present when communicating. Another option, when using a binder, is to narrow the pages so that the core vocabulary (also referred to as the "always section") is always present (see Figure 8–18).

Students who are eye-pointing or eye-gazing may use a clear frame to mount the symbols. The original eye-

FIGURE 8–19
(a) ETRAN frame; (b) ETRAN method of communication

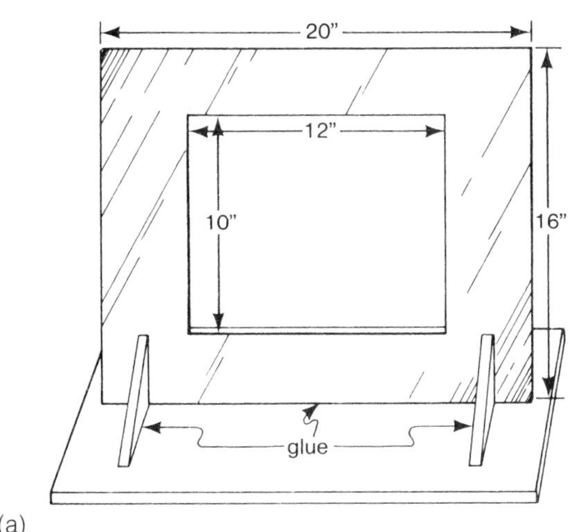

(a)

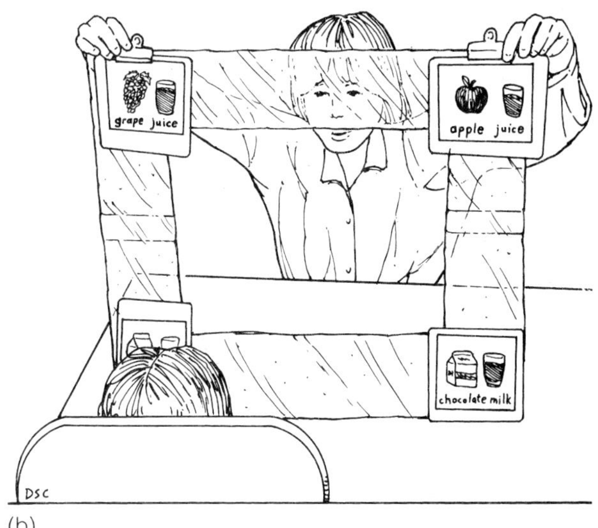

(b)

Note. From *Teaching Individuals with Physical and Multiple Disabilities* (3rd ed., p. 291) by J. L. Bigge, Upper Saddle River, NJ: Prentice Hall.

pointing display is an ETRAN (Eye Transfer Communication Device). The ETRAN is a clear, rectangular, plastic frame that stands on its base between a user and the communication partner (see Figure 8–19). A piece is cut from the middle through which the communication partners look so that voice and eye contact can be made. Symbols or objects are attached to the outer edges. There are several variations on these eye-gaze boards. A soft, folding, plastic eye-pointing frame can be used in the community and other locations in which it is physically awkward to use the acrylate or Plexiglas frames. The foldable plastic material can be carried in a purse or pocket and brought out when needed, so that a user can use eye pointing to access selections in the natural environment. Another variation uses several cardboard rectangles with the middle cut out that are color-coded and bound together with rings. The communication partner holds up one of the cardboard rectangles, allowing the others to dangle below. The student eye-gazes the desired symbol, as with the more traditional ETRAN boards. When the student wants a different overlay, he or she eye-gazes a "change overlay" symbol and then eye-gazes a color strip that is placed between the pictures, indicating which colored overlay to change to. This has the advantage of allowing several pages of symbols. It has been found that children as young as 5 years old can hold this type of eye-gaze board, determine which symbol is being eye-gazed, and interpret the pictures when they are very iconic (Heller, 1993).

Another possible display aimed at those who eye-gaze is having eight tic-tac-toe boxes arranged on an eye-gaze board (see Figure 8–20a). Each tic-tac-toe box contains seven pictures or words (see Figure 8–20b). To indicate which picture the student wants, the student would first look at the tic-tac-toe box that contains the desired picture or word (e.g., Box 3). Then the student looks at the corresponding location on the eye-gaze board (Figure 8–20a) to indicate which square within that box contains the desired picture or word. For example, the student may look at the upper right corner at Box 3, then look at the lower right corner of the eye-gaze board to indicate that the picture she is referring to is in the lower right-hand corner of the number 3 tic-tac-toe box. In this figure, the child would have indicated "drink." To avoid confusion, some boxes will have blank spaces in locations that would require the user to look in the same place twice. (For example, Box 3 would have a blank space in the upper right-hand corner of the box to avoid the confusion of the student's looking at the same place for the desired box and the location in the box). The middle space on the tic-tac-toe box display is also kept blank since it corresponds to the hole in the middle of the eye-gaze board. Using a color-coding system is often an easier encoding method. In a color-coding system,

FIGURE 8–20
(a) A tic-tac-toe format on a placard gives 56 selections on a display; (b) close-up of Box 3

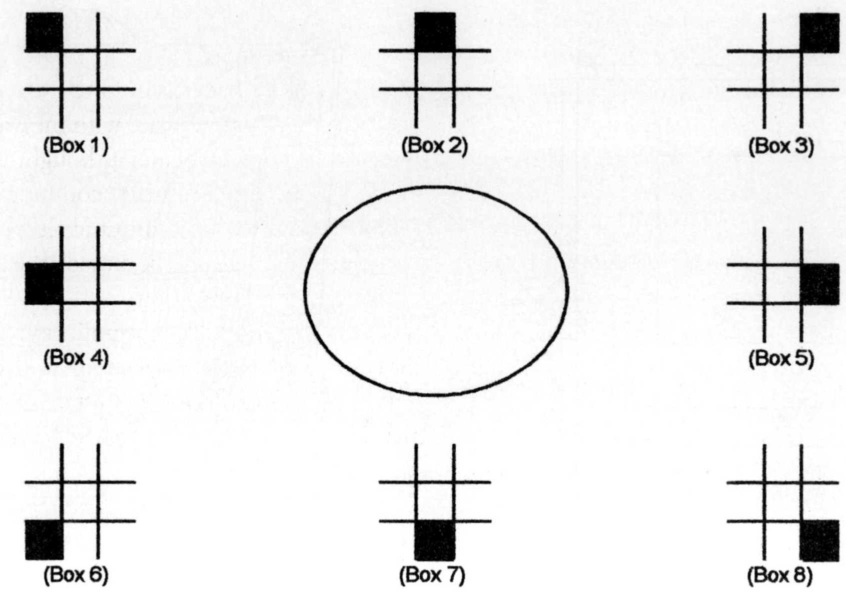

(a)

(b)

each individual picture position is outlined in a different color and these color choices are put around the outside of the board. After eye-gazing the desired box, the student eye-gazes the color corresponding to the desired picture. Another strategy is to first ask the student, "Which box?" and then "Which position in the box?"

Displays on Dedicated Devices and Computers

Displays on dedicated communication devices and on computers are determined with many of the same considerations as nonelectronic assistive devices. Often the number, size, and arrangement of the symbols displayed at one time can be chosen on electronic devices. The type of display will in part also depend upon the type of device. Because of this, it is important that the needs of the student are determined first, followed by determining whether the device fits the student's needs. One should never try to get the student to fit the requirements of the communication device.

INSTRUCTIONAL STRATEGIES

When teaching a student to communicate using AAC, there are certain guidelines that need to be followed. First, communication should always be taught in a meaningful way in the context of an actual situation. This is because communication is a tool, not an end result. While teaching communication in actual situations, students should receive the end product of what they have communicated, whenever possible. For example, if the teacher is holding a glass of the student's favorite drink and asks the student, "What do you want?" when the student points to the drink picture, he or she should receive the drink. It would be inappropriate to make this a labeling activity in which the teacher holds up a drink and says, "What's this?" and the student points to the drink symbol and the teacher says "Good."

A second guideline is that communication instruction should occur throughout the day in meaningful and appropriate situations. Since communication naturally occurs throughout the day, so should communication instruction. Often teachers will target specific activities throughout the day in which the student needs to communicate. For example, the student may be taught to use her communication system to greet the teacher and classmates upon arriving, call for assistance when she runs out of material during an activity, choose what she wants to eat or drink during lunch, choose the leisure skill, and so forth.

A third guideline is that the student should have a means to communicate with him at all times and communication partners should respond accordingly. If the student has no means to communicate when he wants or needs to, he can become frustrated, as well as being cut off from participating in life experiences requiring communication. Therefore there should be some means to communicate provided for the student across situations and activities. For example, Tanya uses an electronic communication device, but she is not permitted to take it outside during recess due to the fear that she might get sand in it. This resulted in her being unable to communicate with her friends about what she wanted to do, or to ask them about certain activities. Since it is important to always have a means to communicate, a simple paper board was constructed that could be folded into a pocket and used to communicate with her friends. It is important that several situations, environments, and individuals interact with the AAC user to promote generalization (ability to use the AAC system across settings, people, and activities).

A fourth guideline deals with the need to examine and expand the components of the student's total communication system. The communication system should be examined to see if it allows communication across a variety of functions, such as requesting, commenting, questioning, refusing, and answering. Communication systems should be expanded in regard to vocabulary, and typically the system itself eventually needs to be revised. Students can outgrow more-simple systems and require more-complex systems to meet their communicative needs.

The fifth guideline deals with the importance of teaching a student to initiate. First, the student may need to have a way to signal someone that she wants to communicate, especially if a nonelectronic device is used. Secondly, students need to learn to initiate what they want to communicate without waiting for someone to ask them. One line of thought is that a student hasn't really learned to really communicate unless she is able to initiate the communication on her own. Instruction should always be aimed at teaching a student to initiate communication.

To effectively teach communication and the ability to initiate, there are certain techniques that may be used. These include the following: establishing want/no, response prompt strategies, milieu teaching procedures, environmental arrangement strategies, interrupted-chain strategies, conversational skill training, and breakdown strategies.

Establishing Want/No

When a student is beginning to communicate using augmentative communication, he or she may be taught to communicate using "want" and "no." This may be targeted as one of the first vocabulary areas, or taught later, after the student has learned some individual symbols for highly reinforcing items. Teaching a generalized "want" and "no" gives the student a way to request/accept or reject an item. When an item is presented, or the student sees an item, he or she can indicate that he or she wants it by indicating "want" or can reject it by indicating "no."

Any symbolic or nonsymbolic form may be selected for "want" and "no." For example, a student may use a happy face for "want" and a red circle with a line through it for "no." (It should be noted that a sad face was not selected for the "no" because it is important that the two symbols be visually distinct.) Another student may make motor movements or gestures indicating "want" or "no." Whatever form is used, it needs to be consistent and responded to appropriately. If it is not an easily identifiable movement, there should be a written explanation for communication partners to read to understand the movements.

The "want" and "no" system is a variation of "yes" and "no." However, "want" may be more appropriate than "yes" for beginning communication or for students who have severe intellectual disabilities. The reason for this is threefold. First, questions directed to the student who is learning beginning communication systems are of the requesting nature, such as "Do you want this?" A student can point to (or access) the "want" symbol in reply, which is understandably a positive response. Second, as the student's communication develops into other functions, the student will need to combine "want" and "juice" to request juice (and learn to combine other functions such as "Do you want" and "juice," or "like" and "juice"). Having already learned the "want," it makes it easier to learn to use it in combination when the student's communication is being expanded. Third, and most importantly, writing "want" above the symbol instead of "yes" allows students to initiate. If the student stares at a desired item that is somewhere in the classroom, and then touches the "want" symbol (or makes the "want" sign or gesture), the communication partner will immediately understand that there is something the student wants and should be able to determine it based on where the student is looking. Unfortunately, this author has seen several instances where students actually made beginning attempts to initiate by looking at a desired item and touching a "yes" symbol. The teacher's or paraprofessional's response in these instances was to say, "I haven't asked you anything yet." Communication was thus ignored. This would not happen if the symbol was a "want."

There are several different ways to teach "want"/"no." The following method is outlined for "want" and "no" symbols, but other forms could be used. It also uses direct selection, with the student pointing (although other methods can be used). It is taught as follows:

Want:

1. Put a large WANT sign (symbol, object, etc.) in front of the student.
2. Show the student a reinforcing item (highly desired) and say, "Do you want this? Touch WANT."
3. Prompt or guide the student's hand to touch WANT, then give the item to the student.
4. When the student independently touches WANT, move sign off to the side (upper left corner).
5. When the student learns to touch the sign, make it smaller until it is the desired size.

No:

6. Put a large NO sign in front of the student (you may put it in front, then later move it, or just begin with it in upper right-hand corner).
7. Show the student something she hates and say, "Do you want this? Touch NO."
8. Prompt or guide the student's hand to touch NO, then remove the undesirable item. (Only do NO for a few trials, then switch back to WANT with reinforcing item. Then go back to NO).
9. When the student has learned to touch the sign, make it smaller until it is the desired size (and move it to the desired location).

Response Prompt Strategies

Augmentative communication is often taught by using a variety of response prompt strategies. These strategies provide guidance and assistance in the actual performance of the behavior. As noted in Chapter 6, there are many different types of response prompts. Some of these are verbal cues (telling the student the step), verbal instructions (providing more direction on how to do the step), gesturing, modeling, partial physical prompts (partially physically guiding the student), and full physical prompts (completely guiding the student through the step). Teachers choose the response prompts most effective with the student to use with instruction and determine whether they will use them singularly (e.g., the time delay strategy) or in combination (e.g., the system of least prompts) to provide a predictable pattern of assistance to a student.

Time Delay. In a **time delay** procedure, the teacher selects one prompt that is effective for the student and applies the prompt after waiting a specific amount of time (Snell & Gast, 1981). For example, Joey has a history of responding well to gestures. If Joey is going to be taught to touch the picture for "cookie," the teacher would first provide the gesture of pointing toward the "cookie" picture while asking him if he wanted a cookie. After a beginning session (or sessions) where the prompt (e.g., gesture) and instruction are given simultaneously, the teacher would then ask the student, "Do you want a cookie?" and wait a specified period of time (e.g., four seconds) for the student to perform the task. If he did not do so within that time frame, the teacher would provide the selected prompt (e.g., gesture) to help him perform the task. If Joey did it incorrectly, he would be corrected. Students with physical disabilities may require longer time periods between instructions and prompts to allow for physical performance of the task.

System of Least Prompts. For some students a multiple prompting strategy may be used. As discussed in Chapter 6, these may involve using increasing or decreasing amounts of assistance. First the prompts that are going to be used are selected based upon what is effective for the student. If, for example, the student does not respond to a model (demonstration), then this prompt is not selected. The prompts are arranged in increasing order of intrusiveness (e.g., verbal cues, verbal instructions, gesturing, modeling, partial physical prompts, and full physical prompts). In the **system of least prompts** (increasing amounts of assistance), the teacher first sees if the student will communicate the appropriate response (e.g., Teacher provides the natural cue "Do you want a cookie?"). Then, after waiting three to five seconds (or whatever is appropriate for the student), the teacher gives a verbal cue of what to do (e.g., "Touch cookie picture"). If the student does not respond within the designated time, the teacher proceeds with the next level of prompt (e.g., gesture) paired with the verbal cue. The teacher continues to provide more-intrusive prompts until the student either touches the picture or the teacher arrives at a full physical prompt in which the teacher takes the student's hand and touches the cookie picture.

System of Maximum Prompts. For students who require more-intrusive prompts first, the teacher may select the **system of maximum prompts** (decreasing amounts of assistance). In this multiple-prompting strategy, after selecting the prompts to be used, the teacher starts with the most intrusive (intensive), and as the student shows mastery over several sessions, a less intrusive prompt level is provided. Unlike the system of least prompts, which gives the opportunity for the student to perform at his or her highest level of independence on each trial, this system provides repeated practice using a prompt over sessions until mastery on that prompt level is achieved before moving to a less intrusive prompt.

Milieu Teaching Procedures

Another instructional strategy that uses multiple prompts is the milieu teaching procedure that was specifically designed to promote initiation of communication (Kaiser, 2000). It is a four-part process of (1) modeling, (2) manding (verbally instructing) (Warren, McQuarter, & Rogers-Warren, 1984), (3) time delay (Halle, Marshall, & Spradlin, 1979), and (4) incidental teaching (Hart & Risley, 1975). In this strategy, the teacher presents the student with a highly reinforcing item and models the correct communicative response to the teacher question "Want this?" After the student is correctly responding to modeling, the teacher moves to the next teaching step of manding, by asking "Want this?" without modeling. After the student correctly responds at this step, the teacher uses a time delay procedure by showing the object without asking and then allowing the student to initiate a request or comment. After being successful at this step, the teacher moves on to incidental teaching across learning environments and using predictable routines in which the communication response is expanded in some way. This milieu teaching procedure has been shown to be an effective strategy in teaching sign language, spoken words and phrases, and the use of electronic and nonelectronic communication devices (Kaiser, Ostrosky, & Alpert, 1993; Kaiser, Yoder, & Keetz, 1992; Romski & Sevcik, 1993). The procedure is described in brief as follows:

Step 1. Model (Imitation)

a. Teacher holds up a desired object.
b. Teacher says, "Want this?" Teacher then points to a corresponding picture on the communication device and says, "Point to __________ [name of picture]."
c. *If student points to picture,* student receives the item.
d. *If student does not point to picture,* student is partially or completely guided to point to the appropriate picture on the communication device and receives item.
e. When the student has a high rate of accuracy at this step, move to step 2.

Step 2. Mand (Requesting)

a. Teacher holds up a desired object.
b. Teacher says, "Want this?"
c. If student points to a corresponding picture on the communication device, he or she receives item.
d. If student points to a picture of an item that is not being presented, he or she receives the item represented by the picture he pointed to.

e. If student does not point at all, go back to step 1.
f. When the student has a high rate of accuracy at this step, move to step 3.

Step 3. Time Delay (Initiation)
a. Teacher presents a desired object where student can see it, but not acquire it.
b. Teacher waits a specified amount of time for student to initiate.
c. If student initiates by pointing to the corresponding picture on his or her device, he or she receives the item.
d. If student initiates by pointing to a different picture, he or she receives the item represented by the picture he or she pointed to.
e. If student does not initiate, go back to step 2.
f. When the student has a high rate of accuracy at this step, move to step 4.

Step 4. Incidental Teaching (Expand Language)
Through use of a combination of the above procedures, the student's communication is expanded. Often the teacher arranges the environment to promote communication. (For example, the student may have been touching a symbol of "drink," and now that is being expanded to touching "want" and then "drink.")

Environmental Arrangement Strategy

Environmental arrangement strategies create communicative opportunities for students to initiate and use their communication system. These strategies are based on arranging certain situations which require the student to communicate in order to achieve an end result. This may range from having a reinforcing item in sight and unobtainable, to having a favorite windup toy stop moving. In these instances, it is important to set up the situation and wait for a response. If no response occurs after a predetermined amount of time, then the teacher should help guide the student to make the desired response (by manding, modeling, or physical prompting).

There are several environmental strategies that have been shown to increase communicative attempts (Kaiser, 2000). These are as follows:

1. *Interesting materials.* In order to encourage communication, it is important that interesting materials and activities are presented to the student. This will help encourage the student to communicate about items he or she wants.

2. *Out of reach.* One way to encourage students to make requests is to put desired objects out of reach. For children with severe physical impairments, the item may be placed out of the child's range of motion, but where he or she can see it. Students who are more mobile may have the item placed up on a shelf. As the student communicates that he or she wants the item, the teacher will either recognize the student's request and give the item to the student, or teach a targeted communicative response. For example, if the student's favorite ball is out of reach, the student may reach out and make an "aahh" sound. The teacher may take this opportunity to model (or prompt) touching the symbol for "ball" and, upon the student's touching the symbol, give the ball to the student.

3. *Assistance.* In this situation, the teacher presents the student with a desired item that he or she needs assistance operating. This may range from giving a student a windup toy that stops to giving the student a carton of milk that needs to be opened. The teacher is trying to teach the student to indicate he or she needs help with an item.

4. *Small portions.* Students are provided small or inadequate portions to encourage them to request more. For example, the student may be given a small amount of snack or an inadequate number of blocks.

5. *Missing material.* Another strategy is to not provide all the material needed or to have the student run out of material. In one study (Heller, Allgood, Ware, Arnold, & Castelle, 1996), students were taught to request missing or insufficient materials at four community-based vocational sites when the teacher purposefully set up situations in which the students would run out of material (e.g., run out of staples, run out of trash bags, run out of grocery bags) or would have material missing (e.g., missing twist ties, tools, tags for the dry cleaner, watering can, rake) at the various jobs they were assigned. The students were able to initiate with their communication systems with 80% to 100% accuracy. In the classroom, a teacher could leave a student's pencil on the floor and wait for it to be requested.

6. *Unwanted actions.* In this strategy, the teacher does something that the student does not want the

teacher to do. For example, the teacher may take a cracker away from the student while he is eating it. This strategy is aimed at teaching the student to protest by indicating "no" or "I don't like that" or some other form of negation.

7. *Unexpected situations.* Unexpected situations may be arranged in which the teacher violates the child's expectation. This is often aimed at teaching the child to comment on a particular situation. For example, the teacher may wind up a toy and let it unexpectedly fall off of the table. The student is taught to communicate "That's funny" or "Silly!"

8. *Choice making.* Students should be exposed to choices throughout the day to allow them to indicate their preferences. Typically two or more choices are presented. For beginning choice making, one choice is typically something the child really likes and the other is something that the child does not care for (Kaiser, 2000). This encourages the child to make a selection and not just point (or however she indicates her choice) to whatever is put in front of her. It is also important that if the child chooses the item she doesn't like, she is given it. This teaches the concept that what the student chooses is what she gets.

Interrupted-Chain Strategy

In the interrupted-chain strategy, the teacher selects a routine that is very familiar to the student, and interrupts with a communication instructional trial while the student is performing the routine (Alwell, Hunt, Goetz, & Sailor, 1989). For example, if the student is making a peanut butter and jelly sandwich, the teacher may interrupt the chain of behaviors and delay giving the student the peanut butter or have the peanut butter out of reach. The teacher waits the predetermined number of seconds for a response, such as pointing to a "want" picture or signing "want." If the student gives the correct response, he is given the peanut butter and continues with the routine. If the student does not make the response, then he is guided through the response. Goetz, Gee, and Sailor (1985) found interrupting a routine in this manner to be more effective than targeting communication before a routine. Students with moderate to severe intellectual disabilities have also been able to generalize requesting to different routines utilizing the behavior chain interruption strategy (Grunsell & Carter, 2002).

Conversational Skill Training

Conversational skill training typically requires instruction to the communication partner as well as to the student. As with the teaching of vocabulary, it is important that the topics are important to the communication partner as well as the student. In this type of instruction, the student is taught to initiate a question or comment (e.g., "How are you?" or "What did you do last night?") and the communication partner is to answer and then pose a question back to the student. The student is then taught to answer the question and pose another question back to the communication partner. This type of turn taking promotes a flow of conversation. In some instances, students may be taught a pattern to follow, such as greeting, asking about school, asking about what they did last night, asking if they liked it, and closing. Over time, the pattern will need to be varied to allow more flexibility and true conversation.

Breakdown Strategies

Sometimes communication problems occur in which the communication partner is really unsure of what the student is trying to say. This often occurs when the student does not have the necessary vocabulary on the communication device. In these instances, the communication partner must use such strategies as narrowing the options, clarifying and verifying messages, and recognizing deadlocks.

Narrow the Options to Find a Category. Sometimes a student's communication will be unclear, especially if it is not within the student's communication system. One of the quickest ways to determine what the student is trying to say is to use listener-assisted auditory scanning strategies and narrow the options. In this strategy, the communication partner provides a series of questions and options, starting with a general category and narrowing to more specific areas. First, the communication partner begins by finding the category. This is done by first asking "Are you thinking of telling something? Or asking something?" "Telling?" "Asking?" Once that is decided, repeat the strategy. Ask, "Do you want to talk about somebody, some place, some things or feelings, or none of these?" If the answer is a place, narrow the options further by asking, "Is it about home? School? Or someplace else?" Then repeat each of the questions one at a time to allow individuals to indicate which category best describes their communication. For very young students, start with the basic questions ("Is it about home? Is it about school?"), since most communications will center on one of these two places. For older students, add helpful questions concerning time. "Is it something that has already happened, is happening, or will happen?" "Is it about the past? The present? The future?"

Clarify and Verify to Ensure Messages Are Received Correctly. Effectiveness of those communication interactions limited to "yes" and "no" responses hinge upon a communication partner's use of the clarification strategy. It is a great temptation to ask an individual only dead-end and fact-level yes-or-no questions when communication is unclear. However, speakers with unclear speech have ideas, feelings, and reactions to share with those who will listen. Some of their ideas may be only partially formulated. Their feelings and reactions may not be completely understood, even by themselves. This may be true for many, but it is a particular problem to students without speech who must decide if their teachers and other communication partners reflected their thoughts correctly.

It is relatively easy to understand what students without speech are trying to say when conversation is restricted to those topics to which responses can easily be anticipated. This frequently occurs because communication partners, anticipating that they will not understand the response, tend to ask three kinds of questions. They ask dead-end, yes-no questions ("Do you have brothers and sisters?" "Do you like school?"). They ask questions for which they already know or can easily anticipate the answer ("What is the name of your school?" "What is your favorite TV show?"). Finally, they ask in such a way that they feel they can deal with unclear answers without the nonspeaking student's realizing their response was not understood ("What is the name of your pet?" . . . "Oh, that's a good name.") It is harder, however, to understand the message when the student attempts to add one more detail, to express his or her opinion about something, to tell how he or she feels as a result of it, to tell about a better way to do something, or to initiate a topic of conversation. These kinds of message exchanges depend very much upon clarification strategies of communication partners.

To clarify and verify, communication partners repeat the perceived messages in their entirety or by segments to see if the message was received correctly. The strategy involves stating first what they think has been communicated so far. If the message was received correctly and verified by a positive answer to the question "Is this exactly right?" then the conversation may move on. If the message is not verified as being correct, then more clarification is necessary. The strategy now involves repeating the message in segments. After each segment, ask "Am I close?" "Is there more to it than that?" "Do you want to change part of what I said?" "Is this too specific or too general?" Partners must base further questions and comments on their interpretations of what individuals with severe speech impairment mean to say. Therefore, to avoid "getting off track" or to use a conversational repair strategy to "get back on track," partners may prefer to question to clarify each segment of the communication as it develops. Then, if necessary, they seek more information from the nonspeaking student to assist in rephrasing the message until it correctly reflects what was intended. "Is that exactly right?" is repeatedly asked until a final and correct message can be verified.

The following conversation shows why persistence and periodic clarification are vital. The teacher (T) has established that the student (S) is speaking of a new wheelchair she is getting and that she is worried about it.

T: Is that right?
S: Yes.
T: Is there more to it?
S: Yes.
T: Do you want to talk about why you're worried?
S: Yes.
T: You're worried that it won't be ready on time?
S: No.
T: Are you worried it won't work?
S: Yes.
T: You won't be able to run it?
S: No.
T: Wait! Do you think you'll have trouble making it run?
S: No.

T: Steering it?
S: No.
T: Stopping it?
S: No.
T: So it doesn't have anything to do with getting from place to place. Is that right?
S: Yes.
T: Oh. But you are worried that it won't work?
S: Yes.
T: Let's see . . . what "works" on a wheelchair?
S: (looks at lap)
T: Your seating?
S: Yes.
T: Do you think you'll be uncomfortable?
S: Yes-no.
T: Wait. Did you say yes and no?
S: Yes.
T: Um, did you just say yes?
S: No.
T: You're worried about the seating.
S: Yes.
T: About whether you'll be comfortable?
S: Yes.
T: Is it that sometimes it will be uncomfortable?
S: No.
T: Always?
S: No.
T: Do you think it will ever be uncomfortable?
S: Yes.
T: A specific time?
S: Yes.
T: One or several times each day?
S: No.
T: Do you mean after you've had your chair for a while?
S: Yes.
T: A week?
S: No.
T: Several weeks?
S: No.
T: Months?
S: Yes. (looks at body)
T: Are you worried about growing?
S: Yes.
T: You've been getting taller, haven't you?
S: Yes.
T: Let me see if I understand your concern. You're afraid that, after you've had your chair a couple of months, you will start outgrowing it and you'll be uncomfortable. Is that exactly right?
S: Yes.
T: Is there more?
S: Yes. (with emotion)
T: You seem agitated.
S: Yes.
T: Do you think you'll have to stay uncomfortable?
S: Yes.
T: Do you mean that you're afraid they won't modify it in case you grow?
S: Yes.
T: You're afraid they won't modify your new chair when you grow?
S: Yes.
T: Is that exactly it?
S: Yes.
T: That's what you want people to know you've thought about.
S: Yes.

As the conversation continued, the teacher assisted the student in developing ideas on what questions to ask the people who were designing her new wheelchair and how to communicate her concern. Notice how many times in this short conversation the teacher had to repeat to clarify what she thought the student was saying to avoid distorting the message. Notice attempts to verify each message before moving on.

Shades of feeling are particularly difficult for nonspeaking students to express. Because of physical limitations, individuals may have a relatively small repertoire of facial expressions. Feelings of anger, hurt, anxiety, or eagerness are difficult to communicate and may be mistaken for each other. Therefore, check impressions before pursuing the reasons for feelings. Since anger, disappointment, and hurt are difficult feelings to deal with, individuals who do not speak need the opportunity to have feelings put into words and to be accepted without criticism and with understanding. "Is that exactly what you feel?" If the answer is no, pursue with "Let's see if I can say it better." "Am I close?" Paraphrasing the feelings of another, all the while clarifying to the speaker's satisfaction, is a difficult task, but the effort to do so will yield valuable insight.

Recognize Deadlocks. In conversations with students who do not speak clearly, communication partners often meet barriers. But communication partners can learn to recognize and correct barriers. In communication breakdowns communication partners can use conversational repair strategies (Blackstone, Cassatt-James, & Bruskin, 1988; Kraat, 1986). For example, the student may wish to say something, but a partner does not reflect the correct message. Sometimes the student may realize that a block has been reached over an unimportant topic and would rather drop the subject than waste time pursuing it. Or the opposite may be true. The message may be very important and partners can help the speaker by saying "I'm really stuck. Do you want to go on trying?" Be certain that the student does not feel pressured into changing topics. Sometimes partners simply cannot decipher what a person is trying to say. Both parties may feel highly frustrated. But partners should persist if the student indicates it is important to do so. If partners must terminate a conversation before both partners are satisfied, partners can keep the communication open by saying "I have to leave, but I'll think about it. You think too, and maybe you'll find another way of telling me."

The most frequent mistake that leads to a deadlock is reaching premature conclusions based on incorrect interpretations of the communications "heard." The nonspeaking person realizes there is a deadlock, but the communication partner does not. A boy told about a party at school: the refreshments, activities, and people invited. The Boy Scout master (BSM) "heard" all the details and said, "You must have enjoyed that."

S: No.
BSM: You didn't?
S: No.
BSM: But you told me all about it. Did something bad happen?
S: No.
BSM: But you didn't enjoy it.
S: No.
BSM: Well, you did go, didn't you?
S: No.
BSM: You didn't! Why not? Were you somewhere else?
S: No.
BSM: Were you ill?
S: No.
BSM: I don't get it, then.

The student was attempting to tell the scout master about a party that his class had planned, but that had not yet taken place. The scout master assumed that the party was a past event.

The best method for identifying erroneous assumptions that block conversation is by clarifying, or checking information, phrase by phrase with the speaker. (For example: "We're talking about a party?" "Yes." "At school?" "Yes." "That your class had?" "No.") If this strategy fails, ask, "Am I missing something? Is it about someone? Some place? A time? A thing? A feeling?" Erroneous assumptions do not always leave the student dissatisfied, but they always leave the teacher with false information. "Is that exactly right?" is again the important question.

If communication partners try to ask questions that individuals do not wish to answer, a barrier is created. These questions might concern feelings, personal concerns, events the student is not ready to discuss, or topics that draw the conversation away from where the speaker wishes to go. Individuals may have no way to say, "I don't want to talk about that right now," or to head the conversation in another direction. The sensitive teacher can ask, "Do you feel like going into this?"

SUMMARY AND CONCLUSION

This chapter presented information on the range of expressive and receptive augmentative and alternative communication options, from nonsymbolic to symbolic AAC. The various forms, functions, and content of communication must be carefully considered in order to promote effective communication. The concept was stressed that a communication system is not limited to just one assistive device or technique, but often consists of multiple aided and unaided forms. Students often need their communication system to accommodate various functions of communication, such as requesting, questioning, and commenting. Careful selection of the content of the communication was stressed, with strategies of using reinforcing items, ecological inventories, school topic considerations, and non-task-related communication. Various symbols need to be considered when an aided system is used (e.g., objects, pictures), as well as storage and retrieval options (i.e., levels, picture-based acceleration techniques, abbreviation expansion, and predictive techniques). Students must find a way to access their communication system, such as using direct selection, scanning, and/or encoding, and various board arrangements and displays must also be considered. The end of the chapter presented a variety of systematic instructional strategies to promote communication and student initiation of communication.

QUESTIONS FOR DISCUSSION

1. When would a nonsymbolic form of communication be appropriate for a student? Discuss various expressive and receptive forms of communication that would be considered and how they would be used.
2. A student will be participating in community-based instruction that includes going to a drugstore. Discuss how the vocabulary would be determined.
3. Mary, a 7-year-old student with cerebral palsy, uses a walker for mobility and a DynaVox for communication. Her parents do not want her to take the DynaVox outside for recess. Construct a possible nonelectronic system that you could make for the student. What would some of the content be? What communicative functions would you include?
4. Divide up into pairs and with a made-up communication board (overlay) demonstrate each of the following instructional techniques: establishing want/no, milieu teaching procedure, response prompt strategy, environmental arrangement strategy, interrupted-chain strategy, and conversational skill training. Discuss advantages and disadvantages of each.
5. Communication breakdowns often occur when talking with augmentative communication users. Divide into pairs and discuss a topic. Then have one person think of something they want to say about the topic, but only be able to answer yes-or-no questions. Have the other person use communication breakdown strategies to determine what their partner wanted to communicate. Discuss how successful this was.

FOCUS ON THE NET

Abledata
http://abledata.com

This site is sponsored by the National Institute on Disability and Rehabilitation Research and provides a searchable database on augmentative communication and adaptive devices, news, and links.

Closing the Gap
http://www.closingthegap.com/

This site specializes in computer technology in special education and rehabilitation, and it includes a sample copy of the *Close the Gap* newspaper and a yearly resource directory that teachers find helpful across many topics.

Companies that sell AAC devices

AbleNet, Inc.
http://www.ablenetinc.com

ADAMLAB, LLC
http://www.adamlab.com

Crestwood Communication Aids, Inc.
http://www.communicationaids.com

Don Johnston Inc.
http://www.donjohnston.com

DynaVox Systems, LLC
http://www.dynavoxsys.com

Enabling Devices, Toys for Special Children
http://www.enablingdevices.com

IntelliTools
http://www.intellitools.com

Mayer-Johnson Inc.
http://www.mayer-johnson.com

Prentke Romich Co.
http://www.prentrom.com

Zygo
http://www.zygo-usa.com

REFERENCES

Alwell, M., Hunt, P., Goetz, L., & Sailor, W. (1989). Teaching generalized communicative behaviors within interrupted behavior chain contexts. *Journal of the Association for Persons with Severe Handicaps, 14*, 91–100.

Austin, J. (1962). *How to do things with words.* Cambridge, MA: Harvard University Press.

Baker, B. R. (1982, Sept.). Minspeak: A semantic compaction system that makes self-expression easier for communicatively disabled individuals. *Byte*, pp. 186–202.

Banajee, M., Dicarlo, C., & Stricklin, B. (2003). Core vocabulary determination for toddlers. *Augmentative and Alternative Communication, 19*, 67–73.

Bates, E. (1979). The emergence of symbols: *Cognition and communication in infancy.* New York: Academic.

Blackstone, S. W. (1988). Vocabulary selection: Current practices and a glimpse at the future. *Augmentative Communication News, 1*(5), 2.

Blackstone, S. W., & Hunt-Berg, M. (2003). Social networks: A communication inventory for individuals with complex communication needs and their communication partners. Monterey, CA: Augmentative Communication.

Blackstone, S. W., Cassatt-James, E. L., & Bruskin, D. B. (Eds). (1988). *Augmentative communication implementation strategies.* Rockville, MD: American Speech-Language-Hearing Association.

Brown, L., Branston-McLean, M. B., Baumgart, D., Vincent, L., Falvey, M., & Schroeder, J. (1979). Using the characteristics of current and subsequent least restrictive environments as factors in the development of curricular content for severely handicapped students. *AAESP Review, 4*, 407–424.

Clark, C. R. (1981). Learning words using traditional orthography and the symbols of Rebus, Bliss, and Carrier. *Journal of Speech and Hearing Disorders, 46*, 191–196.

Cook, A. M., & Hussey, S. M. (2002). Assistive technologies: Principles and practice (2nd ed.). St Louis, MO: Mosby.

Daehler, M. W., Perlmutter, M., & Myers, N. A. (1976). Equivalence of pictures and objects for very young children. *Child Development, 47*, 96–102.

Decoste, D. C. (1997). AAC and individuals with physical disabilities. In S. L. Glennen & D. C. DeCoste (Eds.), *Handbook of augmentative and alternative communication* (pp. 363–389). San Diego, CA: Singular.

Doster, S., & Politano, P. (1996). Augmentative and alternative communication. In J. Hammel (Ed.), *AOTA Self-Paced Clinical Course: Technology and occupational therapy: A link to function.* Bethesda, MD: American Occupational Therapy Association.

Duncan, J. L., & Silverman, F. H. (1977). Impacts of learning American Indian sign language on mentally retarded children: A preliminary report. *Perceptual and Motor Skills, 44*, 11–38.

Fallon, K. A., Light, J., & Achenbach, A. (2003). The semantic organization patterns of young children: Implications for augmentative and alternative communication. *Augmentative and Alternative Communication, 19*, 74–85.

Foulds, R. (1980). *Communication rates for nonspeech expression as a function of manual tasks and linguistic constraints.* Proceedings of the International Conference on Rehabilitation Engineering, Toronto, Canada.

Glennen, S. L. (1997). Augmentative and alternative communication systems. In S. L. Glennen & D. C. DeCoste (Eds.), *Handbook of augmentative and alternative communication* (pp. 59–96). San Diego, CA: Singular.

Goetz, L., Gee. K., & Sailer, W. (1985). Using a behavior chain interruption strategy to teach communication skills to students with severe disabilities. *Journal of the Association for Persons with Severe Handicaps, 10*, 21–30.

Goossens, C. (1989). Aided communication intervention before assessment: A case study of a child with cerebral palsy. *Augmentative and Alternative Communication, 5*(1), 14–26.

Goossens, C., & Crain, S. (1986). *Augmentative communication: Intervention resource.* Wauconda, IL: Don Johnston Developmental Equipment.

Grunsell, J., & Carter, M. (2002). The behavior chain interruption strategy: Generalization to out-of-routine contexts. *Education and Training in Mental Retardation and Developmental Disabilities, 37*, 378–390.

Halle, J. W., Marshall, A. M., & Spradlin, J. E. (1979). Time delay: A technique to increase language use and facilitate generalization in retarded children. *Journal of Applied Behavior Analysis, 12,* 431–439.

Hart, B., & Risley, T. R. (1975). Incidental teaching of language in the preschool. *Journal of Applied Behavior Analysis, 8,* 411–420.

Heller, K. W. (1993). *Promoting communication using eye-gaze boards.* Unpublished manuscript.

Heller, K. W., Alberto, P. A., & Bowdin, J. (1995). Interactions of communication partners and students who are deaf-blind: A model. *Journal of Visual Impairments and Blindness, 89,* 391–401.

Heller, K. W., Alberto, P. A., & Romski, M. (1995). Effect of object and movement cues on receptive communication by preschool children with mental retardation. *American Journal on Mental Retardation, 99,* 510–521.

Heller, K. W., Allgood, P., Davis, B., Arnold, S., Castelle, M., & Taber, T. (1996). Promoting nontask-related communication at vocational sites. *Augmentative and Alternative Communication, 12,* 169–178.

Heller, K. W., Allgood, P., Ware, S., Arnold, S., & Castelle, M. (1996). Initiating requests during community-based vocational training by students with mental retardation and sensory impairments. *Research in Developmental Disabilities, 17,* 173–184.

Heller, K. W., Ware, S., Allgood, P., & Castelle, M. (1994). Use of dual communication boards with students who are deaf-blind. *Journal of Visual Impairments and Blindness, 88,* 368–376.

Heller, K. W., Ware, S., Allgood, P., & Castelle, M. (1996). Use of dual communication boards at vocational sites by students who are deaf-blind. *Rehabilitation and Education for Blindness and Visual Impairments, 27,* 180–192.

Hetzroni, O. E., & Roth, T. (2003). Effects of a positive support approach to enhance communicative behaviors of children with mental retardation who have challenging behaviors. *Education and Training in Developmental Disabilities, 38,* 95–105.

Hurlbut, B. I., Iwata, B. A., & Green, J. D. (1982). Nonvocal language acquisition in adolescents with severe physical disabilities: Blissymbol versus iconic stimulus formats. *Journal of Applied Behavior Analysis, 15,* 241–258.

Kaiser, A. P. (2000). Teaching functional communication skills. In M. E. Snell & F. Brown (Eds.), *Instruction of students with severe disabilities* (5th ed., pp. 453–492). Upper Saddle River, NJ: Merrill/Prentice Hall.

Kaiser, A. P., Ostrosky, M. N., & Alpert, C. L. (1993). Training teachers to use environmental arrangement and milieu teaching with nonvocal preschool children. *Journal of the Association for Persons with Severe Handicaps, 18,* 188–199.

Kaiser, A. P., Yoder, P. J., & Keetz, A. (1992). Evaluating milieu teaching. In S. F. Warren & J. Reichle (Eds.), *Causes and effects in communication and language intervention* (pp. 9–47). Baltimore: Brookes.

Kraat, A. W. (1985). *Communication interaction between aided and natural speakers: A state of the art report.* Toronto: Canadian Rehabilitation Council for the Disabled.

Kraat, A. W. (1986). Developing intervention goals. In S. W. Blackstone & D. M. Bruskin (Eds.), *Augmentative communication: An introduction* (pp. 197–266). Rockville, MD: American Speech-Language-Hearing Association.

Lafontaine, L. M., & DeRuyter, F. (1987). The nonspeaking cerebral palsied: A clinical and demographic database report. *Augmentative and Alternative Communication, 3*(2), 153–162.

Levin, J., & Scherfenberg, L. (1987). *Selection and use of simple technology in home, school, work, and community settings.* Minneapolis, MN: ABLENET.

Lloyd, L. L., & Karlan, G. R. (1984). Non-speech communication symbols and systems: Where have we been and where are we going? *Journal of Mental Deficiency Research, 28,* 3–20.

Matas, J. A., Mathy-Laikko, P., Beukelman, D. R., & Legresley, K. (1985). Identifying the nonspeaking population: A demographic study. *Augmentative and Alternative Communication, 1,* 17–31.

Millikin, C. C. (1997). Symbol systems and vocabulary selection strategies. In S. L. Glennen & D. C. DeCoste (Eds.), *Handbook of augmentative and alternative communication* (pp. 97–148). San Diego: Singular.

Mirenda, P., & Locke, P. (1987). A comparison of symbol transparency in nonspeaking persons with intellectual disabilities. *Journal of Speech and Hearing Disorders, 54*(2), 131–140.

Mirenda, P., & Schuler, A. L. (1988). Augmenting communication for persons with autism: Issues and strategies. *Topics in Language Disorders, 9*(1), 24–43.

Musselwhite, C., & St. Louis, K. (1988). *Communication programming for the severely handicapped.* San Diego, CA: College-Hill.

Owens, R. E. (1988). *Language development: An introduction.* Upper Saddle River, NJ: Merrill/Prentice Hall.

Romski, M. A., & Sevcik, R. A. (1993). Language learning through augmented means: The process and its products. In A. P. Kaiser & D. B. Gray (Eds.), *Enhancing children's communication: Research foundations for intervention* (pp. 85–104). Baltimore: Brookes.

Rowland, C., & Schweigert, P. (2000). Tangible symbols, tangible outcomes. *Augmentative and Alternative Communication, 16,* 61–78.

Sevcik, R. A., & Romski, M. A. (1986). Representational matching skills of persons with severe retardation. *Augmentative and Alternative Communication, 2,* 160–164.

Siegel, E., & Wetherby, A. (2000). Nonsymbolic communication. In M. E. Snell & F. Brown (Eds.), *Instruction of students with severe disabilities* (5th ed., pp. 409–451). Upper Saddle River, NJ: Merrill/Prentice Hall.

Sigafoos, J. (2000). Communication development and aberrant behavior in children with developmental disabilities. *Education and Training in Mental Retardation and Development Disabilities, 35,* 168–176.

Silverman, F. (1980). *Communication for the speechless.* Upper Saddle River, NJ: Prentice Hall.

Skelly, M., & Schinsky, L. (1979). *Ameri-Ind gestural code based on universal American Indian Hand Talk.* New York: Elsevier North Holland.

Snell, M., & Gast, D. (1981). Applying delay procedure to the instruction of the severely handicapped. *Journal of the Association of the Severely Handicapped, 6,* 3–14.

Sternberg, L., & McNerney, C. (1988). Prelanguage communication instruction. In L. Sternberg (Ed.), *Educating students with severe or profound handicaps* (2nd ed., pp. 311–341). Austin, TX: PRO-ED.

Stillman, R. D., & Battle, C. W. (1984). Developing prelanguage communication in the severely handicapped: An interpretation of the Van Dijk method. *Seminars in Speech and Language, 4,* 159–170.

Struck, M. (1996). Augmentative communication and computer access. In A. S. Allen, J. Case-Smith, & P. N. Pratt (Eds.), *Occupational therapy for children* (3rd ed., pp. 545–562). St. Louis, MO: Mosby.

Vanderheiden, G. C., & Kelso, D. D. (1987). Comparative analysis of fixed vocabulary communication acceleration techniques. *Augmentative and Alternative Communication, 3*(4), 196–206.

Vanderheiden, G. C., & Lloyd, L. L. (1986). Communication systems and their components. In S. W. Blackstone & D. M. Bruskin (Eds.), *Augmentative communication: An introduction* (pp. 29–162). Rockville, MD: American Speech-Language-Hearing Association.

Verberg, G. (1987). A wholistic approach. *Communicating Together, 5*(1), 17–18.

Warren, S. F., McQuarter, R. J., & Rogers-Warren, A. K. (1984). The effects of mands and models on the speech of unresponsive socially isolated children. *Journal of Speech and Hearing Disorders, 47,* 42–52.

Westling, D. L., & Fox, L. (2004). *Teaching students with severe disabilities* (2nd ed). Upper Saddle River, NJ: Merrill/Prentice Hall.

Wetherby, A. M., Yonclass, D. G., & Bryan, A. A. (1989). Communicative profiles of handicapped preschool children: Implications for early identification. *Journal of Speech and Hearing Disorders, 54*(2), 148–158.

Yovetich, W. S., & Young, T. A. (1988). The effects of representativeness and concreteness on the "guessability" of Blissymbols. *Augmentative and Alternative Communication, 4,* 35–39.

PART III

SPECIALIZED CURRICULA

CHAPTER 9 Feeding and Swallowing

CHAPTER 10 Adaptations for Personal Independence

CHAPTER 11 Adaptations in Physical Education, Leisure Education, and Recreation

CHAPTER 12 Transition and Self-Determination

Feeding and Swallowing

RONA ALEXANDER

CHAPTER 9

KNOWLEDGE AND SKILLS

After you have read this chapter, you will be able to:

1. **Understand the variety of variables that impact a child's feeding abilities.**
2. **Differentiate between the activities described by the terms *feeding* and *swallowing*.**
3. **Identify the primary areas to be investigated during a clinical oral-motor, feeding/swallowing, and respiratory coordination evaluation.**
4. **Discuss key questions to be explored in each area of the clinical evaluation process.**
5. **Appreciate the need for a team approach to intervention programming for children with feeding and swallowing management needs.**
6. **Describe the differences between oral-motor, feeding/swallowing, and respiratory coordination treatment and carryover activities such as mealtime feeding.**
7. **Recognize the importance of carryover activities as part of the child's intervention programming and the need to carry over strategies that do not compromise the child's overall nutritional intake.**
8. **Discuss how positioning, feeding utensil selection, sensory aspects of foods and liquids, and oral sensory awareness and preparation can impact the spoon-feeding, cup-drinking, and solid food intake abilities of a child with neuromotor involvement.**

As children with physical or multiple disabilities are integrated into regular school programming through the current emphasis on inclusive education, professionals and paraprofessionals working in the schools have been challenged by new areas of function in which they have had to obtain knowledge and special training. This has certainly occurred in the areas of feeding and swallowing as children with significant medical feeding and swallowing problems are being integrated into all aspects of the school setting. Which aspects of feeding and swallowing intervention programming must be incorporated into a child's school day are dependent upon the individual child's needs for treatment and management and the appropriateness of the implementation of certain strategies for that child into his or her educational setting. If a child is in school all day, his or her teacher and other designated school personnel will need to be trained in the appropriate procedures to be used at mealtime.

In pediatrics, the term **feeding** is used to describe "a functional process which involves the interactions of a variety of factors including the child's environment; caregiver-child interactions; integrity of the child's medical, developmental, sensorimotor, neuromotor, and cognitive status; feeding techniques/procedures; feeding utensils; positioning needs; swallowing; and the interaction of swallowing variables with respiratory and gastrointestinal factors; nutritional requirements; and specific oral and pharyngeal activity" (Alexander & Beecher, 1992). **Swallowing** (i.e., deglutition) is a complex series of finely timed motor acts that transport material from the oral mechanism through the pharynx and esophagus to the stomach. Safe swallowing implies that the movement of material from the mouth through to the stomach occurs without aspiration (Jones & Donner, 1991).

Aspiration refers to the entrance of material into the trachea, below the level of the true vocal folds. Aspiration may occur on all foods and liquids presented during oral feeding or only on one specific texture. It may occur only when liquids are presented by open-rimmed cup and not when they are presented by soft-spouted cup. It can occur due to oral-motor dysfunction and problems of coordination with pharyngeal activity, or it can occur when there is coordinated, organized oral-motor function, but significant pharyngeal sensory and motility problems. Aspiration may not occur during feeding activities, but only on saliva and secretions. Coughing may occur in response to material entering the airway, and yet it may be too weak to actually clear the material and prevent it from entering the lungs.

When a child has physical or multiple disabilities, elements of the oral feeding process and the act of swallowing may be affected. If airway management is compromised during swallowing by the occurrence of aspiration, and this has been documented using clinical and instrumental evaluation procedures, specific feeding and swallowing management strategies will need to be followed. This needs to occur whether the child receives no food or liquids by mouth and is fed totally by gastrostomy tube or the child receives very specific textures by mouth during oral feeding activities with supplemental nutritional intake provided by tube feeding. If aspects of a child's feeding and swallowing function place the child at risk for aspiration, as documented by findings of a comprehensive evaluation, the child may continue to be orally fed. However, there will be very specific mealtime management strategies that will need to be carried over into feeding-related activities the child is involved in during the school day as well as at home.

Although this chapter will focus on the feeding/swallowing, oral-motor, and respiratory coordination function of children with neuromotor involvement, children with a wide variety of diagnoses and conditions may have problems in these areas. Physical conditions that may be associated with pediatric feeding and swallowing problems include the following:

- Prematurity;
- Upper airway anomalies (e.g., cleft lip and palate, laryngomalacia);
- Congenital defects of the larynx, trachea, and esophagus (e.g., tracheoesophageal fistula, esophageal strictures);
- Acquired anatomical defects due to traumatic injury; and
- Neurological conditions due to central nervous system diseases, peripheral nervous system diseases, neuromuscular diseases, or other neurologically based problems (Rogers, 1996; Tuchman & Walter, 1994; Weiss, 1988).

Of course, not all children with medical diagnoses falling within any of these condition areas reveal feeding and swallowing problems. Some of these conditions are so broad that the actual reason for one child's feeding and swallowing problem may be different from another child with the same basic medical diagnosis. It is only through the comprehensive evaluation of feeding and swallowing function that appropriate management and intervention strategies can be developed for an individual child.

Children with physical/medical conditions underlying the cause of their feeding and swallowing problems may develop behavior management issues related to the fears, frustrations, procedures, and, sometimes, physical discomfort they have learned to associate with mealtime feeding. However, these behavior management issues, which have developed due to significant physical/medical causes, are different from behavioral feeding disorders. Behavioral feeding disorders are described by Babbitt, Hoch, and Coe (1994) in terms of whether they are motivationally based or skill-deficit based. In either case, the child with a true behavioral feeding disorder possesses the physical abilities to feed and swallow in a typical manner with no medical reasons (e.g., gastroesophageal reflux, food allergies, medication interactions, sensorimotor processing issues) for the behaviors. A child with a behavioral feeding disorder will require a comprehensive behavioral assessment and subsequent development of appropriate management strategies to be incorporated into his or her daily activities.

Although oral-motor function plays a very significant role in feeding and swallowing, other factors (e.g., pharyngeal activity, gastrointestinal function, respiratory function) may be more influential in terms of a child's ability to eat and drink safely. Therefore, the procedures, equipment, positioning, and types of food or liquid provided during mealtime must be determined after careful evaluation of all factors related to feeding and swallowing, recognizing that the primary goal at every mealtime is maximum nutritional intake presented in as safe a manner as possible.

Oral-motor, feeding/swallowing, and respiratory coordination treatment focusing on changes in specific oral-motor activity, oral sensory awareness and organization, pharyngeal activity, postural alignment and activity, and respiratory coordination with oral and pharyngeal activities cannot be provided at mealtime. Such treatment, generally provided by a qualified pediatric speech/language pathologist, must be provided on an individual basis with the carryover of activities into mealtime as the child begins to exhibit more spontaneous changes during treatment. Intervention programming in feeding and swallowing requires that all members of the child's team be in communication to assure continuity of programming when new strategies that encourage new movements to enhance nutritional intake need to be integrated into daily programming.

WHY ARE WE CONCERNED WITH FEEDING AND SWALLOWING?

It is easy to see the relationship between the development of oral and laryngeal movements in early sound production and the development of coordinated oral and pharyngeal activities for connected, articulate speech. It is more difficult to recognize the relationship between the oral and pharyngeal development in feeding and swallowing and the development of speech. However, feeding and swallowing activities are important not only because they are related to speech production, but also because they have significant effects on nutrition, dental care, communication, and personal-social, perceptual, cognitive, and sensorimotor development.

The influence of nutritional intake on brain growth, learning, and behavior has been examined extensively (Palmer, 1978). If children are unable to consume the amounts and types of food necessary to supply their daily nutritional requirements because of the inability to coordinate feeding, swallowing, and breathing, or because they cannot initiate a sucking or swallowing motion, or because poor oral-motor activity does not permit them to drink from a cup or to bite and chew solid foods, their brain growth and intellectual function may be compromised.

There is an important relationship between feeding and swallowing activities and the development of teeth and maintenance of healthy gums. When teething begins, at about 4 or 5 months of age, rubbing of the gums or munching on foods such as teething crackers appears to help the baby tolerate the pain and swelling (Brazelton, 1969). Teething crackers, hard solids, fingers, toys, or other objects that are put in the mouth during teething help maintain the health of the gums for the eventual development of teeth, and also help integrate sensorimotor responses to oral stimulation as preparation for later chewing of solid foods. For the child with neuromotor impairment who is unable to tolerate oral tactile stimulation from objects or food, the pain of teething cannot easily be reduced and the child is even more irritable. Such children will have a much more difficult time developing the ability to bite and chew solids.

Moyer (1971) has stated that the sensory stimulation provided by the contact of the teeth with other things is one of the most important elements in the development of coordination for chewing. Feeding activities and dental health are interrelated; if the child cannot tolerate tactile stimulation to keep the gums healthy, the eruption of teeth and the tolerance for stimulation in the mouth may be affected. This will, in turn, affect the child's ability to handle solid foods and possibly adversely affect the development of a mature, coordinated chewing pattern.

The development of communication and personal-social skills can be traced to the foundation established during early feeding. The child learns that through crying, fussing, or body movement, he or she can get a response from people. By picking up or cuddling him or her, the caregiver reinforces the child's use of sound and movement as a means of communicating his or her needs. The child also communicates likes and dislikes of certain foods through sounds and movements, which, because they elicit responses from the feeder, are reinforced, further supporting the child's development of communication.

As the infant is being fed in the caregiver's arms, feelings of security and attachment develop. The parent learns to respond to the infant's signals during feeding, and the infant learns to respond to the parent's actions by making signs of contentment, which reinforce the parent's behavior. When the child establishes eye contact with the parent, an even stronger bond is developed. When the child smiles, the parent becomes even more comforting and reassuring. The entire process leads to bonding, or attachment, one of the initial phases of personal-social development.

Although the parent of a child with neuromotor impairment begins by responding to the sounds and movements of the child, the child's problems in reinforcing the behavior of the caregiver may lead to a breakdown in personal-social interaction. The child may respond to being picked up for feeding by increasing his or her body tension and strongly pushing his or her head back. In response to these negative cues, the parent may try to avoid many of the situations that cause increased tension in the child, consequently increasing the caregiver's own tension during feeding. This breakdown in the interaction between child and parent leads to problems in the child's early development of communication and personal-social skills.

Such breakdowns in communication and personal-social interactions can also occur when educators, support personnel, and other service providers are not properly trained in the mealtime feeding methods to be used for a specific child and do not have an understanding of the overall special needs of the child. Responses by the child may be misinterpreted and may be viewed as negative behavioral responses requiring behavior management, rather than responses that the child uses due to specific sensory processing or neuromotor problems. The child who does not let the toothbrush into his or her mouth may be having difficulty dealing with the visual or tactile stimulation related to the presentation of the toothbrush or may have gastroesophageal reflux (GER) and therefore will try to avoid any sensory input to the tongue that may trigger the GER to occur. If caregivers believe that the child is just being negative and has no real reason for this response, they may implement inappropriate methods to change behaviors rather than establishing programming to deal with the real causes of the response through strategies to increase tolerance for the regulation of sensory input or through strategies to reduce the negative impact of GER.

The interrelationship of perceptual, cognitive, and sensorimotor development is strong, as noted in the works of Piaget (Ginsburg & Opper, 1969) and Uzgiris and Hunt (1975). Feeding of the infant or young child involves a vast amount of stimulation, which is necessary for successful development. For example, as food is brought by spoon toward the mouth, the child learns to focus on the spoon and begins to track its movement toward him or her. An association is soon established between the visual presentation of the spoon and receiving of food; cognitively, the child begins to recognize that seeing the spoon means getting something to eat. He or she also learns that the sensory stimulation provided by the spoon and the food is pleasurable and that certain kinds of movements of the mouth allow him or her to take the food in easily. Therefore, as the child is fed, he or she obtains a great deal of positive perceptual, cognitive, and sensorimotor stimulation that leads to continued growth. On the other hand, the child with neuromotor problems may respond to this situation with body stiffening, increased head and body extension, or strong biting on the spoon because he or she cannot tolerate the visual or tactile stimulation. This will result in a breakdown in the child's perceptual, cognitive, and sensorimotor development and will cause the parent or caregiver to become frustrated and tense during feeding.

It should be evident that feeding and swallowing activities play a significant role in the child's overall development not only because of their influence on oral-motor function, but also because of their importance in providing the stimulation that leads to the development of many other skills. Even when sensory, neuromotor, or medical problems exist which make feeding and swallowing and early sound production experiences difficult, children need opportunities to experience these or similar activities in order to enhance their educational experiences.

Whether working with a 6-month-old infant with a suspected neuromotor disorder or a 10-year-old child with a diagnosed sensory-processing disorder, professionals must have a valid concept of oral-motor, feeding/swallowing, and respiratory coordination development in the typical infant or young child in order to assess a child's abilities and to develop appropriate intervention strategies. All professionals providing services for the infant or child with a disability must have an extensive grasp of both typical and atypical aspects of development in these important areas.

FIGURE 9–1
Terms related to typical oral-motor function in feeding

Automatic Phasic Bite-Release Pattern. A response to tactile input presented on the biting surfaces of the gums or teeth, composed of a small, rhythmical series of up/down jaw movements; occurs until approximately 5 months of age.

Chewing. The process used to break up solid foods in preparation for swallowing, is characterized by rotary movements of the jaw; lateral, spreading, and rolling movements of the tongue to propel and maintain food between the teeth; and lip and cheek activity to help hold food between the biting surfaces.

Controlled, Sustained Bite. Easy, graded closure of the teeth through the food with an easy, graded release for chewing; seen by approximately 11 to 12 months of age.

Gag Response. A response to tactile input presented to the back of the tongue or pharyngeal area, composed of jaw extension, forward/downward tongue movements, and pharyngeal constriction with eye widening and head and neck extension; very strong at birth, reducing in strength by approximately 7 months of age; persists throughout adulthood.

Jaw Stabilization. Active, internal jaw control with minimal up/down jaw movements, especially significant in cup drinking; initially obtained by biting on the cup rim at about 13 to 15 months of age; gradually develops using active jaw musculature by 24 months of age.

Munching. Early chewing activity composed of rhythmical up/down jaw movements with spreading, flattening, and some up/down tongue movements; begins at approximately 5 months of age with the introduction of solids.

Rooting Response. A food-seeking movement that occurs in response to tactile input presented on the lips or cheeks, characterized by mouth opening and head turning in the direction of the touch; occurs until approximately 4 to 5 months of age; stronger just before feeding and when the infant is in a position generally associated with feeding.

Rotary Jaw Movements. Activity used in chewing, increases from 15 to 36 months of age; reflects the integration of up/down, forward/backward, lateral-diagonal, diagonal-rotary, and circular-rotary movements of the jaw.

Sucking. A rhythmical method for obtaining liquid and food, characterized by the active coordination of small up/down jaw movements, up/down tongue movements, lip approximation, and cheek activity; negative pressure is built up in the oral cavity due to the more closed mouth position.

Suckling. An early lick-type of sucking pattern composed of rhythmical forward/backward tongue movements, large rhythmical up/down jaw movements, and minimal cheek and lip activity; the tongue moves forward and down as the jaw depresses, and moves up and slightly back as the jaw elevates.

Tongue Lateralization. Active movements of the tongue to the sides of the mouth to maintain and propel food between the biting surfaces during the chewing process; begins at about 6 to 7 months of age with horizontal shifts or gross rolling movements of the tongue when food is placed on the side gums.

TYPICAL FEEDING AND SWALLOWING DEVELOPMENT

Characteristics of Typical Oral-Motor Development

Infants are born with primary repertoires of movement that are responses to sensory stimulation (e.g., visual orientation to moving objects, orientation to sound, reciprocal kicking) (Howle, 2002). Due to the sensory-rich nature of the feeding experience, it would be expected that newborns exhibit many of their unique movements during feeding.

When touched along the outside of the mouth, the infant's head turns in the direction of the touch and the mouth opens. This is called the **rooting response** and is the infant's food-seeking movement. Any touch around the face, except right after feeding, will stimulate a rooting response in an infant from birth until approximately 4 to 5 months of age. Figure 9–1 displays terms related to typical oral-motor function in feeding. Refer to this table throughout the chapter to become familiar with the developmental progression of feeding and eating.

Babies often look as if they are chewing, because when someone or something touches the biting surfaces of the gums, a rhythmical opening and closing of the lower jaw can be seen. Actually, this is an automatic, uncontrollable action of the infant. It is called the **automatic phasic bite-release pattern** and is seen in the baby as a pumping movement, which starts the liquid flowing into the mouth. It is easily observed in the infant until approximately 6 months of age, when the infant begins experiencing a greater variety of oral tactile stimulation, including hard solids for scraping on the biting surfaces of the gums to reduce the discomfort of teething.

The **gag response** is a survival response that is present throughout life. The newborn has a very strong gag response when anything touches the back of the tongue or the throat (i.e., pharyngeal area). As the baby brings fingers or toys into the mouth and starts to tolerate more solid foods, the strength of the gag decreases until it appears more like an adult protective gag at approximately 7 months.

Bottle Drinking. During the first 2 to 4 weeks of life, the full-term newborn uses a total pattern of **sucking** to take in liquids from the bottle or breast. This sucking activity, with intra-oral negative pressure used to draw liquid into the mouth, appears to be directly related to the generally flexed position of the infant's head and body (i.e., physiological flexion); the close approximation of the jaw and the upper rib cage providing a limited amount of space for jaw and tongue movements; and the small size of the oral space with the tongue filling up a significant amount of the intra-oral area.

During feeding, as the infant begins to turn and extend his or her head, moving the chin away from the chest, the mouth biomechanically opens in a larger vertical range of movement. In this position, jaw, tongue, and cheek/lip activity characteristic of **suckling** takes place more often than sucking. This mixture of suckling and sucking continues until approximately 6 months, when more-mature sucking movements of the oral mechanism appear. Most children can start to be weaned from the bottle at about 12 months and are usually totally off bottle drinking by 24 to 30 months.

Initially, when the baby is using mostly suckling movements, he or she will make about two suckles before he or she has to pause to swallow and breathe. During swallowing, the tongue will either move forward and backward, or it will protrude from the mouth. By about 3 months, the child can perform more suckling/sucking activity before having to pause to swallow and breathe. It is not until the child is using predominantly sucking movements, at around 6 months, that no real pauses between the sucking and swallowing of liquids from the bottle are noted and longer sequences can be produced in coordination with breathing.

Spoon-Feeding. The introduction of spoon-feeding often depends upon the age at which the parent, caregiver, or pediatrician believes the baby should begin to eat pureed foods (see Figure 9–2). Oral motor activity characteristic of suckling is used during spoon-feeding until about 5 months, when sucking activity begins. Up to this time, swallowing movements during spoon-feeding consist basically of forward and backward tongue movements with tongue protrusion, frequently resulting in some of the food being pushed out of the mouth.

At 6 months the lower lip begins to move upward and protrude outward while stabilizing under the bowl of the spoon. This provides an active base of stability for the jaw and tongue, quieting the mouth and allowing for the downward movement of the upper lip to close on the spoon. By about 7 months the upper lip becomes more active in removing food from the spoon and then gradually develops more-precise forward-downward-backward movements so that removal of food from the spoon becomes an active process. By 9 months swallowing shows some up-and-down tongue movements along with occasional tongue protrusion or forward and backward tongue movement. By 12 months the child is able to clean food from the lower lip, make much more precise tongue-lip movements, and accomplish more active lip closure during the spoon-feeding process.

Cup Drinking. Children often start to receive liquids from a cup at approximately 6 months, although they continue to receive their primary liquid intake by bottle or breast. Suckling activity with forward/backward tongue movements or tongue protrusion will be noted in swallowing. The child may occasionally cough or choke on the liquid because of the poor coordination of suckling, swallowing, and breathing. Not until approximately 9 months of age can the child take one to three sips of liquid before stopping to swallow and breathe.

At 10 to 12 months of age, the baby will begin to protrude his or her tongue under the cup, elevate the lower lip to surround the tongue to stabilize against the cup surface, and draw larger amounts of liquid into the mouth and back to the pharyngeal area for swallowing. This often causes gulping sounds to be heard during swallowing. Young children soon discover that biting on the cup rim and closing the lips on the cup can provide a more efficient means for quieting their jaw movements while allowing them to use the tongue more effectively for guiding liquid in and

FIGURE 9–2
Descriptions of different textures of food and liquids

1. **Liquid** (material that flows and takes the shape of its container)
   Thin: unrestricted flow; no cohesiveness (e.g., water, milk, juice)
   Nectar: slight reduction of flow rate; slight cohesiveness (e.g., fruit nectars)
   Syrup: moderate reduction of flow rate; some cohesiveness (e.g., pancake syrup)
   Honey: significant reduction of flow rate; good cohesiveness (e.g., honey, milk shakes)
2. **Pureed**
   Thin pureed: smooth, slippery with some cohesiveness, does not separate, but will spread out without pressure (e.g., strained pears, strained carrots)
   Pureed: smooth, moist with good cohesiveness, will not separate or spread out without some pressure (e.g., commercially prepared pureed baby foods, not meats)
   Thick pureed: smooth, little moisture, cohesive (sticky), resists separation and pressure (e.g., puddings, smooth peanut butter)
3. **Soft mechanical** (cohesive, textured, soft solid foods)
   Thin: junior baby food, lumpy applesauce, thick soups
   Medium: canned stew, most casseroles
   Thick: macaroni and cheese; thick stew
4. **Solids**
   Quick dissolving: materials that dissolve in saliva or are dissolved after one to three chews (e.g., crackers, cheese puffs, Crispix cereal)
   Soft chewy: soft, breaks apart with little pressure (e.g., chicken, pasta, many cookies)
   Chewy: firm, requires more than five chews to become swallow-safe, dissolves somewhat with repeated chewing (e.g., beef, gummy candies)
   Hard: breaks into smaller pieces when chewed, but does not dissolve (e.g., nuts, uncooked vegetables, hard candies)
5. **Combination:** any food that separates quickly when placed in the mouth (e.g., soups, meat with gravy, cookies with nuts)

Note. Adapted from workshop handout, "Descriptions of Food Textures," developed by Robert Beecher (1998).

back for swallowing. Biting on the cup rim may be seen until 24 months of age or until internal jaw musculature control for active jaw stability has been developed. Active lip closure with no liquid loss during swallowing will also be achieved by 2 years of age.

Solid Food Intake. Infants of 5 to 6 months of age begin to prepare for solid foods while attempting to reduce the swelling and soreness of the gums due to teething by putting toys, fingers, furniture, hard solid foods, and other objects into their mouths. They scrape the solid foods or other objects on the biting surfaces and use their automatic phasic bite-release pattern on the hard solid, providing themselves with new tactile/proprioceptive sensory information directly impacting through the gums to the erupting teeth. Contact is made with the tongue surface, centrally and laterally, providing new sensory information to prepare the tongue for new movements and new sensorimotor experiences in the near future.

When a 5-to-6-month-old is given a soft cracker, piece of cereal, or other quickly dissolving solid, the child will try to bite using movements like the automatic phasic bite-release pattern or he or she will use a sucking or suckling pattern. By 8 to 9 months, the child will close the jaw, posture on the solid (hold the jaw closed on the solid), and then the child or the feeder will break off a piece of the cracker since there is not yet enough musculature strength or grading of the jaw to actually bite through the soft solid. At 10 to 12 months the child is using a more **controlled, sustained bite** through the quickly dissolving solid. This controlled, sustained bite will not be integrated for a hard solid until 20 to 21 months of age.

When the child begins to receive solid food at 5 to 6 months, the chewing process actually begins. He or she uses a **munching** pattern that consists of a combination of up-and-down tongue movements, like those seen in sucking, and rhythmic small up-and-down jaw movements, like those seen in the automatic phasic bite-release pattern. Suckling movements or tongue protrusion will be used to complete the swallow process. Gagging or choking may occur. Some pieces of solid will be swallowed whole, as the child is not yet able to move food from the center of the tongue back to the biting surfaces for more chewing.

Changes in the chewing process begin at approximately 7 months. When food is placed on the side biting surfaces, the tongue starts to make some shifting or rolling movements to the sides of the mouth. If food gets to the center of the tongue, the infant will suckle it or may swallow it whole. At about 9 months he or she starts to use lateral and diagonal movements of the jaw as food is moved from the side to the middle of the mouth for swallowing. Even with these changes in jaw and tongue movements when food is on the side, the child may still use a munching pattern when food gets to the center of the mouth.

By 12 months the child is able to use his or her tongue to transfer food from the center to the sides of the mouth and is able to use the upper front teeth to clean food off the lower lip. Swallowing may be accomplished by using some tongue elevation or tongue protrusion. More-frequent diagonal movements of the jaw are seen by approximately 13 to 15 months, and the corners of the lips now actively draw inward to assist in controlling the movement of food. By approximately 2 years of age the child is using more controlled, **rotary jaw movements** to break up solids, more controlled, active tongue movements to transfer food from one side of the mouth to the other, and more active lip movements to prevent the loss of food or saliva while chewing. However, it is not until at least 3 years of age that the child begins to exhibit some rotary grinding, providing the tearing and shearing motions needed to adequately break up the toughest foods.

This review of typical oral feeding development demonstrates that, by 2 years of age, the typically developing child is capable of eating a wide variety of foods of many different textures. However, throughout oral-motor development in feeding, the child has had to learn to control and coordinate the different parts of his or her mouth in each different feeding situation. Although the 6-month-old infant was able to actively suck from a bottle, he or she could not automatically start sucking from a cup. Children learn to coordinate all parts of the oral mechanism in each different situation in order to ultimately be able to coordinate the mechanisms for all of them.

CHARACTERISTICS OF TYPICAL RESPIRATORY DEVELOPMENT

The newborn's predominant respiratory pattern is that of belly (i.e., diaphragmatic, abdominal) breathing. This breathing pattern is a result of the newborn's physiological flexion; elevated position and alignment of the rib cage and shoulder girdle within the trunk; and activation of the diaphragm musculature within the rib cage for inhalation. When the newborn inhales, taking air in through the nasal cavity, the diaphragm pushes against the abdominal wall and lifts and pushes out on the lower ribs, creating belly breathing with lower rib expansion or rib flaring. Even with changes starting to occur in the size and alignment of the structures within the oral and pharyngeal mechanisms at 3 to 4 months and modifications in the skeletal alignment and musculature activity within and between the shoulder girdle and rib cage at 4 to 6 months, belly breathing with belly expansion, rib flaring, and limited rib cage/thoracic cavity movement continues to be the predominant respiratory pattern for the infant until approximately 8 to 9 months of age.

As the nasal, oral, and pharyngeal cavities begin to modify in size and shape and as the infant begins to develop more active antigravity movements and postural control through musculature of the head, neck, shoulder girdle, rib cage, pelvis, and hips, the infant changes aspects of his or her basic respiratory function as well as how respiratory function is coordinated with general and upper extremity movements, feeding and swallowing tasks, and early sound production activities. By approximately 3 to 4 months, the baby has changed from an obligatory nose breather to an individual who can also breathe through the mouth. Newly developing gross-motor activities are leading to more active antigravity movements and control at the head, neck, shoulder girdle, and trunk.

More experiences with movement and positioning in supine, prone, sitting, and standing at 4 to 6 months results in changes in the alignment of the skeletal framework of the head, neck, rib cage, shoulder girdle, and pelvis/hips. As the rib cage begins to descend within the trunk and the ribs begin to angle downward in their relationship to the thoracic spine, the depth of belly breathing increases and the abdominal muscles begin to take on a more active role in the respiratory process. By 8 to 9 months the infant is actively using the shoulder girdle as a point of stability for movements of the structures of the oral and pharyngeal mechanisms from above and of the upper rib cage from below; the abdominal musculature to stabilize the lower rib cage; and upward and rotational movement of the ribs to expand the thoracic cavity during inhalation, increasing respiratory depth. Greater abdominal musculature activity will assist in reducing the occurrence of rib flaring and increasing the length and control of exhalation. This begins the young child's use and further development of a more adultlike respiratory pattern of abdominal-thoracic breathing.

Typical Respiratory Coordination with Oral and Pharyngeal Activities

Over the first 2 years of life, respiratory coordination with oral and pharyngeal activity in feeding and swallowing modifies significantly due to a variety of factors, including increased postural activity against gravity; greater overall postural control; growth of the oral and pharyngeal mechanisms; changes in skeletal and structural alignment throughout the body as well as the oral and pharyngeal mechanisms; experiences with a greater variety of sensory information (e.g., new tastes, new textures, new smells, oral proprioceptive/tactile experiences); and changes in respiratory function. In order to prevent aspiration from occurring, the opening to the airway in the pharynx must be protected or closed as swallowed material moves from the posterior oral area (i.e., oropharyngeal area) through the pharynx to the esophagus. Appropriate timing of pharyngeal airway closing and opening during swallowing must occur in order for eating and drinking activities to be safe.

The full-term, typically developing newborn begins life with upper airway protection during bottle drinking or breastfeeding. The small oral mechanism space; elevated position of the pharyngeal structures; close approximation of the posterior tongue, soft palate/uvula, epiglottis, and pharyngeal wall; physiological flexion throughout the body; and the alignment and limited range of movement of the mouth/head/neck/shoulder girdle all help to create protection for the opening to the airway as material is swallowed by the newborn. However, as soon as any aspect of this early protection mechanism changes due to body movement, maturation, growth, or sensorimotor experiences, the infant must be developing and integrating a more active foundation of musculature activity and responses to sensory information in the oral and pharyngeal areas to prevent aspiration from occurring.

The gag response helps to protect the airway from material that may occlude it. Coughing or choking may also occur in an attempt to expel materials entering the laryngeal area. When a baby is first learning to handle a new texture, requiring integration of new sensory as well as new movement information, some loss of respiratory coordination or organization may occur. However, in short time the infant integrates this new information and organizes it so that there is less risk of aspiration with this texture in the future.

As babies develop deeper, more controlled lower respiratory system function, they have a better foundation on which to organize upper respiratory, oral-motor, and pharyngeal activity. Sequencing of sucking-swallowing-breathing becomes longer and more coordinated for breastfeeding or bottle drinking and later for cup drinking. Pureed or soft mechanical (food that is cohesive, textured, soft solid) foods can be removed from the spoon and moved back by the tongue for swallowing without gagging, reducing the risk of aspiration. Greater active coordinated movements of the tongue, jaw, and cheeks/lips to break up solids in the mouth reduces the risk that larger pieces of solids will be swallowed and compromise the airway.

Although differences exist between feeding and swallowing activities and sound production, there are significant areas in common, which can be observed as the infant learns to use his or her oral and pharyngeal muscles and structures and learns to coordinate these movements with respiratory function. Therefore, it is important to know how these areas develop coordinated function in sound production as well as feeding and swallowing activities.

From birth to approximately 8 to 9 months of age, there is a direct relationship between body movement and sound production. The infant must actively move his or her body in order to generate adequate musculature activity to support sufficient respiratory airflow and laryngeal activity to create sound. Therefore, it is not until the infant is about 8 to 9 months of age that he or she can separate body movement from sound production.

The typical newborn automatically produces phonation (sounds) with respiration. The first sounds are limited to crying characterized by much nasality. The loudness and speed of the infant's cry changes by approximately 1 month of age. For example, the pain cry is higher in pitch, longer in duration, and louder than it was earlier, allowing it to be more easily differentiated from the hunger cry. It is more intense than the hunger cry. The infant may also make some cooing sounds when moving his or her body.

Between 2 and 4 months, the cry becomes differentiated so that the caregiver can identify whether the crying signifies hunger or fussing or, eventually, pain or anger. Actual vowel-like sounds begin with movement and in response to the child's changing physiological state. By 3 months nasality begins to decrease, and changes in the intonation patterns of the vowels can be heard. As the child's body position and movements change at about 4 months, definite changes in sounds can be heard. If a child is on his or her back, he or she will tend to produce throaty or gurgly sounds. When on his or her stomach, he or she will produce sounds with the lips. While in a supported sitting position, he or she will produce sounds with the tongue and jaw.

By approximately 6 months the young child is using a deeper belly-breathing pattern with greater air intake, which allows for the production of sounds of longer duration and greater variation in intonation with movements, especially those which stimulate some activation of the abdominal musculature for support during exhalation. Sound production changes not only because of the new, more advanced body movements and new respiratory musculature activity, but also because of other developments occurring throughout the body.

The eruption of the first teeth at about 6 months influences new sounds. The child may start to produce sounds that require lip-to-teeth or tongue-to-teeth movements. As greater head and trunk control are developed for sitting, lip and tongue sounds tend to increase. This is also the time when the child begins to imitate repetitive sounds such as *bah-bah* and *ma-ma.*

As the child develops more active control of his or her body for movement against gravity at around 8 to 9 months, sounds begin to be produced that are separate from body movements, with a general increase in babbling activity during play. By 9 months most children are producing chains of repeated vowel and consonant combinations, using some bilabials such as *b* and *m*, and reproducing consonants formed with the front or back of the tongue. The child's first spontaneous word may be produced at this time, although he or she may not realize what he or she has done.

By the time the child is 12 months old, more thoracic expansion with active abdominal control is evident in the respiratory pattern. The child attempts to produce new words but does not always get them out correctly. Note that at this time the child is also learning motor patterns such as walking; therefore, the phenomenon of plateauing may occur, in which speech development slows down, as the child is more involved in these new motor tasks. At approximately 12 to 15 months the child has developed the basics of the respiratory control needed for more-mature speech production. However, it will be about another year before the more adult abdominal-thoracic breathing pattern becomes a more consistent part of the child's respiratory function.

Growth and maturation have significant influences on the development of respiratory coordination with oral feeding and swallowing and sound production activities. Each growth spurt requires the reorganization of sensory information and motor activities and the development of new, more coordinated movements for function using musculature that has greater length and modified skeletal and structural alignment. Children learn to coordinate their respiratory function with each new movement experience, requiring a period of time to recognize new sensory cues and musculature activity and to practice ways to most efficiently and effectively integrate changes in activity. This sensory and motor learning process is seen throughout development. A child's typical development of feeding and swallowing as well as sound production function is no exception. For further information on significant aspects of typical development, the following resources are suggested: Alexander, Boehme, and Cupps (1993), Bly (1994), Cech and Martin (1995), and Morris and Klein (2000).

FEEDING AND SWALLOWING IN CHILDREN WITH NEUROMOTOR INVOLVEMENT

Atypical Oral-Motor Activity

Recent years have seen an increase in our knowledge of the development of atypical movement and, consequently, in our understanding of the influence of early atypical postural tone and atypical movement patterns on the child's total development. We have learned that except for a small percentage of children with suspected or diagnosed neuromotor impairment who are born with extremely severe hypertonicity, most such children are hypotonic at birth. When the hypotonic child begins to move his or her head and body against gravity, he or she has to use atypical postural tone along with atypical body movements to reach the desired position. The more these atypical movements are used, the greater the postural tone may be at certain key areas and the more these movements become a part of the child's total motor repertoire. These experiences affect the postural tone and movement of the child throughout the body and throughout the process of development. Eventually the child's total body becomes involved in attempts at movement during a wide variety of functional activities.

Since motor development is generally accepted as progressing from head to toe (or cephalo-caudal) and since the oral mechanism is actively used by the infant from the very beginning for feeding/swallowing and phonation (crying), it is logical to expect the head, neck, oral and pharyngeal mechanisms, shoulder girdle, and upper rib cage to exhibit the initial problems with body movements. Therefore, a child with head and neck hyperextension will often reveal atypical oral movements, including jaw thrusting with retraction, cheek/lip retraction, and tongue retraction, as part of this atypical movement pattern (see Figure 9–3). When a child has pronounced asymmetry with strong head and neck hyperextension, jaw thrusting with retraction and deviation to the side and cheek/lip retraction with deviation to the side can be expected to be seen in the oral mechanism.

FIGURE 9–3
Atypical oral movements

Cheek/Lip Retraction. The atypical pulling back of the cheeks and lips for stabilization; the lips appear thin as they form a tight line across the mouth; initially seen in conjunction with atypical head and neck hyperextension and tongue retraction.

Exaggerated Jaw Closure. Excessive closure of the jaw on feeding utensils used to obtain external jaw stability during feeding; occurs as a compensation for excessive jaw instability; not due to problems in tolerating oral tactile stimulation.

Exaggerated Tongue Protrusion. An exaggerated amount of forward tongue movement as the tongue moves forward/backward in a pattern similar to suckling; tongue may have a thickened appearance.

Jaw Thrusting. The strong depression of the lower jaw with a greater extent and force than seen in typical suckling activity; the jaw may become stuck in an open position; reinforces atypical head and neck hyperextension.

Jaw Thrusting with Protrusion. The strong depression with forward pushing of the lower jaw; often seen initially with attempts to close an unstable jaw that opened using thrusting with retraction; occurs as a compensatory jaw movement.

Jaw Thrusting with Retraction. The strong depression with backward movement of the lower jaw; initially seen in conjunction with atypical head and neck hyperextension and tongue retraction.

Lip Pursing. A purse-string positioning of the lips and cheeks; the cheeks and lip corners are slightly retracted for atypical holding/stability while the central portions of the lips are semiprotruded and appear to be puckering.

Tongue Retraction. Strong pulling back of the tongue body to the oral-pharyngeal area for atypical holding/stability; the tongue appears thick in contour; reinforces atypical head and neck hyperextension.

Tongue Retraction with Anterior Tongue Elevation. Stabilization of the tongue back in the oral cavity with the anterior portion of the tongue elevated, pushing up against the alveolar ridge or hard palate; the back of the tongue is lowered due to the anterior tongue elevation; occurs as a compensation for excessive tongue instability.

Tongue Thrusting. The strong forward pushing of the tongue, which is bunched and thick in appearance; generally occurs in an attempt to compensate for tongue retraction.

Tonic Biting. The strong closure of the jaw in response to tactile input presented on the biting surfaces of the gums or teeth; stronger jaw closure with increased atypical head, neck, and trunk extension occurs as attempts are made to remove the stimulation; the jaw is stuck in a closed position.

These atypical patterns of movement dramatically impact on the child's functional activities. He or she tries to overcome the original pattern through the production of other atypical movements that require the use of greater increases in postural tone and atypical movements. The child who has an original pattern of jaw thrusting with retraction, cheek/lip retraction, and tongue retraction may, with greater hypertonicity, strongly push his or her tongue forward, which results in tongue thrusting. This compensatory tongue thrusting may become so pronounced that it camouflages the child's original problems with tongue retraction.

A child with atheotsis will exhibit uncontrolled, ungraded fluctuations in body tone and movements, which also occur throughout the face and mouth, creating great instability in oral-motor activity. The child with hypertonicity may show tightness throughout the oral mechanism, greatly restricting his or her oral-motor function and future development. Problems in postural control and movement will make it difficult for the child to develop independent, coordinated oral movements for feeding and swallowing function as well as for sound production activities.

Atypical oral-motor activity creates major difficulties in feeding and swallowing. The child with severe hyperextension throughout his or her body may exhibit strong tongue retraction or tongue thrusting. Strong tongue retraction will interfere with the child's use of rhythmic forward-and-backward tongue movements for suckling or up-and-down tongue movements for sucking and will, therefore, inhibit the child's ability to handle liquids, pureed foods, and solids. Tongue movements for swallowing will be minimal, and material will flow down the throat with little control, which may result in choking. Tongue thrusting, as demonstrated by the children in Figure 9–4, will hinder the development of lip and jaw closure and will force food and liquids to be pushed out of the mouth. Habitual tongue thrusting during feeding and other activities may eventually lead to major deformities of the teeth and upper jaw.

Cheek/lip retraction interferes with the development of functional, active movements of the lips and cheeks, making it extremely difficult for the infant to drink from a bottle without biting on the nipple. The lips cannot close and actively remove food from the spoon, so food must be scraped off on the upper teeth. A child with cheek/lip retraction may have great difficulty drawing liquid into the mouth from a cup without biting on the cup rim to establish greater mouth

FIGURE 9–4
Tongue thrusting prevents active lip and jaw movements in spoon-feeding and solid food intake

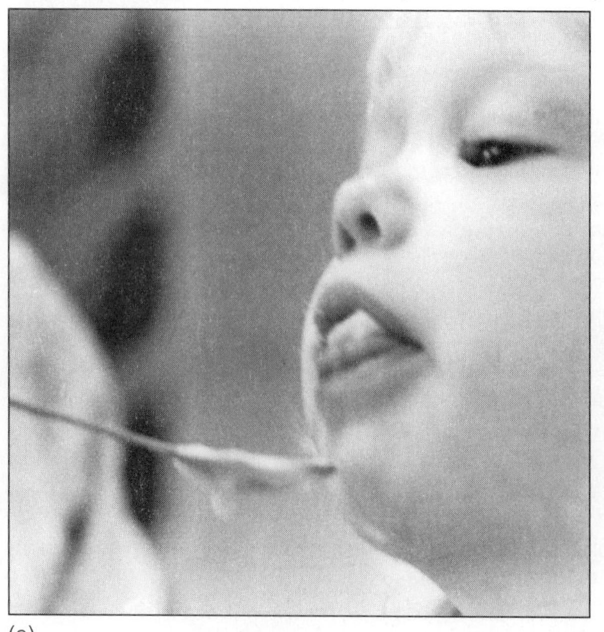
(a)

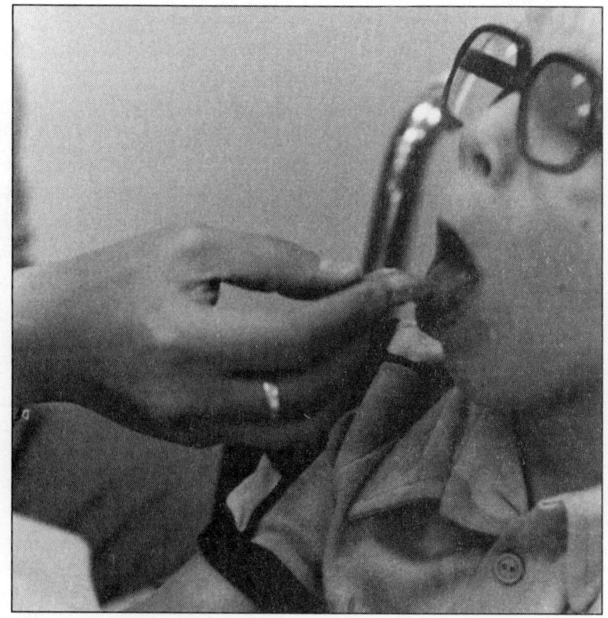
(b)

closure or by thrusting his or her tongue into the cup to limit the amount of liquid that can come into his or her mouth at one time for airway protection. Controlling pieces of solids during biting and chewing activities is extremely difficult with the existence of cheek/lip retraction (see Figure 9–5).

Strong jaw thrusting with protrusion as seen in Figure 9–6, jaw thrusting with retraction, or exaggerated jaw closure will greatly affect the development of graded jaw movement for biting and chewing. The child in Figure 9–6 with excessive jaw thrusting with protrusion will also have problems grading his jaw closure as the spoon enters his mouth, making active closure of the lips around the spoon impossible.

Strong exaggerated jaw closure with spoon-feeding or cup drinking will negatively impact the child's ability to move the tongue to control the food or liquid within the mouth and to move the material back for safe swallowing. Continual use of jaw thrusting with retraction, jaw thrusting with protrusion, or exaggerated jaw closure may lead to deformities of the jaw and significant problems at the temporomandibular joints.

Children with strong patterns of asymmetry, or patterns of head and neck hyperextension with pushing back of the shoulders, rarely have the opportunity to enjoy oral sensory stimulation by bringing hands, feet, and toys to the mouth. Without oral sensory experiences, responses to any type of oral tactile stimulation will become more atypical. If the child with hypertonicity does not experience a variety of food textures over time, he or she will continue to exhibit a strong gag in response to any change in texture. Some extremely hypotonic infants and children have an absent or weak gag response, so that as objects or pieces of food are brought into the mouth, they may become lodged in the throat and obstruct the upper airway.

With limited oral sensory stimulation, a child may begin to respond to all oral tactile stimulation with greater head/neck extension, cheek/lip retraction, tongue retraction, and jaw thrusting. Habitual atypical oral-motor responses to oral tactile stimulation will strongly interfere with the child's overall development of oral-motor function. Therefore, even children who are prevented from being oral feeders should receive oral tactile sensory stimulation to limit their development of atypical oral-motor responses to other necessary daily oral activities such as toothbrushing.

FIGURE 9–5
Active lip closure is impossible when cheek/lip retraction exists

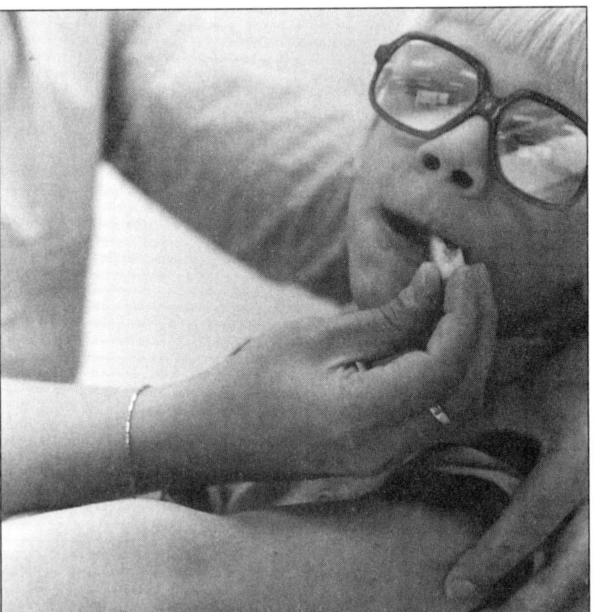

FIGURE 9–6
Jaw thrusting with head and neck extension may occur when solids are presented

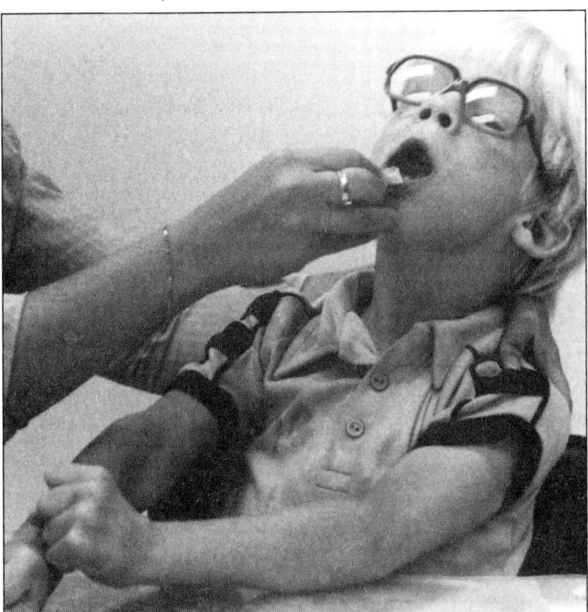

Atypical Respiratory Function

Atypical postural control and movements have a direct impact on respiratory function. Children with hypotonicity or significant inactivity of the trunk musculature will often exhibit a belly-breathing pattern in which belly expansion is limited and the sternum (breastbone) is retracted or pulled inward toward the thoracic spine during inhalation. Children with strong hyperextension of the head and neck often exhibit elevation and internal rotation of the shoulder girdle and significant shortening of the musculature between the sternum and pelvis, which creates flattening of the anterior chest wall, rib cage, and abdominal area. If these patterns are allowed to persist, excessive flaring of the lower ribs and flattening of the upper rib cage will result, which will greatly reduce the amount of air a child can inhale, so that breathing will be very shallow.

When respiratory function is limited due to skeletal alignment or musculature activity problems, the child's overall respiratory function will be restricted and his or her coordination of respiration with oral and pharyngeal activities will be limited. During feeding and swallowing activities, this can lead to aspiration of food, liquid, or saliva, compromising the safety of oral feeding. During sound production activities, this can result in the child's inability to initiate phonation, sustain vocal production, or produce a variety of different sounds on one inhalation-exhalation cycle. Wet or gurgly respirations or sound productions may be heard, reflecting a problem with the coordination of respiration with saliva management and laryngeal activity. Whenever there is incoordination of respiration with oral and pharyngeal activity, the child is at greater risk for problems in the areas of feeding and swallowing.

The Comprehensive Evaluation Process

A comprehensive evaluation of a child's oral-motor, feeding/swallowing, and respiratory coordination function should be conducted by a professional who has extensive knowledge of typical and atypical development in these functional areas and an understanding of the function of other body systems (e.g., gastrointestinal, pulmonary, cardiac) that may be impacting upon the child's ability to function in these areas. A qualified pediatric speech/language pathologist generally conducts these evaluations. An occupational therapist with extensive pediatric oral-motor and feeding experience may also be involved in the evaluation process.

Many children with diagnosed or suspected physical or multiple disabilities with feeding and swallowing problems entering regular school programming have had evaluations conducted during their birth-to-3 or early childhood education programs. These children generally will not require a new complete assessment of their feeding and swallowing function by school professionals. However, all aspects of a child's mealtime feeding—oral sensory needs, nutritional needs, medication needs, and positioning/handling needs—will need to be reviewed and discussed with family members and other treatment service providers to assure appropriate carryover of procedures that have presently been found successful for mealtime, snack time, and toothbrushing activities into school programming.

If a teacher or caregiver suspects that a child is having a previously unobserved problem impacting on oral-motor, feeding/swallowing, and respiratory function, the child should be referred for a clinical evaluation. A clinical evaluation will include the gathering of case history (e.g., medical, feeding, pulmonary, gastrointestinal) information and the observation of the child during a variety of activities, including eating and drinking activities as managed by the child's parent or caregiver (Alper & Manno, 1996; Arvedson, 2002; Arvedson & Lefton-Greif, 1998; Lefton-Greif, 1994; McCurtin, 1997; Morris & Klein, 2000; Pinder & Faherty, 1999; Wolf & Glass, 1992). The primary areas of investigation during clinical observations and some key questions to be asked in each of these areas are:

Postural Control and Movement

1. What is the child's basic postural activity at rest?
2. Are there changes in the child's postural activity with volitional movement or with attempts at communication or speech?
3. What is the child's head control and trunk activity like in different positions and with movement?
4. Does the child's head or trunk control change during activities such as feeding, speech, communication, and volitional movement?
5. How do movements of the head or trunk affect movements of the lips, jaw, tongue, and cheeks?
6. Does asymmetry affect movements of the lips, jaw, tongue, and cheeks?

Responses to Sensory Stimulation

1. Can the child tolerate loud noises?
2. How does the child respond to different visual stimuli?
3. Is there a difference in postural activities when the child is moved slowly or rapidly?
4. Does the child adapt easily to new tastes? new smells?
5. With social and emotional stimulation does the child react with strong changes in postural activity?
6. What is the child's response to tactile stimulation of the trunk, legs, arms, hands, and feet? Is there a difference between responses to a firm touch and those to a light touch?
7. What is the child's response to touch on the forehead, cheeks, and lips? Is there a difference between responses to a firm touch and those to a light touch?
8. What is the child's response to touch on the teeth, gums, tongue, and hard palate?

Respiratory Function

1. What is the breathing pattern at rest? (Describe.)
2. How does the breathing pattern change with general movement? with upper extremity movements? with sound production? with feeding and swallowing activities?
3. Does breathing get noisier or sound wet/gurgly during feeding and swallowing activities? general movement?
4. Does the child initiate sound production easily?
5. Are sounds loud or soft?

Feeding Position(s)

1. What position(s) is the child usually fed in for liquid intake? for spoon-feeding or solids?
2. Do changes in the child's postural control and movement occur during feeding?
3. Does the feeder make adaptations in the child's position during feeding?
4. Does the feeder make adaptations in his or her position during feeding in response to changes in the child's position?

Bottle Drinking/Breastfeeding/ Other Methods of Liquid Intake

1. Does the child easily initiate sucking or suckling from the bottle or breast?
2. What type of nipple is used on the bottle, and has the hole been enlarged by the feeder? Has formula been thickened?
3. Is the child tube-fed? If so, what kind and is it total or supplemental?
4. Does the child suck or suckle from the cup? Use a spouted cup or open-rimmed cup?
5. Are there atypical oral movements evident during bottle drinking or cup drinking? (Describe.)
6. Does the child choke, cough, gag, or spit up liquids?
7. Is head and neck extension observed during drinking?
8. Can the child coordinate sucking, swallowing, and breathing?

Spoon-Feeding of Pureed/Soft Mechanical Foods (Cohesive Textured, Soft Solid Food)

1. What types of foods does the child eat by spoon?
2. Does the child use suckling or sucking movements to eat foods presented by spoon?
3. Can the child use the upper lip to remove food from the spoon?
4. Are there atypical oral movements evident during spoon-feeding? (Describe.)
5. Does the child choke, cough, gag, or spit up foods?
6. Does the child show tongue protrusion or tongue thrusting with swallowing?
7. Does the child lose large amounts of food from the mouth during eating?

Biting and Chewing of Solids

1. What type(s) of solids does the child have experience with?
2. Does the child use a suck, suckle, or phasic bite-release pattern to bite?
3. Is there a sustained, controlled bite through soft and hard solids?
4. Does the child suck or suckle instead of chewing?
5. Does the child use an early munching pattern?
6. Is there tongue lateralization when food is on the side of the mouth?
7. Can the child transfer food from the center of the mouth to the side or from side to side with the tongue?

8. Are there atypical oral movements evident during biting? chewing of soft solids? chewing of hard solids?
9. Does the child gag, choke, cough, or spit up when eating solids?

Drooling

1. Does the child drool in different positions?
2. Does the child drool when actively involved in gross-motor or fine-motor activities?
3. Is the child cutting teeth?
4. Does the child show any awareness of the saliva?

Oral-Motor Function During Sound/Speech Production

1. Does the child use sounds to communicate?
2. When are sounds produced by the child?
3. Are atypical oral movements evident during sound production activities? (Describe.)
4. Is sound production wet or gurgly in quality?
5. Is sound production tense, hoarse, nasal, or breathy?

Use of Communication

1. Does the child try to communicate?
2. Does the child use any atypical body movements to communicate?
3. How does the child communicate with the feeder during mealtime activities?
4. Does the child use facial expressions to communicate?
5. Does the child use eyes, arms, or hands for communication?
6. Does the child have an augmentative communication system?

Additional pertinent case history information should be obtained from the child's parents and caregivers, as it is necessary to determine whether or not the child's problems in feeding and swallowing are due to oral-motor dysfunction, pharyngeal sensory or motility problems, gastrointestinal issues, respiratory/airway issues, or other underlying physical or neurological problems. Decreased oral sensory awareness, pharyngeal sensory and motility problems, and reduced appetite may be the result of medications the child is receiving, suggesting the need to obtain a thorough record of the medications a child is presently receiving.

If the child has a history of frequent respiratory illness and pneumonia, an increased wet, gurgly quality to respiration and sound production during feeding, or consistent coughing or sputtering during feeding, aspiration may exist. More definitive analysis of the child's oral and pharyngeal function will be required through instrumental examination. In pediatrics the two most often used procedures are the videofluoroscopic study of swallowing (i.e., oral-pharyngeal motility study; modified barium swallow) (Arvedson & Lefton-Greif, 1998; Benson & Lefton-Greif, 1994) and the fiberoptic endoscopic evaluation of swallowing (FEES) (Willging, Miller, Link, & Rudolph, 2001).

If the child has a history of consistent spitting up or vomiting during or after feeding; fussiness about the types of foods he or she will eat, which does not appear to be related to oral sensory issues; poor weight gain; increased irritability after a certain amount of food intake on a fairly consistent basis; chronic constipation; or periods of suckling/sucking activity occurring significantly after mealtime, problems with gastrointestinal system function may exist. The child's pediatrician or a pediatric gastroenterologist must be contacted by the evaluator so that he or she can determine if tests that more discretely examine the function of the upper and/or lower gastrointestinal tracts are required (Mascarenhas & Dadhania, 1995; Putnam, 1997; Rossi, 1993; Tuchman, 1994).

The evaluator must contact the child's primary physician if any questions arise based upon medical, feeding, and respiratory history information and clinical observations that suggest the need for additional specialized medical evaluations or additional instrumental evaluations of the feeding and swallowing processes. Problems in feeding and swallowing can result from many different causes that may have no relationship to the child's oral-motor function. In order to determine the best intervention for a specific child, it is necessary to investigate all possible areas that may be creating the feeding and swallowing problems. A comprehensive evaluation points out areas in need of further investigation, recommends whether treatment is required, and may provide recommendations regarding mealtime feeding strategies.

FEEDING AND SWALLOWING INTERVENTION

An intervention program that focuses on the areas of feeding and swallowing must develop goals and strategies for direct treatment as well as goals and strategies for carryover activities such as mealtime feeding, snack time feeding, and toothbrushing. Such a program will have to be developed and periodically modified based upon information obtained during the comprehensive clinical evaluation, instrumental evaluations of the feeding and swallowing processes, and any additional medical, behavioral, and educational evaluations.

Although a qualified pediatric speech/language pathologist may have conducted the clinical evaluation, all members of a child's team at school, at home, and in the community must be involved in setting up and implementing aspects of a child's feeding and swallowing intervention program. Since feeding and swallowing function is part of and has such direct influences on the child's overall nutritional status, growth, and medical/health status, it is most appropriately discussed as an aspect of medical speech/language pathology, especially in terms of the goals and strategies established for individual direct treatment. Carryover activities, which are part of the child's daily routine, must be discussed in terms of the appropriate strategies to be used consistently in preparation for or during mealtime, snack time, and toothbrushing activities. Dependent upon an individual child's school programming, he or she may need to participate in each of these carryover activities at least once each school day.

Carryover Activities

Mealtime feeding has a predetermined primary goal of adequate nutritional intake provided in as safe a manner as possible. Any caregiver who feeds at breakfast, lunch, or dinner knows that his or her job is to get in as much food and liquid as possible to meet the child's nutritional needs. It is not the time for implementing new feeding strategies that have never been used before. It is not the time for the use of strategies that upset the child to such an extent that nutritional intake is significantly compromised. New strategies (e.g., procedures, textures, tastes, and equipment) must be initiated outside of the mealtime feeding situation and can be integrated into mealtime as long as they do not negatively impact the child's overall nutritional intake and medical/health status. Therefore, direct treatment that focuses on introducing, stimulating, and assisting in the integration of new or intermittently produced oral-motor, feeding/swallowing, and respiratory coordination components and activities is not appropriate at mealtime.

Snack time can more easily be used to begin incorporating some newer strategies into an actual feeding situation without having to be overly concerned about amounts of intake. It can also be more appropriately used as a time to focus on the social aspects of eating or to begin some self-feeding activities for a child when it is not essential that an adequate amount of food be eaten.

Toothbrushing is important to include in a child's daily routine because of the need to maintain good oral hygiene and to make sure that no residual food remains in the child's mouth after eating. Any food left in the mouth could eventually lead to dental and gum problems or choking and coughing as the remaining food dislodges and falls into the oropharyngeal or laryngeal areas. Through toothbrushing, the child can also be provided with important oral sensory stimulation to enhance the child's readiness for greater oral-motor activity for feeding and swallowing as well as for sound/speech production.

Positioning for Mealtime Feeding

Finding the most appropriate ways of positioning a child for mealtime feeding is often the first and the most difficult aspect of mealtime feeding carryover programming. Appropriate positioning for feeding must take into account the individual child's age, size, and present status in terms of postural activity and alignment; head, neck, and trunk control; typical and atypical general and oral movement activities; pharyngeal sensory and motor function; respiratory function, gastrointestinal function, and overall sensorimotor processing. Establishing positions that encourage body symmetry, trunk elongation, neck elongation, and neutral head flexion generally provides a foundation of proper body alignment for better oral-motor function for feeding and swallowing. However, what happens to the child with feeding and swallowing problems who has more significant pharyngeal sensory and motility issues for whom neck elongation and neutral head flexion may actually increase his or her risk of aspiration rather than reduce it? A position requiring neck elongation and neutral head flexion may not be appropriate for this child.

There is no one proper feeding position for all children with feeding and swallowing problems. Some children need to have a small amount of head/neck extension, which helps to protect the upper pharyngeal airway when taking in liquids and some thin pureed foods. Many children with primary oral-motor problems place themselves at greater risk for aspiration when they use head/neck hyperextension and shoulder girdle elevation in order to stabilize their upper body during feeding. Some children use head/neck extension and tongue protrusion during feeding due to obstructions in the upper airway, such as enlarged adenoids and tonsils. When children consistently resist certain changes in position, even into positions that we expect to be helpful for them during mealtime feeding, it is essential to further investigate possible physical reasons for this inability to handle the change in position and not just treat it as a behavioral issue.

Note that a single position will not provide the variety of stimulation needed by the child with neuromotor involvement. Establishing proper body alignment with more static positioning for a carryover activity (such as mealtime feeding) will provide a foundation for better oral movements for that activity, but will not necessarily be generalized to other functional activities for which the child may need to use his or her oral mechanism. Direct treatment, which encourages active oral-motor and respiratory coordination through dynamic handling with the stimulation of active antigravity movements by the child, is essential for the development of more generalized, integrated functional movements.

All people who feed the child must have an understanding of the child's movement patterns and responses to certain sensory stimulation so they can respond to the changes or differences that may occur from day to day or hour to hour. If a child has been receiving treatment services focusing on the feeding, swallowing, and respiratory areas prior to entering regular school programming, it will be essential to observe the parent or caregiver feeding the child a meal to see what strategies have already been found to be most successful, especially in terms of body alignment or positioning and food presentation. The following are suggestions for positioning during feeding:

1. The infant or young child with severe neuromotor involvement can be positioned in a way that provides greater external body stability, fosters symmetry, and increases the potential for eye contact. The caregiver sits at a table placed against a stable surface such as a wall. A wedge that slopes downward toward the feeder is placed so that it rests partly on the table and partly in the feeder's lap. The child is placed on the wedge facing the feeder so that his or her legs can be positioned around the feeder's body, providing abduction (a movement of the extremities away from the center of the body) and external rotation (see Figure 9–7).

To assist the child in maintaining better head and trunk alignment, neck elongation, and neutral head flexion, the feeder can use the lateral portion of the hand or the forearm to exert slight downward pressure on the child's breastbone. Initially, it may be necessary to keep the child in a more reclined position during feeding, although symmetrical body alignment should still be maintained. As the child becomes better able to

FIGURE 9–7
The child is positioned on a wedge to face the feeder

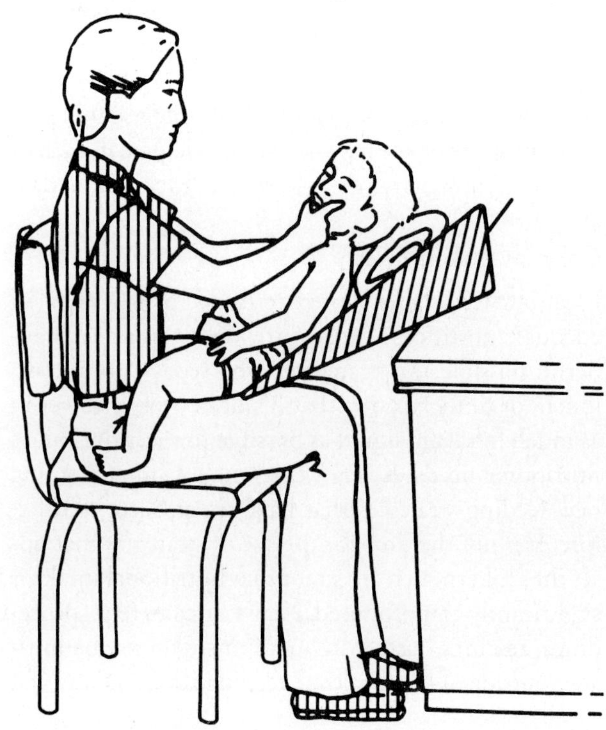

maintain a more upright posture, the incline of the wedge can be changed, with the feeder sitting closer to the table so that the wedge is at a steeper angle.

2. As shown in Figure 9–8, the infant or young child can also be positioned for feeding in an infant seat, car seat, or feeder seat, which allows for the adjustment of the child's angle of recline. A towel roll may be placed under the child's thighs to facilitate more stable hip flexion, counteract extension, and encourage better body alignment. If the seat is too large for the child, so that the child tends to fall to the side, towel rolls can be placed on each side to provide more stable trunk support. The feeder should sit in front of the child to foster symmetry and better eye contact. Special care should be taken when placing a small pillow or towel roll behind the head, because pressure to the back of the head will often stimulate extensor thrusting. As the infant or young child becomes more capable of maintaining an upright position, the seat should be adjusted accordingly to facilitate continued improvement.

Some older children are at considerably less risk for aspiration during mealtime when fed at a slight recline rather than upright at 90 degrees. In this slight recline, they can be positioned with neutral head flexion, neck elongation, and symmetry throughout the trunk to allow for less stressful feeding and swallowing. There are tilt-in-space wheelchairs that have adjustments allowing the whole chair to be tilted back at the angle needed by the child to be safe during mealtime. Many children and adolescents with significant neuromotor involvement need to have the ability to be tilted back slightly for eating and drinking activities, but not for all other functional activities.

FIGURE 9–8
The child is positioned in a car seat for feeding

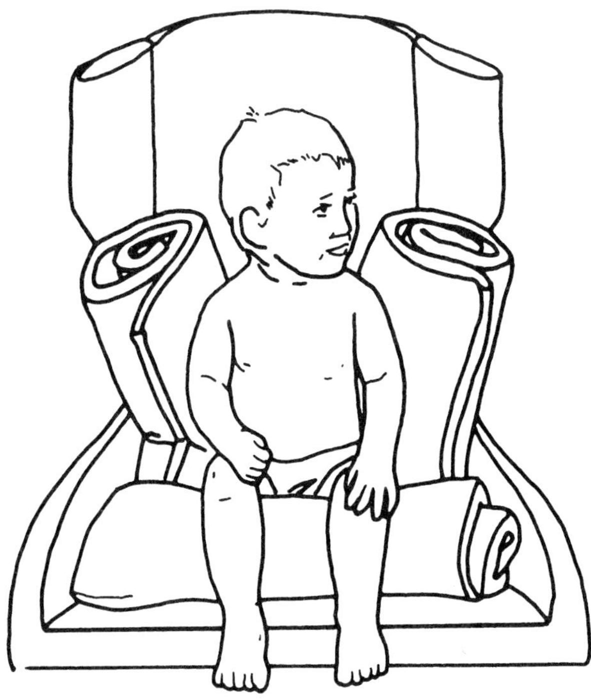

3. As the baby begins to develop more active head and trunk control for better upright positioning, feeding may be accomplished with the child positioned in an adapted highchair. Reduce possible extension and stimulate better head and trunk alignment by providing increased hip flexion with appropriate abduction through the use of a foam wedge or a rolled towel. The wedge is placed in the seat of the chair so that the thicker part of the wedge is toward the child's knees. The rolled towel is placed under the child's thighs. The size of the wedge or rolled towel depends on the size of the child and the amount of hip flexion needed to prevent extension. If the child requires assistance for maintaining stable hips with more-neutral hip flexion, a special insert can be purchased to help maintain more stable, abducted hips, or two neckties can be used to maintain this position (see Figure 9–9). Each tie is placed around the upper part of the child's legs and is tied around the back of the highchair. The ties should be fastened in a bow to allow for easy release. If the child tends to lean to one side, so that midline orientation is difficult, small towel rolls can be placed between the sides of the child's body and the highchair to provide more support for symmetry and trunk control.

The tray of the highchair should be at the proper height to encourage more active stability of the arms, shoulders, and trunk. This may initially require the adjustment of the tray to "nipple height" if the child is unable to actively use forearm weight-bearing on a tray. A stable footplate that can be attached to the highchair and provides more stability for the legs and feet may also be needed (see Figure 9–9).

4. Similar modifications to those discussed for positioning in the highchair should be considered for the school-age child or adolescent with neuromotor involvement who eats while sitting in a wheelchair.

FIGURE 9–9
Positioning a child in a highchair using ties, towel rolls, and a tray

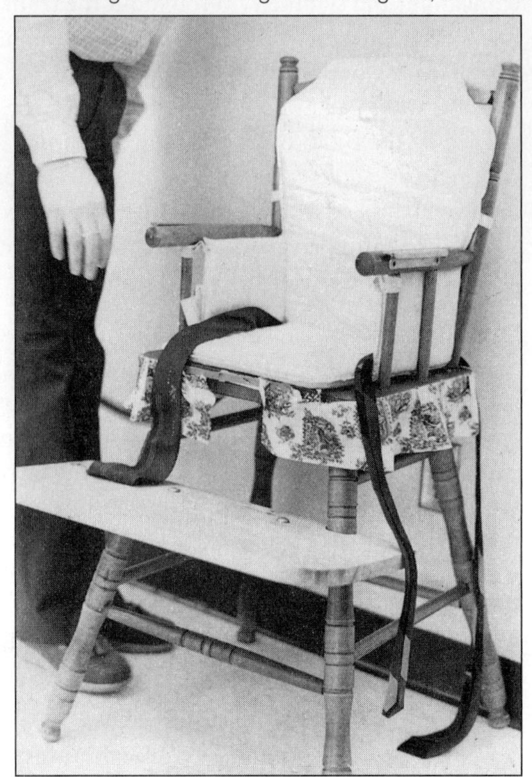

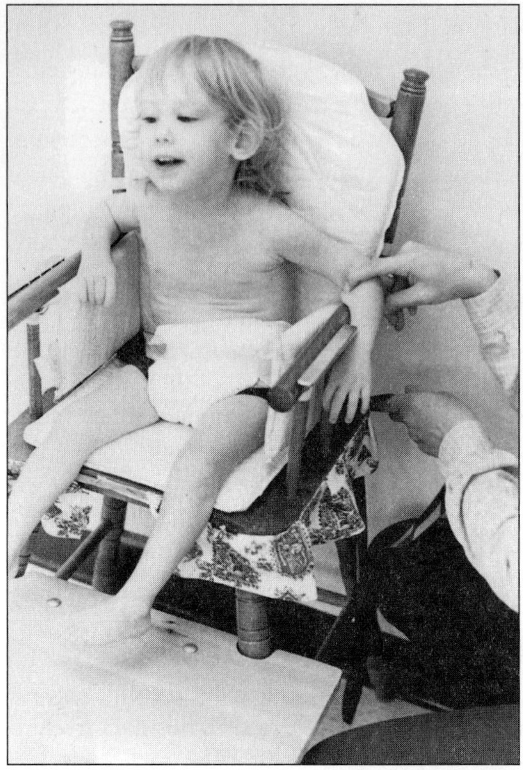

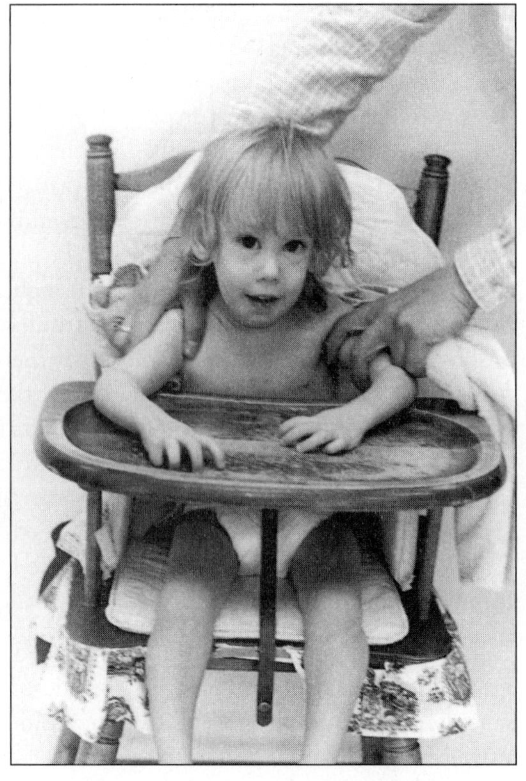

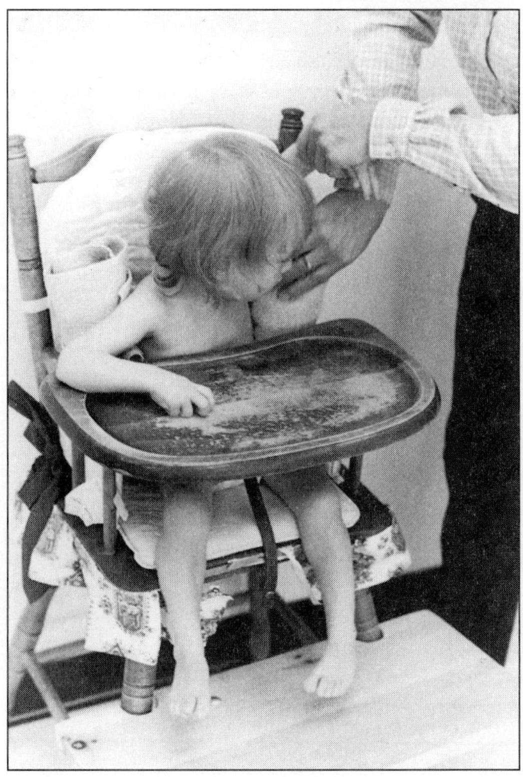

FIGURE 9–10
Positioning a school-age child in a wheelchair

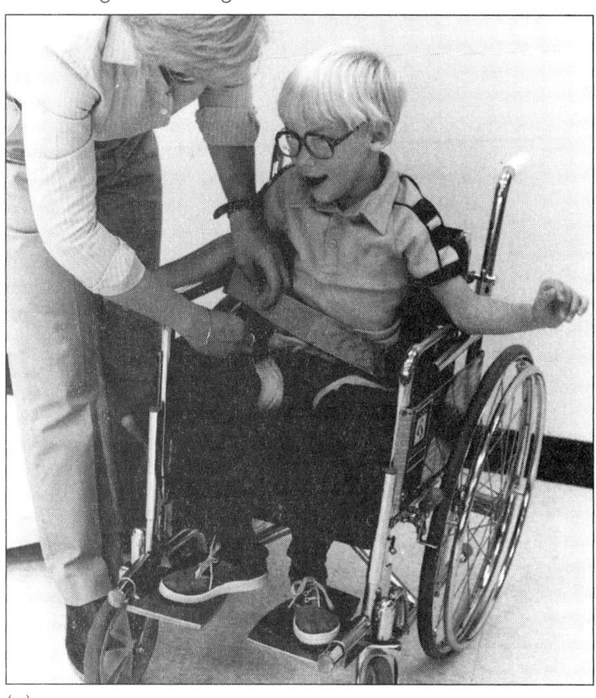
(a)

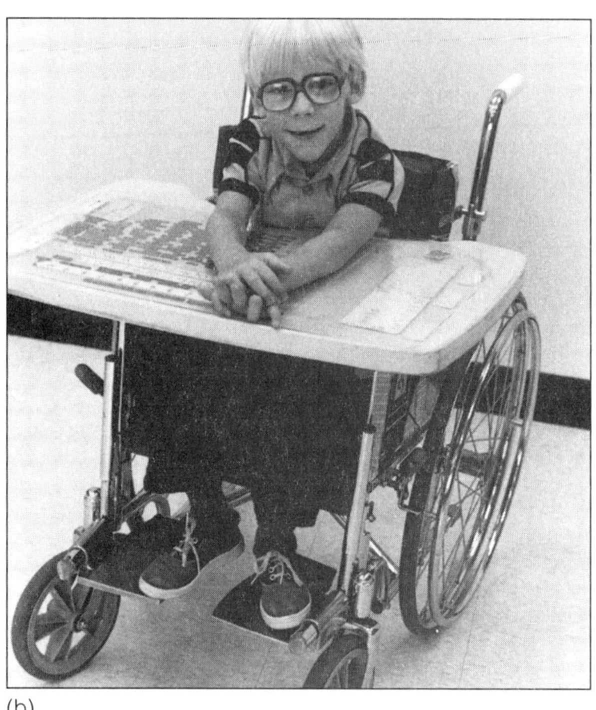
(b)

Establishing proper body alignment with neck elongation and neutral head flexion as a foundation for better oral-motor activity during feeding is essential no matter what the age of the individual with neuromotor involvement (see Figure 9–10). If there are pharyngeal, respiratory, or gastrointestinal problems causing difficulties at mealtime, this proper body alignment may not be easily tolerated and may not help to improve feeding and swallowing. Of course, fixed physical deformity in an older child may restrict the caregiver's ability to obtain proper body alignment and, therefore, will limit the modifications that can be expected in oral-motor activity for feeding. Remember that many wheelchair adaptations made specifically for feeding may be unnecessary for the child at other times. These adaptations should, therefore, be easy to remove when the child is sitting in the wheelchair for other activities.

5. Positioning the child for feeding on a prone board, in a prone stander, or in a standing frame may stimulate active head and trunk control for more effective oral movements (see Figure 9–11). The equipment should be brought up to a table or have a tray attached;

FIGURE 9–11
Use of a prone board for feeding

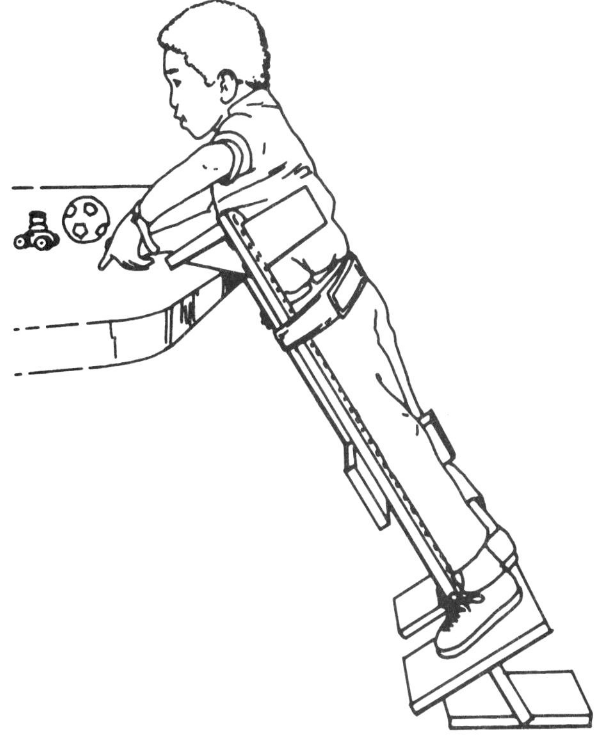

this encourages the child to bring his or her arms forward for shoulder and arm stability. Often the child can come closer to controlling trunk activity and stability if he or she is freer to use more-typical movements of the arms and hands to touch the food and thus provide himself or herself with new and finer (more graded) levels of tactile stimulation during the feeding process. Other feeding positions and more extensive descriptions of some of the positions just discussed can be found in Alexander (1987, 1993); Finnie (1997); Morris and Klein (2000), Mueller, (1997); Snyder, Breath, and DeMauro (1999); and Woods (1995).

Selection of Feeding Utensils

An inappropriate feeding utensil can foster the use of atypical motor patterns. If a child is drinking from a bottle, try a variety of nipples to see whether a different shape or texture improves the ability to suck. Examine the flow of liquids, since a nipple that allows liquids to flow out too rapidly may only stimulate greater tongue retraction, tongue thrusting, or exaggerated jaw closure. An angled bottle may help to reduce air intake and effort during bottle drinking. Remember that some older children continue to be fed by bottle because it is the safest way for the child to receive liquids to prevent dehydration and is the only way the child can continue oral feeding at a level for adequate nutritional intake.

A spoon of the proper size and shape will fit within the child's mouth without touching the side gums or teeth, since such touching may stimulate a tonic bite. Do not let the child's age dictate the size of spoon to be used, but rather the size and shape of the jaw. Use a spoon with a very shallow bowl so that minimal lip movement is needed. Never put brittle plastic spoons in the mouth of a child who has a strong bite. A shallow, soft-bowled spoon often works nicely for children who have significant malocclusions or who are very sensitive to oral sensory input. Shallow, narrow metal spoons are often better to use than plastic-coated spoons, because children often bite harder and longer into the flexible plastic coating.

If the child is not ready for drinking from an open cup, a soft-spouted cup may provide the child with the help he or she needs in controlling the amount and flow of the liquid while allowing him or her to use greater oral activity during the drinking process. A soft plastic cutout cup is often a good first cup, as the feeder can assist in guiding and grading the flow of the liquid as the child uses more appropriate lip closure on the cup rim. The cutout allows the cup, rather than the child's head, to be tipped back, reducing the risk of head/neck hyperextension leading to aspiration.

Choosing Appropriate Foods and Liquids

The sensory aspects of the foods and liquids given to a child at mealtime may affect his or her ability to eat or drink them successfully and safely. Certain children may handle different textures and consistencies of foods and liquids (see Figure 9–2) more easily with less risk of aspiration. Children with pharyngeal motility problems generally have more difficulty with thicker foods and liquids that require greater strength of the musculature moving material through the pharynx and esophagus to the stomach. Children with significant oral sensory problems often respond with greater oral activity when crunchier foods are presented.

Choosing a certain taste, smell, or temperature of food often heightens a child's awareness of the food or liquid in the mouth, stimulating more active oral and pharyngeal movements for eating, drinking, and swallowing. There are some children who can drink any consistency of liquid safely as long as the liquid is cold. Some children with very inactive oral areas show significantly greater lip and tongue activity when spicy or sour flavors, rather than sweet flavors, are presented by spoon. The smell of a particular food or liquid may also be a defining characteristic by which a child chooses the food or liquid he or she will eat or drink, resulting in everything the child eats or drinks having the same general smell.

It will be important to analyze the foods and liquids a child is presently eating in regard to all sensory factors involved and to use that information to determine what sensory information the child uses to determine which foods and liquids he or she will or can eat or drink more effectively. Better analysis of the sensory factors involved in food and liquid selection plays a significant role in stimulating more active oral and pharyngeal movements during mealtime and increasing a child's nutritional intake at a meal.

Acid-based thin liquids such as orange juice may be difficult for a child to handle, not only because of their thinness, but also because the acid increases saliva production, which is already a major difficulty for many children. Milk increases the amount of mucus in the child's system and thus is difficult to drink without increased congestion, coughing, or choking. The intake of milk could be decreased while that of solid milk products such as cheese could be increased. It may be helpful to give only small amounts of milk at a time by cup throughout a meal to decrease mucus or saliva production.

Many children find thin pureed foods more difficult to control orally and obtain more sensory cues when these foods are thickened slightly. Special care must be taken not to create lumps when using materials such as graham cracker crumbs for thickening, since this will result in a mixed or combination texture that is more difficult for the child to handle. When thickening foods or liquids, it is important to make sure that there is a uniform consistency that allows the child to eat or drink the material more effectively and with less risk of aspiration. Often it is better to grind up table foods than to try to thicken thin pureed foods when trying to create the most uniform texture.

Choosing solid foods may be difficult. Carefully analyze the type of solid the child is now taking into his or her mouth. Do not expect the child to be able to handle all types of solids simply because he or she has shown some ability for chewing. Quick-dissolving solids such as crackers are more easily broken up by early chewing movements and, because they mix with saliva, are more easily swallowed. Solids such as soft chicken stick together better and can be more easily chewed and swallowed. Although hard solids such as teething crackers and bread sticks may be difficult for the child if broken apart into many large pieces, scraping these hard solids on the side gums or teeth will allow for a greater mixing with saliva so that the child can handle them more effectively. Children with lower sensory awareness and reduced activity often do better with solids that provide more-distinctive tactile information, such as harder solids and cereals when they are scraped on the side gums or teeth or are presented in smaller pieces, stimulating more active movements for chewing. Further suggestions concerning modifying foods and liquids are discussed by Arvedson and Lefton-Greif (1998); Kovar (1997); Morris and Klein (2000); and Murphy and Caretto (1999).

Preparation of the Oral Mechanism

Alexander (1987), Morris and Klein (2000), Mueller (1972), and Murphy and Caretto (1999) discuss the importance of activities that help to modify the child's response to oral tactile stimulation. Overresponsiveness or underresponsiveness to oral tactile sensory input has a negative effect on the child's development of more coordinated and refined oral movements. Having limited opportunities to experience oral sensory exploration activities as a baby results in greater sensitivity to oral stimulation in children with neuromotor involvement.

An infant or child with oral and facial overresponsiveness (i.e., hypersensitivity) will first need to tolerate tactile stimulation in body areas away from the mouth before he or she can be expected to tolerate tactile stimulation on the face or within the oral cavity. New sensory stimulation can be presented through movement to music and other games typically played with a baby. Firm rubbing or stroking of the child's trunk, shoulders, neck, and face with a washcloth, the baby's own hand, or squeeze toys can be incorporated into play for tactile stimulation. The caregiver can gradually bring this tactile stimulation closer and closer to the mouth.

As the child learns to accept tactile stimulation on the cheeks, forehead, and lips, stimulation of the oral cavity can be introduced. Note that even with greater acceptance of stimulation on the outside of the mouth, stimulation within the oral cavity may be extremely upsetting to the child. Therefore, touching, stroking, or rubbing in the mouth must be done with firm pressure through a slowly graded process. Only in this way will the child begin to tolerate the stimulation and learn to respond to it with more-typical oral movements.

Oral tactile stimulation to the cheeks/lips, teeth/gums, hard palate, and tongue can be provided in various ways in order to maximize the child's ability to accept the stimulation and to use it to produce greater active oral-motor function. Some children may only be able to tolerate their own fingers in their mouth, while others can handle the caregiver's presentation of stimulation using an infant gum massager, a massage toothbrush, a soft, small, child's toothbrush, or an automatic toothbrush. Some children respond best if oral tactile/pressure input is presented with changes in temperature in conjunction with vibratory input or with distinctive flavors. Oral exploration of toys and feeding tasks are functional activities that help the child to integrate new functional oral activities with greater oral sensory awareness.

Two important ways of providing typical oral stimulation include wiping the child's mouth and during

FIGURE 9–12
Cleaning the face

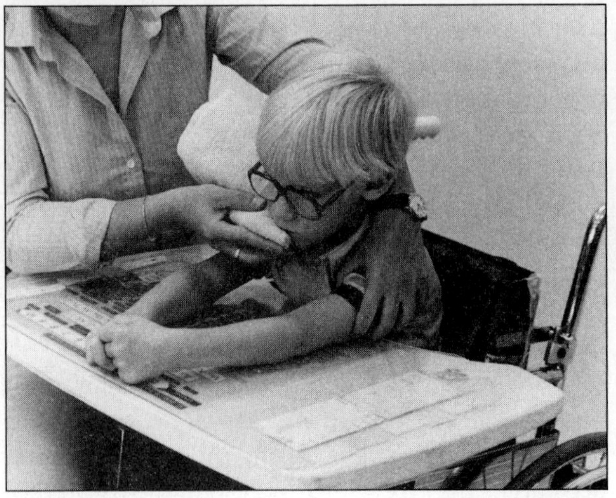

toothbrushing. When wiping a child's mouth, use a lukewarm, soft, damp cloth. Use firm, slow pressure to dab or pat areas around the face (see Figure 9–12). Proper positioning must also be maintained during this process. As soon as a child starts to develop teeth, toothbrushing should be introduced. A soft, small toothbrush can be used to provide firm and well-graded tactile stimulation to the hard palate, gums, teeth, and tongue. This early and consistent oral stimulation can help the child learn to tolerate touch in the mouth and can reduce or eliminate tonic biting.

Mueller (1972) discusses a procedure for older children called oral digital stimulation, which involves a systematic, graded use of oral stimulation that helps to coordinate swallowing movements and to decrease oral hypersensitivity. Remember that the typically developing baby learns to tolerate tactile stimulation in the mouth through movement, bringing fingers to the mouth, bringing toys to the mouth, and feeding. When providing services to the infant or young child with neuromotor involvement, keep the typical developmental process in mind.

Direct Help for the Jaw, Lips, and Tongue

If changes in postural control and alignment, feeding utensils, and the sensory aspects of food and liquids do not elicit desired improvements toward active, controlled oral movements, direct assistance, which is called **oral control,** can be provided. The caregiver, therapist, or teacher can use oral control to stimulate lip closure, coordinate swallowing, and influence graded jaw movement while reducing the influence of tongue and jaw thrusting. The use of oral control should be discussed by the team, and it should be determined as to whether it would be useful for an individual child before it is implemented for mealtime carryover activities.

Before using oral control, always establish proper body alignment through positioning with neutral head flexion, neck elongation, stable, depressed shoulder girdle, symmetrically elongated trunk, and good pelvic/hip alignment. Oral control is useful only if this body alignment can be established and is not effective if asymmetry is a significant problem. Oral control can be performed from two different positions:

1. If the child with neuromotor involvement has a tendency to push his or her head back during feeding or has extremely poor head control, side positioning for the feeder is preferable. The caregiver, therapist, or teacher should be seated next to and slightly behind the child.
   a. As shown in Figure 9–13, the caregiver should bring the arm of his or her nondominant side around the back of the child's shoulders and head, avoiding putting pressure on the child's head. The index finger should be placed on the child's chin just below the lower lip. This placement will stimulate lip closure.
   b. The middle finger should be placed under the child's chin just in back of the jawbone. The entire length of the side of the middle finger should lie flat under the chin. Pressure upward with the middle of the finger at the base of the tongue will help to inhibit tongue retraction and thrusting. The caregiver should not use oral control simply for the sake of opening and closing the child's jaw, but rather to provide assistance during feeding and sound productions that will stimulate more active, coordinated oral movements.
   c. The caregiver's thumb should not touch the child's facial area. This can be accomplished by lacing the thumb in the palm of the hand or by bringing the thumb out to the side, not touching the child's face and not entering the child's visual field. Many children respond negatively to touch

FIGURE 9–13
Oral control from the side

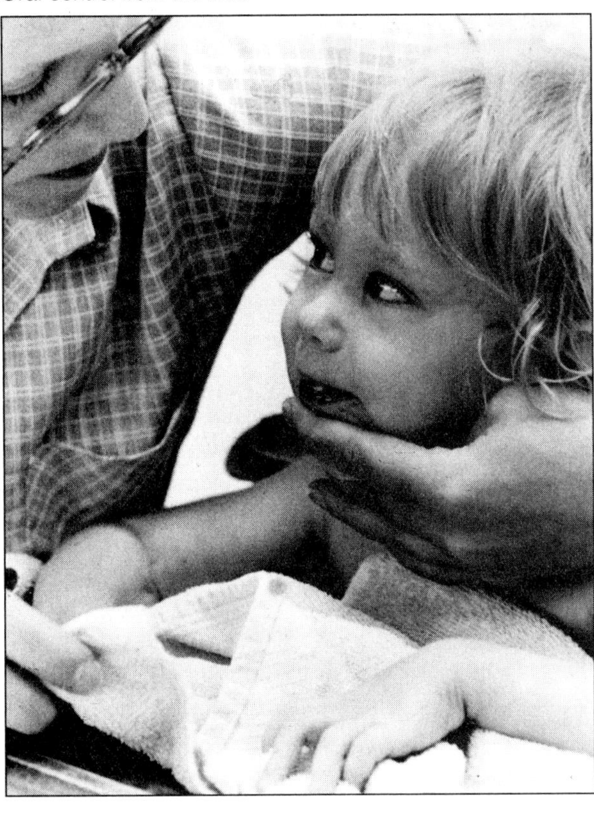

FIGURE 9–14
Oral control from the front

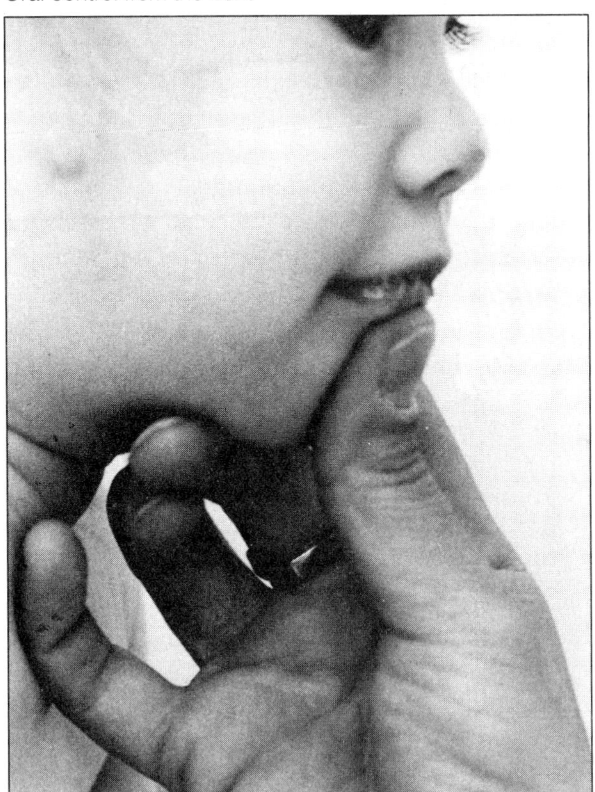

on the cheek or to the sight of the thumb when it is allowed to stay on the cheek.

2. If the child with neuromotor involvement has good head control or is being fed in a semireclined or upright position in a car seat or infant seat, the feeder will have to sit in front of the child and perform the oral control from the front (see Figure 9–14).
   a. The caregiver's thumb should be placed upright against the chin, underneath the lower lip, to stimulate lip closure.
   b. As with oral control from the side, the middle finger should be placed on its side, lengthwise under the chin, just behind the jawbone, to inhibit tongue thrusting and jaw thrusting.
   c. If the child is not overresponsive to tactile stimulation, the index finger can be placed on the cheek. If the child is overresponse to tactile input, the finger should not be allowed to touch the cheek and should be kept out of the child's visual field.
   d. The little finger, or pinky, can provide light pressure to the child's breastbone to help maintain better head and trunk alignment.

Oral control is only one method of stimulating more active jaw, lip, and tongue movements during feeding and swallowing activities. The goal, as with all intervention programming, is to help the child develop more active control of his or her own oral mechanism without outside assistance. Therefore, if oral control is used initially, it should eventually be reduced or eliminated so that the child is actively controlling his or her oral movements.

Oral control must never be used to keep the child's mouth totally closed with no active oral movements. The caregiver, therapist, and teacher should always bear in mind the movements that the typical baby must experience to achieve active oral coordination. The purpose of oral control is to reduce or eliminate the effects of atypical oral movements while at the same time fostering the use of more-coordinated oral activity.

Cup Drinking

The typically developing child can begin to receive liquid by cup as early as 6 months of age. This does not mean that at 6 months the child can take in liquids by cup in an efficient, coordinated, and controlled manner. However, it does mean that early experience with cup drinking will allow the child to learn to use his or her lips, jaw, tongue, and cheeks for development of this ability. As is true in typical development, the early introduction of cup drinking is extremely important for the child with neuromotor involvement, for it will help stimulate more active lip movements, internal jaw control, and coordinated tongue movements with minimal internal oral tactile stimulation required.

As children are introduced to different methods of receiving liquids, they are often initially presented with liquids by spouted cup as well as a few sips of water or juice by open-rimmed cup. Soft spouts help to control the flow, amount, and direction of liquid while allowing the child to use activity of the jaw, tongue, and cheeks/lips to pump the liquid into the mouth. Hard spouts are generally smaller than soft spouts and are more effectively used once the child can maintain a more graded, controlled oral mechanism to establish good intra-oral negative pressure to draw the liquid in with active holding of the lips around the spout. Of course, if a child with neuromotor involvement has significant problems handling oral tactile sensory input to the teeth/gums, a spouted cup will be more difficult for him or her, resulting in greater tongue retraction, exaggerated jaw closure, jaw thrusting with protrusion, or cheek/lip retraction. Therefore, presenting liquids by open-rimmed cup may be preferable.

As described in the section on feeding utensils, a flexible plastic cutout cup is often used initially, so that the cup, and not the child's head, is tipped back during the drinking process (see Figure 9–15). The flexibility of the cup will allow the caregiver to better direct the liquid flow. The cup rim should be placed between the child's lips, resting, but not pressing down, on the lower lip. Be careful to keep the cup rim from contacting the teeth, which might stimulate a tonic bite or jaw thrusting. If too much pressure is applied to the lower lip, the chances of stimulating good active lip closure are reduced.

FIGURE 9–15
Cup drinking with graded lip movements and graded liquid presentation

(a)

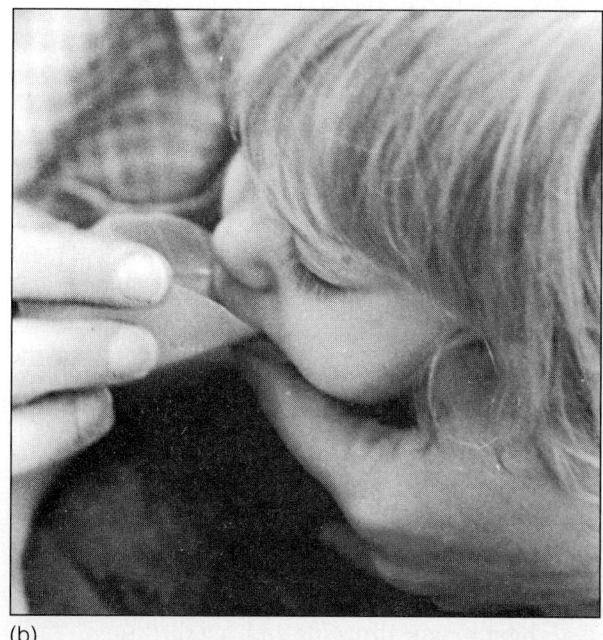

(b)

The caregiver should tilt the cup slightly toward the child so that the liquid comes in contact with the lips. Liquid should not be poured into the child's mouth, but rather should be brought to the lips to encourage the child to move his or her lips to draw the liquid in.

If the child appears to be having trouble controlling the liquid, the caregiver can lessen the tilt of the cup, which will stop the flow and give the child the opportunity to handle the liquid that is already in the mouth. Reducing the tilt provides less visual stimulation than might occur if the cup were continually removed and replaced. It is essential that the child's head be in neutral flexion and the neck elongated during the cup drinking process. If the head is allowed to tilt back, there is a greater chance that liquid will flow into the mouth and pharynx too quickly, which may cause problems in swallowing and in coordinating swallowing with breathing, and increase the risk for aspiration.

If the child displays little or no active movements of the upper lip, the cup rim can be brought up slightly toward the upper lip so that the liquid touches the lip, which often helps to stimulate upper lip activity. Thickened liquids may also help to stimulate greater upper lip activity and more-coordinated tongue movements for swallowing.

If a wet/gurgly respiratory quality is heard or coughing and choking often occur during cup-drinking activities at mealtime, the speech/language pathologist providing oral-motor, feeding/swallowing, and respiratory coordination treatment services for the child should be contacted immediately. Changes can then be made in the strategies being used at mealtime, and the reasons for problems can be further investigated in order to limit the child's risk for aspiration.

Spoon-Feeding

The caregiver must remember several points when feeding by spoon at mealtime:

1. Place a small amount of food on the front of the spoon. A large amount will only cause more food to be lost and will not help the child consume more.
2. The spoon should be presented at the center or front of the mouth. The caregiver should never present or remove the spoon with a motion that stimulates the child to extend the head back. In other words, the spoon should always be brought in and out of the front of the mouth, below the child's eye level.
3. To encourage more active lip closure around the spoon and to inhibit tongue retraction, the bowl of the spoon can be pressed flat down upon the middle of the tongue. Make sure that the tongue is resting on the floor of the mouth before pressing down. As the pressure is applied, the lips should automatically begin to close around the spoon. When this closure begins, the spoon should be removed from the middle of the mouth without scraping the child's teeth or gums.
4. Oral control may be used throughout the spoon-feeding process to provide more consistent jaw stability and to stimulate more active lip closure. If used, oral control should be maintained throughout the spoon-feeding process, even after the spoon is removed from the mouth, to reduce the possibility of tongue and jaw thrusting (see Figure 9–16).
5. Thick pureed foods will often be easier for the child with primary oral-motor problems to remove from the spoon and move back in the oral mechanism for swallowing than thin pureed foods. Children who have significant pharyngeal problems interfering with feeding and swallowing at mealtime may have trouble with thickened pureed foods as they move through the pharynx and esophagus and may actually find pureed or thin pureed foods easier to handle.
6. Always give the child sufficient time to swallow a spoonful of food before presenting the next one. Look for signs from the child that he or she is ready for the next spoonful. It often takes the child with oral-motor problems, limited oral and pharyngeal sensory awareness, or pharyngeal motility problems longer to completely move the food from the mouth back and down through the pharynx and esophagus to the stomach. Feeding too quickly will only lead to a child who pulls away from the feeder after just two to three spoonfuls of food, refusing to take in any more at mealtime.

Solid Food

Generally, children start receiving some experiences with hard solids as early as 5 months of age, as part of the teething process. Such hard solid food input assists in establishing a foundation of early oral tactile/proprioceptive sensory input essential to the development of oral sensory awareness and integration, oral-motor activity, and oral-motor coordination with

FIGURE 9–16
Spoon-feeding using oral control

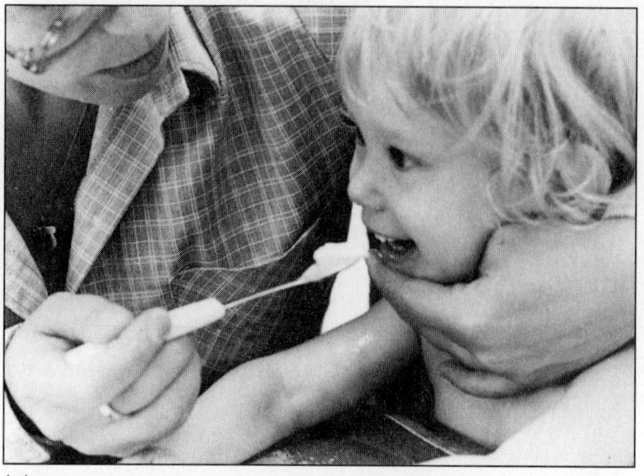
(a)

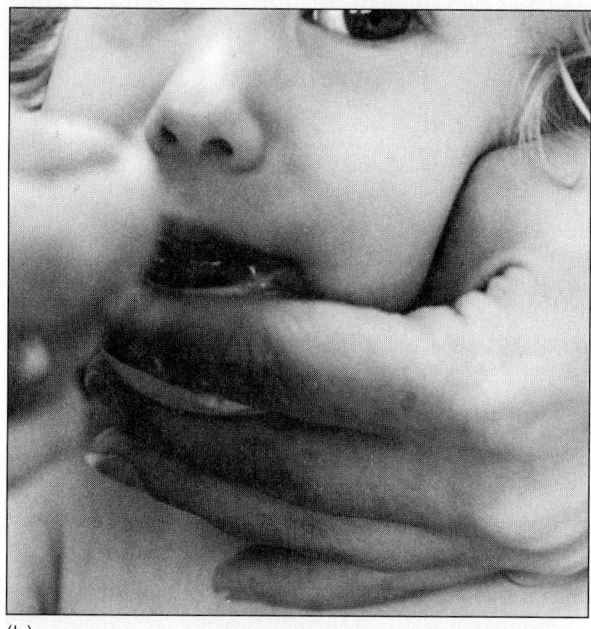
(b)

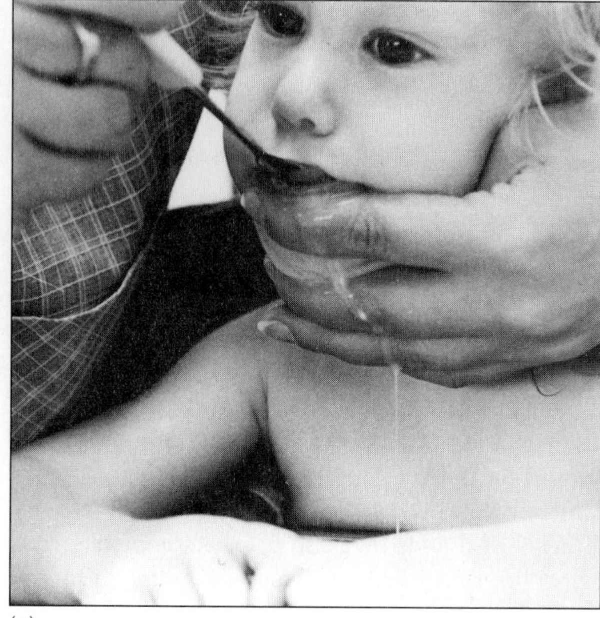
(c)

respiration. Early input to the gums and hard palate also appears to positively impact tooth eruption and the overall health of the oral mechanism. Therefore, the longer we wait to introduce solids to children with neuromotor involvement, the greater the likelihood the child will have difficulties in learning to tolerate solids foods, to handle a variety of food textures, and to move the tongue and jaw for more advanced, coordinated activities. Teeth are often slow to erupt in children who have very limited experiences with solids (e.g., food, toys) and other areas of oral exploration.

The presentation of solid foods must reflect the development of the typical chewing process. Solid foods are initially handled with more advanced oral movements when presented on the sides of the mouth (see Figure 9–17). Solid foods presented to the front will result in more-primitive oral movements, such as sucking or suckling. Once proper body alignment is established, solid foods can be placed on the side of the mouth between the gums or teeth. If jaw instability is noted, oral control can be used. The stimulation of jaw stability along with the proper food placement should help the child to respond automatically with active jaw and tongue movement (see Figure 9–17).

Remember that the child typically begins by scraping hard solids such as teething crackers on the gums and by eating quick-dissolving and soft chewy solids such as crackers, cheese, soft chicken, cereal, and pastas. The development of mature chewing is a long process, and the ultimate use of rotary jaw movement with intricate tongue and lip patterns does not come until later in the child's development (until approximately 3 years of age). Therefore, we cannot expect such movements to occur automatically in children with neuromotor involvement and must focus on presenting them with opportunities, during snack times

FIGURE 9–17
The presentation of solid food

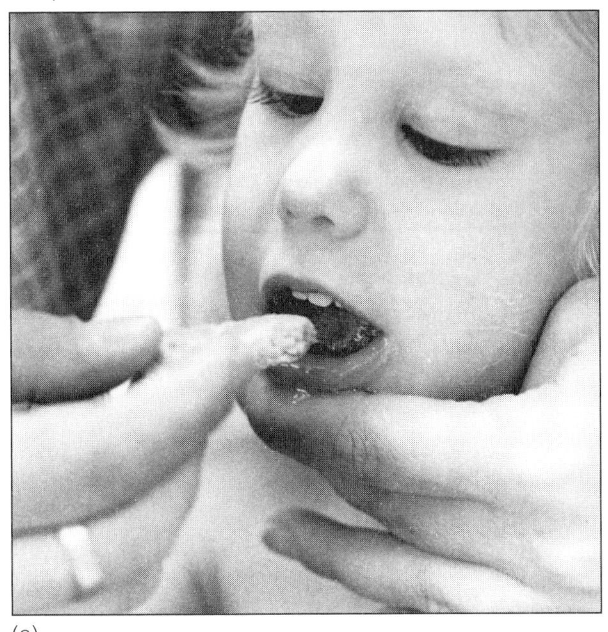
(a)

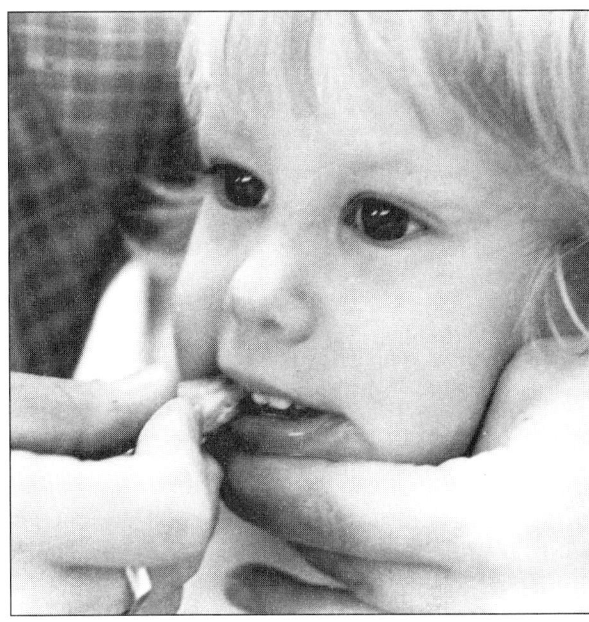
(b)

or other activities, to experience these types of textures as preparation for future mealtime changes.

Stimulating Respiratory Coordination with Oral and Pharyngeal Activities

Children with neuromotor involvement may exhibit problems in feeding and swallowing directly related to their difficulties in coordinating respiratory function with oral and pharyngeal activities. Similar problems may also be seen in their ability to coordinate breathing with sound production and other communication activities as well as general and fine-motor, upper extremity activities. When rib cage mobility and alignment, respiratory musculature activity, and respiratory coordination issues exist, it will be essential that the child's programming recognize the importance of handling/movement facilitation activities, as well as proper body alignment through positioning, to the child's future development of a respiratory foundation supportive of oral and pharyngeal function. Handling and movement facilitation that stimulate active antigravity movements and more active abdominal musculature control will help the child achieve deeper and more sustained respiratory patterns as a foundation for more coordinated oral and pharyngeal activities for feeding, swallowing, and sound production.

Handling techniques directed toward modifying respiratory function must provide input that helps to increase rib cage and shoulder girdle skeletal mobility and alignment; stimulate respiratory musculature activity, including rib cage, abdominal, and other supportive respiratory musculature; increase oral and pharyngeal musculature activity; and encourage the integration of this information by the child into functional movement activities such as feeding, swallowing, and sound production. Carryover activities that include body alignment through positioning that encourages improved respiratory coordination with oral and pharyngeal activities are essential to the child's intervention programming. The speech/language pathologists, physical therapists, and occupational therapists who use handling and movement facilitation techniques during their treatment sessions with a child should discuss with teachers and their assistants ways in which proper positioning and some useful handling techniques might be incorporated into different aspects of a child's school day. This will help to provide the child with a foundation on which he or she can be more active during his or her classroom-based activities as well as reinforcing a postural foundation on which greater progress with more advanced, integrated activity can be stimulated in treatment. Everyone who participates in the care of the child must incorporate techniques that focus on postural control and movement in coordination with oral-motor, feeding/swallowing, and respiratory coordination function to ensure that the child receives maximum exposure to and carryover of activities throughout each day.

SUMMARY AND CONCLUSION

Children with physical or multiple disabilities often present with feeding and swallowing problems. Each child may have different causes for the specific problems he or she is having in feeding and swallowing. Subsequent to a comprehensive evaluation of a child's oral-motor, feeding/swallowing, and respiratory coordination function, appropriate intervention programming will need to be implemented based upon clinical and instrumental examination findings and the findings of any other medical or educational areas recommended for further investigation. Activities will need to be incorporated into the child's daily programming involving all members of the intervention team at home, at school, and in the community. If the child has needs in the areas of feeding and swallowing requiring treatment, a qualified pediatric speech/language pathologist with an understanding of the medical base of feeding and swallowing problems will be needed to initiate treatment services and to assist in implementing appropriate management strategies during carryover activities such as mealtime, snack time, and toothbrushing. Key professionals and paraprofessionals involved in the child's school programming will need to be trained in the procedures to be used during a child's carryover activities.

QUESTIONS FOR DISCUSSION

1. Give some examples of variables impacting on a child's feeding and swallowing activities other than oral-motor function.
2. Discuss the different sensory characteristics that food and liquids may have and how modifying the sensory aspects of a child's diet may positively impact overall feeding and swallowing activities.
3. What are some strategies that can be implemented by the intervention team to help maintain a consistent level of communication regarding a child's progress in feeding and swallowing treatment and modifications that need to be implemented during carryover activities to help the child to integrate newly developing activities?

FOCUS ON THE NET

Dysphagia Mail List

http://lists.b9.com/mailman/listinfo/dysphagia

This online mail list serves as a forum for various medical professionals to discuss clinical cases and to pose questions regarding a variety of clinical and research topics related to swallowing and swallowing disorders. To subscribe, complete the subscription form on the Web site. To post a message to all subscribers, send e-mail to dysphagia@b9.com.

Dysphagia Resource Center

http://www.dysphagia.com

The Dysphagia Resource Center is an important source for resources regarding swallowing and swallowing disorders. Links are provided to sites in the areas of anatomy and physiology, diseases and dysphagia, organization and foundations, research information and funding, Internet journals, reference lists, book lists and reviews, and conference announcements. A list of vendors for materials related to swallowing and swallowing disorders is also provided. "Tutorials and Articles" provides links to an extensive list of swallowing disorders and other swallowing-related topics. The Dysphagia Resource Center also serves as the site for the Dysphagia Mail List Archive, which contains all correspondence from the Dysphagia Mailing List from November 1995 to the present.

GTube Mailing List

http://www.gtube.org

This online mailing list is an active list for parents of children with feeding tubes, adults with feeding tubes, and professionals working with individuals with feeding and swallowing problems. The GTube Mailing List archives provide access for subscribers to messages posted since July 2000. To subscribe, follow subscription instructions posted on the Web site.

New Visions
http://www.new-vis.com

New Visions was established in 1985 by its founder-director, Suzanne Evans Morris, Ph.D. Its primary focus is to provide "continuing education and therapy services to professionals and parents working with infants and children with feeding, swallowing, oral-motor, and prespeech problems." One can learn about New Visions workshops and clinical services online through its Web site.

New Visions' Web site also provides information about Mealtimes, which is a catalog with an extensive variety of therapy materials, tapes, and books related to some aspect of pediatric feeding, oral-motor function, and mealtime behaviors and activities. Information regarding the placement of orders for materials found in the Mealtimes catalog is provided.

One of the most valuable sections of the Web site is its section called "Feed Your Mind." A listing of articles by Dr. Morris addressing special issues in pediatric feeding and oral-motor function is found under "Information Papers." "Links We Like" provides a series of annoted links to other Web sites in the areas of information resources, anatomy and physiology, feeding development, feeding and swallowing, gastrointestinal resources, respiratory resources, health and nutrition, sensorimotor challenges, and educational and therapy resources. Link resources for professional associations, products and services, parenting resources, and mailing lists (online) provide both the professional and parent with valuable sources in a well-organized, informative manner.

REFERENCES

Alexander, R. (1987). Prespeech and feeding development. In E. McDonald (Ed.), *Treating cerebral palsy: For clinicians by clinicians* (pp. 133–152). Austin, TX: PRO-ED.

Alexander, R. (1993). Respiratory and oral-motor function. In B. Connolly & P. Montgomery (Eds.), *Therapeutic exercise in developmental disabilities* (2nd ed., pp. 125–135). Hixson, TN: Chattanooga Group.

Alexander, R., & Beecher, R. (1992). Definition developed and used in workshops on pediatric feeding and swallowing and pediatric oral-pharyngeal motility studies. Unpublished handout.

Alexander, R., Boehme, R., & Cupps, B. (1993). *Normal development of functional motor skills: The first year of life.* San Antonio, TX: Therapy Skill Builders.

Alper, B. S., & Manno, C. (1996). Dysphagia in infants and children with oral-motor deficits: Assessment and management. In J. Arvedson & M. Lefton-Greif (Eds.), Pediatric dysphagia: Complex medical, health, and developmental issues. *Seminars in Speech and Language, 17,* 283–310.

Arvedson, J. (2002). Oral-motor and feeding assessment. In J. Arvedson & L. Brodsky (Eds.), *Pediatric swallowing and feeding: Assessment and management* (2nd ed.) (pp. 283–340). Albany, NY: Singular.

Arvedson, J., & Lefton-Greif, M. (1998). *Pediatric videofluoroscopic swallow studies: A professional manual with caregiver guidelines.* San Antonio, TX: Communication Skill Builders.

Babbitt, R., Hoch, T., & Coe, D. (1994). Behavioral feeding disorders. In D. Tuchman & R. Walter (Eds.), *Disorders of feeding and swallowing in infants and children: Pathophysiology, diagnosis and treatment* (pp. 77–95). San Diego, CA: Singular.

Beecher, R. (1998). *Descriptions of food textures.* Workshop handout.

Benson, J., & Lefton-Greif, M. (1994). Videofluoroscopy of swallowing in pediatric patients: A component of the total feeding evaluation. In D. Tuchman & R. Walter (Eds.), *Disorders of feeding and swallowing in infants and children: Pathophysiology, diagnosis and treatment* (pp. 187–200). San Diego, CA: Singular.

Bly, L. (1994). *Motor skills acquisition in the first year.* San Antonio, TX: Therapy Skill Builders.

Brazelton, T. B. (1969). *Infants and mothers: Differences in development.* New York: Dell.

Cech, D., & Martin, S. (1995). *Functional movement development across the life span.* Philadelphia: Saunders.

Finnie, N. (1997). *Handling the young child with cerebral palsy at home* (3rd ed.). Boston: Butterworth-Heinemann.

Ginsburg, H., & Opper, S. (1969). *Piaget's theory of intellectual development: An introduction.* Upper Saddle River, NJ: Prentice Hall.

Howle, J. (2002). *Neuro-developmental treatment approach: Theoretical foundations and principles of clinical practice.*

Laguna Beach, CA: Neuro-Developmental Treatment Association.

Jones, B., & Donner, M. (1991). Interpreting the study. In B. Jones & M. Donner (Eds.), *Normal and abnormal swallowing: Imaging in diagnosis and therapy* (pp. 51–75). New York: Springer-Verlag.

Kovar, A. (1997). Nutrition assessment and management in pediatric dysphagia. In J. Arvedson & M. Lefton-Greif (Eds.), Pediatric dysphagia II: A team approach for assessment, management, and special problems. *Seminars in Speech and Language, 18,* 39–49.

Lefton-Greif, M. (1994). Diagnosis and management of pediatric feeding and swallowing disorders: Role of the speech-language pathologist. In D. Tuchman & R. Walter (Eds.), *Disorders of feeding and swallowing in infants and children: Pathophysiology, diagnosis, and treatment* (pp. 97–113). San Diego, CA: Singular.

Mascarenhas, M., & Dadhania, J. (1995). Gastrointestinal problems. In S. Rosenthal, J. J. Sheppard, & M. Lotze (Eds.), *Dysphagia and the child with developmental disabilities: Medical, clinical, and family interventions* (pp. 253–282). San Diego, CA: Singular.

McCurtin, A. (1997). *The manual of paediatric feeding practice.* Bicester, Oton, United Kingdom: Winslow.

Morris, S. E., & Klein, M. D. (2000). *Pre-feeding skills: A comprehensive resource for feeding development* (2nd ed.). San Antonio, TX: Therapy Skill Builders.

Moyer, R. (1971). Postnatal development of the orofacial musculature. *ASHA Reports, 6,* 37–47.

Mueller, H. (1972). Facilitating feeding and pre-speech. In P. Pearson & C. Williams (Eds.), *Physical therapy services in the developmental disabilities* (pp. 283–310). Springfield, IL: Charles C. Thomas.

Mueller, H. (1997). Feeding. In N. Finnie, *Handling the young child with cerebral palsy at home* (3rd ed., pp. 209–221). Boston: Butterworth-Heinemann.

Murphy, S. M., & Caretto, V. (1999). Sensory aspects of feeding. In D. K. Lowman & S. M. Murphy, *The educator's guide to feeding children with disabilities* (pp. 111–125). Baltimore: Brookes.

Palmer, S. (1978). Normal nutrition, growth, and development. In S. Palmer & S. Ekvall (Eds.), *Pediatric nutrition in developmental disorders* (pp. 3–20). Springfield, IL: Charles C. Thomas.

Pinder, G. L., & Faherty, A. S. (1999). Issues in pediatric feeding and swallowing. In A. Caruso & E. Strand (Eds.), *Clinical management of motor speech disorders in children* (pp. 281–318). New York: Thieme.

Putnam, P. (1997). Gastroesophageal reflux disease and dysphagia in children. In. J. Arvedson & M. Lefton-Greif (Eds.), Pediatric dysphagia II: A team approach for assessment, management, and special problems. *Seminars in Speech and Language, 18,* 25–38.

Rogers, B. (1996). Neurodevelopmental presentation of dysphagia. In J. Arvedson & M. Lefton-Greif (Eds.), Pediatric dysphagia: Complex medical, health, and developmental issues. *Seminars in Speech and Language, 17,* 269–281.

Rossi, T. (1993), Pediatric gastroenterology. In J. Arvedson & L. Brodsky (Eds.), *Pediatric swallowing and feeding: Assessment and management* (pp. 123–156). San Diego, CA: Singular.

Snyder, P., Breath, D., & DeMauro, G. (1999). Positioning strategies for feeding and eating. In D. K. Lowman & S. M. Murphy, *The educator's guide to feeding children with disabilities* (pp. 65–109). Baltimore: Brookes.

Tuchman, D. (1994). Gastroesophageal reflux. In D. Tuchman & R. Walter (Eds.), *Disorders of feeding and swallowing in infants and children: Pathophysiology, diagnosis, and treatment* (pp. 231–250). San Diego, CA: Singular.

Tuchman, D., & Walter, R. (1994). Disorders of deglutition. In D. Tuchman & R. Walter (Eds.), *Disorders of feeding and swallowing in infants and children: Pathophysiology, diagnosis, and treatment* (pp. 53–75). San Diego, CA: Singular.

Uzgiris, I., & Hunt, J. (1975). *Assessment in infancy.* Urbana: University of Illinois Press.

Weiss, M. (1988). Dysphagia in infants and children. *The Otolaryngologic Clinics of North America, 21,* 727–741.

Willging, J. P., Miller, C., Link, D., & Rudolph, C. (2001). Use of FEES to assess and manage pediatric patients. In S. Langmore (Ed.), *Endoscopic evaluation and treatment of swallowing disorders* (pp. 213–234). New York: Thieme.

Wolf, L., & Glass, R. (1992). *Feeding and swallowing disorders in infancy: Assessment and management.* San Antonio, TX: Therapy Skill Builders.

Woods, E. (1995). The influence of posture and positioning on oral motor development and dysphagia. In S. Rosenthal, J. J. Sheppard, & M. Lotze (Eds.), *Dysphagia and the child with developmental disabilities: Medical, clinical, and family interventions* (pp. 153–187). San Diego, CA: Singular.

Adaptations for Personal Independence

KATHRYN WOLFF HELLER
JUNE L. BIGGE
PEGGY ALLGOOD

CHAPTER 10

KNOWLEDGE AND SKILLS

After you have read this chapter, you will be able to:

1. **Assess and teach hygiene skills, such as hand washing, face washing, hair brushing, oral hygiene, tissue use, and feminine hygiene.**
2. **Know how to teach using a target strategy or a quadrant strategy for personal care activities.**
3. **Describe adaptations and methods of teaching toilet training.**
4. **Discuss health care procedures as instructional objectives that students may learn to perform independently or with assistance.**
5. **Discuss the impact of time-limited steps and caution steps on instructional methodology and selection of student objectives.**
6. **Discuss guidelines for promoting successful dressing skills and possible adaptations.**
7. **Describe home care management skills and possible adaptations that may be necessary for students with physical or multiple disabilities.**
8. **Discuss considerations for successful community-based instruction.**

The necessity of teaching personal management skills to students with physical, health, or multiple disabilities cannot be stressed enough. If teachers, parents, and therapists do not teach these skills when students are young or if they lose skills because of an injury, students may become unnecessarily dependent on others. By teaching and fostering personal management skills, teachers provide students with an opportunity for personal independence. Dealing with these skills directly and in collaboration with other professionals and parents results in outcomes that are as important for some students as is a focus on academics. Until individuals can care for personal needs or have effective ways of directing others to assist with their personal care, they may not be able to acquire desired living and working opportunities.

Personal management skills cover a broad range of skills including self-care skills, home management skills, and community-based skills. Depending upon the disability, students may learn (a) to independently perform these skills (with or without adaptations), (b) to partially perform these skills, (c) to direct another person to help them with skill performance, or (d) knowledge and skills about the task (Heller, Forney, Alberto, Schwartzman, & Goeckel, 2000). Although independent performance of a skill is optimal, some students will only be able to participate in some parts of a skill due to physical or cognitive limitations. Promoting this type of partial participation is important to do when a student cannot independently perform the skill, since it assists with task completion, decreases learned helplessness, and provides the student some control of the activity. In some situations, the student may have such severe physical involvement that he or she is unable to physically perform the task. In these situations, the student may learn to direct another person in performing the task. In the last category, knowledge of the skill, the student may learn more in-depth information about the task and its implications, such as learning about infections in addition to learning about proper hand washing. Regardless of which type of task participation is targeted, increasing student performance of these skills increases independence and self-esteem.

*

ASSESSMENT AND INSTRUCTION OF PERSONAL MANAGEMENT SKILLS

Prior to teaching personal management skills, it is important to assess the student's current abilities and, from there, to determine how the skill will be taught. One type of assessment aimed at determining a student's performance capability is a **discrepancy analysis.** A discrepancy analysis consists of four parts: (a) performing a task analysis of the skill, (b) observing and scoring student performance of the steps of the task analysis, (c) recording the student's errors and doing a performance discrepancy, and (d) determining whether the skill will be taught directly, require an adaptation, or require an alternative performance strategy (Heller, Forney, et al., 2000).

After selecting a personal management skill to assess, the skill is broken down into small steps. This process is referred to as a **task analysis** (see Chapter 6 on task analysis). The steps are initially recorded as a nondisabled person would perform them. As seen in Figure 10–1, these would be recorded in the first column. Next, the student is directed to perform each step of the task. Assistance is given as necessary for steps the student has difficulty performing due to physical difficulty, lack of knowledge, or other problems. Based on the student's performance, the teacher will record in the second column an "I" if he or she does the step independently, a "V" for verbal prompts, and a "P" for any other type of prompt, such as gesturing, modeling (showing how to do it), or providing physical assistance.

When the student is unable to do a step independently, the teacher records the error the student made in the third column. Information in this column will help in analyzing why the error occurred. The teacher will next decide why the student was unable to perform the step independently. Based on observation of the error and student assistance, the teacher will determine if the error was due to learning, physical, health, sensory, communication, or motivational reasons. (See Chapter 6 for more information on distinguishing motor from cognitive difficulties.) This information will help guide the teacher and educational team in determining whether the student needs some type of adaptation or alternate performance strategy, or needs to be taught the skill directly.

Adaptations range from changing the skill sequence (by expanding or changing the task analysis) to changing the material (by modifying existing material or using assistive devices) (Heller, Forney, et al., 2000). As seen in Figure 10–1, modifications were needed regarding the faucet handles and type of soap dispenser to assist the student in the hand-washing activity. Colored dots also needed to be added to help the student distinguish between the cold and hot faucets. If an alternate performance strategy had been needed, the task would have changed, but the same outcome would have been accomplished. (For example, using an AAC device to ask for assistance in washing hands is an alternate performance strategy when speaking is not possible.)

After completing a performance discrepancy and making any necessary modifications, the teacher will need to determine the most appropriate instructional strategy to use. Although there are many types of instructional strategies that can be used to teach personal management skills, four major types are often used. These include antecedent prompts, learning strategies, demonstration–guided-practice–independent model, and response prompts.

Antecedent Prompts. Antecedent prompts are materials and instructions that are presented to a student to encourage the correct performance of a behavior when the naturally occurring cues are not sufficient to produce correct behavior. For example, a student may be unable to distinguish the front from the back of the shirt, even though the natural cue is to look for the tag and be sure it is in the back. In this situation, the teacher may use an antecedent prompt in which the tag-recognition part of the task is the one upon which the student should focus. In this example, the teacher may place a piece of red ribbon on the tag to help draw the student's attention to it. As the student learns the

FIGURE 10–1
An example of a discrepancy analysis for a student with a disability who is washing his hands

Student:
Domain:

Teacher:
Environment:

Date:
Subenvironment:

Task Analysis (Nondisabled person inventory) for activity of: Hand washing	Score I = Independence V = Verbal Prompt P = Prompt	Student Error	Performance Discrepancy L = Learning P = Physical H = Health S = Sensory C = Communication M = Motivation	Adaptation or Alternative Performance Options
1. Go to bathroom	I			
2. Position body for hand washing	V	Not getting close enough to sink	L	Provide practice
3. Turn on faucet	P	Difficulty manipulating	P	Try elongated handles
4. Adjust water temperature	P	Unsure which is hot	L	Mark hot and cold with red and blue marks
5. Thoroughly wet hands	I			
6. Put soap on hands	P	Difficulty manipulating	P	Change dispenser
7. Rub together, creating lather	P	Difficulty moving hands together	P	Provide elbow support, for now
8. Continue rubbing, count to 15 slowly (15 seconds)	V	Kept stopping	M	Continue counting and use sticker chart
9. Rinse soap off hands thoroughly	P	Did not get all of soap off	L	Provide practice, point out soapy areas
10. Dry hands	P	Did not thoroughly dry	L	Provide more practice
11. Turn off water with paper towel	V	Wanted to turn off water without towel	L	Provide more practice

Note. Adapted from *Meeting Physical and Health Needs of Children with Disabilities: Teaching Student Participation and Management,* 1st edition, by Heller/Forney/Alberto/Schwartzman/Goeckel. © 2000. Reprinted with permission of Wadsworth, a division of Thomson Learning: www.thomsonrights.com. Fax 800 730-2215.

task, the red ribbon will be cut shorter and shorter until it is no longer there, so that the student will learn to look for the tag as the natural cue. Placing a red mark on the washing machine showing where to set the dial is another example. In this situation, the teacher may decide to leave this antecedent prompt permanently.

Self-Operated Prompting System. In this system the steps of the task analysis are visually presented through pictures (self-operated picture prompts) or recorded on a tape recorder (self-operated verbal prompt) (Alberto, Sharpton, Briggs, & Stright, 1986; Alberto & Troutman, 2003; Martin, Rusch, James, Decker, & Trytol, 1982). For example, a student who is learning to clean a bathroom may refer to a series of pictures showing the supplies to get and showing each of the steps needed to clean each of the items in the bathroom. The student learns to follow the pictures to reinforce initial instruction, or may always use the pictures to perform the task if the student has significant cognitive impairments.

Learning Strategies. Another type of instructional strategy, known as a learning strategy, focuses on how the student learns, rather than specific content. Steps in this strategy include describing the strategy, modeling the strategy, practicing the strategy, and showing how to apply the strategy (Ellis & Sabornie, 1986; Polloway & Patton, 1993). There are many different types of learning strategies. One that may be used for some self-management skills is the use of mnemonics. For example, when teaching tube feeding, the teacher may teach the student the mnemonic "Feeding is the four *F*'s: flush the tube, food goes in the tube, fill the tube before it's empty, flush the tube when you are done" (Heller, Forney, et al., 2000). Learning strategies are typically used with students who have mild to no cognitive impairments.

Demonstration–Guided-Practice–Independent-Practice Model. Another type of instructional strategy is known as the demonstration–guided-practice–independent-practice model (Polloway & Patton, 1993). As discussed in Chapter 15, this form of instruction begins with a demonstration of the skill by the teacher. Next, the teacher provides support to the student and helps the student learn the steps of the selected personal management skills through guided practice. In guided practice, the teacher may use a continuum of assistance, based upon individual student needs (Mercer & Mercer, 2001). In the last step of independent practice, the student practices the skill without assistance, but still receives feedback as needed. For example, if the student is learning how to use a vending machine, the teacher may first demonstrate its use, then systematically guide the student through using it. After the student is showing competence, the teacher will allow the student to practice the skill independently, providing feedback as needed.

Response Prompts. Response prompts are another type of instructional strategy. This strategy provides guidance and assistance in the actual performance of the behavior. There are many different types of response prompts. Some of these are verbal cues (telling the student the step), verbal instructions (providing more direction on how to do the step), gesturing, modeling, partial physical prompts (partially physically guiding the student), and full physical prompts (completely guiding the student through the step). These prompts are either used singularly (e.g., the time delay strategy) or in combination (e.g., the system of least prompts or system of maximum prompts) to provide a predictable pattern of assistance to a student (see Chapters 6 and 8 for additional detail on prompting).

All of these different types of instructional strategies may be used to teach personal management skills. The selection of the instructional approach will depend upon the student's individual needs, as well as the selected skill. Regardless of which strategy is selected, it is important that appropriate settings and times are used and the targeted skills are socially valid, age appropriate, and culturally appropriate (Farlow & Snell, 2000). The remainder of the chapter will provide further information on teaching and adapting specific physical management skills, including hygiene skills, basic self-help skills (e.g., toileting), health care procedures, dressing, home care management, and community-based instruction.

HYGIENE SKILLS

Students with physical or multiple disabilities may have decreased hygiene due to the physical difficulties or cognitive demands of correctly washing hands, manipulating tissues, or performing other hygiene skills. Individualized instruction may be needed on hygiene skills to teach the student how to effectively carry out these activities. Learning how to perform these essential hygiene skills can help decrease infection and illness, maintain health, and promote socialization and acceptability to others (Westling & Fox, 2004). This section will discuss specific strategies, adaptations, and adaptive equipment to teach appropriate hand washing, face and body washing, hair brushing, oral hygiene, tissue use, and feminine hygiene.

Hand Washing

Hand washing is the single most effective means of infection control. However, few elementary-age students actually wash their hands after using the restroom (Pete, 1987). Learning when and where hand washing should occur is important in order for it to become routine (Loumiet & Levack, 1993). Hand washing should be taught as part of a daily routine before preparing food, before eating, after using the restroom, and before taking oral medications. To wash hands correctly, students need to be taught this skill, and many students with physical or multiple disabilities will require adaptations to make hand washing accessible.

The first step in assessing and teaching hand-washing skills is to do a task analysis in which the process of hand washing is broken into small steps. As presented earlier in Figure 10–1, these steps included turning off the water by using a paper towel on faucet handles to prevent recontaminating the hands, and scrubbing hands with soap for at least 10 to 15 seconds (Medcom Trainix, 1993; Smith, 1992). A discrepancy analysis is then performed in which the student performs the tests, and the teacher records and analyzes the type of error and determines what adaptations are needed.

To make hand washing accessible, the student may require a sink that allows the wheelchair to slide under it or a different type of handle for turning on the water (e.g., elongated handles, one-handle control). An antecedent prompt may be needed to help with temperature control (such as using red fingernail polish or tape to indicate where the handle(s) should be placed for optimal temperature). Different types of dispensers are available for dispensing soap that can be operated by pushing down, pulling up, or pulling out, and they can be mounted by suction cups or hardware mounts. The type of adaptations will depend upon the student's motoric ability.

For students who cannot rotate their hands upward (supinate), an adapted method of hand washing may be used. In this instance, the student pumps the soap with the palm of the left hand onto the back of the right hand. The student rubs the hands together by placing the right hand over the left and moving them back and forth, then repeating with the left hand over the right. The hands are then placed under running water for rinsing. In some instances, sponges may be stabilized on the sink rim to rub against, or the soap dispenser can be positioned/stabilized for ease of use (see p. 216). After adaptations have been determined, the teacher will select the appropriate instructional strategy and monitor for any additional needed modifications.

Face and Body Washing

Part of teaching students face and body washing is teaching them when washing is needed. Face washing may be taught to occur in the morning and night, as well as when dirty. In the school setting, teaching the student to recognize when the face is dirty and needs washing can occur after such activities as eating messy foods that the napkin can't wipe up or removal of face-painting paints. The student should be positioned in front of a mirror to identify what parts of the face are dirty.

Many hygiene skills are taught using a target or quadrant strategy. A **target strategy** involves washing only the area that is dirty. For this to be successful, the student must be able to identify the area that is dirty. For some students, this will take repeated trials and systematic instruction. In a **quadrant strategy,** the entire area is washed and the task is broken down by dividing the area into quadrants to be washed. For face washing, the quadrants are right cheek, left cheek, chin, mouth area, nose, and forehead. For body washing, this would be various parts of the body (e.g., arms, legs, stomach, and chest). Some students will benefit from using a prompting strategy that consists of pictures of the different quadrants, while others will do well with other instructional strategies. Students may be taught to use this systematic face-washing strategy using all quadrants in all situations, while other students will be taught to use the quadrant strategy when washing the face in the morning and evening, but use a target strategy when there is something directly on the face. Figure 10–2 provides a task analysis for face washing that uses the quadrant strategy.

FIGURE 10–2
Task analysis for face washing

1. Go to designated area to wash.
2. Get washcloth/mitt, soap and dry towel.
3. Position body for washing face.
4. Turn on the faucet.
5. Adjust water temperature.
6. Wet the washcloth/mitt.
7. Put soap on the washcloth/mitt.
8. Identify the area to be washed in the mirror.
9. Touch the right cheek with the wet washcloth/mitt.
10. Gently rub in a counterclockwise motion. (Be careful not to get soap in the eyes!)
11. Repeat #s 8, 9, and 10 with left cheek, chin, mouth area, nose, and forehead.
12. Thoroughly rinse the soap from the washcloth/mitt. (You may want to use a second washcloth/mitt with no soap on it with which to rinse.)
13. Repeat #s 9, 10, and 11 to remove residual soap.
14. Repeat #s 9, 10, and 11, gently blotting to remove remaining water.

FIGURE 10–3
A washmitt and a long-handled sponge are common adaptations for washing

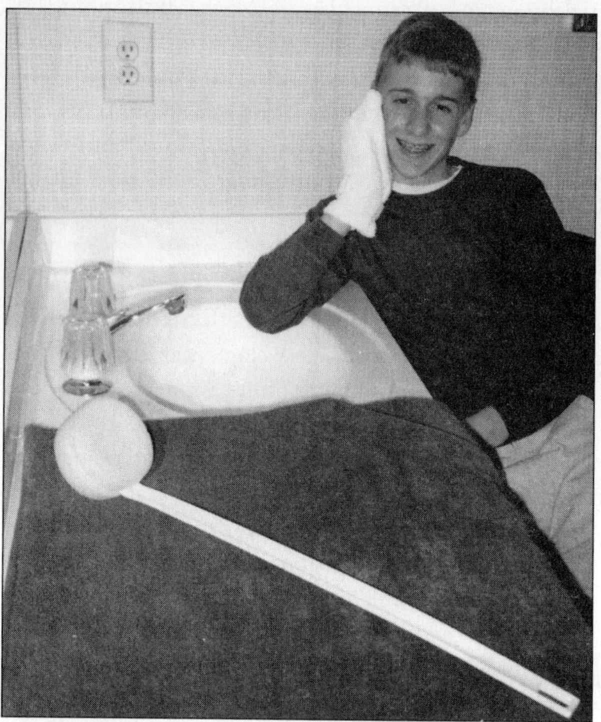

Several adaptations may be needed for face or body washing, depending upon the outcome of the discrepancy analysis. Some students will benefit from using a wash mitt, especially if they have difficulty grasping. Some mitts have pockets with Velcro® closures to hold soap. Long-handled sponges may also be used for hard-to-reach places when bathing (see Figure 10–3). To assist bathing and transferring, a bathtub chair may be used to make sitting more comfortable and secure.

When teaching face washing (and in some cases body washing), the procedure may first be taught using only water; then, after that is accomplished, the student may be taught to add soap. Soap can be irritating to the eyes if it inadvertently comes into contact with them while washing. Some students will find this aversive and be less inclined to engage in the washing task due to the experience. By first learning to wash without soap, students can become proficient at the task and will be less likely to get soap in their eyes when soap is added as part of the procedure.

Hair Brushing

Hair brushing may also be taught throughout the day for maintenance of the hairstyle after such activities as gym and recess. Depending upon the person's hairstyle, the direction the hair is brushed will vary. The task analysis will need to be based upon the student's own hairstyle. A target or quadrant strategy may be used. Quadrant strategies may vary depending upon the hairstyle, but will often involve dividing the hair into top, right side, left side, and back. A variety of hair adornments such as hair bands, ribbons, and barrettes may be used and their application taught.

Brushing one's own hair requires a range of motion in the shoulder, arms, and wrists, as well as a certain amount of muscular strength that can be difficult for individuals with physical disabilities. Several adaptations may help, such as providing larger grips on the brush or using a brush with a handle extension to adequately reach the top and back of the head (see Figure 10–4). Adaptations will need to be determined based on the discrepancy analysis and data.

Oral Hygiene

Good oral hygiene maintains the teeth, mouth, and gums in a healthy condition and lessens offensive mouth odor. Part of good oral hygiene is regular toothbrushing. In many instances, teachers may in-

FIGURE 10–4
A long-handled brush can help reach the hair for grooming

struct students on how to brush their teeth during appropriate times during the day, such as after lunch or a snack. There are many varieties of toothbrushing techniques that are acceptable. The American Dental Association (1991) recommends placing the head of the toothbrush at a 45-degree angle to the gums and moving the brush back and forth with short, gentle strokes. They also recommend that the brush be tilted vertically to clean the inside surfaces of the front teeth and that the tongue be brushed to freshen the breath.

Effective toothbrushing may target individual teeth or use a quadrant method. When using the individual-tooth method, students are taught to brush each tooth. However, since the toothbrush often covers more than one tooth at a time, it is often easier to divide the mouth into quadrants. In the quadrant method, toothbrushing is taught across the (a) front, (b) upper outer right, (c) far back right, (d) upper outer left, and (e) far back left. This is repeated across the outer surfaces of the bottom teeth. The inner teeth are brushed next in the same sequence (upper teeth, lower teeth). The grinding surfaces are brushed last. The student is encouraged to spit throughout the task. For students who do not like to spit, a target (e.g., a piece of paper) may be placed in the sink to help encourage the student. A sample task analysis is shown in Figure 10–5.

FIGURE 10–5
Task analysis for toothbrushing

Student is to wet toothbrush, get more toothpaste, and spit as needed and planned for the individual student.

1. Pick up toothbrush.
2. Place toothpaste on toothbrush.
3. Bring toothbrush to mouth.
4. Brush with an up-and-down movement the outer front teeth.
5. Brush upper outer right.
6. Brush upper outer far back right.
7. Brush upper outer left.
8. Brush upper outer far back left.
9. Brush lower front teeth.
10. Brush lower outer right.
11. Brush lower outer far back right.
12. Brush lower outer left.
13. Brush lower outer far back left.
14. Brush upper inner front teeth.
15. Brush upper inner right.
16. Brush upper inner far back right.
17. Brush upper inner left.
18. Brush upper inner far back left.
19. Brush lower inner front teeth.
20. Brush lower inner right.
21. Brush lower inner far back right.
22. Brush lower inner left.
23. Brush lower inner far back left.
24. Brush right top grinding surfaces.
25. Brush right bottom grinding surfaces.
26. Brush left top grinding surfaces.
27. Brush left bottom grinding surfaces.
28. Remove brush and rinse it out.
29. Put away toothbrush.

A discrepancy analysis may determine that a student needs adaptive equipment to assist with toothbrushing. A toothbrush handle can be enlarged with a sponge, rubber ball, or handle grip. Some toothbrushes have handles that fit around the student's hand if gripping is a problem (see Figure 10–6). Students with limited mobility may benefit from an electric toothbrush with a small, soft brush and an adaptive handle. The student may have difficulty squeezing the toothpaste onto the toothbrush. A special dispenser may be used in which the toothbrush is aligned with the guide under the nozzle and the toothpaste is dispensed by pressing a long lever down with the hand or arm.

FIGURE 10–6
An adapted toothbrush can make holding a toothbrush possible for individuals who are unable to grasp

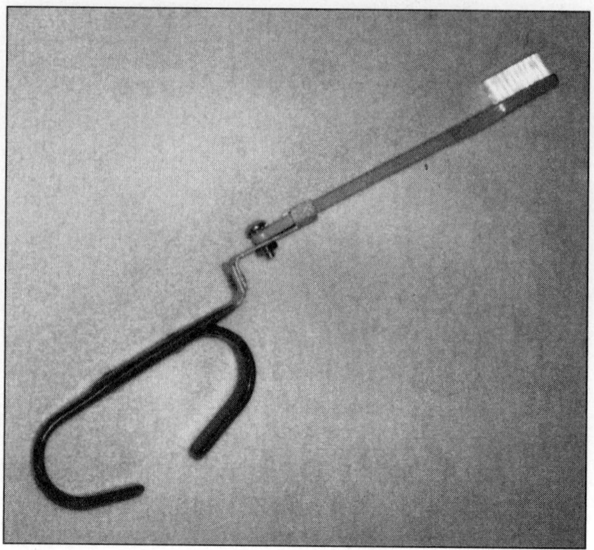

FIGURE 10–7
Task analysis for tissue use

1. Become aware of the need for a tissue.
2. Position body for tissue use.
3. Reach/ask for tissue.
4. Grasp tissue in hand.
5. Turn wrist toward body.
6. Raise hand/arm to mid-face area.
7. Bring hand/arm to face.
8. Place tissue over nose and mouth.
9. Blow through nostrils into tissue.
10. Gently wipe area with tissue.
11. Dispose of tissue appropriately.
12. Wash hands.

Tissue Use

To maintain a healthy environment, it is important that students learn to use a tissue to wipe and blow the nose, as well as to cover the mouth and turn the head away from other people when coughing or sneezing. The steps of bringing a tissue to the nose and mouth may be broken down into a task analysis (see Figure 10–7). The tissue may be grasped with a pincer grasp or a full hand grasp, then it is brought to the position over the nose. If the student has very limited motor control, he or she may need assistance and should be taught to ask for help.

To master tissue use, the student may need to be taught how to blow the nose. Some students will have difficulty understanding the act of blowing. To help teach this concept, place a loose tissue over the nose and have the student blow with his or her mouth closed to make the tissue blow in the air. Proper positioning to allow for chest expansion and diaphragmatic use to expel air is important to give enough power behind the expelling of air to effectively blow one's nose.

Feminine Hygiene

Menstrual care is considered a highly private matter, and there is much concern regarding the manner in which menstrual hygiene is taught and by whom. The involvement of a parent or legal guardian is essential, as is instructional approval by the student (as much as is feasible). It is a good practice to obtain written permission signed by the student and guardian, and to explain the procedures orally and in written form.

One of the most effective ways to teach feminine hygiene is by on-self instruction. For students with mental retardation, teaching menstrual care on-self was found to be more effective than using simulation training with dolls (Epps, Stern, & Horner, 1990). Students with physical disabilities also would benefit with on-self instruction, since the motions required for doing the procedure on oneself are different from practicing on a doll. Although training should occur when the student is having her period, role-playing may also be used in order to have enough practice of these skills.

To learn when to use a pad, practice sessions showing stained versus nonstained underwear may be helpful. During these sessions, the student identifies which underwear is stained, indicating that a pad is needed. For students having difficulty recognizing when a pad is needed, they are taught to change the pad at certain times of the day, such as getting up in the morning, midmorning break, lunch, before going home, dinner, and bedtime. Many students will benefit from marking a calendar showing when the menstrual cycle should occur. This usually occurs every 28 days, counting from the first day of onset (Guyton, 1995).

Steps for putting on a pad or changing to a new one should be broken down into small steps. As seen in

FIGURE 10–8
Task analysis for changing a menstrual pad

1. Identify need for menstrual bag.
2. Take bag to bathroom.
3. Remove necessary clothing.
4. Pull down underwear.
5. Sit on toilet.
6. Remove small sandwich sack from menstrual bag.
7. Remove soiled pad.
8. Place in sandwich sack.
9. Fold over sack two times.
10. Determine if underwear is soiled.
11. If soiled, take plastic bag from menstrual bag.
12. Remove soiled underwear.
13. Place soiled underwear in plastic bag.
14. Take clean underwear from menstrual bag.
15. Put on clean underwear.
16. Take clean sanitary napkin from menstrual bag.
17. Remove adhesive strips.
18. Place sanitary napkin in crotch of underwear.
19. Clean vaginal area.
20. Pull up underwear.
21. Examine external clothing for soiled areas.
22. Replace clothes as necessary.
23. Place soiled clothes in plastic bag with soiled underwear.
24. Flush toilet.
25. Place soiled napkin (in folded sandwich bag) in appropriate trash container.
26. Place adhesive strips in appropriate trash container.
27. Place plastic bag with soiled underwear in menstrual bag.
28. Wash hands.
29. Return to locker/personal storage area.
30. Remove plastic bag with soiled clothing and place in appropriate place for cleaning.
31. Replace used items in menstrual bag.
32. Return to class/work.

Figure 10–8, the task analysis for changing a pad involves undressing, positioning, disposing of the used pad, cleaning the vaginal area, putting on a new pad, and redressing. At the start of menstruation, the student would need to identify that a pad was needed, redress, and retrieve her spare pads. Some students will benefit from using a picture prompting system that is kept within the cosmetic bag containing the supplies. It is important that proper hand washing be followed after the completion of any feminine hygiene task. If the student is unable to independently perform the procedure due to physical disabilities, she may participate by indicating that she needs her pad changed, by holding needed supplies, or by directing her care through the use of augmentative communication. The person assisting with the procedure should provide her with a private location, use gloves, and maintain the student's dignity at all times.

BASIC SELF-HELP SKILLS: EATING AND TOILETING

Students may be taught the most basic self-help skills of eating and using a toilet in the school setting. Students may have difficulties with both of these due to the impact of physical, health, or multiple impairments. Eating may be difficult due to abnormal reflexes, and eating patterns and specialized strategies may be needed to teach the student eating skills. Due to the complexity of this area, a separate chapter addresses feeding and swallowing (see Chapter 9). Another complex area is teaching toileting skills to students with physical or multiple disabilities. With systematic instruction and adaptations, most students can learn to achieve these skills.

Toileting consists of both bowel and bladder training. The purposes of bowel and bladder training are to teach self-care, to provide maximum cleanliness and comfort, to prevent skin breakdown due to urinary or fecal soilage, to prevent changes in kidney and bladder functions that can become severe or life-threatening problems, and to alleviate emotional problems associated with incontinence. For bowel and bladder programs to be successful, it is important that the student learns to relax. In many cases, this involves using adaptive equipment.

The most common adaptations used in toileting for students with physical or multiple disabilities are adaptive toilets. Students with disabilities must be properly positioned to use the toilet. Adaptive toilets will provide appropriate positioning and support to allow the student to relax and not be concerned about falling off the toilet seat. There are many different types of adaptive toilets. Some are stand-alone toilets, while others are devices that fit over the existing toilets. They range from simple box-style potty chairs to those with backs, headrests, and armrests for students who are more physically involved (see Figure 10–9). The physical therapist will help determine the most appropriate toilet for the student.

FIGURE 10–9
Special equipment provides physical security and privacy

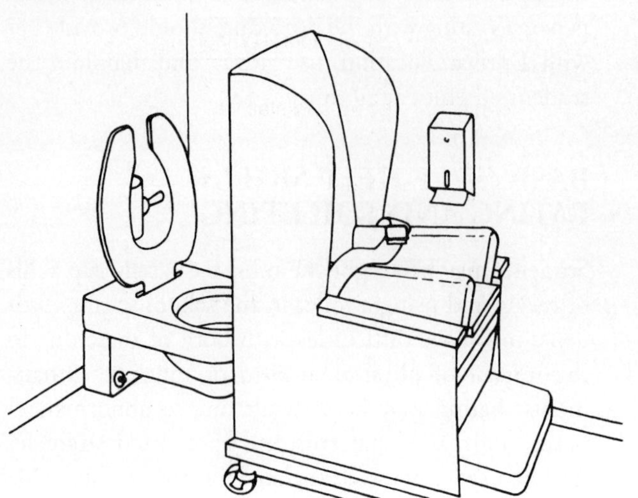

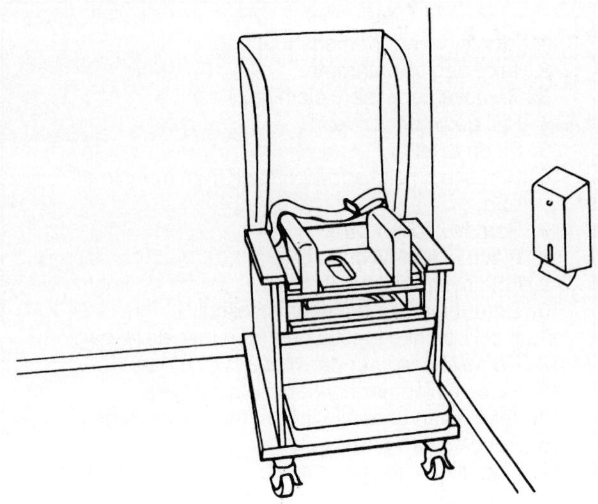

Some students may use other adaptive devices for toileting. For example, some students may use a bed-pan for urination or defecation. Some students have removable seat portions of their wheelchairs that allow a container to be attached for toileting purposes. Some students may use a urinal. For boys who cannot stand to urinate and who are wheelchair users, a hand-held urinal may be an appropriate solution.

Toileting involves a long series of skills that the individual needs to learn as one single task. The task begins when the individual feels the need to use the bathroom and ends when he or she dries his or her hands after washing them. To foster independence in this task, we must teach each of the skills of toileting and supply all equipment that will enable the individual to complete this task either without help or with as little help as possible. As with other personal management tasks, the process should be task-analyzed. Table 10–1 shows sample task analyses for a student who is ambulatory and a student with a physical disability who is a wheelchair user. Task analysis can vary widely based upon the student's motoric abilities. Students should be helped and encouraged to tell others how to help them with toileting if they cannot carry out the entire procedure themselves.

There are several methods of toilet training. One of the most successful programs involve some components of the **trip training method.** A trip training program uses scheduled times for the student to go the bathroom, based on student request, presence of student cues, and data taken on toileting times. Data is often taken two weeks prior to beginning a trip training program to determine the student's pattern of urination. This often consists of checking the student every half hour and recording whether the student is dry, wet, or had a bowel movement. Once a pattern emerges, a schedule is set, with the student often being taken to the restroom 10 minutes prior to when he or she typically urinates. Once the schedule is set, instruction begins. The student is placed on the toilet according to the schedule. If the student does not urinate after 5 minutes, he or she is removed from the toilet and returned to class. The student should never be reprimanded if he or she does not use the toilet at the scheduled time or if an accident occurs. This only results in the student's becoming tense during toileting time and may result in more accidents. Upon correct performance, the student receives reinforcement. For more in-depth information on teaching toileting skills and the trip training method, the reader is referred to the chapter on toilet training in *Meeting Physical and Health Needs of Children with Disabilities: Teaching Student Participation and Management* (Heller, Forney, et al., 2000).

Bowel training involves teaching the student to empty the bowels completely on a regularly scheduled basis. Appropriate diet and exercise play an important part in helping this to occur. Teaching a student to

TABLE 10–1
Sample Task Analyses for Toileting for Children with and without a Physical Impairment

Ambulatory	Physical Impairment—Wheelchair User
1. Request to use restroom.	1. Request to use restroom.
2. Go into restroom into stall.	2. Move into restroom and stall.
	2.1 Position chair.
	2.2 Lock brakes.
	2.3 Undo seat belt.
	2.4 Move to edge of seat.
	2.5 Assist with assisted standing.
	2.6 Hold on to handrail.
3. Unfasten pants and pull down.	3. Help unfasten pants and pull down.
3.1 Unfasten belt.	
3.2 Undo zipper.	
3.3 Pull down pants.	
3.4 Pull down underwear.	
4. Sit on toilet.	4. Sit up on toilet.
5. Urinate.	5. Urinate.
6. Wipe self.	6. Call for assistance to wipe.
6.1 Take toilet paper.	
6.2 Pull off roll.	
6.3 Wipe self from front to back.	
7. Stand up.	7. Request assistance to stand.
	7.1 Hold handrail and assist with standing.
8. Pull up clothing.	8. Assist in pulling up pants and fastening.
8.1 Pull up underwear.	
8.2 Pull up pants.	
8.3 Zip up zipper.	
8.4 Fasten belt.	
9. Reach for handle and flush.	9. Move into chair and reach for handle.
	9.1 Assist with turning and sitting on wheelchair seat.
	9.2 Move back into seat.
	9.3 Put on seat belt.
	9.4 Unlock brakes.
	9.5 Move wheelchair near handle and push to flush.
10. Go wash hands.	10. Go wash hands.

Note. From *Meeting Physical and Health Needs of Children with Disabilities: Teaching Student Participation and Management,* 1st edition, by Heller/Forney/Alberto/Schwartzman/Goeckel © 2000. Reprinted with permission of Wadsworth, a division of Thomson Learning: www.thomsonrights.com. Fax 800 730-2215.

empty his or her bowels on a schedule can occur in conjunction with the trip training program used for teaching bladder control. Typically, bowel evacuation is targeted to occur 30 minutes after a meal and at a time when the student is not rushed, but can relax on the toilet. However, some students with spinal cord injuries and other abnormalities will need suppositories, mild laxatives, and/or digital stimulation to assist with evacuation (Reid, 1996). The appropriate health care professional will need to direct the use of any medication or stimulation to be used as part of a bowel-training program.

To prevent unnecessary irritation to the buttocks and the area between the thighs, the skin should be cleaned with plain soap and water and patted dry when soilage is apparent. Every effort should be made to protect the skin from prolonged contact with waste matter. Prolonged contact will cause skin breakdown and skin irritation. Certain greaseless creams may be used to prevent skin irritation.

TUBE FEEDING, CATHETERIZATION, AND COLOSTOMY CARE

Some students may have specialized health care procedures for providing nutrition or elimination of waste materials. Instead of eating orally, some students may receive tube feedings. Other students may have difficulties or abnormalities with elimination and require urinary catheterization or colostomies. These specialized health care procedures are occurring in schools across the nation, with teachers and paraprofessionals regularly performing them. (Heller, Fredrick, Best, Dykes, & Cohen, 2000). There is much debate regarding who should perform these procedures in the school. More importantly, the educational team must determine if the student will learn to perform the procedure and what constitutes a safe, healthy environment for these procedures to be performed.

Specialized health care procedures are identified as self-help skills or independent living skills which should be considered for inclusion on the Individualized Education Program (IEP) (DPHD Critical Issues and Leadership Committee, 1999). Depending upon the student's abilities and the type of health care procedure, students may learn to independently perform their health care procedure, partially participate in some part of the procedure, or direct someone else in performance of the procedure (Heller, Forney, et al., 2000; Heller & Swinehart-Jones, 2003). The team must decide together if the student will be learning all or part of the procedure. The nurse will bring the expertise on how the procedure is to be performed, while the special education teacher brings the expertise on systematic instructional strategies that may be used to teach the student. The physical therapist may assist with proper positioning, while the occupational therapist may provide input on manipulating materials and adaptations. The speech/language pathologist may program the student's augmentative communication device to include key words or phrases regarding the procedures or possible complications.

In addition to including specialized health care procedures on the IEP, all teachers must strive to maintain a safe and healthy school environment for their students. Part of this includes being knowledgeable about the student's health care procedure, planning for emergencies or problems related to the procedure, and learning to recognize problems and act appropriately should they occur. Teachers should also be knowledgeable about universal precautions, general first aid, and cardiopulmonary resuscitation (CPR) (DPHD Critical Issues and Leadership Committee, 1999).

Tube Feeding

When a student is unable to achieve proper nutrition by ingesting food orally, a tube may be inserted into the student's stomach or intestines through which proper nutritional feedings can be given (Ault, Rues, Graff, & Holvoet, 2000). This is known as **tube feeding.** Tube feeding occurs in place of oral feedings or in addition to them. The most common ways of delivering tube feeding is through a gastrostomy tube (G-tube), which is a tube going directly into the stomach, or through a gastrostomy button (also known as a skin-level device), which is a small silicon device that goes through the abdominal wall and is positioned at skin level. Formula is delivered through a connecting tube that connects to the gastrostomy button. Formula is usually given on an intermittent basis at scheduled times. It is usually poured into a syringe barrel that is connected to the tube, and it flows by gravity through the tube into the stomach (see Figure 10–10). Care must be taken to prevent air from entering the tube to avoid cramping. In some instances the physician may have ordered the tube feeding on a continuous basis, in which case the formula is placed in a bag and flows by gravity or is infused by a mechanical pump.

Catheterization

Certain students may be unable to control urination due to such conditions as spina bifida, and may achieve continence through **clean intermittent catheterization (CIC).** In CIC a clean (not sterile) catheter is gently inserted into the urethra and advanced into the bladder. The catheter remains in place long enough to allow urine to be released from the bladder, and then the catheter is removed. Typically it is performed on a schedule, although new equipment is becoming available that can detect the amount of urine in the bladder, allowing the procedure to be done when needed based on the volume of urine in the bladder (Heller, Forney, et al., 2000).

Some students may not be candidates for toilet training or catheterization, but may wear an **external urinary catheter.** An external urinary catheter is a condom-like device with a tube on the end that allows urine to drain into a leg bag. Although this works well for males, similar devices for females tend to leak and have not had as much success.

FIGURE 10–10
Student receiving nutrition via tube feeding

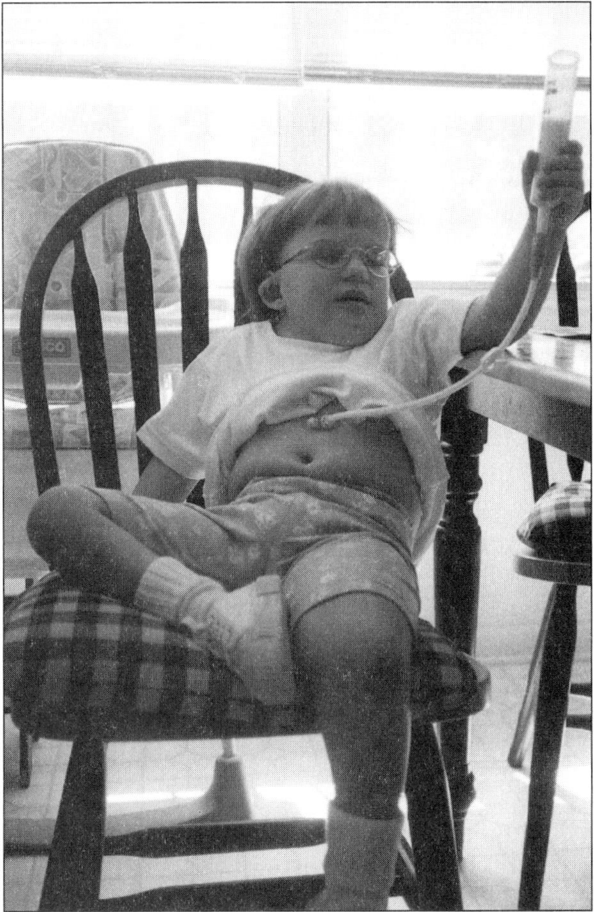

Note. From *Meeting Physical and Health Needs of Children with Disabilities: Teaching Student Participation and Management,* 1st edition, by Heller/Forney/Alberto/Schwartzman/Goeckel © 2000. Reprinted with permission of Wadsworth, a division of Thomson Learning. www.thomsonrights.com. Fax 800 730-2215.

Colostomy Care

Some students may have certain conditions, such as a congenital malformation of the intestines or a disease (e.g., Hirschprung's disease), that prevents feces from exiting the body through the normal anatomical route. These students may have an artificial opening (known as an ostomy) that is surgically created by connecting a section of the intestines through the abdomen. The name of each type of surgical formation is derived from the part of the gastrointestinal or urinary system involved in the process, such as **colostomy** (ostomy of the large intestine), **ileostomy** or **jejunostomy** (ostomies of the small intestine). Feces exits out of the ostomy. Usually a bag is needed to collect the feces. The bag will need to be emptied throughout the school day, and should it leak, the bag itself may need to be reapplied. A skin barrier is used between the bag and the skin to help prevent skin breakdown.

Students Performing Their Own Health Care Procedures

Students requiring tube feeding, catheterization (or other urinary device), or colostomy care (or other type of ostomy) may learn to perform their own health care procedure. As with any other type of self-help skill, the procedure will need to be task-analyzed, and a discrepancy analysis should be performed. Students may be taught to perform all or part of the steps, depending upon their ability. The appropriate instructional strategy will need to be selected.

However, unlike typical self-care skills, each health care procedure will need to be analyzed for time-limited steps and caution steps (Heller, Forney, et al., 2000). **Time-limited steps** are those that must be completed within a certain time frame or injury could result. For example, in the tube-feeding procedure, the step when more formula needs to be added to the syringe barrel before it empties in order to avoid air being introduced into the stomach (which could cause cramping) is a time-limited step. **Caution steps** are those steps in which the student could injure himself or herself by making a quick, jerking, or incorrect movement. For tube feeding, a caution step is attaching the syringe barrel to the G-tube, since the student could inadvertently pull out the G-tube.

If the educational team determines that the student should learn the time-limited steps and caution steps, the adult needs to highlight these steps on the data sheet and provide **shadowing** (keeping adult hands within an inch of the student's hands) in order to allow for quick intervention and prevent errors. For more in-depth information on these and other health care procedures, including task-analyzed procedures, sample IEP and IHPs, teaching techniques, and problems and emergencies, refer to *Meeting Physical and Health Needs of Children with Disabilities: Teaching Student Participation and Management* (Heller, Forney, et al., 2000).

DRESSING

Children who enter school with physical or multiple disabilities may have functional problems that interfere with the mastery of dressing and undressing. Depending upon the type and severity of the impairment, problems dressing or undressing may occur in such areas as positioning, muscle tone and strength, head and trunk control, coordination and motor planning, fine-motor dexterity, and perceptual skills. To meet these problems, children with physical limitations may be taught to participate to the greatest extent by using particular positioning techniques, modified clothing, adaptive equipment, or a combination of these. Some children are often good problem solvers in determining which techniques suit their needs and abilities. However, it is the teacher's role to assist the student in developing the techniques that will enable the child to perform dressing and undressing at the greatest level of independence.

Helping Individuals Learn Dressing Skills

There are several guidelines that may be followed to help students learn to dress themselves. Teachers should (a) analyze current dressing skills, (b) provide assistance only when needed and allow time for the student to plan and execute necessary movements, (c) teach undressing skills prior to teaching dressing skills, (d) teach special techniques in dressing, and (e) teach what to wear and when to wear it. Each of these will be discussed next.

Analyze Current Dressing Skills. Care must be taken to observe individuals as they attempt particular dressing tasks. Individuals should be encouraged to complete as much of the task as possible. Observers should notice when a student faces a task that requires modifications. Ellen, for example, had two physically involved arms and hands. She got stuck at the same point each time she attempted to take off her heavy winter coat with cuffs. After a while she became discouraged and stopped trying. It was observed that when she had slipped the coat off her shoulders with both arms still in the sleeves, she was unable to free either elbow from the elbow of the sleeve. Ellen needed someone to push the armhole of the garment from the upper part of her arm to the lower part in order to free her elbow and allow her to pull the sleeve off (see Figure 10–11).

FIGURE 10–11
A little help at the elbow was all that was needed

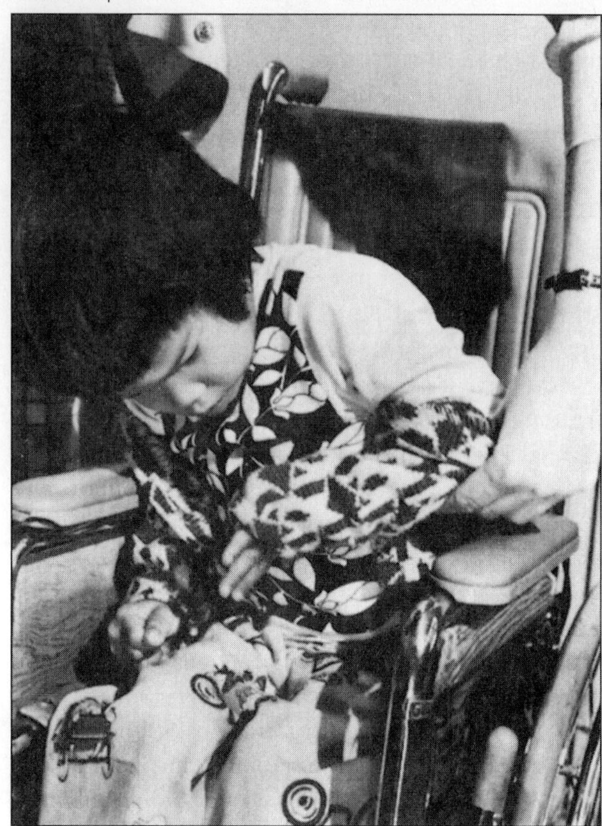

Attempts at dressing should be studied both at home and at school. Notice the student's attempts to dress himself or herself or to help others to dress him or her. Analyze the different subtasks of dressing. Parents and teachers should compare their observations. A particular student may be able to undress herself at school when anticipating a swim or therapy, yet the same student is completely dependent on parental help at home; or the situation may be reversed. The parent may take the time to permit the child to undress herself completely, whereas the teacher may feel rushed and provide assistance even when it is not needed.

At times, it is not enough to know that the individual can make the movements necessary to complete a dressing task. Teachers must notice other characteristics of the individual that influence his or her performance. The student may enjoy dependence and attention from others, or may be unaware of what is expected of him or her. For instance, when a student comes to school with a jacket on, he or she may not realize that the jacket should be taken off in the classroom. Perhaps the student is not willing to ask for help or is unable to receive help graciously. Perhaps the student does not show interest in learning new tasks. A student may have the motor skills for completing a task, but may not be able to plan the movements necessary for that particular task. Finally, a student may not have received enough positive reinforcement when attempting new tasks, consequently becoming easily frustrated and discouraged.

Provide Assistance Only When Needed and Provide Sufficient Time. Some students with motor impairment are able to dress themselves, but adults do not allow enough time for them to complete the tasks. Thus, they do not try or quickly become discouraged. Some students are never given the opportunity to learn that they can complete some tasks without aid. This, of course, causes unnecessary dependence. When helping to dress or undress a young student, the teacher should try to orient his or her own arms in the same direction as the student's arms, so that the student will imitate the teacher's movements and learn to perform the same skills by copying what the teacher does.

Teach Undressing Skills Prior to Teaching Dressing Skills. It is generally agreed that it is easier to undress than to dress. It is easier, for instance, for a student to pull a shoelace and untie a shoe than it is for him or her to put a shoe on and tie the laces. Similarly, it is easier for most individuals to take off shorts and dresses than to put on the same garments. The following description of removal of socks demonstrates the steps in learning an undressing skill:

1. Cooperates passively when being undressed.
2. Moves limbs to aid in removal of clothing, holds out foot for shoe removal, pulls arm from last of sleeve, and withdraws foot from sock.
3. Pulls sock off over toes after adult removes sock to that point.
4. Pulls socks off over sole after socks are removed to that point.
5. Pulls socks off over heel after socks are removed to that point.
6. Pulls socks off completely (Santa Cruz Office of Education, 1973).

Teach Special Techniques in Dressing. Many techniques and special appliances are available to assist with dressing. For example, flipping a coat over one's head is a technique often used by students with coordination or weakness problems. The student lays the garment flat on her lap, the floor, or a table. The collar should be near her body with the front of the coat on top and the lining showing. The student can then either push both arms into the sleeves or push in the involved arm first and the other arm second (see Figure 10–12). Next, the student ducks the head forward while extending the arms over the head. Finally, the coat is slipped into place when the student shrugs her shoulders and pulls down with her arms. Special tools and buttons for moving buttons through the holes should be used when necessary. Other adapted devices and clothing are described in the next section.

Teach What to Wear and When to Wear It. When working with a student on dressing, teach appropriate ways to dress for different types of weather and different kinds of activities. These learning sessions can easily become a part of the daily curriculum. For example, a weather chart can be placed in the classroom, with pictures pasted on the chart to represent different types of weather. This chart can be used for discussion of what should be worn on a rainy day, for example. Young students can dress cutouts of people with different kinds of clothing. Teachers should also help students become aware of suitable color combinations. Discussions between parents and students about appropriate selection of clothing are also helpful.

Adapted Clothing and Adapted Dressing Devices

Beginning Dressers. Full-length, center-front openings such as those found on overalls, jumpsuits, some dresses, jumpers, skirts, blouses, and pantsuit tops are helpful to children just learning to dress themselves. Expandable neck openings of stretchable fabrics are also helpful. Some fastenings are inconvenient or prevent independence of persons with disabilities. The type, size, and location of fasteners on a garment determine how easily they can be managed. Zippers are easy to pull up or down, and large zipper tabs are easy to grasp and may be made of a fabric loop or metal ring. Nylon coil zippers are pliable and less likely to snag. Buttons must be large enough to be grasped and should not be sewn on tightly. A flat, smooth button slips through a buttonhole

FIGURE 10–12
Steps of an alternative method for putting on a jacket

(a) (b) (c) (d) (e) (f)

more easily than does a fancy one. A Velcro® fastening requires minimal hand and finger dexterity to open or close. Hooks and eyes are difficult to fasten unless they are large and sturdy. The type of metal hook and bar used on men's trousers is more manageable on skirts and slacks for those with hand limitations. In addition, the location of fasteners has a great deal to do with ease in dressing. Fasteners should be easy to see, to reach, and to grasp. Fasteners located in the center front of a garment are usually easier to manipulate than are those located on the side or back. Select trousers with a zipper fly and elasticized waist back or garments tailored specially for people with disabilities. Knitted garments with elasticized waistbands and rib-knit expandable necklines eliminate the need for fasteners.

Individuals with Coordination Problems and Limited Use of Hands. Most features helpful to individuals learning to dress themselves are also recommended for those with uncoordinated or insufficient hand use. Nylon zippers and Velcro® are particularly helpful on openings in blouse and shirt fronts, jackets, fly fronts, skirt waists, and cuffs of long sleeves. If side openings are used, they should be on the side opposite the student's stronger hand. Difficulty getting buttons through buttonholes may require the use of a buttonhook. A **buttonhook** is a handled device that has a wire loop on the end. The wire loop is inserted through the buttonhole, going around the button. The child pulls the button through the hole with the buttonhook while the other hand stabilizes the fabric. Often a small hook is attached to the opposite end of the buttonhook to assist with zipping or unzipping clothing when the child is unable to hold the zipper.

Some students who have limited reach may use reachers. **Reachers** have a handle on one end and a gripper jaw on the other. They can be purchased in a variety of lengths from 18 to 33 inches long and have a variety of gripper jaws. The activating handles can be purchased with a squeeze-to-open or squeeze-to-close gripper, depending upon the strength and skill of the child. A reacher is used when full range of movement is not available to reach particular parts of the body. For example, when putting on pants, reachers may be used to hold on to the waistband to lower pants toward the feet (Goeckel, Heller, Forney, & Cohen, 2000).

Students who have difficulty maintaining a grasp on the clothing item may use a **dressing stick.** Dressing sticks are usually make of a wooden dowel 12 to 34 inches long with a push/pull hook on one end and a C hook on the other end (see Figure 10–13). For the child with a limited shoulder range of movement, shortened limbs, or limited grasp, the dressing stick hook can be used to pull the waistband up to the hip or used to push the pants down to knee level (Goeckel et al., 2000). Schwartz (1995) describes making a dressing stick by using a wooden hanger with the hook removed.

FIGURE 10–13
Student uses a sock aid to help put on a sock. A dressing stick (on the right) can be used to assist with dressing

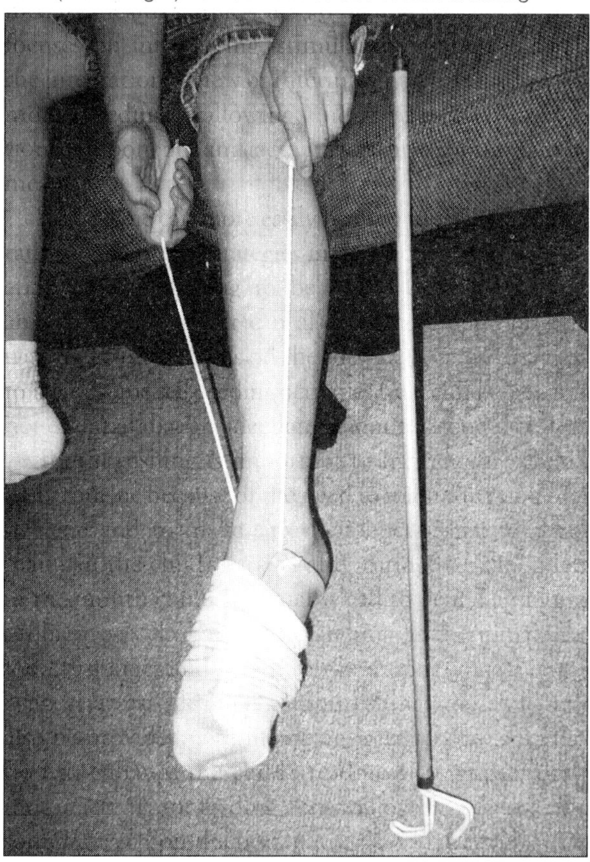

A cup hook is screwed into one end for grasping and a thimble is placed on the other end to push clothing into place.

Socks and shoes may also require adaptations. Selection of the size, type, and fabric of the sock should be considered. Socks with stretchable cuffs may be easier to put on for children with weak hands. Tube socks that do not have heel seams can help decrease concern about orienting the sock to the heel of the foot (Shepard, Procter, & Coley, 1996). A **sock aid** may assist a child in putting on socks if the child has difficulty placing the sock over the foot or pulling the sock up. Figure 10–13 shows a typical sock aid made out of plastic that allows the foot to more easily slide into an open sock. Shoes may also be put on with the assistance of such devices as long shoehorns. Shoelaces can be particularly difficult for students with physical impairments. There are a variety of adaptations that may be used with or in place of shoelaces to help the student to be independent in this task, such as using lace locks, shoe buttons, or Velcro fasteners instead of laces.

Individuals with Braces. Full-length crotch openings are helpful for students wearing braces, particularly for those who need to have diapers changed. The inseam is opened and Velcro® or a zipper is inserted. Wide pant legs are more comfortable for individuals wearing braces. If trouser or slack legs are too narrow to slip over braces, zippers or Velcro® strips can be inserted in the seams (see Figure 10–14). Elastic bands on skirts, trousers, or slacks add the flexibility needed to accommodate braces. Knitted fabrics tend to catch on brace locks. Undergarments should fit snugly if worn under braces or be large enough to allow room for braces if worn over them. Underwear should be reinforced in spots where braces may rub.

Crutch Users. Students who use full-length crutches need garments that will not tear along underarm seams. Garments with double-stitched underarm seams are more durable. Certain fabrics, such as those that are stretch-woven, tolerate more abuse than others. Stress points in a garment can be reinforced before use. Choose garments so that underarm crutches fit comfortably under the arms without changing the lines of the clothing. If Canadian or Loftstand crutches are used, select coats that allow the crutches to fit over the sleeves.

FIGURE 10–14
Dark strips of Velcro® down the side of trousers permit ease in dressing when braces are worn

Wheelchair Users. Culottes also allow ample room for body movement and allow transfer to and from a wheelchair without the embarrassment of exposure. Slim, straight skirts tend to ride up, and full skirts tend to get caught in the wheels or bunch up as the person sits. Wraparound skirts are easy to put on and facilitate toileting. Skirts with some flare permit both wrinkle-free sitting and room for movement.

Trouser seats are more comfortable if they are fuller than usual and if they do not contain the useless bulk of pockets. Heavy belts in strong trouser loops allow helpers to lift and support students who cannot support themselves. Long sleeves often get dirty when worn by wheelchair users; therefore, short sleeves are desirable.

In cold weather an easily made wool cape with a front zipper and a hood can eliminate the need for struggling with sleeves and getting the back of a jacket down between the person and the chair. The process of using the cape is simple, which greatly benefits students who go outdoors several times a day. The zipper can be opened and the sides and the hood can be thrown around the back of the wheelchair. The sides can be brought to the front and zipped when needed. Students can "sit in" the cape all day even when it is not needed over their shoulders. A large loop can be added to the zipper so that the student with a disability can pull the zipper up and down.

Figure Irregularities and Prosthetic Arm Considerations. Blouses and shirts designed to be worn outside skirts and trousers help disguise figure irregularities. Dress and trouser hemlines can be adjusted so that they are balanced in spite of postural or other figure irregularities. Hemline imbalance with irregularities of the upper part of the body can be avoided by choosing two-piece dresses. Long-sleeved dresses and shirts are often desired by individuals with prosthetic arms. Sources for manufacturers of adapted clothing and other independence items are listed at the end of this chapter.

HOME CARE AND MANAGEMENT

"Plan ahead" should be the motto for people with physical disabilities who attempt household tasks. Many cannot carry out household tasks without substantial preplanning. Menus are an example. Individuals must learn what they are able to cook and how to prepare a well-balanced meal. They should consider what they have on their shelves, what they need to purchase, where they must go to buy food, how they will travel there, the availability of various foods, the value of their money (its purchasing power), the time required to cook a specific food, and the time that cooked and uncooked foods will remain fresh. Finally, they need to plan the exact steps they will take to complete the meal. Will they need to allow extra time to cut the vegetables with one hand? Will they need any special appliances or any adaptations to expedite the task? Many individuals with disabilities can do all the planning, though some may need help in carrying out the plan. To teach specific home care skills, skills can be task-analyzed and a discrepancy analysis should be performed. Specific adaptations and instructional strategies can be selected based upon student need. This section will concentrate on kitchen tasks and housecleaning, since they often present the largest problems.

Kitchen Tasks

There are many objects and techniques that individuals can use as aids in accomplishing kitchen tasks. Individuals with severe coordination problems or physical weakness, or who use crutches or a wheelchair, may wish to use unbreakable dishes (see Figure 10–15). By placing a platform inside a sink, it can be made shallower for easier use by those in wheelchairs. A dishwasher increases accessibility for a wheelchair user, provided there is sufficient space to position the wheelchair near the open door. Pullout cupboard shelves are desirable for reaching dishes, bowls, and pots. A broom closet may be converted into an easy-reach pantry. For some students, dishwashing may be accessed by having the student use his or her prone stander at the sink to do dishes, or by using a strap to help maintain balance at the sink (see Figure 10–16).

Menu Selection. Menu selections may be limited somewhat if cooks have limited reading ability and difficulty remembering recipes. Teachers and parents should teach young students how to cook so that they have acquired sufficient cooking skills by the time they need to be independent. Some cookbooks are available (or can be made) that use pictures to represent the ingredients and steps needed to make simple meals.

FIGURE 10–15
Debra's mother purchased unbreakable dishes and encouraged Debra's independence and responsibility from her early childhood

FIGURE 10–16
With the security of the strap, Stacy enjoys washing dishes

Many manufacturers are now using pictures to illustrate how to cook their product. Besides using pictures, students may also be taught to read frequently encountered words in recipes. Typically, simple recipes will be selected that the student likes and can easily learn to make. The teacher looks through the recipes for key words that occur frequently. The words are taught using one of the reading approaches discussed in Chapter 13 on literacy and language arts.

Cooking. Cooking must be done safely as well as efficiently. If stove burners are at the eye level of the wheelchair user, a mirror may be hung with a forward tilt behind the burners to permit viewing pot interiors. Knobs must be in safe locations, such as on the front of the stove, to prevent injury caused by reaching over burners. If the stove is unsuitable, cooking can be done with immersible frying pans, microwave ovens, and tabletop broilers. All of these appliances can be placed on low counters or tables. Individuals lacking accurate sensation of hot or cold must protect all exposed parts of the body with padding. If hot pans are to be carried on the lap of a wheelchair user, aprons made with two layers of crib pads or wheelchair lapboards can be used.

Storage and Counter Space. Ample space is very important for wheelchair users. They should be able to maneuver their wheelchairs with ease within the kitchen. Individuals who have trouble standing and walking may prefer to have a smaller floor space with items in easy reach. Counters should be designed so that wheelchair users can bring themselves closer to the work area. Adequate location and amount of storage space for equipment and supplies may require a great deal of preplanning. It is generally recommended that equipment and supplies be placed at the "point of first use." Cooking utensils should be stored near the stove. Baking utensils should be stored near the place where baked goods are prepared. Frequently used items can be reached most easily if they are hung on the front of cupboards. Pegboards are handy for hanging utensils.

Ample counter space is important to any cook. Cooks with motor impairment appreciate counter space that enables them to slide, instead of lift, pans and other items. Individuals in wheelchairs usually prefer counters low enough to permit them to rest their elbows on them and deep enough for their legs to fit underneath (see Figure 10–17).

FIGURE 10–17
A shelf grooved to fit firmly on opened cupboard doors creates a low counter with leg room for a wheelchair.

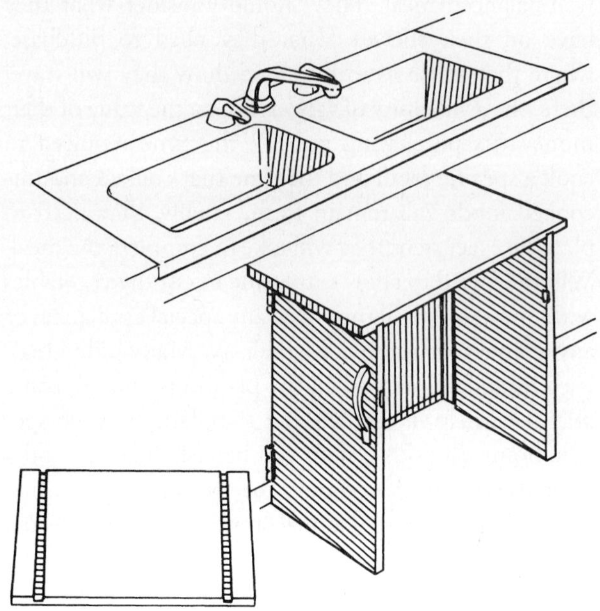

Utensils. Nearly every utensil a cook needs is available commercially. A person with a disability needs only to anticipate desired features of utensils before shopping. Funnels help prevent spilling when hands are weak or unsteady. Large spoons with holes prevent spilling liquid overflow while serving. Wedge-type jar openers prevent needless turning and twisting of jar lids. Screw-handled pans facilitate steadiness. Heavy pots and pans help counteract excess motion.

Special needs that cannot be met by commercial utensils and equipment can often be accommodated with simple homemade adaptations. Accidents can also be prevented with homemade adaptations. Bowls can be stabilized when they are placed into a simple wooden frame to prevent spillage when mixing (see Figure 10–18). Food items can be placed between two nails protruding from a board to prevent them from turning or rolling while they are being cut. A potato, apple, or other round food item can be impaled on the nails and managed easily by a person with weak or uncoordinated movements. When using this strategy, be sure to use rustproof nails!

Appliances. Appliances come in many different designs and weights. Electric appliances that have a plug that can be pushed into the socket on the appliance

FIGURE 10–18
Beaters that "went wild" are now confined

rather than pushed into a wall socket are better for those for whom weakness is a problem. Some electric appliances, such as electric skillets, are heavier than others. Extra weight helps reduce excessive motion. Lightweight appliances may be preferred for those with weakness problems. An important aspect of electrical appliances is the location and size of knobs and controls. Select electrical appliances on which knobs and controls are located away from the heated areas. If knobs are not long enough, they can be extended so that the person with a disability can operate them more easily. People with severe physical disabilities often demonstrate skill in personal engineering. They have come up with ideas and plans for counteracting inconveniences and dependencies resulting from their disabilities. They have suggested ways of adapting the control systems available for radio, television, and other electronic devices. They have found ways to use free and inexpensive supplies to make wands, mouth sticks, extensions to switches, and enlarged surfaces on switches.

Housecleaning

It is unrealistic to expect a person with extensive paralysis, limited energy, or severe coordination difficulty to do major housecleaning. Too much energy is expended by a

FIGURE 10–19
Simple household tasks can be adapted, such as making a bed from a kneeling position (a) and vacuuming using a scooterboard (b). Baking soda may be sprinkled on the carpet for practice

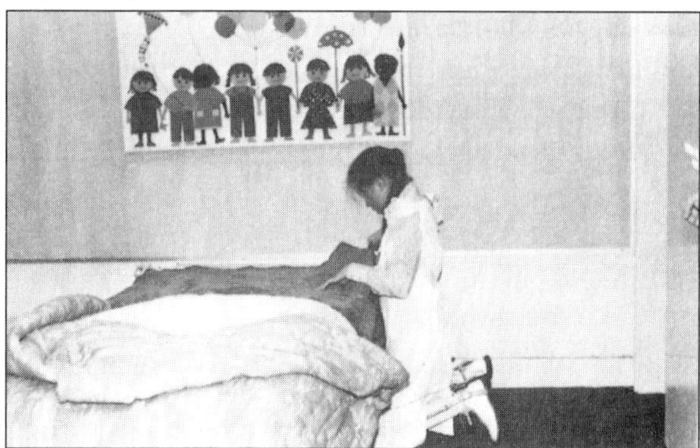

(a)

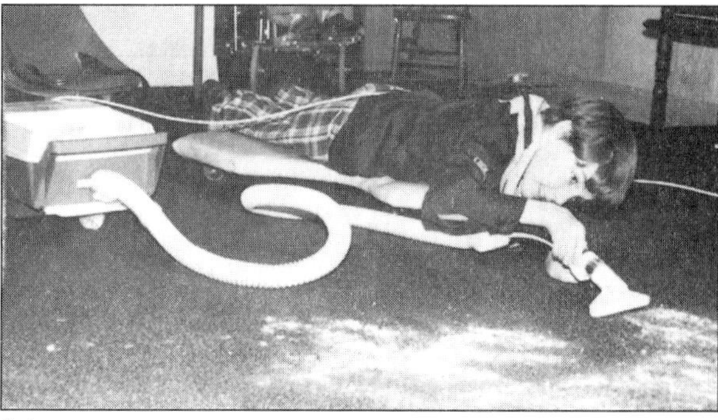

(b)

person with a significant physical disability in simply lifting his or her body, using crutches, walking with braces, or propelling a wheelchair. Some individuals, however, can find ways to do many household tasks (see Figure 10–19). Homes adapted or designed to be barrier-free reduce inconvenience caused by the combination of a disability and a home full of physical barriers.

To manage fatigue, heavy jobs can be spread throughout the week rather than being undertaken all in one day. Long and complex tasks can be divided over several days, so that the work on each day will be as varied and as interesting as possible. There will generally be some housekeeping tasks that individuals will be unable to do and some that will be accomplished only with extreme difficulty.

Individuals should assume leadership in establishing agreement among members of the household about who will do what. This strategy will relieve the anxiety of others regarding the appropriate kind and amount of help to be given. A list of homemaking jobs that can be performed by individuals with disabilities might include dusting, sweeping with a lightweight or electric broom, use of a canister vacuum cleaner that swivels easily in all directions, and cleaning with various homemade and commercial reaching devices (e.g., long-handled brushes or sponges for cleaning bathtubs and sinks). Homemade, custom-designed tools are often the most useful.

Technology and Environmental Control

Some individuals have so little motor function that they can do little for themselves without aid from others or from technology. No discussion of means for teaching individuals to take control over their personal care can be complete without including technological advances that allow individuals with physical disabilities to exercise more control over things in their environment. Research in robotics, for instance, holds much promise for the development of assistive devices that allow individuals with limited physical capabilities to take physical control over the performance of activities in their everyday living. Environmental control devices and strategies also hold much promise.

Environmental control devices are available that will allow users to activate or deactivate any appliance controlled by electricity. The young adult in Figure 10–20 is able to accomplish a variety of activities to help himself. He is able to do so with an environmental control unit that was designed especially for that purpose. Computers, to the surprise of many, can also be used as a means to environmental control. William, a 15-year-old youth who has control only of the eyebrows and forehead, was supplied with a communication device for speech and a computer for academics and written communication; however, he was dependent on others to control the lights, stereos, televisions, and heat in his environment. An environmental control device was connected to his computer, and through the use of his single switch, William could operate six different electrically powered devices in his room.

FIGURE 10–20
By puffing and sipping, this young man controls TV channels and the radio, and draws his living room curtains

(Prentke Romich Environmental Control Unit. Prentke Romich, 1022 Heyl Road, Wooster, Ohio 44691.)

COMMUNITY-BASED INSTRUCTION

Students with physical or multiple disabilities need to access and perform various activities in the community. In order to do so, they will need systematic instruction in the actual task in the environment in which it takes place. A community-based instruction program should be in place at school to give students the opportunity to learn how to shop, eat, and perform numerous activities in the community (for information on community-based vocational training, see Chapter 12, "Transition and Self-Determination"). Students with physical disabilities who are on an academic track may also benefit from some instruction to learn how to get assistance at a grocery store, how to get around, and other areas. As with all activities, a task analysis and a discrepancy analysis may need to be performed to determine strategies and adaptations.

One of the first areas to address in community-based instruction is how the student will get to the desired destination in the community. Although the school may provide a school bus, this is not how the student will get around after graduation. Discussing and determining appropriate modes of transportation will be important. The student will also need to anticipate architectural barriers as well as shopping considerations.

Anticipating Architectural Barriers

Individuals may have special kinds of problems depending on whether they use crutches, canes, walkers, or wheelchairs. However, shopping can be an adventure for those willing to explore different kinds of stores. Check by phone about any possible barriers before going to unfamiliar stores. Since crowds become barriers to shoppers with disabilities, shop at slow times when possible. Doors are prime architectural barriers. Are they wide enough? Are they automatic or manually operated? Does one have to push or pull? Is there a handle, a doorknob, a lever, or nothing at all to grab? Does a door swing in one or both directions? Does it swing freely, is it on a spring, or is it pressurized? Turnstiles are another problem. These obstacles are impossible to overcome in a wheelchair and are very awkward for those using crutches. Ask if there are other ways for a customer to enter the store. Aisles should also be checked. Are they wide enough? Do they take you to all parts of the store? Do the aisles connect smoothly, or are they a maze? Do racks or displays project into the aisles? Is merchandise stacked in places where it can be easily knocked over? Shelves and counters often present problems. Can customers in wheelchairs see and reach the merchandise? Are some shelves so high that it is impossible to reach the items? Are the items stacked too high on shelves? Are the meat counters and freezer shelves too deep? Is the aisle leading to the checkout counter wide enough for someone in a wheelchair?

Restrooms. Individuals often need to use restrooms while shopping. For customers using wheelchairs, this can be a nightmare. They need to learn adaptive strategies for using public restrooms that are not totally accessible. For instance, when it is difficult for them to get into the restroom, they may have to make adjustments such as making the wheelchair narrower while sitting in it, or they may have to ask strangers for assistance with this task. Many wheelchairs are at least 28 inches wide. Is the door wide enough for it to pass through? Does the door have to be pulled or pushed? (Pulling can be difficult for a person on crutches.) Does the door have handles, a doorknob, or a push plate? (Doorknobs require superior fine-motor control.) Is there a spring on the door that causes it to close too rapidly for the person to pass through safely? Similar questions can be raised about entrance hallways and passageways. Is there a series of doors? Is the space from one door to the next adequate for a wheelchair? Are the doors equipped with time delay or self-closing devices?

Once inside the restroom area, can the person in a wheelchair locate an empty stall, get into the stall, and maneuver to a toilet? Is one toilet freestanding, or are they all in stalls? Are there privacy screens? Are there handrails in convenient places? Does the door to the stall provide clearance for the wheelchair? Hopefully, shoppers with mobility difficulties and other citizens will encourage businesspeople to place the "wheelchair-accessible" logo on the front of the store so that individuals will know that their shop is wheelchair accessible (see Figure 10–21).

FIGURE 10–21
This barrier-free restroom is designated with a logo

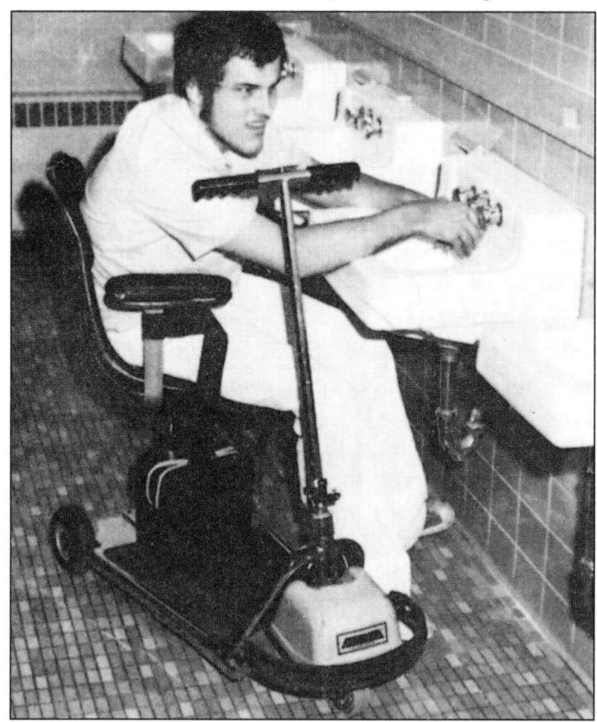

Shopping

Before individuals with motor and perhaps other disabilities can begin to shop, they must formulate a plan. After determining transportation needs and architectural barriers, they need to decide how to shop. The floor plan of targeted stores should be studied so that the person can go to the desired areas with the least amount of movement. They may find it more efficient to go to certain sections of the store while continuously scanning the shopping list to see if any items they pass are on the list. A person who shops item-by-item from the list may cover the whole store many times. Individuals may want to try to shop repeatedly at the same stores so they can become familiar with how the merchandise is arranged. Problems involved in finding merchandise, reaching for it, carrying it, and paying for it should also be anticipated. Some individuals may prefer to shop by the computer, telephone, or television. Many products can now be ordered by computer and delivered to the person's home. Department stores and many local grocers also provide delivery services.

Finding and Managing Merchandise. When people go shopping, they often formulate a list of items they wish to purchase. Students should be taught to make and use lists to help them remember the items they are shopping for. The list may be a written list of items or a picture list that shows the desired items (see Figure 10–22). Picture lists may have several items on a page with corresponding pictures or symbols, or may show one item at a time. Students are taught to mark off the item (or to move the picture into a "finished" area) once they have taken the item.

FIGURE 10–22
Mike uses pictures instead of a shopping list to remind himself what to buy

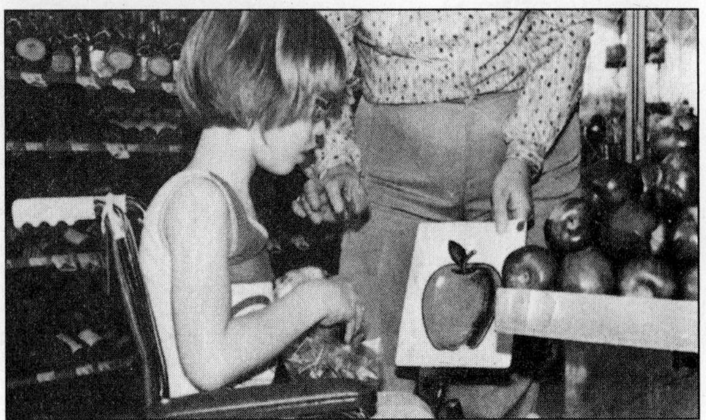

From early childhood, individuals should be taught categorizations and groupings of merchandise. Whenever possible, parents should take children with them to stores and point out ways that store merchandise is grouped. Some groupings are more obvious than others. At times, it may be necessary to teach individuals certain definitions that describe groupings. *Dairy*, for instance, is a word that is not self-descriptive. The dairy section is where one finds items such as milk, cream, and eggs. Shoppers who can read should be taught how to use the signs above the aisles in grocery stores, store directories, and signs on counters in department stores. Knowing how merchandise is grouped, the location of groupings in a store, and the floor plan of the store will conserve the time and effort of shoppers.

Individuals who cannot read need to know ways of finding items in the stores. Meat and cheese are easy to find in grocery stores because shoppers are able to see the product through glass on display cases or through plastic wrap on individual packages. Items in cans, such as vegetables and fruits, often have pictures on the labels. Shoppers can associate pictures with products. Items in cartons, such as cottage cheese and yogurt, may be difficult to identify, since they lack picture representation on the outside of the carton. Nonreaders need to be taught which kinds of foods are found in which kinds of containers and in which sections of stores.

Even when shoppers can identify items they wish to purchase, they may have difficulty reaching them. They may wish to employ a neighborhood child as a "basket pusher and can reacher." In department stores, clerks can be asked to hold the merchandise so that it can be seen.

In grocery stores, wheelchair occupants might use baskets placed on their laps for light articles. A low shopping cart on rubber swivel casters can be pulled easily by a wheelchair user. Wheelchair users may prefer to have a large cloth bag attached to the back of the wheelchair. For a person who has difficulty walking, large shoulder bags are sometimes helpful. The shoulder bag shifts the weight from the hands and arms and distributes it over the trunk and shoulders. Shoulder bags and backpacks are also useful for people using canes or crutches, since the bags allow the hands to be free.

Paying for Merchandise. Shoppers must be able to determine the price of items and the amount of merchandise their money will buy. Games such as Count

Your Change (Milton Bradley) and Pay the Cashier (Dolch), along with classroom lessons, will provide practice in handling money and buying items. Shoppers often must add up the prices of items as they proceed in order to be sure they have enough money. Calculators can be a helpful device for this task. Students can practice in the classroom on problems anticipated in actual shopping. (See Chapter 16 for teaching money counting.) For a person with hand-control or weakness problems, a calculator can be adapted to fit on the wrist like a watch or can be carried on a tray or in the lap.

Shoppers who are unsure of the value of coins can compensate for their lack of knowledge by paying with dollar bills only. They can be taught to read the number of dollars posted or registered and not worry about the number of cents on a given total. They then need to learn to count out and give a cashier one more dollar than the stated total or than the number of dollars on a price placard or on the register. In this manner, confidence is gained by the shopper because it never becomes obvious that he or she does not know the value of coins. (See Chapter 16 for more information.)

Restaurants. Eating establishments are varied and require a different set of skills in order to correctly acquire food, pay for the food, and find a place to sit. For example, eating at a fast-food restaurant involves ordering food from a counter, paying at the counter, and finding a place to sit. This is different from a buffet-style restaurant, in which the customer may be seated, go to a buffet counter to select the food, and pay on the way out. At a formal restaurant the customer is seated, selects from a menu, and pays at the table after eating. It is important that students learn about different types of restaurants and learn the skills necessary to succeed in eating at these establishments.

Eating out also requires advanced planning. First, there are accessibility issues as to whether the student can easily move to the table and whether a wheelchair will easily fit up to the table. It is also important to find out about bathroom accessibility. If the student requires an adaptive plate or utensil, advance planning is needed to determine how these will be transported and used in the restaurant. In some situations, the student may be able to manage with the eating utensils the restaurant provides, while in other cases food may be transferred into an adapted plate and the student may use his or her own utensils. Food selections may need to be preprogrammed into the student's augmentative communication device. If this is not possible, the student should be allowed to select his or her choice.

SUMMARY AND CONCLUSION

This chapter presented information on a range of adaptations to promote personal independence. Use of a discrepancy analysis was stressed for assessment of students' current skills and determining needed adaptations. Various systematic instructional strategies for promoting the learning of personal management skills were described. Hygiene skills were discussed utilizing various adaptations and the use of target and quadrant strategies, and toileting considerations were described. Students can be taught physical health care procedures as skills which they perform independently, partially participate in, or direct another person to perform. It is critical that students be encouraged to participate as fully as possible. Teachers need to learn about these procedures in order to maintain a safe, healthy environment. Other personal management skills such as dressing, home management, and community tasks were discussed in terms of adaptations and considerations for individuals with physical or multiple disabilities. The importance of teaching personal management skills and providing appropriate adaptations cannot be stressed enough in order to promote personal independence in home, school, and community environments.

QUESTIONS FOR DISCUSSION

1. Select a hygiene skill (such as face washing or toothbrushing) and perform a task analysis and discrepancy analysis with a student with physical or multiple disabilities. Discuss possible problems and adaptations. What instructional strategy would you use to teach the student?

2. Discuss roles and responsibilities of tube-feeding a student during school hours. What would a teacher need to know about tube feeding to maintain a safe, healthy environment?
3. Mary, a 7-year-old student with severe spastic quadriplegic cerebral palsy, wants to learn how to put her coat on and how to take it off. What would you teach first and how?
4. Select a recipe and adapt it using pictures. Discuss how it would be taught. For students who cannot independently follow a recipe, describe how partial participation could be used.
5. Select a store in your community and assess it for accessibility issues and organization of items. Discuss how accessible it would be for a person who uses a wheelchair or crutches. Describe several possible adaptations and strategies to make shopping in the store possible.

FOCUS ON THE NET

Abledata
http://www.abledata.com

Abledata is a federally funded project that provides information on assistive technology and rehabilitation equipment available from various national and international sources. Searches can be done by keyword, product type, company, or brand. Products that promote personal independence can be found under such categories as home management, controls, personal care, and architectural elements.

Ableware
http://www.maddak.com or
http://63.125.198.12/index.asp

This company manufactures a wide range of products for daily living activities. New products and featured products are described as well as the products of the month. There are also links to related resources.

Attainment Company
http://www.attainmentcompany.com

This company provides life skill curricula and hands-on materials on personal hygiene, keeping house, selecting a meal, shopping, home cooking, and planning the day. This company also has software for teaching money concepts and social skills for the community, as well as a picture dictionary.

Independent Living Aids
http://www.independentliving.com

This company provides a variety of adapted devices for individuals with visual impairments, many applicable for students with physical and multiple disabilities. Several independent living products are available as well as magnifiers and educational and recreational products.

Sammons Preston, Inc.
http://www.sammonspreston.com

This company provides a wide range of adapted devices for daily living. Adapted devices are provided across several daily living areas such as dressing, personal care, kitchen and dining, resting comfortably, and home health. Products can be searched by category and item. Description and pictures are available.

Adapted Clothing

Accessible Threads
http://www.accessiblethreads.com

Adaptive Designs Apparel
http://www.adaptiveapparel.com

Adrian's Closet
http://www.adrianscloset.com

REFERENCES

Alberto, P., Sharpton, W., Briggs, A., & Stright, M. (1986). Facilitating task acquisition through the use of a self-operated auditory prompting system. *Journal of the Association for Persons with Severe Handicaps, 11*, 85–91.

Alberto, P. A., & Troutman, A. C. (2003). *Applied behavior analysis for teachers* (6th ed.). Upper Saddle River, NJ: Merrill/Prentice Hall.

American Dental Association. (1991). *Dental care for special people.* Chicago: Author.

Ault, M. M., Rues, J. P., Graff, J. G., & Holvoet, J. F. (2000). Special health care procedures. In M. Snell & F. Brown (Eds.), *Instruction of students with severe disabilities* (5th ed., pp. 245–290). Upper Saddle River, NJ: Merrill/Prentice Hall.

DPHD Critical Issues and Leadership Committee. (1999). Position statement on specialized health care procedures. *Physical Disabilities: Education and Related Services, 18*(1), 1–2.

Ellis, E. S., & Sabornie, E. J. (1986). *Teaching learning strategies to learning disabled students in postsecondary settings.* Unpublished manuscript, University of South Carolina, Columbia.

Epps, S., Stern, R. J., & Horner, R. H. (1990). Comparison of simulation training on self and using a doll for teaching generalized menstrual care to women with severe mental retardation. *Research in Developmental Disabilities, 11,* 37–66.

Farlow, L. J., & Snell, M. E. (2000). Teaching basic self-care skills. In M. Snell & F. Brown (Eds.), *Instruction of students with severe disabilities* (5th ed., pp. 331–380). Upper Saddle River, NJ: Merrill/Prentice Hall.

Goeckel, T., Heller, K. W., Forney, P., & Cohen, E. (2000). *Dressing skills for students with physical disabilities.* Atlanta: Bureau for Students with Physical and Health Impairments.

Guyton, A. (1995). *Textbook of medical physiology.* Philadelphia: Saunders.

Heller, K. W., Forney, P. E., Alberto, P. A., Schwartzman, M. N., & Goeckel, T. M. (2000). *Meeting physical and health needs of children with disabilities: Teaching student participation and management.* Belmont, CA: Wadsworth.

Heller, K. W., Fredrick, L., Dykes, M. K., Best, S. J., & Cohen, E. T. (2000). Specialized health care procedures in schools: Training and service delivery. *Exceptional Children, 66,* 173–186.

Heller, K. W., & Swinehart-Jones, D. (2003). Supporting the educational needs of students with orthopedic impairments. *Physical Disabilities: Education and Related Services, 22,* 3–24.

Loumiet, R., & Levack, N. (1993). *Independent living: A curriculum with adaptations for students with visual impairments: Volume 2. Self-care and maintenance of personal environment.* Lubbock: Texas School for the Blind and Visually Impaired.

Martin, J., Rusch, F., James, V., Decker, P., & Trytol, K. (1982). The use of picture cues to establish self-control in the preparation of complex meals by mentally retarded adults. *Applied Research in Mental Retardation, 3,* 105–119.

Medcom Trainex. (1993). *Universal precautions: AIDS and Hepatitis B prevention for healthcare workers.* Garden Grove, CA: Medcom, Inc.

Mercer, C. D., & Mercer, A. R. (2001). *Teaching students with learning problems* (6th ed.). Upper Saddle River, NJ: Merrill/Prentice Hall.

Pete, J. M. (1987). Hand washing practices among various school age students. *Health Education, 17,* 37–39.

Polloway, E. A., & Patton J. R. (1993). *Strategies for teaching learners with special needs.* New York: Merrill.

Reid, S. R. (1996). Bowel and bladder function in neuromuscular disorders. In L. A. Kurtz, P. W. Dowrick, S. E. Levy, & M. L. Batshaw (Eds.), *Handbook of developmental disabilities: Resources for interdisciplinary care* (pp. 427–430). Gaithersburg, MD: Aspen.

Santa Cruz Office of Education. (1973). Santa Cruz BCP Observation Chart: Special Education Management System Project document. (ESEA Title III Project No. 1328). Santa Cruz, CA: Author.

Schwarz, S. P. (1995). *Dressing tips and clothing resources for making life easier.* Madison, WI: AJ Press.

Shephard, J., Procter, S. A., & Coley, I. L. (1996). Self-care and adaptations for independent living. In A. S. Allen, J. Case-Smith, & P. N. Pratt (Eds.), *Occupational therapy for children* (3rd ed., pp. 461–503). St. Louis, MO: Mosby.

Smith, D. P. (1992). Preventing transmission of infection in an acute care setting. In D. P. Smith, K. S. Nix, J. Y. Kemper, R. Liguori, D. K. Brantly, J. H. Rollins, N. V. Stevens, & L. B. Clutter (Eds.), *Comprehensive child and family nursing skills* (pp. 307–312). St Louis, MO: Mosby Year Book.

Westling, D. L., & Fox, L. (2004). *Teaching students with severe disabilities* (3rd ed.). Upper Saddle River, NJ: Merrill/Prentice Hall.

CHAPTER 11

Adaptations in Physical Education, Leisure Education, and Recreation

SHERWOOD J. BEST
JUNE L. BIGGE
PENNY MUSANTE
CATHERINE MARY MACIAS

KNOWLEDGE AND SKILLS

After you have read this chapter, you will be able to:

1. **Define adapted physical education, leisure education, and recreation.**
2. **Describe legislative mandates relevant to the inclusion of individuals with disabilities in sports, recreation, and leisure activities.**
3. **Collaborate with adapted physical education professionals to deliver appropriate services for individuals with physical or multiple disabilities.**
4. **Identify the more commonly used adapted physical education assessment instruments and the possible means of authentic assessments.**
5. **Adapt sports and other physical education activities.**
6. **Select and develop appropriate leisure education activities for individuals with physical or multiple disabilities.**
7. **Become familiar with contraindications for some sports activities for individuals with physical or multiple disabilities.**

Historically, individuals with physical disabilities were relegated to the sidelines of sports, recreation, and leisure events, forced to watch their nondisabled peers partake in such activities. This was not merely a matter of misconception regarding the potential of people with disabilities to participate in sports, recreation, and leisure activities, but was also the lack of needed accommodations that placed limits upon individuals with physical or multiple disabilities. However, in 1973, Section 504 of the Rehabilitation Act (PL 93–112) designated the inclusion of individuals with disabilities in all programs and activities that were federally funded, including sports, recreation, and leisure events and programs. In 1990 the American with Disabilities Act (ADA) established specific criteria for the design and construction of barrier-free buildings and transport systems for both government and private sectors. Because of this legislation, sports, recreational, and leisure settings had to be modified for accessibility for individuals with disabilities. The result has been an explosion of adaptations and technology that have been specifically designed for individuals with disabilities to have unlimited access to sports, recreation, and leisure activities.

The instruction of students in sports and recreation is covered under the domain of physical education. **Adapted physical education (APE)** is the area of instruction for children with exceptionalities. APE is an individualized program provided by individuals who have studied the needs of physical education instruction for children with disabilities. As outlined by the Education for All Handicapped Children Act in 1975, children with exceptionalities must receive related services that will facilitate their instructional program. APE is considered a related service because it addresses physical skill

FIGURE 11–1
Example of a rubric scale (using throwing for force and/or distance as a skill)

Exemplary

- The student stepped in the direction of the target being thrown to him/her with the *nonthrowing* leg.
- The student visually focused on the target being thrown to him/her.
- The student sequentially coordinated musculature to maximize motor function relative to the throwing task.
- The student adjusted the force with which he/she threw to maximize both distance and accuracy.

Acceptable

- The student stepped with the *nonthrowing* leg.
- The student visually focused on the target.
- The student used entire body (legs, torso, and arm) in the throwing motion.

Needs Improvement

- The student did not step when throwing (kept the feet planted).
- The student used only the arm to throw.

Note. From "Authentic Assessment: Using a Portfolio Card in Physical Education" by T. K. Smith, 1997, *The Journal of Physical Education, Recreation, and Dance, 68*(4),49. Copyright 1997 by American Alliance on Health, Physical Education, Recreation, and Dance. Reprinted with permission.

can be very creative as long as evaluation is well defined and developed. More commonly used authentic assessments include the following:

1. *Rubrics.* Teachers can design benchmarks for skills and behaviors. It is important to word the criteria for a benchmark carefully, in order to have clearly defined levels for skill or activity performance. For instance, a higher level of throwing a ball can include a specified length the ball travels and the manner in which the ball is thrown (either in feet or a statement such as "from the pitcher's mound to the catcher"). Figure 11–1 displays an example of a rubric designed to assess throwing for force and distance.

2. *Portfolios.* A portfolio is a collection that showcases a child's improvement and achievement. It highlights events that demonstrate progress and exemplifies performance, much as a graph can display changes over a period of time. The portfolio is not a mess of papers, photographs, and so forth just thrown into a folder. Rather it is an orderly selection of material that can be viewed as a child's calendar of various points of success or regression in relation to specified goals. Figure 11–2 shows portfolio ideas.

3. *Portfolio Cards.* Portfolio cards are a combination of rubrics and portfolios. A basic index card can be used to record data obtained on the basis of teacher observation, student self-evaluation, and peer evaluation. Selected daily physical activities can be evaluated according to rubric benchmarks by a variety of involved individuals. The card is designed based upon teacher and student objectives. Space can be allowed for comments, scoring notes, and recording milestone achievements (Smith, 1997).

Teachers should examine students and their individual interests and needs in an effort to choose the most useful type of assessment. For example, students in secondary-level classrooms frequently move between classes. Rubric files, therefore, may be most useful for maintaining records. However, portfolios and portfolio cards are a good way to enhance self-esteem and independence as students take an active part in designing and evaluating their own progress. Portfolios in a variety of formats, from videos to binder collections, can help a child feel proud as he or she sees the assemblage of work. The best rule to remember is that any combination of authentic assessments may be incorporated in customizing an assessment program.

Individualized Education Program Planning

Including APE in the IEP should be collaboratively decided between the classroom and APE teachers. It may seem less time-consuming to have only one instructor decide upon what goals need to be included in the IEP, but it is more fruitful if both teachers come together to provide a thorough analysis of the student's needs. Discussion prior to the IEP meeting can focus on ways to complement skills a particular student needs to be

FIGURE 11–2
Possible portfolio projects to demonstrate national standards for physical education

- Written self-evaluation of current skill level and playing ability with individual goals for improvement
- Ongoing self- and peer evaluation of skill performance and playing performance (Process/Product—checklists, rating scales, criterion-referenced tasks, task sheets, game-play statistics)
- Graph or chart and explanation, which show performance of a particular skill(s), strategies across time
- Analysis of student's game-playing performance (application of skills and strategies) through the collection and analysis of individual game statistics (i.e., shooting percentage, assists, successful passes, tackles, steals, etc.)
- The creation and performance of an aerobic dance, step aerobic, or gymnastic routine, with application of knowledge and skills. Evidence: a routine script and/or videotape of performance
- Provide documentation participation in practice, informal game play and/or organized competition outside of class
- Keep a daily PE journal in which the student sets daily goals, records successes, setbacks, and progress, analyzes the situation and makes recommendations for present and future work
- Complete a written scouting report of potential opponents in class tournament prior to play (must demonstrate knowledge of offensive and defensive strategies which apply to opponent's strengths and weaknesses)
- Based on self-analysis or preassessment, select or design appropriate practice program and complete schedule, record results
- Set up, conduct, and participate in a class tournament for assigned group. Keep group and individual records and statistics (as individual or as a part of a group)
- Write a newspaper article reporting on the class tournament, or a game, as if a sports reporter (must demonstrate knowledge of the game)
- Develop and edit a class sports or fitness magazine
- Complete and record a play-by-play and color commentary of a class tournament game, as if a radio (audiotape) or a television announcer (videotape)
- Interview a successful competitor about his/her process of development as an athlete and current training techniques and schedule (audio or videotape)
- Interview an athlete with a disability about his/her experience of overcoming adversity. Apply what you have learned to your situation (audio, videotape or article)
- Write an essay entitled "What I Learned and Accomplished during Gymnastics (or any activity unit . . .) and What I Learned about Myself in the Process"

Note. From "Using Portfolios to Enhance Student Learning and Assessment" by M. F. Kirk, 1997, *The Journal of Physical Education, Recreation, and Dance, 68*(7), 31. Copyright 1997 by American Alliance on Health, Physical Education, Recreation, and Dance. Reprinted with permission.

taught or have strengthened. The skills covered by the APE teacher can be further touched upon with a classroom curriculum that would incorporate those skills. IEP goals should be based on assessment results and be stated for the student's program. The goals are broad, general descriptions rather than detailed outlines. Examples of IEP goals could include improvement in physical and motor fitness, aquatic skills, leisure skills, game and sport skills, dance skills, perceptual motor function, and affective areas such as self-concept and social competency.

Short-term performance objectives should be matched to goals. The objective contains the components of performance (observable behavior), conditions, and criteria (extent or accuracy of performance). The objective serves as a specific educational guide for the instructor and also determines the sequence of material to be taught. Guidelines for selection of objectives are as follows:

1. The objectives are generalized to the majority of the physical education curriculum.
2. The objectives have relevance to the everyday life of the individual.
3. The objectives are sequenced throughout the school education to enhance the attainment of the long-term goal (Sherrill, 1998).

ADAPTING PHYSICAL EDUCATION ACTIVITIES

Not all individuals with physical or multiple disabilities require a separate adapted physical education program. It is ideal to have children with disabilities included in the general physical education program. Equally, these students should be able to participate in schoolwide and community sports and recreation events that are scheduled apart from the physical education program. However, it is often necessary to make adaptations or modifications of typical physical activities.

Educators must teach students about adaptations and access technology and equipment, and are obligated to instill in them independence and self-confidence. It is important to discuss with students the barriers and constraints that may prevent involvement in some activities. However, numerous other physical activities can be introduced and practiced as a way to help students understand they still have a wealth of participation options.

Planning for Adaptations

The development of adaptations is contingent upon and will vary with the individual's abilities, needs, and limitations, as well with the environment in which the physical activity takes place. In some cases, adaptations will focus upon available access technology, such as in skiing. In other instances, adaptations may need more creative, hands-on effort, such as lowering a pool table. The following list offers examples of factors to consider in the planning of adaptations for students:

1. *Using All the Senses*—techniques to stimulate sensory systems.
   - Verbally describe and physically demonstrate.
   - Verbally describe and touch or move students' body parts.
2. *Sequencing Tasks*—utilizing the task analysis format.
   - Start with the first movement required in a task. Build on from that point.
   - Give auditory cues to coincide with each movement.
3. *Modifying Facilities*—making alterations to accommodate the program.
   - Construct temporary ramps.
   - Remove hazardous obstacles to create a clear space.
4. *Assessing Placement*—choosing positions to suit abilities.
   - When needed, place students in safer areas of play.
   - Ensure equality during rotations and selection of positions.
5. *Timing Participation*—adjusting time of activity to suit abilities.
   - Provide rest intervals for students with limited strength and endurance.
   - Utilize substitutions to ensure rest and participation.
6. *Modifying Rules*—cooperative understanding that rules can be changed.
   - Apply a classification system like that of the United States Cerebral Palsy Athletic Association so that students compete in approximation to their physical condition (see Table 11–2).
   - Have able-bodied individuals walk instead of run, or use one hand instead of two.
7. *Modifying Equipment*—a means of meeting the individual's needs.
   - Use longer or shorter striking equipment.
   - Change net, basket, or target heights.
   - Suspend objects to be hit or use tees.
   - Use different weights and sizes of equipment.
8. *Purchasing Specialized or Access Technology and Equipment.*
   - Research access technology and equipment manufacturers to see what they have to offer.
   - Have a set of access technology equipment, such as racing wheelchairs, on hand for students to use in much the same way a school has storage of general physical activity equipment.
9. *Awareness of Medical Implications*—being familiar with the implications of disabilities.
   - Be alert to the possible hazards of twisting, bending, falling, and lifting movements.
   - Substitute sitting or lying positions when necessary.
10. *Modifying Teaching Methods*—providing a successful atmosphere for learning.
    - Utilize peer teaching and cooperative learning.
    - Use a circuit of rotating stations for lessons (Sherrill, 1998; Seaman, 1995).

The following list of adaptive words can serve as a useful guide to facilitate the process of selecting and designing appropriate adapted physical activities:

Increase or *decrease*

Reduce or *enlarge*

Raise or *lower*

Inflate or *deflate*

TABLE 11–2
USCPAA's Eight-Level Classification System

Class	Challenge
1	Severe involvement in all four limbs. Limited trunk control. Unable to grasp a softball. Poor functional strength in upper extremities, often necessitating the use of an electric wheelchair for independence.
2	Severe to moderate quadriplegic, normally able to propel a wheelchair very slowly with arms or by pushing with feet. Poor functional strength and severe control problems in the upper extremities.
3	Moderate quadriplegic, fair functional strength and moderate control problems in upper extremities and torso. Uses wheelchair.
4	Lower limbs have moderate to severe involvement. Good functional strength and minimal control problem in upper extremities and torso. Uses wheelchair.
5	Good functional strength and minimal control problems in upper extremities. May walk with or without assistive devices for ambulatory support.
6	Moderate to severe quadriplegic. Ambulates without walking aids. Less coordination. Balance problems when running or throwing. Has greater upper extremity involvement.
7	Moderate to minimal hemiplegic. Good functional ability in nonaffected side. Walks/runs with noted limp.
8	Minimally affected. May have minimal coordination problems. Able to run and jump freely. Has good balance.

This classification system is used in all individual sports—including track and field, swimming, cycling and cross country—where athletes compete only against athletes with their same classification. In the remaining sports, athletes are grouped in divisions according to classification.

Note. Reprinted with permission of United States Cerebral Palsy Athletic Association Web site: http://www.uscpaa.org.

Widen or *narrow*
Farther or *closer*
Smaller or *larger*
Heavier or *lighter*
Assistive
Substitute
Alternate
Protective

Planning for adaptations with this vocabulary list might include the following:

Increase: Rest period between sets of tennis; points scored for a basketball goal.

Decrease: Number of sets and repetitions while weight-lifting; time for each quarter of a football game.

Reduce: Size of court for a basketball game; distance between bases for a softball game.

Enlarge: Goals for a soccer game; wickets for a croquet game; score boxes in a shuffleboard game.

Raise: The limit on three strikes and out in a kickball game; the amount of attempts needed to throw a bocce ball successfully.

Lower: The hurdles in a track unit; the balance beam for a gymnastics unit.

Deflate: A soccer ball to shorten distance kicked; a volleyball to make a softer blow.

Widen: The lanes of a bowling alley; the size of the holes in golf.

Narrow: The playing floor of a hockey game; the distance between basketball goals.

Farther: Spaces between equipment in weight room.

Closer: Targets for throwing games; partners in reciprocal activities (catching, throwing, etc.).

Smaller: Balls available to ensure good grip; hockey sticks to be used from wheelchairs; baseball diamond.

Larger: Targets to be hit; lanes for swimming; hoop in basketball.

Lighter: Bowling pins to be knocked over easier; bats for softball.

Assistive: Bowling frame to guide the bowling ball; batting tee in baseball; softballs on strings to reel them in.

Substitute: Scooter boards for ambulation; carpeted surfaces for slick ones.

Alternate: Playing positions in games; partners in square dance.

Protective: Shin guards; eye protectors.

Modification strategies have an impact upon whether individuals with physical and perhaps multiple disabilities

TABLE 11–3
Yearlong Physical Education Curriculum Plan A: Physical Skill Units

PLAN A			
Month	Physical Skills Unit	Sport/Rec Activity	Fitness Plan
September	Locomotor skills	Track and field	Jogging/stretching
October	Eye-foot coordination	Soccer	Low-impact aerobics
November	Rhythm and movement	Creative dance production	Rubber band workout
December	Fine motor skills	Table tennis	Isometrics
January	Axial skills	Gymnastics meet	Aerobics/yoga
February	Perceptual motor	New games	Circuit training
March	Dance	International dance days	Aerobics
April	Eye-hand coordination	Softball	Jogging
May	Sensory motor	Cooperative games	Relaxation
June	Outdoor education exploration	Nature day	Aerobics
July	Aquatics	Swim meet	Stretching

Note. Developed by Darcy Thompson, adapted physical education specialist. Reprinted with permission.

TABLE 11–4
Yearlong Physical Education Curriculum Plan B: Physical Skill Units

PLAN B			
Month	Physical Skills Unit	Sport/Rec Activity	Fitness Plan
September	Eye-hand coordination	Horseshoes and croquet	Isometrics
October	Dance	Square dance—hoedown	Aerobics
November	Locomotor skills	Floor hockey	Jogging
December	Fine motor skills	Shuffleboard	Rubber band workout
January	Eye-hand coordination	Bowling	Circuit training
February	Axial skills and tumbling	Parachute play	Stretching
March	Rhythm and movement	Frisbee golf	Jogging
April	Eye-foot coordination	Kick ball	
May	Perceptual and sensory motor	Lacrosse	Rubber band workout
June	Outdoor education exploration	Nature games	Aerobic relays
July	Aquatics	Swim meet	Stretching

Note. Developed by Darcy Thompson, adapted physical education specialist. Reprinted with permission.

will be able to participate in natural kinds of activities and situations. The extra planning required to adapt a lesson pays off with the rewards of individuals involved in total participation and meaningful inclusion in a physical activity with their nondisabled peers.

Instructional Program

A degree of flexibility must be built into the physical educational program. It is advantageous to have several yearlong curriculum plans to choose from that reflect varying abilities and interests. When designing curriculum plans, the following guidelines are suggested:

1. Focus on 11 physical skills to be developed, each one being the basis for a unit. This allows a monthly unit rotation plan (see Physical Skills Units in Tables 11–3 and 11–4).
2. Pair the physical skill with an appropriate sport or recreational activity. This facilitates the acquisition of the physical skill by reinforcing the learned behavior in a rewarding activity. The physical skill can be that which is designated in the IEP and is part of the APE program.
3. Provide individual fitness and wellness unit plans to correspond with each physical skill unit.

Instructional Strategies

The success of a curriculum unit relies heavily on instructional style. The most critical factor in adopting an instructional strategy is the ability to utilize an individualized instructional approach. Every step of the lesson focuses on each individual's ability and needs. Remember that individualized instruction does not al-

TABLE 11–5
Example of a Unit Plan

Unit Plan			
Physical skill: Sport activity: Fitness unit:	Eye-hand Coordination Softball Jogging—strength development		
Week 1 **Task Analysis**	**Modified Games**	**Fitness**	**Cognitive Skills**
Throwing Catching	"Throw and go" "I can"	Jog bases	Learn the meaning of strikes, fouls
Week 2 **Task Analysis**	**Modified Games**	**Fitness**	**Cognitive Skills**
Batting Pitching	"Three flys up" "Target pitch"	Bat aerobics Jogging	Learn the meaning of walks, base running
Week 3 **Task Analysis**	**Modified Games**	**Fitness**	**Cognitive Skills**
Base running Fielding	"Base tag" "Simon says"	Base sprints Jogging	Learn the meaning of scoring, out, innings
Week 4			
Game play—softball tournament			

Note. Developed by Darcy Thompson, adapted physical education specialist. Reprinted with permission.

ways mean one-to-one instruction. An entire class may be participating in the same activity, but the expectation levels, evaluation standards, and adaptations are different from one student to another. When possible, schedules and instruction are integrated with that of students participating in the general education curriculum.

Progressive Parts Method. The instructional strategy of the progressive parts method allows greater success in skill acquisition and a lower frustration level. The smaller the steps, the greater the chances are of acquiring the skill. Combine the smaller steps with a slower pace of instruction and a greater number of repetitions for more successful skill acquisition.

The progressive parts method focuses on teaching the skills needed sequentially and then putting them together progressively until the whole sequence is attained. The task analysis method of instruction follows this method and is highly recommended for teaching physical skills. A yearlong instructional strategy based on the progressive parts method would utilize:

1. Individual task analysis for each separate physical educational skill used in the unit.
2. Daily modified game play based on the unit game.
3. A fitness plan unit that focuses on the acquisition of the skills.
4. Cognitive tasks that facilitate learning of the unit game or recreational activity.
5. Culminating activities such as participation in the unit game or recreation activity.

A unit plan example of this method is illustrated in Table 11–5.

Students with severe physical or multiple disabilities may require additional time and planning. For example, the unit plan for a nonambulatory student with severe spastic cerebral palsy can focus on attaining part or all of certain task-analyzed skills, such as batting and throwing. Games and fitness activities need appropriate modifications to ensure success. Cognitive skill tasks are acquired depending upon cognitive ability. Each student should participate in the cumulative sport or recreation activity.

Strategies for Inclusion. Block and Conaster (2002) have proposed three strategies for supporting students with disabilities in general physical education. The first strategy is *Multilevel Curriculum Selection,* which involves applying different curricular objectives to the same educational domain. A related strategy is

Curriculum Overlapping, which involves setting goals from different curricular areas within the same activity. A final strategy is *Alternatives,* in which an activity must be adapted for the student with a disability but still has relevance to other students. An example is one in which an aquatic volleyball game is moved to the shallow end of the pool to accommodate the student who was unable to tread water. The game of volleyball remained relevant to all players.

Safety Issues

The nature of some disabilities (e.g., cerebral palsy) is such that they are visible and remind the educator to be alert to issues of safety. Other impairments (e.g., diabetes, asthma) are not visible but are affected by exercise (Block, 2000). Lack of awareness of the implications of disability can lead to unsafe participation. Block (2000), Porreta (2000), and Surburg (2000) provide ideas for implementing safe adaptive physical education programs. These include:

1. Learning about the disability from students' files, professionals such as the school nurse, and parents.
2. Getting acquainted with students' needs. Some students are more robust than others and some may have conditions for which certain activities are contraindicated. Some students may need to premedicate before specific activities.
3. Attending IEP meetings.
4. Assessing students' physical ability to protect themselves when they fall, their attention to personal physical space, and their balance and coordination. Remember that some students react to sudden movement or loud noises with reflexive reponses.
5. Assessing the physical environment. This includes checking to make sure that the activity area is free from restrictive equipment, arranging boundaries to keep activities safely contained, and reducing distractions. Other environmental considerations include checking air quality and temperature extremes for outdoor activities.
6. Checking equipment. Broken materials should be replaced. Padding may be added to standards and other hard surfaces.
7. Using safe techniques. This includes teaching students how to handle equipment, reviewing and enforcing activity rules, and supervising appropriately.
8. Implementing modifications such as alterations in intensity, duration, and type of exercise, reducing emphasis on the competitive nature of activities, providing rest periods, and providing time for thorough warm-ups and cool-downs. (Block, 2000, pp. 291–299; Porreta, 2000, pp. 190–194; Surburg, 2000, pp. 240–242)

From the Classroom to the Community

One of the tremendous benefits of physical education is the opportunity to take the physical education program into the community. Organizations dedicated to the physical and recreational endeavors of individuals with exceptionalities are located in many communities. Athletic clubs and organizations may be general, such as Disabled Sports USA (*http://www.dsusa.org*), or specific as with the United States Quad Rugby Association (*http://www.quadrugby.com/toc.htm*). Getting in contact and becoming involved with local organizations and events provide opportunities to take a physical education unit, extend it, and provide a tangible community-based reward. In school, training and preparation for a track and field meet becomes charged with excitement and desire when the end result is participation in a "real" track meet and a chance to go off campus, to interact with new friends, and to bring home the blue ribbon. A few other organizations to be contacted are listed in "Focus on the Net" at the end of this chapter.

LEISURE EDUCATION AND RECREATION

An important part of classroom instruction, whether it is a special day class or a general education setting, is the introduction of various leisure and recreational interests. Recreation is fun, it provides opportunities for social interactions, it promotes fitness and teaches skills that are applicable to other areas, and it can be a satisfying way to spend time (Westling & Fox, 2000). Although most students in a class may enjoy a certain leisure or recreational activity for the duration it is presented in school, some students may find the activity enjoyable enough to continue with it as a lifelong pursuit. Just as we instruct in history and mathematics, so educators need to address leisure and recreational activities as a way to produce well-rounded individuals.

Given the unlimited resources that are available for participation in leisure and recreation, there are endless possibilities for dynamic and engaging leisure education curricula.

Leisure is oftentimes thought of as something we do in our spare time for our own personal satisfaction. However, there are a number of forces interacting when a person undertakes a leisure pursuit. Leisure is an activity of choice. What causes us to choose a particular leisure activity? We make decisions based on a search for an "experience" such as solitude or excitement (Hull, Michael, Walker, & Roggenbuck, 1996). We may choose a certain activity because we want to maintain the sense of enjoyment or satisfaction that we remember gaining from it. Some of us want to find socialization opportunities in the pursuit of leisure, while others are seeking a pleasurable way to stay healthy and fit (Laverie, 1998). Leisure choice involves what we have experience in and what we are knowledgeable about. Our personal likes and dislikes determine what we will engage in, and the accessibility to the activity will play a significant role. For example, if someone enjoys the solace of a stroll but hates the beach, he or she will perhaps choose to walk in the woods or along the path of a park.

Leisure Activities Are Learned Rather Than Something Done Naturally. Leisure education provides an opportunity to develop a positive attitude toward leisure and enhances awareness of the options for activities, skills, and knowledge. Choice is the most crucial element. Without choice, activities become simply tasks rather than providing elements of control that lead to leisure satisfaction. If television is the only offering, choice is negated (Bouchard et al., 1993).

Recreational Activities Tend to Be Activities People Choose to Do in a Noncompetitive Atmosphere. Aerobics and kickboxing performed for fitness are recreational. People choose different recreational activities because they anticipate the activity will restore their sense of well-being. They are activities people choose to do in their free time because they have memories of feeling better or more balanced after the last time they participated in the activity. Mental well-being can be achieved through recreation, with the exception of intense activity participation. Slowing down and calming our inner feelings can come about through leisurely recreation versus spending hours in vigorous exercise (Zuzanek, Robinson, & Iwasaki, 1998).

Traditionally, there has been relatively little meaningful articulation between school districts and the available community agencies and services that represent a less restrictive environment in which a student with a disability could engage in leisure and recreational activities. Teachers must be proactive in their search for local resources in this area of education. Exploring the Internet, visiting local agencies, and collaborating with fellow colleagues and parents are required efforts in order to establish a fine, useful leisure and recreation program.

Leisure Education Program Development

Comprehensive leisure and recreation program development includes four major components: leisure awareness, social interaction, leisure activity skills, and leisure resources. **Leisure awareness** involves knowledge and understanding of leisure and the importance of a healthy leisure lifestyle to overall life satisfaction. This component also includes development of personal concepts of choice and related participatory and decision-making skills. **Social interaction** is easily included in leisure education programs within general and special education curricula because social-skill development is an important aspect of all programs. Such skills are vital because individuals need these skills to participate appropriately in dyads, small groups, and large groups for a successful leisure lifestyle. **Leisure activity skills** include choice as an important component and assume that students will be introduced to a wide variety of activity options, not just the traditional activities or those that are the favorite of the teacher. **Leisure resources** include exploration of personal resources, including skills, finances, and experience, as well as home and community resources.

Leisure education programs should focus on development of all of the knowledge, skills, and attitudes necessary to facilitate choice—not only traditional group activity skills but also those individual skills that will have lifetime application. This includes specific activity skills as well as how to access home and community resources and use decision-making skills.

Leisure Education Program Areas

In the development of activity programs, it is important to consider current activities as well as exploration of new leisure options. The following are examples of traditional and nontraditional aspects of leisure.

Traditional Recreation Activities

- Aquatics and water-related activities
- Arts and crafts
- Dance
- Drama
- Hobbies
- Mental games and activities
- Music
- Outdoor activities
- Sports and games

Nontraditional Categories of Adult Leisure

- Social interaction
- Spectating and appreciating
- Leadership and community service
- Fitness
- Relaxation and meditation
- Food preparation
- Shopping
- Home improvement
- Home maintenance
- Living-things maintenance (pets and plants)
- Self-development
- Education
- Self-care
- Travel (Peterson and Stumbo, 1999)

These are only some of the possible choices. The only limitations for exploration and skill development should be the interests of the students and their facilitators. Teachers need not be limited by what they think the students are capable of doing. Both need to be willing to explore all options creatively. It is also important for teachers to remember that they are enablers, not demonstrators. A teacher does not need to be a star in ceramics, for example, in order to provide students an opportunity to try their own skills.

The next several sections present examples of leisure programs that enhance student learning and participation. Choice of actual programs will be influenced by available community options, student abilities and choice, finances, and environmental surroundings. Examples have been organized within several domains: creative, special interests, science/technology, and recreation.

Creative Domains

Photography. Photography can be an artistic endeavor, a career, or a tool of journalism. As a leisure activity it can be the reason for travel and can lead one into hours of human analysis. Photography requires astute observational skills and a desire to express oneself through a medium that lends itself to realism as well as to the creative manipulations of special lighting and effects. Photography, being a subject of the art field, can best be enjoyed by individuals who themselves are creative. The design of an in-class darkroom and the development of a photography program can engage students whose artistic inclinations may lead them to embrace the world of photography.

Through research and practice, photography can be a cross-curriculum project. Studying the events of World War I, for example, can include a discussion of the role of photojournalism in the recording of this monumental event in history. The unique viewpoints of Ansel Adams can be presented within ecology and nature units. The options for introducing the subject of photography are abundant. In addition, the advances in digital photography allow students with disabilities the option of scanning photos into their computers and using them for many purposes.

Crafts. Crafts have been made throughout the history of the world for a variety of reasons. Craftspeople have handed down cultural and familial identities by the nature of their projects. In some parts of the world, crafts are a means of economic survival. The crafts are sold not just for display, but also for practical uses, such as pottery containers for food. Crafts are also a means of creative expression, which makes them a favored leisure activity for many (Herald, 1993). Crafts activities in classrooms have frequently been used as a "filler" in the last school hour of a Friday afternoon or when weather conditions keep students indoors. This dilutes the distinct cultural, historical, and artistic relevance of crafts. Crafts can be studied singularly or they can become part of an instructional unit, such as basket weaving of Native American peoples. The many options for pairing a craft activity with a curriculum should be part of lesson planning.

In addition to planning crafts activities as an important element in the class curriculum, adaptations for making the crafts have to be considered as well. For example, many crafts require the use of fine-motor skills (for example, cutting, pasting, and folding). The type and degree of a student's disability is foremost in deciding the adaptations needed to complete a particular craft. Planning a project over several days may be necessary if more severe motor delays are involved. Although craft activities can be a means of refining motor skills, their enjoyment can be lost if they become physically and mentally tedious.

When deciding upon a craft activity, it is important to focus on the meaningfulness it has to the student's life. For example, students who are learning about face masks worn at masquerade dances in the Democratic Republic of the Congo can create masks with their own designs and then wear them at a class masquerade luncheon. Embroidery projects can result in logos of students' names, and pottery can be gifts for family. Students learn the pleasure of making crafts for enjoyment and to reflect their talent, time, and effort. The value of crafts does not need to be measured only by their utility. A wood bowl does not need to be for food, but can simply sit upon a living room shelf as a decorative piece. Time spent in creation is pleasurable in itself.

The following suggestions assist teachers to make appropriate choices for crafts projects for students with physical, health, or multiple disabilities. These suggestions are followed by examples of specific crafts projects.

Early Childhood Through Approximately 6 Years of Age

- Plan crafts that accommodate a short attention span.
- Try colorful materials.
- Develop and refine adaptive responses.
- Use the concrete properties of crafts in order to explore two- and three-dimensional objects.
- Consider the visual-motor integration requirements of activities.
- **Examples:** Finger painting or block printing onto cloth, grasping and rolling wet clay, crafts related to holidays, simple necklace stringing such as plastic bear claws, gluing rather than sewing materials, puppets, wood collages, fantasy chalk drawings, and constructing models out of a variety of materials such as paper towel tubes.

Seven Years Through Approximately 11 Years of Age

- Consider more-complex crafts to refine fine-motor skills.
- Use crafts for clustering and classifying new information.
- Some crafts are associated with game playing or storytelling. These develop skills such as sequencing and memory.
- Themes of friendship and bonding may be explored through crafts.
- **Examples:** Simple sewing, basic pottery, cryptic drawings and paintings using symbols such as from Native American tribes, more-advanced puppets, masks, hats, sand structures and design, dioramas, game pieces, kites, and wind chimes with special meaning in the items.

Early Adolescence Through Approximately 17 Years of Age

- Plan projects of utility.
- Plan some crafts projects that use more detail and skill.
- Strive for self-expression coming through in design and projects.
- Use a longer time frame of activity, especially for more intricate crafts.
- Support manipulation of all tangible two- and three-dimensional designs.
- Design crafts to promote independence.
- **Examples:** Birdhouses, figurines, weaving, baskets, pottery and ceramics, sewing, embroidery, wallets, wood projects, musical instruments, more advanced face masks, carving, appliqué, dyeing, spinning, collages of many mediums, and small furniture items such as CD holders. (Herald, 1993)

Special Interests

Card Games. Individuals of all ages and abilities can enjoy card games. Card games provide opportunities for competition, problem solving, and experiencing success and failure. They also provide a means for individuals with and without disabilities to enjoy social interactions.

Using task analysis, we can study skills needed to play card games, abilities needed for cognitive tasks, and props necessary for making adaptations for physical needs. The process of analyzing cognitive tasks required for different card games leads to the definition of which tasks, if any, need to be taught. The game of Concentration, for instance, requires that players have the ability to match numbers or pictures. Rummy requires an ability to (1) match suits, (2) match numbers, (3) identify number of cards in a group, (4) recognize number of card groups in the hand, (5) place cards in consecutive order within suits, (6) recognize the value by face number, and (7) add points held in each hand. The following are some suggestions for handling cards if players are either unable to hold the cards themselves or unable to indicate verbally what manipulations they wish to make.

FIGURE 11–3
Try whatever works

Note. From *Teaching Individuals with Physical and Multiple Disabilities* (3rd ed.) by J. L. Bigge, 1991, New York: Macmillan.

Use of special cards. Various kinds of cards are available from toy and department stores. Cards with large numbers, magnetic cards, or crooked cards may be easier for some individuals to use. Jumbo cards, with oversized symbols and numbers, and Braille playing cards are available in pinochle and regular decks from the American Foundation for the Blind.

Use of pointers. For a person who uses a pointer for communication, experiment with the tip of the pointer by surrounding the tip with masking tape or another adhesive so as to adhere the pointer to the cards. A sticky pointer can lift cards from stock piles, designate cards to discard, or pass cards to someone else. A plain pointer can be used to point to cards that players want to discard or to pass to someone else. It also can be used to hit something in such a way as to signal "start," "stop," or "I win."

Card management. A card holder may be used for a student with poor coordination. If adapted equipment is not available or properly individualized, a card holder can be devised from a flat brush with bristles approximately 3 inches high. When the back of the brush is placed on a flat surface, the cards can be placed upright in the bristles (see Figure 11–3).

For players unable to speak and who cannot handle cards, the tic-tac-toe communication system can be used. One of each card of an extra deck of cards can be placed in each cell of a plastic photo holder. Instead of asking for a card, the nonvocal player can signal which card he or she wants. In the game of Authors, for instance, a player can ask for a card by signaling the position corresponding to the desired author. Then he or she can signal the position of the letter that begins the name of the desired book by that author. If the cards in Concentration are placed in the nine-cell, tic-tac-toe format, a player can again signal the two positions that he or she hopes will match. Figure 11–4 illustrates how the tic-tac-toe system is implemented (Sirvis, Musante, & Bigge, 1991).

Signals. Special signals will be necessary for the following types of communication:

1. Signal for help in arranging cards in desired order.
2. Signal which card(s) to pick up or put down.
3. Signal a win.
4. Signal when a player wants to group cards and lay them facing up or down.
5. Signal a pass rather than a turn in which the person will play.
6. Signal or point to a card in the opponent's hand.

All players explore ways to help the players with disabilities find suitable signals. For some games, all players use the same signals. In Slapjack, for instance, all players give the same signal (such as a kick on the floor) when the jack is exposed. With ingenuity, each game can be adjusted to suit the needs of the players. Some means for communicating plays in the game must be devised for each player who communicates in a different way.

Collecting. Almost anything can be collected, from valuable antiques and stamps to bottles and mugs. As with crafts, collecting can be a cross-curriculum activity. History and science, for example, can easily be matched with collecting. Slogan buttons can be related to presidential campaigns, and seashells can be

FIGURE 11–4

(a) Twelve choices of author. Student signals middle, right, or left, then the position of the card. (b) Choice of the book: student signals which box and then position for the beginning letter of a book title

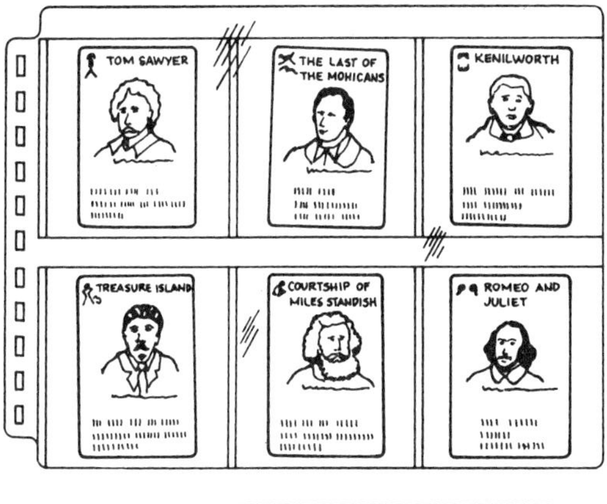

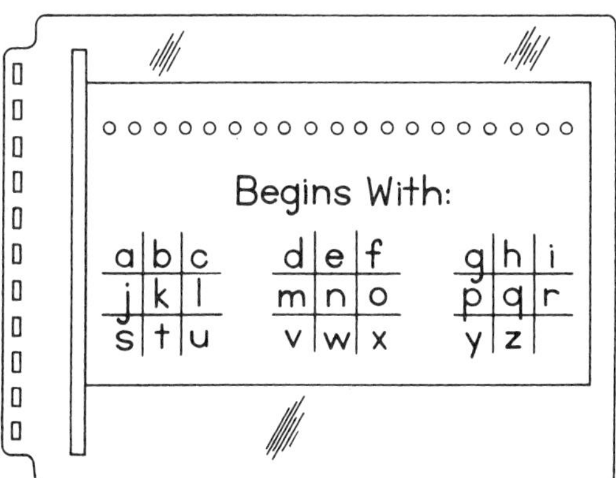

Note. From "Leisure Education and Adapted Physical Education," by B. Sirvis, P. Musante, & J. L. Bigge, in *Teaching Individuals with Physical and Multiple Disabilities* (3rd ed., pp. 428–459), editor J. L. Bigge, Upper Saddle River, NJ: Merrill/Prentice Hall.

included in marine lesson plans. The beauty of collecting is that few adaptations are needed. However, how one obtains the item for a collection may require some accommodations. Traveling along the beach and searching among tidepools presents unique difficulties for individuals with physical or multiple disabilities.

Teaching students about collectibles includes (a) establishing a focus area of collecting, (b) discussing the value and pleasure of collecting, and (c) choosing an area of collecting. Focus involves selecting a period of time, an individual, or a type of item (such as buttons or turtles). The focus area can be related to an academic part of instruction within a cross-curriculum project. It can also be based on the interests of all class members. If students are interested in the Olympic Games, for instance, then this can be a theme and students can collaboratively collect articles. Students can also become acquainted with what makes collecting particular items significant and the various ways people develop collections that have historic or other significance. Finally, choosing an area for collecting enhances student motivation. Students need to be taught how to display and care for their collections. Since more pieces may be added over time, the style and manner of showcasing collections have to accommodate the new arrivals. Ideas for displaying collectibles can be unlimited. Some people have collectibles placed throughout the house, while others have them in one designated room. For collectibles such as stamps or spoons, albums and wooden cases are often used for showcasing. Equally important is the care of articles that may lose color, break, or tarnish over extended periods of time. Students can be taught about materials and what agents are best to clean them. The placement of articles can have an impact as well. Color can fade in the sunlight and photographs can turn yellow without proper protection. Cloth materials are susceptible to moths, and mice love to nibble on older woolen pieces.

Caring for and maintaining collections will make a difference in the time and effort that individuals spend in enjoying this intriguing hobby. Teaching students how to enjoy items that are somehow related to their lives can lead to collecting as a lifelong leisure activity.

Science and Technology Domains

Robotics. Leisure time does not always mean something artistic or recreational. Some individuals enjoy the scientific world and many different leisure domains.

Robotics is an area that can provide hours of work and fun for individuals who are interested in technology, computers, construction, mechanics, remote controls, and physics. Robotics refers to the science or study of robot design, construction, and operation. Robots do not have to resemble human beings, but they have mechanical functions to perform a variety of tasks. Simple machines can be utilized and combined to create fundamental or complex robots. The technology of robotics may intimidate some people, but in time, anyone can become fascinated with robotics. Planning and designing require the ability to be inventors and collaboraters. Sharing ideas can create social opportunities. Robotics can foster individualism as students compete in science and technology fairs or try to outwit each other with the most ingenious design. Good sportsmanship can be a lesson as students showcase their projects.

Robotics can be taught at all grade levels because there are many types of robots. Simple machines such as the wedge, lever, pulley, and inclined plane can be introduced at earlier grade levels, while a combination of these machines can be taught during the upper-grade-level years (Franklin Institute Online, 1996). Computers and electrical mechanisms can be added. The process of developing an idea for a robot has no age limit. Students can think of uses for robots as they explore the concepts of discovery and invention as ways of making life easier. Presenting historical figures in the area of technology can help students learn why it is important to have a constant flow of new inventions. Teaching about electricity, for example, can include an introduction to Thomas Edison. Follow-up projects can concentrate on the many inventions that are associated with the use of electricity.

A robotics workshop can be created either in a section of the classroom or by using the entire classroom. Materials, which can be anything from tools and computer chips to metal, rubber, and batteries, should be properly stored and labeled. Safety is also an issue. Students should be taught rules of caution and have access to safety equipment and first-aid kits. Students need to have good eye-protection glasses. An adequate safety plan is also important. Most robotic projects are not dangerous, but being safe and prepared is the best strategy. Prior to robotic design, consider:

- Situations or tasks for which it makes sense to use robots rather than humans, and vice versa.
- Why has it been difficult to build robots that replicate human characteristics?
- Will it ever be possible to build a robot whose intelligence is close to that of a person?

It will be useful to:

- List robots from movies, literature, toys, etc. Why are they considered to be robots?
- How can one tell something is a robot? Is it by looks, behavior, or something else?
- How might one communicate with a robot? By speech, gestures, pressed buttons, or typed words?

When considering robotic construction and design features, consider:

- **Looks.** What does the robot look like? Is there a reason for it to look as it does?
- **Sensing.** How does the robot "know" or figure out what is in its environment? If put in a different environment, would it be able to figure out this new environment?
- **Movement.** How does the robot move? If placed in a different environment, would it be able to move within this new space?
- **Manipulation.** How does the robot move or manipulate other objects within its environment? Can a single robot move or manipulate more than one kind of object?
- **Energy.** How is the robot powered? Can it have more than one energy source?
- **Intelligence.** How does the robot "think"? What does it mean to say the robot "thinks"? (See "Focus on the Net.")

Based on the student's capabilities, robotics can be a solo or a group project. The design does not always have to be complex. A good basic teaching strategy is to assign one utility target and have student groups collaborate on design and construction. For example, perhaps the target is to design a way to pick up trash from the floor or to create a system to shuffle a deck of cards. This provides a focal point for students and allows them to pool their thoughts and talents. One author of this chapter was involved in designing an instructional unit on mechanics in which students needed to design and build a simple machine using the principles of the pulley, lever and fulcrum, and inclined plane. A "potato chip crusher" was designed by one group of students. Evaluation of the machine was based on use of a combination of simple machines, whether the machine performed its function, student collaboration during project development and construction, and the knowledge displayed by students when they explained its use.

Ham Radio Operation. Ham radio operation is the amateur use of radio transmission to communicate, and is a fun hobby that can provide local and international communication and socialization opportunities. "Hams" communicate with people from around the world out of their homes. Ham radios differ from the Internet because people are able to speak to each other as opposed to typing words and never hearing a live voice. For individuals with physical disabilities, and especially more severe impairments, ham radio operation can be an excellent leisure time activity. Although the construction of a transmission system can be facilitated by the use of ready-made kits, part of the fun for some "hams" is designing, building, and maintaining a viable transmission system.

Ham radio operation is a diverse hobby in which individuals can choose to work with low-power communication or more-sophisticated, computer-involved systems. The following list includes a number of fun ham radio operation activities:

- Talk to people in foreign countries.
- Help in emergencies by providing communications.
- Provide communications in parades and walkathons.
- Help other people become hams.
- Hook a computer system to the radio and communicate by computer.
- Collect QSL cards (cards from other hams) from all over the world and receive awards.
- Participate in contests or field-day events.
- Provide radio services to the local civil defense organization through ARES (Amateur Radio Emergency Service) or RACES (Radio Amateur Civil Emergency Service).
- Aid members of the military by joining MARS, the Military Affiliate Radio System.
- Participate in transmitter hunt games and build direction-finding equipment.
- Receive weather pictures.
- Build radios and antennas, and learn about electronics and radio history and theory.
- Send and receive live television pictures. (Conejo Valley Amateur Radio Club, 1999)

Every country has a set of regulations for ham radio licensing and operations. In order to become a ham in the United States, one must pass a qualifying examination. Currently there are three ham radio operation categories: the novice-level Technician Class, the mid-level General Class, and the top-level Extra Class. The exams are easy, only a "D" is required to pass, and even if someone has no previous knowledge of ham radio operation, it is simple to learn about it. Anyone from a young student to an older adult can enjoy being a ham. The exams are administered by volunteers (American Radio Relay League, 2000). If needed, a person may have a medical release so that an adapted version of the multiple-choice exam may be taken. The modifications may be based upon the specific physical disability limitations.

The best way to introduce ham radios is for the teacher to become a certified ham radio operator. Transmission units can be built as a class effort, and the results can be a product of students' ideas. The instruction of how ham radio operation works and how the technology is created can be a cross-curriculum project. There are also many ways to build a ham radio and therefore many options for student projects. Some people use handheld VHF or UHF radios, while others enjoy mobile units that can be mounted on a car. If a class project is assigned, building a more elaborate system may be the most fun option (Ham Radio Online, 1999).

Communicating with other hams can be a class-time activity. Talking to people from regions related to the curriculum can provide firsthand learning experiences. As a class project, ham radio operation can become an enjoyable collaboration that leads to socialization and service opportunities. The technological knowledge involved is not the most complex, but for the student who has a scientific inclination, ham radio operation may be a lifelong leisure pursuit.

Leisure Time Computer Use. Computers offer many leisure opportunities that appeal to a wide range of ages and interests. Students with physical or multiple disabilities can take full advantage of computers. Adaptive equipment such as pointers and eye scanners not only provide physical input access, but can alter the speed of the program presentation to allow individuals time to respond. Some exciting alternatives include arcade-type games, interactive fantasy and fiction, creative arts, simulator programs, and computerized board games.

Games. Initially, a large percentage of computer games were home versions of the violent arcade programs with the object of killing aliens or other undesirables. Although there are still many of these programs available, there are an increasing number of nonviolent arcade programs and games. There are some unique games that provide hours of fun, such as the wonderful railroad tycoon and construction games created by both Pop Top Software and Knowledge Adventure.

Sports. For individuals who enjoy sports, Sierra Attractions and Electronic Arts have created a number of programs that offer digital sports interaction such as Infogames' snowboarding program, Boarder Zone. Rather than spend the weekend watching football on television, children and adults can coach their own team with John Madden Football from Electronic Arts. If indoor sports such as darts, pool, and bowling are preferred, Mindscape and Interplay offer software for this type of entertainment.

Board and family games. Popular board games are also available in computer form. Hasbro has Jeopardy, Wheel of Fortune, Scrabble, and Life, while Jellyvision has Who Wants to Be a Millionaire? Some companies offer packages that include sets of popular family games. Encore Software puts out the Family Megahits Edition that features Monopoly, 3D Mini Golf, Asteroids, Myst, and Sim City 2000, while Sierra Attractions' Hoyle Board Games package has over 15 games, including Parcheesi, Chinese Checkers, Dominoes, and Backgammon. There are sets that have more than board games, such as Interplay's Family Favorites, which has a variety of puzzles, games, and clip art activities.

Simulator programs. If getting off the ground is the objective, flight simulators such as those created by Looking Glass Studios, Microprose, Empire Interactive, and the Digital Combat Series by TLC Multimedia provide such realistic piloting programs that even professionals try their hand at mastering them. Maybe racing around a track is interesting. The Sierra Sports' Nascar Racing Series, Infogames' Test Drive, Wizard Works' Dirt Track Racing, and Speedvisions' Superbike programs can boost one's energy level. Younger players will enjoy Mattell's Hot Wheels racers and stunt programs.

Storytellers and fantasy. Software that is based on fantasy or literary characters can provide hours of enjoyment. Popular literary characters such as Madeline, Winnie-the-Pooh, and the Cat in the Hat all have series of programs with games, puzzles, print-art kits, and learning activities. For youngsters who cannot miss out on their favorite cartoon or fantasy television shows, Scooby Doo, Blue's Clues, Stuart Little, the Lion King, and Cruella can give them a fun time with programs that feature these characters in a variety of situations. Disney offers a collection of programs that feature almost every Disney character that exists.

Creative arts. Children can create art and crafts projects using bright graphics and logos. Broderbund offers a number of art programs including Click Art, Print Master, and Print Shop. American Greetings allows the creation of cards, signs, crafts, and banners with Print Premium and Crafts. For people who enjoy designing and construction, Lego has a series of programs in which users can explore, build, and destroy, such as the Robotics Invention System, Robo Sports, and Extreme Creatures.

Recreation Domains

Exploring Nature

> When we try to pick out anything by itself, we find it hitched to everything else in the universe.
>
> —John Muir

The outdoors offers an environment where individuals use their senses of seeing, hearing, touching, smelling, and tasting. They can satisfy their own inquisitive and adventurous natures by learning about nature and the interactions that take place outdoors. Fresh air, different surroundings, and the closeness of the plants and animals can also provide a wonderful opportunity for mental relaxation and physical refreshment.

The outdoors experience of wilderness hiking and camping is no longer limited to able-bodied individuals. In the past 10 years, there have been significant structural changes in the National Parks hiking trails and campsites, in an effort to meet the mandates of the Americans with Disabilities Act. Where once there

FIGURE 11–5
Many national parks have renovated trails for wheelchair use

were uneven, dirt trails, now there are selected trails that have been paved for smooth riding by wheelchair (see Figure 11–5). Some routes have been modified with handrails, while others have information boards posted at eye level for wheelchair users. Bathrooms and phone booths have been renovated, and water fountains have been added throughout campsites. From Yellowstone National Park in Montana to the redwood forests of California, these alterations allow for the enjoyment of wilderness camping, hiking, and nature study by individuals with disabilities.

Nature study is one of those areas of curriculum in which coursework in science can be combined with leisure education goals, or nature study can be taught as a life management component of curriculum. Nature study offers one of the best opportunities for individuals with physical disabilities to be involved in the direct-experience approach to learning. Adaptations may be needed to solve access challenges. Extra people can assist wheelchair users on hikes. Different avenues to physical participation can be explored to accommodate seating positions and hand-use problems. Peers and others may need to provide full or partial physical assistance for experiences that require fine motor coordination. Students who cannot participate in hiking activities for health reasons may be involved in other activities in which the same concepts can be studied. If the class is studying animal locomotion, teachers can have these students study animals that live near the classroom, home, yard, or campgrounds. Teachers may obtain graphic copies, plaster castings, or models of different animal tracks so that these students can study animal travel.

One approach lending itself to leisure pursuit over a lifetime is placing emphasis on plants and animals native to one's community. Libraries, education departments, museums, zoos, regional and national parks, and organizations such as Sierra Club, Audubon, etc., are good sources of information on local nature studies.

Knowing the potential of nature study to contribute to leisure, how can teachers provide a program of study as well as take advantage of incidental learning opportunities? What is important for students to learn, experience, and be able to do? How can teachers plan a program of study instead of a series of splinter lessons? In all areas of nature study, emphasis should be placed on concepts and interrelationships among natural phenomena rather than on scientific names and facts. Scientific facts may change rapidly, but concepts remain stable over many years. For some students it is more meaningful to understand concepts centered on how and why than merely to memorize names.

Basically, a nature study program should encourage the following in each student:

- Awareness of the student's natural surroundings;
- Appreciation and knowledge of living things and their interrelationships;
- Respect for the environment engendered through discovering how other creatures live, and how one's surroundings may be preserved both by and for oneself and for other living things;
- Knowledge that humans actually are a part of the environment, not just observers or manipulators; and
- Realization that the interrelationships of the environment are a necessary requisite to one's survival.

Several key nature study concepts can provide the base for a nature study program. The same concepts will be found in science courses and are equally applicable to nature study for recreational use. The concepts and activities of nature study involve animals, plants, earth science, conservation/ecology, predator-prey relationships, natural communities (interrelationships of plants and animals), weather, altitude, Native American peoples' uses of plants, animals, and natural resources, astronomy, microorganisms in ponds, creeks, and puddles, and solar energy. Study of these can be a valuable introduction to sources of enjoyment for both present and later use of leisure time. Use ingenuity to develop and explain concepts suggested here and to evolve new activities to expand options for students' recreation. Select learning experiences that promote active student involvement leading to discovery (the hands-on approach).

Many community resources, such as libraries, museums, botanical gardens, and park departments, can be very helpful. Materials from these agencies can be used in the classroom. Some agencies may have field trips or speakers and some zoos operate a traveling animal exhibit. Students can be encouraged to pursue their particular interests through books or recordings.

Horseback Riding. Teachers and parents involved with students with physical or multiple disabilities must not overlook horseback riding. Rarely is this activity even considered because it is perceived as being impossible or too dangerous. If properly conducted, it is no more dangerous for individuals with disabilities than for those without physical problems. Reading about therapeutic horsemanship convinces us that it is not only a possible but also an exciting sport. It also reminds us that certain safety standards and procedures must be followed for success in any sport.

Riding horses can be done purely for recreation or for therapeutic reasons. **Hippotherapy** is physical therapy which uses the horse as a therapy tool (STRIDES Therapeutic Riding, 1999). There are thousands of stables throughout the country that provide hippotherapy for individuals with physical disabilities. However, not all horseback riding programs must be structured as therapeutic, and many local horseback riding programs also provide beneficial leisure activities.

Children with a variety of physical or multiple disabilities can benefit from a horseback riding program. Riding can improve total gross-motor functioning, such as increasing range of motion in the extremities and improving muscle tone and strength. Horseback riding can also help with posture, balance, and flexibility for the individual when off the horse (STRIDES Therapeutic Riding, 1999). It can also develop pleasurable use of leisure and improve self-concept. Riding is a major accomplishment. Learning to control an animal that is four times one's size is a significant and rewarding achievement.

Therapeutic horsemanship. The popularity of therapeutic horsemanship began in Europe in the 1940s when a small group of therapists began using the gentle movement of the horse to help individuals with physical disabilities (Banbury Cross Therapeutic Equestrian Center, 2000). The first therapeutic riding school was opened in Chigwell, England, under the directorship of John Davies. In 1967 the British Advisory Council on Riding for the Handicapped (now the National Riding for the Disabled Association) was formed.

Before students receive equine therapy, they must have a written referral from their physicians and the therapist and riding instructor must evaluate them. During the first lesson, the instructor evaluates and records the student's riding abilities: position, recovery of balance, attitude, and intelligence. Instructors understand that each student will progress at an individual rate and that each lesson should be individualized according to the student's ability.

John Davies, foremost authority on therapeutic horsemanship, has elaborated procedures for the riding lessons. The English saddle is usually used, because it offers greater opportunity for independent balance. However, some students require another type of saddle, such as a western, a Portuguese, or a sidesaddle. Students first sit on a dummy horse (made from an oil drum) in order for them to get the feel of the new position. Prior to mounting a horse, students are fitted with a safety helmet (mandatory) and harness. They then meet, pet, and groom their horse.

Before mounting, students check the tack (make sure the bridle is on properly, all buckles are fastened, and the saddle girth is secure). Each student is taught to mount, if able, properly. Other methods of mounting are used according to individual abilities.

After mounting, students are instructed in the correct position for riding. To achieve the correct seat takes a lot of hard work and concentration for nondisabled riders as well as students with physical disabilities. If students cannot extend their arms to hold the reins or cannot put their feet in the stirrups, volunteers are a necessity. Some students, in their initial stages of riding, may require three volunteers: one to lead the horse and one on each side of the student to add support.

Adaptive equipment is essential to a therapeutic horsemanship program. Probably the most necessary and back-saving piece of equipment is the mounting ramp (see Figure 11–6). These examples of adaptive equipment should be used as long as necessary:

- Safety or body harness: leather shoulder straps and handholds
- Leading reins: used by the leader of a horse for control, but does not interfere with a rider's control
- Safety stirrup: prevents a foot from falling through the stirrup
- Fleece saddle cover: goes over the saddle to provide extra padding and a softer seat for a student who has spina bifida or other loss of sensation below the waist and who may be more susceptible to pressure sores

FIGURE 11–6
Mounting with a ramp

- Bareback pad: a foam pad placed on the horse, cinched up, and used in place of a saddle for a student with scissoring of the legs that prevents the legs from opening wide enough to sit on a saddle. The warmth from the horse will be felt through the horseback pad and will help to relax the tight muscles.
- Handhold: a strap attached to D rings on the saddle that helps in stabilizing riders
- Ladder reins: used mainly by one-handed riders for rein control, these are leather straps stitched at intervals

The most important part of a therapeutic horsemanship program is the hero of it all: the horse. Horses and ponies are selected and trained carefully. If a horse exhibits even one bad habit (kicking or biting), it is not suitable for the program. It must be patient, quiet, and willing to respond. The horses are trained to tolerate crutches, wheelchairs, chattering students, riders flailing around in the saddle, movement around their bodies, being led by another horse on a ride, and standing by a mounting ramp.

The objective for the students is to increase function. The goal of therapeutic horsemanship is to teach students to ride with enough confidence, coordination, and strength to participate and compete with their nondisabled peers. Horseback riding is a great equalizer of people: when on a horse, individuals with physical, health, or multiple disabilities have just as much strength and power as nondisabled riders.

Travel

Travel extends from an overseas experience that entails extensive planning to a daylong field trip to the local art museum. Travel opens doors into the unknown and leads to better cultural and historical understanding of the world and fellow human beings. Travel can be a functional event when it is related to visiting family or involves work-related excursions. Travel is also the perfect leisure activity for many. In recent years travel has increasingly become accessible for individuals with disabilities, so that they can visit and sightsee in almost any part of the world.

It is necessary to teach students with physical, health, or multiple disabilities they can go out into the world and enjoy it. Travel as part of leisure instruction allows them to see firsthand the many accommodations that exist in order to better serve them and will help them learn how to access these adaptations. Most importantly, it can help students with disabilities become more independent and gain self-confidence in themselves as they witness a world that is increasingly becoming an accessible one.

The beginning point in planning class trips should be the destination, and might include exploration of one's city or town. Chicago, for example, has become "-wheelchair-friendly," with its many museums, stores, and fine architecture that can be seen in the Loop. There are wheelchair-accessible lifts and entrances to buildings (Johnson-Wright & Wright, 2000). Philadelphia is another city with many accessible attractions. In order to prevent damage to historic Independence Hall and Congress Hall, accessibility has been created to the first floors and photos are provided of the second floors (Harrington, 1999).

Travel planning for individuals with disabilities also requires proper precautions. The Moss Rehab Resource Net Internet site (*www.mossresourcenet.org*) details tips to consider when traveling. The following is a summary listing of some ideas the site offers:

Medical Needs

- Have a proper supply of medications.
- Have prescriptions for medications.
- Have appropriate medical supplies and equipment.
- Have extra glasses or contact lenses.
- Know how to obtain medical help at your destination, as well as en route to it.
- Be aware of the general physical condition of students as determined by their physician.

Wheelchair Considerations

- Do a maintenance check of wheelchairs prior to the trip date.
- Have tools and extra parts on hand.
- Find out about wheelchair rentals at the destination for students who may use wheelchairs intermittently.

Travel Considerations

- Find out about accommodations on the means of travel (boat, bus, train, airplane, cruise ship, tour group).
- Know all the special accommodations that will be needed, such as help with the wheelchair at the airport or restaurant, special seating, and special meals.
- Have planned rest stops.
- Schedule trip days so that they will not be so tiring.
- Be aware of special assistance that can be offered by hotels, restaurants, tours, and so forth.
- Discuss the possibility of getting travel insurance.

Travel is a leisure activity that can mean a lifetime of socialization and discovery, and it can be a fulfilling experience for individuals with disabilities. Inviting students to explore their accessibility rights and options via travel activities can lead to exciting class trips and valuable lessons in developing positive self-esteem.

SPORTS

No chapter on physical education, recreation, and leisure would be complete without discussion of the current trends in sports for individuals with physical disabilities. Adaptations for physical activity participation were previously viewed as matching the limitations of the individual to the demands of the activity. For instance, an individual with a disability could merely sit in his or her wheelchair as a nondisabled peer pushed him or her around the basketball court. Now an individual has the range of freedom to decide on a physical activity based on personal interest, and then adaptations are considered. Individuals with disabilities can skydive or hang glide. They can scuba dive deep in the ocean and climb up mountainsides. With the technological advancement and cost deflation of wheelchairs and with the development of sports access equipment, individuals with physical or multiple disabilities are now able to enjoy an unlimited variety of physical activities. The evolution of organizations such as the National Sports Center for the Disabled and the rapid growth of the disability sports equipment industry have advocated for the inclusion of individuals with disabilities in every area of physical activity. Sports and recreation for individuals with disabilities has become a serious competitive and financial business.

Wheelchair Racing

Wheelchair racing has been a catalyst in wheelchair sports and is featured in marathons, track-and-field events, and other athletic affairs. Even young children can participate in wheelchair racing.

The sport of wheelchair racing requires access to asphalt or concrete turf or a racetrack. A good pair of racing gloves is vital to avoid serious hand blisters. Proper sets of gloves are made specifically for wheelers; these fit snugly, are durable and padded, and are seamless to avoid blistering. For example, individuals with paraplegia tend to blister on their forefingers, thumbs, and palms, whereas individuals with quadriplegia or tetraplegia have difficulties with their little fingers and palms (Shanahan, 1998). Prior discussion with parents about purchasing gloves and the care of hand blisters is important.

The type of wheelchair must also be considered. Some chairs may be too heavy for pushing to higher speeds or are simply not advanced enough to make sharp turns. In such cases it may be an alternative to switch to chairs that are lighter or more geared to racing. If finances permit, sets of racing chairs can be purchased as physical education equipment.

Wheelchair racing events are held nationwide. Local organizations will host events for all age groups and ability levels. Sports clubs and community recreation programs can also provide training. With time, practice, and training, students can become strong athletes.

FIGURE 11–7
Individuals with disabilities can excel in arm sports such as archery

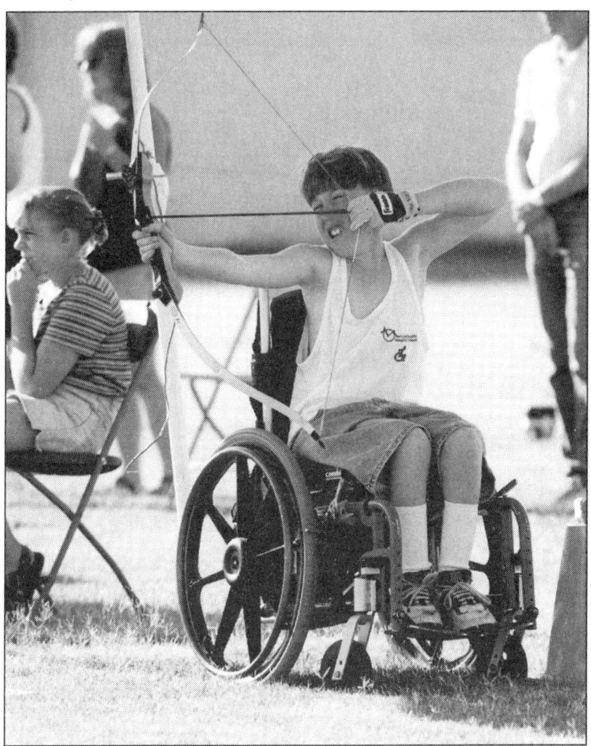

Racquet and Arm Sports

For students with disabilities who dream of being professional athletes, participating in racquet and arm sports can lead to competition, socialization, and travel. For example, a recent international tennis match drew over 243 athletes with disabilities from 19 countries (Snow, 1999). This highlights the growing professionalism of sports for individuals with physical disabilities. It also supports the need for competitive school programs that include students with disabilities.

Racquet sports include tennis, racquetball, badminton, and table tennis (Ping-Pong). Individuals with physical disabilities have long favored these sports because they can be played in wheelchairs. Using wheelchairs with advanced designs, athletes with physical disabilities have more range of upper body or arm movement and can travel between points on court at a more rapid speed (Snow, 1999). The enjoyment of Ping-Pong can also be experienced inside the classroom. A great activity would be to hold matches between students or to have teams drawn from different classrooms throughout the school.

Arm sports, including archery, as shown in Figure 11–7, involve the use of one or both arms to engage in an event from a wheelchair. Each of these sports requires the same instructional approaches in rules and forms of play as in a general education setting. Adaptability concerns can be discussed according to each student's needs, as well as the nature of their wheelchair. The same concerns about hand blisters mentioned in wheelchair racing are important in racquet and arm sports. If there are not enough students at a school to make a team, joining local organizations and sports clubs may be the answer.

Winter or Summer

Whether you live in an area of winter snowfalls or year-long sunshine, sports can be played at all times, in any setting. A few hours' drive to the mountains should not rule out a class snow-sporting trip, and the absence of an on-campus swimming pool should not prohibit a visit to the local pool. Whether it is climbing, archery, or ice-skating, a class-based sporting trip can be included to enhance physical education, recreation, and leisure education programs. Planning trips provides students with experience, knowledge, and confidence.

FIGURE 11–8
Students with physical, health or multiple disabilities can enjoy a range of outdoor sports activities with the proper instruction and accommodations

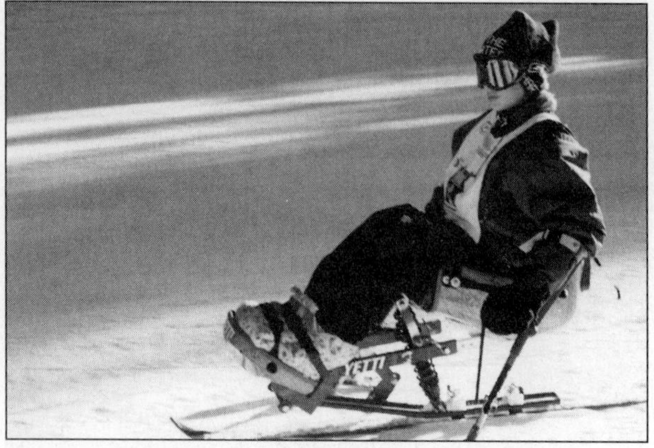

Organizing activities through local sport clubs and groups designed for individuals with physical or multiple disabilities can increase the quality of training and the level of participation (see Figure 11–8).

Individuals with physical or multiple disabilities have long participated in winter sports such as ice hockey and downhill and cross-country skiing. Ski and skate rentals at most resorts and rinks now include specially designed equipment and training to meet disability needs. The degree of physical ability will decide what type of modified snow-sport equipment an individual will use. Some individuals with cerebral palsy, for instance, may only require modified ski poles, whereas persons with spinal cord injury may need to engage in "sit-skiing." In sit-skiing, the person sits in a specially made seat that can slide downhill and uses shortened ski poles that have wide edges at the tips. For individuals who prefer to skate, sled-type equipment with blades underneath allow participation in many different ice sports.

For summertime sports, aquatic events are a popular choice. Individuals with physical or multiple disabilities can participate in both team and individual competitions. An aquatics lesson is not just having students splash about in the pool. The local pool or local sports group staff can probably offer assistance and suggestions about a training program (Rowland, 1990).

The only limitations to sports participation are health or medical restrictions. Some students may not be able to participate in specific sports. The type of sport should be considered with respect to its endurance and impact levels. For example, skiing is considered to be a high-contact sport that involves the body hitting and bouncing against solid ground. This sport, therefore, is not an option for someone with osteogenesis imperfecta. Contraindications for students with spina bifida include bobsledding, jump skiing, and waterskiing. Students with arthritis cannot participate in diving, downhill skiing, speed skating, or hockey (Goldberg, 1995). Even with restrictions, introducing and educating students with physical, health, or multiple disabilities in new physical experiences can open up worlds of participation that can be enjoyed for many years beyond school.

SUMMARY AND CONCLUSION

With guidance, encouragement, and creativity, individuals with physical or multiple disabilities can engage in physical education, recreation, leisure, and sports activities throughout childhood and into adult life. The opportunities for leisure for individuals with physical or multiple disabilities are as broad as their imaginations.

QUESTIONS FOR DISCUSSION

1. What are the legislative justifications for including individuals with disabilities in physical education, recreation, and leisure activities?
2. Respond to the following statement: "Leisure is not an important activity."
3. How would you begin a wheelchair sports club for students in your school district?
4. You are a high school history teacher. Discuss how you would infuse crafts studies into an instructional unit related to studying indigenous peoples of North and South America.
5. What sports activities would you recommend for someone with spastic quadriplegia? spina bifida? osteogenesis imperfecta? paralysis? asthma? What sports would you not recommend for these individuals, and why?

FOCUS ON THE NET

Disabled Sports, U.S.A.
http://www.dsusa.org

Founded in 1967, Disabled Sports U.S.A. is a national center for sports and recreation services for individuals with disabilities. A member of the United States Olympic Committee, the DSUSA maintains a Web site that offers extensive educational and recreational program information.

National Association for Sport and Physical Education (NASPE)
http://www.aahperd.org/naspe-contact.html

APE information, standards, publications, and resources.

National Center for Equine Facilitated Therapy
http://www.nceft.com

"Hippotherapy" (from the Greek word *hippo,* meaning "horse") has helped many children and adults to gain confidence and physical skills. Founded in 1971, the National Center for Equine Facilitated Therapy (NCEFT) has helped thousands of individuals experience the enjoyment of therapeutic horseback riding. Serving people of all ages and with a variety of disabilities, the NCEFT explains the benefits of therapeutic riding.

National Center on Accessibility
http://www.indiana.edu/~nca/nca.htm

Excellent site that provides information on accessibility for a variety of outdoor activities.

The National Center on Physical Activity and Disability
http://www.ncpad.org

The National Center on Physical Activity and Disability (NCPAD) is affiliated with the University of Illinois at Chicago, the Rehabilitation Institute of Chicago, and the National Center on Accessibility. The NCPAD promotes a healthful lifestyle and the prevention of secondary conditions through participation in "regular physical activity." Most outstanding is their extensive collection of fact pages that cover a range of sports activities as related to individuals with physical disabilities. They also provide great links, a newsletter, and access to a disability Web ring.

National Sports Network
http://www.nsnsports.org

A nonprofit organization to provide people of all ages with recreational opportunities.

Sports and Outdoor Assistive Recreation (SOAR)
http://www.wind.uwyo.edu/soar/

From the University of Wyoming, this site is an excellent resource on adaptive recreation.

United States Organization for Disabled Athletes
http://www.wwws.net/usoda

Provides sport opportunities for dwarf athletes. This site has extensive links to other organizations.

Winter Sports

AbilityPLUS
http://www.abilityplus.org

A nonprofit adaptive skiing and recreation organization that provides a great informative site.

Sitski
http://www.sitski.com

Wonderful site that addresses adaptive winter sports.

United States Sled Hockey Association
http://www.SledHockey.org

The national governing body for sled hockey in the United States.

Summer Sports

Freedom's Wings International
http://www.fly.to/fw

Information for flying activities.

Handcycling.Com
http://www.handcycling.com

Information, links, and extensive contact list for anyone interested in handcycling.

Handicapped Scuba Association International
http://www.hsascuba.com

Worldwide authority in the field of scuba diving sports for individuals with disabilities.

The Moray Wheels
http://www.moraywheels.org

Scuba diving classes, information, activities, and vacations are covered in this great site.

National Wheelchair Basketball Association (NWBA)
http://www.nwba.org

Want information on the Chicago Wheelchair Bulls Team? This group is partner to the NBA.

National Wheelchair Poolplayers Association
http://www.nwpainc.com

Fun Web site that covers everything related to wheelchair pool-playing.

National Wheelchair Softball Association
http://www.wheelchairsoftball.com

Great site for information on wheelchair softball.

Sailing Alternatives
http://www.sailingalternatives.org

This group offers information, instruction, and environmental support for sailing experiences.

Trips Inc.
www.tripinc.com

Trips Inc. provides travel adventures for adults with physical and developmental disabilities. Package prices include airfare and all meals.

United States Disabled Volleyball Team (USDVT)
http://www.volleyball.org

This is the first team of athletes with disabilities to face able-bodied athletes in competition.

United States Electric Wheelchair Association (USEWHA)
http://www.usewha.org

Excellent resource that provides support and knowledge for anyone interested in wheelchair sports.

United States Quad Rugby Association (USQRA)
http://www.quadrugby.com

This great site has extensive information, resources, links, and online library.

Wheelchair Hockey League (WCHL)
http://www.scorezone.com

Great site with news, information, contacts, and links.

Wheelchair Sports and Recreation Association
http://www.wheelchairinc.com

Events, newsletter, information, and services make this a great site.

Creative Domain

Aunt Annie's Crafts
http://www.auntannie.com

Offers ideas and products for a variety of children's crafts ideas.

National Arts and Disability Center
http://www.nadc.ucla.edu

Terrific resources and library search system.

The Rainy Day Resource Page
http://www.cp.duluth.mn.us/~sarah/index.html

A fun-filled online guide to creative activities for children.

Science and Technology

The American Radio Relay League (ARRL)
http://www.arrl.org/hamradio.html

The national organization of amateur radio.

Kiss Institute for Practical Robots
http://www.kipr.org

Robotics courses for all ages, including professional development classes.

Robot Science and Technology Online Supplement
http://www.robotmag.com

Great Web site of the premier robotics magazine.

Science Made Clear with Robots
http://www.mobilerobots.com

Information and services regarding robots.

Recreation Domain

The Access Board
http://www.access-board.gov

The site of the United States Architectural and Transportation Barriers Compliance Board.

Global Access Disabled Travel Network
http://www.geocities.com/Paris/1502/

Complete listing of travel-related links and information for individuals with physical disabilities.

Great Outdoor Recreation Page
http://www.gorp.com

Covers a variety of recreational interests, with reviews of renovated hiking trails and campsites.

Horses Unlimited
http://www.psln.com/zipper

Terrific organization that offers a Web site filled with information on therapeutic riding.

Mobility International U.S.A.
http://www.miusa.org

Offers information on exchange programs for individuals with physical disabilities.

New Horizons: Information for the Traveler with a Disability
http://www.faa.gov/acr/dat.htm

The official Web site of the U.S. Department of Transportation and Aviation.

Pal-O-Mine Equestrian
http://www.pal-o-mine.org

A terrific Web site that offers an online newsletter, extensive links, and valuable information.

Wilderness Inquiry
http://www.wildernessinquiry.org

Has a lot of information on outdoor adventure recreation, including dog sledding and sea kayaking.

REFERENCES

American Radio Relay League. (2000). http://www.arrl.org/hamradio.html

Anderson, A., & Goode, R. (1997). Assessment informs instruction. *Journal of Physical Education, Recreation, and Dance, 68*(3), 42–49.

Banbury Cross Therapeutic Equestrian Center. (2000). "Program Information." http:// www.banburycrosstec.com

Block, M. E. (2000). *A teacher's guide to including students with disabilities in general physical education* (2nd ed.). Baltimore: Brookes.

Block, M. E., & Conaster, P. (2002). Adapted aquatics and inclusion. *Journal of Physical Education, Recreation, and Dance, 73*(5), 31–34.

Bouchard, S., Shepard, R. J., & Stephens, T. (1993). *Physical activity, fitness, and health.* Champaign, IL: Human Kinetics Books.

Brigance, A. (1977). Brigance Diagnostic Inventory of Basic Skills. North Billerica, MA: Curriculum Associates.

California Department of Education: (1994). *Physical education framework.* Sacramento: Author.

Conejo Valley Amateur Radio Club. http://www.cvarc.org

Franklin Institute Online. (1996). "Simple Machines." http://www.sln.fi.edu

Gabbard, C., LeBlanc, B., & Lowry, S. (1994). *Physical education for children: Building the foundation* (2nd ed.). Upper Saddle River, NJ: Prentice Hall.

Goldberg, B. (Ed.). (1995). *Sports and exercise for children with chronic health conditions.* Champaign, IL: Human Kinetics.

Graham, G., Holt-Hale, S. A., & Parker, M. (1998). *Children moving: A reflective approach to teaching physical education* (4th ed.). Mountain View, CA: Mayfield.

Ham Radio Online. (1999). "Welcome to Amateur Radio." Virtual Publishing Co. http://hamradioonline.com

Harrington, C. B. (1999). Historic Philadelphia. *Emerging Horizons, 2*(3), 11.

Herald, J. (1993). *World crafts.* Asheville, NC: Lark.

Huettig, C., & Roth, K. (2002). Maximizing the use of APE consultants: What the general physical educator needs to know. *Journal of Physical Education, Recreation, and Dance, 73*(1), 32–35.

Hull, B., Michael, S. E., Walker, G. J., & Roggenbuck, J. W. (1996). Ebb and flow of brief leisure experiences. *Leisure Sciences, 18:* 299–314.

Johnson, L. V., Kasser, S. L., & Nichols, B. A. (2002). Including all children in standards-based physical education. *Journal of Physical Education, Recreation, and Dance, 73*(4), 42–46.

Johnson-Wright, H., & Wright, S. (2000). "Bright Light, Big Cities." New Mobility Online. http://www.newmobility.com

Kasser, S. L., Collier, D., & Solava, D. G. (1997). Sports skills for students with disabilities: A collaborative effort. *Journal of Physical Education, Recreation, and Dance, 68*(1), 50–53.

Kirk, M. F. (1997). Using portfolios to enhance student learning and assessment. *Journal of Physical Education, Recreation, and Dance, 68*(7), 29–33.

Laverie, D. A. (1998). Motivations for ongoing participation in a fitness activity. *Leisure Sciences, 20,* 277–302.

Miller, D. K. (1998). *Measurement by the physical educator: Why and how.* San Francisco: McGraw-Hill.

National Association for Sport and Physical Education, (1995). *Moving into the future: National physical education standards.* Philadelphia: Mosby.

Peterson, C. A., & Stumbo, N. J. (1999). *Therapeutic recreation program design: Principles and procedures* (3rd ed.). Needham Heights, MA: Allyn & Bacon.

Porreta, D. L. (2000). Cerebral palsy, stroke, and traumatic brain injury. In J. P. Winnick (Ed.), *Adaptive physical education and sport* (pp. 181–198). Champaign, IL: Human Kinetics.

Rowland, T. (1990). *Exercise and children's health.* Champaign, IL: Human Kinetics.

Safrit, M. J., & Wood, T. M. (1995). *Introduction to measurement in physical education and exercise science* (3rd ed.). Philadelphia: Mosby.

Seaman, J. (1995). *Physical best and individuals with disabilities.* Reston, VA: American Alliance for Health, Physical Education, Recreation, and Dance.

Shanahan, N. (1998). Get a grip. *Sports 'N Spokes, 24*(5), 26–28.

Sherrill, C. (1998). *Adapted physical activity, recreation, and sport* (5th ed.). Boston: WCB/McGraw-Hill.

Sirvis, B., Musante, P., & Bigge, J. L. (1991). Leisure education and adapted physical education. In J. L. Bigge (Ed.), *Teaching individuals with physical and multiple disabilities* (3rd ed., pp. 428–459). Upper Saddle River, NJ: Merrill/Prentice Hall.

Smith, T. K. (1997). Authentic assessment: Using a portfolio card in physical education. *Journal of Physical Education, Recreation, and Dance, 68*(4), 46–52.

Snow, R. (1999). A new tradition. *Sports 'N Spokes, 25*(8), 22–26.

STRIDES Therapeutic Riding. (1999). http://www.strides.org

Strommer, P. (1996). Assessments used by adapted physical education specialists in California. *California Association for Health, Physical Education, Recreation, and Dance, Journal/Times, 58*(6), 11.

Surburg, P. R. (2000). Other health-related impairments. In J. P. Winnick (Ed.), *Adaptive physical education and sport* (pp. 235–250). Champaign, IL: Human Kinetics.

Ulrich, D. (1985). Test of gross motor development, Austin, TX: Pro-Ed.

Westling, D. L., & Fox, L. (2000). *Teaching students with severe disabilities* (2nd ed.). Upper Saddle River, NJ: Merrill/Prentice Hall.

Zuzanek, J., Robinson, J. P., & Iwasaki, Y. (1998). The relationships between stress, health, and physically active leisure. *Leisure Sciences, 20,* 253–275.

Transition and Self-Determination

GARY M. CLARK
JUNE L. BIGGE

CHAPTER 12

KNOWLEDGE AND SKILLS

After you have read this chapter, you will be able to:

1. **Identify some of the barriers that contribute to difficulties for individuals with physical or multiple disabilities in obtaining and maintaining employment.**
2. **Describe ways teachers can plan and provide for students with physical or multiple disabilities to make it easier for the students to surmount barriers to employment.**
3. **Describe the stages of career education and instructional goals that follow a career development approach.**
4. **Identify the major occupational clusters and some of the strategies and considerations for providing occupational guidance to students in gaining awareness of themselves and alternatives related to their interests and preferences.**
5. **Describe and discuss the advantages and disadvantages of strategies educators can use with students with physical or multiple disabilities in preparing for and entering employment.**
6. **Discuss some of the applications of different curricular options for enhancing the employability and employment success of individuals with physical or multiple disabilities.**

One of the most important responsibilities of educators and other allied professionals is to help pupils with physical or multiple disabilities prepare for present and future life work endeavors. *Work is defined broadly here as directing physical or mental effort toward the achievement of something productive.* Work, in this sense, not only pertains to jobs for pay but also encompasses tasks related to schoolwork, daily living, personal growth, and leisure time. Since other chapters addressed these latter areas, the focus of this chapter will be preparation for paid employment and the knowledge and skills in the area of self-determination that make that preparation more successful and satisfying.

Information in this text is consistent with the view that "a comprehensive model of transition education and services must take into account the idea that success in one transition increases the likelihood of success in later transitions" (Sitlington, Clark, & Kolstoe, 2000, p. 26). Teachers can integrate information in this chapter with information throughout the text to organize and implement transition programs, services, and experiences that prepare students for their varying roles throughout their school lives and into adulthood. Information in this text complements the model of Sitlington et al. discussed in Chapter 5. Curriculum options and sub-options in this chapter cover many of the same knowledge and skill domains or curricular areas. Whether teachers choose to teach content or performances that lead to outcomes in these areas is often an individual decision. In some instances, school administrators and teacher committees make this choice and there is a collective commitment to this important and high-stakes concept.

Like any graduates, young adults with physical or multiple disabilities are leaving educational programs and encountering major decisions that may influence the entire course of their lives. When deciding to pursue employment instead of, or along with, higher education and perhaps volunteer pursuits, individuals are confronted with some very real questions. Individuals inquire: What would I enjoy doing? What jobs are available, and do I have or could I develop the skills for those jobs? Where can I obtain training that will lead to a job? Will I be able to get to and from a job? Will I be able to advocate for myself in terms of accommodations or supports? Will I be able to function in the work environment? Will I want to do the particular kind of work that is available to me? What difference will my disability make?

Unlike other graduates, some young adults with physical or multiple disabilities may encounter additional degrees of challenge in obtaining and maintaining work. Some common barriers to employment include the following:

1. Independence difficulties may influence the ease of gaining employment because a high degree of extra support is needed. Some examples of extra support would be special transportation needs, accessibility modifications, assistive technology devices, communication supports, and possible need for a personal attendant.
2. Some physical conditions or chronic health problems raise questions regarding regular attendance, strength and stamina, side effects of medications, and the need for emergency health care.
3. Lack of experience in self-care or personal health management due to overprotection or unrelinquished control by family and professional caregivers can slow self-determination development.
4. Limited social experiences with peers and adults outside of school or home may influence the level of social competence, self-confidence, and desire to expand social contacts and interactions.

To prepare individuals and families to deal with these impending challenges, educators can provide educational and vocational experiences that help individuals with physical or multiple disabilities become as socially competent, physically self-sufficient, and economically self-sufficient as possible. Preparation of students to choose vocations and become workers begins in early childhood. Neglect of this preparation encourages attitudes of psychological, social, and physical dependency and makes it impossible for individuals to develop the self-determination and self-reliance needed by successful workers. Addressing this preparation directly allows students to find success in directing their physical and mental efforts toward the achievement of paid work.

The first section of this chapter develops teacher awareness of ways in which students can surmount or avoid barriers to employment. The way teachers and others treat students with physical or multiple disabilities from early childhood on can eliminate or reduce potential barriers to employment. In the place of barriers, skills that result in employment can be built. These skills, usually referred to as work-related skills, address the major problem areas of employability: physical self-reliance, valid self-evaluation, and self-adaptability or self-determination.

The second section focuses on the aspects of career education that lead toward preparing students for work. Stages in a career education curriculum are (a) career awareness, (b) career exploration, (c) career preparation, and (d) career placement/follow-up and continuing education. Generalized goals by school levels are identified to provide direction to teachers and to let teachers see goals for a career education continuum.

The third section introduces teachers to occupational clusters into which the myriad of current occupations are divided. With this framework, guidelines are presented for providing practical career/vocational experiences using occupational clusters as guides. Experiences, particularly those in natural settings, help students develop awareness and appreciation of the jobs of others and to examine them as possible jobs for themselves. Situational illustrations are presented for basic and advanced skills and for teaching students to (a) observe people on the job, (b) evaluate self/job compatibilities, and (c) consider possible assistive modifications. A second set of illustrative practical activities and accompanying procedures illustrates how to help students assess their own abilities to complete components of school tasks that must be done to achieve an understanding of the connection between school and working someday after leaving school.

Transition from school to community-based competitive employment is the topic of the fourth section of this chapter. It addresses recommended practices designed and implemented on behalf of students with disabilities who are seeking employment at the highest level possible. A range of strategies is suggested to account for the wide range of abilities and needs of students with physical and multiple disabilities.

The fifth section describes seven job design or redesign strategies to allow students with physical or multiple disabilities to work with maximum independence. The Oregon Research Institute, as part of the Oregon Transition to Employment Project, developed these strategies.

The final section of the chapter teaches about vocational uses of the computer and other electronic office equipment. Software, hardware, and shortcut strategies to save movement and maintain or expedite productivity of individuals with movement difficulties are described.

SURMOUNTING BARRIERS TO EMPLOYMENT

Many people meet not only their economic needs but also their needs for social status and self-esteem through their roles in work. Many people with physical and perhaps additional disabilities wish to meet precisely the same needs in the same ways.

Individuals with physical or multiple disabilities often encounter numerous barriers in trying to achieve equal social status, self-esteem, and acceptance as a worker. The more obvious barriers may result from the mere presence of the disability. The less obvious barriers may result from social prejudices or from the injurious barriers presented by our society's preoccupation with health, youth, and beauty, and its fear and avoidance of sickness, aging, and disability. In addition to these possible obstacles, myriad problems may arise when people with and without disabilities are educated at separate sites, when they receive totally separate education on the same sites, or even when they are in the same classroom but are separated within it. These service delivery models tend to prohibit students with and without disabilities from having natural opportunities for forming peer relationships and mutual understanding and acceptance of one another.

Isolation not only has negative effects on the students, but it may also distort the perception of teachers and counselors working with these students in isolated settings. Unfortunately, inclusive education settings may result in equally negative outcomes when teachers "overassist," fail to hold students to high standards of performance and independence, or fail to make adaptations that are required to accommodate disabilities. As a result, these teachers may fail the people they most want to help in three growth areas: (a) physical self-reliance and self-management, (b) valid self-evaluation, and (c) self-adaptability or self-determination. Underdevelopment of these three qualities adds to the barriers that must be overcome if one is to achieve status and acceptance as a competent worker.

Physical Self-Reliance

Bowe (2000), Sowers and Powers (1991), and Rubin and Roessler (2001) have all identified and discussed work-related skill areas in which individuals with physical or multiple disabilities frequently encounter difficulties and which can pose major problems for employability. These are psychological coping, physical capacity and stamina, mobility, communication, bathroom use, eating, and drinking. Wehman and Kregel (1988) wrote an entire book chapter responding to the underemployment situation of individuals with cerebral palsy. It is obvious that Wehman and Kregel are identifying the physical self-reliance challenge when they write of teenagers with cerebral palsy: "Motor and communication impairments frequently mask real potential and abilities" (p. ix). Transportation to and from work or as a part of job requirements has also been cited as a work-related skill barrier affecting physical self-reliance (Bowe, 2000).

It is safe to predict that individuals with disabilities will face challenges in employment situations. It is becoming increasingly obvious that educators and advocates cannot wait for a favorable "employment climate." Educational services that contribute to the development of marketable vocational skills for students with severe vocational handicaps should be included in the curriculum and course of study options. As our society becomes more creative in adjusting work environments and the work tasks for workers with special needs, and as students' schooling for physical self-reliance and self-determination improves, individuals making their transitions from school to work will be more prepared than ever to meet the challenges.

Valid Self-Evaluation

Appropriate self-evaluation is an important practice for a worker. Field and Hoffman (1998), in fact, identify "Know Yourself" as the first component of their self-determination model. Appropriate self-evaluation is more than merely repeating, "I can do anything anyone else can do; I can do anything better than you." Appropriate self-evaluation means an honest look at one's interests, preferences, strengths, and needs. It then might require a comparison of one's own abilities and performances to the abilities of others or the demands of different situations.

Inappropriate self-evaluation can often be traced to a lack of experience in seeing for oneself how one measures up to others in different situations. Some individuals with disabilities may have enjoyed only limited opportunities to interact with other students or to participate in situations where certain standards are expected. How, for instance, can students who are still experiencing only a special center or class of only pupils with physical or multiple disabilities ever gain valid and reliable evaluations of how ready they are to participate in regular classes and society with their peers? Without ample opportunities for interacting with others or participating along with others (such as most programs now provide), there is little opportunity to see what is expected, how their skills compare, and where improvement is needed.

Inappropriate self-evaluation may also result from inappropriate feedback sent from well-meaning adults. Students with disabilities often receive inaccurate messages in the form of inappropriate praise from others. Overzealous praise fosters inaccurate self-evaluation. The receiver, for example, does not always place verbal praise in its proper perspective. It may transmit meanings quite different from those intended by a sender. Artwork described by an overpraising teacher as "marvelous," "beautiful," "fabulous," or "fantastic" is not necessarily of genius quality. Is it any wonder that a 17-year-old with quadriplegic cerebral palsy who receives an abundance of such praise eventually feels he has the ability to become another Michelangelo? An enthusiastic comment about the student's proud attitude toward his finished product would seem far less risky or deceiving; for example, "You really feel good about this picture!" "I really like the way you blended your tones!" or "This must be your favorite!" As with any other student, these individuals would benefit from helpful suggestions for further improvement or additional information to expand the learning experience. Without honest appraisal and constructive suggestions for improvement, individuals are opened to disappointing future realizations that they were not nearly as "good" as they thought they were. Overzealous feedback in comments or grading has the potential for eventually developing invalid self-evaluation, which, in the competitive workforce, leads to disappointment and frustration.

Enhanced Self-Adaptability and Self-Determination

Adaptability means depending upon one's "strategies for making choices for [oneself] and managing [one's] own behavior" (Agran, Martin, & Mithaug, 1989, p. 4). Agran et al. view adaptability skills as vital to success in achieving transition from school to community-based employment.

Self-adaptability, as used here, includes students' exercising of their own abilities and judgment. To illustrate, several years ago a therapist was involved in a special research project with young, school-age children who were disabled by cerebral palsy and, in some cases, by intellectual impairment. A short time later the therapist began to work in a rehabilitation center with adults with cerebral palsy as well as other disabilities. While working with these adults, the therapist reflected upon her past experiences with students and realized how she might have contributed to their lack of self-adaptability as adults.

The therapist had previously viewed the unexpected absence of one of her student clients with relief. She appreciated the extra time gained to write progress notes, devise rehabilitation plans, and prepare for the next day's work schedule. The next time she saw the client, the therapist did not take the opportunity to approach him and suggest the importance of notifying people when appointments had to be canceled. Moreover, she realized that over time, she had allowed the child's parents to take full responsibility for cancellations. They either called in or wrote a note; any tardiness or absence was because they did not get the child up on time, or they did not get him dressed, or they forgot to get his lunch ready, or they did not get him to the bus on time. It was sadly evident that the child was not even expected to set his own alarm or to remind someone else to help him if he could not do it himself. No one regularly expected any significant assistance or personal responsibility from the child regarding his own daily schedule.

This simple vignette depicts how early in a child's life caring persons can unwittingly cheat youngsters with disabilities by not letting them learn the adaptability skills they will need as adults. In this case, the therapist missed an opportunity to help the child develop adaptability responses that eventually would be expected by employers. Without meaning to at all, this therapist was contributing to the child's lack of learning opportunities for at least one adaptability skill.

Agran et al. (1989) offered an adaptability instructional model for enhancing the adaptability and problem-solving skills of students in work environments. They presented a model based on the assumption that "for students to function adequately in dynamic work environments their instructions should focus on generic adaptability skills" (p. 4).

The adaptability instructional model, designed to improve postschool success, is directed toward instruction of students with mild to severe learning needs. Therefore, it is also appropriate for most students with physical, health, or multiple disabilities. Stressing the reduction of dependence upon coworkers and supervisors on the job, the model can also be used for the reduction of excessive student dependency upon teachers in the educational setting. The model consists of four components:

1. **Decision making** (e.g., indicating which job(s) he can perform best; clarifying unclear instructions);
2. **Independent performance** (e.g., reporting to appropriate site; begining work on time; working at job continuously without disruption; following time schedule; selecting antecedent and/or consequent self-management procedure to facilitate task performance);
3. **Self-evaluation** (e.g., maintaining a record of arriving at work or returning from break/lunch on time; responding appropriately to criticism);
4. **Autonomy** (e.g., correcting own work to conform to job expectations or standards; adapting to change in work schedule; adapting to changes in supervisory staff).

Recent literature in the area of reducing dependency on teachers, coworkers, or supervisors stresses the importance of teaching the use of self-directed instruction and self-management procedures (Wehmeyer, Agran, & Hughes, 1998). Learned helplessness, or overdependence on others, is a hurdle that the approaches of some teachers and other members of society unknowingly make larger for students with physical or multiple disabilities.

Self-determination, a concept encompassing self-adaptability, is a term that is used widely in the area of transition (refer to Chapter 5 on self-determination and self-advocacy content). Self-determination curriculum and instruction is infused throughout this text because of its importance. We assume that readers agree with Seymour Sarason's (1990) statement about the essential purpose of the educational process, which is to "produce responsible, self-sufficient citizens who possess the self-esteem, initiative, skills and wisdom to continue individual growth and pursue knowledge" (p. 163), and that this statement "articulates the intent of initiatives to promote the self-determination of children and youth with disabilities" (Wehmeyer, Palmer, Agran, Mithaug, & Martin, 2000, p. 439). These authors went on to declare that "teachers seeking to promote the self-determination of their students must enable them to become self-regulated problem-solvers." The authors did not stop with their commitment to talking about self-determination. Rather, they accompanied it with a research-based model of teaching, the "Self-Determined Learning Model of Instruction." We refer teachers to their article (Wehmeyer, Palmer, et al., 2000) about the model to learn how to teach students "to become causal agents in their lives" (p. 440). Most intriguing about the article is the specificity of the process and the specificity of educational supports (or instruction bases) for each step in the process.

Conceptually, self-adaptability and self-determination are basically the same. Self-determination, the more common term now, gained national visibility when the U.S. Department of Education's Office of Special Education Programs funded an initiative for a series of self-determination projects. Field, Martin, Miller, Ward, and Wehmeyer (1997) presented an excellent description of the current major models of self-determination (including the self-adaptability model) and existing curricula and materials in *A Practical Guide for Teaching*

Self-Determination. Readers will find this publication rich in specific information on this topic. One component of the book provides a helpful framework for the self-determination outcomes educators should be working toward. Field, Martin, Miller, Ward, and Wehmeyer (1998, p. 3), in a position statement of the Division on Career Development and Transition, described some characteristics of self-determined people. The characteristics they included are as follows:

- Awareness of personal preferences, interests, strengths, and limitations;
- Ability to differentiate between wants and needs;
- Ability to make choices based on preferences, interests, wants, and needs;
- Ability to consider multiple options and to anticipate consequences for decisions;
- Ability to initiate and take action when needed;
- Ability to evaluate decisions based on the outcomes of previous decisions and to revise future decisions accordingly;
- Ability to set and work toward goals;
- Problem-solving skills;
- A striving for independence while recognizing interdependence with others;
- Self-advocacy skills;
- Ability to self-regulate behavior;
- Self-evaluation skills;
- Independent performance and adjustment skills;
- Persistence;
- Ability to use communication skills such as negotiation, compromise, and persuasion to reach goals;
- Ability to assume responsibility for actions and decisions;
- Self-confidence;
- Pride; and
- Creativity.

Three self-determination project products of particular note are *Steps to Self-Determination* (Field & Hoffman, 1996), *Next S.T.E.P.: Student Transition and Educational Planning* (Halpern et al., 1997), and *Take Charge* (Powers, Singer, & Sowers, 1992). The first two may be implemented in general education classes that are inclusive settings with students who have physical, sensory, mild cognitive, learning, or behavioral disabilities. *Take Charge* is based on a program designed specifically for adolescents with physical disabilities. They have all been field-tested extensively and give similar, yet distinctive, instructional strategies for teachers to use in teaching self-determination skills. Teachers will find the detailed lesson plans, teacher guides, and student materials easy to follow and exceptionally helpful.

In summary, students can get a "running start" on many of the barriers in the work world if teachers deliberately teach for added strengths that students can use to cope with those barriers. This happens when teachers encourage students from early childhood on to develop and strengthen physical self-reliance, valid self-assessment, and self-adaptability or self-determination.

TEACHING CAREER AND TRANSITION EDUCATION FROM EARLY CHILDHOOD

The notion of life-span transition education is obvious when one thinks about it, but because of federal initiatives and the legislative requirements for transition services at only two age levels (at age 3 and ages 14 and older), most educators continue to think in those terms only. Patton and Dunn (1998) presented their perspective on the continuum of need across the life span with their discussion and an illustration of vertical and horizontal transitions in life. Sitlington, Clark, et al. (2000) also affirmed the life-span approach in their transition education and transition services models. There are numerous time periods and events that require individuals to adjust to or cope with changes in their lives and the demands and expectations that come with those changes. Career and transition education is about preparation for those changes.

Preparation for work cannot suddenly begin when an intense desire arises for employment. Physical therapy started at the age of 18 does not make the body of a person with a crippling condition reach its optimal potential; nor does beginning preparation for vocational job placement at age 18 allow students with disabilities opportunities to reach their optimal job potential. Career education and transition education focusing on employability skills should address the needs of all students with disabilities (Brolin, 1995; Sitlington, Clark, et al., 2000), and this definitely includes students with physical disabilities. This chapter focuses on preparation of students for careers in paid employment situations. This section will stress the importance of life-centered career education instruction and transition education as a foundation for satisfying employment outcomes.

Brolin's (1995, 1997) long-standing position on the developmental nature of career development is well documented. He described four stages of career development and how he used those stages for designing his Life-Centered Career Education (LCCE) curriculum (Brolin, 1992). His four stages include:

1. Career awareness
2. Career exploration
3. Career preparation
4. Career placement/follow-up and continuing education

Although these four stages suggest a sequential, developmental model, students can and should be given experiences and opportunities to learn in more than one stage at a time. Astute educators develop awareness of the importance of infusing career education concepts, materials, and experiences at all levels and in all areas of students' education.

Integrated with these four stages of career development are three main career education curriculum areas. Brolin's curriculum model (1992, 1995, 1997) includes *daily living skills, personal-social skills*, and *occupational skills.* Although these three areas may be thought of separately in curriculum planning, they often are blended together in school-based and community-based teaching situations. For example, a student learning how to buy items for personal care (a daily living skill) may at the same time be taught how to use augmentative communication to interact with people in a store (a personal-social skill) and how to count change (an occupational skill). In the context of this chapter on employment, a teacher's main focus may be on occupational skills, but other kinds of skills (daily living and personal-social) may also be work-related and supportive of independence in maintaining a job. It is both natural and desirable for teachers to infuse instruction into the important tasks at hand.

Career Awareness

Career awareness starts during early childhood education in learning that people have a variety of roles and jobs that require different skills. Students also learn that someday they may fulfill some of these roles. This exposure to a variety of roles starts to build knowledge and appreciation about jobs and the roles of work and workers in society. Career education at the elementary-school level should include these two general objectives: to convey the positive value of work and to instill a self-concept that offers opportunities for pride, recognition, and reward for work achievements. As students notice the manual, physical, and academic skills needed by workers, they will begin to assess themselves in terms of these standards. As a guide, teachers can introduce many ways in which students can begin to think of themselves now as future valuable workers in their community. This is a time to start students thinking about the other ways jobs can be done by people who cannot do them in usual ways. For example, field trips or in-class simulations of a store, office, or laboratory may help them visualize themselves in worker roles, but at the same time give them opportunities to see how accommodations or task modifications need to be made. Career awareness can also be provided through different areas of the curriculum: in language arts, the study of people's roles in picture books and other literature; in geography, the study of workers around the world; and in science, the study of the lives of discoverers and inventors. It is provided when workers with and without disabilities visit as classroom guests, and through videos or films in which students can observe people doing different jobs. Along with developing awareness and appreciation of workers in many ways in the curriculum, teachers can begin to orient students toward kinds of behavior, such as appropriate dress and grooming, work habits, and social behavior, that will be required of them when they take on roles in the adult world.

Career Exploration

Career exploration starts at a basic level in the elementary years but becomes more important in middle/junior high school. Whereas career awareness provides a general understanding of the nature of work, career exploration gives specific opportunities for students to examine their abilities and needs as potential workers. Career exploration was one of the original purposes of junior high schools. With emphasis on academics now and the elimination of exploratory courses, it is more difficult to provide students opportunities to explore music, drama, speech, art, graphic arts, sewing, cooking, industrial arts, and a variety of other occupationally related subjects. This makes the challenge of providing career exploration much more difficult. Schools have to think in terms of special before- or after-school programs, summer programs, community service and volunteer activities, and looking to community youth organizations and churches for alternative career exploration options.

At the exploration stage, students examine different occupational clusters. Because it is impossible to expose students to the 20,000 or more occupations that exist, students can develop some awareness and do some exploring more efficiently by looking at occupational clusters. A major listing of occupations can be found in the *Occupational Outlook Handbook* (*www.stats.bls.gov/oco/home.htm*) on the Internet. In it, approximately 250 occupations are categorized into the following job clusters:

1. Management Occupations
2. Professional and Related Occupations
3. Service Occupations
4. Sales Occupations
5. Administrative Support Occupations
6. Farming and Related Occupations
7. Construction Occupations
8. Installation and Related Occupations
9. Production Occupations
10. Transportation Occupations
11. Job Opportunities in the Armed Forces

The Occupational Information Network (O*NET; *www.doleta.gov/programs.onet/*) is another source of information from the Department of Labor that provides a comprehensive database system for collecting, organizing, describing, and disseminating data on job characteristics and worker characteristics. Viewing sources like these helps students, families, teachers, and counselors think about a range of options for exploration or training. Individuals with physical or multiple disabilities can be found in every one of the cluster areas. Even persons with multiple disabilities that include moderate to severe cognitive deficits can work in most of these cluster areas through what is called "job creation" and supported employment (Hagner & Dileo, 1993). There should be no stereotyping of occupational clusters as obvious or workable matches for individuals with disabilities. A job is made up of a collection of tasks, and many tasks can be performed in a variety of work settings, regardless of the occupational area. Occupational clusters are not just ability areas, but interest areas as well. A person with a disability might not be able to perform the role of a company president or plant manager (executive, administrative, and managerial occupations), but could work in the office area or be a support person to a manager or executive. Military service might be impossible for anyone with physical or multiple disabilities, but jobs can be found or created in the civilian support sector on a military base. Technology, as an interest area, cuts across every one of the 11 occupational cluster areas.

Whenever possible, students should be given hands-on experiences in and out of school, observing their parents and others in various occupations and comparing occupations in more depth than they did in earlier studies of awareness. All subjects and extracurricular activities become avenues for a student to test personal aptitudes, interests, and preferences. In rural areas, participation in 4-H Club activities, in scouting, and in county fairs is one way to find out what local people do for work and leisure (see Figure 12–1). In urban areas, street festivals, art in the park, music festivals, Boys and Girls Clubs, scouting, and countless activities sponsored by schools, public museums, libraries, colleges and universities, and civic organizations provide children with multiple opportunities to explore.

Students can be encouraged to explore jobs (a) in natural situations in the classroom and at school (see Figure 12–2), (b) through attention to people's jobs while reading newspapers or magazines, watching television, and going about their daily lives with families and friends, and (c) through visits to actual job sites in the community (see Figure 12–3). Whenever appropriate and safe, students should be given opportunities for on-the-job tryouts or for job shadowing. Through such firsthand experiences in natural situations, students will be better able to assess task requirements and other features of an occupation or occupational cluster.

FIGURE 12–1
Teachers guide students into participation in community activities

FIGURE 12–2
Students can be given opportunities to try different actual job tasks at school

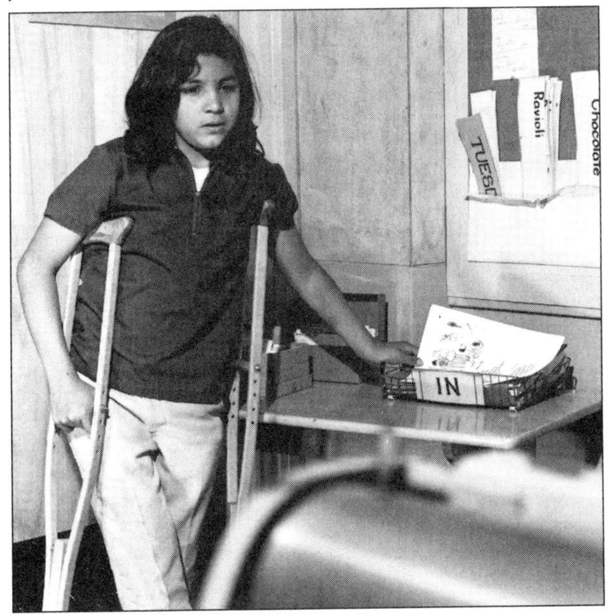

FIGURE 12–3
On a planned field trip, students investigate jobs clustered around their special interest in cars

Students and teachers can explore individual occupational clusters using the questions in Table 12–1 as a guide. These nine questions, when applied to the job cluster of food service jobs, for example, illustrate how exploration of one occupational area of the Service Occupations cluster can provide career exploration experience. Note and compare the basic activities for young or less experienced students to advanced activities for older or more experienced students in exploring the nine questions. These questions could be expanded into a task analysis of job exploration, then further refined into actual job-training analyses.

As older students study what specific jobs really entail, they are often eager to try some of them. Students need opportunities to try simulated or actual jobs to further assess their abilities and interests. They also need to experience firsthand the thinking they might have to do regarding modifications of work environments, accessibility techniques, accommodations in hours or schedules, and ways to advocate for themselves in job interviews and after being employed. Cooperation among school personnel and community employers is necessary to arrange formal or informal observations, job shadowing, or on-the-job tryouts. This takes effort, but it results in a meaningful exploration approach for students.

In addition to information about occupations, the exploration process involves self-assessment. Students engaging in exploration activities should be encouraged to think in terms of whether or not certain occupations are a good match with their strengths.

TABLE 12–1
Sample Guide Illustrating Career Exploration in the Area of Food Services

Question	Activity	Basic	Advanced
1. What are the occupations within food services?	Visit a restaurant and conduct a survey of all the different jobs people are doing.	Find those who are cooking (chef), bringing customers food (servers), taking money (cashier or server/cashier).	For the following workers, define the roles observed or perceived: server, salad worker, bus person, dishwasher, pot and pan washer, prep cook, line cook, chef, hostess, cashier, manager, and maintenance person. Compare jobs in different kinds of restaurants (e.g., 24-hour coffee shop, fast-food restaurant, family restaurant, cafeteria, specialty restaurant). Explore the vocabulary (or jargon) related to jobs in food services.
2. Who works in these occupations?	Find out what backgrounds and preparation workers in different occupations must have.	Ask the workers how they learned to do their jobs, what they like to do best in the jobs, and what they like to do least in the jobs.	Ask the workers to state what qualifications they perceive to be the most important for their jobs. Compare qualifications of service personnel in different kinds of restaurants.
3. What is the lifestyle of food service personnel?	Find out how the jobs and the job schedules affect the lives of the workers, or how their lifestyles are influenced by their job selections.	Compare the days of the week that students go to school and the days a restaurant worker works. Compare the hours of work and the time a student spends in school and on homework.	Interview an employee and ask questions about how the work affects the way he/she lives. Ask what influenced his/her job selection.
4. Where are the jobs?	Study how to find jobs.	Ask teachers or working parents how they found their jobs.	Study employment ads in newspapers, on bulletin boards in supermarkets, etc., and find out where jobs are located. Study city map and transportation systems that can be used to get to these different locations.
5. How do workers perform their jobs?	Describe or demonstrate what each person does as part of the job.	Role-play, taking a part as a customer, waiter or waitress, and cashier.	Watch any one restaurant worker and list all the activities and skills demonstrated. Notice what communication skills the worker uses. List activities not seen but assumed to be part of the job, including those involving computers and other high-technology devices, interpersonal communication, and interpersonal relationships.

TABLE 12–1
(Continued)

Question	Activity	Basic	Advanced
6. How might workers accomplish their jobs if they could not talk/walk/use their hands in usual ways?	Describe or demonstrate how different food service workers might do their jobs if they could not talk, move around, or use their hands in usual ways.	Identify which workers could still do their jobs if they were wheelchair users or used a communication device.	Pretend to be the manager and describe how you and potential workers would explore their needs for environmental modifications, opportunities to use assistive aids, and other techniques which makes it possible for a person to do the job.
7. How does this job contribute to others?	Discuss different ways food service jobs make a contribution to a larger group or to society.	Evaluate the significance and the effect of some of the food service workers at school, such as cafeteria workers.	Discuss the roles, for example, Board of Education members, personnel directors, building (kitchen) maintenance personnel, contract officers, and health standards officers in the school district in making policy about food service in the school and in making all the business operational arrangements for food service to students. This may be studied in whatever degree is appropriate to provide an opportunity to develop positive and respectful feelings about the contributions of many other occupations.
8. What is the vocabulary of the work world?	Teach vocabulary used by workers in food service settings.	Teach work-setting vocabulary and relate it to present school activities, such as: *time card*—class attendance roll; *time clock*—school bell; *performance review*—report card; *restaurant safety*—fire drill; *disciplinary layoff*—suspension from school; *work history*—transcript; *employee handbook*—school policies/rules; *termination*—graduation or drop out; *break*—recess; *work holidays*—school holidays.	The list of vocabulary words can be enlarged to include vocabulary and concepts used by workers in food service in general and vocabulary specific to all the various jobs roles in food service. For example, words used in cooking: *boil, fry, grill, sauté, broil, bake, roast, garnish, blend, stir, chop, slice, layer, thaw, season,* etc.
9. How might a given job be done more effectively?	Find ways to evaluate how well individual food service jobs are done.	Set up a small assembly-line operation in the classroom and relate it to teamwork needed in food service. After making some timed practice runs, evaluate how it might be altered to increase speed and quality.	Visit a local café or fast-food restaurant that is busy. Have the students work from an industrial analysis form to evaluate what is required in performing a particular job operation. Discuss how the job operation could be done more easily or more effectively.

Note. Adapted from *Career Awareness for the Handicapped in the Elementary Schools* by C. Kokaska, 1974, Des Moines: Iowa Department of Public Instruction; and from "Work and Transition Education" by J. L. Bigge, 1991, in *Teaching Individuals with Physical, Health, or Multiple Disabilities* (3rd ed., p. 468–470). J.L. Bigge, editor, New York: Macmillan.

However, any process of self-assessment must be tailored cautiously so that it does not become a demeaning or discouraging experience. White (1997) suggested that fears of the unknown can be a major barrier in life transitions. It is vital that these processes of self-assessment through exploration help students assuage their fears as well as realize their assets and abilities. A teacher's knowledge of possible adaptations, modifications, and assistive aids can often offset a student's discouragement or giving up on an occupational choice when their disabilities seem insurmountable. For example, one young man with spina bifida wanted to work in television. His use of a wheelchair prevented the mobility and activity required of a cameraperson, but the teacher investigated the television production process well enough to learn that the young man could be a technical director who directs the camera work or video filming in angles, framing, zooming, and composition. He learned that job and was able to perform it well.

In summary, teachers' responsibilities are to offer students opportunities to explore vocation-related tasks, analyze vocations and work settings, evaluate themselves, and come to understand some of the requirements for specific jobs. Teachers also provide support for students as they discover their own strengths and weaknesses, including physical capabilities and needs for assistive strategies and technology, their own aptitudes and capacities, and their own interests.

Career Preparation

Career preparation also occurs at all levels of the curriculum but is emphasized more directly in high school and continues to play a part in career development throughout life. Career preparation is particularly important in a student's course of study for students who do not choose to pursue postsecondary education goals. Regular vocational education classes or special education career/vocational programs are available in many schools, but others have to send students to vocational or technical training centers. Focus is upon training students for very specific kinds of vocations or for a specific job in their own communities. For some students, the next step may be postsecondary vocational training, community college, or four-year college or university before seeking a job. Sitlington, Clark, et al. (2000) identified major career/vocational education service delivery systems. These include secondary vocational education, secondary special-needs vocational education, postsecondary vocational and technical education, apprenticeship programs, and vocational rehabilitation programs.

Wehman (1996) divided the major vocational alternatives for adults with disabilities into **competitive employment** and **supported employment.** Competitive employment is working full-time or part-time in any competitive labor market job or position without any support person. It might include job modifications or accommodations, but no support person is needed to ensure that the job is done properly or to provide assistance when needed. Supported employment can be part-time to full-time with supports and includes the individual placement model and group placement models (e.g., mobile work crews, industrial enclaves, and small businesses). In these models a designated support person provides ongoing or "as-needed" supports to keep work activity productive and satisfactory. These support persons can be paid support workers or natural support persons within the work setting. Readers are encouraged to study existing literature for more information on career/vocational education transition to employment, and vocational alternatives for adults with disabilities.

Some vocational programs are designed to include student participation as employees in community-based work sites. When students participate in and/or observe a variety of jobs at a specific work site, employment choices and current occupational skills will be better identified. Students will be able to make real choices and determine very specific training needs for maintaining actual jobs. Vocational assessments should emphasize strengths particular to specific work-setting demands, just as was suggested for the career exploration stage.

Career/vocational programs and curricular experiences help develop attitudes and skills needed for the successful employment of individuals with disabilities. The suggestions that follow illustrate ways of preparing students so that they have successful job acquisition (placement) and job maintenance (follow-up) experiences.

Train Students for Job Tasks Exactly as the Supervisor or Employer Wants. Some work tasks generalize from job to job without deviation, but some vary slightly due to specific preferences at the work site.

While doing this, remember to provide prompts as needed for learning the tasks, provide consistency in prompts, keep verbal directions and explanations to a minimum so that students can concentrate on following through with what you said, fade prompts as soon as feasible, give positive feedback, and stress safe work habits right from the beginning (Hagner & Dileo, 1993).

Train Students for the Work Site Environment. This includes learning to get around the work setting to perform tasks and learning where to get supplies or materials, where personal telephone calls can be made, where break times occur, where restrooms are located, and where the supervisor's office is. The environment also has a culture that needs to be explained, and the student needs to learn the social "rules" of the work site for interactions with employers, coworkers, and, when appropriate, customers/clients/patrons of the work site.

Find a Mentor for the Student from Among Coworkers or from Supervisory Staff. These mentors are frequently the best people to teach the student the work site culture and "tricks of the trade," make introductions to others, pass on inside information about customs or traditions, assist with terms or language unique to the job, and give support beyond the initial training period.

After Specific Work Task Learning Has Occurred, Train the Student to Increase His or Her Speed and Accuracy of Performance of the Task. One of the primary reasons that some individuals are not kept on a job after the initial training and adjustment period is that the work production rate is not acceptable. Training for work where production is important should not stop at learning the work task, but continue on so that the student achieves an acceptable work rate and continued accuracy or quality.

Monitor Work Behavior and Identify Any Behaviors That Interfere with the Quality and Quantity of Work Expected. Some behaviors are allowed at a work site that would never be allowed at school and vice versa. Be sure to determine what behaviors are truly interfering with work expectations and what behaviors the work site will permit.

Train the Student in Knowing When and How to Ask for Assistance. Practice this at the work site, using role-play if necessary. The student needs to learn early that trying to "fake" understanding almost always backfires.

Sowers and Powers (1991) identified nine strategies that have been acknowledged as critical components of successful vocational preparation programs for students with severe and multiple disabilities. The eight strategies most appropriate for discussion in this section of the book include:

1. Identify and train for jobs and tasks that reflect the local community job market.
2. Train for work-related skills that are critical to job success.
3. Train students in community settings.
4. Use systematic instructional procedures to train students.
5. Identify adaptive strategies that will increase student independence.
6. Involve parents in the vocational preparation of their children.
7. Establish paid employment for students before they leave school.
8. Coordinate and collaborate with adult service programs.

Each of these strategies is discussed briefly below to give the reader a better understanding of the importance that each plays and some insight into how to implement such strategies.

Identify and Train for Jobs and Tasks That Reflect the Local Community Job Market. The strategy of focusing on local community job market skills rather than broad, general prevocational readiness or employability skills is based on research that confirms that direct instruction in actual job tasks is more effective. Not only is it more effective, it permits the placement of students for training at work sites in the community, where the likelihood of being employed by the employer is much higher than if training is done at school or some rehabilitation facility. This approach also recognizes that students can, for example, learn to assemble products or produce microfilm records without first learning the alphabet, counting to 10, or matching items in a match-to-sample activity. Another reason for going directly into the local community job market is simply that that is where the jobs are.

School districts should conduct surveys of the local employment market, identify those tasks that occur with frequency, and then target those which their students with physical or multiple disabilities could perform if provided direct instruction, adaptations, and support. Results from job surveys that are especially appropriate for people who use wheelchairs, for instance, reveal a number of possibilities in computer science, graphic design, various professional occupations (law, architecture, accounting, etc.), counseling, basic computer data entry, word processing, simple form typing, telephone answering (telephone answering service, dispatchers, etc.), photocopying, microfilming, mailroom service, filing, seated light-assembly tasks, and packaging/unpackaging/pricing. Accessibility to these jobs would be enhanced by appropriate assistive technology. Students assisted by keyboard or mouse control (see Chapter 8) or for whom materials are stabilized (see Chapter 7) will be more successful.

The number, type, and availability of different jobs in a community vary considerably from region to region. Small rural towns have a much more restricted range of job opportunities than urban and suburban areas. The rise of the use of computer technology and assistive technology, however, is creating new opportunities in rural areas. It is important to watch trends in a community or region and be ready to enter new training arenas for individual students who do not find a match with old training sites.

Train for Work-Related Skills Critical to Job Success. Work-related skills and behaviors are those that ultimately may be the most important factor in keeping a job. Just as there is no standard list of job tasks for training all students, there is no standard list of work-related skills. There are some work-related skills that are unique to a given job or type of work setting. For example, the social skills needed to deal with customers in a retail store are unrelated to the skills that are critical for someone doing microfilming in a relatively isolated location. There is no need to waste individual student time by teaching customer relations skills unless that is the type of job or work setting that is selected.

There are, however, some work-related skills that are generic or common across a number of work settings. Some examples of these are grooming, sequencing tasks, attendance and punctuality, following directions, taking supervisory criticism, appropriate conversations and interactions with coworkers, and skills getting to and from work. Some other work-related skills that may not be needed for all students with physical or multiple disabilities, but which occur with greater frequency, include communication skills, eating and drinking, mobility, and bathroom use.

While some of these work-related skills may be part of school-based work training, direct instruction or training in specific work settings is much more effective. Students who use wheelchairs need to learn accessibility routes for a particular work site, including special maneuvering procedures for getting on and off buses or vans, negotiating specific curb cuts, and how to open specific doors and move around in a particular business. They need to learn the specific transfer demands of particular restroom facilities or whether assistance will be needed. Learning to interact with specific coworkers in a particular work setting is more valuable than learning in the classroom about how to interact with coworkers in general, because of the different and unique personalities within work groups.

Schools need to assist students through training and adaptive strategies to perform needed work-related skills as independently as possible. This may require the school (teachers and related-services personnel) to reconceptualize their roles, become knowledgeable about the work world, and become involved in issues related to local community employment. At times, this means assuming the role of a job coach—someone who works one-on-one to train a student in all job tasks, monitor performance, make corrections as needed, and provide formal and informal evaluations of progress. At other times, the teacher supervises a paraprofessional or job coach. In any case, it is critical to know what a student needs to know or be able to do in a specific work setting to be as independent as possible. The more independent a student becomes in a job setting, the less support he or she needs to maintain employment at that site.

Train Students in Community Settings. This strategy addresses some of the features of the previous two strategies. In essence, this strategy advocates for training students in real work settings, not the artificial settings of schools, hospitals, or rehabilitation centers. Research and experience demonstrate that the extent to which students can or will generalize skills they learn at school is directly related to how similar the learning setting is to the setting in which they will be expected to perform those skills.

School districts find it challenging, to say the least, to provide those students with significant physical or multiple disabilities with the opportunity to gain work experience and training in the community. Transportation difficulties, time required for one-on-one staff supervision, and liability issues are common reasons for resisting community-based training. However, there are solutions to some of these barriers. For students' first work experiences, "real" work experiences in school settings are, of course, not only acceptable, they are desirable. Working in the school office doing data entry, photocopying, answering the phone, and filing records is similar to working in a community office setting doing those same tasks. Similarly, the nurse's office, the counselor's office, the athletic office, the library, audiovisual center, or computer laboratory can be positive training sites that provide real work. Another solution is to place several students in the community in one site, relieving the school of the problem of transportation scheduling and multiple staff assignments for individual job coaching and supervision.

Ultimately, community-based training is essential. It can be provided after a student has explored work settings within the school and may not be scheduled until the student's final year of school. Before leaving school, every student should have this opportunity for real employment training for competitive employment in the community, even if it is a summer work experience. Every effort should be made to place every student in the community, regardless of the presenting problems of mobility, communication, or dependence. As in inclusion practices for academic instruction, all students deserve chances to be included and learn employment skills in the community before ever being considered for a sheltered work program.

Use Systematic Instructional Procedures to Train Students. Systematic instruction for performing work tasks may be needed for those who have discrimination and learning problems or those who have neuromuscular or musculoskeletal difficulties in movement. There is a current body of literature on vocational training techniques that have been successful in training persons with disabilities on a wide range of skills (i.e., Moon, Inge, Wehman, Brooke, & Barcus, 1990; Renzaglia & Hutchins, 1990; Rusch & Mithaug, 1980; Unger, Parent, Gibson, & Kane-Johnston, 1998). Most of these techniques come out of the philosophy and methods of applied behavior analysis. Task analysis, instructional cues, shaping, reinforcement, and fading are the common elements of most of these procedures, and they are effective. The reader is encouraged to review Chapter 6 for in-depth discussion of these valuable strategies.

Impairment in movement for task achievement, as opposed to impairment in discrimination and learning, has posed a different problem for vocational trainers. Physical therapy has been one strategy used to improve an individual's central nervous system and thus improve motor performance. Biofeedback has also been used as a strategy for individuals with excessive body or muscle tension or pain. Sowers and Powers (1991) suggested that some of the behavioral techniques that were developed early on for people with cognitive disabilities also have something to offer those with motor difficulties. Among the behavioral techniques that they used effectively were task analysis, whole-task versus part-task training, reinforcement, and assistance prompts. In addition, they proposed using relaxation training, one-step movement strategies, physical warm-up strategies before the motor task, graduated work periods to increase stamina, use of videotaping for modeling and feedback, and imagery. For more detail, readers are encouraged to refer to the Sowers and Powers book.

Identify Adaptive Strategies That Will Increase Student Independence. A critically important activity for school programs is to attempt to identify the strategies that are the most successful in assisting a student to perform tasks as independently as possible. It often is not feasible for a student with severe motor impairments to perform a job task as it is currently designed and performed by other individuals. Through the use of redesign, adaptations, and modifications, the difficult requirements of many job tasks can be eliminated or decreased.

Sowers and Powers (1991) identified some strategies for redesign, adaptation, or modification. They include:

- Redesign the task or task sequence to eliminate a difficult step.
- Identify alternative response strategies to the ones ordinarily used that are not feasible.
- Change the equipment, furniture, room arrangement, or other environmental barriers to permit access and freedom of movement.
- Position the individual or the equipment the individual uses in a way to make task performance efficient and comfortable.
- Provide environmental cues to assist in sequencing or decision making.
- Identify and provide assistive devices to alleviate difficulties in task performance.

Readers are encouraged to find detailed suggestions in such sources as Sowers and Powers (1991), Wehman (2001), and Wehman and Kregel (1998) as well as in Chapter 6 of this text.

Involve Parents in the Vocational Preparation of Their Children. Some parents are reluctant to think about vocational and functional training during school years. Many parents may even believe that work, and especially competitive employment, is simply not possible for their child. Teachers and school staff need to counsel parents about the importance of work in their children's futures and the importance of starting early to prepare them. Parents need to have hope in regard to their children's work potential, and reassurance from information about the concept of supported employment.

One way of opening the eyes of parents who have never really believed that work is an option is to have them see or hear directly from working people who have disabilities similar to their son's or daughter's. Sometimes, simply providing parents with an opportunity to observe their children at a community-based work training site, working side by side with nondisabled workers, is sufficient for them to see their children in a new way in relationship to work. It may also be helpful to make sure that parents observe individuals with severe physical limitations working in both competitive and sheltered settings. This will give them a basis for comparison of the possibilities and for setting goals with the school in the IEP.

Beyond awareness and a vision for the vocational futures of their children, parents can be important partners with the school in working at home with their sons or daughters on goals that need continuous monitoring and reinforcement. Parents can assist particularly in helping their children learn the work-related skills and behaviors that were discussed earlier in the chapter, such as grooming, communication skills, task sequences, value of attendance and punctuality, and transportation skills. They can also work with teachers and job coaches in developing positive interpersonal relationships with people at work and, when possible, forming friendships.

Establish Paid Employment for Students Before They Leave School. Paid employment in a community work setting should be the ultimate goal and measure of success of a school program for students with disabilities. From a practical standpoint, it is a more important goal than a high school diploma. To ensure that this outcome is achieved, school programs should attempt to obtain jobs for their students *before* they leave school if students are not going on to higher education or postsecondary vocational-technical training. This idea highlights the difference between community-based vocational training and community-based employment. Many community-based vocational training programs are unpaid situations and operate under specific Fair Labor Standards Act provisions for student learners. School program staff should make sure that there is a specific plan to move a student out of a student learner status with an employer into an employee status before graduation or exiting school. If that is not possible at the training site, the school should plan for a timely placement of the student out of the training setting into an employment setting. This should occur during the last year of school under the IEP, before a change-of-placement IEP occurs with graduation or school exit. Frequently, the arrangement for paid employment has long-term implications and requires collaborative planning with one or more adult service agencies. That process is the essence of the next and final strategy.

Coordinate and Collaborate with Adult Service Programs. Many, if not most, students with severe physical or multiple disabilities are going to require ongoing support after leaving school. This is especially true in relation to employment. Consequently, it is absolutely essential that school program staff work closely with local vocational rehabilitation agencies and, for those who are also eligible for developmental disabilities services, with the local community developmental disabilities organization (CDDO). Good school transition programs will have established ongoing communication with agencies like these, and good coordination in making referrals and good collaboration in joint planning through the IEP are routine.

The provisions of the IDEA of 1997 clearly establish the expectation that the delivery of transition services is not solely a school responsibility (Sitlington, Clark, et al., 2000). However, the law does charge the school with ensuring that linkages with nonschool agencies occur, rather than waiting for those agencies to initiate something. Schools have no authority to compel nonschool agencies to participate in the IEP process during the final planning and "hand-off" stage unless a service contract is in place between the school and that agency. Some adult service agencies are reluctant to engage in collaborative IEP planning because they do not want to expend their funds for services that they believe the school is obligated to provide under the law. Similarly, schools resist paying for services that they believe are the responsibility of adult providers. The regulations are clear, though, that there is nothing in the provisions of the law that relieves any participating agency, including a state vocational rehabilitation agency, of the responsibility to provide or pay for any transition service that the agency would otherwise provide to students with disabilities who meet the eligibility criteria of that agency.

Teachers are one of the essential ingredients in a successful career preparation program. Teachers work as instructors, trainers, job coaches, public relations experts, counselors, and guidance workers. In these varied roles, teachers draw on resources of the school, the family, the local education agency, the community, and adult service agencies to design a plan for employment while students are in the school program. Teachers may be like students at times in that different work situations with different students demand new responses. Teachers may need to find their own mentors to go to for help when career preparation situations are difficult and get beyond their levels of experience or expertise.

Career Placement/Follow-up and Continuing Education

Career placement and follow-up may take place fairly early, but the usual timetable for involving students in on-the-job training and work experiences is during high school or during extended programs for students who are 18 to 21 years of age and need additional training. Sometimes the placements made during schooling years extend into adulthood for long-term employment. In other instances, actual employment placement may occur after leaving school. The last stage of schooling for those students not entering formal postsecondary training should include a "final" employment placement whenever possible. Hopefully, by the time students exit school, they will have experienced several job situations and be ready for a decision on a job placement that represents their first postschool employment.

Launching students with severe disabilities into the world of work or into the services of adult agencies is a highly complex process. Many planned and intensive transition activities are important, particularly in making sure families know they must assume the role of service managers and coordinators at times. Wehman (2001) suggested that preparation for the career placement and follow-up process works best if the process combines community-based vocational training and supported-employment training models. Supported employment is one of the most effective models for occupational placement and follow-up with persons for whom competitive employment has not traditionally occurred. For this population, supported employment can offer real jobs, wages and benefits equal to those received by other workers performing the same jobs, the right to opportunity, a focus on abilities, and ongoing supports (Parent, Cone, Turner, & Wehman, 1998; Sitlington, Clark, et al., 2000; Unger et al., 1998; Wehman, 1996). Although supported employment has many advantages for individuals with moderate to severe and/or multiple disabilities, it may not be the appropriate model for those with mild disabilities or even some individuals with moderate to severe levels of disability.

Teachers and other school personnel must take leadership roles in the development of school-to-work transition planning for individual students. Transition planning is required as part of the IEP for all students 14 years of age and older. After students leave school, a similar plan might be developed for them if they are accepted for services under a state's designated agency for vocational rehabilitation services. The vocational rehabilitation plan is now referred to as the Individual Plan for Employment (IPE), replacing the old term, Individual Written Rehabilitation Plan (IWRP). Keep in mind that vocational rehabilitation services are not mandated for young adults who are no longer part of the educational system. Graduates and school leavers must apply for services, be found eligible for those services, and then be accepted for provision of services under their respective state's order of selection policies. It is absolutely critical that the linkage is made, though, between a student (and his/her family) and state rehabilitation services prior to graduation or exit from school.

There are very specific steps that rehabilitation counselors must follow to determine eligibility before providing any services. The school needs to be involved actively in the referral process and in providing assistance in seeing that all the evaluation information the agency needs is obtained. If the rehabilitation counselor determines that the student is eligible for services, the student's IPE will specify what services the student needs and will receive. These may include extended evaluation, counseling, training or postsecondary education, maintenance and transportation while in training or school, physical restoration procedures, prostheses or other assistive devices, vocational placement assistance, supported employment, and follow-up. None of these services are guaranteed. Each case is developed for the unique needs of the individual. More important to remember, however, is that economic conditions may override individual service delivery and the process can vary considerably in quality and efficiency based on personnel and economic factors.

During the career placement and follow-up stage, teachers have a chance to see the rewards of student involvement in a career education continuum from early childhood to young adulthood. Teachers, job coaches, and other support personnel working with students at this stage are the ones who help students make their transitions into the world of work or other productive work activities that benefit themselves and others. The following section introduces teachers to some of the strategies and programmatic activities that they can use for providing that help to students.

MAKING THE TRANSITION FROM SCHOOL TO EMPLOYMENT

Of all disability groups, those identified as having physical or multiple disabilities present the widest range of cognitive and physical characteristics. Students with these disabilities are identified for special education services and may have more severe impairments and a high frequency of combinations of primary and secondary disabilities. However, there is still a range of ability that defies simple or single program solutions. For that reason, any presentation of the best ways to prepare young people in this population for employment after exiting school must include a range of options.

Students with High Abilities

Starting from the assumption that a high percentage of students with physical or multiple disabilities will spend considerable instructional time in general education classes, the standards that are proposed for employment preparation in general education should be a starting place for curriculum planning. Table 12–2 provides the foundation skills and basic competency areas proposed for all students in public education, as set forth in *What Work Requires of Schools: A SCANS Report for America 2000* (Secretary's Commission on Achieving Necessary Skills, 1991). Unfortunately, only a few schools use the SCANS curriculum model and only a few states that received School-to-Work Opportunity Act (STWOA) of 1994 (PL 103–239) planning funds are offering some of the creative alternatives that came out of the STWOA initiative. This means that each secondary teacher advocating for his or her students with physical or multiple disabilities will have to look for the best possible programs at hand. If a student has the cognitive and academic skills to aim high for skilled, technical, or professional employment, the general education alternatives for career preparation should be the focus. The choice should

TABLE 12–2
Foundation Skills and Basic Competency Areas Identified by the Secretary's Commission on Achieving Necessary Skills (SCANS)

A Three-Part Foundation

Basic Skills: Reads, writes, performs arithmetic and mathematical operations, listens and speaks
A. *Reading*—Locates, understands, and interprets information in prose and in documents such as manuals, graphs, and schedules
B. *Writing*—Communicates thoughts, ideas, information, and messages in writing; and creates documents such as letters, directions, manuals, reports, graphs, and flow charts
C. *Arithmetic/Mathematics*—Performs basic computations and approaches practical problems by choosing appropriately from a variety of mathematical techniques
D. *Listening*—Receives, attends to, interprets, and responds to verbal messages and other cues
E. *Speaking*—Organizes ideas and communicates orally

Thinking Skills: Thinks creatively, makes decisions, solves problems, visualizes, knows how to learn, and reasons
A. *Creative Thinking*—Generates new ideas
B. *Decision Making*—Specifies goals and constraints, generates alternatives, considers risks, and evaluates and chooses best alternative
C. *Problem Solving*—Recognizes problems and devises and implements plan of action
D. *Seeing Things in the Mind's Eye*—Organizes and processes symbols, pictures, graphs, objects, and other information
E. *Knowing How to Learn*—Uses efficient learning techniques to acquire and apply new knowledge and skills
F. *Reasoning*—Discovers a rule or principle underlying the relationship between two or more objects and applies it when solving a problem

Personal Qualities: Displays responsibility, self-esteem, sociability, self-management, and integrity and honesty
A. *Responsibility*—Exerts a high level of effort and perseveres toward goal attainment
B. *Self-Esteem*—Believes in own self-worth and maintains a positive view of self
C. *Sociability*—Demonstrates understanding, friendliness, adaptability, empathy, and politeness in group settings
D. *Self-Management*—Assesses self accurately, sets personal goals, monitors progress, and exhibits self-control
E. *Integrity/Honesty*—Chooses ethical courses of action

Five Competencies

Resources: Identifies, organizes, plans, and allocates resources
A. *Time*—Selects goal-relevant activities, ranks them, allocates time, and prepares and follows schedules
B. *Money*—Uses or prepares budgets, makes forecasts, keeps records, and makes adjustments to meet objectives
C. *Material and Facilities*—Acquires, stores, allocates, and uses materials or space efficiently
D. *Human Resources*—Assesses skills and distributes work accordingly, evaluates performance and provides feedback

Interpersonal: Works with others
A. *Participates as Member of a Team*—Contributes to group effort
B. *Teaches Others New Skills*
C. *Serves Clients/Customers*—Works to satisfy customer's expectations
D. *Exercises Leadership*—Communicates ideas to justify position, persuades and convinces others, responsibly challenges existing procedures and policies
E. *Negotiates*—Works toward agreements involving exchange of resources, resolves divergent interests
F. *Works with Diversity*—Works well with men and women from diverse backgrounds

Information: Acquires and uses information
A. *Acquires and Evaluates Information*
B. *Organizes and Maintains Information*
C. *Interprets and Communicates Information*
D. *Uses Computers to Process Information*

Systems: Understands complex interrelationships
A. *Understands Systems*—Knows how social, organizational, and technological systems work and operates effectively with them
B. *Monitors and Corrects Performance*—Distinguishes trends, predicts impacts on system operations, diagnoses systems' performance and corrects malfunctions
C. *Improves or Designs Systems*—Suggests modifications to existing systems and develops new or alternative systems to improve performance

Technology: Works with a variety of technologies
A. *Selects Technology*—Chooses procedures, tools or equipment including computers and related technologies
B. *Applies Technology to Task*—Understands overall intent and proper procedures for setup and operation of equipment
C. *Maintains and Troubleshoots Equipment*—Prevents, identifies, or solves problems with equipment, including computers and other technologies

Note. From *What Work Requires of Schools: A SCANS Report for America 2000* (pages 12 and 16) by Secretary's Commission on Achieving Necessary Skills, 1991, Springfield, VA: National Technical Information Service, Operations Division. NTIS Number: PB92-146711.

be made on the basis of the student's preferences and interests first, awareness of strengths second, and finally, the program alternatives and the accommodations and supports that will be needed in that program.

Students with Severe Physical and/or Multiple Disabilities

Students who find it difficult at the high school level to be successful academically in meeting district or state standards, even with supports, should not be relegated to either weak segregated programs or unproductive inclusive programs. Just because the students' strengths do not lie in academic performance does not mean that they cannot be prepared to find meaningful work in competitive employment or competitive supported employment.

One of the shining achievements of advocates for persons with severe disabling conditions in the past three decades has been their clear demonstration of employability for many who were believed to be unemployable by teachers and families (Bellamy, Rhodes, Mank, & Albin, 1988; Gold, 1972; Rhodes & Valenta, 1985; Rusch & Mithaug, 1980; Wehman, Kregel, & Shafer, 1990). The notion that systematic training and ongoing support can be effective with people with severe cerebral palsy, spina bifida, muscular dystrophy, or other severe physical, health, or multiple disabilities is no longer questioned.

Assessment for Transition Planning

There are many ways of assessing students' needs, interests, and preferences for transition planning, and the major approaches have been described elsewhere (Clark, 1998; Clark, Patton, & Moulton, 2000; Sitlington, Neubert, Begun, Lombard, & Leconte, 1996). It is important to keep in mind that the success of the transition process and its outcomes depend upon the transition planning process that preceded it. That said, it could be argued that the transition planning process and its outcomes depend upon the adequacy of the information that was used to develop the plans. In other words, the transition process from early childhood on through adulthood depends upon accurate, relevant information that has been obtained through planned and systematic question-asking.

Assessment is nothing more than question-asking. Teachers can ask those questions through informal and formal assessment procedures and techniques. Observations and other assessments by parents, teachers, and related services staff often yield information on a student that is adequate to develop some academic goals for an IEP. What is not often addressed with nearly enough adequacy is the transition component of the IEP. In all likelihood, the primary reason this is the case is that the IEP members are not familiar enough with the IDEA-mandated areas for transition planning, much less the broad scope of transition-planning areas representing quality programming from recommended practice. Without such knowledge, it is understandable that there would be little planned or systematic effort to assess "transition service needs or needed transition services," as prescribed in the IDEA and its regulations. School programs should at least attempt a general assessment that screens for transition service needs and needed transition services. Two examples of assessment instruments that are designed to do that are the Enderle-Severson Transition Rating Scales (Enderle & Severson, 1991) and the Transition Planning Inventory (Clark & Patton, 1997). Both of these inventories are rating scales rather than tests. The Enderle-Severson scales (two forms based on level of severity) use teachers and family raters across five transition planning areas, and the Transition Planning Inventory draws its rating information from the student, home, and school across nine planning areas.

It is common that screening inventory responses in areas that are less familiar to teachers and parents (e.g., self-determination, certain aspects of sexuality, knowledge of how to apply for admission to a postsecondary program, etc.) may lead to an awareness that little or nothing is known about the student's knowledge or skill in that particular area. In such cases, further assessment is needed. A comprehensive informal screening inventory is available for further assessment in *Informal Assessment for Transition Planning* (Clark, Patton, & Moulton, 2000). Students, parents, and teachers can use this instrument to arrive at a better perspective of what the student knows or can do in the areas where there is little or no existing evaluation information. In addition, there are 43 selected informal assessment instruments that offer a variety of procedures for obtaining more information in certain transition knowledge and skills areas.

Two instruments that show promise in assessing vocational interests are *Your Employment Selections (Y.E.S.)* (Morgan, Ellerd, Gerity, & Tullis, 2000) and the Occupational Aptitude Survey and Interest Schedule—3 (OASIS—3)(Parker, 2002). Y.E.S. is a computerized assessment that provides video images of persons working in a variety of jobs and settings. It was designed especially for nonreaders and persons with communication difficulties. The OASIS—3 has two assessment survey features, interest and aptitude, and is used frequently by vocational counselors and vocational evaluation personnel in rehabilitation settings. Another assessment approach that should be mentioned is ecological assessment. This assessment is of a job setting and assesses the demands and expectations of a particular environment and work situation rather than assessing the individual. It does provide a set of skills, expectations, or environmental demands that make a job match much easier when one focuses on what a person needs to succeed in a particular situation. One example of this type of assessment is the Environmental Job Measure (E-JAM) (Waintrup, Kelley, & Bullis, 1999).

The provisions of the IDEA require a statement of transition service needs and needed transition services for each student receiving special education services. In the area of employment for students with physical and multiple disabilities, it is important to be able to state annually what students need to know or be able to do by the end of the year in relation to career awareness, career exploration, career preparation, and/or career placement and follow-up goals and objectives. The IEP team must take responsibility for gathering the assessment information it needs in order to develop the statement of needs and services and the goals that will be set in order to meet those needs and service requirements. The brief case study that follows is an example of how one can take data from an instrument such as the Transition Planning Inventory (Clark & Patton, 1997) and develop a statement of transition service needs and annual goals on the IEP to work toward meeting those transition needs. Included in the case study is a brief description of Andrea, her Transition Planning Inventory Profile and Further Assessment Recommendation Form, a Planning Notes Form that can serve as a Statement of Transition Needs and Needed Transition Services for Andrea's IEP, and, finally, a present level of educational performance and sample goals that are suggested for the transition planning area of Employment.

CASE STUDY

Transition Services Planning for Andrea in the Area of Employment

Andrea is a 17-year-old junior in a suburban high school who has cerebral palsy. She takes most of her classes in general education, receiving average grades in most and higher-than-average grades in math. Because motor movement difficulties make it laborious for her to complete academic performances that require dexterity and speech, and because she has to work so hard academically to keep up with everything but math, she does not carry a full academic load. She has difficulty in oral speech and in cursive writing. She receives instruction from the special education teacher both in her general education classes and in the Resource Room. This instruction and collaboration with general education teachers is designed to help Andrea keep up with her classes, to build self-determination skills and attitudes, and to prepare her for transition to the world of work after completing high school.

Andrea does not want to go to college and her mother is very concerned that "she not come home and become a 'couch potato,' with the only places she goes by herself is moving back and forth in her walker from the TV to the refrigerator." Her mother (single parent) and adult service providers have had preliminary discussions about the process to help Andrea and themselves to plan to meet goals for the rest of her schooling and for the years immediately following her schooling.

Planning Notes Form

Student: Andrea | Date: April 30, 2002

Likely Postschool Settings:[1]
Employment/Further Education: University
Living Arrangement: Dormitory

Directions: List the important strengths and suggested transition needs on this page that you conclude from your analysis of the TPI Profile. Under the needs section, add any *new* transition needs *after* further assessment on TPI items, showing discrepancies, "Don't Know" responses, or the need for more specification.

If desired, each need can be coded as an instructional need (I), a linkage need (L), or both (I/L).

	Relative Strengths	Transition Needs	
		Initial Analysis	**After Further Assessment**
Employment	• Knowledge about applying for and maintaining employment	• Awareness of own career interests • Knowledge of job requirements • Vocational training in area of interest	
Further Education/ Training	• Knowledge and skills for success in postsecondary employment program	• Understanding of application processes • Awareness of postsecondary program requirements	
Daily Living	• Money management • Transportation	• Completing household tasks	• Personal hygiene • Laundry
Leisure Activities	• Participation in community entertainment settings • Interest in indoor recreational activities	• Development of outdoor recreational interests	
Community Participation	• Knowledge of basic rights and responsibilities • Access to some community resources	• Ability to make legal decisions • Knowledge of rights as a person with disabilities	• Knowledge about right to privacy • Access to legal assistance
Health			

Planning Notes Form (continued)

	Relative Strengths	Transition Needs	
		Initial Analysis	**After Further Assessment**
Self-Determination	• Knowledge of own strengths and weaknesses • Expresses self appropriately/ confidently	• Goal setting	
Communication	• Reading and writing	• Spoken communication skills	
Interpersonal Relationships	• Family relationships • Social skills	• Meeting people • Maintaining friendships	

Additional Comments:
Andrea needs to work on her technology/computer related skills. Although she has accomplished basic computer skills, she needs to develop skills needed to use augmentative communication devices.

Present Level of Educational Performance and Sample Goals for Andrea

Employment	PLEP: Andrea knows how to look for employment and participate in the application process. She needs to identify personal interests and related career options.	
	Instructional Goals: 1. Andrea will identify at least three personal interests and relate these to each of two career or occupational options as one personal outcome of the careers class. 2. In a summer community-based job trial, Andrea will demonstrate satisfactory job skills and work attitude as measured on the Job Trial Rating Form. 3. By the end of a summer community-based job trial, Andrea will demonstrate acquisition of entry-level job skills as determined by her employer. 4. In a summer community-based job trial, Andrea will use, with the aid of AAC procedures/equipment, appropriate social interaction skills as an employee on the job and as a consumer when using transportation and restaurants on workdays.	*Linkage Goals:* 1. Andrea will meet with the vocational counselor to take the Y.E.S., a career interest inventory, and the OASIS-2 Interest and Aptitude Surveys and then discuss potential occupational choices. 2. The teacher will refer Andrea to the WIA office director for a summer youth job program interview. 3. The teacher will arrange enrollment for Andrea in a self-determination curriculum that is being offered as part of the general education Teen Living class during the fall semester.

SUMMARY AND CONCLUSION

Preparation for work begins early and continues well into adulthood. Transition service needs and needed transition services for employment must be considered annually as a part of each student's IEP planning and IEP meeting no later than age 14. The IEP team and those teachers responsible for instruction should ensure that students move through the stages of career awareness, exploration, preparation, and placement in their schooling from elementary school on through graduation or school exit. There are numerous strategies for planning curricula and instructional activities that support a student working toward the important adult outcome of satisfactory and satisfying employment.

The curricular options described in Chapter 5 provide a framework for schools to determine for each student what approach or combination of approaches is needed to ensure that the student is prepared to enter employment or move directly from public school into postsecondary education/training. The general education curriculum has much to offer through its core academic courses, electives (including vocational and technical education), and basic skills instruction. The general education curriculum with modifications may be needed for some students who have needs that require special accommodations or modifications in the entire curriculum or in only some parts of the curriculum. Special modifications in general education course syllabi for course assignments or projects, for example, may provide special motivation and focus for a student in relation to exploring an occupational area or identifying special vocabulary or math skills that are used in certain occupational clusters. Other students might not be able, even with modifications and supports, to complete enough high school core academic credits for graduation and/or to pass the state's minimum standards examination. These students need access to a life skills curriculum that provides systematic and direct instruction in employability and specific occupational skills. Finally, some students will need special curricular opportunities in modified means of communication and performance that go beyond the general education curriculum or life skills curriculum options. Those students will also need instruction in the following areas: (a) modifying the physical task performance requirements for working; (b) acquiring language and communication skills for specific work settings; (c) operating and using assistive technology related to their work training or employment; (d) acquiring self-determination knowledge and skills, and (e) finding information that will enhance their career development and ability to manage their lives effectively and efficiently.

Curriculum options in transition education involve content related to knowledge and skills. The curriculum models described in Chapter 5 presented clear examples of transition education content or content domains. Readers need to remember, however, that teaching content is not an end in itself. The instruction of needed content must always keep student outcomes for knowledge and skill acquisition as the goal. We do not know if we have taught knowledge and skills until they are demonstrated and used. The emphasis on student outcomes helps teachers stay "on track" with their aim to prepare students for adult life, even with the many accountability issues and barriers that will impede their efforts.

Readers of this textbook will encounter many issues in the delivery of transition education and services. Readers can fortify themselves for this challenge through further study in transition education, coupled with interactions with representative groups of people at the national, state, and local levels who organize to promote, develop, maintain, and improve transition services for students and graduates with disabilities. Sitlington, Clark, et al. (2000) identified some of these issues. They are:

Issue 1: "Life skills education and the inclusive education movement are often seen as two different approaches" (p. 326).

Issue 2: "The assessment of the transition education needs of individuals with disabilities and their involvement in state and district-wide assessment programs is left to chance" (p. 328).

Issue 3: "Minimum competency testing and standards may adversely affect the graduation and type of exit document(s) of students with disabilities" (p. 329).

Issue 4: "Transition education and services are still an add-on in many IEPs" (p. 331).

Issue 5: "Formal training in self-determination is often not provided" (p. 331).

Issue 6: "Dropout prevention among students with disabilities remains a low priority activity by public schools" (p. 333).

Issue 7: "The involvement of individuals with disabilities in general education initiatives such as school-to-work programs and vocational education varies greatly across states and districts" (p. 334).

Issue 8: "Postsecondary education programs are placing increasing emphasis on standard psychological tests to provide documentation of a disability, whereas programs at the secondary level are moving toward curriculum-based assessments and noncategorical labels" (p. 335).

Issue 9: "A firm research base is needed for transition in terms of what works and whether transition education and services are making a difference" (p. 337).

Issue 10: "In the area of transition to adult life, there is little formalized preparation of special education personnel" (p. 337).

Issue 11: "No recognized certification mechanism is in place for personnel whose primary responsibility is the provision of transition education and services" (p. 337).

If transition education and services appear to you to be challenging for teachers, they are. As someone once said, "Teaching is not for wimps." In the classroom, there is no room for individuals who are not committed to making school a place where students have every opportunity possible to learn what they need to learn to be self-determined, self-reliant, and satisfied individuals in their various life roles of family members, citizens, and workers. Through putting to work the curriculum adaptations and instructional strategies in this book, teachers can prepare students with disabilities (such as the one in Figure 12–4) who transfer to post-high-school ventures to gain the knowledge and skills to take on their roles in the adult world. Through their own efforts and those of special and general educators, families, and others, students with physical, health, or multiple disabilities should leave their school programs prepared to meet and take on the major demands of adulthood.

FIGURE 12–4
Off to meet the demands of adulthood

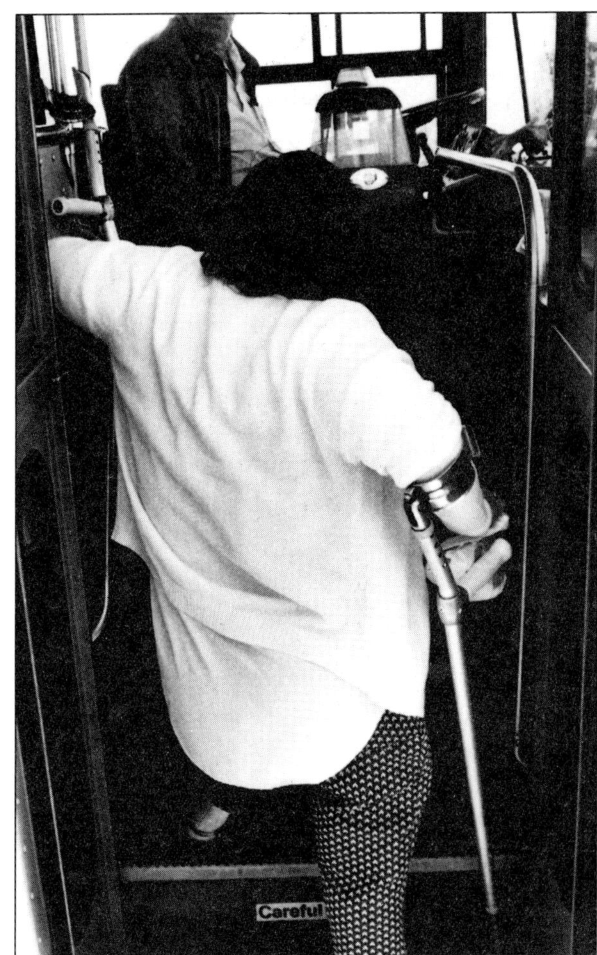

QUESTIONS FOR DISCUSSION

1. Discuss three reasons why transition education and preparation for individuals with physical or multiple disabilities should begin in early childhood.
2. Describe several ways that preschool and elementary-level teachers can infuse career awareness into their curricula.

3. Why is valid self-evaluation important for career success for individuals with physical or multiple disabilities? How can teachers assist students with disabilities to make valid self-evaluations?
4. How could teachers infuse the characteristics of self-determined people across their classroom activities?
5. You are a middle school teacher who provides special education services to a female student with severe asthma. She is making average academic progress in school, but has many absences due to her chronic condition. What barriers does she face to successful transition education and preparation, and how can you help her meet her challenges?
6. A male student in your high school class is very interested in forestry as a career. You suspect that this student (who has spastic diplegic cerebral palsy) is being discouraged from pursuing this interest by his parents. How could you intervene in ways that would support both the student and his family?
7. How are social competence and self-determination linked to transition education and vocational preparation? Should students with progressive and terminal illnesses participate in vocational preparation? Why or why not?

FOCUS ON THE NET

America's JobBank

http://www.ajb.dni.us/

This Web site provides information for job searches and current information on job markets.

Assessment for Transition Planning

http://www.transitioncoalition.org/assessment

Information, resources, links, and technical assistance in the area of transition assessment are offered.

Courage Center

http://www.courage.org/

Rehabilitation, enrichment, and other services for people with special needs are provided by this nonprofit organization.

Job Accommodations Network

http://www.janweb.icdi.wvu.edu

The network, a service of the Office of Disability Employment Policy of the U.S. Department of Labor, provides publications and facts about job accommodations.

Microsoft Enable Production

http://www.microsoft.com/enable/productions

At this Web site, you can order a complimentary copy of an excellent video entitled "Enable: People with Disabilities and Computers."

National Center on Secondary Education and Transition

http://www.ncset.org/

This center coordinates national resources, offers technical assistance, and disseminates information related to secondary education and transition for youth with disabilities.

National Institute on Life Planning for Persons with Disabilities

http://www.sonic.net/nilp

The institute helps families with information on transition, life and person-centered planning, government benefits, advocacy, guardianship, housing, and supported employment.

National Program Office on Self-Determination

http://www.self-determination.org

This Web site offers a newsletter, discussion forum, resource links, and publications.

National Transition Network

http://ici2.umn.edu/ntn

This is a federally funded network system for communicating about transition services in states, publications, and links.

Through the Looking Glass

http://www.lookingglass.org

This national center provides families of children and youth with disabilities with information on research, training, and services.

Transition Coalition
http://www.transitioncoalition.org/index.html/

This site offers information, support, and linkages to professionals, families, individuals with disabilities, and others interested and involved in the transition from school to adult life.

TransitionLink
http://www.transitionlink.com

An online community for sharing ideas, resources, and information concerning the transition to life after high school for adolescents with disabilities.

Western Regional Resource Training
http://interact.uoregon.edu/WRRC/transitiondocument.html

This regional resource center provides information on transition services, publications, links.

REFERENCES

Agran, M., Martin, J. E., & Mithaug, D. E. (1989). Achieving transition through adaptability instruction. *Teaching Exceptional Children, 21* (2), 4–7.

Bellamy, G. T., Rhodes, L. E., Mank, D. M., & Albin, J. M. (1988). *Supported employment: A community implementation guide.* Baltimore: Brookes.

Bowe, F. (2000). *Physical, sensory, and health disabilities: An introduction.* Upper Saddle River, NJ: Merrill/Prentice Hall.

Brolin, D. E. (1992). *Life centered career education (LCCE) curriculum program.* Reston, VA: Council for Exceptional Children.

Brolin, D. E. (1995). *Career education: A functional life skills approach* (3rd ed.). Upper Saddle River, NJ: Prentice Hall.

Brolin, D. E. (1997). *Life centered career education: A competency based approach* (5th ed.). Reston, VA: Council for Exceptional Children.

Clark, G. M. (1998). *Assessment for transitions planning.* Austin, TX: PRO-ED.

Clark, G. M., & Patton, J. R. (1997). Transition Planning Inventory. Austin, TX: PRO-ED.

Clark, G. M., Patton, J. R., & Moulton, L. R. (2000). *Informal assessment for transition planning.* Austin, TX: PRO-ED.

Enderle, J., & Severson, S. (1991). Enderle-Severson Transition Rating Scales. Moorhead, MN: Practical Press.

Field, S., & Hoffman, A. (1996). *Steps to self-determination.* Austin, TX: PRO-ED.

Field, S., Martin, J., Miller, R., Ward, M., & Wehmeyer, M. (1997). *A practical guide for teaching self-determination.* Reston, VA: Council for Exceptional Children.

Field, S., Martin, J., Miller, R., Ward, M., & Wehmeyer, M. (1998). Self-determination for persons with disabilities: A position statement of the Division on Career Development and Transition. *Career Development for Exceptional Individuals, 21,* 113–128.

Gold, M. (1972). Stimulus factors in skill training of the retarded on a complex assembly task: Acquisition, transfer, and retention. *American Journal of Mental Deficiency, 76,* 517–526.

Hagner, D., & Dileo, D. (1993). *Working together: Workplace culture, supported employment, and persons with disabilities.* Cambridge, MA: Brookline.

Halpern, A., Herr, C. M., Wolf, N., Doren, B., Johnson, M., & Lawson, J. (1997). *Next S.T.E.P.: Student transition and educational planning.* Austin, TX: PRO-ED.

Moon, S. M., Inge, K., Wehman, P., Brooke, V., & Barcus, J. M. (1990). *Helping persons with severe mental retardation get and keep employment.* Baltimore: Brookes.

Morgan, R. L., Ellerd, D. A., Gerity, B. P., & Tullis, M. D. (2000). *Your employment selections.* Logan, UT: Technology, Research, and Innovation in Special Education (TRI-SPED), Utah State University.

Parent, W. S., Cone, A. A., Turner, E., & Wehman, P. (1998). Supported employment: Consumers leading the way. In P. Wehman & J. Kregel (Eds.), *More than a job: Securing satisfying careers for people with disabilities* (pp. 183–216). Baltimore: Brookes.

Parker, R. M. (2002). Occupational Aptitude Survey and Interest Schedule—3. Austin, TX: PRO-ED.

Patton, J. R., & Dunn, C. (1998). *Transition from school to young adulthood: Basic concepts and recommended practices.* Austin, TX: PRO-ED.

Powers, L. E., Singer, G., & Sowers, J. (1992). *A student directed model for the promotion of self-determination* (CFDA Grant No. 84.158K: Model demonstration projects to identify and teach skills necessary for self-determination). Lebanon, NH: Department of Education, Office of Special Education and Rehabilitative Services, Dartmouth Medical School.

Renzaglia, A., & Hutchins, M. (1990). A community-referenced approach to preparing persons with disabilities for employment. In P. Wehman & S. Moon (Eds.), *Vocational rehabilitation and supported employment* (pp. 91–110). Baltimore: Brookes.

Rhodes, L. E., & Valenta, L. (1985). Industry-based supported employment: An enclave approach. *Journal of the Association for Persons with Severe Handicaps, 10,* 10–12.

Rubin, S. E., & Roessler, R. T. (2001). *Foundations of the vocational rehabilitation process* (5th ed.). Austin, TX: PRO-ED.

Rusch, F. R., & Mithaug, D. E. (1980). *Vocational training for mentally retarded adults.* Champaign, IL: Research Press.

Secretary's Commission on Achieving Necessary Skills. (1991). *What work requires of schools.* Washington, DC: U.S. Government Printing Office.

Sarason, S. (1990). *The culture of the school and the problem of change.* New York: Teachers College Press.

Sitlington, P. L., Clark, G. M., & Kolstoe, O. P. (2000). *Transition education and services for adolescents with disabilities.* Needham Heights, MA: Allyn & Bacon.

Sitlington, P. L., Neubert, D. A., Begun, W., Lombard, R. C., & Leconte, P. J. (1996). *Assess for success: Handbook on transition assessment.* Reston, VA: Council for Exceptional Children.

Sowers, J., & Powers, L. (1991). *Vocational preparation and employment of students with physical and multiple disabilities.* Baltimore: Brookes.

Unger, D. D., Parent, W. S., Gibson, K. E., & Kane-Johnston, K. (1998). Maximizing community and workplace supports: Defining the role of the employment specialist. In P. Wehman & J. Kregel (Eds.), *More than a job: Securing satisfying careers for people with disabilities* (pp. 183–216). Baltimore: Brookes.

Waintrup, M., Kelley, P., & Bullis, M. (1999). The Environmental Job Assessment Measure. In M. Bullis & C. D. Davis (Eds.), *Functional assessment in transition and rehabilitation for adolescents and adults with learning disorders* (pp. 59–62). Austin, TX: PRO-ED.

Wehman, P. (1996). *Life beyond the classroom: Transition strategies for young people with disabilities.* Baltimore: Brookes.

Wehman, P. (2001). *Supported employment in business: Expanding the capacity of workers with disabilities.* St. Augustine, FL: Training Resources Network.

Wehman, P., & Kregel, J. (1988). Adult employment programs. In R. Gaylord-Ross (Ed.), *Vocational education for persons with handicaps* (pp. 205–233). Mountain View, CA: Mayfield.

Wehman, P., & Kregel, J. (1998). *More than a job: Securing satisfying careers for people with disabilities.* Baltimore: Brookes.

Wehman, P., Kregel, J., & Shafer, M. (1990). *Emerging trends in the national supported employment initiative: A preliminary analysis of twenty-seven states.* Richmond: Rehabilitation Research and Training Center, Virginia Commonwealth University.

Wehmeyer, M. L., Agran, M., & Hughes, C. (1998). *Teaching self-determination to students with disabilities: Basic skills for successful transition.* Baltimore: Brookes.

Wehmeyer, M. L., Palmer, S., Agran, M., Mithaug, D., & Martin, J. (2000). Promoting causal agency: The self-determined learning model of instruction. *Exceptional Children, 66,* 439–453.

White, P. H. (1997). Success on the road to adulthood: Issues and hurdles for adolescents with disabilities. *Pediatric Rheumatology, 23,* 697–707.

PART IV

CORE CURRICULUM ADAPTATIONS AND INSTRUCTIONAL STRATEGIES

CHAPTER 13 Adaptations and Instruction in Literacy and Language Arts

CHAPTER 14 Adaptations and Instruction in Writing

CHAPTER 15 Adaptations and Instruction in Science and Social Studies

CHAPTER 16 Adaptations and Instruction in Mathematics

Adaptations and Instruction in Literacy and Language Arts

KATHRYN WOLFF HELLER

CHAPTER 13

KNOWLEDGE AND SKILLS

After you have read this chapter, you will be able to:

1. Identify several barriers that contribute to reading difficulties for students with physical or multiple disabilities.
2. Discuss how to address communication barriers, physical efficiency areas, experiential deficits, learning environment problems, and instructional barriers.
3. Provide strategies in promoting book awareness, print awareness, phonemic awareness, and letter-sound correspondence.
4. Discuss the use of the Nonverbal Reading Approach for phonics and reading instruction.
5. Discuss strategies to promote vocabulary, fluency, and comprehension skills.
6. Describe an ecological assessment for functional reading skills and discuss four approaches for teaching functional literacy skills.

LITERACY BARRIERS

One of the most basic academic skills taught by every school system is reading. When students have severe physical or multiple disabilities, significant reading difficulties are often present (V. W. Berninger & Gans, 1986b; Pierce & McWilliam, 1993; Smith, Thurston, Light, Parnes, & O'Keefe, 1989). Their reading skills are poorer than would be predicted based on intelligence and educational levels (Foley, 1993; Seidel, Chadwick, & Rutter, 1975), and often these deficits continue into adulthood (Smith et al., 1989). Several barriers may exist that contribute to difficulty reading: restricted language and participation, lack of motor ability, individual factors, lack of experience, and problems with the learning environment and instruction.

Restricted Language and Participation

The first barrier that may affect literacy development is the impact of restricted language experiences and restricted participation in typical literacy activities. This occurs when the disability results in a lack of understandable speech. For example, a child who has limited speech will be unable to talk about an activity or event with another person, thus missing the opportunity to effectively convey ideas, practice correct grammar, learn new information, and acquire new vocabulary words. Students with AAC systems may still lack these experiences due to the restricted number of pictures/symbols, slow rate of communication exchanges, and alternate communication patterns (Fried-Oken, 1988). This in turn may interfere with literacy development (Stratton & Wright, 1991).

Students with severe speech impairments may also have restricted opportunities to develop literacy skills. These students are often unable to retell stories, read aloud, or say the sounds of the letters while decoding words. Participation in literacy activities, such as providing an original sentence for a chart story, is not possible. An inability to ask questions regarding literacy activities will further impede learning. When students are unable to ask questions about sounds, words, stories, or ideas, the results are unanswered questions, ineffective learning, and interference with typical literacy development (Blischak, 1995; Katims, 1993). Having an AAC system will help students to participate in literacy activities. However, the AAC system may not be sufficient to allow the student to fully participate in these activities or ask questions on specific areas. This is especially the case for children who are just beginning to learn to read, write, and communicate using an AAC system. Unless the student can already write and spell out specific questions with an AAC device, there will always be unanswered questions.

Lack of Motor Ability

A second barrier to developing reading skills is the impact of limited motor skills on accessing books. Some children may have decreased contact with books, due to an inability to independently retrieve and manipulate books because of their physical impairments. Once a book is retrieved by another person, there may be difficulties positioning the book and the student for optimal contact. Even if correct positioning is achieved, the child may be unable to turn the pages, indicate when he or she is ready to turn a page, go back to a previous page, or maintain the book in a good position (Light & Smith, 1993). This can have a negative impact on learning to read. Reading literacy experiences may be lost without appropriate adaptations.

Individual Factors

The third barrier to acquiring reading skills for students with physical, health, or multiple disabilities consists of the category known as individual factors. These include (a) increased absenteeism due to health factors; (b) lack of attending to the literacy activity due to problems with pain, discomfort, or fatigue; and (c) medication or treatment effects that can interfere with learning (Heller, Alberto, Forney, & Schwartzman, 1996; Heller & Swinehart-Jones, 2003b). Additional problems include visual and auditory perceptual problems, language deficits, poor self-esteem, and passive learning patterns that may influence literacy development (McNaughton, 1993; Smith, 1992). Additional disabilities may also accompany the physical disability, such as learning disabilities or mental retardation, requiring additional instructional techniques to teach reading and writing.

Lack of Experiences

A fourth barrier to literacy development is a lack of broad experiences. Individuals with physical, health, or multiple disabilities may be limited in gaining broad experiences concerning the world around them due to difficulty ambulating and exploring interesting items or activities (Blischak, 1995). Transportation problems may also limit students' ability to learn about common places such as movie theaters and shopping malls. Everyday experiences such as sitting on the grass and having a picnic with ants may be missed due to never being positioned on the ground. When students with disabilities encounter reading material dealing with these broad experiences or are assigned to write about them, they may lack comprehension and knowledge. As a result, they may have difficulty with the reading material and may even be perceived as less intellectually capable than their peers.

A student's lack of experiences may also result in construction of inaccurate concepts. When a student has difficulty manipulating objects, inaccurate perceptions or missed perceptions regarding their properties may occur. For example, certain items may be mistaken as heavy (e.g., an apple), when they are light in weight, or certain items may be mistaken as hard (e.g., a sponge), when they are squeezable and soft. Lacking the opportunity to feel the item or hold it can create many misconceptions. If the student also has a visual impairment, further misconceptions can occur from a lack of visual information.

Learning Environment and Instruction

The last barriers affecting literacy development are problems in the learning environment and inadequacies in instruction. In some home and school environments, there may be reduced expectations of children with speech and physical impairments in acquiring literacy skills (Koppenhaver, Evans, & Yoder, 1991; Light & Smith, 1993). Low expectations do not provide a positive environment for the child. Another problem within the learning environment is the amount of time students with speech and physical impairments receive in literacy instruction. These students appear to receive less literacy instruction than their peers without disabilities, experience frequent and regular interruptions while receiving literacy instruction, lack interaction with peers during instruction, and respond to instruction in a passive manner (Harris, 1982; Koppenhaver et al., 1991; Koppenhaver & Yoder, 1993; Mike, 1987). Inadequate instructional strategies, lack of adaptations, and inappropriate use of assistive technology all have a negative impact upon the acquisition of literacy skills for students with physical or multiple disabilities.

In spite of these barriers, the acquisition of literacy skills is crucial, especially for students who are nonverbal and use augmentative and alternative communication (W. S. Berninger, 1986; Blackstone & Cassatt-James, 1988; McGinnies & Beukelman, 1989; Smith et al., 1989; Yoder & Kraat, 1983). Literacy skills "unlock the doors to independent communication and offer access to more complete, comprehensible, and self-initiated interactions" (Koppenhaver et al., 1991, p. 20). This is especially true in the area of communication. Only a student who is able to spell can communicate whatever he or she wants to and is not limited by the programming of the communication device. Being able to effectively spell out questions, ideas, and comments is critical for effective communication and learning. Literacy skills will also broaden job opportunities. This is especially crucial since the presence of physical impairments will preclude many jobs requiring certain physical abilities. Literacy skills will also increase academic skills, leisure skills, independent living skills, and opportunities for personal fulfillment.

Due to the barriers confronting students with physical, health, or multiple disabilities and the critical need for obtaining literacy skills, teachers will need to learn specialized skills to adapt instruction. Prior to teaching these areas, it is crucial that a thorough literacy profile of the student is obtained to determine modifications, adaptations, and assistive technology needs for reading and writing.

ADDRESSING LITERACY BARRIERS

It is important to consider which barriers may impede a student's ability to read and ways of addressing them. This includes assessing the child's communication, motor ability (i.e., physical efficiency), individual factors, experiential deficits, and the learning environment and instruction as it relates to reading, and determining appropriate adaptations and strategies to address these areas.

Addressing Communication Barriers

As noted earlier, restricted participation due to speech constraints is a significant barrier to acquiring literacy skills. It is important that students with severe speech and physical impairments are included in discussions and encouraged to participate in literacy activities. This is often done by putting questions in a multiple-choice format (e.g., Where did the girl go? beach . . . mountains . . . forest . . . ? What is this word? cat . . . catch . . . dog . . . cot?). The multiple-choice format may be given verbally or in written form. It is important to determine whether the student can respond well to both oral and written choices. In addition, a careful analysis should be conducted of the number of choices that can be handled by the student.

When questions are provided in a multiple-choice format, the student then needs to answer these questions using the most **reliable means of response (RMR).** The most reliable means of response refers to the most reliable, accurate, and consistent way the student can respond. For example, the student may be able to vocalize some words, head nod for "yes," use an AAC device, or eye-gaze a choice on an E-Tran board (see Figure 13–1). Once all of the forms of communication that the student uses are identified, it is then important to determine which is the most reliable response. This is done by recording how accurately the student is able to use various types of responses to questions. Whichever method has the highest accuracy rate is the most reliable means of response. If the student performs equally well on several responses, then other factors are considered, including degree of effort, fatigue, speed of response, and readability of the response to unfamiliar people. It is important that the

FIGURE 13–1
Directions for using an eye-gaze board

Using an Eye-Gaze Board

An eye-gaze board (E-tran board) should be constructed of see-through material, such as Plexiglas. Usually a hole is cut out of the middle to reduce glare and to make it more personal (so that a piece of Plexiglas is not in the student's face). Items are Velcroed around the edges of the eye-gaze board. (Sometimes rectangles of erasable whiteboard material will be put along the edges to allow the teacher to quickly write the choices.)

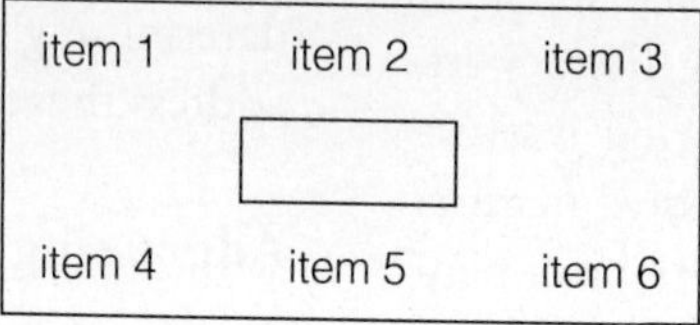

The number of items and their arrangement will depend upon the student, the size of the board and the size of the material. Items may be letters, vocabulary words, pictures, or whatever is being taught. The board is held in front of the student, with the teacher looking through the hole in the middle of the board at the student's eyes.

Students are taught to

1. look at the items (they often need to look at each one)
2. look at the desired item
3. look at the teacher

The teacher knows that the last item the student looked at before looking back at him or her, was the selected item. It is important to have the student look back at the teacher, otherwise it is difficult to know when the student has made a selection, since the student may spend some time looking at the choices (e.g., sounding out the words to himself or herself to determine the correct answer). The teacher may also verify the student's choice (e.g., the teacher points to the item and asks, "Is this the one you chose?")

response selected is the most accurate, so that when the student makes an error, the error has to do with the content of the question, rather than an unreliable motor response or a partially learned communication device. Verifying the student's response by asking the student "Is this the one you want?" can also help determine if the error was a response error or a content error.

Another barrier to literacy is a lack of language experiences. Language experiences can be increased by utilizing early, multimodal AAC interventions (Carlson, 1987), and responding to students' natural attempts at communication (Rogow, 1988). The social nature of communication should also be stressed (Koppenhaver et al., 1991) by encouraging question asking and social language play routines (Rogow, 1988). If possible, vocabulary on the AAC device should include messages such as "My turn to read," "Please read this," "Your turn to read," "Please repeat that," "I don't know that word," "I want to press the computer keys," and other phrases that will quickly allow the student to participate in literacy activities and get assistance when needed. Often the AAC device will have a **generic reading display** that contains these messages that will allow the student to participate in the reading process across a wide variety of stories (see Figure 13–2). It is important to develop and provide phrases that promote participation, ask questions, and allow the student to comment about a book. However, it must be stressed that students also need to have access to specific book content on their device as well as a generic reading display in order to promote participation and benefit from the entire literacy process (Musselwhite & King-DeBaun, 1997).

As students gain proficiency on an AAC system and the AAC system expands to include more vocabulary, it is important to consider setting up the AAC system to support literacy. To determine if the current AAC system will support literacy, there are some fundamental questions that may be asked:

FIGURE 13–2
An example of a generic reading display to be used across a wide range of books

1. Can the student answer and ask questions regarding reading and writing using the current AAC system?
2. Can the AAC system be used to construct reading pages or picture pages to support vocabulary instruction?
3. Can the AAC system be used to write or spell?
4. Does the AAC system hook up to a computer for computer access?
5. Does the AAC system allow the student to read through construction of reading pages for reading and writing activities?

The AAC system should also be examined regarding its graphic representational system (symbols), since this can promote or interfere with literacy (McNaughton, 1993). On a simple AAC device, the printed words above the symbols on the AAC device should be made large enough for the student to easily see and notice, if the aim is for the student to eventually learn to read printed words. For more advanced AAC systems, it should also be determined whether (a) the symbols provide semantic information relating to the concepts represented, (b) linguistic features (e.g., verb tense, possession, plurality) are represented, (c) the layout of the symbols resembles that of oral and written language, (d) word classes are well organized, (e) provision is made for sound-symbol correspondence, (f) vocabulary selection is useful and the student has the ability to produce new vocabulary, and (g) the system promotes metalinguistic awareness (McNaughton, 1993).

Addressing Physical Efficiency Areas

The second barrier to literacy acquisition consists of physical and motor constraints. Students with physical or multiple disabilities typically have physical impairments that interfere with motor aspects of reading (e.g., book handling, following words with a finger) and writing (e.g., manipulating a pencil, using a standard keyboard). This may be due to contractures, a limited range of motion, or the physical impairment itself (such as a limb deficiency). It is important to assess a student's **physical efficiency areas** in order to make appropriate modifications to promote literacy. Physical efficiency refers to the student's motor abilities in naturally occurring activities (e.g., turning pages in a book, pointing to a picture about a story). There are five major physical efficiency areas: (a) student positioning, (b) movement and work surface adaptations, (c) fine-motor movement and accessing material, and (d) range of motion for material placement, and (e) fatigue and endurance issues.

Student Positioning. Without proper positioning, there can be great variability as to the reliability of a response. Proper positioning will allow the student to have maximum control over his or her arm and hand movement, whereas poor positioning may impede accessing a keyboard, manipulating a book, handwriting, or activating a switch. Some basic considerations when evaluating positioning are as follows:

- Do the student's feet touch the ground or are they supported in some way? Do they need to be?
- Is the student seated in the back of the chair (with strap over hips) to prevent the student from falling out or going into extension?
- Is the student in midline position in the chair?
- Is the student able to maintain proper position or are more or less supports needed?
- Is the student's position at 90 degrees at the ankles, knees, and hips? Should they be? (Heller & Swinehart-Jones, 2003a).

Movement and Work Surfaces. In order to use arm and hand movements to access reading and writing materials, appropriateness of the work surface must be examined. For example, the chair (including the wheelchair) needs to be at an appropriate height for the student, since this can affect accessing items on the table surface and lead to muscle strain and fatigue. Often the table will need to be raised or lowered. Some students will require their work surface to be slanted. This can be achieved with adjustable slant boards or book easels. It is important to remember that the slant needed to read or point to parts of a book can be very different than the slant needed to write or type on a keyboard.

Other work surface considerations include material stabilization and contrast. Slippery materials must be secured to surfaces. If the student has a visual impairment, a sharp color or texture contrast is often needed between the items on the table and the color of the material. Contrast can easily be changed by placing contrasting construction paper under the material.

Fine-Motor Movement and Accessing Material. Hand use is important for literacy instruction. If the student is unable to access material with his or her hands due to severe physical impairment (e.g., missing arms and no prosthetic, arms with severe contractures), alternate access will be important through the use of assistive technology and modifications. An AT assessment will be needed (see Chapter 7 on Assistive Technology). If hand use is present but impaired, it is important to first determine which hand is more dominant to use in such activities as pointing to an answer, following a line of print, picking up items, and handwriting (or accessing a keyboard). This can be accomplished by observing the student. Sometimes the student's disability will result in one hand or arm being more affected than the other. When this occurs, assumptions should not be made that the least impaired hand is always the best one to use. Students should have both hands assessed for use. Careful observation and the evaluation by an OT will assist in this area.

Some students will be unable to manipulate books. To assist, pieces of double-sided foam tape can be placed between book pages ("page fluffers") to create a space for inserting the finger and flipping the page. Another option is to scan the books into a computer and have the student change the pages by pressing a switch. Pictures of book pages can be placed on slides and the student can control the slide projector (King-DeBaun, 1995). Books may also be difficult to manipulate because of their size and need to be enlarged. Print size can also be changed as well as symbols added to make them more accessible.

Another consideration is whether the student will be able to point with his or her hand at the print when reading. It is common for young children to use their hands to point to the words as they are reading to help keep their place. Beginning readers who have physical disabilities may lose their place if they are unable to point to the words while reading. Initially, the teacher may point to each word as it is being read. However, it is important to replace this modality with another that allows the teacher freedom of movement and the student to have increased independence. Two alternative strategies are the colored-line prompting strategy and computer highlighting. Chapter 7 contains additional extensive discussion of environmental and object modification.

The **colored-line prompting strategy** is based on the premise that by pairing the print with colored lines under the words, students will be able to maintain their place by pairing the word or line they are reading with a colored line. For students who lose their place on the line, a clear plastic sheet of paper (such as a transparency used with overhead projector) is prepared with multicolored lines, each of which is composed of 1-inch strips of different colors (see Figure 13–3). Each word does not require its own color, so the sheet of paper can be used across different pages, just so it fits under each line. Students are often easily able to make the transition from someone's finger pointing to the words, to following along with colored lines under the words. Over time, colored lines can be **faded** (gradually removed). The first step to fading the colored line is to eliminate every other line. In this way the student uses the colored line under the words for the first line of print, and the same colored line on top of the words for the second line of print. One colored line serves every two lines. (Some students actually start with the color lines set at every other line and fade the lines from this point.) After the student gains competency, the line may be further faded by elongating each color to about 2 inches. Later, each color is elongated to 3 inches. Over time, half the sentence may have one color and the other half another color, with the first two sentence lines having half red and half green be-

FIGURE 13–3
Colored line prompting strategy

Can the student follow a line of print?
Does he get lost between words or between lines?

Color Line Prompting Strategy

Using color lines for word placement

The boy then turned and saw his friend holding his puppy. He was so happy that his lost puppy was found. Tears began to swell in his eyes. He now knew how much the puppy meant to him and how he would always take good care of him.

Fading to using one color line for every two lines of print

The boy then turned and saw his friend holding his puppy. He was so happy that his lost puppy was found. Tears began to swell in his eyes. He now knew how much the puppy meant to him and how he would always take good care of him.

Fading color line

The boy then turned and saw his friend holding his puppy. He was so happy that his lost puppy was found. Tears began to swell in his eyes. He now knew how much the puppy meant to him and how he would always take good care of him.

Further fading the color line

The boy then turned and saw his friend holding his puppy. He was so happy that his lost puppy was found. Tears began to swell in his eyes. He now knew how much the puppy meant to him and how he would always take good care of him.

Using color lines for line placement

The boy then turned and saw his friend holding his puppy. He was
so happy that his lost puppy was found. Tears began to swell in his
eyes. He now knew how much the puppy meant to him and how he
would always take good care of him.

tween them and the next two sentence lines having half blue and half orange between them.

As the reader matures, the problem may no longer be keeping the place on the line, but staying on the correct line. A colored line is no longer used between the lines, but a vertical colored line is placed down the side of the written lines (see Figure 13–3). The student pairs the line he or she is reading with the green colored line in front, and then moves to the next line with the blue in front of it. Over time, the colored line may be faded when the student's competency has increased. The colored vertical line may be faded by elongating the vertical line so that the first two lines have a green mark and the next two lines have a red mark. Eventually the length of color will be increased until there is only one color, and then the line is removed. This colored-line prompting strategy has been used successfully with dozens of students with severe speech and physical impairments who have successfully moved from a teacher pointing to each word, to the student using colored lines, to not needing this prompt.

An alternative to the colored-line prompting strategy is using computer software. Stories can be scanned into the computer and software programs will highlight each sentence or word (e.g., WYNN, manufactured by Arkenstone, and Kurzweil 3000, manufactured by Lernout & Hauspie). Most of these programs also have voice output that can be turned off. Other features include changing the spacing between words, lines, or characters and masking distracting sections of a page.

Range of Motion (ROM) for Material Placement. Some students will have limited range of motion (how far they can reach). Their range of motion may be fixed (e.g., due to contractures) or fluctuate (e.g., increases in tone due to excitement, startle, or fatigue). Determining a student's range of motion is important in order to ensure that the student will be able to reach everything needed in an activity. For example, some students' range of motion may be limited, resulting in an inability to point to an item or a word in a book, reach an item on the table, access a standard keyboard, or reach certain symbols on an AAC device. Due to limitations in range of motion, a student's answers can be mistakenly recorded as wrong due to a problem with the student's range of motion, rather than a learning error.

To help avoid errors due to motor ability, it is important that items be placed in the student's range of motion. Range of motion can be assessed in several ways. One way is to make a grid (a piece of paper with horizontal and vertical lines) and put the grid directly in front of the student. Ask the student to touch different parts of the paper, such as top right, top left, top, right, left, bottom right, bottom left, bottom. (An alternative would be to have the student draw with a marker or pick up reinforcing items scattered on the grid.) Map out on the grid how far the student was able to reach by making marks with a pen. Repeat the process with the grid positioned to the right or left of the student's midline (if the student appears to be able to move farther to one side than another) and at different slants. When examining the results on the grid, the slant and position providing the student the most range should be selected. The results of the grid should also provide concrete information on how materials should be positioned (e.g., place book about 3 inches to the left of midline, with bottom of book 4 inches from student, and book should be placed at 30-degree angle). Since a student's tone may fluctuate and sizes of books vary, it may be necessary to reassess by having the student try to touch the top, left, right, and bottom of a book before starting to read it.

When determining placement, it is also important to determine the print size and spacing for physical access. For example, when attempting to touch a word (or symbol) out of an array of four items, some students lack the fine-motor ability to point, but will use their entire hand. If the items are placed too closely together, the student's hand can cover several words, making it difficult to discern which word the student selected. This can be modified by (a) making the words larger so that the student can easily touch the one he or she wants, or (b) spacing the words farther apart to make touching the intended word more accurate. The number of words (items or symbols) a student will be able to access will depend on the student's range of motion, vision, and cognitive ability. Some students will only be able to touch four items due to a restricted range of motion and needing them spaced apart. Some students will cognitively only be able to handle three choices. The teacher will need to determine the optimum number of items that can be displayed at one time. For students unable to touch, alternate access may be used (e.g., eye gaze, teacher points to selection and student voices or moves to indicate choice).

Fatigue and Endurance Issues. If students become fatigued or have limited endurance, decisions will need to be made regarding length of work sessions, whether changing response modes will help, and how the lesson can be adapted for fatigue. Some students will benefit from short periods of instruction in which they need to motorically respond, followed by breaks when they just listen. Others may need actual breaks in the lesson. For students who respond in several ways, their initial response may be through an AAC device, but as they become fatigued, they may change to answering yes-or-no questions. For students who access writing through using a switch, changing the switch placement to an equally effective location may decrease fatigue.

Addressing Individual Considerations

Individual factors constitute the third barrier area to the development of literacy skills. Individual considerations are any conditions or problems that may interfere with learning literacy. If students have problems with distractibility, interfering behaviors, or perceptual problems, these should be recorded. Any additional disabilities such as visual impairments, hearing impairments, learning disabilities, or mental retardation should also be noted.

Strategies used to address these problems or additional disabilities will need to be identified. For example, students who are distractible may need to have distractions decreased by eliminating clutter or moving to a less distracting area. Students with visual impairments or perceptual difficulties may require a certain size font or font style. (See Figure 8–13 in Chapter 8 on teacher tips for determining what size font to use.) Students with learning disabilities may require the incorporation of special techniques to address the learning disability in addition to those techniques used to address the physical impairment. Other students may require additional instruction when there is increased absenteeism. Changes in instructional sequence or amounts of instruction may be used to accommodate fatigue or endurance problems (Heller, Alberto, et al., 1996).

Students with mental retardation may require a different approach to literacy instruction. Depending upon their current skills and abilities, they may receive instruction in conventional literacy skills or receive instruction in functional literacy instead. **Conventional literacy** refers to typical, formal, academic literacy instruction that is taught in general education. For some students, conventional literacy may not be feasible or appropriate. An alternative form of instruction is teaching functional literacy skills. **Functional literacy** refers to learning to read and write key words that are needed in functional tasks.

Addressing Experiential Deficits

Since students with physical disabilities often lack experiences due to motor issues, it is important that assumptions are not made regarding the student's exposure to common concepts. Teacher of students with physical disabilities typically anticipate that there is a lack of general knowledge due to a lack of experience. Teachers need to provide missing concepts through explanations, pictures, or actual experiences. Asking a student if he or she knows what a concept is and taking "yes" at face value is a poor technique. (For example, when learning the word "beach," the teacher should not just ask the student if he or she knows what a beach is.) Students often do not want to be different or are used to saying "yes" to teachers' questions. Teachers should either probe more deeply or provide information to the student along with the concept.

To increase common experiences, every effort should be made to involve the student in everyday routines (Kekelis & Anderson, 1984). Increasing common experiences begins with providing appropriate positioning to increase participation (Foley, 1993; McEwen & Lloyd, 1990), using adapted toys and devices (Carlson, 1987), and describing and bringing experiences to the student (Kekelis & Anderson, 1984). Exposing students to print and involving students in reading contribute to learning to read (Light & Smith, 1993). Growing up in home and school environments with abundant reading and writing materials and being immersed in literacy activities contributes to the success of children with severe speech and physical impairment in learning to read and write (Koppenhaver et al., 1991).

Addressing the Learning Environment and Instructional Barriers

The last barrier to affect literacy acquisition consists of problems in the learning environment and instructional issues. The learning environment should be designed to promote learning for all students. It is important that preconceived notions, not based on data and assessment, should be avoided regarding a student's capability of learning literacy skills. Teachers should ask themselves if expectations are in place that the student will learn to read. Reduced expectations may be addressed through providing high expectations in literacy (Light & Smith, 1993).

Another problem is the amount of time devoted to teaching literacy skills to students with physical disabilities. There is often less time to learn and inadequate individual and classroom instruction may contribute to the problem (V. W. Berninger & Gans, 1986b; Koppenhaver et al., 1991). The learning environment must include time blocks dedicated to providing literacy instruction in which interruptions are minimized. In addition, interaction with peers and encouragement to participate in class discussion pertaining to literacy activities need to be systematically planned (Mercer & Mercer, 2001). Students who take a long time to respond, due to their physical impairment, may need longer periods of time devoted to literacy activities in order to promote learning. Teachers should also be sure that the learning environment is able to support any modifications or assistive technology that are needed by the student.

There are many different instructional strategies that may be used to support instruction of students with physical disabilities. Due to the specialized nature of each literacy area, each of these areas is presented as a separate section in this chapter. These sections are (a) emergent and beginning literacy, (b) conventional literacy: approaches and assessment, (c) conventional literacy: phonics, (d) conventional literacy: vocabulary instruction, (e) conventional literacy: fluency, (f) conventional literacy: text comprehension, (g) specialized curricula and software, and (h) functional literacy: reading. Each area specifically targets students with physical or multiple disabilities, including those who have limited speech. Writing and spelling techniques are discussed in Chapter 14.

EMERGENT AND BEGINNING LITERACY

Literacy can be viewed as a process which often begins in the crib as parents read books to their children and which continues throughout life (Teale & Sulzby, 1989). Emergent literacy skills are the very beginning skills in literacy. These skills are observed in children who have a lot of exposure to print and who actively participate in storybook reading and other early literacy experiences. For students with severe speech and physical disabilities, systematic adaptations will need to be put in place to promote active participation in early literacy experiences.

There is no formal assessment of emergent literacy skills. However, a checklist has been developed that can help determine which emergent skills the student possesses. As seen in Figure 13–4, emergent literacy skills have been divided into seven stages. The skills range from beginning to attend to pictures to recognizing words and word parts. For students who are nonverbal or are beginning to use an AAC device, this checklist will need to be modified by determining whether the child is looking at or pointing to pictures or words that the adult is reading. Questions may be given in a yes/no or multiple-choice format to help determine how well the student is attending to the story.

To help promote emergent literacy, young children should be in an environment that promotes early interactions with books and awareness of print as a medium to communicate stories, ideas, and information. Activities promoting emergent literacy should be programmed for the young child in home and school environments. Young children should also engage in structured activities that develop their familiarity with books and their phonemic awareness.

Book and Print Awareness

From an early age, students without physical disabilities have picked up books, turned the book pages, and pointed to words or pictures in these books. Students with severe physical disabilities may not have had that opportunity. This may impede their book knowledge. Early exposure to books should include pointing out how the book should be oriented, how to open the book, location of the first page, where reading begins, and which way the pages are turned. Teachers should assess for this knowledge. This can be easily assessed through yes-or-no questions (e.g., Do you start here or here or here?) Appropriate modifications to books (e.g., page fluffers), discussed under physical efficiencies areas, should also be implemented.

As children gain exposure to books and printed material, they will also have increased exposure to print. Eventually children will move from identifying where print is on a page, to being able to identify what a word is (has spaces on either side), to eventually picking out letters and known words. Teachers should be sure to point out the print and help the child understand that what is being read is conveyed in print.

Some students with physical disabilities may have perceptual problems or memory difficulties that interfere with such areas as orthographic awareness, visual memory, and component processing. Teachers should determine if the student has problems in these areas so that appropriate intervention can be given. **Orthographic awareness** refers to the ability to identify same and different letters. For example, some students may have difficulty visually discriminating the letters "b" and "d" or "c" and "e." If that is the case, further instruction will be needed. Another area some students have difficulty in is visual memory. Assessing a student's visual memory for a printed whole word (which utilizes global

FIGURE 13–4
Checklist of emergent literacy development

Stage 1: Early Connections to Reading—Describing Pictures
- ____ Attends to and describes (labels) pictures in books
- ____ Has a limited sense of story
- ____ Follows verbal directions for this activity
- ____ Uses oral vocabulary appropriate for age/grade level
- ____ Displays attention span appropriate for age/grade level
- ____ Responds to questions in an appropriate manner
- ____ Appears to connect pictures (sees as being interrelated)

Stage 2: Connecting Pictures to Form Story
- ____ Attends to picture and develops oral stories across the pages of the book
- ____ Uses only childlike or descriptive (storyteller) language to tell the story, rather than book language (i.e., Once upon a time . . . There once was a little boy . . .)

Stage 3: Transitional Picture Reading
- ____ Attends to pictures as a connected story
- ____ Mixes storyteller language with book language

Stage 4: Advanced Picture Reading
- ____ Attends to pictures and develops oral stories across the pages of the book
- ____ Speaks as though reading the story (uses book language)

Stage 5: Early Print Reading
- ____ Tells a story using the pictures
- ____ Knows print moves from left to right, top to bottom
- ____ Creates part of the text using book language and knows some words on sight

Stage 6: Early Strategic Reading
- ____ Uses content to guess at some unknown words (guesses make sense)
- ____ Notices beginning sounds in words and uses them to guess unknown words
- ____ Seems to sometimes use syntax to help identify words in print
- ____ Recognizes some sound parts, such as root words and affixes

Stage 7: Moderate Strategic Reading
- ____ Sometimes uses context and word parts to decode words
- ____ Self-corrects when making an oral reading miscue
- ____ Retells the passage easily and may embellish the story line
- ____ Shows some awareness of vowel sounds

Note. From *Reading Inventory for the Classroom* 3/e by Flynt/Cooper, © 1998. Adapted by permission of Prentice-Hall, Inc., Upper Saddle River, NJ.

processing) is important, since acquisition of sight word vocabulary depends on the ability to attend to and remember whole-word patterns (V. W. Berninger & Gans, 1986b). A third area of difficulty may be with component processing (which is selective attention of a letter). This is also important to assess since phonics rules of letter-phoneme correspondence require the reader to attend to letter information, and memory for a letter sequence (serial processing) requires attention to the serial order of letters for spelling patterns and orthographic rules. Teachers can informally assess for any problems in these areas or use a standardized test. One test that is appropriate for students with severe speech impairments is the Matching Subtest of the Metropolitan Reading Readiness Test, Level II (Nurss & McGauvran, 1976). In this test, words (or wordlike stimuli) are presented and the task is to match one of four whole patterns to a target whole pattern. This test can be used by students who are nonverbal and have physical impairments. Problems may be targeted for instruction.

Orthographic awareness, visual memory, and component processing may be directly taught. Children need to be able to visually discriminate between pictures, letters, words, phrases, and sentences, and to distinguish the spaces between words and the orientation of words on a page. Students may be involved in any number of activities involving matching pictures, letters, words, or sentences. This can be accomplished by providing very gross discriminations to very fine ones. For example, when matching letters, the student may initially need to match the letter "a" and be given choices of a picture of a tree, an abstract symbol, and the letter "a." Finer and finer discriminations are made over time. Any confusion between letters can be highlighted by color or size and specifically taught. Component processing is taught in a similar manner, except a sequence of letters or items is used. Visual memory instruction often involves showing the student a letter or picture and then removing it before the choices are made available.

When there is visual confusion, it is important that a visual impairment is ruled out or corrected if needed. If an uncorrectable visual impairment is present, the student may need such adaptations as enlarged print, decreased visual clutter, high contrast, or lighting changes. If Braille is a consideration, the Braille Assessment Checklist for Persons with Multiple Disabilities (Heller, D'Andrea, Soucy, & Caruso, 1997) may be a useful tool to determine the appropriate modifications to accommodate both visual and physical impairment.

Storybook Reading with Adaptations

Young children are often first exposed to reading through exposure to story reading in the home. Storyreading experiences have been identified as critical for preparation to classroom literacy instruction (Cazden, 1983; Heath, 1982; Snow & Ninio, 1986; Wells, 1987). In one study (Light & Smith, 1993), the home experience of preschool children with speech and physical impairments was compared to that of preschool children who did not have disabilities. There was no significant difference between ownership of books, library use, tape usage, or story reading between the two groups of children. However, some differences were found in their story-reading experiences. First, there was a difference in how actively the students participated in the reading experience. Eighty percent of parents of children without disabilities reported that their children asked questions during the story reading, while only one parent of a child with a speech and physical disability reported that her child participated. This lack of participation by students with speech and physical impairments could be attributed to lack of an effective AAC system, severe restrictions in vocabulary on their AAC devices, or an inability to access their AAC systems during story reading, especially when being positioned on the parent's lap, where access is often difficult.

It is important that children's exposure to storybook reading continue, but with more active participation. Stories can be adapted with pictures or symbols that can be moved onto the corresponding book page and attached with Velcro®. Children can select the appropriate picture (through yes/no, eye gaze, or pointing), and the picture can be placed on the page by the child when possible. This type of interactive storybook can be made or purchased. One example of commercial books made for this purpose is *Breakstone's Interactive Stories,* distributed by Mayer-Johnson, Inc. For example, in the interactive storybook about making the bed, the pillow can be selected from a variety of items and moved onto the bed (and attached with Velcro®).

Predictable books, or **patterned books,** are often used to promote emergent literacy. A predictable or patterned book is a book that uses a predictable sequence of words. For example, in the book *Goodnight Moon* (Brown, 2002), the word "goodnight" occurs frequently and in a fairly predictable pattern. Children with speech and physical impairments may increase participation in literacy activities when the book's predictable or pattern phrase is accessible to the student. This may be a symbol to touch, either in the book or on an AAC device (such as a symbol for "goodnight" or the symbol "goodnight" with additional symbols that "goodnight" is combined with, such as "goodnight" "room") (Rogow, 1988). As the rest of the children say the pattern or repetitive phrase in a group story-reading situation, students with AAC devices can also have the words or phrase programmed into their device (or spoken into a tape recorder or Big Mac switch) and "say" the phrase along with the rest of the class.

Books can also be adapted to have symbols associated with the pictures and words. Symbols can be attached to the book page or placed on an AAC device for the child to select. In this manner, the child actively participates by selecting the symbol. The child can also begin learning to recognize the word that is paired with the symbol. Some books come with symbols already on each page. One example of a book with symbols is shown in Figure 13–5 and is taken from *Quick Tech: Readable, Repeatable Stories and Activities* (McNairn & Shioleno, 1994).

FIGURE 13–5
An example of a storybook with symbols provided

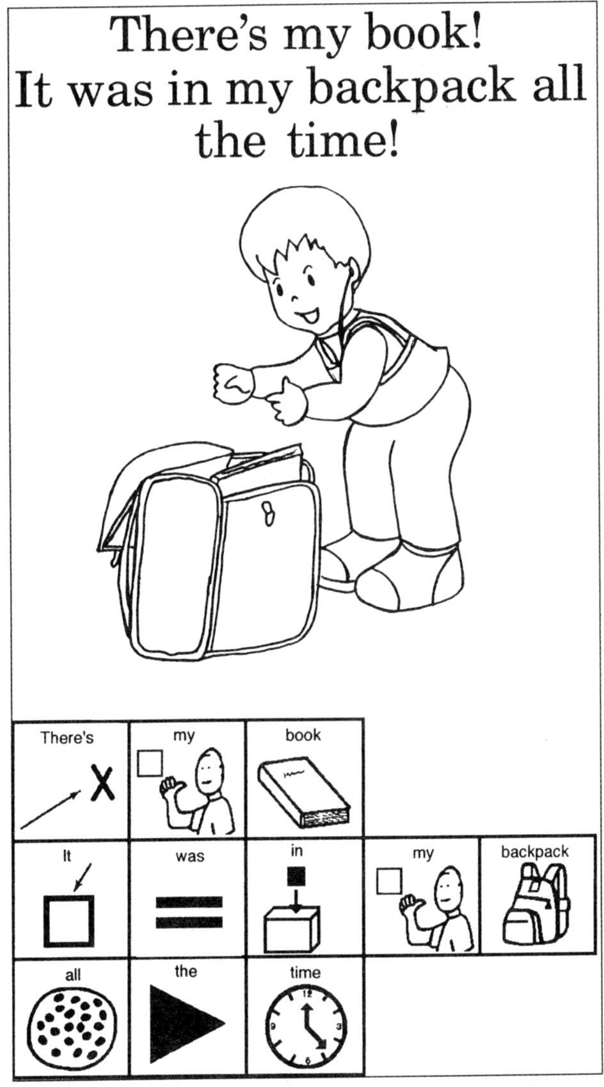

Note. From *Quick Tech: Readable, Repeatable Stories and Activities* by P. McNairn and C. Shioleno. © 1994, Mayer-Johnson, Inc., P.O. Box 1579, Solana Beach, CA 92075.

Another series that uses fewer words and more simplistic sentences with symbols is the "Learning to Read" series (Creative Teaching Press, adapted by Mayer-Johnson). In their books, each picture symbol is presented in the book with print above it, with sentences such as "It's my birthday." Eight- and 36-cell overlays for AAC devices come with each book for immediate use. An example overlay for a story about a birthday is found in Figure 13–6. The books also have page fluffs (pieces of foam) between the pages to assist with page turning.

Similar books pairing words and symbols include *Tools for Literacy and Communication: A Collection of Stories* (Simmons & Young, 1994) and *Hands-on Reading* (Kelly & Friend, 1993). *Quick Tech Magic: Music-Based Literacy Activities* (Coleman, McNairn, & Shioleno, 1995) contains stories with AAC symbols and is designed to be put to music and used with flash cards to teach corresponding words (see Figure 13–7). It should be noted that this book provides a combination of print and symbols, allowing targeting of specific words that have both symbol and print.

When books are used that have symbols paired with words, the student may learn the words over time. However, the words often need to be systematically taught. This can occur by making the symbol smaller over time until it is finally eliminated. The word can also be systematically taught using phonics or sight-word approaches and then can be replaced with the symbol with only the word once it is learned.

Repeated Reading and Promoting Choice

Young children often benefit from repeated readings of a story to allow them to anticipate the content and more directly participate in the reading process. According to Light and Smith (1993), parents of children without disabilities more often read the same stories repeatedly, whereas parents of children with disabilities were more inclined to read new books. This difference may be due to reading initiation. Children without disabilities may initiate story reading and select favorite books with which they are more comfortable, whereas parents of students with disabilities may initiate the story reading and select books that they have not grown tired of. It is therefore important to allow

FIGURE 13–6
An AAC overlay to use with a storybook about a birthday. This is provided in addition to stories with symbols on each page

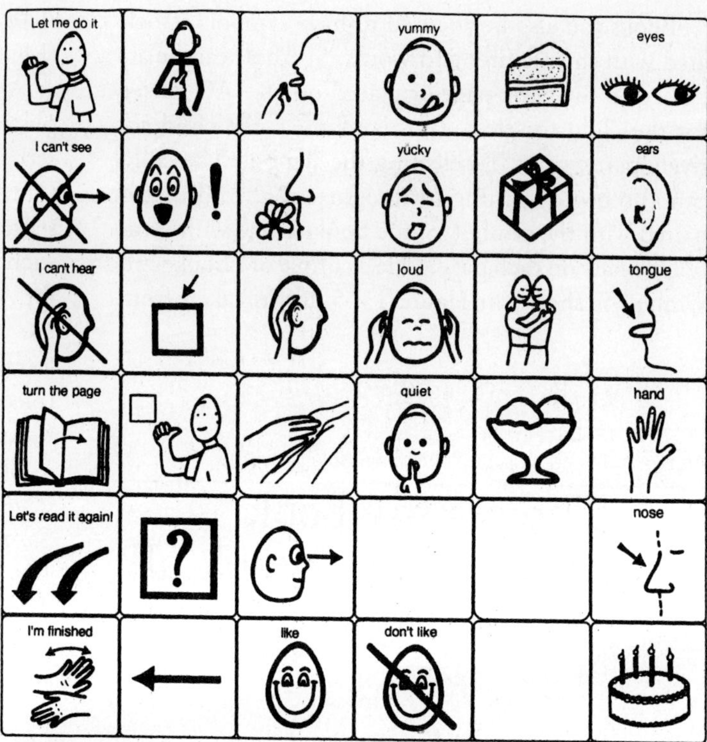

Note. Adapted from Boardmaker™ & the Picture Communication Symbols. © 1981–2000, Mayer-Johnson, Inc., P.O. Box 1579, Solana Beach, CA 92075. Adapted with permission.

students the choice of book selection and promote repeated reading to enhance literacy.

Phonemic Awareness

Instruction in phonemic awareness has been suggested for improving literacy (Armbruster, Lehr, & Osborn, 2001). **Phonemic awareness** refers to the ability to discriminate, identify, and manipulate individual sounds (phonemes) in spoken words. Phonemic awareness lays the foundations for helping students to later sound out words and to spell. It is important to note that phonemic awareness deals only with sounds, not with sounds as they relate to letters (which is phonics).

To determine a student's phonemic ability, the teacher may use one of several different tests out on the market or construct her own. The Metropolitan Reading Readiness Test, Level II (Nurss & McGauvran, 1976), is an example of one test that also includes tests of phonemic analysis and vocabulary knowledge that can be used with students who lack speech and have physical impairments. Another test of phonemic ability suited for students with severe speech and physical impairments is the Auditory Discrimination Subtest of the Stanford Diagnostic Reading Test—Red Level (Karlsen, Madden, & Gardner, 1976).

There are several different phonemic awareness activities that can be used to teach phonemic awareness. Some of these include:

- Phoneme isolation—recognizing sounds in words (e.g., What is the first sound in the word "man"?);
- Phoneme identification—identifying the same sounds in different words (e.g., What sound is the same in the words "man," "mat," and "more"?);
- Phoneme categorization—identifying the word that has the sound that doesn't belong (e.g., What word doesn't belong? Man, mat, or rag?);
- Phoneme blending—combining the phonemes to make a word (e.g., What word is "mmm," "aaa," "nnn"?);
- Phoneme segmentation—identification of the different sounds in a word (e.g., How many sounds in the word "man"? What are they?);

FIGURE 13–7
(a) Words are paired with symbols to facilitate reading, and (b) flash cards are used to reinforce the words

I like to go 

I like to go 

here

here

(a)

summer

hot

swimming

(b)

Note. From *Quick Tech Magic: Music-Based Literacy Activities* by K. Coleman, P. McNairn, and C. Shioleno. © 1995, Mayer-Johnson, Inc., P.O. Box 1579, Solana Beach, CA 92075.

- Phoneme deletion—identification of a word that remains when a phoneme is removed. (e.g., What is smile without the "sss"?);
- Phoneme addition—ability to make a new word by adding a phoneme (e.g., What word do you have when you add "sss" to "mile"?); and
- Phoneme substitution—ability to substitute a phoneme for another one to make a new word (e.g., The word is "man." Change "mmm" to "t.") (Armbruster, Lehr, & Osborn, 2001).

Usually only a few of the phonemic awareness activities listed above are chosen. Often phonemic blending and phonemic segmentation are stressed due to their importance in sounding out words (using blending) and spelling (using segmentation).

Students who are unable to speak will need adaptations when teaching phonemic awareness. Some of these strategies include (a) giving verbal choices of the targeted phonemic awareness activities and having the student choose, (b) categorizing pictures on the basis of shared initial, medial, or final sounds (Bradley & Bryant, 1983, 1985), (c) having the student make a movement (or other response) for each phonemic sound of a word that the teacher slowly pronounces (Foley, 1993), and (d) using symbols on the AAC device to match the spoken phonemes of a word (e.g., s-u-n, and the AAC device shows a picture of a sun) (Ball & Blachman, 1991). When teaching discrimination of phonemes, students are usually first taught gross discriminations, such as different environmental sounds or different sounding words. Eventually finer discriminations are made, such as discriminating between short vowel sounds. Students with physical disabilities may also engage in activities in which they program different sounds into an AAC device. Specific phonemic awareness programs may also be used and adapted for children with physical disabilities.

Letter-Sound Correspondence

To promote effective reading, children are taught letter-sound correspondence in which they are able to identify the sound or sounds that go with each letter or certain combination of letters (e.g., sh). Without this knowledge, they will have difficulty sounding out words during phonics instruction. If it is not known whether the student knows all of the letter-sound correspondences, it can easily be assessed by showing the student a letter and asking the student to make the corresponding sound. If the student is nonverbal, he or she can be given choices to choose from. (For example, the student is directed to look at the card with the "m" on it and is asked, Does this make the sound "sss," "mmm," or "nnnn"?) It is important to also assess the student's knowledge of lowercase letters, uppercase letters, manuscript, and cursive. Knowledge of basic letter sounds will be important for any reading approach or reading curriculum that includes phonics instruction.

There are several approaches to teaching letter-sound correspondence. Some students are taught using direct instruction in which the teacher follows a script and the students are shown the letter and repeat the sounds. Some students may need additional visual antecedent prompts. For example, letters can be made to look like something representing their sounds, and then the picture is faded, leaving only the letter. For example, an "a" can be made to look like an apple, an "s" can be made to look like a snake, a "z" can have a bee on it that makes the "zzz" sound. An example program that uses visual cues on the letters to promote learning the sounds is *Reading by the Rules* (Kapp & Kravitz-Zodda, 1997). (See Figure 13–8.)

When learning the sounds, it is important that the teacher correctly pronounces each sound that corresponds to the letter. Some sounds are **continuous sounds** that can be held, while others are **stop sounds.** Continuous sounds are those you can hold without distorting the sound (e.g., "mmm," "sss," "lll"), whereas stop sounds are those that cannot be held (e.g., "c," "b," "t"). When a letter sound is continuous, it is important to hold it. Phonics instruction will often stress holding the sounds (that are continuous) and blending them into the next sound in order to help the student to learn to put the sounds together to make a word. When a stop sound is encountered, most approaches will stress saying the stop sound and quickly moving into the next sound to also help with putting the sounds together to make a word.

FIGURE 13–8
Using visual imagery on letters to teach letter sound correspondence

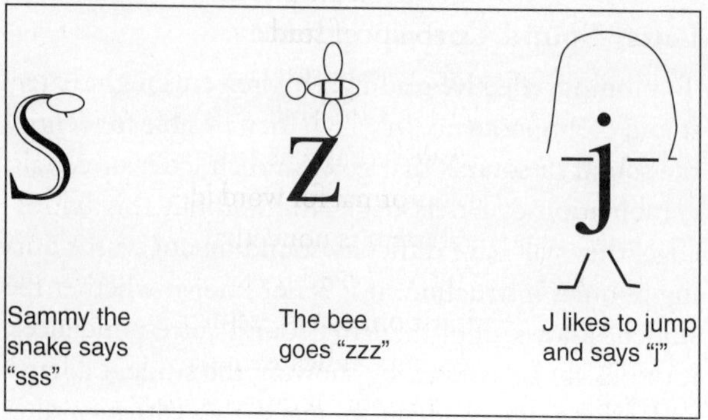
Sammy the snake says "sss"
The bee goes "zzz"
J likes to jump and says "j"

Software Programs Addressing Beginning Literacy Skills

There are numerous computer programs that are aimed at promoting emergent literacy skills. Many early literacy software programs allow the student to listen to the story as the words are highlighted. Usually, the student can also click on the words for them to be spoken. One example is the program "Just Grandma and Me Deluxe" (manufactured by Riverdeep–The Learning Company). This beginning early interactive program reads the story to the child, allows the child to click on words to be spoken, and allows the child to click on the scenery in the pictures. When the pictures are selected, an animated feature results in an action sequence. In the UkanDu Little Books series (manufactured by Don Johnston, Inc.), stories are presented in which the child chooses who or what some of the characters are doing. The story is read back to them highlighting the words as they are being read. Several programs also promote learning the letters of the alphabet, letter sounds, and word reading. Some sample programs include Early Learning Suite (published by Marblesoft), Reading Blaster Ages 4–6 (manufactured by Knowledge Adventure), Reader Rabbit Reading (manufactured by Riverdeep–The Learning Company), and Bailey's Book House (manufactured by Edmark, Riverdeep Family). Many of these programs support alternate access such as scanning and switch use or alternate mouse use.

CONVENTIONAL LITERACY: APPROACHES AND ASSESSMENT

Students in general education are taught conventional (i.e., regular or academic) literacy skills with the expectation that they will learn to read. Many students with physical disabilities will become readers, although many will have reading levels below their grade level or age. Students with more-severe cognitive impairments may only learn words that they will typically encounter in their environment (see the Functional Literacy section later in this chapter).

There are several approaches to teaching reading, including the basal approach, language experience approach, literature-based approach, whole language approach, and direct instruction. Often these can be divided into two major categories: whole-language-type approaches and phonics-type approaches. Whole language works from the premise that learning to read is as natural as learning to speak. Therefore, rather than teaching students rules for reading, or specific letter-sound relationships, the whole language approach provides students with a print-rich environment in which they may interact with print in many ways. Children listen as stories are read to them, they write their own stories either through dictation or with invented spelling, they tell stories, they look at picture books and create a story based on the pictures, they follow along in books as stories are read, and they are exposed to literature. While some children will learn to read with this approach, many children need to be systematically and explicitly taught (Snow, Burns, & Griffin, 1998) and this typically requires systematic instruction in phonics instruction (Honig, 1996).

For students with severe physical or multiple disabilities, two of the problems of a pure whole language approach is that it assumes the child has attained a high level of mastery of the forms and functions of language and has a rich experiential language base. These assumptions cannot be made for students with severe speech and physical impairments, as they ignore differences in broad experiences, linguistic competence, literary experience, and physical ability that influence learning to read (Foley, 1993). Instead, many students with severe speech and physical impairments will need a systematic approach that explicitly teaches reading skills and provides strategies to read unknown words and acquire new vocabulary independently and teaches generalizable skills for decoding unknown words (Jorm & Share, 1983; Vandervelden & Siegel, 1995).

Because of the recognized need for phonics instruction, many approaches include varying degrees of phonics instruction, and many reading curricula are phonetically based. Skills such as phonemic awareness, phonics, blending, and comprehension are systematically taught. Often a conventional literacy approach will include instruction in phonics, vocabulary, fluency, and comprehension. Before addressing these areas, it is important to ascertain the level at which the student is currently functioning.

Assessment of Conventional Reading Skills

There are several ways in which reading ability can be assessed. One of the best ways to determine reading ability is to have the student read passages at various grade levels. Errors such as omissions, substitutions, mispronunciations, and insertions are noted. To help determine the appropriate reading level for the student, the number of errors that are made are counted. Students are considered to be at an independent reading level when they can read with less than 1 error per 100 words with 90% comprehension or better. An instructional reading level is no more than 5 errors per 100 words and at least 75% comprehension level. A frustration level is more than 10 errors per 100 words and less than 50% comprehension (Spache, 1976). Current reading material may be assessed by using this technique to determine if it is too difficult. Informal reading inventories are especially valuable in the content areas (such as science and social studies) where the student may be struggling with the reading and missing the content. The informal reading inventory can lead to modifications that result in enhanced ability to learn the content.

Reading rates are another important assessment component. Students with physical impairments may be such slow readers that they will require extra time or need some alternative modality for content reading. Figure 13–9 provides oral and silent reading rates to which the student's own rate can be compared.

One of the most difficult areas of assessment is determining the reading ability of students who are nonverbal. Formal reading tests assess such areas as word decoding, word identification abilities, vocabulary comprehension, and passage comprehension. Tests that provide a multiple-choice format for word identification are required when the student is nonverbal. Test items may be placed on an ETRAN board (or a piece of Plexiglas) for eye-gaze identification, or test items may be spoken aloud for the student to indicate choice. Two formal instruments that do not require speech are the

FIGURE 13–9
Oral and silent reading rates

Oral reading speeds—words per minute
(Guszak, 1985)

Grade 1 = over 60
Grade 2 = over 70
Grade 3 = over 80
Grades 4, 5, & 6 = over 90

Silent reading speeds—words per minute
(Carver, 1989)

Grade 3 = 109–130 words
Grade 4 = 131–147
Grade 5 = 148–161
Grade 6 = 162–174
Grade 7 = 175–185
Grade 8 = 186–197
Grade 9 = 198–209
Grade 10 = 210–224
Grade 11 = 225–240
Grade 12 = 241–255

Gates-MacGinitie Comprehension Test, 4th edition (MacGinitie, MacGinitie, Maria, & Dreyer, 2000) and the Reading Comprehension subtest of the Peabody Individualized Achievement—Revised Test (Markwardt, 1997). The Peabody Picture Vocabulary Test III (PPVT, III) by Dunn and Dunn (1997) may be used to help determine word comprehension.

A close examination of the student's phonetic ability is helpful if the student will be taught reading using a phonetic approach. Students may be informally assessed regarding their ability to decode words and determine their meaning. First, students are assessed regarding their phonetics abilities. Student abilities are assessed in the following areas: alphabet sounds, consonant blends (e.g., "cl," "fl"), consonant digraphs (e.g., "ch," "sh"), diphthong sounds (e.g., "ow," "oi") and vowel digraphs (e.g., "ai," "oa," "ea"). Whether the student can blend phonemes into words and read unknown or made-up words will indicate the strength of phonic abilities. A multiple-choice format is required for nonverbal students.

The student's abilities in structural and semantic analysis of written words also provide important information for instruction. **Structural analysis** involves breaking down the word into smaller parts, such as identifying common prefixes and suffixes. Whether the student can break the word down into segments (syllables) should be noted as well. **Semantic analysis** is the student's ability to use picture clues as word identification. It also includes the ability to predict unknown words by using context in combination with letter-sound relationships. Information from these areas, as well as the other areas of reading, should help determine current abilities and where reading instruction should begin.

CONVENTIONAL LITERACY: PHONICS

There are numerous reading programs that focus on phonics. However, not all phonics programs are good. Some general guidelines that indicate an effective reading program that focuses on phonics has the following characteristics:

- The reading program explicitly and systematically instructs students on relating letters and sounds, breaking spoken words into sounds, and blending sounds to form words.
- The reading program helps students understand the reasons for learning the relationship between letters and sounds.
- The reading program helps students apply their knowledge of phonics as they read words, sentences, and text.
- The reading program helps students apply what they learn about sounds and letters to their own writing.
- The reading program allows for adaptations to meet the student's needs.
- The reading program includes systematic phonics instruction as well as a wide variety of skills (e.g., alphabetic knowledge, phonemic awareness, vocabulary development, reading of text). (Armbruster, Lehr, & Osborn, 2001)

Regardless of the precise program being used to teach phonics and reading, it can be very difficult to teach students with severe speech and physical impairments phonics. One approach that adapts phonics instruction for students with severe speech and physical impairments is the Nonverbal Reading Approach (Heller, Fredrick, & Diggs, 1999).

FIGURE 13–10
Use of Nonverbal Reading Approach with guided practice for initial instruction

GUIDED PRACTICE	
Process	**Example Script**
	1. T: "Let's look at some new words together."
	2. T: "Look at this word." (Teacher shows student entire word.) *Example: man*
Active participation	3. T: "Let's sound it out loud together." Teacher points to each letter saying the letter sound out loud, along with the student making the sounds, approximations, or noises.
Internal speech: letter sounds	4. T: Teacher shows only the first letter of the word (by covering other letters with a piece of paper) and says, "Say in your head this sound." Teacher says the sound out loud, and student looks at card without making any sound. (Note: If the word has a blend (*st, sh,* etc.), these are shown together and pronounced as one sound.) *Example: m* *Teacher says "mmm." Student says "mmm" in his head.*
	5. T: Shows the next letter of the word by moving the paper, and repeats Step 4 for each letter (phoneme) for the entire word. *Example: ma (Teacher uncovers next letter.)* *Teacher says "aaa." Student says "aaa" in his head.* *Example: man (Teacher uncovers next letter.)* *Teacher says "nnn." Student says "nnn" in his head.*
Internal speech: blending slowly	6. T: "Now, in your head, say it all together. Don't stop between sounds." Teacher points to each sound and slowly sounds out the word out loud as student sounds out word using internal speech. *Example: man* *Teacher says "mmmaaannn" while pointing to each letter sound, and the student says "mmmaaannn" in his head.*
Internal speech: blending fast	7. T: "Now, say it in your head fast." Teacher says the entire word out loud. *Example: Teacher says "man" as student says "man" in his head.*
Additional instruction	8. Teacher may do additional instruction here: comparing the word to other learned words, pointing out certain sounds, showing picture of what a man is, etc. *Example: Student had learned the word "mat" and teacher shows how the words begin in a similar fashion and how the ending sound makes it different.*

Adapting Phonic Instruction: The Nonverbal Reading Approach

There are few reading strategies adapted specifically for students with severe speech and physical impairments that address phonics instruction. One strategy is the Nonverbal Reading Approach, which utilizes active participation, internal speech, diagnostic distractor arrays, error analysis, and additional instruction in conjunction with specific adaptations and assistive technology to promote reading skills (Heller, Fredrick, & Diggs, 1999; Heller, Fredrick, Tumlin, & Brineman, 2002).

Active Participation. Some students with severe speech and physical impairments are able to make noises or approximations of letter sounds. In the first part of the Nonverbal Reading Approach, students are shown the word and the teacher instructs the student to sound it out loud along with the teacher, who makes the appropriate letter sounds (see Figure 13–10). This step allows the student to actively participate in the process (and for some students, may actually help improve their pronunciation, although no correction is usually given of the student's attempt to say a letter sound). Since students with severe physical disabilities usually lack the motor ability to correctly pronounce the letter sounds and they are often concentrating on the physical effort to make sounds, this step does not necessarily help students learn the correct letter sounds or sound out the targeted word. However, it does show the teacher that the student is actively engaged. For students who are unable to speak at all (e.g., those with anarthria), this step may be omitted.

Internal Speech. When students are not physically able to correctly verbalize phonemes for sounding out words, they can be taught to use internal speech. **Internal speech** is the process of silently speaking to oneself or saying something "in your head." Since there has been research demonstrating the development of sound-blending skills in the absence of speech production abilities (Smith, 1989), internal speech is a useful strategy to teach students to say the sound "in their head" or "to themselves" as they are sounding out words. It is important that when students say a word using internal speech, they do not verbalize, but concentrate on saying it in their head to "hear" the sounds internally the way the letter(s) should be pronounced.

Students are initially guided through the process of using internal speech (see Figure 13–10). The student is shown the first letter (by covering the rest of the word with paper or pointing to the first letter) and is told to "say in your head this sound." When guiding the student, the teacher says the sound aloud while the student is saying it to himself or herself. The next letter is shown and the student is instructed to "say in your head this sound" as the teacher says it aloud. This continues until the word is completely sounded out. The next step is to blend the word slowly. The student is then told to "say it in your head, all together" while the teacher sounds it all out together. Lastly, the word is blended quickly and the student is told to "say it in your head fast" as the teacher says the word.

Additional Instruction. Additional instruction may be given after the student sounds out the word using internal speech. This may include comparing that word to a previously learned word, pointing out prefixes or suffixes, explaining a rule or way to think of the word, giving a definition, and/or using the word in a sentence, as well as writing and spelling activities. Since the emphasis on reading should be reading more than single words, using the words within sentences becomes important. The teacher follows the selected reading curriculum using the Nonverbal Reading Approach.

Evaluation: Guiding Through the Process. When evaluating the student, the above sequence is used, but the teacher does not provide the sounds or say the word. The teacher begins by guiding the student through actively saying the sounds aloud to promote active participation. The teacher continues with the next part of the Nonverbal Reading Approach, by showing the student each letter of the word and having the student use internal speech to sound out the letters. The teacher then instructs the student to blend the sounds together slowly, then blend the sounds together fast, all while using internal speech. By continuing to take the student through this process, the student is learning a strategy to sound out words (see Figure 13–11).

Evaluation Using Diagnostic Distractor Arrays. Up to this point, the teacher really doesn't know if the student is learning the word or actually using the method to sound out words using internal speech. In order to determine if the student is learning the word, the teacher will give the student a **diagnostic distractor array.** Since students are unable to verbally produce their answers, they need to be given an array of choices from which to select their answers to the teacher's questions during reading activities. A diagnostic distractor array is a list of alternative choices provided to the student, either orally or in writing, which are designed to evaluate the student's acquisition of the targeted material (i.e., targeted words). The student's selected choice from the array should indicate that the student does or does not know the answer. In addition, if the student does not know the answer, the selection from the diagnostic distractor array should indicate the student's error patterns.

Diagnostic distractor arrays typically consist of the correct answer and two or more additional items that have been explicitly selected to determine that the student knows the target word. For example, if the student was learning the word "ball" and the choices in the array were "cat," "ball," "dog," and "tree," the selection of the word "ball" tells us only that the student can accurately select the correct first letter ("b") of the word, but may not know the word "ball" from the word "big." If the distractor array was "bill," "ball," "bell," and "bail," the correct selection may tell us only that the student could select the correct vowel sound of the word.

Diagnostic distractor arrays should be carefully chosen to assure the teacher that the student knows the word. Initially, a diagnostic distractor array may begin by including a very similar word, a word with a different ending, and a word with just the vowel sound dif-

FIGURE 13–11
Use of Nonverbal Reading Approach for evaluation

EVALUATING STUDENT KNOWLEDGE	
Process	Example Script
	1. T: "I'm going to give you some words to read. First, you will sound out the word, then I'll give you some spoken choices and you tell me which is correct. OK? Here we go."
	2. T: "Look at this word." (Teacher shows student entire word.)
Active participation	3. T: "Sound it out loud" (Teacher points to each letter as student makes sounds, approximations, or noises.)
Promoting internal speech	3. T: Teacher shows only the first letter of the word (by covering other letters with a piece of paper) and says, "Say in your head this sound."
	4. T: Teacher shows the next letter of the word by moving a card and repeats steps for each letter (or phoneme) of the entire word.
	5. T: "Now, in your head, say it all together. Don't stop between sounds." (Teacher points to each sound.)
	6. T: "Now, say it in your head fast."
Diagnostic distractor array	7. T: "I'll give you four choices. Listen to your choices. Your choices are: [choice 1], [choice 2], [choice 3], [choice 4]. Is it [choice 1]? [Waits for student's response]. Is it [choice 2]?" etc.
Data	8. Student indicates his or her answer and teacher writes student's selection on the data sheet.
Error analysis and correction	9. T: If student gives correct answer, confirm correct selection. If student gives incorrect answer, reteach using guided practice to sound out the word together and reteach any specific area missed based on the word selected from the distractor array. (For example, if student selected "mat" for "man," teacher would reteach "n" and "t" and emphasize looking at the last part of the word. Next time this word is evaluated, the distractor array will contain "mat" as a distractor, as well as other words with "t" and different ending sounds.
	10. Look across data for any error patterns and reteach problem areas.

ferent. For example, if the target word was "ball," the distractor array could consist of "bill," "ball," "doll," and "bat." The distractor array would later be changed based upon the types of errors the student is making. One study (Heller, Fredrick, & Diggs, 1999) demonstrated the dramatic differences in words the students chose to select, based upon indiscriminate, dissimilar distractor arrays and diagnostic distractor arrays. This study showed that inadequate distractor arrays can leave the false impression that the student knows the word, when he or she may only know the first letter or some other aspect of it.

Error Analysis and Correction. After the student selects his or her choice from the diagnostic array, any incorrect answers are corrected. However, it is important to determine the type of error the student is making, which can be done by conducting an error analysis. An **error analysis** is a careful examination of the type of errors the student is making, as well as the presence of any error patterns occurring across time. Detection of errors and error patterns will help guide the teacher to select correction strategies and reevaluate the student's knowledge by changing the diagnostic distractor array. In the previous example, suppose the student selects "bat" instead of "ball." The student is either confusing "t" and "l" sounds, not sounding out the entire word and blending it, or not attending. Correction may take the form of providing more instruction with the "l" and "t" sounds, reinforcing blending skills, and/or teaching the student to attend to all of the sounds in the word (see Figure 13–11). When reevaluating the student, the distractor array should be changed to include more differences in the last sound, such as "ball," "ban," "bat," "back."

Sometimes the student may confuse the vowels. Vowels are often the most difficult to learn, and the student may require additional prompts. This is especially true when using words with short vowel sounds and dialects that make it difficult to hear the difference. The teacher may provide more-intense instruction, or teach the student to temporarily use a vowel sheet (showing the vowel and a picture representing its sound) or an auditory vowel sheet (in which the vowel sounds are on an AAC device, so when it's pushed, the correct sound is made). When evaluating the word again, the distractor array may be changed to show words with different vowel sounds to determine if the student really knows the word.

Analysis of the student's errors may show a directional error. For example, a student may confuse "ma" and "am" and "ton" and "not." In this case, the student is reading from the right to left instead of the left to right. A red dot can be placed under the first letter until the student has more practice reading.

Assistive Technology and Modifications. The final aspect of the Nonverbal Reading Approach is the use of assistive technology and any needed modifications to ensure proper assessment, instruction, comprehension, and practice of target reading material. Assistive technology to promote reading may include the use of augmentative communication devices, devices to allow access to choices, and computer programs to facilitate responses. Each of these must be individually selected and assessed as to its accuracy and effectiveness in facilitating the reading process.

Nonverbal Reading Approach Using Direct Instruction. The components of active participation, internal speech, additional instruction, diagnostic distractor arrays, error analysis and correction, and assistive technology of the Nonverbal Reading Approach can be used within most reading curricula. In one study (Heller, Fredrick, & Diggs, 1999), the Nonverbal Reading Approach was used with direct instruction curricula (Reading Mastery by SRA and Corrective Reading by SRA) for three students with severe speech and physical impairments. The components of the program were incorporated with learning to decode words. Overall, all three students were found to make dramatic gains as compared to their previous reading progress. The students in the study learned a strategy to decode (sound out) words, and over time they learned to automatically recognize words without needing to decode them. This is the goal of phonics instruction: to provide a strategy for students to decode words and learn them and, once having learned them, to be able to automatically recognize them. There was a high level of satisfaction from the teachers, parents, and students using this approach. Comprehension was assessed through questioning and other modalities (see the section entitled "Conventional Literacy: Text Comprehension," which appears later in this chapter).

Nonverbal Reading Approach with Sight-Word Instruction. The Nonverbal Reading Approach can also be used when a sight-word reading approach is being used for high-frequency words, or words that do not follow the rules of phonics. When using these approaches, the student is shown the entire word and is instructed to "say in your head this word" as the teacher says the entire word aloud. The student is also typically instructed to spell the word on his or her AAC device. When evaluating whether the student has learned the word, the teacher tells the student to look at the word and say it in his or her head. A diagnostic distractor array is given (as described above). Any errors are immediately corrected. An error analysis is performed and any errors or error patterns are addressed through systematic instruction. Any needed assistive technology is incorporated within reading instruction.

Students have been successfully taught to look at the word as the teacher says it and type it, without sounding it out. This method, however, has not been found as effective for beginning readers as using a phonics approach in which the student views each phoneme sequentially and then synthesizes them into a real word (Berninger, 1986). However, a sight-word approach that emphasizes the student's saying the word in his or her head and spelling the word may be very appropriate for students who are unable to learn words phonetically or for words that do not follow phonics rules. Also, students who use AAC devices that display symbols and printed words may learn some words by a sight word approach, due to the continual exposure of the word and its association to a symbol.

Sequence of Teaching Using the Nonverbal Reading Approach. Over time, the student will begin to learn the process of sounding out words using the

Nonverbal Reading Approach. He or she will also gain competency with some words and progress from words to sentences. There is a six-part competency process that the student will need to be guided through to improve his or her reading skills. These six areas are (a) being guided to sound out words using the Nonverbal Reading Approach, (b) sounding out words using the Nonverbal Reading Approach independently, (c) recognizing words without sounding out (automaticity) (d) reading a line of print and stopping at unknown words, (e) checking for accuracy and comprehension, and (f) spelling and writing target words.

In this sequence, students are first guided to learn the process of sounding out words using internal speech as taught through the Nonverbal Reading Approach. Over time, the student should learn to do this process without the teacher guiding the student. Some students have programmed on their AAC device the steps of the process (i.e., active participation, sounding out each sound using internal speech, blending slowly using internal speech, blending fast using internal speech). The AAC device is then used to inform the teacher of what steps are being performed or as a reminder of what to do.

As the student learns words, he or she will be able to recognize certain words without sounding them out (automaticity). When the word has been taught, the student may be shown a word and be asked, "Do you know what this word is?" If no, the teacher may say, "What do we need to do? We need to sound it out." The teacher then guides the student through the protocol with guided practice using the Nonverbal Reading Approach (or instructs the student to do so if he or she has learned the process). If the student indicates that he or she knows the word, the teacher may assess whether the student actually does and follow the protocol for evaluating student knowledge (by using diagnostic distractor arrays).

It is important that learned words are put together into sentences (especially those words with which the student has achieved automaticity). If the student can point as he or she reads, this will help the teacher know where the student is when reading the sentence, as well as help the student keep his or her place. If the student is unable to point, the teacher may initially point to the words with the student nodding or making a motion as he or she is ready to go to the next word. This will help give the teacher an idea of how quickly the student is moving from word to word. When several sentences are put together, the student may get lost as to which line he or she is reading. The teacher may use the underline strategy discussed under the Physical Efficiency section, so that the student can read independently without losing his or her place.

When moving to reading sentences and later paragraphs, it is important to teach the student to stop at unknown words and sound them out using the Nonverbal Reading Approach. If the student is unsure of the word, it is important that he or she learns to alert the teacher. If the student is pointing, he or she may stop on the word, and if he or she can't figure it out, make a noise or alert the teacher with his or her AAC device. If the student is unable to point, the teacher can ask if the unknown word is on this line, this line, or this line while pointing to each line. When the student indicates which line it is on, the teacher can then point to each word until the student indicates the word he or she is having problems with. To help teach students to develop these skills, teachers will often put in unfamiliar words or words that do not follow phonics code in order to teach the student to ask for help.

Teaching reading also involves checking for accuracy and comprehension. When a student is reading a sentence using internal speech, it is important to verify that the student is actually reading the words correctly. When the student is unable to speak, it can be assessed in several different ways. Some of these include the teacher asking the following types of questions:

- Point to __________ [the word].
- What word is this? (Uses a diagnostic distractor array—e.g., *cat, can, con, kit.*)
- Where did the boy go? (Questions for comprehension.)
- Point to a picture that describes what this means.

Further information on comprehension is found later in this chapter.

In addition to teaching phonics and comprehension, it is critical that the student is also taught to spell and write targeted words. In the next chapter, spelling strategies are presented to help teach students to spell the words being taught. Students who have learned to use internal speech through the Nonverbal Reading Approach can also use this approach to aid with spelling. Students are taught to say the word in their head that they want to spell (using internal speech). Next, students say the word slowly using internal speech, by elongating the phonemes. (Instead of blending slowly, they are segmenting the word slowly.) Students are next encouraged to say the phonemes even slower so they can be identified. Finally, students write the sounds they hear.

Teaching Multiple-Syllable Words

As students gain reading competency and the vocabulary gets more difficult, they often encounter difficulty decoding longer words. One strategy, developed by Archer, Gleason, and Vachon (2000), is as follows:

1. Circle the word parts (prefixes) at the beginning of the word.
2. Circle word parts (suffixes) at the end of the word.
3. Underline the letters for vowel sounds in the rest of the word.
4. Say the parts of the word.
5. Say the parts fast.
6. Make it a real word.

Learning to look at the root for meaning, as well as learning prefixes and suffixes, can also aid in comprehension of these longer words. Archer, Gleason, and Vachon's specialized reading program, "REWARDS: Reading Excellence: Word Attack and Rate Development Strategies" is one example of a program that targets teaching decoding long words.

CONVENTIONAL LITERACY: VOCABULARY INSTRUCTION

There are four types of vocabulary: listening vocabulary, speaking vocabulary, reading vocabulary, and writing vocabulary. Students often learn vocabulary through engaging in daily oral language, listening to adults reading to them, and reading on their own. Although children learn much of their vocabulary indirectly, students still need to have direct vocabulary instruction (Armbruster, Lehr, & Osborn, 2001). For many students with severe speech and physical impairments, direct systematic instruction of vocabulary is crucial since they may not indirectly pick up vocabulary as readily when they are not engaging in oral language or lack ability to ask for meanings of words.

Teachers should systematically teach specific vocabulary as well as methods for students to learn word meanings. Specific word instruction may include introduction of the vocabulary for the week (or appropriate period of time) as well as teaching specific vocabulary that the student will encounter in a story, book, or lesson. Presenting the target vocabulary in several different contexts and activities will often help the student to learn the word. In addition to specific instruction, students should be taught to use a dictionary (book or computer based) to find the meaning of unknown words. Teaching students how to determine the word meaning from context clues or from prefixes and suffixes can also aid in word learning.

Promoting Vocabulary Development with Symbols

Symbol Reading Page. Symbol reading pages may be used to verify that students who are nonverbal are reading the words correctly. A symbol reading page consists of pictures or symbols that represent the words the student is learning to read. (The page may be constructed of paper, or be included on an AAC device as a separate page or overlay, or be programmed into a computer.) The symbol reading page does not have any print on it, only symbols or pictures. Upon reading a written sentence, the student demonstrates his or her reading ability by choosing a series of the pictures or symbols on the symbol reading page that represent each word (and word ending) that was read. For example, if a student read the written sentence, "She is petting the sheep and singing," he or she would point to each corresponding picture or symbol on the symbol reading page: "she" symbol, "is" symbol, "pet" symbol, "ing" symbol, "the" symbol, "sheep" symbol, "and" symbol, "sing" symbol, "ing" symbol. (Notice that the student had separate "ing" ending symbols that were used in addition to the nouns.) (See Figure 13–12a.) A second sheet is often made by the teacher as a reference for others who are unfamiliar with the symbols or for use in various reading activities. (See Figure 13–12b.)

Reference Symbol Page. Another type of reading page or overlay is one that is used for reference to look up unknown words (also referred to as a picture dictionary). This type of reading page or overlay has both symbols and print together and is used for reference, or as a dictionary for students who do not recall the word.

FIGURE 13–12

An example of a reading page. (a) After the student reads a written sentence, he or she points to the corresponding symbol to demonstrate correct word identification. (b) The reading page with words can be used as a reference or for reading activities

(a)

	truck	for	had	did	
he	sheep	the	has	get	
his	cash	a	is	got	yes
she	clock	and	up	go	pet
her	gas	no		sent	sing
I	hill	not		this	-ing

(b)

Note. Made with Boardmaker™ and the Picture Communication Symbols. © 1981–2000, Mayer-Johnson, Inc., P.O. Box 1579, Solana Beach, CA 92075 U.S.A. Phone (619) 550-0084. Reprinted with permission.

These reference reading pages help with learning the meaning, as well as being used for reference to remember the word or help with spelling. They are especially helpful for students who have difficulty reading the printed definition (and lack software with voice output to read the definition) and for students who were initially introduced to the word combined with a symbol. These reference pages or overlays can easily be constructed with appropriate software, photographs, drawings, or pictures.

Word and Sentence Construction Page. A word or sentence construction page may also be used to promote learning vocabulary and using vocabulary. These pages or overlays can be used to construct and read words, phrases, or sentences. These overlays consist of words or parts of words that are used to group together to make words or sentences. When used with an AAC device or computer, voice output can confirm the construction of the new word or sentence. For example, in Figure 13–13, the student is asked to construct and read words from the word group "at" (words rhyming with "hat"). The student is encouraged to make and read different words within the group, such as "hat," "cat," "sat." This particular configuration can be used in conjunction with reading *The Cat in the Hat* by Dr. Seuss (Musselwhite & King-DeBaun, 1997). For AAC devices with voice output, the student has immediate feedback if the selected word was the desired one.

FIGURE 13–13

An example of a word display overlay that can be used with the book, *The Cat in the Hat*

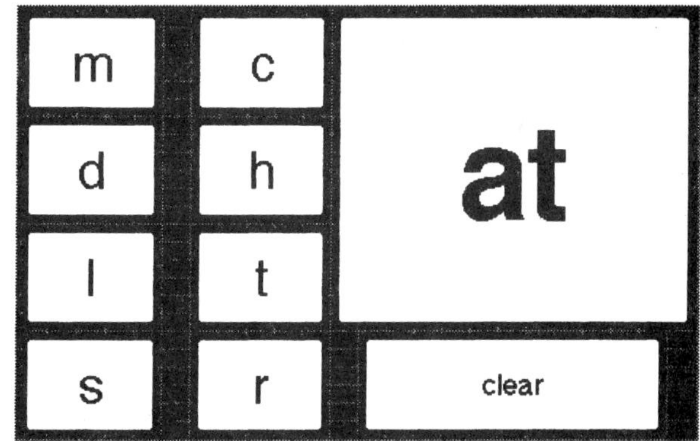

Note. From *Emergent Literary Success: Merging Technology and Whole Language for Students with Disabilities* by C. Musselwhite and P. King-DeBaun, 1997, Park City UT: Creative Communicating. Reprinted with permission.

CONVENTIONAL LITERACY: FLUENCY

Fluency refers to the ability of a student to read the word, sentence, or text in an accurate and quick manner. Students who are reading fluently are usually recognizing the words and exhibiting automaticity. Students demonstrate fluency when they read quickly, effortlessly, and with meaning. Readers who are not reading the material at a fluent level typically read word by word, often having difficulty with comprehension since so much time is spent on decoding the words. The reading rates listed in Figure 13–9 provide some guidelines as to typical reading rates.

Teachers should systematically teach and encourage fluent reading. This often requires selecting material at an appropriate reading level (often at an independent reading level as discussed under Assessment of Conventional Reading Skills) and having the student orally read and reread the material several times until a certain level of fluency is reached. Rereading as many as four times is sufficient for most students without disabilities (Armbruster, et al., 2001). For students who are unable to read aloud because of their speech impairments, the teacher should encourage rereading of materials silently with actively timing students and checking that the material is actually being read.

There are several activities that may assist with increasing fluency. One way is for the student and adult to read the material together, with the adult providing a model of fluent reading. Reading aloud in a group is another strategy, as is reading with another classmate. Repeated readings of the textual material with the use of computer software programs that read the text aloud has been shown to increase fluency as well (Patillo, Heller, & Smith, 2004). A low-tech solution would be reading along with a tape recorder.

Providing Sufficient Practice. Students with severe speech and physical impairments may not receive sufficient practice to decode, learn vocabulary, or increase fluency. This is especially the case when they have a slow rate of response. For any reading program to be successful, it is important that enough instructional time and practice be provided. In some situations, the student will be in a regular reading class, but may also need some individualized time or concentrated instruction in a small reading group to learn to read. Careful assessment of progress will determine how to best meet the student's needs.

Students should also be provided a means to practice on their own. Some students may benefit from the use of a card reader, in which they read the word, then put the card through the card reader to check if they were right. This can also be done on a computer with voice output. After reading the story, students can have the story read to them using software (e.g., Write:Outloud, manufactured by Don Johnston, Inc.) that highlights the words or sentences as they are read aloud by the computer.

Students should also be motivated to read and be provided time to read on their own. Having easy-to-read books available that are of interest to the student can help promote reading. High-interest, low-vocabulary books are ideal. Books can also be scanned into the computer for ease of access. Once on the computer, voice output support can be used as needed. For older readers, teachers can use series that provide high-interest books that are designed to highlight the words as they are being read and motivate children to want to read (e.g., the Start-to-Finish Books manufactured by Don Johnston, Inc.).

CONVENTIONAL LITERACY: TEXT COMPREHENSION

Students with severe speech and physical disabilities may have experiential deficits that interfere with their comprehension abilities. The determination of a student's comprehension of written material begins with the assessment of whether the student comprehends individual words, and progresses to determine whether the student understands phrases and sentences. Lastly, the student's comprehension of paragraphs, passages, and stories is assessed.

There are several different types of information that can be checked for comprehension, including detail, vocabulary definition and application, figurative language definition and application, main idea, summary, sequence, comparative relationships, cause/effect relationships, conclusions, applications, analysis, synthesis, and evaluation. Students may be evaluated on whether they understand these various types of information or relationships found within the story. However, different types of comprehension ability are often required to extract the intended meaning.

Comprehension can be divided into three main categories. These categories of comprehension are textually explicit (literal) comprehension, textually implicit comprehension, and scripturally implicit comprehension (Bos & Vaughn, 2002). **Textually explicit comprehension** refers to literal understanding of what is written. It is also known as literal comprehension. This typically includes understanding the meaning of words, identifying the facts in the text and the sequence of events, and being able to summarize the material. **Textually implicit comprehension** (or inferential comprehension) refers to the ability to infer information. In some stories, this may include identifying the main idea, drawing conclusions, and making predictions based upon the material presented. **Scripturally implicit comprehension** requires the reader to draw upon background knowledge to aid in comprehension of the material. Scripturally implicit comprehension questions often include application, analysis, synthesis, and evaluation. Often these three types of comprehension may overlap in several areas. It is important for the teacher to understand the type of comprehension being requested.

Teaching Comprehension

Providing Experiences, Explanations, and Materials. It should never be taken for granted that students with physical, health, or multiple disabilities have the same experiences on which to build literacy. A student can easily decode a word and not know its meaning. A student can also match a word to a symbol and still be unsure of what it actually means. It is therefore important to provide information and material on the words, sentences, and concepts being presented. Continual checking for understanding is crucial so that the student will understand what is being read.

Checking for Literacy Comprehension. After students have read a sentence or passage, their comprehension can be assessed through questions about factual information from the story. For students who are nonverbal and have a long response time accessing their AAC device, response time can be increased by numbering the words in the passage. For example, when asked who went to the beach, the student can quickly answer by indicating number 1 on his AAC device or number board. When asked what she was doing there, the student can reply "7" and "10." When asked if Mary was happy at the beach, the student can answer yes or no. When asked how he knows Mary was not happy, the student can answer "19."

1 2 3 4 5 6 7 8 9 10
Mary went to the beach to find her lost dog.
11 12 13 14 15 16 17 18 19
She couldn't find him, so she started to cry.

Other forms of literal comprehension can easily be checked as well. To check for sequencing, the student can be given a series of numbered or lettered sentences. The student would indicate (by pointing, scanning, etc.) the order by giving the number (e.g., 3, 4, 1, 5, 2). To check the main idea, the student can be given several sentences to choose from and select the one that gives the main idea.

When checking for textually implicit comprehension (inference), choices can again be provided. However, if the student has a comprehensive AAC device and has literacy skills (and so can spell out words not on the device), it is often preferred that the student answer with the AAC device to express original thoughts. However, constructing messages does take time. Waiting for the student to construct the message may put undue pressure on the student, as everyone may stare at the student, waiting for a response. In some situations it may be preferable for the teacher to ask the student the comprehension question and state that while the student is getting the answer ready on the AAC device, the teacher will proceed and ask a few other questions of other students. If this technique of going on while the student constructs the message is used, it is critical that the teacher's following questions be very easy or unimportant questions. This is because the student will not be able to fully listen to the teacher or the discussion while constructing the answer to the question he or she was asked. In some instances, a different technique of providing the student with questions ahead of time so that the answers can already be programmed into the AAC device may be used.

Scripturally implicit comprehension can be most difficult for students who lack common experiences. When a student misses comprehension questions that are scripturally implicit, it is important that the teacher determines whether the student lacked the background knowledge to know the answer. This missing knowledge should be taught and the wrong answer not be counted against him or her. The question can be asked again once the necessary background information is taught.

Students should be taught to be active readers for comprehension. When teaching and assessing comprehension, the teacher must first ensure that the student has already mastered decoding the words. If the student is still struggling with decoding, he or she will be unable to read for comprehension. The material being read should be at an appropriate level to accurately assess for comprehension.

Basic Comprehension Strategy

There are many comprehension strategies that can easily be used by teachers. The most basic strategy is a three-part process, represented by the saying "Let's get the BIG picture." BIG stands for: Before reading, Investigate what's going on during reading, and Get the big picture when you're done. At each of these steps, the teacher may encourage the student and provide experiences and instructions to enhance comprehension abilities.

Before Reading. Prior to reading, reading passages should be previewed and the student's background knowledge tapped. Discussions regarding the text's topic should occur and experiences or information to enrich the student's background can be provided. Brainstorming activities regarding the upcoming topic may also occur. Time should be given to allow students with AAC devices to give their input.

Students may also be given advanced organizers to aid in their reading. The teacher may tell them things to look for: "Read closely for what Mary was doing on the beach," or "I'm going to ask you who the main characters are." These can help students focus on the relevant information while reading and prepare them to answer comprehension questions.

When difficulties are anticipated with specific sections of the text, teachers may provide some advanced instruction. Unknown or potentially difficult vocabulary should be identified. These words and their meanings can be placed on a separate list for teaching and reference. Any difficult text can be preceded by advance organizers that summarize the upcoming content and relate it to earlier textual material. It is crucial that students using AAC devices have access to appropriate vocabulary or symbols to allow them to ask questions about what will be read and what they do not understand.

During Reading: Investigate What's Going On. During reading, students should learn to self-question and monitor their understanding of the text. One type of monitoring strategy is self-questioning. A strategy suggested by Alvermann and colleagues (1989) uses a series of questions. Students are taught to think ahead (with such questions as "What do I already know about the topic?" and "What do I want to find out?"), and to think while reading (with such questions as "What have I read about so far?" "Do I understand it?" and "If not, what should I do?") and think back (with such questions as "Have I learned what I wanted to learn?" and "How can I use what I read?"). These questions can be listed out on a card for the student to access. Some students with AAC may program them into the device as an auditory reminder of each step.

Another questioning strategy teaches students to think of the *wh* and *how* questions when reading a story (Clark, Deshler, Schumaker, Alley, & Warner, 1984; Nolan, Alley, & Clark, 1980). These would include who, what, where, when, and how questions. Students may think of these as they read the material, and answer the *wh* and *how* questions after completing the material. For younger students, an answer sheet with each of the *wh* and *how* questions and their corresponding pictures may be used (see Figure 13–14). The pictures used to represent the *who* and *how* questions may be programmed into the AAC device to help the student communicate about them.

A more expanded version of using the *wh* and *how* questions for comprehension uses a combination of a summarization strategy and self-monitoring instructions (Jitendra, Hoppes, & Xin, 2000). In this strategy, the students are first taught to name the person in a single passage and categorize the action (by telling the main thing they did). Next, they are taught a main-idea-generation rule in which they name the group and tell the main thing the group did (over a series of passages). Next, they also examine the passage utilizing the *wh* and *how* questions. A prompt card is used by the students to remind them to look for the subject of group and the action of the group

FIGURE 13–14
This questioning strategy may be used as a prereading activity

Student Name: ______________________

Title: ______________________

Who?	
What?	
Where?	
When?	
Why?	
How?	

Note. From C. S. Bos & S. Vaughn, *Strategies for Teaching Students with Learning and Behavior Problems* (4e). Copyright © 1998 by Allyn & Bacon, Reprinted by permission.

as well as the *wh* and *how* questions. To help students perform the procedure correctly, a self-monitoring checklist can be used in which students place a check mark on the card after reading the passage, using the prompt card, applying the strategy, and writing the main idea.

A third strategy uses story maps (Baumann & Bergeron, 1993; Emery, 1996; Idol, 1987) (see Figure 13–15). A story map provides a visual outline of information for students while they are reading. It is based on the idea that stories are composed of fairly predictable components that can be organized in a set fashion, such as identification of the setting (characters, time, place), the problem, the goal, the action, and the outcome.

Mnemonic strategies have been used to foster comprehension abilities. For example, STORE is a mnemonic that aids with retelling a story and finding relevant information in it. It stands for:

Setting (who, what, when, where),

Trouble (what is the trouble to be solved),

Order of action (what happened when),

Resolution (or outcome), and

End (what is the ending of the story) (Bos & Vaughn, 2002).

FIGURE 13–15
This story map can be filled out and used to provide a visual outline of information to help reading comprehension

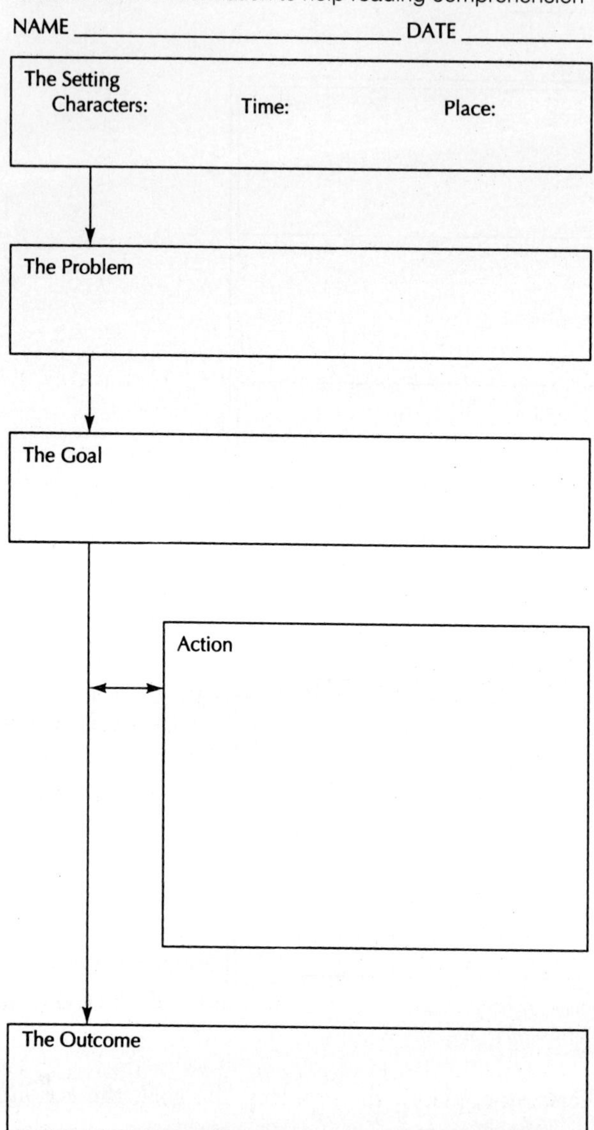

Note. From "Group Story Mapping: A Comprehension Strategy for Both Skilled and Unskilled Readers" by L. Idol, 1987, *Journal of Learning Disabilities, 20,* p. 196–205. Copyright 1987 by PRO-ED, Inc. Reprinted with permission.

After Reading: Get the BIG Picture When You're Done. After reading, students should determine whether they are able to answer the questions or organizers used to assist them in comprehending the material. Teachers may ask a variety of questions and model how that information can be obtained through reading strategies. Teachers may generate discussions after reading the material to encourage the students to generate more questions and ideas. Students may also be encouraged to summarize or restate the story. For students with AAC devices who take a long time to respond, they may be offered multiple-choice answers to identify main ideas, or specific events or sequences of events.

SOFTWARE AND SPECIALIZED CURRICULA FOR READING

There are many software programs that may be used in supplemental reading instruction. For example, Reader Rabbit Reading (manufactured by Riverdeep–The Learning Company) helps build functional reading and spelling skills, as well as word recognition, spelling, and vocabulary skills, through a fun game format. The Stickybear software (manufactured by Optimum Resource) has separate programs in such areas as phonics, spelling, typing, learning the alphabet, reading comprehension, science, and math. Phonics Based Reading (manufactured by Lexia Learning System, Inc.) provides hundreds of exercises in phonemic awareness, sound-symbol correspondence, word-attack skills, and comprehension skills, and includes about 2,000 vocabulary words.

One beginning reading software program that is fully supportive of alternate access and integrates both sight words and phonics is Balanced Literacy (manufactured by IntelliTools). It is a full-year program in beginning literacy that integrates guided reading, supported writing, and phonics activities. It targets kindergarten to second grade. A core vocabulary of 100 sight words and 500 decodable words are taught and built around animal themes.

Increasing automaticity of word recognition and vocabulary knowledge has been suggested through the use of educational software programs that use speech output and provide students with experience in manipulating sounds and syllables and hearing the results of their efforts (Foley, 1993). Computers and word-processing programs may be used to promote literacy through educational software that develops decoding and encoding skills and that can be "read aloud" to students (Foley, 1993; Steelman, Pierce, & Koppenhaver, 1993). The Start-to-Finish book series (published by Don Johnston) provides high-interest books at a lower reading level. Words are highlighted and read through voice output as they are displayed on the computer screen. Individual words can be selected and read aloud. To increase vocabulary knowledge, students may be taught to use a dictionary or thesaurus that is online or a print version. Additional software is available that targets vocabulary acquisition, such as First Words—Sterling Edition (manufactured by Laureate Learning Systems, Inc.).

There are several different programs that may be used to enhance comprehension skills. For example, Comprehension Connection (manufactured by Milliken Publishing Co.) assists the student to study the story from different perspectives and provides several types of assistance such as graphic organizers, vocabulary assistance, and an easier version of the text. Questions for the student cover such areas as vocabulary comprehension, finding the main idea, and recalling inferential and literal facts. Another software program is Comprehension Power (manufactured by Taylor Associates), which consists of 180 reading selections that are aimed at increasing comprehension and study skills. Lessons cover vocabulary review, skimming, timed reading, and comprehension activities.

There are numerous reading curricula that are successfully used with students with physical disabilities. Often these curricula are the same ones used in the general education class. However, sometimes additional or more specific instruction is needed. For example, Reading Mastery (published by SRA) has been used in both general education and special education. It uses a Direct Instruction reading approach to teach explicit phonics and comprehension through a special alphabet designed to decrease confusion between letters and letter sounds.

Some curricula are specifically targeted for students with mental retardation. For example, the Phonics Remedial Reading Lesson (Kirk, Kirk, & Minskill, 1985) was designed to teach phonic skills to students with mild mental retardation through the use of overlearning, corrective feedback, verbal mediation, and multiple sensory learning. It is primarily used as a means for teaching students to identify unknown words. Another curriculum that targets students with mental retardation is the Edmark Reading Program (published by Pro-Ed). This is a sight-word approach curriculum that is designed to teach 150 sight words, plus the endings. An errorless approach is used, in which the student must make gross discriminations, then finer ones (as seen in

FIGURE 13–16
Example of an errorless discrimination strategy

1. ____	milk	____
2. milk	____	____
3. km	____	milk
4. milk	xid	mli
5. klm	il	milk
6. mk	milk	mlk
7. milk	ilk	mil
8. mill	milk	mark

Figure 13–16). These may be adapted for students with physical and multiple impairments.

FUNCTIONAL LITERACY: READING

Some students may be candidates for a functional literacy program. Functional literacy programs focus on reading and writing skills that are needed to increase independence in daily living (Koenig & Holbrook, 1993). Since students vary as to their involvement in differing environments, and the literacy requirements for these environments vary, selection of key words to teach may be based upon an ecological assessment.

Vocabulary Selection: Ecological Assessment

An ecological assessment is an inventory of environments and activities in which the student engages, now or in the future. Identified in these environments is the print the student will encounter and need to be able to read to succeed in the task.

An ecological assessment is developed for each of the following broad curriculum domains: personal and domestic; community; leisure; and vocational. The ecological inventory consists of conducting a four-step sequence: (1) listing current and future student environments, (2) identifying the relevant subenvironments within each environment, (3) listing the priority activities that occur within each subenvironment, and (4) identifying the written words the student will encounter (by needing to either read the words or write the words).

Identification of Environments and Subenvironments. Through interviews with the student, parents, and the other education team members, the teacher identifies (a) current school, home, and community environments in which the student needs or wants to function, (b) next environments in which the student must function (e.g., specialty rooms in the school, the next school which the student will attend, community settings in which the student does not currently participate), and (c) identification of postschool environments in which the student may participate, including postsecondary education settings, job settings, residential settings, and leisure settings, as the student advances to transition planning.

School environments might include general education and special education classrooms and labs; bathrooms; the cafeteria; specialty rooms such as home-living units; the nurse's room; the gymnasium; hallways (including corners and doorways); stairwells; elevators; the school yard (land contours, play equipment); and the surrounding neighborhood streets. Community environments might include fast-food and cafeteria-style restaurants, large and small department stores, groceries, drugstores, card shops, laundromats, medical services, public bathrooms, malls, and parking lots.

Subenvironments are areas, rooms, or departments within an environment where different activities take place. For example, in the home, each room, such as the kitchen, bedroom, or bathroom, is a subenvironment because different activities are performed in each. In a grocery the entranceway, the dairy section, the produce section, and the checkout are each a subenvironment because different activities are performed in each.

Identification of Activities. Within each selected subenvironment, the teacher identifies the activities or functions that take place. For example, in fast-food restaurants there are the activities of entering through the front door, locating and approaching the counter, waiting in line to order, ordering and paying, locating supplies (napkins, straws, etc.), dispensing a drink, locating and moving to an empty seat, sitting down, eating, disposing of tray and trash, and exiting.

Identification of Literacy Tasks. Within each activity, the teacher identifies the written words the student will need to read or write in order to perform the task. All of the possible words are listed. The teacher examines the words for frequency of use, importance of the words, and need for reading or writing the words. Some of the words are then targeted for present instruction, while other words will be taught at a later time. Examples may be grocery lists, reading environmental print (such as "drugstore," "men's restroom"), or reading the numbers on a form at a vocational site.

Instructional Strategies

There are several strategies that may be used to teach literacy skills to students with multiple impairments. A few of the more common ones include the sight-word approach, sign language facilitation, symbol support, environmental print, and phonics.

Sight-Word Approach. Sight-word approaches have been used for some time to successfully teach students with moderate mental retardation to read nouns and adjectives and short sentences (Brown & Perlmutter, 1971). A sight-word approach does not utilize phonics to sound out the word, but has the student learn the word as a whole-word entity. Some curricula have been based upon this approach. For example, one curriculum that was specifically designed to teach students with mild to moderate mental retardation to read is the Edmark Reading Program (see the discussion in the previous section).

There have been various strategies used to teach students with mental retardation to read using a sight-word approach. For example, peer tutors have been trained to teach sight words to students with moderate mental retardation using a time delay approach (Koury & Browder, 1986). Due to problems with generalization, sight-word instruction of environmental print is often conducted in the environment in which the sight word is usually found. With the increase in technology, more high tech methods of instruction have been used. In one study (Mechling, Gast, & Langone, 2002), computer-based video instruction was used to teach grocery aisle signs to students with moderate mental retardation, and the students successfully generalized to reading the print in actual grocery stores.

Sign Language Facilitation of Reading. For many years, sign language has been successfully used to facilitate reading in students with mental retardation and other disabilities and has been found to be more effective than teaching sight words alone (Sensenig, Mazeika, & Topf, 1989). In most procedures, words are presented in conjunction with their corresponding signs. Upon being presented with a word to read, students are asked to verbally say the word or sign the word to the teacher. As the student learns to read the word, signing of the word is often faded. This technique may be used with students with severe physical or multiple disabilities. Although motor impairments may prevent signing by a student, he or she may benefit from the additional signed input paired with the written word. Using signs with speech supports a multimodal learning approach.

Symbol Support and Environmental Print. Pictures have often been used in conjunction with written words to facilitate learning the words. This occurs through pairing with pictures, changing the print (by adding pictures, etc.), and using environmental print/logos. The pairing-with-picture approach consists of presenting the picture and word simultaneously, then fading the picture so that only the word remains. Fading may occur by making the picture smaller and the word bigger over time, or making the picture fainter to see and the word bolder. The word may be placed next to the picture (paired) or the word may be embedded in the picture. Embedding the picture (in which the word is placed in the picture) has the advantage over placing the word next to the picture, since the student does not have to shift attention from one to another (Westling & Fox, 2004). For example, in Figure 13–17 the picture of the coffee cup has the word embedded in it and the cup is faded over time.

Changing the print or using environmental print/logos is another reading strategy. Often print is exaggerated, colored, or made to look like what the word represents. This has the advantage of drawing the student's attention to the word itself. The cue is slowly faded until the print remains. In some instances, it may be preferable to keep the visual cue in the print, especially if this is how it appears in the environment. For example, the "M" in "McDonald's" is made up of yellow arches. Learning it in this format makes it readily identifiable and is how it is naturally found.

Students may benefit from using symbols and words together to read recipes, messages, stories, or other materials. Pairing symbols with words also promotes writing skills. There are several symbol-based programs and books as discussed earlier in the chapter under Emergent and Beginning Literacy. There are also publications designed for older school-age children, such as *News-2-You* (published by News-2-You). *News-2-You* is a weekly newspaper, about 13 to 20 pages in length, with simple up-to-date stories with symbol support. More-simplified editions and those supporting AAC devices are also available.

FIGURE 13–17
This picture-association reading strategy presents a picture with the written word, then fades the picture over time, leaving the written word.

Note. From *Instruction of Students with Severe Disabilities* 5E by Snell/Brown, © 1993. Reprinted by permission of Prentice-Hall, Inc., Upper Saddle River, NJ.

Teachers may decide to also make their own symbol-supported material using such software as Writing with Symbols 2000 (manufactured by Mayer-Johnson, Inc.). Writing with Symbols 2000 is a talking-picture and word-processing program, which puts a symbol above each word when the words are typed. This allows for the creation of books, lists, recipes, or support of any written material by having symbols associated with each word. This and similar

FIGURE 13–18
This software program puts a symbol above each word when the word is typed

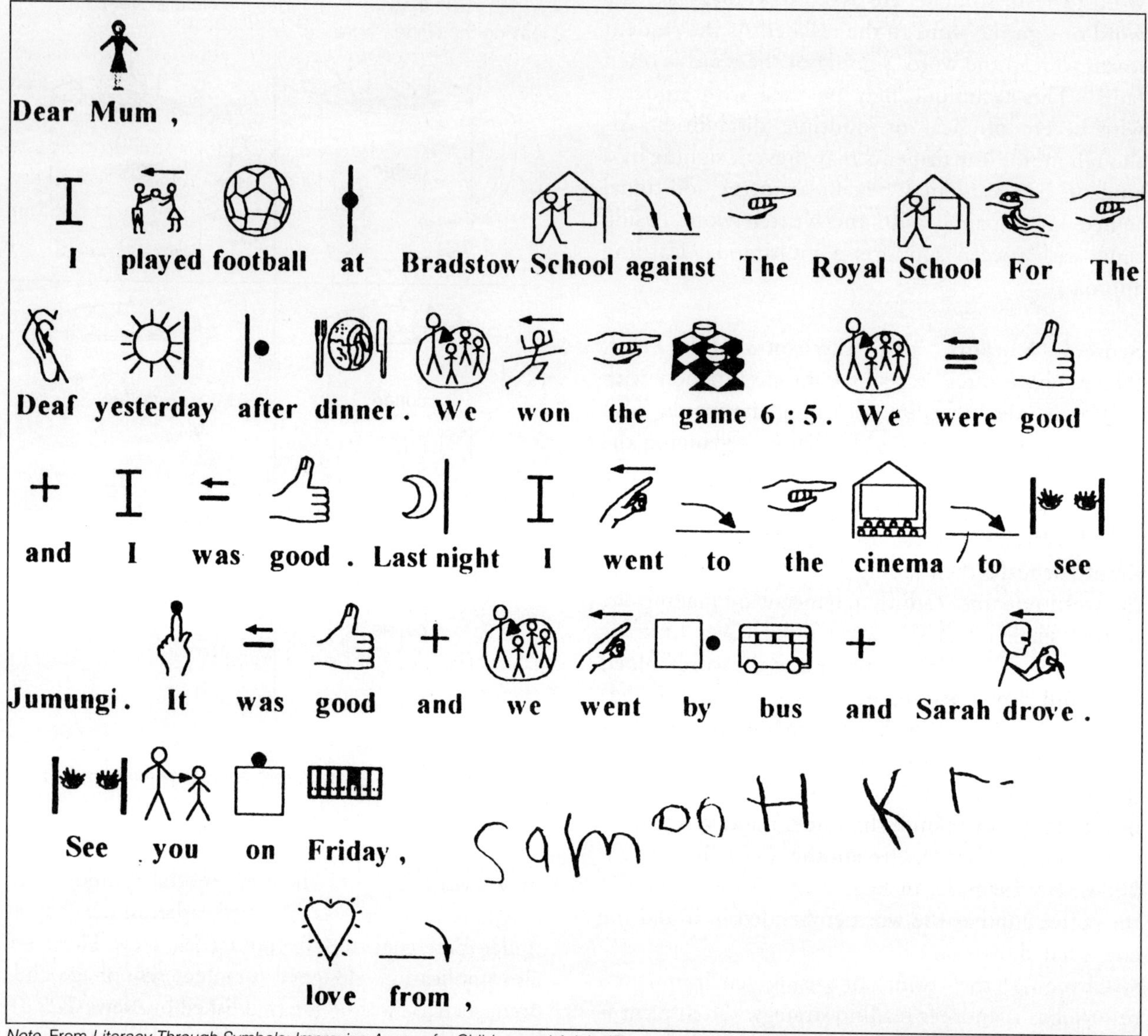

Note. From *Literacy Through Symbols: Improving Access for Children and Adults* (Fig. 1.6, p. 6) by T. Detheridge and M. Detheridge, 1977, London: David Fulton Publishers. Reprinted by permission.

programs can assist in facilitating reading and writing through symbol support (see Figure 13–18).

Phonics Approaches. It has often been thought that sight-word recognition skills are the foundation for functional literacy skills (Worrall & Singh, 1983). Although sight-word instruction has been successful with students with mental retardation, it does not provide the skills necessary to generalize reading to unfamiliar words as does a phonics-based approach (Barudin & Hourcade, 1990). Phonics approaches are not often used with students with moderate to severe mental retardation, based on the assumption that phonics is somehow more cognitively demanding. This is not necessarily the case. It is important that assumptions regarding reading instruction not be made in this area, and that limitations not be placed on students who could benefit from such an approach. Students may be taught phonics skills to assist them in learning and recognizing targeted words.

SUMMARY AND CONCLUSION

Students with physical or multiple disabilities are often behind in literacy skills and need special adaptations and systematic instruction. Teachers need to assess each student's abilities and make informed decisions regarding adaptations, use of specialized strategies, and instructional targets. Reading can be divided into the areas of emergent and beginning literacy, conventional literacy, and functional literacy. Emergent literacy often requires adaptations such as adapted books and use of AAC devices to promote active participation. When teaching conventional reading to students who have speech and physical impairments, the Nonverbal Reading Profile may be used; it incorporates active participation, internal speech, diagnostic distractor arrays, error analysis, additional instruction, and assistive technology. This strategy may be used along with the curriculum the teacher is presently using. In the area of functional literacy, students may be taught using strategies such as a sight-word approach, sign language facilitation of reading, picture/symbol association reading strategy, or a phonics approach.

QUESTIONS FOR DISCUSSION

1. Discuss the phonics approach versus the whole language (or sight-word) approach to reading and discuss the advantages and disadvantages of these approaches as they relate to students who are nonverbal and have severe physical disabilities.
2. Compare various reading curricula and discuss how the Nonverbal Reading Approach can be used to teach the curriculum to students with physical and speech impairments.
3. Examine some of the software for phonics and/or reading. What are the advantages and disadvantages? How can you determine the appropriateness of the software for a specific student?
4. Explain how words are selected for instruction using an ecological assessment for students with multiple impairments. Select a specific environment and discuss the words that would be selected for an activity in that environment.

FOCUS ON THE NET

ABLEDATA
http://www.abledata.com

This site is sponsored by the National Institute on Disability and Rehabilitation research and offers searchable databases on assistive technology, devices, news, and links to pertinent sites.

Blue Web'n Learning Applications
http://www.kn.pacbell.com/wired/bluewebn

This site offers curriculum ideas from which reading assignments can be drawn.

Carol Hurst's Children's Literature
http://www.carolhurst.com

Provides reviews of books and suggests book-related activities. A newsletter and a listing of professional resources are included.

Closing the Gap
http://closingthegap.com

This site provides a searchable database on assistive technology and software that can be used to support literacy and other areas in special education and rehabilitation.

Education World
http://www.education-world.com

Curriculum ideas for teaching reading are provided here.

Library of Congress National Library Service for the Blind and Physically Handicapped
http://lcweb.loc.gov/nls/

This site offers books on tape. After listening to a story, the student can be given a writing assignment.

News-2-You
http://www.news-2-you.com

Teachers (or anyone) can subscribe to a weekly newspaper that uses symbol support. This 15-or-so-page newspaper provides easy-to-understand stories on current events. More-simplified versions and communication boards can also be requested.

Project Gutenberg Index
http://promo.net/pg/

This site includes a tremendous number of literary works that can be accessed on screen and then read by using a reading program. All of the works are in the public domain and out of copyright. Although they are not very contemporary works, they can be useful and enjoyable.

REFERENCES

Alvermann, D., Bridge, C., Schmidt, R., Seafoss, L., Winograd, P., Paris, S., Priestly, C., & Santeusanio, N. (1989). *Heath reading.* Lexington, MA: Heath.

Armbruster, B., Lehr, F., & Osborn, J. (2001). *Put reading first: The research building blocks for teaching children to read.* Jessup, MD: National Institute for Literacy.

Archer, A., Gleason, M., & Vachon, V. (2000). REWARDS. Longman, Co: Sopris West.

Ball, E. W., & Blachman, B. A. (1991). Does phoneme awareness training make a difference in early word recognition and developmental spelling? *Reading Research Quarterly, 26,* 49–66.

Barudin, S. I., & Hourcade, J. J. (1990). Relative effectiveness of three methods of reading instruction in developing specific recall and transfer skills in learners with moderate and severe mental retardation. *Education and Training in Mental Retardation, 21,* 286–291.

Baumann, J. F., & Bergeron, B. S. (1993). Story map instruction using children's literature: Effects on first graders' comprehension of central elements. *Journal of Reading Behavior, 25,* 407–437.

Berninger, V. W., & Gans, B. M. (1986a). Language profiles in nonspeaking individuals of normal intelligence with severe cerebral palsy. *Augmentative and Alternative Communication, 2,* 45–50.

Berninger, V. W., & Gans, B. M. (1986b). Assessing word processing capability of the nonvocal, nonwriting. *Augmentative and Alternative Communication, 2,* 56–63.

Berninger, W. S. (1986). Comparison of two microcomputer-assisted methods of teaching word decoding and encoding to non-vocal, non-writing and learning disabilities students. *Programmed Learning and Educational Technology, 23*(2), 124–129.

Blackstone, S. W., & Cassatt-James, E. L. (1988). Augmentative communication. In N. J. Lass, L. V. McReynolds, J. L. Northern, & D. E. Yoder (Eds.), *Handbook of speech-language pathology audiology* (pp. 986–1013). Toronto: Decker.

Blischak, D. M. (1995). Thomas the Writer: Case study of a child with severe physical, speech, and visual impairments. *Language, Speech, and Hearing Services in the Schools, 26,* 11–20.

Bos, C. S., & Vaughn, S. (2002). *Strategies for teaching students with learning and behavior problems* (5th ed.). Boston: Allyn & Bacon.

Bradley, L., & Bryant, P. (1983). Categorizing sounds and learning to read: A causal connection. *Nature, 301,* 419–421.

Bradley, L., & Bryant, P. (1985). *Rhyme and reason in reading and spelling.* Ann Arbor: University of Michigan Press.

Brown, L., & Perlmutter, L. (1971). Teaching functional reading to trainable level retarded students. *Education and Training of the Mentally Retarded, 6,* 74–84.

Brown, M. W. (2002). *Goodnight moon.* New York: Harper Festival.

Carlson, F. (1987). Communication strategies for infants. In E. T. McDonald (Ed.), *Treating cerebral palsy* (pp. 191–207). Austin, TX: PRO-ED.

Cazden, C. B. (1983). Adult assistance to language development: Scaffolds, models, and direct instruction. In R. P. Parker & F. A. Davis (Eds.), *Developing literacy: Young children's use of language* (pp. 3–18). Newark, DE: International Reading Association.

Clark, F. L., Deshler, D. D., Schumaker, J. B., Alley, G. R., & Warner, M. M. (1984). Visual imagery and self-questioning: Strategies to improve comprehension of written materials. *Journal of Learning Disabilities, 17,* 145–149.

Coleman, K., McNairn, P., & Shioleno, O. C. (1995). *Quick tech magic: Music-based literacy activities.* Solana Beach, CA: Mayer-Johnson.

Dunn, L. M., & Dunn, L. M. (1997). PPVT-III: Peabody Picture Vocabulary Test (3rd ed.). Circle Pines, MN: American Guidance Service.

Emery, D. W. (1996). Helping readers comprehend stories from the characters perspectives. *Reading Teacher, 49,* 534–541.

Foley, B. E. (1993). The development of literacy in individuals with severe congenital speech and motor impairments. *Topics in Language Disorders, 13,* 16–32.

Fried-Oken, M. (1988). The auditory scanner for visually impaired, non-speaking persons. In L. E. Bernstein (Ed.), *The vocally impaired: Clinical practice and research* (pp. 249–264). Philadelphia: Grune & Stratton.

Harris, D. (1982). Communicative interaction processes involving nonvocal physically handicapped children. *Topics in Language Disorders, 2,* 21–37.

Heath, S. B. (1982). What no bedtime story means: Narrative skills at home and school. *Language in Society, 11,* 49–76.

Heller, K. W., Alberto, P. A., Forney, P. E., & Schwartzman, M. N. (1996). *Understanding physical, sensory, and health impairments: Characteristics and educational implications.* Pacific Grove, CA: Brooks/Cole.

Heller, K. W., D'Andrea, F. M., Soucy, L., & Caruso, M. B. (1997). *Braille Assessment Checklist for Persons with Multiple Disabilities.* New York: American Foundation for the Blind.

Heller, K. W., Fredrick, L. D., & Diggs, C. A. (1999). Teaching reading to students with severe speech and physical impairments using the Nonverbal Reading Approach. *Physical Disabilities: Education and Related Services, 18,* 3–34.

Heller, K. W., Fredrick, L. D., Tumlin, J., & Brineman, D. G. (2002). Teaching decoding for generalization using the Nonverbal Reading Approach. *Journal of Physical and Developmental Disabilities, 14,* 19–35.

Heller, K. W., & Swinehart-Jones, D. (2003a). *Strategies for promoting literacy in students who have physical disabilities.* Atlanta: Bureau for Students with Physical and Health Impairments, Georgia State University.

Heller, K. W., & Swinehart-Jones, D. (2003b). Supporting the educational needs of students with orthopedic impairments. *Physical Disabilities: Education and Related Services, 22,* 3–24.

Honig, B. (1996). *Teaching our children to read: The role of skills in a comprehensive reading program.* Thousand Oaks, CA: Corwin.

Idol, L. (1987). Group story mapping: A comprehension strategy for both skilled and unskilled readers. *Journal of Learning Disabilities, 20,* 196–205.

Jitendra, A. K., Hoppes, M. K., & Xin, Y. P. (2000). Enhancing main idea comprehension for students with learning problems: The role of a summarization strategy and self-monitoring instruction. *Journal of Special Education, 34,* 127–139.

Jorm, A. F., & Share, D. L. (1983). Phonological recoding and reading acquisition. *Applied Psycholinguistics, 4,* 103–147.

Kapp, S., & Kravitz-Zodda, J. (1997). *Reading by the rules.* Burlington, MA: Wisnia-Kapp Reading Programs.

Karlsen, B., Madden, R., & Gardner, E. (1976). Standford Diagnostic Reading Test—Red Level. New York: Harcourt Brace Jovanovich.

Katims, D. S. (1993, January.) *The emergence of literacy in preschool children with disabilities.* Paper presented at the Third Annual Carolina Literacy Center Symposium, Research Triangle Park, NC.

Kekelis, L., & Anderson, E. (1984). Family communication styles and language development. *Journal of Visual Impairment and Blindness, 78,* 54–56.

Kelly, J., & Friend, T. (1993). *Hands-on reading.* Solana Beach, CA: Mayer-Johnson.

King-DeBaun, P. (1995). *Merging whole language and technology strategies for children with severe disabilities.* Paper presented at the Annual International Convention of the Council for Exceptional Children. (ERIC Document Reproduction Service No. ED 3831254)

Kirk, S. A., Kirk, W. S., & Minskill, E. (1985). *Phonic remedial reading lessons.* Novato, CA: Academic Therapy.

Koenig, A. J., & Holbrook, N. C. (1993). *Learning media assessment of students with visual impairments: A resource guide for teachers.* Austin: Texas School for the Blind and Visually Impaired.

Koppenhaver, D. A., Evans, D. A., & Yoder, D. E. (1991). Childhood reading and writing experiences of literate adults with severe speech and motor impairments. *Augmentative and Alternative Communication, 7,* 20–33.

Koppenhaver, D. A., & Yoder, D. E. (1993). Classroom literacy instruction for children with severe speech and physical impairments (SSPI): What is and what might be. *Topics of Language Disorders, 13,* 1–15.

Koury, M., & Browder, D. M. (1986). The use of delay to teach sight words by peer tutors classified as moderately mentally retarded. *Education and Training of the Mentally Retarded, 21,* 252–258.

Light, J., & Smith, A. K. (1993). Home literacy experiences of preschoolers who use AAC systems and of their nondisabled peers. *Augmentative and Alternative Communication, 9,* 10–25.

MacGinitie, W. H., MacGinitie, R. K., Maria, K., & Dryer, L. G. (2000). Gates-MacGinitie Reading Tests (4th ed.). New York: Riverside.

Markwardt, F. C. (1997). *Peabody Individual Achievement Test-Revised/Normative Update.* Circle Pines, MN: American Guidance Service.

McEwen, I. R., & Lloyd, L. L. (1990). Positioning students with cerebral palsy to use augmentative and alternative communication. *Language, Speech, and Hearing Services in Schools, 21,* 15–21.

McGinnies, J. S., & Beukelman, D. R. (1989). Vocabulary requirements for writing activities for the academically mainstreamed students with disabilities. *Augmentative and Alternative Communication, 5,* 183–191.

McNairn, P., & Shioleno, C. (1994). *Quick tech: Readable, repeatable stories and activities* (1994). Solana Beach, CA: Mayer-Johnson.

McNaughton, S. (1993). Graphic representational systems and literacy learning. *Topics in Language Disorders, 12,* 58–75.

Mechling, L. C., Gast, D. L., & Langone, J. (2002). Computer-based video instruction to teach persons with moderate intellectual disabilities to read grocery aisle signs and locate items. *Journal of Special Education, 35,* 224–240.

Mercer, C. D., & Mercer, A. R. (2001). *Teaching students with learning problems.* New York: Merrill.

Mike, D. G. (1987, October). *Literacy, technology, and the multiply disabled: An ethnography of classroom interaction.* Paper presented at the meeting of the National Reading Conference, St. Petersburg Beach, FL.

Musselwhite, C., & King-DeBaun, P. (1997). *Emergent literacy success: Merging technology and whole language for students with disabilities.* Park City, UT: Creative Communicating.

Nolan, S., Alley, G. R., & Clark, F. L. (1980). *Self-questioning strategy.* Lawrence: University of Kansas, Institute of Research in Learning Disabilities.

Nurss, J., & McGauvran, M. (1976). Metropolitan Reading Readiness Test, Level II. New York: Harcourt Brace Jovanovich.

Patillo, S. T., Heller, K. W., & Smith, M. (2004). The impact of a modified repeated-reading strategy paired with optical character recognition on the reading rates of students with visual impairments. *Journal of Visual Impairments and Blindness, 98* (1) 28–46.

Pierce, P. L., & McWilliam, P. (1993). Emerging literacy and children with severe speech and physical impairments (SSPI): Issues and possible intervention strategies. *Topics in Language Disorders, 13,* 47–57.

Rogow, S. M. (1988). *Helping the visually impaired child with developmental problems.* New York: Teachers College Press.

Seidel, U. P., Chadwick, O., & Rutter, M. (1975). Psychological disorders in crippled children with and without brain damage. *Developmental Medicine and Child Neurology, 17,* 563–573.

Sensenig, L. D., Mazeika, E. J., & Topf, B. (1989). Sign language facilitation of reading with students classified as trainable mentally-handicapped. *Education and Training of the Mentally Retarded, 24,* 121–125.

Simmons, T., & Young, C. (1994). *Tools for literacy and communication: A collection of stories.* Solana Beach, CA: Mayer-Johnson.

Smith, A., Thurston, S., Light, J., Parnes, P., & O'Keefe, B. (1989). The form and use of written communication produced by physically disabled individuals using microcomputers. *Augmentative and Alternative Communication, 5,* 115–124.

Smith, M. (1989). Reading without speech: A study of children with cerebral palsy. *Irish Journal of Psychology, 10,* 601–614.

Smith, M. (1992). Reading abilities of nonspeaking students: Two case studies. *Augmentative and Alternative Communication, 8,* 57–66.

Snow, C. E., Burns, M. S., & Griffin, P. (Eds.). (1998). *Preventing reading difficulties in young children.* Washington, DC: National Academy Press.

Snow, C., & Ninio, A. (1986). The contracts of literacy: What children learn from learning to read books. In W. H. Teale & E. Sulzby (Eds.), *Emergent literacy* (pp. 116–138). Norwood, NJ: Ablex.

Spache, G. D. (1976). *Investigating the issue of reading disabilities.* Boston: Allyn & Bacon.

Steelman, J. D., Pierce, P., & Koppenhaver, D. (1993). The role of computers in promoting literacy in children with severe speech and physical impairments (SSPI). *Topics in Language Disorders, 13,* 76–88.

Stratton, J. M., & Wright, S. (1991). On the way to literacy: Early experiences for young visually impaired children. *RE:view, 23,* 55–63.

Teale, W., & Sulzby, E. (1989). Emergent literacy: New perspective. In D. Strickland & L. Morros (Eds.), *Emergent literacy: Young children learn to read and write* (pp. 1–15). Newark, NJ: International Reading Association.

Vandervelden, M. C., & Siegel, L. S. (1995). Phonological recoding and phoneme awareness in early literacy: A developmental approach. *Reading Research Quarterly, 30,* 854–875.

Wells, G. (1987). The learning of literacy. In B. Fillion, C. Hedley, & E. Dimartino (Eds.), *Home and school: Early language and reading* (pp. 27–45). Norwood, NJ: Ablex.

Westling, D. L., & Fox., L. (2004). *Teaching students with severe disabilities,* 3rd ed. Upper Saddle River, NJ: Merrill/Prentice Hall.

Worrall, N., & Singh, Y. (1983). Teaching TMR children to read using integrated picture cuing. *American Journal of Mental Deficiency, 87,* 422–429.

Yoder, D. E., & Kraat, A. (1983). Intervention issues in nonspeech communication. In J. Miller, D. E. Yoder, & R. Schiefelbusch (Eds.), *Contemporary issues in language intervention* (pp. 27–51). Rockville, MD: American Speech and Hearing Association.

Adaptations and Instruction in Writing

KATHRYN WOLFF HELLER

CHAPTER 14

Writing is not only one of the most basic and fundamental skills taught in schools, it is a critical skill for students with physical or multiple disabilities. Learning to write is especially critical for the 31.5% to 47.3% of students with physical or multiple disabilities who are also nonverbal (Lafontaine & DeRuyter, 1987; Matas, Mathy-Laikko, Beukelman, & Legresley, 1985). The ability to write allows these students to express their thoughts without being restricted by the vocabulary on their AAC device. The ability to write also opens up opportunities and helps them achieve success in academic, community, and vocational environments.

KNOWLEDGE AND SKILLS

After you have read this chapter, you will be able to:

1. **Identify barriers that contribute to writing difficulties for students with physical or multiple disabilities.**
2. **Describe instructional strategies and modifications for promoting handwriting skills.**
3. **Describe computer adaptations such as keyboard modifications, keyboard layout modifications, alternative keyboards, alternate input devices, and output modifications.**
4. **Describe considerations in teaching keyboarding skills and computer tools.**
5. **Describe strategies for teaching spelling and spelling tools that may be used to promote correct spelling.**
6. **Discuss written expression considerations and instructional strategies.**
7. **Discuss strategies for promoting functional writing skills.**

IDENTIFYING AND ADDRESSING WRITING BARRIERS

As with reading, there are many barriers that students with physical disabilities may encounter that interfere with the mechanics and process of writing. Teachers need to closely observe their students with physical or multiple disabilities to determine if any of these barriers are interfering with a student's writing ability. Once identified, barriers can then be addressed through adaptations and instruction. Barriers can include lack of motor ability, restricted participation and practice, individual factors, lack of experiences, loss of the reading and writing connection, and problems with the learning environment and instruction.

Lack of Motor Ability. Students with physical or multiple disabilities will often encounter significant literacy difficulties (Berninger & Gans, 1986; Pierce & McWilliam, 1993; Smith,

Thurston, Light, Parnes, & O'Keefe, 1989). These can be attributed to several barriers that interfere with effective writing for students with physical or multiple disabilities. One of the first barriers that can interfere in writing is a lack of motor ability. Often students with physical or multiple disabilities are unable to manipulate traditional writing tools, resulting in their having little experience scribbling, drawing, or writing. For some students, traditional computers may be inaccessible without adaptations or assistive technology. Teachers will need to be certain that appropriate assistive technology and adaptations are put in place. Closely examining the physical efficiency areas (as discussed in Chapter 13) will also help pinpoint problems and determine adaptations.

Restricted Participation and Practice. Another barrier to writing proficiency is a lack of participation and practice. In some instances, there is so much emphasis on other aspects of a student's education and care that writing instruction is minimized, resulting in fewer opportunities to practice writing. It is important that this area is not overlooked. It will be especially critical for AAC users who may need to write out messages not on their AAC device.

Another problem resulting in restricted participation and practice is the slow speed at which some students write. Once students are given access to appropriate adapted writing tools, they often write much slower due to their motoric ability or means of accessing the writing task (e.g., onscreen keyboard with scanning). This can result in the production of fewer writing drafts and fewer rewriting assignments to improve writing skills. With less practice, students are unable to develop their writing skills. Teachers need to provide sufficient practice and time for students with severe physical impairments to go through the writing process of writing a draft and rewriting their product. This may require providing the student with a longer time frame to complete the written paper, as well as possibly needing to reduce the number of writing assignments to allow the student to complete a well-written paper. If the number of writing assignments is reduced, alternate assignments may be given that result in a different product but meet the targeted objective.

Students who use AAC and communicate by combining words or using short phrases will often be inexperienced with the structure of a sentence. Often these students will write in a way similar to how they "talk" with their AAC system. This often results in incomplete sentences, less-complex sentences, and grammatically incorrect sentences. It is important that systematic instruction is provided to teach proper sentence construction and improve their writing skills.

Individual Factors. Another barrier that may have a negative impact on literacy development for students with physical, health, or multiple disabilities consists of individual factors. This barrier includes (a) increased absenteeism due to health factors, (b) lack of attending to the literacy activity due to problems with pain, discomfort, or fatigue, and (c) medication or treatment effects that can interfere with learning (Heller, Alberto, Forney, & Schwartzman, 1996). Additional problems include visual and auditory perceptual problems, language deficits, poor self-esteem, and passive learning patterns that may influence literacy development (McNaughton, 1993; Smith, 1992). The teacher will need to use adaptations and instructional strategies designed to address these problems (e.g., providing breaks when fatigue is present, encouraging more active learning patterns).

Additional disabilities such as learning disabilities and mental retardation may also accompany the physical disability. When additional disabilities are present, the student will often require additional instructional techniques to teach writing in addition to the techniques used to accommodate the physical impairment.

Lack of Experiences. Almost 50% of 3-year-old children who do not have disabilities scribble and use letter-like forms and converse about the purposes of writing (DeCoste, 1997). These early scribbling or pretend-writing experiences are gradually refined into standard writing, which over time incorporates the rules of spelling and composition. Many of these beginning writing experiences are missed by students with physical, health, or multiple disabilities, which can put them at a disadvantage.

Students with physical or multiple disabilities often lack broad experience of the world around them due to difficulty in mobility or fatigue, which limits exploration of interesting items and activities (Blischak, 1995). These difficulties may also limit students' ability to go to different places in their environment, such as moving across a room to see an interesting item or going to a location in the community. This may restrict the content they have to write about. It is often necessary to broaden students' experiences and provide activities to give the students ideas to write about.

Loss of the Reading and Writing Connection. Reading and writing involve many of the same mechanisms and should be taught in an integrated manner, not as separate subjects (Kucer, 1985). Writing provides practice in letter-sound relationships and word analysis, and writing helps focus the child's attention on the visual details of the letters (Chomsky, 1970; Clay, 1975). As young children begin to refine their writing, they apply this knowledge to storybook reading (Dobson, 1989). For students with physical or multiple disabilities, writing may not be taught until after reading instruction has begun, due to motoric problems accessing writing tools. This can put these children at a disadvantage. Adaptations and assistive technology may be used to address access issues.

Problems with the Learning Environment and Instruction. Reduced expectations in the home and school environments in the area of literacy can negatively contribute to a student's literacy skills. In order to help develop writing skills, it is important to promote positive expectations. Also, these students tend to receive less literacy instruction than their peers without disabilities, experience frequent and regular interruptions while receiving literacy instruction, lack interaction with peers during instruction, and respond to instruction in a passive manner (Harris, 1982; Koppenhaver, Evans, & Yoder, 1991; Koppenhaver & Yoder, 1993; Mike, 1987). Therefore, it is crucial that these students be allowed enough time to develop writing skills, and that they experience increased peer interaction and active instructional techniques. One of the first steps is to provide access to writing tools.

LITERACY SKILLS: ACCESSING WRITING TOOLS

Children are typically exposed to writing at an early age through drawing, painting, and scribbling with crayons. Often children will scribble on paper and pretend that they wrote a message, just as they have seen their parents and older siblings do. Some children will master writing some letters and simple words at an early age. Some of them will have early exposure to computers and enjoy pretend writing as they push the keys of a keyboard or draw with the mouse. Using and playing with writing tools promotes the assignment of meaning through (a) writing or drawing, (b) organizing information on a page, and (c) reinforcing sound-symbol relationships. Access to writing materials in the preschool years is critical to literacy development (Chomsky, 1981; Ferreiro, 1986).

Students with physical impairments have difficulty using standard writing tools. In one study by Light and Smith (1993), most children with speech and physical disabilities were found to be interested in writing and drawing activities, but many lacked access to these activities. Students with cerebral palsy may have difficulty grasping a standard writing tool and lack fine-motor control to manipulate it. Students with spina bifida may have difficulty with handwriting due to visual-perceptual and fine-motor coordination difficulties. Some students have accompanying tremors, ataxia, and muscle weakness that interfere with writing (Anderson & Plewis, 1977; Hancock & Alston, 1986; Wallace, 1973). Not only will these difficulties impede writing, but these children may enter school with a much more limited foundation for literacy activities than their nondisabled counterparts.

To help promote literacy, it is important to provide access to writing and writing activities at an early age by using appropriate assistive technology and providing experiences in using writing tools and writing with them. As the child matures, writing tools can be used to promote writing stories, letters, journals, and eventually more complex writing such as research papers and newsletter articles. Competency in using appropriate writing tools will be crucial to help students become mature writers.

In order to have access to writing tools and develop writing skills, many students will need adaptations and the use of assistive technology. There are two primary categories of writing tools that may require adaptations to be accessible to students with physical disabilities. These are handheld writing tools (such as pencils, crayons, pens, paintbrushes, and markers) with some type of paper, and computers (or other devices with some type of keyboard, such as an AlphaSmart, which is a portable notetaking device). The first type typically requires the development of handwriting skills, while the second requires keyboarding skills or alternate input skills (such as scanning skills).

It is important that students are properly positioned prior to assessing or teaching. Proper positioning can often promote shoulder stability and better control of the forearm through proper seating and trunk placement (Kangas, 1987). Positioning of materials and use of needed work surface modifications are also critical.

Handheld Writing Tools and Paper Adaptations

Writing with a handheld tool (such as a pencil) requires proper positioning of the tool in the hand and good fine-motor abilities. Some students with physical impairments will lack the ability to use handheld tools for legible writing. However, at an early age, they may benefit from drawing with the tool, to promote some early literacy experience, then learning to access a computer for written expression. Other students with physical impairments may be able to write with a pencil with adaptations. In either case, it is important that appropriate adaptations be used as needed.

Tool Adaptations. Typically, students are taught to hold their pencil or writing tool with the index finger on top, the middle finger below, and the thumb opposite the index finger in a bent position. The last two fingers touch the paper. The pencil is near the big knuckle, and the end of the pencil points toward the shoulder (Milone & Wasylyk, 1981). However, some students with physical impairments may lack fingers or have poor stability of the writing tool when it is held in this traditional manner. The teacher and occupational therapist may explore alternate ways to hold the writing tool. Often the child will have already adapted the position when using crayons or other tools for drawing. For example, some children may hold the pencil with different fingers; others may place the pencil between the index and middle finger for stability. These alternate positions will need to be assessed as to efficiency and legibility of handwriting.

Interference with writing and accessing written material due to motoric constraints can be addressed by the provision of adaptive writing devices (Bigge, 1991; Doherty, 1987). Some students will have difficulty gripping the writing tool, holding the tool at the correct angle, or maintaining smooth strokes of the pencil. The writing tool can be adapted in many different ways to overcome many of these problems. Pencils may be adapted to provide a larger or better gripping surface through adding clay, standard pencil grips, balls, or foam material (see Figure 14–1a). The writing tool may be adapted completely to allow an alternate grip (Figure 14–1b). Some tools come with an attachment that holds the writing tool at the proper angle (Figure 14–1c). Sometimes splints may be used to hold the writing tool in place for access and greater stabilization (Figure 14–1d). Some students with athetoid cerebral palsy have extraneous movements and difficulty writing. In some situations, weights may be used to inhibit excessive and uncoordinated movements. Weights may be worn on the wrist, or the writing tool may itself be weighted.

In situations in which students have severe impairments affecting their arms, they may not be able to access the writing tool using their hands. Students with limb deficiencies who have a prosthesis may be taught to use the prosthesis for writing (Figure 14–2a), and some students may write using their feet. Some students will be unable to use their hands *or* arms for writing due to the severity of their physical impairments. These students may use a mouth stick or head stick with a pencil or writing tool attached to the end of it (see Figure 14–2b). Students who have good head movement and neck range of motion may be able to write using a different body part to manipulate the writing utensil. Some artists have done tremendous artwork in this manner.

Paper Adaptations. Another consideration concerns the need for paper stabilization or adapted paper to promote writing. Students without disabilities are typically able to stabilize the paper by using their nonwriting hand. Students with physical disabilities that affect arm use may be unable to hold and stabilize the paper. This results in paper movement and interferes with legible writing. Paper may need to be taped to the

FIGURE 14–1
Writing tools may be adapted by (a) adding gripping material, (b) changing the grip, or (c and d) using attachments or supports to hold the tool at the right angle

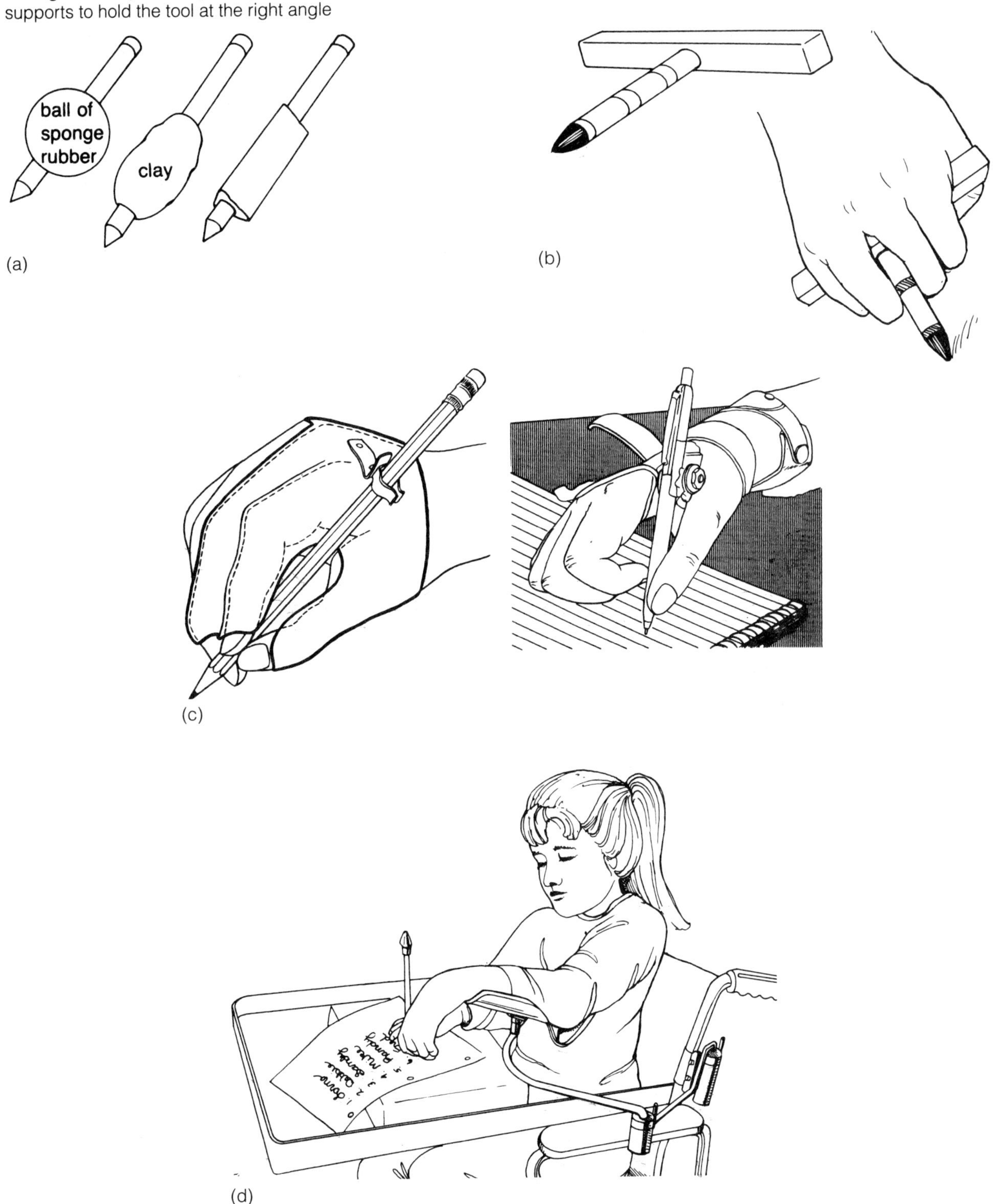

FIGURE 14–2
Students may hold writing tools in several ways, including using (a) a prosthesis and (b) a head stick

(a)

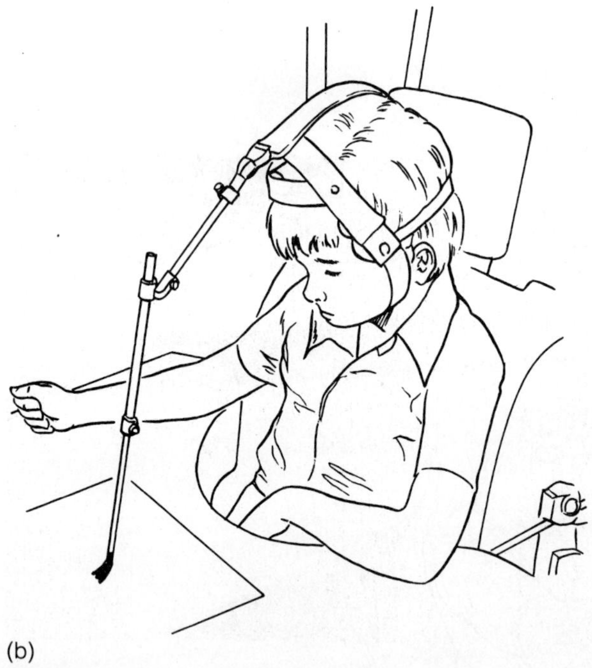

(b)

desk for stabilization. Other options include using clipboards or adapted paper holders (Bigge, 1991). (See Figure 14–3.)

Paper placement is an important consideration for promoting good handwriting skills. The angle of the desk (or paper holder) and the use of boundaries (so that pencils do not roll off the desk) are important considerations. Equally important is the angle at which the paper is placed to promote legible writing. Standard paper position for manuscript right-handed writing is straight toward the person, while left-handed manuscript writing is angled. Cursive writing also uses an angled paper position (see Figure 14–4). It is important that paper is consistently positioned in the correct place, to ensure consistency of the writing (Milone & Wasylyk, 1981). Students with physical impairments may benefit from a different positioning of the paper. Teachers may need to experiment with different paper angles before an optimum angle is achieved. Once the angle is determined, a template may be used. A template can be made by drawing the outline of the paper at the correct angle on a piece of construction paper. The construction paper is placed directly in front of the student, and the paper is placed on top of the outline to achieve the optimum angle of the paper every time. The construction paper can be secured to the work surface with tape so it does not slip.

In some instances, the paper will need to be elevated at an angle to allow for easy access. Various types of handmade and commercial angled writing surfaces may be used to promote writing. These include such devices as clipboards that are raised in the back to produce an angle, using thick three-ring binder notebooks with clips to hold the paper, adjustable easels, desks that angle, and freestanding angled surfaces (see Figure 14–5).

The paper itself may need to be modified. Some students will perform better with larger spaces between the lines to allow for larger strokes of the letters. Other students may benefit from dark-lined paper or raised-line paper that provides better visualization or tactile feedback of where the lines are located. Sometimes the entire size of the paper needs to be enlarged. Students who cannot see their own handwriting due to visual impairments may use a CCTV when they write to enlarge their print (see Figure 14–6).

Handwriting Skills

Instructional Strategies and Modifications. Students need to be taught handwriting skills directly. In one study (Hancock & Alston, 1986), students with spina bifida were taught handwriting with an emphasis on proper table height and slant, good posture, warm-up finger exercises, and correct pencil length,

FIGURE 14–3
Assistive paper holders and work space modifications: (a) rulers taped over paper and continuous roll of paper allow one-handed advancing and tearing off of paper; (b) elastic bands secure papers; (c) drafting tape holds papers and does not tear paper when pulled off; (d) clipboards hold papers; (e) clear plastic over worksheets protects writing surface to avoid tearing, wrinkling, and moisture damage from drool; (f) students may be able to mark widely spaced answers better than closely spaced ones; (g) APH signature guide

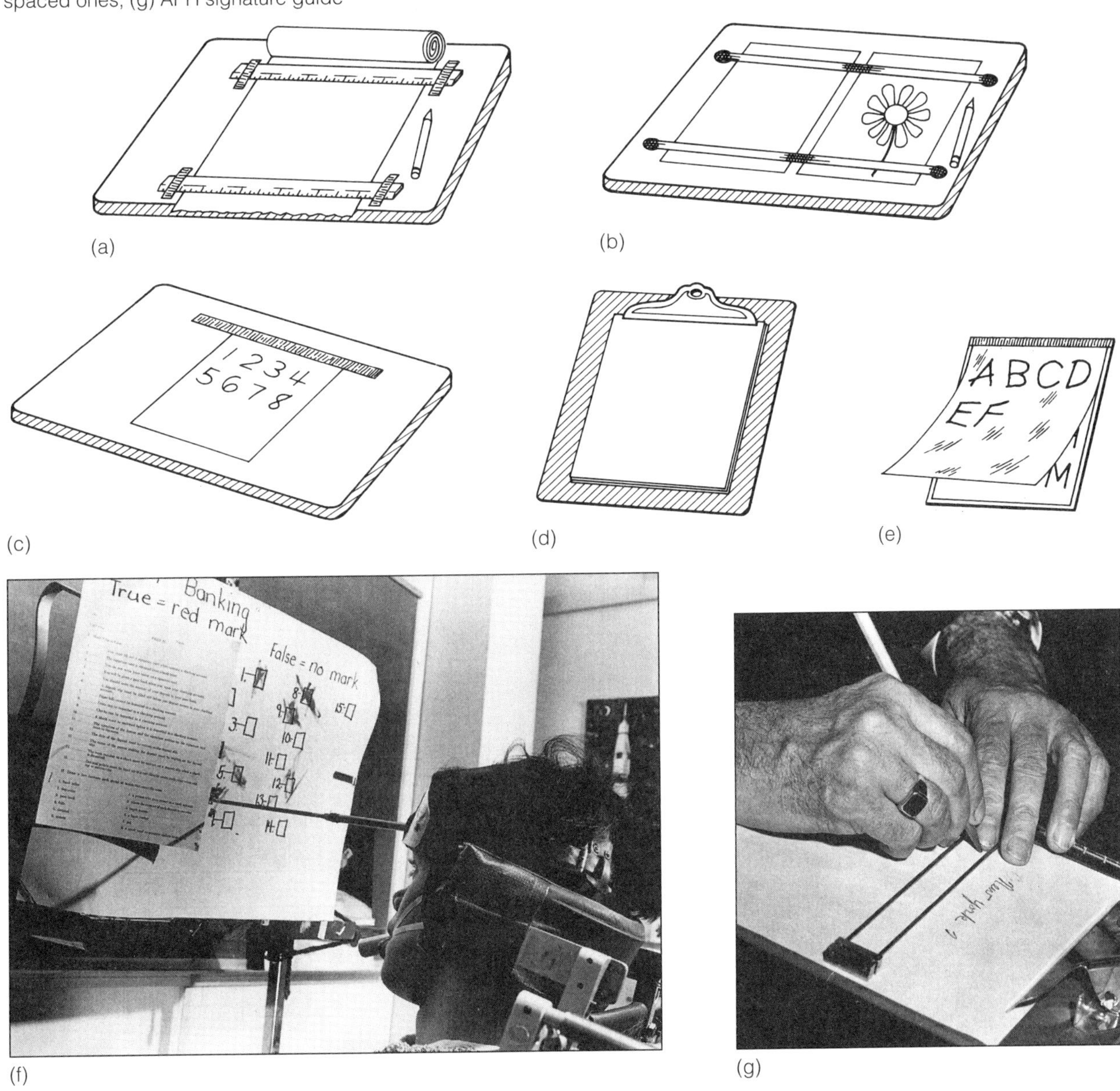

pencil grip, and paper position. Students were reminded of the 3 S's: "spacing, size, and sitting on the line." Students were initially assessed on their letter formation when writing the letters on a grid (which provided a line and a large space to write) and were provided tracing exercises that they practiced on three-line writing paper. A fluorescent pen was used to highlight the bottom line. Improvements were seen across letter formation, alignment, letter slant, and word spacing.

FIGURE 14–4
Standard paper placement for left-handed and right-handed students

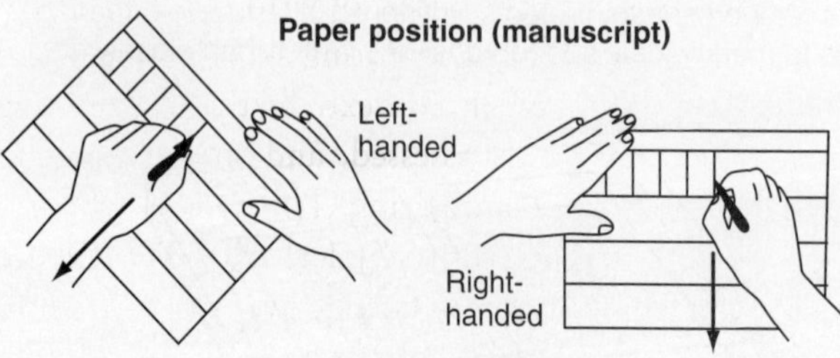

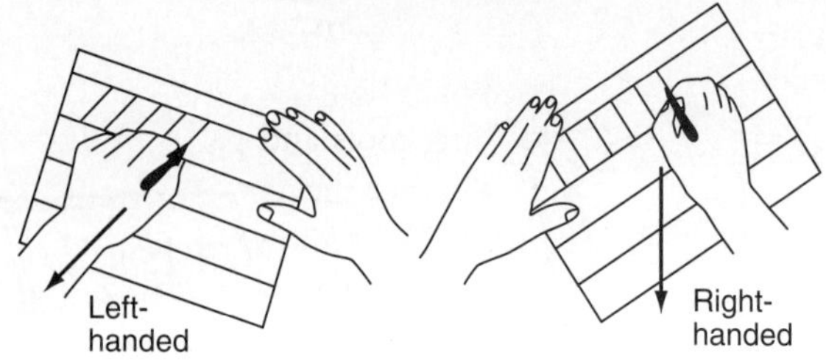

Note. Copyright 1981 by Zaner-Bloser. Inc., Columbus, Ohio. Reproduced with permission from Zaner-Bloser, Inc.

FIGURE 14–5
Writing surfaces may need to be elevated and angled to allow for easy access.

FIGURE 14–6
Student using a CCTV to enlarge his print as he writes

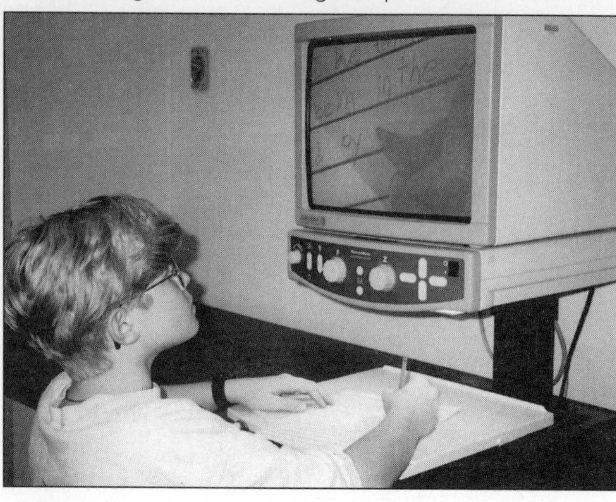

FIGURE 14–7
Preparatory activities that may be used prior to teaching actual letter formation

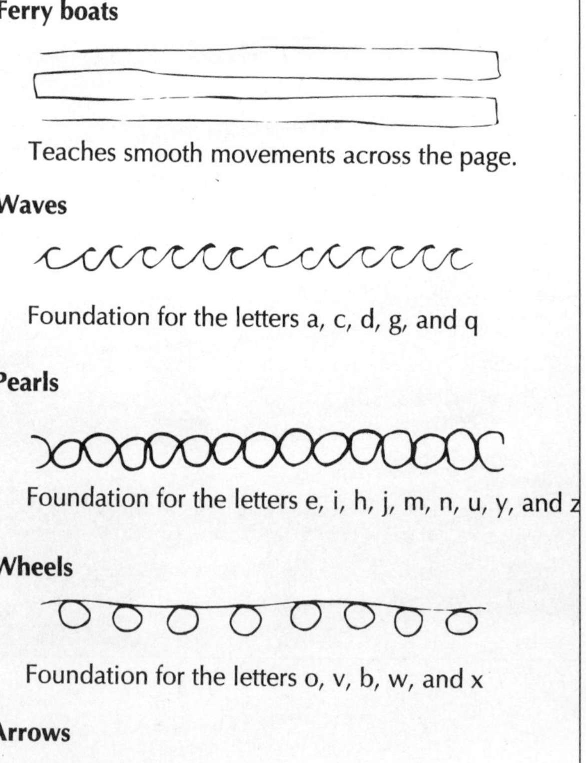

Ferry boats
Teaches smooth movements across the page.
Waves
Foundation for the letters a, c, d, g, and q
Pearls
Foundation for the letters e, i, h, j, m, n, u, y, and z
Wheels
Foundation for the letters o, v, b, w, and x
Arrows
Foundation for the letters k, l, t, r, and f

Note. Adapted from "Write Right or Left: A Practical Approach to Handwriting" by R. H. Hagin, 1983, *Journal of Learning Disabilities*, 16, 266–271. Copyright 1983 by PRO-ED, Inc. Reprinted with permission.

Writing is typically taught through teaching basic strokes that compose the more complex formation of the letters. Published handwriting series provide guidance on how to make the strokes and help guide the student in the correct formation of the letters. There are several different approaches to teaching handwriting. Many programs teach preparatory activities of drawing waves (to prepare for writing letters such as "a," "c," and "d"), drawing connected circles (to prepare for writing letters such as "o," "b," "v"), drawing connected arrows (to prepare for letters such as "k," "l," and "r") (see Figure 14–7). When teaching the actual

TABLE 14–1
Teaching Printing Using Similar Configurations

Type	Fun Name	Letters
Straight lines	Trees	l, t, i
Diagonals	Slides	y, v, w, x, z, k
Circular	Balls	o, c, a, e
Lines and circles	Stick and balls	d, b, p, q
Rounded	Mountains	m, n, u, r, h, f
Ends are rounded	Hooks	g, h
Curvy	Snake	s

letter formation, some programs will teach writing "a" through "z." Other programs will group together letters that are similar in shape. For example, the "c" and "o" may be taught at the same time (see Table 14–1). Some students benefit from the D'Nealian Handwriting Program (Thurber & Jordan, 1981), which provides a transition between manuscript and cursive. Lowercase manuscript letters are formed like their corresponding cursive letters. Because the letters are formed with continuous strokes, the writing tool does not have to be lifted off the paper and then re-placed, as happens with more traditional configurations such as diagonals or lines and circles (see Table 14–1). Students with poor hand and finger stability can control movements of writing tools when using the D'Nealian approach. In addition, they do not need to learn manuscript and then learn cursive formation. Another popular program is Handwriting Without Tears (manufactured by Handwriting Without Tears). This program has a readiness, printing, and cursive program, is developmentally based, and easy to use (*http://www.hwtears.com/*).

Several major companies (e.g., Allyn & Bacon; Doubleday; Macmillan; Charles E. Merrill; and Scott, Foresman) produce handwriting materials, and teachers will need to determine the adequacy of the program for the individual student. There are several software programs that can assist with teaching handwriting skills, such as School Fonts for Beginning Writers (manufactured by Mayer-Johnson, Inc.).

There are certain principles that should be used in conjunction for any effective handwriting program. First, teachers should use direct instruction and provide individualized instruction in this skill. Second, a variety of techniques and methods should be used that match the student's individual needs. Third, handwriting should be taught frequently, typically several times a week. Fourth, short handwriting lessons should be given in the context of writing assignments. Fifth, overlearning of handwriting skills should occur before being applied in context. Sixth, handwriting should be periodically assessed, and students should evaluate their own handwriting. This is especially important for students with physical disabilities, since their motoric abilities may change over time. Seventh, handwriting should be taught as a visual and a motor task (Bos & Vaughn, 2002; Hagin, 1983).

Identifying and Correcting Problems. Students will need to be assessed as to their handwriting legibility. Adaptations of writing tools and paper should be made where needed. Whether they are effective in assisting students to have legible handwriting as a means of written expression will need to be determined. There are several published handwriting assessments that may be used to assess handwriting, such as Basic School Skills Inventory (Hamill, Pearson, & Maddox, 1997), Denver Handwriting Analysis (Anderson, 1983), Test of Legible Handwriting (Larsen & Hammill, 1989), and Zaner-Bloser Evaluation Scales (1984). Informal assessments can also occur by examining such areas as (a) letter formation, (b) letter size, proportion, and alignment, (c) line quality, (d) slant, (e) spacing, (f) proper joining of cursive letters, and (g) writing in a left-to-right order (Mercer & Mercer, 2001). By identifying areas of difficulty, further instruction or modifications may be targeted. The teacher and occupational therapist should first evaluate whether physical access problems are resulting in poor handwriting. The work surface or adapted writing tool may need to be modified or changed. If physical access problems are ruled out, other, more typical problems should be investigated. Table 14–2 provides several common problems and typical remediation strategies that may be tried to improve handwriting.

Electronic Writing Tools: Computers

Students with legible handwriting may be required to use a computer to submit their schoolwork. Students whose handwriting is illegible or who cannot use handheld writing utensils need to use mechanical or electronic writing tools for writing. Interference with writing and accessing written material due to motoric

TABLE 14–2
Diagnostic Chart for Manuscript and Cursive Writing

Factor	Problem	Possible Cause	Remediation
		MANUSCRIPT WRITING	
Shape	Letters slanted	Paper slanted	Place paper straight and pull straight-line strokes toward center of body.
	Varies from standard	Improper mental image of letter	Have student write problem letters on chalkboard.
Size	Too large	Poor understanding of writing lines	Reteach size concept by pointing out purpose of each line on writing paper.
		Exaggerated arm movement	Reduce arm movement, especially on circle and part-circle letters.
		Improper mental image of letter	Have student write problem letters on chalkboard.
	Too small	Poor understanding of writing lines	Reteach size concept by pointing out purpose of each line on writing paper.
		Overemphasis on finger movement	Stress arm movement; check hand–pencil and arm–desk positions to be sure arm movement is possible.
		Improper mental image of letter	Have student write problem letters on chalkboard.
	Not uniform	Adjusting writing hand after each letter	Stress arm movement; move paper with nonwriting hand so writing hand can remain in proper writing position.
		Overemphasis on finger movement	Stress arm movement; check arm–desk and hand–pencil positions.
Space	Crowded letters in words	Poor understanding of space concepts	Reteach uniform spacing between letters (finger or pencil width).
	Too much space between letters	Improper lowercase letter size and shape	Review concepts of size and shape; provide appropriate corrections under size and shape.
Alignment	Letters not sitting on baseline	Improper letter formation	Evaluate work for letter shape; stress bringing straight-line strokes all the way down to baseline.
		Poor understanding of baseline concept	Review purpose of baseline on writing paper.
		Improper hand–pencil and paper–desk positions	Check positions to make sure student is able to reach baseline easily.
	Letters not of consistent height	Poor understanding of size concept	Review concept of letter size in relationship to lines provided on writing paper.
Line quality	Too heavy or too light	Improper writing pressure	Review hand–pencil position; place wadded paper tissue on palm of writing hand to relax writing grip; demonstrate desired line quality.

TABLE 14–2
(Continued)

Factor	Problem	Possible Cause	Remediation
		CURSIVE WRITING	
Shape	Letters too oval	Overemphasis of arm movement and poor image of letter	Check arm–desk position; review letter size and shape.
	Letters too narrow	Finger writing	Check positions to allow for arm movement.
		Overemphasis of straight-line stroke	Make sure straight-line stroke does not come all the way down to baseline in letters such as *l*, *b*, and *t*.
		Poor mental image of letter shape	Use transparent overlay for student's personal evaluation of shape. In all problems of letter shape, review letters in terms of the basic strokes.
Size	Letters too large	Exaggerated arm movement	Check arm–desk position for overmovement of forearm.
		Poor mental image of letter size	Review base and top line concepts in relation to ¼ space, ½ space, and ¾ space; use transparent overlay for student's personal evaluation of letter size.
	Letters too small or letters not uniform	Finger movement	Check arm–desk and hand–pencil positions; stress arm movement.
		Poor mental image of letter size	Review concept of letter size (¼ space, ½ space, and ¾ space) in relation to base and top lines; use transparent overlay for student's personal evaluation of letter size.
Space	Letters in words crowded or spacing between letters uneven	Finger movement	Check arm–desk, hand–pencil positions; stress arm movement.
		Poor understanding of joining strokes	Review how letters are joined; show ending stroke of one letter joined to beginning stroke of following letter; practice writing letters in groups of five.
	Too much space provided between letters and words	Exaggerated arm movement	Check arm–desk position for over-movement of forearm.
		Poor understanding of joining strokes	Review joining strokes; practice writing groups of letters by rhythmic count.
	Uneven space between words	Poor understanding of between-word spacing	Review concept of spacing between words; show beginning stroke in second word starting under ending stroke of preceding word.

(Continued)

TABLE 14–2
(Continued)

Factor	Problem	Possible Cause	Remediation
Alignment	Poor letter alignment along baseline	Incorrect writing position; finger movement; exaggerated arm movement	Check all writing positions; stress even, rhythmic writing movement.
		Poor understanding of baseline concept	Use repetitive exercise with emphasis on relationship of baseline to written word.
		Incorrect use of joining strokes	Review joining strokes.
	Uneven letter alignment in words relative to size	Poor understanding of size concept	Show size relationships between lower- and uppercase, and ¼ space, ½ space, and ¾ space lowercase letters; use repetitive exercise with emphasis on uniform height of smaller letters.
Speed and ease	Writing becomes illegible under stress and speed (grades 4, 5, and 6)	Degree of handwriting skill is insufficient to meet speed requirements	Improve writing positions; develop more arm movement and less finger movement.
	Writing becomes illegible when writing activity is too long	Handwriting positions have not been perfected to allow handwriting ease	Improve all writing positions, especially hand–pencil position; stress arm movement.
Slant	Back slant	Left-handedness	Correct hand–pencil and paper–desk positions.
	Vertical	Poor positioning	Correct hand–pencil and paper–desk positions.
	Too far right	Overemphasis of finger movement	Make sure student pulls slant strokes toward center of body if right-handed and to left elbow if left-handed.
			Use slant line instruction sheets as aid to teaching slant.
			Use transparent overlay for student's personal evaluation.
			Review all lowercase letters that derive their shape from the slant line.
			Write lowercase alphabet on chalkboard; retrace all slant strokes in color chalk.

Note. From *Teaching Students with Learning Problems* 5/e by Mercer/Mercer, © 1998. Reprinted by permission of Prentice-Hall, Inc., Upper Saddle River, NJ.

constraints can be addressed by provision of adapted computer keyboards or other input devices (e.g., a switch) for the computer, or specialized software (e.g., word prediction) that promotes story and journal dictation (Katims, 1993). In one case study, by Steelman, Pierce, and Kopenhaver (1993), two students were able to increase their writing ability by using computers to practice writing twice weekly. They used such adapted devices as mini-keyboards, keyguards, and dedicated communication devices, along with specialized software (word prediction software). Another study by Smith (1989) and Smith et al. (1989) confirms the usefulness of adapted computers and software for written communication. These adaptations or assistive technology devices that can improve access to the computer include accessibility options, keyboard modifications, keyboard layout options, alternative keyboards, mouse alternatives, alternative input devices, and different forms of output (Heller & Swinehart-Jones, 2003).

Accessibility Options. Accessibility options can be particularly helpful for students with physical disabilities. Many computers come with standard accessibility options that can modify how the keyboard functions (most accessibility options can be found by looking under "My Computer" and then under "Control Panel"). There are several different accessibility options, such as **filter keys**, which makes the computer ignore repeated keystrokes or slows down the repeat rate (e.g., a student who holds the key too long will get an "s" when this option is used instead of "ssssssssss"). Another option is often known as **sticky keys**, which will allow the student to press one key at a time, instead of having to press two at a time when using "ctrl," "shift," or "alt." Other examples of accessibility options (often found under "Mouse") will slow down the mouse or give it a trail to increase visibility. If the computer lacks these and other options, they can often be downloaded or purchased.

Keyboard Modifications. There are several adaptations that allow access to the standard keyboard. Some students will benefit from using moveable forearm rests or adjustable arm supports that clamp onto the computer or table. These reduce the effects of repetitive motion and assist people with limited motion. Some students may benefit from standard gel pads, which enable them to rest their wrists and improve their stability while typing.

Adaptations to standard keyboards can be made with either hardware or software. Some hardware changes are moisture guards and keyguards. For students who drool, a moisture guard may be used. This is a clear protective covering that is placed over the keys to protect them from fluids. Keyguards are hard plastic grids that fit over the keyboard, with holes over each of the keys. Keyguards allow students to drag their hands across the keyboard without activating other keys. When the student is able to move his or her hand to the desired letter, he or she puts a finger into the hole over the desired key and presses the key.

Other modifications to the standard keyboard include modifying the print on the keys. For students with visual impairments, large print and Braille keytop labels may be applied over the regular keys. However, this may not be desirable for students learning to touch-type, since typing is taught by position, not by reading each key.

Keyboard Layout Options. Some students may benefit from having a different keyboard layout than the standard "QWERTY" layout. A keyboard layout is how the keys are arranged on the keyboard. The arrangement is determined by computer software, and the keys are labeled to correspond to the software. Typically the keyboard layout is in QWERTY format, which corresponds to the top line of letters, which begins with "Q," "W," "E," "R," "T," "Y." However, many computer programs and writing devices (e.g., AlphaSmart) allow for different keyboard layouts. The Dvorak keyboard layout, for example, was designed by Dr. August Dvorak to speed up typing and reduce fatigue by arranging the keys by the most common letter combinations. Keyboard layouts have also been devised by Dvorak and others for one-handed typists and for people accessing the keyboard using a mouth stick or head stick. In these layouts, the keyboard is arranged to allow for quicker, less fatiguing one-handed typing (see Figure 14–8). Computer users may download Dvorak's keyboard layouts from the Internet onto their computers; they do not need to modify their hardware keyboards to use these layouts. After selecting the type of keyboard layout, labels may be attached to the keys to show the corresponding letters.

Alternative Keyboards. Students unable to access the standard keyboard may benefit from alternative keyboards. As seen in Figure 14–9, alternative keyboards may be larger for students requiring larger targets to make their selection (e.g., Intellikeys by Intellitools) or smaller for students with a limited range of motion (e.g., WinMini by TASH), or who are accessing the keyboard using a mouth stick or head stick (and have good control). Keyboards also come in different shapes and configurations. If a student is unable to use a standard keyboard due to its size or configuration, he or she can be assessed for an alternative keyboard.

Mouse Alternatives. Some students with physical impairments will have difficulty manipulating a standard mouse. This may occur even when accessibility modifications have been made to the computer (e.g., slowing down the mouse, having a mouse trail). Alternatives to the mouse may be used, such as a joystick, touchpad, or a trackball. A careful evaluation will determine if these are feasible alternatives for the student.

Alternative Input Devices. When keyboards or alternative keyboards (or mouse alternatives) are not effective options for the student, the computer can be accessed by

FIGURE 14–8
Different types of keyboard layouts

(a) QWERTY keyboard layout.

(b) Dvorak keyboard layout.

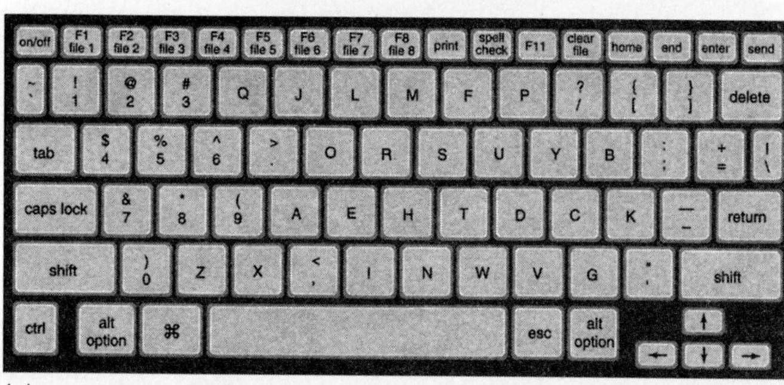

(c) Right one-handed keyboard layout.

(d) Left one-handed keyboard layout.

Note. KEYTIME, Inc., 5512 Roosevelt Way N.E., Seattle, WA 98105-3631. See http://www.microsoft.com/enable/products/dvorak.htm for Dvorak keyboard downloads. These are available from the Internet, and no permission is required to download them.

FIGURE 14–9
Two examples of alternative keyboards are the large IntelliKey keyboard produced by Intellitools and the mini keyboard produced by TASH International, Inc.

FIGURE 14–10
A variety of different switches that may be used instead of a keyboard to access the computer

using alternative input devices. Alternative input devices are used as substitutes to the standard computer input devices. There are three main categories of alternative input devices: switches, pointing devices, and voice recognition (Lewis, 1993). A switch is a device that can be connected to the computer and used in place of a keyboard. Switches come in all shapes and sizes (see Figure 14–10) and are made to be accessed by any number of different body parts. The student's position, the placement of the switch, and the type of switch must be considered. For literacy activities on the computer, switches are usually used in combination with software programs that permit scanning of pictures, letters, words, phrases, stories, or documents onto the keyboard. After highlighting the desired item (i.e., the picture or letter), the student activates the switch and the selection is made.

Often switches are used in combination with **on-screen keyboards**, such as EZ Keys (Words + Inc.), and REACH Scan Plus (Applied Human Factors, Inc.). An on-screen keyboard can be displayed directly on the computer monitor. The software program allows scanning of the keyboard, and the student makes a selection by activating (e.g., pushing, touching, or pulling) a switch. Many of these on-screen keyboards are also accessed through other means, such as a standard keyboard, mouse, trackball, various switches, and Morse code. Some programs also have word prediction and abbreviation expansion (i.e., when an abbreviation is typed in, an entire word or phrase substitutes automatically).

There are several different types of **pointer devices**. Unlike switches, these devices work by direct selection, in which the student points to his or her choice in some manner. Many of these devices (e.g., Optical Headpointer and HeadMaster, manufactured by Prentke Romich) use some type of optical sensor or reflector that is mounted on a headband. By moving his or her head, the student points the sensor or reflector (often appearing as a light) on a letter on an on-screen keyboard to make a selection. Some alternative input devices are made to control the computer completely through eye gaze. These systems track the movements of the student's eye as he or she looks at the computer screen. The eye movements are then converted into computer input.

Another device that is used in combination with pointing devices is a **TouchWindow** (by Edmark). A TouchWindow is a transparent plastic screen that is placed over the computer monitor screen. Programs using compatible software will allow the student to touch the screen (with a finger, mouth stick, or head stick) to provide input into the computer and make a selection.

The last category of alternative input devices is **voice recognition software**. Instead of using an alternative input device, the student speaks and the software converts that speech into words on the computer screen. The software requires each student to "train" the software to recognize his or her voice. Students with cerebral palsy who have dysarthric speech had some difficulty having their speech recognized by earlier voice recognition software (Coleman & Meyers, 1991). Although improvements have made this technology far more feasible than in the past, careful assessment of the voice recognition software and the student is needed to determine its effectiveness (Koester, 2001; Rosen & Yampolsky, 2000). Voice recognition software programs include Dragon Naturally Speaking (L & H Speech Products) and ViaVoice (IBM).

Output Modifications. There are several types of output modifications that may accommodate students who have additional sensory impairments. Most computers will allow the color of the print and the background color to be changed for better contrast and easier viewing to accommodate students with visual impairments or to accommodate viewing preferences. Screen enlargement programs such as ZoomText Xtra (by Ai Squared) may enlarge the screen for better viewing. Large-screen monitors may also be selected. For students who are blind or have learning disabilities, voice output software, such as JAWS for Windows Screen Reading Software (by Freedom Scientific, Inc.), can be used to allow the screen to be read aloud. Printers can also provide large printouts or material can be printed in Braille using a **Brailler embosser** (another name for a Braille printer).

Keyboarding Skills and Computer Tools

Keyboarding Skills and Learning to Use Alternative Input Devices. Students who use a computer with standard or alternative access will require instruction in its use. For students using a standard keyboard, there are several keyboarding programs that can be used to teach keyboard awareness and touch-typing skills. These include Type + Learn Jr., for kindergarten to grade 2 (manufactured by Sunburst); Learn to Type 3, for age 3 to adult (manufactured by Sunburst); Typing Tutor 9 (manufactured by Knowledge Adventure); and Read, Write, & Type (manufactured by The Learning Company).

Students who are only able to access the computer with one hand will require alternate instruction. Instruction may be aimed at using a different keyboard layout, or if the standard QWERTY layout is used, the typing hand is placed in the middle of the middle row and the student is taught to access the surrounding keys with the certain fingers (see Figure 14–11). Software programs, such as 5 Finger Typist (manufactured by Mayer-Johnson), are available to help teach this skill. Another option is changing the keyboard layout to a one-handed (right or left) Dvorak layout, which is geared toward promoting the speed of one-handed typists. A third option is to use a program such as Half-QWERTY (manufactured by Matias Corporation), which allows the student to keep his or her hand over one side of the keyboard and, by holding down the space bar, to access the keys on the other side of the keyboard. (For example, if the student has only right hand use, he presses the key under the right index finger [in typical typing position] to type a "j," and when he holds down the space bar and presses the exact same key, it will type an "f," which is in the mirror-image position to the "j" on the keyboard.)

Students who are learning to use alternative input devices will need practice to develop accuracy and speed. To promote effective learning of these devices, instruction in their use will need to be broken into small steps. Data should be taken on writing accuracy and speed over time to assess for improvement.

Word-Processing Programs. Word-processing programs, e.g., Microsoft Word (manufactured by Microsoft) and ClarisWorks (manufactured by Claris Corporation), are used to assist with the writing process by creating, editing, and saving text. Often these programs come with a spell-checker, thesaurus, and grammar-checker. Selection of a word-processing program should be based on such factors as (a) ease of use, (b) transparency to the user (which allows the student to focus on writing instead of the word processor) and (c) writing effectiveness.

There are several word processors that are available with voice output (e.g., Write:OutLoud, manufactured by Don Johnston, Inc.; IntelliTalk II, manufactured by Intellitools). These talking word-processing programs read the text that has been entered by the student. In some instances, students with severe speech and physical impairments have been found to make fewer errors in their final drafts and more self-corrections when using a word processor with speech feedback (Koke & Neilson, 1987; Koppenhaver & Yoder, 1993).

Word Prediction Programs. Word prediction programs were originally designed to improve the typing rate of students with physical disabilities. As a student types, the word prediction program provides a chang-

FIGURE 14–11
When using a standard keyboard layout, the student who can only use one hand will be taught to place the hand on the "F," "G," "H," and "J" keys. For a right hand, the index finger pushes all keys in the area labeled "1," the middle finger pushes all keys in the area labeled "2," and so forth

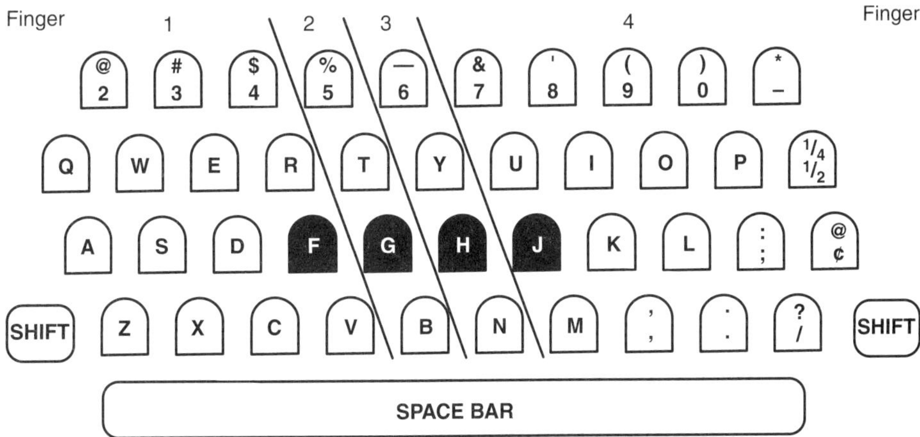

ing list of possible words that the student may be typing based on the letters being typed. When a student types the first letter in a word, several selections of words come up on the screen. The word may be selected by typing the word's corresponding number. If none of those are a match, when the second letter is typed, a new set of words comes up on the screen with the same two beginning letters. When the word prediction program displays the desired word, the student selects the word instead of typing out the rest of the word, thus resulting in less keystrokes (which may increase typing speed and reduce fatigue for some students). Word prediction programs include Co:Writer (manufactured by Don Johnston, Inc.), EZ Keys (manufactured Words+, Inc.), and Key Rep (manufactured by Prentke Romich).

Students with physical disabilities may take much longer to type an assignment than their nondisabled peers due to (a) speed limitation from their physical impairments, (b) the use of alternative access devices that use scanning, or (c) fatigue factors that reduce the amount that can be typed at one time. One study (Tumlin & Heller, in press) found some increases in typing speed when using word prediction with students who were very slow typists due to their physical disabilities. However, for the students with physical disabilities who were able to type fast, word prediction made no impact or slowed the typing rate, possibly due to the time it took to scan the list of words provided by the word prediction program. In another study, focusing on students with spina bifida (Tam, Reid, Naumann, & O'Keefer, 2002), word prediction use increased accuracy of text entry.

Programming Abbreviations to Substitute for Words. One alternative to word prediction programs is to program the computer to substitute words for abbreviations. For example, the autocorrect can be modified by adding abbreviations for high-frequency words. For example, a student may type in "sw," and then hit the space bar, which triggers the autocorrect to replace it with his name, "Stephen Williamson." In another example, if the student is learning about the Statue of Liberty, the student may type "sl" and the autocorrect writes out "Statue of Liberty." This can be a time saver and eliminate unnecessary physical effort. Many writing software programs also have this feature, and refer to it as abbreviation expansion.

LITERACY SKILLS: SPELLING

Assessing Spelling

Students with severe speech and physical impairments should be able to demonstrate spelling ability using a computer (with assistive technology when needed), AAC device, and/or an alphabet page that is accessed through a reliable response mode. When determining a student's spelling ability, it is important to be sure that errors are due to a lack of knowledge rather than access problems.

Several formal spelling assessments and diagnostic tests are available to assess spelling levels (e.g., Iowa Test of Basic Skills, Peabody Individual Achievement Tests—Revised, Wide Range Achievement Test 3). Some tests provide diagnostic detailed information about the type of student spelling errors (Diagnostic Spelling Potential Test, Test of Written Spelling). The teacher can also informally assess the student's spelling.

Spelling errors should undergo a spelling error analysis. Spelling errors are examined for the type of errors being made, and additional instruction is provided based upon the errors. There are several different types of spelling errors. Teachers should examine the misspellings for any error patterns such as:

1. missing certain letters consistently due to mistaken letter-sound knowledge,
2. using incorrect blends, digraphs, or diphthongs,
3. using incorrect prefixes or suffixes,
4. omitting silent letters,
5. doubling a consonant when not needed,
6. deleting letters in words,
7. inserting unneeded letters,
8. reversing letters in words, or
9. using the wrong homonym for the intended meaning (Bos & Vaughn, 2002; Hitchcock, 1989; Mercer & Mercer, 2001).

Once errors are identified, additional spelling instruction should occur on the targeted errors.

Spelling Instruction

Phonetically Based Approaches. There are many different approaches to teaching spelling. Most spelling methods are phonetically based. In 1977, Stephens identified nine phonetically based spelling competencies that enabled a student to be a good speller. These are auditory discrimination, knowledge of consonants, phonographs, plurals, syllabication, structural elements, ending changes, vowel digraphs and dipthongs, and silent "e." Today, teaching these spelling competencies is important to promote spelling, as well as teaching words that are exceptions to phonic rules and are frequently encountered in writing (Ekwall & Shanker, 1993). There is typically very little modification needed of spelling programs for use with students who have severe speech and physical impairments. The student is encouraged to sound out the words "in his or her head" as he or she spells them on the computer, AAC device, and/or alphabet board. A careful error analysis is performed so that instruction can target the areas of difficulty.

Multisensory Approaches. Another strategy for teaching spelling is to use one of the multisensory approaches (Fernald, 1943). Spelling words are taught through a combination of visual, auditory, kinesthetic, and tactile modalities. Multisensory approaches emphasizing tactile and kinesthetic modalities will have limited benefit to many students with physical disabilities who are unable to approach the letters tactually or kinesthetically due to their impairments. Other methods that stress word tracing may be inappropriate for students with severe physical impairments.

Visual Mnemonics and Word Associations. Spelling instruction may be supplemented by teaching visual mnemonics and word associations. Visual mnemonics involve adding pictures or symbols to the words (such as adding eyes to the word "look," drawing the "ch" together as one ongoing letter, or marking out silent letters). Typically the visual mnemonic (also referred to as the antecedent prompt) is presented along with the unchanged word for the student to learn to spell. Word associations to promote spelling may also be used, such as "The principal is a 'pal'" (Mercer & Mercer, 2001).

Independent Study Strategies and Instruction for Spelling. Many independent spelling approaches can be taught with little modification. The most basic word study approach involves teaching the student to:

1. Look at the word carefully and say the word. (The student who lacks speech would say it in his or her head using internal speech.)
2. Close his or her eyes and visualize the word.
3. Look again at the word to verify that he or she was visualizing it correctly.
4. Cover the word and write it.
5. Check to see if he or she wrote the word correctly and, if not, start the process over.

Independent study methods that rely on the student only saying the word and spelling aloud limit active student participation. Writing and visualizing the word will give more-concrete practice. There are many variations on this approach, such as the number of times the student writes the word, looks at the word, or says the word.

Other strategies to improve spelling involve showing the student the spelling words and then teaching the student how to spell the word by filling in missing letters. This directs student attention to relevant features of the word. For example, in the **cloze spelling approach**, after the student studies the word, it is presented with the vowel(s) missing and the student must write the entire word with the missing vowel (i.e., cat, c_t). Next the word is presented with the consonants missing and the student must write the entire word with the correct consonants (cat, _a_). Last, the student writes the entire word (Mercer & Mercer, 2001). Other techniques involve having letters missing and providing spaces, then gradually increasing the number of missing letters (i.e., cat, c_t, ca_, _at, c_ _, _ _ _).

Whichever spelling approach, curriculum, or programs are used, it is important that students are actively engaged in the spelling process and that they receive sufficient practice and feedback. Error analysis and specific direct instruction will help remediate any errors that are occurring.

Spelling Tools

Several spelling tools may be used to aid in spelling. Learning how to use a dictionary is one standard tool for enhancing spelling. Also available are handheld spell-checkers that come with and without voice output. Word-processing programs also typically contain spell-checkers. Some of these perform real-time spell-checking that underlines or highlights a misspelling immediately after the word is typed. Typically a selection of correctly spelled words is provided for the student to select the correct word. Word processors with voice output, such as Write:Outloud (manufactured by Don Johnston, Inc.), provide auditory feedback when the word is written. Misspelled words will often not sound correct, which signals the student that there is an error. Often these word-processing programs with speech output also provide spell-checkers with voice output.

Computer Programs for Spelling

Several software programs are available to enhance spelling instruction. Auditory and phonological programs such as Earobics Step 1 (manufactured by Cognitive Concepts) and Simon Sounds It Out (manufactured by Don Johnston, Inc.) may be used to provide instruction and practice in phonological awareness of the different sounds. There are several spelling programs that practice sounding out the words (e.g., Simon Spells, manufactured by Don Johnston, Inc.), teach basic rules of spelling (e.g., Spelling Blaster, manufactured by Knowledge Adventure; Spelling Rules, manufactured by Optimum Resource Inc.), and provide drill and practice of the words the user enters (e.g., Spell-a-Word, manufactured by JR Cooper and Associates).

LITERACY SKILLS: WRITTEN EXPRESSION

Assessing Written Expression

Some students with speech and physical impairments have been found to have difficulty in written expression skills. Part of this may be attributed to lack of access to writing tools in early years. Other problems have been attributed to the habit of using telegraphic messages (often reinforced by some AAC systems), reluctance to use appropriate language structures for fear of not being understood, and slowness in composing written assignments (Smith et al., 1989). A lack of practice may also contribute to problems in written skills, due to lack of time to properly edit and correct a piece of written work when the student writes slowly.

Students should be assessed on their level of written expression skills, and any significant problems should be targeted for individualized instruction. Students' work should be evaluated for grammar as well as written expression. Grammar includes such areas as capitalization, punctuation, and syntax. For written expression ability, one of the first areas to assess is whether students know simple sentence structure and can write a complete sentence. Students who are accustomed to writing telegraphic messages due to their AAC device may need additional instruction on complete sentence structure. Sentences should be evaluated regarding the variety of sentences used (declarative, interrogative), as well as acceptable length, clarity, and content.

When writing a paragraph, or multiple paragraphs, the text is evaluated for effective communication and a logical order. Writing is also evaluated for appropriate quantity of writing, given the student's age and

FIGURE 14–12
Checklist of written expression

Student's Name ____________ Grade ______ Examiner ____________ Date ______

I. PENMANSHIP
(1 = it's a mess, 5 = beautiful)
A. Spacing on the page ____
B. Spacing of the sentences ____
C. Spacing of the words ____
D. Spacing of letters ____
E. Slant ____
F. Letter formations ____
G. Pressure on the paper ____
H. Pencil grip ____

II. SPELLING
____% misspelled
(Check areas in which the student has problems.)
A. Miscalled rule ____
B. Letter insertion ____
C. Letter omission ____
D. Letter substitution ____
E. Phonetic spelling ____
F. Directional confusion ____
G. Schwa or *r*-controlled vowels ____
H. Letter orientation ____
I. Sequence ____
J. Other ____

III. GRAMMAR
(TA = too advanced or not appropriate, A = adequately used in the sample, I = skills needed to be introduced to improve writing, R = needs remediation or review)

	TA	A	I	R	Notes
A. Capitalization					
1. Proper noun					
2. Proper adjective					
3. First word in a sentence					
4. First word in a line of verse					
5. First word in a quotation					
6. Principal words in a title					
7. Personal title					
8. Use of "I" or "O"					
9. Salutation in a letter					
10. Complimentary close in a letter					
11. Other					
B. Punctuation					
1. Period					
2. Comma					
3. Apostrophe					
4. Quotation marks					
5. Question mark					
6. Semicolon					
7. Exclamation mark					
8. Colon					
9. Dash					
10. Parentheses					
11. Brackets					
12. Slash					
C. Syntax					
1. Parts of speech					
a. Verbs					
b. Nouns					
c. Pronouns					
d. Adjectives					
e. Adverbs					
f. Prepositions					
g. Conjunctions					
h. Interjections					

functioning level. Some students who have alternate access devices or who are slow accessing their writing device have deficits in this area. The duration of writing should be timed to determine if the rate improves, or if intervention is needed. In some instances in which the rate is too slow, some of the previously described writing tools may be used to enhance the rate (i.e., word prediction). Figure 14–12 shows a detailed checklist of written expression that may help analyze the student's writing problems.

FIGURE 14–12
(Continued)

	TA	A	I	R	Notes
2. Agreement					
3. Case					
4. Pronoun reference					
5. Order/position of words					
6. Parallelism					
7. Abbreviations/numbers					
8. Paragraph					
9. Tense					

IV. IDEATION
A. Type of writing
1. Story _____ 2. Poem _____ 3. Letter _____ 4. Report _____ 5. Review _____
B. Substance
1. Naming _____ 2. Description _____ 3. Plot _____ 4. Issue _____
C. Productivity
1. Number of words written _____
a. Acceptable number _____ b. Too few _____
D. Comprehensibility
1. Easy to understand _____ 2. Difficult to understand _____ 3. Incomprehensible _____
a. Perseveration of words _____ b. Perseveration of ideas _____ c. Illogical _____ d. Disorganized _____
E. Reality
1. Accurate perception of stimulus or task _____ 2. Inaccurate perception of stimulus or task _____
F. Style
(Tallies)
1. Sentence sense
a. Completeness
(1) Complete sentences _____
(2) Run-on sentences _____
(3) Sentence fragments _____
b. Structure
(1) Simple _____
(2) Compound _____
(3) Complex _____
(4) Compound/complex _____
c. Types
(1) Declarative _____
(2) Interrogative _____
(3) Imperative _____
(4) Exclamatory _____
2. Tone
a. Intimate _____ b. Friendly _____ c. Impersonal _____
3. Word choice
(N = none, F = few, S = some, M = many)
a. Formality
(1) Formal _____ (2) Informal _____ (3) Colloquial _____
b. Complexity
(1) Simple _____ (2) Multisyllable _____ (3) Contractions _____
c. Descriptiveness
(1) Vague _____ (2) Vivid _____ (3) Figures of speech _____
d. Appropriateness
(1) Inexact words _____ (2) Superfluous words/repetitions _____ (3) Omissions _____

Note: Reprinted, with changes in notation, with permission of the publisher and author from J. A. Poteet, "Informal Assessment of Written Expressions," *Learning Disability Quarterly*, 1980, *3*(4), pp. 90–92. © Council for Learning Disabilities.

Early Written Expression

Children should be encouraged to manipulate writing tools (or adapted writing tools) from an early age. As children "scribble" with a pencil or computer, they should be encouraged to tell about their writing. This helps to reinforce the connection between "scribbling" (or pretend writing) and meaning. For students who are AAC users, this means that their AAC device needs to accommodate a range of vocabulary. If that is not possible, children can also be given a topic to "write" about and through a series of yes-or-no questions determine what they are writing.

As children's writing develops, many teachers will have their students work on journal writing each day. Children either think of a topic or are given one, and are encouraged to write a few sentences about it. Younger students are often encouraged to draw a picture about what they have written. Software programs designed for students who are transitioning from pictures to words promote writing by having the student select pictures, words, or phrases from a series of grids on the computer (e.g., Clicker 4 manufactured by Don Johnston; Writing with Symbols 2000, manufactured by Mayer-Johnson, Inc.).

As a student's writing develops, he or she will no longer need grid support, but be able to write a sentence on his or her own. The teacher may help support the student by writing a word or two for the student to use in the sentence to help build vocabulary and spelling. Often, giving a story or a topic to write about produces more-complex writing than letting students write about topics of their own choosing (Dobson, 1989).

Written Expression Instruction

Students with physical impairments are taught conventional writing skills in much the same manner as individuals without disabilities. Writing is often taught as a process, in which a topic is selected, ideas are brainstormed or researched, ideas are organized, a first draft is written, editing occurs, and a second draft is written. Emphasis is placed on learning the process, rather than giving excessive corrective feedback that may interfere with learning the process (Isaacson, 1988). Students with physical disabilities may require extensive support in several of these areas.

Brainstorming. The first steps—topic selection and brainstorming or researching—can be problematic for some students with physical disabilities. Some students with physical impairments will lack the basic, broad experiences of students without disabilities, due to transportation or mobility problems. These students may lack information with which other students are very familiar. It then becomes important that the topic selected for beginning the writing process is familiar or can be experienced with the rest of the students in a prewriting activity. For the more mature writer, a topic may be selected that requires research. With Internet access, many students are able to obtain information without the problems of manipulating books, encyclopedias, and journals. Teaching a student research skills on the Internet becomes a priority when physical impairments interfere with accessing other forms of materials.

Editing. Another difficulty encountered by students with physical disabilities is the editing process. This is especially the case when a student with physical impairment has very slow writing due to problematic physical movements or the use of alternate input modes that tend to be slow (i.e., scanning). It may take a student a class period to write two sentences, while the rest of the class writes the first draft of an entire paper. Although it is tempting to skip the revision part of writing for the student with physical impairments due to the time involved, this omission will reduce practice and result in limited writing skills. The educational team needs to assess whether the student's writing rate would improve with more practice or through the use of other forms of assistive technology.

As previously discussed, word prediction programs may help increase students' writing speed. An abbreviation expansion approach may also be used to increase writing speed. Students can use abbreviations and short codes to recall longer words, phrases, and sentences by programming the autocorrect or spell-checker. In other cases, an alternate form of access to the computer may also be warranted. If assistive technology is found to be appropriate, modifications may need to be made in the assignments. One suggestion is to decrease the number of required papers and have alternate assignments for other material. The required papers would have to have the necessary editing and rewrites to help the student learn good writing skills. Extended deadlines for turning in edited work typically are necessary.

Syntax and Content. Beginning writing depends upon learning how to construct a sentence, then a paragraph, and then a paper. When writing sentences, some students may need assistance to develop appropriate syntax and content. One beginning strategy is to provide the student with several words that they must arrange in order to make a sentence. For example, the student may be given the words "I cat have a." If the student is unable to physically arrange the words, he or she could point to (or otherwise indicate) which word should start the sentence, and a partner could move the word to a first-word slot and continue until the student has selected all of the words. Another strategy is to pair words with numbers over them. The student selects the number and a partner arranges the words in order. Typing out the words is also an option, but the emphasis should be on sentence construction, and typing may take a long time, depending upon the student's physical abilities and means of typing.

A second strategy for teaching beginning syntax is providing incomplete sentences for the student to complete. For example, when teaching the subject of a sentence, the teacher could provide the sentence "__________ is playing ball" and the student would complete it. Later sentences could have verbs missing (e.g., "Tommy __________ candy"). More-complex parts of sentences can be taught in the same manner. Over time, less and less of the sentence may be provided to encourage more-independent writing skills (i.e., "The bird __________"). Eventually, the student may be provided only a topic or may need to develop one independently.

Simple Sentences. Once a student is able to produce correct syntax and write comprehensible sentences, the complexity of the sentence should be examined. Some students use very few adjectives and adverbs in their sentences. One way to encourage more-complex sentences is to first write out the student's sentence. Next, the teacher provides a card that lists the words "size," "shape," "kind," "color," "how many," "when," "where," "how," and "how much." The student examines the sentence to see if it can be expanded to include any of these. The sentence is rewritten as more information is added to it. This can be done as a game in which the student makes a check next to the descriptor category that he or she was able to use in the sentence and he or she receives points for each added word.

Mnemonics. There are several mnemonics that may be used to help a student remember basic writing steps. For sentence writing, Schumaker and Sheldon (1985) developed the mnemonic PENS (Pick a sentence type and formula, Explore words to fit the formula, Note the words, and Search for verbs and subjects and check). Students can be taught to use the mnemonic to assist them in writing a sentence.

Paragraph writing may be taught using mnemonic strategies, visual strategies, and outliners. One mnemonic strategy adapted from Welch (1992) is PLEASE, which is: Pick a topic and format, List information, Evaluate if list is complete and organize the list, Always start your paragraph with a topic sentence, Supply the supporting sentences, End with a concluding sentence that rephrases the topic sentence, and Evaluate for errors. As seen in Figure 14–13, visual strategies that teach basic paragraph writing may be initially used, including guided paragraphs with fill-in-the-blank formats or visual strategies to help learn basic paragraph format.

Paper writing with multiple paragraphs may be taught using any number of strategies. Some students may be taught the mnemonic POWER, which stands for: Plan, Organize, Write, Edit, and Revise (Englert,

FIGURE 14–13
Two ways of promoting early paragraph writing

a. *Guided Paragraph Writing*

This story is about ______________________ (who).
In the story the two girls argue about ______________
______________. After that happens, ______________
______________________. Then, ______________
______________________. The girls stop arguing when
______________________________. The story
end ______________________________.

b. *Beginning Paragraph Planner*

The Lamp Paragraph—Filled with bright ideas.

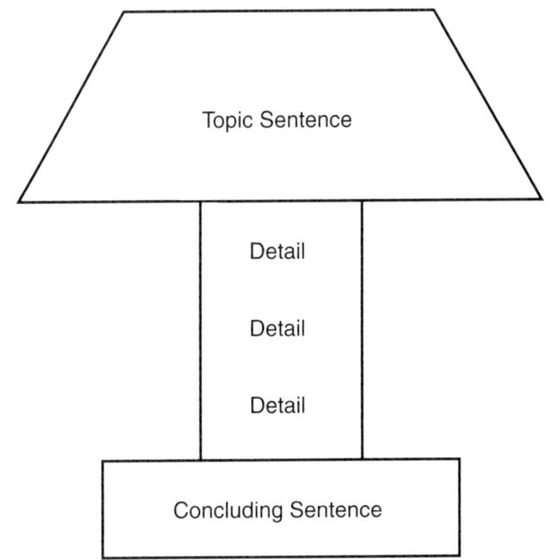

Raphael, Anderson, Anthony, & Stevens, 1991). Another variation is the strategy TOWER, which stands for Think about content, Order topics and details, Write the draft, Look for Errors, and Revise/rewrite (Mercer & Mercer, 2001). Paper writing typically builds on good sentence and paragraph writing. Editing and looking for errors typically involves looking at the sentence structure, logical order of the paragraphs, punctuation, spelling, capitalization, and appearance of the paper. One popular mnemonic used for error monitoring is COPS (Schumaker, Nolan, & Deshler, 1985). COPS is a series of self-questions regarding Capitalization, Overall appearances, Punctuation, and Spelling.

When mnemonics are used, students with AAC systems may program the mnemonic into their AAC device as a reminder. This also allows quick access to the mnemonic if the student has questions for the teacher regarding its use.

To improve writing skills, students should write frequently and in a number of different formats. Some students may be required to keep journals, write letters, write newsletter articles, or write informational reports.

Software Support for Written Expression

Software to Assist with Grammar. Some students will need assistance to learn grammar and parts of speech. There are several useful software programs, ranging from those that teach beginning grammar skills (e.g., learning proper nouns, tenses) to those that teach more advanced skills (e.g., word order, punctuation). Programs include Grammar (manufactured by Optimum Resource Inc.), Grammar Fitness (manufactured by Merit Software), Grammar Play with Alps and Droops (manufactured by Optimal-Education Learning Materials), and Word Order Plus (manufactured by Parrot Software).

Outliners, Process Tools, Editing Tools, and Style Aids. There are several software programs that may be used to assist with the writing process. Some of these include outliners, process tools, editing tools, and style aids. **Outliner software** programs provide a written and/or graphic outline to assist students in planning what they are going to write. Examples of outliner programs are Kidspiration (manufactured by Inspiration Software), Inspiration (manufactured by Inspiration Software), and Draft:Builder (manufactured by Don Johnston Inc.). **Process tool software** programs assist the student in starting stories, offer questions to evaluate what is written, and/or provide editing assistance. Some software programs with process tools include Writing Process Workshop (manufactured by Educational Activities Software) and Writing Workshop (manufactured by Milliken Publishing Co.). **Editing tools** include spell-checking, a thesaurus, and grammar-checking. **Style aid software** provides the student with information about different types of writing.

Desktop Publishing and Multimedia. For more advanced presentations, students will be instructed in desktop publishing and multimedia programs. Desktop publishing programs are used to combine text and graphics in several different formats, especially newsletters, reports, and flyers. Multimedia programs can also add sound and video, in addition to text and graphics. Some multimedia programs include Kid Pix Studio Deluxe (manufactured by Riverdeep–The Learning Company), Kid Works Deluxe (manufactured by Knowledge Adventure) and Kid's Media Magic (manufactured by Humanities Software).

LITERACY SKILLS: FUNCTIONAL WRITING

Assessment of Functional Writing

Students with additional cognitive impairments are usually taught functional writing, which focuses on skills in the natural environment (Westling & Fox, 2004), rather than use conventional written expression, which targets more academic uses of writing. To determine what should be taught as functional writing skills, an ecological assessment is used. This follows the same procedure as described under functional reading, but it examines what needs to be written in each activity to provide success to the individual. Functional writing will range from writing a grocery list or phone message to more-complex writing skills such as filling out an application. The requirements of each activity need to be examined, and the requisite writing skills need to be targeted for instruction. It should also be noted that students with moderate mental retardation have been taught to write letters (Collins, Branson, Hall, & Rankin, 2001), and other types of writing for socialization, leisure, and fun may also be stressed for students with physical and cognitive impairments.

Functional Writing Strategies

There are many types of functional writing strategies that may be used to teach students functional writing skills. Some of the functional writing strategies that should be considered for students with physical and cognitive impairments include writing tools, pictures for writing, matching to sample, and forms.

Writing Tools. As with conventional writing strategies, the first consideration is access to writing tools. This would follow the same considerations as discussed under conventional writing. One additional consideration is whether the student would benefit from a signature stamp that allows the student to stamp his or her name instead of writing it. Stamps may be composed of a variety of words or pictures for writing lists, addresses, and other ideas. This can be a nice alternative to the computer, which may be difficult for some students to learn. Signature stamps reduce the need to perform unnecessary writing tasks, which is especially critical for students who become fatigued easily.

Pictures for Writing. Functional writing may include using pictures instead of or in addition to written words. Grocery lists, recipes, messages, and other types of functional writing may be replaced or augmented with the use of symbols. Some adapted cookbooks include pictures that represent aspects of shopping steps in meal preparation. These pictures can also be produced with appropriate software. For students who have difficulty writing with traditional orthography, using pictures and symbols may be an appropriate alternative.

Match-to-Sample Strategy. Writing skills may also be promoted through having students copy a sample of writing. This may occur through handwriting, computer, or AAC access. Initially students may be prompted to copy a word or sentence through tracing lines. To aid in copying a writing sample, the letters may be highlighted on the keyboard, or irrelevant keys may be blocked out. This is especially useful as the student is learning the layout of the keyboard. Eventually, written material may be available for students to copy without prompts. Through repetition and systematic training, students will often attain writing skills. They may do so by being able to copy (which can lead to some job opportunities) or, over time, by learning to independently engage in some functional writing tasks. A dictionary in which each word is defined by a picture may remain available to assist students.

Forms. Functional writing involving applications or forms will require systematic instruction. It is important that actual forms be used. Some students will be unable to access these forms unless they are available on the computer. Specific instruction on what to look for on a form and what is being asked is necessary, as well as training in the writing skills needed to complete the forms. The teacher may acquire forms or use curricula that address this type of written instruction.

SUMMARY AND CONCLUSION

Writing is a critical skill that may pose challenges for students with physical or multiple disabilities. Several modifications and adaptations may be needed to allow these students access to writing tools. This may result in using handheld adapted writing tools or electronic writing tools, such as a computer with adaptations. Word-processing programs and word prediction programs may assist with the writing process, as may spell-checkers. As these children are provided access, they should be encouraged from a young age to "scribble" or pretend write with an adapted pencil or computer, and to talk about what they have written in order to learn the connection between writing and meaning. As writing becomes more developed, written expression is systematically taught through the use of any number of methods to promote writing sentences, paragraphs, and finally papers. Functional writing strategies may include using pictures for writing or a match-the-sample writing technique.

QUESTIONS FOR DISCUSSION

1. You have a student with severe spastic cerebral palsy. Discuss possible ways to make writing accessible.
2. Examine the following passage written by a student. Identify the problems and discuss possible interventions: "I swim. the pool coold. I fun. Go tommoro."
3. You have a student in your class who accesses the alphabet through a scanning program. He currently writes approximately four words per minute. What are some of the possible ways to help the student?
4. Examine some of the software for written expression. What are the advantages and disadvantages? How can you determine the appropriateness of the software for a specific student?
5. Explain how words are selected for instruction using an ecological inventory for students with multiple impairments. Select a specific environment and discuss the words that would be selected for an activity in that environment.

FOCUS ON THE NET

ABLEDATA

http://www.abledata.com

Abledata is a federally funded project that provides information on assistive technology and rehabilitation equipment available from various national and international sources. Searches can be done by keyword, product type, company, or brand. Adapted keyboards, input devices for the computer, and writing tools can be found at this site, as well as numerous other assistive technology devices. This site also offers resource centers, a consumer forum, a reading room, and links.

Carol Hurst's Children's Literature Site

http://www.carolhurst.com

This site contains a collection of reviews of great books for students; ideas about ways to use them in the classroom; and collections of books and activities about particular subjects, curricular areas, themes, and professional topics. These book reviews often contain questions for discussion and writing. Books can be searched by titles or by curriculum areas (such as U.S. history, world history, math, geography, cultures, science, literature, art, reading, writing).

Closing the Gap

http:closingthegap.com

Closing the Gap provides up-to-date information on thousands of assistive technology products, including hardware and software. Descriptions of the products are given as well as manufacturers' contact information.

Education World

http://www.education-world.com

Education World is a Web site created for educators. It contains daily school news articles, monthly site reviews, and employment listings. The daily school news articles contain lesson plans on a variety of topics, with writing assignments and projects. The site covers content and lesson plans across several subject areas: the arts, foreign language, history, language and literature, math, PE and health, science, social science, and technology. Each lesson plan specifies how it relates to national education standards. This site allows users to search over 120,000 Web sites that can be located through title or subject.

Knowledge Network Explorer

http://www.kn.pacbell.com/wired

This site contains Web-based lessons and activities. Examples of activities on this site include Eyes on Art (introduction to art, art history, humanities, and critical thinking from kindergarten to college level), Searching for China (which demonstrates a variety of Web-based activity approaches), and Look Who's Footing the Bill (which uses interactive budget simulations, the national debt clock, and online articles). Various projects that students can learn about or participate in (e.g., Rainforest Action Network, 54 Ways You Can Help the Homeless) are described. Several resources, links, and a searchable library are also provided by this Web site.

Trace Research and Development Center
http://www.trace.wisc.edu

This site provides information on products to improve accessibility. To make the computer accessible for individuals with physical, sensory, and multiple disabilities, look under the Computer category. Information is provided under the subcategories of Computer and Software Developers, Computer Access Programs at Trace, Software Toolkits, and Other Computer Access Resources.

REFERENCES

Anderson, E. M., & Plewis, I. (1977). Impairment of motor skills in children with spina bifida cystica and hydrocephalus: An exploratory study. *British Journal of Psychology, 68,* 61–70.

Anderson, P. L. (1983). Denver Handwriting Analysis. Novato, CA: Academic Therapy.

Berninger, V. W., & Gans, B. M. (1986). Assessing word processing capability of the nonvocal, nonwriting. *Augmentative and Alternative Communication, 2,* 56–63.

Bigge, J. L. (1991). *Teaching individuals with physical and multiple disabilities* (3rd ed.). Upper Saddle River, NJ: Merrill/Prentice Hall.

Blischak, D. M. (1995). Thomas the Writer: Case study of a child with severe physical, speech, and visual impairments. *Language, Speech, and Hearing Services in the Schools, 26,* 11–20.

Bos, C. S., & Vaughn, S. (2002). *Strategies for teaching students with learning and behavior problems* (5th ed.). Boston: Allyn & Bacon.

Chomsky, C. (1970). Reading, writing, and phonology. *Harvard Educational Review, 40,* 284–309.

Chomsky, C. (1981). Write now, read later. In C. B. Cazden (Ed.), *Language in early childhood education* (pp. 141–149). Washington, DC: National Association for the Education of Young Children.

Clay, M. M. (1975). *What did I write?* Auckland, NZ: Heinemann.

Coleman, C. L., & Meyers, L. W. (1991). Computer recognition of the speech of adults with cerebral palsy and dysarthria. *Augmentative and Alternative Communication, 7,* 34–42.

Collins, B. C., Branson, T. A., Hall, M., & Rankin, S. W. (2001). Teaching secondary students with moderate disabilities in an inclusive academic classroom setting. *Journal of Developmental and Physical Disabilities, 13,* 41–59.

DeCoste, D. (1997). The role of literacy in augmentative and alternative communication. In S. Glennen & D. DeCoste (Eds.), *Handbook of augmentative and alternative communication* (pp. 283–333). San Diego, CA: Singular.

Dobson, L. N. (1989). Connections in learning to write and read: A study of children's development through kindergarten and first grade. In J. M. Mason (Ed.), *Reading and writing connections* (pp. 83–103). Boston: Allyn & Bacon.

Doherty, J. M. (1987). Handling, positioning, and adaptive equipment. In E. T. McDonald (Ed.), *Treating cerebral palsy* (pp. 191–207). Austin, TX: Pro-Ed.

Ekwall, E. E., & Shanker, J. L. (1993). *Locating and correcting reading difficulties* (6th ed.). Upper Saddle River, NJ: Merrill/Prentice Hall.

Englert, C. S., Raphael, T. E., Anderson, L. M., Anthony, H. M., & Stevens, D. D. (1991). Making strategies and self-talk visible: Writing instruction in regular and special education classrooms. *American Educational Research Journal, 23,* 337–372.

Fernald, G. (1943). *Remedial techniques in basic school subjects.* New York: McGraw-Hill.

Ferreiro, E. (1986). The interplay between information and assimilation in beginning literacy. In W. H. Teale & E. Sulzby (Eds.), *Emergent literacy* (pp. 15–49). Norwood, NJ: Ablex.

Hagin, R. A. (1983). Write right or left: A practical approach to handwriting. *Journal of Learning Disabilities, 16*(5), 266–271.

Hammill, D. D., Pearson, N. A., & Maddox, T. (1997). Basic School Skills Inventory (3rd ed.). Austin, TX: Pro-Ed.

Hancock, J., & Alston, J. (1986). Handwriting skills in children with spina bifida: Assessment, monitoring, and measurement. *British Journal of Special Education, 13*(4), 155–158.

Harris, D. (1982). Communicative interaction processes involving nonvocal physically handicapped children. *Topics in Language Disorders, 2,* 21–37.

Heller, K. W., Alberto, P. A., Forney, P. E., & Schwartzman, M. N. (1996). *Understanding physical, sensory, and health impairments: Characteristics and educational implications.* Pacific Grove, CA: Brooks/Cole.

Heller, K. W., & Swinehart-Jones, D. (2003). *Promoting literacy in students with physical disabilities.* Atlanta: Georgia Bureau for Students with Physical and Health Impairments.

Hitchcock, M. E. (1989). *Elementary students' invented spellings at the correct stage of spelling development.* Unpublished doctoral dissertation, University of Oklahoma, Norman.

Isaacson, S. (1988). Teaching written expression. *Teaching Exceptional Children, 20*(2), 21–39.

Kangas, K. (1987). Writing aids. *Assistive Device News, 4*(2), 11–12.

Katims, D. S. (1993, January). *The emergence of literacy in preschool children with disabilities.* Paper presented at the Third Annual Carolina Literacy Center Symposium, Research Triangle Park, NC.

Koester, H. (2001). User performance with speech recognition: A literature review. *Assistive Technology, 13,* 116–130.

Koke, S., & Neilson, J. (1987). *The effect of auditory feedback on the spelling of nonspeaking physically disabled individuals.* Unpublished master's thesis, University of Toronto, Toronto, Ontario.

Koppenhaver, D. A., Evans, D. A., & Yoder, D. E. (1991). Childhood reading and writing experiences of literate adults with severe speech and motor impairments. *Augmentative and Alternative Communication, 7,* 20–33.

Koppenhaver, D. A., & Yoder, D. E. (1993). Classroom literacy instruction for children with severe speech and physical impairments (SSPI): What is and what might be. *Topics of Language Disorders, 13,* 1–15.

Kucer, S. L. (1985). The making of meaning: Reading and writing as parallel processes. *Written Communication, 2,* 317–336.

Lafontaine, L. M., & DeRuyter, F. (1987). The nonspeaking cerebral palsied: A clinical and demographic database report. *Augmentative and Alternative Communication, 2,* 153–162.

Larsen, S. C., & Hammill, D. D. (1989). Test of Legible Handwriting. Austin, TX: Pro-Ed.

Lewis, R. (1993). *Special education technology: Classroom application.* Pacific Grove, CA: Brooks/Cole.

Light, J., & Smith, A. K. (1993). Home literacy experiences of preschoolers who use AAC systems and of their nondisabled peers. *Augmentative and Alternative Communication, 9,* 10–25.

Matas, J. A., Mathy-Laikko, P. B., Beukelman, D. R., & Legresley, K. (1985). Identifying the nonspeaking population: A demographic study. *Augmentative and Alternative Communication, 1,* 17–31.

McNaughton, S. (1993). Graphic representational systems and literacy learning. *Topics in Language Disorders, 12,* 58–75.

Mercer, C. D., & Mercer, A. R. (2001). *Teaching students with learning problems.* New York: Merrill.

Mike, D. G. (1987, October). *Literacy, technology, and the multiply disabled: An ethnography of classroom interaction.* Paper presented at the meeting of the National Reading Conference, St. Petersburg Beach, FL.

Milone, M. N., & Wasylyk, T. M. (1981). Handwriting in special education. *Teaching Exceptional Children, 58*(2), 58–61.

Pierce, P. L., & McWilliam, P. (1993). Emerging literacy and children with severe speech and physical impairments (SSPI): Issues and possible intervention strategies. *Topics in Language Disorders, 13,* 47–57.

Rosen, K., & Yampolsky, S. (2000). Automatic speech recognition and a review of its functioning with dysarthric speech. *Augmentative and Alternative Communication, 16,* 48–60.

Schumaker, J. B., Nolan, S. M., & Deschler, D. D. (1985). *The error monitoring strategy.* Lawrence: University of Kansas, Institute for Research in Learning Disabilities.

Schumaker, J. B., & Sheldon, J. (1985). *The sentence writing strategy.* Lawrence: University of Kansas, Center for Research on Learning.

Smith, A., Thurston, S., Light, J., Parnes, P., & O'Keefe, B. (1989). The form and use of written communication produced by physically disabled individuals using microcomputers. *Augmentative and Alternative Communication, 5,* 115–124.

Smith, M. (1989). Reading without speech: A study of children with cerebral palsy. *Irish Journal of Psychology, 10,* 601–614.

Smith, M. (1992). Reading abilities of nonspeaking students: Two case studies. *Augmentative and Alternative Communication, 8,* 57–66.

Steelman, J. D., Pierce, P., & Koppenhaver, D. (1993). The role of computers in promoting literacy in children with severe speech and physical impairments (SSPI). *Topics in Language Disorders, 13,* 76–88.

Stephens, T. M. (1977). *Teaching skills to children with learning and behavior disorders.* Upper Saddle River, NJ: Merrill/Prentice Hall.

Tam, C., Reid, D., Naumann, S., & O'Keefe, B. (2002). Effects of word prediction and location of word prediction list on text entry with children with spina bifida and hydrocephalus. *Augmentative and Alternative Communication, 18,* 147–162.

Thurber, D. N., & Jordan, D. R. (1981). *D'Nealian handwriting.* Glenview, IL: Scott, Foresman.

Tumlin, J., & Heller, K. (in press). The use of word prediction software to increase typing fluency and reduce spelling errors of students with physical disabilities. *Journal of Special Education Technology.*

Wallace, S. J. (1973). The effect of upper limb function on mobility of children with myelomeningocele. *Developmental Medicine and Child Neurology, 29* (Suppl.), 84–91.

Welch, M. (1992). The PLEASE strategy: A metacognitive learning strategy for improving the paragraph writing of students with mild learning disabilities. *Learning Disability Quarterly, 15,* 119–128.

Westling, D. L., & Fox, L. (2004). Teaching students with severe disabilities (3rd ed.). Upper Saddle River, NJ: Merrill/Prentice Hall.

Zaner-Bloser Evaluation Scales. (1984). Columbus, OH: Zaner-Bloser.

Adaptations and Instruction in Science and Social Studies

KATHRYN WOLFF HELLER

CHAPTER 15

KNOWLEDGE AND SKILLS

After you have read this chapter, you will be able to:

1. **Identify the steps necessary to evaluate current instructional material and make appropriate adaptations.**
2. **Discuss methods of making textbooks accessible for students with physical and multiple disabilities.**
3. **List important components of prelesson activities and considerations for students with physical or multiple disabilities.**
4. **Discuss effective lesson presentation strategies and adaptations to promote learning in students with physical or multiple disabilities.**
5. **Discuss possible adaptations needed to evaluate student learning.**
6. **Identify specific skills needed in social studies and methods of adapting instruction for students with physical or multiple disabilities.**
7. **Identify specific skills needed in science and methods of adapting instruction for students with physical, health, or multiple disabilities.**

When students with physical or multiple disabilities enroll in social studies, science, and other content courses, appropriate adaptations and strategies may need to be provided to facilitate learning. Students with physical or multiple disabilities may be at a disadvantage in content courses due to a lack of experiences (Blischak, 1995), possible deficits in reading (Berninger & Gans, 1986; Foley, 1993), or inability to access certain materials or activities (Heller, Alberto, Forney, & Schwartzman, 1996). Knowing how to adapt for these problems is necessary to maximize students' learning.

This chapter will begin by providing information on general guidelines for lesson preparation, lesson presentation, lesson evaluation, and adaptations applicable to all content area learning. The next sections will specifically address the two content areas of social studies and science. Social studies is often challenging for students with physical and multiple disabilities when they lack background information, have lower reading skills, and have limited research skills that are necessary for learning social studies content. Science poses additional challenges due to its manipulation of materials during lab experiments that may be motorically difficult for students with physical disabilities.

LESSON PREPARATION

Prior to beginning instruction, teachers will need to systematically prepare the lesson. Lesson preparation includes (a) determining the content of the lesson, (b) evaluating the materials to be used to deliver content, (c) assessing students' background knowledge, and (d) determining appropriate adaptations for students with physical and multiple disabilities. Lesson preparation will be necessary for the general education teacher (when that teacher is teaching the course). The special education teacher may support the general education teacher through co-teaching or providing the student additional support, or directly teaching the content himself or herself. The special education teacher is also responsible for determining appropriate adaptations and instructional strategies needed to meet each student's specific needs.

Determining Content

Prior to instruction, teachers need to determine the major concepts that are important to learn from the chapter. This advance planning enables the teacher to know what material to emphasize during instruction. Deciding what materials should be emphasized is often based on a combination of factors. Teachers will base this on their own knowledge and expertise, especially if they majored in the area of instruction (e.g., a teacher who is teaching biology and who has a degree in this area). Teachers less familiar with the content area tend to rely on textbook and curriculum guides (Bos & Vaughn, 1998). Often teachers will draw from both their experiences and curriculum guides.

Special education teachers who are providing additional instruction to students with physical, health, or multiple disabilities in social studies or science classes will need to know which concepts are being targeted, and the level and degree of skill required for the student at grade level. Close collaboration between the general and special education teacher is essential for this to occur. This is especially crucial if the student needs a reduction in the level or amount of the material to be learned, due to endurance, fatigue, health, or learning problems.

The content to target in a subject will also be driven by the type of diploma the student is seeking. Some students with physical or multiple disabilities will be seeking an academic diploma, while others will be seeking a different type of diploma (e.g., special education diploma). Those students seeking academic diplomas will be expected to pass state- and national-level tests, so the teacher has the obligation to see that all necessary information and skills are taught. Therefore, only certain types of modifications will be appropriate for these students.

Evaluating and Adapting Instructional Material

The primary instructional tool for teaching social studies and science in elementary and middle school classrooms is the textbook. However, there has been a great deal of criticism regarding the content, design, and difficulty level of such books (Bean, Zigmond, & Hartman, 1994; Beck, McKeown, & Gromoll, 1989; Gagnon, 1987; Sewall, 1987). The reading difficulty of social studies texts has often been found to be substantially higher than those of basal reading texts of the same grade (Chall & Conrad, 1991). When textbooks are written above students' reading ability level, achievement in the subject area declines (Martin, Sexton, Wagner, & Gerlovich, 1997). Social studies and science textbooks have been found to have poor scope and sequence, inadequate presentation, boring presentation, too much detail and not enough overall concept, poor readability, insufficient content, and inadequate application of higher-level thinking skills (Armbruster & Anderson, 1988; Bean et al., 1994; Elliott, Nagel, & Woodward, 1985). Texts that are difficult in organization or readability will impede comprehension. Texts with inadequate presentation or insufficient content can result in poor concept acquisition. Because of these difficulties, the textbook being used for the course should be evaluated for readability and ease of use. Some general features of the textbook that should be evaluated include the genre (including the type of text as well as the linguistic features, structuring of the text, and graphic representation of ideas), content (including accuracy and complexity), and visual features (including illustrations, diagrams, and text) (Donovan & Smolkin, 2002). Other types of items to evaluate include appropriate reading level; logical ordering of content; sufficient explanatory information; formatting with headings and subheadings to promote appropriate organization of information; highlighting of key terms; advance organizers; special interest items; highlighting key concepts in figures or box format; and follow-up summaries.

Adaptations will be needed when textbooks have flaws that impede learning or the student's disability interferes with textbook use. These adaptations include changing textbook sequence, simplifying textbooks' content, substituting textbooks, accessing textbooks, and using supplementary materials.

Changing Textbook Sequence. Sometimes changing the chapter order or organization of the material will help improve students' understanding of the material. Simple resequencing may bring about improvements in social studies and science achievement and help make stronger conceptual connections. Learning theory emphasizes the importance of tying new concepts to concepts that have already been learned. Restructuring the material in such a way as to relate new ideas to old information can improve learning (Martin et al., 1997).

Content restructuring should follow several principles. First, students should be provided assistance in clarifying content structure. Students should be introduced to the "big picture" and how all the smaller ideas fit within it. Second, the overall structure of content should be provided to help students organize the sequence of what is being taught. This may be provided as a visual display in the classroom or be given as a student handout. Third, content should follow a logical progression and be ordered from the simple to the complex. This allows information to build in a logical fashion (Martin et al., 1997). Table 15–1 shows how a textbook could be resequenced to provide a logical pattern from which students can build their knowledge base. In the new sequence the chapters are arranged from basic components to more complex systems (e.g., from matter to living organisms and the climates affecting them). The chapters also build on the concepts gained from the prior chapters (e.g., presenting information on matter prior to energy sources; presenting information on energy for living things prior to the plant chapter).

Simplifying Textbooks. One of the ways textbooks may be adapted is by simplifying their content. Examples include highlighting pertinent content, skipping over irrelevant sections, and using a study guide (Bean et al., 1994). When the key concepts of a text have been identified, the text may be highlighted to emphasize these concepts. Highlighting textual information may be used to draw the student's attention to the relevant information. For students who have difficulty reading certain quantities of information, due to physical, health, or learning problems, highlighting may be used to direct the student to the relevant information. Highlighting may occur through using a colored highlighter on the relevant text, underlining the relevant text with a pen, or scanning the chapter into a computer and bolding the relevant text or using software that will provide highlighting and bookmarking (e.g., Kurzweil 3000, manufactured by Kurzweil Educational Systems; and WYNN, manufactured by Freedom Scientific, Inc., Learning Systems Group). In some instances when students require a reduction in the amount of textual material, teachers will mark out the sections of the text that are irrelevant.

TABLE 15–1
A Sample Comparison of Unrevised and Revised Textbook Content Sequence

Textbook Sequence	Revised Content Sequence
Animals with backbones	Matter (elements and compounds)
Classifying animals without backbones	Sources of energy
Plants	Light
Life cycles	Electricity and magnetism
Matter (elements and compounds)	Communications
Electricity and magnetism	Energy outcomes and the future
Sources of energy	Energy for living things
Light	Plants
Communications	Life cycles
Climates of the world	Classifying animals without backbones
Energy for living things	Animals with backbones
Energy outcomes and the future	Climates of the world

Note. From "Influence of Resequencing General Science Content on the Science Achievement, Attitudes Toward Science, and Interests in Science of Sixth Grade Students" by L. Hamrick and H. Harty, *Journal of Research in Science Teaching, 24*(1), 20. Copyright © 1987 Wiley-Liss, Inc. Reprinted by permission of Wiley-Liss, Inc., a subsidiary of John Wiley & Sons, Inc.

Substituting Textbooks. In some instances, an alternate textbook (or material) that provides greater readability and better organization may be used. When selecting a social studies or science textbook, teachers should evaluate the book across content, processes, format, readability, and general considerations. Figure 15–1 provides several guiding questions that help evaluate the usefulness and appropriateness of textbooks.

For students whose reading level precludes using the textbook (even when textbooks with lower reading levels are selected), alternative approaches must be used. Some students will benefit from having the textbook on tape (or scanned into the computer and presented auditorily). The student can listen while looking at each page, rather than struggling with the reading and missing the content. Another alternative is to have the textbook read aloud in class or to use a peer tutor to read the book aloud with the student with limited literacy skills.

In some instances a textbook may not be used at all. Instead, the teacher may use outlines and notes to decrease student frustration. Some teachers may rewrite the material to emphasize key concepts. This allows the material to be presented at an appropriate reading level with clear and concise organization of the material, and emphasizes the important information to learn.

Accessing Textbooks. Students with severe physical disabilities may have difficulty accessing textbooks. Physical impairments may not allow students to hold books or turn their pages. The textbook may be adapted to allow for easier manipulation of the pages

FIGURE 15–1
Screening textbooks

Content
1. Is there a balance in emphasis among the different topics?
2. Do the materials include study of the problems that are important to us now and in the future?
3. Do the materials require students to apply major science or major social studies concepts to everyday life situations and/or current events?
4. If different text is being used for students with special needs, how does the content compare to the regular textbook? Are key concepts included?

Processes: Social Studies
1. Does the material emphasize hands-on experiences?
2. Does the textbook build bridges to other subjects?
3. Does the textbook focus on people?
4. Does the textbook encourage reflective thinking?
5. Does the textbook encourage historical, descriptive, survey, and experimental research?

Processes: Science
1. Does the material include liberal amounts of hands-on investigations and activities?
2. Is scientific inquiry an important part of the material?
3. Does the material encourage students to explore, discover, and find answers for themselves?
4. Does the material require students to apply science processes to problem-solving situations and construct conclusions?

General Considerations
1. Are materials consistent with science and social studies goals of school district?
2. Are materials clearly written and current?
3. Do the textbook and materials proceed from the simple to the complex and are they designed for the students' developmental levels?
4. Is information written at an appropriate reading level?
5. Does the textbook follow a logical sequence?
6. Do topics appear interesting and relevant?
7. Are valid evaluation materials used or included?
8. Is the teacher's guide included and helpful?
9. Do materials include enough application of content and process to make science and social studies meaningful to students?

Note. Adapted from Martin, R., Sexton, C., Wagner, K., & Gerlovich, J. (1997). *Teaching Science for All Children.* Boston: Allyn & Bacon, Also from Mechline, K. R., & Oliver, D. L. (1983). *Characteristics of a Good Elementary Science Program.* Washington, DC: National Science Teacher Association. Reprinted with permission from the National Science Teachers Association, 1840 Wilson Boulevard, Arlington, VA 22201-3000.

by using page fluffers or paper clips between each page to allow easier turning. Simple page-turning devices that fit on the hand and "grab" the page may also be used. In some instances a mechanical page turner may be available. Another option is to scan textbooks (or material) into the computer and access them through a mouse, trackball, or alternative input device.

Another accessibility consideration relates to stamina and fatigue. Students may be unable to carry all the needed textbooks between home and school due to the material's weight and bulkiness. To solve this problem, a second set of textbooks or computer access to the content can be provided at home. Another consideration is the need to carry books between classes. Some students will have difficulty managing their books between classes due to an inability to carry them, or will experience fatigue from trying to move them between classes. In these situations, needed textbooks may be kept in each of the classrooms for the student to use, with another set at home for homework.

Using Supplementary Activities and Materials. The textbook should not be used as the sole basis for information (Fernstrom & Goodnite, 2000). Exclusive use or overuse of the textbook discourages students from thinking about the important issues in social studies and from generalizing scientific concepts to everyday life (Allen & Stevens, 1998). A wider, more integrated experience is necessary to promote learning. In social studies, additional activities such as cooperative learning, inquiring learning, role-playing, and simulations are often used (Chapin & Messick, 1989). In science, demonstrations and experiments will play an important role (Martin et al., 1997).

Additional resources, such as the Internet and newspapers, can supplement instruction. Internet use for both social studies and science can provide immense learning experiences, although students need to be taught to consider source authority in their evaluation of Internet material (Clark & Slotta, 2000). Newspapers may be used to link science or social studies to everyday life. However, teachers are not adequately instructing their students to critically read and respond to how science is portrayed in the newspaper (Jarman & McClune, 2002), which is an important skill when evaluating for bias or source reliability. Supplementary activities can be designed to promote learning, as well as critical evaluation skills, in a fun, interesting, and relevant manner.

Assessing Students' Background Knowledge

Students with physical, health, or multiple disabilities often have deficits in background knowledge that may have an impact upon their content learning. However, even students without disabilities may be unaware of some of the concepts to be taught. Assessing prior knowledge will help the teacher provide meaningful information and determine whether additional information is needed to fill in any blanks.

One common way to assess prior knowledge of a group of students is to collectively write their ideas related to the topic, through a technique known as **semantic mapping** (Johnson, Pittelman, & Heimlich, 1986). A semantic map is a pictorial collection of ideas surrounding a target topic. It serves to both assess current knowledge and to activate prior knowledge. A semantic map is developed by writing the topic on the board or on a computer using mapping software (e.g., Inspiration, manufactured by Inspiration Software, Inc.). Students provide associations regarding the topic, and those are placed in logical groupings. For example, in Figure 15–2 the topic is the desert. In this semantic map, students provided information regarding examples of deserts and descriptions of desert conditions, although they did not provide any definitions.

FIGURE 15–2
Semantic map of fifth-grade students' knowledge of deserts

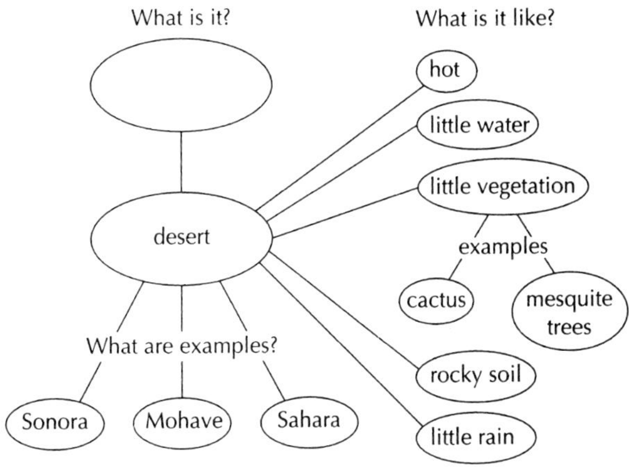

Note. From C. S. Bos and S. Vaughn, *Strategies for Teaching Students with Learning and Behavioral Problems.* Copyright © 1998 by Allyn & Bacon. Reprinted by permission.

Also, the language was rather simplistic and contained information that was only partially correct. From the semantic map, the teacher could deduce that definitions, technical vocabulary, and more information regarding climate conditions and different types of deserts would enhance student knowledge.

Individualized assessment of prior knowledge is also important. For example, students in wheelchairs may have little experience moving over various types of terrain and no idea of what rocky soil really means. Also, students who have limited speech will need to have their AAC devices programmed with ideas that can be included in the semantic map. The more influence students have on selecting ideas to be preprogrammed, the better. Before the lesson, the student can indicate some ideas on the topic to be programmed into the AAC device. the teacher can say a list of relevant and irrelevant choices from which the student can select what should be programmed for use in the semantic mapping activity.

In addition to determining modifications for physical disabilities, teachers will need to consider the need for further modifications when students also have diverse cultural and linguistic needs. Students' knowledge and vocabulary, use of cognitive strategies, and sociocultural influences must be taken into account (Watson & Houtz, 2002). For example, mismatches can arise when a student has been socialized to be told what to do and to rote-memorize information, but is being asked to do independent work on a hands-on assignment. Teachers need to identify and address these mismatches through modifying lessons and utilizing appropriate instructional strategies to meet the student's needs.

Determining Modifications for Students with Physical or Multiple Disabilities

Students with physical or multiple disabilities will often need several modifications in order to learn and participate in the class. The need for modifications is determined upon examining the student's ability to perform a task or activity. After breaking the task down into small steps (see Chapter 6 on task and situational analysis), the student is assessed on each step to determine the areas in which instruction or modification is needed. Errors for each step are recorded and the special education teacher determines if the error was due to learning (or cognitive), physical (or motor), health (or endurance), sensory, communication, or motivational reasons (Heller, Forney, Alberto, Schwartzman, & Goeckel, 2000). Based upon the type of error, modifications may be needed. For example, if the student is unable to handle a certain type of laboratory equipment due to a physical impairment, the equipment may be modified by attaching handles to it or securing it to a worktable.

When teaching science, social studies, or other content areas, the teacher must not only consider specific modifications to the lesson and equipment, but more general areas as well. There are typically 10 areas to consider for modifications: type of condition the student has, physical/health monitoring, environmental arrangement, communication, instructional and curricular modification, modifications and assistive technology, class participation, assignments and classroom tests, other general modifications, and sensory and perceptual modification (Heller, 2000). As seen in Figure 15–3, these areas are part of a Classroom Modifications Checklist for Students with Physical and Health Impairments (Heller, 2000). The purpose of this checklist is to provide a summary of the modifications needed for individual students in school based upon the special education teacher's and the educational team's recommendations. The checklist can serve as a written reference for school personnel working with the student, to ensure that consistent, appropriate modifications are being made across activities, settings, and personnel. Depending upon the student's condition, the modifications may change over time and may need to be updated throughout the year. Check marks are placed next to areas that require modifications, and comments are written to the right of each area to provide more complete information. A cover sheet is usually part of the checklist and includes the student's name, area of exceptionality, current educational placement, date the checklist was completed, and the name of the person completing the checklist.

When students with disabilities are participating in science and social studies in general education classrooms, teachers may also need to provide students with the necessary social support (Palinscar, Magnusson, Collins, & Cutter, 2001). Part of providing access

FIGURE 15–3
Classroom modifications checklist for students with physical and health impairments

Area *Comments*

I. Type of Condition and Effects

II. Physical/Health Monitoring

_____ Pain/discomfort
_____ Fatigue/endurance
_____ Functional physical limitations
_____ Medication or treatment effects
_____ Health care procedures
_____ Seizure monitoring
_____ Absenteeism
_____ Activity restrictions
_____ Diet restrictions
_____ Allergy
_____ Other (specify)

III. Environmental Arrangement

_____ Modified day
_____ Scheduled rest breaks
_____ Proximity of classrooms
_____ Need for homeroom to be near an exit
_____ Special bathroom accommodations
_____ Need to leave early to get to next class
_____ Preferential seating
_____ Widened aisles
_____ Student requires special chair, desk, other
_____ Work surface modifications
_____ Materials need to be specially positioned. Location:
_____ Materials need to be stabilized. How:
_____ Assistance needed in manipulating materials
_____ Specialized Emergency Evacuation Plan (specify)
_____ Other (specify)

IV. Communication

_____ No adaptations in this area
_____ Needs a longer time to respond
_____ Uses an alternate form of response (specify)
_____ Uses AAC system (specify)
_____ Communicates correct answer with multiple choice format (with __ number of choices) by
  _____ pointing to answer
  _____ eye-gazing
  _____ marking with pencil
  _____ signaling when oral choices given
  _____ using switch to scanning device
  _____ other
_____ Other means of communication

V. Instructional and Curricular Modifications

_____ Provide study outline
_____ Provide extra repetition
_____ More frequent feedback from teacher
_____ Directions should be: _____ written down, _____ read orally, _____ demonstrated
_____ Provide material in lower-grade reading level
_____ Requires individualized instruction
_____ Alter material
_____ Alter curriculum
_____ Organizational modifications
_____ Requires extra set of books
_____ Other (specify)

(Continued)

FIGURE 15–3
Continued

VI. Modifications and Assistive Technology (AT) for Specific Content Areas

_____ Computer modifications (specify)
  _____ Keyboard modifications
  _____ Alternative keyboard
  _____ On-screen keyboard
  _____ Alternative input device (e.g., switch)
  _____ Voice recognition
  _____ Output modifications
_____ Writing modifications/AT needs:
_____ Spelling modifications/AT needs:
_____ Reading modifications/ AT needs:
_____ Math modifications/AT needs:
_____ Specific content areas_______________ (specify) modifications/AT needs:
_____ Life management/daily living modifications/AT needs:
_____ Recreation/leisure modifications/AT needs:
_____ Prevocational areas modifications/AT needs:
_____ Other areas modifications/assistive technology needs:

VII. Class Participation

_____ Requires extended time to respond
_____ Give student question(s) to answer in advance
_____ Uses modified response/communication system
_____ Gains teacher attention by: _____ raising hand, _____ signaling device, _____ AAC system
_____ Works best _____ individually, _____ teams of two, _____ small group, _____ large group
_____ Needs encouragement to participate in class discussions
_____ Other (specify)

VIII. Assignments/Classroom Tests

_____ Abbreviate assignments/tests
_____ Break up into shorter segments
_____ Provide extended time
_____ Modify reading level
_____ Reduce paper/pencil tasks
_____ Allow computer use for assignments
_____ Allow alternate responding (see communication)
_____ Alternate test/assignment format
_____ Peer helper for assignments
_____ Alternate grading
_____ Other (specify)

IX. Other Modifications

_____ Assistance needed in transferring
_____ Assistance needed in moving chair up to desk
_____ Assistance needed in mobility
_____ Assistance needed in bathroom
_____ Assistance needed in eating
_____ Other (specify)

X. Sensory and Perceptual Modifications

_____ Need to decrease visual clutter
_____ Needs extra lighting or low lighting (specify)
_____ Needs material to be high contrast
_____ Materials need to be modified visually or tactually (specify)
_____ Student uses an LVD (low vision device), CCTV, or other adaptations (specify)
_____ Student needs everything described orally
_____ Student uses hearing aids or other adaptations (specify)
_____ Student requires visual presentation
_____ Student requires set of notes in appropriate format
_____ Other (specify)

XI. Other

Note. From Classroom Modification Checklist for Students with Physical and Health Impairments by K. W. Heller, 2000, Atlanta: Georgia Bureau for Students with Physical and Health Impairments.

to the curriculum is assisting students to gain successful entrée into small-group activities. Teachers need to be observant for situations in which students have difficulty gaining acceptance or participating in the science or social studies small-group activity and provide appropriate intervention (e.g., practicing working in a small group through rehearsal strategies, or programming key messages in the student's communication device to promote participation).

LESSON PRESENTATION

Lesson presentation begins with a sequence of prelesson activities, followed by presentation of new materials, and independent practice of the material. Within this structure, students are guided through a process of acquisition, fluency, maintenance, and generalization (see Table 15–2). **Acquisition** refers to the ability to correctly perform the task. During an acquisition phase, the teacher presents new information and guides students through correct performance. Students have obtained acquisition of the task when they demonstrate they can perform the task correctly. As students continue to practice the task, they gain speed in their performance of the task. Being able to complete a task correctly and with appropriate speed is known as **fluency**. **Maintenance** refers to the ability to perform the task over time, and not forget how to do it several weeks later, for example. To ensure maintenance of a task, the teacher will need to periodically revisit the task. The last type of learning is **generalization**, which refers to the ability to apply what was learned in the task to other, similar situations. Teachers will need to provide examples and guide students in application of the task to promote generalization. These types of learning principles are applicable to all content areas, including social studies and science.

Prelesson Activities

Prelesson activities are designed to motivate the learner, preview the lesson, tie existing information to new information, and help guide the student by emphasizing what should be learned (Hudson, 1996; Kindsvatter, Wilen, & Ishler, 1988). Prelesson activities typically can be divided into two categories: review and introduction.

Review. Review of the past material should occur to provide a link to the new information being presented in the upcoming lesson. Successful reviewing typically includes (a) involving all students in the discussion, (b) providing positive feedback for correct responses, and (c) correcting any erroneous information (Hudson, 1996; Rosenshine & Stevens, 1986). Review is important to help the student understand where the new information will fit in relation to the old information. Also, review is critical if the new information builds on the previous information. Students who use AAC devices should have previously programmed information to ensure meaningful participation in this part of the lesson.

Introduction. Prelesson activities also include an introduction to the lesson. One of the first components to lesson introduction is the lesson opening in which the teacher tries to pique students' interest in the upcoming lesson. Students may also be given advance organizers or prelesson components. Advance organizers may include an outline or series of questions to help prepare students for reading, focus on important concepts, or assist in simplifying the textbook content. Prelesson components consist of any number of strategies to help the student prepare for the lesson. These may include stating the purpose of the lesson, providing lesson objectives and task or content expectations, clarifying the concepts to be learned, providing background knowledge, identifying topics and subtopics of the lesson, providing rationales, and providing an organizational framework (Hudson, 1996; Lenz, Alley, & Schumaker, 1987).

In one study (Hudson, 1996) a group of prelearning activities, referred to as a learning set, resulted in significantly better outcomes than the absence of prelearning activities. The prelearning activities included a review of the previous content, a statement linking the review to the new material, a statement of new lesson objectives, a rationale of the importance of the content, and a statement of performance expectations.

Within the introduction to the new material, related vocabulary is often introduced. Social studies and science have their own vocabularies specific to the content being taught. When the vocabulary is introduced prior to the lesson, the student will understand the word meanings upon encountering them. New vocabulary should be programmed into students' AAC devices to be used appropriately during lessons.

TABLE 15–2
Instructional Model

Instructional Step	Teacher	Student	Type of Learning
Prelesson Activities	Teacher reviews previous material. Teacher introduces lesson.	Student engages in review. Student attends to prelesson.	
Presentation & Guided Practice	Teacher presents information and promotes active participation. Teacher promotes meaningful discussions and meaningful reading. Teacher monitors students' learning and provides immediate feedback.	Student attends and participates. Student participates in discussions and activities with supervision and assistance.	Acquisition
Independent Practice	Teacher monitors student performance and provides feedback.	Student performs task independently. Student performs task independently and without difficulty.	Fluency
Mastery	Teacher revisits previous information. Teacher monitors student performance and provides feedback.	Student performs task independently at a later time.	Maintenance
Application	Teacher guides student in applying information to similar situations. Teacher monitors student performance and provides feedback.	Student performs similar tasks using mastered material.	Generalization

TABLE 15–3
Cues to Listen and Watch for in Lectures

Type of Cue	Examples
Organizational Cues	Today, we will be discussing . . . The topic I want to cover today . . . There are (number) points I want you to be sure to learn . . . The important relationship is . . . The main point of this discussion is . . . Any statement that signals a number or position (e.g., first, last, next, then). To review/summarize/recap . . .
Emphasis Cues	
Verbal	You need to know/understand/remember . . . This is important/key/basic/critical . . . Let me repeat this . . . Let me check. Now do you understand . . . Any statement is repeated. Words or terms are emphasized. Teacher speaks more slowly, loudly, or with more emphasis. Teacher stresses certain words. Teacher spells words. Teacher asks rhetorical question.
Nonverbal	Information written on overhead/board. Information handed out in study guide. Teacher emphasizes point using gestures.

Note. Adapted from "Notetaking Strategy Instruction" by S. K. Suritsky and C. A. Hughes, 1996, in D. D. Deshler, E. S. Ellis, and B. K. Lenz, (Eds.), *Teaching Adolescents with Learning Disabilities* (2nd ed., p. 275), Denver: Love. Copyright 1996 by Love Publishing Company. Reprinted with permission.

Presenting New Materials and Guided Practice

The primary way of presenting information in content area classes such as social studies is through lecturing (Crank & Bulgren, 1993; Crawley, 1994). On average, lectures have been found to occur for approximately 70% of the class time (Nolet & Tindel, 1993). For science, there tends to be more hands-on experimentation, resulting in less lecture time.

Many students will benefit from systematic strategies to help them gain the most from the lecture and lesson presentation. Some systematic strategies for helping students learn content information include (a) using effective lecture techniques, (b) providing guided practice and the pause procedure, (c) using cooperative learning groups, and (d) learning to read for content by utilizing appropriate learning strategies and study guides. Adaptations may be necessary to promote classroom discussion, notetaking, and access to the material by students with physical, health, or multiple disabilities.

Effective Lecturing. It is important that the teacher incorporate good lecturing techniques to promote student learning. Some of these techniques involve organizational cues and emphasis cues. As seen in Table 15–3, organizational cues can help direct students by emphasizing what the topic will be about, stressing the points to look for, ordering the key points, and summarizing the main points. Emphasis cues stress the important information verbally (by explicitly telling students what is important or stressing certain material) and nonverbally (by writing on the board, giving study guides, and using pictures, diagrams, and semantic maps to show key relationships and information).

Lecture approaches often are more effective when students take notes. For students with severe physical disabilities, several modifications can be used to accommodate the student. First, the teacher can provide a copy of his or her own notes for the student. Another possibility is for another student or person to take notes for the student during lecture. If possible, notetaking by another individual on the computer is often the most effective, since it allows the student with a physical disability to easily access and embellish the notes. In some instances the class can be taped, but the notes may need to be transcribed for the student.

Guided Practice. One technique to enhance learning information during presentation is guided practice. Guided practice consists of breaking the lecture into several naturally occurring units of information, asking students oral questions about the units of information after the teacher's presentation, and providing feedback to student responses. Students with learning problems were found to perform significantly better on evaluation measures after using a guided-practice technique than after receiving only lecture and study time (Hudson, 1997).

A different guided-practice technique involves having students read small sections of the text, then highlighting key concepts or facts. Oral reading can be used to direct students where to highlight relevant information and to assist with comprehension and readability of the material (Bean, Zigmond, & Hartman, 1994). Highlighting helps to direct students to important information. Students with physical disabilities who are unable to highlight their own text will require assistance. A student without disabilities can be paired with the student with a physical disability to help highlight the textbook. If the textbook or material was placed on the computer for the student with a physical disability, then he or she will be able to highlight his or her own material by using the underline function or appropriate software (e.g., WYNN).

For students who use AAC, another consideration of the guided-practice technique is determining how to adapt class discussion to allow the student to participate. Unless the AAC device has been preprogrammed with ideas and concepts pertaining to the lesson and these have been explained to the student during a prelesson preview, it can be difficult to participate in the discussion. There are two techniques that can be used. The first technique involves providing time for the student to preconstruct an answer or construct an answer during class. In this technique, the teacher gives the student the question that he or she will be asked during class time ahead of time. During prelesson time with another teacher, the student finds the answer and prepares a response for class discussion. However, this approach can be difficult since it requires the student to be pretaught concepts that may be better explained during the regular class time. Another possibility is to ask the student the question during class time, go on and ask other students nonvital questions while the student is constructing a message on his or her AAC device, and then return to the student for an answer. If this approach is used, it must be stressed that the questions or discussion occurring during message construction be nonvital or previously discussed so that the student does not miss any information. A second approach is to number the lines in the textbook or handout material. When the teacher asks a factual comprehension question, the student can indicate his or her answer by replying with the appropriate number to indicate which line contains the answer. This approach can benefit all class members, since they are redirected to the material and can count down to the appropriate line to which the student is referring.

Pause Procedure. Another technique that may be used is the pause procedure (DiVesta & Smith, 1979; Ruhl, Hughes, & Gajar, 1990; Ruhl, Hughes, & Schloss, 1987). This is a variation on the guided-practice technique. In this procedure, the teacher pauses during naturally occurring breaks in the lecture. During the pause, students work with partners for about two minutes to discuss the topic and review notes. After the pause, the students ask the teacher any questions they may have about the material and receive clarification. Lecture then resumes. This strategy allows frequent feedback and creates opportunities for "chunking" information by organizing it into groups. The teacher can also elicit more student responses in this manner and be alert to current student misunderstanding in a timely manner.

For students with physical and speech impairments, two minutes may not be sufficient to formulate questions on a communication device. It is important that AAC devices have a symbol or phrase stating that the student has a question or doesn't understand. The partner (or teacher during this pausing time) then needs to go through the categories of presented information to determine which area was not understood. After ascertaining the category, the teacher can ask the student other questions to pinpoint the misunderstanding or question. If the teacher is unable to pinpoint the problem, the student should have the opportunity to construct a question to be asked at a later time or as soon as it is constructed.

Cooperative Learning Groups. Some students may be placed in groups to formulate questions, discuss information, or perform experiments. The idea behind the use of cooperative learning groups is to create a diverse group of students, often intermixing academically strong students with weaker ones, in order to allow the stronger students to help clarify information. It is important, however, that each student be viewed as contributing to the group in some way, including the student with a physical or multiple disability. Sometimes students with physical disabilities can assist with guiding discussions or making outlines, while other students provide assistance with some of the mechanical aspects of a task that the student with a physical impairment is unable to perform.

Reading for Content: Learning Strategies and Study Guides. Part of the lesson may require students to read part of their textbooks, either silently or aloud. Students may need guidance on how to read meaningfully. The use of learning strategies and study guides may help facilitate learning.

There are numerous types of learning strategies that may be used to help students read for content. Students may be taught to use self-questioning while reading, along with summarization or paragraph reinstatement. A common strategy that has been used for decades is **SQ3R**, which stands for survey, question, read, recite, review (Bean et al., 1994; Robinson, 1946). In this technique the student first surveys the material by reading through the headings. Next, each heading is changed into a question to provide guidance for what should be learned in that section. The student reads the section to answer the question. After reading each section, the student recites to himself or herself what was read and may make notes about the reading. When the entire selection is read, the student reviews the main points by recitation or reviewing his or her notes. An adapted version of SQ3R has been used successfully with secondary students with disabilities (Powell & Zalud, 1982). In this adapted version, worksheets are used to help the students identify the main and supporting ideas, clarify text structure, and link key ideas (see Figure 15–4). From that point, questions are formed and the students continue with the read, recite, and review process. For students with physical disabilities, worksheets may be entered into the computer for easier access. If the student has difficulty locating main and supporting ideas, these can be highlighted in the text for visual reference. Students who become confused about changing statements into questions will require prior practice in who, what, why, when, and how formulations.

Another strategy is known as **Multipass** (Schumaker, Delsher, Alley, Warner, & Denton, 1982). In this strategy, the student makes multiple passes in going through the text, without ever actually reading the text in its entirety. The text is studied to learn the main ideas, framework, and related detail and to answer study questions. This technique is meant to address the issue of not struggling to read textual material that is above the student's reading level. The Multipass strategy consists of three passes over the text. In the first pass, the students survey the text by becoming familiar with the title, introduction, summary, organization, figures and tables, and the table of contents. On the second pass, the students size up the information by looking more closely at the information, including the illustrations, chapter questions, vocabulary words, and headings. In the last pass, students read the study questions. Questions that are known are checked off, and those that are not known require students to scan back to the appropriate section and/or headings to find the answer. Questions that cannot be answered are marked for help. Both the SQ3R and Multipass strategies must be carefully taught for their full benefit. These techniques can easily be used by students with speech and physical disabilities. The steps of these strategies are typically programmed into the student's AAC device and/or computer for reference.

Another learning strategy is the **K-W-L** strategy (Ogle, 1986). In this strategy, the students make three columns. In the first column, they write "What We Know" about the topic. Ideas are jotted down. In the second column, the students write out "What We Want to Learn." In the last column is written "What We Learned." Sometimes the strategy is presented with an "H" on the end (i.e., K-W-L-H strategy), which stands for "How are we going to find out the answers (to what we wanted to learn that we could not answer)? The K-W-L (or K-W-L-H) strategy, allows students to activate prior knowledge, read for meaning based on the questions formulated in the second column, and summarize the information that was learned. It can also help them figure out what to do next for missing information.

The use of **visual spatial displays** may be helpful for some students to promote comprehension of the material. These may take the form of graphic organizers, discussion webs (Alvermann, 1991), or semantic maps

FIGURE 15–4
The aSQ3R strategy helps students read meaningfully

aSQ3R Worksheet

Page 1.
Subject: ______
Main Idea (chapter heading/title): ______
Supporting Ideas (subsection headings/titles):
1. ______
2. ______

Subheadings: Found in section no.
1. ______ ______
2. ______ ______

Page 2.
Special Terms. If you can, define each term in your own words using ten words or less.
Found in section no.
1. ______ ______
2. ______ ______

Page 3.
List supporting ideas and subheadings and special terms found in each section.
______
______
______

Page 4.
Change supporting ideas and subheadings into who, what, why, where, when, or how questions. Be sure to use all special terms found in that section when answering the question.
1. ______
______
2. ______
______

Note. From "aSQ3R for Secondary Handicapped Students" by G. Powell and G. Zalud, *Journal of Reading*, 26(3), 1982, 262–263. Copyright 1982 by the International Reading Association. Reprinted with permission.

(Pearson & Johnson, 1978). All of these are similar in that they use some type of visual display to help students categorize and identify important information. Visual spatial display may be put together with class participation, be partially completed for the students to finish, or be given in a fully constructed format. Examples of visual spatial displays are shown in Figure 15–5.

The use of **study guides** may help decrease the complexity of the textbook and increase comprehension. In a study by Horton and Lovitt (1989), the use of study guides in social studies and science classes was found to result in significantly higher performance than self-study. Study guides may be used in several formats. They may be presented in an outline form or as a series of teacher-generated questions. Outlines may be teacher generated, or students may learn to develop their own. Each time new content is introduced, the teacher prompts the students to complete a partial outline and, over the year, expects the student to supply more headings and details so that by the end of the year they are capable of producing their own study guide. This process can be programmed on a

FIGURE 15–5
These two examples of visual spatial displays help promote comprehension. A graphic organizer (a) helps organize information while a discussion web (b) promotes ideas and discussion

(a)

A. Vegetation

B. Animals

C. Industries

D. Vegetation changes as you go up the mountain.

J. Deer

K. Elk

O. Mining, lumber, and tourism

G. No trees just meadows

H. Snow

L. Bear

M. Bighorn sheep

N. Mountain goat

F. Smaller trees

2

E. Bigger trees at the bottom of the west side

I. Desert at the bottom of the east side

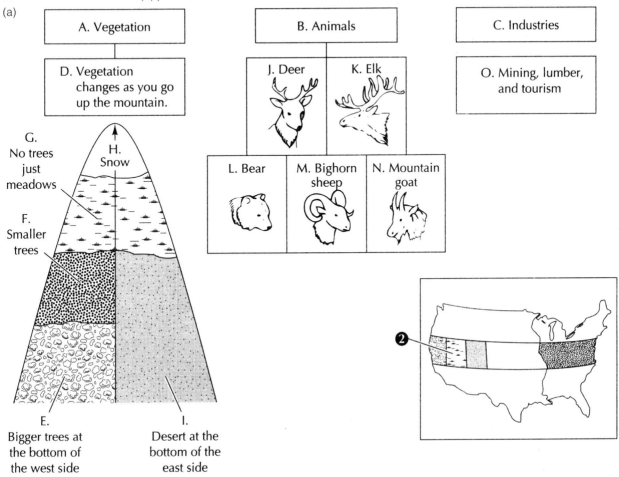

Note. From "Teaching Content Area Material to Learning Disabled Students," by C. Darch and D. Carmine. *Exceptional Children*, 53, 1986, p. 243. Copyright 1986 by The Council for Exceptional Children. Reprinted with permission.

(b)

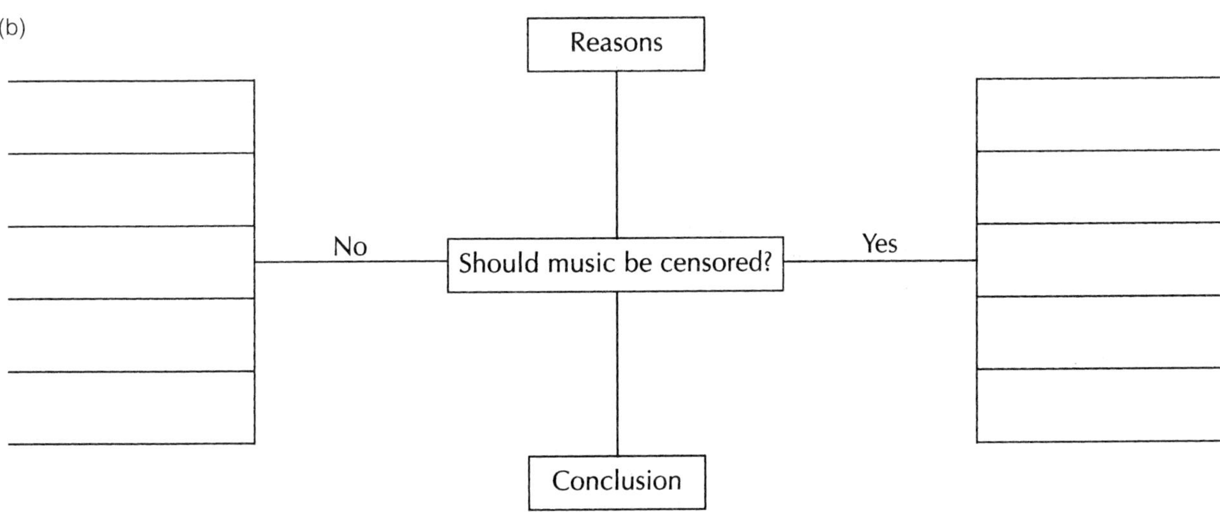

Note. Adapted from "The Web: A Powerful Tool for Teaching and Evaluation of the Expository Essay" by J. Duthie, *The History and Social Science Teacher, 21*, 232–236.

computer to allow students easy access to constructing and using their study guides.

Other Techniques. Studying techniques may include using the above strategies, such as study guides, visual spatial organizers, and the Multipass technique. Studying may also involve using mnemonics to remember information. Mnemonics is a technique of improving the memory by using associations for the target material (such as "My Dear Aunt Sally" for the order of mathematical operations [multiply, divide, add, subtract] or "HOMES" for the names of the Great Lakes [Huron, Ontario, Michigan, Erie, Superior]). Also, mental imagery may be used: the material is visualized or an associated picture is visualized in addition to the concept. A rehearsal technique may also be used, in which the student says it aloud (Bos & Vaughn, 1998) or, if the student is nonverbal, says it to himself or herself using internal speech or programs it into an AAC device. Whichever study strategy is used, it should be systematically taught and include information on organizational skills and scheduling techniques.

Independent Practice of Material

Independent practice of the material helps students to develop fluency. Class assignments, seatwork, and homework provide opportunities for independent practice. Independent practice work should be required only after the student has been taught the information, has been guided through learning the information, and has demonstrated understanding of the content. Assigning independent practice of the material is beneficial only after the student has acquired a learning level of the material and is working on reinforcing concepts, increasing the rate of performance (fluency), or generalizing concepts.

Several adaptations may be needed for students with physical disabilities to be able to practice the material independently. Some students may need to be paired with a paraprofessional or another individual to record their answers on the worksheet or on a computer or tape recorder. Students may need extended time lines as to when assignments or tests need to be completed due to fatigue or slowness in accessing the computer (or response time). In some instances the number of questions or assignments may be decreased based on the student's status. When work is decreased, it is important to be sure that the students have learned the information well, despite having completed a lesser number of questions or assignments than their peers.

EVALUATING CONTENT KNOWLEDGE

A variety of evaluation measures are used with students to ensure they have learned the academic content. The most traditional form of evaluation is a test. Students with physical disabilities may need adaptations in (a) the method of accessing and responding to test questions, (b) the format of the test, and (c) the testing procedure. The type of adaptations will depend upon the effects of the physical disabilities.

There are several modifications that may be necessary to permit students with physical disabilities to read and respond to test items. Students who are unable to use pencil and paper to respond may need to have tests scanned into a computer to allow them to answer the questions on the computer. A student may need a scribe or typist to record the student's spoken answers when hand function and typing function are too limited or slow to allow the student to write the answers. If the student's reading level is considerably below that of peers or is very slow, the student may need the test to be read aloud. This can be done by a computer program that reads text aloud, a tape recording of the test (with stop, start, and rewind functions easily available), or a person reading the test. Some students may have visual impairments and require the size of the print to be enlarged (and/or bolded). This may be easily accomplished on the computer, or by using a copy machine that enlarges. Some students may use low-vision devices to allow them access (e.g., a magnifier or CCTV).

The format of the test may need to be modified due to access and response-time issues. Students who are nonverbal may require a multiple-choice format to allow them to select an answer, especially if they have poor literacy skills or take a very long period of time to type out an answer. This occurs especially for students who are not using direct selection to access the alphabet to spell out answers, or those who use direct selection very slowly. (See Chapter 8 on AAC for more information on access techniques.) Discussion questions may need to be decreased in number or content, shortened, placed in a modified form, or changed to an alternate format.

The testing procedure may also need to be modified. Students with physical disabilities will typically need longer periods of time to take the test, based upon the student's response time. It is not unusual for some tests to be taken over days, due to the time it takes for the student to completely respond. Sometimes discussion questions may be given as take-home questions in order to accommodate the length of time the student requires to answer questions. Students with endurance and fatigue problems may also need breaks during the test.

Teachers need to be flexible and allow modification of teacher-made tests in order to accurately assess student knowledge. However, when standardized tests are modified, their validity becomes questionable. Teachers may be able to discuss individual student outcomes, but comparing a student's scores against their peers or a standardized norm is not always valid, depending upon the types of modifications made. On the other hand, forcing a student to respond to test materials by using an access method that is incompatible or fails to accommodate for slow motor response will not result in test scores that reflect the student's true abilities.

FIGURE 15–6
Disciplines found in social studies

Anthropology: The study of culture and the scientific study of humans.
Archaeology: The study of historic or prehistoric people and their culture.
Economics: The study of the production and consumption of goods and services.
Geography: The study of regions or places.
History: The study of the past and current human experience.
Law: The study of the rules and regulations that govern societies.
Philosophy: The study of truths and principles of being and knowledge.
Political science: The study of the governing processes and power structure found in those processes.
Psychology: The study of the mind and mental states.
Religion: The study of belief systems.
Sociology: The study of groups and norms of human behavior that persons exhibit due to their group memberships.

SOCIAL STUDIES CURRICULUM CONSIDERATIONS

Social studies instruction is an important part of the general education curriculum. It helps teach students about the people around them and promotes citizenship. Students with physical disabilities may encounter some difficulties with the social studies content material due to their reduced reading levels and experiential backgrounds. However, with appropriate adaptations, the social studies curriculum can be made accessible.

Social Studies Defined

Social studies involves the study of human beings, their interactions, their cultures, and their contributions. The National Council for the Social Studies (*http://www.socialstudies.org*) defined social studies as the integrated study of the social sciences and humanities to promote civic competence. The primary purpose of social studies is to help young people develop the ability to make informed decisions for the public good. Although this view of social studies as citizen transmission is the oldest and most widely accepted view, there are other views. These views include that social studies should be taught as a social science, that it should be taught as reflective inquiry, or that its emphasis should be on personal development (Allen & Stevens, 1998).

Several disciplines are included in social studies, such as anthropology, archaeology, economics, geography, history, law, philosophy, political science, psychology, religion, and sociology. Also, appropriate content is taken from the humanities, mathematics, and natural sciences (Ellis, 1998). Figure 15–6 provides brief definitions of the various disciplines found within social studies.

Process Skills for Social Studies

Several skills are needed to process information in the social studies curriculum. These process skills describe types of thinking and reasoning required to succeed in social studies. Seven different process skills have been identified:

1. The ability to make connections between previously learned information and new information in the social studies curriculum.
2. The ability to think about and analyze information through different logical patterns and perspectives obtained through the study of social studies.

3. Recognition that new knowledge is created by the interaction of new information from social studies.
4. The ability to communicate with others about the data and interpretation of social studies as it applies to the student's studies and the real world.
5. The ability to acquire information from reading, study, references, and information search from electronic devices.
6. The ability to organize and use information through thinking, decision-making, and metacognitive skills.
7. The ability to use interpersonal relationship skills, such as personal and group interaction and social and political participation skills (Allen & Stevens, 1998; Bragaw & Hartoonian, 1988; "In Search of a Scope and Sequence," 1989).

Some students with or without disabilities may have weaknesses or gaps in these areas. Teachers may need to provide additional instruction, guided practice on the implementation of these skills, or simplification of the material to help guide students through effective implementation of these processes.

Social Studies Curriculum Design and Adaptations

Widening Horizons and the Spiral Curriculum. The social studies curriculum is based on two concepts: widening horizons and the spiral curriculum. Widening horizons refers to the idea that material is taught from the familiar to the unfamiliar, the known to the unknown, and the simple to the complex. Students may be taught about families and self-awareness on a kindergarten and first-grade level, then expand to neighborhoods, communities, cities, regions, nations, and the world.

A spiral curriculum is one in which topics are revisited at a much greater depth as the student progresses from elementary to middle to high school. For example, the neighborhood, discussed in first grade, may be revisited in middle school at sixth grade in conducting sophisticated neighborhood studies (Ellis, 1998). The spiral curriculum then reinforces knowledge and ideas, helps develop new concepts and skills, and draws from previous learning.

It is important that students are taught not only content, but historical thinking. Historical thinking requires understanding people who lived in different cultures and different times. Students can easily misinterpret historical information when they base their viewpoint on their own experiences and present-day standards. Students need to learn to understand the perspectives of multiple groups within the times they lived. Historical thinking also includes examining who authored the text as well as the purpose of the text, possible biases, and the sources of the information used (La Paz & MacArthur, 2003). Teachers can help promote this understanding through systematic teaching, discussions, and examples.

Considerations and Adaptations. For students with physical and multiple disabilities, this widening-horizons and spiral curriculum may cause some difficulties. Assumptions about what is known at a starting point may be quite different for students with severe physical and speech impairments than they would be for their typically developing peers, due to lack of similar experiential backgrounds. It therefore becomes important to check for prior knowledge in social studies courses and to teach the student any missing information.

Another consideration is the effect of a spiral curriculum. If the student has high absenteeism due to health problems (or due to attendance at PT, OT, or SLP sessions), there may not be as strong a foundation to draw from when returning to the content on a more sophisticated level. Assumptions should never be made regarding whether the student has had the content before, especially if there has been significant absenteeism. Again, missing information will need to be taught, especially if it included key concepts or was the basis for new information. In some instances, decisions must be made to reduce the amount of content or to skip over areas. It becomes crucial to consider how these omissions will impact future content and the potential to pass state-level standard tests, high school competency exams, and national exams such as the ITBS or SAT.

Students with physical or multiple disabilities may have difficulty with the material due to literacy issues, weaknesses in determining key points of lessons or readings, or the amount of content. A careful determination of the student's literacy skills, comprehension skills, and ability to deal with large amounts of material is crucial. Problems in these areas can be addressed through the strategies discussed in the previous section.

Since social studies is the study of people, the social studies curriculum can provide a unique opportunity to include discussions regarding individuals with disabilities. When discussing similarities found across people, discussions on how individuals with disabilities are the same as individuals without disabilities can occur. The contributions of individuals with disabilities may also be pointed out. It is important that these discussions not be limited to a designated time, such as "Disability Awareness" week or month. The natural inclusion of individuals with disabilities should be stressed.

Social Studies Software

Numerous software programs that address various areas of social studies are available. For example, on the elementary school level, many students enjoy "Where in the World Is Carmen Sandiego?" (manufactured by Riverdeep–The Learning Company). This software program takes the student through various countries as the student deciphers clues relating to the geography, history, and culture of the area using a fun game format. Another program by Riverdeep–The Learning Company, "The Oregon Trail," uses a fun game format to teach the student about the Oregon Trail and how the people survived on the trail. Edmark/Riverdeep Family's Imagination Express Series (e.g., "Imagination Express, Destination: Time Trip USA"; "Imagination Express, Destination: Ocean"; "Imagination Express, Destination: Pyramids"; "Imagination Express, Destination: Rain Forest") teaches elementary students about various areas as they create their own interesting stories or read about the places in a Fact Book.

There are many other software programs supporting instruction in social studies from elementary school to college. Approximately 400 software titles addressing various areas of social studies (e.g., African-American history, geography, American history) can be found at such software stores as Educational Resources *(http://www.edresources.com).* This particular site allows searching by title, topic, and age range and provides a description of each software program.

SCIENCE CURRICULUM CONSIDERATIONS

Science teaches students about their environment. Through presentation of information, observation, experimentation, and analysis of outcomes, students gain scientific knowledge. However, students with physical disabilities may encounter several barriers to learning science. Some of these barriers are stereotypes and low expectations, poor accessibility to manipulative experiences that are critical for basic learning, lack of modification or adaptations of the science program, and teachers who harbor negative attitudes or are overprotective (Stefanich, 1985). Fortunately, most of these barriers can be overcome by a commitment to meet the student's needs and the implementation of appropriate adaptations.

The importance of science for students with physical disabilities cannot be overstressed. The study of science may help fill in some experiential gaps due to extensive hospital stays, overprotectiveness, or lack of community access. Learning the process of inquiry can help develop students' mental and manipulative readiness for new technology use. Finally, many job opportunities will require greater use of technological devices, as well as some science skills, and education in these areas can aid students in obtaining and retaining their jobs (Martin et al., 1997).

Science Defined

Science is the systematic knowledge of the physical or material world gained through observations and experimentation (*Webster's New Universal Unabridged Dictionary,* 1996). Knowledge is gained through a group of processes that are used to systematically make discoveries about the natural world. Science may be characterized as having a set of values including truth, order, originality, communication, skepticism, and freedom. These values help guide the scientist to not accept things at face value, to promote construction of unbiased conclusions, and to disseminate these conclusions to others (Abruscato, 1996).

There are several disciplines represented in science. These may be categorized as physical sciences, life sciences, earth sciences, and space science. The physical sciences include such areas as chemistry and physics. The life sciences (also known as biological sciences) include

FIGURE 15–7
Disciplines found in science

Physical Science
Chemistry: The study of natural and artificial substances to determine their composition and structure, and examination of changes that occur in their composition and structure when combined with other substances.
Physics: The study of light and energy. Typically includes areas such as mechanics, heat, light, sound, electricity, magnetism, and properties of matter.

Life Sciences (Biology)
Botany: The study of plants.
Zoology: The study of animals (including humans).

Earth Sciences
Geology: The study of the composition and structure of the earth.
Meteorology: The study of the earth's atmosphere and weather conditions.

Space Science
Astronomy: The study of stars, planets, comets, meteors, galaxies, and other objects in space.
Cosmology: The study of the structure and origins of the universe.

botany and zoology. Earth sciences include geology and meteorology. Space science comprises the area of astronomy and other areas such as cosmology. Figure 15–7 provides definitions of these areas of science.

Process Skills for Science

Several process skills are identified as being critical in the area of science. These process skills consist of the reasoning and thinking skills that are used in this field. They may be divided into basic skills and integrated skills (Martin et al., 1997). Basic skills include observing, classifying, communicating, measuring, estimating, predicting, and inferring. Integrated skills include identifying, controlling variables, operationally defining, hypothesizing, experimenting, graphing, interpreting, modeling, and investigating. As seen in Table 15–4, the integrated skills are not typically introduced until 3rd grade, and all skills continue being developed up through 12th grade.

Students who have difficulty with these process-skill areas will need to have these taught. Teachers may need to provide additional instruction or guided practice on the implementation of these skills. Checking for comprehension of these process skills will help teachers know which skills should be targeted for systematic instruction.

Science Curriculum Design and Adaptations

Scientific Inquiry. Science is often taught as a process in which students pursue answers to questions using a list of steps. This list may contain the following steps: (1) define the problem, (2) find out what is already known, (3) form a hypothesis, (4) conduct an experiment to test the hypothesis, and (5) use the results to formulate a conclusion. Unfortunately, this is often treated as a recipe for doing science and does not necessarily provide students with skills necessary to become independent inquirers about their world. The National Science Education Standards (NSES) encourages a broader approach that promotes understanding of science concepts, takes a "know how we know" approach, develops independent inquiry skills, and develops mental habits of using their skills (Martin et al., 1997).

One scientific inquiry method, by Fields (1989), provides a method that is used to motivate and provide interactive instruction and meets the demands of the NSES. There are five steps in this process:

1. Formulate a question from a topic of interest and have students conclude that experimenting will provide the best answer to the question. For example, the teacher may provide a demonstration or discussion that motivates the students to ask why something occurs the way it does. Students then decide that experimenting is needed to answer the question.
2. Focus the science question. Class members brainstorm about what they want to find out and what they are asking. From this brainstorming, the question is narrowed and refined.
3. Guess the answer to the science question, and use references to find out if the answer is already known. Students are guided to determine whether they can find the answer in their book or whether they know anyone who knows the answer. If the answers are not clear, then the students are asked how they can design an experiment to find out the answer. Variables that may affect the outcome of the experiment can be discussed at this point.

TABLE 15–4
Science Process Skills

Basic skills can be emphasized at the primary grades and then serve as a foundation for using the integrated skills at the intermediate grades and higher.

	GRADES								
Basic Skills	K	1	2	3	4	5	6	7	8
Observing	X	X	X	X	X	X	X	X	X
Classifying	X	X	X	X	X	X	X	X	X
Communicating	X	X	X	X	X	X	X	X	X
Measuring	X	X	X	X	X	X	X	X	X
Estimating	X	X	X	X	X	X	X	X	X
Predicting	X	X	X	X	X	X	X	X	X
Inferring	X	X	X	X	X	X	X	X	X
Integrated Skills	K	1	2	3	4	5	6	7	8
Identifying				X	X	X	X	X	X
Controlling variables				X	X	X	X	X	X
Defining operationally				X	X	X	X	X	X
Hypothesizing				X	X	X	X	X	X
Experimenting				X	X	X	X	X	X
Graphing				X	X	X	X	X	X
Interpreting				X	X	X	X	X	X
Modeling				X	X	X	X	X	X
Investigating				X	X	X	X	X	X

Note. Adapted from R. Martin, C. Sexton, K. Wagner, J. Gerlovich, *Teaching Science for All Children*. Copyright © 1997 by Allyn & Bacon. Adapted by permission.

4. Find the answer to the science question. Use resources or experiment to find out the answer.
5. Interpret the results and apply these results. After interpreting the results, the main idea of what was learned is discussed in terms of other everyday experiences. Concepts are applied to other pertinent areas (Fields, 1989; Martin et al., 1997).

This process can be used for students with physical and multiple disabilities. For students who use AAC devices, it is crucial that they have sufficient vocabulary to express ideas during classroom discussions. It is also important to ensure that the student is provided enough time to respond.

When the results of scientific inquiry contradict the student's own notions, the results of the experiment may not necessarily restructure the student's incorrect existing ideas. For example, when seeing heavier and lighter objects falling at the same speed, students often "protect" their own concept that heavier objects fall faster (e.g., arguing that one was not really heavier, or that the objects were not released from a high enough point). The teacher needs to anticipate this by (a) providing concepts in an understandable manner, (b) designing a critical event that addresses the student's misconception and using scientific concepts to explain the student's concept, (c) teaching other scientific concepts supporting the one being taught, and (d) using additional perceptual activities to sustain the targeted concepts. To aid in this process, teachers may create conflict maps, which are graphic representations (much like the semantic map in Figure 15–2) of the targeted scientific concept being taught, the student's alternate concept, the experiment resulting in a conflict between what is being taught and what the student thinks, supporting perceptions, and additional relevant concepts. These maps can be used as a planning guide to help teachers construct lessons addressing possible misconceptions, as well as used by students as a metacognitive strategy to monitor their understanding (Tsai, 2000).

Literacy Issues in Science. Students with physical or multiple disabilities may also have difficulty with the material due to literacy issues, weaknesses in determining key points, or an inability to handle the required amount of content. As previously discussed, many of these problems can be addressed through general strategies in teaching and adapting content presented in the first part of this chapter. However, the diversity of reading skills required for success in science should be emphasized. See Table 15–5 for a summation of how literacy pertains to various science skills.

TABLE 15–5
Relationship of Science and Reading Skills

Science Skills	Reading Skills	Examples
Observation	Discriminating shapes, sounds, syllables, and word accents	Break words in syllables and list on chalkboard. Class pronounces new words aloud. Teacher mispronounces some words and rewards students who make corrections.
Identification	Recognizing letters, words, prefixes, suffixes, and base words	Select a common science prefix, suffix, or base word, define it, and list several words in which it may be used. Example: *kilo* (1,000): *kilometer, kilogram, kiloliter.*
Description	Isolating important attributes and characteristics Enumerating ideas Using appropriate terminology and synonyms	Ask students to state the purpose of an activity. Construct keys for student rock collections, etc. Play vocabulary games. Use characteristics to identify an object or animal.
Classification	Comparing and contrasting characteristics Arranging ideas and ordering and sequencing information Considering multiple attributes	List in order the steps of a mealworm's metamorphosis. Construct charts that compare and contrast characteristics. Put concepts in order.
Investigation design	Asking questions Investigating possible relationships Following organized procedures	Use library resources and design an experiment from an outline. Write original lab reports. Outline facts and concepts.
Data collection	Notetaking Using reference materials Using different parts of a book Recording information in an organized way Being precise and accurate	Prepare bibliographies from library information. Use tables of contents, indexes, and organizational features of chapters. Use quantitative skills in lab activities. Have students compare and discuss notes.
Interpretation of data	Recognizing cause-and-effect relationships Organizing facts Summarizing new information Varying reading rate Thinking inductively and deductively	Discuss matters that could affect the health of an animal. Teach students to preview and scan printed text. Have students organize notes in an outline. Have students construct concept maps, flow-charts, and new arrangements of facts.
Communication of results	Using graphs Arranging information logically Sequencing ideas Describing clearly	List discoveries through a time line. Ask for conclusions from graphed data or tables and figures. Describe chronological events.
Conclusion formation	Generalizing Critically analyzing Identifying main ideas Establishing relationships Using information in other situations	Ask "What if?" questions. Have students scrutinize conclusions for errors. Use case studies to develop conclusions through critical thinking.

Note. From R. Martin, C. Sexton, K. Wagner, J. Gerlovich, *Teaching Science for All Children.* Copyright © 1997 by Allyn & Bacon. Adapted by permission.

Adapting the Physical and Learning Environment. Science tends to be a very hands-on type of curriculum in which students manipulate and experiment with a wide variety of materials. Because of this emphasis on manipulating and experimenting with materials, there is a need for extensive adaptations for many students with physical disabilities. To meet these students' needs, the physical environment must be examined for safety and for accessibility for students with physical and multiple disabilities. This can be examined in three areas: access, facility and furniture, and equipment and instruction. (See Figure 15–8 for a checklist of these areas.)

As with all school environments, ramps, accessible doorways, and barrier-free corridors are a must. If possible, safety glass and carpeting should also be used. All facilities and furniture should also be accessible. Ensuring that the aisles are wide enough for maneuverability and that students are able to get to the materials is the first step. Individual equipment should be examined next. The laboratory bench (or desk) should be at an appropriate height; modifications in it and in other furniture may be needed. This is critical so that the student with a physical disability can see what is going on and participate to the maximum extent possible. Typical elements

FIGURE 15–8
Checklist for classroom safety

Access

- Ramps should be both inside and outside to facilitate entry to the school building.
- Smooth industrial-type carpeting reduces noise and slipping and cushions inevitable falls.
- Barrier-free corridors are a must for emergency and fire protection.
- Classroom doorways should be at least 35 inches wide to allow access of wheelchairs.
- Reevaluate the size, weight, and hardware of all doors. The doors should be single effort, opened with a force of eight pounds or less, and have lever hardware and no sill (Operation Overcome, 1987).
- Use of safety glass on all windows and doors is recommended.

Facilities and Furniture

- Classroom aisles should be wide enough for easy maneuverability (dependent on the type of wheelchair). Rearrange the furniture to create bigger aisles and remove extra furniture to create more open space.
- Lower mounting of chalkboards to 3 feet from floor. Most students use the chalkboards at one time or another. The wheelchair occupant (whose maximum reach is no more than 5 inches) can comfortably reach only the lower 2 feet of a standard mount chalkboard.
- The laboratory bench is the basic provision for laboratory work and should adjust to a height of 24 inches to 36 inches (Brindle, 1981).
- Look for flexibility in all classroom elements to accommodate the limited reach of a disabled person. Gas, water, air, vacuum, and electric outlets should be accessible to all, with easy-to-operate hardware on these fixtures.
- Eye-wash stations and shower pulls must be placed at suitable heights.
- Cables, wires, and power sources should be placed to eliminate dangling wires (Frinks & McNamara, 1985).
- Modify standard furniture (large laboratory tables with separate chairs that fit underneath) by adjusting the table height with wooden blocks so that a wheelchair can be pulled up to the table comfortably.

Equipment and Instruction

For the Wheelchair Occupant:

- To help a wheelchair occupant transport equipment, trays can be made from heavy gauge stainless steel, with spring clips that snap onto the sides of the wheelchair (Brindle, 1981).
- Microscopes with angled oculars are more convenient for wheelchair occupants.

For the Visually Impaired:

- Visually impaired students should be taught using models and hands-on activities since they usually spend more time exploring objects than do sighted students (Hofman & Ricker, 1979).
- Good diction and clear descriptions must be used for the visually impaired.
- Students with limited vision must be seated in the front of the classroom.
- Blind students often tape-record lectures; therefore, it is essential to place them where there is minimum background noise.
- Orient students to the location of safety equipment, storage, emergency stations, and facilities prior to the first class (Hofman & Ricker, 1979).

Note. From "Safe Science Classrooms for Students with Disabilities" by J. A. Bazler and R. Roberts, *The American Biology Teacher*, 55, 1993, 302–303. Reprinted with permission.

on the bench, such as gas, water, air, vacuum, and electric outlets, should be within easy reach for the student with physical disabilities. For safety reasons, eye-wash stations and shower pulls need to be placed at appropriate heights, which are often lower than those designed for students who can stand (Bazler & Roberts, 1993).

In the area of equipment and instruction, further modifications may be needed. To allow the student to transport equipment, for example, heavy-duty trays may be placed on the wheelchair. Careful assessment of how the student will access the material is imperative. For example, microscopes may need to have angled oculars in order for the student to see. Other students with physical disabilities may be unable to look through a microscope and may require alternate access. Systems such as the Video Flex (by Ken-a-Vision) use a microscope eyepiece adapter that fits over the microscope eyepiece and connects to a TV monitor. The image on the microscope is displayed on the monitor for easy viewing. Other students may not be able to optimally position themselves to closely view dissection or examine items. In these instances, the Video Flex or a CCTV (see Figure 14–6 in Chapter 14) may be used to enlarge an item and display it on a monitor for easy viewing.

Using lab partners is a classic grouping strategy in science activities, and one that works well for a student who has physical limitations. This pairing allows the nondisabled student to help the student with a disability in areas that he or she cannot perform. It is still important that the student with the physical disability receive direct physical experience with the science activities to the greatest extent possible. For example, when doing an experiment with magnets, the magnet may be taped on the student's arm or leg and another student can bring objects in close contact with the magnets (Martin et al., 1997). Students who are unable to physically access the material (e.g., who are unable to dissect) due to very severe physical disabilities can direct the partner, jot down observations, or work collaboratively in other ways. In some instances the student may be able to access dissection or biology computer programs as an adjunct to what is being taught in class.

Some adjunct science curricula have been developed to provide access to science materials that would otherwise be inaccessible. One of these is the SAVI/SELPH curriculum (*www.lawrencehallofscience.org/cml/saviselph/index.html*) (Malone, De Lucchi, & Thier, 1984). This curriculum was originally developed as the SAVI program (Science Activities for the Visually Impaired), but was expanded to include students with physical impairments and learning disabilities in SELPH (Science Enrichment for Learners with Physical Handicaps). This program was originally designed for students in grades 4 to 7, but has been used from 1st grade through 10th grade. It is designed to be a multisensory science enrichment program that is typically used in conjunction with the student's current science program. There are nine SAVI/SELPH modules: Measurement; Scientific Reasoning; Communication; Structures of Life; Magnetism and Electricity; Environments; Mixtures and Solutions; Kitchen Interactions; and Environmental Energy. Each module comes with all of the supplies and equipment needed, and the equipment is adapted to provide access to students with limited motor and/or visual ability. For example, scales are enlarged and hold items in cups so that they will not spill, plungers cannot be inadvertently pulled out of the syringe barrel and they are marked tactually, containers are oversized and are made to stabilize equipment and promote ease of access, and oversized thermometers can easily be placed in liquid (see Figure 15–9). Each module also has a series of experiments based upon the process of science, and includes an overview, background information, purpose of the experiment, materials list, pre-experiment activities, follow-up activities, enrichment activities, language development section, and general application skills.

Many other science curriculums may be adapted to meet the needs of students with disabilities. For example, the Full Option Science System (FOSS) curriculum (which was developed at University of California at Berkeley) is a carefully planned and coordinated science curriculum for students in grades K–6. It comes with teacher guides, equipment kits, teacher preparation videos, reading resources, science stories, and a Web site (*http://www.fossweb.com*). Although adapted equipment is not included, many of the activities can be modified to allow students with physical disabilities to participate.

Another approach will be needed for students who have difficulty with science due to cognitive or organizational demands. One approach that was adapted for students with mild disabilities was the FAST I Program (Sasaki & Serna, 1995). FAST I (Foundational Ap-

FIGURE 15–9
Students with visual or physical disabilities can access science materials through the SAVI/SELPH curriculum

Note. From *SAVI Leadership Trainer's Manual* by L. Malone, L. D. DeLucchi, and H. D. Thier, 1984, Berkeley: Center for Multisensory Learning, University of California. Reprinted with permission.

proach to Science Teaching) (Pottenger & Young, 1992) is a hands-on, practical inquiry approach to learning physical science, ecology, and other related areas. Students are placed in teams of three or four and a leader is assigned. In Sasaki and Serna's use of this approach with students with mild disabilities, they included one student who was good in reading and one student who was good in math in each group. Teachers served as facilitators by encouraging group interaction, answering questions with other questions, and helping students evaluate and draw conclusions from data. Emphasis on behavior management procedures, such as time-out for breaking a lab rule, as well as earning points for participation, was found to be effective. The adaptations to this approach also included more-structured laboratory notebooks, which had checklists covering the inclusion of problem statements, equipment lists, vocabulary lists, procedures, data and observations, and a summary and conclusion for each experiment.

In addition to ensuring that the physical environment and the curricula are modified as needed, teachers must create a positive learning environment in which students' strengths are utilized and the expectation is that all students can learn. It should be emphasized that students with physical disabilities can learn science concepts and that most will develop higher levels of reasoning skills if given the opportunity. To develop these skills, it is important that the student receive direct, experiential opportunities in science. Hands-on, inquiry-based, and real-life experiences must be stressed (Martin et al., 1997). Students should not be relegated to the back of the room in isolation, but be part of the class by participating in the science curriculum with appropriate adaptations.

Science Software

There are many software programs available that can be used along with traditional science curriculums. Young children may enjoy "Sammy's Science House" (manufactured by Edmark/Riverdeep Family), which introduces preschool and elementary school students to plants, animals, seasons, and other concepts, while allowing students with physical disabilities to access the program using an adapted keyboard or switch access. "Thinkin' Science" (manufactured by Edmark/Riverdeep Family) teaches basic science concepts and information and also allows alternate access for students needing adapted keyboards or switch access. Edmark also manufactures "Thinkin' Science Zap," a voice output program that provides 3rd to 6th graders the opportunity to observe, experiment, and solve problems in learning labs. Students can learn as they manipulate circuits, sound waves, and light.

There are several other programs that can provide useful information to elementary students, although they are not manufactured to accommodate alternate input devices such as switch interfaces. For example, Optimum Resources, Inc., manufactures the popular "Stickybear's Science Fair: Light," which allows elementary (and secondary) students to explore and experiment with light through manipulating prisms, lenses, and color mixing. The topics of refraction and reflection are also included. Sunburst Communications manufactures several software programs that teach students about insects, plants, and animals. In "Learn About Insects," students learn about the growth, homes, and movement of many types of insects. In "Learn About Plants," students plant a garden and watch it grow and are taught about plant anatomy and pollination. In "Learn About Animals," students can explore habitats, foods, and animal characteristics.

Software and supplementary videos and books are available that specifically target students in the secondary grades. For example, Educational Activities, Inc. (*http://www.edact.com/*), provides multiple videos and instructional material over a wide range of science fields in both elementary and secondary education (as well as other subject materials). Multimedia programs, such as "A.D.A.M. The Inside Story Complete" or "A.D.A.M. Essentials High School Suite" (both manufactured by Adam.com) provide information on human anatomy and physiology and help students explore major body systems and identify over 3,600 anatomic structures. Several other products are available from this company, such as "A.D.A.M. Interactive Physiology," "A.D.A.M. Interactive Anatomy," and "A.D.A.M. Anatomy Practice." Other science software can be found through contacting individual companies or using a software store such as Educational Resources (*http://www.edresources.com*), which has over 500 titles of science software for the preschool to adult learner.

SUMMARY AND CONCLUSION

Students with physical or multiple disabilities can benefit from instruction in social studies and science when appropriate curricular adaptations amd instructional strategies are provided. Careful lesson preparation is needed to determine adaptations and to prepare the student for success. A clear understanding of the general format for instruction, including prelearning activities, lesson presentation, and evaluation and possible adaptations at each level, will help the teacher make the material accessible for each student. Social studies adaptations often incorporate providing and adapting material for a lower reading level, programming appropriate content into an AAC device, and providing appropriate experiential background information. Science adaptations typically address adapting for motoric constraints that can interfere with experiments and lab participation. Several adaptations have been presented, but the student's requirements must be carefully and individually assessed to determine that the adaptation meets the student's needs.

QUESTIONS FOR DISCUSSION

1. Discuss how a student's physical or multiple disability may have an impact on learning a science or social studies unit.
2. Select a social studies or science textbook and examine the textbook for readability, organization, and usefulness. Use the checklist in Figure 15–1.
3. Select a unit from a social studies textbook and discuss how the techniques discussed in this chapter could be utilized.
4. Select a science experiment and discuss which aspects of the science experiment could be difficult for a student with a limited range of motion and poor fine-motor skills. Discuss possible adaptations that will facilitate learning.

FOCUS ON THE NET

C-span
http://www.c-span.org

This provides access to the House of Representatives, allowing the teacher to tie in a unit on the democratic process with the actual process of debating and voting.

Educational Resources
http://www.edresources.com

This particular site allows searching by subject, title, topic, and age range and provides a description of each software program.

Globe Program
http://www.Globe.gov

This site provides information on environmental issues through a combination of social studies, science, and other areas. Research scientists use the student data and provide feedback.

National Science Teachers Association
http://www.nsta.org/

Provides current information on science for elementary, middle, high school, and college students.

NCSSonline
http://www.socialstudies.org/

This is the official site of the National Council for the Social Studies. Information and networks in the area of social studies are provided.

Teacher Network
http://www.teachnet.org

This is a database of approximately 500 classroom projects that are ready for use. Also included is a bulletin board that allows teachers to share ideas.

REFERENCES

Abruscato, J. (1996). *Teaching children science: A discovery approach.* Boston: Allyn & Bacon.

Allen, M. G., & Stevens, R. L. (1998). *Middle grades social studies.* Boston: Allyn & Bacon.

Alvermann, D. E. (1991). The discussion web: A graphic aid for learning across the curriculum. *Reading Teacher, 45,* 92–99.

Armbruster, B. B., & Anderson, T. H. (1988). On selecting "considerate" content area textbooks. *Remedial and Special Education, 9,* 47–52.

Bazler, J. A., & Roberts, R. (1993). Safe science classrooms for students with disabilities. *American Biology Teacher, 55,* 302–303.

Bean, R. M., Zigmond, N., & Hartman, D. K. (1994). Adapted use of social studies textbooks in elementary classrooms. *Remedial and Special Education, 15,* 216–226.

Beck, I. L., McKeown, M., & Gromoll, E. W. (1989). Learning from social studies texts. *Cognition and Instruction, 6*(2), 99–153.

Berninger, V., & Gans, B. (1986). Language profiles in nonspeaking individuals of normal intelligence with severe cerebral palsy. *Augmentative and Alternative Communication, 2,* 45–50.

Blischak, D. M. (1995). Thomas the Writer: Case study of a child with severe physical, speech, and visual impairments. *Language, Speech, and Hearing Services in the Schools, 26,* 11–20.

Bos, C. S., & Vaughn, S. (1998). *Strategies for teaching students with learning and behavior problems* (4th ed.). Boston: Allyn & Bacon.

Bragaw, D., & Hartoonian, H. M. (1988). Social studies: The study of people in society. In R. Brandt (Ed.), *Content of the curriculum, 1988 yearbook* (pp. 9–29). Alexandria, VA: Association for Supervision and Curriculum Development.

Chall, J. S., & Conrad, S. S. (1991). *Should textbooks challenge students?* New York: Teachers College Press.

Chapin, J. R., & Messick, R. G. (1989). *Elementary social studies: A practical guide.* New York: Longman.

Clark, D. B., & Slotta, J. D. (2002). Evaluating media-enhancement and source authority on the Internet: the knowledge integration environment. *International Journal of Science Education, 22,* 859–871.

Crank, J. N., & Bulgren, J. A. (1993). Visual depictions as information organizers for enhancing achievement of students with learning disabilities. *Learning Disabilities Research and Practice, 8,* 140–147.

Crawley, J. F. (1994). Science for students with disabilities. *Remedial and Special Education, 15,* 67–71.

DiVesta, F. J., & Smith, D. A. (1979). The pausing principle: Increasing the efficiency of memory for ongoing events. *Contemporary Educational Psychology, 4,* 288–296.

Donovan, C. A., & Smolkin, L. B. (2002). Considering genre, content, and visual features in the selection of trade books for science instruction. *Reading Teacher, 55,* 502–520.

Elliott, D. L., Nagel, K., & Woodward, A. (1985). Do textbooks belong in elementary social studies? *Educational Leadership, 42*(7), 21–28.

Ellis, A. K. (1998). *Teaching and learning elementary social studies* (6th ed.). Boston: Allyn & Bacon.

Fernstrom, P., & Goodnite, B. (2000). Accommodate student diversity in the general education social studies classroom. *Intervention in School and Clinic, 35,* 244–245.

Fields, S. (1989, April). The scientific teaching method. *Science and Children,* p. 15.

Foley, B. E. (1993). The development of literacy in individuals with severe congenital speech and motor impairments. *Topics in Language Disorders, 13,* 16–32.

Gagnon, P. (1987). *Democracy's untold story: What world history textbooks neglect.* Washington, DC: American Federation of Teachers.

Heller, K. W. (2000). Classroom Modifications Checklist for Students with Physical and Health Impairments. Atlanta: Georgia Bureau for Students with Physical and Health Impairments.

Heller, K. W., Alberto, P. A., Forney, P. E., & Schwartzman, M. N. (1996). *Understanding physical, sensory, and health impairments: Characteristics and educational implications.* Pacific Grove, CA: Brooks/Cole.

Heller, K. W., Forney, P. E., Alberto, P. A., Schwartzman, M. N., & Goeckel, T. M. (2000). *Meeting physical and health needs of children with disabilities.* Belmont, CA: Wadsworth.

Horton, S. V., & Lovitt, T. C. (1989). Using study guides with three classifications of secondary students. *Journal of Special Education, 22,* 447–462.

Hudson, P. (1996). Using a learning set to increase the test performance of students with learning disabilities in social studies classes. *Learning Disabilities Research and Practice, 11,* 78–85.

Hudson, P. (1997). Using teacher-guided practice to help students with learning disabilities acquire and retain social studies content. *Learning Disabilities Quarterly, 20,* 23–32.

In search of a scope and sequence for social studies: Report of the National Council for Social Studies Task Force on Scope and Sequence. (1989). *Social Education, 53,* 386–387.

Jarman, R., & McClune, B. (2002). A survey of the use of newspapers in science instruction by secondary teachers in Northern Ireland. *International Journal of Science Education, 24,* 997–1020.

Johnson, D. D., Pittelman, S. D., & Heimlich, J. E. (1986). Semantic mapping. *Reading Teacher, 39,* 778–783.

Kindsvatter, R., Wilen, W., & Ishler, M. (1988). *Dynamics of effective teaching.* New York: Longman.

La Paz, S., & MacArthur, C. (2003). Knowing the how and why of history: Expectations for secondary students with and without learning disabilities. *Learning Disability Quarterly, 26,* 142–154.

Lenz, B. K., Alley, G. R., & Schumaker, J. B. (1987). Activating the inactive learner: Advance organizers in the secondary content classroom. *Learning Disability Quarterly, 10,* 53–67.

Malone, L., De Lucchi, L. D., & Thier, H. D. (1984). *SAVI leadership trainer's manual.* Berkeley: Center for Multisensory Learning, University of California.

Martin, R., Sexton, C., Wagner, K., & Gerlovich, J. (1997). *Teaching science for all children* (2nd ed.). Boston: Allyn & Bacon.

Nolet, V., & Tindel, G. (1993). Special education in content area classes: Development of a model and practical procedures. *Remedial and Special Education, 14*(1), 36–48.

Ogle, D. M. (1986). K-W-L: A teaching model that develops active reading of expository text. *Reading Teacher, 39,* 564–570.

Palinscar, A. S., Magnusson, S. J., Collins, K. M., & Cutter, J. (2001). Making science accessible to all: Results of a design experiment in inclusive classrooms. *Learning Disability Quarterly, 24,* 15–32.

Pearson, P. D., & Johnson, D. D. (1978). *Teaching reading comprehension.* New York: Holt, Rinehart, & Winston.

Pottenger, F. M., & Young, D. B. (1992). *Foundational approaches in science teaching (FAST I Program).* Honolulu: Curriculum Research and Development Group, University of Hawaii. (ERIC Document Reproduction Service No. ED 365 549)

Powell, G., & Zalud, G. (1982, December). aSQ3R for secondary handicapped students. *Journal of Reading,* pp. 262–263.

Robinson, F. P. (1946). *Effective study.* New York: Harper.

Rosenshine, B., & Stevens, R. (1986). Teaching functions. In M. D. Wittrock (Ed.), *Handbook of research in teaching* (pp. 376–391). New York: Macmillan.

Ruhl, K. L., Hughes, C. A., & Gajar, A. H. (1990). Efficacy of the pause procedure for enhancing learning disabled and nondisabled college students' long and short term recall of facts presented through lecture. *Learning Disability Quarterly, 13,* 55–64.

Ruhl, K. L., Hughes, C. A., & Schloss, P. J. (1987). Using the pause procedure to enhance lecture recall. *Teacher Education and Special Education, 10,* 14–18.

Sasaki, J., & Serna, L. A. (1995). FAST Science: Teaching science to adolescents with mild disabilities. *Teaching Exceptional Children, 27*(4), 14–16.

Schumaker, J. B., Delsher, D. D., Alley, G. R., Warner, M. M., & Denton, P. H. (1982). Multipass: A learning strategy for improving reading comprehension. *Learning Disability Quarterly, 5,* 295–304.

Sewall, G. T. (1987). *American history textbooks: An assessment of quality.* New York: Educational Excellence Network.

Stefanich, G. P. (1985). *Addressing orthopedic handicaps in the science classroom.* (ERIC Document Reproduction Service No. ED 258 802)

Tsai, C. (2000). Enhancing science instruction: the use of conflict maps. *International Journal of Science Education, 22,* 285–302.

Watson, S. M., & Houtz, L. E. (2002). Teaching science: Meeting the academic needs of culturally and linguistically diverse students. *Intervention in School and Clinic, 37,* 267–278.

Webster's new universal unabridged dictionary. (1996). New York: Barnes & Noble.

Adaptations and Instruction in Mathematics

KATHRYN WOLFF HELLER

CHAPTER 16

KNOWLEDGE AND SKILLS

After you have read this chapter, you will be able to:

1. **Describe several barriers that students with physical or multiple disabilities encounter when learning math skills.**
2. **Describe several different methods to assess math skills and how these methods pertain to students with physical or multiple disabilities.**
3. **Describe five general approaches and principles of math instruction to promote effective learning.**
4. **Describe and demonstrate instructional techniques for precomputational skills.**
5. **Describe and demonstrate systematic instructional techniques for computational skills, including math facts, algorithms, sequencing instruction, computer software, and adaptations.**
6. **Describe instructional strategies for functional math skills and adaptations across money, time, and calendar use.**

One of the most common skills that pervade everyday life is the application of mathematics. Math is used in such common activities as handling money, telling time, cooking, keeping score in recreational activities, and counting items. It is also present in more-advanced activities such as analyzing data, budgeting money, calculating income tax, and designing architectural structures. Math is encountered across home, community, leisure, and vocational domains. Students will be expected to learn an array of mathematical concepts and skills throughout their school experience, whether they are learning academic or functional skills.

BARRIERS IN MATHEMATICS

Students with physical or multiple disabilities may encounter several barriers that negatively affect learning and performing math skills. First, most students with physical or multiple disabilities have poor motor skills, which can result in an inability to manipulate objects when counting, illegible and inaccurate writing of numbers, incorrect alignment of numbers, and/or inability to access math materials (e.g., math book, protractor). These types of difficulties can negatively affect performance (Miller & Mercer, 1997). Adaptations, assistive technology, and specialized instructional strategies are needed to accommodate for the effects of poor motor skills.

Students with physical or multiple disabilities may have severe speech impairments that interfere with learning and performing math skills. Severe speech impairments typically decrease participation and the ability to effectively ask questions. Even when students have an AAC system, they may still be learning the system or have a system that limits their ability to ask questions regarding the math concepts being presented. It may also be difficult to determine the type of errors students are making if they are unable to explain how they arrived at their answer.

Another barrier to math learning and performance consists of the poor literacy skills and/or low language abilities that are often found in students with physical or multiple disabilities (French, 1995; Tew, 1979). This may result in difficulty with certain types of math problems, such as calculations and word problems. When performing computational math problems, language skills are required to systematically recall and apply the many steps, math facts, and rules. In the problem 73×96, for example, there are about 33 steps for the student to go through in order to answer the problem (Miller & Mercer, 1997; Strang & Rourke, 1985). Certain levels of reading ability are also required in word problems. The ability to comprehend the word problem and decipher the relevant information is critical to correctly solving the problem. Literacy problems will affect the student's ability to solve the problem without assistance in reading it.

Distractibility, short attention span, and disorganization are found to occur in physical disabilities such as spina bifida and can result in barriers to math learning and performance (Anderson & Spain, 1977; Horn, Lorch, Lorch, & Culatta, 1985; Hunt, 1981; Land, 1977; Tew, 1979). Difficulty in sustaining attention to the teacher's instruction during math can interfere with gaining information. Also, poor math performance may occur when the student is unable to sustain attention to the sequential steps required in algorithm use or problem solving (Miller & Mercer, 1993a).

Many students with physical or multiple disabilities may have frequent absences or increased fatigue due to their impairment, which can create a barrier to math learning and performance (Heller, Alberto, Forney, & Schwartzman, 1996). Since math is a hierarchical skill that builds on previous information, absences or fatigue can result in missing important information. Unlike some academic subjects in which certain material is less important and may be omitted if necessary due to prolonged illness, the area of math often builds on itself, requiring that the student be taught all of the math concepts before proceeding to new material. Without additional instruction to help the student learn the missed material, the student may be confused and not prepared for the material currently being targeted in his or her class.

Cognitive and/or perceptual problems that can create a barrier to learning and performing math are present in some students with physical, health, or multiple disabilities. Some students may have mental retardation or learning disabilities that require the teacher to provide specialized instructional strategies and appropriate curriculum options in addition to the strategies used for physical disabilities. For example, visual-spatial deficits can interfere with differentiating between numbers, writing in a straight line, relating to directional aspects of math (such as solving problems in columns), and using such tools as number lines. Auditory processing difficulties may result in difficulties in counting on from a number from within a sequence (Miller & Mercer, 1993a). Appropriate strategies will be needed to address these barriers.

ASSESSING MATH SKILLS

An effective mathematics curriculum prepares students for solving problems as they participate in school, home, and work activities. It challenges students to learn increasingly difficult concepts and skills as they progress in their studies and their life activities. Math studies and accompanying assessment of student progress are organized in the curriculum by topical strands, which often are highly interconnected with each other (National Council of Teachers of Mathematics, 2000).

Topical strands generally cover content and processes stemming from some set of adopted standards such as the standards for mathematics education proposed by the National Council of Teachers of Mathematics (NCTM). Five of the proposed standards identify mathematical *content* goals in the areas of number and operations, algebra, geometry, measurement, and data analysis and probability. Five more standards identify *processes* of problem solving, reasoning and proof, communication, connections, and representation (National Council of Teachers of Mathematics, 2000). Table 16–1 conveys each standard and its main ideas that permeate the mathematics curriculum over four grade-bands: prekindergarten–grade 2, grades 3–5, grades 6–8, and grades 9–12.

TABLE 16–1
Standards 2000 (National Council of Teachers of Mathematics)

Content Standards	Process Standards
1. Number and Operations Instructional programs from prekindergarten through grade 12 should enable all students to ■ understand numbers, ways of representing numbers, relationships among numbers, and number systems ■ understand meanings of operations and how they relate to one another ■ compute fluently and make reasonable estimates **2. Algebra** Instructional programs from prekindergarten through grade 12 should enable all students to ■ understand patterns, relations, and functions ■ represent and analyze mathematical situations and structures using algebraic symbols ■ use mathematical models to represent and understand quantitative relationships **3. Geometry** Instructional programs from prekindergarten through grade 12 should enable all students to ■ analyze characteristics and properties of two- and three-dimensional geometric shapes and develop mathematical arguments about geometric relationships ■ specify locations and describe spatial relationships using coordinate geometry and other representational systems ■ apply transformations and use symmetry to analyze mathematical situations ■ use visualization, spatial reasoning, and geometric modeling to solve problems **4. Measurement** Instructional programs from prekindergarten through grade 12 should enable all students to ■ understand measurable attributes of objects and the units, systems, and processes of measurement ■ apply appropriate techniques, tools, and formulas to determine measurements **5. Data Analysis & Probability** Instructional programs from prekindergarten through grade 12 should enable all students to ■ *formulate* questions that can be addressed with data and collect, organize, and display relevant data to answer them ■ *select and use* appropriate statistical methods to analyze data ■ *develop and evaluate* inferences and predictions that are based on data ■ *understand and apply* basic concepts of probability	**6. Problem Solving** Instructional programs from prekindergarten through grade 12 should enable all students to ■ build new mathematical knowledge through problem solving ■ solve problems that arise in mathematics and in other contexts ■ apply and adapt a variety of appropriate strategies to solve problems ■ monitor and reflect on the process of mathematical problem solving **7. Reasoning & Proof** Instructional programs from prekindergarten through grade 12 should enable all students to ■ recognize reasoning and proof as fundamental aspects of mathematics ■ make and investigate mathematical conjectures ■ develop and evaluate mathematical arguments and proofs ■ select and use various types of reasoning and methods of proof **8. Communication** Instructional programs from prekindergarten through grade 12 should enable all students to ■ organize and consolidate their mathematical thinking through communication ■ communicate their mathematical thinking coherently and clearly to peers, teachers, and others ■ analyze and evaluate the mathematical thinking and strategies of others ■ use the language of mathematics to express mathematical ideas precisely **9. Connections** Instructional programs from prekindergarten through grade 12 should enable all students to ■ recognize and use connections among mathematical ideas ■ understand how mathematical ideas interconnect and build on one another to produce a coherent whole ■ recognize and apply mathematics in contexts outside of mathematics **10. Representation** Instructional programs from prekindergarten through grade 12 should enable all students to ■ create and use representations to organize, record, and communicate mathematical ideas ■ select, apply, and translate among mathematical representations to solve problems ■ use representation to model and interpret physical, social, and mathematical phenomena

Note. Adapted from National Council of Teachers of Mathematics. (April 2000). *Electronic Edition of Principles and Standards for School Mathematics.* Reston, VA: National Council of Teachers of Mathematics. All rights reserved. For Internet: http://standards.nctm.org/document. Adapted with permission.

Standards describe what students should be enabled to know and do as a result of the curriculum, assessment, and instruction. Standards identify what is valued for the curriculum. They guide curriculum content and processes that are important for students at large, as well as provide opportunities for individuals with different characteristics and needs to learn what is of personal importance to them. Skills and concepts in curriculum "are not taught as isolated topics but rather as valued, connected and useful parts of students' experiences" (National Council of Teachers of Mathematics, 2000, p. 46).

This chapter on adaptations and instruction in mathematics focuses on instruction and assessment of some of the most fundamental and basic content and processes consistent with the NCTM and other standards. It covers math skills that are required for everyday living and functioning at home, in school, and, when appropriate, in the workplace. These functional math skills include such skills as telling time and handling money.

When considering mathematics assessment, it is important to determine the appropriateness of student assessment measures and to make the necessary modifications for students with physical or multiple disabilities. Students with physical or multiple disabilities may require significant modifications to obtain an accurate assessment, and some types of assessment may be more appropriate than others. Student assessment via standardized math achievement tests, diagnostic math tests, curriculum-based measurement, informal teacher-constructed tests, portfolio assessment, and error analysis will be discussed.

Standardized Achievement Tests for Mathematics

Standardized achievement tests are norm-referenced tests designed to compare how well the student is performing in regard to a large population of students. These types of tests provide different types of information such as math grade level, math age score, percentile, and stanine scores. Often the test may cover a range of subjects, such as reading, math, written language, and science, and is typically given in a group setting. School systems often require certain standardized tests to determine how well their students are doing. Some examples of standardized achievement tests that include math sections are the Wide Range Achievement Test-3 (Wilkinson, 1993), Peabody Individual Achievement Test-Revised (Markwardt, 1989), and the Kaufman Test of Educational Achievement (Kaufman & Kaufman, 1985).

Students with physical or multiple disabilities who are on an academic track may take these tests as a requirement of their school system or as a way to assess how well they are doing in regard to other students. However, the test scores of students with physical disabilities often have limited applicability and must be interpreted with caution due to the impact of the student's motor, speech, and additional (e.g., sensory) impairments. Students with physical disabilities who respond in a slow and laborious manner will be at a disadvantage when time limits are imposed. Due to the nature of the test, it can also be difficult to determine whether missed items are due to the physical disability or to not knowing the answer to an item (Sattler, 1992). Test adaptations are often needed to get a more accurate score. Accommodations and modifications that may be made include extending time limits; allowing the student to use his or her AAC device or computer for providing responses; and/or enlarging the test or reading test items to the student to provide visual and/or motor access to the material.

In order for the test score to remain valid, only the manufacturer's test modifications discussed in the test manual can be used. For example, changing the amount of time it takes to take a timed test may invalidate the results. However, in many instances, standard test procedures are not applicable to all children. Often, more information can be obtained regarding student performance by departing from standard procedures, especially when the student has a severe physical impairment. In these instances, the teacher must carefully document all adaptations and make a notation if the adaptations used are not approved by the manufacturer and could violate test norms.

Diagnostic Tests of Math Performance

Diagnostic tests are those that cover a narrower range of skills and are designed to give more information regarding the student's strengths and weaknesses in certain math skill areas. The test may be norm-referenced, providing comparative information just like norm-referenced achievement tests. However, most diagnostic tests are criterion-referenced, which means that they provide information regarding student knowledge of specific content, unrelated to peer performance (Hammill & Bryant, 1991). Diagnostic criterion-referenced tests are the most suited for identifying specific math problems (Mercer & Mercer, 2001). Some examples of diagnostic tests for math are Key Math Revised: A Diagnostic Inventory of Essential Skills (Connolly, 1988); Stanford Diagnostic Mathematics Test-Fourth Edition (Beatty, Madden, Gardner, & Karlsen, 1995); Diagnostic Mathematics Inventory/Mathematics System (Gessell, 1983); and Diagnostic Test of Arithmetic Strategies (Ginsburg & Mathews, 1984). As with standardized achievement tests, diagnostic tests may need to be modified to accommodate the student's physical impairments. All modifications should be documented.

Curriculum-Based Measurement

Curriculum-based measurement (CBM) is ongoing assessment of student performance when compared to the curricular outcomes of the school system (Bryant & Rivera, 1997; Fuchs & Fuchs, 1988; Shinn & Hubbard, 1993). Student performance is monitored as the student progresses through the curriculum to determine the effectiveness of math instruction and intervention. This type of assessment allows for in-depth examination of the student's specific math skills based on the problems encountered by the student in the instructional setting. It is the most instructionally useful method of assessment, since it diagnoses math problems based upon the curriculum being used.

Curriculum-based measurement typically begins by giving a survey test of a span of math skills. A survey test is developed using five steps: (1) identifying a sequence of skills in the curriculum being used (which typically involves the scope and sequence of skills identified in the school's curriculum), (2) selecting a span of math skills within the scope and sequence of skills to be assessed, (3) selecting items for each skill within the span of skills selected (typically having a minimum of three items per skill), (4) administering and scoring the test, and (5) displaying the results in graph form, interpreting the results, and planning instruction (Mercer & Mercer, 2001). Based upon the student's errors, further instruction in poorly understood math concepts is given and specific skill monitoring is used to determine skill mastery. All testing is graphed to determine whether each student is making progress toward the intended goal. An example of a survey test of third-grade computational skills is shown in Figure 16–1.

Informal Teacher-Constructed Tests

Teacher-constructed tests are crucial for individualizing instruction and pinpointing students' errors. Often students may show difficulty in a particular area, and the teacher can construct a test to gain further information. Teacher-constructed tests can also be used to determine the student's level of understanding and monitor student progress. As with other types of tests, appropriate modifications for testing and instruction are implemented to accommodate the student's physical or multiple impairments.

Portfolio Assessment

Portfolio assessment consists of a collection of student work that exhibits the student's efforts, progress, and achievements (Paulson, Paulson, & Meyer, 1991). It is used to monitor student progress and make instructional decisions. Since portfolio assessment tends to focus more on the way the student responds to math problems, rather than on the student's answers, it helps guide the teacher in making instructional decisions for the individual student.

Although assessment portfolios range in composition, the portfolio content should (a) represent student work on curricular goals, (b) be collected in a specific period of time, (c) show a variety of student work utilizing different instructional techniques, and (d) show a variety of student work across a variety of situations (Bryant & Rivera, 1997; Rivera, 1994). The student's IEP math goals should be reflected in the portfolio. Other information gained from standardized tests, diagnostic tests, informal teacher-made tests, and curriculum-based tests may be included in the portfolio as well.

Error Analysis

Much can be learned regarding the student's knowledge of and skill in mathematical concepts and calculations when the teacher does a careful error analysis. An error analysis consists of closely examining the student's work to determine the types of errors the student is making. Teachers should determine if the student is:

a. making random responses,
b. making computation errors (e.g., $6 + 8 = 13$),
c. missing a basic math rule (e.g., the zero rule: $6 \times 0 = 6$),
d. using a faulty algorithm in which the steps are performed incorrectly or out of sequence (e.g., $6\,(2 + 2) = 14$),

FIGURE 16–1
Survey test of third-grade computation skills

1. 476 + 200	2. 807 + 407	3. 9000 + 3010
4. 3168 + 5426	5. 4727 + 2761	6. 7964 + 385
7. 604 − 237	8. 704 − 369	9. 501 − 269
10. 7134 − 3487	11. 5094 − 4630	12. 8751 − 2683
13. 9 × 8	14. 9 × 6	15. 8 × 7
16. 7 × 8	17. 6 × 9	18. 9 × 0
19. 8 × 0	20. 6 × 1	21. 1 × 8
22. 34 × 2	23. 26 × 1	24. 31 × 8
25. 24 ÷ 3 = _____	26. 12 ÷ 2 = _____	27. 4)16
28. 5)16	29. 4)34	30. 7)58
31. 17 × 5	32. 49 × 2	33. 16 × 4
34. 82 × 4	35. 74 × 2	36. 81 × 5
37. 342 × 2	38. 637 × 1	39. 312 × 3
40. 436 × 3	41. 578 × 6	42. 638 × 7
43. 3)36	44. 4)44	45. 2)28
46. 3)51	47. 4)72	48. 7)84
49. $\frac{1}{3}$ of 6 = _____	50. $\frac{1}{4}$ of 8 = _____	51. $\frac{1}{2}$ of 12 = _____
52. $\frac{1}{2} = \frac{\ }{4}$	53. $\frac{2}{3} = \frac{\ }{6}$	54. $\frac{2}{5} = \frac{\ }{5}$

Note. From *Teaching Students with Learning Problems* 5/e by Mercer/Mercer, © 1998. Reprinted by permission of Prentice-Hall, Inc., Upper Saddle River, NJ.

e. making grouping errors (e.g., 28 + 4 = 22),
f. using an incorrect operation (e.g., 6 − 2 = 8), or
g. setting up the problem incorrectly (e.g., using irrelevant information from a word problem).

Performing an error analysis will pinpoint the student's areas of difficulty and will determine the focus of instruction. Keeping track of the types of errors and their corrections will provide an important record of past difficulties and intervention techniques.

Sometimes it is difficult to determine the type of error the student is making by looking at a student's work. In these situations, the teacher may ask the student to explain how he or she obtained specific answers in order to pinpoint the error the student is making. Nonverbal students can answer using their AAC devices. If the student is not proficient in using the device, the teacher may need to closely observe the student while he or she is doing the problem to detect the error. Another option would be to stop the student after a specific error and ask the student a series of yes/no or multiple-choice questions to uncover types of possible errors in basic math facts, algorithms, or computations. In some cases, further informal testing may help to pinpoint the error. As this chapter presents specific math facts and algorithms, the reader should note these as possible types of errors to be looking for when performing an error analysis.

GENERAL APPROACHES AND PRINCIPLES OF MATH INSTRUCTION

Teachers need to incorporate into their instruction appropriate principles and methods to facilitate learning math. Some of these general approaches to promote learning math include building on previous learning; systematic and explicit instruction; active involvement of students; learning strategies; computer-assisted instruction; and adaptations and attitudes. If one of these approaches is not effective for a specific student, another one should be tried. Students with physical or multiple disabilities will also need appropriate adaptations for math instruction. Each of these general approaches is described next. Specific strategies are incorporated in the following sections.

Building on Previous Learning

Of all the various disciplines that students will be exposed to in school, mathematics plays the most critical role in utilizing students' previous knowledge (Reys, Suydam, Lindquist, & Smith, 1998). This is due to the hierarchical nature of mathematics and the need to utilize relational understanding between the various types of mathematics being learned. It is therefore critical that teachers link students' previous learning to the new information being taught.

In order to effectively link previously learned information to new information, the material to be learned should first be presented in a logical, organized fashion that allows building of information. An advance organizer should be used, in which teachers begin the lesson by discussing what was previously learned and how this relates to the new information being presented that day (Miller, Mercer, & Dillon, 1992). Written advance organizers may also be used. Within this introduction, the teacher should discuss how the new math material relates to everyday life, within the realm of the students' experiences and knowledge, in order to help establish relevance and promote generalization of the material.

Systematic and Explicit Instruction

Systematic and explicit instruction has been found to effectively promote learning of mathematics. This type of instruction has been found to incorporate four specific elements (Christenson, Ysseldyke, & Thurlow, 1989; Mercer & Miller, 1992). The first element is the use of the **demonstration–guided-practice–independent-practice model** (Polloway & Patton, 1993). In this approach, the teacher provides demonstration of what is being targeted for instruction that day. During guided practice, the teacher provides support to the student and carefully helps the student through the concept being learned. In guided practice, the teacher may use various prompts such as a permanent model or a display of the steps of the procedure. This form of instruction typically occurs with an interaction format that promotes active participation, close monitoring by the teacher, and immediate corrective feedback. In the final step of independent practice, the student practices the skill without assistance or guidance, but still receives feedback from the teacher as needed.

The second element in providing systematic and explicit instruction involves **providing highly organized, step-by-step presentations.** This typically takes advance planning to be sure that the presentation of information and methods being used to teach the student are occurring in a logical, consistent sequence. In these presentations the target skill is identified and the skill's importance and usefulness is stressed. How to apply the skill is also discussed.

Checking for understanding is the third element in providing systematic and explicit instruction. Teachers should not assume that the student understands the directions and the task. Periodic checks should be conducted to be sure the student understands (Good, 1983). Frequent questioning is a critical aspect of checking for understanding. If students are unable to answer the questions correctly, the teacher should give immediate feedback and reteach the concept.

The last element is the **emphasis on positive student outcomes.** The teacher tries to maintain high motivation. Often positive reinforcement will be used. This may be in the form of praise, stickers, activities, or other forms of reinforcement that are specifically reinforcing to the student and doable in the classroom setting.

Active Involvement of Students

An effective strategy to promote learning mathematics is to actively involve the student. Active involvement may include interaction with other students, hands-on experimentation, use of manipulatives, or use of special learning materials (e.g., the Internet, textbooks) (Reys et al., 1998). For example, when teaching fractions, two- or three-dimensional cutouts may be used to help teach the concept.

When teaching basic math skills, teachers can promote the active involvement of students through the use of a sequence of concrete, semiconcrete, and abstract levels, also referred to as CSA. For example, to solve addition problems, students would first be taught on a concrete level, manipulating three-dimensional objects to solve problems. On a semiconcrete level, the student may draw items to promote understanding. On an abstract level, the student works the problems without objects or drawings (Miller & Mercer, 1993b; Miller et al., 1992). This progression allows the student to begin with actively using objects to promote understanding math concepts and to gradually move to more abstract uses of numbers and math concepts.

Learning Strategies

There are several different learning strategies that can help students learn mathematics. Learning strategies are "behaviors and thoughts that the learner engages in during learning and that are intended to influence the learner's encoding progress" (Weinstein & Mayer, 1986, p. 315). Learning strategies include a wide range of techniques, such as **self-monitoring** and metacognition. Students have increased their accuracy and speed in math using such self-monitoring techniques as self-recording, self-evaluation, and self-reinforcement (Miller, Strawser, & Mercer, 1996). In one study (Hughs, Ruhl, & Peterson, 1988), students recorded how many problems they had completed and evaluated their performance using a point system. They would provide themselves with reinforcement when their answers reached a certain level of accuracy.

Self-monitoring can also incorporate metacognitive strategies. **Metacognition** refers to what one knows or believes about oneself as a learner and how to control and change one's behavior. Students are aware of their weaknesses, strengths, and behaviors. They observe themselves as they work, and they think about what they are thinking. For example, a metacognitive strategy is to continually ask, "What am I doing? Why am I doing it? How will it help me?" (Reys et al., 1998). Metacognitive strategies have been used to help solve word problems and complex forms of mathematics. Encouraging students to think about their thinking and what they are doing and why comprises most metacognitive strategies.

Another learning strategy is the use of **mnemonics**. A mnemonic is used to help students learn and be able to recall information. Acronym mnemonics form a word from the initial letters of other words. For example, the mnemonic "DRAW" stands for Discover the sign, Read the problem, Answer (or draw and check), and Write the answer (Mercer & Miller, 1992; Miller et al., 1996). Other types of acronyms may use phrases, such as "Please Excuse My Dear Aunt Sally," which provides the order in which math operations should occur (parentheses, exponents, multiplication, division, addition, and subtraction).

Effective instruction of mnemonics includes carefully discussing and modeling each step of the mnemonic and providing sufficient practice using it (Miller & Mercer,

1993a). The student should have enough practice to ensure that the steps of the strategy are learned at an automatic level to avoid the student's struggling to remember the mnemonic. Equally important is teaching the student when the mnemonic should be used. Having sufficient practice using the mnemonic across a variety of problems will help teach its application.

Another type of learning strategy that has been used to promote math learning is **self-instruction**. The purpose of this strategy is to modify thinking and behavior through the development of inner speech. Although there are several variations on self-instruction, it usually follows a four-part process. First, the teacher performs the task and verbalizes the steps aloud. Second, the student performs the task as the teacher verbalizes the steps. Third, the student performs the task and whispers the self-instruction. Fourth, the student performs the task and self-instructs using inner speech (Fulk, 1992; Meichenbaum, 1977).

Computer-Assisted Instruction

Computer-assisted instruction (CAI) has become a popular tool to use to promote learning and extended practice. CAI can be individualized, repetitive, and systematic in its presentation of material, as well as provide immediate feedback and reinforcement (Hofmeister, 1984; Podell, Tournaki-Rein, & Lin, 1992). It is used for all types of students, ranging from those having intellectual disabilities to those who are gifted. For students with mild intellectual disabilities, CAI has shown to be an effective method in teaching students a broad array of skills from promoting automatization of addition and subtraction problems (Podell et al., 1992) to learning multiplication and division word problems (Gleason, Carnine, & Boriero, 1990). When using CAI, it is critical that teachers select the appropriate type of software for the student's needs. For example, drill and practice software has a goal of improving proficiency, while instructional games can provide further information and instruction on a concept. CAI can be a positive tool to allow repeated practice for students who can easily access a computer, but have difficulty accessing a book or other materials due to the severity of their physical disabilities.

Adaptations and Attitudes

Students with physical or multiple impairments will typically need adaptations in order to benefit from math instruction. As seen in Table 16–2, there are eight

TABLE 16–2
Adaptations for Students with Physical and Multiple Disabilities for Math Instruction

Adaptation Category	Adaptation for Physical/Multiple Impairment	Examples for Math Instruction
Physical environment	Modify environment to allow access.	Student needs to sit close to board to see and aisles are widened.
Adapted device/assistive technology (AT)	AT or device is used to compensate for physical/multiple disability.	Math software is used that allows the student to carry when doing addition problems.
Student response	Use alternate response form or modified response, such as allowing more time.	Student eye-gazes answers to multiple choice math answers and aide writes in response.
Alter material/activity	Change material/activity so student can access it and/or promote learning.	Manipulatives are changed and made bigger to allow for physical manipulation.
Teamwork	Work in teams to assist with physical aspects of task.	Student with physical disabilities works with a peer in drawing geometric angles.
Instructional modification	Teacher modifies instruction to meet learner's needs.	Teacher provides more guided practice and repetition to ensure student masters the math skill.
Behavior management	Teacher provides motivational strategies and encourages independence to promote learning and combat learned helplessness.	Teacher and student set goals and student receives reinforcing items for learning multiplication tables.
Alter curriculum	Curriculum is altered to address student's needs.	Curriculum is changed to a functional math curriculum. Curriculum is modified for student to learn how to use special math AT.

categories of adaptations for students with physical impairments. These are (1) adaptations to the physical environment, (2) adapted device/assistive technology use, (3) change in student response, (4) alteration of the material or activity, (5) teamwork, (6) instructional modifications, (7) behavior management, and (8) alteration of the curriculum (Heller, Dangel, & Sweatman, 1995). Some students may need only one category of adaptations for a certain math task, while other students may need several different types of adaptations. The student's individual need for adaptations must be determined and evaluated for effectiveness after implementation.

Equally important to the effective and appropriate use of adaptations is the teacher's attitude. Teachers who enjoy teaching mathematics and show this enjoyment tend to produce students who like mathematics (Renga & Dalla, 1993). Teachers should be careful to promote this positive attitude toward all members of the class. It is important to be sure that there is no gender bias, cultural bias, or disability bias occurring in the class. A willingness to make appropriate adaptations to promote effective math instruction for students with physical or multiple disabilities is critical to promote success in math.

BEGINNING MATH SKILLS

Before students are taught computational skills, such as addition and subtraction, there are several basic precomputational skills that need to be mastered. These include the prenumber skills of one-to-one correspondence, classification, and seriation. Other early math skills include counting and numeration.

Prenumber Skills

Students with physical or multiple disabilities often come to school with few experiences regarding prenumber skills. This is especially the case when the student lacks fine-motor skills and is nonverbal. It becomes important for the teacher to provide instruction in these skills, making appropriate adaptations so that the student can actively participate.

One-to-one correspondence is the idea that every one thing seen can be matched to one other thing that may or may not be seen (Polloway & Patton, 1993). One-to-one correspondence is used in a wide range of tasks, such as putting one sock on one foot, setting the table with one plate for each person, distributing one book to each student, matching one quarter to one quarter on a money chart to buy a soda, and counting one item one time. Without this crucial concept, the student will be unable to learn more-advanced math skills.

Teachers may teach this concept by engaging the student in activities in which the student pairs up one item with another item or person. Common activities include handing out one set of instructional materials to each student or giving one juice pack to each student for snack. It may also include matching items together or putting one item in each circle or square. Students who lack motor control may eye-gaze where each item is to go or indicate through answering yes/no questions if it is being placed correctly (e.g., Does this go here? Does another one go here? Does this go here or here?).

Classification is grouping or sorting like items, based on one or more common properties. Students need to learn to group by such properties as size, shape, and color. It is an important prenumber skill since it focuses on common properties and teaches students to reduce large numbers of items into smaller groups (Bos & Vaughn, 2002). Students are often taught first to make gross discriminations, such as sorting large round red balls and small blue blocks. Finer and finer discriminations are made until students are able to sort by a number of different properties. If students do not have the motor control to physically sort items, they can indicate their choice through eye-gaze, AAC, or yes/no answers to questions.

Teaching **patterns** helps students develop number sense, ordering, counting, and sequencing (Coburn et al., 1992). Most pattern instruction requires the student to use both cognitive and motor abilities. For students unable to manipulate items in a pattern, they can indicate which item is next in a pattern when given a choice. There are three types of patterns that may be taught. These are copying an existing pattern, finding the next one in a pattern, and making their own patterns (Reys et al., 1998). Each one of these can provide valuable experience to help students develop their mathematical abilities.

Comparisons of quantities is an important step toward number awareness and counting. Comparisons can occur across a wide range of attributes, such as size and number. Children are taught to compare items to determine who has more, less, or the same. Also, items can be compared to determine which item is bigger, smaller, longer, shorter, taller, thinner, wider, darker, and so forth. In order for comparisons to be made, the student needs to understand the term being used, such as "bigger." Due to differences in experiential backgrounds, many students, especially those who have disabilities, may not have learned some of these terms or basic concepts. It is important that many examples be given of each concept so that the student learns how to attend to the important attribute and disregard irrelevant features.

Some students will be learning their symbols for their AAC device as they are learning math concepts. Teaching these symbols within the math lesson can help the student attain instructional objectives. For example, in Figure 16–2, questions are presented in printed and symbol format. This combines learning AAC symbols and learning the concept of "more."

Seriation is the ordering of items by some attribute. It can occur across size, height, length, weight, color, or number. For example, items may be placed from smallest to largest, tallest to shortest, longest to shortest, lightest to heaviest, darkest to lightest, or least number of items to most number of items. After the student has an understanding of the concept being targeted (e.g., size, height, length, weight, color, number), the teacher may give the student a few items that are the same except their size (for example), and ask the student to put the smallest at the top of the desk and the next biggest one beside it, and the largest one last. The teacher can expand on the number of items and the various attributes. Students with physical impairments can indicate their selection of each item to be put next in the sequence, and another individual can help to move it into place. It is important that seriation of such attributes as weight be taught by allowing the student to hold or feel different weights. If the student is unable to hold the item, items with large differences in weight can be placed on the arm or leg for the student to feel the difference (with care not to put any strain on a contracture).

Students who are learning prenumber skills benefit from practice with manipulatives. One program that is based on manipulation of common household items to reinforce prenumber skills is *Mathematics Their Way* (Baratta-Lorton, 1976). This program contains many motivating lessons in areas such as patterns, sorting, classifying, counting, comparing, and graphing. Teachers who use manipulatives with students who have physical or multiple disabilities may need to adapt some lessons by employing work surface modifications, object stabilization, and containment strategies (see Chapters 7 and 13).

Counting

Rote Counting. When children are learning to count, they first learn to count by rote (without understanding the meaning), then they learn to count sets of objects using one-to-one correspondence, and last they learn to associate the numeral with the number of items they counted. Learning to **rote count** teaches children the names of the numbers and the order they are in. Students who are verbal will have often heard the numbers modeled for them and had some practice repeating them in sequence. Asking a student "How far can you count?" will ascertain to what extent the student has this skill. For students having difficulty remembering the numbers, the teacher can make up a jingle or chant to facilitate memory (similar to the alphabet song children learn to remember the letters of the alphabet).

For students who are nonverbal, rote counting can be assessed by telling the student to count aloud (as best the student can) while saying the number "in his or her head" (i.e., using internal speech). The teacher will say the numbers with the student up to a point and then ask, "What number comes next?" The teacher will then give verbal choices for the student to choose. Having the student select a numeral on an AAC device or on a number chart is a different skill, requiring the student to know the numeral and match it to the spoken number. Although numeral identification is an important task and also needs to be taught, it is a different task than rote counting.

Rational Counting. Rational counting is counting items in succession and providing the correct number name. When students are taught to count objects, they are learning one-to-one correspondence as they apply the number name in sequential order to each item they are counting. Students need to practice saying the correct number name as they touch each object. Students with severe speech impairments should be taught to say the number name "in their head" using internal speech.

FIGURE 16–2
Symbols may be used to teach math concepts

Teacher Directions: Read question with student pointing to the words and pictures. Use real objects and situations if possible. Have student circle correct answer. Model and redirect as needed.
Which one
???
has
more
?
Which one
???
has
more
?
Which one
???
has
more
?
© 1994 by the Mayer-Johnson Co.
This page may be copied for instructional use.

Note. From *Math Exercises for Non-Readers* by A. M. Johnson. ©1994, Mayer-Johnson, Inc., P.O. Box 1579, Solana Beach, CA 92075. Reprinted with permission.

Students may be taught the use of a jingle or chant to say to themselves to reinforce memory. Students who are nonverbal and have not yet learned numerals can be provided verbal choices of answers and indicate their choice.

It is important that students with physical disabilities have the opportunity to manipulate the items. Manipulating the items provides more active interaction and allows the student to avoid counting an item twice. Adaptations may include changing the material so that larger items are used with handles for easier grasp, knocking down items in succession, or moving items across a computer screen.

When counting semiconcrete items, such as a group of items in a picture, young students often point to each item or cross it off in order to assist with the counting process and help preclude the chance of counting the same item twice. Students with physical disabilities may need the item set redrawn with adequate spacing to allow the student to point or mark off each one. For students with very severe physical disabilities, the teacher may need to point as the student counts. If the student's physical condition precludes vocalization, it is important that the student does some type of motion to indicate that he or she is counting each item. For example, one student who could not vocalize or make any controlled movement except with her tongue, would slightly stick her tongue out with each item being counted, and this was found to facilitate her learning the counting process (Heller, 1999).

There are four main principles to counting that students need to learn in order to be effective counters. First, the student must learn that each object to be counted can be assigned only one number name. This uses the concept of one-to-one correspondence. Second, the student must learn that the number-name list must be used in the same, fixed order. When counting, the person always starts with "one," followed by "two," and so forth. Skipping around is not permitted. Third, items can be counted in any order. Students need to learn that there is no set order of how items are counted. They can start counting items at the top of the grouping, bottom, left, right, or however they choose. (However, some students may be taught some systematic means of counting to avoid missing items.) Fourth, students must learn that the last number-name used gives the number of objects (Reys et al., 1998). Students can easily confuse this concept. For example, when presented with a set of four balls, the teacher may provide multiple-choice answers for the student who is nonverbal to answer. When asked if there are three balls, the student may indicate yes. This is because there are three balls there, but there are four altogether. It is important to clarify this concept at the very beginning.

Another key concept to teach about counting is the principle of "one more" or "one less." As students are able to count items with a high rate of accuracy (from numbers one to five), the teacher should introduce having one more or less of an item. For example, for snack time, she gives out two cookies to each student and then she points out that she gives John "one more" cookie. (After discussing this, each student gets "one more" cookie.) Concrete examples of these principles need to be given to facilitate understanding of the concept. Learning the concept will help with learning addition and subtraction in the future.

Patterned Counting. Students will often be taught set patterns of dots to represent particular numbers. Students who have had exposure to a lot of games using dice, for example, learn over time that each pattern of dots on the dice represents a number. Instant recognition of the number the pattern represents can usually be learned over time through repeated exposure to the pattern. Figure 16–3 shows several patterns that can be taught. For students with physical disabilities, learning patterns may later assist with computational skills.

Counting On. After students are able to count from one to the desired number, it is important that students learn to count on from numbers other than one. For example, if asked to start at three, the student needs to learn to continue counting "four," "five," etc. It will take students some practice to be able to do this, but this skill will help later when learning to add. Students who are nonverbal can be asked what number comes next. For example, the teacher may ask, "What number comes after five?" The student then has four different numbers to choose from that are presented orally (or in written format if the student has learned the numerals). When assessing whether the student knows what number comes next, it is important that

FIGURE 16–3
Different patterns of dots may be used to represent numbers and assist with counting

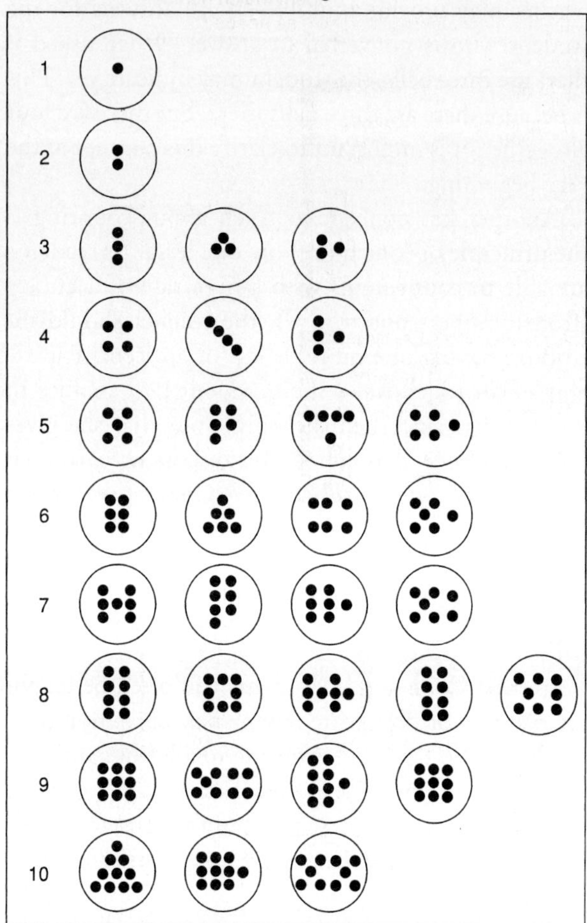

Note. From John A. Van De Walle, *Elementary and Middle School Mathematics: Teaching Developmentally,* 3e. Published by Allyn and Bacon, Boston, MA. Copyright © 1997 by Pearson Education. Reprinted by permission of the publisher.

the student does not have the numerals written out in sequential format. It would be very easy for the student to just point to the next numeral after the one given. This type of response does not indicate whether the student actually knows what number is next.

Skip Counting. Skip counting is counting by multiples of a base number, such as counting by 10s, 5s, and 2s. Skip counting will make counting large numbers faster. It also lays the foundation for multiplication, learning to count change, and counting the 10s and 100s places when moving on to large numbers. Most difficulties in counting change are attributed to problems with this type of counting.

Numerals and Place Values

Matching Numerals. As students are learning to count, they typically are also learning numerals, the written representation of the spoken number. Teaching numeral identification typically goes through a sequence of (a) teaching the student to match numerals, (b) teaching the name of the numeral, and (c) teaching the student to match the numeral to the number of items that are counted. It is important to start by matching numerals to be sure that the student is attending to the relevant features of the numeral. For students with physical or multiple disabilities, it is also an important task since many students with multiple disabilities have visual impairments. Successfully matching numerals will indicate that the student can visually see the numerals at the size provided. If the student is unable to match, vision should be initially ruled out as a cause.

As with other math objectives, AAC symbols may be used in addition to print for those students who are not print readers. As seen in Figure 16–4, a useful activity, such as matching a locker number to a number on a locker, can be used.

Identification of Numerals. Students should be exposed to the numerals and their names once they can rote count to 8 (Stein, Silbert, & Carnine, 1997). Many children will start kindergarten being able to rote count to 8 and will immediately begin instruction with numeral identification. Students need to be taught numeral names in a systematic manner by being shown the numeral, modeling the name, and having the students repeat the name. Review of the previously learned numerals should occur within the lesson, and the new numeral should be introduced several times in the lesson. Students can be assessed for numeral identification by asking them individually to name the numeral. Students who are nonverbal can be shown the numeral and be given verbal choices as to possible numeral names. When the student gives an answer, he or she should receive immediate reinforcement if correct. Students should receive immediate corrective feedback if an error is made, and the teacher should note which

FIGURE 16–4
A functional math activity using symbols

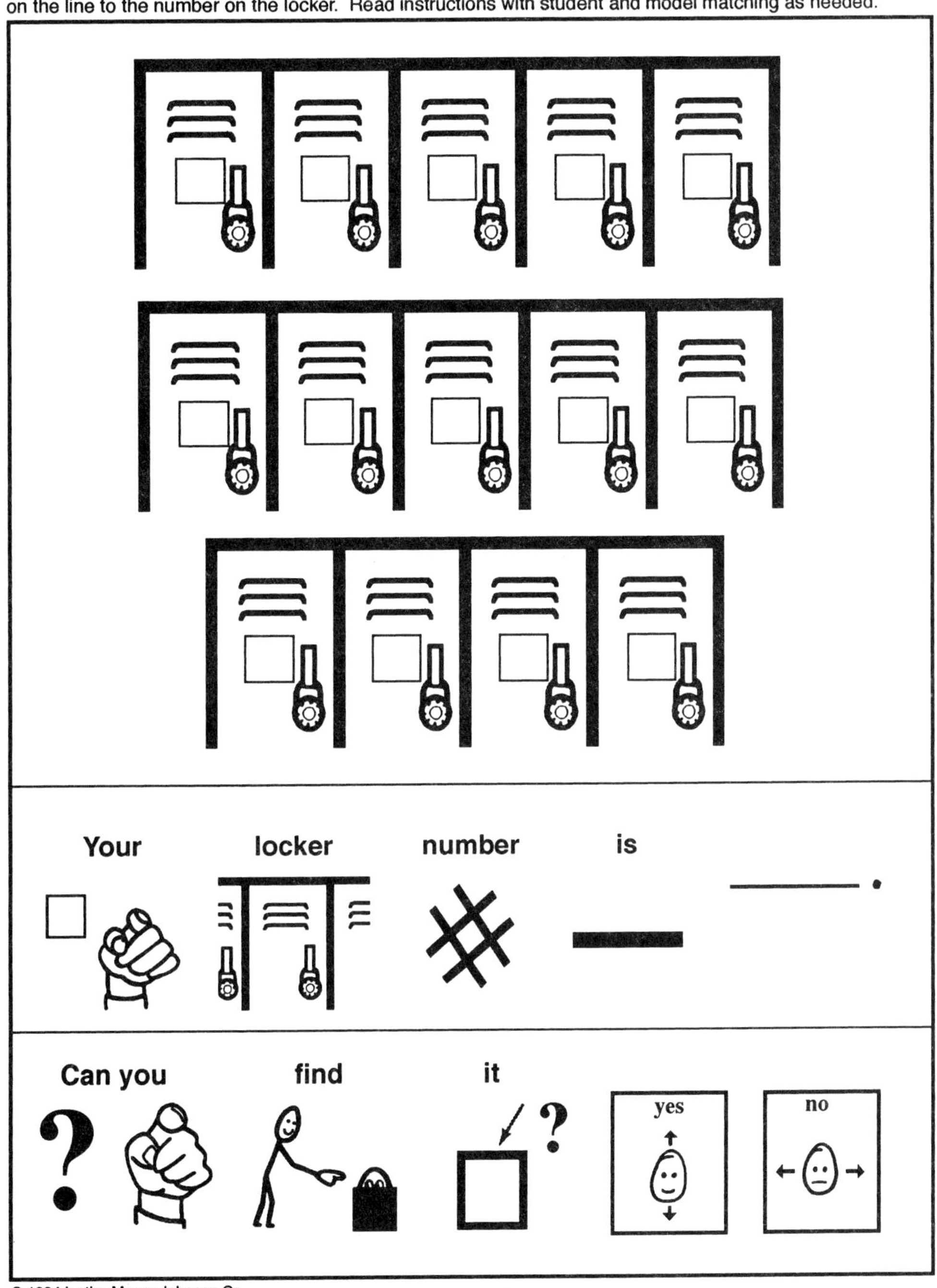

Teacher's Directions: Fill in locker number on the line. Put numbers on lockers. Have student match number on the line to the number on the locker. Read instructions with student and model matching as needed.
Your
locker
number
is
Can you
find
it
yes
no
© 1994 by the Mayer-Johnson Co.
This page may be copied for instructional use.

Note. From *Math Exercises for Non-Readers* (p. 16) by A. M. Johnson. © 1994, Mayer-Johnson, Inc., P.O. Box 1579, Solana Beach, CA 92075. Reprinted with permission.

numerals the student is not identifying correctly, so that follow-up instruction and evaluation can occur.

Numerals are often not taught in sequential order. Numerals that are similar in shape or sound are usually taught separately from each other. For example, the 6 and 9 appear similar and should be taught separately; the numerals 4 and 5 sound similar and should be taught separately. Separating these pairs of numerals by several lessons would be best. A possible sequence of teaching numeral identification would be: 4, 2, 6, 1, 7, 3, 0, 8, 5, 9, 10. This provides a separation of 6 and 9; 4 and 5; and 1, 0, and 10 (Stein et al., 1997).

There is some variation in how numerals appear in different text and material. Showing some of the different forms, such as the two ways the number 4 appears, should be discussed to avoid confusion. However, this point does not need a lot of attention until the student has a firm grasp on numeral identification and other forms of numerals are encountered. Students should practice writing numerals in the traditional format. For students who do not have fine-motor control, numerals may be written using a computer or accessed by pointing or scanning to a number on a number page on an AAC device.

As students learn to count and use numerals over 10, a number chart may be used. To help with later concepts, it is usually easier if the number chart is displayed with 0 as the first number and 9 as the last number in the row, rather than the row ending with 10. In this way all of the 10s are together, 20s are together, and so forth. For example:

0	1	2	3	4	5	6	7	8	9
10	11	12	13	14	15	16	17	18	19
20	21	22	23	24	25	26	27	28	29
30	31	32	33	34	35	36	37	38	39
40	41	42	43	44	45	46	47	48	49
50	51	52	53	54	55	56	57	58	59
60	61	62	63	64	65	66	67	68	69
70	71	72	73	74	75	76	77	78	79
80	81	82	83	84	85	86	87	88	89
90	91	92	93	94	95	96	97	98	99
100	101	102	103	104	105	106	107	108	109

Match Numerals and Items. After counting out a certain number of items, the student should be able to indicate the number by writing or pointing to a numeral. This can be accomplished only if the student knows how to rationally count and can identify numerals. Although this is a basic skill from which other math skills will be built, it is especially crucial for students with speech and physical disabilities to learn as quickly as possible, since it will allow responses to be made in written or AAC format, instead of through spoken choices only. Students should learn how to count out the specified number of items when presented with a numeral, as well as count out the specified items and select the corresponding numeral.

Some students may benefit from the use of a **number line** to facilitate rational counting and numeral use. When first counting concrete items, the student is given a number line and moves each item onto the number line while saying the numbers aloud (or saying the number "in their head" for students who are nonverbal). The student then indicates how many items by saying the last number or selecting an oral or written choice from an array of numbers. As the student becomes familiar with counting, the number line is moved to where it is in sight for reference, but the items are not put on the number line. After counting the items, the student selects the appropriate numeral that matches the number of items. Eventually the number line will not be necessary for certain numbers and will be faded (gradually moved away until it is not present). One student using this technique was able to successfully learn to rationally count from 1 to 7 using the number line technique, internal speech, and a number jingle. The number line was gradually faded to where she could count to 7 without it. She continued to use the number line for numbers 8 to 20 with a high rate of accuracy. A self-checking procedure was also taught to promote student independence. Once the student counted out the specified number of objects, she would record her choice, and then check herself by moving each item to the number line. Most of the time, she would catch her error before the teacher checked her (Heller, 1999).

Place Value. Children need to learn that the position of a number represents its value. For example, the 1 in \$14 represents "ten," whereas the 1 in \$41 represents "one." Equally important is the concept that our number system is based on groupings of 10. In this system, 10 is the value that determines a new collection, and the system has ten digits of 0 through 9 (Reys et al.,

1998). To help teach this concept, students should practice placing items into groups of 10, counting them by 10, and indicating the remainder. Students should start with concrete items, then move to pictures, and finally numerals. Students can use a wide variety of manipulates such as Popsicle sticks, erasers, or connecting cubes to group into groups of 10 (see Figure 16–5). Many motivating lessons involving place value are contained in *Mathematics Their Way* (Baratta-Lorton, 1976).

For students who are unable to physically manipulate objects—even after larger objects are tried—the teacher or peer can point to each object as the student counts (aloud or using internal speech). The student then indicates when a group of 10 is made, so that the teacher or peer can move it together into a group. The number of groups and number of items can be expressed by the student by providing questions in a yes or no format or in a multiple-choice format. When working with pictures, students who are unable to circle 10 items may have another person touch each of the items as the student counts (aloud or using internal speech), and then the student indicates when a line needs to be made around the group.

FIGURE 16–5
Place-value models

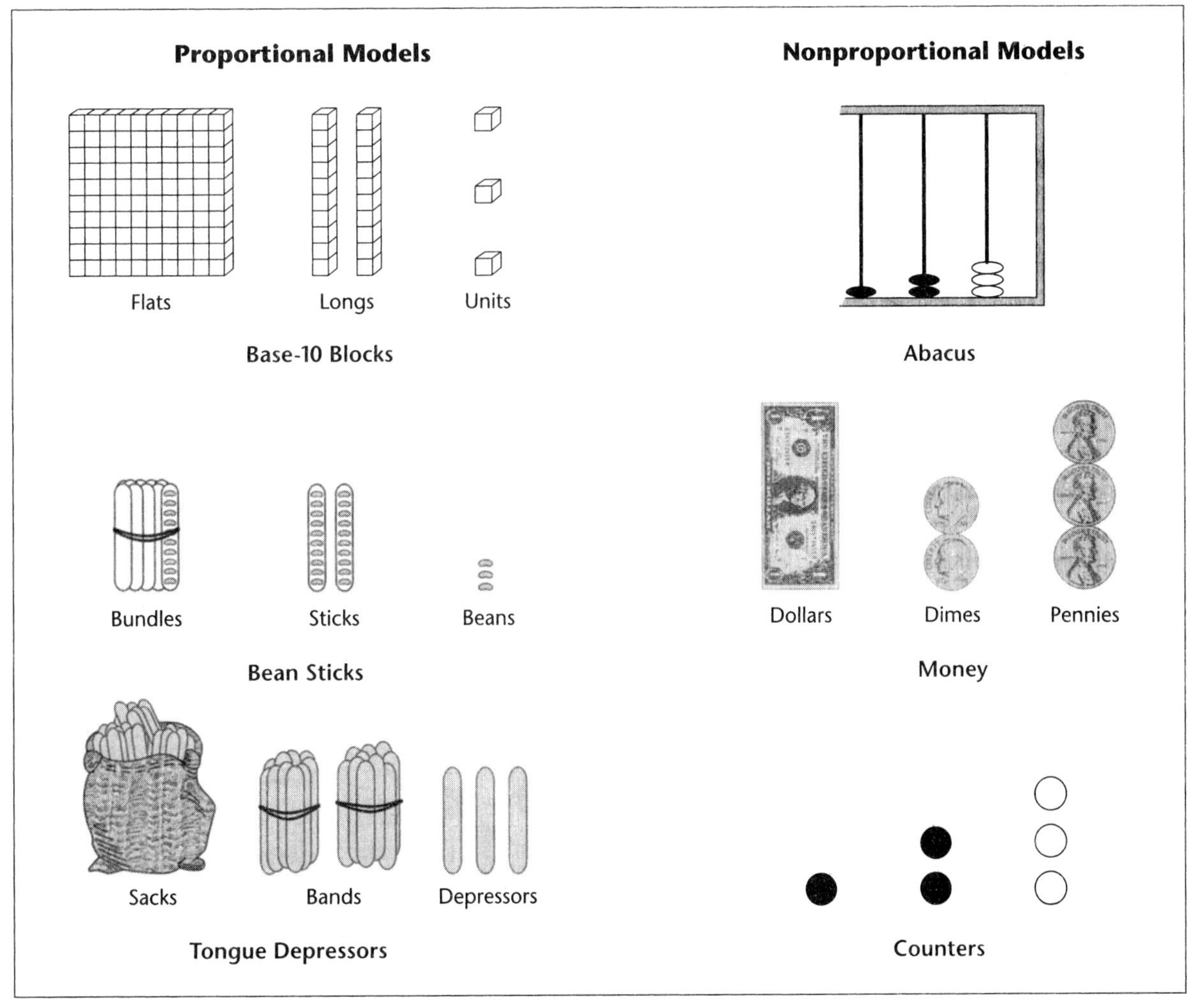

Note. From *Helping Children Learn Mathematics,* 5th ed., by R. E. Reys, N. Suydam, M. M. Lindquist, and N. L. Smith. Copyright 1998 by John Wiley & Sons, Inc. This material is used by permission of John Wiley & Sons, Inc.

After learning 10s and 1s, students need to expand to learning about 100s and 1,000s. After counting off 10 piles of 10 rods, a group of 100 is made. As the items are grouped, students should have practice writing down the corresponding numeral. It is important that students understand that 324 means 300 + 20 + 4. Teaching this type of **expanded notation** helps ensure that the student understands the meaning behind the numeral. Care should be taken that the student is taught the use of "0" as representing the absence of something, since students often make "0" mistakes when later learning to add.

Software for Early Math Skills

There are numerous math programs that teach beginning math skills such as matching, discrimination, and counting. Often these begin at a discovery level and move from matching and identification to simple addition. For example, Early Learning I, II, III (manufactured by Marblesoft) begins with number and shape recognition and moves to early addition and subtraction. These programs have scanning capability and can be accessed through adapted keyboards and switches. Stickybear's Early Learning Activities (manufactured by Optimum Resource, Inc.) features counting, grouping, and shapes, along with other skills. Math Magic (manufactured by MindPlay) has beginner lessons that allow counting objects with the space bar. Edmark (Riverdeep Family) has several software programs such as Millie's Math House that provide early math concepts and are accessible with alternate input devices.

COMPUTATIONAL SKILLS: ADDITION AND SUBTRACTION

In the early elementary grades, students will be spending considerable time learning computational skills such as addition and subtraction. As with teaching counting skills, initial instruction in addition and subtraction should begin with the use of concrete objects. Students should be exposed to a variety of experiences and discussions using concrete items. When teaching the operation of addition, the teacher should present various groups of objects and ask the students to "find how many in all" and explain what they are doing. After gaining competency in this skill, students should be introduced to the term "addition," followed by instruction on the addition symbol. Continuing to talk about what is being done aloud as a class as the operation is being performed will help reinforce learning the symbol.

Subtraction also begins with using concrete items. It is usually taught as "take away" or "separation." It is best approached by first having one amount of something (or quantity), removing a specified amount (or quantity) away from it, and noting what is left (Reys et al., 1998). The term "subtraction" and the minus sign are usually introduced after the students have learned the concept of take away. As students are being taught how to subtract, the concept that addition and subtraction are inverse to each other (i.e., one undoes the other) may be introduced. Examples such as $5 + 3 = 8$ and $8 - 3 = 5$ are often used to teach the relationship between addition and subtraction.

After manipulating items on a concrete level, students will need to move to a semiconcrete level. On the semiconcrete level, students may be taught to add or subtract using two-dimensional drawings, tally marks, or symbols. When moving from concrete items to the semiconcrete level, students with physical or multiple disabilities may be assisted by several visual approaches to help learn addition and subtraction. Some of these include touch math, pattern use, math marks, and a number line.

TouchMath. The *TouchMath* program (manufactured by Innovative Learning Concepts, Inc.) uses a series of dots that are placed directly on the numerals. As seen in Figure 16–6, each numeral has a dot or dots) placed on the numeral that equal the value of the numeral. Some numerals have a dot with a circle that indicates two dots at that point. When using TouchMath, students are taught to touch the dots (touch points) with a pencil while looking at the number and counting. If touching a dot with a circle, they touch the circled dot twice as they count two numbers.

When performing addition problems, students are taught to count forward as they touch each dot on the numerals. For students who can count on from a number, students are taught to say the larger number and continue counting by touching the dots on the next number. For example, in $6 + 4$, the student would say "6" and then count on as he or she touches each of the four dots on the 4 ("7," "8," "9," "10"). In subtraction, students are often taught to touch the dots and count

FIGURE 16–6
The TouchMath program helps students learn numerals, add, and subtract by touching the dots (touch points) that are on the numerals

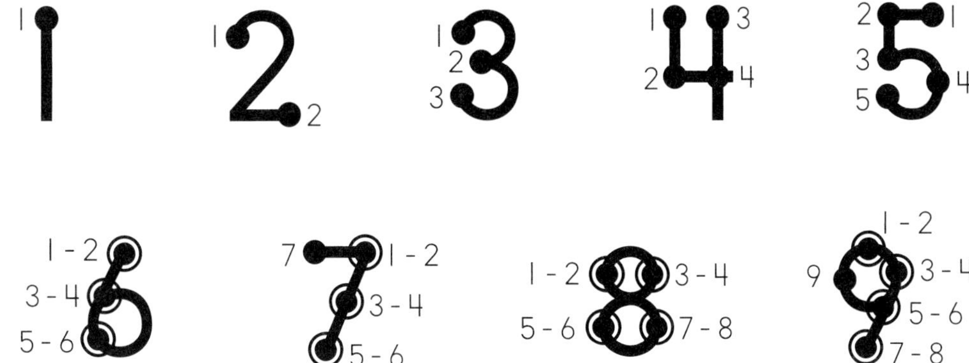

Note. From Bullock, J., *TouchMath: The Touchpoint Approach for Teaching Basic Math Computation* (4th ed.). Colorado Springs, CO: Innovative Learning Concepts. Reprinted with permission.

backwards to find the answer. Over time, the dots may be faded by gradually decreasing their size until they are no longer there. Students who learn this strategy may continue to touch the points on the numerals where the dots once were with their pencils from memory. This multisensory approach has been used across single-digit addition, two-digit addition with regrouping, single-digit subtraction, double-digit subtraction with regrouping, and three-digit subtraction with regrouping, as well as multiplication and division problems (Scott, 1993a, 1993b). Although this approach is effective for many students, it may be difficult to use with students with physical disabilities when a lack of fine-motor control is present.

Pattern Dot Use. Pattern dot use is similar to TouchMath, except that a particular pattern is taught that is not placed on the number. For example, the dot pattern used on dice may be taught as an addition and subtraction aid. Students are first introduced to the number and pattern together and students are taught to touch each dot as they are counting. Addition and subtraction are taught similarly to TouchMath. Over time, students are taught to draw the patterned dots and count the dots. After a high degree of success, students are taught to move their pencil in the configuration of the dots from memory as they count each dot. Eventually the student may use the patterns to count in their head. Students who learn the patterns easily and have a physical disability prohibiting pencil use may use the pattern to count either in their head or by moving a body part in the pattern configuration.

Math Marks. Math Marks is an adaptation designed specifically for students who lack fine-motor skills, but are able to use a pencil with larger writing movements (Heller, 1999). In an addition problem, the student is taught to find the small number and put marks corresponding to the number (e.g, put four marks by the number 4). The student then says the larger number aloud and touches each mark that he or she made for the smaller number as he or she counts on from the larger number. Any type of mark will work, although slash marks are typically used since they are usually the easiest to make for many students with a physical impairment.

Addition

```
  8
+ 4  \ \ \ \
```

1. Student puts marks beside the smaller number (four marks by the 4).
2. Student says the larger number, "8."
3. Student touches each mark and counts "9," "10," "11," "12."
4. Student writes (or indicates) the answer is 12.

When using the Math Marks method, the student is taught to subtract by adding up. When using this method, the student finds the small number and begins counting to the larger number while making marks for each number said. The marks are made where the answer goes, as seen below:

Subtraction

```
  9
- 5
----
   \ \ \ \
```

1. Student says the small number, "5."
2. Students says "6" and puts a mark below the line, says "7" and puts a mark, says "8" and puts a mark, and says "9" and puts a mark.
3. Student counts the marks and writes (or indicates) the answer as 4.

Number Line. For students who need some visual help with computations, a number line may be used (Polloway & Patton, 1993). This is especially useful for students who used a number line for counting, as previously described. When using a number line for addition, the student marks the larger number and then counts over to the smaller number.

For example:

In the addition problem:

```
  6      1 2 3 4 5 6 7 8 9 10
+ 3      |_|_|_|_|_|*|_|_|^|_|
----
```

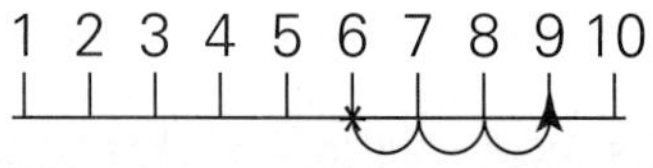

The student makes a mark on the 6, then counts up the number line three numbers while touching each number. The student ends on the answer, which is a 9 in this example.

In the subtraction problem:

```
  9      1 2 3 4 5 6 7 8 9 10
- 4      |_|_|_|_|^|_|_|_|*|_|
----
```

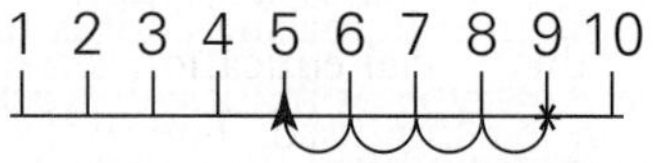

The student makes a mark on the 9, then counts down the number line four numbers while touching each number. The student ends on the answer, which is a 5 in this example.

For students with physical disabilities, the number line may need to be bigger to allow them to touch each number when counting. For students with very limited arm ability, they can direct an assistant as to where the mark should go and how many numbers to count up or down the number line. Although the number line is a very effective method for teaching addition and subtraction, it is imperative that it be faded from use as quickly as possible if the expectation is for the student to add and subtract without it in the future.

Mnemonics. A mnemonic can be a useful tool to help cue students to answer a math fact from memory, or use previously learned strategies to solve the problem. Mnemonics are any type of verse, formula, or abbreviation that is intended to assist the memory. One example of a mnemonic used for computation is "SOLVE," which stands for the following:

1. See the sign.
2. Observe and answer (but if unable to answer, continue).
3. Look and draw.
4. Verify your answer.
5. Enter your answer. (Miller & Mercer, 1993a, p. 79)

The student using this mnemonic is to first "see the sign" to determine the operation to perform (e.g., addition, subtraction, multiplication). In the "observe and answer" step, the student is to look at the numbers and answer the problem if he or she can. If the student does not automatically know the answer, he or she continues to step 3. In step 3, "look and draw," the student figures out the answer by looking at the numbers and using whatever method the student has been taught, such as drawing tally marks, Math Marks, TouchMath, number line, or making a graphic representation. In the fourth step, the student verifies his or her answer by rechecking each number (and drawing) and the answer (and drawings). In the last step, the student is to enter his or her answer (Miller & Mercer, 1993a).

A simpler computation mnemonic that has less complex vocabulary is "DRAW." It stands for:

1. Discover the sign.
2. Read the problem.
3. Answer or draw counting marks and check.
4. Write the answer. (Miller & Mercer, 1993a, p. 79).

In this mnemonic, the student first looks at the sign and determines the operation he or she is to perform. In the next step, the student reads the problem (aloud or silently). In the third step, the student answers the problem, or draws and then rechecks the drawing. In the last step, the student writes the answer.

Students with severe speech impairments may have the mnemonic programmed into their AAC device for reference and to facilitate participation in class when asked by the teacher, "How do we remember this?" Keeping the mnemonic on a card on the student's desk or wheelchair tray may also be a good idea, especially when it is difficult to see it posted on the board or other location in the room.

Math Rules for Addition and Subtraction

There are several basic math rules that students should be taught to help them become proficient in math. Teachers will need to be sure students learn these rules and are able to apply them. When analyzing the types of errors the student is making, the teacher should check for errors due to a lack of understanding of one of these rules and reteach the concept when rule errors occur. For addition, these rules are:

1. *Order Rule:* The answer is the same regardless of which order is used to add the numbers together.
2. *Zero Rule:* Adding a zero (nothing) to a number keeps the number the same (e.g., $6 + 0 = 6$).
3. *One Rule:* Adding a 1 to a number is one more than the number (e.g., $4 + 1 = 5$). The student may count up by one to arrive at the answer.
4. *Nine Rule:* Think of the 9 as a 10 and then subtract 1 from the answer.

$$\begin{array}{r} 9 \\ +\ 5 \\ \hline \end{array} \quad \text{equals} \quad \begin{array}{r} 10 \\ +\ 5 \\ \hline 15 \end{array} - 1 = 14$$

   An alternative nine rule is that the number in the ones column is always one less than the number they are adding to the 9.

$$\begin{array}{r} 9 \\ +\ 5 \\ \hline 14 \end{array} \qquad \begin{array}{r} 9 \\ +\ 8 \\ \hline 17 \end{array}$$

5. *Ten Rule:* Ten plus any single number changes the 0 in the 10 to the number being added to it.
6. *Doubles Rule:* When students are taught doubles, (e.g., $6 + 6 = 12$, $7 + 7 = 14$) they can use their knowledge of doubles to answer near doubles.

$$\begin{array}{r} 6 \\ +\ 7 \\ \hline \end{array} \quad \text{equals} \quad \begin{array}{r} 6 \\ +\ 6 \\ \hline 12 \end{array} + 1 = 13$$

There are also several basic rules for subtraction:

1. *Order Rule:* The order cannot be changed when calculating subtraction problems.
2. *Zero Rule:* Subtracting a zero (nothing) from a number keeps the number the same (e.g., $5 - 0 = 5$).
3. *One Rule:* Subtracting a 1 from a number is one less than the number (e.g., $6 - 1 = 5$). The student may count backwards by one to arrive at the answer.
4. *BBB Rule.* If the Bottom number is Bigger than the top number, the student should Break down the top number by trading it for 10 units and then subtracting (Mercer & Mercer, 2001).

$$\begin{array}{r} 24 \\ -\ 6 \\ \hline \end{array} \qquad \begin{array}{r} \overset{1}{\not{2}}\,{}^{1}4 \\ -\ 6 \\ \hline \end{array}$$

5. *Relationship-of-Addition-and-Subtraction Rule:* The answer of a subtraction problem (difference) added to the number that is subtracted (subtrahend) equals the top number (minuend). For example:

$$\begin{array}{r} 9 \\ -\ 4 \\ \hline 5 \end{array} \quad \text{is the same as } 5 + 4 = 9$$

   Students can use this to calculate the answer by starting at 4 and adding up to 9. They can also use this to check their answers. (Bos & Vaughn, 2002; Mercer & Mercer, 2001).

Addition and Subtraction Algorithms

There are several different algorithms that may be used to teach addition and subtraction. When the student is taking math in the general education math class, it is important that the special education teacher find out which algorithm is being used. The special education teacher can then provide additional training on that algorithm or select one that may be more appropriate for the student in collaboration with the general education teacher. Also, when analyzing student's math errors, it is important to determine whether the student is making an algorithm error that needs further instruction. Some select algorithms are presented in this section, especially those that may help facilitate regrouping or assist students with physical disabilities who are unable to easily put numbers on top of columns or mark out numbers for regrouping on a computer.

Expanded-Notation Algorithm. In this algorithm, the problem is rewritten to demonstrate the actual place values that the numbers represent. The purpose of this is to enhance understanding of the tens, hundreds, and so on. For example, when adding the 4 and the 2 in the hundreds column, this approach emphasizes that a 400 and a 200 are being added. Some teachers will begin with this algorithm, then move to a more standard approach. For example,

$$\begin{array}{r} 436 \\ +\ 248 \\ \hline \end{array} \quad \text{is the same as:} \quad \begin{array}{rrr} 400 & 30 & 6 \\ +\ 200 & 40 & 8 \\ \hline \end{array}$$
$$600 + 20 + 14 = 684$$

Standard Approach for Addition. In the standard approach, the student is taught to add the numbers together without using expanded notation. When the number exceeds the column, students are taught to put the number at the top of the appropriate column. (Depending upon the approach being used, this is called regrouping, renaming, trading, or carrying.) One example presented follows Stein et al.'s (1997) suggestions of presenting a standard algorithm for addition of two-digit plus two-digit numbers using a direct instruction approach.

Partial Sum for Addition. The partial sum algorithm avoids having to place numerals on top of tens, hundreds, or other columns. Instead, when the number is equal to or greater than 10, it is written as a two-digit numeral at the bottom of the tens and ones columns. In the example of 56 + 37, when 6 + 7 are added together, the 13 is written at the bottom of the columns, with the 3 under the ones column and the 1 under the tens column. When adding 5 tens + 3 tens, the answer is 8 tens, or 80. This is placed below and the two partial sums are added together (Mercer & Mercer, 2001).

$$\begin{array}{r} 56 \\ +\ 37 \\ \hline 13 \\ 80 \\ \hline 93 \end{array}$$

For students with physical disabilities who are performing calculations on a computer, the partial sum algorithm may be faster and easier. This is because the student does not have to position the cursor at the top of the tens column to put the 1. (However, there is software available to aid in regrouping problems. See the section titled "Software for Computational Skills," which appears later in this chapter.)

Left-to-Right Addition from Memory. The left-to-right addition algorithm is another algorithm that allows students to regroup in the answer (Pearson, 1986). What is unique about this algorithm is that students add from left to right and this particular form of left-to-right algorithm is designed for them to add "in their head" without using paper. As seen in the next example, the student would first add the hundreds column of 200 + 100 = 300. Next, the student would add the largest ten (80) to the number to get 380. Then the student adds the second ten (50) to get 430. Then the largest ones is added to get 437. Finally, the other number in the ones column is added to get the answer.

	Teacher	*Students*
$\begin{array}{r} {}^{1} \\ 37 \\ +\ 25 \\ \hline \end{array}$	1. Read this problem.	37 + 25 = how many?
	2. What column do we start?	The ones column.
	3. What are the first 2 numbers we are going to add?	7 + 5
	4. 7 + 5 equals what?	12
	5. Twelve equals 1 ten and 2 ones. We put the 2 in the ones column. We can't put a ten in the ones column, so we put the 1 ten at the top of the tens column. Where do we put the ten?	On top of the tens column.
	6. What are the first two numbers in the tens column that are to be added?	1 + 3
	7. What does 1 + 3 equal?	4
	8. Now what two numbers do we add?	4 + 2
	9. What does 4 + 2 equal?	6
	10. How many tens do we end up with? We write the 6 here under the tens column.	6 tens
	11. We are finished. What does 37 + 25 equal? Read the problem and say the answer.	37 + 25 = 62

```
  285
+ 157
  300  Add hundreds first (200 + 100)
  380  Add the largest ten (300 + 80)
  430  Count other ten (380 + 50)
  437  Add largest one (430 + 7)
  442  Add other one (437 + 5)
```

Antecedent Prompts. Some students may have difficulty remembering where to start computing a math problem, where to place a number on top of the tens column, or even how to line up the columns. In these instances, the student may benefit from the use of antecedent prompts. Several different antecedent prompts may be used to assist a student. In the addition example in Figure 16–7, antecedent prompts are shown for helping with column alignment and placing the 1 on the tens column. Other types of visual prompts could have been used, such as placing a colored dot for where to start addition, or circling the sign. Whichever type of antecedent prompt is used, the minimal number of prompts should be used and they should be faded as quickly as possible to avoid dependence on them. In Figure 16–7, one way to fade certain prompts is shown. These types of prompts may also be used across other computational problems.

Standard Algorithm for Subtraction. There are several different algorithms that may be used for computing subtraction problems. In the most commonly taught subtraction algorithm, subtraction is taught from right to left. When the number on top is smaller than the number on bottom, the student is taught to regroup the numbers through renaming, trading, or borrowing from the next column, depending upon the method being used to teach this algorithm. One example presented next follows Stein et al.'s (1997) suggestions on presenting a standard algorithm for subtraction using a direct instruction approach.

FIGURE 16–7
Fading prompts from the learning task

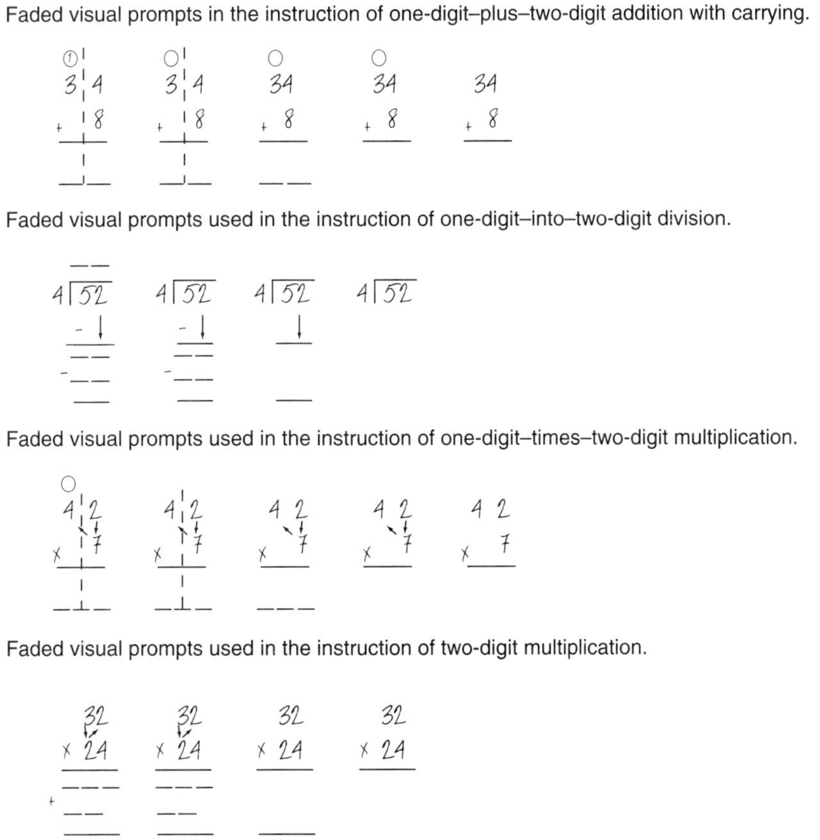

Faded visual prompts in the instruction of one-digit–plus–two-digit addition with carrying.

Faded visual prompts used in the instruction of one-digit–into–two-digit division.

Faded visual prompts used in the instruction of one-digit–times–two-digit multiplication.

Faded visual prompts used in the instruction of two-digit multiplication.

Note. From *Teaching the Mildly Handicapped in the Regular Classroom,* 2/e by Affleck/Lowenbraun/ Archer, © 1980. Reprinted by permission of Prentice-Hall, Inc., Upper Saddle River, NJ.

$$\begin{array}{r} {\scriptstyle 3\,1} \\ \not{4}2 \\ -\ 16 \\ \hline \end{array}$$

Teacher	Students
1. Read the problem.	42 − 16 =
2. Where do we start?	In the ones column.
3. What do we do first?	Start with 2 and take away 6.
4. Do we rename (trade, regroup, borrow)?	Yes.
5. What do we do first to rename?	Borrow a ten from the 4 tens.
6. So I cross out the 4 and write a 3 to show that 3 tens are left.	
7. We borrowed a ten. What is next?	Put the 10 with the 2 ones.
8. Right. So I put a little one beside the 2. We have a 12 in the ones column.	
9. We now subtract 12 − 6. What is that?	6
10. We write a 6 in the ones column.	
11. The tens column now says 3 tens minus 1 one. How many is 3 tens minus 1 ten?	2
12. So we write a 2 under the tens column.	
13. What is 42 take away 16?	26

Changing-the-Numbers Subtraction Algorithm. To avoid regrouping, students may be taught to change the numbers by adding or subtracting a constant. In the examples below, students are taught to add or subtract the same number from each of the numbers in the problem to arrive at the correct answer. In the first problem, the student adds a 3 to each number, and in the second example, the student subtracts 1 from each number.

$$\begin{array}{rcr} 53 + 3 = & & 56 \\ -\ 27 + 3 = & & -\ 30 \\ \hline & & 26 \end{array} \qquad \begin{array}{rcr} 300 \quad -\ 1 & = & 299 \\ -\ 158 \quad -\ 1 & = & -\ 157 \\ \hline & & 142 \end{array}$$

Students who are unable to use pencil and paper due to a physical disability often have the problem of how to cross out and add numbers to the appropriate column on the computer. Without specific software, many students will be unable to mark out numbers. The changing-number algorithm avoids the physical problems of regrouping. Other algorithms, such as subtracting from left to right, will not be addressed since they require the physical task of crossing out numbers and placing small ones in several columns, which is typically difficult for most students with physical disabilities.

Addition and Subtraction Sequences

Students should be taught a logical sequence from basic to more advanced addition and subtraction skills. One possible sequence consists of teaching as follows:

1. Precomputational skills (see the previous section).
2. Adding numbers together with sums less than 10.
3. Adding numbers together with sums less than 18 (with each number being added being less than 10).
4. Adding two-digit plus one-digit numbers without regrouping.
5. Adding two-digit plus two-digit numbers without regrouping.
6. Adding two-digit plus one-digit numbers with regrouping.
7. Adding two-digit plus two-digit numbers with regrouping.
8. Adding two-digit plus two-digit plus two-digit numbers with grouping.
9. Adding three-digit plus three-digit numbers with regrouping.
10. Advancing to larger sums.

Subtraction may be taught simultaneously with addition or sequentially after addition. Subtraction can be sequenced in a similar manner to addition. After learning the precomputational skills, the student learns to

1. Subtract single digits from 0 to 9.
2. Subtract two-digit numbers of 18 and below from a single number without regrouping.
3. Subtract the difference between two-digit and one-digit numbers without regrouping.
4. Subtract the difference between two-digit and two-digit numbers without regrouping.
5. Subtract using three-digit and two-digit numbers without regrouping.
6. Subtract three-digit from three-digit numbers without regrouping.
7. Subtract two-digit and one-digit numbers with regrouping.
8. Regroup the tens column with two-digit and two-digit numbers.
9. Regroup the tens column with three-digit and two-digit numbers.
10. Double-regroup between three-digit and two-digit numbers.
11. Subtract three-digit from three-digit numbers with regrouping (regrouping is first introduced in the tens column, followed by teaching double regrouping [tens and hundreds]).
12. Subtract using numbers with zeros in the top number, or minuend (first put zeros in the ones column, and later the tens and ones).
13. Subtract using more-complex numbers.

COMPUTATIONAL SKILLS FOR MULTIPLICATION AND DIVISION

As with addition and subtraction, it is very important that students be taught the meaning of multiplication and division. If multiplication and division are taught only in a drill fashion, students may be unable to apply these operations while problem-solving or in practical situations. As with addition and subtraction, multiplication and division should be taught using concrete, semiconcrete, and then abstract symbols. Some teachers will teach multiplication as repeated addition (4×5 being the same as $5 + 5 + 5 + 5$) and division ($12 \div 3$) as repeated subtraction is the same as $12 - 3 - 3 - 3 - 3$. (It takes four 3s subtracted from twelve to arrive at zero, so the answer is 4.) An example of using a semiconcrete strategy is as follows:

```
         / / / / /
3 × 5 =  / / / / /  = 15
         / / / / /
```

Multiplication and Division Rules

As with addition and subtraction, there are several rules that students will need to learn to help them make correct computations. For multiplication these rules are as follows:

1. *Order Rule:* The order of the numbers can be changed.
2. *Zero Rule:* When multiplying a number by 0, the answer is always 0.
3. *One Rule:* When multiplying a number by 1, the answer is always the number.
4. *Two Rule:* When multiplying a number by 2, the answer is double the number (e.g., 6×2 is the same as $6 + 6$).
5. *Five Rule:* When multiplying by 5, the student can count by 5s to arrive at the answer. For example, in the problem 5×6, the student would count by 5s six times: "Five, ten, fifteen, twenty, twenty-five, thirty."
6. *Nine Rule:* When multiplying by 9, first subtract 1 from the number being multiplied by 9 and write the answer in the tens column. Then figure out what number added to that number equals 9, and write the answer in the ones column. For example, to use this method to calculate 9×6, the student would subtract $6 - 1 = 5$. The 5 goes in the tens column. $5 + 4 = 9$, so the 4 would go in the ones column. The answer would be 54 (Mercer & Mercer, 2001).

Another way of calculating this is to spread out all 10 fingers, with each finger being 1 through 10. If the problem is 9×4, fold under the fourth finger from the left. To its left there are 3 fingers (which is the tens) and to its right there are 6 fingers (which is the ones), making the answer 36. This can be done with any number times 9. For students with physical disabilities, this shortcut strategy may not be very successful due to poor fine-motor control. Some students have a modification in which they have a line drawing of 10 fingers on a piece of paper and they put a mark on the finger that would be folded under and derive the answer as another student would using his or her fingers.

There are also several different rules that are taught in division:

1. *Order Rule:* The order of the numbers in division is important and cannot be changed.
2. *Zero Rule:* You cannot divide a number by 0.
3. *One Rule:* When dividing a number by 1, the answer is the number.
4. *Two Rule:* When dividing a number by 2, it is half of the number.
5. *Relationship of Multiplication and Division:* The answer to a division problem (quotient) multiplied by the divisor equals the dividend. For example:

   21 (dividend) ÷ 3 (divisor) = 7 (quotient) is the same as 7 × 3 = 21

   This can be used to help calculate the answer or check whether the answer is correct.

Heuristic Strategies

It should be noted that students often use a variety of heuristic strategies for multiplication and division. Heuristic strategies are alternate techniques, generated by the student to simplify and augment the standard procedures used in arithmetic. In multiplication and division, these strategies are especially useful for students who do not successfully memorize the multiplication tables. Some heuristic strategies are skip counting, repeated addition, adding one more set, building on known facts through the use of an anchor point, calculation of twice as much as a known fact, use of patterns, and use of manipulatives (including finger counting). It has been recommended to teach students having computational deficiencies a variety of heuristic procedures, with ample opportunities for practice and generalization, to increase performance and application of basic computational facts (Erenberg, 1995).

Multiplication and Division Algorithms

There are several different algorithms that may be taught to students with physical or multiple disabilities. Although standard algorithms are typically taught, alternate algorithms may be easier to comprehend and to physically perform. Both standard and alternate algorithms are presented as follows.

Standard Algorithm for Multiplication. In the standard algorithm for multiplication, the student multiplies right to left, carrying numbers as needed. One example, presented next, follows Stein et al.'s (1997) suggestions for presenting a standard algorithm using a direct instruction approach.

	Teacher	*Student*
36 Order × 24	1. Read this problem.	24 times 36
	2. First we multiply 4 × 6.	
	3. What do we multiply first?	Multiply 4 times 6
	4. Next we multiply 4 × 3. What do we do next?	Multiply 4 times 3
	5. Next we multiply 2 × 6.	
	6. Next we multiply 2 × 3.	

Calculate	5. What is 4×6? We can't write 24 in the ones column. We carry the tens.	24
	6. How many tens are there?	2 tens
	7. We put the 2 above the tens column, and put a plus sign in front to remind us to add.	
$\begin{array}{r} ^{+2} \\ 36 \\ \times\ 24 \\ \hline 144 \end{array}$	8. Twenty-four has 2 tens and how many ones?	4
	9. We write the 4 under the ones column.	
	10. Next we multiply 4×3. What is 4×3?	12
	11. Now we add the 2. What is $12 + 2$?	14
	12. There are no more numbers on the top to multiply, so we write the 14 next to the 4 under the line.	
	13. We multiplied 4×36. What is 4×36? Now we cross out the 2 we carried to show we are through with that number.	144
	14. Next we multiply 2 tens $\times$ 36. Tens numbers have a zero, so we put a 0 in the ones column. That shows we are multiplying by 20. How do we show we are multiplying by 20?	Put a 0 in the ones column
$\begin{array}{r} ^{+1} \\ ^{\not+\not2} \\ 36 \\ \times\ 24 \\ \hline 144 \\ 720 \\ \hline 864 \end{array}$	15. Next we multiply 2×6, then 2×3. What do we multiply first?	2×6
	16. What is 2×6?	12
	17. Write the 1 above the tens column and the 2 next to the 0. Where do I write?	(Students repeat)
	18. Now we multiply 2×3. What is 2×3?	6
	19. What do we do now?	Add 1 in tens column
	20. What is $6 + 1$?	7
	21. Write the 7 next to the 2.	
	22. First we multiplied 4×36 and ended with 144. Next, we multiplied 20×36 and ended with 720.	
	23. Now we add those numbers together. What is $4 + 0$? What is $4 + 2$? What is $1 + 7$?	4 6 8
	24. What does 36×24 equal?	864

Partial Products Algorithm. A partial products algorithm reduces the regrouping requirement and is thus easier to perform for some students because it alleviates the physical and cognitive challenges of carrying numbers. Notice that this algorithm has the student multiply the top number by the bottom number, while the standard algorithm above had the student multiply the bottom number by the top number. It is important that when initially teaching this method, the teacher be consistent within and across algorithms to avoid confusion. An example of using this algorithm is as follows:

$$\begin{array}{rl} 49 & \\ \times\ \ 6 & \\ \hline 54 & (9 \times 6) \text{ partial product} \\ 240 & (40 \times 6) \text{ partial product} \\ \hline 294 & \end{array}$$

Antecedent Prompts. As seen in Figure 16–7, small arrows can be used to guide students to multiply the correct numbers. Other prompts assist with the process of multiplication and division.

Standard Division Algorithm. In the standard algorithm for division, the student divides left to right. One example, presented below, follows Stein et al.'s (1997) suggestions on presenting a standard algorithm using a direct instruction approach.

	Teacher	*Student*
7)224	1. When a division problem has a lot of digits, we work the problem one part at a time. We begin a problem by underlining the part we will work on first. Sometimes we underline the first digit and sometimes we underline the first two digits.	
	2. Read the problem.	
7)<u>22</u>4	3. We are dividing by 7. If the first digit is as big as or bigger than 7, we underline the first digit in 224. If it is smaller, 7 can't go into it, so we underline the first two digits. The first digit we're dividing into is 2. Is 2 at least as big as 7? So we underline the first two digits.	7 goes into 240 No
	4. The underlined problem says 7 goes into 22. What does the underlined problem say?	7 goes into 22
	5. How many times does 7 go into 22?	3
3	6. We write the 3 over the last digit underlined.	
7)224	7. Now we multiply 3×7. What is 3×7?	21
21	8. Now write the 21 under the line.	
1	9. Now subtract $22 - 21$. What is $22 - 21$?	 1
	10. What is the next digit to bring down?	4
	11. We bring down the 4 and write it next to the 1.	
32	12 What number is now under the line?	14
7)224	13. The next part of the problem says 7 goes into 14. What does it say?	7 goes into 14
21	14. How many times does 7 go into 14?	2
14	15. We write the 2 above the digit we brought down.	
14	16. Now, what numbers do we multiply?	2×7
	17. What is 2×7?	14
	18. Write 14 under the 14 and subtract.	
	19. What is $14 - 14$?	0
	20. Is there a remainder?	No
	21. Is there another number to bring down?	No
	22. The problem is finished. Every digit after the underlined part has a number over it. How many times does 7 go into 224?	 32

Adjusting-Computations Division Algorithm. Sometimes students miscalculate in determining how many times one number goes into another number by computing too low. One easy method is to allow the student to use the adjusting-computations division algorithm. This algorithm is helpful for students with physical disabilities who have difficulty erasing or take too long deleting and redoing it on the computer. For example:

```
   1
  22 = 32
7)224
  14
  --
   8
   7
   -
  14
  14
```

1. Seven goes into 22 by how many? The student selected a 2.
2. Put the 2 above the 22; $2 \times 7 = 14$; $22 - 14 = 8$.
3. 7 can still go into 8. Put a 1 above the 2; $1 \times 7 = 7$.
4. Bring down the 4; 7 goes into 14 two times.
5. Add each column in the quotient to get the answer of 32.

Multiplication and Division Sequences

Instruction in multiplication and division must occur from basic to complex, building on the concepts that are learned. One possible sequence for multiplication is as follows:

1. Teaching the meaning of multiplication, the signs, and basic multiplication facts.
2. Multiply one digit by one digit with each digit being less than 5.
3. Multiply one digit by one digit with one of the digits being greater than 5 and less than 10.
4. Multiply a two-digit number by a one-digit number without regrouping problems.
5. Multiply a two-digit by a one-digit number with regrouping, with a product less than 100.
6. Multiply with products more than 100.
7. Multiply a two-digit by a two-digit number with regrouping.
8. Multiply a three-digit by a one-digit number with regrouping.
9. Multiply a three-digit by a two-digit number with regrouping.
10. Multiply more-complex problems.

A similar sequence is followed in division. One possible sequence is as follows:

1. Learn the meaning of division, the signs, and the basic division facts.
2. Compute basic division facts using division problems without a remainder.
3. Divide one digit by one digit with a remainder.
4. Divide a two-digit by a one-digit number without a remainder.
5. Divide a two-digit by a one-digit number with a remainder.
6. Divide a three-digit by a one-digit number and use estimation.
7. Divide one-digit into multiple-digit numbers.
8. Divide a three-digit by a two-digit number.
9. Use division in more-complex problems.

SOFTWARE FOR COMPUTATIONAL SKILLS

There are several software programs available to assist students in learning addition, subtraction, multiplication, and division. These programs typically utilize a drill and practice technique within a game format. Some programs provide animated characters to help understand the operation they are using. For example, Show Me Math CD (manufactured by Attainment) addresses addition, subtraction, multiplication, and division. In the instructional mode, the student is presented with random math problems. The student has the option of typing an answer from the keyboard or selecting an answer from a moving parade of numbers with a mouse (or switch). If the student requires some help understanding the problem, the student can push the "Show Me" button, which will play a short animated movie illustrating the math problems with ants, sheep, or jumping beans. Another program, Math Blasters (manufactured by Knowledge Adventure), is available for grades 1 through 5 and presents math problems in an exciting game format. MathPad by Voice (manufactured by Metroplex Voice Computing) allows students to do addition, subtraction, division, and multiplication by voice. A calculator is also included that can be accessed by speech. Other examples of programs targeting computations skills are Stickybear's Math Town and Stickybear's Math Word Problems (manufactured by Optimum Resource, Inc.), Math Sequences (manufactured by Milliken Publishing Co.), Math Magic (manufactured by MindPlay), and Math Workshop Deluxe (manufactured by Riverdeep–The Learning Company). IntelliMathics (manufactured by IntelliTolls, Inc.) contains on-screen manipulatives to help increase understanding of computational skills, as well as other areas of math (e.g., sorting, fractions, decimals).

Other types of computer software allow students to do computations on the computer. This is especially important for students who are physically unable to access paper. These **electronic worksheet programs** also feature auditory review of the problem, visual accommodations (size, colors, numbers of problems displayed), on-screen keyboards, and printing capabilities. Access to Math (manufactured by Don Johnston, Inc.), for example, makes customized worksheets for addition, subtraction, multiplication, and division. It shows number borrowing and carrying just as they would appear on paper and can guide students step-by-step using talking numbers and speech feedback. It also informs students of incorrect entries. Another electronic worksheet program is MathPad (manufactured by IntelliTools, Inc.). MathPad contains many accessibility features (e.g., built-in scanning, speech output, text size options) and is designed to use other assistive technology such as IntelliKeys or other alternative input devices.

CALCULATOR USE

Calculator use is recommended when computations need to be made and computational skills are not the main focus of the instruction (Reys et al., 1998). This includes using a calculator as an adjunct to teaching math concepts (e.g., place value), to assist with learning math facts, to focus on meaning and process when learning more-advanced math skills (e.g., algebra), and to promote functional and applied skills for students in a functional curriculum (e.g., grocery shopping or balancing a checkbook).

In the elementary grades, learning the basic math facts continues to be an important goal. However, calculators may be used to assist learning these facts and help with the development of number sense. It is a myth that calculators harm student achievement or do all the thinking for the student. The National Council of Teachers of Mathematics (NCTM) Standards make an analogy between using calculators for math and using word processors for writing; both are tools that simplify but do not perform the work. The NCTM position statement on calculators recommends that appropriate calculators should be available to all students. Besides stressing calculator use, this also refers to the need for calculators that match students' growing knowledge. Students can outgrow calculators and need more-advanced ones as they master various math skills (NCTM, 1989).

There are several guidelines for early calculator instruction. First, students should be encouraged to press the Clear key twice before beginning each problem on the calculator. Second, the sequential order of the numbers on the calculator should be pointed out. Sometimes using a calculator designed for demonstration on an overhead projector can be a helpful tool to point out the features of the calculator. Third, students should check their entries by checking the display panel after each entry. Fourth, students should know that weak batteries or a broken calculator may show wrong answers. Last, students can benefit by learning to use the calculator with the nondominant hand (e.g., the hand not used for writing) so that they can record the results while operating the calculator (Heddens & Speer, 1997; Mercer & Mercer, 2001).

There are several modified calculators and software programs targeting calculator use. Some calculators have large buttons to assist with fine-motor problems and/or visual impairments. Large-print calculators and talking calculators may be selected to accommodate for visual or perceptual problems. Several of these are available from such companies as MaxiAids, LS&S, and Texas Instruments. Graphing calculators are also available and are often a requirement in middle or high school. Some calculators offer a tilting LED display of the numbers, which can promote better visualization of the display and less glare.

Computer software offers on-screen calculators that can be accessed in an application or in isolation. One example of an on-screen calculator is Big:Calc (manufactured by Don Johnston, Inc.). Big:Calc includes six different calculator layouts for different needs, and the equations can be viewed horizontally or vertically. Big:Calc can talk and scan, and the font size and colors/backgrounds can be changed to increase visibility and contrast. This on-screen calculator can be accessed by a mouse, keyboard, or alternate access method. On-screen calculators are also standard features of Windows 95, 98, ME, and XP, as well as Macintosh computers. VoiceEZcalc (manufactured by Metroplex Voice Computing) operates the 95/98/ME/XP calculator by voice.

WORD PROBLEMS

In the special education literature, there has been an increased emphasis on teaching students computation and problem-solving skills (Butler, Miller, Lee, & Pierce, 2001). Problem-solving skills often are presented in the form of word problems. However, many students have difficulty applying correct math operations and applications when performing word problems. This can be especially difficult for students with physical or multiple disabilities when reading ability is below grade level and/or there is confusion over the vocabulary being used. Also, students with physical or multiple disabilities may have a lack of experiences resulting in faulty or incomplete concepts that can negatively impact academic performance (Heller et al., 1996). This includes performance on word problems. Therefore, it is important that the teacher be sure that the student first understands what the word problem is about. This can occur through discussion, using actual items and real-life application examples. Beginning with word problems that have no extraneous information can also be helpful.

It is important to use systematic strategies to help students learn how to answer word problems. Word problem instruction has occurred using many strategies, such as manipulative use (Marsh & Cooke, 1996), diagrammatic strategies (Walker & Poteet, 1990), mnemonics (Mercer & Miller, 1994; Miller & Mercer, 1993a), direct instruction (Wilson & Sindelar, 1991), diagnostic teaching (Parmar & Crawley, 1994), cognitive and metacognitive strategies (such as reading aloud, paraphrasing, visualizing, stating problems, hypothesizing, estimating, calculating, and self-checking) (Montague & Bos, 1986), self-regulated cognitive strategies (Case, Harris, & Graham, 1992), sequencing word problem strategy (Stein et al., 1997), video-based and anchored instruction (Bottge, Heinrichs, Chan, Mehta, & Watson, 2003), and word problem context strategy (Bottge & Hasselbring, 1993). Teaching students a variety of strategies can often be helpful in providing them more options to figure out the answer. Also, supplementary practice can be provided by software programs specifically addressing word problems, such as Math Word Problems Series (manufactured by Optimum Resource Inc.).

GENERAL AND ADVANCED MATH SKILLS

Depending upon students' abilities, they will learn to calculate percent, rations, fractions, and decimals as they learn computational skills. Many students with physical or multiple disabilities will progress in their mathematics instruction and go on to learn geometry, algebra, trigonometry, statistics, probability, and/or calculus. By the time students are learning advanced math skills, issues such as AAC use and access to basic math materials have been addressed. New issues, such as access to tools used in geometry, will need to be determined. Some adaptations would include having the student with severe physical impairments direct a peer in use of tools (i.e., a protractor or compass), software use, or adaptation of the material being used. Solutions to these problems will depend upon the needs of each individual student.

Software may be used to support a variety of math skills. At the elementary grade levels, MathPad Plus: Faction and Decimal (manufactued by IntelliTools, Inc.) targets fractions and decimals, and IntelliMathics (manufactured by IntelliTools, Inc.) provides on-screen manipulations to teach fractions and decimals (as well as other math skills). Math Workshop Deluxe (manufactured by Riverdeep) provides math problems that include fractions, geometry, and spatial relations.

Besides the standard tutorial software for more-advanced math (e.g., algebra, geometry, calculus), there is specialized software that can be used by students with physical disabilities. For example, Math Type 5 (by Design Science, Inc.) is an excellent tool for writing mathematical equations. Since it can be used through the word processor and allows for a customized toolbar, alternate access (e.g., joystick) is possible. It contains over 500 math symbols to allow for making complex equations. MathTalk/Scientific Notebook (manufactured by Metroplex Voice Computing) allows the user to voice such math areas as pre-algebra, algebra, trigonometry, calculus, and statistics. It also includes voicing graphs.

Some students will not be able to progress to more-advanced math skills or, in some cases, may have been unable to learn traditional computational skills. For these students, functional math skills should be stressed. In some situations, students with physical or multiple disabilities will be taught functional math skills in addition to the more traditional academic skills.

FUNCTIONAL MATH SKILLS

Functional math skills lessons stress the everyday application of math to help students function in home, community, vocational, and school environments. As seen in Table 16–3, functional math skills of money, time, capacity/volume, length, weight/mass, and temperature are required across many functional adult skills. Students with physical or multiple disabilities may learn a few or most of these types of skills, depending upon the students' abilities and needs. Some software is available to support these functional math skills, such as Math for Everyday Living (manufactured by Educational Activities Software), which teaches the real-life

TABLE 16–3
Math Skills Typically Encountered in Adulthood

Life demand	APPLIED MATH SKILLS					
	Money	Time	Capacity/Volume	Length	Weight/Mass	Temperature
Employment						
Transportation	x	x		x		
Pay						
■ wages	x	x				
■ deductions	x					
■ taxes	x					
■ retirement	x	x				
■ investment	x	x				
■ savings	x					
Commission						
■ straight or graduated	x					
Hours worked		x				
Overtime	x	x				
Breaks/lunch	x	x				
Deadlines		x				
Further education						
Budgeting	x	x				
Costs	x					
Financing	x					
Time management						
■ requisite course hours		x				
■ scheduling		x				
■ extra curricular		x				
■ meetings		x				
Home/family						
Budgeting	x	x				
Bills						
■ payment options	x	x				
■ day-to-day costs	x					
■ long-term purchases	x					
Locating a home						
■ rental or purchase	x	x	x	x		
■ moving	x	x	x		x	
■ insurance	x	x				
■ contracts	x	x				
■ affordability	x					
■ utilities	x	x				
Mortgage	x	x				
Home repair/maintenance	x	x	x	x	x	x
Financial management						
■ checking/savings account	x					
■ ATM	x			x		
■ credit cards	x	x				
■ insurance	x	x				
■ taxes	x	x				
■ investment	x	x				
Individual/family scheduling		x		x		
Automobile						
■ payments	x	x				
■ maintenance	x	x	x	x	x	x
■ repair	x					
■ depreciation	x					
■ fuel costs	x		x			
Thermostat		x				x
Cooking	x	x	x	x	x	x
Yard maintenance	x	x	x	x	x	x

TABLE 16–3
Continued

Life demand	APPLIED MATH SKILLS					
	Money	Time	Capacity/Volume	Length	Weight/Mass	Temperature
Home remodeling	x	x	x	x	x	x
Decorating	x	x	x	x	x	x
Shopping						
■ comparing prices	x	x	x		x	
Laundry	x	x	x			x
Leisure pursuits						
Travel	x	x		x	x	x
Membership fees	x	x				
Subscription costs	x	x				
Reading newspaper	x	x	x	x	x	x
Equipment costs						
■ rental or purchase	x	x				
Sports activities	x	x		x	x	x
Entertainment (e.g., movies, videos, performances, sporting events, cards, board games, electronic games)	x	x		x		x
Lottery	x	x				
Hobbies	x	x	x	x	x	x
Personal responsibility and relationships						
Dating	x	x				
Scheduling		x				
Anniversaries/birthdays, etc.	x	x				
Correspondence	x	x	x		x	
Gifts	x	x				
Health						
Physical development						
■ weight					x	
■ height				x		
■ caloric intake				x		
■ nutrition	x	x			x	
Physical fitness program	x	x		x	x	
Doctor's visits	x	x		x	x	x
Medications	x	x				
Medically related procedures (e.g., blood pressure)		x	x			x
Community involvement						
Scheduling		x		x		
Voting		x		x		
Directions				x		
Public transportation	x	x		x		
Menu use	x	x				
Tipping	x					
Financial transactions						
■ making/receiving change	x					
■ fines/penalties	x	x				
Phone usage	x	x				
Using specific community services	x	x		x		
Emergency services	x	x		x		x
Civic responsibilities						
■ voting		x		x		
■ jury duty		x				

Note. From "A Life Skills Approach to Mathematics Instruction: Preparing Students with Learning Disabilities for the Real-Life Demands of Adulthood" by J. R. Patton, M. E. Cronin, D. S. Bassett, and A. Koppel, 1997, *Journal of Learning Disabilities, 30,* 178–187. Copyright 1997 by PRO-ED, Inc. Reprinted by permission.

math skills used in activities such as paying for meals, filling out time cards, calculating sales tax, and finding a job; and Math in the Workplace (manufacted by Educational Activities Software), which targets math activities in business, health occupations, home economics, agriculture, and other areas.

Some of the building blocks of teaching functional math skills revolve around the three basic areas of money, time, and calendar use. This section will discuss strategies that are applicable for students with normal cognitive ability as well as strategies for students with severe intellectual disabilities in learning these basic skills.

Money

Traditional Money Instruction. One of the most important skills students will need to learn is the use of money. Money use includes a wide range of skills, from identifying and counting money to consumer skills with money. A typical scope and sequence for teaching money is as follows:

1. *Matching Like Coins.* The student is presented with several different coins and is taught to place all the same coins in the same group. This is taught with the front and back of the coin. Students who are nonverbal may have a request on their AAC device to turn over a coin to help them match it. It will be important that the student learn to match them regardless of which side of the coin is visible. It is important that actual coins be used when teaching matching and later identification. Students with cognitive impairments should always use the actual coin. Students without cognitive impairments may eventually move to simulation coins or coins on worksheets.

2. *Identifying the Name and Value of a Penny and the Name and Value of a Nickel.* Most teachers will begin with the penny and the nickel, since they are so visually distinct. The student is usually taught the name and value of the coin at the same time. For example, the teacher may present a penny and say, "This is a penny and it is worth one cent." Students who have difficulty remembering names and values may be taught little sayings, such as "knuckle nickel," which is accompanied by the student's looking at the knuckles of one of his or her hands and opening the hand to show five fingers (which represent the 5 cents the nickel is worth).

3. *Identifying the Name and Value of a Dime.* Typically a dime is introduced next. After teaching about the dime, the teacher should point out the differences between the penny, nickel, and dime by size, edges (rough or smooth), and picture. The student should learn to identify the penny, nickel, and dime when presented together. A mnemonic for the dime is saying "dizzy dime" while the 10 fingers go up in the air. This saying refers to the idea that the dizzy dime fell down with 10 fingers pointing in the air (and the dime is worth 10 cents). Some teachers may take this further and say, "Dizzy dime fell in a sticker bush and has little marks on her," (referring to the marks on the side of a dime).

4. *Identifying the Name and Value of a Quarter.* Quarters are often introduced last. Although quarters are the biggest coin (excluding half-dollars and dollars), students often confuse them when presented with nickels or dimes. Pointing out distinctive features on the quarter can be helpful. Also, comparing the size of the quarter to the student's own fingers (e.g., "It covers all of your little and ring fingers") can be helpful. However, more than size needs to be stressed for students who cannot manipulate the coin due to a physical impairment.

5. *Identifying and Counting Dollar Bills.* Students will also need to know how to identify the various dollar bills (e.g., 1-, 5-, 10-, and 20-dollar bills) and how to add them together. Students should be familiar with the newer and the older bills, since the older bills are still in circulation.

6. *Counting Like Coins.* Students first learn to count like coins. They are taught to count pennies by ones, count nickels by 5s, count dimes by 10s, and count quarters by 25. If the student has already been taught how to count by 5s and 10s, this will help the student to learn how to count like coins.

7. *Counting Unlike Coins.* Students are typically taught to count two unlike coins, followed by three or four unlike coins. One strategy is to teach the student to first group like coins together and then start counting the coins with the highest value, then the coins of the next highest value, and so on (Stein et al., 1997). For example, if the student is given one nickel, two quarters, and three dimes, the student would first count the two quarters, then the dimes, then the nickels.

8. *Making Equivalent Change.* To make equivalent change, the student first learns the various combina-

tions of smaller coins that equal larger coins. For example, the student learns that two dimes and one nickel equal a quarter. After that is accomplished, the student is taught to count various sets of coins to determine whether the change is the desired amount. An example is to determine whether two quarters is the same as four dimes and two nickels.

9. *Verifying Change.* To verify change, students are taught to begin with the price and count the coins received as change, beginning with the coin of smallest value. The derived number is then compared to the amount given to pay for the item. For example, if the student bought an item for 26 cents, paid 50 cents, and received four pennies and two dimes, the student would say "26" and count the four pennies (27, 28, 29, 30) and then count the two dimes (40, 50). The student knows the change is correct since she got the same amount she paid for the item. Creating situations in which the student needs to verify change after making a purchase in a pretend school store or during community-based instruction will help reinforce this skill.

10. *Decimal Notation.* Students are first taught the cent sign and dollar sign, as in 35¢ and $5. When teaching decimal notation, the student is taught that the two numbers to the right of the decimal are cents and the numbers to the left of the decimal are dollars. After practice with this, students should be shown examples in which there are no dollars ($ .45) or no cents ($6.00). Typically, showing students cents between 1 and 9 is not done until later because of the need to have a zero after the decimal (e.g., $1.07). This is confusing to many students and should be introduced after students have a good grasp of this skill (Stein et al., 1997). Giving students many examples to read from, such as price lists, menus, and clothing tags, will help students apply this skill. As students learn to read, it is important that money is expressed in the story to reinforce the skill.

11. *Making Purchases with Money.* Besides being able to read decimal notation, it is important that students understand how much money to give a cashier after they read (or hear) the amount requested. For example, if an item costs $1.42, students need to be able to give an appropriate amount, based upon the coins that they have available (whether this is $1.50, two $1 bills, or the exact change). Creating exercises in which the students are given certain amounts of money and need to indicate how much they would give for a purchase will help reinforce this skill. Having the student verify the change afterward will help with the previous skill.

12. *Word Problems.* Students will eventually be taught to answer word problems that deal with money. It is important that this occur after students have had experience with basic word problems dealing with single digits.

Software for Money Calculations. There is a lot of different software available for students to learn how to identify, count, and use money. For example, Dollars & Cents Series (manufactured by Attainment Co.) provides instruction in identification and value of coins and bills up to $50; grouping of money and what it is worth; shopping trips to a "Money Mall" in which there are items to purchase and students must select the correct amount of dollars and coins to make purchases; and exercises in which the student is a cashier and must select the correct amount of change to return, with hundreds of purchasing situations available. Some other examples of money programs are Coin Critters (manufactured by Nordic Software, Inc.), Touch Money (manufactured by Riverdeep), Money Skills 1.4.1 and 2.0 (manufactured by Marblesoft), Money Challenge (manufactured by GAMCO Educational Software) and Money Town (manufactured by Knowledge Adventure). Many of these programs come with alternate access options (e.g., scanning with switch use).

To the greatest extent possible, students should be taught money management and checkbook skills. This may be done manually, or software may be used both to teach the skill and as a money management tool. For example, in a study by Davies, Stock, and Weymeyer (2002), specially designed software was used to improve management of personal checking accounts. Software use was found to reduce errors and be more effective than the traditional manual method when used with students with mental retardation. Teachers will need to carefully consider the effective use of software for instruction and as a management tool as more-sophisticated software continues to become available.

Calculator Use for Money. Some students may be taught to use a calculator for various problems involving money, such as budgeting and checkbook use. However, some students with cognitive impairments may be taught to use a calculator in lieu of learning to count change. In this latter situation, the student may be taught to use either a count-up or a count-down method.

When a student is making purchases, a calculator may be used to keep track of the amount so that the student has enough money when arriving at the cashier. In the **count-up** method, the student adds together the amount of each purchase until coming to or going over a predetermined number. For example, if the student has $20.00, the predetermined amount may be $18.00 (because of tax). The student enters the amount of each item, and must stop getting items and put the last item back if the amount goes over $18.00. (Depending upon the student's ability, he or she may return a different item if he or she knows how to subtract its price.) In order for this method to be effective, the student must recognize when the amount displayed on the calculator is over the predetermined amount.

An easier way to use the calculator for shopping is to use the **count-down method**. In this method, the calculator is set at the amount of money available for spending. When the student finds an item to purchase, the student presses the minus sign and enters the price of the item. The student then presses the equals sign. The student is taught to check the display on the calculator to determine if there is enough money to buy more items (Westling & Fox, 2004). If the calculator goes to zero (or less than zero), the student is taught to put back the last item (or a different item if the student knows how to add an amount back). The advantage to this method is that the student does not have to recognize whether the number displayed on the calculator is larger than the predetermined amount. He only needs to recognize the zero. One word of caution is that some calculators will show negative numbers instead of a zero. In this situation, either a different calculator should be used, or the student is taught to look for the minus sign (and treat it like a zero).

Give-to-Next-Dollar Strategy. The give-to-next-dollar strategy is designed for students who are unable to count change or use a calculator. Students are taught to count dollar bills and give one more dollar than the amount heard. For example, if the cashier said that the amount was $4.32, the student would count out four dollars and then one more dollar (equaling $5.00). This strategy requires students to be able to count out dollar bills. (Some students also may be able to learn to use this strategy using $5 and $10 bills.)

Money Card Strategy. Some students are unable to count change or dollars, but can match coins and dollar bills. In these instances, cards are made up with the proper amount of money attached to them and a symbol for what they represent. For example, the soda machine in the community-based vocational setting that the student uses for break costs 55 cents for a soda. The student may have a card with two quarters and a nickel and a symbol of a soda on the card. In this method the student matches the amount to the card. Cards can be made for the bus, coin-operated washing machines, snack machines, public telephones, and other items. (It should be noted that there are alternative strategies for soda and snack machines, such as putting in a coin and pushing the desired item after each coin is dropped in until the machine releases the soda or snack and then checking for change.)

Predetermined-Amount Strategy. Some students will need to use a predetermined-amount strategy. In this strategy the student is given a certain amount to give the cashier or machine. When grocery shopping, the student has a $20 bill that is given to the cashier, regardless of the amount. (The person giving the money needs to be certain that the items on the picture shopping list will not exceed the amount.) When operating a soda machine, the student is given $1.00 to put into the machine. This is the least complex strategy and is typically used for students who are unable to master other strategies.

Time

Traditional Time Instruction. Students are taught to tell time as a part of the traditional and functional math curricula. Students will need to learn both analog and digital forms of clocks, since both are encountered in various settings. A typical scope and sequence of learning to tell time is as follows:

1. *Basic Clock Identification.* Basic clock identification includes discriminating the hour hand from the minute hand (by showing how one is short and the other is long), knowing which way the clock hands move, and knowing that the numbers on the clock represent hours. A clock that has notch marks repre-

senting the minutes is often used. Clocks whose hands can be moved should be used for instruction. It is especially helpful to use a clock whose minute hand moves automatically when the hour hand is moved, so that the students can see the actual movement of the clock hands.

2. *Telling Time to the Hour.* When the hour hand points to a number and the minute hand is on the twelve, students are taught that it is __________ o'clock. Some teachers will teach the hour hand only, without referring to the minute hand. Referring to activities that occur on the hour or pointing out each time it is another hour will help students understand the length of time of one hour. Many teachers will teach how this looks on a digital clock, while others will wait to teach this after learning the analog clock. Whichever sequence is used, it is important that students be able to read both types of clock, match the equivalent times (clock time to written time), and know how to write out the time.

3. *Telling Time to the Half Hour.* Although it is relatively easy for most students to learn that the minute hand pointing to the 6 means 30 minutes, some students will have difficulty learning which hour it is. Knowing the direction that the hands move will help students understand that when the hour hand is between the 5 and the 6, for example, it is 5:30, since it was 5:00 and is not yet 6:00.

4. *Telling Time to the Quarter Hour.* Typically students learn how to tell time to the quarter hour next. For example, 5:15, 5:30, and 5:45. For some students, terms such as "15 minutes before 6" (or any amount of minutes *before* an hour) are taught after they learn to tell time by expressing it as minutes *after* the hour, in order to avoid confusion. Teachers may have students count the notches to show that there are 15 minutes when the minute hand is pointing to the 3, for example. Some teachers will introduce counting by 5s at this time (if they did not introduce it when telling time by the half hour).

5. *Telling Time in 5-Minute Increments.* Being able to count by 5s will help students identify the minutes. Students are typically taught to say "zero" at the top of the clock and then count by 5s until reaching the minute hand. Over time, students are taught to do this automatically.

6. *Telling Time to the Minute.* When teaching time to the minute, students are taught to first count by 5s, until they reach a numeral before the minute hand, then switch to counting by minutes to get the correct number.

7. *Alternate Ways of Expressing Time.* If the student was not taught the digital way of reading a clock along with the analog, it would be introduced at this time. Students are taught that another way of saying "18 minutes after 3" is 3:18. Other terms used in expressing time are also introduced at this time, such as "quarter after" (meaning 15 minutes after) and "half past" (meaning 30 minutes).

8. *Minutes before an Hour.* Stein et al. (1997) suggest teaching minutes before an hour in a scope and sequence to prevent confusion. For example, teaching students to identify that it is 15 minutes before the hour or 10 minutes before the hour is accomplished by teaching students to count counterclockwise (i.e., starting at 12, but counting in the opposite direction). Since many people give the time as minutes before an hour, this skill will be important for students to learn.

Software. There are several software programs available that provide opportunities for students to practice telling time. For example, Clock Shop (manufactured by Nordic Software) is designed for the elementary and secondary student and teaches digital and analog time with lessons ranging from one-minute to hour intervals. Clockworks (manufactured by William K. Bradford Publishing Co.) is designed for preschool and elementary grades and teaches time in hour to five-minute increments.

Antecedent Prompts. Some students may have difficulty learning to tell the minutes on an analog clock. One strategy to assist students is the use of a circular number line that is placed around the clock face in order to show the minute numbers (see Figure 16–8). This may be used for initial instruction for telling time and then faded, or kept in place. Some clocks and wristwatches are available with the minute numbers on the clock face to assist with telling time.

Identifying Specific Times When Unable to Tell Time. Some students may not be able to learn to tell the time. However, it is important that they be able to tell when it is time for breaks, lunch, and other events

FIGURE 16–8
Clock face with a circular number line

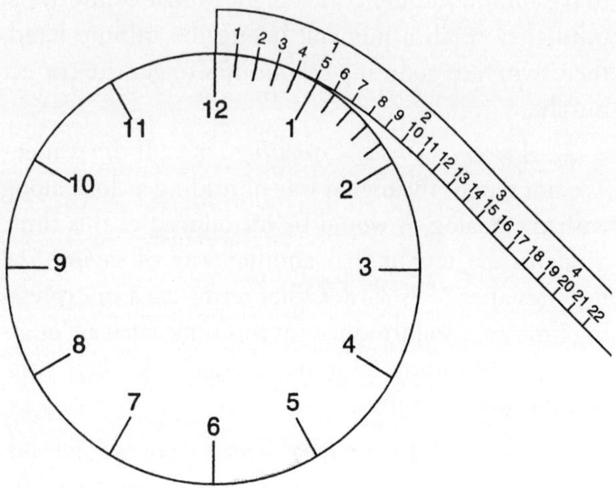

Note. From *Teaching Students with Learning Problems*, 5/e, by Mercer/Mercer. © 1998. Reprinted by permission of Prentice-Hall, Inc., Upper Saddle River, NJ.

during the work or school day. One approach is to have the student wear a digital watch, and have a card indicating when it is lunchtime (e.g., a lunch symbol and "12:00"). The problem with this strategy is that some students will miss the 12:00 time and not know that when it is 12:01 they can still leave for lunch. If lunchtime is indicated as occurring from 12:00 to 12:30 and the student cannot count, then it will still be difficult to know what to do when it is 12:01. To overcome this problem when using a digital clock, cards with all the times occurring during lunchtime or break time can be used. In some situations, students may keep their watch beeping on the hour and learn to check the card indicating breaktime or lunchtime each time they hear the watch beep. An alarm could also be set as to when lunch break occurs. However, this may not always be feasible. A different approach is using an analog watch.

Learning to determine break time and lunchtime or other specific times when the individual cannot tell time is usually easiest with a modified analog watch. Analog watches can be modified by placing color coding along the period of time the hour hand would be pointing to indicate a specific time. For example, if the student should take his lunch between 12:00 and 12:30 at the community-based vocational site, he would have a color-coded card (e.g., blue) with the lunch symbol and the watch would be marked with blue at the numeral 12 and halfway between the 12 and 1 (corresponding to the area in which the small hand is located when it is 12:00 to 12:30). Some teachers put the color just between the numbers, and others will put the color like a pie wedge coming from the center out between the numbers. Coloring the watches can occur by adding color along the outer ring of the numbers, on top of the plastic cover, or directly to the number area underneath the plastic cover area. These types of modifications can be made to regular watches or to watches made for individuals who are blind, which allow the plastic cover to be removed so the hands can be touched.

High-tech devices may also be used to assist students with time management skills. For example, Davies, Stock, and Wehmeyer (2002) used a palmtop computer with automated schedule-prompting software to increase the independence of students with mental retardation in performing daily living tasks. As with all types of technology, it is important to ascertain that it will be accessible for students with physical disabilities.

Calendar Use

Besides learning about the time of day, students also need to learn about the time of week, month, and year. Students will typically learn the names of the days of the week first, followed by the names of the months, and the year. From this they are taught how many days are in a week and how many months in a year. Finally they are taught how to use a calendar to answer questions about the date, day, and month (Bos & Vaughn, 2002).

Modified Calendar. Some students may be unable to learn the names of the days and months of the traditional calendar. Students can still learn about the progression of time. Although this may be done as a group activity, teaching students to manage their own individual calendar more closely approximates adult calendar use and can be helpful to the student in anticipating events. Modified calendars may consist of calendars for the day, week, or month.

Some students will benefit from having their own calendar or schedule for the day. These are referred to as **object calendars**, **anticipations shelves**, or **picture schedules** (Rowland, Schweigert, & Prickett, 1995). This type of calendar includes objects, pictures, symbols, and/or words that represent major activities that occur throughout the day. Pictures or objects for morning circle, functional reading skills, break time, and so forth are represented. One way of teaching daily object calendar use is to teach the student to select the object/picture for the current activity, take it to the location of the activity, and perform the activity. When the activity is over, the object/picture is placed in a "Finished" box or bag and the next activity is selected from the object calendar. This type of modified day calendar assists students with transitioning between activities and helps students to follow a schedule.

Just as many students and adults have their own personal calendars, many students will benefit from having their own personal **week strip**. A week strip shows the seven days of the week and is marked with symbols representing the events that will be occurring that week. For example, the week strip may include birthdays, school activities (assembly, pep rally, community trip), home activities (movie, visits to a friend), or other events symbolized by pictures, symbols, or small objects. Parents are encouraged to put items on the week strip as well. Students are taught to mark out the days that have occurred with a simple X or slash. (It is important that the activities on the calendar remain visible for the student to refer to.) The current day may be highlighted with a moving circle. Students are taught to look for upcoming events, events occurring that day, and past events. Not only does this help students learn the passage of time, it also provides a topic of conversation. Students can use week strip calendars to show people what they have been doing or will be doing, as well as ask on their AAC device such questions as "What did you do yesterday?" and "What are you doing later this week?" (See Chapter 8 on AAC for more information on conversational skills in this area.) Some students who master weekly strips will move on to two-week strips. From there, some students may go on to a three-week and then a one-month calendar. Some will be able to use a full-year calendar.

SUMMARY AND CONCLUSION

Depending upon their capabilities, students with physical or multiple disabilities may be taught academic math skills, functional math skills, or both. Several possible barriers to learning and performing math skills may be encountered, such as poor motor skills; restricted language ability; poor literacy skills; distractibility and disorganization; absences and fatigue; and cognitive or perceptual problems. These barriers may be lifted through the use of adaptations, systematic strategies, and assistive technology.

Students will need careful assessment of their math skills. This can occur through standardized achievement tests, diagnostic tests, curriculum-based measurement, informal tests, portfolio assessment, and error analysis. Each of these has various uses, and care must be taken that adaptations are in place for the students with physical or multiple disabilities. It is also important that the teacher's instruction is carefully examined to be sure that general principles of math instruction are in place, such as building on previous learning, providing systematic and explicit instruction, promoting active student involvement, using appropriate learning strategies, using appropriate computer-assisted instruction, and promoting proper adaptations and attitudes.

There are a variety of math skills that may be taught, including precomputational skills, computational skills, word problems, advanced math skills, and functional math skills. All of these various skills may need various adaptations and alternate teaching strategies to assist with learning and accessing the material. Teachers who provide services to individuals with physical or multiple disabilities must carefully determine the best approach to take for each student and closely monitor the student's progress to determine when further modifications or instruction is needed.

QUESTIONS FOR DISCUSSION

1. You have a fourth-grade student with myelomeningocele (spina bifida) transfer into your classroom in the fall. You do not have any information on the student, nor are you sure what the student has retained over the summer. What type of assessment(s) would you select to determine how the student is functioning in math?
2. Several students in your class were making the following addition errors. What is an error

analysis and what type of errors are these? What should you do as a teacher to correct them?

$$\begin{array}{r} 58 \\ +\ 34 \\ \hline 812 \end{array} \quad \begin{array}{r} 43 \\ +\ 20 \\ \hline 80 \end{array} \quad \begin{array}{r} 12 \\ +\ 6 \\ \hline 6 \end{array} \quad \begin{array}{r} 6 \\ +\ 7 \\ \hline 12 \end{array} \quad \begin{array}{r} 4 \\ +\ 3 \\ \hline 6 \end{array}$$

3. You are working with a young student with cerebral palsy who is unable to match a numeral to a set of items (e.g., the numeral 5 to five erasers). What skills are necessary to do this? What student skills would you check as a teacher?
4. One of your students lacks fine-motor skills. What are some possible ways to help the student be able to calculate addition problems requiring regrouping? What about multiplication problems?
5. There are several different strategies for teaching money. For a student with multiple disabilities who has a cognitive impairment, what are the possible strategies that can be used to teach money? What would determine which one would be selected?

FOCUS ON THE NET

Closing the Gap
http://closingthegap.com

This site provides searchable database on assistive technology and software that can be used to support literacy and other areas in special education and rehabilitation.

Educational Resources
http://www.edresources.com

This particular site allows searching by subject, title, topic, and age range and provides a description of each software program.

Eisenhower National Clearinghouse
http://www.enc.org

This site offers mathematics and science curriculum resources from kindergarten to 12th grade. The user can be linked to lesson plans and activities in math and science, professional development opportunities, and reference sources. There are a variety of math topics categorized by subject areas within mathematics (e.g., advanced mathematics, data analysis and probability, algebra, geometry, applied mathematics, measurements, number and operations, problem solving). Education bulletins are also available.

The Math Forum
http://www.forum.swarthmore.edu/index.js.html

This site offers information for students and teachers alike. Students in grades kindergarten through 12 may ask Dr. Math math questions, answer problems of the week, participate in an Internet math hunt or math magic. Activities, software, organizations, and reference materials are available. Teachers may join in discussion groups, check out user-contributed Web-based classroom materials and lessons, and link to many resources and materials. There is also a research division and a parents' and citizens' section on this Web site.

The National Council of Teachers of Mathematics
http://standards.nctm.org/document

The National Council of Teachers of Mathematics (NCTM) is the largest nonprofit professional association of mathematics educators in the world. NCTM offers vision, leadership, and avenues of communication for mathematics educators at the elementary school, middle school, high school, and college and university levels.

PlaneMath
http://www.planemath.com

This site provides activities pertaining to math and aeronautics. It was originally designed for students with physical disabilities who have difficulty manipulating objects and may not consider aeronautics a career possibility. Through carefully arranged activities and the use of multimedia, children with and without disabilities learn about math concepts and aeronautics. Parent and teacher information is provided as well as links to other sites. PlaneMath is currently funded through NASA.

REFERENCES

Anderson, P. J., & Spain, B. (1977). *The child with spina bifida.* London: Oxford University Press.

Barratta-Lorton, M. (1976). *Mathematics their way.* Menlo Park, CA: Addison-Wesley.

Beatty, L. S., Madden, R., Gardner, E. F., & Karlsen, B. (1995). Stanford Diagnostic Mathematics Test—Fourth Edition. San Antonio, TX: Harcourt Brace Educational Measurement.

Bos, C. S., & Vaughn, S. (2002). *Teaching students with learning and behavior problems* (5th ed.). Boston: Allyn & Bacon.

Bottge, B. A., & Hasselbring, T. S. (1993). A comparison of two approaches for teaching complex, authentic mathematics problems to adolescents in remedial math classes. *Exceptional Children, 59,* 556–566.

Bottge, B. A., Heinrichs, M., Chan, S., Mehta, Z. D., & Watson, E. (2003). Effects of video-based and applied problems on the procedural math skills of average- and low-achieving adolescents. *Journal of Special Education Technology, 18,* 5–22.

Bryant, B. R., & Rivera, D. P. (1997). Educational assessment of mathematics skills and abilities. *Journal of Learning Disabilities, 30,* 57–68.

Butler, F. M., Miller, S. P., Lee, K., & Pierce, T. (2001). Teaching mathematics to students with mild-to-moderate mental retardation: A review of the literature. *Mental Retardation, 39,* 20–31.

Case, L. P., Harris, K. R., & Graham, S. (1992). Improving the mathematical problem-solving skills of students with learning disabilities: Self-regulated strategy development. *Journal of Special Education, 26,* 1–19.

Christenson, S. L., Ysseldyke, J. E., & Thurlow, M. L. (1989). Critical instructional factors for students with mild handicaps: An integrative review. *Remedial and Special Education, 10*(5), 21–31.

Coburn, T. G., Bushey, B. J., Holton, L. C., Latozas, D., Mortimer, D., & Shotwell, D. (1992). *Patterns.* Reston, VA: National Council of Teachers of Mathematics.

Connolly, A. J. (1988). *Key math—revised: A diagnostic inventory of essential mathematics.* Circle Pines, MN: American Guidance Service.

Davies, D. K., Stock, S. E., & Wehmeyer, M. L. (2002). Enhancing independent time-management skills of individuals with mental retardation using a palmtop personal computer. *Mental Retardation, 40,* 358–365.

Erenberg, S. R. (1995). An investigation of the heuristic strategies used by students with and without learning disabilities in their acquisition of the basic facts of multiplication. *Learning Disabilities, 6,* 9–12.

French, K. (1995). Mathematics performance of children with spina bifida. *Physical Disabilities: Education and Related Services, 14,* 9–27.

Fuchs, L., & Fuchs, D. (1988). Curriculum-based measurement: A methodology for evaluating and improving student programs, *Diagnostique, 14,* 3–13.

Fulk, B. M. (1992). Math: Individualized instruction for students with mild handicaps. *Intervention in School and Clinic, 27,* 236–240.

Gessel, J. K. (1983). Diagnostic Mathematics Inventory/Mathematics System. Monterey, CA: CTB/McGraw-Hill.

Ginsberg, H. P., & Mathews, S. C. (1984). Diagnostic Test of Arithmetic Strategies. Austin, TX: Pro-Ed.

Gleason, M., Carnine, D., & Boriero, D. (1990). Improving CAI effectiveness with attention to instructional design in teaching story problems to mildly handicapped students. *Journal of Special Education Technology, 10,* 129–136.

Good, T. L. (1983). Classroom research: A decade of progress. *Educational Psychologist, 18,* 127–144.

Hammill, D. D., & Bryant, B. R. (1991). Standardized assessment and academic intervention. In H. L. Swanson (Ed.), *Handbook on the assessment of learning disabilities: Theory, research, and practice* (pp. 373–406). Austin, TX: Pro-Ed.

Heddens, J. W., & Speer, W. R. (1997). *Today's mathematics. Part II: Activities and instructional ideas* (9th ed.). Upper Saddle River, NJ: Merrill/Prentice Hall.

Heller, K. W. (1999). *Instructional modifications in beginning math skills for students with severe speech and physical impairments.* Unpublished manuscript.

Heller, K. W., Alberto, P. A., Forney, P. E., & Schwartzman, M. (1996). *Understanding physical, sensory, and health impairments.* Pacific Grove, CA: Brooks/Cole.

Heller, K. W., Dangel, H., & Sweatman, L. (1995). Systematic selection of adaptations for students with muscular dystrophy. *Journal of Physical and Developmental Disabilities, 7,* 253–265.

Hofmeister, A. M. (1984). The special educator in the information age. *Peabody Journal of Education, 62,* 5–21.

Horn, D. [illegible] (1985). [illegible] spina bifida [illegible]. *Developmental Medicine and Child Neurology, 27,* 713–720.

Hughes, C. [illegible] (1988). Teaching self-management skills: Promising practices. *Teaching Exceptional Children,* [illegible]

Hunt, G. M. (1981). Spina bifida: Implications for 100 children at school. *Developmental Medicine and Child Neurology, 23,* 160–172.

Kaufman, A. S., & Kaufman, N. L. (1985). Kaufman Test of Educational Achievement. Circle Pines, MN: American Guidance Service.

Land, L. C. (1977). [illegible] children with [illegible] (Ed.), *Myelomeningocele* (pp. 115–140). New York: Grune & Stratton.

[illegible] students with learning disabilities. *Learning Disabilities Research and Practice, 11,* 58–65.

Meichenbaum, D. (1977). *Cognitive-behavior modification.* [illegible]

Mercer, C. D., & Mercer, A. R. (2001). *Teaching students* [illegible] Upper Saddle River [illegible]

Mercer, C. D., & Miller, S. P. (1992). Teaching students with learning problems in math to acquire, understand, and apply basic math facts. *Remedial and Special Education, 13*(3), 19–35, 61.

Mercer, C. D., & Miller, S. P. (1994). Implications of constructivism for teaching math to students with moderate to mild disabilities. *Journal of Special Education, 28,* 290–306.

Miller, S. P., & Mercer, C. D. (1993a). Mnemonics: Enhancing the math performance of students with learning difficulties. *Intervention in School and Clinic, 29,* 78–82.

Miller, S. P., & Mercer, C. D. (1993b). Using data to learn about concrete-semiconcrete-abstract instruction for students with math disabilities. *Learning Disabilities Research, 8*(2), 89–96.

Miller, S. P., & Mercer, C. D. (1997). Educational aspects of mathematics disabilities. *Journal of Learning Disabilities 30,* 47–56.

Miller, S. P., Mercer, C. D., & Dillon, A. S. (1992). Acquiring and retaining math skills. *Intervention in School and Clinic, 28,* 105–110.

Miller, S. P., Strawser, S., & Mercer, C. D. (1996). Promoting strategic math performance among students with learning disabilities. *LD Forum, 21*(2), 34–40.

Montague, M., & Bos, C. S. (1986). The effect of cognitive strategy training on verbal math problem solving performance of learning disabled adolescents. *Journal of Learning Disabilities, 19,* 26–33.

National Council of Teachers of Mathematics (NCTM). (1989). *Curriculum and evaluation standards for school mathematics.* Reston, VA: Author.

National Council of Teachers of Mathematics (NCTM). (2000). *Electronic edition of principles and standards for school mathematics.* [illegible]

Paulson, F. L., Paulson, P. R., & Meyer, C. A. (1991). What makes a portfolio a portfolio? *Educational Leadership, 48*(5), 60–63.

[illegible]

Polloway, E. A., & Patton J. R. (1993). *Strategies for teaching learners with special needs.* New York: Merrill.

Renga, S., & Dalla, L. (1993). Affect: A critical component of mathematical learning in early childhood. In R. Jensen (Ed.), *Research ideas for the classroom: Early childhood mathematics* (pp. 22–39). New York: Macmillan.

Reys, R. E., Suydam, N., Lindquist, M. M., & Smith, N. L. (1998). *Helping children learn mathematics.* Boston: Allyn & Bacon.

Rivera, D. (1994). Portfolio assessment. *LD Forum, 19*(4), 14–17.

Rowland, C., Schweigert, P. D., & Prickett, J. G. (1995). Communication systems, devices, and modes. In K. M. Heubner, J. G. Prickett, T. R. Welch, & E. Joffee (Eds.), *Hand in hand: Essentials of communication and orientation and mobility for your students who are deaf-blind* (pp. 219–259). New York: AFB Press.

Author Index

Abruscato, J., 489
Accardo, P. J., 34
Achenbach, A., 254
Agran, M., 370, 371
Aksu, F., 88, 93
Alberman, E., 88
Alberto, P. A., 8, 15, 31, 40, 51, 60, 61, 76, 88, 89, 91, 174, 232, 238, 309, 311, 312, 319, 321, 402, 409, 442, 471, 476, 502
Albin, J. M., 386
Albright, A. L., 97
Alcouloumre, D. S., 170
Alexander, M. A., 88
Alexander, R., 277, 286, 298, 299
Algatt-Bergstrom, P., 63
Allen, M. G., 475, 487, 488
Alley, G. R., 428, 479, 483
Allgood, P., 251, 255, 259, 266, 309
Alper, B. S., 290
Alper, S., 169, 170
Alpert, C. L., 265
Alston, J., 443, 446
Alvermann, D., 428, 483
Alwell, M., 267
American Dental Association, 315
American Radio Relay League, 355
Andersen, R. D., 71
Anderson, A., 341
Anderson, E., 409, 443
Anderson, L. M., 464
Anderson, P. J., 502
Anderson, P. L., 449
Anderson, T. H., 472
Anthony, H. M., 464
Archer, A., 424
Armbruster, B., 414, 415, 418, 424, 426, 472
Arnold, S., 251, 266
Arvedson, J., 290, 292, 299
Ault, M. M., 320
Austin, J., 228
Avery, M. E., 62
Avezaat, C., 40
Azcue, M. P., 88

Babbitt, R., 278
Badley, E. M., 6
Baker, B. R., 246
Baker, S., 134
Bale, J. F., 71
Balfar, H., 88
Ball, E. W., 415
Banajee, M., 248, 255
Banbury Cross Therapeutic Equestrian Center, 358
Banit, D. M., 34
Banta, J., 34
Baratta-Lorton, M., 511, 517
Barcus, J. M., 381
Barnard, D., 13
Barnhart, H. X., 73
Bartel, N. R., 151, 154
Barth, J., 38
Barudin, S. I., 434
Bassett, D. S., 533
Bates, E., 228
Batshaw, M. L., 71, 72
Battle, C. W., 233
Bauer, R. E., 88
Baumann, J. F., 429
Baumgart, D., 249
Bazler, J. A., 493, 494
Bean, R. M., 472, 473, 482, 483
Beatty, L. S., 505
Beaulieu, C. L., 39, 42
Beck, I. L., 472
Beecher, R., 277, 283
Begun, W., 386
Behrman, B., 38
Behrman, R. E., 68, 93
Beilke, R. L., 34
Bell, S., 36
Bellamy, G. T., 386
Belman, A. L., 74
Benson, J., 292
Berg, M. H., 238
Bergeron, B. S., 429
Berman, B., 98
Berninger, V. W., 401, 409, 411, 441, 471
Berninger, W. S., 403, 422
Berry, D. H., 69
Best, G. A., 16
Best, S. J., 3, 16, 20, 22, 25, 31, 50, 59, 76, 87, 151, 152, 164, 179, 320, 337
Beukelman, D. R., 103, 227, 233, 403, 441
Bierle, T., 76, 92
Bierman, C. W., 61
Bigge, J. L., 4, 16, 23, 24, 50, 87, 105, 113, 114, 115, 121, 123, 124, 133, 134, 135, 137, 142, 143, 144, 145, 146, 151, 152, 153, 156, 157, 158, 159, 161, 163, 164, 169, 172, 174, 175, 179, 227, 261, 309, 337, 352, 353, 367, 377, 444, 446
Blachman, B. A., 415
Blackman, M. D., 71
Blackstone, S. W., 237, 238, 239, 248, 270, 403
Bleck, E. E., 36, 51, 61, 65
Blickstein, I., 88
Blischak, D. M., 402, 442, 471
Block, M. E., 347, 348
Bloomberg, G. R., 61
Blosser, J. L., 45
Blum, R. W., 35
Bly, L., 90, 286
Boehme, R., 286
Bolden, S., 68
Boos, M. L., 51
Boriero, D., 509
Bos, C. S., 427, 429, 449, 458, 472, 475, 486, 510, 521, 531, 538
Bottge, B. A., 531
Bouchard, S., 338, 349
Bowdin, J., 232, 238
Bowe, F., 369

Bowser, G., 186, 192
Braakman, R., 40
Bradley, B., 80
Bradley, L., 415
Bragaw, D., 488
Branson, T. A., 465
Branston-McLean, M. B., 249
Brazelton, T. B., 279
Breath, D., 298
Brigance, A., 340
Briggs, A., 312
Brineman, D. G., 419
Brolin, D. E., 129, 141, 372, 373
Brooke, V., 381
Brouwers, P., 74
Browder, D. M., 432
Brown, F., 156, 230
Brown, L., 157, 169, 248, 432
Brown, L. K., 61, 73
Brown, L. W., 93
Brown, M. W., 412
Brown, R. T., 69
Bruce, D. A., 34
Bruskin, D. M., 237, 270
Bryan, A. A., 229
Bryant, B. R., 504, 505
Bryant, P., 415
Bulgren, J. A., 481
Bullis, M., 387
Bullock, J., 519
Burkhart, L. J., 218, 219
Burleson, D., 346, 347
Burns, M. S., 417
Butler, C., 97, 98, 204
Butler, F. M., 530
Butterworth, J., 117
Buzan, T., 174
Byrne, M. R., 22, 25

Caldwell, D., 69
Caldwell, T. H., 76, 77, 79, 92
California Department of Education, 123, 124, 338
Campbell, M., 202, 214, 216
Campbell, S., 97, 98
Caretto, V., 88, 299
Carlson, B. C., 141
Carlson, F., 404, 409
Carnine, D., 509, 514
Carson, R. A., 13
Carter, M., 267
Caruso, M. B., 412
Case, L. P., 531
Cassatt-James, E. L., 270, 403
Castelle, M., 251, 255, 259, 266
Catlin, F. I., 71
Caton, W., 40
Cazden, C. B., 412
Cech, D., 286
Centers for Disease Control and Prevention, 80
Chadwick, D., 39, 42
Chadwick, O., 401
Chall, J. S., 472
Challenor, Y. B., 52
Chan, S., 531
Chapin, J. R., 475
Charney, E. B., 34
Chomsky, C., 443
Christenson, S. L., 507
Church, G., 199, 215, 218, 219
Cimera, R. E., 5
Clancy, R. R., 93
Clark, C. R., 240
Clark, D. B., 475
Clark, D. R., 54
Clark, F. L., 428
Clark, G. M., 114, 137, 141, 367, 372, 378, 383, 386, 387, 388, 394
Clay, M. M., 443
Clippard, D., 39
Coburn, T. G., 510
Coe, D., 278
Cohen, E., 325
Cohen, E. L., 20
Cohen, E. T., 76, 320
Cohen, M., 157
Cole, J. S., 37
Coleman, C. L., 456
Coleman, K., 413, 415
Coley, I. L., 325
Collier, D., 340
Collins, B. C., 465
Collins, K. M., 476
Com, A. L., 22, 25
Conaster, P., 347
Cone, A. A., 383
Conejo Valley Amateur Radio Club, 355
Conlon, C. J., 72
Connolly, A. J., 505
Conrad, S. S., 472
Cook, A., 220, 234
Cook, I. D., 141
Cooke, N. L., 531
Cooke, T., 88
Cordell, R. L., 72
Corr, C., 50
Corr, D., 50
Council for Exceptional Children, 20–21, 60
Covey, H. C., 3, 4, 5
Crain, S., 231
Crank, J. N., 481
Crawley, J. F., 481, 531
Cronin, M. E., 126, 128, 129, 133, 533
Crooks, G. M., 68–69
Cropp, G. J., 66
Culatta, B., 502
Cupps, B., 286
Cusick, B., 36, 53, 54, 93, 98
Cutter, J., 476
Cystic Fibrosis Foundation, 65, 66

Dadhania, J., 292
Daehler, M. W., 232
Dalla, L., 510
D'Alonzo, B. J., 141
Dammann, O., 88
D'Andrea, F. M., 412
Dangel, H., 510
Darbee, J., 204
Davidson, R. C., 22, 25
Davies, D. K., 535, 538
D'Avignon, J., 36
Davis, A., 38, 39
Davis, B., 251
Davis, H., 13
Davy, P., 32, 33
Decker, P., 312
DeCoste, D., 103, 218, 227, 442
Deitz, J. C., 204
De Lucchi, L. D., 494, 495
DeMauro, G., 298
Demchak, M. A., 152, 156, 161, 163, 164
Demmler, G. J., 71
Denti, L. G., 69
Denton, P. H., 483
DePaepe, P., 60
DePompei, R., 45
DeRuyter, F., 227, 441
Deshler, D. D., 428, 464, 481, 483
Detheridge, M., 434
Detheridge, T., 434
Dettmer, P., 188
Dias, L. S., 34
Dicarlo, C., 248, 255
Diette, G. B., 63
Diggs, C. A., 418, 419, 421, 422
Dileo, D., 374, 379
Dillon, A. S., 507
Disabato, J., 32
DiScala, C., 38
DiVesta, F. J., 482

Do, T., 46, 49
Dobson, L. N., 443, 462
Doelling, J., 60
Doherty, J. M., 444
Donaldson, J. S., 34
Donner, M., 277
Donovan, C. A., 472
Dorman, C., 36
Doster, S., 228, 234, 238
Downing, J. E., 152, 156, 161, 163, 164
DPHD Critical Issues and Leadership Committee, 320
Dryer, L. G., 418
Duhaime, A., 38
Duncan, J. L., 232
Dunn, C., 372
Dunn, L. M., 418
Duthie, J., 485
Dyck, N., 188
Dykes, M. K., 20, 22, 25, 76, 320
Dynes, M. C., 34

Easterbrooks, S. R., 22, 25
Edwards, M., 13
Eigen, H., 62
Ekwall, E. E., 458
Ellerd, D. A., 387
Elliott, D. L., 472
Ellis, A. K., 487, 488
Ellis, E. S., 312, 481
Elmayan, M. M., 68
Emery, A. E. H., 46, 49
Emery, D. W., 429
Enderle, J., 386
Englert, C. S., 463
Epilepsy Foundation of America, 93
Epps, S., 316
Epstein, L., 74
Erenberg, S. R., 526
Erikson, M. A., 34
Esscher, E., 90
Eule, J. M., 34
Evans, D. A., 403, 443

Faherty, A. S., 290
Fallon, K. A., 254
Falvey, M., 120, 165, 166, 249
Farlow, L. J., 312
Fay, G. C., 39
Fein, A. M., 61
Feinsilver, S. H., 61
Feldman, J., 63
Fernald, G., 458
Fernstrom, P., 475
Ferreiro, E., 443
Field, S., 136, 137, 141, 370, 371, 372
Fielder, K., 116
Fields, S., 490, 491
Fiewell, E., 32, 33
Finnie, N., 101, 214, 215, 298
First, L. R., 62
Fisher, S., 141
Flodmark, O., 90
Foley, B. E., 401, 409, 415, 417, 430, 471
Folzer, S. M., 38, 39, 40, 42
Forney, P. E., 8, 15, 31, 40, 51, 60, 61, 76, 88, 89, 91, 174, 309, 310, 311, 312, 318, 319, 320, 321, 325, 402, 442, 471, 476, 502
Fougeyrollas, P., 6
Foulds, R., 245
Fox, L., 120, 164, 229, 249, 313, 348, 433, 464, 536
Frank, G., 106
Franklin Institute Online, 354
Franks, C., 204
Fredrick, L., 20, 76, 320, 418, 419, 421, 422
French, K., 502
Fried-Oken, M., 401
Friedrich, W. N., 34, 35, 38
Friend, T., 413
Frinks, 493
Fuchs, D., 505
Fuchs, L., 505
Fulk, B. M., 509

Gabbard, C., 339
Gagnon, P., 472
Gahm, N., 34
Gajar, A. H., 482
Galbraith, S., 40
Gans, B. M., 401, 409, 411, 441, 471
Gardner, E., 414, 505
Gardner, H., 136
Garrison-Kane, L., 60
Gast, D., 264, 432
Gates, A. J., 76
Gee, K., 267
Gerity, B. P., 387
Gerlovich, J., 472, 474, 491, 492
Gersten, R., 134
Gessel, J. K., 505
Giangreco, M. E., 115, 120, 122
Giardina, R. G., 72, 80
Giardino, N., 63
Gibson, K. E., 381
Ginsburg, H., 280, 505
Glass, R., 290
Gleason, M., 424, 509
Gleeson, R. M., 37
Glennen, S. L., 103, 218, 243, 245, 246, 247, 260
Glennen, S. R., 215, 218
Goeckel, T., 40, 76, 309, 311, 319, 321, 325, 476
Goetz, L., 267
Goffman, E., 12, 13
Gold, M., 386
Goldberg, B., 362
Goldberg, M. J., 51
Golden, D., 181
Good, T. L., 508
Goode, R., 341
Goodnite, B., 475
Goossens, C., 231, 254, 255
Gordon, T., 188
Gortmaker, S. L., 61
Graff, J. G., 320
Graham, G., 339
Graham, S., 531
Grandinette, S., 42
Grant, H., 40
Gray, D. B., 6
Green, J. D., 240
Grenot-Scheyer, M., 120
Grether, J. K., 88
Griebel, M. L., 34
Griffin, P., 417
Groce, N., 4
Gromoll, E. W., 472
Gross, P., 157
Grossman, J. H., III, 71
Grubman, S., 74
Grunsell, J., 267
Gustafson, K. E., 65
Guyton, A., 316

Haas, M. B., 77
Hagberg, B., 90
Hagberg, G., 90
Haggerty, M. C., 62
Hagin, R. H., 448, 449
Hagner, D., 117, 374, 379
Hale, A. R., 72, 73
Hale, C. M., 72
Hall, D. M., 39
Hall, D. M. B., 197, 208
Hall, M., 465
Halle, J. W., 265

Halpern, A. S., 141, 372
Hamlett, K. W., 65
Hammill, D. D., 154, 449, 504
Ham Radio Online, 355
Hamrick, L., 473
Hancock, J., 443, 446
Handler, M., 34
Hanshaw, J. B., 71
Hanson, S. L., 39
Haring, N., 157
Harrington, C. B., 360
Harris, D., 403, 443
Harris, K. R., 531
Harryman, S., 198, 199
Hart, B., 265
Hartford, J., 34
Hartman, D. K., 472, 482
Hartoonian, H. M., 488
Hartwick, P., 45
Harty, H., 473
Harvey, B., 61, 65
Hasselbring, T. S., 531
Haynie, M., 76, 92
Heath, S. B., 412
Heddens, J. W., 530
Heiden, J., 40
Heilman, D. K., 62
Heimlich, J. E., 475
Heinrichs, M., 531
Heller, K. W., 8, 15, 20, 21, 22, 25, 31, 32, 37, 38–39, 40, 46, 48, 51, 60, 61, 62, 63, 64, 65, 67, 68, 71, 73, 76, 77, 88, 89, 91, 92, 93, 96, 97, 174, 215, 227, 232, 238, 251, 254, 255, 259, 261, 266, 309, 310, 311, 312, 318, 319, 320, 321, 325, 401, 402, 405, 409, 412, 418, 419, 421, 422, 426, 441, 442, 452, 457, 471, 476, 478, 501, 502, 510, 513, 516, 519, 530
Hemsley, R. E., 16
Hemyari, P., 38
Hendrick, I., 5
Hennessy, E., 88
Herald, J., 350, 351
Hetzroni, O. E., 231
Hill, J. L., 36, 42, 47, 48, 62, 63, 65, 66, 69, 79, 88, 90, 92
Hitchcock, M. E., 458
Hoch, T., 278
Hoffman, A., 136, 137, 370, 372
Hofmeister, A. M., 509
Hogan, M. B., 62
Holbrook, C., 22, 25
Holbrook, N. C., 431
Holt-Hale, S. A., 339
Holvoet, J. F., 320
Honig, B., 417
Hoppes, M. K., 428
Horn, D., 502
Horner, R. H., 316
Horton, S. V., 484
Hourcade, J. J., 434
Houtz, L. E., 476
Howle, J., 89, 90, 92, 281
Hubbard, D. D., 505
Hudson, P., 479, 482
Huettig, C., 340
Hughes, C., 371, 481, 482, 508
Hull, B., 349
Hunt, G. M., 502
Hunt, J., 280
Hunt, P., 267
Hurlbut, B. I., 240
Hurley, A. D., 36
Hussey, S., 220, 234
Hutchins, M., 381

Iannaccone, S. T., 46, 48
Idol, L., 429, 430
Inge, K., 381
Isaacson, S., 462
Ishler, M., 479
Iwasaki, Y., 349
Iwata, B. A., 240
Iwinski, H. J., 34

Jaffe, K. M., 39, 40
James, V., 312
Janvier, K. W., 51
Jarman, R., 475
Jarvis, W. R., 37
Jenkins, C., 160, 211
Jennett, B., 40
Jitendra, A. K., 428
Johnson, A. M., 512, 515
Johnson, D. D., 475, 484
Johnson, L. V., 339
Johnson, M., 34
Johnson, S. L., 39
Johnson-Wright, H., 360
Jones, B., 277
Jones, D., 64
Jones, M. H., 88, 90
Jones, M. W., 89
Jordan, D. R., 449
Jorm, A. F., 417
Joy, J. H., 63

Kaiser, A. P., 265, 266, 267
Kane-Johnston, K., 381
Kangas, K., 444
Kapp, S., 416
Karlan, G. R., 234
Karlsen, B., 414, 505
Kasser, S. L., 339, 340
Katims, D. S., 402, 452
Katz, C., 138
Kaufman, A. S., 504
Kaufman, N. L., 504
Keetz, A., 265
Kekelis, L., 409
Kelker, P. H., 75
Kelley, P., 387
Kelly, J., 413
Kelso, D. D., 246
Kermoian, R., 204
Khan, J. H., 89
Kiernan, W. E., 117
Kindsvatter, R., 479
King-DeBaun, P., 404, 406, 425
Kirk, M. F., 343
Kirk, S. A., 431
Kirk, W. S., 431
Klein, G. L., 64
Klein, M. D., 286, 290, 298, 299
Koch, K. D., 38, 49
Koch, L., 38
Koenig, A. J., 431
Koester, H., 456
Kokaska, C. J., 377
Koke, S., 456
Kolstoe, O. P., 114, 137, 141, 367
Koontz-Lowman, D. K., 88, 92
Koppel, A., 533
Koppenhaver, D. A., 403, 404, 409, 430, 443, 452, 456
Koreska, J., 48
Korsten, J., 192
Koury, M., 432
Kovar, A., 299
Kraat, A. W., 245, 270, 403
Kraemer, M. J., 61
Kraus, J. F., 38
Kravitz-Zodda, J., 416
Krebs, L., 88
Kregel, J., 369, 382, 386
Kucer, S. L., 443
Kurtz, L. A., 88

Kurze, T., 40
Kushner, D. S., 38

Laatsch, L. K., 36
Lafontaine, L. M., 227, 441
Lahm, E., 186
Land, L. C., 502
Langhoff-Roos, J., 88
Langone, J., 432
La Paz, S., 488
Larsen, J. W., Jr., 71
Larsen, S. C., 449
Laverie, D. A., 338, 349
Lazar, M. F., 38
LeBlanc, B., 339
Leconte, P. J., 386
Lee, K., 530
Lefton-Greif, M., 290, 292, 299
Legresley, K., 227, 441
Lehr, F., 414, 415, 418, 424
Lehrer, P., 63
Lemire, R. J., 32
Lenz, B. K., 479, 481
LeRoy, C. H., 75
Levack, N., 313
Levin, J., 198, 200, 218, 242
Levy, L. D., 88
Lewis, R., 455
Liao, S., 39
Light, J., 102, 254, 401, 402, 403, 409, 412, 413, 442, 443
Lin, A., 509
Lindgren, S., 63
Lindquist, M. M., 507, 517
Link, D., 292
Liptak, G. S., 32, 34, 35, 37, 38
Lloyd, L. L., 234, 236, 237, 240, 243, 245, 247, 409
Locke, P., 240
Lombard, R. C., 386
Lorch, E., 502
Lorch, R., 502
Lord, J., 38
Loumiet, R., 313
Lourie, K. J., 61, 73
Lovejoy, M. C., 34
Lovitt, T. C., 484
Lowry, S., 339
Loyd, R. J., 129
Lubkin, I. M., 4, 13
Lynch, R., 38

Maas, A., 40
MacArthur, C., 488
Macciocchi, S., 38
MacGinitie, R. K., 418
MacGinitie, W. H., 418
Macias, C. M., 337
MacMillan, D. L., 5
Madan-Swain, A., 69
Madden, R., 414, 505
Maddox, T., 449
Magnusson, S. J., 476
Majer, L. S., 63
Male, M., 14
Malone, L., 494, 495
Malouf, D. B., 14
Mank, D. M., 386
Manno, C., 290
Maria, K., 418
Markson, L., 63
Markwardt, F. C., 418, 504
Marsh, L. G., 531
Marshall, A. M., 265
Marshall, L. F., 38
Martin, J., 88, 312, 370, 371, 372
Martin, R., 472, 473, 474, 475, 489, 490, 491, 492, 494, 495
Martin, S., 286
Martinez, F. D., 61
Mascarenhas, M., 292
Mason, K. J., 53
Matas, J. A., 227, 441
Mathews, S. C., 505
Mathy-Laikko, P., 227, 441
Matlock, L., 116
Mayer, B., 508
Mazeika, E. J., 432
McClune, B., 475
McCuaig, M., 106
McCurtin, A., 290
McEwen, I. R., 409
McGauvran, M., 411, 414
McGinnies, J. S., 403
McIlvain-Simpson, G. R., 51
McKeown, M., 472
McLaughlin, M. J., 113, 146
McLone, D. G., 34
McLoughlin, J. A., 63
McMurray, J. L., 89, 90
McNairn, P., 413, 415
McNaughton, S., 402, 405, 442
McNerney, C., 233
McQuarter, R. J., 265
McWilliam, P., 401, 441
Mechline, K. R., 474
Mechling, L. C., 432
Medcom Trainex, 313
Meeropol, E., 37
Mehta, Z. D., 531
Meichenbaum, D., 509
Meier, F. E., 153
Melamed, B. G., 70
Mercer, A. R., 152, 312, 409, 449, 452, 458, 459, 464, 505, 506, 521, 522, 525, 530, 538
Mercer, C. D., 152, 312, 409, 449, 452, 458, 459, 464, 501, 502, 505, 506, 507, 508, 520, 521, 522, 525, 530, 531, 538
Merz, M., 38
Messick, R. G., 475
Meyer, C. A., 505
Meyers, A., 72
Meyers, B. S., 69
Meyers, L. W., 456
Michael, S. E., 349
Michaud, L., 38, 39
Middleton, J., 39
Mike, D. G., 403, 443
Miller, C., 292
Miller, D. K., 341
Miller, F., 48
Miller, R., 371, 372
Miller, S. P., 501, 502, 507, 508, 520, 530, 531
Millikin, C. C., 239
Milone, M. N., 444, 446
Minderhoud, J., 40
Minskill, E., 431
Mira, M., 45
Mirenda, P., 103, 233, 240
Mishra, A., 61
Mitchell, C. C., 32, 33, 35, 36
Mithaug, D. E., 370, 371, 381, 386
Molnar, G. E., 52
Montague, M., 531
Moon, S. M., 381
Morgan, R. L., 387
Morgan, W. J., 61
Morris, C., 97
Morris, S. E., 286, 290, 298, 299
Morton, A. A., 49
Moseley, C. F., 48
Moulton, L. R., 386
Moyer, R., 279
Mueller, G. A., 62
Mueller, H., 298, 299, 300
Muir, J., 356
Murph, J. R., 71
Murphy, S. M., 88, 92, 299
Musante, P., 337, 352, 353

Musselwhite, C., 245, 404, 425
Myers, N. A., 232
Myhr, U., 198, 199
Myles, B. S., 129

Nabe, C., 50
Nagel, K., 472
Nagels, D. A., 51, 61, 65
Nall, M., 63
National Association for Sport and Physical Education, 338
National Council of Teachers of Mathematics, 502, 503, 504, 530
National Institute of Allergy and Infectious Diseases, 73
National Institutes of Health, 39, 64
National School Boards Association, 192
Naumann, S., 457
Nehring, W. M., 88
Neilson, J., 456
Nelson, K. B., 88
Nelson, R., 35
Neubert, D. A., 386
Nguyen, T. T. H., 63
Nichols, B. A., 339
Nikiforuk, A., 4
Ninio, A., 412
Nolan, S., 428, 464
Nolet, V., 113, 146, 481
Norrlin, S., 198
Nurss, J., 411, 414

Oakes, W. J., 34
O'Brien, M. F., 34
Occupational Exposure to Blood-Borne Pathogens, 80
O'Connell, E. J., 62
Ogle, D. M., 483
O'Keefe, B., 401, 442, 457
Oliver, D. L., 474
Opper, S., 280
Osberg, J., 38
Osborn, J., 414, 415, 418, 424
Osborne, A. G., 21, 181
O'Shea, T. M., 88
Ostrosky, M. N., 265
Owen, J. H., 98
Owens, R. E., 245

Packer, B., 202
Palfrey, J. S., 76, 92
Palinscar, A. S., 476
Palisano, R., 204
Palmer, S., 279, 371
Pao, M., 61, 73
Parent, W. S., 381, 383
Park, K., 4
Park, T. S., 98
Parker, M., 339
Parker, R. M., 387
Parker, S. L., 68, 70
Parmar, R. S., 531
Parnes, P., 401, 442
Patillo, S., 426
Patton, J. R., 114, 115, 126, 128, 129, 133, 141, 312, 372, 386, 387, 388, 507, 510, 520, 533
Paulson, F. L., 505
Paulson, P. R., 505
Peacock, W. J., 98
Pearson, 522
Pearson, M. L., 37
Pearson, N. A., 449
Pearson, P. D., 484
Pellegrino, L., 88, 89, 90, 92, 97, 98
Pencharz, P. B., 88
Percy, A. K., 71
Perin, B., 99
Perlmutter, L., 432
Perlmutter, M., 232
Perret, Y. M., 71
Perrin, J. M., 61
Pete, J. M., 313
Peterson, C. A., 350
Peterson, S. K., 508
Pharoah, P. O., 88
Pickard, J., 40
Pierce, P., 401, 430, 441, 452
Pierce, T., 530
Pierz, K., 34
Pinder, G. L., 290
Pittelman, S. D., 475
Pless, I., 13
Plewis, I., 443
Poblete, X., 92
Podell, D. M., 509
Polakoff, R. J., 49, 50
Polissar, N. L., 39
Politano, P., 228, 234, 238
Polloway, E. A., 114, 115, 312, 507, 510, 520
Porreta, D. L., 348
Porter, S., 76, 77, 79, 80, 92
Poteet, J. A., 461, 531
Pottenger, F. M., 495
Powell, G., 483, 484
Powell, T. H., 75
Powers, A. R., 22, 25
Powers, L., 160, 211, 369, 372, 379, 381, 382
Powers, S. W., 66
Prentice, R., 188
Prickett, J. G., 538
Procter, S. A., 325
Protection and Advocacy, Inc., 180
Psota, C. E., 72, 80
Putnam, J., 120, 122
Putnam, P., 292

Radabaugh, 10
Radell, U., 196, 198, 199
Raikhy, E., 18
Raj, A., 61
Rankin, S. W., 465
Raphael, T. E., 464
Reed, P., 179, 184, 185, 186, 189, 192
Reid, D., 457
Reid, M. J., 62
Reid, S. R., 319
Reigel, D., 34
Reilly, S., 92
Remer, E. M., 34
Renga, S., 510
Renzaglia, A., 381
Resnick, M. D., 35
Reys, R. E., 507, 508, 510, 513, 516, 517, 518, 530
Rhodes, L. E., 386
Rios, C. M., 49
Risley, T. R., 265
Rivera, C., 134
Rivera, D., 152, 505
Roberts, R., 493, 494
Robinson, F. P., 483
Robinson, J. P., 349
Rock, A., 38
Roessler, R. T., 369
Rogers, B., 278
Rogers, M. F., 72
Rogers-Warren, A. K., 265
Roggenbuck, J. W., 349
Roghmann, K., 13
Rogow, S. M., 404, 412
Romski, M., 227, 232, 240, 265
Roscigno, C. I., 98
Rosen, K., 456
Rosenshine, B., 479
Rossi, T., 292
Roth, K., 340
Roth, T., 231
Rourke, B. P., 502
Rowland, C., 238, 538

Rowland, T., 362
Rowley-Kelly, F. C., 34
Rubin, S. E., 369
Rudolph, C., 292
Rues, J. P., 320
Ruhl, K. L., 482, 508
Runkel, P., 188
Rusch, F., 312, 381, 386
Russman, B. S., 90
Russo, C. J., 21, 181
Rutstein, R. M., 72, 73, 74
Rutter, M., 401
Ryndak, D. A., 169, 170
Ryndak, D. L., 170

Sabornie, E. J., 312
Safrit, M. J., 341
Sailor, W., 267
Sanford, C. C., 51
Santa Cruz Office of Education, 323
Sarason, S., 371
Sasaki, J., 494, 495
Sattler, J. M., 504
Savage, R. C., 38, 40, 41, 45
Schaeffler, C., 214, 215
Schalock, R. L., 117
Scheer, J., 4
Scheerenberger, R. C., 5
Schenk-Rootlieb, A. J. F., 88
Scher, M. S., 88
Scherer, M., 192
Scherfenberg, L., 198, 200, 218, 242
Scherzer, A. L., 89
Schinsky, L., 232
Schloss, C. N., 170
Schloss, P. J., 170, 482
Schmaling, K., 63
Schmuck, R., 188
Schrag, C., 98
Schroeder, J., 249
Schuler, A. L., 240
Schumaker, J. B., 428, 463, 464, 479, 483
Schut, L. B., 34
Schwartzman, M. N., 8, 15, 31, 40, 51, 60, 61, 76, 88, 89, 91, 174, 309, 311, 319, 321, 402, 442, 471, 476, 502
Schwarz, S. P., 325
Schweigert, P., 238, 538
Schwenn, M. R., 70
Scott, C. I., 51
Scott, K. S., 519
Seaman, J., 344
Secretary's Commission on Achieving Necessary Skills, 384, 385
Seidel, U. P., 401
Sensenig, L. D., 432
Serna, L., 114, 115, 494, 495
Sevcik, R. A., 227, 240, 265
Sever, J. L., 71
Severson, S., 386
Sewall, G. T., 472
Sexton, C., 472, 474, 491, 492
Shafer, M., 386
Shaffer, J., 34
Shames, R. S., 66
Shanahan, N., 361
Shanker, J. L., 458
Shapiro, J. P., 4, 6
Share, D. L., 417
Sharpton, W., 312
Sheldon, J., 463
Shepard, R. J., 338
Shephard, J., 325
Sherrill, C., 343, 344
Shinn, M. R., 505
Shioleno, O. C., 413, 415
Shurtleff, D. B., 32, 34
Shurtleff, H., 34
Siegel, E., 230
Siegel, L. G., 70
Siegel, L. S., 417
Sigafoos, J., 230
Silberman, R. K., 105, 114, 121, 135, 153
Silbert, J., 514
Silkworth, C. S., 64, 80
Silverman, F., 232, 245
Simmons, T., 413
Simonds, R. J., 72
Simpson, R. L., 129
Sindelar, P. T., 531
Singer, G., 372
Singh, Y., 434
Sirvis, B., 16, 50, 170, 352, 353
Sitler, A., 80
Sitlington, P. L., 114, 117, 137, 141, 367, 372, 378, 383, 386, 394
Skelly, M., 232
Skinner, E. A., 63
Skuse, D., 92
Slotta, J. D., 475
Small, R., 40
Smets, E. M., 69
Smith, A., 401, 403, 441, 452, 459
Smith, A. K., 402, 403, 409, 412, 413, 443
Smith, D. A., 482
Smith, D. D., 6, 12, 152
Smith, D. P., 313
Smith, M., 170, 402, 420, 426, 442, 452
Smith, N. L., 507, 517
Smith, T. K., 340, 342
Smolkin, L. B., 472
Snell, M., 120, 156, 230, 264, 312
Snow, C., 412, 417
Snow, R., 361
Snyder, P., 298
Sobol, A. M., 61
Solava, D. G., 340
Solomon, S. L., 72
Song, H. S., 63
Soucy, L., 412
Sowers, J., 160, 211, 369, 372, 379, 381, 382
Spache, G. D., 417
Spagna, M. E., 105, 114, 121, 135, 153
Spain, B., 502
Speer, W. R., 530
Spence, G. T., 69
Spencer, P., 188
Spock, A., 65
Spradlin, J. E., 265
Sprague, J. B., 98
Steele, S., 88
Steelman, J. D., 430, 452
Steensma, M., 46
Stefanich. G. P., 489
Stein, M., 514, 516, 522, 523, 526, 528, 531, 534, 535
Steinbok, P., 98
Stephens, T., 338, 458
Stern, R. J., 316
Sternberg, L., 233
Sterne, F., 90
Stevens, D. D., 464
Stevens, R., 475, 479, 487, 488
Stewart, K., 99
St. Germaine, A., 35
Stillman, R. D., 233
St. Louis, K., 245
Stock, S. E., 535, 538
Stoller, L. C., 202
Strang, J. D., 502
Stratton, J. M., 401
Strawser, S., 508
Stricklin, B., 248, 255
STRIDES Therapeutic Riding, 358
Stright, M., 312
Strommer, P., 340, 341
Struck, M., 235
Strunk, R. C., 61
Stumbo, N. J., 350

Stump, C. S., 4, 23, 24, 105, 113, 114, 115, 121, 123, 124, 134, 135, 137, 142, 143, 144, 146, 153, 161, 163
Sulzby, E., 410
Surburg, P. R., 348
Suritsky, S. K., 481
Sutton, L. N., 34
Suydam, N., 507, 517
Sweatman, L., 510
Swinehart-Jones, D., 20, 21, 215, 320, 402, 405, 452
Szekeres, S. F., 45

Taber, T., 251
Talwalkar, V., 34
Tam, C., 457
Teale, W., 410
Teasdale, G., 40
Tew, B. J., 502
Thier, H. D., 494, 495
Thiers, N., 204
Thompson, J., 34
Thompson, R. L., 65
Thurber, D. N., 449
Thurlow, M. L., 507
Thurston, L., 188
Thurston, S., 401, 442
Timmerman, V., 64
Tindel, G., 481
Todaro, A. W., 76
Todis, B., 205
Tong, T., 68
Toombs, S. K., 13
Topf, B., 432
Topp, M., 88
Tournaki-Rein, N., 509
Treanor, R. B., 4, 5, 6, 7
Troutman, A. C., 312
Truesdell, A., 202, 214, 216
Trytol, K., 312
Tsai, C., 491
Tuchman, D., 278, 292
Tucker, B., 45
Tullis, M. D., 387
Tumlin, J., 419, 457
Turner, E., 383
Tworek, P., 45
Tyler, J., 42, 45

Ulrich, D., 340
Umbreit, J., 33
Unger, D. D., 381, 383
U.S. Architectural and Transportation Barriers Compliance Board, 211
U.S. Department of Education, 20
Utah State Office of Education, 80
Uzgiris, I., 280

Vachon, V., 424
Valenta, L., 386
van der Graaf, Y., 88
Vanderheiden, G. C., 234, 236, 237, 240, 243, 245, 246, 247
Vandervelden, M. C., 417
Van de Walle, J. A., 514
van Nieuwenhuizen, O., 88
Varzos, N., 38
Vaughan, C. L., 98
Vaughn, S., 427, 429, 449, 458, 472, 475, 486, 510, 521, 538
Vecht, C. J., 40
Verberg, G., 240
Vincent, L., 249
Visser, M. R., 69
von Wendt, L., 198

Wade, G., 51
Wagner, K., 472, 474, 491, 492
Waintrup, M., 387
Walker, D. W., 531
Walker, G. J., 349
Wallace, S. J., 92, 93, 443
Walsh, D., 116
Walsh, J. M., 116
Walter, R., 278
Ward, M., 371, 372
Ware, S., 255, 259, 266
Warner, M. M., 428, 483
Warren, L., 198, 199
Warren, S. F., 265
Wasylyk, T. M., 444, 446
Watson, E., 531
Watson, S. M., 476
Wehman, P., 126, 127, 369, 378, 381, 382, 383, 386
Wehmeyer, M. L., 371, 372, 535, 538
Weiland, S., 13
Weinberger, S. E., 65
Weinstein, R. S., 508
Weiss, M., 278
Weitzman, M., 61, 72
Welch, M., 463
Weller, S. C., 34
Wells, G., 412
Westcott, M. A., 34
Westling, D. L., 120, 164, 229, 249, 313, 348, 433, 464, 536
Wetherby, A., 229, 230
White, P. H., 378
Whitman, B. Y., 34
Wicks, D., 38
Wicks, J., 38
Wilen, W., 479
Wilkinson, G., 504
Willemse, J., 88
Willging, J. P., 292
Williams, J., 69
Williams, K., 88
Williams, S. M., 51
Williamson, G. G., 34
Williamson, W. D., 71
Wilson, C., 531
Wilson, N. W., 62
Wingo, P. A., 68
Wisconsin Assistive Technology Initiative, 181, 183, 185, 186, 189, 190, 191
Wittebol-Post, D., 88
Wolcott, G., 38, 40, 41, 45
Wolf, L., 290
Wong, F. W. H., 39
Wood, T. M., 341
Woods, E., 298
Woodward, A., 472
World Health Organization (WHO), 6, 7, 13
Worley, G., 34
Worrall, N., 434
Wright, S., 53, 360, 401
Wright-Ott, C., 207
Wu, A. W., 63
Wulf, J., 32
Wulz, S. V., 46

Xin, Y. P., 428

Yampolsky, S., 456
Ylvisaker, M., 45
Yoder, D. E., 403, 443, 456
Yoder, P. J., 265
Yonclass, D. G., 229
Young, C., 413
Young, D. B., 495
Young, T. A., 240
Yovetich, W. S., 240
Ysseldyke, J. E., 507

Zalud, G., 483, 484
Zaner-Bloser Evaluation Scales, 449
Zello, G. A., 88
Zigmond, N., 472, 482
Zolten, A. J., 69
Zuzanek, J., 349

Subject Index

Note: An italic *f* indicates a figure. An italic *t* indicates a table.

AAC. *See* Augmentative or alternative communication (AAC)
Abbreviation expansion, 246, 457
Abbreviations to substitute for words, 457
Abductor, 201, 201*f*
ABLEDATA database, 193
Accessibility
designing for, 211*f*
legal requirement of, 10
uniform, 211
Accessibility Guidelines for Buildings and Facilities, 211
Access to Math, 529
Accommodation. *See also* Assistive technology
appropriate, 13–14
defined, 117
in general education curriculum, 117, 118*t*–119*t*, 119*f*
legal requirement of, 10, 11
Acquired disabilities, 31
Acquired immune deficiency syndrome. *See* HIV/AIDS
Acquired limb deficiencies, 51
Acquisition, 479
Activities of daily living: cerebral palsy and, 105–106
Acute disabilities, 13, 31
ADA. *See* Americans with Disabilities Act of 1990 (ADA)
Adaptability: self-, 370–372
Adaptability instructional model, 371
Adapted physical education (APE), 337–343. *See also* Leisure education; Sports
activity adaptation in, 343–348
assessment in, 340–342, 343*f*
classification system in, 345*t*
collaboration with specialists in, 339–340
in community, 348
defined, 337, 339
individualized education program in, 342–343, 346
instructional strategies in, 346–348, 347*t*
safety issues in, 348
standards-based, 338–339
Adapted Physical Education Assessment Scale (APEAS), 340–341
Adaptive physical educator, 24
Addition, 518–525
algorithms for, 521–524
math rules for, 521
sequencing in, 524–525
task analysis with, 168*f*
Adult service programs: career education and, 382–383
Aided symbolic communication, 234, 235–236
means of access, 240–245
direct selection, 240–242
encoding, 243–245, 244*f*
scanning, 242, 243*f*
multicomponent system of, 236*f*–237*f*
output methods in, 247–248
selecting system of, 236–238
storage and retrieval in, 245–247
symbol type in, 238–240, 239*f*
vocabulary in, 245–247
Airborne disease transmission, 70
ALDS (assistive listening devices), 220–221
Alerting devices, 221
Algorithms
for addition and subtraction, 521–524
for multiplication and division, 526–528
Alignment: positioning and, 197
Alveoli: asthma and, 62
Ambulation: with neural tube defects, 34
Amelia, 51
American Indian Hand Talk, 232
American Sign Language (ASL), 234
Americans with Disabilities Act of 1990 (ADA) (PL 101-336), 5, 10–11, 37, 46, 181, 211, 337
Amer-Ind gestural system, 232
Anencephaly, 32
Antecedent prompts, 310, 312
in mathematics, 523, 528
for time skills, 537
Antecedents, 42
Anthropology, 487*f*
Antibodies: asthma and, 61
Anticipation shelves, 232, 538–539
Antigens: asthma and, 61
APE. *See* Adapted physical education
APEAS (Adapted Physical Education Assessment Scale), 340–341
Appliances: kitchen, 328–329
Approximations of behaviors, 164
Archaeology, 487*f*
Architectural access modifications, 211, 211*f*
Architectural and Transportation Barriers Compliance Board, 5–6
Architectural barriers
in community, 330–331
to education, 19
Architectural Barriers Act of 1968, 5
ASL (American Sign Language), 234
Aspiration, 278
Assessment
in adapted physical education, 340–342, 343*f*
for assistive technology, 184–192
authentic, 341–342, 342*f*
of background knowledge, 475–476
of content knowledge, 486–487
of feeding and swallowing, 290–292
formative, 153, 167, 169
of literacy, 417–418
of math skills, 168*f*–169*f*, 502–507
of personal management, 310–312
summative, 153, 167, 169

(Assessment, *cont.*)
task analysis as, 152–153
for transition planning, 386–393
Assistance needs identification, 163–165, 164*t*, 166f
Assistive listening devices (ALDs), 220–221
Assistive technology
acquiring, 192–194
architectural access modifications, 211, 211*f*
cerebral palsy and, 102–103, 105
curriculum in operation and use of, 134–135
defined, 14, 21, 180–181
devices, 179, 180, 181–184
environmental and object modification with, 211–217
environmental control and, 217–220, 218*f*, 219*f*, 330
in individualized education programs, 194–196
for information acquisition and management, 135–136
legal basis for, 180–181
for literacy instruction, 406, 422
for mobility, 204–211
need assessment, 184–186, 185*f*
need assessment process, 186–192
decision making, 188–190, 191*f*
extended assessment, 190, 192
gathering information, 187–188, 189*f*
trial use, 190, 192
overview, 179–180
positioning with, 196–198, 197*f*, 198*f*, 201–203, 201*f*, 202*f*
Quick Wheel, 184
as related service, 195
seating with, 196, 198–203, 199*f*–202*f*
selecting, 192–194
for sensory impairments, 220–221
services, 179, 180, 181–184
in special education, 194
as supplementary aids and services, 195
as support for school personnel, 195–196
transfers from, 203
for visual impairments, 221
Wisconsin Assistive Technology Checklist, 181, 182*f*–183*f*, 184
for writing. *See* Writing tools
Assistive Technology Consideration Guide, 185, 185*f*
Associated-object cue, 238
Asthma, 61–65, 61*f*
autonomy and, 64
career/adult outcomes and, 64–65
cognitive development and, 63
definitions and descriptions, 61–62
education and, 63–64
medical conditions associated with, 62
physical development and, 63
psychosocial development and, 63
treatments for, 62–63
Astronomy, 490*f*
Ataxic cerebral palsy, 89, 90
managing, 101
Athetoid cerebral palsy, 90
managing, 100–101
Audiologist, 24
Auditory processing disability: with cerebral palsy, 92, 104
Augmentative and alternative communication specialist, 24
Augmentative or alternative communication (AAC)
board arrangement, 253–259
cerebral palsy and, 92, 102–103, 105
content of, 228, 248–251, 252*f*
non-task related, 250–251, 252*f*
school topic, 250, 251*f*
social, 250–251, 252*f*
task-specific, 248–250
verifying, 251
curriculum in, 135
defined, 227–228
display types for, 259–262, 260*f*–262*f*
forms of, 228
functions of, 228
generic reading display, 404, 405*f*
for information acquisition and management, 135–136
instructional strategies, 262–270
breakdown, 267–270
conversational skill training, 267
environmental arrangement, 266–267
establishing want/no, 263–264
guidelines for, 262–263
interrupted-chain, 267
for milieu teaching, 265–266
response prompt, 264–265
literacy and, 401–402, 403–405, 412–414, 414*f*
nonsymbolic communication, 228–234
defined, 228
expressive, 232
form, function, and content of, 228–229
moving from noncommunicative behaviors to, 231
moving to symbolic communication, 234
receptive, 232–234
recognizing, 229–231, 230*f*
symbolic communication. *See* Symbolic communication
Authentic assessment, 341–342, 342*f*
Automatic phasic bite-release pattern, 281, 281*f*
Automatic scanning, 242
Autonomy. *See* Independence; Personal management skills

Backward chaining: in task analysis, 153
Baclofen (Lioresal): for cerebral palsy, 97
Barriers
architectural, 19
to employment, 368, 369–372
literacy, 401–403
addressing, 403–410
mathematics, 501–502
philosophical, 20
tangible, 19–20
training, 20
Behavior regulation: communication for, 229
Benchmarks, 113
Benign tumor, 68
BigCalc, 530
Biology, 490*f*
Biopsy, 68
Bite, 281*f*, 283, 287*f*
Bladder control
loss of, 33
myelomeningocele and, 37
Boardmaker, 239
Boards, communication. *See* Vocabulary boards
Body mechanics: for lifting and transfer, 101–102, 101*f*, 102*f*
Body washing, 313–314, 314*f*
Bone cancer, 69
Bone marrow transplants, 69
Books. *See also* Textbooks
awareness of, 410–412

patterned, 412
predictable, 412
story, 412–414, 413*f*, 414*f*
Botany, 490*f*
Botox (botulinum toxin): for cerebral palsy, 98
Bottle drinking, 282, 298
Boundaries: object, 215, 216*f*
Bowel control
loss of, 33
myelomeningocele and, 37
Braces: dressing and, 326, 326*f*
Braille Assessment Checklist for Persons with Multiple Disabilities, 412
Brain damage: diffuse, 90
Brain injury
defined, 38
traumatic. *See* Traumatic brain injury (TBI)
Brainstorming: written expression and, 462
Breakdown instructional strategies, 267–270
Brigance Diagnostic Inventory of Basic Skills, 340
Bronchodilators: for asthma, 62
Brown v. Board of Education, 5
Bruininks-Oseretsky Short and Long Forms, 341
Buttonhook, 325

CAI (computer-assisted instruction), 509
Calculators, 530, 535–536
Calendar/schedule system, 233*f*
Calendar skills, 538–539
Cancer, 61, 68–70
autonomy and, 70
career/adult outcomes and, 70
cognitive development and, 69
definitions and descriptions, 68
education and, 70
medical conditions associated with, 68
physical development and, 69
psychosocial development and, 69–70
treatments for, 68–69
Cancerous tumor, 68
Card games, 351–352, 352*f*, 353*f*
Career/transition education, 367–369
assessment for, 386–393
barriers to employment, 368, 369–372
career awareness stage, 373
career exploration stage, 373–378, 376*t*–377*t*
career placement/follow-up stage, 383–384
career preparation stage, 378–383
case study, 387–393
continuing education stage, 383–384
curricular domain of, 114, 137, 141–143, 141*t*, 142*f*
high-ability students and, 384–386
issues in, 394–395
from school to employment, 384–393
severe/multiple disabilities and, 386
teaching, 372–382
Carl D. Perkins Vocational and Applied Technology Education Act of 1990 (PL 101-392), 11
Carryover activities: for feeding and swallowing, 293
Car seat: positioning in, for feeding, 295, 295*f*
Catheterization
clean intermittent, 34, 37, 320
external urinary, 320
self-care for, 321
Caution steps, 321
CCTV (closed-circuit television), 221, 448*f*
Centers for Disease Control (CDC): universal precautions issued by, 79, 80
Cerebral palsy, 87–88
ataxic, 89, 90, 101
athetoid, 90, 100–101
autonomy and, 105–106
career/adult outcomes and, 106
causes and risk factors associated with, 89*t*
classification of, 89–90, 91*f*
cognitive deficits with, 92
communication development and, 102–103, 103*f*
communication impairments with, 91–92
definitions and descriptions, 88–89
dyskinetic, 89, 90
education and, 104–106
learning disabilities with, 92–93
medical conditions associated with, 90–93
mixed, 89, 90, 101
nutrition and feeding needs with, 92
orthopedic deformities with, 92
physical development and, 98
physical management of, 98–102
seizures with, 93, 94*t*–96*t*
sensory impairments with, 91
social/emotional development and, 103–104
spastic, 89–90, 99–100
therapeutic management of, 93, 97
treatments for, 97–98
CF. *See* Cystic fibrosis
Cheek/lip retraction, 287*f*, 289*f*
Chemistry, 490*f*
Chemotherapy, 68
Chewing, 281*f*
Chronic disabilities, 13, 31
CID (cytomegalic inclusion disease), 71
Circular scanning, 242, 243*f*
Civil Rights Act of 1964, 5
Classification: in mathematics, 510
Classroom Modifications Checklist for Students with Physical and Health Impairments, 476, 477*f*–478*f*
Clean intermittent catheterization (CIC), 34, 37, 320, 321
Closed captioning, 221
Closed-circuit television (CCTV), 221, 448*f*
Cloze spelling approach, 459
Clustering, 17
CMV. *See* Cytomegalovirus
Cognitive development
asthma and, 63
cancer and, 69
cerebral palsy and, 92
cystic fibrosis and, 66
cytomegalovirus and, 71
HIV/AIDS and, 74
limb deficiencies and, 53
muscular dystrophy and, 49–50
neural tube defects and, 34–35
traumatic brain injury and, 40, 42, 43*t*–45*t*
Cognitive difficulties: motor vs., 158–160, 160*f*
Collaboration
with adapted physical education specialists, 339–340
with adult service programs, 382–383
curriculum development through, 143–145, 143*f*, 145*f*
as professional role, 21–26
questions to ask specialist, 21*f*–22*f*, 25*f*
Collaborative and consultative services, 17

Collecting, 352–353
Color-line prompting strategy, 406–407, 407*f*
Colostomy, 321
Colostomy care, 321
Coma, 40
Communication. *See also* Augmentative or alternative communication (AAC)
cerebral palsy and, 91–92, 102–103, 103*f*
developmental stages of, 228
literacy and, 401–402, 403–405
modified, in curriculum, 114, 129, 133–136
nonsymbolic. *See* Nonsymbolic communication
receptive, 232–234, 258–259
symbolic. *See* Symbolic communication
Community ambulators, 34
Community-based instruction, 17–18
in career education, 380–381
for personal independence, 330–333
in physical education, 348
Comparisons: in mathematics, 510–511
Competitive employment, 378
Component processing, 411, 412
Comprehension
scripturally implicit, 427
software programs for, 431
strategies for, 428–430, 429*f*, 430*f*
teaching, 427–428
text, 426–430
textually explicit, 427
textually implicit, 427
Comprehensive Transition Education Model, 137, 141–142, 141*t*
Computer-assisted instruction (CAI), 509
Computerized tomography scan (CT scan): for traumatic brain injury, 39
Computers. *See also* Software programs
accessibility options on, 452–453
displays on, 262
input devices, 453, 455–456, 455*f*
keyboard alternatives, 453, 455*f*
keyboarding skills, 456–457, 457*f*
keyboard layout options, 453, 454*f*
keyboard modifications, 453
leisure activities on, 355–356
mouse alternatives, 453
muscular dystrophy and, 50
output modifications, 456
positioning at, 203
visual impairments and, 221
as writing tools, 449, 452–457
Concussion, 38
Congenital disabilities, 31
Congenital limb deficiencies, 51
Contact disease transmission, 70
Content
evaluating knowledge of, 486–487
lesson, 472
reading for, 483–486
of written expression, 462–463
Content-specific vocabulary, 255, 257*f*
Continuing education, 383–384
Continuous sounds, 416
Controlled, sustained bite, 281*f*, 283
Contusion, 38
Conventional literacy
approaches to, 416–417
assessment of, 417–418, 418*f*
defined, 409
fluency, 426
phonics, 418–424, 419*f*, 421*f*
text comprehension, 426–430
vocabulary instruction, 424–425
Conversational skill training, 267
Cooking, 328
Cooperative learning groups, 482–483
Core vocabulary, 255, 257*f*, 260
Cortical visual impairment (CVI), 39
Cosmology, 490*f*
Council for Exceptional Children (CEC), 184
certification standards of, 20–21
Counselor, 24
rehabilitation, 24
Count-down method: for money skills, 536
Counting
money, 534, 536
from numbers other than one, 513–514
patterned, 513, 514*f*
rational, 511, 513
rote, 511
skip, 514
Counting on, 513–514
Count-up method: for money skills, 536
Coup and contracoup, 38
Courses of study: developing, 145–147, 146*t*
Crafts, 350–351
Created-associations cues, 238
Crutches, 210*f*, 211
dressing and, 326
CT scan: for traumatic brain injury, 39
Cue fading, 165
Cues: lecture, 481
Cup drinking, 282–283, 298, 302–303, 302*f*
Curricula map: developing, 145–147, 147*t*
Curriculum. *See also* Lesson preparation
analysis of, 121–123, 125*t*
collaborative work on, 143–145, 143*f*, 145*f*
fundamental domains, 113, 114, 115*f*
general education with accommodations, 114, 115–117, 118*t*–119*t*
general education with accommodations and modifications, 114, 120–126, 121*f*–125*f*, 125*t*
learning strategies, 126, 126*f*
life skills, 105, 114, 126–129, 127*t*, 128*t*, 129*f*
modified means of communication and task performance, 114, 129, 133–136
options, 113–114, 115*f*
SAVI/SELPH, 494, 495*f*
science, 489–496
scope of, 151
self-determination, 114, 136–137, 137*f*, 138*f*–140*f*
social studies, 487–489
spiral, 488
study skills, 126, 126*f*
task analysis and, 167–169
thinking and problem-solving skills, 123, 125*f*
transition education, 114, 137, 141–143, 141*t*, 142*f*
CVI (cortical visual impairment), 39
Cystic fibrosis (CF), 61, 65–68
appearance of, 65*f*
autonomy and, 67
career/adult outcomes and, 67–68
cognitive development and, 66
definitions and descriptions, 65–66
education and, 67
medical conditions associated with, 66
physical development and, 66
psychosocial development and, 66–67
treatments for, 66
Cytomegalic inclusion disease (CID), 71
Cytomegalovirus (CMV), 70–72

autonomy and, 72
career/adult outcomes and, 72
cognitive development and, 71
definitions and descriptions, 71
education and, 72
medical conditions associated with, 71
physical development and, 71
psychosocial development and, 71–72
treatments for, 71

Daily living skills, 373
Dantrium (dantrolene): for cerebral palsy, 97
Dantrolene (Dantrium): for cerebral palsy, 97
Decimal notation, 535
Dedicated augmentative communication devices, 235, 262
Degenerative diseases, 46. *See also* Muscular dystrophy
Demonstration, 165
Demonstration—guided-practice—independent-practice model, 312
Desktop publishing software, 464
Developmental approach to vocabulary, 248
Developmental sequences: task analysis and, 156–157, 157*f*
Diagnostic distractor array, 420–421
Diagnostician, 24
Diazepam (Valium): for cerebral palsy, 97
Diffuse brain damage, 90
Diffuse damage in traumatic brain injury, 42
Digitized speech, 247
Diplegia, 89
Diplopia, 39
Directed scanning, 242
Direct selection of communication symbols, 240–242
Disability. *See also* Cerebral palsy; Physical disability
acute and chronic, 13
alike and different, 12
defined, 6–9, 7*t*
federal categories of, 8–9
historical perspectives on, 4–6
labeling persons with, 6–8
legal aspects of, 9–12
service intensity and independence issues, 15
visible and invisible, 12–13
Disability rights movement, 5–6
Discrepancy analysis, 310, 311*f*
Discrimination skills, 158–160, 160*f*
Diseases, infectious. *See* Infectious diseases
Displays
on dedicated devices and computers, 262
for nonelectronic communication devices, 259–262, 260*f*, 261*f*, 262*f*
visual spatial, 483–484, 485*f*
Distal stability, 197
Distance education, 17
District special education administrator or coordinator, 24
Division, 525–529
algorithms for, 526–528
heuristic strategies for, 526
math rules for, 525–526
sequencing in, 529
task analysis with, 169*f*
DMD. *See* Duchenne Muscular dystrophy
D-Nealian Handwriting Program, 449
Domains of Adulthood Model, 129, 130*t*–133*t*, 133*f*
Double hemiplegia, 89
Dressing, 322–326
clothing adaptations, 323–326
devices for, 323–326, 325*f*
helping individuals learn, 322–323, 322*f*, 324*f*
Dressing stick, 325, 325*f*
Drinking
bottle, 282, 298
cup, 282–283, 298
selecting liquids for, 298–299
Duchenne muscular dystrophy (DMD), 46. *See also* Muscular dystrophy
Dvorak keyboard, 453, 454*f*, 456
Dynamic display method of symbol sequencing, 246
DynaVox, 246
Dyskinetic cerebral palsy, 89, 90
Dystrophin, 46

EADLs (electronic aids to daily living), 218–220, 219*f*
Earth sciences, 490*f*
Ecological inventories, 169–173, 170*f*, 172*f*
for functional literacy, 431–432
for vocabulary selection, 248–250, 249*f*
Ecologies, 169
Economics, 487*f*
ECUs (environmental control units), 218
Editing tools, 464
Editing written expression, 462
Edmark Reading Program, 431, 432
Education. *See also* Career/transition education; Curriculum
asthma and, 63–64
cancer and, 70
cerebral palsy and, 104–106
continuing, 383–384
cystic fibrosis and, 67
cytomegalovirus and, 72
goals of, 16
HIV/AIDS and, 74–75
limb deficiencies and, 53–54
muscular dystrophy and, 50–51
neural tube defects and, 35–37
service delivery systems, 16–20
traumatic brain injury and, 45–46
Educational psychologist, 24
Educational therapist, 24
Education for All Handicapped Children Act of 1975 (PL 94-142), 8, 10, 337, 339
E-JAM, 387
ELD (English-language development), 134
Electronic aids to daily living (EADLs), 218–220, 219*f*
Electronic worksheet programs, 529–530
Element dimensions: with assistive technology, 193
Element placement: with assistive technology, 193
Emergent literacy, 410–416
assessment checklist for, 410, 411*f*
book and print awareness, 410–412
letter-sound correspondence, 415–416, 416*f*
phonemic awareness, 414–415
repeated reading and, 413–414
software programs for, 416
storybook reading, 412–414, 413*f*, 414*f*
Emotional lability, 42
Emotional/social development
cerebral palsy and, 103–104
Employment. *See also* Career/transition education
barriers to, 368, 369–372
competitive, 378
as school goal, 382
supported, 374, 378
transition from school to, 384–393

Encephalocele, 32
Encephalopathy, 73
Encoding
 letter, 246
 in symbolic communication, 243–245, 244*f*
Enderle-Severson Transition Rating Scales, 386
English-language development (ELD), 134
English-language learners, 134
Entire object cue, 238
Environment
 home, 330
 light sources in, 203
 literacy and, 402–403, 409–410, 431–432
 location of materials and equipment in, 211–213, 212*f*
 modifications to, 211–217
 object modifications in, 214–215, 216*f*, 217*f*
 in science education, 493–496
 situation analysis and, 169
 sounds in, 203
 student placement in, 203–204
 teaching and learning, 16
 work site, 379
 work surface modifications in, 213–214, 213*f*, 214*f*
 writing and, 443
Environmental approach to vocabulary, 248
Environmental arrangement instructional strategies, 266–267
Environmental control, 217–220, 218*f*, 219*f*, 330
Environmental control units (ECUs), 218
Environmental Job Measure (E-JAM), 387
Environmental print, 433
Error analysis
 in mathematics, 505, 507
 in Nonverbal Reading Approach, 421–422
Errorless discrimination strategy, 431, 431*f*
ETRAN (Eye Transfer Communication Device), 261, 261*f*, 403, 404*f*
Evaluation. *See* Assessment
Exaggerated jaw closure, 287*f*
Exaggerated tongue protrusion, 287*f*
Expanded notation, 518
Expanded-notation algorithm, 521–522
Expressive communication: nonsymbolic, 232
Extended assessment, 190, 192
External urinary catheter, 320
Eye-gazing, 243, 260–262, 403, 404*f*, 455
Eye pointing, 241, 260–261
Eye Transfer Communication Device (ETRAN), 261, 261*f*, 403, 404*f*

Face washing, 313–314, 314*f*
Fading
 in color-line prompting, 406–407, 407*f*
 in math prompting, 523, 523*f*
Failure to thrive, 73
FAPE (free appropriate public education), 181, 184
FAST I (Foundational Approach to Science Teaching), 494–496
Feature match: with assistive technology, 193
Feeding and swallowing, 277–279
 aspiration, 278
 carryover activities for, 293
 cerebral palsy and, 92
 concerns with, 279–280
 conditions associated with problems in, 278
 cooking, 328
 cup drinking, 282–283, 298, 302–303, 302*f*
 defined, 277
 development of, 281–284, 281*f*
 evaluation of, 290–292
 food/liquid selection, 298–299, 327–328
 interventions for, 293–306
 neuromotor impairments and, 287–292
 oral control of, 300–306, 301*f*–305*f*
 positioning for, 293–298, 294*f*–297*f*
 preparation of oral mechanism for, 299–300
 respiratory coordination with, 285–286, 305–306
 respiratory development and, 284–286
 solid food, 283–284, 288*f*, 303–305, 305*f*
 spoon-feeding, 282, 288*f*, 298, 303, 304*f*
 textures of food and liquids, 283*f*
 tube, 319–320, 321, 321*f*
 utensils for, 298
Feminine hygiene skills, 316–317, 317*f*
Filter keys, 453
First aid: for seizures, 94*t*–96*t*
Flexion: with athetoid cerebral palsy, 100
Fluency, 426
 task, 479
Food:
 selecting, 298–299, 327–328
 solid, 283–284, 288*f*, 303–305, 305*f*
 textures of, 283*f*
Formative assessment, 153, 167, 169
Forms: filling out, 465
Forward chaining: in task analysis, 153
FOSS (Full Option Science System), 494
Foundational Approach to Science Teaching (FAST I), 494–496
Fractures: myelomeningocele and, 37
Free appropriate public education (FAPE), 181, 184
Full Option Science System (FOSS), 494
Functional academics, 126, 128, 128*t*, 129*f*
Functional approach to vocabulary, 248
Functional literacy
 defined, 409
 ecological assessment for, 431–432
 instructional strategies for, 432–434
 reading, 431–434
 vocabulary selection for, 431–432
Functional writing, 464–465
Function classification of cerebral palsy, 89, 90, 91*f*
Fundamental curricular domains
 self-determination, 114, 136–137, 137*f*, 138*f*–140*f*
 transition, 114, 137, 141–143, 141*t*, 142*f*
Fusion, 48

Gag response, 281–282, 281*f*, 285
Games. *See also* Leisure education
 card, 351–352, 352*f*, 353*f*
 computer, 356
Gastroesophageal reflux (GER), 280
Gastrostomy tube (G-tube), 92, 320, 321
GCS (Glasgow Coma Scale), 40, 40*t*
General education class, 16

General education curriculum with accommodations, 114–119
accommodations, 117, 118*t*–119*t*
curriculum elements, 116–117
natural supports, 117, 119*f*
General education curriculum with accommodations and modifications, 114, 120–126
applying modification approach, 121–123, 125*f*, 125*t*, 126, 126*f*
curricular modifications, 120
determining need for modifications, 120–121, 121*f*–124*f*
Generalization: of learning, 479
Generic reading display, 404, 405*f*
Geography, 487*f*
Geology, 490*f*
Gestures, 232
Glascow Coma Scale (GCS), 40, 40*t*
Goals: defined, 113
Grammar: software for, 464
Graphic organizer, 174, 485*f*
Grasping aids, 215, 217*f*
Group-item scanning, 242, 243*f*
G-tube, 92, 320, 321
Guided practice
in lesson presentation, 482
in phonic instruction, 419*f*

Hair brushing, 314, 315*f*
Ham radio operation, 355
Handheld writing tools, 444, 445*f*, 446, 446*f*
Handicap: defined, 6–7, 7*t*
Handwashing
assessing and teaching, 310, 311*f*, 313
infectious diseases and, 80–81, 80*f*
Handwriting skills, 446–449, 449*t*
assessment of, 449, 450*t*–452*t*
preparatory activities for, 448*f*
Hard copy output: of communication system, 248
Head injury, 38
Head sticks, 240–241
writing with, 446*f*
Health care
meeting special needs in, 76–79
student self-, 321
Health impairments, 59–61
asthma, 61–65
cancer, 68–70
categories of, 60*f*
cystic fibrosis, 65–68
defined, 8–9
Hearing loss: assistive technology and, 220–221
Hemiplegia, 89
Herniates, 32
Heuristic strategies: for mathematics, 526
Highchair: positioning in, 295, 296*f*
Hippotherapy, 358
History, 487*f*
HIV/AIDS, 70–76
autonomy and, 75
career/adult outcomes and, 75–76
cognitive development and, 74
definitions and descriptions, 72–73
education and, 74–75
medical conditions associated with, 73
physical development and, 74
psychosocial development and, 74
stages of, 73
transmission of, 72–73
treatments for, 73–74
Home care and management, 326–330
Horseback riding, 358–359, 359*f*
Hospital-based programs, 17, 18*f*
Housecleaning, 329–330, 329*f*
Household ambulators, 34
Human immunodeficiency virus. *See* HIV/AIDS
Hydrocephalus, 34
Hygiene skills. *See* Personal management skills
Hypertonia, 89, 100
Hypotonia, 90, 100

Iconicity of symbols, 240
IDEA. *See* Individuals with Disabilities Education Act of 1990
IEP. *See* Individualized education programs
IHCP (individualized health care plan), 77, 78*f*–79*f*, 79
Ileostomy, 321
Illness accommodation, 14
Illocutionary stage of communication development, 228
Immunotherapy: asthma and, 62
Impairment
defined, 6–7, 7*t*
health. *See* Health impairments
neuromotor, 32
orthopedic. *See* Physical disability
Inclusion: strategies for, 347–348
Inclusion specialist/inclusion facilitator, 24
Independence. *See also* Personal management skills
asthma and, 64
cancer and, 70
cerebral palsy and, 105–106
cystic fibrosis and, 67
cytomegalovirus and, 72
HIV/AIDS and, 75
issues related to, 15
limb deficiencies and, 54
muscular dystrophy and, 50–51
neural tube defects and, 35–37
traumatic brain injury and, 45–46
Individualized education programs (IEPs)
in adapted physical education, 342–343, 346
assistive technology in, 194–196
curricular modifications in, 120
goal alignment with general education benchmarks, 116
legal requirement of, 10
Individualized health care plans (IHCPs), 77, 78*f*–79*f*, 79
Individual Plan for Employment (IPE), 384
Individuals with Disabilities Education Act of 1990 (IDEA) (PL 101-476), 8, 9, 11, 14, 45, 180–181, 184, 387
Amendments of 1997 (PL 105-17), 11–12, 115, 134, 181, 195, 383
Individual Written Rehabilitation Plan (IWRP), 384
Infectious diseases, 59, 70–71
categories of, 60*f*
cytomegalovirus, 71–72
HIV/AIDS, 72–76
precautions with, 79–81
transmission of, 70
Informal Assessment for Transition Planning, 386
Information acquisition and management
curriculum modification for, 135–136
task analysis for, 174, 175*f*
Injury-related factors in traumatic brain injury, 40
Input devices: computer, 453, 455–456, 455*f*
Input method: with assistive technology, 193
Instructional Model, 480*t*

Instructional strategies. *See also under specific subject areas*
in adapted physical education, 346–348, 347*t*
for augmentative and alternative communication, 262–270
for handwriting, 446–449
for literacy. *See* Literacy
in mathematics, 507–510, 509*t*
for personal management skills, 310–312
Intercalary limb deficiencies, 51
Internal speech, 420
Interrupted-chain instructional strategy, 267
Intrathecal baclofen therapy: for cerebral palsy, 97
Inventory of Task Performance, 161, 162*f*–163*f*
IPE (Individual Plan for Employment), 384
Itinerancy services at home, 17
Itinerant special education instructor, 17
Itinerant teacher, 24
IWRP (Individual Written Rehabilitation Plan), 384

Jaw
exaggerated closure of, 287*f*
oral control of, 300–301
rotary movement of, 281*f*, 284
stabilization of, 281*f*
Jaw thrusting, 287*f*, 289*f*
with protrusion, 287*f*
with retraction, 287*f*
Jejunostomy, 321
Job clusters, 374–375
Job creation, 374
Joint attention: communication for, 229

Keyboarding skills, 456–457, 457*f*
Keyboards
alternative, 453, 455*f*
layout options for, 453, 454*f*
modifications for, 453
Kitchen tasks, 327–329, 328*f*
K-W-L strategy, 483
Kyphosis, 34

Language. *See also* Communication
curriculum modification for, 134
literacy and, 401–402, 403–405
Language arts. *See* Literacy
Language development
myelomeningocele and, 36
vocabulary boards for, 255, 258, 258*f*
Latex allergy: myelomeningocele and, 37
Law, 487*f*
LCCE. *See* Life-Centered Career Education (LCCE)
Learning disabilities: cerebral palsy and, 92–93, 104–105
Learning strategies
in curriculum, 126, 126*f*
in mathematics, 508–509
for personal management skills, 312
for reading for content, 483–486
Least prompts: system of, 265
Least restrictive environment (LRE)
assistive technology and, 195
legal interpretation of, 12
Lecturing, 481, 481*t*
Leisure
activity skills for, 349
awareness of, 349
defined, 338
resources for, 349
Leisure education, 338, 348–349. *See also* Adapted physical education (APE); Sports
card games, 351–352, 352*f*, 353*f*
collecting, 352–353
computer use, 355–356
crafts, 350–351
creative domains in, 350–353
ham radio operation, 355
horseback riding, 358–359, 359*f*
nature exploration, 356–358
photography, 350
program areas in, 350
program development in, 349
recreation domains in, 356–360
robotics, 353–356
science and technology domains in, 353–356
travel, 359–360
Lesson preparation, 471–472, 480*t*
background knowledge assessment, 475–476, 475*f*
content selection, 472
modification determination, 476, 477*f*–478*f*, 479
supplementary materials, 475
textbook evaluation and adaptation, 472–475
Lesson presentation, 479, 480*t*
cooperative learning groups in, 482–483
cues in, 481, 481*t*
guided practice in, 482
independent practice in, 486
lecturing, 481, 481*t*
pause procedure in, 482
prelesson activities in, 479
reading strategies, 483–486
Lesson response requirements, 161
Letter-encoding techniques, 246
Letter-sound correspondence, 415–416, 416*f*
Leukemia, 69
Life-Centered Career Education (LCCE), 373–384
career awareness stage, 373
career exploration stage, 373–378, 376*t*–377*t*
career placement/follow-up stage, 383–384
career preparation stage, 378–383
continuing education stage, 383–384
Life sciences, 490*f*
Life skills curriculum, 105, 114, 126–129, 128*t*, 129*f*
across grades, 127*t*
daily and community living skills, 128–129, 130*t*–133*t*, 133*f*
functional academics, 126, 128, 128*t*, 129*f*
Lightening, 40
Light sources, 203
Limb deficiencies
autonomy and, 54
career/adult outcomes and, 54
cognitive development and, 53
definitions and descriptions, 51
education and, 53–54
medical conditions associated with, 52
physical development and, 53
psychosocial development and, 53
treatments for, 52–53
Linear scanning, 242, 243*f*
Lioresal (baclofen): for cerebral palsy, 97
Lip/cheek retraction, 287*f*, 289*f*
Lips
oral control of, 300–301
pursing, 287*f*
Literacy
barriers to, 401–403
addressing, 403–410
book and print awareness, 410–412
communication barriers, 401–402
addressing, 403–405

conventional
approaches to, 416–417
assessment of, 417–418
defined, 409
fluency, 426
phonics, 418–424
text comprehension, 426–430
vocabulary instruction, 424–425
curricula for, 430–431
emergent, 410–416
experience barriers, 402
addressing, 409
functional, 409, 431–434
functional writing, 464–465
generic reading displays for, 404, 405*f*
individual barriers, 402
addressing, 408–409
learning environment and instructional barriers, 402–403
addressing, 409–410
letter-sound correspondence, 415–416, 416*f*
motor ability barriers, 402
addressing, 405–408
phonemic awareness, 414–415
reading rates, 417–418, 418*f*
reading strategies, 483–486
science and, 491–492, 492*t*
software programs for, 407–408, 416, 430–431
spelling, 457–459
storybook reading, 412–414, 413*f*, 414*f*
writing. *See* Writing
Location classification of cerebral palsy, 89
Locutionary stage of communication development, 228
LRE. *See* Least restrictive environment

Magnetic resonance imagery (MRI): for traumatic brain injury, 39
Maintenance: task, 479
Malignant tumor, 68
Manipulation aids, 215, 217*f*
March of Dimes, 6
Match-to-sample writing strategy, 465
Mathematics
achievement tests for, 504
addition and subtraction, 518–525
algorithms for, 521–524
math rules for, 521
sequencing in, 524–525
advanced skills, 531
assessing skills in, 168*f*–169*f*, 502–507
barriers in, 501–502
calculator use in, 530, 535–536
calendar skills, 538–539
computer-assisted instruction, 509
counting, 511, 513–514, 514*f*, 534
curriculum-based measurement for, 505, 506*f*
decimal notation, 535
diagnostic tests for, 504–505
error analysis in, 505, 507
functional skills, 531–539, 532*t*–533*t*
instructional strategies in, 507–510, 509*t*
money skills, 332–333, 534–536
multiplication and division, 525–529
algorithms for, 526–528
heuristic strategies for, 526
math rules for, 525–526
sequencing in, 529
numerals, 514, 515*f*, 516
place values, 516–518, 517*f*
portfolio assessment for, 505
prenumber skills, 510–511, 512*f*
software for, 518, 529–530, 531, 534, 535, 537
teacher-constructed tests for, 505
time skills, 536–538, 538*f*
word problems in, 530–531, 535
Math Marks, 519–520
MathPad, 529–530
MathPad by Voice, 529
Maximum prompts: system of, 265
Meningocele, 32, 33*f*
Menstrual care, 316–317, 317*f*
Mentor: in career education, 379
Metacognition, 508
Metastasize, 68
Meteorology, 490*f*
Metropolitan Reading Readiness Test, Level II, 411, 414
Microcephaly, 71
Midrange movement: with athetoid cerebral palsy, 100
Milieu teaching procedures, 265–266
Minispeak, 246
Mixed cerebral palsy, 89, 90
managing, 101
Mnemonics, 312
for mathematics instruction, 508–509, 520–521
as memory technique, 486
for reading comprehension, 429
for spelling instruction, 458
for writing instruction, 463–464
Mobility, 204–211
age-related aids for, 208*f*
toys as aids for, 209*f*
travel stroller chairs, 207, 207*f*
walkers, 209, 210*f*, 211
wheelchairs
manual, 204–205, 205*f*
power, 205–207, 205*f*, 206*f*
Modified means of communication and task performance curriculum, 114, 129, 133–136
assistive technology, 134–135
augmentative or alternative communication, 135
information acquisition and management, 135–136
modified physical task performance, 133–134
speech and language, 134
Money skills, 332–333, 534–536
Motor impairment
cognitive vs., 158–160, 160*f*
literacy and, 402, 405–408
writing and, 441–442
Motor pattern classification of cerebral palsy, 89–90
Motor planning: with ataxic cerebral palsy, 101
Mouse alternatives for computers, 453
Mouth sticks, 240–241
Movement classification of cerebral palsy, 89–90
Movement cues, 232
Moving into the Future: National Standards for Physical Education, 338
MRI (magnetic resonance imagery): for traumatic brain injury, 39
Multimedia software, 464
Multipass strategy, 483
Multiple disabilities. *See also* Cerebral palsy
defined, 9
Multiplication, 525–529
algorithms for, 526–528
heuristic strategies for, 526
math rules for, 525–526
sequencing in, 529
task analysis with, 168*f*
Munching, 281*f*, 283
Muscle tone: positioning and, 196
Muscular dystrophy
autonomy and, 50–51

(Muscular dystrophy *cont.*)
career/adult outcomes and, 51
cognitive development and, 49–50
definitions and descriptions, 46, 48
Duchenne, 46
education and, 50–51
medical conditions associated with, 48
physical development and, 49
psychosocial development and, 50
treatments for, 48–49
Musculoskeletal conditions, 51–54
Myelomeningocele, 33*f*
academic impact of, 35–36
autonomy and, 36–37
bladder and bowel control and, 37
career/adult outcomes and, 37–38
cognitive development and, 34–35
defined, 32
fractures and, 37
language issues and, 36
medical conditions associated with, 33–34
physical development and, 34–35
psychosocial development and, 34–35
skin care and, 36–37
treatments for, 34

National Association for Sport and Physical Education (NASPE): standards of, 338
National Council of Teachers of Mathematics (NCTM):
position on calculator use, 530
standards of, 502, 503*t*, 504
National Science Education Standards (NSES), 490–491
Natural supports, 117, 119*f*
Nature exploration, 356–358
Nebulizer: for asthma, 62
Neoplasms, 68
Neural tube defects (NTDs), 32–38, 33*f*
autonomy and, 35–37
career/adult outcomes and, 37–38
cognitive development and, 34–35
defined, 32
descriptions and characteristics, 32–33
education and, 35–37
medical conditions associated with, 33–34
physical development and, 34–35
psychosocial development and, 34–35
treatments for, 34
Neuroanatomy classification of cerebral palsy, 89
Neuromotor impairments, 32
feeding and swallowing and, 287–292
Nonambulators, 34
Noncommunicative behaviors: moving to nonsymbolic communication from, 231
Nonelectronic communication devices: displays on, 259–262
Nonfunctional ambulators, 34
Nonsymbolic communication, 228–234
defined, 228
expressive, 232
form, function, and content of, 228–229
moving from noncommunicative behaviors to, 231
moving to symbolic communication, 234
receptive, 232–234
recognizing, 229–231, 230*f*
Non-task related communication, 250–251, 252*f*
Nonverbal Reading Approach to phonics, 418–424, 419*f*, 421*f*
NSES (National Science Education Standards), 490–491
NTD. *See* Neural tube defects
Number line, 516, 520
Numerals, 514, 515*f*, 516
Nutrition: cerebral palsy and, 92
Nystagmus, 39, 91

OASIS—3, 387
Object calendar, 233, 233*f*, 538
Object cues, 232, 238
Objective evaluation approach to curricular modification, 120–121, 123*f*, 124*f*
Objects
boundaries and, 215, 216*f*
grasping aids for, 215, 217*f*
manipulation aids for, 215, 217*f*
modifications to, 214–215, 216*f*, 217*f*
stabilization of, 215, 216*f*
Occupational Aptitude Survey and Interest Schedule—3 (OASIS-3), 387
Occupational clusters, 374–375
Occupational Information Network (O*NET), 374
Occupational Outlook Handbook, 374
Occupational Safety and Health Administration (OSHA)
standard for prevention of infection by bloodborne diseases, 79–80
Occupational skills, 373, 380
Occupational therapist (OT), 24, 93
Occupational therapy: with cerebral palsy, 93, 97
O*NET, 374
One-to-one correspondence: in mathematics, 510
On-screen keyboards, 455
Optical pointers, 241, 241*f*
Oral activities: respiratory coordination with, 285–286, 305–306
Oral control, 300–306, 301*f*–305*f*
Oral digital stimulation, 300
Oral hygiene, 293, 300, 314–315, 315*f*, 316*f*
Oral-motor activity
atypical, 287–289, 287*f*, 288*f*, 289*f*
evaluation of, 290–292
Oral-motor development, 281–284, 281*f*
Orientation and mobility specialist, 24
Orthographic awareness, 410, 412
Orthopedic impairments, 51–54. *See also* Physical disability
cerebral palsy and, 92
defined, 8
Orthotics: cerebral palsy and, 97, 97*f*
Outcomes
asthma and, 64–65
cancer and, 70
cerebral palsy and, 106
cystic fibrosis and, 67–68
cytomegalovirus and, 72
HIV/AIDS and, 75–76
limb deficiencies and, 54
muscular dystrophy and, 51
myelomeningocele and, 37–38
student learning, 113
traumatic brain injury and, 46
Outliner software, 464
Output methods
with assistive technology, 193
of communication systems, 247–248
computer, 456

Paper adaptations for writing, 444, 446, 447*f*, 448*f*
Paragraph construction, 463–464, 463*f*
Parenteral transmission of HIV/AIDS, 72

Parents: involving in vocational preparation, 382
Partial object cue, 238
Partial participation strategy, 174
Patient-related factors in traumatic brain injury, 40, 42
Pattern dot use: in mathematics, 519
Patterned books, 412
Patterned counting, 513, 514*f*
Pattern instruction in mathematics, 510
Pattern method of analyzing information, 174
Pause procedure in lectures, 482
PCS (Picture Communication Symbols), 239
Peer assistance, 15
Peer questionnaire in situation analysis, 172–173, 172*f*
Performance requirements, 161
Perinatal period:
  cerebral palsy and, 88, 89*t*
  HIV/AIDS transmission and, 72–73
Perlocutionary stage of communication development, 228
Personal access problems: task analysis for, 174–176, 175*f*
Personal independence. *See* Independence; Personal management skills
Personal management skills, 309–310
  assessment and instruction of, 310, 311*f*, 312
  body washing, 313–314, 314*f*
  catheterization, 320, 321
  colostomy care, 321
  community-based, 330–333
  dressing, 322–326, 322*f*, 324*f*–326*f*
  eating. *See* Feeding and swallowing
  face washing, 313–314, 314*f*
  hair brushing, 314, 315*f*
  hand washing, 310, 311*f*, 313
  health care procedures, 321
  home care, 326–330
  hygiene, 312–317
    feminine, 316–317, 317*f*
    oral, 314–315, 315*f*, 316*f*
  task analysis with, 155*f*, 173–174, 174*f*, 310, 311*f*
  tissue use, 316, 316*f*
  toileting, 317–319, 318*f*, 319*f*
  tube feeding, 319–320, 321, 321*f*
Personal-social skills, 373
Person-first language, 8
Pharyngeal activities: respiratory coordination with, 285–286, 305–306
Philosophical barriers, 20
Philosophy, 487*f*
Phocomelia, 51, 51*f*
Phonemic awareness, 414–415
Phonics, 418
  functional literacy instruction with, 434
  nonverbal reading approach to, 419–424, 419*f*, 421*f*
  spelling instruction with, 458
Photography, 350
Physical development
  asthma and, 63
  cancer and, 69
  cerebral palsy and, 98–102
  cystic fibrosis and, 66
  cytomegalovirus and, 71
  HIV/AIDS and, 74
  limb deficiencies and, 53
  muscular dystrophy and, 49
  neural tube defects and, 34–35
  traumatic brain injury and, 40, 42
Physical disability
  acquired, 31
  acute, 13, 31
  chronic, 13, 31
  congenital, 31
  defined, 8
  degenerative diseases, 46
  limb deficiencies, 51–54
  muscular dystrophy, 46–51
  neural tube defects, 32–38
  neuromotor impairments, 32
  orthopedic and musculoskeletal conditions, 51
  traumatic brain injury, 38–46
Physical education, adapted. *See* Adapted physical education (APE)
Physical educator: adaptive, 24
Physical efficiency areas: literacy and, 405–408
Physical science, 490*f*
Physical task performance. *See* Task performance
Physical therapist (PT), 24, 93
Physical therapy: with cerebral palsy, 93
Physics, 490*f*
Picture-association reading strategy, 433, 433*f*
Picture-based acceleration techniques, 245–246
Picture Communication Symbols (PCS), 239
Pictures: for writing, 465
Picture schedules, 538–539
PL 93-112 (Rehabilitation Act of 1973), 6, 10, 181, 337
PL 94-142 (Education for All Handicapped Children Act of 1975), 8, 10, 337, 339
PL 100-407 (Technology-Related Assistance for Individuals with Disabilities Act of 1988), 10, 14, 180
PL 101-336 (Americans with Disabilities Act of 1990), 5, 10–11, 37, 46, 181, 211, 337
PL 101-392 (Carl D. Perkins Vocational and Applied Technology Education Act of 1990), 11
PL 101-476 (Individuals with Disabilities Education Act of 1990), 8, 9, 11, 14, 45, 180–181, 184, 387
PL 103-239 (School-to-Work Opportunity Act), 384
PL 105-17 (IDEA Amendments of 1977), 11–12, 115, 134, 181, 195, 383
Place value: in mathematics, 516–518, 517*f*
Pointer devices, 455
Political science, 487*f*
Portfolio assessment
  in adapted physical education, 342, 343*f*
  in mathematics, 505
Portfolio cards: in adapted physical education, 342
Positioning, 196–198. *See also* Seating
  assistive devices for, 201–203
  changing, 198, 198*f*
  in classroom, 203–204
  for feeding, 293–298, 294*f*–297*f*
  for literacy instruction, 405
  of needed items, 203–204
  proper vs. improper, 197*f*
  transfers from, 203
Postnatal period: cerebral palsy and, 88–89, 89*t*
Postural drainage: for asthma, 62
Posture: positioning and, 196, 197*f*
A Practical Guide for Teaching Self-Determination, 371–372
Practice, 165
  guided, 419*f*, 482
  independent, 486
Predictable books, 412
Predictive techniques in symbolic communication, 246–247, 247*f*
Prenatal period: cerebral palsy and, 88, 89*t*

Problem-solving skills: in curriculum, 123, 125*f*
Processing: with assistive technology, 193
Process skills
- for science, 490, 491*t*
- for social studies, 487–488

Process tool software, 464
Progressive parts method of instruction, 347, 347*t*
Prompting, 163–164, 164*t*
- antecedent, 310, 312, 523, 528, 537
- color-line, 406–407, 407*f*
- least, 265
- maximum, 265
- in milieu teaching, 265–266
- response, 264–265, 312
- self-operated, 312

Prone board: positioning in, for feeding, 297–298, 297*f*
Prone scooter board, 209*f*
Proprioception: cerebral palsy and, 92, 104–105
Prosthesis, 51, 52*f*
- dressing and, 326

Proximal stability, 197
Proximal support: positioning and, 197
Pseudohypertrophy, 46
Psychology, 487*f*
Psychosocial development
- asthma and, 63
- cancer and, 69–70
- cystic fibrosis and, 66–67
- cytomegalovirus and, 71–72
- HIV/AIDS and, 74
- limb deficiencies and, 53
- muscular dystrophy and, 50
- neural tube defects and, 34–35
- traumatic brain injury and, 42–45

Public law notation, 9
Pull-out, 17
Pulmonary percussion: for asthma, 62

Quadrant strategy, 313
Quadriplegia, 89
Question and analysis approach to curricular modification, 120, 121*f*
Question and choice approach to curricular modification, 120, 122*f*
QWERTY keyboard, 453, 454*f*, 456, 457*f*

Racing: wheelchair, 360–361
Racquet and arm sports, 361
Radiation, 69
Rancho Los Amigos Cognitive Scales, 40, 41*t*
Range of motion (ROM)
- cerebral palsy and, 99
- for material placement, 408

Rational counting, 511, 513
Reachers, 325
Reading. *See* Literacy
Reasonable accommodation, 10, 11
Receptive communication
- nonsymbolic, 232–234
- vocabulary boards for, 258–259

Recommendations for Accessibility Standards for Children's Environments, 211
Recreation, 348–349. *See also* Adapted physical education (APE); Leisure education; Sports
- horseback riding, 358–359, 359*f*
- nature exploration, 356–358
- travel, 359–360

Reentry classes, 46, 47*f*
Reference symbol page, 424–425
Rehabilitation Act of 1973 (PL 93-112), 6, 10, 181, 337
Rehabilitation counselor, 24
Related service: assistive technology as, 195
Reliable means of response (RMR), 403
Religion, 487*f*
Resource room teacher, 24
Resource services, 17
Respiratory development, 284–286
Respiratory function
- atypical, 290
- coordination with oral and pharyngeal activities, 285–286, 305–306
- evaluation of, 290–292

Response difficulties: task analysis and, 160–161
Response prompt instructional strategies, 264–265, 312
Response units in task analysis, 152
Restaurants, 333
Restrooms: public, 331
Retinopathy of prematurity (ROP), 91
Reverse scanning, 242
Rigidity: in cerebral palsy, 90
RMR (reliable means of response), 403
Robotics: in leisure education, 353–356
ROM. *See* Range of motion
Roosevelt, Franklin Delano, 5
Rooting response, 281, 281*f*
ROP (retinopathy of prematurity), 91
Rotary jaw movements, 281*f*, 284
Rote counting, 511
Row-item scanning, 242, 243*f*
Rubrics: in adapted physical education, 342, 342*f*

Safety
- in adapted physical education, 348
- positioning and, 198
- in science classroom, 493*f*
- wheelchair, 206

Salient letter encoding, 246
SAVI/SELPH curriculum, 494, 495*f*
Scanning: in symbolic communication, 242, 243*f*
SCANS (Secretary's Commission on Achieving Necessary Skills), 384, 385*t*, 386
Schedules
- calendar and, 233*f*
- picture, 538–539

School topic content, 250, 251*f*
School-to-Work Opportunity Act (STWOA) (PL 103-239), 384
Science
- curriculum design and adaptations for, 490–496
- defined, 489–490
- disciplines in, 490*f*
- environment adaptation for, 493–496
- inquiry skills in, 490–491
- in leisure education, 353–356
- literacy issues in, 491–492, 492*t*
- process skills for, 490, 491*t*
- safety checklist, 493*f*
- software for, 496
- textbooks in, 472–475

Scoliosis, 34, 48
Scooter, 206*f*
Scooter board, 209*f*, 329*f*
Scope of curriculum, 151
Screening performances: using task analysis, 167, 168*f*–169*f*
Scripturally implicit comprehension, 427
Seating, 198–203. *See also* Positioning
- assistive devices for, 201–203
- components of, 199*f*
- consequences of poor, 200–201
- foot support, 199
- pelvic position, 199, 199*f*
- shoulder and upper trunk support, 199–200, 200*f*
- transfers from, 203

Second impact syndrome, 38
Secretary's Commission on Achieving Necessary Skills (SCANS), 384, 385*t*, 386
SEE (Signing Exact English), 234
Segregation: educational, 104
Seizures: cerebral palsy and, 93, 94*t*–96*t*
Selective dorsal (posterior) rhizotomy: for cerebral palsy, 98
Self-adaptability, 370–372
Self-Advocacy Notebook, 136
Self-care skills. *See* Personal management skills
Self-determination, 367, 370–372. *See also* Career/transition education
  curricular domain of, 114, 136–137, 137*f*, 138*f*–140*f*
  defined, 136
Self-Determined Learning Model of Instruction, 371
Self-evaluation, 370
Self-instruction, 509
Self-monitoring, 508
Self-operated prompting system, 312
Self-reliance: physical, 369–370
Semantic analysis of written words, 418
Semantic letter encoding, 246
Semantic mapping, 475–476, 475*f*
Sensation: decreased or absent, 33
Sensory impairments
  assistive technology for, 220–221
  cerebral palsy and, 91
Sentence construction, 463
Sequencing
  in addition and subtraction, 524–525
  defined, 151
  in multiplication and division, 529
  in Nonverbal Reading Approach, 422–424
  in task analysis, 155–157
  in textbooks, 473, 473*t*
Seriation: in mathematics, 511
Service delivery systems, 16–20
  challenges to, 18–20
Service intensity: issues related to, 15
Sexual transmission of HIV/AIDS, 72
Shadowing, 321
Shaping, 164–165
Shared-feature cue, 238
Shopping, 332–333
Show Me Math, 529
Shunt
  defined, 34
  malfunction indicators, 36*f*
Sidelyer, 198*f*
Sight-word instruction, 422, 432
Signing Exact English (SEE), 234
Sign language: reading and, 432–433
Situation analysis, 169–173, 170*f*, 172*f*
  peer questionnaire in, 172–173, 172*f*
  purposes of, 152–153
  steps in, 169–170
  teacher recollections in, 171
Skin care: myelomeningocele and, 36–37
Skip counting, 514
Slant devices, 214*f*
Social communication, 250–251, 252*f*
Social/emotional development
  cerebral palsy and, 103–104
Social interaction
  communication for, 229
  in leisure education program, 349
Social Security Act, 5
Social studies
  curriculum design and adaptations for, 488–489
  defined, 487
  disciplines in, 487*f*
  process skills for, 487–488
  software for, 489
  textbooks in, 472–475
Social worker, 24
Sociology, 487*f*
Software programs. *See also* Computers
  abbreviations expansion, 457
  computer-assisted instruction, 509
  desktop publishing, 464
  editing, 464
  for emergent literacy, 416
  for functional literacy, 433–434, 434*f*
  for grammar, 464
  for handwriting, 449
  for highlighting and bookmarking, 473, 482
  for keyboarding skills, 456
  for literacy instruction, 407–408
  for mathematics
    computational, 529–530
    functional, 531, 534
    general and advanced, 531
    money, 535
    precomputational, 518
    time, 537
  multimedia, 464
  outliner, 464
  process tool, 464
  for reading comprehension, 430–431
  for science, 496
  for social studies, 489
  for spelling, 459
  style aid, 464
  voice recognition, 455–456
  word-prediction, 456–457
  word-processing, 456
  for written expression, 462, 464
Solid food, 283–284, 288*f*, 303–305, 305*f*
Sound
  continuous, 416
  stop, 416
Sound production: development of, 285–286
Space science, 490*f*
Spastic cerebral palsy, 89–90
  managing, 99–100
Special day classes, 17
Special education: assistive technology in, 194
Special education instructor
  defined, 24
  itinerant, 17
Special health care needs, 76–79
Special sites, 17
Speech. *See also* Communication
  curriculum modification for, 134
  digitized, 247
  internal, 420
  synthesized, 247
Speech-language pathologist, 24
Speech recognition, 242
Spelling
  assessment of, 457–458
  computer programs for, 459
  instructional strategies for, 458–459
  tools for, 459
Spina bifida, 32
Spina bifida occulta, 32, 33*f*
Spiral curriculum, 488
Splints, 240–241
Spoon-feeding, 282, 288*f*, 298, 303, 304*f*
Sports. *See also* Adapted physical education (APE); Leisure education
  on computer, 356
  racquet and arm, 361
  wheelchair racing, 360–361
  winter or summer, 361–362
SQ3R strategy, 483, 484*f*
Stability
  of objects, 215, 216*f*
  positioning and, 197–198

Standards
  accessibility, 211
  CEC certification, 20–21
  defined, 113
  mathematics, 502, 503*t*, 504
  physical education, 338–339
  science, 490–491
Stanford Diagnostic Reading Test—Red Level, 414
Step scanning, 242
Stereotyping persons with disabilities, 8
Sticky keys, 453
Stop sounds, 416
STORCH infections, 71
Storybook reading, 412–414, 413*f*, 414*f*
Story maps, 429, 430*f*
Strabismus, 91
Stroller chairs, 207, 207*f*
Structural analysis of written words, 418
Student learning outcomes: defined, 113
Study guides, 484, 486
Study skills: in curriculum, 126, 126*f*
Style aid software, 464
Subtraction, 518–525
  algorithms for, 521–524
  math rules for, 521
  sequencing in, 524–525
  task analysis with, 154*t*, 168*f*
Sucking, 281*f*, 282
Suckling, 281*f*, 282
Summative assessment, 153, 167, 169
Supplementary aids and services
  assistive technology as, 195
Supported employment, 374, 378
Supports
  natural, 117, 119*f*
  for school personnel, 195–196
Swallowing. *See* Feeding and swallowing
Switches, 218
  as communication access devices, 242
  as computer input devices, 455, 455*f*
  mounting of, 220
  selection of, 218–219
  types of, 219*f*
Symbolic communication, 234–238. *See also* Augmentative and alternative communication (AAC)
  aided, 234, 235–236
    direct selection in, 240–242
    encoding in, 243–245, 244*f*
    means of access in, 240–245
    multicomponent system of, 236*f*–237*f*
    output methods in, 247–248
    scanning in, 242, 243*f*
    storage and retrieval in, 245–247
    symbol type in, 238–240, 239*f*
    vocabulary in, 245–247
  moving toward, 234
  selecting system of, 236–238
  unaided, 234–235
Symbol reading pages, 424, 425*f*
Symbols
  in aided communication, 238–240, 239*f*
  board placement of, 253
  display forms for, 259–262
  math concepts through, 511, 512*f*
  vocabulary development through, 424–425, 425*f*
Syntax: of written expression, 462–463
Synthesized speech, 247
Systemic condition, 66
System of least prompts, 265
System of maximum prompts, 265

Tangible symbols, 238
Target strategy, 313
Task analysis
  as assessment tool, 152–153
  assistance needs and, 161, 163–165, 164*t*, 166*f*
  comparison of student skills with, 167, 169*f*
  curriculum development and, 167–169
  defined, 152
  for face washing, 314*f*
  for feminine hygiene, 317*f*
  for hand washing, 311*f*
  motor vs. cognitive difficulties and, 158–160, 160*f*
  order of tasks in, 153, 154*t*, 155*f*
  of personal management skills, 310, 311*f*
  process of, 152, 153–166
  as product, 152, 167–169, 168*f*, 169*f*
  purposes of, 152–153
  response difficulties and, 160–161
  screening with, 167, 168*f*–169*f*
  sequencing in, 155–157
  student strategies for, 173–176
  for tissue use, 316*f*
  for toileting, 319*f*
  for toothbrushing, 315*f*
  of unsuccessful trials, 157–158, 159*f*
Task ladder, 155, 156*f*, 157*f*
Task performance: modified, in curriculum, 114, 129, 133–134
Task redesign, adaptation, or modification, 381–382
Task-specific content, 248–250
TBI. *See* Traumatic brain injury
TDD (telecommunication devices for the deaf), 221
Teachers
  knowledge and skills of, 3–4, 20–21
  recollections of, in situation analysis, 171
  resources for, 26
  roles of, 21–26, 21*f*–22*f*, 24*f*–25*f*
Technology
  assistive. *See* Assistive technology
  in leisure education, 353–356
Technology-Related Assistance for Individuals with Disabilities Act of 1988 (PL 100-407), 10, 14, 180
Telecommunication devices for the deaf (TDD), 221
Telecommunication equipment, 221
Teletypewriter (TTY), 221
Terminal limb deficiencies, 51
Testing. *See also* Assessment
  of content knowledge, 486–487
Test of Gross-Motor Development (TGMD), 340
Tethered cord, 34
Textbooks
  accessing, 474–475
  evaluating, 472–473
  screening, 474*f*
  sequencing of, 473, 473*t*
  simplifying, 473
  substituting, 474
  supplementary materials with, 475
Text comprehension, 426–430
  software programs for, 431
  strategies for, 428–430, 429*f*, 430*f*
  teaching, 427–428
Textually explicit comprehension, 427
Textually implicit comprehension, 427
Textures of food and liquids, 283*f*
TGMD (Test of Gross-Motor Development), 340
Thalidomide, 51
Therapeutic horsemanship, 358–359
Thinking skills: in curriculum, 123, 125*f*
Tic-tac-toe boxes, 261–262, 262*f*, 352, 353*f*
Time delay, 264–265

Time-limited steps, 321
Time skills, 536–538, 538*f*
Tissue use, 316, 316*f*
Toileting, 317–319, 318*f*, 319*f*
Tongue: oral control of, 300–301
Tongue lateralization, 281*f*
Tongue protrusion: exaggerated, 287*f*
Tongue retraction, 287*f*
  with anterior tongue elevation, 287*f*
Tongue thrusting, 287*f*, 288*f*
Tonic biting, 287*f*
Toothbrushing, 293, 300, 314–315, 315*f*, 316*f*
Topography classification of cerebral palsy, 89
Touch cues, 232
TouchMath, 518–519, 519*f*
TouchWindow, 455
Toys: as mobility aids, 209*f*
Training: as barrier, 20
Trajectories: of health impairments, 61
Transfers: from assistive devices, 203
Transition classes, 46, 47*f*
Transition education. *See also* Career/transition education
  curricular domain of, 114, 137, 141–143, 141*t*, 142*f*
Transition Planning Inventory, 386, 387–393
Translucency of symbols, 239
Transparency of symbols, 239
Traumatic brain injury (TBI):
  autonomy and, 45–46
  career/adult outcomes and, 46
  cognitive development and, 40, 42, 43*t*–45*t*
  defined, 9, 38
  descriptions and characteristics, 38–39
  education and, 45–46
  medical conditions associated with, 39
  physical development and, 40, 42
  psychosocial development and, 42–45
  treatments for, 39–40
Travel, 359–360
Travel stroller chairs, 207, 207*f*
Treatment-related factors in traumatic brain injury, 40
Tremor: in cerebral palsy, 90
Trial use, 190, 192
Tricycles, 198*f*
Trip training method, 318
TTY (teletypewriter), 221
Tube feeding, 319–320, 321, 321*f*
Tumors, 68

Unaided symbolic communication, 234–235
Uniform accessibility, 211
United Cerebral Palsy, 6
Unity, 246
Universal precautions, 79, 80
U.S. Architectural and Transportation Barriers Compliance Board (ATBCB), 211
U.S. Cerebral Palsy Athletic Association: classification system of, 345*t*
Utensils
  for cooking, 328, 329*f*
  for feeding, 298

Valium (diazepam): for cerebral palsy, 97
Vectorborne disease transmission, 70
Vehicle route of disease transmission, 70
Ventilator: portable, 77*f*
Visual cues, 165
Visual impairments: assistive technology for, 221
Visual memory, 410–411, 412
Visual outputs: of communication system, 247
Visual processing disability: with cerebral palsy, 92, 104
Visual spatial displays, 483–484, 485*f*
Vocabulary
  approaches for determining, 248
  in communication system, 245–247, 248–251, 252*f*
  content-specific, 255, 257*f*
  core, 255, 257*f*
  ecological assessment of, 431–432
  teaching, 424–425
Vocabulary boards, 253–259
  activity-based, 255
  category-based, 254–255
  font size on, 254*f*
  index of, 255, 256*f*
  language-development-based, 255, 258, 258*f*
  organization of, 253–258
  portable, 259–260
  receptive communication arrangement on, 258–259
  symbol placement on, 253
  theme-related, 255
Voice outputs: of communication system, 247
Voice recognition software, 455–456

Wait time, 164
Walkers, 209, 210*f*, 211
Wands, 241
Warning devices, 221
Washing
  face and body, 313–314, 314*f*
  hand, 80–81, 80*f*, 310, 311*f*, 313
Waste disposal, 81
Wedge, 198*f*, 294–295, 294*f*
Week strip, 539
Wheelchairs
  dressing and, 326
  kitchen adaptation for, 328*f*
  manual, 204–205, 205*f*
  muscular dystrophy and, 49
  positioning in, for feeding, 295, 297, 297*f*
  power, 205–207, 205*f*, 206*f*
  racing in, 360–361
  storing materials on, 212*f*
  toileting from, 318, 331
  transfers to and from, 203
  travel and, 360
  travel stroller chairs, 207, 207*f*
  variations on, 208–209, 209*f*
Wheeler: hand-propelled, 209*f*
Widening horizons, 488
Wisconsin Assistive Technology Initiative, 184–186
  Assistive Technology Checklist, 181, 182*f*–183*f*, 184
  Assistive Technology Consideration Guide, 185, 185*f*
  Assistive Technology Decision-Making Guide, 186, 189–190, 191*f*
  Assistive Technology Trial Use Guide, 186, 190, 192
  Assistive Technology Trial Use Summary, 186
  Environmental Observation Guide, 186, 188, 189*f*
  Student Information Guide, 186, 187–188
  Trial Use Guide, 186
Word associations: spelling instruction with, 458
Word-prediction programs, 456–457
Word problems in mathematics, 530–531, 535
Word-processing programs, 456

Word/sentence construction page, 425, 425*f*
Work: defined, 367
Work surface
- for literacy instruction, 406
- modifications to, 213–214, 213*f*, 214*f*
- for writing, 446, 448*f*

World Health Organization: classifications by, 6–7, 7*t*
Writing. *See also* Written expression
- barriers to, 441–443
- functional, 464–465
- handwriting skills, 446–449, 448*f*, 449*t*, 450*t*–452*t*
- reading connected to, 443
- spelling, 457–459

Writing tools
- accessing, 443–457
- computer, 449, 452–457
  - accessibility options, 452–453
  - input devices, 453, 455–456, 455*f*
  - keyboard alternatives, 453, 455*f*
  - keyboarding skills, 456–457, 457*f*
  - keyboard layout options, 453, 454*f*
  - keyboard modifications, 453
  - mouse alternatives, 453
  - output modifications, 456
- for functional writing, 465
- handheld, 444, 445*f*, 446, 446*f*
- head sticks, 446*f*
- paper adaptations, 444, 446, 447*f*, 448*f*

Written expression
- assessing, 459–460, 460*f*–461*f*
- early, 461–462
- software programs for, 462, 464
- teaching, 462–464

Your Employment Selections (Y.E.S.), 387

Zoology, 490*f*